Contents

BFI FILM AND TELEVISION HANDBOOK 2004

www.bfi.org.uk/handbook

bfi British Film Institute

Editor: Eddie Dyja

Project Manager: David Sharp
Production: Tom Cabot

Information Services
Manager: Peter Todd
Statistics Research: Erinna Mettler, Phil Wickham, Elena Marcarini
Statistics Tabulation: Ian O'Sullivan

Additional Research/Editorial Assistance
Nigel Arthur, Sean Delaney, Jose de Esteban, Allen Eyles, Patrick Fahy, Christie Quinn, Matt Ker, Anastasia Kerameos, Ayesha Khan, Lavinia Orton, David Reeve, Nathalie Sergent, David Sharp, Kristy Widdicombe
Database Consultant: Lavinia Orton
Marketing: Claire Milburn, Sarah Prosser
Cover Design: Jethro Clunies-Ross
Advertising Consultant: Ronnie Hackston

Website: www.bfi.org.uk/handbook

With thanks to bfi – Stills Posters and Designs who provide many of the images used in the Handbook. For more details Tel. 0207 957 4797 or email stills.films@bfi.org.uk

Many thanks to those who also assisted with images: BBC, Buena Vista International, Carlton, Channel 4 Television, Columbia TriStar, Entertainment Film Distributors, Granada, Icon, Miramax, Momentum Pictures, Pathé Distribution, Twentieth Century Fox, United International Pictures (UK), The Walt Disney Company, Warner Bros, Yash Raj, Yorkshire Television

21 Stephen Street
London W1T 1LN

Printed in the UK by the Bath Press, Bath & Glasgow

A catalogue record for this book is available from the British Library.

ISBN 0 85170 990 7

Price: £22.50

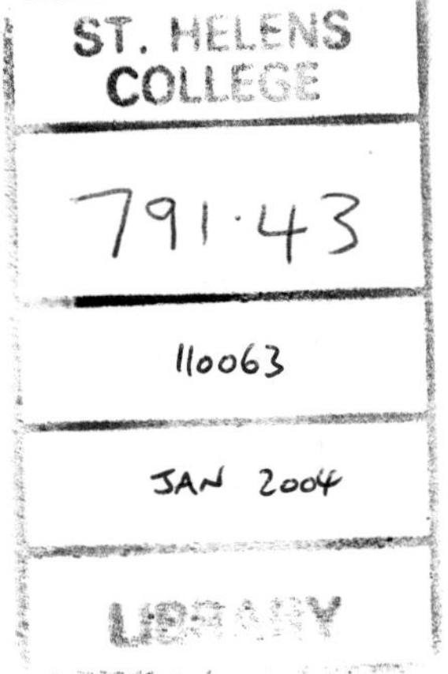

ACKNOWLEDGMENTS

In 1982 the *bfi* published the Film and Television Yearbook 1983 as part of its 50th year anniversary celebrations. The Yearbook filled a yawning gap by providing information and analysis of the British film and television industries and led the way as a reference work of some repute. This is the 21st edition of the Handbook and my sincere thanks goes out to all those who have supported and contributed to its success throughout those years. Reflecting this mood of triumphalism I would like to issue the following Handbook awards.

The Matter of Life and Death Award: Goes to Peter Todd, Phil Wickham, Erinna Mettler and Ian O'Sullivan for the heady days of Handbook stats and the peculiar inbetween staircase world that they managed to work through cheerfully this year.

The Whisky Galore! Award: Goes to the following intrepid group who have managed to hoodwink the authorities by smuggling in the Handbook booty – Sean Delaney, Jose de Esteban, Allen Eyles, Patrick Fahy, Matt Ker, Anastasia Kerameos, Ayesha Khan, Elena Marcarini, Danielle O'Connor, Lavinia Orton, David Reeve, Christie Quinn, Nathalie Sergent, David Sharp and Kristy Widdicombe.

The Licence to Kill Award: Goes to suave, sophisticated agent Tom Cabot who has earned his Oh, Oh, status on many occasions but always manages to complete his assignments.

The Carry On Regardless Award: Goes to all our beloved Publishing colleagues over the years who have shared in the fun and the laughter that producing such a phenomenally successful series of books entails. Thanks in particular to Andrew Lockett, Claire Milburn and Sarah Prosser for keeping it up.

The Wicker Man Award: Goes to Danny Birchall and Gareth de Walters for their jiggery pokery on the website. Let's hope for a good harvest, eh lads?

The Truly, Madly, Deeply Award: This year's Cello goes to the following spirits who have managed to lift mine Nina Bishop, Maureen Brown, Karen Cattini, Christophe Dupin, Mike Elrick, Eugene Finn, Lucia Hadjiconstanti, Guy Hinton, Richard Holford, Alex Hogg, Alison Kirwan, Tina McFarling, Ivan Mowse, Sean Perkins, Mandy Rosencrown, Joe Sieder, Lucy Skipper, Emma Smart, Sara Squire and Tise Vahimagi.

The Blow Up Award: Goes to Tessa Quinn and Nigel Arthur from Stills for their photo opportunism.

The Drowning By Numbers Award: Goes to designer Jethro Clunies-Ross for his pop art, popcorn cover design which sadly only a few will ever see

The Flash Harry Award: Goes to our resident spiv Ronnie Hackston, working out of the St Trinian's office, for getting us those nice half-pages.

Special Award for unswerving loyalty and support: Nielsen EDI Ltd, *Screen Finance, Screen International,* British Videogram Association (BVA), European Audiovisual Observatory and the former ITC for allowing access to their statistics and industry news – their cooperation is deeply appreciated.

The Four Weddings and a Funeral Award: Thanks also go to all the organisations over the years who have helped us produce the Handbook – The Arts Council of Wales, The Arts Council of Northern Ireland, the BBC, The British Council Film and Literature Department, the British Film Commission (BFC), Central Statistical Office (CSO), the Cinema Advertising Association (CAA), the Department for Culture, Media and Sport (DCMS), Media +, Scottish Screen and TaRiS Taylor Nelson Sofres.

The Gosford Park Award: Goes to the UK Film Council for their interest in the Handbook over the past year and their valuable input in the statistical section.

Special Mention: Markku Salmi, for his guidance, tireless pursuit of excellence and for demanding the highest standards at all times.

Eddie Dyja, Handbook Editor, July 2003

{be here}

VFS
Vancouver Film School

FOREWORD

by Anthony Minghella,
Chair of the British Film Institute

"We propose to concentrate our efforts upon encouraging those entertainment films which have some unusual merit about them, those which we think may not receive the backing from the public which they deserve..."

Colonel J Buchan, chairman *bfi* advisory council, 1 February, 1934.

It is salutary but also pertinent that those aspirations seem as urgent today as they did when the *bfi* was created seventy years ago this year. Throughout its history the *bfi* has been a champion of the forgotten film, an advocate of the treasures of international cinema, a vital resource of film preservation and restoration, and a reservoir of specialised information about classics of the cinema and their creators.

It would also be fair to say that it has remained a controversial body, a public service, which, like another essential cultural institution, the BBC, has been buffeted by criticism, frequently challenged as to the exact nature of its remit and its ability to make a difference. As the Institute's new Chairman I find myself intrigued by the early documents which informed the establishment of the *bfi*, conscious that little has changed in the interim, how easy it can be for the *bfi* to drift into the territory of cultural hegemony, of telling people off about their taste, of retreating into a position of remote authority, content with speaking to a decreasing constituency of cineastes.

I come to the *bfi* as someone who has profited, profoundly, from its existence. My love of cinema was fuelled by visits to Regional Film Theatres, as was my understanding that cinema could be an art form as well as the equivalent of a fairground ride, capable of harnessing the most pungent elements of music, literature, theatre and the visual arts into a single medium capable of crossing boundaries of country, class and creed. The *bfi* introduced me to the wonders of Fellini, Visconti, Kurosawa, Kieslowski and Bunuel, to the joys of Keaton, Chaplin and Hitchcock.

Dramatic Fiction plays a complex role in our culture; unquestioned, and barely explored. There is so much of it, infiltrating our living rooms, occupying our imaginations, and it would be well to remember its strengths: that it can enlarge our view of the world; confront our prejudices; reflect our own actions back to ourselves and, most significantly, shift our perspective, allowing us to consider events through the eyes of others. Conversely, it is capable of distortion, simplification and lies; reinforcing the shabby gestures of bigotry and ignorance. If nothing else, I believe the *bfi* should reassert its initial premise, of providing an enthusiastic, contextualised and informed presentation of the cinema overlooked by the mainstream. To do this effectively, we must look to our audience, serve our audience, and listen to them. To do that effectively, we must get better at letting them know what we do, where we do it, how to use our resources. The *bfi* does not belong to its staff or to the privileged few with access to the South Bank. It belongs to everybody.

The Institute has endured many reviews, internal and external, in recent years, as well as several changes of regime and I'm certain that its staff, who form a deep but often secret pool of film knowledge and passionate advocacy, have been bruised by rigorous scrutiny, but a lack of acknowledgment of their legion achievements. The *bfi* has to survive in a cultural landscape which has less money available for its work, fewer outlets for serious cinema, fewer opportunities for people to fall in love with movies beyond those forcefed us by the might of Hollywood's brilliant industrial machine.

As a film-maker who profits from that system I have no desire to criticise its effectiveness but, to borrow from *Alice in Wonderland*, you might as well say you like what you get is the same as you get what you like. Or, to put it another way, it is to imagine a bookshop which only stocks the most recent clutch of bestsellers. For me, the *bfi* must represent the film equivalent of those other shelves, history, poetry, art, politics, philosophy and anthropology – the beautiful shelves which make demands on the imagination, that inform as they entertain. And our advocacy must be in tune with the audience, not only in London, but in the whole of the nation.

Amanda Nevill, the Institute's new Director, has joined us from her marvellous stint at Bradford's National Museum of Film, Photography and Television, and brings with her a shared desire to turn the Institute over to our audience, to grow a younger audience, to insist that we are not a marginal establishment but a treasure-trove for everybody, regardless of age, colour, social territory or creed.

I am delighted that the NFT continues to serve an enthusiastic audience who are revisiting the seminal works of cinema. I also want to see audiences filling our buildings who are watching *The Seven Samurai* for the first time, *Kes* for the first time, *The Philadelphia Story* for the first time, who are seeing the best of recent world cinema and of the movies made in this country, but not supported by mainstream distribution.

As this new regime commences yet another review, the Board of Governors has asked Amanda to do two things, to change the *bfi* from within, by learning from the fantastic staff who serve the Institute, and from without, by using all our energy and vision to provide an irresistible service to the widest constituency possible, so that the changes we make are the ones which transform us into a friendly, welcoming and accessible Institute, one equipped to sustain and develop the enduring principles of the *bfi* for another seventy years.

This is also an opportunity for me to record my thanks to Adrian Wootton who, in the hiatus before Amanda's appointment, guided the Institute through turbulent months with care and distinction. Adrian has since gone on to be the first director of the newly formed Film London. Their gain is the *bfi*'s great loss.

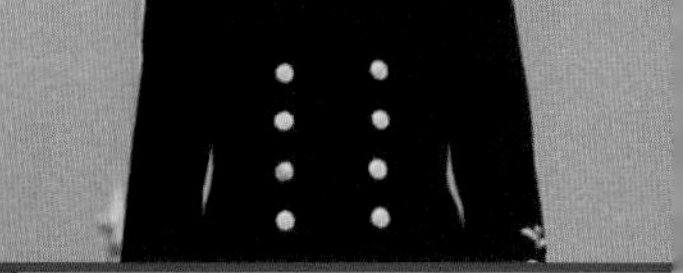

INTRODUCTION

by Amanda Nevill
Director of the British Film Institute

Though new, I am certainly no stranger to the *bfi*, its reputation and its extraordinary range of activity. Nine weeks in, however, the *bfi* continues to unfurl in front of my eyes every day like a classic film that you always thought you knew, but are seeing with new eyes and enjoyment.

The uniting passion which guides everyone at the *bfi* is the stuff that we are about – that film and television culture is a major art form to be studied, disseminated and enjoyed. This passion is stamped through to the core like the name on a stick of seaside rock.

HG Wells once suggested that there was no such thing as a bad film – it was just wonderful that everyone moves! The wonder and awe which fuelled the spectacle of early film was played out in front of my eyes in my first weeks, with a conference launching The Mitchell and Kenyon Collection. This Collection of early material being restored by the Archive, was the Alton Tower ride of its day. Mitchell and Kenyon filmed every-day events, screening later to paying customers curious to see themselves and family 'moving' on screen. Mitchell and Kenyon were a late Edwardian film company based in Blackburn in Lancashire. The collection consists almost entirely of actuality films commissioned by travelling fairground operators for showing at local fairgrounds or other venues across the UK. The collection was stored for many decades in two large barrels following the winding up of the firm and was discovered in Blackburn in the 1990s by Peter Worden. The *bfi* systematically restored the entire collections of film, transferring the images from fragile original nitrate to new masters and viewing copies for distribution. This expansive and painstaking work will enable the films to be seen for the first time in a century. The collection opens not only an unprecedented window on to the society of a bygone era, it shows how the *bfi* can share this window in new ways. In a joint project between the University of Sheffield's National Fairground Archive, the *bfi*, and the Arts and Humanities Research Board, a panel of top academic film and social historians have been commissioned to write a book for *bfi* Publishing on the significance of this collection. Also a major BBC series will be airing on this collection in 2004. Stemming from these engagements will be significant opportunities for other partnerships with film organisations throughout the UK. The acquisition of this collection also stimulates questions at the *bfi* about the nature of a National archive and how we respond to this core responsibility to future generations.

The role of the curator was once described to me as legalised kleptomania. A more accurate description might be oracle or clairvoyant. A curator, to a certain extent, shapes the way in which the future populace will view history. Some of the responsibility is dissipated by the knowledge that future curators will be very selective choosing (as curators do today) from the riches laid down by previous generations.

The *bfi* has this year already restored, often in ingeniously brokered international partnerships, three important films, David Lean's *Summer Madness* which showed at the Berlin Film Festival, EA Dupont's *Piccadilly* a lavish example of one of the last silent films from 1929 generously sponsored by a supportive *bfi* patron (and due to screen at the New York Film Festival before an international tour) and *Sunrise*. At the first Academy Award Ceremony in 1929, *Sunrise* won awards for the Best Picture for Cinematography and the Best Actress Award went to Janet Gaynor. This exquisite film by Murnau was one of the early examples of Fox's sound-on-film process. The original negative was destroyed in 1937 but in partnership the Academy Film Archive in Los Angeles and 20th Century Fox, and the *bfi* Archive examined prints from international cinema texts around the world to find the best possible existing material. Care was taken to retain the flaws and limitations inherent in the original movie process and to only remove any of those defects caused by the ravages of time. It was screened at the Berlin Film Festival before a UK tour. Possibly one of the most influential movies of all time, *Sunrise* has inspired filmmakers such as Neil Jordan and Baz Luhrmann (who based the look of *Moulin Rouge* on *Sunrise*) and cinematographer, John Bailey, whose credits include *As Good As It Gets*. In 2002, *Sunrise* was still placed 7th on the *bfi*'s *Sight and Sound* magazine critic poll of the best films of all time more than 70 years on from its release. Filmmakers among you might ponder awhile – a good opening weekend might not necessarily be the only cultural legacy!

So, the *bfi*'s work is as equally relevant to the present as it is engaged in the past and the future. The *bfi* carefully weaves between the past the present and the future, deliberately creating cultural 'worm holes' where anyone can slip from one film dimension through to another to discover new delights. Much of the *bfi*'s activity is engaged in taking the film out to as wide an audience as possible. The bookings department alone regularly supports up to 500 screens a year, sending films to venues across the UK and providing a one-stop expert access to a cultural reservoir of films not available in any other way. It is a service which can – and does – reach places no other film achieves exemplified by the dedicated programmer in the north of Scotland who flies film and projector to the Shetland Islands – a salutory lesson to those of us who complain about having insufficient time to take in all that is on offer. For those seeking to view film at home, the *bfi* offers classics from the world's most influential directors, specialist releases from the *bfi*'s own collections and a pioneering archive TV strand through its DVD and video publishing label. In total the catalogue now offers a list of over 1,000 titles with releases in recent weeks of Jean Renoir's *Regle de Jeu*, Anup Singh's *The Name of a River*, Ken Loach's *Cathy Come Home* and Peter Watkins' *Culloden*. The development of the *bfi* DVD and video label is a huge success story, this year alone 140,000 DVDs and videos will be sold.

For all its outreach, the *bfi* is still committed to the opportunity to see films as they were intended to be seen, on the big screen, and in the case of IMAX, very big. Highlights have included the Disability Festival, a huge success which rightly challenges perceptions through irreverent programming. Crime Scene is now in its fourth year and has created a distinct flavour and this year offered a joint celebration of the centenary of legendry novelist Georges Simenon and a major retrospective of the influential noir filmmaker Jean Pierre Melville. The Cool World – Towards a Mod Cinema taps into the current 60s retro zeitgeist whilst *The Matrix Reloaded* – seen as never before on IMAX – provides the hot adrenalin rush!

Preparations for the London Film Festival are at full steam as are celebrations in early autumn for the 80th birthday of Lord Attenborough and a major season of Chaplin projects which will extend over two years including theatrical re-releases, new video and DVD releases and a series of screenings with live orchestral accompaniment.

The *bfi* recognises the exciting potential for new film distribution vehicles enabled by digital technology. The National Film Theatre is the host and home to the main UK and European Digital Test Bed facility set up in partnership by the DTI with a host of leading commercial backers. This will allow exploration, piloting and evaluation of digital distribution and exhibition of film. The launch to a capacity NFT audience with a live link onto the set of *The Lord of the Rings* in New Zealand was but a tantalising glimpse of future possibilities.

Every healthy organisation is so because it constantly evolves in order to adapt to new societal and audience needs. The *bfi* hums with activity and my first few weeks here have shown that its armoury of fireworks is robust. The months to come will be about how we collectively choreograph the future display to maximise enjoyment for the widest possible audiences with visibility across the nation. Prepare to be dazzled some more.

UK FILM, TELEVISION AND VIDEO: OVERVIEW

by Eddie Dyja

Scrutiny and control were two common threads interweaving through both the UK film and television industries over the past year. A parliamentary select committee was set up to discover whether there is a British film industry and as such, what influence organisations such as the UK Film Council and the British Film Institute have in persuading UK audiences to occasionally turn their gazes away from Hollywood's global monopoly.

On the broadcasting side the Communications Act finally became law in July 2003 and the new broadcasting regulator Ofcom (Office of Communications) was formed. The undignified spat between the Government and the BBC over the Iraq dossier provided an uncomfortable prologue to Ofcom's review of the BBC's charter.

While all this was going on, home entertainment systems ensured that DVDs/Videos were having an extraordinary rise in fortunes, with UK consumers digging deep into their pockets to buy their favourite films and TV programme box sets.

FILM

There are many assumptions made about the British film industry, which might be summed up by borrowing a famous line from the film *Sunset Boulevard* – "I am big. It's the pictures that got small." In essence the belief exists that UK films can still pack a powerful punch, when in reality the UK industry is almost entirely dependent on the patronage of America and European producers. By taking away UK partners from the equation the home-grown UK film industry is indeed small. While the Americans and Europeans are quite happy to pick up the tab for some of the UK's most successful films, such as *Harry Potter*, they also manage to pocket the profits from these films. As a result, while the UK film industry benefits from inward investment it loses control over the profits of the investment.

Things were looking up for Harry Potter and UK film industry

Building a sustainable UK film industry

In November 2002, Sir Alan Parker, Chairman of the UK Film Council, made a keynote speech to the UK film industry community. In it he talked through priority areas which needed attention in order to build a sustainable UK film industry. Parker suggested that no amount of money allocated to British producers would cure the industry of its real ills, an unhealthy level of parochialism and the lack of any distribution infrastructure to support UK film releases.

He admitted that the UK Film Council initially had to focus on what it could directly control and reform – the use of public subsidy. This resulted in the production of distinctive British films like *Gosford Park*, *Bloody Sunday*, *The Magdalene Sisters* and *Bend It Like Beckham*. However, he was adamant that direct subsidy solely to production could never form the basis of a successful film industry.

He urged that attention should now turn to establishing tax breaks for distributors, which would allow them to invest in and acquire British films. "The Hollywood studios' mathematics are simple: money spent on production is more than earned back in distribution, profits are taken and the balance is used to help finance the production and distribution of more films."

He drew fire from some critics with his view that the industry should not get bogged down with issues surrounding the nationality of money and the definition of what constitutes a British film.

"We need to abandon forever the 'little England' vision of a UK industry comprised of small British film companies delivering parochial British films. That, I suspect, is what many people think of when they talk of a 'sustainable' British film industry. Well, it's time for a reality check. That 'British' film industry never existed, and in the brutal age of global capitalism, it never will."

"We need to stimulate the growth of an industry that embraces the international market. At the same time, we must maintain an environment which supports the production of British films of enduring cultural significance. It's not either/or. It's both."

Parker's sentiments were echoed by Stewart Till, Chairman and CEO of major distributor, UIP, in another keynote speech made in February 2003: "The message is stop worrying about out of date, geographical parameters. Stop worrying about the nationality of money. We are all operating in a worldwide marketplace and the successful European companies and individuals will be the ones who act locally and think globally."

It was ironic that in June 2003 one of the parochial UK hit films of the year *Bend It Like Beckham,* was racking up a surprisingly strong box office across America, passing the $20m mark, and this mainly as a result of word of mouth recommendations.

To emphasise the problem facing the UK film industry it is worth noting that while Gurinder Chandha's *Bend It Like Beckham* was doing remarkable box office business, other British directors such as Mike Leigh, Ken Loach, Stephen Frears, Lynne Ramsey and Shane Meadows were experiencing poor box office returns on their typically British films.

Parker's speech reminded producers that the UK's influential film tax breaks for production were due to run out by July 2005. Some believe that the Treasury had noted that a minority of producers were abusing the tax mechanism by using it to fund overseas productions with only a minimal UK interest. Nevertheless, the conundrum remained, that while tax breaks had supported films being made in the UK, they had not led on to the creation of a robust sustainable industry.

It is within this context that the Government chose to launch an investigation into the current state of the British film industry under the title: *Is there a British Film Industry?* It seems that never before has the British film industry had so much navel-gazing in a genuine attempt to discover its true identity. The Select Committee didn't dodge difficult questions including the following hot potato: *Is it important to seek to preserve a capacity to make British films about Britain in the UK?*

Director Alex Cox, who gave evidence to the Select Committee, vehemently defended the case by stating: "Our culture is not the same as that of the US. The great British film successes – whether *Billy Elliot, The Full Monty, Trainspotting, Women in Love, The Devils, If, Kes, Brighton Rock* or *Brief Encounter* – talk about our own unique experiences...To lose our capacity to make British films about Britain in the UK is like losing our capacity to paint, or to write poetry."

At Cannes actor Ewan McGregor expressed irritation about how difficult it had been to gain funding for his film *Young Adam*. He also lamented the fact that, after his ground-breaking Brit films *Shallow Grave* and *Trainspotting*, UK filmmakers seemed once again intent on making films to please the American market.

Bend It Like Beckham was a parochial UK hit

The Hours won acclaim and awards for the UK film industry

It may be that the Select Committee realises that the aim of a sustainable film industry in the UK is more of an aspiration than an achievable goal.

Some of the blame for misconceptions about the UK film industry should be placed with the UK press who tend to perpetuate myths about British film successes particularly at the time of awards ceremonies. Typical is the following opening paragraph from a *Guardian* report on the Baftas:

"The British film industry was given a much-needed boost last night when Stephen Daldry's *The Hours* won two awards at the Baftas, the UK's answer to the Oscars, against stiff competition from big budget Hollywood blockbusters such as *Chicago* and *Gangs of New York*."

The Hours was an excellent example of the muddy waters of film definition. The film was made by US giant Paramount, who formed a British company specifically for the production. The majority of the film was made in the Home Counties with a British crew, a British screenwriter, David Hare and a British director, Stephen Daldry. Yet, the film boasted Meryl Streep, Julianne Moore and Nicole Kidman in the lead roles. To the public this was just another American film. The 'much-needed boost' was critical acclaim rather than money to bankroll other productions.

The main qualification for classification as a British film is spending 70 per cent of a film's budget in the UK - still allowing effectively a third of the film's budget on location abroad. The system requires filmmakers to spend 70 per cent of their labour costs (for personnel involved in the film) on European and Commonwealth citizens, although it has flexibility to take account of the fact that filmmakers may need to employ foreign talent.

Global domination

In 2003, Hollywood went into formulaic overdrive issuing the worldwide audience with sequels, franchises and remakes. Nearly 30 of the major Hollywood films were sequels, and it came as no surprise to learn that US ticket sales were down over the first half of the year.

The Matrix Reloaded, *Charlie's Angels: Full Throttle* and *Terminator 3: Rise of the Machines* all came with prerequisite hype and mass marketing. However, despite big box office business, cinema audiences appeared to be growing wary (if not weary) of the constant breathless hyping of blockbusters.

It should be noted that the UK has two pretty good franchises of its own in *Harry Potter* and *James Bond* (neither of which have to rely on numbers to sell them to audiences). However, delays on the set of the third *Harry Potter* film meant that it would not be released until 2004 thereby allowing the final episode in *The Lord of the Rings* trilogy to take a larger slice of the Christmas market.

The US studios also began global simultaneous movie releases (day and date releases) breaking with the long studio tradition of staggered releases. The threat of internet piracy was one of the factors influencing this development. *The Matrix Reloaded* was available online days after its simultaneous release in 63 countries. The music industry has seen sales of CDs hit by a dramatic increase

The Matriz Reloaded just became bigger and bigger

in online piracy, costing it upwards of £2.6bn last year, and Hollywood film studios are twitching at the prospect of similar exploitation of their products. The threat will become more apparent once broadband and compression technology makes it easy for everyone to download films.

Meanwhile, back in Britain the Greater London Authority launched an investigation into the diversity of product shown on cinema screens in London. No doubt they will discover the extent of Hollywood's dominance – something akin to the *Monty Python* spam sketch. Londoners, like inhabitants of most major cities around the world, are offered generous helping of spam, spam, spam and more spam.

Roger Michell, director of *Notting Hill*, put it a bit more eloquently in an article in the *Guardian* whose headline read *Let's make movies about our own life and times.* "People don't necessarily like McDonald's more than anything else they eat, but if that's what's on the high street and almost thrust down their throats, it is hard to go to the wholefood restaurant round the corner".

Easy Cinema

Perhaps the most remarkable move in the cinema industry over the past year was the audacious attempt by Stelios Haji-Ioannou, founder of easyJet, to establish a similar no frills concept in British cinema in the form of Easy Cinema. Claiming that Hollywood studios set prices too high, Easy Cinema was offering tickets online priced as low as 20p if booked early (with prices rising as screening time nears). Not surprisingly, the Hollywood majors were not impressed and withheld their films from the scheme. Nevertheless, Easy Cinema secured four titles from Pathé for the opening of its first cinema in Milton Keynes in May 2003. The four films were *Bulletproof Monk*, *Evelyn*, *The Heart Of Me* and *L'Homme Du Train* – and not a hint of popcorn.

It is hard to see how Easy Cinema will be able to sustain itself (particularly without the support of distributors), but then again if it does succeed then perhaps there may be a glimmer of hope for all those low-budget British movies that nobody ever sees.

Digital Cinema

The long-heralded digital cinema revolution appears closer now than ever before. The ability to screen digital data from optical discs or satellite feeds, offers for some the mouth-watering prospect of entertainment venues capable of showing films on demand, not to mention live events. The savings in terms of the cost of prints and transportation will be phenomenal. For those able to dominate the digital cinema market the advantages are obvious – digital films won't suffer from the wear and tear problems encountered by 35mm prints that have been passed in and out of sprockets around the UK's cinema circuits.

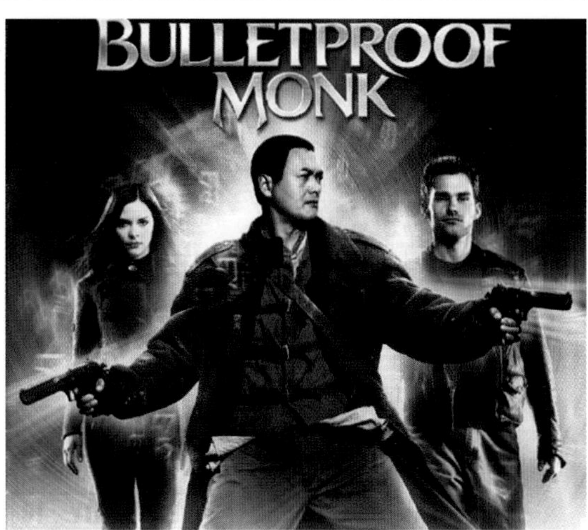

Bulletproof Monk was screened at Easy Cinema, Milton Keynes

This news will not please film purists who will always believe that film should be shown in its original format and are likely to shake their heads at digital restorations of classic films. It also poses a problem for the UK exhibition sector. Those with money will no doubt invest in digital cinema technology, while those without will risk the potentially disastrous situation of having to close down, as 35mm prints for blockbuster films gradually become phased out. The question is: how long will it take before digital becomes the industry standard?

Whether Digital Cinema will widen the diversity of distribution and provide more choice remains to be seen. In theory digital distribution will also help smaller, niche films escape the burden of print costs, but whether there will be an arthouse sector to show them is another matter.

COMMUNICATIONS ACT

While the microscopes were peering at the UK film industry a similar soul-searching scrutiny was occurring in relation to the UK broadcasting industry. On 17 July 2003, after over three-and-a-half years' worth of deliberation, the Communications Act finally became law. The new media regulator Ofcom will take up its powers on 29 December 2003.

Will Ofcom, the broadcast regulator, have too much power?

Before the Bill became law there was extensive consultation through Lord Puttnam's joint scrutiny committee which resulted in vigorous lobbying and, as a result, a plethora of amendments (120 out of 146) were accepted.

The delicate issue of cross-media ownership which aimed to prevent a media group with more than 20 per cent of the market from owning terrestrial TV stations were relaxed but not abolished. The fear was that media giants such as Robert Murdoch's News Corporation, which owns four national newspaper titles, could take Channel Five, thereby acquiring too much power.

To safeguard against this, a 'plurality' test was introduced. In the event of a proposed merger which raises "specified public interest concern in relation to media plurality", the Secretary of State for Trade and Industry can call upon media regulator Ofcom to scrutinise the proposed merger and report upon whether it has public interest implications. If Ofcom decides that the new company would have too much power across all media sectors, it can recommend that the merger be blocked.

The move was designed to prevent the spectre of a media monopoly in the hands of a media mogul. However, it does not prevent the same media moguls from testing the water. It will be interesting to see how soon the plurality test is taken and how watertight it proves to be.
The new act also attempted to support the country's independent television producers with the creation of codes of practice regulating terms of trade between public service broadcasters and independent producers. In essence, the intellectual property rights would stay with the producer, which would in theory give them a stronger position when negotiating deals and give them a much bigger share of revenue.

Ofcom

The formation of Ofcom from the bones of the Independent Television Commission (ITC), the Broadcasting Standards Commission (BSC), the Radio Authority and Oftel, has provoked nervousness from some in the industry who fear that a single body will gain too much power. Its scope for overseeing the entire media and telecoms landscape including the public service responsibilities of broadcasters, taste and decency issues and competition questions is wide ranging.

Its first task will be a review of public service broadcasting, which will inform the debate for the renewal of the BBC's royal charter. In theory Ofcom has the power to take broadcasters to task for not fulfilling their public service remits but as yet it is unclear how sharp Ofcom's regulatory teeth will be. The Government has said that Ofcom will carry out its duties with a light touch. Perhaps its real role is to bark rather than bite. It will be interesting to see how Ofcom copes with the combined complaints that would normally have been fielded by the ITC, BSC and Oftel.

Ant and Dec prepare for a quiet night in front of the Telly

TELEVISION

While Ofcom will open up the debate about public service remits and what the BBC is for, many might like to broaden the question and ask what has happened to the quality of television programmes over the last decade. A report by the outgoing ITC revealed that nearly half of Britain's viewers think the quality of TV programmes is getting worse rather than better. Only 12 per cent of people interviewed thought that the quality of British television was improving. Just under half those questioned said there were too many repeats, while nearly one in five bemoaned the lack of quality on television. Nearly one in five said there was 'not enough quality' on television, up from 6 per cent two years ago.

In 2003 Reality TV shows still dominated prime time slots with karaoke programmes like *Fame Academy* and *Pop Idol* generating unworthy levels of mass adulation for their starry-eyed contestants. New dramas and sitcoms were largely bypassed in favour of feature films and repeats and the best cutting edge TV seemed to come from America. The TV audience was also exposed to the conflict in Iraq where suddenly, instead of a diet of TV murder mysteries, real death and carnage was reported, or not, by embedded reporters who travelled with coalition troops. The ramifications of the standards of reporting and attacks on the integrity of news sources continue today. There was an Orwellian irony to all this, while *Big Brother 4* was limping off the screens to hysterical applause, the Government was slamming the BBC over its reporting on the dossier on Iraq.

The BBC

After a couple of years of growth and triumph the BBC is about to face its most challenging time when its charter comes up for renewal in 2006. Some have urged the Government to review the whole concept of public service broadcasting and are baying for the licence fee to be abolished. The argument follows that, with the offshoots of its digital and online services, the BBC has been given a licence to operate commercially. Indeed, the BBC's annual report showed that for the first time in 10 years, each of the corporation's five commercial businesses reported a profit.

Ofcom has been assigned the task of looking at the public service remit of the BBC and others, and this will be followed by the charter renewal review. The two leading issues that are likely to dominate proceedings are to do with the accountability of the BBC and the exact nature of public service broadcasting.

The BBC's public service remit will be scrutinised by Ofcom

All this is taking place against a backdrop of suscpicion and mistrust, with the Government on the one hand appearing to rein in some of the BBC's power, while on the other hand the BBC is stubbornly insisting that it remains independent. The arguments in favour of public service broadcasting were emphasised during the Iraq crisis when the world media could assess its own standards. While American channels like Fox News, CBS, ABC and NBC appeared muzzled by economic and political factors, the BBC was praised for its objectivity – its charter states that BBC News must aim to reflect every significant strand of opinion in the UK. Ironically, any complaints about anti-war bias were also dispelled when an analysis by Cardiff University on reporting showed that the corporation was more reliant than any of its UK counterparts on Government and military sources. Nevertheless, many fear that abolishing the notion of public service broadcasting would be the slippery slope to broadcasters being in the pockets of huge multinational companies.

In the meantime, the BBC was consolidating its operations. As might have been expected the BBC's two new digital channels, BBC3 (the channel aimed at Twentysomethings launched in February 2003) and BBC4 (the arts channel) have made slow and unimpressive starts. Many thought that there was no need for the creation of BBC3, as viewers in their 20s and 30s were already over-catered for on other channels.

ITV1 made some big scale literary adaptations like Dr Zhivago

BBC4 has had a particularly tough time, leading some commentators to suggest that the TV public really do like mind-numbing game shows and soaps after all. The channel's target audience, those interested in arts and culture, are more likely to hold the opinion that there is nothing worth watching on television in the first place. It is more likely that this is merely a bedding-in period for all digital channels. Once audience levels rise significantly, so too will expectations about audience share.

ITV

ITV suffered another torrid year, losing out comprehensively to the BBC in the ratings battles and seeming unsure of its own programme strategy. An example of this was moving the *Fortysomething* comedy drama from a prime time Sunday slot to a late night Saturday evening slot and replacing it with a repeat of *Midsomer Murders*. Bold attempts at tackling literary adaptations in the shape of *Sons and Lovers* and *Dr Zhivago* have relied too heavily on sexing-up the action which made some hanker for costume dramas of the past. However, it appears that ITV has completely lost its nerve in the sitcom department when you would be hard pressed to name the titles of the shows currently on offer. There is little prime time laughter to be had on ITV – unless you count camcorder calamity shows.

ITV's successes came in the form of *Pop Idol, Popstars: The Rivals* which created Girls Aloud, and *I'm a Celebrity Get Me Out of Here!* which made an unexpected star of ex-cricketer Phil Tufnell and provided nice cameos for Ant and Dec to enhance their TV reputations. As the second series of *Pop Idol* hits the screens in the summer of 2003 executives will be hoping that the public's appetite for manufactured pop stars has not become satiated.

ITV in particular has suffered over recent years as niche channels have eaten into its overall share of viewing. This year the combined viewing share of digital channels overtook ITV's share for the first time.

The proposed merger between Carlton and Granada has been stalled over the issue of how advertising rates are determined. Rival broadcasters Channel 4, Five and BskyB believe a single ITV could abuse its control over the UK's television advertising market since its share would amount to over 50 per cent. As a result Carlton and Granada had an option of selling their sales houses, which both were loath to do. The alternative option is that Channel 4, Five and BskyB would combine their sales operations, in effect creating a duopoly in airtime sales. This thorny issue was being mulled over by the Competition Commission, much to the frustration of Carlton and Granada.

Big Brother 4 struggled to capture the public's imagination

Channel 4

While *Big Brother* is clearly the flagship programme of the channel, under chief executive Mark Thompson, the channel has gained audiences by demoting *Brookside* to a Saturday afternoon slot and putting in its place a series of quirky property and lifestyle programmes of which *How Clean is Your House?* became an unexpected cult hit. Other programmes included *Grand Designs* and *Relocation, Relocation*. Channel 4 could also point to comedy drama *Teachers*, *Smack the Pony* and *Phoenix Nights* on its list of successes.

There were mixed fortunes in its entertainment department. Graham Norton still had award-winning pulling power but executives must have been concerned at the performance of *Big Brother 4* and *Boys and Girls*.

While the *Big Brother 4* final drew in a peak audience of 7.4 million viewers it fell some 2 million short of last year's final. For the first time since Channel 4 started showing *Big Brother* three years ago, the final attracted fewer viewers than the debut show. Channel 4 is committed to at least two more series of Big Brother but whether the format endures beyond that remains to be seen.

At least *Big Brother 4* was able to claim a dedicated audience whereas *Boys and Girls* merely succeeded in making *Big Brother 4* look intelligent.

Five

It is predicted that Five (or Channel 5 for those who missed the rebranding exercise) will face its hardest year in 2004. Despite valiant attempts to smarten up the quality of its programmes, investing in *Home and Away*, and pulling out a range of watchable movies, commentators remain sceptical about the channels ability to increase its market share.

After year on year rises in audience share many feel that Five has reached its plateau. The problem for Five is that it is a channel which joined the terrestrial table at a time when all of its competitors were eyeing up the digital television trolley offering the delights of ITV2, E4, and an array of BBC channels.

Rather like Channel 4 last year, Five has a new chief executive, Jane Lighting, who has been entrusted with steering the channel away from potentially choppy waters ahead. The Communications Act may have made Five less likely to be bought up by a big media giant due to the 'plurality' clause but, nevertheless the channel may seek a partnership with a digital ally.

Freeview

After the trauma of OnDigital and ITV Digital Freeview, the digital television service run by the BBC, in conjunction with transmission business Crown Castle and BSkyB, launched in October 2002, announced in July 2003 that it had almost doubled its digital terrestrial TV audience.

Digital viewing now occurs in over 40 per cent of homes in the UK. The attraction is that people just pay a one-off fee and then receive 30 digital channels through an existing aerial without having to pay a subscription. Research has shown that 75 per cent of Freeview customers are over the age of 35 and 40 per cent are over the age of 55. The Government will be pleased with the uptake since it puts their plans to switch off the analogue signal, back on track. Indeed, Culture Secretary Tessa Jowell, hinted that the 2006 and 2010 deadlines are achieveable. It is likely that by the end of 2003 the total number of multichannel TV viewers will pass the 50 per cent mark.

Surprisingly, the growth of Freeview does not appear to be harming the progress of SkyDigital, which has taken its total of paying customers to around the 6.5 million mark in 2003. At the bottom of the pile lie cable operators Telewest and NTL, who are expected to merge finally in 2004. Both companies have had to overcome debts and falling subscriber numbers, as well as the emergence of Freeview.

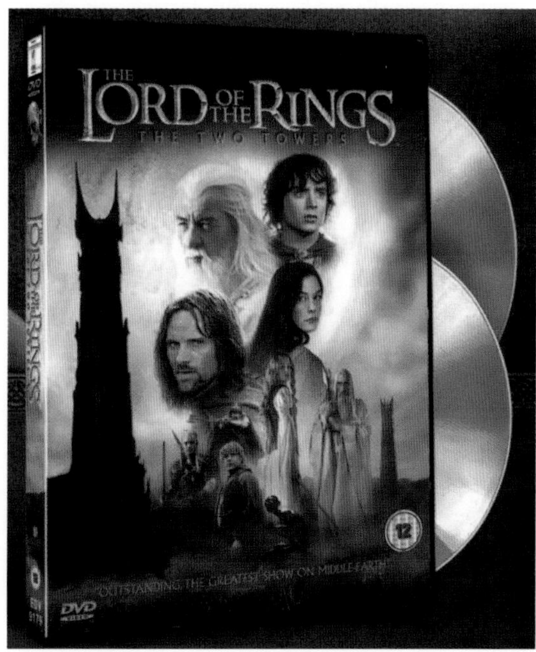

DVD sales experienced an un precedented boom

DVD

In February, 2003 the British Video Association (BVA) reported that for the first time in its history the British video industry had overtaken the music business in terms of retail sales.

The phenomenal rise of DVD, witnessed sales increase by 111 per cent last year. As well as blockbuster movies such as *Harry Potter* and *Lord of the Rings*, cult TV hits like *The Office* and *Buffy the Vampire Slayer* and even music releases such as Led Zepplin's 1972 concert, have helped drive DVD into the leading position in home entertainment.

In fact, so strong has the perfomance of DVD been, coupled with the growth of MP3 files and online music, that some are even suggesting that the days of the music CD are numbered. Remarkably, the VHS format has yet to wither away with as many as 2.2 million *Harry Potter* VHS videos making their way to grateful homes around the country.

By 2006, *Screen Digest* predicts that the DVD explosion will have increased by a further 150 per cent. It is will be interesting to see whether this growth will be arrested with the development of broadband technology. At present, downloading feature films is still likely to take hours rather than minutes.

Mass distraction

It was over two years ago when a leaked memo from Jo Moore, then political adviser to Stephen Byers, the Transport Secretary, suggested that the Government should take advantage of the world crisis caused by 11 September attacks on America to bury any controversial news. In the context of the horrific events of that day the memo was entirely inappropriate, although others would argue that she was just doing her job.

Manipulating the public is what the media industries seem increasingly good at. Over the last year fear has dominated the media agenda, from the banal issue of trading in your mobile phone so as not to embarrass yourself, to the sinister threat posed by terrorist groups and weapons of mass destruction. These threats are hardly new: countries around the world have always been threatened by terrorist groups and there have always been weapons of one sort or another, but the difference is how much news coverage is devoted to them. The threat of global terrorism has gone hand in hand with the advances in technology which have given us the globalisation of the world's media, whether it be the BBC Worldwide, CNN or Al-Jazeera.

In this way the media has ensured that we live in a state of perpetual panic. A section in Michael Moore's Oscar - winning *Bowling For Columbine* shows a sequence of news reports which illustrate graphically how easy it is to create an atmosphere of fear and paranoia. In London, *Evening Standard* news hoardings must break some sort of record for their overuse of the words 'crisis', 'chaos' or 'misery'. None of this serves to make people feel better about their lives but merely makes us all feel anxious. It is a form of control.

The danger with all this spin-doctoring, whether it is to hype the next blockbuster, promote the next pop idol, or, on a more serious level, report from a war-torn area, is that sooner or later the public will become immune to the information and cease to believe what they are told.

1 Number and Value of UK Films 1981–2002

Year	Titles produced	Current prices (£m)	Production cost (£m) (2003 prices*)
1981	24	61.2	146.4
1982	40	141.1	308.1
1983	51	251.1	529.9
1984	53	270.4	506.6
1985	54	269.4	510.8
1986	41	165.8	304.1
1987	55	195.3	343.2
1988	48	175.2	296.4
1989	30	104.7	163.2
1990	60	217.4	305.9
1991	59	243.2	321.6
1992	47	184.9	235.0
1993	67	224.1	284.8
1994	84	455.2	566.6
1995	78	402.4	497.0
1996	128	741.4	885.1
1997	116	562.8	656.3
1998	88	509.3	574.7
1999	100	549.2	601.3
2000	98	804.3	867.8
2001	96	592.3	620.4
2002	105	536.7**	618.5**

UK films are defined here as films produced in the UK or with a UK financial involvement, they include majority and minority co-productions

* based on calendar year inflation figure of 2.9 per cent

** Figure includes estimated budgets

Source: Screen Finance/bfi

Die Another Day was produced and released in the same year

Film Production

In 2002 film production in the UK was bolstered considerably by the presence of *Die Another Day* and *Tomb Raider 2*. Although more films were produced, the total value of films dropped from £592.3m in 2001 to approximately £536.7m in 2002 (Table 1). The average budget of all UK films fell from £6m to around £5m. However, these figures would have been greater had disputes on the set of the third *Harry Potter* film not meant that the film production would be delayed until early in 2003.

Indeed, film studios such as Pinewood and Shepperton which were kept busy during 2002 look likely to stay that way with a handful of potential blockbusters such as *Troy* and *Thunderbirds* going into production in 2003. Pure economics have persuaded US filmmakers to cast their nets further then their traditional film studios with New Zealand, the Czech Republic and Romania offering attractive alternatives. Within this context the UK film production sector has experienced a couple of solid years.

An interesting development over the past couple of years has been the reluctance of some UK producers to reveal their budgetary information for publication. In previous years the Handbook has relied on information supplied by *Screen Finance* and plugged the gaps by going directly to the producers. While the gates haven't exactly slammed shut on the information, the Handbook tables now have occasional gaps. As a result it has become harder to analyse the proportional extent of budgets in the UK film production industry on a film by film basis.

Unfortunately, the majority of UK films are destined for a miserable existence. In terms of 2002 UK productions, it is probable that over half of the films will remain unreleased a year after production (Table 6). If recent trends continue then less than a quarter of UK films will receive a wide release (which constitutes opening on 30 screens or more). It is interesting to consider that in 1984 there were only 53 films made in the UK. However, 50 per cent of those films received a wide release which was around 26 films – roughly the same number that made the grade in 2002.

As a rule of thumb only half a dozen will make any real box office impact, with possibly another handful performing reasonably well. This news isn't exactly new but does reflect how difficult it is for UK film productions to crack the global market.

UK Film Production 2002 - Category A

Feature films where the cultural and financial impetus is from the UK and where the majority of personnel are British.

Title	Production company(ies)	Production cost (£m)
AKA	Third Rock/UK Film Council/Bard Entertainments	n/a*
American Cousins	Little Wing Films/Scottish Screen/Glasgow Film Fund	3.00
Ashes and Sand	Open Road Films	3.50
Bitter Sweet	West Coast Productions	n/a*
Blackball	Midfield Films/Inside Track	4.00
Bright Young Things	Revolution Films/Doubting Hall/Film Consortium/Vision View	7.60
The Bone Hunter	Palm Tree Productions	2.70
The Calcium Kid	WT2	4.00
Cheeky	Xingu Films	3.90
Cloud Cuckoo Land	Airborne Pictures/EIS	1.50
Day of the Sirens	Imaginary Films	n/a*
Devil's Gate	Alchemist Films/Shetland Island UK Film Council	2.00
The Day I Will Never Forget	Channel 4	n/a*
Fallen Angels	Avrio Filmworks	n/a*
Fakers	Faking It Prods/Klepowski and Bee/Janes Films	1.70
Finding Fortune	Palm Tree Productions	1.50
The Football Factory	Vertigo Films/Matrix Film Finance	0.50
Gladiatress	Mission Pictures/Stock Productions	3.50
In This World	Revolution Films/The Film Consortium/BBC Films/UK Film Council	1.30
Kiss of Life	Wild Horses/BBC Films/UK Film Council/Baker St.Media	2.00
The Last Horror Movie	Prolific Films	1.00
LD50	Four Horsemen Films/Random Harvest/Matrix Film Finance	5.20
Lighthouse Hill	Carnaby Films/EIS	2.40
Live Forever	Passion Pictures	n/a*
Living in Hope	Fluidity Films	n/a*
Mandancin	Festival Films/1a Productions/Saltire Films	n/a*
The Mother	Free Range Films/BBC Films	2.00
Neil's Party	Twothreefive	1.20
Nine Lives	A+A Films	2.00
Oh Marbella	VF Versatile Film	n/a*
One for the Road	One for the Road Films/FilmFour/UK Film Council/East Midlands Media Iniative	0.69
The Prodigal	Tiger Films/Fusion Tristar	1.30
Pure	Little Wing Films/Kudos Productions	3.00
16 Years of Alcohol	Tartan Films/Scottish Screen	0.60
Solid Air	Elemental Films/Scottish Screen/Glasgow Film Office	0.90
Suzie Gold	Greenwolf Films/UK Film Council/Inside Track/Sky Movies/Isle of Man Film Commission	3.50
Sylvia	Ruby Films/BBC Films/UK Film Council	8.00
Team One	Imaginary Films 2000	0.90
This Little Life	Common Features Ltd, BBC Films, UK Film Council, Yorkshire Media Production Agency, Northern Production Fund	3.50
To Kill a King	Natural Nylon/VisionView	14.00
Touching the Void	FilmFour/Darlow Smithson/UK Film Council/PBS	n/a*
Wanted	Footprint Films	0.45
Wondrous Oblivion	Kuhn and Co/Apt Films	3.50
Young Adam	Recorded Picture Company/UK Film Council/Scottish Screen	4.50

TOTAL NUMBER OF FILMS **44**
APPROXIMATE TOTAL COST **£111.34m**
APPROXIMATE AVERAGE COST **£2.5m**

* Where budgets are not available an appromiate total has been estimated based on average total of £1m per film.

Source: Screen Finance/Screen International/bfi

UK Film Production 2002 - Category B

Majority UK Co-Productions. Films in which, although there are foreign partners, there is a UK cultural content and a significant amount of British finance and personnel.

Title	Production companies/participating countries	Production cost (£m)
The Actors	Company of Wolves/Film Four/Irish Film Board/Four Provinces Films(Republic of Ireland)	15.00
The Bum's Rush	Hero Films/Scottish Screen/Glasgow Film Office/Motlys(Norway)	2.80
Chaos and Cadavars	Matador Pictures/Zodiac Pictures International(Switzerland)	2.20
Dot the I	Arcane Pictures/Summit Entertainment/Alquima(Spain)	3.00
The Dreamers	Recorded Picture Company/ Penisula Films/Fiction Films (France/Italy)	6.00
Girl with a Pearl Earring	Archer Street Films/UK Film Council/Inside Track/DeLux (Luxembourg)	11.50
Hoover Street Revival	Amoeba Films/Allarts/Ideale Audience (Netherlands/France)	n/a*
The I Inside	RCD Productions/MDP(Germany)	7.00
Loving Glances	Film and Music Entertainment/Yodi (Yugoslavia)	1.00
Luger	Luger the Movie/Stray Dogs Films(Romania)	0.60
The Motorcycle Diaries	FilmFour/Southfork Pictures/Tu Vas Voir (France)	10.00
The Night We Called It a Day	Scala Productions/ Ocean Pictures(Australia)	3.70
Octane	Four Horsemen/DeLux(Luxembourg)	8.00
One Love	Scala Productions/UK Film Council/Baker St. Media Finance/ Exposed Film Productions/Euromax Films (Norway)	1.60
Rivers and Tides	Skyline/Scottish Screen/Scottisn Arts Council/FilmFernsehFondsBayern/Metropolis/ Arte/FilmFonds Berlin-Brandenburg(Germany)	n/a*
S Club Seeing Double	Double Vision Ltd/ 19 Entertainment/ Mediapro (Spain)	n/a*
The Virgin of Liverpool	The Mob Film Company/Senator Entertainment(Germany)	2.00
The Water Giant	Barry Films/MBP(Germany)	12.66

TOTAL NUMBER OF FILMS 18
APPROXIMATE TOTAL COST £94.56m
APPROXIMATE AVERAGE COST £5.25m

* Where budgets are not available an appromiate total has been estimated based on average total of £2.5m per film.

Source: Screen Finance/Screen International/bfi

The advent of digital technology has enabled many first-time filmmakers to make their films. As a result the UK film production sector is flooded with feature films with budgets of £1m or under (Table 2). Nearly half of the films have budgets of £2m or under. The cumulative value of the 15 films with budgets of between £2-£5m works out at £47.08m. This figure is roughly the average cost of a US movie, which, according to the Motion Picture Association of America is $80m (£48m).

At present the UK distribution and exhibition sector is in no position to gamble on releasing these type of films. Low-budget filmmakers are reliant on film festivals in order to promote their work. The advent of digital cinema may be an opportunity in the future for these films. However, in most cases for first-time filmmakers, their first films will also be their last. Those who have worked for free on low-budget films will testify that there is a lot of pain with very little gain.

To Kill a King – big budget for a UK production

UK Film Production 2002 - Category C

Minority UK Co-productions. Foreign (non US) films in which there is a small UK involvement in finance or personnel.

Title	Production company(ies)/participating countries	Production cost (£m)
Absolon	Studio Eight/GFT Entertainment(Canada)	4.50
Baltic Storm	Top Story/Smile Entertainment/IAC Films/Arte/FFA/FBB/Med Filmstudios/ A2 Media/Normedia Fonds (Germany/Denmark/Malta)	3.80
Bl,.m	What's the story/Stalheim (Republic of Ireland)	2.20
The Blue Butterfly	Galafilm Productions/Global Arts (Canada)	1.70
Emile	Meltemi Entertainment/BV International(Norway)	7.00
The Great Goose Caper	Voice Pictures/Les Prod. Colin Neale/Studio Eight/Telefilm Canada (Canada)	3.40
Intermission	Parallel Films/Company of Wolves/UK Film Council/Irish Film Board (Republic of Ireland)	2.50
Jericho Mansions	Spice Factory/Milagro Films/Snowfalls Film(Canada)	3.86
Love's Brother	Great Scott/Sarah Radclyffe Productions(Australia)	n/a?
Luminal	Dreyco Productions/Imago(Italy)	2.00
The Magic Roundabout	bolexbrothers/UK Film Council/Pathe/Sky Movies/Films Action (France)	12.80
Mrs.Ritchie	Nomadic Pictures/Amafi/Visionview (Canada)	n/a*
Piazza of the Five Moons	Soice Factory/Martinelli Productions/Blue Star/Box! Film/Istituto Luce (Italy/Germany)	6.40
The Poet	Maltemi Entertainment/Mediafonds 1/Vienna FilmFund/ Nord Rhine Westfalia(Germany/Austria)	3.15
The Republic of Love	Triptych Media/Dan Films/Film Consortium/UK Film Council/Telefilm Canada (Canada)	2.50
Skaggerak	Umbrella Productions/BBC Films/Scottish Screen/Nimbus Film (Denmark)	3.00
Song for a Raggy Boy	Subotica Ent/Moviefan/Zoma Films/Zentropa/Irish Film Board/ Danish Film Institute (Republic of Ireland/Denmark)	2.40
Swimming Pool	Fidelite Productions/Headforce(France)	3.70
Three Blind Mice	Baker Street Media Finance/Kcraft/Canal +(France)	3.20
The Tulse Luper Suitcase:The Early Years	Kasander Film/Sgrin/DeLux(Netherlands/Luxemburg)	2.21
Underworld	Subterranean Productions/Underworld Productions/ Laurin Productions (Germany/Hungary)	n/a*
Wanted	Studio Eight/GFT Entertainment(Canada)	5.50
Wilbur Wants to Kill Himself	Sigma Films/Scottish Screen/Glasgow Film Fund/Zentropa/ Danish Film Institutr/Nordisk(Denmark)	n/a*
TOTAL NUMBER OF FILMS	**23**	
APPROXIMATE TOTAL COST	**£89.82m**	
APPROXIMATE AVERAGE COST	**£3.9m**	

* Where budgets are not available an appromiate total has been estimated based on average total of £3.5m per film.

Source: Screen Finance/Screen International/bfi

Swimming Pool was released during the record-breaking summer temperatures of 2003

UK Film Production 2002 – Category D

American financed or part-financed films made in the UK. Most titles have a British cultural content.

Title	Production company(ies)	Production cost (£m)
Calendar Girls	Harbour Pictures	8.00
Cold Mountain	Mirage Enterprises	48.00
Die Another Day	Eon Productions/Mandalay Pictures/MGM/UA	62.50
I Am David	Film and General/WaldenMedia	5.00
If Only	Intermedia/Box Films/Outlaw Productions/Lovespell Productions	7.50
I'll Be There	Morgan Creek/Warner Bros	4.00
I'll Sleep When I'm Dead	Will and Co/Revere Pictures	6.00
Johnny English	Working Title/Universal	15.00
Leo	Scala Films/Freewheel International/Joy Films/Vortex International	n/a*
Love Actually	Working Title/Universal	20.00
Masked and Anonymous	Spitfire/Intermedia/BBC Films	3.20
Ned Kelly	Working Title Films/Universal/Endymion Films	20.00
Neverland	Film Colony/Miramax	8.00
Nicholas Nickleby	Cloud Nine Films/Hart Sharp	6.80
Sandmother	Focus Films/Persistence Pictures/Imaginarium/Matrix Film Finance	2.00
Shanghai Knights	Spyglass Entertainment/Touchstone	40.96
Stella Street	Absolutely Productions/Columbia Tristar	0.60
Tomb Raider 2	Paramount	65.00
What a Girl Wants	Dinovi Films/Gaylord Productions/Warner Brothers	13.00

TOTAL NUMBER OF FILMS **19**
APPROXIMATE TOTAL COST **£340m**
APPROXIMATE AVERAGE COST **£17.89m**

* Where budgets are not available an appromiate total has been estimated based on average total of £5m per film.

Source: Screen Finance/Screen International/bfi

Johnny English – typically British?

Types of Release for UK films 1984–2001

Proportion of films with a UK involvement which achieved;

a) Wide release. Opening or playing on 30 or more screens around the country within a year of production

b) Limited release, mainly in art house cinemas or a short West End run within a year of release.

c) Unreleased a year after production

Year	(a)%	(b)%	(c)%
1984	50.00	44.00	6.00
1985	52.80	35.90	11.30
1986	55.80	41.90	2.30
1987	36.00	60.00	4.00
1988	29.50	61.20	9.30
1989	33.30	38.90	27.80
1990	29.40	47.10	23.50
1991	32.20	37.30	30.50
1992	38.30	29.80	31.90
1993	25.40	22.40	52.20
1994	31.00	22.60	46.40
1995	23.10	34.60	42.30
1996	19.00	14.00	67.00
1997	15.50	19.00	65.50
1998	22.70	21.60	55.70
1999	30.00	10.00	60.00
2000	22.50	12.20	65.30
2001	24.50	10.60	64.90

7.5 per cent of 2001 UK film productions were released on 300 screens or more

17.9 per cent of 2001 UK film productions were released on 100 screens or more

40.42 per cent of 2001 UK film productions had received some kind of theatrical release by 1st June 2003

Source: Screen Finance/Nielsen EDI/*bfi*

Love Actually – actually Hugh Grant is also in it

The undeniable truth is that solely UK-funded films are not robust enough to sustain themselves. Once in a while a film such as *East is East* might appear, but these films make it largely by luck rather than design. Indeed, few films are funded out of one country anymore. Any real successes for UK films lie in co-productions (Tables 3, 4, and 5).

In the past the UK's 'arthouse' directors such as Ken Loach, Mike Leigh and Peter Greenaway , whose film *The Tulse Luper Suitcases: Life History in 16 Episodes* was the only UK film in competition at Cannes in 2003, have sought European partners for their funding. The budgets for these films tend to be twice the amount spent on solely UK productions.

The cream of the UK film production industry comes with UK/US co-productions (Table 5). According to research from the UK Film Council, the US accounted for a staggering 98 per cent of inward feature investment in the UK which translates to £230.11m. At the time of writing in August 2003 *Die Another Day*, *Johnny English* and *Tomb Raider 2* had all been released, with *Calendar Girls* not far behind.

In essence here we see what constitutes the half a dozen or so typically successful British UK films of the past few years. *Die Another Day* is a UK franchise film which is guaranteed worldwide success. *Harry Potter* is a home-grown franchise with global appeal made possible by US finance. (There was a time when *Harry Potter* would have been snapped up and serialised by the BBC on Sunday afternoons – rather like *The Borrowers* in the 1990s).

Johnny English follows the tradition of taking a familiar TV personality (in this case Rowan Atkinson) and producing a vehicle film for them. In the past we have seen *Ali G Indahouse, Kevin and Perry Go Large*, and *Bean* (back to Rowan Atkinson). Also coming up in this tradition will be a cluster of films featuring Johnny Vegas, *Gladiatress* featuring the team of *Smack the Pony*, and *Stella Street* which is based on the TV series.

Tomb Raider 2: Cradle of Life (which was filmed at Pinewood Studios) follows hard on the heels of *Resident Evil* as a film, gaining its UK status by being filmed in the UK (as well as being a UK computer game).

Love Actually joins the list of typically British films based purely on the box office pulling power of Hugh Grant. A glance at the top box office UK films of all time will bear witness to the actor's global appeal.

What Happened to 2001 UK Films?

Distribution of 2001 UK productions and foreign films made in the UK up to 1 June 2003. Where approriate the numbers of screens that the film opened on is shown beside the title

Released theatrically in 2002

28 Days Later	318
About a Boy	446
Ali G in da House	396
All or Nothing	55
Anita and Me	226
Before You Go	65
Beginner's Luck	1
Bend it Like Beckham	384
Biggie and Tupac	6
Bloody Sunday	3
Bundy	3
Butterfly Man	3
Charlotte Gray	217
Death Watch	193
Dirty Pretty Things	50
Dog Soldiers	313
Gosford Park	156
Harry Potter and the Chamber of Secrets	524
The Importance of Being Earnest	215
Iris	84
The Magdalene Sisters	31
The Mapmaker	5
The Mean Machine	313
Mike Bassett: England Manager	264
Morvern Callar	17
My Little Eye	255
Nobody Someday	8
Once Upon a Time in the Midlands	74
Resident Evil	264
Sweet Sixteen	66
Thunderpants	356
24 Hour Party People	118
Two Men Went to War	6
The Warrior	19

Released theatrically by 1st June 2003

The Good Thief	20
The Heart of Me	41
Heartlands	31
The Hours	209
I Capture the Castle	76
The Last Great Wilderness	8
Hope Springs (New Cardiff)	303
Revengers Tragedy	7
Spider	19

Awaiting release at 1 June 2003

An Angel For May
And Now Ladies and Gentlemen
Baby Juice Express
Below
Black and White
Bodysong
Bollywood Queen
The Book of Eve
Callas Forever
Carolina
The Case
Conspiracy of Silence
Crust
Death to Smoochy
The Devil's Tattoo
Doctor Sleep
Don't Look Back
The Engagement
The Escapist
The Gathering
The Hawk and Dove
Honour Thy Father
The Intended
It's All About Love
Jimmy Fizz
Married/Unmarried
Mavahlatur (The Seagull's Laughter)
Max – (released 20 June 2003)
Miranda
Moonlight
Mr.In-Between
Napoleon
Never Say Never Mind
Owning Maloney
Plotz with a View
The Principles of Lust
Redemption Road
Reinventing Eddie
The Rocket Post
The Secret Passage
Secrets
Shoreditch
Silent Cry
Simon
South Kensington
$teal
Swept Away
Teenage Kicks
Three Guesses
The Ticking Man
This is Not a Love Song
Tomorrow La Scala!

Titles in paranthesis indicate former title of film

Source: bfi/Nielsen EDI/Screen Finance

Calendar Girls and *Blackball* follow the recent tradition kicked off by *The Full Monty* of quirky British films which are often regional, or reflect cultural diversity (or both in the case of *East is East*).

Finally, *Nicholas Nickleby* doffed its cap to the costume drama tradition exemplified by *Sense and Sensibility*, *Shakespeare in Love* and even *Gosford Park*. However, it should be noted that last year *The Importance of Being Earnest*, despite on paper looking like a sure-fire hit perfomed poorly at the domestic box office.

In effect the preceding list is a marketing executive's demographic delight. In a year where winning formulas were given priority there seems little room for an explosion of edgy, ground-breaking, distinctive UK hits. BFI re-releases over the past couple of years of classics British films such as *Saturday Night and Sunday Morning*, *the Loneliness of The Long Distance Runner*, *If...*, *Kes* and *Get Carter* merely serve as reminders of the type of films Britain was capable of producing alongside the *Carry Ons* and the *Bonds*.

Tomb Raider 2: Cradle of Life, already released in the UK

Nicholas Nickleby an example of UK costume drama

8 Number of UK Feature Films Produced 1912–2002

Year	Films	Year	Films
1912	2	1960	122
1913	18	1961	117
1914	15	1962	114
1915	73	1963	113
1916	107	1964	95
1917	66	1965	93
1918	76	1966	82
1919	122	1967	83
		1968	88
1920	155	1969	92
1921	137		
1922	110	1970	97
1923	68	1971	96
1924	49	1972	104
1925	33	1973	99
1926	33	1974	88
1927	48	1975	81
1928	80	1976	80
1929	81	1977	50
		1978	54
1930	75	1979	61
1931	93		
1932	110	1980	31
1933	115	1981	24
1934	145	1982	40
1935	165	1983	51
1936	192	1984	53
1937	176	1985	54
1938	134	1986	41
1939	84	1987	55
		1988	48
1940	50	1989	30
1941	46		
1942	39	1990	60
1943	47	1991	59
1944	35	1992	47
1945	39	1993	67
1946	41	1994	84
1947	58	1995	78
1948	74	1996	128
1949	101	1997	116
		1998	88
1950	125	1999	100
1951	114	2000	98
1952	117	2001	96
1953	138	2002	105
1954	150		
1955	110		
1956	108		
1957	138		
1958	121		
1959	122		

Source: Screen Digest/Screen Finance/bfi

National Lottery
by Phil Wickham

The most contentious area of debate in the British film industry in the last decade has been over the role of the State. In 2003 this subject remains as problematic as ever. Commentators share little consensus on the matter and fail to agree on basic principles such as whether the Government should offer more financial support to the film industry or whether such subsidy is an inappropriate use of our hard earned taxes, let alone on what shape such funding from Government should take.

At the end of the 1980s funding was feeble indeed. The old Eady levy, a complex arrangement returning ticket money to producers, was abolished in the Films Act of 1985. The only direct national subsidies in place were either through a private company set up under the act, British Screen Finance, assisting mainly in medium budget pictures or the British Film Institute's Production Board. The financial support to the National Film and TV School (still maintained) performed a similar role in realising new talent, from Terence Davies to their latest star alumus, Lynne Ramsey. Similarly, the regional funds that Ramsey was able to take advantage of in making her first short through Scottish Screen have given small amounts of money for very low-budget filmmaking. However, to make bigger projects the indirect funding that came through subsidised TV stations like Channel 4 was the only realistic option for many producers to obtain funds in the early 1990s.

Cultural subsidy was thought by many to be against the principles of the then Thatcher Government. However, various film dignitaries (including Richard Attenborough and David Puttnam) were called to a seminar at Downing Street on 15th June 1990. The one concrete achievement was the formation of the British Film Commission (now part of the UK Film Council) to encourage foreign investment into UK facilities – a strategy that continues to this day and has had some success in attracting overseas spend and ensuring a co-ordinated service for foreign film shoots in Britain. There were also plans to increase opportunities for co-production but the Government resisted entry into the EC's Eurimages programme, much to the chagrin of producers.

Britain's approach to film funding lies somewhere in the middle of the range of possibilities adopted over the world by Governments. Those who believe in production funding from the state at all have tended to fall into two camps. The first believe that money should come through direct grants to particular productions, or as became more fashionable later in the decade, to a slate of productions that could build up towards a sustainable industry. The second school of thought has considered tax to be the most effective instrument of change, particularly write-offs on production costs. At various times the powers that be have listened to the tax arguments and provided legislative backing for investors – notably in Section 48 Finance (No.2) Act of 1997. However, fears of abuse by crafty producers has led to a pattern of useful loopholes opening only to be swiftly closed again. Non-film specific breaks like the Enterprise Investment Scheme and the Business Expansion Scheme have also been used by filmmakers at different times.

The direct grant idea in various forms has developed into the fairly complex funding landscape that faces us in 2003, which by its nature seems to be in a process of constant change and refinement. The motor for this system proved to be the establishment of the National Lottery in 1994, with its promise of bounty for deserving causes. Film productions were taken to be, in effect, the capital projects that lottery rules dictated money had to be put towards. The Arts Councils of the home nations were entrusted with the allocation of monies and from 1995 started to grant awards. The underwhelming results of the first couple of years of this led people to conclude that what was lacking was any kind of cohesion.

One of the first acts of the new Labour government after their election in May 1997 was to announce at the Cannes Film Festival that much of the lottery grants would now go through three new film franchises. Although nominally overseen by the Arts Council of England these three companies - DNA Films, The Film Consortium and Pathé Pictures – would nurture a slate of films from development to screen. The idea was that these conglomerates of various producers would come to resemble mini-studios, working towards that all-important critical mass that would allow good material to reach an audience through some sort of sustainable structure. Needless to say this was easier said than done.

The Labour Government's cinema working group published a strategy document on the industry called *A Bigger Picture* in March 1998, replete with prodigious action plans full of good intentions about all-industry contributory funds and greater training support. The Department of Culture, Media and Sport (as the overseeing Whitehall department was now known) picked up on *A Bigger Picture's* vague call for 'sustainable industry structures' and set up a rationalised film body incorporating the myriad of film organisations under one direct controlling hand. This body became the Film Council, officially launched in October 1999 and active from January 2000. In May 2003 it was renamed the UK Film Council.

The main function of the UK Film Council is to build up structures to enable a cohesive film industry to take shape. They have attempted to do this through setting up a trio of funds – the big budget Premiere Fund, the New Cinema Fund for edgier, less mainstream work and a Development Fund.

After nearly three years they can claim some success. In 2002 *Gosford Park*, *Bend it Like Beckham* and *Mike Bassett: England Manager*, all proved to be box office hits and films like *Morvern Callar* won critical plaudits. In November 2002 there was also the irony of a fully-fledged hit from the much-criticised lottery franchises, DNA Films' *28 Days Later* reaching number one at the box office just as the end of their contracts hove into view.

The issue of State funding gets caught in the same cleft stick every time. What kind of films should be funded? If you fund films that large numbers of people wish to see and that will do well at the box office there may be some return to the exchequer (and ultimately the taxpayer) but if they are going to make money wouldn't the industry make them anyway?

Alternatively the State could support filmmaking that would not otherwise be funded by a market driven industry, as indeed the BFI Production Board did do for many years. However, the problem here is that a large number of people end up contributing their money to work that is often not to their liking. This perhaps makes for a better economic and cultural argument but there is an understandable political sensitivity to the suggestion that the earnings of the masses should keep the loft- dwellers of Shoreditch in clover. Until we resolve these philosophical dilemmas about the State funding of film the controversy will keep on raging.

Edited extracts on Government funding taken from Producing The Goods? UK Film Production Since 1991. Produced by bfi Information Services. Reproduced by kind permission

9

Top 25 All-time Lottery Funded List by UK Box Office

	Title	Award (£m)	Budget (£m)	Box Office (£)
1	Billy Elliot	0.85	2.83	18,230,000
2	Gosford Park	2.00	13.50	12,259,248
3	Bend it Like Beckham	0.95	2.70	11,551,538
4	28 Days Later	3.23	10.40	6,243,656
5	Shooting Fish	0.98	2.90	4,020,000
6	The 51st State	2.00	16.34	3,789,865
7	This Year's Love	0.75	2.75	3,600,636
8	Mike Bassett: England Manager	1.20	3.50	3,568,492
9	The Importance of Being Earnest	1.32	10.50	3,519,574
10	The Parole Officer	2.00	5.99	3,283,870
11	An Ideal Husband	1.00	6.50	2,893,170
12	Plunkett and MacLeane	0.95	9.30	2,779,315
13	The Hole	1.50	4.16	2,302,126
14	Thunderpants	2.05	5.00	1,969,798
15	Anita and Me	0.68	2.98	1,848,620
16	Long Time Dead	1.00	3.27	1,774,552
17	Land Girls	1.50	5.50	1,573,783
18	A Christmas Carol-The Movie	1.18	6.85	1,412,399
19	Topsy Turvy	2.00	13.50	1,163,994
20	Hilary and Jackie	0.95	4.90	1,040,788
21	24 Hour Party People	2.00	4.20	1,035,114
22	My Name is Joe	0.50	2.50	949,228
23	Still Crazy	1.89	7.00	933,574
24	Hideous Kinky	1.00	2.00	793,538
25	Mansfield Park	1.00	6.46	566,450

Figures as of 7 March 2003

Source: Nielsen EDI/Screen Finance/bfi/RSU analysis

Funding of Film Productions by National Lottery Awards 2002/03

Development Awards

Title	Award (£)
Above The Clouds	45,000
Being Me	6,500
Between the Frames	32,000
Black Ice	34,500
Bob's Ark	10,000
Bomber	71,500
Boney & Betsy	10,000
Box of Delights	69,833
Canteen Culture	44,750
The Chosen	24,750
China To Me	15,500
Crime of the Century	9,000
The Dead Wait	4,500
Devils Assassin	16,500
DJ Plum	36,000
The Dope Priest	5,500
Du Quesne's Boys	23,800
Dust - Cloud 9	8,500
Eustace Diamonds	31,433
Fever	3,480
Friends Forever	24,500
Girls at War	30,210
Godparents	49,500
Gods of War	16,000
Hendrix	94,000
Hijra	16,000
Untitled Hunter/Hunsinger	5,000
Ideal World	58,137
In Every Dream Home	27,600
Kiss It	13,265
The Liar, The Bitch...	8,000
Lifesaving aka Adult Behaviour	6,000
Man and the Mysteries...	27,430
Mapping the Edge	67,000
Memoirs of a Geezer	13,600
Mistress of Spices	36,583
Mrs Darwin	38,583
Mrs Radcliffe's Revolution	70,000
Nero	3,000
Newlyn Project	4,000
Northern F&M Script Devlpt	25,000
The Night Train	9,349
One Fine Day....	12,600
One Love	31,380
Patrick Robertson	27,000
The Prince of Dalston	8,250
Peacock Manifesto	69,750
Rent-a-Wife	5,000
Revolving Doors	74,000
Rose of Tralee	13,500
Run	17,857
Sex Lives of the Potato Men	42,150
So What 12,250	
Steerwood	24,500
Swim to America	1,620
Tashkent Girls	16,000
These Things Stay	1,395
The Third Day	18,250
Ugly Streakers	18,750
Urban Legends	2,500
VIY	19,000
Waterloo Sunset	16,869
The Witchfinder General	91,000
Witch	500
You Don't Know My Kids	27,000
Young Santa	13,395

Development Slate Deal

Shona Development	44,200
Tall Stories	50,000
CHX Development	60,000
Gabriel Films	66,000
Autonomous	216,000
Bend It Films	115,000
Company Films	100,000
Ecosse	250,000
Fox Philips Devpt	120,000
Fragile Films	400,000
Gruber Development	200,000
Kuhn 250,000	
Littlebird	150,000
Mission Pictures	250,000
New Steps/Scifi	94,000
October Films	75,000
Passion Pictures	100,000
Recorded Pictures	300,000
Ruby Films	170,000
Tigerlily	73,750

New Cinema - Features

AKA	101,250
Blind Flight	450,000
Entering Blue Zone	241,000
Helen of Peckham	510,000
Intermission	570,000
Live Forever	202,249
Noi the Albino	90,000
One for the Road	240,000
One Love	899,827
Touching the Void	335,000

New Cinema - Other

A Way of Life	10,000
The Carnal Artist	20,000
Cinema Extreme	62,500
A Changed Man	25,000
Championship	33,060
God's Tax	30,440
Home Movie	9,999
List Cubed	4,500
Love me or leave me alone	25,000
The Most Beautiful Man...	30,440
Purifiers	10,000
Signal to Noise	10,000
Sportsman of the Century	10,000
Stones in his Pockets	10,000

New Cinema Digital Shorts

LFVDA	40,000
Moving Image	40,000
Northern F&M	40,000
South West Film	40,000
Lighthouse	44,000
Screen West Mid.	44,000
Shine Comedy Shorts	75,000
Screen East	84,000
Sgrin	100,000
Mayavision Shorts Completion	30,914
Viral Shorts	27,500

Premiere

Code 46	1,565,063
L'Homme du Train	500,000
Sex Lives of the Potato Men	1,766,222
Sylvia	2,460,000
Valiant	2,580,645

The Film Consortium

24 Hour Party People	500,000 (P&A)
Bright Young Things	3,000,000
Bugs	1,000,000
Truth (Country of My Skull)	2,425,000
Dust	32,500 (P&A)
Republic of Love	1,022,222
In this World	12,804 (Post Production)
The Best Man	23,000 (Development)
The Other Half	27,000 (Development)
An Instant in the Wind	9,615 (Development)
How to rob banks without violence	17,500 (Development)

Pathe Pictures Ltd

Thunderpants	53,824 (Post Production)
Suzie Gold	510,000
Natural History	900,000
Girl With A Pearl Earring	2,000,000
Churchill, the Hollywood Years	1,100,000
The Mushroom Prince	4,650 (Development)
A Romantic Comedy about Divorce	100,000 (Development)
The Seven Fires of Mademoiselles	100,000 (Development)
A Semester Abroad	34,250 (Development)
The Blitz	100,000 (Development)
Tunnel Vision	36,500 (Development)
Untitled - Bollywood	41,500 (Development)
With Prejudice	46,530
Development	

DNA

28 Days Later 225,000	Post Production

Films

L'Amour Fou	15,500
The Anarchists	15,828
Blind Flight	18,750
Blood Relative	5,500
Boney and Betsy	10,000
Braids, Twists and Tales	50,000
By the Shore	27,500
Canteen Culture	36,500
Carol	10,000
Carrion	32,250
China to Me	15,500
Chocolate Vanilla	15,525
The Chosen	4,750
Comes the Time	19,163
Crime of the Century	9,000
Cross Your Heart	12,650
The Dead Wait	6,500
The Devil's Assassin	33,500
DJ Plumm	36,000
The Dope Priest	26,000
The Emperor's Babe	5,250
Family Entertainment	5,600
Godparents	14,000
Gods of War	24,000
Grand Ambition	45,721
The Hangman's Apprentice	32,700
Holy Land	24,420
Hostage 2 Fortune	7,500
In Every Dream House	27,600
Julia	75,000
Just the Two of Us	33,000
A Kind of Warfare	28,000
Kisses After Dark	65,000
The Last Man	14,750
Mapping the Edge	57,500
Memoirs of a Geezer	18,000
The Monday Club	20,000
One Fine Day in the Middle of the Night	35,500
Panic Beach	7,850
Patrick Robertson: A Tale of Adventure	26,000
The Prince of Dalston	8,250
The Revolving Door	10,000
The Rivals	2,500
The Rose Grower	85,000

Salsa Con Fusion	11,500
Sensation	23,315
Smokescreen	45,000
Straight to Video	20,000
Straightheads	8,500
Thanksgiving	21,950
These Things Stay	6,000
The Third Day	13,500
This is Not a Love Song	8,383
Timbuktu	3,750
Ultramaroon	4,000
Unknown Rider	1,000
Untitled Black Comedy	5,000
Urban Legends	2,500
VIY	10,000
Wooden Camera	12,000

LOTTERY FILM FRANCHISES

DNA FILMS

28 Days Later 3,000,000
(Total Budget 6,000,000)
Heartlands 1.430,000
(Total Budget 2,800,000)

THE FILM CONSORTIUM

Production

Dr.Sleep 1,375,000
(Total Budget 4,900,000)
The Intended 1,150,000
(Total Budget 3,000,000)

Post-Production/p+a Costs

A Christmas Carol	425,000
Dust	59,410
Gabriel and Me	101,243
Large	80,000
Room to Rent	80,000
24 Hour Party People	247,842

Development

Charlie Noads RIP	11,795
Dead Souls	6,000
Dr.Sleep	8,500
Fourth Wall	15,000
Innocence	16,750
Shame	10,000

PATHÉ PICTURES

Production

Max 1,971,830
(Total Budget 7,000,000)
The One and Only 1,500,000
(Total Budget 3,500,000)
Thunderpants 2,000,000
(Total Budget 5,000,000)

Development

The Blitz	100,000
Drunken Monkey	10,250
Hawksmoor	36,670
The Mushroom Prince	20,900
The Season	47,515
Ugly Streakers	2,500

Source: UK Film Council

SCOTTISH SCREEN

Features

All American Man	500,000
Away Days	20,000
The Bothy	500,000
The Boy David	146,000
The Devil's Tattoo	100,000
The Last Great Wilderness	105,000
Magdalene	150,000 (additional funding)
Outlanders	130,000
16 Years of Alcohol	200,000
Sweet Sixteen	500,000
The Ticking Man	25,000
Young Adam	500,000

Documentaries

A Beginner's Guide to Dying	22,833
Blanketmen and Dreamers	40,000
Fellini-A Life in Film	90,000
Ferry Up the Amazon	80,000
Sightseer	4,080
Through Hell and High Water	82,500

Shorts

Blackout	12,500
Bye Child	21,000
Cry for Bobo	20,000
Dingwall and the Mouse	25,000
Does God Play Football?	10,000
Drama Queen	15,000
4 Minute Wonders	75,000
Last Legs	12,500
Leonard	12,500
Lost	12,500
Manji	20,000
Rank	25,000
Saved	12,500
Small Love	12,500
Tangerine	20,000
The Turning Tide	25,000
Unscrew	24,000
The Window Cleaner	45,000

Development

The Bothy	25,000
The Bum's Rush	20,000
Change of Fortune	10,000
Child of Air	14,950
The Cone Gatherers	25,000
The Cove Shivering Club	12,000
The Dark Island	20,000
Every Third of June	14,750
Fergus Lamont	18,000
Fly me to Dunoon	20,000
The Great Beyond	6,000
Harvey and Joan	5,000
Heartbeat	12,000
The Heist	5,000
House in Berlin	19,300
Last Post	12,000
Little Sisters	7,000
Maud	25,000
The Meat Trade	25,000
Mondo Desperado	5,000
Oracle	12,250
Poor Things	24,800
Red Sub Diaries	25,000
The Ring	25,000
Scottsville	14,000
Skaggerak	21,580
The Soldier's Return	5,000
Solid Air	15,000
Solo	20,000
Sweet Sixteen	15,895
Theory	10,000

Television

Gas Attack	15,000

Company Development

4 Way Pictures	100,000

Source: Scottish Screen

ARTS COUNCIL OF WALES

Features

The Owl Service	250,000

Prints

Diwrnod Hollol Mindblowing	30,782

Shorts

Animation Scheme (10 films)	57,800
The Adventures of Mohammed Ali	61,105
Dad and Boy	42,972
One,Dau,Trois	33,223
Screen Gems (10 films)	90,000
Song of a Pole	18,095
The Vampire Craig	19,532

Development

Abraham's Point	7,500
Acting Up	9,647
Bassoon Children	15,000
Being Mr.Black	15,000
Bruised	15,000
Caitlin	13,787
Calling	5,363
Don't Kiss Me	18,994
Dust Town Girl	10,500
Everything Must Go	15,000
The Hiding Place	15,000
Little Sisters	15,000
The Rabbit	10,525
Stalin's Fridge	15,000
Telepathy	15,000
The Waterfall	14,962

Source: Arts Council of Wales

ARTS COUNCIL OF NORTHERN IRELAND

Award

Shorts

Coronation Day 29,808
(Total Budget 59,808)
Crossing 3,000*
(Total Budget 4,300)
(*Award for Distribution)
Short Back & Sides 29,000
(Total Budget 59,000)
The Two Williams 22,492
(Total Budget 29,990)
The Wayfarer 30,000
(Total Budget 60,000)

Feature Development

Borderland	7,800
If I Were Me	9,305
Middletown	20,000
Mohammed Maguire	20,000
Plan B	17,250
Reading Turgenev	20,000

TV Series Development

The Borderline	12,000

Source: Arts Council of Northern Ireland

Bend it Like Beckham

Gosford Park

28 Days Later

European Funding

For the second year running, we are also able to show details of funding through the European Commission. The EC runs a MEDIA Programme to encourage the audiovisual industry within the European Union. After a number of configurations this is now called MEDIA Plus and there are UK bases at the UK Film Council, Scottish Screen, Sgrîn and the Northern Ireland Film and Television Commission. In 2002 50 per cent of applications to MEDIA Plus from the UK were successful.

Media Plus provides funding to two main areas. As with the National Lottery, production funding is now based largely around development – there is also a growing concentration on slate funding, hoping to build up sustainable companies that can nurture a range of projects. There are also funds available for distribution and exhibition. The distribution awards are to ensure that films from other European countries can reach audiences when Hollywood blockbusters dominate the marketplace. British films receive the same assistance in other territories.

A wider audience for works that otherwise might not be seen is also encouraged by the funding support for a range of films which cover such unsung areas as documentary (Sheffield Documentary Festival), short films (Brief Encounters in Bristol) and Children's films (Cinemagic).

MEDIA Plus Funding: UK Beneficiaries - 2002

Development
Single Project Awards

Company	Country	Amount in Euros
Absolute Features	England	30,000
Beryl Productions International	Wales	30,000
Bloom Street Productions	Wales	30,000
Dundella Properties Ltd/ Rogue Rocket	N.Ireland	30,000
Earthly Delights Films	England	30,000
Flick Media Limited	England	30,000
Forget about It Film + TV	Wales	30,000
Red Fox Productions	England	30,000
Richard Ollive animation	England	30,000
Shining Pictures	England	50,000
Smoking Dogs Films	England	20,000
Spectre Films	England	30,000
Straight Forward Film & Television Productions	N.Ireland	20,000
The Bridge	England	20,000
Treehouse Films	Wales	40,000
True TV & Film	Scotland	10,000
TV4C	England	50,000

Slate Awards

Company	Country	Amount in Euros
Agenda Production	Wales	80,000
APT Films	England	90,000
Artists Independent Films	England	90,000
Assassin Films	England	100,000
Caledonia,Sterne & Wyld	Scotland	110,000
Ecosse Films	England	125,000
Feelgood Fiction	England	125,000
Free Spirit Films	England	60,000
Greenpoint Films	England	125,000
Kuhn and Co	England	90,000
October Films	England	80,000
Picture Palace Films	England	80,000
Ruby Films	England	90,000
Spice Factory	England	100,000
Stampede	England	60,000
Studio Eight Productions	England	100,000
Teledu Elidir	Wales	60,000
Teledu Telesgôp Cyf	Wales	60,000
The Illuminated Film company	England	125,000
Tigress Productions	England	80,000
TowerCreate	Scotland	90,000
Ugh!	Wales	90,000
		2,520,000

Distribution Selective Scheme

Company	Film	Amount in Euros
Artificial Eye	Sma Ulykker	28,000
Artificial Eye	Une Hirondelle a fait Le Printemps	25,000
Artificial Eye	Le Fils	25,000
Artificial Eye	Divine Intervention	30,000
Artificial Eye	Japon	20,000
Axiom Films	Tosca	27,000
Axiom Films	El Bola	30,000
ICA Projects	Man Without a Past	35,000
Metro Tartan	Irreversible	45,000
Metro Tartan	Sex and Lucia	45,000
Metropolis Films	Okay	18,000
Parasol Peccadillo Releasing	Le Fate Ignoranti	15,000
Pathe	Ma Femme est une Actrice	60,000
Pearlshine (Blue Dolphin)	Moro No Brasil	20,000
UGC Films	8 Women	130,000
		553,000

Distribution Automatic Scheme

Company	Amount in Euros
Artificial Eye	117,241
Cinefrance	5,396
	122,637

Sales Agents	
The Works	29,382
Vine International	15,000
	44,382

Festivals

Festival	Amount in Euros
Cinemagic	20,000
International festival of Wales	10,000
Leeds IFF	25,000
Onedotzero	10,000
Sheffield	10,000
	75,000

Promotion and Market Access

Event	Amount in Euros
Exchange at Celtic Film and Television Festival	15,000

Training

Training provider	Amount in Euros
Draft Zero: The European Development Network	294,031

i2i Growth & Audiovisual

Company	Amount in Euros
Scala Productions	50,000

Source: Media Plus

12 Cinema Admissions 1933–2001 (millions)

Year	Admissions	Year	Admissions
1933	903.00	1970	193.00
1934	950.00	1971	176.00
1935	912.33	1972	156.60
1936	917.00	1973	134.20
1937	946.00	1974	138.50
1938	987.00	1975	116.30
1939	990.00	1976	103.90
		1977	103.50
1940	1,027.00	1978	126.10
1941	1,309.00	1979	111.90
1942	1,494.00		
1943	1,541.00	1980	101.00
1944	1,575.00	1981	86.00
1945	1,585.00	1982	64.00
1946	1,635.00	1983	65.70
1947	1,462.00	1984	54.00
1948	1,514.00	1985	72.00
1949	1,430.00	1986	75.50
		1987	78.50
1950	1,395.80	1988	84.00
1951	1,365.00	1989	94.50
1952	1,312.10		
1953	1,284.50	1990	97.37
1954	1,275.80	1991	100.29
1955	1,181.80	1992	103.64
1956	1,100.80	1993	114.36
1957	915.20	1994	123.53
1958	754.70	1995	114.56
1959	581.00	1996	123.80
		1997	139.30
1960	500.80	1998	135.50
1961	449.10	1999	139.75
1962	395.00		
1963	357.20	2000	142.50
1964	342.80	2001	155.91
1965	326.60	2002	176.00
1966	288.80		
1967	264.80		
1968	237.30		
1969	214.90		

Source: Screen Digest/CAA/Nielsen EDI/Screen Finance

13 UK Box Office 2002

Admissions	176 million
Total Cinema Sites	668
Total Cinema Screens	3,258
Total Multiplex Sites	222
Total Multiplex Screens	2,215
Box Office Gross	£755m
Average Ticket Price	£4.29

Source: Screen Finance/Dodona Research/CAA/Nielsen EDI/RSU analysis

Cinema

While the UK film production sector was having a year of mixed fortunes cinema admissions soared to 176 million in 2002, the highest number since 1971 and represented a rise of 13 per cent (Table 12). What was remarkable about this rise was the drop in attendances across France, Germany and Spain during the same period. This put the UK second to France in terms of cinema attendances but far and away the European market leader in terms of box office revenue, which rose by 17 per cent to £755m in 2002 (Table 13).

It is curious, in what appears to be a boom time for cinemas, that two major cinema chains – Odeon and Warner Villages were sold in 2003. The Odeon chain was sold in March 2003 by Cinven for £431m to a consortium of investors comprising German investment bank WestLB, the UK's Entertainment Film Distributors and the private property group Rotch. Shortly after that,

About a Boy (left) and Anita and Me (right) had contrasting box office fortunes in 2002

14 UK Sites and Screens 1984–2002

Year	Total Sites	Total Screens
1984	660	1,271
1985	663	1,251
1986	660	1,249
1987	648	1,215
1988	699	1,416
1989	719	1,559
1990	737	1,685
1991	724	1,789
1992	735	1,845
1993	723	1,890
1994	734	1,969
1995	743	2,019
1996	742	2,166
1997	747	2,383
1998	759	2,564
1999	692	2,758
2000	686	2,954
2001	692	3,164
2002	668	3,258

Source: Screen Finance//Dodona Research

Independent UK exhibitor SBC International Cinemas acquired Warner Village Cinemas for £250m. The acquisition created the second largest cinema circuit in the UK behind Odeon Cinemas: adding 36 Warner Village sites to SBC's existing four. Table 27 shows the cinema circuits prior to the acquisitions. The new cinema venture will go under the title of Vue and a rebranding programme is expected to be completed early in 2004.

It will be interesting to see if this flurry of buying and selling is an ominous indicator that the cinema sector bubble might be about to burst.

The number of multiplexes in the UK fell by two for the first time in 2002 from 224 to 222. However, the number of multiplex screens increased from 2,170 to 2,215 (Table 13). Indicators that the multiplex slow-down had finally arrived were shown by the fact that there were only five new multiplexes proposed or being built in 2003 compared with 19 in 2002. As a whole the number of UK sites fell by 24 although paradoxically the number of screens actually rose by 94.

15 Frequency of Cinema-going 2002

Age group	4 to 14	15 to 24	25 to 34	35+	ABC1	C2DE	Male	Female	Total
No. of people (millions)	**8.06**	**6.99**	**8.09**	**31.35**	**28.03**	**26.46**	**26.43**	**28.07**	**54.49**
Once a month or more	32	50	35	17	31	21	27	25	26
Less than once a month but at least twice a year	52	35	39	32	38	35	35	38	36
Once a year or less	10	11	18	25	17	23	19	20	20
Total who ever go to the cinema	**94**	**97**	**92**	**74**	**86**	**78**	**81**	**84**	**82**

Source: CAA/CAVIAR 20 (2002)

16 Cinemagoing – 18 Year Trends

	1984	1987	1990	1993	1996	1997	1998	1999	2000	2001	2002
People who ever go to the cinema											
7+	38%	58%	64%	69%	72%	75%	83%	78%	86%	82%	82%
7 to 14	73%	88%	85%	93%	95%	95%	97%	955%	97%	97%	98%
15 to 34	55%	74%	83%	86%	90%	94%	96%	93%	95%	94%	94%
35+	21%	42%	49%	535%	58%	60%	74%	66%	79%	73%	74%
Regular Cinemagoers											
7+	5%	8%	11%	14%	15%	22%	24%	25%	24%	25%	26%
7 to 14	10%	12%	18%	22%	25%	34%	39%	37%	32%	38%	37%
15-34	10%	17%	23%	26%	27%	42%	42%	46%	41%	38%	42%
35+	1%	1%	3%	5%	6%	10%	11%	12%	14%	15%	17%

Regular cinemagoers are defined as those that go to the cinema once a month or more

Source: CAA/CAVIAR 20 2002

Top 20 Films at the UK Box Office 2002

	Title	Distributor	Country of Origin	Box Office Gross (£m)
1	**Lord of the Rings: Two Towers**	Entertainment	USA/NZ	53,972,693
2	**Harry Potter and the Chamber of Secrets**	Warner Bros.	UK/US	53,667,056
3	**Monsters, Inc.**	Warner Bros.	US	37,907,451
4	**Star Wars: Episode II Attack of the Clones**	Twentieth Century Fox	US	37,539,932
5	**Die Another Day**	Twentieth Century Fox	UK/US	35,982,997
6	**Spider Man: The Movie**	Columbia TriStar	US	29,025,619
7	**Ocean's Eleven**	Warner Bros.	US/AUS	26,473,267
8	**Austin Powers in Goldmember**	Entertainment	US	23,428,992
9	**Scooby-Doo**	Warner Bros.	US/AUS	22,596,370
10	**Men in Black 2**	Columbia TriStar	US	22,212,394
11	**Minority Report**	Twentieth Century Fox	US	20,685,587
12	**About a Boy**	UIP	UK/US	16,935,159
13	**Signs**	Buena Vista International	US	16,245,914
14	**Ice Age**	Twentieth Century Fox	US	15,058,648
15	**My Big Fat Greek Wedding**	Entertainment	US	13,569,577
16	**Lilo & Stitch**	Buena Vista International	US	13,025,297
17	**Gosford Park**	Entertainment	US/UK	12,259,248
18	**Bend it Like Beckham**	Helkon SK	UK/Germany	11,551,538
19	**xXx**	Columbia TriStar	US	11,508,703
20	**Stuart Little 2**	Columbia TriStar	US	11,186,038

Source: Nielsen EDI/Screen Finance/bfi/RSU Analysis

Top 20 UK Films at the UK Box Office 2002

	Title	Distributor	Country of Origin	Box Office Gross (£m)
1	**Harry Potter and the Chamber of Secrets**	Warner Bros.	UK/US	53,667,056
2	**Die Another Day**	Twentieth Century Fox	UK/US	35,982,997
3	**About a Boy**	UIP	UK/US	16,935,159
4	**Gosford Park**	Entertainment	UK/US	12,259,248
5	**Bend it Like Beckham**	Helkon SK	UK/Germany	11,551,538
6	**Ali G Indahouse**	UIP	UK/France/Germany/US	10,296,604
7	**The Guru**	UIP	UK/US	6,497,236
8	**28 Days Later**	Twentieth Century Foxs	UK/Netherlands/US	6,243,656
9	**40 Days and 40 Nights**	UIP	UK/US/France/Canada	5,259,975
10	**Iris**	Buena Vista International	UK/US	4,226,477
11	**The Importance of Being Earnest**	Buena Vista International	UK/France/US	3,519,574
12	**Resident Evil**	Pathé Distribution	UK/Germany/France	2,768,130
13	**My Little Eye**	Momentum Pictures	UK/US/France	2,693,396
14	**Dog Soldiers**	Pathé Distribution	UK/Lumembourg	2,070,441
15	**Thunderpants**	Pathé Distribution	UK/Germany/Italy	1,969,798
16	**Anita & Me**	Icon	UK	1,848,620
17	**Long Time Dead**	UIP	UK	1,774,552
18	**Charlotte Gray**	FilmFour	UK/Germany/Australia	1,567,185
19	**The Count of Monte Cristo**	Buena Vista International	UK/US	1,433,043
20	**24 Hour Party People**	Pathé Distribution	UK	1,035,114

Source: Nielsen EDI/Screen Finance/bfi/RSU Analysis

UK Box Office for UK Feature Films released in 2002 – UK Films

	Title	Distributor	Country of Origin	Box Office Gross (£m)
1	Anita & Me	Icon	UK	1,848,620
2	Long Time Dead	UIP	UK	1,774,552
3	24 Hour Party People	Pathé Distribution	UK	1,035,114
4	Lost in La Mancha	Optimum	UK	233,383
5	Before You Go	Entertainment	UK	134,102
6	Biggie and Tupac	Optimum	UK	93,835
7	Nobody Someday	UIP	UK	70,971
8	Biggie and Tupac	Optimum	UK	93,835
9	If ....(re)	BFI	UK	19,090
10	Revelation	Miracle	UK	18,678
11	Two Men Went to War	Guerilla	UK	16,168
12	Brighton Rock (re)	BFI	UK	15,687
13	Club Le Monde	Screenprojex	UK	8,800
14	Saturday Night and Sunday Morning (re)	BFI	UK	7,436
15	AKA	City Screen	UK	6,404
16	Lighthouse	Feature Film Co	UK	5,536
17	The Loneliness of the Long Distance Runner (re)	BFI	UK	5,286
18	A Taste of Honey (re)	BFI	UK	5,161
19	Lava	Feature Film Co	UK	4,501
20	Beginner's Luck	Guerilla	UK	2,819
21	Offending Angels	Guerilla	UK	89
Total				**5,400,067**

UK Box Office for UK Feature Films released in 2002 – Other UK Co-productions

	Title	Distributor	Country of Origin	Box Office Gross (£m)
1	Bend it Like Beckham	Helkon SK	UK/Germany	11,551,538
2	Ali G Indahouse	UIP	UK/France/Germany/US	10,296,604
3	28 Days Later	Twentieth Century Fox	UK/Netherlands/US	6,243,656
4	40 Days and 40 Nights	UIP	UK/US/France/Canada	5,259,975
5	The Importance of Being Earnest	Buena Vista International	UK/France/US	3,519,574
6	Resident Evil	Pathé Distribution	UK/Germany/France	2,768,130
7	My Little Eye	Momentum Pictures	UK/US/France	2,693,396
8	The Quiet American	Buena Vista International	US/Germany/UK	2,231,737
9	Dog Soldiers	Pathé Distribution	UK/Lumembourg	2,070,441
10	Thunderpants	Pathé Distribution	UK/Germany/Italy	1,969,798
11	Rabbit-Proof Fence	Buena Vista International	UK/Luxembourg	1,645,875
12	Charlotte Gray	FilmFour	UK/Germany/Australia	1,567,185
13	Deathwatch	Pathé Distribution	UK/Germany	967,748
14	Last Orders	Metrodome	UK/Germany	946,719
15	The Magdelene Sisters	Momentum Pictures	UK/Ireland	887,673
16	K-19	UIP	UK/Germany/US	844,665
17	Sweet Sixteen	Icon	UK/Germany/Spain	824,821
18	All or Nothing	UGC Films	UK/France	672,605
19	Slap Her, She's French	Winchester Films	UK/Germany/US	633,040
20	Once Upon a Time in the Midlands	FilmFour	UK/Germany	494,281
21	The Musketeer	Buena Vista	UK/Germany/Lux	432,443
22	Morvern Callar	Momentum Pictures	UK/Canada	384,049
23	Heaven	Buena Vista International	UK/France/Germany	233,690
24	Dark Blue World	Columbia TriStar	UK/Czech/Ger/Denmark/Itay	198,538
25	No Man's Land	Momentum Pictures	UK/Slov/Fr/Bel/It	196,873
26	Crush	FilmFour	UK/Germany/US	169,724

	Title	Distributor	Country of Origin	Box Office Gross (£m)
27	**The Warrior**	FilmFour	UK/France/Germany/India	147,365
28	**The Eye**	Metro Tartan	UK/Hong Kong	125,211
29	**The Abduction Club**	Pathé	UK/France/Ireland/Germany	61,593
30	**The Mystic Masseur**	Miracle Comms	UK/India	42,235
31	**How Harry Became a Tree**	Buena Vista	UK/Ireland/Italy/France	38,674
32	**11'09'01 September 11**	Artificial Eye	UK/France/Mexico/Egypt/US	26,046
33	**Tosca**	Axiom	UK/France/Germany/Italy	16,763
34	**Invincible**	Film Four	UK/Germany/Irleand/US	13,572
35	**My Kingdom**	Metro Tartan	UK/Italy	13,566
36	**Shooters**	Universal	UK/Netherlands/US	6,983
37	**The War Bride**	Miracle Comms	UK/Canada	5,933
38	**Bloody Sunday**	Feature Film Co	UK/Ireland	5,087
39	**Villa Des Roses**	Miracle Comms	UK/Belgium/Netherlands/Luxembourg	4,891
40	**Butterfly Man**	De Warrenne Pictures	UK/Thailand	4,830
41	**Hijack Stories**	Momentum Pictures	UK/France/Germany	4,015
42	**Kin**	Feature Film Co	UK/Sout Africa	310
Total				**60,221,844**

UK Box Office for UK Feature Films released in 2002 – US/UK Co-productions

	Title	Distributor	Country of Origin	Box Office Gross (£m)
1	**Harry Potter and the Chamber of Secrets**	Warner Bros.	UK/US	53,667,056
2	**Die Another Day**	Twentieth Century Fox	UK/US	35,982,997
3	**About a Boy**	UIP	UK/US	16,935,159
4	**Gosford Park**	Entertainment	UK/US	12,259,248
5	**The Guru**	UIP	UK/US	6,497,236
6	**Iris**	Buena Vista	UK/US	4,226,477
7	**The Count of Monte Cristo**	Buena Vista	UK/US	1,433,043
8	**Birthday Girl**	FilmFour	UK/US	783,575
9	**Dirty Pretty Things**	Buena Vista	UK/US	717,876
10	**Possession**	Warner Bros.	UK/US	321,907
11	**The Lawless Heart**	Optimum Releasing	UK/US	321,263
12	**Ivans XTC**	Metro Tartan	UK/US	140,341
13	**Killing Me Softly**	Pathé	UK/US	69,330
14	**Dancing at the Blue Iguana**	Miracle Comms	UK/US	18,419
15	**Bundy**	Metro Tartan	UK/US	10,304
Total				**133,384,230**
Total Box Office Gross:				**199,006,144**

Source: Nielsen EDI/Screen Finance/bfi

The best served audience for the cinema are those aged between 7–14 who have plenty of blockbusters to keep them on the edge of their seats (Table 15). Those over 35 are least well served and may experience opened-mouth disbelief at the inane quality of film served up to their children and grandchildren.

Most people in the UK (71 per cent) went to the cinema at least once last year, and 26 per cent went at least once a month. Children and teenagers most commonly visited every two to three months or more often, young adults once a month, people aged between 35 and 44 two or three times a year. Sadly, as many as 41 per cent of people aged 55 and over never went to the cinema at all.

Five UK co-productions managed to make it into the UK box office in 2002 – *Harry Potter and the Chamber of Secrets, Die Another Day, About a Boy, Gosford Park* and *Bend It Like Beckham* (Table 17). Top of the list was *The Lord of the Rings: Two Towers,* which just pipped the UK's top film, *Harry Potter and the Chamber of Secrets* to the top spot.

Top 20 EU Films at the UK Box Office 2002

	Title	Distributor	Country of Origin	Box Office Gross (£m)
1	Red Dragon	UIP	US/Germany	9,594,844
2	Blade 2	Entertainment	US/Germany	9,118,147
3	The Bourne Identity	UIP	US/Germany	7,848,011
4	Shallow Hal	Twentieth Century Fox	US/Germany	5,779,232
5	We Were Soldiers	Icon	US/Germany	2,288,856
6	Monsoon Wedding	FilmFour	US/Italy/Germany/France	2,270,404
7	Van Wilder	Momentum Pictures	US/Germany	1,810,970
8	Bowling For Columbine	Momentum Pictures	US/Germany/Canada	1,667,625
9	K-Pax	FilmFour	US/Germany	1,588,410
10	Hable Con Ella (aka Talk to Her)	Pathé Distribution	Spain	1,461,569
11	Big Fat Liar	UIP	US/Germany	1,272,242
12	Mulholland Drive	Pathé Distribution	US/France	1,231,719
13	Lantana	Winchester Films	Australia/Germany	1,165,894
14	Boat Trip	Entertainment	US/Germany	1,005,410
15	Just Visting	MomentumPictures	US/France	726,158
16	Slap Her, She's French	Winchester Films	US/Germany	633,040
17	8 Women	UGC Films	France/Italy	523,470
18	I am Sam	Entertainment	US/Germany	519,421
19	Lucía y el Sexo (aka Sex and Lucia)	Metro Tartan	Spain/France	376,037
20	Italiensk For Begyndere (aka Italian for Beginners)	Pathé	Denmark	374,324

Films exclude UK and UK co-productions

Source: Nielsen EDI/Screen Finance/bfi/RSU analysis

Top 20 Foreign Language Films Released in the UK 2002

	Title	Distributor	Country of Origin	Box Office Gross (£)
1	Devdas	Eros	India	1,742,553
2	Y Tu Mamá También (aka And Your Mother Too)	Icon	Mexico	1,621,560
3	Hable Con Ella (aka Talk to Her)	Pathé	Spain	1,461,569
4	Mujhse Dosti Karoge!	Yash Raj Films	India	831,000
5	Hum Tumhare Hain Sanam	Eros	India	671,215
6	Huit Femmes (aka 8 Women)	UGC	France/Italy	523,470
7	Le Placard (aka The Closet)	Optimum	France	435,432
8	Nueve Reinas (aka Nine Queens)	Optimum	Argentina	410,973
9	Haan Maine Bhi Pyar Kiya	Shree Krishna	India	405,108
10	Kaante	Bollywood Pictures	India	398,912
11	Lucía y el Sexo (aka Sex and Lucia)	Metro Tartan	Spain/France	376,037
12	Italiensk For Begyndere (aka Italian for Beginners)	Pathé	Denmark	374,324
13	Sur Mes Lèvres (aka Read My Lips)	Pathé	France	359,572
14	Dil Hai Tumhaara	Sovereign Sirroco	India	313,644
15	Shakti – the Power	Eros	India	305,609
16	La Stanza Del Figlio (aka The Son's Room)	Momentum	Italy/France	292,251
17	Saathiya	Yash Raj Films	India	288,004
18	Mere Yaar Ki Shaadi Hai	Yash Raj Films	India	260,590
19	Na Tum Jaano Na Hum	Eros	India	226,836
20	Aankhen	Gurpreet Video	India	213,662

Source: Nielsen EDI/Screen Finance/bfi/RSU analysis

22 Breakdown of UK Box Office by Country of Origin 2002

Country of Origin	No. of releases	Box office	%
UK and UK co-productions (non US)	54	50,550,000	15.0
UK US	22	147,010,000	18.2
US solo	122	415,840,000	51.4
US co-productions (other)	38	178,130,000	10.0
Europe	47	5,900,000	0.7
India	60	8,160,000	1.0
Rest of the world	26	3,740,000	0.5
Total	**369**	**809.36**	

Source: Nielsen EDI/RSU analysis

23 Top 10 UK Films Released in the US in 2002 by US Box Office Revenue

	Title	Distributor (US)	Country of Origin	Box Office Gross ($m)
1	Harry Potter and the Chamber of Secrets	Warner	UK/US	261,979,634
2	Die Another Day	MGM/UA	UK/US	160,941,207
3	The Count of Monte Cristo	Buena Vista	UK/US	54,234,062
4	Reign of Fire	Buena Vista	UK/US/Ireland	43,061,982
5	The Hours	Paramount	UK/US	41,608,003
6	About a Boy	Universal	UK/US	40,683,240
7	Resident Evil	Sony Pictures	UK/Germany/France	39,665,330
8	40 Days and 40 Nights	Miramax	UK/US	37,950,822
9	The Pianist	Focus Features	UK/France/Germany/Netherlands/Poland	32,543,587
10	Feardotcom	Warner	UK/Lumembourg/Germany/US	13,221,308

Source: Neilsen EDI/RSU analysis

Hable Con Ella (left) and Y Tu Mamá También (right) – two foreign language films that were actually in a foreign language

Top 20 of Admissions of Films Distributed in the European Union in 2002

Provisional ranking on the basis of data from 12 countries (79 per cent of admissions analysed)

	Title	Country of Origin	Admissions
1	Harry Potter and the Chamber of Secrets	UK/US	39,651,450
2	Spider-Man	US	29,839,465
3	Lord of the Rings: Fellowship of the Ring*	US/New Zealand	28,715,509
4	Star Wars: Episode II - Attack of the Clones	US	27,771,038
5	Lord of the Rings: The Two Towers	US/New Zealand	23,727,624
6	Ocean's Eleven**	US/Australia	22,446,379
7	Monsters, Inc.	US	22,235,989
8	Men In Black II	US	20,321,708
9	Asterix and Obelix: Mission Cleopatra	France/Germany	19,679,380
10	Die Another Day	UK/US	18,616,042
11	Ice Age	US	18,491,750
12	Minority Report	US	16,282,652
13	Signs	US	13,613,469
14	A Beautiful Mind	US	11,589,454
15	Red Dragon	US/Germany	9,670,347
16	Scooby-Doo	US	9,567,873
17	XXX	US	9,434,712
18	About a Boy	UK/US/France/Germany	8,744,433
19	Blade II	US/Germany	8,179,053
20	Harry Potter and the Philosopher's Stone***	UK/US	8,074,317

* 21,609,078 admissions in EU in 2001
** 1,201,828 admissions in EU in 2001
*** 43,579,135 admissions in EU in 2001

Source : European Audiovisual Observatory/LUMIERE/RSU analysis

Harry Potter had the world at his feet

Top 20 of Admissions of European Films Distributed in the European Union in 2002

Provisional ranking on the basis of data from 12 European Union States (ca. 79 per cent of admissions analysed)

	Title	Country of Origin	Admissions
1	Harry Potter and the Chamber of Secrets	UK/US	39,651,450
2	Asterix and Obelix: Mission Cleopatra	France/Germany	19,679,380
3	Die Another Day	UK/US	18,616,042
4	About a Boy	UK/US/Germany/France	8,744,433
5	Harry Potter and the Philosopher's Stone***	UK/US	8,074,317
6	Huit Femmes (aka 8 Women)	France/Italy	5,792,990
7	Hable con Ella (aka Talk to Her)	Spain	5,368,790
8	Gosford Park	UK/US/Germany/Italy	4,938,785
9	Pinocchio	Italy/France/Germany	4,545,841
10	Resident Evil	UK/Germany/France	3,469,703
11	Le boulet (aka Dead Weight)	France/UK	3,372,782
12	L'auberge espagnole	France/Spain	3,347,579
13	Bend It Like Beckham	UK/Germany	3,333,867
14	La leggenda di Al, John e Jack	Italy	3,306,124
15	Ali G Indahouse	UK/France/Germany/US	3,105,662
16	Natale sul Nilo (aka Christmas on the Nile)	Italy/Spain/UK	3,088,387
17	The Pianist	UK/France/Germany/Netherlands/Poland	2,986,410
18	El otro lado de la cama	Spain	2,697,314
19	Le fabuleux destin d'Amelie Poulain* (aka Amelie)	France/Germany	2,504,636
20	Los otros** (aka The Others)	Spain/France/US	2,298,268

* 14,094,971 admissions in the EU in 2001
** 11,121,175 admissions in the EU in 2001
*** 43,579,135 admissions in EU in 2001

Source : European Audiovisual Observatory/LUMIERE/RSU analysis

Harry Potter and the Chamber of Secrets also recorded the biggest-ever opening weekend in the UK with earnings of £18.9 million, and was the best-performing UK film worldwide, taking $728.2m (£436.92m) at the box office.

The top six UK co-produced films scored box office totals in excess of £10m each with the top three leaping straight into the Top 20 UK films of all time (Table 18 & 29).

The picture for home-grown UK films was entirely different. No film broke the £2m barrier and only three films broke through the £1m mark. Top film was *Anita and Me* which grossed £1.8m, followed by *Long Time Dead* at £1.7m and *24 Hour Party People* at just over £1m (Table 19). Co-productions with mainly European partners proved more successful with *Bend It Like Beckham* proving to be a surprise hit and scoring an impressive £11.5m at the box office. The top 12 co-productions managed to break the £1m mark.

German/US co-productions are a feature of the Top EU films at the UK box office. (Table 20). *Red Dragon* leads this table which excludes any UK involvement. Only four films in the top twenty are spoken in a language other than English (although *Monsoon Wedding* does contain some English dialogue).

A total of 131 films, (36 per cent of the total released) were foreign language films and Hindi was the most dominant foreign language. The top three foreign language films in the UK were *Devdas* (India), *Y Tu Mama Tambien* (Mexico) and *Talk to Her* (Spain); (Table 21). Despite making up a third of the release schedules foreign language films rarely find big audiences. Only the top three foreign language films *Devdas, Y Tu Mama Tambien* and *Talk to Her* managed to bring in over £1m at the UK box office.

Over half the films released in the UK are from America. This figure rises to nearly 80 per cent when taking into account co-productions. In comparison, UK films including co-productions register a modest 33 per cent share of the market (Table 22).

UK films performed well in the US with *Harry Potter* topping the chart and asserting its global box office clout

Breakdown of UK Box Office by Distributor in 2002

Box office for all films on release in 2002 by distributor in the period from 4 January 2002 to 2 January 2003. This includes films released in 2001 and still showing in 2002. Film released in 2002 are shown in brackets

Distributor	Titles		Box Office
20th Century Fox	(25)	28	146,073,008
Buena Vista International	(28)	36	124,616,590
Warner	(18)	24	122,652,671
UIP	(27)	29	101,410,216
Columbia TriStar	(27)	31	100,936,712
Majors		**148**	**595,689,197**
Entertainment	(15)	19	135,891,670
Pathé	(14)	22	17,283,748
Momentum	(16)	20	15,517,313
Redbus/Helkon SK	(4)	4	14,022,487
Icon	(6)	6	7,222,162
FilmFour	(9)	13	7,212,431
Eros International	(13)	13	3,487,420
Metrodome	(10)	12	3,166,069
Optimum Releasing	(12)	16	2,065,772
Yash Raj Films	(3)	4	1,817,831
Winchester Films	(2)	3	1,784,382
UGC Films	(2)	2	1,113,935
Metro Tartan	(15)	16	916,166
Artificial Eye	(13)	16	876,587
Tip Top Entertainment	(4)	4	697,170
Spark Entertainment	(6)	6	640,498
Gurpreet Video Intl.	(13)	13	610,975
Sovereign Sirroco	(4)	4	434,908
Venus Entertainment	(5)	5	382,656
BFI	(17)	20	331,485
Bollywood Pictures	(1)	1	321,849
Bollywood Films	(6)	6	146,874
Feature Film Co	(5)	5	138,933
Miracle Communications	(5)	5	90,156
Sunny Super Sounds Ltd	(1)	1	86,823
Diva Films	(6)	5	32,735
Set Singapore	(-)	1	27,433
Eclipse Pictures	(1)	1	21,133
Guerilla Films	(3)	3	19,076
Axiom Films	(1)	1	16,763
Blue Dolphin	(1)	1	15,276
Cinefrance	(1)	1	13,146
Gala	(2)	2	12,462
Arrow Films	(1)	1	11,819
Screenprojex	(1)	1	8,800
NFT	(3)	3	7,856
Blue Light	(1)	1	7,758
Universal Pictures	(1)	1	6,983
City Screen	(1)	1	6,404
Millennium Film Dist	(2)	2	5,350
De Warrenne Pictures	(1)	1	4,830
Twenty First Century Film	(1)	1	4,806
Contemporary	(1)	1	4,416
Rasks Brothers Ltd	(1)	1	4,259
Life Media Ltd	(1)	1	4,106
Salvation Films	(1)	1	3,744
ICA Projects	(2)	2	2,465
Barbican	(1)	1	1,539
Life Films		(1)	1
336			
Thurkka Films Intl	(1)	1	126
Total (independents)		**272**	**216,503,921**
Total		**420**	**812,193,118**

Sorce:Nielsen EDI/bfi/RSU analysis

(Table 24). It is interesting to note the difference between the top 10 UK films in the US with their UK counterpart (Tables 20 & Table 25). Five of the top 10 UK films in the US had earlier release dates, hence the presence of *Reign of Fire* and *The Hours* in the top five.

In Europe, UK films accounted for 16.5 per cent of the market in Germany, while in France they took 12.3 per cent of the market and 12.2 per cent in Spain. The two *Harry Potter* films top and tail the table of admissions throughout Europe with *the Chamber of Secrets* lording over other predictable Hollywood fare (Table 25). *Harry Potter* also dominates the admissions for European films within the European Union (Table 26). Perhaps the one surprise is the success of *Asterix and Obelix: Mission Cleopatra* which is placed as the second favourite European film in Europe.

The UK Distribution sector is dominated by US majors who are responsible for almost 75 per cent of the entire UK releases (Table 26). 20th Century Fox topped the table largely due to the consistent performance of its top releases *Star Wars: Episode II Attack of the Clones, Die Another Day,* and *Minority Report.*

Entertainment is the only UK-based distributor which is able to live in the same company. Indeed, in 2002 Entertainment finished second behind 20th Century Fox, despite having released nine fewer films. However, it could boast at least three crowd-pleasing releases beginning with *Lord of the Rings: The Two Towers, Austin Powers in Goldmember* and picking up the surprise US comedy hit of the year *My Big Fat Greek Wedding.*

Despite having family favourites such as *Harry Potter, Monsters, Inc* and *Scooby Doo,* Warner Brothers finished fourth behind Buena Vista whose top film was *Signs.* Entertainment and Helkon SK (which is now Redbus) were the only two independent distributors in the Top 20. The independent distribution sector consists of 50 companies of which about a fifth distribute Hindi films.

The Hindi film market in the UK is often overlooked, certainly by the film magazines who rarely manage to review Bollywood releases, yet do manage to pick up releases from France, China or Iran. Yet the Bollywood market, while by no means dominating the UK sector, perhaps deserves equal attention. *Devdas* was the highest grossing Indian film in the UK, which placed it as third best Indian movie in the UK of all time, behind *Kabhi Khushi Kabhie Gham,* and *Kuch Kuch Hota Hai* (Table 30).

27

UK Cinema Circuits 1984-2002

s (sites) 668 scr (screens) 3,258

	ABC**		UGC *(ex-Virgin)		Cine UK		Odeon**		Showcase		UCI		Warner Village		Small Chains		Independents	
	s	scr	s	scr	s	scr	s	scr	s	scr	s	scr	s	scr	s	scr	s	scr
1985	-	-	158	403*	-	-	76	194	-	-	3	17	1	5	-	-	-	-
1986	-	-	173	443*	-	-	74	190	-	-	3	17	1	5	-	-	-	-
1987	-	-	154	408*	-	-	75	203	-	-	5	33	1	5	-	-	-	-
1988	-	-	140	379*	-	-	73	214	7	85	12	99	1	5	-	-	-	-
1989	-	-	142	388*	-	-	75	241	7	85	18	156	3	26	-	-	-	-
1990	-	-	142	411*	-	-	75	266	7	85	21	189	5	48	-	-	-	-
1991	-	-	136	435*	-	-	75	296	8	97	23	208	6	57	-	-	-	-
1992	-	-	131	422*	-	-	75	313	9	109	25	219	7	64	-	-	-	-
1993	-	-	125	408*	-	-	75	322	10	127	25	219	9	84	-	-	-	-
1994	-	-	119	402*	-	-	76	327	11	141	26	232	10	93	-	-	437	631
1995	-	-	116	406*	-	-	71	320	11	143	26	232	12	110	-	-	469	716
1996	92	244	24	162*	2	24	73	362	14	181	26	232	16	143	58	139	437	679
1997	80	225	29	213*	5	66	73	362	15	197	26	263	17	152	68	166	434	739
1998	81	234	34	290*	10	116	79	415	15	199	29	287	22	200	73	100	416	633
1999	58	180	36	312	13	146	79	415	16	221	31	320	28	200	55	170	376	794
2000			41	363	20	219	118	634	19	244	35	345	33	331	54	159	366	659
2001			41	386	25	276	103	597	19	244	35	355	41	364	81	209	351	733
2002			43	405	30	333	97	608	19	244	39	375	42	405	72	252	326	636

*** figures from 1985 to 1998 indicate Virgin Cinemas**

** Odeon bought up the ABC chain in 2000

Source: Screen Finance

Lord of the Rings: The Two Towers slugged it out with Harry Potter for box office supremacy

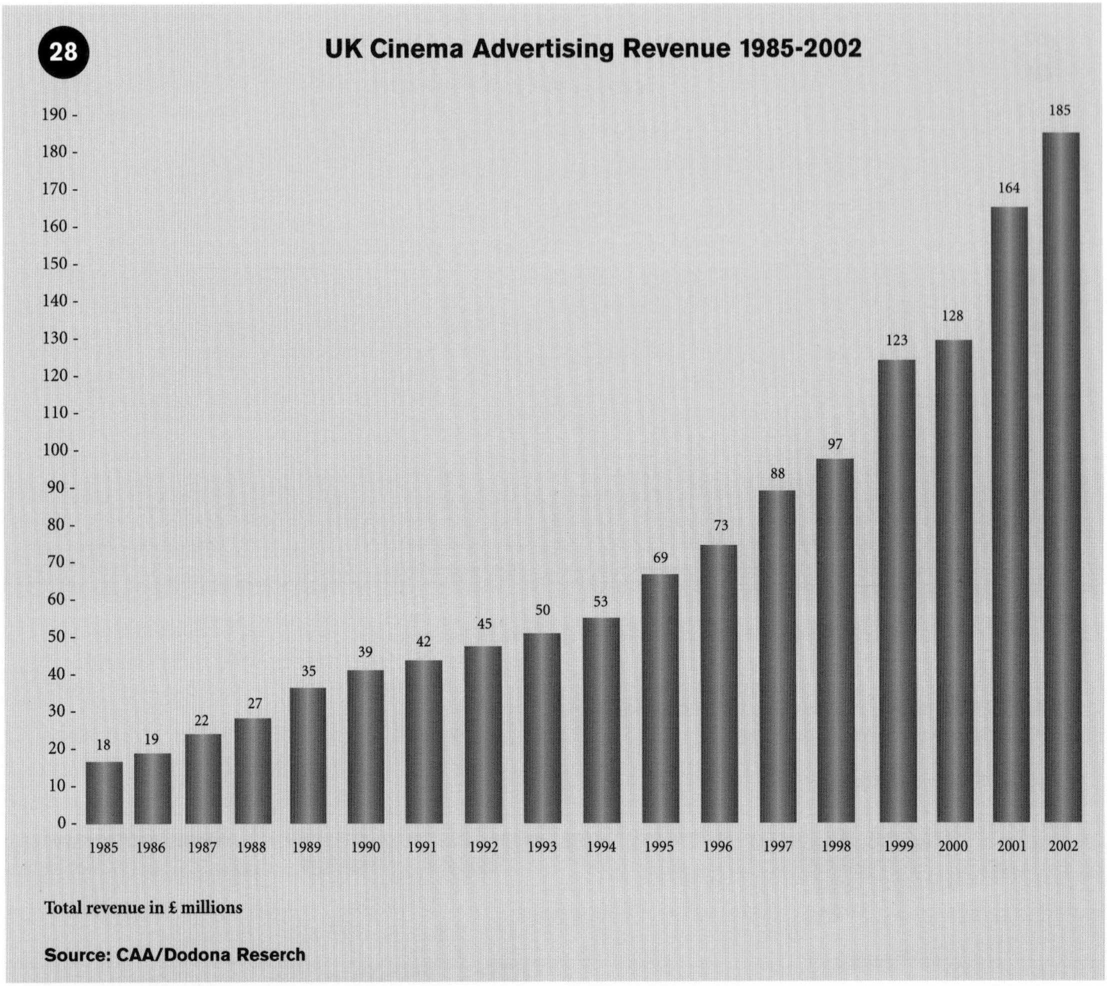

28 UK Cinema Advertising Revenue 1985-2002

Year	1985	1986	1987	1988	1989	1990	1991	1992	1993	1994	1995	1996	1997	1998	1999	2000	2001	2002
Revenue	18	19	22	27	35	39	42	45	50	53	69	73	88	97	123	128	164	185

Total revenue in £ millions

Source: CAA/Dodona Reserch

Devdas was the leading film from India in the UK

The exceptional rise in cinema audiences has been matched by cinema advertisers eager to capitalise on the popularity of film. Cinema advertising rose from £164m in 2001 to £185m in 2002.

In terms of the all-time box office chart, the first two *Harry Potter* films lead the way in a neat order of appearance, with the second *Harry Potter* film falling a good £10m short of displacing *Harry Potter and the Philosophser's Stone. Johnny English* arrives unexpectedly in the chart by virtue of its release in Spring 2003. It will be a surprise if any UK film dislodges *Harry Potter's* top two positions during the course of 2003, as the third *Harry Potter* film is due out in 2004.

29 All-time Top 20 UK Films at the UK Box Office

	Title	Year of Release	Box Office Gross (£)
1	Harry Potter and the Philosopher's Stone	2001	64,268,932
2	Harry Potter and the Chamber of Secrets	2002	54,138,718
3	The Full Monty	1997	52,232,058
4	Bridget Jones' s Diary	2001	42,007,008
5	Die Another Day	2002	36,044,960
6	Notting Hill	1999	31,006,109
7	Chicken Run	2000	29,509,150
8	The World is Not Enough	1999	28,576,504
9	Four Weddings and a Funeral	1994	27,762,648
10	Shakespeare in Love	1999	20,814,996
11	Tomorrow Never Dies	1997	19,884,412
12	Johnny English	2002	19,064,424
13	Billy Elliot	2000	18,386,715
14	GoldenEye	1995	18,245,572
15	Bean	1997	17,972,562
16	About a Boy	2002	16,935,159
17	Lara Croft: Tomb Raider	2001	12,822,883
18	Sliding Doors	1998	12,457,984
19	Trainspotting	1996	12,443,450
20	Snatch	2000	12,337,505

Box office figures as of 7 March 2003

Source: Nielsen EDI/bfi/RSU analysis

N.B. Star Wars Episode 1 The Phantom Menace (1999) £51,063,811; The Mummy Returns (2002) £20,390,060; Sense and Sensibility (1996) 13,632,700 were partially produced in the UK, but for these purposes have been treated as US films

30 Top 10 Indian Movies in the UK

	Title	Distributor	Year of Release	Total Box Office (£)
1	Kabhi Khushi Kabhie Gham	Yash Raj	2001	2,080,040
2	Kuch Kuch Hota Hai	Yash Raj	1998	1,750,000
3	Devdas	Eros	2002	1,742,553
4	Mohabbatein	Yash Raj	2000	1,100,000
5	Dil To Pagal Hai	Yash Raj	1997	990,000
6	Mujhse Dosti Karoge!	Yash Raj	2002	831,000
7	Hum Tumhare Hain Sanam	Eros	2002	671,215
8	Lagaan	Sony	2001	656,184
9	Hum Saath-Saath Hain	Eros	1999	651,797
10	Taal	Eros	1999	604,800

Source: AC Nielsen EDI/Screen International

DVD/Video

It has been another phenomenal year for the DVD and video industry. The video market in 2002 was worth £2.5 billion at retail prices. It has become the largest market for consumer leisure spending – outselling the failing music industry and digital terrestrial television and Pay-Per-View.

DVD has caused this explosion: consumers have embraced the disc in the same way that they did CDs in the late 1980s. It is estimated that 1 in 4 homes have a DVD player. No doubt this figure will continue to shoot up, particularly as stores stock more titles on DVD than VHS.

2002 was the first year in which DVD sales exceeded those of VHS (Table 32). Remarkably the VHS market may not be killed off as quickly as the vinyl market. The BVA indicate that DVD players are currently seen as part of a complementary technology.

Some years ago the Handbook predicted the rise in Music DVD as an exciting prospect to fans. News that Led Zeppelin had reached number 1 in the charts with a release of a concert from the 1970s illustrates this point. Back catalogues and archival footage of classic performances by old rock and pop artists are likely to continue with sophisticated abandon.

31 BBFC Censorship of Videos 2002

Certificate	Number of Films Submitted	Number of Films Cut
Uc	117	0
U	1619	6
PG	1832	26
12	1096	8
15	1559	15
18	879	106
R18	1061	163
Rejected	2	
Total	**8165**	**324**

Source: BBFC

Piracy is the main issue however, because with every improvement in technology comes the opportunity for effective pirating. Indeed, DVD has become the pirate's favourite choice of format. The BVA reckons that video pirating is currently worth around £400m. The Federation Against Copyright Theft declared that they had experienced their busiest ever year, seizing around 700,000 illegally pressed DVDs in 2002.

32 The UK Video/DVD Market 1986–2002

Year	Retail Transactions (million)		Value (£m)		Rental Transactions (millions)		Value (£m)	
1986	6		55		233		284	
1987	12		110		251		326	
1988	20		184		271		371	
1989	38		345		289		416	
1990	40		374		277		418	
1991	45		440		253		407	
1992	48		506		222		389	
1993	60		643		184		350	
1994	66		698		167		339	
1995	73		789		167		351	
1996	79		803		175		382	
1997	87		858		161		369	
1998	100		940		186		437	
1999	96	(4)	882	(68)	174		408	
2000	114	(16.6)	1104	(264)	186		444	
2001	93.5	(41.3)	844	(646)	162	(24.6)	399	(65)
2002	79.0	(90.0)	745	(1,305)	119	(57)	312	(164)

DVD retail/rental transactions in parentheses

Source: BVA

33 Top 20 Rental VHS Videos in the UK 2002

	Title	Distributor	Country
1	**The Others** (12)	Buena Vista	US/Spain
2	**Swordfish** (15)	Warner	US/Austalia
3	**American Pie 2** (15)	Universal	US
4	**Legally Blonde** (12)	MGM	US
5	**Jurassic Park III** (PG)	Universal	US
6	**The 51st State** (18)	Momentum	Canada/UK
7	**A Knight's Tale** (PG)	Columbia TriStar	US
8	**The Fast and the Furious** (15)	Universal	US/Germany
9	**Moulin Rouge** (12)	Fox Pathé	US/Australia
10	**Shallow Hal** (12)	Fox Pathé	US/Germany
11	**Planet of the Apes** (12)	Fox Pathé	US
12	**AI: Artificial Intelligence** (12)	Warner	US
13	**Jeepers Creepers** (12)	Helkon SK	US/Germany
14	**Scary Movie 2** (18)	Buena Vista	US
15	**Rush Hour 2** (12)	EV	US
16	**Lord of the Rings: Fellowship of the Ring** (PG)	EV	US/New Zealand
17	**Spy Game** (15)	EV	US/Germany/ Japan/France
18	**Harry Potter and the Philosopher's Stone** (PG)	Warner	US/UK
19	**Don't Say a Word** (15)	Fox Pathé	US/Australia
20	**Miss Congeniality** (12)	Warner	US/Australia

Source: Rental Monitor/BVA

The Others beat all the others in the rental charts

35 Top 20 Rental Videos VHS & DVD in the UK 2002

	Title	Distributor	Country
1	**The Others** (12)	Buena Vista	US/Spain
2	**Swordfish** (15)	Warner	US/Australia
3	**American Pie 2** (15)	Universal	US
4	**The 51st State** (18)	Momentum	Canada/UK
5	**Legally Blonde** (12)	MGM	US
6	**Jurassic Park III** (PG)	Universal	US
7	**The Fast and the Furious** (15)	Universal	US/Germany
8	**Shallow Hal** (12)	Fox Pathé	US/Germany
9	**AI: Artificial Intelligence** (12)	Warner	US
10	**A Knight's Tale** (PG)	Columbia Tristar	US
11	**Planet of the Apes** (12)	Fox Pathé	US
12	**Jeepers Creepers** (12)	Helkon SK	US/Germany
13	**Moulin Rouge** (12)	Fox Pathé	US/Australia
14	**Scary Movie 2** (18)	Buena Vista	US
15	**Black Hawk Down** (15)	Columbia Tristar	US
16	**Spy Game** (15)	EV	US/Germany/ Japan/France
17	**Lord of the Rings: Fellowship of the Ring** (PG)	EV	US/New Zealand
18	**Rush Hour 2** (12)	EV	US
19	**Don't Say a Word** (15)	Fox Pathé	US/Australia
20	**Vanilla Sky** (15)	Paramount	US

Source: Rental Monitor/BVA

34 Top 20 Rental DVD Videos in the UK 2002

	Title	Distributor	Country
1	**The Others** (12)	Buena Vista	US/Spain
2	**Swordfish** (15)	Warner	US/Australia
3	**The 51st State** (18)	Momentum	Canada/UK
4	**American Pie 2** (15)	Universal	US
5	**Shallow Hal** (12)	Fox Pathé	US/Germany
6	**Black Hawk Down** (15)	Columbia TriStar	US
7	**The Fast and the Furious** (15)	Universal	US/Germany
8	**AI: Artificial Intelligence** (12)	Warner	US
9	**Panic Room** (15)	Columbia TriStar	US
10	**Jurassic Park III** (PG)	Universal	US
11	**Jeepers Creepers** (12)	Helkon SK	US/Germany
12	**About a Boy** (12)	Universal	UK/US/France Germany
13	**Spy Game** (15)	EV	US/Germany/ Japan/France
14	**Blade II** (18)	Buena Vista	US/Germany
15	**Minority Report** (12)	EV	US
16	**Vanilla Sky** (15)	Paramount	US
17	**Legally Blonde** (12)	MGM	US
18	**Scary Movie 2** (18)	Buena Vista	US
19	**A Knight's Tale** (PG)	Columbia TriStar	US
20	**Planet of the Apes** (12)	Fox Pathé	US

Source: Rental Monitor/BVA

DVD/VIDEO 54

36 Top 20 Retail VHS Titles in the UK 2002

	Title	Distributor	Country
1	**Harry Potter and the Philosopher's Stone** (PG)	Warner	US/UK
2	**Lord of the Rings: Fellowship of the Ring** (PG)	EV	US/New Zealand
3	**Monsters Inc.** (U)	Buena Vista	US
4	**Scooby Doo – The Movie** (PG)	Warner	US
5	**Ice Age** (U)	20th Century Fox	US
6	**Cinderella 2** (U)	Buena Vista	US
7	**Spider-Man** (12a)	Columbia TriStar	US
8	**Star Wars Episode 2: Attack of the Clones** (PG)	20th Century Fox	US
9	**Shrek** (U)	Universal	US
10	**Moulin Rouge** (12)	20th Century Fox	US/Australia
11	**Stuart Little 2** (U)	Columbia TriStar	US
12	**Cats & Dogs** (PG)	Columbia Tristar	US/Australia
13	**Barbie As Rapunzel** (U)	Universal	US
14	**Bridget Jones' Diary** (15)	VVL	US/UK
15	**Atlantis** (12)	Buena Vista	US/Australia
16	**The Office – first series**	BBC	UK
17	**Beauty and the Beast** (U)	Buena Vista	US
18	**Ocean's Eleven** (12)	Warner	US
19	**Peter Pan – Return to Neverland** (U)	Buena Vista	UK/US
20	**What Women Want** (12)	Warner	US

Source: BVA/Official UK Charts

37 Top 20 Retail DVD Titles in the UK 2002

	Title	Distributor	Country
1	**Lord of the Rings: Fellowship of the Ring** (PG)	EV	US/New Zealand
2	**Harry Potter and the Philosopher's Stone** (PG)	Warner	US/UK
3	**Star Wars Episode 2: Attack of the Clones** (PG)	20th Century Fox	US
4	**Monsters Inc.** (U)	Buena Vista	US
5	**Ocean's Eleven** (12)	Warner	US
6	**Spider-Man** (12a)	Columbia TriStar	US
7	**The Fast and the Furious** (15)	Columbia Tristar	US
8	**Scooby Doo – The Movie** (PG)	Warner	US
9	**Ice Age** (U)	20th Century Fox	US
10	**Minority Report** (12)	Paramount	US
11	**Shawshank Redemption** (15)	VCI	US
12	**The Office – first series**	BBC	UK
13	**Grease** (PG)	Paramount	US
14	**Moulin Rouge** (12)	20th Century Fox	US/Australia
15	**Blade II** (18)	EV	US
16	**Swordfish** (15)	Warner	US/Australia
17	**Planet of the Apes** (12)	20th Century Fox	US
18	**Gladiator** (15)	Columbia TriStar	US
19	**American Pie 2 – Unseen** (15)	Columbia TriStar	US
20	**Bridget Jones's Diary** (15)	Columbia TriStar	US

Source: BVA/Official UK Charts

38 Top 20 Retail VHS & DVD Titles in the UK 2002

	Title	Distributor	Country
1	**Lord of the Rings: Fellowship of the Ring** (PG)	EV	US/New Zealand
2	**Harry Potter and the Philosopher's Stone** (PG)	Warner	US/UK
3	**Monsters Inc.** (U)	Buena Vista	US
4	**Scooby Doo – The Movie** (PG)	Warner	US
5	**Star Wars Episode 2: Attack of the Clones** (PG)	20th Century Fox	US
6	**Ice Age** (U)	20th Century Fox	US
7	**Spider-Man** (12a)	Columbia TriStar	US
8	**Ocean's Eleven** (12)	Warner	US
9	**Moulin Rouge** (12)	20th Century Fox	US/Australia
10	**The Fast and the Furious** (15)	Columbia Tristar	US
11	**The Office – first series**	BBC	UK
12	**Shawshank Redemption** (15)	VCI	US
13	**Shrek** (U)	Universal	US
14	**Minority Report** (12)	Paramount	US
15	**Grease** (PG)	Paramount	US
16	**Bridget Jones's Diary** (15)	Columbia TriStar	US
17	**Stuart Little 2** (U)	Columbia TriStar	US
18	**American Pie 2 – Unseen** (15)	Columbia TriStar	US
19	**Cinderella 2** (U)	Buena Vista	US
20	**Planet of the Apes** (12)	20th Century Fox	US

Source: BVA/Official UK Charts

Lord of the Rings fought off Harry to claim top spot

39 Distributors' Share of UK Rental Transactions (%) 2002

	Distributor	% share
1	Fox-Pathe/MGM	19.7
2	Universal	14.9
3	Warner	13.5
4	Buena Vista	13.3
5	Columbia Tristar	13.0
6	EV	9.6
7	Paramount	5.0
8	Momentum	4.0
9	FilmFour	2.1
10	High Fliers	1.4

Includes DVD and VHS

Source: Rental Monitor/BVA

Video home entertainment has matured to the extent that home cinema systems have become as desirable status symbols (rather like 4 by 4 drive vehicles), in homes big enough to accommodate them.

Intellectual Property (IP) protection issues have come to the fore as part of a proposed campaign to educate the public that ripping off someone's work is wrong and that copyright theft is theft.

One of the consequences of an increase in the VHS and DVD markets has been the additional workload undertaken by the British Board of Film Classification. This is particularly true in light of the reissue of old films with their obligatory reams of added-value material.

The BBFC only refused a certificate to two videos – *Hooligans*, glorifying football violence and *Love Camp 7*, a film depicting sexual violence against women in a Nazi prison camp. The 324 videos which received cuts increased marginally to 3.6 per cent compared with last year's total of 3.4 per cent. Over half of these cuts came from the R18 category (Table 31).

The BBFC have also spent some in clarifying the meaning of each classification, with consumer advice lines explaining the degree of swearing or violence that people might expect. The organisation also acquired a new President with Sir Quentin Thomas taking over from Andreas Whittam Smith.

A rather peculiar phenomenon occurred in the rental charts of 2002. Usually the rental charts are slaves to box office hits. However, the two top films – *The Others* and *Swordfish* – were not what you might call blockbusters (Tables 33,34 and 35). Part of the explanation for this is

40 Video Retail Company Market Share by Volume (%) 2002

	Distributor	% share
1	Warner	22.7
2	Columbia TriStar	15.4
3	20th Century Fox	11.8
4	Universal	11.0
5	EV	8.7
6	Buena Vista	8.1
7	MGM	6.7
8	Paramount	6.1
9	VCI	3.2
10	Momentum	1.7

Includes DVD and VHS

Source: BVA/CIN

the tendency for big films to be available for purchase at the same time as rental.

Nevertheless the rental VHS and DVD charts contain most of the same movies with the exception of more recent releases such as *Black Hawk Down*, *Panic Room* and *About a Boy* in the DVD chart.

2002 was the year that sales records tumbled. *Lord of the Rings* rang up sales of more than four million, whilst *Harry Potter and the Philosopher's Stone* smashed the all-time single day record with 1.2 million units, sold temporarily satisfying the insatiable appetites of *Harry Potter* fans of all ages, on the Saturday of its release.

Of the top 20 videos the first series of the BBC's slow burning comedy hit *The Office* made an impact on the chart (Tables 36, 37 and 38). *Cinderella 2* was the other anomaly in the chart as it had not received a cinema release in the UK. Interestingly, *Bridget Jones's Diary* and *Shrek*, hits on the chart in 2001, spent another year entertaining home users.

The Lord of the Rings vs *Harry Potter* ding dong battle is well illustrated with *Lord of the Rings* on top of the retail DVD chart while *Harry Potter* sits on top of the VHS retail chart. There are some subtle differences between these two charts. The VHS chart contains titles such as *Cinderella 2, Barbie as Rapunzel and Peter Pan – Return to Neverland* which were essentially straight-to-video releases.

In contrast the DVD chart offers a couple of reissues in the form of *The Shawshank Redemption* (the perennial top five favourite of IMDb), and the 25th anniversary repackaging of Grease. The BVA states that all of the Top

41 All Time Top 20 Rental VHS & DVD Video in the UK 2002

	Title	Distributor	Country
1	Four Weddings and a Funeral	Columbia TriStar	US/UK
2	Dirty Dancing	First Independent	US
3	Basic Instinct	Guild	US
4	Crocodile Dundee	Fox	US/Australia
5	Gladiator	Universal/Columbia	US
6	Sister Act	Buena Vista	US
7	Forrest Gump	CIC	US
8	The Sixth Sense	Buena Vista	US
9	Home Alone	Fox	US
10	Ghost	CIC	US
11	The Green Mile	Universal/Warner	US
12	Speed	FoxVideo	US
13	Pretty Woman	Buena Vista	US
14	Braveheart	Fox Guild	US
15	Jurassic Park	CIC	US
16	Pulp Fiction	Buena Vista	US
17	The Silence of the Lambs	Columbia TriStar	US
18	Bridget Jones's Diary	Universal	US
19	Robocop	VVL	US
20	A Fish Called Wanda	MGM	US/UK

Source: BVA

42 All Time Top 20 Retail VHS & DVD Video in the UK 2002

	Title	Distributor	Country
1	The Jungle Book	Buena Vista	US
2	Titanic	20th Century Fox	US
3	Snow White and the Seven Dwarfs	Buena Vista	US
4	Lord of the Rings: Fellowship of the Ring	EV	US/New Zealand
5	Toy Story	Buena Vista	US
6	The Lion King	Buena Vista	US
7	Shrek	Universal	US
8	Gladiator	Universal/Columbia	US
9	Harry Potter and the Philosopher's Stone	Warner	US/UK
10	Beauty and the Beast	Buena Vista	US
11	Fantasia	Buena Vista	US
12	The Full Monty	20th Century Fox	US/UK
13	101 Dalmatians	Buena Vista	US
14	Star Wars	20th Century Fox	US
15	Return of the Jedi	20th Century Fox	US
16	Lady and the Tramp	Buena Vista	US
17	The Empire Strikes Back	20th Century Fox	US
18	The Matrix	Warner	US
19	Dirty Dancing	Columbia TriStar	US
20	Star Wars 1 - The Phantom Menace	20th Century Fox	US

Source: BVA

20 DVD titles sold at least 400,000 units compared with only seven titles in the top 20 last year.

In the light of the protracted debate about the current health of the UK film industry it is worth noting that there are only two UK films in the top 20 retail chart, namely *Harry Potter* and *Bridget Jones*, and these are of course UK/US co-productions. The rental chart also reveals the dearth of home grown products being selected by the UK public. The three exceptions were the co-produced *51st State, About a Boy*, and the ubiquitous *Harry Potter and the Philosopher's Stone.*

Warners were by far the most successful company in terms of market share for the video retail sector (Table 39). They could boast seven films in the top 20 including *Harry Potter*. EV leapt from a 3.1 per cent share in 2001 to 8.7 per cent, while 20th Century Fox also improved from a 8 per cent share in 2001 to 11.8 per cent in 2002.

Fox Pathé/MGM achieved a first, topping the rental chart with a 19.7 per cent share of the market (Table 40). This was achieved with another record of having 12 different titles at No1 in the weekly rental charts. This same feat is not replicated in the top 20 rental charts which show Fox Pathé/MGM products such as *Moulin Rouge, Shallow Hal* and *Planet of the Apes* in mid-table positions.

Harry Potter broke records upon its video release

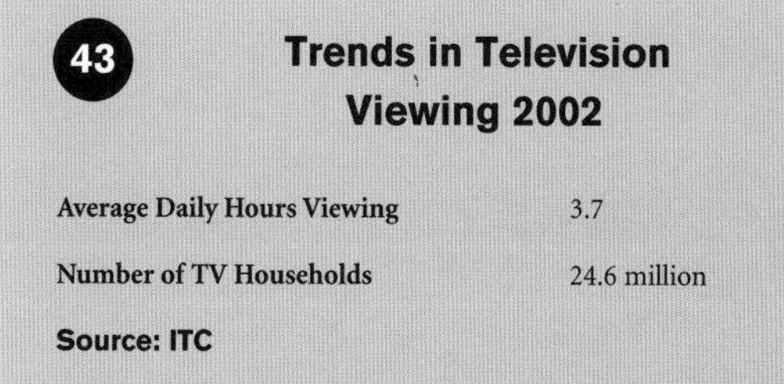

43 Trends in Television Viewing 2002

Average Daily Hours Viewing	3.7
Number of TV Households	24.6 million

Source: ITC

44 Average TV Audience Share (%) of TV Channels 2002

BBC1	BBC2	ITV1	C4	Five	Cab/Sat
26.4	11.5	24.3	10.1	6.3	21.4

	BBC1	BBC2	ITV1	C4	Five	Cab/Sat
2001	26.8	11.1	26.7	9.6	5.7	19.8
2000	27.1	10.7	29.4	10.1	5.7	17.0
1999	28.4	10.8	31.2	10.3	5.4	14.0
1998	29.5	11.3	31.7	10.2	4.3	13.0
1997	30.8	11.6	32.9	10.6	2.3	11.8
1996	32.5	11.5	35.1	10.7	-	10.2
1995	32.2	11.1	37.2	10.9	-	8.6
1994	32.4	10.0	39.3	10.0	-	6.9
1993	32.7	10.2	40.0	11.0	-	6.1

Source: ITC

Eastenders was the top rating drama programme on TV

45 Multichannel Subscriber Numbers 2002

Number of Households (millions)

Operator	Analogue	Digital	Total
BSkyB	-	6.30	6.30
Freeview	-	1.30	1.30
Cable	1.33	2.04	3.37
Total	1.33	9.64	10.97

Source: ITC

Television

While cinema was experiencing its best year since 1971, TV companies were entering the beginning of a twilight zone with the introduction of new digital services while maintaining existing services. The Communications Act and the subsequent arrival of industry super regulator Ofcom served to herald a new era for broadcasting. It was also the year when the public began to embrace Digital TV services in earnest and multichannel viewers crept ever closer to the 50 per cent mark.

The paradox was that by and large it was business as usual for the TV companies, and the public actually increased its average viewing time to nearly 4 hours per day (Table 43). A report suggested that children in particular could not envisage a home environment where the television was not on at all times.

BBC and ITV1 both surrendered viewers to Satellite/cable and digitial viewers (Table 44). Despite a small drop BBC1 still took the largest share of the TV audience. ITV1 experienced over a 2 per cent drop in audience share while BBC2, Channel 4 and Five all registered slight increases.

It is firmly predicted that half of UK homes will have multichannel TV next year. The total number of multichannel homes was just below the 11 million barrier in 2002 (Table 45). Part of this increase must be attributed to the successful launch in October 2002 of Freeview, the successor to the hapless ITV Digital. Freeview's entrance came at a time when Digital TV take-up had appeared to have levelled out.

Six in 10 multichannel homes currently receive TV via digital satellite. Three in 10 watch via analogue or digital cable, with around one in 10 through digital terrestrial TV.

46 Top 25 Programmes for all Terrestrial Channels 2001

Only top rated episodes of each series are included

	Title	Channel	TX date	Audience (m)
1	Only Fools and Horses	BBC1	25-Dec	17.4
2	EastEnders	BBC1	25-Dec	16.97
3	Coronation Street	ITV1	17-Nov	15.01
4	Pop Idol Live Final	ITV1	9-Feb	13.34
5	Jubilee 2002: Party at the Palace	BBC1	3-Jun	12.54
6	England V Denmark	BBC1	15-Jun	12.47
7	England V Brazil	BBC1	21-Jun	12.46
8	Auf Wiedersehen Pet	BBC1	28-Apr	12.41
9	A Touch of Frost	ITV1	27-Jan	12.37
10	England V Nigeria	BBC1	12-Jun	12.22
11	England V Sweden	ITV1	2-Jun	12.21
12	Heartbeat	ITV1	17-Nov	12.1
13	England V Argentina	BBC1	7-Jun	12
14	Emmerdale	ITV1	27-Dec	11.79
15	Who Wants to be a Millionaire?	ITV1	3-Feb	11.61
16	The Mummy	BBC1	24-Dec	11.1
17	EastEnders: Ricky and Bianca	BBC1	13-May	11.04
18	I'm a Celebrity Get Me Out of Here!	ITV1	8-Sep	10.95
19	Indiana Jones and the Last Crusade	BBC1	24-Jan	10.34
20	Indiana Jones and the Temple of Doom	BBC1	17-Jan	10.11
21	Outtake TV	BBC1	27-Dec	10.11
22	Germany V Brazil: World Cup Final	BBC1	10-Jan	10.08
23	Foyle's War	ITV1	17-Nov	10.04
24	Big Brother	C4	26-Jul	10.09
25	Blood Strangers	ITV1	4-Feb	9.68

Source: TARiS Taylor Nelson Sofres/BARB/bfi

However, the total number of cable subscribers fell by 2 per cent to 3.37 million, and this, coupled with the fact that cable subscribers have gone down, it appears to suggest that the cable sector is in freefall.

Meanwhile, on television the Christmas day episode of *Only Fools and Horses* brought in the top audience for all terrestrial channels with 17.4m enjoying the Trotters' latest annual installment (Table 46). However, the audience was nearly 4 million lower than the previous year, when *Only Fools and Horses* had also topped the chart. The Christmas *Eastenders* episode brought BBC1 a neat 1-2 while ITV1's two strongest challenges came from its hardy perennial *Coronation Street*, and the new kid on the block, the final of *Pop Idol.*

Also of interest were the appearance of two other Reality TV shows – the first, Tony Blackburn's victory in the final of *I'm a Celebrity... Get Me Out of Here!* was watched by almost 11 million. Just inside the top 25 was

Only Fools and Horses proved a Christmas cracker with audiences

47 Television Advertising 2002

	£m
Net TV Advertising Revenue	3146
ITV (inc GMTV)	1727
C4 (inc S4C)	623
C5	221
Programme Sponsorship	82
Non Terrestrial TV Advertising Revenue	575

Source: ITC

Channel 4's first entry on to the chart with the final of *Big Brother* which brought in just over 10 million fascinated viewers.

Readers may be puzzled at the World Cup figures in the table. England's World Cup clash against Brazil actually gained a combined audience of 16 million viewers between BBC1 and ITV1. Similarly, England's 3-0 win over Denmark registered 15.6 million viewers. However, this table reflects the top rated programme, which in both cases went to BBC1. This was not the only good news related to football experienced by the Corporation.

In August 2003 the BBC won back the right to show highlights of Premier League matches after an absence of two years. The three-year deal starting from the 2004/05 season was, worth £105m and meant that the familiar theme tune to *Match of the Day* would return to households. BSkyB in the meantime went football crazy by bagging the right to show live Premiership matches. Their package worth £1.024 billion allowed them to show 138 out of the Premier League's total of 380 games. So ended ITV1's brief flirtation with televised Premiership action.

Other programmes of note were the BBC's live coverage of *the Party at the Palace*, part of the Queen's Golden Jubilee celebrations, and the first episode of *Auf Wiedersehen, Pet* which had switched channels from BBC to ITV after two decades off air, attracting 12.4 million.

Net TV revenue, the lifeblood of the commercial channels, made a marginal improvement from £3,119m in 2001 to £3,146m in 2002 (Table 47).

This year the Handbook has tried to extend its net slightly wider to include TV films and single dramas (not all of which have managed audience ratings over 4 million). The dearth of UK film screenings have been noted, particularly by the UK Film Council, which reported with some justifiable exasperation that ITV1 screened only two UK films less than eight years old last year, while fellow commercial station Channel 5 came in with just one. Indeed, the UK Film Council pressed successfully for ammendments in the Communications Bill that broadcasters should show more UK films on television.

Overall, Channel 4 was the biggest network broadcaster of recent UK films, airing 31 features compared to 26 on BBC1 and BBC2 combined.

As might have been expected Channel 4 and BBC 2 were able to premiere some of their own recent productions. BBC2 could boast *Wonderland, This Year's Love* and *Ratcatcher* among its collection, while Channel 4 waded in with some late-night screenings including *The War Zone, Beautiful People* and *Janice Beard 45 wpm.* ITV1 however, could boast the screening of the award-winning *Bloody Sunday* which was unusual since it received a theatrical release after it had been shown on television.

The top 25 original drama productions reveal the usual suspects, led off by *Eastenders* and followed by *Coronation Street* (Table 48). Only nine BBC programmes feature in the the top 25, suggesting that ITV1 has a wider range of popular programmes from regulars such as *A Touch of Frost, Heartbeat* and *Midsomer Murders* to programmes such as *The Forsyte Saga, Foyles War* and *The Swap*. ITV1 has attempted to arrest its ratings slide by experimenting with showing an extra episode of *Coronation Street* on Monday nights and *Emmerdale* on Sundays.

Back to films, and BBC1 enjoyed the lion's share of the feature films screened on television (Table 50). Most of them were Hollywood box office giants from the past led surprisingly by *The Mummy* which gained an audience of just over 11 million. The top UK film was the Christmas screening of *Chicken Run* which brought in over 9.5 million viewers. ITV1's best performer was *Home Alone*, although, ITV1's ratings favourite is without doubt James Bond. James Bond seasons crop up on ITV1 as regularly as repeats of *Dad's Army, Fawlty Towers* and *Only Fools and Horses* appear on the BBC. The top Bond screened in 2002 was *Moonraker* which attracted 6.8 million viewers. This is not a patch on *The World is Not Enough* which was the top Bond film in 2001 gaining a dedicated audience of 9.8m.

UK TV Films Premiered 2002

British TV films and single dramas and drama-documentaries shown on UK terrestrial TV during 2002. Those marked * are films partly produced by broadcasters that have had a release at cinemas prior to transmission. BARB rating is for over 4m only

Title	Tx date	BARB rating (m)	Writer	Director
BBC1				
Murder in Mind: Passion	5-Jan	6.5	Simon.J.Sharkey	Gerry Poulson
Murder in Mind: Disposal	26-Jan	5.0	J.C.Wilsher	Frank.W.Smith
Night Flight	2-Feb	4.1	William Ivory	Nick Renton
Murder in Mind:Rage	2-Mar	5.8	Anthony Horowitz	David Innes Edwards
Strange	9-Mar	5.6	Andrew Marshall	Joe Ahearne
Murder in Mind:Swan Song	20-Mar	4.7	Anthony Horowitz	Frank.W.Smith
Murder in Mind:Flashback	23-Mar	5.6	Anthony Horowitz/Stephen Leather	Ferdinand Fairfax
The Many Lives of Albert Walker	25-Mar	6.3	Philip Palmer	Harry Hook
Sinners	26-Mar	5.5	Lizzie Mickery	Aisling Walsh
Man and Boy	30-Mar	4.6	Kevin Hood	Simon Curtis
Murder in Mind:Victim	6-Apr	5.1	Guy Burt	Audrey Cooke
Murder in Mind: Memories	20-Apr	6.2	Stephen Leather	Nick Jones
Murder in Mind:Regrets	28-May	5.3	Simon Sharkey	Gerry Poulson
Out of Control	15-Sep	4.1	Dominic Savage	Dominic Savage
Jeffrey Archer-The Truth	1-Dec	4.2	Guy Jenkin	Guy Jenkin
George Eliot: A Scandalous Life	24-Dec		Steve Attridge	Mary Downes
The Hound of the Baskervilles	26-Dec	7.6	Allan Cubitt	David Attwood
The Real Jane Austen	30-Dec		Claire Tomalin	N/A
BBC2				
Last Resort*	23-Jan		Pawel Pawlikowski	Pawel Pawlikowski
Conspiracy	25-Jan	4.4	Loring Mandel	Frank.R.Pierson
This Year's Love*	2-Feb		David Kane	David Kane
As the Beast Sleeps	3-Feb		Gary Mitchell	Harry Bradbeer
Smallpox 2002-Silent Weapon	5-Feb		Simon Chinn and Daniel Percival	Daniel Percival
About Adam*	27-Feb		Gerard Stembridge	Gerard Stembridge
Surrealissimo	2-Mar		Matthew Broughton	Richard Curson Smith
Wonderland*	9-Mar		Laurence Coriat	Michael Winterbottom
A Room for Romeo Brass*	16-Mar		Paul Fraser and Shane Meadows	Shane Meadows
Ratcatcher*	23-Mar		Lynne Ramsay	Lynne Ramsay
Get Carmen: The Trials of George Carmen QC	5-Apr		Colin Barr	
The Falklands Play	4-Jun		Ian Curteis	Michael Samuels
The Gathering Storm	12-Jul	4.4	Hugh Whitemore	Richard Loncraine
Little Angels	13-Aug		Devised Project	Paul McGuigan
Flesh and Blood	25-Sep		Peter Bowker	Julian Farino
Born Romantic*	15-Oct		David Kane	David Kane
Tomorrow La Scala!	10-Dec		Francesca Joseph	Francesca Joseph
Cruise of the Gods	23-Dec		Tim Firth	Declan Lowney
No Night is too Long	27-Dec		Kevin Elyot	Tom Shankland
ITV1				
Dick Whittington	1-Jan	5.3	Simon Nye	Geoff Posner
Happy Together	1-Jan	7.6	Sue Teddern	David Wheatley
Bloody Sunday	20-Jan		Paul Greengrass	Paul Greengrass
The Quest	31-Mar	8.4	Douglas Livingstone	David Jason
Poirot: Murder in Mesopotamia	2-Jun	6.1	Clive Exton	Tom Clegg
Bertie and Elizabeth	4-Jun	4.8	Nigel Williams	Giles Foster
The Law	12-Jun	5.1	Matthew Hall	Juliet May
Shipman	9-Jul	7.3	Michael Eaton	Roger Bamford
A Good Thief	22-Jul	5.7	Kay Mellor	Douglas McKinno
A is for Acid	9-Sep	6.0	Glenn Chandler	Harry Bradbeer
Daddy's Girl	23-Sep	7.0	Philomena McDonagh	Bill Eagles
Rogue Trader*	11-Oct		James Dearden	James Dearden
Dead Gorgeous	21-Oct	5.5	Andrew Payne	Sarah Harding
The Safe House	28-Oct	6.5	David Pirie	Simon Massey
Poirot:Evil Under the Sun	15-Dec	7.7	Anthony Horowitz	Brian Farnham
Birthday Girl	22-Dec	6.6	Jonathan Harvey	Morag Fullerton
Goodbye Mr.Chips	26-Dec	6.2	Frank Delaney	Stuart Orme
Bait	27-Dec	5.2	Daniel Boyle	Nicholas Rento
Channel 4				
The War Zone*	15-Jan		Alexander Stuart	Tim Roth
Sunday	28-Jan		Jimmy McGovern	Charles McDougall
With or Without You*	5-Mar		John Forte/Andrew Eaton	Michael Winterbottom
Beautiful People*	11-Mar		Jasmin Dizdar	Jasmin Dizdar
Janice Beard 45 wpm*	8-Sep		Clare Kilner/Ben Hopkins	Clare Kilner
Falling Apart	17-Oct		Anna Maloney	Brian Hill
Solid Geometry	28-Nov		Denis Lawson	Denis Lawson
Some Voices*	3-Dec		Joe Penhall	Simon Cellan Jones
Hotel Splendide*	6-Dec		Terence Gross	Terence Gross
Darwin's Daughter	28-Dec		James Runcie	James Runcie

Source: BARB/bfi

Top 25 Original Drama Productions 2002

Includes Soap Operas, Series, Serials and UK TV Movies. Audience figures are for highest rated episodes of each production

	Title	Producer/Sponsor	Tx date	Audience(m)
1	EastEnders	BBC	25-Dec	17.40
2	Coronation Street	Granada	17-Nov	15.01
3	Auf Wiedersehen Pet	Ziji Productions/BBC	28-Apr	12.41
4	A Touch of Frost	Yorkshire	27-Jan	12.37
5	Heartbeat	Yorkshire	17-Nov	12.10
6	Emmerdale	Yorkshire	27-Dec	11.79
7	EastEnders: Ricky and Bianca	BBC	13-May	11.04
8	Foyle's War	Greenlit Prods/Channel TV	17-Nov	10.04
9	Blood Strangers	Granada	4-Feb	9.68
10	The Bill	Thames/Carlton	9-Jan	9.62
11	Spooks	Kudos/BBC	13-May	9.60
12	Midsomer Murders	Bentley Prods/LWT	22-Sep	9.52
13	Casualty	BBC	9-Nov	9.42
14	The Forsyte Saga	Granada	7-Apr	9.07
15	The Swap	Greenlit Prods/Channel TV	11-Feb	8.95
16	Waking the Dead	BBC	4-Nov	8.92
17	Monarch of the Glen	Ecosse/BBC	29-Sep	8.91
18	Where the Heart Is	United/Anglia	30-Jun	8.68
19	Holby City	BBC	21-May	8.61
20	London's Burning	LWT	7-Jul	8.47
21	Silent Witness	BBC	6-Oct	8.46
22	The Quest	Yorkshire	1-Apr	8.39
23	Poirot	LWT	15-Dec	8.30
24	Born and Bred	BBC	19-May	8.28
25	Wire in the Blood	Coastal Prods/Yorkshire	14-Nov	8.08

Source: BARB/BFI

Coronation Street murdered most of the opposition in the battle for ratings

Top 25 Feature Films Shown on Terrestrial TV 2002

	Title	Country	Year	Channel	Audience (m)
1	The Mummy	BBC1	1999	US	11,102.7
2	Indiana Jones and the Last Crusade	BBC1	1989	US	10,335.9
3	Indiana Jones and the Temple of Doom	BBC1	1984	US	10,115.2
4	Chicken Run	BBC1	2000	UK/US	9,610.6
5	Home Alone	ITV1	1990	US	8,845.4
6	Raiders of the Lost Ark	BBC1	1981	US	8,826.6
7	Mission: Impossible	BBC1	1996	US	8,261.7
8	A Bug's Life	BBC1	1998	US	8,128.0
9	Men In Black	BBC1	1997	USA	8,096.3
10	Entrapment	BBC1	1998	US/UK/GER	6,983.2
11	Small Soldiers	BBC1	1998	US	6,761.2
12	Robin Hood: Prince of Thieves	BBC1	1991	US	6,698.0
13	Moonraker	ITV1	1979	UK/US	6,892.9
14	Live And Let Die	ITV1	1973	UK/US	6,879.3
15	The Italian Job	BBC1	1969	UK	6,671.1
16	Dante's Peak	ITV1	1997	US	6,664.9
17	Volcano	ITV1	1997	US	6,661.4
18	Mansfield Park	BBC1	1999	UK	6,539.7
19	Star Wars: Ep. I – Phantom Menace	ITV1	1999	US	6,520.1
20	Grease	ITV1	1978	US	6,478.1
21	Octopussy	ITV1	1983	UK/US	6,421.2
22	A View To A Kill	ITV1	1985	UK/US	6,409.8
23	Rush Hour	BBC1	1998	US	6,343.0
24	Enemy of the State	BBC1	1998	US	6,325.8
25	Speed 2: Cruise Control	ITV1	1997	USA	6,306.8

Source: TARiS Taylor Nelson Sofres/BARB

Indiana Jones (left) and The Mummy (right) were the most popular films screened on terrestrial TV in 2002

Further Reading

Statistics sources

AC Nielsen/EDI Database Reports
London: AC Nielsen/EDI.
Key source for UK and US Box Office.

British Films Catalogue 2002
British Council, 2002.
Annual listing of features, documentary, short, and animation films made in the UK. (Available at www.britfilms.com).

BVA Yearbook 2003
London: British Video Association, 2001.
Key source for UK video/DVD data.

Cinema exhibition and distribution in Europe: market assessment and forecast
Screen Digest, 2001.
Useful but expensive resource.

Cinemagoing 11
Cinemagoing Western Europe
Leicester: Dodona Research, 2003
Key report on cinema attendance and the state of the exhibition sector.

Developing UK film talent: a comprehensive skills survey of the UK film industry
Skillset/Film Council, 2003.

European Audiovisual Yearbook 2002
EAO, 2002
Formerly known as: Statistical Yearbook: cinema, television and new media in Europe. Now a 5-volume set. Key source for European audiovisual industry with summaries and tables on the film production, distribution, admissions, television, multimedia, home video, and advertising.

European cinema yearbook [2002]
Only available to download:
www.mediasalles.it

European Video Yearbook 2000/2001
Screen Digest: 2001.
Contains brief national market summaries with accompanying tables for VHS/DVD.

Film in the UK 2002 Statistical Yearbook
UK Film Council, 2003.
Compilation of handbook style statistics for the UK film industry.

GB Cinema exhibitors
Office for National Statistics, 2001.

Overseas Transactions of the Film & Television Industry
National Statistics.
(www.statistics.gov.uk)

Statistical Yearbook: cinema, television and new media in Europe 2001
European Audiovisual Observatory, 2002
Key source for European audiovisual industry with summaries and tables on the film production, distribution, admissions, television, multimedia, home video, and advertising.

Suggested further reading and other useful sources

Annuals Guide 2002, by Christophe Dupin and Andrea King
Excellent guide to frequently used sources held in the bfi National Library.
(Available at:
www.bfi.org.uk/library/collections)

The Arts funding guide (6th ed)
Directory of Social Change, 2002

British Cinema of the 90s, edited by Robert Murphy
bfi , 1999.

The British cinema Book (2nd ed), ed by Robert Murphy.
bfi, 2001.
Expanded survey with a new section on contemporary British cinema.

The British film business, by Bill Baillieu and John Goodchild
Chichester: John Wiley & Sons, 2002.
Useful introduction on the workings of the British film industry since 1896.

Building a sustainable UK film industry: a presentation to the UK film industry, by Alan Parker, (5th November 2002).

Cable & Satellite Yearbook 2003
Informa Media, 2003
Standard directory for the sector.

Cinemas & theatres (Key Note report)
Key Note, 2001.

Developing UK film talent: a comprehensive skills survey of the UK film industry
Skillset/Film Council, 2003.

Digital television 2002: final report
Department for Culture, Media and Sport/MORI, May 2002

Entertainment industry economics: a guide for financial analysis (5th ed), by Harold L. Vogel.
Cambridge University Press, 2001.

European feature animation: report, by Tim Westcott.
Cartoon, October 2002

European film industries, by Anne Jackel
bfi, December 2002

The Film Industry Market Report (Keynote Report)
Keynote, 2000.

Film in England: a development strategy for film and the moving image in the English regions
Film Council, 2000. (Available at www.filmcouncil.org.uk/).

Global Film: Exhibition & Distribution (4th ed), by Andy Thomas & Stuart O'Brien
Informa Media Group, 2001.
Analysis and tables on exhibition, admissions, box office & distribution.

The media guide 2003
Atlantic Books, 2002.
Handy and comprehensive guide.

A New Future For Communications.
HMSO, 2001.
White paper on communications and OFCOM.

Producing the Goods? UK film production since 1991: an information briefing,
Phil Wickham.
bfi National Library, 2003.
New survey of the British film industry in the 1990s with useful statistics.

The Relph report: a study for the Film Council examining the costs of lower budget UK films and their value in the world market.
UK Film Council, 2002.

The researcher's guide: film, television, radio and related documentaion collections in the UK.
British Universities Film & Video Council, 2001.

Screen Digest report on the implication of digital technology for the film industry.
Department for Culture, Media & Sport/Screen Digest, 2002.

Striking a balance: the control of children's media consumption, by Pam Hanley.
BBC/Broadcasting Standards Commission, 2002.

TBI Yearbook 2003
Informa Media, 2002.
Long established reference source for international TV.

Towards a Sustainable UK Film Industry
Film Council, 2000.

White sticks, wheels and crutches: disability and the moving image.
bfi, 2003.

Selected annual reports

Arts Council of England annual report 2001

BBC annual report & accounts 2002/3

British Board of Film Classification annual report 2002

BFI annual review 1999/2000

Broadcasting Standards Commission annual report 2002

Independent Television Commission annual report & accounts 2002

UK Film Council Annual Review 2001/2002

Periodicals

Broadcast (UK, weekly)
PACT Magazine (UK, monthly)
Screen Digest (UK, monthly)
Screen Finance (UK, fortnightly)
Screen International (UK, weekly)
Sight and Sound (UK, monthly)
Television (UK, monthly)
Televisual (UK, monthly)
Variety (US, weekly)

Compiled by Sean Delaney

ARCHIVES AND FILM LIBRARIES

International Organisations

FIAF (International Federation of Film Archives)

1 Rue Defacqz
B-1000 Brussels
Belgium
Tel: 32 2 538 3065
Fax: 32 2 534 4774
email: info@fiafnet.org
Website: www.fiafnet.org
Christian Dimitriu
Founded in 1938, FIAF is a collaborative association of the world's leading film archives whose purpose is to ensure the proper preservation and showing of motion pictures. More than 120 archives in over 65 countries collect, restore, and exhibit films and cinema documentation spanning the entire history of film. It also publishes handbooks on film archiving practice which can be obtained from the above address

FIAT/IFTA (International Federation of Television Archives)

email: office@fiatifta.org
Website: www.fiatifta.org
President:
Emmanuel Hoog (INA, France)
Vice Presidents:
Peter Dusek (ORF, Austria)
Branko Bubenik (HRT, Croatia)
Dominique Saintville (INA, France)
General Secretary:
Steve Bryant (BFI, UK)
FIAT membership is mainly made up of the archive services of broadcasting organisations. It also encompasses national archives and other television-related bodies. The aim of the association is to set up local seminars and a worldwide conference annually. Information of the activities of the association is published on the website

European Archives

Below are some European Film Archives of countries in the European Union. For more specialised information consult *Film and Television Collections in Europe – The MAP-TV Guide* published by Blueprint

Austria

Filmarchiv Austria(Austrian Film Archive)

Obere Augartenstraße 1
A-1020 Wien
Austria
Tel: 0043 1 216 1300
Fax: 0043 1 216 1300-100
email: augarten@filmarchiv.at
Website: www.filmarchiv.at
Mag. Ernst Kieninger (Head of Archive)

Belgium

Cinémathèque Royale/Koninklijk Filmarchief (Royal Film Archives)

Palais des Beaux Arts
Rue Baron Horta 9
1000 Bruxelles
Belgium
Tel: 32 02 507 83 70
Fax: 32 02 513 12 72
email: filmarchive@ledoux.be
Website: www.ledoux.be
Film preservation. The collection can be consulted on the Archive's premises for research purposes

Denmark

Danish Film Institute

Archive and Cinematheque
Gothersgade 55
DK - 1123 Copenhagen K
Denmark
Tel: 45 33 74 34 00
Fax: 45 33 74 35 99
email: museum@dfi.dk
Website: www.dfi.dk
Contact: Dan Nissen, Director

Finland

Suomen Elokuva-Arkisto (Finnish Film Archive)

PO Box 177
Fin 00151 Helsinki
Finland
Tel: 35 8 9 615 400
Fax: 35 8 9 615 40 242
email: sea@sea.fi
Website: www.sea.fi
Matti Lukkarila

France

Les Archives du Film du Centre National de la Cinématographie

7 bis rue Alexandre Turpault
78390 Bois D'Arcy Cedex
France
Tel: 33 1 34 14 80 00
Fax: 33 1 34 60 52 25
email: michelle.aubert@cnc.fr
Website: www.cnc.fr
Michelle Aubert, curator

Germany

Deutsche Rundfunkarchiv (DRA)/German Broadcast Archive

Bertramstraße 8
D-60320 Frankfurt/M
Germany
Tel: Tel.: (069) 15 687 - 0
Fax: (069) 15 687 - 100
email: dra@hr-online.de
Website: www.dra.de

Greece

Teniothiki Tis Elladas (Greek Film Archives)

1 Canari Street
Athens 10761
Greece
Tel: 30 1 361 2046
Fax: 30 1 362 8468
email: tain@otenet.gr
Website: www.tte.gr
Theodoros Adamopoulos, Director

Ireland

Irish Film Archive
Film Institute of Ireland
6 Eustace Street
Dublin 2
Republic of Ireland
Tel: 353 1 679 5744
Fax: 353 1 677 8755
email: archive@ifc.ie
Website: www.fii.ie
Kasandra O'Connell, Head of Archive
Sunniva O'Flynn, Archive Curator
Eugene Finn, Keeper
Emma Keogh, Librarian/Paper Archivist

Italy

Cineteca Nazionale (National Film Archive)
Centro Sperimentale di Cinematografia
Via Tuscolana 1524
I-00173 Roma
Italy
Tel: 39 06 722 941
Fax: 39 06 7211619
email: info@snc.it
Website: www.snc.it
Angelo Libertini, General Director

Luxembourg

Cinémathèque Municipale de Luxembourg/Ville de Luxembourg (Luxembourg National Film Archive/City of Luxembourg
10 rue Eugène Ruppert
2453 Luxembourg
Tel: (352) 4796 2644
Fax: (352) 4075 19

The Netherlands

Nederlands Filmmuseum, Stichting (Nederlands Film Museum)
Vondelpark 3
1071 AA Amsterdam
The Netherlands
Tel: 31 20 589 1400
Fax: 31 20 683 3401

Portugal

Cinemateca Portuguesa - Museu do Cinema (Portuguese Film Archive and Museum)
Rua Barata Salgueiro, 39
1269-059 Lisboa
Portugal
Tel: 351 21 359 62 00
Fax: 351 21 352 31 80
email: cinemateca@cinemateca.pt
João Bérnard da Costa, President
José Manuel Costa, Vice President
Rui Santana Brito, Vice President

Spain

Filmoteca Espanola (Spanish National Film Archive)
Caalle Magdalena 10
28012
Madrid
Spain
Tel: 34 91 467 26 00
Fax: 34 91 467 26 11
Website: www.mcu.es

Sweden

Svenska Filminstitutet (Swedish Film Institute) - Cinemateket
PO Box 27 126
S-102 52 Stockholm
Sweden
Tel: 46 0 8 665 11 00
Fax: 46 0 8 661 18 20
email: info@sfi.se
Website: www.sfi.se
Jan-Erik Billinger, Head of Cinemateket

National Archives

bfi National Film and Television Archive
British Film Institute
J. Paul Getty Jnr. Conservation Centre
Kingshill Way
Berkhamsted
Herts HP4 3TP
Tel: 01442 876301
Fax: 01442 289112
Website: www.bfi.org.uk
David Pierce (Curator NFTVA)
The National Film and Television Archive contains more than 275,000 films and 210,000 TV programmes, dating from 1895 to the present. Related collections of stills, posters, designs, scrips and printed ephemera such as marketing materals, technology, props and costumes have been assembled alongside the software to give added context and meaning

Imperial War Museum Film and Video Archive
Lambeth Road
London SE1 6HZ
Tel: 020 7416 5000
Fax: 020 7416 5374
email: film@iwm.org.uk email: film-commercial@iwm.org.uk (commercial enquiries)
Website: www.iwm.org.uk
Paul Sargent/Jane Fish
The national museum of modern conflict, illustrating and recording all aspects of modern war. The Archive reflects these terms of reference with an extensive collection of film and video material, which is widely used by historians and by film and television companies

Scottish Screen Archive
1 Bowmont Gardens
Glasgow G12 9LR
Tel: 0141 337 7400
Fax: 0141 337 7413
email: archive@scottishscreen.com
Website: www.scottishscreen.com
Janet McBain: Curator
Enquiries Tel: 0141 337 7400 (or email)
Almost exclusively non-fiction film, the collection dates from 1896 to the present day and concerns aspects of Scottish social, cultural and industrial history. Available to broadcasters, programme makers, educational users and researchers. Access charges and conditions available on request

The National Screen and Sound Archive of Wales
The National Library of Wales
Aberystwyth
Ceredigion SY23 3BU
Tel: 01970 632828
Fax: 01970 632544
email: agssc@llgc.org.uk
Website: screenandsound.llgc.org.uk
Contact: Iestyn Hughes
The Archive locates, preserves and catalogues film and video material relating to Wales. The collection is made accessible where possible for research and viewing. The Archive is part of The National Library of Wales, Aberystwyth

Regional Archives

East Anglian Film Archive
The Archive Centre
Martineau Lane
Norwich NR1 2DQ
Tel: 01603 592664
Fax: Fax. 01603 593475
email: eafa@uea.ac.uk
Website: www.uea.ac.uk/eafa/
David Cleveland, Director
Jane Alvey, Deputy Director
Phil Butcher, Film Archivist
Preserving both fiction and non-fiction, amateur and professional films, television and video material showing life and work in Bedfordshire, Cambridgeshire, Essex, Hertfordshire, Norfolk and Suffolk. Expertise in the repair, conservation, printing and telecine of small gauge film, up to 16mm. Eafa also teaches future film archivists on its MA in Film Archiving, in conjunction with English and American Studies at UEA

North West Film Archive
Manchester Metropolitan University
Minshull House
47-49 Chorlton Street
Manchester M1 3EU
Tel: 0161 247 3097
Fax: 0161 247 3098
email: n.w.filmarchive@mmu.ac.uk
Website: www.nwfa.mmu.ac.uk
Marion Hewitt, Acting Director
Enquiries: Jo Abley
Preserves moving images showing life in the North West and operates as a public regional archive. Urban and industrial themes are particularly well illustrated. Online film and video catalogue at the Archive's website

Northern Region Film and Television Archive
Blanford House
Blanford Square
Newcastle upon Tyne NE1 4JA
Tel: 0191 232 6789 ext 411
Fax: 0191 230 2614
email: isa@nrfta.org.uk
Website: www.nrfta.org.uk
Director: Leo Enticknap
Middlesbrough Office:
Northern Region Film and Television Archive
c/o School of Arts and Media
University of Teesside
Middlesbrough
Tees Valley TS1 3BA
Tel: 01642 384022
Fax: 01642 384099
Contact: For access enquiries and depositing material
contact Lisa Bond
Tel: 0191 232 6789 ext. 411
email: lisa@nrfta.org.uk
For all other enquiries
contact Leo Enticknap
Tel: 01642 384022 email: leo@nrfta.org.uk
The NRFTA was founded in 1998 in order to collect, preserve and provide access to moving images of historical, social and cultural relevance to an area covering Tyneside, Teesside, Cumbria, Northumberland and County Durham. The bulk of its current holdings (almost entirely non-fiction) consist of BBC North-East news footage from 1958-72, the news and documentary output of Tyne-Tees and Border Television and the productions of Trade Films, a Newcastle-based unit whose output is concerned with industry, in particular coal mining and its community.

South East Film & Video Archive
University of Brighton
Grand Parade
Brighton BN2 OJY
Tel: 01273 643213
Fax: 01273 643214
email: sefva@brighton.ac.uk
Website: www.bton.ac.uk/sefra/
Jane King, Administrator
Established in 1992 the function of this regional film and video archive is to locate, collect, preserve and promote films and video tapes made in the four counties of Surrey, Kent, East Sussex and West Sussex and the unitary authorities of Brighton & Hove and Mcdway

The South West Film and Television Archive
Melville Building
Royal William Yard
Stonehouse
Plymouth
Devon PL1 3RP
Tel: 01752 202650
Fax: 01752 205025
email: enquiries@tswfta.co.uk
Website: www.tswfta.co.uk
Elayne Hoskin
The official film archive for the South West of England. Holds south western film material and includes three television collections covering the period 1961 to 1992 - Westward Television, Television South West and BBC South West

Wessex Film and Sound Archive

Hampshire Record Office
Sussex Street
Winchester SO23 8TH
Tel: 01962 847742
Fax: 01962 878681
email: david.lee@hants.gov.uk
Website: www.hants.gov.uk/record-office/film.html
David Lee
Preserves and makes publicly accessible for research, films, video and sound recordings of local interest to central southern England

Yorkshire Film Archive

York St John College
Lord Mayor's Walk
York YO31 7EX
Tel: 01904 716550
Fax: 01904 716552
email: yfa@yorksj.ac.uk
Sue Howard
The Yorkshire Film Archive exists to locate, preserve and show film about the Yorkshire region. Material dates from 1897 and includes newsreels, documentaries, advertising and amateur films
Yorkshire Film Archive. Website details will be available from September 2003

Newsreel, Production and Stock Shot Libraries

Archive Film Agency

21 Lidgett Park Avenue
Roundhay
Leeds LS8 1EU
Tel: 0113 2662454/0113 2698635
Fax: 0113 2662454
email: acrchivefilmagency@email.com
Website: www.archivefilmagency.com
Agnèse Geoghegan
Film from 1898 to present day, including a current worldwide stock shot library. Specialists in early fiction, newsreel, documentary, Music Hall, Midlands, Yorkshire, British 1930s stills. Cassette services

Associated Press Television News (APTN)

The Interchange
Oval Road
Camden Lock
London NW1 7DZ
Tel: 020 7482 7400
Fax: 020 7413 8302
email: aptnbroadcastservices@ap.org
Website: www.aptn.com
Chris Stocking, Director of Client Operations
APTN Broadcast Services are the leading experts at providing worldwide crewing, editing, live and tape facilities for broadcasters

BBC Information & Archives - Television Archive

Wood Lane
London W12 7RJ
Tel: 020 8576 9222
Rachel Mulligan
The largest collection of broadcast programmes in the world reflecting the whole range of BBC output

bfi Archival Footage Sales

21 Stephen Street
London W1P 2LN
Tel: 020 7957 4842
Fax: 020 7436 4016
email: footage.films@bfi.org.uk
Website:
www.bfi.org.uk/collections/afs
Jan Faull or Simon Brown
Material from the largest collection of film footage in Britain - the National Film and Television Archive. Television, films, documentaries, newsreels and animation are all covered with over 350,000 titles to choose from, including material dating back to 1895. First stop for serious research on subjects that have shaped the 20th century. Research facilities available

Boulton-Hawker Films

Hadleigh
near Ipswich
Suffolk IP7 5BG
Tel: 01473 822235
Fax: 01473 824519
Educational films and videos: health education, social welfare, home economics, P.S.E., P.E., Maths, biology, physics, chemistry, geography

The Bridgeman Art Library

17-19 Garway Road
London W2 4PH
Tel: 020 7727 4065
Fax: 020 7792 8509
email: london@bridgeman.co.uk
Website: www.bridgeman.co.uk
Jenny Page
The Bridgeman Art Library is the world's leading source of fine art images for reproduction. From iconic classics to contemporary art, all styles and periods are represented. Images can be viewed and ordered online and a free printed catalogue is available

British Artists' Film and Video Study Collection

Room 203
Central Saint Martins College of Art and Design
Southampton Row
London WC1B 4AP
Tel: 020 7514 8159
Fax: 020 7514 7071
Website:
www.bftv.ac.uk/projects/csm.htm
The Study Collection contains ore than 1,000 individual film and video works on VHS tape from the Arts Council of England's Reference Collection of funded works, the ICA's former Videotheque collection, exhibition compilations from the Film & Video Umbrella, the former LEA and other organisations and includes many tapes donated by individual artists. Over 500 'artist' files of paper documentation containing published and unpublished writings by artists, writings about artists, and other ephemera (letters, promotional cards, etc). Some files are extensive, others contain as little as a single postcard.
* Fliers and programme notes relating to screenings and exhibitions since 1966, still images and posters

The British Defence Film Library

SSVC, Chalfont Grove
Narcot Lane
Chalfont St. Peter
Gerrards Cross
Bucks SL9 8TN
Tel: 01494 878278/878252
Fax: 01494 878007
email: robert.dungate@ssvc.com
Website: www.ssvc.com
Robert Dungate: BDFL Library Manager
SSVC has many years experience in providing both entertainment and support for the military. The British Defence Film Library (BDFL) is an independent department within SSVC which holds and distributes audio visual training materials for use by the armed forces which have been specifically commissioned by the Ministry of Defence. The Library also supplies this footage to the film and television industry offering a unique collection of British military material

British Movietonews

North Orbital Road
Denham
Middx UB9 5HQ
Tel: 01895 833071
Fax: 01895 834893
email: library@mtone.co.uk
Website: www.movietone.com
Barbara Heavens
One of the world's major film archives featuring high quality cinema newsreels from the turn of the century, with an emphasis on 1929-1979. the library now represents on an exclusive basis the TV-AM News Library with over 1,100 hours of British and World news covering the period 1983-1991. This material is available on re-mastered digital tape

British Pathé Plc

New Pathé House
57 Jameston Road
London NW1 7DB
Tel: 020 7424 3650/020 7424 3636
Fax: 020 7485 3606
email: larry.mckinna@britishpathe.com
Website: www.britishpathe.com
Larry McKinna: Chief Librarian
50 million feet of newsreel and social documentary from 1896 to 1970. Rapid research and sourcing through computerised catalogue. British Pathe footage sales are now managed by ITN archive

Canal + Image UK Ltd

Pinewood Studios
Pinewood Road, Iver
Bucks SL0 0NH
Tel: 01753 631111
Fax: 01753 655813
John Herron
Feature films, TV series, stock shots and stills, b/w and colour, 35mm, 1925 to present day

Chain Production Ltd

2 Clanricarde Gardens
London W2 4NA
Tel: 020 7229 4277
Fax: 020 7229 0861
Website: www.chainproduction.com
Specialist in European films and world cinema, cult classics, handling European Film Libraries with all rights to over 1,000 films - also clip rights and clip search

Channel Four Clip Library

124 Horseferry Road
London SW1P 2TX
Tel: 020 7306 8490
Fax: 020 7306 8362
email: clipsales@channel4.co.uk
Website: www.4clipsales.com
Paul McAllister
An ever growing portfolio of programmes and a diverse collection of library material. Also access to feature films when the copyright has been cleared with original copyright holders

Clips & Footage

2nd Floor
80a Dean Street
London W1D 3SN
Tel: 020 7287 7287
Fax: 020 7439 4886
email: clipsetc@easynet.co.uk
Website: www.clipsfootage.uk.com
Alison Mercer
Supplies historical and modern colour footage of every description to broadcast, commercial and corporate producers. Special colections include B-movies, feature film trailers, newsreels, 35mm stock shots and time-lapse. Free research. Free viewing at our Soho premises

COI Footage File

2 The Quadrant
135 Salusbury Road
London NW6 6RJ
Tel: 020 7624 3388
Fax: 020 7624 3377
email: research@film-images.com.
Website: www.film-images.com
Tony Dykes
Crown copyright films produced for the British Government spanning the last 75 years featuring a number of film greats such as John Grierson, Humphrey Jennings, Alfred Hitchcock and Richard Massingham. The COI Footage File collection has been managed by Film Images since 1997 and a full on-line catalogue is available

Contemporary Films

24 Southwood Lawn Road
Highgate
London N6 5SF
Tel: 020 8340 5715
Fax: 020 8348 1238
email: inquiries@ contemporary-films.com
Website: www.contemporaryfilms.com
Eric Liknaitzky
Documentaries on China, USSR, Cuba, Nazi Germany, South Africa. The library also covers areas like the McCarthy witch hunts in the '50s, the civil rights movements of the '60s, hippie culture, feminism

Editions Audiovisuel Beulah

66 Rochester Way
Crowborough TN6 2DU
Tel: 01892 652413
Fax: 01892 652413
email: bfi@eavb.co.uk
Website: www.eavb.co.uk/library
Beulah publish the following videos Vintage Music, Royal Navy, Military Transport, Yesterday's Britain, operate a stock shot and sound effects library, and provides film and video restoration services

Environmental Investigation Agency

62-63 Upper Street
London N1 ONY
Tel: 020 7354 7960
Fax: 020 7354 3961
email: info@eia-international.org
Website: www.eia-international.org
Extensive and exclusive library of video and stills showing the exploitation of wildlife and the environment worldwide. Subjects include dolphin and whale slaughter, the bird trade, bear farms, animal products illegally on sale in shops and to undercover investigators, and other aspects of endangered species trade. All film sales help to fund future investigations and campaigns

Film and Video Umbrella

52 Bermondsey Street
London SE1 3UD

Tel: 020 7407 7755
Fax: 020 7407 7766
email: info@fvu.co.uk
Website: www.fvumbrella.com
Film and Video Umbrella curates and produces film, video and new media projects by artists which are commissioned and presented in collaboration with galleries and venues across England

Film Images
2 The Quadrant
135 Salusbury Road
London NW6 6RJ
Tel: 020 7624 3388
Fax: 020 7624 3377
email: research@film-images.com
Website: www.film-images.com
Angela Saward
Thousands of hours of classic and contemporary film images from hundreds of different sources around the world. All fully catalogued and immediately available for viewing on VHS or U-Matic. Suppliers include Central Office of Information and Overseas Film and Television

Fred Goodland Archives
81 Farmilo Road
Leyton
London E17 8JN
Tel: 020 8539 4412
Fax: 020 8539 4412
Fred Goodland MBKS
An eclectic collection of actuality and entertainment subjects on high quality film prints and broadcast format video (1890s-2000). The Film Archive includes a wide range of often rare musical material (1920s-1960s), plus examples of early sound and colour film systems, personalities, vintage fashion, animation, amateur footage, adverts and trailers. VHS preview tapes with BITC are available to researchers. Broadcast format transfers are personally supervised. The Sound Archive, containing thousands of recordings on shellac, vinyl and tape, reproduces many musical styles of the 20th century. Transfers for professional use are available on CDR

Fremantle Archive Sales
1 Stephen Street
London W1T 1AL
Tel: 020 7691 6733
Fax: 020 7691 6080
email: archive@fremantlemedia.com
Website: www.freemantlemedia.com
Massimo Moretti
One of the most comprehensive television archives worldwide with moving images from 1950's to the present day. Award winning programmes including light entertainment, drama, game shows, documentaries and current affairs

FRPS (Film Research & Production Services Ltd)
PO Box 28045
London SE27 9WZ
Tel: 020 8670 2959
Fax: 020 8670 1793
email: frps@aol.com
Website: filmresearch.co.uk
Amanda Dunne
Film Research provides both contemporary and archive moving footage and stills sourced from all genres including:- news, sport, wildlife, feature films and television programmes. Footage is supplied for use in all media production formats, including:- commercials, feature films, corporate films, pop promos, documentaries and television series

GB Associates
7 Marion Grove
Woodford Green
Essex 9TA
Tel: 020 8504 6340
Fax: 020 8505 1850
email: filmview@dial.pipex.com
Malcolm Billingsley
An extensive collection, mainly on 35mm, of fact and fiction film from the turn of the century. The collection is particularly strong in vintage trailers, the early sound era, early colour systems and adverts

Granada Visual
48 Leicester Square
London WC2H 7FB
Tel: 020 7633 2700
Fax: 020 7633 2701
email: granada.visual@granadamedia.com
Website:
www.granadamedia.com/visual
Mark Leaver, Head of Sales and Marketing
Granada Visual represents an ever increasing catalogue of over 100,000 hours of diverse programming and materials covering every genre, from entertainment and music to drama and documentaries or news and personalities to wildlife and stockshots. Granada Visual provides access to footage from the libraries of Anglia TV, Border TV, Granada TV, Granada Wild, HTV Network, LWT, Meridian, Tyne Tees TV and Yorkshire TV

Huntley Film Archives
191 Wardour Street
London W1F 82E
Tel: 020 7287 8000
Fax: 020 7287 8001
email: films@huntleyarchives.com
Website: www.huntleyarchives.com
Amanda Huntley, John Huntley, Sarah King
Archive film library for broadcast, corporate and educational purposes, specialising in documentary footage 1900-1980. Phone to make an appointment or write for brochure detailing holdings. Now also 50,000 stills from films and film history, online film catalogue now available for research via website

Index Stock Shots
Highgate Business Centre
33 Greenwood Place
London NW5 1LD
Tel: 020 7482 1953
Fax: 020 7482 1967
email: index@indexstockshots.com
Website: www.indexstockshots.com
Philip Hinds
Unique stock footage on 35mm film and tape. Including time-lapse and aerial photography, cities, landmarks, aviation, wildlife

ITN Archive
200 Gray's Inn Road
London WC1X 8XZ
Tel: 020 7430 4480
Fax: 020 7430 4453
email: sales@itn.co.uk
Website: www.itnarchive.com
Linda Reeve
ITN Archive is one of the largest commercial archives in the world, providing access to over 250 000 hours of high quality news and feature material and dating back to 1986. The holdings comprise of all ITN's output, including award-winning reports and selected rushes since 1955. ITN Archive has exclusive world rights to the entire Reuters Television Archive whichincludes historical newsreel such as British Paramount News, Empire News Bulletin , Gaumont Graphic and Gaumont British.The entire full integrated database is available free online and much of the material is grouped into themed collections to aid research. ITN Archive also represents French Pathé in the UK. British Pathe footage sales are now managed by ITN archive

London Film Archive
c/o 191 Wardour Street
London W1F 82E
Tel: 020 7287 8000
Fax: 020 7287 8001
email: info@londonfilmarchive.org
Website: www.londonfilmarchive.org
Robert Dewar
Dedicated to the acquisition and preservation of film relating to the Greater London region. The collection consists of material from 1895 to the present day and represents professional and amateur produced features and documentary films

The London Jewish Cultural Centre
The Old House
c/o King's College London
Kidderpore Avenue
Lonon NW3 7SZ
Tel: 020 7431 0345
Fax: 020 7431 0361
email: admin@ljcc.org.uk
Website: www.ljcc.org.uk
The LJCC is an educational organisation with an extensive library of feature, documentary and Israeli film containing rare and previously unseen documentary footage, eductational compilation tapes, and a vast archive of material on the Holocaust. It offers some consultancy services to researchers and producers working in this field and organises regular showings of films from the collection. The Centre also uses documentary and feature film widely in all its academic programmes and teaches a variety of film courses

Moving Image Communications
61 Great Titchfield Street
London W1W 7PP
Tel: 020 7580 3300
Fax: 020 7580 2242
email: mail@milibrary.com
Website: www.milibrary.com
Contact: Michael Maloney & Nathalie Banaigs
Moving Image Communications is a well established film and video library
which represents collections consisting of approximately 17 000 hours of material. The collections cover an ever increasing range of subjects both archival and contemporary. Footage ranges from early silent movies to celebrity chat shows; from sport to travelogues; and British imagery. Collections include: TVAM, Channel X, Filmfinders, British Tourist Authority, National Trust, Flying Pictures, Wild Islands, Lonely Planet, Freud Home Movies, Cuban Archives and more. Comprehensive on-line database
available on the website.

Nova Film and Video Library
62 Ascot Avenue, Cantley
Doncaster DN4 6HE
Tel: 0870 765 1094
Fax: 0870 125 7917
email: library@novaonline.co.uk
Website:
www.novaonline.co.uk/library.html
Andrew White, Gareth Atherton
An extensive and unrivalled collection of unique archive material of Britain and the world. The Library holds a huge selection of amateur cine film documenting the changing social life of Britain dating back to 1944 and has a dedicated collection of transport footage from 1949 to the present day. The library also holds a wide selection of specially shot modem footage & interviews. A catalogue and showreel is available, and a selection of video clips are available from the website

The Olympic Television Archive Bureau
Axis Centre
Burlington Lane
Chiswick
London W4 2TH
Tel: 020 8233 5353
Fax: 020 8233 5354
email: webmaster@otab.com
Website: www.otab.com
Contact: Philippa Moore
OTAB was established in 1995 by the International Olympic Committee in order to streamline the commercial management of the audiovisual library of the Olympic Games. The archive contains imagery from the first Olympic Games of the Modern Era, Athens 1896, through to comprehensive coverage of the most recent Olympic Games

OSF (Oxford Scientific Films)
Lower Road
Long Hanborough
Oxford OX29 8LL
Tel: 01993 881881
Fax: 01993 883969 or 01993 882808
email: film.library@osf.uk.com
Website: www.osf.uk.com
Sandra Berry, Victoria Turner, Jane Mulleneux, Rachel Wakefield
Stock footage on 16mm, 35mm film and video. Wide range of wildlife, special fx, timelapse, slow motion, medicine, industry, scenics, world locations, macro, micro etc. Catalogue and showreel available. Extensive stills library

Reuters Television Library
(Managed and Distributed by ITN Archive)
200 Grays Inn Road
London WC1X 8XE
Tel: 020 7430 4480
Fax: 020 7430 4453
email: archive.sales@itn.co.uk
Website: www.itnarchive.com
Alwyn Lindsey, Sales Director
Original newsreel, television news and feature footage from 1896 to present day. Special Collections. Online database (free access) and expert researchers

Ronald Grant Archive
The Cinema Museum
The Master's House
2 Dugard Way (off Renfrew Road,Kennington)
London SE11 4TH
Tel: 020 7840 2200
Fax: 020 7840 2299
email: martin@cinemamuseum.org.uk
Website:
Martin Humphries
15 million feet of fact and fiction film, mainly 35mm, from 1896 on. Also 1 million film stills, posters, programmes, scripts and information. The museum is a FIAF subscriber

Royal Mail Film and Video Archive
PO Box 145
Sittingbourne
Kent ME10 1NH
Tel: 01795 426465
Fax: 01795 474871
email: info@edist.co.uk
Barry Wiles, Linda Gates
Holds a representative selection of documentary programmes made under the GPO Film Unit, including the classic Night Mail, together with programmes produced from 1970s onwards

RSPB Film Unit
The Lodge
Sandy

Bedfordshire SG19 2DL
Tel: 01767 680 551
Fax: 01767 683 262
email: mark.percival@rspb.org.uk
Website: www.rspb.org.uk/films
Mark Percival: Producer and Unit Manager
Lynda Whytock: Film Library Manager
Natural history film-makers specialising in UK birds and other plant and animal wildlife. The RSPB Film Unit has produced over 120 wildlife films generating a film archive of over 750 hours available for commercial library sales via our on-line streaming video, preview, ordering and delivery services. For commercial library sales. The RSPB Film Unit currently produces about one new wildlife film per year and a range of corporate programming

Sky News Library Sales
British Sky Broadcasting Ltd
6 Centaurs Business Park
Grant Way
Isleworth
Middlesex TW7 5QD
Tel: 020 7705 3132
Fax: 020 7705 3201
email: libsales@bskyb.com
Website: www.sky.com/skynewslib-sales
Ben White, Susannah Owen
Extensive round the clock news and current affairs coverage since 1989. Entire library held on Beta SP on site. Library operates 24 hours a day

TWI Archive
Trans World International
McCormack House
Burlington Lane
Chiswick
London W4 2TH
Tel: 020 833 5500
Fax: 020 8233 6476
email:twiarchive@imgworld.com
Website: www.twiarchive.com
Charles Hope-Dunbar, Sales Manager
TWI Archive is one of the leading sporting and non-sporting archives, represents over 60 of the most prestigious federations in the World. Combining professional sales expertise, consultancy, acquisitions and archive management with state-of-the-art storage facilities, TWI Archive provides a one-stop service for its clients and customers.

Undercurrents Archive
16b Cherwell Street
Oxford OX4 1BG
Tel: 01865 203661
Fax: 08701 316103
email: underc@gn.apc.org
Website: www.undercurrents.org
Paul O'Connor
Undercurrents is an archive of grassroots environmental and social protest and dissent and community issues from 1990 to present day. Over 2,000 hours archived and supplied on Betacam SP

World Backgrounds Film Production Library
Millennium Studios,
Elstree Way,
Borehamwood, Herts, WD6 1SF
Tel: 020 8236 1345
Fax: 020 8236 1344
email: films@worldbackgrounds.com
Website:
www.worldbackgrounds.com
Ralph Rogers
Locations around the world. Fully computerised. All 35mm including 3,000 back projection process plates. Numerous video masters held. Suppliers to TV commercials, features, pop promos, TV series, corporate videos etc

Photographic Libraries

BBC Photograph Library
B116 Television Centre
Wood Lane
London W12 7RJ
Tel: 020 8225 7193
Fax: 020 8576 7020
Jaki Faulkner
The BBC's unique archive of radio and television programme stills, equipment, premises, news and personalities dating from 1922. B/w and colour. Visits by appointment

bfi Stills, Posters and Designs
21 Stephen Street
London W1T 1LN
Tel: 020 7957 4797
Fax: 020 7323 9260
email: Website: www.bfi.org.uk/stills/
The world's most comprehensive collection of film and television stills, posters & designs, capturing both on and off-screen moments. The collection illustrates every aspect of the development of world cinema and television - featuring scene stills, star portraits and behind-the-scenes - in addition to original movie posters and designs. Rapid access is available by photographic and digital reproduction or visits by appointment

Corbis
111 Salusbury Road
London NW6 6RG
Tel: 020 7644 7400
Fax: 020 7644 7401
email: info@corbis.com
Website: www.corbis.com
Photographic stills agency/library

The FremantleMedia Stills Library
Teddington Studios
Broom Road
Teddington TW11 9NT
Tel: 020 8781 2789
Fax: 020 8614 2250
email:
stills.library@fremantlemedia.com
Website:
www.fremantlemediastills.com
Colleen Kay
The Library contains over a million images available in all formats including digital. Classic comedy images can be found in the Library's large archive, incorporating programmes both old and new made by some of

the biggest names in television production; Thames (Morecambe and Wise, Benny Hill, Pop Idol, The Bill), Grundy (Neighbours) and Talkback (House Doctor, They Think It's All Over)

Getty Images Film
17 Conway Street
London W1T 6EE
Tel: 0800 279 9255
Fax: 020 7391 9123
email: motion.sales@gettyimages.com
Website: www.gettyimages.com
Business Development Executive: Nikole Ramsey
Includes Archive Films and Image Bank Film

Hulton Archive
Unique House
21-31 Woodfield Road
London W9 2BA
Tel: 020 7266 2662
Fax: 020 7266 3154
email: hultonresearch@getty-images.com
Website: www.hultonarchive.com
One of the world's largest stills archives with over 15 million photographs, prints and engravings covering the entire history of photojournalism

Image Diggers Picture and Tape Library
618b Finchley Road
London NW11 7RR
Tel: 020 8455 4564
Fax: 020 8455 4564
email: ziph@macunlimited.net
Website: imagediggers.netfirms.com
Neil Hornick
35mm slides, stills, postcards, sheet music, magazine and book material for hire. Cinema, theatre and literature clippings archive. Audio/visual tape resources in performing arts and other areas, plus theme research

image.net
1 Hardwick Street
London, EC1R 4RB
United Kingdom
Tel: 020 7841 0550Tel: 020 7841 0550Tel: +44 20 7841 0550
email: sales@image.net
Website: www.image.net
Exclusive on-line access to pre-release publicity material on behalf ofleading entertainment companies

Imperial War Museum
Photograph Archive
All Saints Annexe
Austral Street
London SE11 4SL
Tel: 020 7416 5333/8
Fax: 020 7416 5355
email: photos@iwm.org.uk
Website: www.iwm.org.uk
David Bell
A collection of some 6 million images illustrating all aspects of 20th century warfare. Film stills can also be made from material held by the IWM's Film & Video Archive, by prior arrangement

Institute of Contemporary History & Wiener Library
4 Devonshire Street
London W1W 5BH
Tel: 020 7636 7247
Fax: 020 7436 6428
email: Library@Wienerlibrary.co.uk
Website: www.wienerlibrary.co.uk
Katharina Hübschmann, Senior Librarian
Romsemarie Nief: Photo Archive
The Wiener Library is a private research library and institute specialising in contemporary European and Jewish history, especially the rise and fall of the Third Reich, Nazism and fascist movements, anit-Semitism, the Holocaust and post-war Germany. It holds Britain's largest collection of documents, testimonies, books and videos on the Holocaust. The photographic archive contains stills, postcards, posters and portraits, illustrated books, approx. 2,000 videos and recordings

Joel Finler Collection
7A Belsize Square
London NW3 4HT
Tel: 020 7794 7175
Fax: 020 7813 2965
Joel Finler
Large selection of film stills, posters, slides and transparencies covering the entire history of world cinema, with a special emphasis on colour, Hollywood, production and behind-the-scenes shots of film-makers and stars

Kobal Collection
2 The Quadrant
135 Salusbury Road
London NW6 6RJ
Tel: 020 7624 3300
Fax: 020 7624 3311
email: kobal.info@picture-desk.com
Website: www.picture-desk.com
David Kent
One of the world's leading film photo archives in private ownership. Film stills and portraits, lobby cards and posters, from the earliest days of the cinema to modern times

The Moviestore Collection Ltd
3 Jonathan Street
London SE11 5NH
Tel: 020 7733 9990
email: sales@moviestorecollection.com
Website: moviestorecollection.com
Provider of film and television imagery to the media publishing industry

Mckenzie Heritage Picture Archive
Room 226
Station House
49 Greenwich High Road
London SE10 8JL
Tel: 020 8469 2000
Fax: 020 8469 2000
email: info@mckenziehap.com
Website: www.mckenziehpa.com
Anita Mckenzie
Mckenzie Heritage picture archive specialises in pictures of black communities from Britain and abroad. The images span the 19th and 20th centuries

Retrograph Nostalgia Archive
Number Ten
Hanover Crescent
Brighton BN2 9SB
Tel: 01273 687 554
email: retropix1@aol.com
Website: www.retrograph.com
Jilliana Ranicar-Breese
Vintage worldwide consumer advertising. Decorative labels, magazine advertisements, posters and prints. Commercial and Fine Art (1860-1960). Supplier to CD, film and TV companies. Transparencies, slides, high resolution colour lasers or digital images either by email or CD supplied. Search and service fees. Free colour literature on request

Museums

The Bill Douglas Centre for the History of Cinema and Popular Culture

University of Exeter
The Old Library
Prince of Wales Road
Exeter EX4 4PX
Tel: 01392 264321
Fax: 01392 263871
email: info@billdouglas.org
Website: www.billdouglas.org
Dr Hester Higton
The core of the Centre's collection was assembled over many years by film-maker Bill Douglas and his friend Peter Jewell. Since the original donation, important additions have come from film-makers Roy Fowler, Don Boyd and James Mackay and from cinematographer Ossie Morris. The collections comprise a very extensive range of books, periodicals, programmes, posters, sheet music, cards, toys and games related to the cinema, in addition to 19th century pre-cinema artefacts such as zoetropes, magic lanterns, panoramas, peepshows and other optical toys and devices

The Cinema Museum

The Master's House
2 Dugard Way (off Renfrew Road,Kennington)
London SE11 4TH
Tel: 020 7840 2200
Fax: 020 7840 2299
email:
martin@cinemamuseum.org.uk
Martin Humphries
The museum is a FIAF subscriber

Imperial War Museum Film and Video Archive

Lambeth Road
London SE1 6HZ
Tel: 020 7416 5291/5292
Fax: 020 7416 5299
email: film@iwm.org.uk
Website: www.iwm.org.uk
Paul Sargent/Jane Fish
The national museum of modern conflict, illustrating and recording all aspects of modern war. The Archive reflects these terms of reference with an extensive collection of film and video material, which is widely used by historians and by film and television companies

Laurel and Hardy Museum

4C Upper Brook Street
Ulverston
Cumbria LA12 7BH
Tel: 01229 582292
Website:
www.cumbrialakedistrict.com/stanmuse.htm
The is in Ulverston, Cumbria, Stan Laurel's birthplace. Open all year 7 days a week for talks about Laurel and Hardy. It contains photos, letters, and memorabilia

National Museum of Photography Film & Television

Bradford BD1 1NQ
Tel: 0870 70 10 200
Fax: 01274 723155
email: Website: www.nmpft.org.uk
Bill Lawrence, Head of Film
The world's only museum devoted to still and moving pictures, their technology and history. Features Britain's first giant IMAX film system; the world's only public Cinerama; interactive galleries and 'TV Heaven', reference library of programmes and commercials

AWARDS

Film Awards 2002

This section features some of the principal film festival prizes and awards from 1 January 2002 to 31 December 2002. Compiled by Christie Quinn

BAFTA FILM AWARDS

The Orange British Academy Awards
Awarded on 24 February 2002 at The Odeon Leicester Square, London

BAFTA

195 Piccadilly
London W1V OLN
Tel: 020 7734 0022
Fax: 020 7734 1792
Website: www.bafta.org

Best Film:
THE LORD OF THE RINGS (US/New Zealand) Dir Peter Jackson
Academy Fellowship:
Merchant Ivory Productions, Warren Beatty
Michael Balcon Award For Outstanding British Contribution to Cinema:
Vic Armstrong
Alexander Korda Award For Outstanding British Film of the Year:
Gosford Park (UK/US) Dir Robert Altman
David Lean Award For Achievement in Direction:
Peter Jackson THE LORD OF THE RINGS (US/New Zealand)
Best Screenplay (Original):
Guillaume Laurant/Jean-Pierre Jeunet for AMELIE FROM MONTMARTRE (France/Germany) Dir Jean-Pierre Jeunet

Best Screenplay (Adapted):
Ted Elliott, Terry Rossio, Joe Stillman, Roger S.H. Schulman for SHREK (US) Dir Andrew Adamson, Vicky Jenson
Performance by an Actress in a Leading Role:
Judi Dench for IRIS (UK/US) Dir Richard Eyre
Performance by an Actor in a Leading Role:
Russell Crowe for A BEAUTIFUL MIND (UK) Dir Ron Howard
Performance by an Actress in a Supporting Role:
Jennifer Connolly for (A BEAUTIFUL MIND (UK) Dir Ron Howard
Performance by an Actor in a Supporting Role:
Jim Broadbent for MOULIN ROUGE (US/Australia) Dir Baz Luhrmann

Film Not in the English Language:
AMORES PERROS (Mexico) Dir Alejandro Gonzalez Inarritu
Anthony Asquith Award For Achievement in Film Music:
Craig Armstrong, Marius De Vries for MOULIN ROUGE (US/Australia) Dir Baz Luhrmann
Carl Foreman Award For Most Promising Newcomer to British Film:
Joel Hopkins/Nicola Usborne Writer & Director/Producer: Jump Tomorrow (UK/US)
Best Cinematography:
Roger Deakins for THE MAN WHO WASN'T THERE (US/UK) Dir Joel Coen
Best Production Design:
Aline Bonetto for AMELIE FROM MONTMARTRE (France/Germany) Dir Jean-Pierre Jeunet
Best Costume Design:
Jenny Beavan GOSFORD PARK (UK/US) Dir Robert Altman
Best Editing:
Mary Sweeney for MULHOLLAND DRIVE (France/US) Dir David Lynch
Best Sound:
Andy Nelson, Anna Behlmer, Roger Savage, Guntis Sics, Gareth Vanderhope, Antony Gray for MOULIN ROUGE (US/Australia) Dir Baz Luhrmann
Achievement in Special Visual Effects:
Jim Rygiel, Richard Taylor, Alex Funke, Randall William Cook, Mark Stetson for THE LORD OF THE RINGS (US/New Zealand) Dir Peter Jackson
Best Make Up/Hair:
Peter Owen, Peter King, Richard Taylor for THE LORD OF THE RINGS (US/New Zealand) Dir Peter Jackson
Best Short Film:
ABOUT A GIRL (UK) Dir Brian Percival
Best Short Animation:
DOG (UK) Dir Suzie Templeton
Special Award:
Eon Productions
Orange Audience Award:
THE LORD OF THE RINGS (US/New Zealand) Dir Peter Jackson

52nd BERLIN INTERNATIONAL FILM FESTIVAL

Held 7th-18th February 2002, Berlin
Internationale Filmfestpiele Berlin

Berlin International Film Festival

Potsdamer Strafle 5
D-10785 Berlin
Tel: (49) 030 25 920
Fax: (49) 030 25 920 299
email: info@berlinale.de
Website: www.berlinale.de
Golden Berlin Bear:
SEN TO CHIHIRO NO KAMIKAKUSHI aka Spirited Away (Japan) Dir Hayao Miyazaki
and Golden Berlin Bear:
BLOODY SUNDAY (UK/Ireland) Dir Paul Greengrass
Jury Grand Prix, Silver Berlin Bear:
HALBE TREPPE (Germany) Dir Andreas Dresen
Silver Berlin Bear for the Best Director:
Otar Iosseliani for his film LUNDI MATIN (France/Italy)
Silver Berlin Bear for the Best Actress:
Halle Berry for her role in the film MONSTER'S BALL (US) by Marc Forster
Silver Berlin Bear for the Best Actor:
Jacques Gamblin for his role in the film LAISSEZ-PASSER

(France/Germany/ Spain) Dir Bertrand Tavernier
Silver Berlin Bear for an individual artistic contribution:
Catherine Deneuve, Isabelle Huppert, Fanny Ardant, Emmanuelle Béart, Virginie Ledoyen, Firmine Richard, Danièlle Darrieux, Ludivine Sagnier for 8 FEMMES (France) Dir François Ozon
Silver Berlin Bear for the best film music:
Antoine Duhamel for his music in the film LAISSEZ-PASSER (France/Germany/Spain) Dir Bertrand Tavernier
The AGICOA award The Blue Angel for the best European film:
SMÅ ULYKKER (Denmark) Dir Annette K. Olesen
The Alfred Bauer Prize:
BAADER (Germany) Dir Christopher Roth
The Piper Heidsieck New Talent Award to the best young actress for his first major role:
Dannielle Hall for her role in the film BENEATH CLOUDS (Austria) Dir Ivan Sen
The Piper Heidsieck New Talent Award to the best young actor for his first major role:
Hugh Bonneville for his role in the film IRIS (UK/US)Dir Richard Eyre
Golden Berlin Bear:
AT DAWNING by Martin Jones
Jury Prize, Silver Berlin Bear:
BROR MIN by Jens Jonsson
The PREMIERE First Movie Award:
BENEATH CLOUDS (Austria) Dir Ivan Sen
Special Mentions:
THE LARAMIE PROJECT (US) Dir Moisés Kaufmann
CHEN MO HE MEITING by Liu Hao
INDEPENDENT JURIES PRIZE
OF THE CHURCHES OF THE ECUMENICAL JURY:
BLOODY SUNDAY (UK/Ireland) Dir Paul Greengrass
The award for a film screened in the 17th Panorama:
L'ANGE DE GOUDRON (Canada) Dir Denis Chouinard
The award for a film screened in the 32nd Forum:
É MINHA CARA – THAT'S MY FACE by Thomas Allen Harris
FIPRESCI PRIZES
The prize for a film screened in the Competition:
LUNDI MATIN (France/Italy) Dir Otar Iosseliani
The prize for a film screened in the 32nd Forum:
LES SOVIETS PLUS L'ÉLECTRICITÉ by Nicolas Rey
PRIZE OF THE GUILD OF GERMAN ART HOUSE CINEMAS
HALBE TREPPE (Germany) Dir Andreas Dresen
READER'S PRIZE OF THE BERLINER MORGENPOST
8 FEMMES (France) Dir François Ozon
C.I.C.A.E. PRIZE
PIÑERO (US) Dir Leon Ichaso
O GOTEJAR DA LUZ (Portugal) Dir Fernando Vendrell
and
ALL ABOUT LILY CHOU CHOU (Japan) Dir Shunji Iwai
The members of the jury for a film screened in the 32nd Forum are: ELÄMÄN Ä IDIT by Anastasia Lapsui and Markku Lehmuskallio
PRIX UIP BERLIN
RELATIVITY by Virginia Heath
LVT - MANFRED-SALZGEBER-PRIZE
HEAD KÄED by Peeter Simm

VARUH MEJE by Maja Weiss
PANORAMA AWARD OF THE NEW YORK FILM ACADEMY
The prize for the best short film goes to: GOLDEN GATE by Fernando Meirelles, Kátja Lund
The New York Film Academy Scholarship goes to:
BABIES ON THE SUN by Gariné Torossian
Special Mention: JAZIREH by Safoura Ahmadi
PANORAMA AUDIENCE PRIZE
IM TOTEN WINKEL. HITLERS SEKRETÄRIN by André Heller and Othmar Schmiderer
PRIZE OF THE DEUTSCHES KINDERHILFSWERK
GLASSKÅR (Sweden/Norway) Dir Lars Berg
A Special Mention goes to
SEND MERE SLIK by Cæcilia Holbek Trier
The Deutsches Kinderhilfswerk Special Prize for the best short film donated with the sum of EUR 2,500 goes to
BALLETT IST AUSGEFALLEN by Anne Wild
A Special Mention goes to
DELIVERY DAY (Australia) by Jane Manning
CRYSTAL BEAR
The Crystal Bear for best feature film of the 25th Kinderfilmfest goes to
GLASSKÅR (Sweden/Norway) Dir Lars Berg
A Special Mention goes to
KLATRETØSEN by Hans Fabian Wullenweber
A Special Mention also goes to A PASSAGE TO OTTAWA (Canada) Dir Gaurav Seth
The Crystal Bear for the best short film goes to MABUL by Guy Nattiv
A Special Mention goes to
TORNEHEKKEN
The Hedge of Thorns by Anita Killi
A Special Mention also goes to
DELIVERY DAY (Australia)Dir Jane Manning
PEACE FILM PRIZE
AUGUST – A MOMENT BEFORE THE ERUPTION by Avi Mograbi
TEDDY 2002
The TEDDY for the best feature film goes to
WALKING ON WATER (Australia) Dir Tony Ayres
The TEDDY for the best documentary goes to
ALT OM MIN FAR (Norway) Dir Even Benestad
The TEDDY for the best short film goes to
CELEBRATION by Daniel Stedman
The TEDDY Jury Prize goes to
JUSTE UNE FEMME by Mitra Farahani
READER'S PRIZE OF THE SIEGESSÄULE
WALKING ON WATER (Australia) Dir Tony Ayres
WOLFGANG STAUDTE AWARD 2002
WESH WESH, QU'EST-CE QUI SE PASSE? by Rabah Ameur-Zaïmeche
CALIGARI FILM PRIZE 2002
This year's Caligari Film Prize goes to
UN DÍA DE SUERTE by Sandra Gugliotta
NETPAC PRIZE
CHEN MO HE MEITING by Liu Hao
And a Special Mention goes to
JIN NIAN XIA TIAN by Li Yu
DON QUIXOTE PRIZE OF THE INTERNATIONAL FEDERATION OF FILM SOCIETIES
The prize goes to WA DONG REN by Ho Ping1
Special Mentions go to
UN DÍA DE SUERTE by Sandra Gugliotta

and
ALEXEI TO IZUMI by Motohashi Seiichi
READERS' PRIZE OF THE BERLINER ZEITUNG
ALEXEI TO IZUMI by Motohashi Seiichi

BFI Fellowship

Awarded on 20 October 2002
Bob and Harvey Weinstein
Jack Cardiff

BLACK FILMMAKERS MAGAZINE (BFM) FILM AND TELEVISION AWARDS

Awarded on 9 September 2002 at Grosvenor House Hotel, London

BFM

Suite 13
5 Blackhorse Lane
London E17 6DS
Tel: 020 8531 9111
email: bfm@teleregion.co.uk
Website: www.blackfilmmakermag.com

Best Film: TRAINING DAY (US/Australia) Dir Antoine Fuqua
Male Screen Personality: Denzel Washington
Female Screen Personality: Angela Bassett
Best Soundtrack: ALI (US) Dir Michael Mann
Best Female Performance in Film:
Marsha Thomason
Female Performance in Television:
Diane Parish
Best Male Performance in Film: Lennie James
Best Male Performance in Television: Eammon Walker
Emerging Talent Award: Zak Ove
Best Presenter: Angelica Bell
The Edric Connor Inspiration Award (UK): Lenny Henry
The Lifetime Achievement Award:
Pam Grier

BRITISH INDEPENDENT FILM AWARDS

The 5th Annual BRITISH INDEPENDENT FILM AWARDS sponsored by Park Caledonia were held on Wednesday 30 October 2002 at Pacha, London, SW1

British Independent Film Awards

81 Berwick Street
London WLF 8TW
Tel: 020 7287 3833
Fax: 020 7439 2243
email: info@bifa.org.uk
Website: www.bifa.org.uk
Best British Independent Film: SWEET SIXTEEN (UK/Germany/Spain/France/Italy) Dir Ken Loach
Best Foreign Film (Foreign Language):
MONSOON WEDDING (US/Italy/Germany/France) Dir Mira Nair
Best Foreign Film (English Language):
LANTANA (Australia/Germany) Dir Roy Lawrence
Most Promising Newcomer:
Martin Compston for SWEET SIXTEEN (UK/Germany/Spain/France/Italy) Dir Ken Loach
The Douglas Hickox Award (Debut Director):
Lindy Heymann & Christian Taylor for SHOWBOY (UK/US)
Best Technical Achievement:
Alwin Kuchler DoP for MORVERN CALLAR (UK/Canada) Dir Lynne Ramsay
Special Jury Prize:
Brian Tufano
Best Screenplay:
Tom Hunsinger & Neil Hunter for LAWLESS HEART (UK/US) Dir Neil Hunter
Outstanding Contribution by an Actor:
Richard Harris
Most Effective Distribution Campaign:
CHRISTIE MALRY'S OWN DOUBLE ENTRY (Netherlands/Luxembourg/UK) Dir Paul Tickell
Best Actor:
James Nesbitt for BLOODY SUNDAY (UK/Ireland) Dir Paul Greengrass
Best Achievement in Production:
24 HOUR PARTY PEOPLE (UK) Dir Michael Winterbottom
The Lifetime Achievement Award:
George Harrison
Best Actress:
Samantha Morton for MORVERN CALLAR (UK/Canada) Dir Lynne Ramsay
Best Director:
Paul Greengrass for BLOODY SUNDAY (UK/Ireland)
The Variety UK Personality Award:
Ewan McGregor

55TH CANNES FESTIVAL

Awards film feature 15 -26 May 2002

Festival International du Film de Cannes

Departement Films
3, rue Amelie
F-75007 Paris
Tel: (33) 1 53 59 61 20
Fax: (3)3 1 53 59 61 24
email residence@festival-cannes.fr
Website: www.festival cannes.org
Palme d'Or:
THE PIANIST (France/Poland/Germany/UK/US) Dir Roman Polanski
Prix de la mise en scène (Ex-aequo):
CHIHWASEON by Im Kwon-Taek (Korea)
PUNCH-DRUNK LOVE by Paul-Thomas Anderson (USA)
Prix d'interprétation féminin:
Kati Outinen for THE MAN WITHOUT A PAST (Finland)
Prix d'interprétation masculine:
Olivier GOURMET for THE SON (Belgium)
Prix du scénario:
Paul Laverty for SWEET SIXTEEN (UK)
Prix du Jury:
DIVINE INTERVENTION by Elia Suleiman (Palestine)
Grand Prix
THE MAN WITHOUT A PAST by Aki Kaurismäki (Finland)
Prix Caméra d'Or:
BORD DE MER by Julie Lopes-Curval (France)
(Mention Spéciale)
JAPAN by Carlos Reygadas (Mexico)
Prix spécial du 55ème anniversaire:
BOWLING FOR COLUMBINE by Michael Moore (USA)
Awards short films
Palme d'Or du Festival de Cannes:
ESO UTAN by Peter Meszaros (Hungary)
Prix du Jury (Ex-aequo):
THE STONE OF FOLLY by Jesse Rosensweet (Canada)
A VERY VERY SILENT FILM by Manish Jha (India)
Awards Cinéfondation
Premier Prix de la Cinéfondation:
UM SOL ALARANJADO (Quatre jours) de Eduardo Valente (Brazil)
Deuxième Prix de la Cinéfondation:
SEULE MAMAN A LES YEUX BLEUS de Eric Forestier (France)
K-G I NOD OCH LUST (K-G pour le meilleur ou pour le pire) by Jens Jonsson (Sweden)
Troisième Prix de la Cinéfondation:
SHE'ELOT SHEL PO'EL MET (Questions d'un ouvrier mort) by Aya Somech (Israel).

27th CÉSARS

Selected by L'Académie des Arts et Techniques du Cinéma. Awarded in Théâtre du Châtelet, Paris. 2 March 2002

Académie Des Arts et Technique du Cinéma

19, rue Lauriston
75116 Paris
Tél. : +33 1 53 64 05 25
Fax. : +33 1 53 64 05 24
email: info@lescesarducinema.com
Website: www.lescesarducinema.com

Best French Film:
Le Fabuleux Destin d'Amélie Poulain (France/Germany) Dir Jean-Pierre Jeunet
Best Actor:
Michel Bouquet in Comment J'ai Tué Mon Père (France/Spain) Dir Anne Fontaine
Best Actress:
Emmanuelle Devos in Sur Mes Lèvres (France) Dir Jacques Audiard
Best Supporting Actor:
André Dussollier in La Chambre Des Officiers (France) Dir François Dupeyron
Best Supporting Actress:
Annie Girardot in La Pianiste (France/Austria/Germany) Dir Michael Haneke
Best Director:
Jean-Pierre Jeunet for Le Fabuleux Destin d'Amélie Poulain (France/Germany)
Best Foreign Film:
Mulholland Drive (France/US) Dir David Lynch
Best First Feature Film:
No Man's Land (France/Italy/Belgium/UK/Slovenia/Bosnia-Herzegovina)Dir Danis Tanovic
Best Short Film:
Au Premier Dimanche d'Août (France) Dir Florence Miailhe
Best Original or Adapted Screenplay:
Jacques Audiard and Tonino Benacquista for Sur Mes Lèvres (France) Dir Jacques Audiard
Best Art Direction:
Aline Bonetto for Le Fabuleux Destin d'Amélie Poulain (France/Germany) Dir Jean-Pierre Jeunet
Best Cinematography:
Tetsuo Nagata for La Chambre Des Officiers (France) Dir François Dupeyron
Best Costume Design:
Dominique Borg for Le Pacte Des Loups (france) Dir Christophe Gans
Best Editing:
Marie-Josèphe Yoyotte for Le Peuple Migrateur Dir Jacques Perrin (France/Germany/Switzerland/Italy/Spain)
Best Music:
Yann Tiersen for Le Fabuleux Destin d'Amélie Poulain (France/Germany) Dir Jean-Pierre Jeunet
Best Sound:
Cyril Holtz and Pascal Villard for Sur Mes Lèvres (France) Dir Jacques Audiard

Best Newcomer, Actor:
Robinson Stévenin for Mauvais Genres (France) Francis Girod
Best Newcomer, Actress:
Rachida Brakni for Chaos (France) Dir Coline Serreau
Honorary Cesars:
Anouk Aimée, Jeremy Irons, Claude Rich

EDINBURGH INTERNATIONAL FILM FESTIVAL AWARDS

Awards announced on 26 August 2002

Edinburgh International Film Festival

Filmhouse
88 Lothian Road
Edinburgh EH3 9BZ
Tel: (44) 131 228 4051
Fax: (44) 131 229 5501
email: info@edfilmfest.org.uk
Website: www.edfilmfest.org.uk

The Michael Powell Award for Best New British Feature:
OUT OF CONTROL (UK)Dir Dominic Savage
Produced by Ruth Caleb for BBC FILMS
Saltire Society Grierson Award for Short Documentary supported by BAILLIE GIFFORD:
SKY HIGH (UK) Dir Anna Jones
The Guardian New Director's Award:
Carlos Reygadas for JAPÓN (Mexico/Spain/Nethrelands/Germany)
Special mention:
Marius Holst for DRAGONFLIES (Norway/Sweden)
The Standard Life Audience Award:
RABBIT PROOF FENCE (Australia/UK) Dir Philip Noyce
The Kodak and Short Film Bureau Award for Best British Short Film:
PROCTER (UK) Dir Joachim Trier
The European Short Film Award: Prix UIP:
PROCTER (UK) Dir Joachim Trier
The McLaren Animation Award for New British Animation:
AN EYE FOR AN EYE (UK)Dir Shynola with Ruth Lingford

EMPIRE FILM AWARDS

Held at the Dorchester Hotel, Tuesday, 5 February 2002

Empire Magazine

4th Floor
Mappin House
4 Winsley Street
London W1W 8HF
Tel: 020 7437 9011
Fax: 020 7859 8613
email: empire@ecm.emap.com
Website: www.empireonline.co.uk/magazine

Best Film:
THE LORD OF THE RINGS THE FELLOWSHIP OF THE RING (US/New Zealand) Dir Peter Jackson
Best British Actor:
Ewan McGregor for MOULIN ROUGE (US/Australia) Dir Baz Luhrmann
Best British Actress:
Kate Winslet for ENIGMA (Netherlands/US/UK/Germany) Dir Michael Apted
Best British Film:
BRIDGET JONES'S DIARY (US/France/UK) Dir Sharon Maguire
Best Debut:
Orlando Bloom for THE LORD OF THE RINGS THE FELLOWSHIP OF THE RING (US/New Zealand) Dir Peter Jackson
Best Actor:
Elijah Wood for THE LORD OF THE RINGS THE FELLOWSHIP OF THE RING (US/New Zealand) Dir Peter Jackson

Best Actress:
Nicole Kidman for MOULIN ROUGE (US/Australia) Dir Baz Luhrmann
Best Director:
Baz Luhrmann for MOULIN ROUGE (US/Australia)
Independent Spirite Award:
Alejandro Amenábar for THE OTHERS (Spain/US)
The Empire Inspiration Award:
Michael Mann
The Empire Lifetime Achievement Award:
Christopher Lee

EUROPEAN FILM AWARDS

Held at Teatro dell'Opera di Roma on 7th November 2002

European Film Academy

Kurfürstendamm 225
107 19 Berlin
Tel: 49 (30) 887 167 0
Fax: 49 (30) 887 167 77
Website: www.europeanfilmacademy.org

European Film:
HABLE CON ELLA aka Talk to Her (Spain) Dir Pedro Almodóvar
European Director:
Pedro Almodóvar for Hable Con Ella HABLE CON ELLA aka Talk to Her (Spain)
European Actor:
Sergio Castellitto for BELLA MARTHA aka Mostly Martha (Germany/Austria/Switzerland/Italy) Dir Sandra Nettlebeck and
& L' ORA DI RELIGIONE: IL SORRISO DI MIA MADRE aka My Mother's Smile (Italy) Dir Marco Bellocchio
European Actress:
The ensemble cast of 8 Femmes:
Catherine Deneuve
Isabelle Huppert
Emmanuelle Béart
Fanny Ardant
Virginie Ledoyen
Danielle Darrieux
Ludivine Sagnier
Firmine Richard
European Screenwriter:
Pedro Almodóvar for Hable Con Ella HABLE CON ELLA aka Talk to Her (Spain)
European Cinematographer:
Pawel Edelman for THE PIANIST (France/Poland/Germany/UK/US) Dir Roman Polanski
Screen International Award - for a non-European Film:
DIVINE INTERVENTION (France/Germany/Morroco/Netherlands/US) Dir Elia Suleiman
European Discovery - Fassbinder Award:
HUKKLE (Hungary) Dir György Palfi
European Short Film Award - Prix UIP:
10 MINUTA (Bosnia and Herzegovina) Dir Ahmed Imamovic
European Documentary Award - Prix Arte:
ETRE ET AVOIR (France) Dir Nicolas Philibert
European Achievement in World Cinema:
Victoria Abril
European Film Academy Lifetime Achievement Award:
Tonino Guerra, Screenwriter, Italy
European Critics' Award - Prix Fipresci:
Sweet Sixteen (UK/Germany/Spain/France/Italy) Dir Ken Loach

The People's Choice Awards (voted for by film fans across Europe):
Best European Director: Pedro Almodóvar for Hable Con Ella HABLE CON ELLA aka Talk to Her (Spain)
Best European Actor:
Javier Camara for Hable Con Ella HABLE CON ELLA aka Talk to Her (Spain) Dir PedroAlmodóvar
Best European Actress:
Kate Winslet for IRIS (UK/US) Dir Richard Eyre

28th EVENING STANDARD BRITISH FILM AWARDS

Awarded in London 3rd February 2002

Evening Standard

Northcliffe House
2 Derry Street
London W8 5EE
Tel: 020 7938 600
Website: www.thisislondon.co.uk

Best Film:
Gosford Park (UK/US) Dir Robert Altman
Actor:
Linus Roache for Pandemonium (UK/US) Dir Julien Temple
Best Actress:
Kate Winslet for Iris (UK/US) Dir Richard Eyre, Enigma (Netherlands/US/UK/Germany) Dir Michael Apted and Quills (Germany/US) Dir Philip Kaufman
Peter Sellers Award for Comedy:
Hugh Grant for BRIDGET JONES'S DIARY (US/UK/France) Dir Sharon Maquire
Best Screenplay:
Helen Fielding, Andrew Davies, Richard Curtis for BRIDGET JONES'S DIARY
The Carlton Television Most Promising Newcomer:
Ben Hopkins for The Nine Lives Of Thomas Katz (Germany/UK) Dir Ben Hopkins

Technical Achievement:
Stuart Craig for Harry Potter And The Philosopher's Stone (UK/US) Dir Chris Columbus
Special Award:
Christopher Lee

59th GOLDEN GLOBE AWARDS

Awarded 20th January 2002, Los Angeles

Golden Globes

Hollywood Foreign Press Association
646 North Robertson Boulevard
West Hollywood
California 90069
Tel: (310) 657 1731
Fax: (310) 657 5576
email: hfpa95@aol.com
Website: www.hfpa.com

Best Motion Picture - Drama:
A BEAUTIFUL MIND (US) Dir Ron Howard
Best Motion Picture - Musical or Comedy:
MOULIN ROUGE (US/AUSTRALIA) Dir Baz Luhrmann
Best Director:
Robert Altman for GOSFORD PARK (UK/US)
Best Foreign Language Film:
NO MAN'S LAND (France/Belgium/Italy/UK/Slovenia/Bosnia-Herzegovina) Dir Danis Tanovic

Best Performance by an Actor in a Motion Picture - Drama:
Russell Crowe in A BEAUTIFUL MIND (US) Dir Ron Howard
Best Performance by an Actor in a Motion Picture - Comedy or Musical:
Gene Hackman in THE ROYAL TENENBAUMS (US) Dir Wes Anderson
Best Performance by an Actor in a Supporting Role in a Motion Picture:
Jim Broadbent in IRIS (UK/US) Dir Richard Eyre
Best Performance by an Actress in a Motion Picture - Comedy or Musical:
Nicole Kidman in MOULIN ROUGE (US/AUSTRALIA) Dir Baz Luhrmann
Best Performance by an Actress in a Motion Picture - Drama:
Sissy Spacek in IN THE BEDROOM (US) Dir Todd Field
Best Performance by an Actress in a Supporting Role in a Motion Picture:
Jennifer Connelly in A BEAUTIFUL MIND (US) Dir Ron Howard
Best Screenplay - Motion Picture:
Akiva Goldsman for A BEAUTIFUL MIND (US) Dir Ron Howard
Best Original Score - Motion Picture:
Craig Armstrong for MOULIN ROUGE (US/AUSTRALIA) Dir Baz Luhrmann
Best Original Song - Motion Picture:
UNTIL Music and Lyrics:
Sting from Kate & Leopold (US) Dir James Mangold

INDIAN INTERNATIONAL FILM ACADEMY AWARDS

Awarded 6th April 2002
Genting Highlands Resort, Kuala Lumpar, Malaysia

Indian International Film Academy

Website: www.iifa.com

Best Picture:
LAGAAN (India) Dir Ashutosh Gowariker
Direction: Ashutosh Gowariker for LAGAAN (India)
Actor In A Leading Role:
Aamir Khan for LAGAAN (India) Dir Ashutosh Gowariker
Actress In A Leading Role:
Tabu for CHANDNI BAR (India) Dir Madhur Bhandarkar
Actor In A Supporting Role:
Saif Ali Khan for DIL CHAHTA HAI (India) Dir Farhan Akhtar
Actress In A Supporting Role:
Jaya Bachchan for KABHI KHUSHI KABHI
Lyrics:
Javed Akhtar LAGAAN (India) Dir Ashutosh Gowariker
Performance In A Negative Role:
Akshay Kumar for AJNABEE Dir Abbas-Mustan
Performance In A Comic Role:
Govinda for JODI NO.1 Dir David Dhawan
Music Direction:
A. R. Rahman for LAGAAN (India) Dir Ashutosh Gowariker
Male Playback Singer:
Sonu Nigam for Suraj Jua Maddham KABHI KHUSHI KABHI GHAM
Female Playback Singer:
Asha Bhosle for Radka Kaise Na Jale LAGAAN (India) Dir Ashutosh Gowariker
Best Story:
Ashutosh Gowariker for LAGAAN (India) Dir Ashutosh Gowariker
Sound Recording:
H. Shridhar
Costume Designer:
Manish Malhotra
Song Recording:
Vijay Benegal
Art Direction:
Sharmista Roy
Dialogue:
Karan Johar Shaktiman
Choreography:
Farah Khan
Cinematography:
Santosh Sivan
Background Score:
Babloo Chakvorty
Editing:
Bhallu Saluja
Screenplay
Farhan Akthar
Sound Re - recording:
Anil Mathur and Nakul Kamte
Make-up:
Mickey Contractor
Special Effects (Visual):
Paul Sims
Outstanding Indian Contribution to International Cinema:
Waheeda Rehman
Lifetime Achievement Award:
Sadhana
Electrolux Kelvinator Personality of the Year:
Amitabh Bachchan
Sony Faces of the Year:
Bipasha Basu, Gracy Singh, Arjun Ramphal
Invaluable Contribution To Indian Cinema:
Shammi Kapoor

37TH KARLOVY VARY INTERNATIONAL FILM FESTIVAL

Held at Karlovy Vary, Czech Republic between 4th July and 13th July

Karlovy Vary

Film Servis Festival Karlovy Vary
Panská 1110 00 Prague
Tel: (420) 221 411 011
Fax: (420) 221 411 033
email: festival@iffkv.cz
Website:www.iffkv.cz

Grand Prix – Crystal Globe:
ROK DÁBLA (Czech Republic) Dir Petr Zelenka
Special Jury Prize:
NIRGENDWO IN AFRIKA aka Nowhere in Africa (Germany) Dir Caroline Link
Best Director Award:
Asghar Massombagi for KHALED (Canada)
Best Actress Award:
Ugla Egilsdóttir
for MAVAHLATUR (Iceland) Dir Ágúst Gudmundsson
Best Actor Award:
William H. Macy for FOCUS (US) Dir Neal Slavin
Special Jury Mentions:
YIRLAMA, BARI YAKHSHI! (Korea) Dir Min Boung-hun
SMOKING ROOM (Spain) Dir Julio Wallovits, Roger Gual
DOCUMENTARY FILMS IN COMPETITION
Best Documentary Film Above 30 Minutes in Length:
En´an no musume (Japan) Dir Kaoru Ikeya

Best Documentary Film Lasting 30 Minutes or Less:
Obec B. (Czech Republic) Dir Filip Remunda
Special Mention:
Devil´s Playground (USA)Dir Lucy Walker
Hunting Down an Angel or Four Passions of The Soothsayer Poet (Russia) Dir Andrei Osipov
OTHER PRIZES AWARDED AT THE FESTIVAL
Award for Outstanding Artistic Contribution to World Cinema:
John Boorman, Great Britain
Vlastimil Brodsky, Czech Republic (In Memoriam)
Sean Connery, Great Britain
Prize of the Mayor of the Town of Karlovy Vary:
Michael York, Great Britain
Mladá Fronta Dnes Audience Prize:
L´AUBERGE ESPAGNOLE (France) Dir Cédric Klapisch
Eurotel Audience Prize:
SMRADI (Czech Republic) Dir Zdenek Tyc
NON-STATUTORY AWARDS
The Philip Morris Freedom Award:
SESTRY (Russia)Dir Sergei Bodrov Jr.
Award of International Film Critics (FIPRESCI)
NIRGENDWO IN AFRIKA aka Nowhere in Africa (Germany) Dir Caroline Link
Special Mention:
YIRLAMA, BARI YAKHSHI! (Korea) Dir Min Boung-hun
The Don Quijote Prize (FICC - International Federation of Film Societies)
Cuento de hadas para dormir cocodrilos (Mexico)Dir Ignacio Ortíz Cruz
The Ecumenical Jury Award:
Cisza (Poland) Dir Michal Rosa
Ecumenical Jury Special Mention:
Filament (Japan) Dir Jinsei Tsuji
STUDENT FILMS
Best Student Film:
Broken (US) Dir Patrick Downs
Best collection of student films:
FAMU, Czech Republic
Special Prizes Best Documentary Film:
Make Me Proud (UK) Dir Moby Longinotto
Best Animation Film:
Pirát (Czech Republic)Dir Jan Bubenícˇek
Special Mention:
See No Evil (Greece) Dir Aris Bafaloukas
Viktor och hans bröder (Sweden) Dir Martin Klingberg
Tego lata ... (Poland) Dir Emil Graffman

LOCARNO INTERNATIONAL FILM FESTIVAL

Held, at Locarno, Switzerland

Locarno International Film Festival

Via Luini 3a
CH-6601 Locarno
Switzerland
Tel: (41) 91 756 2121
Fax: (41) 91 756 2149
email: info@pardo.ch
Website: www.pardo.ch

Golden Leopard:
Das VERLANGEN (Germay) Dir Ian Dilthey
Silver Leopard (New Cinema):
TAN DE REPENTE (Argentina) Dir Diego Lerman
Special Jury Prize:
MAN TARANEH PANZDAH SAL DARAM (Iran) Dir Rasoul Sadr-Ameli
Silver Leopard (Young Cinema):
SZEP NAPOK (Hungary) Dir Kornél Mundruczó
Bronze Leopard (Actress):
Taraneh Allidousti for MAN TARANEH PANZDAH SAL DARAM (Iran) Dir Rasoul Sadr-Ameli
Bronze Leopard (Actor):
Giorgos Karayannis for DISKOLI APOCHERETISMI: O BABAS MOU (Greece/Germany) Dir Penny Panayotopolou
Special Mentions:
Acting ensemble of TAN DE REPENTE (Argentina) Dir Diego Lerman
FIPRESCI Prize:
LA CAGE (France) Dir Alain Raoust
Ecumenical Jury:
Alain Raoust for LA CAGE (France)
Special Mention:
DISKOLI APOCHERETISMI: O BABAS MOU (Greece/Germany) Dir Penny Panayotopolou
INTERNATIONAL FEDERATION OF CINEMA CLUBS
Don Quijote Prize
TAN DE REPENTE (Argentina)
CICAE/ART Prize:
Dorothée Van den Berghe for MEISJE (Belgium/Holland/France)
Special Mention:
OKAY (Denmark) Dir Jesper W.Nielsen
NETPAC JURY (to promote Asian Cinema)
Aparna Sen for MR & MRS IYER (India)
Sobi al-Zobaidi for OBOR KALANDIA (Palestine)
Rakhshen Bani-Etemad for RUZ-EGAR-E MA (Iran)
CRITICS WEEK
FORGET BAGHDAD-JEWS AND ARABS-THE IRAQI CONNECTION (Swiss/Germany) Dir Samir
PRIX DU PUBLIC UBS:
BEND IT LIKE BECKHAM (UK/Germany) Dir Gurinder Chadha
VIDEO COMPETITION
Golden Leopard Video Sony:
JEON JANG KEU I HU (South Korea) Dir Nobuhiro Suwa, Moon Seong-Wok, Wang Xiaoshuai
LOVE AND DIANE (USA/France) Dir Jennifer Dworkin
Special Distinction:
UN'ORA SOLA TI VORREI (Italy/Switzerland) Dir Alina Marazzi
LEOPARDS OF TOMORROW
NEW SWISS TALENT CATEGORY
Golden Leopard SRG SSR idé suisse:
NUIT DE NOCES (Switzerland) Dir Olga Baillif
Silver Leopard Kodak Prize:
SWAPPED (Switzerland) Dir Pierre Monnard
The Action Light Prize for Best Swiss Newcomer:
DUST (Switzerland) Dir Ruxanra Zenide
Special Mention:
PETITS GESTES (Switzerland) Dir Francois Rossier
AUSTRALIAN AND NEW ZEALAND FILM CATEGORY
Golden Leopard SRG SSR idé suisse:
DELIVERY DAY (Australia) Dir Jane Manning
Silver Leopard Kodak Prize:
LOST (Australia) Dir Jo Kennedy
The Film and Video Prize for Subtitles:
VITALOGY by Greg Williams
Special Mention:
STILL LIFE by Sima Urale)

74th OSCARS – ACADEMY OF MOTION PICTURE ARTS AND SCIENCES

Awarded on 24th March 2002, Kodak Theatre Hollywood, Los Angeles
Website:www.oscar.com and www.oscars.org

Best Film:
A BEAUTIFUL MIND (US) Dir Ron Howard
Best Director:
Ron Howard for A BEAUTIFUL MIND (US)
Best Actor:
Denzil Washington for TRAINING DAY (US/Austrailia) Dir Antoine Fuqua
Best Supporting Actor:
Jim Broadbent for IRIS (UK/US) Dir Richard Eyre
Best Actress:
Halle Berry for MONSTER'S BALL (US) Dir Marc Forster
Best Supporting Actress:
Jennifer Connley for A BEAUTIFUL MIND (US) Dir Ron Howard
Best Art Direction:
Catherine Martin (Art Direction) and Brigitte Broch (Set Decoration) for MOULIN ROUGE (US/Australia) Dir Baz Luhrmann
Best Cinematography:
Andrew Lesnie for The LORD OF THE RINGS THE FELLOWSHIP OF THE RING (US/New Zealand) Dir Peter Jackson
Best Costume Design:
Catherine Martin and Angus Strathie for MOULIN ROUGE (US/Australia) Dir Baz Luhrmann
Best Documentary Short:
Sarah Kernochan and Lynn Appelle for THOTH
Best Documentary Feature:
Jean-Xavier de Lestrade and Denis Poncet for MURDER ON A SUNDAY MORNING
Best Film Editing:
Pietro Scalia for BLACK HAWK DOWN (US) Dir Ridley Scott
Best Foreign Language Film:
NO MAN'S LAND (France/Italy/Belgium/UK/Slovenia/Bosnia-Herzegovina) Dir Danis Tanovic
Best Make Up:
Peter Owen and Richard Taylor for The LORD OF THE RINGS THE FELLOWSHIP OF THE RING (US/New Zealand) Dir Peter Jackson
Best Music (Score):
Howard Shore The LORD OF THE RINGS THE FELLOWSHIP OF THE RING (US/New Zealand) Dir Peter Jackson
Best Music (Song):
"If I Didn't Have You" Music and Lyric by Randy Newman MONSTERS, INC. (US) Dir Peter Docter
Best Animated Feature:
SHREK (US) Dir Andrew Adamson and Vicky Jensen
Best Short - Live Action:
Ray McKinnon and Lisa Blount for THE ACCOUNTANT
Best Short Animated:
Ralph Eggleston for FOR THE BIRDS
Best Sound:
Michael Minkler, Myron Nettinga and Chris Munro for BLACK HAWK DOWN (US) Dir Ridley Scott
Best Sound Editing:
George Watters II and Christopher Boyes PEARL HARBOR (US) Dir Michael Bay
Best Visual Effects:
Jim Rygiel, Randall William Cook, Richard Taylor and Mark Stetson for The LORD OF THE RINGS THE FELLOWSHIP OF THE RING (US/New Zealand) Dir Peter Jackson
Best Screenplay (Adapted):
Akiva Goldsman for A BEAUTIFUL MIND (US) Dir Ron Howard
Best Screenplay (Original):
Julian Fellowes for GOSFORD PARK (US/UK) Dir Robert Altman
Honorary Oscars:
Sidney Poitier. Robert Redford

VENICE FILM FESTIVAL

Held on 29 August– 8 September 2002

59th Mostra Internazionale d'Arte Cinematografica

San Marco, 1364
Ca' Giustinian
30124 Venice - Italy
Tel: (39) 041 5218878
Fax: (39) 041 5227539
email: cinema@labiennale.com
Website: 194.185.28.38

Golden Lion for Best Film:
THE MAGDALENE SISTERS (UK/Ireland0 Dir Peter Mullan
Jury Grand Prix:
DOM DURAKOV (Russia/France) Dir Andrei Konchalovsky
Special Director's Award:
OASIS (Korea) Dir Lee Chang-dong
Award for an Outstanding Individual Contribution:
Ed Lachman, director of photography for FAR FROM HEAVEN (US/France) Dir Todd Haynes
Coppa Volpi for Best Actor:
Stefano Accorsi for Un VIAGGIO CHIAMATO AMORE (Italy) Dir Michele Placido
Coppa Volpi for Best Actress:
Julianne Moore for FAR FROM HEAVEN (US/France) Dir Todd Haynes
"Marcello Mastroianni" Award for Best Young Actor or Actress:
Moon So-Ri for OASIS (Korea) Dir Lee Chang-dong
SHORT FILMS
Silver Lion per il miglior cortometraggio:
Clown by Irina Efteeva
UIP Award for Best European Short Film:
Kalózok Szeretöje (Lover of Pirates) by Zsofia Péterffy
Special Mention:
Tempo by Per Carleson
Controcorrente (Upstream)
San Marco Award:
Xiao Cheng Zhi Chun (Springtime in a Small Town) by Tian Zhuangzhuang
Jury's Special Award:
Rokugatsu No Hebi (A Snake of June) by Shinya Tsukamoto
Special Mentions:
La Virgen De La Lujuria by Arturo Ripstein and Renmin Gongche (Public Toilet) by Fruit Chan
The International Jury of the "Luigi De Laurentiis" Venice Award for a First Film - Lion of the Future: (SIC - International Critics' Week)
DUE AMICI (Italy) Dir Spiro Scimone and Francesco Sframeli
ROGER DODGER (US) Dylan Kidd

2003

This section features some of the principal film festival prizes and awards from 1 January 2003 to 30 June 2003. Compiled by Christie Quinn

BAFTA FILM AWARDS

The Orange British Academy Awards
Awarded on 23 February 2003 at The Odeon Leicester Square, London

BAFTA

195 Piccadilly
London W1V OLN
Tel: 020 7734 0022
Fax: 020 7734 1792
Website: www.bafta.org

Best Film:
THE PIANIST (France/Poland/Germany/UK/US) Dir Roman Polanski
Academy Fellowship:
Saul Zaentz
Michael Balcon Award For Outstanding British Contribution to Cinema:
David Tomblin and Michael Stevenson
Alexander Korda Award For Outstanding British Film of the Year:
THE WARRIOR (UK/France) Dir Asif Kapadia
David Lean Award For Achievement in Direction:
Roman Polanksi THE PIANIST (France/Poland/Germany/UK/US)
Best Screenplay (Original):
Pedro Almodóvar for HABLE CON ELLA (Spain) Dir Pedro Almodóvar
Best Screenplay (Adapted):
Charlie Kaufman/Donald Kaufman for ADAPTATION (US) Dir Spike Jonze
Performance by an Actress in a Leading Role:
Nicole Kidman for THE HOURS (US/UK) Dir Stephen Daldry
Performance by an Actor in a Leading Role:
Daniel Day-Lewis for GANGS OF NEW YORK (US) Dir Martin Scorsese
Performance by an Actress in a Supporting Role:
Catherine Zeta-Jones for CHICAGO (US) Dir Rob Marshall
Performance by an Actor in a Supporting Role:
Christopher Walken for CATCH ME IF YOU CAN (US) Dir Steven Spielberg
Film Not in the English Language:
HABLE CON ELLA (Spain) Dir Pedro Almodóvar
Anthony Asquith Award For Achievement in Film Music:
Philip Glass for THE HOURS (US/UK) Dir Stephen Daldry
Carl Foreman Award For Most Promising Newcomer to British Film:
Asif Kapadia Director/Co-Writer: THE WARRIOR (UK/France)
Best Cinematography:
Conrad L. Hall for ROAD TO PERDITION (US) Dir Sam Mendes
Best Production Design:
Dennis Gassner for ROAD TO PERDITION (US) Dir Sam Mendes
Best Costume Design:
Ngila Dickson and Richard Taylor for The LORD OF THE RINGS THE TWO TOWERS (US/New Zealand) Dir Peter Jackson
Best Editing:
Daniel Rezende for CIDADE DE DEUS (Brazil/Germany) Dir Fernando Meirelles
Best Sound:
Michael Minkle, Dominick R.Tavella, David Lee and Maurice Schell for
CHICAGO (US/Germany) Dir Rob Marshall
Achievement in Special Visual Effects:
Jim Rygiel, Joe Letteri, Alex Funke, Randall William Cook for THE LORD OF THE RINGS THE TWO TOWERS (US/New Zealand) Dir Peter Jackson
Best Make Up/Hair:
Judy Chin, Beatrice De Alba, John Jackson, Regina Reyes for FRIDA (US) Dir Julie Taymor
Best Short Film:
MY WRONGS 8245-8249 AND 117 (UK) Dir Chris Morris
Best Short Animation:
FISH NEVER SLEEP (UK) Dir Gaëlle Dennis
Orange Audience Award:
THE LORD OF THE RINGS THE TWO TOWERS (US/New Zealand) Dir Peter Jackson

53rd BERLIN INTERNATIONAL FILM FESTIVAL

Held 6–16 February 2003, Berlin
Internationale Filmfestpiele Berlin

Berlin International Film Festival

Potsdamer Strafle 5
D-10785 Berlin
Tel: (49) 030 25 920
Fax: (49) 030 25 920 299
email: info@berlinale.de
Website: www.berlinale.de

INTERNATIONAL JURY
Golden Berlin Bear:
IN THIS WORLD (UK) Dir Michael Winterbottom
Jury Grand Prix, Silver Berlin Bear:
ADAPTATION (US) Dir Spike Jonze
Silver Berlin Bear for the Best Director:
Patrice Chereau for SON FREREhis film LUNDI MATIN (France)
Silver Berlin Bear for the Best Actress:
Meryl Streep, Nicole Kidman and Julianne Moore for THE HOURS (US/UK) Dir Stephen Daldry
Silver Berlin Bear for the Best Actor:
Sam Rockwell for CONFESSIONS OF A DANGEROUS MIND Dir George Clooney
Silver Berlin Bear for an individual artistic contribution:
Li Yang as screenwriter and director for MANG JING (Blind Shaft) (Hong Kong/China/Germany)
Silver Berlin Bear for best film music:
Majoly, Serge Fiori, Mamadou Diabaté for MADAME BROUETTE (Canada/Senegal/France) Dir Moussa Sene Absa
AGICOA Blue Angel award for best European film:
GOOD BYE LENIN (Germany) Dir Wolfgang Becker
The Alfred Bauer Prize:
YING XIONG (Hero) (China/Hong Kong) Dir Zhang Yimou
INTERNATIONAL SHORT FILM JURY
Golden Berlin Bear for Best Short Film:
(A)TORZIJA (Slovenia) Dir Stefan Arsenijevic
Jury Prize, Silver Berlin Bear:

EN AUSENCIA (Argentina) Dir Lucia Cedron
ISCHOV TRAMWAI No.9 (Ukraine) Dir Stepan Koval
OTHER AWARDS

Prize of the Churches of the Ecumenical Jury
IN THIS WORLD (UK) Dir Michael Winterbottom
The award for a film screened in the Panorama:
KNAFAYIM SHVUROT (Broken Wings) (Israel) Dir Nir Bergman
Award for a film screened in the Forum:
EDI (Poland) Dir Piotr Trzaskalski
FIPRESCI prizes
Prize for a film screened in Competition:
LICHTER (Germany) Dir Hans-Christian Schmid
Prize for a film screened in the Panorama:
WOLFSBURG (Germany) Dir Christian Petzold
Prize for a film screened in the Forum:
EDI (Poland) Dir Piotr Trzaskalski
Prize of the Guild of German Art House Cinemas
MY LIFE WITHOUT ME Dir Isabel Coixet
Readers' Prize of The Berliner Morgenpost
THE HOURS (US/UK) Dir Stephen Daldry
C.I.C.A.E. Prize
Prize for a film screened in the Panorama:
KNAFAYIM SHVUROT (Broken Wings) (Israel) Dir Nir Bergman
Special Mention:
POLIGONO SUR (Spain/France) Dir Dominique Abel
Prize for a film screened in the Forum:
AMARELO MANGA (Brazil) Dir Claudio Assis
Special Mention:
POWER TRIP (US) Dir Paul Devlin
Prix UIP Berlin
(A)TORZIJA (Solvenia) Dir Stefan Arsenijevic
LVT – Manfred Salzgeber Prize:
PURE (UK) Dir Gillies MacKinnon
Special mention for acting:
Harry Eden for PURE (UK) Dir Gillies MacKinnon
Panorama Short Film Award
Best Short Film:
MISDEMEANOR (US) Dir Jonathan LeMond
New York Film Academy Scholarship:
MOGLEM BYC CZLOWIEKIEM (I Could Have Been Human) (Poland) Dir Barbara Medajska
Special Mention:
UNDERDOG by Eran Merav
Panorama Audience Prize
KNAFAYIM SHVUROT (Broken Wings) (Israel) Dir Nir Bergman
Prize of the Deutsches Kinderhilfswerk
Grand Prix for Best Feature:
KALD MIG BARE AKSEL (Denmark) Dir Pia Bovin
Special Mention:
ELINA – SOM OM JAG INTE FANNS (Sweden/Finaland) by Klaus Haro
DRENGEN DER VILLE GORE DET UMULIGE (The Boy Who Wanted to Be a Bear) (France/Denmark/Norway) by Jannik Hastrup
Special Prize for Best Short film:
LE TROP PETIT PRINCE (France) Dir Zoia Trofimova
Special Mention:
HOUDINS HUND by Sara Johnsen
Crystal Bear
Crystal Bear for best feature film of the Kinderfilmfest:
ELINA – SOM OM JAG INTE FANNS (Sweden/Finland) Dir Klaus Haro
Special Mention:
MISS ENTEBBE (Israel) Dir Omri Levy
EL VIAJE DE CAROL (Carol's Journey) by Imanol Uribe
Crystal Bear for best short film:
LE TROP PETIT PRINCE (France) Dir Zoia Trofimova
Special Mention: BIRJU by Heeraz Marfatia
Peace Film Prize
IN THIS WORLD (UK) Dir Michael Winterbottom
Teddy 2003
Teddy for best feature film:
MIL NUBES DE PAZ CERCAN EL CIELO, AMOR, JAMAS ACABARAS DE SER AMOR (Mexico) Dir Julián Hernández
Teddy for best documentary:
ICH KENN KEINEN – ALLEIN UNTER HETEROS (Gemany) Dir Jochen Hick
Teddy for best short film:
FREMRAGENDE TIMER (Precious Moments) (Norway) Dir Lars Daniel Krutzkoff and Jan Dalchow
Special Teddy:
Friedrich Wilhelm Murnau (1888–1931)
Readers' Prize of The Siegessaule
THE EVENT (Canada/US) Dir Thom Fitzgerald
Wolfgang Staudte Award 2003
RENGETEG (Forest) (Hungary) Dir Benedek Fliegauf
Caligari Film Prize 2003
SALT (Iceland/US) Dir Bradley Rust Gray
NETPAC Prize
KOUFUKU NO KANE (The Blessing Bell) (Japan) Dir Sabu
Special Mention:
AKU INGIN MENCIUMMU SEKALI SAJA (Bird-Man Tale) (Indonesia) Dir Garin Nugroho
Don Quixote Prize of the International Federation of Film Societies
EDI (Poland) Dir Piotr Trzaskalski
Readers' Prize of The Berliner Zeitung
POWER TRIP (US) Dir Paul Devlin

56th CANNES FESTIVAL
Held in Cannes 14-25 May 2003

Festival International du Film de Cannes
Departement Films
3, rue Amelie
F-75007 Paris
Tel: (33) 1 53 59 61 20
Fax: (3)3 1 53 59 61 24
email residence@festival-cannes.fr
Website: www.festival cannes.org

Feature Film Palme d'Or:
ELEPHANT (US) Dir Gus Van Sant
Grand Prize:
UZAK (Turkey) Dir Nuri Bilge Ceylan
Best Director Award:
Gus Van Sant for ELEPHANT (US)
Jury Prize:
FIVE IN THE AFTERNOON (Iran) Dir Samira Makhmalbaf
Best Screenplay:
BARBARIAN INVASIONS (Canada) Dir Denys Arcand
Best Actress Award:
Marie Josée Croze for BARBARIAN INVASIONS (Canada) Dir Denys Arcand
Best Actor Award:
Muzaffer Ozdemir and Mehmet Emin Toprak for UZAK (Turkey) Dir Nuri Bilge Ceylan
Camera d'Or:
RECONSTRUCTION (Denmark) Dir Christoffer Boe

Special Mention:
OSAMA (Afghanistan) Dir Sedigh Barmak
Cinéfondation Award (First Prize):
BEZI ZEKO BEZI (RUN RABBIT RUN) (Serbia) Dir Pavle Vuckov
Cinéfondation Award (Second Prize):
STORY OF THE DESERT (Spain) Dir Celia Galan Julve
Cinéfondation Award (Third Prize):
TV CITY (Germany) Dirs Alberto Couceiro and Alejandra Tomel
(Ex-aequo) AT THAT POINT (Mexico) Dir Luciana Jauffred Gorostiza

27th CÉSARS

Selected by L'Académie des Arts et Techniques du Cinéma. Awarded in Paris. 22 February 2003

Académie Des Arts et Technique du Cinéma

19, rue Lauriston
75116 Paris
Tél. : +33 1 53 64 05 25
Fax. : +33 1 53 64 05 24
email: info@lescesarducinema.com
Website: www.lescesarducinema.com

Best French Film:
LE PIANIST (France/Poland/Germany/UK/US) Dir Roman Polanski
Best Actor:
Adrien Brody for THE PIANIST (France/Poland/Germany/UK/US) Dir Roman Polanski
Best Actress:
Isaballe Carre for SE SOUVENIR DES BELLES CHOSES (France) Dir Zabou Breitman
Best Supporting Actor:
Bernard Le Coq for SE SOUVENIR DES BELLES CHOSES (France) Dir Zabou Breitman
Best Supporting Actress:
Karin Viard for EMBRASSEZ QUI VOUS VOUDREZ (France/UK/ Italy) Dir Michel Blanc
Best Director:
Roman Polanski for THE PIANIST (France/Poland/Germany/UK/US)
Best Foreign Film:
BOWLING FOR COLUMBINE (Canada/Germany/US) Dir Michael Moore
Best European Union Film:
HABLE CON ELLA (Spain) Dir Pedro Almodóvar
Best First Feature Film:
Se Souvenir Des Belles Choses (France) Dir Zabou Breitman
Best Short Film:
PEAU DE VACHE Dir Gerald Hustache-Mathieu
Best Original or Adapted Screenplay:
Costa-Gavras, Jean-Claude Grumberg for AMEN (France/Germany) Dir Costa-Gavras
Best Art Direction:
Allan Starski for THE PIANIST (France/Poland/Germany/UK/US) Dir Roman Polanski
Best Cinematography:
Pawel Edelman for THE PIANIST (France/Poland/Germany/UK/US) Dir Roman Polanski
Best Costume Design:
Philippe Guillotel, Tanino Liberatore, Florence Sadaune for ASTERIX ET OBELIX: MISSION CLEOPATRA (France/Germany) Dir Alain Chabet
Best Editing:
Nicolas Philibert for ETRE ET AVOIR (France) Dir Nicholas Philibert
Best Music:
Wojciech Kilar for THE PIANIST (France/Poland/Germany/UK/US) Dir Roman Polanski
Best Sound:
Jean-Marie Blondel, Gerard Hardy, Dean Humphreys for THE PIANIST (France/Poland/Germany/UK/US) Dir Roman Polanski
Best Newcomer, Actor:
Jean-Paul Rouve for MONSIEUR BATIGNOLE (France) Dir Gerard Jugnot
Best Newcomer, Actress:
Cecile de France for L'AUBERGE ESPAGNOLE (France) Dir Cédric Klapisch
Honorary Cesars:
Berndadette Laffont, Spike Lee and Meryl Streep

EMPIRE FILM AWARDS

Held at the Dorchester Hotel, London, 2003

Empire Magazine

4th Floor
Mappin House
4 Winsley Street
London W1W 8HF
Tel: 020 7437 9011
Fax: 020 7859 8613
email: empire@ecm.emap.com
Website: www.empireonline.co.uk/magazine

Best Film:
THE LORD OF THE RINGS THE FELLOWSHIP OF THE RING (US/New Zealand) Dir Peter Jackson
Best British Actor:
Hugh Grant for ABOUT A BOY (Germany/US/France/UK) Dir Paul Weitz
Best British Actress:
Samantha Morton for MINORITY REPORT (US) Dir Steven Spielberg
Sky Movies Best British Film:
28 DAYS LATER (UK) Dir Danny Boyle
Best Newcomer:
Rosamund Pike for DIE ANOTHER DAY (UK/US) Dir Lee Tamahori
Best Actor:
Tom Cruise for MINORITY REPORT (US) Dir Steven Spielberg
Best Actress:
Kirsten Dunst for SPIDER-MAN (US) Dir Sam Raimi
Best Director:
Steven Spielberg for MINORITY REPORT (US)
Independent Spirit Award:
Michael Winterbottom and Andrew Eaton, director and producer of 24 HOUR PARTY PEOPLE (UK)
Sony Ericsson Scene of the Year:
Yoda's duel in STAR WARS EPISODE II ATTACK OF THE CLONES (US)
The Empire Lifetime Achievement Award:
Dustin Hoffman

EVENING STANDARD BRITISH FILM AWARDS

Awarded in London, 5 February 2003

Evening Standard

Northcliffe House
2 Derry Street
London W8 5EE
Tel: 020 7938 600
Website: www.thisislondon.co.uk

Best Film:
DIRTY PRETTY THINGS (US/UK) Dir Stephen Frears
Best Actor: Chiwetel Ejiofor for DIRTY PRETTY THINGS (US/UK) Dir Stephen Frears
Best Actress:
Catherine Zeta-Jones for CHICAGO (US/Germany) Dir Rob Marshall
Best Screenplay:
Tom Hunsinger and Neil Hunter for LAWLESS HEART (UK/US) Dir Tom Hunsinger and Neil Hunter
Peter Sellers Award for Comedy:
LOST IN LA MANCHA (UK) Dir (Keith Fulton)
The Carlton Television Most Promising Newcomer:
Asif Kapadia for directing THE WARRIOR (UK/France)
Technical Achievement: Eve Stuart for production design of ALL OR NOTHING (UK/France) Dir (Mike Leigh)
Special Award:
Barbara Broccoli and Michael G. Wilson for 40 years of James Bond

60th GOLDEN GLOBE AWARDS

Awarded 19 January 2003, Los Angeles

Golden Globes

Hollywood Foreign Press Association
646 North Robertson Boulevard
West Hollywood
California 90069
Tel: (310) 657 1731
Fax: (310) 657 5576
email: hfpa95@aol.com
Website: www.hfpa.com

Best Motion Picture - Drama:
THE HOURS (US/UK) Dir Stephen Daldry
Best Motion Picture - Musical or Comedy:
CHICAGO (US/Germany) Dir Rob Marshall
Best Director:
Martin Scorsese for GANGS OF NEW YORK (US)
Best Foreign Language Film:
HABLE CON ELLA (Talk to Her) (Spain) Dir Pedro Almodóvar
Best Performance by an Actor in a Motion Picture - Drama:
Jack Nicholson for ABOUT SCHMIDT (US) Dir Alexander Payne
Best Performance by an Actor in a Motion Picture - Comedy or Musical:
Richard Gere in CHICAGO (US/Germany) Dir Rob Marshall
Best Performance by an Actor in a Supporting Role in a Motion Picture:
Chris Cooper in ADAPTATION (US) Dir Spike Jonze
Best Performance by an Actress in a Motion Picture - Drama:
Nicole Kidman for THE HOURS (US/UK) Dir Stephen Daldry
Best Performance by an Actress in a Motion Picture - Comedy or Musical:
Renée Zellweger in CHICAGO (US/Germany) Dir Rob Marshall
Best Performance by an Actress in a Supporting Role in a Motion Picture:
Meryl Streep in ADAPTATION (US) Dir Spike Jonze
Best Screenplay - Motion Picture:
Alexander Payne and Jim Taylor for ABOUT SCHMIDT (US) Dir Alexander Payne
Best Original Score - Motion Picture:
Elliott Goldenthal for FRIDA (US) Dir Julie Taymor
Best Original Song - Motion Picture:
THE HANDS THAT BUILT AMERICA Music and Lyrics: U2 from GANGS OF NEW YORK (US) Dir Martin Scorsese
Cecil B. DeMille Award:
Gene Hackman

INDIAN INTERNATIONAL FILM ACADEMY AWARDS

Awarded 17 May 2003
Johannesburg, South Africa
Indian International Film Academy
Website: www.iifa.com

Best Picture:
DEVDAS
Best Director:
Sanjay Leela Bhansali for DEVDAS
Actor in a Leading Role
Shah Rukh Khan for DEVDAS Dir Sanjay Leela Bhansali
Actress in a Leading Role:
Aishwarya Rai for DEVDAS Dir Sanjay Leela Bhansali
Actor in a Supporting Role:
Mohanlal for COMPANY Dir Ram Gopal Verma
Actress in a Supporting Role:
Kiron Kher for DEVDAS Dir Sanjay Leela Bhansali
Lyrics:
Nusrat Badr for DOLA RE DOLA
Performance in a Negative Role:
Akshaye Khanna for HUMRAAZ Dir Abbas-Mustan
Performance in a Comic Role:
Mahesh Manjrekar for KAANTE Dir Sanjay Gupta
Composer:
A.R. Rahman for SAATHIYA Dir Shaad Ali
Male Playback Singer:
Sonu Nigam for SAATHIYA Dir Shaad Ali
Female Playback Singer:
Shreya Ghosal and Kavita Krishnamurthi for DOLA RE DOLA
Best Story:
Jaideep Sahni for COMPANY Dir Ram Gopal Verma
Sound Recording:
Jitendra Chowdhary, Vikram Motwane, Kunal Sharma for DEVEDAS Dir Sanjay Leela Bhansali
Costume Designer:
Neeta Lulla, Abu Jani, Sandeep Khosla, Reza Sharifi for DEVDAS Dir Sanjay Leela Bhansali
Song Recording:
Daman Sood, Bishwadeep Chattarjee, Tanay Gajjar for DEVDAS Dir Sanjay Leela Bhansali
Art Direction: Nitin Chandrakant Desai for DEVDAS Dir Sanjay Leela Bhansali
Dialogue:
Prakash Kapadia for DEVDAS Dir Sanjay Leela Bhansali
Choreography:
Saroj Khan for DEVDAS Dir Sanjay Leela Bhansali

Cinematography:
Binod Pradhan for DEVDAS Dir Sanjay Leela Bhansali
Background Score:
A.R. Rahman for SAATHIYA Dir Shaad Ali
Editing:
Chandan Arora for COMPANY Dir Ram Gopal Verma
Screenplay:
Mahesh Bhatt for RAAZ Dir Vikram Bhatt
Sound Re - recording:
Leslie Fernandes for DEVDAS Dir Sanjay Leela Bhansali
Make-up:
Arun Pillai, Jaywant Parab, Pradeep Nahate for DEVDAS Dir Sanjay Leela Bhansali
Special Effects:
Prime Focus for KAANTE Dir Sanjay Gupta
Action:
Allan Amin for COMPANY Dir Ram Gopal Verma
Outstanding Indian Contribution to International Cinema:
Aparna Sen
Lifetime Achievement Award:
Dev Anand
Special Diva Award:
Rekha
Samsung Style Icon Award:
Fardeen Khan
Sony Face of the Year:
Esha Deol and John Abraham

23RD LONDON CRITICS' CIRCLE FILM AWARDS

Held at Dorchester Hotel, London 12 February 2003

Critics Circle Film Awards

51 Vartry Road
London N15 6PS
email: info@criticscircle.org.uk
Website: www.criticscircle.org.uk

British Film Of The Year:
ALL OR NOTHING (UK/France) Dir Mike Leigh
Film of The Year:
ABOUT SCHMIDT (US) Dir Alexander Payne
British Actor of The Year:
Hugh Grant for ABOUT A BOY (Germany/US/France/UK) Dir Paul Weitz
Actor of The Year:
Michael Caine for THE QUIET AMERICAN (US/Germany/UK) Dir Phillip Noyce
British Actress of The Year:
Lesley Manville for All Or Nothing (UK/France) Dir Mike Leigh
Actress of The Year:
Stockard Channing for The BUSINESS OF STRANGERS (US) Dir Patrick Stettner
British Actor In A Supporting Role:
Kenneth Branagh for HARRY POTTER AND THE CHAMBER OF SECRETS (US/UK/Germany) Dir Chris Columbus
British Actress In A Supporting Role:
Emily Watson for RED DRAGON (US/Germany) Dir Brett Ratner
British Director of The Year:
Christopher Nolan for INSOMNIA (US)
Director of The Year:
Phillip Noyce for THE QUIET AMERICAN(US/Germany/UK)
British Screenwriter of The Year:
Steven Knight for DIRTY PRETTY THINGS (US/UK) Dir Stephen Frears
Screenwriter of The Year:
Andrew Bovell for LANTANA (Australia/Germany) Dir Lawrence
Foreign Language Film of The Year:
Y TU MAMÁ TAMBIÉN (Mexico) Dir Alfonso Cuarón
British Newcomers of The Year:
Martin Compson for SWEET SIXTEEN (UK/Germany/Spain/France/Italy) Dir Ken Loach
Keira Knightley for BEND IT LIKE BECKHAM (Germany/UK) Dir Gurinder Chadha

75th OSCARS - ACADEMY OF MOTION PICTURE ARTS AND SCIENCES

Awarded on 23 March 2003, Kodak Theatre Hollywood, Los Angeles
Website:www.oscar.com and www.oscars.org
Best Film:
CHICAGO (US/Germany) Dir Rob Marshall
Best Director:
Roman Polanski for THE PIANIST (France/Poland/Germany/UK/US)
Best Actor:
Adrien Brody for THE PIANIST (France/Poland/Germany/UK) Dir Roman Polanski
Best Supporting Actor:
Chris Cooper for ADAPTATION (US) Dir Spike Jonze
Best Actress:
Nicole Kidman for THE HOURS (US/UK) Dir Stephen Daldry
Best Supporting Actress:
Catherine Zeta-Jones for CHICAGO (US/Germany) Dir Rob Marshall
Best Art Direction:
John Myhre, Gordon Sim (Set Decoration) for CHICAGO (US/Germany) Dir Rob Marshall
Best Cinematography:
Conrad L. Hall for ROAD TO PERDITION (US) Dir Sam Mendes
Best Costume Design:
Colleen Atwood for CHICAGO (US/Germany) Dir Rob Marshall
Best Documentary Short:
William Guttentag and Robert David Port for TWIN TOWERS (US)
Best Documentary Feature:
Michael Moore for BOWLING FOR COLUMBINE (Canada/ Germany/US)
Best Film Editing:
Martin Walsh for CHICAGO (US/Germany) Dir Rob Marshall
Best Foreign Language Film:
nirgendwo in afrika (Germany) Dir Caroline Link
Best Make Up:
Beatrice DeAlba and John E. Jackson for FRIDA (US) Dir Julie Taymor
Best Music (Score):
Elliot Goldenthal for FRIDA (US) Dir Julie Taymor
Best Music (Song):
Luis Resto, Eminen and Jeffrey Bass for 8 MILE (US) Dir Curtis Hanson
Best Animated Feature:
SEN TO CHIHIRO NO KAMIKAKUSHI (Spirited Away) (Japan) Dir Hayao Miyazaki

Best Short - Live Action:
Mie Andreasen and Martin Strange-Hansen for DER ER EN YNDIG MAND
Best Short Animated:
Eric Armstrong for THE CHUBBCHUBBS!
Best Sound:
David Lee, Michael Minkler and Dominick R. Tavella for CHICAGO (US/Germany) Dir Rob Marshall
Best Sound Editing:
Michael Hopkins and Ethan van der Ryn for THE LORD OF THE RINGS THE TWO TOWERS (US/New Zealand) Dir Peter Jackson
Best Visual Effects:
Jim Rygiel, Randall William Cook, Joe Letteri and Alex Funke for The LORD OF THE RINGS THE TWO TOWERS (US/New Zealand) Dir Peter Jackson
Best Screenplay (Adapted):
Ronald Harwood for THE PIANIST (France/Poland/Germany/UK/US) Dir Roman Polanski
Best Screenplay (Original):
Pedro Almodóvar for HABLE CON ELLA (Spain) Dir Pedro Almodóvar
Lifetime Achievement Award:
Peter O'Toole

This section features some of the principal Television festival prizes and awards from 1 January 2002 to 31 December 2002. Compiled by Christie Quinn

Television Awards 2002

BAFTA

195 Piccadilly
London W1V OLN
Tel: 020 7734 0022
Fax: 020 7734 1792
Website: www.bafta.org

BAFTA TELEVISION AWARDS

Winners announced on Sunday 21 April 2002
Actress:
Julie Walters for My Beautiful Son
Actor:
Michael Gambon for Perfect Strangers
Entertainment Performance:
Graham Norton for So Graham Norton
Comedy Performance:
Ricky Gervais for The Office
The Richard Dimblemby Award for the Best Presenter: (Factual, Features and News)
Louis Theroux for WHEN LOUIS MET...
Single Drama:
When I Was 12 Ruth Caleb, Dominic Savage
Drama Series:
Cold Feet Andy Harries, Spencer Campbell, Mike Bullen
Drama Serial:
The Way We Live Now Nigel Stafford-Clark, David Yates, Andrew Davies
Soap:
EastEnders Production Team
Factual Series or Strand
Horizon Bettina Lerner, Matthew Barrett, John Lynch
The Flaherty Documentary Award
Kelly and Her Sisters Marilyn Gaunt
Features:
Faking It Production Team
The Huw Wheldon Award for Specialist Factual:
The Private Dirk Bogarde (Arena) Anthony Wall, Adam Low
Sport:
Channel 4 Cricket Production Team
News Coverage:
September 11th - 12th (Sky News) Production Team
Current Affairs:
Beneath The Veil (Dispatches) Production Team
Innovation:
Double Take Jemma Rodgers, Alison Jackson
Entertainment Programme or Series
Pop Idol Claire Horton, Ken Warwick, Jonathan Bullen
Situation Comedy Awaard
The Office Anil Gupta, Ash Atalla, Ricky Gervais, Stephen Merchant
Comedy Programme or Series
The Sketch Show Production Team
Lew Grade Audience Award sponsored by RadioTimes
Buried Treasure

BAFTA TELEVISION CRAFT AWARDS

Special Awards Presented to: Edward Mansell - Editor
BBC Natural History Unit
Costume Design sponsored by Allders:
The Life And Adventures Of Nicholas Nickleby (ITV1) Barbara Kidd
Editing Factual:
The Show Must Go On (BBC2) Anna Ksiezopolska
Editing Fiction/Entertainment sponsored by Bentley Productions:
Othello (ITV1) Nick Arthurs
Make Up & Hair Design sponsored by Allders:
The Way We Live Now (BBC1) Caroline Noble
New Director Factual:
Witness: The Train (C4) Donovan Wylie
New Director Fiction:
Tales From Pleasure Beach (BBC2) Edmund Coulthard
New Writer sponsored by AKA Pictures:
Navigators (C4) Rob Dawber
Original Television Music sponsored by Sebastian McLean International:
The Blue Planet (BBC1) George Fenton
Photography Factual:
The Blue Planet (BBC1) Camera Team
Photography & Lighting Fiction/Entertainment sponsored by Kodak Entertainment Imaging:
Othello (ITV1) Daf Hobson
Production Design sponsored by the British Studio Alliance:
The Way We Live Now (BBC1) Gerry Scott
Sound Factual:
Hell In The Pacific (C4) Peter Eason, Craig Butters,Cliff Jones
Sound Fiction/Entertainment:
Clocking Off (BBC1) Sound Team
Visual Effects & Graphic Design sponsored by Oasis Television:
Banzai (C4) Blue Source

28th BROADCASTING PRESS GUILD TELEVISION AND RADIO AWARDS

Presented at the Theatre Royal, Drury Lane, London on Friday 12 April 2002 by the Guild's chairman, Ray Snoddy, Media Editor of The Times.

Best Single Drama:
Othello (LWT/WGBH for ITV1)
Best Drama Series/Serial:
The Way We Live Now (BBC/WGBH/DeepIndigo for BBC ONE)
Best Documentary Series:
The Blue Planet (BBC ONE)
Best Single Documentary:
Arena - The Private Dirk Bogarde (BBC TWO)
Best Entertainment:
The Office (BBC TWO)
Best Actor:
David Suchet (The Way We Live Now)
Best Actress:
Lesley Sharp (Bob and Rose, Clocking Off)
Best Performer (Non-Acting):
Andrew Marr (Political Editor, BBC News)
Writer's Award (joint):
Ricky Gervais and Stephen Merchant (The Office)
Radio Programme of the Year:
The Archive Hour (BBC Radio 4)
Radio Broadcaster of the Year:

Sue MacGregor (Today, BBC Radio 4)
Multichannel Award:
Freestyler (MTV Base)
Harvey Lee Award for Outstanding Contribution to Broadcasting:
Jim Moir

EMMY AWARDS 30th INTERNATIONAL EMMY AWARDS

Awarded in New York City, Monday, 25 November 2002

Arts Programming
DRACULA – PAGES FROM AVIRGIN'S DIARY (Connie von Helmot film in association with /Canadian Broadcasting Corporation – Canada)
Children & Young People Programming
STIG OF THE DUMP: Episodes 1&3 (CBBC/Childsplay Productions for BBC1)
Drama Series
UNIT ONE: Episodes 20&25 (Danish Broadcasting Corporation TV-Drama (Denmark)
Documentary
NICHOLAS WINTON - THE POWER OF GOOD (WIP/Trigon Production,Czech Television/Slovak Television – Slovakia
TV Movies/Mini-series
DIE MANNS – EIN JAHRHUNDERTROMAN (The Manns – Novel of a Century) (Bavaria Film in Co-operation with WDR/BR/NDR/ARTE/ORF/SRG/SFDRS – Germany)
News Coverage
FALL OF KABUL – BBC NEWS (BBC News – UK)
Popular Arts
THE KUMARS AT NO. 42 Series 1: Episode 1 Grant & Parkinson (Hat Trick Productions for BBC2 – UK)
FAKING IT (RDF Media Production for Channel 4 – UK)

54th PRIME TIME EMMY AWARDS

Awarded 22 September 2002 in Los Angeles

Drama Series:
THE WEST WING (NBC)
John Wells Productions in association with Warner Bros. Television
Comedy Series:
FRIENDS (NBC)
Kauffman/Crane Productions in association with Warner Bros. Television
Lead Actor in a Drama Series:
Michael Chiklis in THE SHIELD (FOX)
Fox Television Studios in association with Columbia Tristar Television
Lead Actress in a Drama Series:
Allison Janney in THE WEST WING (NBC)
John Wells Productions in association with Warner Bros. Television
Lead Actor in a Comedy Series:
Ray Roman in EVEREYBODY LOVES RAYMOND (CBS)
Worldwide Pants Inc. and HBO Independent Productions in association with Where's Lunch Productions Inc.
Lead Actress in a Comedy Series:
Jennifer Aniston in FRIENDS (NBC)
Bright/Kauffman/Crane Productions in association with Warner Bros. Television
Lead Actor in a Mini-series or a Movie:
Albert Finney in THE GATHERING STORM (HBO)
A Scott Free Production in association with HBO Films
Lead Actress in a Mini-series or a Movie:
Laura Linney in WILD IRIS (HBO)
Showtime and Paramount Network Television Presents
Made for Television Movie:
THE GATHERING STORM (HBO)
A Scott Free Production in association with HBO Films
Supporting Actor in a Mini-series of a Movie:
Michael Moriarty in JAMES DEAN (TNT)
A Gerber Pictures/Marvin Worth Production in association with Five Mile River Films and Splendid Television
Supporting Actress in a Mini-series or a Movie:
Stockard Channing in THE MATTHEW SHEPARD STORY (NBC)
Alliance Atlantis presentation in association with Cosmic/Clearlight Pictures
Mini-series:
BAND OF BROTHERS (HBO)
Dreamworks SKG and Playtone in association with HBO Original Programming
Writing for a Mini-series or a Movie:
THE GATHERING STORM (HBO)
A Scott Free Production in association with HBO Films
Larry Ramin, Story; Hugh Whitmore, Teleplay, Story
Variety, Music or Comedy Series:
LATE SHOW WITH DAVID LETTERMAN (CBS)
Worldwide Pants Inc.
Variety, Music or Comedy Special:
AMERICA: A TRIBUTE TO HEROES
Tenth Planet Productions
Directing for a Mini-series:
BAND OF BROTHERS (HBO)
Dreamworks SKG and Playtone in association with HBO Original Programming
David Frankel, Director; Tom Hanks, Director; David Leland, Director; Richard Loncraine, Director; David Nutter, Director; Phil Alden Robinson, Director; Mikael Salomon, Director; Tony To, Director
Individual Performance in a Variety or Music Program;
Sting, Performer STING IN TUSCANY ...ALL THIS TIME (A&E)
Richard Frankel Productions for A&E Network
Directing for a Variety or Music Program:
OPENING CEREMONY SALT LAKE 2002 OLYMPIC WINTER GAMES (NBC)
Don Mischer Productions
Ron de Moraes, Director; Kenny Ortega, Director; Bucky Gunts, Director
Writing for a Variety, Music or Comedy Program:
SATURDAY NIGHT LIVE (NBC)
Broadway Video Inc. in association with SNL Studios)
Tina Fey, Head Writer; Dennis McNicholas, Head Writer; Doug Abeles, Writer; James Anderson, Writer; Max Brooks, Writer; James Downey, Writer; Hugh Fink, Writer; Charlie Grandy, Writer; Steve Higgins, Writer; Erik Kenward, Writer; Lorne Michaels, Writer; Matt Murray, Writer; Paula Pell, Writer; Matt Piedmont, Writer; Michael Schur, Writer; Frank Sebastiano, Writer; T. Sean Shannon, Writer; Robert Smigel, Writer; Emily Spivey, Writer; Andrew Steele, Writer; Scott Wainio, Writer
Writing for a Comedy Series:
THE BERNIE MAC SHOW - Pilot (FOX)
Regency Television
Larry Wilmore, Writer
Supporting Actor in a Comedy Series:
Brad Garrett in EVERYBODY LOVES RAYMOND (CBS)
Worldwide Pants Inc. and HBO Independent Productions in association with Where's Lunch Productions Inc.
Supporting Actress in a Comedy Series:

Doris Roberts in EVERYBODY LOVES RAYMOND (CBS)
Worldwide Pants Inc. and HBO Independent Productions in association with Where's Lunch Productions Inc.
Directing for a Comedy Series:
SEX AND THE CITY – THE REAL ME (HBO)
HBO Original Programming
Michael Patrick King, Director
Writing for a Drama Series:
24 – MIDNIGHT – 1:00a.m - Pilot (FOX)
Real Time Productions, Imagine Television in association with 20th Century Fox Television
Joel Surnow, Writer; Robert Cochran, Writer
Supporting Actor in a Drama Series:
John Spencer in THE WEST WING (NBC)
John Wells Productions in association with Warner Bros. Television
Supporting Actress in a Drama Series:
Stockard Channing in THE WEST WING (NBC)
John Wells Productions in association with Warner Bros. Television
Directing for a Drama Series:
SIX FEET UNDER - Pilot (HBO)
The Greenblatt/Janollari Studios and Actual Size Inc. in association with HBO Original Programming
Allan Ball, Director
Bob Hope Humanitarian Award:
Oprah Winfrey

PRIME TIME EMMY AWARDS – CREATIVE ARTS CATEGORIES

Awarded 14 September 2002 in Los Angeles

Animated Program (For Programming Less Than One Hour:
FUTURAMA – ROSEWELL THAT ENDS WELL (FOX)
Animated Program (For Programming One Hour or More)
WALKING WITH PREHISTORIC BEASTS (DISC)
Guest Actor in a Comedy Series
Anthony LaPaglia as Simon in FRASIER (NBC)
Guest Actor in a Drama Series
Charles S. Dutton as Leonard Marshall in THE PRACTICE (ABC)
Guest Actress in a Comedy Series
Cloris Leachman as Ida in MALCOLM IN THE MIDDLE (FOX)
Guest Actress in a Drama Series
Patricia Clarkson as Sarah O'Connor in SIX FEET UNDER (HBO)
Art Direction for a Multi-Camera Series
WILL & GRACE – CHEATIN' TROUBLE BLUES (NBC)
Art Direction for a Single-Camera Series
ALIAS – TRUTH BE TOLD (Pilot) (ABC)
Art Direction for a Mini-series, Movie or a Special
JAMES DEAN (TNT)
Art Direction for a Variety or Music Program
OPENING CEREMONY SALT LAKE 2002 OLYMPIC WINTER GAMES (NBC)
Casting for a Comedy Series
SEX AND THE CITY (HBO)
Casting for a Drama Series
SIX FEET UNDER (HBO)
Casting for a Miniseries, Move or a Special
BAND OF BROTHERS (HBO)
Choreography
THE 74TH ANNUAL ACADEMY AWARDS (ABC)
Cinematography for a Multi-Camera Series
WILL & GRACE – A CHORUS LIE (NBC)
Cinematography for a Single-Camera Series
ALIAS – TRUTH BE TOLD (Pilot) (ABC)
Cinematography for a Mini-series or Movie
SHACKLETON – PART 2 (A&E)
Cinematography for Non-Fiction Programming (Single or Multi-Camera)
BLUE PLANET: SEAS OF LIFE – OCEAN WORLD (DISC)
Costumes for a Series
SEX AND THE CITY – DEFINING MOMENTS (HBO)
Costumes for a Miniseries, Movie or a Special
VICTORIA AND ALBERT – PART 1 (A&E)
Costumes for a Variety or Music Program
OPENING CEREMONY SALT LAKE 2002 OLYMPIC WINTER GAMES (NBC)
Single-Camera Picture Editing for a Series
Chris Willingham, Editor for 24 – 7:00am - 8:00am (FOX)
Single-Camera Picture Editing for a miniseries, Movie or a Special
Frances Parker, Editor for BAND OF BROTHERS – PART 2:Day of Days (HBO)
Multi-Camera Picture Editing for a Series
Ron Volk, Editor for FRASIER – THE PROPOSAL (NBC)
Multi-Camera Picture Editing for a Miniseries, Movie or a Special
A&E IN CONCERT: STING IN TUSCANY… ALL THIS TIME (A&E)
Picture Editing for Non-Fiction Programming (Single or Multi-Camera)
IN MEMORIAM: NEW YORK CITY, 9/11/01 (HBO)
Hairstyling for a Series
ENTERPRISE – TWO DAYS AND TWO NIGHTS (UPN)
Hairstyling for a Miniseries, Movie or a Special
ANNE RICE'S THE FEAST OF ALL SAINTS – PART 1) (SHO)
Lighting Direction (Electronic, Multi-Camera) For VMC Programming
OPENING CEREMONY SALT LAKE 2002 OLYMPIC WINTER GAMES (NBC)
Main Title Design
SIX FEET UNDER (HBO)
Makeup for a Series (Non-Prosthetic)
CSI: CRIME SCENE INVESTIGATION – SLAVES OF LAS VEGAS (CBS)
Makeup for a Series (Prosthetic)
SIX FEET UNDER – A PRIVATE LIFE (HBO)
Makeup for a Miniseries, Movie or a Special (Non-Prosthetic)
THE MISTS OF AVALON – PART 1 (TNT)
Makeup for a Mini-series, Movie or Special (Prosthetic)
JIM HENSON'S JACK AND THE BEANSTALK: THE REAL STORY – PART 2 (CBS)
Music Composition for a Series (Dramatic Underscore)
George Fenton for BLUE PLANET: SEAS OF LIFE – OCEAN WORLD (DISC)
Music Composition for a Miniseries, Movie or a Special (Dramatic Underscore)
Adrian Johnson for SHACKLETON – Part 2 (A&E)
Music Direction
OPENING CEREMONY SALT LAKE 2002 OLYMPIC WINTER GAMES (NBC)
Music and Lyrics
Brian Wallows and Peter Swallows – "You've Got a Lot to See" for FAMILY GUY (FOX)
Main Title Theme Music
SIX FEET UNDER (HBO)

59th GOLDEN GLOBE AWARDS

Awarded 20 January 2002, Los Angeles

Golden Globes

Hollywood Foreign Press Association
646 North Robertson Boulevard
West Hollywood
California 90069
Tel: (310) 657 1731
Fax: (310) 657 5576
email: hfpa95@aol.com
Website: www.hfpa.com
TELEVISION
Best Mini-Series or Motion Picture Made for Television:
BAND OF BROTHERS
HBO; in association with DreamWorks and Playtone of a Band of Brothers Ltd production
Best Performance by an Actor in a Mini-Series or a Motion Picture made for Television:
James Franco for JAMES DEAN
Gerber Pictures; Marvin Worth Productions; in association with Splendid TV; in association with Five Mile River Films
Best Performance by an Actor in a Supporting Role in a Series, Mini-Series or Motion Picture Made for Televison:
Stanley Tucci in CONSPIRACY
BBC Films; HBO
Best Performance by an Actor in a Television Series - Drama:
Kiefer Sutherland for 24 Imagine Television in assoc with 20th Century Fox TV
Best Performance by an Actor in a Television Series - Musical or Comedy:
Charlie Sheen for SPIN CITY
UBU Productions; Lottery Hill; DreamWorks SKG
Best Performance by an Actress in a Mini-Series or a Motion Picture made for Television:
Judy Davis in LIFE WITH JUDY GARLAND: ME AND MY SHADOWS Alliance Atlantis in co-production with IN-motion, In association with Storyline Entertainment
Best Performance by an Actress in a Supporting Role in a Series, Mini-Series or Motion Picture Made for Televison:
Rachel Griffiths in SIX FEET UNDER
Actual Size Productions/Greenblatt Janollari Studio. HBO
Best Performance by an Actress in a Television Series - Drama:
Jennifer Garner in ALIAS
Sisyphus Productions in association with Touchstone Television
Best Performance by an Actress in a Television Series - Musical or Comedy:
Sarah Jessica Parker for SEX AND THE CITY HBO
Best Television Series - Drama:
SIX FEET UNDER
Actual Size Films, Greenblatt/Janollari Studios HBO
Best Television Series - Musical or Comedy:
SEX AND THE CITY HBO

42nd GOLDEN ROSE OF MONTREUX

Awards 2002

Golden Rose:
Pop Idol (Thames Television – UK)
Honorary Rose :
Dawn French and Jennifer Saunders
Comedy :
Silver Rose :
HippHipp! (SVT – Sweden)
Bronze Rose :
The Kumars at No 42 (BBC – UK)
Music : Silver Rose :
One Night with Robbie Williams (BBC – UK)
Bronze Rose:
Walk On By: The Story of Popular Song (BBC – UK)
Special Mntion :
Per Yves Montand (Rai International – Italy)
Sitcom : Silver Rose :
Los Dos Bros (Channel 4 – UK)
Bronze Rose:
Madam & Eve (Penguin Films – South Africa)
Special Mention :
Finanzamt Mitte (Entertainment Factory – Germany)
Games Show : Silver Rose :
Oblivious (Tiger Aspect – UK)
Bronze Rose :
Make My Day (Channel 4 – UK)
Variety :
Silver Rose : Perfect Match (RDF Media – UK)
Bronze Rose:
So Graham Norton (Channel 4 – UK)
Arts & Special: Silver Rose:
Special Prize of the City of Montreux:
A Mere Grain of Nothing My Death
(VPRO - Netherlands)
Special Mention :
We, the Sparrows - About the Scarecrows (BNT – Bulgaria)
Press Prize:
2DTV (2DTV – UK)
e-Rose: Joya Rennt (FaroTV - Switzerland)
Golden Award: Sauna DDB (Czech Republic)

42th MONTE CARLO TELEVISION FESTIVAL

1–6 July, 2002 — Grimaldi Forum – Monaco

Television Films Gold Nymphs: Best Television Film:
"GOKIGEN-IKAGA, TEDDY BEAR?" ("How are you, Teddy Bear?") -
Mainichi Broadcasting System, Inc. - Japan
Best Script
Alberto SIMONE / Silvia NAPOLITANO for "UN DIFETTO DI FAMIGLIA"
- RAI Radiotelevisione Italy
Best Direction
Dimiter PETKOV pour/for "OPACHKATA NA DYAVOLA" ("The Devil's Tail")- Parallax films Ltd - Bulgarie/Bulgaria
Best Performance by an Actor
Jürgen TARRACH dans/in "WAMBO" ("Exposed") - Beta Film GmbH - Germany
Best Performance by an Actress
Anne-Marie DUFF dans/in "SINNERS" - Parallel Films Ltd. - Ireland
Special Mention:
À / To "LA SURFACE DE RÉPARATION" - Stephan Films / Arte France - France
Mini-Series Gold Nymphs: Best Mini Series
"NO TEARS" - Radio Telefis Eireann - Ireland
Best Script
Heinrich BRELOER & Horst KÖNIGSTEIN for "DIE MANNS" -
Westdeutscher Rundfunk Köln - Germany
Best Direction
Diarmuid LAWRENCE pour/for "MESSIAH" -
Messiah Films Ltd. - United Kingdom
Best Performance by an Actor
Colm FEORE dans/in "TRUDEAU" -
CBC Canadian Broadcasting Corporation - Canada

Best Performance by an Actress
Sarah LANCASHIRE dans/in "THE CRY" - Fremantle International Distribution - United Kingdom
News & Current Affairs Programmes
Gold Nymph:
Best Current Affairs Programme
"BENEATH THE VEIL" - CNN and Channel 4 - United Kingdom
Gold Nymph:
Best Current Affairs Programme
"HIBAKUCHIRYO 83 - NICHIKAN NO KIROKU : TOKAIMURA RINKAI GIKO" - ("A Certain Death") - NHK Japan Broadcasting Corporation - Japan
Special Mention
"WITNESS : IN THE LINE OF FIRE" - CBC Canadian Broadcasting Corporation - Canada
News Programmes
Gold Nymph: Best News Programme
MEILLEUR REPORTAGE D'ACTUALITE
"DER AUFSTAND DER TALIBAN" - WDR - Germany
Gold Nymph Best News Programme:
"AFGHANISTAN 2001 - FALL OF THE TALIBAN - BBC 1 - United Kingdom
24-Hour News Programmes Gold Nymph:
Best 24-Hour News Programme
MEILLEUR REPORTAGE D'ACTUALITE 24 HEURES / 24
Breaking News:
BREAKING NEWS : SEPTEMBER 11 TERRORIST ATTACKS - CNN - United Kingdom
Special Prizes Prize of the Monaco Red Cross Colombia: LA COMPASION Y LA INFAMIA - TVE, S.A. - Spain
Amade & UNESCO Prize Fiction Programme:
"GOKIGEN-IKAGA, TEDDY BEAR?" ("How are you, Teddy Bear?") -
Mainichi Broadcasting System, Inc. - Japan
News Programme:
"LA PETITE FÉE DU MALI - TF1 - France
Signis Prize Fiction:
"GOKIGEN-IKAGA, TEDDY BEAR?" ("How are you, Teddy Bear?") - Mainichi Broadcasting System, Inc. - Japan
News Programmes :
"FORTET EUROPA : DÖDEN VID GRÄNSEN" ("Fortress Europe : death on the border") Sveriges Television SVT - Sweden
4th European Television Producer Award
The Prize is awarded to COMPANY PICTURES (UK) for its fiction productions over the last two years.
1st Producer Award For TV Series Drama Category
Producer of the Year
For "WEST WING"
Producers: JohnWELLS, Aaron SORKIN, Thomas SCHLAMME, Llewellyn WELLS, Christopher MISIANO, Alex GRAVES, Michael HISSRICH
European Producer of the Year
For "BOB & ROSE"
Producers : Nicola SHINDLER, Russell T. DAVIES, Annie HARRISON-BAXTER
Actor of the Year:
Alan DAVIES
Actress of the Year:
Lesley SHARP
Comedy Category Producer of the Year
For : "SEX & THE CITY"
Producers : Michael Patrick KING, Sarah Jessica PARKER, Cindy CHUPACK, John P. MELFI.
European Producer of the Year
For "Don MATTEO" - Producer : Alessandro JACCHIA
Actor of the Year
Terence HILL
Actress of the Year
Sarah Jessica PARKER
Grand Prix du Documentarie
(Université Radiophonique et Télévisuelle Internationale)
Trophiée Arman
"Bellaria - as long as we live" WDR (Germany) / ARTE
Director : Douglas Wolsperger
Producer : Martin Dietrich
MÉDAILLE D'ARGENT
"E xercices de Liberté" - TVR - Romania
Director : Stephan Dimitriu
Médaukke de Bronze
"Arbres" - RTBF (Belgium) ARTE
Directors : Sophie Bruneau and Marc-Antoine Roudil
Special Mention:
"For Yves Montand" - RAI International
Director: Nino Bizzarrri - Producer: Daniela Battaglini

ROYAL TELEVISION SOCIETY AWARDS

Presented on Tuesday 19 March 2002 by Graham Norton at Grosvenor House, Park Lane, London W1

PROGRAMME AWARDS
2000/2001

Serials and Single Drama
PERFECT STRANGERS A TalkBack Production for BBC2
Drama Series
CLOCKING OFF Red Production Company for BBC1
Soap
EastEnders BBC1
Writer
Stephen Poliakoff (PERFECT STRANGERS A TalkBack production for BBC2)
Actor - Male
David Suchet (The Way We LiveNow (A BBC/WGBH co-production in association with Deep Indigo for BBC1)
Actor – Female
Diane Parish (BABYFATHER BBC2)
Team
KUMBH MELA A REX MUNDI
Production for Channel Four Television
Network Newcomer-Onscreen
Johnny Vegas (HAPPINESS BBC2)
Network Newcomer Behind The Screen
Marc Isaacs (Director - THE LIFT A DUAL PURPOSE Production for Channel 4 Television)
Regional Programme
Tartan Shorts: Cry for Bobo Forged Films for Scottish Screen and BBC Two Scotland
Regional Presenter
Tam Cowan (TAXI FOR COWAN/OFFSIDE The Comedy Unit for BBC1 Scotland)
Presenter
Anthony McPartlin and Declan Donnelly (SM:TV Live Blaze Television (A Division of Zenith Entertainment) for ITV)
Entertainment Performance
Alistair McGowan (ALISTAIR MCGOWAN'S BIG IMPRESSION Vera Production for BBC1)
Entertainment
BANZAI Radar/RDF Media for E4 and Channel 4 Television
Situation Comedy and Comedy Drama
THE OFFICE BBC2

Children's Drama
MY PARENTS ARE ALIENS Granada Kids for CITV
Children's Factual
NICK NEWS WisedUp for Nickelodeon
Documentary Series – General
LIVING WITH CANCER BBC1
Single Documentary – General
KELLY AND HER SISTERS A Carlton production for ITV
Arts
ARENA: JAMES ELLROY'S FEAST OF DEATH BBC2
Science and Natural History
CONGO SCORER Associates for BBC2.
History
THE GREAT PLAGUE: PLAGUE, FIRE, WAR & TREASON A Juniper Production for Channel 4 Television
Features Primetime
FAKING IT RDF Media for Channel 4 Television
Daytime Programme
THE WEAKEST LINK, BBC2
Cyril Bennett Judges' Award
Nick Elliott
Gold Medal
BBC Natural History Unit

RTS Television Sports Awards 2002

Monday 20 May 2002. Hosted by Jim Rosenthal
The London Hilton, Park Lane, London W1
Sponsors
The Daily Telegraph
Millbank Studios

SPORTS PRESENTER
Sue Barker, BBC Sport
SPORTS COMMENTATOR
Jim McGrath, BBC Sport
SPORTS PUNDIT
John McEnroe, BBC Sport
SPORTS NEWS REPORTER
Gabriel Clarke, ISN/Carlton for ITV Sport
SPORTS DOCUMENTARY
Black Britain Fighting Back - The Michael Watson Story, BBC2
REGIONAL SPORTS DOCUMENTARY
Scott Gibbs: Out On His Own, BBC Sport Wales
REGIONAL SPORTS PROGRAMME OF THE YEAR - ENTERTAINMENT
Offside, A Comedy Unit production for BBC Scotland
REGIONAL SPORTS PROGRAMME OF THE YEAR - ACTUALITY
Y Clwb Rygbi, BBC Sport Wales
REGIONAL SPORTS PRESENTER OR COMMENTATOR
Mark Bolton, Carlton Television
LIVE OUTSIDE BROADCAST COVERAGE OF THE YEAR
Wimbledon Championships, Men's Finals: Rafter v Ivanisevic, BBC Sport
CREATIVE SPORTS SEQUENCE OF THE YEAR
Beckham's Eye (Sports Personality of the Year), BBC Sport
INNOVATION
The Hawk-Eye System (Channel 4 Cricket), A Sunset + Vine Production for Channel 4 Television
SPORTS SHOW OR SERIES
The Morning Line, Highflyer Productions for Channel 4 Racing
SPORTS PROGRAMME OF THE YEAR
Channel 4 Cricket, A Sunset + Vine Production for Channel 4 Television
LIFETIME ACHIEVEMENT AWARD
Reg Gutteridge OBE and
Harry Carpenter OBE
JUDGES' AWARD
Roger Philcox

RTS EDUCATIONAL TELEVISION AWARDS

Wednesday 12 June 2002. Hosted by Reeta Chakrabarti The Savoy, London WC2. Awards presented by Sarah Thane, RTS Chairman

SCHOOLS TELEVISION
PRE SCHOOL AND INFANTS
Sarah and the Whammi: Bullies, A Westway Film Production in association with the Northern Ireland Community Relations Council for 4Learning
PRIMARY ARTS AND LANGUAGE
The Story of Tracy Beaker, CBBC Education for BBC1
PRIMARY HUMANITIES
Focus: Citizenship: A Home from Home (Refugees), Eric Rowan Productions for BBC2
PRIMARY AND SECONDARY SCIENCE, MATHS, DESIGN AND ICT
Megamaths: Shape and Space: Symmetry, CBBC Education for BBC2
SECONDARY ARTS AND LANGUAGES
Reading Media Texts: The Interactive Image, CBBC Education for BBC2
SECONDARY HUMANITIES
The A-Z of Love and Sex: Everything You Are Afraid To Ask, Lambent Productions for 4Learning
PRIMARY AND SECONDARY MULTIMEDIA AND INTERACTIVE
Walking with Beasts Online, BBC Interactive Factual & Learning for BBC1
ADULT EDUCATIONAL TELEVISION
VOCATIONAL TRAINING
Wild Moves: Water & Air, Natural History Unit/BBC Open University for BBC2
SINGLE PROGRAMME
Celebrity Blind Man's Bluff, A Maverick Production for Channel 4 Television
CAMPAIGNS AND SEASONS RTS / NIACE AWARD
Passion for Science, BBC Open University for BBC2
EDUCATIONAL IMPACT IN THE PRIMETIME SCHEDULE
The Private Life of a Masterpiece: The Scream, Fulmar Televison & Film for BBC2
JUDGES AWARD
Paul Ashton

RTS CRAFT & DESIGN AWARDS

Monday 18 November 2002 at the Savoy, London. Hosted by Richard Whiteley

PRODUCTION DESIGN – DRAMA
Michael Carlin for CRIME AND PUNISHMENT (BBC Drama for BBC2)
PRODUCTION DESIGN – ENTERTAINMENT & NON-DRAMA PRODUCTIONS
Richard Plumb for THE EXPERIMENT
ART DIRCTOR
Lynne Hitson and Matt Robinson for SHACKLETON (Firstsight for Channel 4)
VISUAL EFFECTS – DIGITAL
Angus Bickerton and Cinesite (Europe) for BAND OF BROTHERS (sections) (HBO/Dreamworks SKG/Playtone

in association with BBC Television for BBC2)
VISUAL EFFECTS – SPECIAL
Tom Harris for HORNBLOWER (series II) (A United Film and TV Production for Meridian Broadcasting in association with A&E Network)
COSTUME DESIGN – DRAMA
Rosie Hackett for CRIME AND PUNISHMENT (BBC Drama for BBC2)
COSTUME DESIGN – ENTERTAINMENT & NON-DRAMA PRODUCTIONS
Robert Lever for POENIX NIGHTS II (Ovation Entertainment for Channel 4)
MAKE UP DESIGN – DRAMA
Sue Minton, Veytie McLeod and Samantha Marshall for SUNDAY (A Gaslight Production in association with Box TV produced by Sunday Productions for Channell 4)
MAKE UP DESIGN – ENTERTAINMENT AND NON-DRAMA PRODUCTIONS
Veronica Brebner for THE GREAT PLAGUE (Juniper Productions for Channel 4)
GRAPHIC DESIGN – TRAILS & PACKAGING
Guy North for BBC Sport's World Cup 2002 Campaign THE WINNING TEAM FROM THE BBC (BBC Broadcast and Passion Pictures on behalf of Duckworth Finn Grubb Waters)
GRAPHIC DESIGN – TITLES
Steve Burrell and Paul Tigwell for THE CURIOUS GARDENERS (Burrell Durrant Hifle/BBC Television Features for BBC2)
GRAPHIC DESIGN – PROGRAMME CONTENT SEQUENCES
Rob Hifle, Alan Short and Paul Greer (Burrell Durrant Hifle) for LION BATTLEFIELD (BBC Natural History Unit for BBC2/Discovery)
LIGHTING – PHOTOGRAPHY & CAMERA – PHOTOGRAPHY, DRAMA
Daf Hobson for OTHELLO (LWT co-production with WGBH/Boston in association with CBC for ITV1)
LIGHTING, PHOTOGRAPHY & CAMERA – PHOTOGRAPHY, DOCUMENTARY AND NON-DRAMA PRODUCTIONS
Camera Team for THE BLUE PLANET (BBC Natural History Unit for BBC1/Discovery)
LIGHTING, PHOTOGRAPHY & CAMERA – LIGHTING FOR MULTICAMERA
Chris Rigby and Gurdip Mahal for RE:COVERED (Aurora Film & Television Lighting for Blaze Television for BBC Choice/BBC1)
LIGHTING, PHOTOGRAPHY & CAMERA – MULTI-CAMERA WORK
BBC Production Team for THE QUEEN MOTHER'S FUNERAL (BBC Events for BBC1)
TAPE AND FILM EDITING – DRAMA
Chris Gill for CRIME AND PUNISHMENT (BBC Drama for BBC2)
TAPE AND FILM EDITING – DOCUMENTARY & FACTUAL
Martin Elsbury, Jo Payne, Tim Coope and Alan Hoida for THE BLUE PLANET (BBC Natural History Unit for BBC1/DISC)
TAPE AND FILM EDITING – ENTERTAINMENT & SITUATION COMEDY
Pete Hallworth for PHOENIX NIGHTS II (Ovation Entertainment for Channel 4)
SOUND – DRAMA
Maurice Hillier and Colin Martin for OTHELLO (LWT Co-production with WGBH/Boston in association with CBC for ITV1)
SOUND – ENTERTAINMENT & NON-DRAMA PRODUCTIONS
BBC Sound Team for THE QUEEN'S GOLDEN JUBILEE (BBC Events for BBC One)
MUSIC – ORIGINAL TITLE MUSIC
Donald Shaw and Charlie McKerron for GRUTH IS UACHDAR (CRODIE & CREAM) (BBC Scotland for BBC2 Scotland)
MUSIC – ORIGINAL SCORE
Donald Shaw and Charlie McKerron for GRUTH IS UACHDAR (CRODIE & CREAM) (BBC Scotland for BBC2 Scotland)
TEAM AWARD
Framestone CFC for WALKING WITH BEASTS (BBC1)
DESGIN AND CRAFT INNOVATION
Rod Clarke, Stephen James Downer, Tim MacMillan, Howard Jones, Carl Chittenden and Stuart Napier for WEIRD NATURE: MARVELLOUS MOTION (Prog 1) (John Downer Productions for BBC/Discovery)
PICTURE ENHANCEMENT
Howard Jones and Carl Chittenden for WEIRD NATURE (John Downer Productions for BBC1/Discovery)
JUDGES' AWARD
Craft members of the BBC OB department for an year in Event coverage
LIFETIME ACHIEVEMENT AWARD
Eileen Diss

2003

This section features some of the principal festival prizes and awards from 1 January 2003 to 30 June 2003.

BAFTA

195 Piccadilly
London W1V OLN
Tel: 020 7734 0022
Fax: 020 7734 1792
Website: www.bafta.org

BAFTA TELEVISION AWARDS

Winners announced in London, Sunday 13 April 2003

Actress:
Julie Walters for MURDER (Tiger Aspect for BBC2)
Actor:
Albert Finney for THE GATHERING STORM (Scott Free in association with HBO/BBC Films for BBC2)
Entertainment Performance:
Paul Merton for HAVE I GOT NEWS FOR YOU? (Hat Trick for BBC1)
Comedy Performance:
Ricky Gervais for The Office (BBC for BBC2)
Single Drama:
Production team for CONSPIRACY (HBO/BBC Films for BBC2)
Drama Series:
Production Team for SPOOKS (Kudos Productions for BBC1)
Drama Serial:
Selwyn Roberts, Charles Sturridge for SHAcKLETON (Firstsight Films for C4)
Soap:
Kieran Roberts, Carolyn Reynolds for CORONATION STREET (Granada Television for ITV1)
Huw Wheldon Award for Factual Series or Strand:
Production Team for THE TRUST (Hart Ryan Productions for C4)
The Flaherty Documentary Award:
Roger Graef, Brian Hill for FELTHAM SINGS (Century/Films of Record for C4)
Features:
Stephen Lambert for FAKING IT (RDF Media for C4)
Sport:
Production Team for THE COMMONWEALTH GAMES (BBC for BBC1)
News Coverage:
Production Team for SOHAM – AUGUST 16/17 (Sky for Sky)
Current Affairs:
Steve Boulton, David Modell, Richard Fabb for YOUNG, NAZI & PROUD (Steve Boulton Productions for C4)
Entertainment Programme or Series:
Production Team for I'M A CELEBRITY – GET ME OUT OF HERE! (LWT for ITV1)
Situation Comedy Award:
Anil Gupta, Ash Atalla, Ricky Gervais, Stephen Merchant for THE OFFICE (BBC for BBC2)
Comedy Programme or Series:
Charlie Hanson, Gareth Carrick, Alistair McGowan for ALISTAIR McGOWAN'S BIG IMPRESSION (Vera for C4)
Lew Grade Audience Award sponsored by RadioTimes
FOYLE'S WAR (ITV1)
Fellowship:
David Jason
Alan Clarke Award for Creative Contribution to Television
Norma Percy and Brian Lapping

BAFTA TELEVISION CRAFT AWARDS

Costume Design:
Shirley Russell for SHACKLETON (Firstsight Films for C4)
Editing Factual:
Peter Norrey for SAS EMBASSY SIEGE (BBC for BBC2)
Editing Fiction/Entertainment:
Philip Kloss for DANIEL DERONDA (BBC/WGBH Boston for BBC1)
Graphic Design:
Burrell Durrant Hifle for THE DINOSAUR HUNTERS (Granada for C4)
Make Up & Hair Design:
Daniel Parker, Frances Hannon, Stephen Rose for THE GATHERING STORM (Scott Free in association with HBO/BBC Films for BBC1)
New Director Factual:
Alice Yglesias for DEATH (Quality Time for C4)
New Director Fiction sponsored by Sony Pictures Television International:
Brian Hill for FALLING APART (Century Films for C4)
New Writer sponsored by Montblanc:
Anna Moloney for FALLING APART (Century Films for C4)
Original Television Music sponsored by Sebastian McLean International:
Geoffrey Burgon for THE FORSYTE SAGA (Granada for ITV1)
Photography Factual:
Nigel Meakin for SAHARA WITH MICHAEL PALIN (Prominent Television for BBC1)
Photography & Lighting Fiction/Entertainment:
Ivan Strasbourg for BLOODY SUNDAY (Granada for ITV1)
Production Design:
Luciana Arrighi for THE GATHERING STORM (Scott Free in association with HBO/BBC Films for BBC2)
Sound Factual:
Sound Team for THE QUEEN'S GOLDEN JUBILEE (BBC Events for BBC1)
Sound Fiction/Entertainment:
Sound Team for DANIEL DERONDA (BBC/WGBH Boston for BBC1)
Visual Effects & Graphic Design sponsored by Oasis Television:
Max Tyrie, Tim Greenwood, Jez Gibson Harris for THE GIANT CLAW – A WALKING WITH DINOSAURS SPECIAL (Impossible Pictures for BBC1)
Special Award:
Carl Davis

BROADCASTING PRESS GUILD TELEVISION AND RADIO AWARDS

London. Awards 2003

Best Single Drama:
THE GATHERING STORM (BBC2
Best Drama Series/Serial:
DANIEL DERONDA (BBC1)
Best Documentary Series:
JAMIE'S KITCHEN (Channel 4)
Best Single Documentary:

FAKING IT: DRAG QUEEN (Channel 4)
Best Entertainment:
BREMNER, BIRD & FORTUNE: AT HER MAJESTY'S PLEASURE (Channel 4)
Best Actor:
Albert Finney (THE GATHERING STORM)
Best Actress:
Vanessa Redgrave (THE GATHERING STORM)
Best Performer (Non-Acting):
Andrew Marr (BBC)
Writer's Award (joint):
Ricky Gervais and Stephen Merchant THE OFFICE (BBC2)
Radio Programme of the Year:
BROADCASTING HOUSE (BBC Radio 4)
Radio Broadcaster of the Year:
Sue Lawley (BBC Radio 4)
Multichannel Award:
SCRATCHIN' (MEN AND MOTORS)
Harvey Lee Award for Contribution to Broadcasting:
Brian Lapping

60th GOLDEN GLOBE AWARDS

Awarded Sunday, 19 January 2003, Los Angeles

Golden Globes

Hollywood Foreign Press Association
646 North Robertson Boulevard
West Hollywood
California 90069
Tel: (310) 657 1731
Fax: (310) 657 5576
email: hfpa95@aol.com
Website: www.hfpa.com

TELEVISION
Best Mini-Series or Motion Picture Made for Television:
THE GATHERING STORM (HBO)
Best Performance by an Actor in a Mini-Series or a Motion Picture made for Television:
Albert Finney for THE GATHERING STORM
Best Performance by an Actor in a Supporting Role in a Series, Mini-Series or Motion Picture Made for Televison:
Donald Sutherland for PATH TO WAR
Best Performance by an Actor in a Television Series - Drama:
Michael Chiklis for THE SHIELD
Best Performance by an Actor in a Television Series - Musical or Comedy:
Tony Shalhoub for MONK
Best Performance by an Actress in a Mini-Series or a Motion Picture made for Television:
Uma Thurman for HYSTERICAL BLINDNESS
Best Performance by an Actress in a Supporting Role in a Series, Mini-Series or Motion Picture Made for Televison:
Kim Cattrall for SEX AND THE CITY
Best Performance by an Actress in a Television Series - Drama:
Edie Falco for THE SOPRANOS
Best Performance by an Actress in a Television Series - Musical or Comedy:
Jennifer Aniston for FRIENDS
Best Television Series - Drama:
THE SHIELD
Best Television Series - Musical or Comedy:
CURB YOUR ENTHUSIASM

43rdMONTE CARLO TELEVISION FESTIVAL

30 June–5 July, Monaco 2003

TELEVISION FILMS
Gold Nymphs :
Best Television Film
OUT OF CONTROL (BBC1 – UK)
Best Script
Pierre Colin-Thibert and Jean-Claude Islert for UNE FERRARI POUR DEUX (TF1/PM Films – France)
Best Direction
Krisztina Deak for JADVIGA PARNAJA (Jadviga's Pillow) (MTV Hungarian Television – Hungary)
Best Performance by an Actor
Gotz George in DER ANWALT UND SEIN GAST (The Lawyer and His Guest) (Sudwestrundfunk – Germany)
Best Performance by an Actress
Marthe Villalong in NÉS DE LA MERE DU MONDE (Born of the Mother of the World) (Cipango – France)
MINI-SERIES
Gold Nymphs:
Best Mini-Series
WHITE TEETH (Company Pictures – UK)
Best Script
Dan Frank for JEAN MOULIN (Scarlett – France)
Best Direction
Beeban Kidron for MURDER (BBC2 – UK)
Best Performance by an Actor
Thomas Sangster in ENTRUSTED (Le Sabre/Grundy Italia/Simply Committed – France/Germany)
Best Performance by an Actress
Naomie Harris in WHITE TEETH (Company Pictures – UK)
News and Current Affairs Programmes
Gold Nymph:
Best Current Affairs Programme
HUGO CHAVEZ – EIN STAATSSTREICH VON INNEN (Hugo Chavez – Inside the Coup) (ZDF – Germany)
TILBAGE TIL BAGDAD (Back to Bagdad) (Danish Broadcasting Corporation DR/Danish Television – Denmark)
News Programmes
Gold Nymph:
Best News Programme
GUINEA REFUGEES: SEX FOR FOOD (CNN – UK)
IRAQ WAR (BBC1 – UK)
24-Hour News Programmes
Gold Nymph:
Best 24-Hour News Programme
IRAQ WAR (BBC News 24 – UK)
SPECIAL PRIZES
Special Prize of HSH Prince Rainier III
UPPDRAG GRANSKNING : HOTET FRAN OLJAN (Black Sea – Troubled Waters) (SVT Sveriges Television – Sweden)
Prize of the Monaco Red Cross
POUR UNE POIGNÉE DE ROUPIES (TF1 – France)
Prize of the Red Cross International Committee
CORRESPONDENT: KENYA: WHITE TERROR (BBC2 – UK)
AMADE & UNESCO PRIZE
Fiction Programme
DAKISHIMETAI (A Brother for Life) (NHK Broadcasting Corpoation – Japan)
News Programme:
POUR UNE POIGNÉE DE ROUPIES (TF1 – France)
SIGNIS PRIZE
Fiction :

OUT OF CONTROL (BBC1 – UK)
News Programmes:
LES PETITS SOLDATS DE L'ARMÉE RUSSE (Little Russian Soldiers) (Noon – France)
4th European Television Producer Award
The Prize is awarded to SALLY HEAD PRODUCTION (UK) for its fiction productions over the last two years.
2nd Producer Award For TV Series Drama Category
Producer of the Year
For 24
Producers: Brian Grazer, Tony Krantz, Howard Gordon, Robert Cochran, Joel Surnow, Sirus Yavneh
European Producer of the Year
For ABSCHNITT 40
Producers : Marc Conrad, Friedrich Wildfeuer
Actor of the Year
Keiffer Sutherland
Actress of the Year
Allison Janney
Comedy Category Producer of the Year
For: CURB YOUR ENTHUSIASM
Producers : Larry David, Jeff Garlin, Robert B. Weide, Tim Gibbons
European Producer of the Year
For BARBARA
Producers : Mark Bussell, Justin Sbresni
Actor of th e Year
Larry David
Actress of the Year
Marina Orsini
FORMATS
Gold Nymph:
INTERNATIONAL FORMAT OF THE YEAR AWARD
For BIG BROTHER (Endemol International – Netherlands)
Special Mention
For WHO WANTS TO BE A MILLIONAIRE? (Celador – UK)
INTERNATIONAL FORMAT MASTERPIECE AWARD
For THE PRICE IS RIGHT (FreemantleMedia)
GRAND PRIX DU DOCUMENTAIRE
(Université Radiophonique et Télévisuelle Internationale)
TROPHÉE ARMAN
LA LECON DE TOLÉRANCE (RTBB – Belgium)
Director: Roger Beeckmans
MÉDAILLE D'ARGENT
S21, LA MACHINE DE MORT KMERE ROUGE (UNESCO)
Director : Rithy Panh
MÉDAILLE DE BRONZE
ET LES ARBRES POUSSENT EN KABYLIE (ARTE – France)
Director: Djamila Sahraoui
Special Mention
L'ODYSSÉE DE L'ESPACE (France 3)
Director: Jacques Malaterre
Honary Awards
Reg Grundy, Ted Turner

43rd ROSE D'OR - FESTIVAL OF ENTERTAINMENT PROGRAMMES

Montreux, Switzerland. Awards 2003

Golden Rose:
FAKING IT (Channel 4 - UK)
Honorary Rose:
Emil Steinberger (Switzerland)
Comedy
Silver Rose :
THE ALL NEW HARRY HILL SHOW (Avalon Television - UK)
Bronze Rose :
SMACK THE PONY (Channel 4/Talkback Productions - UK)
Special Mentions:
THE RICHARD TAYLOR INTERVIEWS (Channel 4 – UK)
SHOREDITCH TW*T (Channel 4/Talkback Productions – UK)
ALT & DURCHGEKNALLT (Brainpool – Germany)
Music
Silver Rose :
SUSHEELA RAMAN ET CHEB MAMI (ARTE France - France)
Bronze Rose:
PARTY AT THE PALACE (BBC - UK)
Sitcom : Silver Rose :
THE OFFICE (BBC - UK)
Bronze Rose:
PUPPETS WHO KILL (PWK – CDN)
Games Show
Silver Rose :
your face or mine (E4/Talkback - UK)
Bronze Rose :
INTERNATIONAL KING OF SPORTS (Channel 5 - UK)
Variety
Silver Rose :
DERREN BROWN – MIND CONTROL (Channel 4 - UK)
Bronze Rose:
PLUK DE DAG (Tros TV - NL)
Arts & Special/ Special Prize of the City of Montreux
Golden Rose:
TINA IN MEXICO (Rhombus – CDN)
Special Mention :
ROLF ON ART (BBC - UK)
Press Prize
Reality Show:
FAKING IT (Channel 4 – UK)

ROYAL TELEVISION SOCIETY AWARDS

RTS PROGRAMME AWARDS 2002
Presented on Tuesday 18 March 2003 by Kirsty Young at Le Meridien, Grosvenor House, London W1.

SERIALS & SINGLE DRAMA
OUT OF CONTROL (BBC Films for BBC1)
DRAMA SERIES
CLOCKING OFF (Red Production Company for BBC1)
SOAP
CORONATION STREET (Granada Television for itv)
WRITER
Peter Bowker for FLESH & BLOOD (BBC Drama Serials/Red Production Company for BBC2)
ACTOR - MALE
Christopher Eccleston for FLESH & BLOOD (BBC Drama Serials/Red Production Company for BBC2)
ACTOR - FEMALE
Julie Walters for MURDER (Tiger Aspect for BBC2)
NETWORK NEWCOMER - ONSCREEN
Jimmy Carr for YOUR FACE OR MINE (Talkback for E4)
NETWORK NEWCOMER - BEHIND THE SCENES
David Modell (Director) for YOUNG NAZI AND PROUD (Steve Boulton production for Channel 4)

REGIONAL PROGRAMME
AR Y STRYD (Ffilmiau'r Nant for S4C)
REGIONAL PRESENTER
Dewi Pws for BYD PWS (Ffilmiau'r Nant for S4C)
PRESENTER (FACTUAL)
Susannah Constantine and Trinny Woodall for WHAT NOT TO WEAR (BBC General Factual for BBC2)
ENTERTAINMENT PERFORMANCE
Jonathan Ross for FRIDAY NIGHT WITH JONATHAN ROSS/THEY THINK IT'S ALL OVER (Open Mike Productions/Talkback Productions for BBC1)
ENTERTAINMENT
POP IDOL: THE FINAL & RESULTS SHOW (Thames/19 Television production for ITV)
COMEDY PERFORMANCE
Ricky Gervais for THE OFFICE (BBC Comedy for BBC2)
SITUATION COMEDY & COMEDY DRAMA
PHOENIX NIGHTS 2 (Ovation Entertainment for Channel 4)
CHILDREN'S FICTION
DOUBLE ACT (Television Junction for 4Learning)
CHILDREN'S FACTUAL
SERIOUS JUNGLE (CBBC for BBC1)
DOCUMENTARY SERIES - GENERAL
THE HUNT FOR BRITAIN'S PAEDOPHILES (BBC General Factual for BBC2)
SINGLE DOCUMENTARY -GENERAL
HOUSE OF WAR (Berwick Univeral Pictures/Diverse production for Channel 4) ARTS
THE STRANGE WORLD OF BARRY WHO? (Darlow Smithson for BBC4)
SCIENCE & NATURAL HISTORY
SUPERFLY (Oxford Film & Television for BBC4)
HISTORY
DAMBUSTERS: REVEALED (Windfall Films for Five)
FEATURES PRIMETIME
LADS ARMY (Twenty Twenty Televsion for ITV)
DAYTIME PROGRAMME
TODAY WITH DES (Carlton Production for ITV)
JUDGES' AWARD
Peter Bazalgette
GOLD MEDAL
David Liddiment

RTS JOURNALISM AWARDS 2001/2002
Presented on Thursday, 28 February 2003 by Katie Durham at London Hilton, London

NEWS – INTERNATIONAL
TERROR ON TAPE (CNN)
NEWS – HOME
NEWSNIGHT – REPLICA GUNS (BBC2)
REGIONAL DAILY NEWS MAGAZINE
BBC WALES TODAY: THE CLYDACH VERDICT (BBC Wales)
NEWS EVENT
HOLLY AND JESSICA (Sky News)
CAMERA OPRATOR OF THE YEAR
Dodge Billingsley and Damien Degueldre for A HOUSE OF WAR (Diverse Production for Channel 4)
PRESENTER OF THE YEAR
Jon Snow, Channel 4 News
REGIONAL CURRENT AFFAIRS
SPOTLIGHT:
PEOPLE FOR SALE (BBC Northern Ireland)
CURENT AFFAIRS – INTRNATIONAL
AVENGING TERROR (A Brook Lapping production for Channel 4)
CURRENT AFFAIRS – HOME
PANORAMA: THE CORRUPTION OF RACING (BBC1)
INNOVATION
Virtual Reality Graphics THE BURRELL TRIAL (ITV News)
TELEVISION JOURNALIST OF THE YEAR
Peter Taylor, BBC1/BBC2
YOUNG JOURNALIST OF THE YEAR
Lindsey Hilsum, Diplomatic Correspondent, Channel 4 News
NEWS PROGRAMM OF THE YEAR
NEWSNIGHT (BBC2)
NEWS CHANNEL OF THE YEAR
Sky News
PROGRAMME OF THE YEAR
TONIGHT WITH TREVOR McDONALD (Granada Television)
JUDGES' AWARD
David Lloyd

RTS STUDENT TELEVISION AWARDS 2002
Thursday 1 May 2003. Hosted by Paul Watson Centre for Magic Arts, London. Sponsored by JVC Professional

UNDERGRADUATE
Animation:
Sumito Sakakibara for 3 BROTHERS (Kingston University)
Factual:
Nathalie Berry for WHEN YOU DON'T COME HOME (Bournemouth University)
Non-Factual:
Mark Henrichsen and Jamie Goldblatt for DEAD (Edinburgh College of Art)
POSTGRADUATE
Animation:
John Chorlton, Josephine Law, Jon Driscoll, Richard Overall, Bradley Miles, Toni Bates and Philippe Ciompi for LAST RUMBA IN ROCHDALE (National Film & Television School)
Factual:
Saed Andoni for A NUMBER ZERO (Goldsmiths College)
Non-Factual:
Avie Luthra, Victoria Powell, Simon Vickery, Samantha Holgate and Simon Winter for BABY (National Film & Television School)

RTS Television Sports Awards 2002

Monday 19 May 2003, Hosted by Mark Nicholas
The London Hilton, Park Lane, London W1

SPORTS PRESENTER
Gary Linekar, BBC Sport for BBC1
SPORTS COMMENTATOR
Clive Tyldesley, ITV Sport for ITV1
SPORTS PUNDIT
Simon Hughes, Sunset + Vine Productions for Channel 4
SPORTS NEWS REPORTER
Gabriel Clarke, ITV Sport for ITV1
SPORTS DOCUMENTARY
THE GAME OF THEIR LIVES (VeryMuchSo Productions/Passion Pictures for BBC4)
REGIONAL SPORTS PROGRAMME
GRASPING THE THISTLE (Colour Television for BBC Scotland)

REGIONAL SPORTS ACTUALITY PROGRAMME
RUGBY LEAGUE RAW III (Paul Doherty International for Yorkshire Television)
REGIONAL SPORTS PRESENTER OR COMMENTATOR
Roger Johnson, BBC South
LIVE OUTSIDE BROADCAST COVERAGE OF THE YEAR
COMMONWEALTH GAMES (BBC Sport for BBC1 AND BBC2)
SPORTS FEATURE
HOW ARSENAL WON THE TITLE (Carlton/ISN for ITV1)
CREATIVE SPORTS SEQUENCE OF THE YEAR
HOW ARSENAL WON THE TITLE (Carlton/ISN for ITV1)
SPORTS INNOVATION AWARD
CHANNEL 4 WORLD RALLY CHAMPIONSHIP 2002 – VIRTUAL SPECTATOR (Chrysalis Television for Channel 4)
SPORTS SHOW OR SERIES
SKI SUNDAY: KITZBUHEL 2002 (BBC Sport for BBC2)
SPORTS PROGRAMME OF THE YEAR
FORMULA ONE (Chrysalis Sport/Granada Sport for ITV1
LIFETIME ACHIEVEMENT AWARD
Desmond Lynam

RTS Educational Television Awards 2002

Wednesday 11 June 2003. Hosted by Reeta Chakrabarti The Savoy, London WC2. Awards presented by Simon Shaps, RTS Chairman

SCHOOLS TELEVISION
PRE SCHOOL AND INFANTS
STOP, LOOK, LISTEN: OKEY COKEY KARAOKE! – THE RAJA WITH BIG EARS (SFTV for 4Learning)
PRIMARY ARTS AND LANGUAGE
LET'S WRITE A STORY: THE MASTER STORYTELLER (CBBC Education for BBC2)
PRIMARY HUMANITIES
GEOGRAPHY JUNCTION: JAMAICA – THE LOCAL PEOPLE (Wised Up Productions for 4Learning)
PRIMARY AND SECONDARY SCIENCE, MATHS, DESIGN AND ICT
THE MATHS CHANNEL (CBBC Education for BBC2)
SECONDARY ARTS AND LANGUAGES
EXTRA (FRENCH):
L'ARRIVÉE DE SAM (Double Exposure for 4Learning)
SECONDARY HUMANITIES
DEAD DRUNK (Hurricane Films for BBC2) PRIMARY AND SECONDARY MULTIMEDIA AND INTERACTIVE AROUND SCOTLAND: TECHNOLOGY – THINGS WE WEAR (BBC Scotland Commission for BBC Education Scotland) ADULT EDUCATIONAL TELEVISION
LIFELONG LEARNING & MULTIMEDIA
HOW TO BE A GARDENER online course (BBC Factual & Learning for BBC2 & BBCi)
SINGLE PROGRAMME
THE MAN WHO LEARNT TO SEE (Documentaries & Factual for BBC2)
CAMPAIGNS AND SEASONS RTS /FI NIACE AWARD
SPOTLIGHT: SAVE YOURSELF A FORTUNE (Meridian Trust/Meridian Broadcasting)
EDUCATIONAL IMPACT IN THE PRIMETIME SCHEDULE
GEAT BRITONS: BRUNEL (BBC Documentaries for BBC2)
JUDGES' AWARD
John Richmond

British Successes in the Academy Awards 1927–2002

The following list chronicles British successes in the Academy Awards. It includes individuals who were either born, and lived and worked, in Britain into their adult lives, or those who were not born here but took on citizenship. Compiled by Erinna Mettler

(1st) 1927/28 held in 1930

Charles Chaplin
- **Special Award (acting, producing, directing and writing):** THE CIRCUS

(2nd) 1928/29 held in 1930

Frank Lloyd
- **Best Direction:** THE DIVINE LADY

(3rd) 1929/30 held in 1930

George Arliss
- **Best Actor:** THE GREEN GODDESS

(6th) 1932/33 held in 1934

William S. Darling
- **Best Art Direction:** CAVALCADE

Charles Laughton
- **Best Actor:** THE PRIVATE LIFE OF HENRY VIII

Frank Lloyd
- **Best Direction:** CAVALCADE

(8th) 1935 held in 1936

Gaumont British Studios
- **Best Short Subject:** WINGS OVER MT. EVEREST

Victor Mclaglen
- **Best Actor:** THE INFORMER

(11th) 1938 held in 1939

Ian Dalrymple, Cecil Lewis & W.P. Lipscomb
- **Best Screenplay:** PYGMALION

(12th) 1939 held in 1940

Robert Donat
- **Best Actor:** GOODBYE MR. CHIPS

Vivien Leigh
- **Best Actress:** GONE WITH THE WIND

(13th) 1940 held in 1941

Lawrence Butler & Jack Whitney
- **Special Visual Effects:** THE THIEF OF BAGDAD

Vincent Korda
- **Best Colour Set Design:** THE THIEF OF BAGDAD

(14th) 1941 held in 1942

British Ministry of Information
- **Honorary Award:** TARGET FOR TONIGHT

Donald Crisp
- **Best Supporting Actor:** HOW GREEN WAS MY VALLEY

Joan Fontaine
- **Best Actress:** SUSPICION

Jack Whitney & The General Studios Sound Department
- **Best Sound:** THAT HAMILTON WOMAN

(15th) 1942 held in 1943

Noel Coward
- **Special Award:** IN WHICH WE SERVE

Greer Garson
- **Best Actress:** MRS. MINIVER

(16th) 1943 held in 1944

British Ministry of Information
- **Best Documentary:** DESERT VICTORY

William S. Darling
- **Best Art Direction:** THE SONG OF BERNADETTE

(18th) 1945 held in 1946

The Governments of the United States & Great Britain
- **Best Documentary:** THE TRUE GLORY

Ray Milland
- **Best Actor:** THE LOST WEEKEND

Harry Stradling
- **Best Cinematography (b/w):** THE PICTURE OF DORIAN GRAY

(19th) 1946 held in 1947

Muriel & Sydney Box
- **Best Original Screenplay:** THE SEVENTH VEIL

Clemence Dane

- **Best Original Story:** VACATION FROM MARRIAGE

Olivia de Havilland
- **Best Actress:** TO EACH HIS OWN

Laurence Olivier
- **Special Award:** HENRY V

Thomas Howard
- **Best Special Effects:** BLITHE SPIRIT

William S. Darling
- **Best Art Direction (b/w):** ANNA AND THE KING OF SIAM

(20th) 1947 held in 1948

John Bryan
- **Best Art Direction:** GREAT EXPECTATIONS

Jack Cardiff
- **Best Cinematography (col):** BLACK NARCISSUS

Ronald Colman
- **Best Actor:** A DOUBLE LIFE

Guy Green
- **Best Cinematography (b/w):** GREAT EXPECTATIONS

Edmund Gwen
- **Best Supporting Actor:** MIRACLE ON 34TH STREET

(21st) 1948 held in 1949

Carmen Dillon & Roger Furse
- **Best Art Direction (b/w):** HAMLET

Brian Easdale
- **Best Score:** THE RED SHOES

Roger Furse
- **Best Costume Design:** HAMLET

Laurence Olivier
- **Best Picture:** HAMLET

Laurence Olivier
- **Best Actor:** HAMLET

(22nd) 1949 held in 1950

British Information Services
- **Best Documentary:** DAYBREAK IN UDI

Olivia de Havilland
- **Best Actress:** THE HEIRESS

(23rd) 1950 held in 1951

George Sanders
- **Best Supporting Actor:** ALL ABOUT EVE

(24th) 1951 held in 1952

James Bernard & Paul Dehn
- **Best Motion Picture Story:** SEVEN DAYS TO NOON

Vivien Leigh
- **Best Actress:** A STREETCAR NAMED DESIRE

(25th) 1952 held in 1953

T.E.B. Clarke
- **Best Story & Screenplay:** THE LAVENDER HILL MOB

London Films Sound Dept.
- **Best Sound:** THE SOUND BARRIER

(26th) 1954 held in 1955

British Information Services
- **Best Documentary Short Subject:** THURSDAY'S CHILDREN

S. Tyne Jule
- **Best Song:** THREE COINS IN THE FOUNTAIN

Jon Whitely & Vincent Winter
- **Special Award (Best Juvenile Performances):** THE KIDNAPPERS

(29th) 1956 held in 1957

George K. Arthur
- **Best Short Subject:** THE BESPOKE OVERCOAT

(30th) 1957 held in 1958

Malcolm Arnold
- **Best Musical Score:** THE BRIDGE ON THE RIVER KWAI

Alec Guinness
- **Best Actor:** THE BRIDGE ON THE RIVER KWAI

Jack Hildyard
- **Best Cinematography:** THE BRIDGE ON THE RIVER KWAI

David Lean
- **Best Director:** THE BRIDGE ON THE RIVER KWAI

Pete Taylor
- **Best Editing:** THE BRIDGE ON THE RIVER KWAI

(31st) 1958 held in 1959

Cecil Beaton
- **Best Costumes:** GIGI

Wendy Hiller
- **Best Supporting Actress:** SEPARATE TABLES

Thomas Howard
- **Special Visual Effects:** TOM THUMB

David Niven
- **Best Actor:** SEPARATE TABLES

(32nd) 1959 held in 1960

Hugh Griffith
- **Best Supporting Actor:** BEN HUR

Elizabeth Haffenden
- **Best Costume Design (col.):** BEN HUR

(33rd) 1960 held in 1961

Freddie Francis
- **Best Cinematography (b/w):** SONS & LOVERS

James Hill
- **Best Documentary:** GIUSEPPINA

Hayley Mills
- **Special Award (Best Juvenile Performance):** POLLYANNA

Peter Ustinov
- **Best Supporting Actor:** SPARTACUS

(34th) 1961 held in 1962

Vivian C. Greenham

- **Best Visual Effects:** THE GUNS OF NAVARONE

(35th) 1962 held in 1963

John Box & John Stoll
- **Best Art Direction:** LAWRENCE OF ARABIA

Anne V. Coates
- **Best Editing:** LAWRENCE OF ARABIA

Jack Howells (Janus Films)
- **Best Documentary:** DYLAN THOMAS

David Lean
- **Best Director:** LAWRENCE OF ARABIA

Shepperton Studios Sound Dept. (John Cox Sound Director)
- **Best Sound:** LAWRENCE OF ARABIA

Freddie Young
- **Best Cinematography:** LAWRENCE OF ARABIA

(36th) 1963 held in 1964

John Addison
- **Best Score:** TOM JONES

John Osborne
- **Best Adapted Screenplay:** TOM JONES

Tony Richardson
- **Best Director:** TOM JONES

Tony Richardson (Woodfall Films)
- **Best Picture:** TOM JONES

Margaret Rutherford
- **Best Supporting Actress:** THE V.I.P.S

(37th) 1964 held in 1965

Julie Andrews
- **Best Actress:** MARY POPPINS

Cecil Beaton
- **Best Art Direction (col):** MY FAIR LADY

Cecil Beaton
- **Best Costume Design (col):** MY FAIR LADY

Rex Harrison
- **Best Actor:** MY FAIR LADY

Walter Lassally
- **Best Cinematography (b/w):** ZORBA THE GREEK

Harry Stradling
- **Best Cinematography (col):** MY FAIR LADY

Peter Ustinov
- **Best Supporting Actor:** TOPKAPI

Norman Wanstall
- **Best Sound Effects:** GOLDFINGER

(38th) 1965 held in 1966

Julie Christie
- **Best Actress:** DARLING

Robert Bolt
- **Adapted Screenplay:**DOCTOR ZHIVAGO

Frederic Raphael
- **Original Screenplay:** DARLING

Freddie Young
- **Colour Cinematography:** DOCTOR ZHIVAGO

John Box, Terence Marsh
- **Best Art Direction (colour):**DOCTOR ZHIVAGO

Julie Harris
- **Costume (b/w):** DARLING

Phyllis Dalton
- **Costume (col):** DOCTOR ZHIVAGO

John Stears
- **Special Visual Effects:** THUNDERBALL

(39th) 1966 held in 1967

John Barry
- **Best Original Score:** BORN FREE

John Barry & Don Black
- **Best Song:** BORN FREE

Robert Bolt
- **Best Adapted Screenplay:** A MAN FOR ALL SEASONS

Joan Bridge & Elizabeth Haffenden
- **Best Costume (col):** A MAN FOR ALL SEASONS

Gordon Daniel
- **Best Sound:** GRAND PRIX

Ted Moore
- **Best Cinematography (col):** A MAN FOR ALL SEASONS

Ken Thorne
- **Best Adapted Score:** A FUNNY THING HAPPENED ON THE WAY TO THE FORUM

Peter Watkins
- **Best Documentary Feature:** THE WAR GAME

(40th) 1967 held in 1968

Leslie Bricusse
- **Best Song:** DOCTOR DOLITTLE (TALK TO THE ANIMALS)

Alfred Hitchcock
- **Irving Thalberg Memorial Award**

John Poyner
- **Best Sound Effects:** THE DIRTY DOZEN

(41st) 1968 held in 1969

John Barry
- **Best Original Score:** THE LION IN WINTER

Vernon Dixon & Ken Muggleston
- **Best Art Direction:** OLIVER!

Carol Reed
- **Best Director:** OLIVER!

Shepperton Sound Studio
- **Best Sound:** OLIVER!

Charles D. Staffell
- **Scientific, Class I Statuett -**
for the development of a successful embodiement of the reflex background projection system for composite cinematography

John Woolf
- **Best Picture:** OLIVER!

(42nd) 1969 held in 1970

Margaret Furfe
- **Best Costume:** ANNE OF THE THOUSAND DAYS

Cary Grant
- **Honorary Award**

John Schlesinger
- **Best Director:** MIDNIGHT COWBOY

Maggie Smith
- **Best Actress:** THE PRIME OF MISS JEAN BRODIE

(43rd) 1970 held in 1971

The Beatles
- **Best Original Score:** LET IT BE

Glenda Jackson
- **Best Actress:** WOMEN IN LOVE

John Mills
- **Best Supporting Actor:** RYAN'S DAUGHTER

Freddie Young
- **Best Cinematography:** RYAN'S DAUGHTER

(44th) 1971 held in 1972

Robert Amram
- **Best Short:** SENTINELS OF SILENCE

Ernest Archer, John Box, Vernon Dixon & Jack Maxsted
- **Best Art Direction:** NICHOLAS & ALEXANDRA

Charles Chaplin
- **Honorary Award**

David Hildyard & Gordon K. McCallum
- **Best Sound:** FIDDLER ON THE ROOF

Oswald Morris
- **Best Cinematography:** FIDDLER ON THE ROOF

(45th) 1972 held in 1973

Charles Chaplin
- **Best Original Score:** LIMELIGHT

David Hildyard
- **Best Sound:** CABARET

Anthony Powell
- **Best Costume Design:** TRAVELS WITH MY AUNT

Geoffrey Unsworth
- **Best Cinematography:** CABARET

(46th) 1973 held in 1974

Glenda Jackson
- **Best Actress:** A TOUCH OF CLASS

(47th) 1974 held in 1975

Albert Whitlock
- **Special Achievement In Visual Effects:** EARTHQUAKE

(48th) 1975 held in 1976

Ben Adam, Vernon Dixon & Roy Walker
- **Best Art Direction:** BARRY LYNDON

John Alcott
- **Best Cinematography:** BARRY LYNDON

Bob Godfrey
- **Best Animated Short:** GREAT

Albert Whitlock
- **Special Achievement In Visual Effects:** THE HINDENBERG

(49th) 1976 held in 1977

Peter Finch
- **Best Actor:** NETWORK

(50th) 1977 held in 1978

John Barry, Roger Christians & Leslie Dilley
- **Best Art Direction:** STAR WARS

John Mollo
- **Best Costume Design:** STAR WARS

Vanessa Redgrave
- **Best Supporting Actress:** JULIA

John Stears
- **Best Visual Effects:** STAR WARS

(51st) 1978 held in 1979

Les Bowie, Colin Chilvers, Denys Coop, Roy Field & Derek Meddings
- **Special Achievement In Visual Effects:** SUPERMAN

Michael Deeley, John Peverall & Barry Spikings
- **Best Picture:** THE DEER HUNTER

Laurence Oilvier
- **Lifetime Achievement Award**

Anthony Powell
- **Best Costume Design:** DEATH ON THE NILE

Maggie Smith
- **Best Supporting Actress:** CALIFORNIA SUITE

(52nd) 1979 held in 1980

Nick Allder, Denis Ayling & Brian Johnson
- **Special Achievement In Visual Effects:** ALIEN

Alec Guinness
- **Honorary Award**

Tony Walton
- **Best Art Direction:** ALL THAT JAZZ

(53rd) 1980 held in 1981

Brian Johnson
- **Special Achievement In Visual Effects:** THE EMPIRE STRIKES BACK

Lloyd Phillips
- **Best Live Action Short:** THE DOLLAR BOTTOM

Anthony Powell
- **Best Costume Design:** TESS

David W. Samuelson
- **Scientific and Engineering Award - for the engineering and development of the Louma Camera Crane and remote control system for motion picture production**

Jack Stevens
- **Best Art Direction:** TESS

Geoffrey Unsworth
- **Best Cinematography:** TESS

(54th) 1981 held in 1982

Leslie Dilley & Michael Ford
- **Best Art Direction:** RAIDERS OF THE LOST ARK

John Gielgud
- **Best Supporting Actor:** ARTHUR

Nigel Nobel
- **Best Documentary Short:** CLOSE HARMONY

David Puttnam
- **Best Picture:** CHARIOTS OF FIRE

Arnold Schwartzman
- **Best Documentary Feature:** CLOSE HARMONY

Colin Welland
- **Best Original Screenplay:** CHARIOTS OF FIRE

Kit West
- **Special Achievement In Visual Effects:** RAIDERS OF THE LOST ARK

(55th) 1982 held in 1983

Richard Attenborough
- **Best Picture:** GANDHI

Richard Attenborough
- **Best Director:** GANDHI

John Briley
- **Best Original Screenplay:** GANDHI

Stuart Craig, Bob Laing & Michael Seirton
- **Best Art Direction:** GANDHI

Ben Kingsley
- **Best Actor:** GANDHI

John Mollo
- **Best Costume Design:** GANDHI

Sarah Monzani
- **Best Achievement In Make Up:** QUEST FOR FIRE

Colin Mossman & Rank Laboratories
- **Scientific and Engineering Award - for the engineering and implementation of a 4,000 meter printing system for motion picture laboratories**

Christine Oestreicher
- **Best Live Action Short:** A SHOCKING ACCIDENT

Ronnie Taylor & Billy Williams
- **Best Cinematography:** GANDHI

(56th) 1983 held in 1984

Gerald L. Turpin (Lightflex International)
- **Scientific And Engineering Award**
- for the design, engineering and development of an on-camera device providing contrast control, sourceless fill light and special effects for motion picture photography

(57th) 1984 held in 1985

Peggy Ashcroft
- **Best Supporting Actress:** A PASSAGE TO INDIA

Jim Clark
- **Best Editing:** THE KILLING FIELDS

George Gibbs
- **Special Achievement In Visual Effects:** INDIANA JONES AND THE TEMPLE OF DOOM

Chris Menges
- **Best Cinematography:** THE KILLING FIELDS

Peter Shaffer
- **Best Adapted Screenplay:** AMADEUS

(58th) 1985 held in 1986

John Barry
- **Best Original Score:** OUT OF AFRICA

Stephen Grimes
- **Best Art Direction:** OUT OF AFRICA

David Watkin
- **Best Cinematography:** OUT OF AFRICA

(59th) 1986 held in 1987

Brian Ackland-Snow & Brian Saregar
- **Best Art Direction:** A ROOM WITH A VIEW

Jenny Beavan & John Bright
- **Best Costume Design:** A ROOM WITH A VIEW

Michael Caine
- **Best Supporting Actor:** HANNAH & HER SISTERS

Simon Kaye
- **Best Sound:** PLATOON

Lee Electric Lighting Ltd.
- **Technical Achievement Award**

Chris Menges
- **Best Cinematography:** THE MISSION

Peter D. Parks
- **Technical Achievement Award**

William B. Pollard & David W. Samuelson - Technical Achievement Award

John Richardson
- **Special Achievement In Visual Effects:** ALIENS

Claire Simpson
- **Best Editing:** PLATOON

Don Sharpe
- **Best Sound Effects Editing:** ALIENS

Vivienne Verdon-Roe
- **Best Documentary Short:** WOMEN - FOR AMERICA, FOR THE WORLD

(60th) 1987 held in 1988

James Acheson
- **Best Costume Design:** THE LAST EMPEROR

Sean Connery
- **Best Supporting Actor:** THE UNTOUCHABLES

Mark Peploe
- **Best Adapted Screenplay:** THE LAST EMPEROR

Ivan Sharrock
- **Best Sound:** THE LAST EMPEROR

Jeremy Thomas
- **Best Picture:** THE LAST EMPEROR

(61st) 1988 held in 1989

James Acheson
- **Best Costume Design:** DANGEROUS LIAISONS

George Gibbs
- **Special Achievement In Visual Effects:** WHO FRAMED ROGER RABBIT

Christopher Hampton
- **Best Adapted Screenplay:** DANGEROUS LIAISONS

(62nd) 1989 held in 1990

Phyllis Dalton
- **Best Costume:** HENRY V

Daniel Day-Lewis
- **Best Actor:** MY LEFT FOOT

Freddie Francis
- **Best Cinematography:** GLORY

Brenda Fricker
- **Best Supporting Actress:** MY LEFT FOOT

Anton Furst
- **Best Art Direction:** BATMAN

Richard Hymns
- **Best Sound Effects Editing:** INDIANA JONES AND THE LAST CRUSADE

Jessica Tandy
- **Best Actress:** DRIVING MISS DAISY

James Hendrie
- **Best Live Action Short:** WORK EXPERIENCE

(63rd) 1990 held in 1991

John Barry
- **Best Original Score:** DANCES WITH WOLVES

Jeremy Irons
- **Best Actor:**REVERSAL OF FORTUNE

Nick Park
- **Best Animated Short:** CREATURE COMFORTS

(64th) 1991 held in 1992

Daniel Greaves
- **Best Animated Short:** MANIPULATION

Anthony Hopkins
- **Best Actor:** SILENCE OF THE LAMBS

(65th) 1992 held in 1993

Simon Kaye
- **Best Sound:** THE LAST OF THE MOHICANS

Tim Rice
- **Best Original Song:** ALADDIN (A WHOLE NEW WORLD)

Emma Thompson
- **Best Actress:** HOWARDS END

Ian Whittaker
- **Best Art Direction:** HOWARDS END

(66th) 1993 held in 1994

Richard Hymns
- **Best Sound Effects Editing:** JURASSIC PARK

Nick Park
- **Best Animated Short:** THE WRONG TROUSERS

Deborah Kerr
- **Career Achievement Honorary Award**

(67th) 1994 held in 1995

Ken Adam & Carolyn Scott
- **Best Art Direction:** THE MADNESS OF KING GEORGE

Peter Capaldi & Ruth Kenley-Letts
- **Best Live Action Short:** FRANZ KAFKA'S IT'S A WONDERFUL LIFE

Elton John & Tim Rice
- **Best Song:** THE LION KING (CAN YOU FEEL THE LOVE TONIGHT)

Alison Snowden & David Fine
-**Best Animated Short:** BOB'S BIRTHDAY

(68th) 1995 held in 1996

James Acheson
- **Best Costume Design:** RESTORATION

Jon Blair
- **Best Documentary Feature:** ANNE FRANK REMEMBERED

Lois Burwell & Peter Frampton
- **Special Achievement In Make Up:** BRAVEHEART

Emma Thompson
- **Best Adapted Screenplay:** SENSE & SENSIBILITY

Nick Park
- **Best Animated Short:** A CLOSE SHAVE

(69th) 1996 held in 1997

Anthony Minghella
- **Best Director:** THE ENGLISH PATIENT

Rachel Portman
- **Best Original Score Musical or Comedy:** EMMA

Tim Rice & Andrew Lloyd Webber
- **Best Original song:** EVITA (YOU MUST LOVE ME)

Stuart Craig & Stephanie McMillan
- **Best Art Direction:** THE ENGLISH PATIENT

(70th) 1997 held in 1998

Peter Lamont and Michael Ford
- **Best Achievement In Art Direction:** TITANIC

Anne Dudley
- **Best Original Score Musical or Comedy:** THE FULL MONTY

Jan Pinkava
- **Best Animated Short:** GERI'S GAME

(71st) 1998 held in 1999

David Parfitt
- **Best Film:** SHAKESPEARE IN LOVE

Judi Dench
- **Best Actress in a Supporting Role:** SHAKESPEARE IN LOVE

Tom Stoppard
- **Best Original Screenplay:** SHAKESPEARE IN LOVE

Martin Childs and Jill Quertier
- **Best Art Direction:** SHAKESPEARE IN LOVE

Sandy Powell
- **Best Costume Design:** SHAKESPEARE IN LOVE

Jenny Shircore
- **Best Make-up:** ELIZABETH

Stephen Warbeck
- **Best Original Score Musical or Comedy:** SHAKESPEARE IN LOVE

Andy Nelson
- **Best Sound:** SAVING PRIVATE RYAN

(72nd) 1999 held in 2000

Michael Caine
- **Actor in a Supporting Role:** CIDER HOUSE RULES

Peter Young
- **Art Direction:** SLEEPY HOLLOW

Lindy Hemming

- Costume Design: TOPSY-TURVY

Sam Mendes
- Directing: AMERICAN BEAUTY

Kevin MacDonald, John Battsek,
- Documentary Feature: ONE DAY IN SEPTEMBER

Christine Blundell, Trefor Proud
- Make up: TOPSY-TURVY

Phil Collins
- Original Song: TARZAN "You'll Be In My Heart"

(73rd) 2000 held in 2001

Janty Yates
- Costume Design: GLADIATOR

Claire Jennings
- Best Animated Short: FATHER AND DAUGHTER

Ken Weston
- Best Sound: GLADIATOR

Tim Burke
- Best Visual Effects: GLADIATOR

SPECIAL AWARDS

Jack Cardiff
- Honorary Oscar

Vic Armstrong
- Scientific and Technical Award

(74th) 2001 held in 2002

Jim Broadbent
- Actor Supporting: IRIS

Peter Owen
- Make Up

Chris Munro
- Sound:

Julian Fellowes
- Writing (Original): GOSFORD PARK

(75th) 2002 held In 2003

Catherine Zeta-Jones
- Actress, Supporting : CHICAGO

Peter O'Toole
- Lifetime Achievement

Ronald Harwood
- Adapted Screenplay: THE PIANIST

BOOKSELLERS

This listing does not claim to be definitive, or in any way endorse any of the booksellers listed. It aims to list as wide a variety of booksellers and services as possible (within time and space limits) that offer (or even purchase) new, out of print, second hand and rare titles on film and television. The metrocentric emphasis in the listing is purely unintentional but unfortunately inevitable. Compiled by Ayesha Khan

Andromeda Bookshop
1 Suffolk Street,
Birmingham B1 1LT
Tel: 0121 643 1999
Website: www.andromedabook.co.uk
Open: Mon-Sat 10.00am-5.00pm, Telephone enquiries answered 10.30am-4.30pm
Science fiction, horror and fantasy bookshop including some titles on film and television. Books can be ordered online or through mail order.

Arnolfini Bookshop
16 Narrow Quay,
Bristol BS1 4QA
Tel: 0117 929 9191
Fax: 0117 925 3876
email: bookshop@arnolfini.demon.co.uk
Website: www.arnolfini.demon.co.uk/
Open: Mon-Wed, Fri-Sat 10.00am-7.00pm, Thu 10.00am-9.00pm, sun and Bank Holidays 12.00pm-7.00pm
The Arnolfini boasts one of the very best specialist arts bookshops in the country, with an exceptional range of texts on art, film, performance, design, photography, society plus relevant specialist magazines. Bookshop Manager: Peter Begen; Deputy Bookshop Manager: Julian Warren

Cinema Bookshop
13-14 Great Russell Street
London WC1B 3NH
Tel: 020 76370206
Open: Mon-Sat 10.30am-5.30pm
Legendary bookshop containing very large stock of new, out of print and rare books. Excellent source for the non-glossy cinema magazines. Stills and posters held too

Cinema Store (London)
4C Orion House,
Upper St Martin's Lane,
London, WC2H 9NY
Tel: 020 7379 7895
Fax: 020 7240 7689
Shops are based on adjacent premises. This side for film books and videos.
4B Orion House,
Upper St Martin's Lane,
London, WC2H 9NY
Tel: 020 7379 7838 [general enquiries]
Tel: 020 7379 7865 [DVDs]
This half for magazines, toys, t-shirts, collectibles and DVDs
Website: www.the-cinema-store.com
email: cinemastor@aol.com
Open: Mon-Wed 10.00am-6.30pm, Thu-Fri 10.00am-7.00pm, Sat 10.00am-6.30am, Sun 10.00pm-6.00pm

Cinema Store (Nottingham)
Unit T2,
The Cornerhouse Leisure Complex,
Nottingham, NG1 4DB
Tel: 01159 503090
Fax: 01159 508054
Nottingham shop opened in April 2001. Books, magazines, posters, DVDs, videos, ephemera and CD soundtracks

Cornerhouse Bookshop
70 Oxford Street
Manchester M1 5NH
Tel: 0161 228 7621
email: info@cornerhouse.org
Website: www.cornerhouse.org
Open: Everyday 12.00pm-8.30pm
Whereas the bookshop holds mainly film related titles, Cornerhouse Publications' book distribution service distributes contemporary visual arts, architecture, design etc.

Cusack Books
PO Box 17696
London W12 8WR
Tel: 020 8743 0517
Fax:f: 020 870 133 2476
email: queries@cusackbooks
Website: www.cusackbooks.com
Elaine Cusack-O'Connell
For out of print television, film and music-related books. Stock runs from Abba to Z Cars via Bagpuss, Monty Python and Truffaut. Established 1998. Mail order/Internet-based

David Drummond at Pleasures of Past Times
11 Cecil Court
Charing Cross Road
London WC2N 4EZ
Tel: 020 7836 1142
email: Drummond @popt.fsnet.co.uk
Open: Mon-Fri 11.00am - 5.45pm (Closed lunch 2.30-3.30); also open the first Saturday in the month 11.00am-2.30pm. Extended hours and Saturday's by appointment only. Books, memorabilia and other ephemera on the performing arts (including circus, cinema, music hall and conjuring).

Decorum Books
24 Cloudesley Square
London N1 0HN
Tel: 020 7278 1838
Fax: 020 7837 6424
email: decorumbooks@tiscali.co.uk
Website: www.decorumbooks.co.uk
Sue Soames
Mail order only for secondhand books for film and performing arts. 150,000 approx books in stock. Occasional joint ventures with small specialist publishers on cinema and theatre architecture and design. Now includes Decorum Books 2 specialising in books on Indian cinema and performing arts. See website: www.india-cinema.co.uk

Dress Circle
57-59 Monmouth Street
Covent Garden
London WC2H 9DG
Tel: 020 7 240 2227
Fax: 020 7 379 8540
email: info@dresscircle.co.uk
Open: Mon-Sat 10.00am – 6.30pm
Website: www.dresscircle.co.uk/
General enquires: info@dresscircle.co.uk
Order Queries: shopping@dresscircle.co.uk
Specialising in musical theatre books, soundtracks, videos and DVDs. Mail order and online ordering services.

Forbidden Planet
71 New Oxford Street
London WC1A 1DG
Tel: 020 7240 3666
Fax: 020 7240 3663 (Order line)
email: info@forbiddenplanet.com
(Branches in Birmingham, Bristol, Cambridge, Coventry, Croydon, Liverpool, London, Newcastle, Southampton, and in cities in Scotland, Wales and Ireland).
Specialises in all aspects of science fiction, horror and fantasy. London branch has a surprisingly eclectic selection of book on film and television in spite of its specialism.
No website covering all the shops yet, but more information can be found at: www.fpiscotland19.co.uk

Foyles
W & G Foyle Ltd,
113-119 Charing Cross Road,
London WC2H 0EB
Tel: 020 7437 5660
Fax: 020 7434 1580.
email: sales@foyles.co.uk.
Website: www.foyles.co.uk
Open: Mon-Sat 9.30am-8.00pm, Sun and Public Holidays, 12.00pm-6.00pm
One of the largest bookshops in the UK. Has one of the larger film and TV sections for a general bookshop. Some out of print titles held. Online ordering service via the website.

Grant & Cutler
55-57 Great Marlborough Street,
London W1F 7AY
Tel: 020 7734 2012
Fax: 020 7734 9272
email: contactus@grantandcutler.com
Website: www.grantandcutler.com
Open: Mon - Fri, 9.00am-6.00pm, Thu 9.00am-7.00pm, Sat 9.00am-5.30pm.
Foreign language specialists.

Greenroom Books
9 St James Road
Ilkley
West Yorkshire LS29 9PY
Tel: 01943 607662
email: greenroombooks@blueyonder.co.uk
Contact: Geoff Oldham
Mail Order and internet only.
Regular catalogue issued covering film, television, radio, music and theatre

Heffers
20 Trinity Street
Cambridge CB2 1TY
Tel: 01223 568513
Fax: 01223 354936
email: artbooks@heffers.co.uk
Website: www.heffers.co.uk
Large bookshop now part of the Blackwells empire. Specialises in secondhand, rare and collectable books and other items (pressbooks, posters, programmes, journals, etc) relating to cinema, television, theatre and the performing arts. Catalogues are issued regularly

Henry Pordes Bookshop
58-60 Charing Cross Road
London WC2H 0BB
Tel: 020 7836 9031
Fax: 020 7240 4232
email: henrypordes@clara.net
Website: home.clara.net/henrypordes
Secondhand, remaindered and antiquarian booksellers. Their online catalogue can be found via www.AbeBooks.com

ICA Bookshop
The Mall
London, SW1Y 5AH
Tel: 020 7766 1452
email: bookshop@ica.org.uk
Manager: Russell Herron
Open: Mon-Sun 12.00pm-9.00pm
A wide range of books, magazines, videos and DVDs from the cutting edge of popular culture and theory.

Inkt Collections (Flicks Books)
29 Bradford Road
Trowbridge
Wilts BA14 9AN
Tel: 01225 767728
email:
matthew.stevens@dial.pipex.com
Website: antiqbook.com/inktcollections/
Mail order service, specialising in second hand, rare and collectable books and other items (pressbooks, posters, programmes and journals) relating to cinema, television, theatre and the performing arts. They also buy book collections large or small. Catalogues are issued regularly

Irish Film Centre Bookshop
The Film Institute of Ireland.
6 Eustace St., Temple Bar
Dublin 2.
Ireland
Tel:+353 1 6795744
Fax:+353 1 6778755
email: info@ifc.ie
Website: www.fii.ie/index.html
Mary Sherlock
The Irish Film Centre Shop carries a wide range of books, magazine and journals relating to film. It also stocks an extensive collection of videos, DVDs, posters and small gift items

Kelly Books Limited
6 Redlands
Tiverton
Devon EX16 4DH
Tel: 01884 256170
Fax: 01884 252765
email: len@kellybooks.co.uk
Website: www.kellybooks.co.uk
Used books,magazines, pamphlets & ephemera on all aspects of the history and technology of broadcasting and mass media. Also has a small publishing arm – sell their own publications

National Museum of Photography, Bradford
Zwemmer Bookshop
Bradford BD1 1NQ
Tel: 01274 202041
Fax:01274 202041
Open: Tue-Sun & Bank Holidays 10.00am-6.00pm. Entrance to the Gallery is free except for special exhibitions

Offstage Theatre & Film Bookshop
37 Chalk Farm Road
London NW1 8AJ
Tel: 020 7485 4996
Fax: 020 7916 8046
email: offstagebookshop@aol.com
Open: Mon-Fri 10.00am-6.00pm, Sat-Sun 12.00pm-6.00pm
New books only. Stock caters for students, academics and filmmakers. Free catalogues can be sent. Mail order available, but no website

Rare Discs
18 Bloomsbury Street
London WC1B 3QA
Tel: 020 7580 3516
Open: Mon - Sat 10.00pm-6.30am
email: masheter@softhome.net
Contact: Martin Masheter
Holds thousands of soundtracks for films, musicals, shows, films stills, posters, books, magazines etc

Screenwriter's Store
Suite 121 Friars House
157-168 Blackfriars Road
London SE1 8EZ
Tel: 020 7261 1908
Fax: 020 7261 1909
email: info@thescreenwritersstore.co.uk
Webstie: www.screenwriterstore.co.uk
Open: Mon- Fri 10.00am-6.00pm (by prior arrangement only)
Europe's largest authorised reseller and distributor of screenwriting and production software. The website also has over 100 mainly Hollywood titles in proper script format that are available to download

Spread Eagle Bookshop
9 Nevada Street
London SE10 9JL
Tel: 020 8305 1666
Fax: 020 8305 0447
email: books@spreadeagle.org.uk
Website: www.spreadeagle.org/cgi-bin/books.asp
Large second hand bookshop that specialises partly in cinema, design, and the performing arts.

Tate Modern Shop
Bankside
London SE1 9TG
Tel: 020 7401 5167
Tel orders: 020 7887 8870
Shop online:
www.tate.org.uk/shop/default.htm
Open: Sun-Thu 10.00am-6.00pm, Fri-Sat 10.00am-10.00pm
Stocks over 10,000 art books and other materials, including an impressive range of materials on the moving image

Terence H. Kaye
52 Neeld Crescent
London NW4 3RR
Tel/Fax: 020 8208 8188
Specialist in rare and collectable books about cinema, theatre and the performing arts

The European Bookshop
5 Warwick Street
London W1R 5RA
Tel: 020 7734 5259
Fax: 020 7287 1720
email: direct@esb.co.uk
Website:
www.europeanbookshop.com
Open: Mon-Sat 9.30am – 6.00pm
Specialists in foreign language literature and audio visual material their services are aimed at educational users. Ordering services available.

Treasure Chest
61 Cobbold Road
Felixstowe
Suffolk IP11 7BH
Tel: 01394 270717
Open: Mon-Sat 9.30am - 5.30pm.
Large general second hand stock though specialising in cinema and literature

VinMagCo
39-43 Brewer Street
London W1R 9UD
Tel: Telephone: 020 7439 8525
Fax: 020 7439 8527
email: info@vinmag.com
Website: www.vinmag.com
Open: Mon-Wed 10.00am-7.00pm, Thu 10.00am-8.00pm, Fri-Sat 10.00am-10.00pm, Sun 12.00pm-8.00pm
VinMagCo Ltd has been producing movie memorabilia since 1975 and supplies to retailers throughout the world. Items available include posters, photographs, postcards, t-shirts, life-size standups and mouse pads. Availability in some countries may depend on the terms under which an image is licensed. For further details or to place a wholesale order contact Paul Belchamber. There are also stores in Brighton and Oxford, though opening times may vary

Zwemmer Media
80 Charing Cross Road
London WC2H 0BB
Tel: 020 7240 4157
Fax: 020 7240 4186
email: enquiries@zwemmer.com or media@zwemmer.com
Website: www.zwemmer.com
Claire de Rouen
Open: Mon-Wed 10.00am-6.30pm, Thu 10.00am-7.00pm, Fri 10.00am-6.30pm, Sat 10.00am-6.30pm, Sun 12.00pm-5.00pm
A catalogue of new and in-print titles on every aspect of cinema is available on request. Mail order service for all books available through Mail Order Department

Major Chains

Blackwells
One of the smaller, more academically inclined chains. Has online bookshop service with searchable database. The Charing Cross Road branch (100, Charing Cross Road, tel: 020 7292 5100) has a good stock of film and TV.
For other branches, see: www.bookshop.blackwells.co.uk.

Books etc
Re-expansion is planned for of this one time high street fixture. No searchable database or online ordering service available unfortunately.
Website: See: www.booksetc.co.uk

Bookcase
138-140 Charing Cross Road
London WC2H
Tel: 020 7836 8391
Bookshop chain that specialises in remaindered bookshops that often contain pleasant surprises for the browser and unpleasant ones for the acquisitions librarian. Sadly no website or subject listings

Borders
Whether you're a fan or not, the stores usually have useful holdings on film & TV, especially in the 120, Charing Cross Road (020 7379 8877) and 203, Oxford St (020 7292 1600) branches.
See: www.borders.co.uk for other store locations (but as yet no online service)

Waterstones
Numerous stores all over the UK, usually fairly well stocked with film & TV books.
Flagship store is at in Piccadilly, London.203-206 Piccadilly, London, W1J 9LE (020 7851 2400).
Have entered strategic alliance with Amazon.co.uk for online supply and their website links directly to Amazon's searchable database and online ordering services.
For other branches information and ordering online:
www.waterstones.co.uk

Online Services

Advanced Book Exchange

Website: www.AbeBooks.com
Claiming to offer 40 million books from 10,000 booksellers from all over the world, this could described as the Amazon" service for used out of print and rare books. Also a useful to see judge how much your collection may be worth

Amazon

Website: www.amazon.co.uk
The best-known online book ordering service, offering plenty of film and TV titles.

Retro Sellers

Website: www.retrosellers.com
Describing itself as the "definitive site for retro and nostalgia", covering film, TV and popular culture this comprehensive site offers features and newsletters as well as a sourcing and valuation service for those hard to find books, videos, records, CDs and stills

UK Bookworld

Website: www.ukbookworld.com
Provides details of old and out-of-print books from British bookshops. Books mailed out and paid via credit card or cheque. Can search by title, author or subject. eg.'film' which retrieved more than 500 pages of titles. Prices range from £3.50 upwards

CABLE, SATELLITE AND DIGITAL

Information in this section was compiled by Erinna Mettler

As the number of channels and digital services expands, the number of companies involved in delivering multichannel television to UK homes is rapidly diminishing. Following the collapse of ITV Digital, in the satellite orbit there has been currently one dominant operator—British Sky Broadcasting (BSkyB) —for some years. The cable business is moving towards a comparable position now that the third largest operator, NTL, has taken over the domestic cable television operations of the biggest, Cable & Wireless Communications, leaving only two major multiple system operators (MSOs). The second largest MSO, Telewest, is widely expected to become part of one major cable company in due course through a merger with NTL. The cost to NTL of the CWC acquisition is £8.2 billion, whilst Cable & Wireless is paying £6.5 billion to take full ownership of CWC's business operations. These figures indicate the massive financial scale of cable investment and costs.

This process of merger and takeover has radically altered the structure of the UK's broadband cable industry as envisaged when the first franchises were awarded in November 1983. With 12.5m homes already passed by cable systems that are continuing to build—and only 4m homes outside franchise areas—a new phase is beginning as the exclusivity that operators enjoyed as part of their franchises is abandoned. Competition between cable companies is thus possible, although the prospect of operators spending huge sums of money on building competitive cable networks in the foreseeable future is remote. While cable has up to now tended to be the Cinderella partner, its ability to provide broadband facilities has resulted in a range of new - and potentially extremely lucrative - services being added to the cable portfolio.

MULTIPLE SYSTEM OPERATORS

Almost all franchises are held as part of groups of holdings. Such groups are called multiple system operators (MSOs). Extensive consolidation has taken place since 1995 and especially during the first half of 1998, which resulted in the emergence of two dominant groups: NTL and Telewest.

AT&T

US telecom operator, which acquired Tele-Communications Inc (TCI), the largest US cable operator, holder of 50% share in TW Holdings, which owns 53% of Telewest [qv]

Atlantic Telecom Group

Holborn House
475-485 Union St
Aberdeen AB11 6DB
Tel: 01224 454 000
Fax: 01224 454 0111
Website: www.atlantic-telecom.co.uk
Areas: Aberdeen

British Telecommunications (BT)

87-89 Baker Street81 Newgate Street
London W1M 2LPLondon EC1A 7AJ
Tel: 020 7487 12547356 5000
Fax: 020 7487 1259
website: www.bt.com
Areas: as BT New Towns Cable TV Services: Milton Keynes
as Westminster Cable Company: Westminster LB.
Also upgrade systems at Barbican (London), Brackla, Martlesham, Walderslade, Washington
Note: From 1 January 2001 BT will be allowed to compete in delivery of television-related services with existing cable networks.

Cable & Wireless Communications

Cable franchises now owned by NTL

Cox Communications

US cable operator
10% stake in Telewest (23% of preference shares) [qv]

Eurobell (Holdings)Telewest Broadband Eurobell

Eurobell Multi-Media House
Alexandrea RoadLloyds Court,
Manor Royal
Plymouth PL4 7EFCrawley, West Sussex RH10 2PT
Tel: 01293 400444405405
Fax: 01293 400440website:
www.telewest.co.uk/eurobell
Ownership: Detecon (Deutsche Telepost Consulting)Telewest
Areas: Crawley, /Horley, Tunbridge Wells, Sevenoaks, Tonbridge, Plymouth, Exeter, Torbay/Gatwick, Devon South, Kent West

NTL

Bristol House
1 Lakeside Road
Farnborough
Hampshire GU14 6XPBartley Wood Business Park
Bartley Way
Hook
Hampshire RG27 9UP
Tel: 012526 402662752000
Fax 01256 7521002 402665
Website: www.cabletel.co.ukntl.com
HQ: 110 East 59th Street, New York, NY 10022 USA
Tel +1/212 906 8440
Fax +1/212 752 1157
Formerly: International CableTel
Ownership: Rockefeller family, Capital Cities Broadcasting Company (subsidiary of Walt Disney Company), Microsoft, France Télécom (eventually will be largest shareholder with 25%)18.32%, Cable & Wireless plc 11.23%, Capital Research & Management Co. 9.87%
NTL covers the areas in and around Belfast, Cardiff, Glasgow, Newcastle Upon Tyne, Sunderland, Middlesbrough, Leeds, Manchester, Liverpool, Derby, Sheffield, Leicester, Grimsby, Northampton, Milton Keynes, Cambridge, Chelmsford,Ipswich, Coventry, London, Winchester, Lamborough, Brighton, and Folkestone.
NTL has acquired Cable & Wireless Communications cable franchises and is has replacinged that brand

with its own.
Areas: former CableTel franchises
as CableTel Bedfordshire: Bedford
as CableTel Glasgow:
Bearsden/Milngavie, Glasgow Greater, Glasgow North West/Clydebank, Invercylde, Paisley/Renfrew
as CableTel Herts & Bedfordshire:
Luton/South Bedfordshire
as CableTel Hertfordshire:
Hertfordshire Central, Hertfordshire East,
as CableTel Kirklees:
Huddersfield/Dewsbury
as CableTel Northern Ireland:
Northern Ireland
as CableTel South Wales:
Cardiff/Penarth, Glamorgan West, Glamorgan/Gwent, Newport/Cwmbran/Pontypool
as CableTel Surrey: Guildford/West Surrey
former Comcast UK franchises:
as Anglia Cable: Harlow/Bishops Stortford/Stansted Airport
as Cambridge Cable:
Cambridge/Ely/Newmarket,
as Comcast Teesside: Darlington, Teesside
as East Coast Cable:
Colchester/Ipswich/etc,
as Southern East Anglia Cable: East Anglia South,
Sold its 50% stake in Cable London to Telewest (qv) August 1999.
former ComTel franchises:
Andover/Salisbury/Romsey, Daventry, Corby/Kettering/Wellingborough, Hertfordshire West, Litchfield/Burntwood/Rugeley, Northampton, Nuneaton/Bedworth/Rugby, Oxford/Abingdon, Stafford/Stone, Swindon, Tamworth/North Warwickshire/Meriden, Thames Valley, Warwick/Stratford-upon-Avon/Kenilworth/Leamington Spa
former Diamond Cable franchises:
Bassetlaw, Burton-on-Trent, Coventry, East Derbyshire, Grantham, Grimsby/Immingham /Cleethorpes, Hinckley/Bosworth, Huddersfield/Dewsbury, Leicester, Lincoln, Lincolnshire/South Humberside, Loughborough/ Shepshed, Mansfield/Sutton/Kirkby-in-Ashfield, Melton Mowbray, Newark-on-Trent, Northern Ireland, Nottingham, Ravenshead, Vale of Belvoir
fomerly Cable & Wireless Communications franchises
Areas: Aylesbury/Amersham/ Chesham, Bolton, Bournemouth/Poole/Christchurch, Brighton/Hove/Worthing, Bromley, Bury/Rochdale, Cheshire North, Chichester/Bognor, Dartford/Swanley, Derby/Spondon, Durham South /North Yorkshire, Ealing, Eastbourne/Hastings, Epping Forest/Chigwell/Loughton/O_ngar, Fenland, Great Yarmouth/Lowestoft/ Caister, Greater London East, Greenwich/Lewisham, Harrogate/Knaresborough, Harrow, Havering, Hertfordshire South, Kensington/Chelsea, Kent South East, Lambeth/Southwark, Lancashire East, Leeds, London North West, Macclesfield/Wilmslow, Manchester/Salford, Newham/Tower Hamlets, Norwich, Oldham/Tameside, Peterborough, Portsmouth/Fareham/Gosport/Havan t, Southampton/Eastleigh, Stockport, Stoke-on-Trent/Newcastle, Surrey North, Surrey North East, Thamesmead, Totton/Hythe, Waltham Forest, Wandsworth, Wearside, Whittlesey/March/Wisbech, Winchester, The Wirral, York
SBC International
Ownership: Southwestern Bell Telecom [US telecom operator]
10% stake in Telewest (23% of preference shares) [qv]

Telewest Communications

Unit 1, Genesis Business Park
Albert Drive
Woking, Surrey GU21 5RW
Tel: 01483 750900
Fax 01483 750901
Website: www.telewest.co.uk
Ownership: TW Holdings (= Tele-Communications International (TINTA) 50% and US West International 50%) 53%, Microsoft 29.923.6%, Liberty Media (=AT&T) 25.2%, Cox Communications 10%, SBC International (= Southwestern Bell Telecom) 10%Media One 1.3%, the remainer of the shares are distributed.
Acquired NTL's (formerly Comcast UK's) half-share in Cable London in August 1999.
Telewest's network passes more than 4.9 million homes throught the UK, running from London and the South East to Bristol and the South West, Birmingham and the West Midland, Yorkshire, Merseyside, Tyneside and Scotland.
Local franchises acquired by Telewest have been rebranded as Telewest. It has a 100% interest in Cable Corporation Ltd, Yorkshire Cable Ltd, General Cable plc, Cable London Ltd, Eurobell Ltd, and Birmingham Cable Corporation.
Areas formerly:
as Birmingham Cable:
Birmingham/Solihull, Wythall
as Cable Corporation:
Hillingdon/Hounslow, Windsor
as Cable London: Camden, Enfield, Hackney & Islington, Haringey
as Telewest Eurobell: Crawley, Horley, Tunbridge Wells, Sevenoaks, Tonbridge, Plymouth, Exeter, Torbay
as Telewest London & the South East): Croydon, Kingston/Richmond, Merton/Sutton, Thames Estuary North, Thames Estuary South
as Telewest Midlands & the South West: Avon, Black Country, Cheltenham/Gloucester, Taunton/Bridgewater, Telford, Worcester
as Telewest North West):
Blackpool/Fylde, Lancashire Central, Liverpool North/Bootle/Crosby, Liverpool South, St Helens/Knowsley, Southport, Wigan
as Telewest Scotland & North East:
Cumbernauld, Dumbarton, Dundee, Edinburgh, Falkirk/West Lothian, Fife, Glenrothes/Kirkaldy/Leven, Motherwell/East Kilbride/Hamilton/Wishaw/Lanark, Perth/Scone, Tyneside
as Yorkshire Cable Communications:
Barnsley, Bradford, Calderdale, Doncaster/Rotherham, Sheffield, Wakefield/Pontefract/Castleford

US West International

50% share in TW Holdings, which owns 53% of Telewest [qv]

CABLE FRANCHISES

All broadband cable franchises to date were granted by the Cable Authority (apart from 11 previously granted by the Department of Trade and Industry), the role of which was taken over by the Independent Television Commission (ITC) in January 1991, under the Broadcasting Act 1990.

The Act empowered the ITC to grant fifteen-year 'local delivery licences', which can include use of microwave distribution. Licences must be awarded to the highest bidder on the basis of an annual cash bid in addition to forecasts of the sums that will be paid to the Exchequer as a percentage of revenue earned in the second and third five-year periods of the licence.

The biggest change since the last edition of the Handbook is that the major operators, by agreement with the ITC, have each opted for a single non-exclusive local delivery service licence, thus allowing the possibility of competitive marketing and delivery on a potentially national basis. The individual franchise exclusive licences held by NTL were consequently revoked by the ITC on 31 December 1999 and those of Telewest on 31 May 2000.

In some towns an older cable system still exists. These are not franchised but are licensed by the ITC to provide limited services. They are gradually being superseded by new broadband networks

Details of who holds the franchise for a particular town/area can be obtained from the ITC.

SATELLITE AND CABLE TELEVISION CHANNELS

All channels transmitting via cable or satellite within or to the UK, wholly or partly in the English language or intended for viewing by other linguistic groups within the UK. Services are licensed and monitored by the Independent Television Commission (ITC). Channels not intended for reception in the UK are excluded, as are those that are licensed but not actively broadcasting (many licensed channels never materialise).

The television standard and encrypting system used are indicated after the name of the satellite. Services for which a separate charge is made are marked 'premium' after the programming type.Services for which a seperate charge is made are marked "premium" after the programming type. Services which require a subscription is marked "subscription".

The advent of digital television from late 1998 has already created many new channels. Although initially most digital channels are conversions of services already available in analogue form, by 2000 this was no longer the case.many channels are now exclusively in the digital format. Currently, one third of households in the UK receive digital television. In this highly competitive field, new channels are constantly launching, with less successful channels closing down.

MULTIPLE SERVICE PROVIDERS (MSP)

BBC Worldwide

Woodlands
80 Wood Lane
London W12 0TT
Tel: 020 8433 2000
Fax: 020 8749 0538
Services: Animal Planet 50%, BBC News 24%, UK Gold 50%, UK Horizons 50%, UK Style 50%, PLAY UK 50%

British Sky Broadcasting (BSkyB)

6 Centaurs Business Park
Grant Way, Syon Lane
Isleworth
Middlesex TW7 5QD
Tel: 0870 240 3000
Fax: 020 7705 3030
Website: www.sky.com.uk
Ownership: News International Television 39.88 %, BSB Holdings (= Pathé 30.27%, Granada 36.22%, Pearson 4.29%) 12.82 %, Pathé 12.71 %, Granada Group 6.48 %
Services: The Computer ChannelAdventure One 50%, Artsworld 20% (option), attheraces 33.33%, Biography Channel 50%, G Plus 49.5%, The History Channel 50%, Men and Motors 49.5%,Music Choice 36%, MUTV 33.33%, National Geographic Channel 50%, Nickelodeon 50%, Nick Jr 50%, Paramount Comedy Channel 25%, QVC 20%, Sky Box Office, Sky Cinema, Sky MovieMax, Sky News, Sky One, Sky Premier, Sky Soap, Sky Sports1 , Sky Sports 2, Sky Sports 3, Sky Sports Extra, Sky Travel. 40% stake in Granada Sky Broadcasting

Carlton Communications

25 Knightsbridge
London SW1X 7RZ
Tel: 020 7663 6363
Website: www.carlton.com
Services: Taste, Carlton Cinema, ITVDigital (50%)

Discovery Communications

160 Great Portland Street
London W1N 5TB
Tel: 020 7462 3600
Fax: 020 7462 3700
Services: Animal Planet, Discovery Channel Europe, TLC Europe

Flextech Television
160 Great Portland Street
London W1N 5TB
Tel: 020 7299 5000
Fax: 020 7299 5400
Ownership: Telewest (see MSOs)
Services: Bravo, Challenge TV, Living, Trouble, bid-up TV, Screenshop, UK Gold 50%, UK Gold 2 50%, UK Horizons 50%, UK Style 50%, UK Drama, Play UK 50%, TV Travel Shop 37%, Sit-Up TV 38%
Service management: Discovery, Discovery Home & Leisure, Playboy TV, Screenshop

Granada Sky Broadcasting
Franciscan Court
16 Hatfields
London SE1 8DJ
Tel: 020 7578 4040
Fax: 020 7578 4176
email: malcolm.packer@gsb.co.uk
Website:gsb.co.uk
Ownership: Granada Group 60%, British Sky Broadcasting 40%
Services: Granada Breeze, Granada Plus, Granada Men & Motors

Home Video Channel (Playboy TV)
Aquis House
Station Road
Hayes
Middlesex UB3 4DX
Tel: 020 8581 7000
Fax: 020 8581 7007
website: www.playboytv.co.uk
Ownership: Spice Entertainment Companies
Services: The Adult Channel, HVC, Spice

Landmark Communications
64-66 Newman Street
London W1P 3PG
Tel: 020 7665 0600
Fax: 020 7665 0601
Ownership: Landmark Communications Inc
Services: Travel Channel, Travel Deals Direct, Weather Channel

MTV Networks Europe (Viacom)
Hawley Crescent
London NW1 8TT
Tel: 020 7284 7777
Fax: 020 7284 7788
Ownership: Viacom
Services: MTV Base, MTV Dance, MTV in the UK, MTV Hits, MTV2,VH1, VH1 Classic

Portland Enterprises
Portland House
Portland Place
London E14 9TT
Tel: 020 7308 5090
Services: Gay TV, Television X The Fantasy Channel

Turner Broadcasting System (TBS)
CNN House
19-22 Rathbone Place
London W1P 1DF
Tel: 0171 637 6700
Fax: 0171 637 6768
Ownership: Time Warner
Services: Cartoon Network,Cartoon Network Boomerang, CNN International, Turner Network Television

UK Channel Management
160 Great Portland Street
London W1N 5TB
Tel: 020 7765 1959
Ownership: BBC Worldwide, Flextech [qqv]

CHANNELS

3+
Viasat Broadcast Centre
Horton Road
West Drayton
Middlesex UB7 8JD
Tel: 01895 433327
Ownership: Viastat Broadcasting UK Ltd
Programming: general entertainment aimed at Scandinavia

18 Plus Movies
6 Centaurs Business Park
Grant Way
Isleworth TW7 5QD
Tel: 020 7705 3000
Ownership: British Sky Broadcasing
Programming: Adult pay per view programming

Abu Dhabi Television Satellite Channel
PO Box 63
Abu Dhabi
United Arab Emirates
Tel: 971 2 4430000
Fax: 971 2 4435000
Ownership: Emirates Media Inc
Programming: general entertainment, news programming

AC voice TV Ltd
22 Goodwin Road
London W12 9JW
Tel: 0870 770 2467
Programming: General entertainment, Afro- Caribbean focus

Ace TV
7 Peregrine Way
London SW19 4RN
Tel: 020 8947 8841
Programming: general entertainment

The Adult Channel
Aquis House
Station Rd
Hayes UB3 4DX
Tel: 020 8581 7000
Fax: 020 8581 7007
email: adultch@spicecos.com
Website: www.theadultchannel.co.uk
Ownership: Home Video Channel [see MSP above]Playboy TV UK Ltd
Service start: Feb 1992
Satellite: Astra 1B (PAL/Videocrypt)
Programming: 'adult' entertainment ([premiumsubscription)]

Adventure One
NGC-UK Partnership
Grant Way
Isleworth
Middlesex TW7 5QD
Tel: 020 7941 5073
Fax: 020 7941 5103
email: george.jeffrey@bskyb.com
Website: www.nationalgeographic.co.uk
Ownership: National Geographic 50%, British Sky Broadcasting [see MSP above] 50%
Satellite: Astra 2 North
Programming: documentaries on exploration and adventure

Africa Independent Television
3 Archway Close
Archway Road
London N19 3TD
Tel: 0207 233 7965
Fax: 07050153388
Ownership: Dear Communications Ltd.
Programming: General entertainment

Al Mustakillah Television
49 Gorst Rd.
London NW10 6LS
Tel: 0208 8838 2884
Fax: 0208 8838 2928

Al Qula
38 Devonshire Place
London W16 6JT
Tel: 020 7935 7566
Fax: 020 7224 0964
Ownership: Entertainment Distribution Company Ltd.
Programming: Movies

Al Thalita (general Entertainment)
Al Thania (general Ent.) as above

Alpha ETC Punjabi
Units 7-9
Belvue Business Centre
Belvue Road
Northolt UB5 5QQ
Tel: 020 8839 4003
Fax: 020 8841 9950
Ownership: Asia TV Ltd.
Programming: General entertainment

Amateur Babes
117-121 Salusbury Rd.
London NW6 6RG
Tel: 020 7328 8808
Fax: 020 7328 8858
Ownership: Broadcasting (Gaia) Ltd.
Programming: adult entertainment

Amp
British Sky Braodcasting
Grant Way
Isleworth
Middlesex
Tel: 0870 240 3000
Fax: 0870 240 3060
Ownership: BSkyB
Programming: music

Animal Planet
160 Great Portland St
London W1W 5TB
Tel: 020 7462 3600
Website: www.animal.discovery. com
Ownership: BBC Worldwide, Discovery Communications [see MSP above]
Service start: Sep 1998
Satellite: Astra 1E, Hot Bird 1 (PAL/encrypted)2 South
Programming: natural history documentaries

Apna TV
60 Aubert Park
London N5 1TS
Tel: 020 7831 2525
Fax: 020 7242 2860
Website: www.apnatv.com
Programming: entertainment, arts, music programmes from/about India, Pakistan and Bangladesh

Arab News Network
14-17 Wells Mews
London W1P 3FL
Tel: 020 7323 9920
Ownership: Linkchain LTD
Programming: current affairs in Arabic

The Arabic Series Channel
38 Devonshire Place
London W1G 6JT
Tel: 020 7935 7566
Fax: 020 7224 0964
Ownership: Enterainment Distribution Company Ltd.
Programming: drama, soaps, comedy

ARY Digital
AML House
12 Cumberland Ave
Park Royal NW10 7QL
Tel: 020 8961 4911
Fax: 020 7493 1333
Ownership: Pakistani Channel Ltd.
Programming: general entertainment

Artsworld
Artsworld Channels Ltd.
80 Silverthorne Road
London SW8 3XA
Tel 020 7819 1160
Fax 020 7819 1161
email: tv@artsworld.com
Website: www.artsworld.com
Ownership:_BSkyB, Caledonia Investments, Guardian Media Group 20%, and private investors 60%, British Sky Broadcasting [see MSP above] 20% (option)
Service start: 2 Dec 2000
Satellite: Astra 2 North
Programming: arts [premium]

Asia 1 TV
276 Soho Road
Birmingham B21 9LZ
Tel: 0121 558 6600
Programming: programmes in Punjabi

Asia Television Network
Unit 26
Park Royal Metro Centre
Britainnia Way
Coronation Road
London NW10 7PA
Tel: 020 8965 2100
Fax: 01753 673816
Ownership: Gujarat Television Ltd.
Programming: general entertainment with Gujarati focus

Asian Music Channel
Vis Television Media International
Fountain House,
140 Dudley Port
Tipton,
West Midlands. DY4 7RE.
Tel: 08700 110020
Fax: 08700 110030
email: info@vismediaint.com
Website: vismediaint.com
Programming: Material for Asian, African and UK broadcasters

Asianet
PO Box 38
Greenford
Middlesex UB6 7SB
Tel: 020 8566 9000
Fax: 020 8810 5555
Website: www.asianet-tv.com
Cable only from videotape
Programming: movies and entertainment in Hindi, Punjabi and other languages

Asset Television
Management Plus
548 Ley Street
Newbury Park
Ilford
Essex 1G2 7DB
Tel: 020 8554 7766
Fax: 020 8554 8881
Programming: family entertainment with some sport for a multi-cultural audience

Attheraces
Tel: 0870 787 1000
email: team@attheraces.co.uk
Website: www.attheraces.co.uk
Ownership: Arena Leisure 33.33%, Channel 4 33.33%, British Sky Broadcasting [see MSP above] 33.33%
Service start: 1 May 2002
Satellite: Eurobird – Programming: horse races, interactive betting

Auctionworld
Elena House
Unit 6, I/O Centre
Lea Riad
Waltham Cross
Herfordshire EN8 7PG
Tel: 0870 122 6510
Fax: 01992 760888
email: info@auction-world.tv
Website: www.auction-world.tv
Ownership: Auctionworld Ltd
Service start: 1 Nov 2001
Satellite: Eurobird
Programming: teleshopping

Avachat
Unit 6-7
Princes Court, Wapping Lane
London EC1W 2DA
Tel: 020 7942 7942
Fax: 0207942 7943
Ownership: Digital Television Production Company Ltd.
Programming: teleshopping

Avago
Unit 6-7
Princes Court, Wapping Lane
London EC1W 2DA
Tel: 020 7942 7942
Fax: 0207942 7943
email: customercare@avago.tv
Website: www.avago.tv
Ownership: Digital Television Production Company Ltd
Service start: 5 Jul 2002
Programming: light entertainment, interactive game shows

The Baby Channel
40 Claremont Road
London N6 5BY
Tel: 0870 787 7351
Fax: 020 7355 5055
Website: www.thebabychannel.net
Ownership: Baby Communications Ltd.
Programming: baby/child related programmes for parents

Babycare TV
Princes Court
Wapping Lane
London E1W 2DA
Tel: 020 7942 7942
Fax: 020 7942 7943
Ownership: Digital Television Production Co Ltd.
Programming: interactive

Bangla Channel
Imex House
6 Wadsworth Road
Middx UB6 7JJ
Tel: 020 8991 3758
Fax: 020 8991 1442
Programming: general entertainment and information

Bangla TV
Prestige House
Clifford Rd.
London E17 4JW
Tel: 020 8523 4555
Fax: 020 8523 4888
email: postbox@balnglatv.co.uk
Website: www,banglatv.co.uk
Service start: 17 Nov 1999
Satellite: Eurobird, Hot Bird 3
Programming: light entertainment [subscription]

Bazaar TV
Clerkenwell House
67 Clerkenwell Road
London EC1R 5BL
Tel: 020 7693 8405
Fax: 020 7693 8445
Programming: home shopping

BBC Food
Woodlands
80 Wood Lane
London W12 0TT
Tel: 020 8433 2555
Fax: 020 8433 3513
Programming: cookery

BBC Four
BBC Television Centre
London W12 7RJ
Tel: 020 8743 8000
email: info@bbc.co.uk
Website: www.bbc.co.uk/bbcfour
Service start:2 Mar 2002
Satellite: Astra 2 South
Programming: arts

BBC News 24
Woodlands
80 Wood Lane
London W12 0TT
Tel: 020 8433 2000
Fax: 020 8749 0538
email: info@bbc.co.uk
Website: www.bbc.co.uknews.bbc.co.uk
Ownership: BBC Worldwide [See MSP above]
Satellite: Astra 2A, 2B
Programming: news

BBC Parliamentary Channel
BBC Westminster
4 Millbank
London SW1P 3JA
Tel: 020 7973 6048
Fax: 020 07973 6049
email: info@bbc.co.uk
Website: www.bbc.co.uk/bbcparliament
Ownership: British Broadcasting Corporation
Satellite: Astra 2A
Programming: daily coverage of Parliamentary proceedings

BBC Three
BBC Television Centre
Londond W12 7RJ
Tel: 020 8743 8000
email: info@bbc.co.uk
Website: www.bbc.co.uk/bbcthree
Service start: 9 Feb 2003
Programming: general entertainment

Best Direct TV
167 Imperial Drive
Harrow HA2 7SP
Tel: 020 8868 4355
Fax: 020 8868 5024
email: customerservices@bestdirect.co.uk
Website: www.bestdirect.tv
Ownership: Best Direct (International) Ltd
Satellite: Eurobird
Programming: home shopping

Bid-up.tv
4 Warple Way
London W3 0UE
Tel: 020 8600 9700
Fax: 020 8746 0299
email: info@bid-up.tv
Website: www.bid-up.tv
Ownership: sit-up Ltd
Service start: 2 Nov 2000
Satellite: Astra 2B
Programming: home shopping – live auctions

B4U
Bollywood Eros Network
Unit 23, Sovereign Park
19 Heather Park Drive,
Middlesex HA0 1SS
Tel: 020 8963 8400020 8795 7171
Fax: 020 8795 7181
email:b4utv@b4unetwork.comtv.com
Website: www.b4utv.com
Ownership: Bollywood Eros Network
Service start: 26 Aug 1999
Programming: mainstream Hindi feature films [subscription]

B4U Direct
Unit 26, Park Royal
London NW10 7PR
Tel: 020 8963 8700
Fax: 020 8963 0154
email: adminsitrator@b4utv.com
Website: www.b4utv.com/direct
Service start: 15 Feb 2001
Satellite: Astra 2
Programming: Hindi films

The Biography Channel
Grant Way, Syon Lane
Isleworth
Middlesex TW7 5QD
Tel: 0870 240 3000
Fax: 020 7705 3030
email: getin-Touch@thebiography-channel.co.uk
Website:
www.thebiographychannel.co.uk
Ownership: Arts & Entertainment Television Network 5%, British Sky Broadcasting [see MSP above] 50%
Service start: 1 Oct 2000
Satellite: Astra 2 South
Programming: historical biographical programmes biographical material

BIZ4BIZ TV
Avon House
Kensington Village
Avonmore Road
London W14 8TS
Tel: 020 7371 5353
Fax: 020 7371 5355
Programming: Teleshopping

Bloomberg Television
City Gate House
39-45 Finsbury Square
London EC2A 1PQ
Tel: 020 7330 7500
Fax: 020 7661 57487256 5326
email: ukfeedback@bloomberg.net
Website: www.bloomberg.co.uk
Service start: 1 Nov 1995
Satellite: Astra 1E, Eutelsat II-F1Eurobird
Programming: business and finance news and information

Boomerang
see **Cartoon Network Boomerang**
Turner House
16 Great Marlborough St
London W1F 7HS
Tel: 020 7693 1000
Fax: 020 7693 1001
Website: www.cartoonnetwork.co.uk
Ownership: Turner Broadcasting [see MSP above]
Service start: 27 May 2000
Programming: classic cartoons

The Box
Mappin House
4 Winsley Street
London W1W 8HF
Tel: 020 7436 1515
Fax: 020 7312 8227
Website: www.thebox.com
Ownership: Emap
Service start: 2 Mar 1992
Satellite: Astra 1A (PAL/Videocrypt; cable only)
Programming: interactive pop music

BMP TV
PO Box 5249
Brinlow
Milton Keynes MK17 9ZH
Tel: 0870 120 5395
Fax: 0870 120 5391
Programming: youth light entertainment

Bravo
160 Great Portland Street
London W1W 5QA
Tel: 020 7299 5000
Fax: 020 7299 6000
email:
enquiriesenquiries@bravo.co.uk
Website: www.bravo.co.uk
Ownership: Flextech Television [see MSP above]
Service start: Sept 1985
Satellite: Astra 1C (PAL/Videocrypt)2A
Programming: old movies and television programmes general entertainment aimed at men

Bright Entertainment Network
3 Central Hall
Archway
London N19 3TD
Tel: 07050 202 460
Ownership: African Broadcasting Corp.
Programming: genral entertainment African focus

British Eurosport see Eurosport

British Interactive Video
34-35 Faringdon St
London EC4A 4HL
Tel: 020 7332 7000
Fax: 020 7332 7100
email:_name@open-here.co.uk
Website:_www.open-here.co.uk
Programming: interactive television

Business Information Television
11 Marlborough Place
Brighton BN1 1UB
Tel: 01273 728809
Programming: training programmes for travel and tourism

Carlton Cinema
45 Foubert's Place
London W1
Tel: 020 7432 9000
Fax: 020 7494 2841
email: dutyoffice@carltontv.co.uk
Website: www.carltoncinema.co.uk
Ownership: Carlton Communications [see MSP above]
Service start: 2 Sep 1996 2 Sep 1996
Satellite: Intelsat 605
Programming: feature films
Also digital

Carlton Kids
Ownership: Carlton Entertainment [see MSP above]
Programming: children's
Digital, included in ITV Digital

Carlton World
Ownership: Carlton Entertainment [see MSP above]
Programming: documentary
Digital, included in ITV Digital

Cartoon Network
Turner House
16 Great Marlborough St
London W1V 1AFF 7HS
Tel: 020 7693 1000
Fax: 020 7693 1001
email: toon.pressoffice@turner.com
Website: www.cartoon-network.co.uk
Ownership: Turner Broadcasting Systems (TBS) Inc, an AOL Time Warner Company [see MSP above]
Service start: 17 Sept 1993
Satellite: Astra 1C, Astra 1F (PAL/clear)2A, 2B
Programming: children's animation
Also digital

Cartoon Network Boomerang
Turner House
16 Great Marlborough St
London W1F 7HS
Tel: 020 7693 1000
Fax: 020 7693 1001
Website: www.cartoonnetwork.co.uk
Ownership: Turner Broadcasting Systems (TBS) Inc. an AOL Time Warner Company [see MSP above]
Service start: 27 May 2000
Satellite: Astra 2 South
Programming: classic cartoons

CBBC
BBC Television Centre
Wood Lane
London W12 7RJ
Tel: 020 8752 8000
email: cbbc.online@bbc.co.uk
website: www.bbc.co.uk/cbbc
Ownership: BBC Worldwide [see MSP above]
Service start: 11 Feb 2002
Satellite: Astra 2A
Programming: children's

Cbeebies
see above
email: cbeebies@bbc.co.uk
Website: www.bbc.co.uk/cbeebies
Service start: 11 Feb 2002
Satellite: Astra 2A
Programming: young children's

Challenge TV
160 Great Portland Street
London W1N 5TBW 5QA
Tel: 020 7299 5000
Fax: 020 7299 6000
email: challengetv_enquiries@flex-tech.co.uk
Website: www.challengetv.co.uk
Ownership: Flextech [see MSP above]
Service start: 3 Feb 1997
Satellite: Astra 1C (PAL/Videocrypt)2A
Programming: general entertainment, game shows and live interactive competitions

Channel Health
6th floor
Swiss Centre
London W1P 6QF
Tel: 020 7758 3200
Fax: 020 7758 3240
email: contacts@channelhealth.tv
Website: www.channelhealth.tv
Ownership: Channel Health Ltd
Service start: 20 Jun 2000
Satellite: Eurobird
Programming: health related programs

Channel One
PO Box 336
Old Hall Street
Liverpool L69 3TE
Tel: 0151 472 2700
Fax: 0151 472 2702
email: Ch1.lpl@cybase.co.uk
Service start: November 1994
Programming: local news and features

Channel U
18 Soho Square
London W1D 3QL
Tel: 020 7025 8088
Fax: 020 7025 8188
Programming: interactive music video

Chart Show TV
37 Harwood Rd
London SW6 4QP
Tel: 020 7384 2243
Fax: 020 7384 2026
Website: www.chartshow.com
Programming: music

Chelsea TV
Stamford Bridge
Fulham Road
London SW6 1HS
Tel: 020 7915 1951
Fax: 020 7381 4831
email: chelseatv@chelseavillage.com
Website: www.chelseafc.com
Ownership: Chelsea Digital Media Ltd
Service start: Aug 2001
Satellite: Astra 2A
Programming: football coverage and news

Christian Communications
646 Shore Road
Whiteabbey
Northern Ireland BT37 0PR
Tel: 028 9485 3997
email: ccc@ccneurope.org.uk
Website: www.ccneurope.org.uk
Programming: Christian focus

Cinenova
1 Stephen Street
London W1T 1AL
Tel: 020 7691 6960
Fax: 020 7691 5130
OwnershiP: Europe Movieco Partners
Programming: Dutch movie channel

Classic Performance
New Pathe House
57 Jamestown Road
London NW1 7XX
Tel: 020 7424 3688
Fax: 020 7424 3689
Website: www.performancetv.co.uk
Ownership: Arts & Entertainment Ltd.
Programming: arts and culture

Classic Sport
22 Suffolk Street
London SW1Y 4HG
Tel: 020 7930 0003
Fax: 020 7930 1443
email: robert.page@premiumtv.co.uk
Ownership: Premium TV Ltd
Programming: sports

Classics TV
91-93 Cleveland Street
London W1T 6PL
Tel: 020 7636 7474
Fax: 020 7636 7040
Ownership: On-Air Systems Ltd.
Programming: movies and general entertainment

Club
18 Soho Square
London W1D 3QL
Tel: 020 7025 8088
Fax: 020 70258188
Ownership: Video Interactive TV Plc.
Programming: music video

CNBC Europe
10 Fleet Place
London EC4M 7QS
Tel: 0181 653 9300020 7653 9300
Fax: 020 7653 9333
email: feedback@cnbceurope.com
Website: www.cnbceurope.com
Ownership: International General Electrics
Service start: 11 Mar 1996
Satellite: Astra 1E2B
Programming: business news

CNE
Marvic House
Bishops Road
London SW6 7AD
Tel: 020 7610 3880
email: chinesemarkets@cnetv.demon.co.uk
Programming: news and entertainment for the Chinese community

CNN International
CNN House
19-22 Rathbone Place
London W1P 1DF
Tel: 020 7637 6921020 7637 6700
Fax: 020 7637 6868738
email: _cnni@turnercnn.com
Website: www.europe.cnn.comwww.cnn.com
Ownership: Turner Broadcasting Systems (TBS) Inc, an AOL Time Warner IncCompany
Service start: Oct 1985
Satellite: Astra 1B, Intelsat 605 (PAL/clear)2A
Programming: international news

The Community Channel
3-7 Euston Centre
Regents Place
London NW1 3JG
Tel: 020 7874 7626
Fax: 020 7874 7644
email: info@communitychannel.org
Website:

www.communitychannel.org.uk
Ownership: The Media Trust
Service start: 18 Sep 2000
Satellite: Astra 2B
Programming: community affairs and social action programmes

Country Music Television Europe
25 James Street
London W1M 6AA
Tel: 020 7486 7000
Ownership: Westinghouse Electric Ltd
Programming: country music videos

CPD TV
The Prestwood Centre
99 High Street
Prestwood
Bucks HP16 9EU
Tel: 01494 865907
email: cpdental.tv@lineonenet
Website: www.cpddental.tv
Ownership: CPD Dental TV Ltd
Service start: 7 Dec 2001
Satellite: Astra 2B
Programming: professional development programmes for dentists

Create and Craft With Ideal World
Ideal Home House
Newark Road
Peterborough PE1 5WG
Tel: 0870 777 002
Fax: 0870 777003
Ownership: Ideal Shopping Direct plc.
Programming: home shopping

The Crime Channel
Media Matrix
Lutidine House
Newark Lane
Ripley
Surrey GU23 6BS
Tel: 01483 270480
Faxl 01483 270351
email: media@matrix-group.co.uk

CTC
Knightrider House
Knightrider Street
Maidstone ME15 6LU
Tel: 01622 776776
Fax: 01622 776778
Ownership: Christian Television Broadcasting Ltd.
Programming: religion

CTV
83 High Street
Rayleigh
Essex SS6 7ES
Tel: 01268 454748
email: ctvdg@compuserve.com
Programming: culture documentaries

Cube
6-7 Princes Court
Wapping Lane
London E1W 2DA
Tel: 020 7942 7942
Fax: 020 7942 7943
Ownership: Digital Television Production Ltd.
Programming: interactive entertainment

The Dating Channel
124-128 City Road
London EC1V 2NJ
Tel: 020 7748 1500
Fax: 020 7748 1501
email: info@thedatingchannel.com
Website: www.thedatingchannel.co.uk
Ownership: Euro Digital Corporation Ltd
Satellite: Eurobird
Programming: interactive dating service

Deepam TV
176 Franciscan Road
London SW17 8HH
Tel: 020 8814 6565
Ownership: Tele Europe Ltd
Programming: Tamil language entertainment

Deshi Channel
Dame Colet House
Ben Johnson Road
Stepney Green
London E1 3NH
Tel: 020 7375 0345
Website: www.deshbangla.tv
Ownership: Deshbangla Television Ltd.
Programming: general entertainment for the Bengali community

Digital Classics TV
31 Eastcastle Street
London W1W 8DL
Tel: 020 7636 1400
Fax: 020 7637 1355
email: matt@digitalclassics.tv
Website: www.digitalclassics.tv
Ownership: Digital Classics plc
Service start: Jun 2001
Satellite: Eurobird
Programming: classical music and opera performances

The Discovery Channel
160 Great Portland Street
London W1N 5TB
Tel: 020 7462 3600
Fax: 020 7462 3700
email: comments_uk@discovery.com
Website: www.discovery.com
Ownership: Discovery Communications Europe [see MSP above]
Service start: Apr 1989
Satellite: Astra 1C, Hot Bird 1 (PAL/encrypted)2A
Programming: documentaries

Discovery Civilization
see above
Programming: ancient history

Discovery Health
see above
Programming: health

Discovery Home & Leisure
See above
Website: www.homeandleisure.co.uk
Satellite: Eurobird, Astra 2A
Programming: lifestyle

Discovery Kids
see above
Programming: childrens

Discovery Sci-Trek
see above
Programming: science

Discovery Travel & Adventure
see above
Programming: travel

Discovery Wellbeing
see above
Programming:_healthy living

Discovery Wings
see above
Programming: flight

The Disney Channel UK
3 Queen Caroline St
Hammersmith
London W6 9
Tel: 020 8222 1000
Fax: 020 8222 27951144
Website: www.disneychannel.co.uk
Ownership: Walt Disney Company Ltd
Satellite: Astra 1B (PAL/Videocrypt)2D
Programming: family entertainment and films children's (supplied as bonus with Sky Premier and Moviemax)[premium]

E4
124 Horseferry Road
London SW1P 2TX
Tel: 020 7396 4444
Website: www.channel4.co.uk/entertainment
Ownership: 4 Ventures Ltd
Service start: 19 Jan 2001
Satellite: Astra 2 North
Programming: general entertainment

East
Springfield Road
Hayes UB4 0LE
Tel: 020 8573 4000
email: hds-studios@yahoo.com
Ownership: World Channel Ltd.
Programming: Asian subscription channel

EBN: European Business News
10 Fleet Place
London EC4M 7RB
Tel: 020 7653 9300
Fax: 020 7653 9333
Website: www.ebn.co.uk
Ownership: Dow Jones & Co 70%, Flextech 30%
Service start: 27 Feb 95
Satellite: Eutelsat II F6 (PAL/clear)
Programming: financial and business news

The Ecology Channel
100 New Bridge Street
London EC4V 6JA
Tel: 020 7919 1000
Fax: 020 7919 1999
Ownership: CNI UK Ltd
Programming: enviromental and wildlife documentaries

Ekushey TV
91-93 Cleveland Street
London W1T 6PL
Tel: 020 7702 4111
Ownership: On- Air Systems Ltd
Programming: geneneral entertainment

EMMA TV
37 Langford Court
Langford Place
London NW8 9DN
Tel: 020 7636 1233
Fax: 020 7636 1255
Programming: general entertainmet ethnic culture

Er-ban TV
2a Ely Rd
West Croydon
Surrey CR0 2LU
Tel: 020 8671 0660
Ownership: Upfront Broadcasting Ltd
Programming: general entertainment aimed at black audiences

Erotika
Suite 14, Burlington House
St. Saviour's Rd
St Helier
Jersey JE2 4
Tel: 01534 703 700
Fax' 01534 703 760
Ownership: RHF Productions Ltd
Programming: adult entertainment

The European Film Channel
100 New Bridge Street
London EC4V 6JA
Tel: 020 7919 1000
Ownership: CNI UK Ltd
Programming: European cinema

European Network Broadcasting
211 Picadilly
London W1N 9LP
Tel: 020 7917 2731
Ownership: UK Network Sales
Programming: religious

Eurosport
84 Theobalds Road
London WC1X 8RW
Tel: 020 7468 7777
Fax: 020 7468 0024
email: network@eurosport.co.uk
Website: www.eurosport-tv.com.co.uk
Ownership: ESO Ltd = TF1 34%, Canal Plus 33%, ESPN 33%
Service start: Feb 1989
Satellite: Astra 1A, Hot Bird 1 (PAL/clear)2A
Programming: sport
Also digital

Exercise Channel
61 Eccleston Square
London SW1v 1PH
Tel: 020 7630 0225
Fax: 020 7630 0226
Programming: exercise and health channel

Extreme Motion/Urbanchillers.com
29 Conway Street
London W1T 6BW
Tel: 020 7387 8822
Fax: 020 7387 8822
Programming: horror movies

Extreme Sports Channel
The Media Centre
131-151 Great Titchfield Street
London W1W 5BB
Tel: 020 7244 1000
Fax: 020 7244 0101
email: info@extreme.com
Website: www.extreme.com
Ownership: United Pan-Europe Communications and The Extreme Group
Satellite: 13 Oct 2000
Programming: youth oriented sports and lifestyle programs

Fans Channel
Teddington Studios
Broom Road
Teddington
Middlesex TW11 9NT
Tel: 020 8614 2675
Fax: 020 8614 2265
email: doug@thefanschannel.tv
Programming: sports news and entertainment

FilmFour
124 Horseferry Road
London SW1P 2TX
Tel: 020 7396 4444
Fax: 020 7306 8366
email: generalfilmenquiries@filmfour.com
Website: www.filmfour.com
Ownership: Channel Four Television 4 Ventures Ltd
Programming: feature and short films [premium][premium]
Digital

FilmFour Extreme
see above
Programming: extreme and challenging movies [premium]

FilmFour World
see above
Programming: foreign movies [premium]

Fox Kids (FK)UK
338 Euston Road
London NW1 3AZ
Tel: 020 7554 9000
Fax: 020 7554 9005
email: webmaster@foxkids.co.uk
Website: www.foxkids.co.uk
Ownership: Fox Television 50%, Saban 50%
Satellite: Astra 1A (PAL/Videocrypt)2B
Programming: children's

Fox Kids Network
see above
Programming: children's

Fox Kids Play
see above
Programming: interactive games

Fresco Channel
100 New Bridge Rd
London EC4V 65 A
Tel: 020 7919 1000
Ownership: CNI UK Ltd
Programming : cultural for EU member states

Friendly TV
Interxion Building
11 Hanbury Street
London E1 6QR
Tel: 020 7247 8544
Fax: 020 7247 0135
Website: www.friendlytv.com
Programming: interactive general entertainment

Front Row
Front Row Television
64 Newman Street
London W1P 3PG
Tel: 020 7551 5956
Ownership: NTL, Telewest
Programming: films [pay-per-view] movies [pay-per-view]

FTN
160 Great Portland Street
London W1W 5QA
Tel: 020 7299 5203
Fax: 020 7299 6366
Ownership: Flextech Television Ltd
Programming: general entertainment

The Games Channel
61 Eccleston Square
London SW1V 1PH
Tel: 020 7630 0225
Fax: 020 7630 0226
Programming: interactive sports channel

GMTV2
The London Television Centre
Upper Ground
London SE1 9TT
Tel: 020 7928 5884
Fax: 020 7633 0919
email: laura.lewis@gmtv.co.uk
Website: www.gmtv.co.uk
Programming: morning general interest. Digital

Going Places TV
Parkway two
Parkway Business Centre
300 Princess Rd
Manchester M14 7QU
Tel: 0161 232 5883
Website: www.mytravelgroup.com
Programming: travel shopping channel

Golf TV
First Floor
1 Kingsgate
Bradford Business Park
Bradford BD1 4SJ
Tel: 01274 725909
Programming: golf programmes and home shopping

The Gospel Channel
Gospel Channel House
Monkton Park
Chippenham SN15 3XL
Tel: 01249 446210
Programming: religious

Granada Breeze
Franciscan Court
16 Hatfields
London SE1 8DJ
Tel: 020 7578 4040
Fax: 020 7578 4176
Website: www.gbreeze.co.uk
Ownership: Granada Sky Broadcasting
Satellite: Astra 1E (PAL/encrypted)
Programming: lifestyle
Also digital

Granada Men &+ Motors
Franciscan Court
16 Hatfields
London SE1 8DJ
Tel: 020 7578 4040
Fax: 020 7578 4176
email: men@gsb.co.uk
Website: www.menandmotors.co.uk
Ownership: Granada Sky Broadcasting Ltd
Satellite: Astra 1A (PAL/Videocrypt)2A
Programming: male-oriented, motoring
Also digital

Granada Plus
Franciscan Court
16 Hatfields
London SE1 8DJ
Tel: 020 7578 4040
Fax: 020 7578 4176
email: plus@gsb.co.uk
Website: www.gplus.co.uk
Ownership: Granada 50.5 %, British Sky Broadcasting [see MSP above] 49.5%
Satellite: Astra 1A (PAL/Videocrypt)2 North
Programming: classic TV programmes
Also digital

The Hallmark Channel Entertainment Network
3-5 Bateman Street
London W1V 5TT
Tel: 020 7368 91007439 0633
Fax: 020 7368 91017439 0644
Website: www.hallmarkchannelint.com.uk
Service start: 1 Nov 2001
Satellite: Astra 2D
Programming: drama

Healix
Portland House
Aldermaston Park
Aldermaston
Reading RG7 4HR
Tel: 0118 981 6666
Fax: 0118 981 9801
email: info@synigence.net
Website: www.synigence.net
Ownership: Synigence Plc
Programming: educational

Health Zone
345 Ice Wharf
17 New Wharf Rd
London N1 9RW
Tel: 020 7689 5226
Fax: 020 7689 5226
email: health@bizonline.co.uk
Programming: health education

The History Channel
6 Centaurs Business Park
Grant Way, Syon Lane
Isleworth
Middlesex TW7 5QD
Tel: 0870 240 3000020 7705 3000
Fax: 020 7705 3030
email: feedback@thehistorychannel.co.uk
Website: www.sky.co.ukwww.thehistorychannl. co.uk
Ownership: BSkyB 50%, Arts &Entertainment Television Networks 50%, British Sky Broadcasting [see MSP above] 50%
Service start: 1 Nov 1995
Satellite: Astra 1B (PAL/Videocrypt)
Programming: historical and biographical documentariesry
Website: www.thehistorychannel. co.uk
Also digital

The Hits
Mappin House
4 Winsley House
London W1W 8HF
Tel: 020 7348 8737
Fax: 020 7376 1313
Ownership: Box TV
Programming: music and general entertainment

The Home Shopping Channel
Sir John Moores Building
100 Old Hall Street
Liverpool
Merseyside L70 1AB
Tel: 0800 775533
Ownership: The Home Shopping Channel Ltd
Digital

The Horror Channel
50 Riverside
South Church
Bishop Auckland
County Durham DL14 6XT
Tel: 01388 601361
Programming: films and light entertainment with horror focus

Ice Cube TV
1 The Courtyard
Swan Centre
Fishers Lane
London W4 1RX
Tel: 0845 666 77778
Programming: general entertainment

Ideal World Home Shopping
Ideal Home House
Newark Road
Peterborough PE1 5WG
Tel: 01733 777 305
Fax: 01733 777 315
email: website@idealshoppingdirect.co.uk
Website: www.idealworldtv.co.uk
Ownership: Ideal Shopping Direct plc
Service start: 17 Apr 2000
Satellite: Astra 2B
Programming: home shopping

Indus Television
88 Newcourt Street
London NW8 7AA
Tel: 020 7722 2922
Programming: news, entertainment and multicultural programmes

Invest Television Ltd
103a Oxford St
London W1D 2HG
Tel: 020 7758 3100
programming: home shopping

ITN News Channel
200 Gray's Inn Road
London WC1X 8XZZ
Tel: 020 7833 3000
Fax: 020 7430 47004868
email: contact@itn.co.uk
Website: www.itv.co.ukwww.itn.co.uk
Satellite: Astra 2B
Programming: news

ITV Select
346 Queenstown Road
London SW8 4NE
Tel: 020 7819 8000
Fax: 020 819 8100
Website: www.itv-digital.co.uk
Programming: entertainment, movies, sport

ITV Sports Channel
346 Queenstown Road
London SW8 4NE
Tel: 020 7819 8000
Fax: 020 819 8100
Website: www.itv-digital.co.uk
Programming: sport

ITV12
200 Gray's Inn Road
London WC1X 8HF
Tel: 020 7843 8000
Fax: 020 7843 8443
email: dutyoffice@itv.co.uk
Website: www.itv.co.uk
Ownership: ITV companies
Satellite: Astra 2D
Digital; also on analogue cable

ITV2
see above

Japan Satellite TV (JSTV)
3rd floor, Quick House
65 Clifton Street
London EC2A 4JE
Tel: 020 7426 7330
Fax: 020 7426 73393
email: info@jstv.co.uk
Website: www.jstv.co.uk
Ownership: NHK, private Japanese investors – Satellite: Astra 1E (PAL/Videocrypt)Hotbird 5
Programming: Japanese news, drama, documentary, entertainment, sport

The Job Channel
Cheltenham Film Studios
Hatherley Lane
Cheltenham
Gloucestershire GL51 6PN
Tel: 01242 534 500
Fax: 01242 534 502
email: admin@jobchannel.tv
Website: www.jobchannel.tv
Ownership: MultiMedia Television
Service start: October 2000
Programming: job vacancies

Kanal5
Falcon House
115-123 Staines Rd.
Hounslow TW3 3LL
Tel: 020 8814 7520
Fax: 020 8569 5565
Programming: general entertainment

Kerrang!
Mappin House
4 Winsley Street
London W1W 8HF
Tel: 020 7436 1515
Fax: 020 7312 8227
Website: www.thebox.co.uk
Ownership: Box Television Ltd
Service start: 5 Dec 2001
Satellite: Eurobird
Programming: interactive music video programming

Khalifa Television
82 Mortimer Street
London W1W 7HN
Tel: 020 8838 2959
Fax: 020 8961 5050
Programming: news

Kidz Sport
Walton End
Walton Lane
Bosham
West Sussex PO18 8QF
Tel: 01243 575557
Fax: 01243 576657
Programming: children's sport

KT TV
Dovewell Communications
March House
Victoria Trading Estate
Victoria Road
London W3 6VR
Tel: 020 8752 3971
Programming: Christian church services

The Landscape Channel Europe
Landscape Studios
Hye House
Crowhurst,
East Sussex TN33 9BX
Tel: 01424 830900830668
Fax: 01424 830680680
email: info@landscapetv.com
Website: www.landscapetv.com
Service start: Nov 1988 (on videotape); Apr 1993 (on satellite)
Satellite: Orion, Hispasat (PAL/clear)Astra 3A
Programming: music and visual wallpapermusic and visual wallpaper

Let's Go Shop+
167 Imperial Drive
Harrow
Middlesex HA2 7JP
Tel: 020 8868 4355
Fax: 020 8868 5024
Ownership: Best Direct (International) Ltd
Programming: home shopping

Life TV
Westbrook House
18/20 Albion Place
Maidstone
Kent ME14 5DZ
Tel: 01622 776776
Fax: 01622 678080
Programming: light entertainment

Live TV
24th floor
1 Canada Square
Canary Wharf
London E14 5AP
Tel: 0171 293 3900
Fax: 0171 293 3820
email: cable@livetv.co.uk
Ownership: Mirror Group Newspapers
Service start: 12 June 95
Programming: general entertainment
Website: www.livetv.co.uk

Living
160 Great Portland St
London W1N 5TB
Tel: 020 7299 5000
Fax: 020 7299 6000
Website: www.livingtv.co.uk
Ownership: Flextech [see MSP above]
Service start: Sept 1993
Satellite: Astra 1C (PAL/Videocrypt)2A
Programming: daytime lifestyle, evening general entertainment, particularly aimed at women

M4U
19 Heather Park Drive
Wembley HA0 1SS
Tel: 020 8795 7171
Fax: 020 8963 8445
Website: www.b4utv.com
Programming: Indian music and films

Magic
Mappin House
4 Winsley Street
London W1W 8HF
Tel: 020 7436 1515
Fax: 020 7436 1313
Website: www.thebox.co.uk
Ownership: Box Television Ltd
Service start: 5 Dec 2001
Satellite: Eurobird
Programming: interactive music videos

Mars TV
Warton House
3rd Floor
150 High Street
Stratford
London E15 2NE
Tel: 020 8221 2115
Fax: 020 8221 1592
ownership: Asian Vision
programming: general entertainment

Mashriq
227 Gascoigne Road
Barking
Essex IG11 7LU
Tel: 020 8591 5621
Fax: 020 8507 8424
Ownership: TV Asia Ltd
Programming: Asian Music and news

MATV
MPK House
233 Belgrave Gate
Leicester LE1 3HT
Tel: 0116 253 2288
Fax: 0116 253 8900
email: mbc.matv@technocom.com
Ownership: Middlesex Broadcasting Corporation Ltd.
Programming: general entertainment

Maximum Animatrix
Queens Studios
117 Salisbury Road
London NW6 6RG
Tel: 020 7328 8808
Fax: 020 7328 8858
Website: www.zonevision.com
Ownership: Zone Broadcasting
Programming: animation some adult

Maximum Horror
(see above)
programming: horror films

Maximum Reality
(see above)
programming: documentary

Maximum Speed
(as aove)
programming: motor sport

MBC: (Middle East Broadcasting Centre)
80 Silverthorne Road
Battersea
London SW8 3XA
Tel: 020 7501 1111
Fax: 020 7501 1110
email: info@mbc1.tv
Website: www.mbctvsat.com
Service start: 18 Sept 91
Satellite: Hotbird 5
Programming: general news and entertainment in arabic

Media News Network MNN
24 Ullswater Close
Bromley
Kent BR1 4JF
Tel: 020 8464 3383
Fax: 020 8464 3381
email: info@mnn.co.uk
Programming: general entertainment

Mediashop Television
19 Norfolk Road
London NW8 6HG
Tel: 020 7722 0242

Minaj Broadcast International
Suite 3 Berkeley Square House
London W1X 5LE
Tel: 020 7491 2393
email: europe@minaj.com
Website: www.minaj.co.uk
Progarmming: Afro-centric entertainment

MINT
Studio 54
222 Kensal Road
London W10 5BN
Tel: 020 7729 7016
email: alex.wright@tvventures.co.uk
Ownership: TV Ventures
Programming: interactive music channel

Men & Motors see Granada Men & Motors

The Money Channel
Princes Court
Wapping Lane
London E1W 2DA
Tel: 020 7942 7942
Fax: 020 7942 7943
email: reception@themoneychannel.co.uk
Website: www.themoneychannel.co.uk
Programming: financial news

Moviemax
33 New Cavendish Street
London W1G 9TS
Tel: 020 7224 5504
Fax: 020 7224 5506
Ownership: Eclipse Sat Ltd
Programming: feature films

MTV Base
180 Oxford Street
London W1N 0DS
Tel: 020 7284 7777
Fax: 020 7284 7788
email: info@mtv.co.uk
Website: www.mtv.co.uk/base.asp
Ownership: MTV Networks Europe
Satellite: Astra 2A
Programming: music and general entertainment

MTV Dance
see above
Service start: 20 Apr 2001
website: www.mtv.co.uk/dance
Programming: music videos

MTV Hits
see above
Website: www.mtv.co.uk/hits
Programming: music videos

MTV in the UK Channel
see above
Website: www.mtv.co.uk
Programming: music videos
180 Oxford Street
London W1N 0DS
Tel: 020 7478 6000
Website: www.mtv.co.uk
Ownership: Viacom
Service start: Aug 87
Satellite: Astra 1A (PAL/Videocrypt)
Programming: pop music
Also digital

MTV2
see above
email: ViewerFeedback@mtveuro-pean.com
website: www.mtv2europe.com
Programming: music videos

Music Choice
Fleet House
57-61 Clerkenwell Road
London EC1M 5LA
Tel: 020 7014 8700
Fax: 020 7534 2144
Website: www.musicchoice.co.uk
Ownership: Sony 8%, Warner 16%, MCE 13%, private investors 27%, British Sky Broadcasting [see MSP above] 36%
Programming: music (interactive)

Muslim TV Ahmadiyyah
16 Gressenhall Road
London SW18 5QL
Tel: 020 8870 09228517 ext 210
Fax: 020 8870 0684
Website: www.alislam.org/mta
Ownership: Al-Shirkatul Islamiyyah
Service start: Jan 1994
Satellite: Intelsat 601Eurobird
Programming: spiritual, and educational, training programmes for the Muslim community

MUTV
Manchester United Television
274 Deansgate
Manchester M3 4SB
Tel: 0161 930 1968834 1111
Fax: 0161 876 5502
email: mutv@manutd.com
Website: www.manutd.com/mutv
Ownership: Manchester United FC 33.33%, Granada 33.33%, British Sky Broadcasting [see MSP above] 33.33%, Granada
Service start: Satellite: Astra 2B
Programming: Manchester United FC [premium]

Mystery Channel
Templar Lodge
Edinburgh EH31 2AS
Tel: 01620 842275
Fax: 01620 842970
Programming: documentary mysteries

Namaste Television
Unit 11
Forest Business Park
South Access Road
Walthamstow
E17 8BA
Tel: 01603 660783
Website: www.namastev.co.uk
Service start: Sept 92
Satellite: Intelsat 601
Ownership: Gandhi Corporation
Programming: Asian entertainment

NASN Ltd.
52 Haymarket
London SW1Y 4RP
Tel: 020 7389 0771
Fax: 020 7925 0580
Programming: Sport

National Geographic Channel
6 Centaurs Business Park
Grant Way
Isleworth TW7 5QD
Tel: 020 7941 5068
Fax: 020 7805 2295
Ownership: National Geographic 50%, British Sky Broadcasting ([see MSP above)] 50%, National Geographic
email: natgeoweb@bskyb.com
Website: www.nationalgeographic.comco.uk
Service start: 1997
Satellite: Astra 12A (PAL/Videocrypt)
Programming: natural history documentaries

NBC Channel
Harbour Yard
Chelsea Harbour
London SW10 0XD
Tel: 020 7352 9205
email: talkback@nbc.com
Programming: general entertainment

Nickelodeon
15-18 Rathbone Place
London W1P 1DF
Tel: 020 7462 10000800 801 801/020 7462 1000
Fax: 020 7462 10300800 802 802/020 7462 1030
Website: www.nicktv.co.uk
Ownership: British Sky Broadcasting 50% [see MSP above], MTV NetworksViacom 50%, British Sky Broadcasting [see MSP above] 50%
Service start: 1 Sept 93
Satellite: Astra 1C (PAL/Videocrypt)2B
Programming: children's

Nick Jr
15-18 Rathbone Place
London W1P 1DF
Tel: 020 7462 10000800 801 801
Fax: 020 7462 10300800 802 802
email: letterbox@nickjr.co.uk
Website: www.nicktvjr.co.uk
Ownership: Viacom 50%, British Sky Broadcasting [see MSP above] 50% [see MSP above], MTV Networks 50%
Service start: 1 Sept 99
Satellite: Astra 2A, 2B
Programming: young children's

Novashop One
c/o Connexion Exports Ltd
91 Cleveland Street
London W1T 6PL
Tel: 020 7636 7474
Fax: 020 7636 7040
Programming: home shopping

On-Air TV
The Media Centre
131 Great Titchfield Street
London W1W 5BB
Tel: 020 7663 3651
Fax: 020 7663 3664
Programming: general entertainment

Open Acces
2-4 Hoxton Square
London N16 NU
Tel: 0870 744 2041
faxL 0870 054 2891
Ownership: Definition Consultants Ltd.
Progarmming: light entertainment

Out TV
Queens Studios
117 Sakusbury Road
London NW6 6RG
Tel: 020 7328 8808
Fax: 020 7328 8858
Ownership: Zone Broadcasting Ltd.
Programming: general entertainment for gay audiences

Pakistani Channel
65 North Acton Road
London NW1D 6PS
Tel: 020 8838 6300
Fax: 020 8838 2112
Programming: general entertainment and news in Urdu

The Paramount Comedy Channel
3-5 Rathbone Place
London W1P 1DA
Tel: 020 7399 7700
Fax: 020 7399 7730
Website: www.paramountcomedy.co.ukom
Ownership: Viacom 75%, British Sky Broadcasting [see MSP above], 25% Viacom
Service start: 1 Nov 1995
Satellite: Astra 1C (PAL/Videocrypt)2A
Programming: comedy

Performance: The Arts Channel
New Pathe House
57 Jamestown Rd
London NW1P 7DB
Tel: 020 7424 368826
Fax: 020 7424 3689
email: info@performancetv.co.uk
Website: www.performancetv.co.uk-channel.com
Ownership: Arts & Entertainment Ltd
Service start: Oct 1992
Cable only from videotape
Satellite: Telstar 11
Programming: opera, jazz and classical concerts, drama, performing arts

Phoenix Chinese News and Entertainment
7th floor
The Chiswick Centre
414 Chiswick High Road
London W4 5TF
Tel: 020 8987 4320
Fax: 020 8987 4333
email: info@phoenixcnetv.com
Website: www.phoenixtv.com
Ownership: Phoenix Chinese News and Entertainment Ltd
Service start: Nov 1992
Satellite: Eurobird
Programming: general entertainment in Mandarin and Cantonese

Playboy TV
2nd floor, Aquis House
Station Road
Hayes
Middlesex UB3 4DX
Tel: 020 8581 7000
Fax: 020 8581 7007
Website: www.playboytv.co.uk
Ownership: Flextech 51% [see MSP above], BSkyB, Playboy
Service start: 1 Nov 1995
Satellite: Astra 12B (PAL/Videocrypt)
Programming: erotic (premium)adult entertainment [subscription]

Phoenix Chinese News and Entertainment (CNE)
Marvic House
Bishops Road, Fulham
London SW6 7AD
Tel: 020 7610 3880
Fax: 020 7610 3118
email: chinesemarkets@cnetv.demon.co.uk
Website: phoenixtv.com
Ownership: The CNT Group
Service start: Nov 92
Satellite: Astra 1C (PAL/Clear)
Programming: news, current affairs, films, dramas, lifestyle

Playhouse Disney
Beaumont House
Avonmore Road
London W14 8TS
Tel: 020 8222 1000
Fax: 020 8222 1144
email: guest.mail@online.disney.com
Website: www.disney.co.uk/disney-channel/playhouse
Ownership: The Walt Disney Company Ltd
Satellite: Astra 2D
Programming: children's entertainment [premium]

POP
37 Harwood Road
London SW6 4QP
Tel: 020 7384 5999
Fax: 020 7384 2026
Website: ww.chartshow.tv
Ownership: Chart Shows Channels Ltd
Programming: animation and music

The Pop Culture Channel
100 New Bridge Road
London EC4V 6JA
Tel: 020 7919 1000
Fax: 020 7919 1999
Ownership: CNI UK Ltd.
Programming: less well known film and television form overseas

Pout
6 Princes Court
Wapping Lane
London E1W 2DA
Tel: 020 7942 7942
Fax: 020 7942 7943
Ownership: Digital Television Production Ltd.
Programming: adult entertainment

Prime TV
AMC House
12 Cumberland Ave
Park Royal
London NW10 7QL
Tel: 020 8961 4911
Fax: 020 8961 4913
email: info@primetv.freeserve.co.uk
Ownership: Pak Television Ltd
Service start: Nov 1998
Satellite: Intelsat 707, Astra 2B
Programming: family programming aimed at the Pakastani community [subscription]

Private Blue
33 New Cavendish Street
London W1G 9TS
Tel: 020 7328 8808
Fax: 020 7328 8858
email: info@privatebroadcasting.nl
Website: www.privateblue.com
Service start: 2 Mar 2001
Satellite: Astra 2 South
Programming: erotic

Private Girls
see above
Satellite: Astra 2 North
Programming: adult entertainment

P-Rock TV
24 Park Royal Metro Centre
Britannia Way
London NW10 7PA
Tel: 020 8961 5456

Q
Mappin House
4 Winsley Street
London W1W 8HF
Tel: 020 7436 1515
Fax: 020 7376 1313
email: qtv@q4music.com
Website: www.q4musci.com
Ownership: Emap
Service start: 2000
Satellite: Astra 2B
Programming: interactive general entertainment

QVC: The Shopping Channel
Marco Polo House, Chelsea Bridge
346 Queenstown Road
London SW8 4NQ
Tel: 020 7705 5600
Fax: 020 7705 56021
Website: www.qvcuk.com
Ownership: QVC (= Comcast, TCI) 80%, British Sky Broadcasting [see MSP above] 20%

Satellite: Astra 1C (soft scrambled)2B
Service start: Oct 1993
Programming: home shopping

The Racing Channel
Satellite House
17 Corsham Street
London N1 6DR
Tel: 020 7253 2232
Fax: 020 7490 00177608 2229
email: info@satelliteinfo.co.ukwebmaster@racingchannel.com
Website: www.racingchannel.com
Ownership: Satellite Information Services Ltd
Service start: Nov 1995
Satellite: Astra 1D2A
Programming: horse racing [subscription]

Rapture TV
43 Parkhead Loan
Edinburgh EH11 4SJ
Tel: 0131 443 4642
Website: www.powertv.co.uk
Ownership: Power Tv Ltd
Programming: light entertainment

The Reality Channel
100 New Bridge Street
London EC4V 6JA
Tel: 020 7919 1000
Fax: 020 79191999
Ownership: CNI UK Ltd
Programming: documentary

Reality Television
Zone Broadcasting
Queen's Studios
117-121 Salisbury Road
London NW6 6RG
Tel: 020 7328 8808
Fax: 020 7328 8858
email: pobox@zonevision.com
Website: www.zonevision.com
Programming: documentaries/fly-on-the-wall programmes

Red Hot All Girl
Suite 14
Burlington House
St Saviour's Road
St Helier
Jersey JE2 4LA
Tel: 01534 703 720
Fax: 01534 703 760
Website: www.redhottv.co.uk
Ownership: RHF Productions Ltd
Programming: adult entertainment

Red Hot Amateur
see above
Programming: adult films

Red Hot Euro
see above
Programming: adult entertainment

Red Hot Films
see above
Programming: adult films

Refugee Tv
9 Ivatt Way
London N17 6PF
Tel: 020 8881 0869
Programming: community

The Relationships Channel
PO Box 4516
London SW9 7XF
Tel: 020 7732 3521

Revelation
91-93 Cleveland Street
London W1T 6PL
Tel: 020 7636 7474
Fax: 020 7636 7040
Programming: general entertainment

The Revival Channel
Stonehills Shields Road
Gateshead
Tyne & Wear NE10 0HW
Tel: 0191 495 2244
Fax: 0191 568 0808
email: info@god.tv
Website: www.godnetwork.com
Ownership: The Dream Family Network Ltd
Satellite: Eurobird
Programming: Christian

RNTV
6-8 Amwell Street
London EC1R 1UQ
Tel: 020 7278 1105
Fax: 020 7713 7732
Programming: gay

Romance Channel
15 Shadwell Park Court
Leeds
West Yorkshire LS17 8TS
Tel: 07803 743 984
Programming: films and light entertainment

Romantica
Queens Studios
117 Salusbury Rd
London NW6 6RG
Tel: 020 7328 8808
Programming: soap operas

Russian Channel
24 Ullswater Close
Bromley
Kent BR1 4JF
Tel: 020 8464 3383
Website: www.mnn.uk.com
Ownership: Media News Network Ltd.
Programming: Russian language movies

The Sci-Fi Channel Europe
5-7 Mandeville Place
London W1M 5LB
Tel: 020 7535 3500
Fax: 020 7535 3585
email: mail@uk.scifi.com
Website: www.scifi.com
Ownership: Sci-Fi Channel Europe
Service start: 1 Nov 1995
Satellites: Astra 1B, Hot Bird 1 (PAL/encrypted)2A
Programming: science fiction, fantasy, horror programming

Screenshop
4 Warple Way
London W3 0VE
email: screenshop_enquiries@ screenshop.co.uk
Website: www.screenshop.co.uk
Ownership: Sit-UpFlextech
Service start: 30 Sep 1999
Satellite: Astra 2A
Programming: home shopping

Scuzz
Grant Way Isleworth
Middlesex TW7 5QD
Tel: 0870 240 3000
Fax: 0870 240 3060
Ownership BSkyB
Programming: music

Setanta Television
Broadcasting House
3a South Prince's Street
Dublin 2
Eire
Tel: 00 353 1 677 6705
Fax: 00 353 1 671 6671
email: setanta.uktvproduction@setanta.com
Website: www.setanta.com
Ownership: Setanta Sport Ltd
Service start: 1999
Programming: Gaelic sports for pubs Gaelic soccer and rugby

S4C2
Sianel Pedwar Cymru
Parc Ty-Glas
Llanisihen
Cardiff CF4 5DU
Wales
Tel: 029 2074 7444
Fax: 020 2075 4444
email: s4c@s4c.co.uk
Website: www.s4c..co.uk
Service start: 15 Sep 1999
Satellite: Astra 2A
Programming: coverage of the Welsh

Assembly in session initially, news and general entertainment in Welsh and English
Digital

Shop America
1st floor
1 Kingsgate
Bradford Business Park
Canal Road
Bradford BD1 4SJ
Tel: 0800 0821 821
email: info@shopamerica.co.uk
Website: www.shopamerica.co.uk
Ownership: Shop America (Australasia) Ltd
Satellite: Astra 2 South
Programming: home shopping

Shop Smart
Unit 24 Metro Centre
Britania Way
Park Royal
London NW10 7PA
Tel: 0870 124 5656
email: enquiries@shopsmart.tv
Website: www.shopsmart.tv
Ownership: Shop Smart Television Ltd
Satellite: Eurobird
Programming: home shopping

Shop USA
Chalfont Grove
Narcot Lane
Chalfont St. Peter
Buckinghamshire SL9 8TW
Tel: 01494 878078
Fax: 01494 878076
email: info@siriustv.net
Ownership: Sirius Retail TV
Programming: home shopping

Shopping Galore
146 Chase Side
London N14 5PP
Tel: 020 8886 1539
Fax: 020 8838 1173
Programming: home shopping

Shopping Genie
Chalfont Grove
Narcot Lane
Chalfont St Peter
Buckinghamshire SL9 8TW
Tel: 0800 052 0300
Fax: 01494 878076
email: info@shoppinggenie.com
Website: www.shoppinggenie.net
Ownership: Sirius Television Ltd
Satellite: Astra 2 South
Programming: home shopping

Showcase (Magazine Showcase)
Knightrider House
Knightrider Street
Maidstone
Kent ME15 6LU
Tel: 01622 776776
Ownership: Millennium 7 Television Ltd
Service start: Apr 2001
Satellite: Eurobird
Programming: shows based on magazine brands

Showtime (The Movie Channel)
Gulf DTH Productions
117 Salusbury Road
London NW6 6RG
Tel: 020 7328 8808
Fax: 020 7328 8858
Ownership: Zone TV
Programming: feature films

Simply Health
150 Great Portland Stret
London W1W 6QD
Tel: 020 7307 6100
Fax: 020 7307 6101
email: feedback@simplyshoppingtv.co.uk
Website: www.simplyshoppingtv.co.uk
Ownership: Invest TV Ltd
Service start: Dec 2001
Satellite: Astra 2A
Programming: home shopping

Simply Holidays
see above
Service start: Dec 2001
Programming: holidays

Simply Ideas
See above
Programming: home shopping (general)

Simply Jewellery
see above
Service start: Sep 2001
Programming: home shopping (jewerelly)

Simply Music
see above
Service start: Oct 2001
Programming: home shopping (music and entertainment)

Simply Nine
See above
Programming: science and technology

Simply Shopping
See above
Website: www.simplyshoppingtv.comsee above
Programming: home shopping

Simply Ten
See above
Programming: general entertainment with Asian foocus

Sinematurk
See Music Box
Programming: Turkish Film Channel

Sirasa TV
The White House
Barkston Ash
Tadcaster
North Yorkshire LS24 9TT
Tel: 01937 557 029
Fax: 01937 557029
email: sirasatvuk@disc.tv
Website: www.sirasa.com
Ownership: MBC Networks Ltd
Satellite: Eurobird
Programming: entertainment

Sky Box Office
6 Centaurs Business Park
Grant Way
Syon Lane
Isleworth
Middlesex TW7 5QD
Tel: 020 7705 3000
Fax: 020 7705 3030
email: feedback@sky.co.uk
Website: www.sky.co.uk
Ownership: British Sky Broadcasting [see MSP above]
Service start: 1 Dec 97
Satellite: Eurobird, Astra 2A, 2B, 2D1E (PAL/Videocrypt)
Programming: movies, concerts, events (pay-per-view)
Also digital

Sky Movies Cinema
see aboveOwnership: British Sky Broadcasting [see MSP above]
Service start: Oct 92
Satellite: Astra 1C (PAL/Videocrypt)2B
Programming: movies ([premium)]

Sky Movies Max
Ownership: British Sky Broadcasting [see MSP above]see above
Service start: Feb 1989
Satellite: Astra 12A, 2B (PAL/Videocrypt)
Programming: movies ([premium)]
Also digital

Sky Movies Premier
see above

Website: www1.sky.com/movies/premier
Satellite: Astra 2A, 2B
Programming: movies [premium]

Sky News
Ownership: British Sky Broadcasting [see MSP above]see above
website: www.sky.com/skynews
Service start: Feb 1989
Satellite: Astra 12AB (PAL/Videocrypt)
Programming: news

Sky One
Ownership: British Sky Broadcasting [see MSP above]see above
website: www.skyone.co.uk
Service start: Feb 1989
Satellite: Astra 1A (PAL/Videocrypt)2B, 2A
Programming: general entertainment
Also digital

Sky Premier
Ownership: British Sky Broadcasting [see MSP above]
Service start: Apr 91
Satellite: Astra 1B (PAL/Videocrypt)
Programming: movies (premium)
Also digital

Sky Pub Channel
BSkyB
Grant Way
Isleworth
Middlesex TW7 5QD
Tel: 020 7941 5572
Fax: 020 7941 5123
email: generalenquiries@pubchannel.com
website: www.pubchannel.com
Ownership: British Sky Broadcasting [see MSP above]
Satellite: Astra 2B
Programming: food, drink. entertainment programmes

Sky Scottish
Ownership: British Sky Broadcasting [see MSP above]
Programming: Scottish programmes
Satellite: Astra 1A (PAL/Videocrypt)

Sky Soap
Ownership: British Sky Broadcasting [see MSP above]
Satellite: Astra 1B (PAL/Videocrypt)
Programming: entertainment

Sky Sports 1
Ownership: British Sky Broadcasting [see MSP above]see above
website: www.skysports.com
Service start: Apr 1991
Satellite: Astra 1B (PAL/Videocrypt)2A, 2B
Programming: sport (premium)
Also digital

Sky Sports 2
Ownership: British Sky Broadcasting [see MSP above]see above
Service start: Aug 1994
Satellite: Astra 1C (PAL/Videocrypt)2A, 2B
Programming: sport (premium)
Also digital

Sky Sports 3
Ownership: British Sky Broadcasting [see MSP above]see above
Service start: Aug 1994
Satellite: Astra 1B (PAL/Videocrypt)
Programming: sport (premium)[premium]
Also digital

Sky Sports Extra
see aboveOwnership: British Sky Broadcasting [see MSP above]
Service start: Aug 1999
Satellite: Astra 1B (PAL/Videocrypt)2A, 2D
Programming: sports (bonus with premium channels)[premium]
Digital

Sky Sports News
see above
Satellite: Astra 2A
Programming: sports news

Sky Travel
Ownership: British Sky Broadcasting [see MSP above]see above
website: www.skytravel.co.uk
Satellite: Astra 1C (PAL/Videocrypt)2D
Programming: travel documentaries

Sky Venue
Ownership: British Sky Broadcasting [see MSP above]
Programming: general entertainment

Smash Hits
Mappin House
4 Winsley Street
London W1W 8HF
Tel: 020 7436 1515
Fax: 020 7312 8246
email: feedback@smashhits.net
Website: www.smashhits.net
Ownership: Emap Box Television
Service start: 5 Dec 2001
Satellite: Eurobird
Programming: music videos and information (interactive)

Sony Entertainment Television Asia
Molinare
34 Fouberts Place
London W1B 2BH
Tel: 020 7534 7575
Fax: 020 7534 7585
Website: www.setindia.com
Ownership: Sony Pictures Entertainment Inc
Service start: 26 Aug 1999
Satellite: Astra 2 South
Programming: general entertainment [subscription]

Soulvision
Suite 1
Lansdowne House
85 Surbiton Rd.
London KT1 2JQ
Tel: 020 8549 7709
Fax: 020 8949 0563
email: international@hotmail.com
Ownership: International ICON Ltd.
Programming: music and light entertainment

South For You
MPK House
233 Belgrave Gate
Leicester LE1 3HT
Tel: 0116 253 2288
Fax: 0116 253 8900
Ownership: Middlesex Broadcasting Corp.
Programming: Southerna Asia entetainment

Spice
PO Box 690
Hayes
Middlesex UB3 4BR
Tel: 020 8581 7000
Fax: 020 8581 4090
email: enquiry@spicexxx.co.uk
Website: www.spicexxx.co.uk
Ownership: Playboy TV UK Ltd
Service start: 2 Mar 2001
Satellite: Astra 2A, Hot Bird 1
Programming: adult entertainment

Spin TV
Unit 6
Princes Court
Wapping Lane, London E1 9DA
Tel: 020 7492 7492
Fax: 020 7492 7493
Ownership: Digital Television Production Ltd.
Programming: interactive gameshows

Sporting Life TV
See above
Programming: sport and interactive betting

STAR News
8th floor

1 Harbourfront
18 Tak Fung Street
Hungko
Kowloon
Hong Kong
Tel: 00 852 2621 8888
Fax: 00 852 2621 8000
Website: www.startv.com
Ownership: STAR Group, a subsidiary of News Corporation
Service start: Jan 2001
Satellite: Astra 2 South
Programming: news and analysis in English and Hindi [premium]

STAR Plus
see above
Service start: Jan 2001
Programming: general entertainment [premium]

Stara Vision
54 Oswald Street
Glasgow G1 4PL
Tel: 0141 248 2495
Programming: Asian

STEP-UP
University of Plymouth
Notte Street
Plymouth PL1 2AR
Tel: 01752 233635
Programming: educational and business

Sun TV
Unit 15D
Oakcroft Road
Chessington KT9 1RH
Tel: 020 8974 2651
Fax: 020 8974 2652
Website: www.suntvuk.com
Programming: general entertainment

Supershop
See Novashop

SVM Television
29 Windmill Street
London W1P 1HG
Tel: 020 7629 0200
Fax: 020 7629 0229
Ownership: MBS Datacom Ltd.
Programming: music and health

The Talent Channel
Portland Palce
London E14 9TT
Tel: 020 7308 5095
Programming: general light entertainment

Tantalise TV
PO Box 611
Bromley
Kent BR2 9YE
Tel: 0870 046 7759
Fax: 020 8461 8474
email: info@tantalise.com
Website: www.tantalise.com
Ownership: Airtime Leasing Ltd
Satellite: Astra 2B
Programming: adult entertainment

Taste (formerly Carlton Food Network)
Website: www.cfn,co.uk
Ownership: Carlton Communications [see MSP above]
Service start: 2 Sep 1996
Satellite: Intelsat 601 (MPEG2 encrypted)
Programming: food
Also digital

Tel Sell
Unit 5
The Robert Eliot Centre
1 Old Nichol St
London E2 7HR
Tel: 08701 621 942
Website: www.telsell.com
Ownership: Tel Sell UK Ltd
Satellite: Eurobird
Programming: home shopping

Television In Colour
23 Cinderford Way
Bromley BR1 5PR
Tel: 020 8468 1618
email: pearlj@ukf.net
Programming: lifstyle for people of colour

TMF
See MTV

Thane Direct
35-37 Fitzroy Square
London W1T 6DX
Tel: 0870 444 2252
Fax: 020 7323 0396
Website: www.thanedirect.co.uk
Ownership: Thane International Inc
Satellite: Eurobird
Programming: informercials and home shopping

Thomas Cook TV
8 Park Place
Lawn Lane
Vauxhall
London SW8 1UD
Tel: 020 7840 7163
Fax: 020 7820 4471
Website: www.thomascooktv.com
Ownership: Thomas Cook Ltd
Service start: Nov 2001
Satellite: Eurobird
Programming: travel

TCM Turner Classic Movies
Turner House
160 Great Marlborough St
London W1F 7HS
Tel: 020 7693 1000
Fax: 020 7693 1001
email: tcmeurope@turner.com
Website: www.tcmonline.co.uk
Ownership: Turner Broadcasting [see MSP above]
Service start: Sept 93
Satellite: Astra 1C, Astra 1F (PAL/clear)
Programming: movies

TLC Life Unscripted
160 Great Portland Street
London W1N 5TB
Tel: 020 7462 3600
Fax: 020 7462 3700
Website: tlc.discovery.com
Ownership: Discovery Communications
Service start: 1992
Programming: educational/ instructional

Toniq TV
64 The Drive
Acton
London W3 6AG
Tel: 07930 954427
Programming: general entertainmet

Toon Disney
Building 12
566 Chiswick High Rd
London W4 5AN
Tel: 020 8222 1000
Fax: 020 8222 2565
Website: www.disney.co.uk
Ownership: The Walt Disney Company Ltd
Satellite: Astra 2D
Programming: children's entertainment [premium]

Toonami
Turner House
16 Great Malborough Street
London W1F 7HS
Tel: 020 7693 0779
Fax: 020 7693 0780
Ownership: Turner
Programming: animation

The Travel Channel
66 Newman Street
London W1P 3LAW1T 3EQ
Tel: 020 7636 5401
Fax: 020 7636 6424

email: enquiries@travelchannel.co.uk
Website: www.travelchannel.co.uk
Ownership: Landmark Communications [see MSP above]
Service start: 1 Feb 1994
Satellite: Astra 1E
Programming: travel

Travel Deals Direct
Tel: 08705 770063
Ownership: Landmark Communications [see MSP above]
Programming: home shopping (travel)

Trouble
160 Great Portland Street
London W1N 5TB
Tel: 020 7299 5000
Fax: 020 7299 6000
email: webmaster@trouble.co.uk
Website: www.trouble.co.uk
Ownership: Flextech Television [see MSP above]
Service start: February 1997
Satellite: Astra 1C (PAL/Videocrypt)2 South
Programming: general entertainment aimed at teenagers
email: webmaster@trouble.co.uk

Turner Classic Movies
Turner House
16 Great Marlborough St
London W1V 1AF
Tel: 020 7693 1000
Fax: 020 7693 1010
email: tcmmailuk@turner.com
Website: www.tcmonline.co.uk
Ownership: Turner Broadcasting [see MSP above]
Service start: Sept 1993
Satellite: Astra 2A
Programming: movies

TV Job Shop
Units 1-4 Archers Court
48 Masons Hill
Bromley BR2 9JG
Tel: 020 8461 8461
Fax: 020 8461 8403
email: info@tv-jobshop.com
Website: www.tvjobshop.co.uk
Ownership: TV Jobshop Ltd
Service start: Sept 2000
Satellite: Astra 2B
Programming: employment related programming

TV Shop
Admail 68
Plymouth PL1 1AD
Tel: 0800 975 8904
Fax: 01726 816401
email: customerserviceuk@tvshop.com
Website: www.tvshop.com
Ownership: Modern Times Group
Programming: home shopping

TV Travel Shop
45 Homesdale Road
Bromley, Kent BR2 9LY
Tel: 020 7691 6132
Fax: 020 7691 6392
email: admin@tvtravelshop.ltd.uk
Website: www.tvtravelshop.com
Service start: 4 Apr 1998
Satellite: Astra 2A
Programming: holiday and travel home shopping

TV Travel Shop 2
see above
Service start: 2000
Satellite: Astra 2A
Programming: holiday and travel home shopping

TV Warehouse
Chalfont Grove
Narcot Lane
Chalfont St Peter
Buckinghamshire SL9 8TW
Tel: 0800 052 0300
Fax: 01494 878076
email: info@tv-warehouse.co.uk
Website: www.tv-warehouse.co.uk
Ownership: Sirius Television Ltd
Satellite: Astra 2B
Programming: home shopping

TVBS Europe
Teddington Studios
Broom Road
Teddington
Middlesex TW11 9NT
Tel: 020 8614 8300
Fax: 020 8943 0982
Website: www.chinese-channel.co.uk
Satellite: Astra 1E (digital)
Programming: Chinese-language

TV Travel Shop
1st Floor
1 Stephen St
London W1P 1AL
Tel: 020 7691 6112
Website: www.tvtravelshop.co.uk
Service start: 4 April 1998
Satellite: Astra 1C
Also digital

TXT ME ;-)
Chalfont Grove
Narcot Lane
Chalfont St Peter
Buckinghamshire SL9 8TW
Tel: 0800 052 0300
Fax: 01494 878076
email: info@siriustv.net
Website: www.txtmetv.co.uk
Ownership: Sirius Television Ltd
Service start: 11 Dec 2001
Satellite: Astra 2B
Programming: mobile telephone ring tones and logos promotions

u>direct
6-7 Cross Street
London EC1N 8UA
Tel: 020 7242 7770
Fax: 020 7242 7776
Ownership: DBC Television Ltd
Service start: 8 Jul 1999
Programming: feature films, entertainment, sports

UK Bright Ideas
Unit 1 Genesis Business Park
Albert Drive
Woking
Surrey GU21 5RW
Tel: 01483 750 900
Fax: 01483 750901
Programming: documentaries

UK Drama
4th floor
160 Great Portland Street
London W1N 5TB5QA
Tel: 020 7299 5000
Fax: 020 7299 6000
Website: www.telewest.co.uk/flextech/ukdrama
Ownership: UKTV = BBC Worldwide, Flextech [see MSP above]
Service start: 31 March 2000
Satellite: Astra 2A
Programming: drama
Also digital

UK Food
see above
email: info@ukfood.tv
website: www.ukfood.tv
Service start: 5 Nov 2001
Satellite: Astra 2A
Programming: food

UK Gold/UK Gold 2
160 Great Portland Street
London W1N 5TB
Tel: 020 7299 5000
Fax: 020 7299 6000see above
Website: www.telewest.co.uk/flextech-www.telewest.co.uk/flextech/ukGold
Ownership: UKTV = BBC Worldwide, Flextech [see MSP above]
Service start: Nov 1992
Satellite: Astra 1B (PAL/Videocrypt)2A
Programming: entertainment
Also digital

UK History
See above

UK Home Style
See above

UK Horizons
160 Great Portland Street
London W1N 5TB
Tel: 020 7299 5000
Fax: 020 7299 6000see above
email: talkback@ukhorizons.co.uk
Website: www.telewest.co.uk/flex-techukhorizons.co.uk
Ownership: UKTV = BBC Worldwide, Flextech [see MSP above]
Satellite: Astra 1E2A
Programming: documentarieseduca-tional programs on natural history, travel, and science
Also digital

UK Style
160 Great Portland Street
London W1N 5TB
Tel: 020 7299 5000
Fax: 020 7299 6000see above
Website: www.telewest.co.uk/flex-techukstyle.tv
Ownership: UKTV = BBC Worldwide, Flextech [see MSP above]
Satellite: Astra 1E2A
Programming: lifestyle

Urbanchillers.tv
See Extreme Motion

The Vault
37 Harwood Road
London SW6 4QP
Tel: 020 7384 2243
Fax: 020 7384 2026
Website:www.chartshow.com
Ownership: Chartshow TV Channels Ltd.
Programming: music

Vectone TV Channels 1-9
58 Marsh Wall
London E14 9TP
Tel: 020 7170 0400
Fax: 020 7170 0419
Website: www.vectonetv.com
Programming: general entertainment

VH-1
180 Oxford Street
London W1N 0DS
Tel: 020 7284 7777
Fax: 020 7284 7788
Website: www.vh1online.co.uk
Ownership: MTV Networks = Viacom (100%)
Satellite: Astra 1B (PAL/encrypted)Astra 2A
Programming: pop music

VH1 Classic
see above
Satellite: Astra 2A
Programming: music and general entertainment

Viasat Explorer
Horton Road
West Drayton
Middlesex UB7 8JD
Tel: 01895 433211
Website: www.viasat.co.uk
Programming: genneral entertain-ment

Vibe TV
Unit 2D
Eagle Road
Mons Moat North Industrial Estate
Redditch B98 9HF
Tel: 01527 406 108
Fax: 01527 406 112
Ownership: Eagle Road Studios Ltd
Satellite: Astra 2 South
Programming: self-promotional videos

Vision Channel
Vision (SN237)
FREEPOST
Swindon SN1 3SJ
Tel: 01793 511244
Fax: 01795 511211
email: info@visionchannel.co.uk
Website: www.visionchannel.co.uk
Ownership: Vision Broadcasting Communications
Satellite: Eurobird
Programming: Christian

Vision Salon
See Music Box

The Weather Channel
66 Newman Street
London W1P 3PG
Tel: 020 7665 0600
Fax: 020 7665 0601
Website: www.weather.co.uk
Ownership: Landmark Communications
Programming: weather forecasts and information

Wellbeing see Discovery Wellbeing

Zee Cinema
Unit 7-9
Belvue Business Centre
Belvue Road
Northolt
Middlesex UB5 5QQ
Tel: 020 8839 4012
Fax: 020 8841 9550
email: uk@zeetelevision.com
Website: www.zeetelevision.com
Ownership: Asia TV Ltd
Satellite: Astra 2A, 2B
Programming: feature films [sub-scription]

Zee Music
see above
Programming: music [subscription]

Zee TV Europe
Unit 5-97-9
Belvue Business Centre
Belvue Road
Northolt
Middlesex UB5 5QQ
Tel: 020 8839 40000
Fax: 020 8842 32238845 8603
email: info@zeetv.co.uk
Website: www.zeetelevision.com
Ownership: Asia TV Ltd
Service start: March 1995
Satellite: Astra 1E (PAL/Videocrypt)2A, 2B
Programming: films, discussions, news, game shows in Hindi, Punjabi, Urdu, Bengali, Tamil, English, etc [subscription]

DIGITAL TELEVISION

BBC Digital Services

TV Centre
Wood Lane
London W12 7RJ
Tel: 020 8743 800008700 100 123
website: www.bbc..co.uk/digital
All the BBC's digital services are funded by the licence fee and are therefore non-subscription

Freeview

2nd Floor
85 Tottenham Court Road
London W1T 4DU
Tel: 08708 80 99 80
Website: www.freeview.co.uk
Freeview is marketed by DTV Services Ltd which is a company run by its three shareholders the BBC, Crown Castle International and BSkyB. DTV Services Ltd has been established to promote Freeview by utilising the complementary skills and expertise of the BBC, Crown Castle International and BSkyB respectively. Responsibility for the programmes shown on Freeview however remains with the channels providing those programmes.
Crown Castle International
Website: www.crowncastle.com
Crown Castle International is the world's leading independent owner and operator of shared wireless communications and broadcast infrastructure. Crown Castle engineers, deploys, owns and operates technologically advanced shared wireless infrastructure, including extensive networks of towers and rooftops as well as analog and Digital Radio and television broadcast transmission systems.

Sky Digital

6 Centaurs Business Park
Grant Way
Syon Lane
Isleworth
Middlesex TW7 5QD
Tel: 0870 240 3000
Fax: 020 7705 30300870 240 3060
email: skydigital@sky.com
Website: www.skydigital.com.uk

CAREERS AND TRAINING

Compiled by Sean Delaney and David Sharp, with Nina Bishop

Careers

Information about careers in the media industries is available from a number of sources and we have provided details of some of these in this section, but you should note no-one is likely to provide individually-tailored information. The most exciting development for young people hoping to get into the industry is the emergence of the skillsformedia helpline and website (see below).

Many people are attracted to the media industries because they seem glamorous, but they can be difficult to get into, and the recent difficulties that the digital television sector has experienced shows that the market is volatile. Anyone wanting to work in these industries should be open to the idea of using ICT and should anticipate the need to update their skills regularly, and offering a range of skills rather than just one may be to an applicant's benefit.

It is important that anyone considering working in the industry takes care to investigate what courses are available that will help prepare the way, and if possible, although this is rarely easy, talks to someone already doing the kind of job you want.

You may discover that they managed to "get a foot in the door" and then using initiative and skill worked their way towards the job they now have: this may indicate that formal qualifications are only part of the picture, but you can be fairly certain that such people have had to work and train hard, possibly for little reward, and that this kind of opportunity is becoming less common.

Sources for company contacts

It is still a common practice for prospective employees to solicit work through mailing their CV. There are online sources (visit the Contacts section at www.bfi.org.uk/gateway) but these are not as comprehensive as those in the standard directories for the UK film, television and video industries.

These sources include:
BFI Film and Television Handbook
Kay's UK Production Manual
Kemp's Film and Television Yearbook
The Knowledge
PACT Directory
Production Guide

Although the PACT directory contains a modest amount of companies, its listings are very thorough and detailed. They include company personnel and production credits both past and projected. It also contains very handy indexes including one of production company by programme type (eg comedy, documentary etc). It is also a good deal cheaper than its peers but remains steadfastly in hard copy and its contents are not available on the web, unlike some others (eg www.theknowledgeonline.com)

Sources for jobs: Newspapers and Journals

Saturday and Monday edition of the *Guardian* contain a Creative, Media and Sales Jobs section in its Media supplement, which is well worth consulting. The trades such as *Broadcast* and *Screen International* also contain job adverts, but these tend to be aimed at people already in the industry.

The next step is to consult the specialist subscription listings. However, they tend to be very expensive. Below are the four main listings which are available from the *bfi* National Library.

PCR (Production and Casting Report)

PCR
PO Box 100
Broadstairs
Kent CT10 1UJ
Tel: 01843 860885
Fax: 01843 866538
Website: www.pcrnewsletter.com
Weekly detailed listing for upcoming film, television and theatre productions seeking cast. Back page lists casting directors for ongoing feature productions and upcoming/long-running TV programmes. May need to be used in conjunction with Who's Where directory available from PCR

Filmlog

FromPCR (as above)
Brief listing of films in production and pre-production listed as seeking cast and crew. Needs to be used in conjunction with Who's Where directory available from PCR

Film News

Profile Group
6-7 St Cross Street
London EC1N 8UA
Tel: 020 7405 44455
email: info@entnews.co.uk
Website: entnews.co.uk
Contains two sections: A Calendar (including events, releases and birthdays) and an Index of Productions with calendar for UK based and international productions including contact details

Programme News (Bulletin)

Profile Group (as above)
Tel: 020 7440 8558
email: info@programmenews.co.uk
Website: www.programmenews.co.uk
Listing of upcoming television programmes and reported stage of development. Contains contact details

The Jobs

The media industry contains a wide range of jobs, some of which have equivalents in other sectors (eg accountant; librarian), but many of which are highly specialized, some with strange sounding and misleading names (best boy; gaffer). Increasingly, ICT will play a major part in many media industry jobs.

Bibliography

The select list of books below, based on BFI National Library holdings, should give you some guidance about the kinds of jobs that exist and the structure of the industry, and in some cases will offer help preparing a CV. Your local reference library may stock some of these (and others), but some titles are expensive.

Websites

We have listed some organizations that are involved in training in our sector, and where known a web address.

There are two websites we strongly commend: one is skillsformedia, developed jointly by Skillset and BECTU, and the other is that of Skillset themselves (see entries below).

What to read

A CAREERS HANDBOOK FOR TV, RADIO, FILM, VIDEO & INTERACTIVE MEDIA
Llewellyn, **Shiona**
A&C Black, 2000
ISBN 0713656981

GETTING INTO FILMS & TELEVISION
Angell, Robert
How To Books, **7th ed, 2002,**
ISBN 1857037715

LIGHTS, CAMERA, ACTION! CAREERS IN FILM, TELEVISION, VIDEO
Langham, Josephine
BFI, 2nd ed., 1997
ISBN 0851705731

MAKING ACTING WORK
Salt, Chrys
Bloomsbury, 1997
ISBN 0747535957

RESEARCH FOR MEDIA PRODUCTION
Chater, Kathy
2nd ed, Oxford: Focal Press, 2002
ISBN 02405 16486

STORY: SUBSTANCE, STRUCTURE AND STYLE AND THE PRINCIPLES OF SCREENWRITING
McKee, Robert
Methuen, 1998
ISBN 04137 15507

Courses

Part of our website gives information on courses: www.bfi.org.uk/mediacourses

This has replaced Media Courses UK, which is discontinued, and covers short and long course information. You need to consider what balance you need between practical, theory and academic, and plan accordingly. Decide what qualifications and skills you want to acquire, check who validates the course, and for practical courses, what equipment is available to learn with. The location of the course and its cost are also likely to be key factors to check.

MEDIA AND MULTIMEDIA SHORT COURSES
Orton, Lavinia
BFI/Skillset (3 issues per year, but the content is included in the website)

FLOODLIGHT
(covers the Greater London region) available in newsagents and libraries. Other local guides to courses may be worth checking via a local library.

Courses Abroad

VARIETY INTERNATIONAL FILM GUIDE
Cowie, Peter, ed.
This annual guide includes an international film schools section

WHERE TO GET MULTIMEDIA TRAINING IN EUROPE
Institut National de L' Audiovisuel
4th edition CIDJ 1999
ISBN 2869381360

CILECT (Centre International de Liaison Ecoles de Cinema et de Télévision)

8 rue Theresienne
1000 Bruxelles
Belgique
Tel: 00 32 2 511 98 39
Fax: 00 32 2 511 98 39
Website: www.cilect.org
Contact: Executive Secretary, Henry Verhasselt.
email: hverh.cilect@skynet.be

Training Organisations

4 Skills

C/0 4th Floor
Warwick House
9 Warwick Street
London W1R 5LY
Tel: 020 7734 5141
Fax: 020 787 9899
email: ft2@ft2.org.uk
Website: www.ft2.org.uk
Sharon Goode
Managed by ft2, this is Channel 4's biennial training programme for people from ethnic minority backgrounds wishing to train as new entrants in junior production grades

ARTTS Skillcentre

Highfield Grange
Bubwith
North Yorkshire YO8 6DP
Tel: 01757 288088
Fax:01757 288253
email: admin@artts.co.uk
Website: web. www.artts.co.uk
ARTTS Skillcenter offers a fully residential, one-year training course for Theatre, Film, Television and Radio. Trainees have the opportunity to specialise in Acting, Directing or

Production Operations. The courses are 100 per cent practical and hands-on. Courses commence in April and October each year

Cyfle (& Media Skills Wales)

Gronant, Penrallt Isaf
Caernarfon, Gwynedd
LL55 1NS
Tel: 01286 671000
Fax: 01286 678831
email: post@cyfle.co.uk
Website: www.cyfle.co.uk
This organisation supports the training needs of the Welsh film and television industry
Cyfle
Crichton House
11-12 Mount Stuart Square
Cardiff CF10 5EE

Film Education

Film Education
2nd Floor
21-22 Poland Street
London W1F 8QQ
Tel: 020 7851 9450
Fax: 020 7439 3218
email: postbox@filmeducation.org
Website: www.filmeducation.org
Useful general background on how films are put together, generally as part of their study packs on particular titles

FT2 - Film & Television Freelance Training

4th Floor
Warwick House
9 Warwick Street
London W1R 5LY
Tel: 020 7734 5141
Fax: 020 787 9899
email: ft2@ft2.org.uk
Website: www.ft2.org.uk
Sharon Goode
FT2 is the only UK-wide provider of new entrant training for young people wishing to enter the freelance sector of the industry in the junior construction, production and technical grades. Funded by the Skillset Investment Funds, European Social Fund and Channel 4, FT2 is the largest industry managed training provider in its field and has a 100 per cent record of people graduating from the scheme and entering the industry. FT2 is also an approved Assessment Centre and offers assessment to industry practitioners for the Skillset Professional Qualifications

Gaelic Television Training Trust

Sabhal Mor Ostaig
An Teanga
Isle of Skye, IV44 8RQ
Tel: 01471 888 000
Fax: 01471 888 001
Website: www.smo.uhi.ac.uk
Catriona Niclain

Intermedia Film and Video

19 Heathcote Street
Nottingham NG1 3AF
Tel: 0115 955 6909
Fax: 0115 955 9956
email: info@intermedianotts.co.uk
Website: intermedianotts.co.uk
Ceris Morris, Director
East Midlands leading production agency offers training courses, seminars and workshops each year - targeting everyone from new entrants to established producers

Lighthouse

9-12 Middle Street
Brighton BN1 1AL
Tel: 01273 384222
Fax: 01273 384233
Email: info@lighthouse.org.uk
Website: www.lighthouse.org.uk
Training and production centre providing courses, facilities, and production advice. Bursaries offered 3 times a year

Media Training North West

Rm G082
BBC
Oxford Road
Manchester M60 1SJ
Tel: 0161 244 4637
Fax: 0161 2444198
email: info@mtnw.co.uk
Website: www.mtnw.co.uk
Lynne McCadden
Regional training body with a brief to develop a training strategy for those who already have industry experience

National Film & Television School

National Short Course Training Programme
Beaconsfield Film Studios
Station Road,
Beaconsfield,
Bucks, HP9 1LG
Tel: 01494 677903
Fax: 01494 678708
email: info@nfts-scu.org.uk
Website: www.nftsfilm-tv.ac.uk
Deanne Edwards
Short course training for people already working in the industry

Northern Film and Media

Central Square
Forth Street
Newcastle-upon-Tyne NE1 3PT
Tel: 0191 269 9200
Fax: 0191 269 9213
email: training@northernmedia.org
Website: www.northernmedia.org
Annie Wood

Northern Ireland Film and Television Commission (NIFTC)

3rd Floor
Alfred House
21 Alfred Street
Belfast BT2 8ED
Tel: 01232 232444
Fax: 01232 239918
email: info@niftc.co.uk
Website: www.niftc.co.uk

Panico London Ltd

PO Box 496
London WC1A 2WZ
Tel: 020 7485 3533
Fax: 020 7485 3533
email: panico@panicofilms.com
Website: www.panicofilms.com
Panico courses include: Foundations Course - designed to give students an overall view and practical experience of the filmmaking process. It is spread over six days either six saturdays or six sundays. The aim of the course is to give students enough knowledge and practical experience to be able to undertake their own productions. The course also gives students an insight into the working conditions, practices and opportunities in the British Film Industry. Students gain experience working in both video and film formats, and get practical experience in drama and documentary film. Panico also runs a number of advanced courses for individuals who already have some experience of filmmaking

Scottish Screen Training

Second Floor
249 West George Street
Glasgow G2 4QE
Tel: 0141 302 1778
Fax: 0141 302 1711
email: info@scottishscreen.com
Website: www.scottishscreen.com

Screen East Training Department

Anglia House
Norwich NR1 3JG
Tel: 01603 756860
email: training@screeneast.co.uk
Website: www.screeneast.co.uk

Skillsformedia.com

Tel: 08080 300 900
Available to anyone wanting to get in or get on in the media. The website has games, case studies and resources to investigate. A joint initiative from Skillset and BECTU. Scotland only, in partnership with learndirect: Telephone 08081 008 094 for industry careers advice

Skillset

Prospect House
80-110 New Oxford Street
London WC1A 1HB
Tel: 020 7520 5757
Fax: 020 7520 5758
email: info@skillset.org
Website: www.skillset.org
Skillset is the sector skills council for broadcast film and video

Skillstrain South East

c/o Skillset (see above)
Contact: Tricia Bolland

South West Screen

The Regional Training Consortium for the South West
59 Prince Street
Bristol BS1 4QH
Tel: 0117 925 4011
Fax: 0117 925 3511
email: info@swscreenco.uk
Website: www.skillnetsouthwest.com
Jules Channer, Amanda Doughty

Yorkshire Media Training Consortium

40 Hanover Square
Leeds LS3 1BR
Tel: 0113 294 4410
Fax: 0113 294 4989
email: info@ymtc.co.uk
Website: www.ymtc.co.uk
A regional agency, YMTC is concerned to develop a strategy to identify, develop and provide training for those who are already working within the industry in the region

Additionally all the Regional Arts Councils and Media Development Agencies are involved with or have information on training. These are listed in the separate section of this handbook under Funding

Paying Your Way

It is important to be clear on the cost of any course you embark on and sources of grants or other funding. Generally speaking short courses do not attract grants, but your local authority or careers office may be able to advise on this. Check directories of sources for grants at your local library. The main ones are the Directory of Grant-Making Trusts, Directory of Small Grant-Making Trusts, Charities Action Foundation.
Learn Direct may also be able to advise. They are on 0800 100 900 with a (multilingual) website at **www.learndirect.co.uk**. (Learn Direct, PO Box 900, Manchester M60 3LE)

CINEMAS

Listed below are the companies who control the major cinema chains and multiplexes in the UK, followed by the cinemas themselves listed by county and town, and including seating capacities (permanent wheelchair spaces are not generally included in the totals because of the difficulties in obtaining consistent data). The listing also includes some disabled access information. Many websites have now been added and others will follow in future editions. Revised by Allen Eyles

KEY TO SYMBOLS

P/T Part-time screenings
S/O Seasonal openings

DISABILITY CODES

West End/Outer London

E Hearing aid system installed. Always check with venue whether in operation
W Venue with unstepped access (via main or side door), wheelchair space and adapted lavatory
X Venue with flat or one step or lift access to auditoria
A Venue with 2-5 steps to auditoria
G Provision for Guide Dogs

England/Channel Islands/ Scotland/Wales/ Northern Ireland

X Accessible to people with disabilities (advance arrangements sometimes necessary - please phone cinemas to check)
E Hearing aid system installed. Always check with venue whether in operation

The help of Artsline, London's Information and Advice Service for Disabled People on Arts & Entertainment, in producing this section, including the use of their coding system for venues in the Greater London area, is gratefully acknowledged.

CINEMA CIRCUITS

Apollo Cinemas
Houston House
12 Sceptre Court
Sceptre Point
Preston
Lancs PR5 6AW
Tel: 01772 323544
Fax: 01772 323545
Website: www.apollocinemas.co.uk
11 cinemas with 56 screens in the northwest of England, Wales, Yorkshire and the Midlands, and a 9 screen multiplex at Paignton, Devon. A five-screen cinema called the Apollo West End will be opened in the redevelopment of the Plaza Piccadilly Circus site in London's West End. Two further screens will be added at both Leamington and Stafford by December 2003, and new 7-screen cinemas will be opened at Altrincham, Crewe and Worksop in the autumn of 2004

Artificial Eye Film Company
14 King Street
London WC2E 8HN
Tel: 020 7240 5353
Fax: 020 7240 5242
Film distributors operating the Chelsea Cinema and Renoir in London's West End

Cine-UK Ltd
Chapter House
22 Chapter Street
London SW1P 4NP
Tel: 020 7932 2200
Fax: 020 7932 2222
Website: www.cineworld.co.uk
Operates 30 Cineworld multiplexes in mid-2003 with six other sites scheduled to open by December 2004

City Screen
Hardy House
16 -18 Beak Street
London W1F 9RD
Tel: 020 7734 4342
Fax: 020 7734 4027
Website: www.picturehouses.co.uk
Operates Picturehouses at 18 locations: Aberdeen (The Belmont), Bath (Little Theatre), Brighton (Duke of York's), Brixton (Ritzy), Cambridge (Arts), Clapham, East Grinstead, Edinburgh (Cameo), Exeter, Ely (The Maltings), Liverpool (FACT), London West End (The Other Cinema), Notting Hill (Gate), Oxford (Phoenix), Southampton (Harbour Lights) Stratford upon Avon, Stratford East (London) and York (City Screen)

Graves (Cumberland) Ltd
8 Falcon Place
Workington
Cumbria CA14 2EX
Tel: 01900 64791
Fax: 01900 601625
Established 1910. Four sites in Cumbria including a multiplex at Workington

Hollywood Screen Entertainment
41 London Road South
Lowestoft
Suffolk NR33 0AS
Tel: 01502 564567
Website: www.hollywoodcinemas.net
Operate cinemas in Dereham, Fakenham, Great Yarmouth,Lowestoft and Norwich

Mainline Pictures
37 Museum Street
London WC1A 1LP
Tel: 020 7242 5523
Fax: 020 7430 0170
Website: www.screencinemas.co.uk
Screen cinemas at Baker Street, Haverstock Hill, Islington Green, Oxted, Reigate, Walton-on-Thames and Winchester with a total of 11 screens

National Amusements (UK)
Showcase Cinema
Redfield Way
Lenton
Nottingham NG27 2UW
Tel: 0115 986 2508
Website: www.showcasecinemas.co.uk
Operates 19 Showcase multiplex cinemas in July 2003

Northern Morris Associated Cinemas
Eller Howe Farm,

Lindale,
Grange Over Sands
Cumbria LA11 6NA
Tel/fax: 015395 35735
Website: www.nm-cinemas.co.uk
Operates the Royalty Bowness-on-Windermere, Rex Elland, Picture House Keighley, Regal Lancaster and Plaza Skipton as well as booking the Grand Clitheroe

Odeon Cinemas
54 Whitcomb Street
London WC2H 7DN
Tel: 0207 321 0404
Fax: 0207 321 0357
Website: www.odeon.co.uk
97 cinemas with 608 screens in June 2003

Reeltime Cinemas
Carlton
Westgate-on-Sea Kent
St Mildreds Road CT8 8RE
Tel: 01843 834290
Based at the Carlton Westgate-on-Sea, Reeltime also operates Bognor Regis Picturedrome, Bristol Orpheus, Cannock Picture House, Cosham Carlton, Dorchester Plaza, Herne Bay Kavanagh, Margate Dreamland, Ryde Commodore and Sittingbourne New Century

Scott Cinemas
Alexandra
Newton Abbot
Devon
Tel: 01626 65368
West Country circuit

Ster Century Europe
3rd floor, St. George's House
Knoll Road, Camberley
Surrey GU15 3SY
Tel: 01276 605 605
Fax: 01276 605 600
Website: www.stercentury.com
This subsidiary of South Africa's Ster Kinekor operates multiplexes at Basingstoke, Cardiff, Edinburgh (Leith), Leeds, Norwich and Romford

UCI Cinemas
7th Floor, Lee House
90 Great Bridgewater Street
Manchester M1 5JW
Tel: 0161 455 4000
Fax: 0161 455 4076
Website: www.uci-cinemas.co.uk
This American partnership between the Paramount and Universal film companies operates 37 purpose-built multiplexes in the UK plus the Empire in London's West End

UGC Cinemas
6th Floor, Adelaide House
626 High Road, Chiswick
London W4 5RY
Tel: 020 8987 5000
Fax: 020 8742 7984
Website: www.ugccinemas.co.uk
The UK circuit of this leading French film company consists of 37 multiplexes and 5 subdivided traditional cinemas in UK in June 2003 with a total of 390 screens

Vue Entertainment Group
Conduit House
309-317 Chiswick High Road
London W4 4HH
Tel: 01208 996 9920
Fax: 0208 996 9930
Website: www.myvue.com
This combines the SBC (Spean Bridge) multiplexes at Aberdeen, Hamilton, Livingston and Southport with the recently acquired Warner Village circuit (42 cinemas, 405 screens) which will be rebranded as Vue cinemas

Ward-Anderson Cinema Group
Film House
35 Upper Abbey Street, Dublin 1
Ireland
Tel: (353) 1 872 3422/3922
Fax: (353) 1 872 3687
Leading cinema operator in Northern and Southern Ireland. Sites include Ballymena, Belfast, Londonderry, Lisburn and Newry plus one in England at Borehamwood, Hertfordshire

West Coast Cinemas
Studio, John Street
Dunoon
Strathclyde
Scotland
Tel: 01369 704545
Operate cinemas in Dunoon, Greenock and Fort William

WTW Cinemas
Regal, The Platt
Wadebridge
Cornwall PL27 7AD
Tel: 01208 812791
Operates Wadebridge Regal, St Austell Film Centre, Truro Plaza and Padstow Cinedrome

LONDON WEST END

Baker Street
Screen on Baker Street, Baker Street, NW1
Tel: 020 7935 2772
Seats: 1:95, 2:100

Bayswater
UCI Whiteleys, Queensway, W2
WG
Tel: 08700 102030
Website: www.uci-cinemas.co.uk
Seats: 1:333, 2:281, 3:196, 4:178, 5:154, 6:138, 7:147, 8:125

Bloomsbury
Renoir, Brunswick Square, WC1
Tel: 020 7837 8402
Seats: 1:251, 2:251

Chelsea
Chelsea Cinema, Kings Road, SW3
Tel: 020 7351 3742
Seats: 713

UGC, Kings Road, SW3
Tel: 020 737 64744/0870 9070710
Website: www.ugccinemas.co.uk
Seats: 1:220, 2:238, 3:122, 4:111

City of London
Barbican Centre, Silk Street, EC2
WE
Tel: 020 7382 7000
Website: www.barbican.org.uk/film
Seats: 1:288, 2:255

Fulham Road
UGC, Fulham Road, SW10
Tel: 0207 370 2110/0870 9070719
Website: www.ugccinemas.co.uk
Seats: 1:348 X, 2:329 X, 3:173 X, 4:203 X, 5:218, 6:154

Haverstock Hill
Screen on the Hill, Haverstock Hill, NW3
A
Tel: 020 7435 3366/9787
Seats: 339

Haymarket
UGC, Haymarket, SW1
W
Tel: 0207 930 6196/0870 9070712
Website: www.ugccinemas.co.uk
Seats: 1:448, 2:200, 3:201

Islington
Screen on the Green, Upper Street, Islington, N1
A
Tel: 020 7226 3520
Seats: 280

Warner Village, Parkfield Street, Islington, N1
Tel: 0870 240 6020
X
Seats: 1:293, 2:140, 3:150, 4:103, 5:106, 6:159, 7:200, 8:198, 9:446

Kensington

Odeon, Kensington High Street, W8
Tel: 0870 50 50 007
Website: www.odeon.co.uk
Seats: 1:520, 2:66, 3:91, 4:266 X, 5:172 X, 6:204 X

Leicester Square

Empire Leicester Square, WC2
Tel: 08700 102030
Seats: 1:1,330 X, 2:353, 3:77

Odeon Leicester Square, WC2
Tel: 0870 50 50 007
Website: www.odeon.co.uk
Seats: 1,943 EX; Mezzanine: 1:60 W, 2:50, 3:60, 4:60, 5:60

Odeon Panton Street, SW1
Tel: 0870 50 50 007
Website: www.odeon.co.uk
Seats: 1:127 X, 2:143 X, 3:138, 4:133

Odeon Wardour Street, Swiss Centre, W1
Tel: 0870 50 50 007
Website: www.odeon.co.uk
Seats: 1:97, 2:101, 3:93, 4:108

Odeon West End, Leicester Square, WC2
E
Tel: 0870 50 50 007
Website: www.odeon.co.uk
Seats: 1:500, 2:832

Prince Charles, Leicester Place, WC2
X
Tel: 020 7437 8181
Seats: 488

Warner Village West End, Cranbourne Street, WC2
X
Tel: 08702 40 60 20
Seats: 1:187, 2:126, 3:300, 4:298, 5:414, 6:264, 7:410, 8:180, 9:303

The Mall

ICA, The Mall, SW1
AG
Tel: 020 7930 3647
Website: www.ica.org.uk
Seats: 185, C'théque: 45

Marble Arch

Odeon, Edgware Road, W1
E
Tel: 0870 50 50 007
Website: www.odeon.co.uk
Seats: 1:254, 2:119, 3:171, 4:229, 5:239

Mayfair

Curzon Mayfair, Curzon Street, W1
Tel: 020 7495 0500
Website: www.curzoncinemas.com
Seats: 1:320, 2:83

Notting Hill

Coronet, Notting Hill Gate, W11
A
Tel: 020 7727 6705
Seats: 1:388, 2:147

Electric, Portobello Road, W11
X
Tel: 020 7908 9696
Website: www.electriccinema.co.uk
Seats: 220 plus sofas

Gate, Notting Hill Gate, W11
Tel: 020 7727 4043
Seats: 240

Piccadilly Circus

Apollo West End, Lower Regent Street
Seats: 1:202, 2:102, 3:102, 4:85, 5:45 (Scheduled to open in March 2004)

The Other Cinema, Rupert Street, W1
W
Tel: 020 7734 1506
Website: www.picturehouse-cinemas.co.uk
Seats: 1:195, 2:84

Shaftesbury Avenue

Curzon Soho, Shaftesbury Avenue, W1
Tel: 0871 871 0022
Website: www.curzoncinemas.com
Seats: 1:249, 2:110, 3:130

Odeon Covent Garden, Shaftesbury Avenue, WC2
Tel: 0870 50 50 007
Website: www.odeon.co.uk
Seats: 1:153, 2:269, 3:167, 4:152

UGC, Shaftesbury Avenue at The Trocadero, W1
W
Tel: 0207 434 0032/0870 907 0716
Website: www.ugccinemas.co.uk
Seats: 1:548, 2:240, 3:146, 4:154, 5:122, 6:94, 7:89

South Kensington

Ciné Lumiére, French Institute, Queensberry Place, SW7
(P/T)
Tel: 020 7838 2144/2146
Website: www.institut-francais.org.uk
Seats: 350

Goethe Institute, 50 Princes Gate, Exhibition Rd, SW7 (P/T)
Tel: 020 7596 4000
Seats: 170

IMAX, Science Museum, Exhibition Road
Tel: 0870 870 4771
Seats: 450

Tottenham Court Road

Odeon, Tottenham Court Road, W1
Tel: 0870 50 50 007
Website: www.odeon.co.uk
Seats: 1:328, 2:145, 3:137

Waterloo

bfi London IMAX, Charlie Chaplin Walk, SE1
Tel: 020 7902 1234
Seats: 482

National Film Theatre, South Bank, Waterloo, SE1
WE
Tel: 020 7928 3232
Website: www.bfi.org.uk/nft
Seats: 1:450, 2:162, 3:134

Royal Festival Hall, South Bank, Waterloo, SE1 (P/T)
X
Tel: 020 7928 3002
Seats: 2,419

OUTER LONDON

Acton
Warner Village, Royale Leisure Park, Park Royal
W
Tel: 020 8896 0099
Seats: 1:425, 2:159, 3:205, 4:274, 5:314, 6:274, 7:205, 8:159, 9:425

Barnet
Odeon, Great North Road
Tel: 0870 50 50 007
Website: www.odeon.co.uk
Seats: 1:532 E, 2:182, 3:182, 4:187 W, 5:155

Beckenham
Odeon, High Street
Tel: 0870 50 50 007
Website: www.odeon.co.uk
Seats: 1:471, 2:207, 3:113. 4:190, 5:168. 6:119

Bexleyheath
Cineworld, The Broadway
W
Tel: 020 8303 0015
Website: www.cineworld.co.uk
Seats: 1:157, 2:128, 3:280, 4:244, 5:88, 6:84, 7:111, 8:168, 9:221

Brentford
Watermans Arts Centre, High Street
WEG
Tel: 020 8232 1010
Seats: 240

Brixton
Ritzy, Brixton Oval, Coldharbour Lane, SW2
Tel: 020 7733 2229
Seats: 1:353, 2:179, 3:125, 4:108, 5:84

Bromley
Odeon, High Street
Tel: 0870 50 50 007
Website: www.odeon.co.uk
Seats: 1:392, 2:124 X, 3:105 X, 4:277

Camden Town
Odeon, Parkway
Tel: 0870 50 50 007
Website: www.odeon.co.uk
Seats: 1:403, 2:92, 3:238, 4:90, 5:103

Clapham
Picturehouse, Venn Street, SW4
Tel: 020 7498 3323
Website:
www.picturehouse.cinemas.co.uk
Seats: 1:202, 2:153 X, 3:134 X, 4:115

Croydon
(see also Purley Way)
David Lean, Clock Tower, Katherine St
X
Tel: 020 8253 1030
Seats: 68

Fairfield Halls/Ashcroft Theatre, Park Lane (P/T)
Tel: 020 8688 9291
Seats: Fairfield: 1,552 WEG, Ashcroft: 750

Safari, London Road
Tel: 020 8688 3422
Seats: 1:650, 2:399 X, 3:187 X

Warner Village, Grant's
W
Tel: 0870 240 6020
Seats: 1:171, 2:194, 3:178, 4:106, 5:88, 6:398, 7:170, 8:131, 9:167, 10:224

Dagenham
Warner Village, Dagenham Leisure Park, Cook Road
W
Tel: 020 8592 2211
Seats: 1:404, 2:146, 3:189, 4:252, 5:305, 6:252, 7:189

Dalston
Rio, Kingsland High Street, E8
WEG
Tel: 020 7241 9410
Seats: 405

Ealing
UGC, Uxbridge Road, W5
E
Tel: 0208 579 4851/0870 907 0719
Website: www.ugccinemas.co.uk
Seats: 1:576, 2:371, 3:193

East Finchley
Phoenix, High Road, N2
XG
Tel: 020 8444 6789
Seats: 308

East Ham
Boleyn, Barking Road
Tel: 020 8471 4884
Seats: 1:800, 2:250, 3:250

Elephant and Castle
Coronet, New Kent Road (P/T)
Seats: 572
(Awaiting licence in summer 2003)

Enfield
UGC, Southbury Leisure Park, Southbury Road
WE
Tel: 0208 366 1550/0870 90 70 745
Website: www.ugccinemas.co.uk
Seats: 1:156, 2: 270, 3:236, 4:186, 5:156, 6:192, 7:277, 8:522, 9:273, 10:203, 11:156, 12:270, 13:236, 14:186, 15:98

Feltham
Cineworld, Leisure West, Browells Lane
W
Tel: 020 8867 0888
Website: www.cineworld.co.uk
Seats: 1:104, 2:116, 3:132, 4:205, 5:253, 6:351, 7:302, 8:350, 9:265, 10:90, 11:112, 12: 137, 13:124, 14:99

Finchley Road
Warner Village, 02 Centre
W
Tel: 08702 40 60 20/020 7604 3066
Seats: 1:359, 2:324, 3:159, 4:261, 5:376, 6:258, 7:134, 8:86

Fulham Broadway
Warner Village, Fulham Broadway Retail Centre, Fulham Road
W
Tel: 08702 40 60 20
Seats: 1:127, 2:316, 3:316, 4:187, 5:163, 6:560, 7:310, 8:242, 9:136

Greenwich
The FilmWorks, Bugsby's Way
W
Tel: 08700 10 20 30
Seats: 1:115, 2:138, 3:157, 4:178, 5:178, 6:157, 7:138, 8:115, 9:279, 10:338, 11:372, 12:261, 13:44, 14:44

Hammersmith
UGC, King Street, W6
E
Tel: 0208 748 2388/0870 907 0718
Website: www.ugccinemas.co.uk
Seats: 1:322, 2:322, 3:268 A, 4:268 A

Riverside Studios, Crisp Road, W6
E
Tel: 020 8237 1111
Seats: 200

Hampstead
Everyman, Holly Bush Vale, NW3
X
Tel: 020 7431 1777
Seats: 184

Harrow
Safari, Station Road
Tel: 020 8426 0606
Seats: 1:612, 2:133

Warner Village, St George's Centre, St. Anne's Road
W
Tel: 020 8427 9900/9944
Seats: 1:347, 2:288, 3:424, 4:296, 5:121, 6:109, 7:110, 8:87, 9:96

Hayes
Beck Theatre, Grange Road (P/T)
XE
Tel: 020 8561 8371
Seats: 518

Holloway
Odeon, Holloway Road, N7
Tel: 0870 50 50 007
Website: www.odeon.co.uk
Seats: 1:330, 2:315, 3:72, 4:231, 5:183, 6:249, 7:92, 8:103

Ilford
Cineworld, i-scene, Clements Road
WE
Tel: 020 8911 2900/8553 5599
Website: www.cineworld.co.uk
Seats: 1:433, 2:362, 3:278, 4:204, 5:111.6:122, 7:180, 8:191, 9:114, 10:95, 11:146

Kilburn
Tricycle Cinema, High Road
Tel: 020 7328 1000
Seats: 280

Kingston-on-Thames
Odeon, Rotunda Leisure Centre, Clarence Street
W
Tel: 0870 50 50 007
Website: www.odeon.co.uk
Seats: 1:199, 2:431, 3:112, 4:186, 5:178, 6:146, 7:308, 8:118, 9:161, 10:182, 11:256, 12:183, 13:339, 14: 217

Lambeth
Imperial War Museum, Lambeth Road, SE1 (P/T)
X
Tel: 020 7735 8922/7416 5320
Seats: 216

Lee Valley
UCI, Picketts Lock Lane, Meridian Way, Edmonton
W
Tel: 08 700 10 20 30
Website: www.uci-cinemas.co.uk
Seats: 164 (6 screens), 206 (4 screens), 426 (2 screens)

Mile End
Genesis, Mile End Road
Tel: 020 7780 2000
Seats: 1:575, 2:159, 3:159, 4:101, 5:95

Muswell Hill
Odeon, Fortis Green Road, N10
Tel: 0870 50 50 007
Website: www.odeon.co.uk
Seats: 1:400, 2:165 X, 3:164 X

Newham
Showcase, Jenkins Lane, off A13
W
Tel: 020 8477 4500
Website:
www.showcasecinemas.co.uk
Seats: 3,664 (14 screens)

North Finchley
Warner Village, Great North Leisure Park, Chaplin Square, N12
W
Tel: 020 8446 9977/9933
Seats: 1:377, 2:164, 3:219, 4:333, 5:333, 6:219, 7:164, 8:377

Peckham
Premier, Rye Lane
X
Tel: 020 7732 1010
Seats: 1:397, 2:255, 3:275, 4:197, 5:218, 6:112

Purley Way
Warner Village, Valley Park Leisure Complex, Croydon
W
Tel: 020 8680 1968/6881
Seats: 1:253, 2:205, 3:178, 4:396, 5:396, 6:178, 7:205, 8:253

Putney
Odeon, High Street, SW15
AWG
Tel: 0870 50 50 007
Website: www.odeon.co.uk
Seats: 1:434, 2:315, 3:147

Richmond
Filmhouse, Water Lane
WG
Tel: 020 8332 0030
Seats: 150

Odeon, Hill Street
Tel: 0870 50 50 007
Website: www.odeon.co.uk
Seats: 1:406, 2:179 X, 3:179 X

Odeon Studio, Red Lion Street
Tel: 0870 50 50 007
Website: www.odeon.co.uk
Seats: 1:81 X, 2:78 X, 3:78, 4:91

Romford
Ster Century, The Brewery, Waterloo Road
W
Tel: 01708 759100
Seats: 1:160, 2:160, 3:182, 4:198, 5:198, 6:168, 7:160, 8:160, 9:108, 10:132, 11:286, 12:414, 13:464, 14:435, 15:385, 16:264

Shepherds Bush
Warner Village, West 12 Shopping & Leisure Centre, Shepherds Bush Green
W
Tel: 0208 749 5014/08702 40 60 20
Seats: 1:127, 2:137, 3:189, 4:227, 5:287, 6:201, 7:175, 8:114, 9:387, 10:227, 11:201, 12:285

Southall
Himalaya Palace, South Road
Tel: 020 8813 8844
Seats: 1:500, 2:150, 3:150

Staples Corner
UGC Cinemas, Staples Corner Retail Park, Geron Way
W
Tel: 0208 208 1367/0870 907 0717
Website: www.ugccinemas.co.uk
Seats: 1:455, 2:362, 3:214, 4:210, 5:166, 6:166

Stratford
Picturehouse, Gerry Raffles Square, Salway Road, E15
Tel: 020 8555 3366
Seats: 1:260, 2:242, 3:215, 4:151

Streatham
Odeon, High Road, SW16
Tel: 0870 505 000
Website: www.odeon.co.uk
Seats: 1:451, 2:110, 3:110, 4:103 X, 5:237 X, 6:209 X, 7:93 X, 8:172

Surrey Quays
UCI, Redriff Road, SE16
W
Tel: 08700 10 20 30
Website: www.uci-cinemas.co.uk
Seats: 1:411, 2:401, 3:328, 4:200, 5:198, 6:198, 7:164, 8:164, 9:164

Sutton
UCI, St Nicholas Centre, St Nicholas Way
W
Tel: 08700 10 20 30
Website: www.uci-cinemas.co.uk
Seats: 1:305, 2:297, 3:234, 4:327, 5:261, 6:327

Swiss Cottage
Odeon, Finchley Road, NW3
Tel: 0870 50 50 007
Seats: 1:715, 2:111, 3:220 W, 4:120, 5:154 W, 6:156

Wandsworth
Cineworld, Arndale Centre
Seats: 3,000 (14 screens)
(Scheduled to open in April 2004)

West India Quay
UGC, Hertsmere Road
WE
Tel: 0207 517 7860/0870 907 0722
Website: www.ugccinemas.co.uk
Seats: 1:111, 2:168, 3:216, 4: 275, 5:360, 6: 104, 7:164, 8: 216, 9:275, 10:359

Willesden
Belle Vue, Willesden Green Library Centre, NW10
Tel: 020 8830 0822
Seats: 204

Wimbledon
Odeon, The Crescent, The Broadway, SW19
W
Tel: 0870 50 50 007
Website: www.odeon.co.uk
Seats: 1:203, 2:197, 3: 217, 4:383, 5:205, 6:173, 7:378, 8:188, 9:261, 10:172, 11:232, 12:214

Woodford
Odeon, High Road, E18
Tel: 0870 50 50 007
Website: www.odeon.co.uk
Seats: 1:207, 2:154, 3:104, 4:153, 5:161, 6:92, 7:144

Wood Green
Cineworld, Shopping City, High Road
Tel: 020 8829 1400
Website: www.cineworld.co.uk
Seats: 1:267, 2:315, 3:106, 4:152, 5:185, 6:111, 7:180, 8:137, 9:172, 10:140, 11:162, 12:105

Showcase, Spouters Corner, Hollywood Green, High Road
Tel: 0870 162 8960
Website: www.showcasecinemas.co.uk
Seats: 1,600 (6 screens)

ENGLAND

Accrington – Lancashire
Premiere, The Viaduct
X
Tel: 01254 306660
Seats: 1:162, 2:265, 3:266, 4:161

Aldeburgh - Suffolk
Aldeburgh Cinema, High Street
X
Tel: 01728 452996
Seats: 284

Aldershot - Hants
West End Centre, Queens Road (P/T)
X
Tel: 01252 330040
Seats: 98

Alnwick - Northumberland
Playhouse, Bondgate Without (P/T)
Tel: 01665 510785
Seats: 272

Alton - Hants
Palace, Normandy Street
Tel: 01420 82303
Seats: 1: 111, 2: 62

Ambleside - Cumbria
Zeffirelli's, Compston Road
X
Tel: 01539 431771
Seats: 1:110, 2:60

Ashford - Kent
Cineworld, Eureka Leisure Park, Trinity Road
X
Tel: 01233 620568/622226
Website: www.cineworld.co.uk
Seats: 1:344, 2:75, 3:63, 4:89, 5:156, 6:254, 7:254, 8:156, 9:89, 10:63, 11:215, 12:345

Ashton-under-Lyne - Greater Manchester
Cineworld, Ashton Moss
Seats: 2,700 (14 screens)
(Scheduled to open December 2003)

Metro, Old Street
Tel: 0161 330 1993
Website: www.cosmoleisure.com
Seats: 987

Aylesbury - Buckinghamshire
Odeon, The Exchange
X
Tel: 0870 50 50 007
Website: www.odeon.co.uk
Seats: 1:399, 2:283, 3:266, 4:230, 5:205, 6:194

Banbury - Oxfordshire
Odeon, Horsefair
Tel: 01295 262071
Website: www.odeon.co.uk
Seats: 1:428, 2:225

Barnsley - South Yorkshire
Odeon, Eldon Street
Tel: 0870 50 50 007
Website: www.odeon.co.uk
Seats: 1:403, 2:438X

Barnstaple - Devon
Central, Boutport Street
Tel: 01271 342550/342288
Seats: 1:360, 2:80, 3:80, 4:130

Barrow - Cumbria
Apollo, Hollywood Park, Hindpool Road
Tel: 01229 825354
Website: www.apollocinemas.co.uk
Seats: 1:118, 2:103, 3:258, 4:258, 5:118, 6:118

Basildon - Essex
UCI, Festival Leisure Park, Pipps Hill
X
Tel: 0870 010 2030
Website: www.uci-cinemas.co.uk
Seats: 1:361, 2:180, 3:146, 4:164, 5:220, 6:337, 7:246, 8:220, 9:164, 10:146, 11:180, 12:538

Basingstoke - Hants
Ster Century, Festival Place
Seats: 1:199, 2:199, 3:143, 4:275, 5:275, 6:123, 7:319, 8:248, 9:295, 10:175

Warner Village, Basingstoke Leisure Park, Churchill Way West, West Ham
XE
Tel: 0870 240 6020
Seats: 1:427, 2:238, 3:223, 4:154, 5:157, 6:157, 7:154, 8:223, 9:238, 10:427

Bath - Avon
Odeon, Westgate Street
Tel: 01225 461730/462959
Website: www.odeon.co.uk
Seats: 652 X

Little Theatre, St Michael's Place
Tel: 01225 330817
Seats: 1:192, 2:74

Robins, St John's Place
Tel: 01225 461506

Seats: 1:151, 2:126 X, 3:49

Bedford - Bedfordshire

Civic Theatre, Horne Lane (P/T)
Tel: 01234 44813
Seats: 266

UGC, Aspects Leisure Park, Newham Avenue
XE
Tel: 01234 212826/0870 155 5130
Website: www.ugccinemas.co.uk
Seats: 1:334, 2:292, 3:291, 4:289, 5:187, 6:187

Berkhamsted – Hertfordshire
Rex, High Street (P/T)
(Scheduled to re-open in 2003)

Berwick - Northumberland

Maltings Art Centre, Eastern Lane (P/T)
X
Tel: 01289 330999/330661
Seats: 100

Playhouse, Sandgate
Tel: 01289 307769
Seats: 650

Bexhill - East Sussex

Curzon Picture Playhouse, Western Road
Tel: 01424 210078
Seats: 175

Bideford - Devon

College Theatre (P/T)
Tel: 01237 428110
Seats: 181

Billingham - Cleveland

Forum Theatre, Town Centre (P/T)
Tel: 01642 552663
Seats: 494

Birkenhead - Merseyside

Warner Village, Europa Boulevard, Conway Park
X
Tel: 0151 649 8822
Seats: 1:161, 2:204, 3:429, 4:204, 5:161, 6:354, 7:311

Birmingham - West Midlands

AMC, Broadway Plaza, Ladywood Middleway, off Broad Street, Edgbaston
Seats: (12 screens)
(Scheduled to open by end 2003)

Electric, Station Street
X
Tel: 0121 643 7277
Seats: 1:200, 2:100

IMAX Theatre, Millennium Point, Curzon Street
Tel: 0121 202 2222
Seats: 385

MAC
Cannon Hill Park, Edgbaston
Tel: 0121 440 3838
Seats: 1:202, 2:144

Odeon, New Street
Tel: 0870 50 50 007
Website: www.odeon.co.uk
Seats: 1:231, 2:390, 3:298, 4:229, 5:194, 6:180, 7:130, 8:80

Piccadilly, Stratford Road, Sparkhill
Tel: 0121 773 1658

Showcase, Kingsbury Road, Erdington
X
Tel: 0121 382 9779
Website:
www.showcasecinemas.co.uk
Seats: 3,599 (12 screens)

UGC, Arcadian Centre, Hurst Street, China Town
XE
Tel: 0121 6223323/08701 555 177
Website: www.ugccinemas.co.uk
Seats: 1:419, 2:299, 3:275, 4:240, 5:192, 6:222, 7:210, 8:196, 9:168

UGC, Tennant Street (Broad Street)
XE
Tel: 0121 6430631/0870 907 0723
Website: www.ugccinemas.co.uk
Seats: 1:371, 2:330, 3:269, 4:181, 5:287, 6:434, 7:341, 8:185, 9:269, 10: 240, 11:263, 12:167

Warner Village, StarCity, Watson Road, Nechells
X
Tel: 0121 326 0246
Seats: 1:440, 2:138, 3:107, 4:190, 5:243, 6:243, 7:178, 8:138, 9:138, 10:119, 11:119, 12:539, 13:208, 14:208, 15:140, 16:37, 17:52, 18:52, 19:539, 20-28 currently not in use, 29:160, 30:338

Bishop's Stortford - Herts

Cineworld, Anchor Street
Tel: 01279 710 000/659301
Website: www.cineworld.co.uk
Seats: 1:299, 2:104, 3:160, 4:259, 5:230, 6:185

Blackburn - Lancashire

Apollo, King William Street
Tel: 01254 695979
Website: www.apollocinemas.co.uk
Seats: 1:295, 2:205, 3:115, 4:100, 5:95

Blackpool - Lancashire

Odeon, Rigby Road
X
Tel: 0870 50 50 007
Website: www.odeon.co.uk
Seats: 1:417, 2:137, 3:342, 4:151, 5:198, 6:393, 7:158, 8:342, 9:376, 10:199

Bluewater - Kent

Showcase
Tel: 0870 242 7070
Website:
www.showcasecinemas.co.uk
Seats: 1:129, 2:197, 3:361, 4:464, 5:245, 6:176, 7:80, 8:139, 9:298, 10:379, 11:193, 12:132, Studio:86

Blyth - Northumberland

Wallaw, Union Street
Tel: 01670 352504
Seats: 1:850, 2:150, 3:80

Bognor Regis - West Sussex

Picturedrome, Canada Grove
Tel: 01243 841015
Seats: 1:368, 2:100

ABC, Southcoast World
Tel: 0870 841916
Seats: 1:240, 2:240

Boldon - Tyne and Wear

UGC, Abingdon Way, Boldon Leisure Park, Boldon Colliery
XE
Tel: 0191 5360913/08701 5505512
Website: www.ugccinemas.co.uk
Seats: 1:284, 2:197, 3:80, 4:119, 5:263, 6:529, 7:263, 8:136, 9:119, 10:197, 11:284

Bolton - Greater Manchester

Warner Village, Middlebrook Leisure Park, Horwich
X
Tel: 08702 406020
Seats: 1:375, 2:124, 3:124, 4:166, 5:244, 6:269, 7:269, 8:244, 9:166, 10:124, 11:124, 12:368

UGC, Valley Entertainment, Eagley Brook Way
XE
Tel: 01204 366200/0870 907 0714
Website: www.ugccinemas.co.uk
Seats: 1: 143, 2:144, 3:118, 4:155, 5:230, 6:467, 7:635, 8:522, 9:233, 10:156, 11:156, 12:193, 13:193, 14:72, 15:72

Borehamwood - Hertfordshire

Omniplex, The Point, Shenley Road
Tel: 0208 207 2028
Seats: 1:193, 2:157, 3:121, 4:119

Boston - Lincolnshire

Blackfriars Arts Centre, Spain Lane (P/T)
Tel: 01205 363108
Seats: 237

West End, West Street
Tel: 01205 363634/363639
Seats: 1:360, 2::260, 3:150, 4:150, 5:110

Bournemouth - Dorset

ABC, Westover Road
Tel: 0870 5050 007/900 7694
Seats: 1:652, 2:585, 3:223

Sheridan IMAX Cinema, Waterfront Pier Approach
Tel: 01202 200000
Seats: 419

Odeon, Westover Road
Tel: 0870 50 50 007
Website: www.odeon.co.uk
Seats: 1:757, 2:146, 3:266, 4:119, 5:119, 6:354

Bowness-on-Windermere - Cumbria

Royalty, Lake Road
X
Tel: 01539 443364
Seats: 1:399, 2:100, 3:65

Bracknell - Berkshire

South Hill Park Arts Centre
X
Tel: 01344 427272/484123
Seats: 1:60, 2:200

UCI, The Point, Skimpedhill Lane
X
Tel: 0870 010 2030
Website: www.uci-cinemas.co.uk
Seats: 1:177, 2:205, 3:205, 4:177, 5:316, 6:316, 7:177, 8:205, 9:205, 10:177

Bradford - West Yorkshire

Cineworld, Leisure Exchange, Vicar Lane
XE
Tel: 01274 387220/371941
Website: www.cineworld.co.uk
Seats: 1:168, 2:239, 3:161, 4:301, 5:301, 6:192 7:190, 8:311, 9:166, 10:209, 11: 288, 12:106, 13:120, 14:120, 15:154, 16:259

National Museum of Photography, Film & Television
XE
Tel: 0870 70 10 200
Website: www.nmpft.org.uk
Seats: Pictureville: 306, Cubby Broccoli: 108, **IMAX:** 340

Odeon, Gallagher Leisure Park, Thornbury
X
Tel: 0870 50 50 007
Website: www.odeon.co.uk
Seats: 1:126, 2:228, 3:150, 4:233, 5:384, 6:442, 7:442, 8:211, 9:257, 10:157, 11:170, 12:140, 13:148

Braintree - Essex

Cineworld, Freeport Shopping Village
Tel: 01376 554280
Website: www.cineworld.co.uk
Seats: 1:311, 2:169, 3:93, 4:148, 5:170, 6:222, 7:222, 8:170, 9:148, 10:93, 11:207, 12:310

Bridgnorth - Shropshire

Majestic, Whitburn Street
Tel: 01746 761815/761866
Seats: 1:500, 2:86, 3:86

Bridgwater - Somerset

Film Centre, Penel Orlieu
Tel: 01278 422383
Seats: 1:223, 2::232

Bridlington - Humberside

Forum, The Promenade
Tel: 01262 676767
Seats: 1:202, 2:103, 3:57

Brierley Hill - Staffordshire

UCI, Merry Hill Shopping Centre
X
Tel: 0870 0102030
Website: www.uci-cinemas.co.uk
Seats: 1:350, 2:350, 3:274, 4:274, 5:224, 6:224, 7:254, 8:254, 9:178, 10:178

Brighton – East Sussex

Cinematheque, Media Centre, Middle Street
Tel: 01273 384300
Website: www.cinematheque.org

Duke of York's Picturehouse, Preston Circus
Tel: 01273 602503
Website: www.picturehouse-cinemas.co.uk
Seats: 327

Gardner Arts Centre, University of Sussex, Falmer (P/T)
Tel: 01273 685861
Seats: 354

Odeon, Kingswest, West Street
Tel: 0870 50 50 007
Website: www.odeon.co.uk
Seats: 1:389, 2: 220, 3:238, 4:238, 5: 514, 6: 286, 7:232, 8:100

UGC, Brighton Marina
XE
Tel: 01273 818094/0870 155 5145
Website: www.ugccinemas.co.uk
Seats: 1:351, 2:351, 3:251, 4:251, 5:223, 6:223, 7:202, 8:203

Bristol – Avon

Arnolfini, Narrow Quay
XE
Tel: 0117 929 9191
Seats: 176

Cineworld, Hengrove Leisure Park, Hengrove Way
Tel: 01275 831300
Website: www.cineworld.co.uk
Seats: 1:97, 2:123, 3:133, 4:211, 5:264, 6:343, 7:312, 8:344, 9:262, 10:88, 11:113, 12:152, 13:123, 14:98

The Cube, King Square
X
Tel: 0117 907 4190/4191
Seats: 124

IMAX, Canon's Marsh
X
Tel: 0117 915 5000
Seats: 250

Odeon, Union Street
Tel: 0870 50 50 007
Website: www.odeon.co.uk
Seats: 1:399, 2:224, 3:215

Orpheus, Northumbria Drive, Henleaze
Tel: 0117 962 1644
Seats: 1:160, 2:129, 3:125

Showcase, Avon Meads off Albert Road, St Phillips Causeway
Tel: 0117 972 3800
Website: www.showcasecinemas.co.uk
Seats: 3,408 (14 screens)

Warner Village, The Venue, Cribbs Causeway Leisure Complex, Merlin Road
Tel: 0117 950 0222
Seats: 1:385, 2:124, 3:124, 4:166, 5:239, 6:273, 7:273, 8:239, 9:166, 10:124, 11:124, 12:385

Warner Village, Aspects Leisure Park, Longwell Green
Tel: 0117 960 0021

Seats: 1:385, 2:166, 3:124, 4:124, 5:166, 6:293, 7:337, 8:293, 9:166, 10:124

Watershed, 1 Canon's Road, BS1 5TX XE
Tel: 0117 927 6444/925 3845
Website: www.watershed.co.uk
Seats: 1:200, 2:54
(Third screen seating 100 scheduled to open late 2003)

Broadstairs - Kent

Windsor, Harbour Street
Tel: 01843 865726
Seats: 120

Bromborough - Merseyside

Odeon, Wirral Leisure Retail Park, Welton Road
X
Tel: 0870 50 50 007
Website: www.odeon.co.uk
Seats: 1:458, 2:356, 3:238, 4:197, 5:327, 6:162, 7:162, 8:90, 9:133, 10:76, 11:120

Bude - Cornwall

Rebel, off A39, Rainbow Trefknic Cross
Tel: 01288 361442
Seats: 120

Burgess Hill - West Sussex

Orion, Cyprus Road
Tel: 01444 232137/243300
Website: www.orioncinema.com
Seats: 1:150, 2:121

Burnham-on-Crouch - Essex

Rio, Station Road
Tel: 01621 782027
Seats: 1:220, 2:60

Burnley - Lancashire

Apollo, Hollywood Park, Centenary Way, Manchester Road
Tel: 01282 456222/456333
Website: www.apollocinemas.co.uk
Seats: 1:61, 2:238, 3:93, 4:339, 5:93, 6:339, 7:93, 8:238, 9:93

Burton-on-Trent - Staffordshire

Cineworld, Middleway Leisure Park, Guild Street
Tel: 01283 511561
Website: www.cineworld.co.uk
Seats: 1:225, 2:98, 3:136, 4:107, 5:316, 6:289, 7:203, 8:132, 9:98

Bury - Greater Manchester

Warner Village, Park 66, Pilsworth Road
X
Tel: 08702 406020
Seats: 1:559, 2:322, 3:278, 4:434, 5:208, 6:166, 7:166, 8:208, 9:434, 10:278, 11:322, 12:573

Bury St Edmunds - Suffolk

Odeon, Hatter Street
Tel: 0870 5050 007
Website: www.odeon.co.uk
Seats: 1:188, 2:117

Camberley - Surrey

Camberley Theatre, Knoll Road (P/T)
Tel: 01276 707600
Seats: 338

Globe, Hawley (P/T)
Tel: 01252 876769
Seats: 200

Cambridge - Cambridgeshire

Arts Picturehouse, St Andrews Street
Tel: 01223 504444
Website: www.picturehouse-cinemas.co.uk
Seats: 1: 250, 2:150, 3:98

Cineworld
Seats: 1,700 (9 screens)
(scheduled to open in August 2004)

Warner Village, Grafton Centre, East Road
XE
Tel: 0870 240 6020
Seats: 1:162, 2:168, 3:182, 4:205, 5:166, 6:175, 7:321, 8:442

Cannock - Staffordshire

Picture House, Walsall Road
Tel: 01543 502226
Seats: 1:368, 2:185

Canterbury - Kent

Odeon, St Georges Place
Tel: 0870 155 5133
Website: www.odeon.co.uk
Seats: 1:534, 2:385

Cinema 3, Gulbenkian Theatre, Cornwallis South, University of Kent, CT2 7NX
Tel: 01227 769075/764000 x4017
Seats: 300

Canvey Island - Essex

Movie Starr Cineplex, Eastern Esplandade
Tel: 01268 699799
Seats: 1:134, 2:122, 3:104, 4:73

Carlisle - Cumbria

Lonsdale, Warwick Road
Tel: 01228 514654
Seats: 1:375, 2:216, 3:54

City Cinemas 4 & 5, Mary Street
X
Tel: 01228 514654
Seats: 4:122, 5:112

Village Cinemas, Botchergate
X
Tel: 01228 819 104
Seats: 1:148, 2:248, 3:248, 4:148, 5:301, 6:301, 7:340

Castleford – West Yorkshire

Cineworld
Seats: 2,900 (14 screens)
(scheduled to open October 2003)

Chelmsford - Essex

Cramphorn Theatre, High Street (P/T)
Tel: 01245 606 505
Seats: 140

Odeon, Kings Head Walk
EX
Tel: 0870 50 50 007
Website: www.odeon.co.uk
Seats: 1:339, 2:108, 3:158, 4:235, 5:171, 6:143, 7:128, 8:131

Cheltenham - Gloucestershire

Odeon, Winchcombe Street
Tel: 0870 50 50 007
Website: www.odeon.co.uk
Seats: 1:261, 2:184, 3:183, 4:82, 5:129 X, 6:104 X, 7:177 X

Chesham - Buckinghamshire

New Elgiva Theatre, Elgiva Lane (P/T)
XE
Tel: 01494 582900
Seats: 328

Cheshire Oaks - Cheshire

Warner Village, The Coliseum, Coliseum Way, Ellesmere Port
Tel: 0151 356 2261
Seats: 1:341, 2:166, 5:166, 6:245, 7:272, 8:341, 9:272, 11:166, 12:124, 13:124, 14:166, 15:341 (Screens 3, 4 and 10 not in use in summer 2003)

Chester - Cheshire

Odeon, Northgate Street
Tel: 0870 50 50 007
Website: www.odeon.co.uk
Seats: 1:406, 2:148, 3:148, 4:122, 5:122

UGC, Chaser Court, Greyhound Park, Sealand Road

XE
Tel: 01244 380155/08701 555158
Website: www.ugccinemas.co.uk
Seats: 1:366, 2:366, 3:265, 4:232, 5:211, 6:211

Chesterfield - Derbyshire
Cineworld, Derby Road, Alma Leisure Park
Tel: 0246 229172/278000
Website: www.cineworld.co.uk
Seats: 1:245, 2:128, 3:107, 4:150, 5:291, 6:291, 7:150, 8:107, 9:128, 10:237

Chichester - West Sussex
Cineworld, Chichester Gate
XE
Tel: 01243 816800
Website: www.cineworld.co.uk
Seats: 1:222, 2: 222, 3:99, 4:165, 5: 295, 6: 257, 7:154, 8:125, 9:194, 10:222

New Park Film Centre, New Park Road
X
Tel: 01243 786650
Seats: 120

Chippenham - Wiltshire
Astoria, Marshfield Road
Tel: 01249 652498
Seats: 1:215, 2:215

Chipping Norton - Oxfordshire
The Theatre, Spring Street (P/T)
Tel: 01608 642349/642350
Seats: 195

Christchurch - Dorset
Regent Centre, High Street (P/T)
Tel: 01202 479819/499148
Seats: 485

Cinderford - Gloucestershire
Palace, Bellevue Road
Tel: 01594 822555
Seats: 155

Cirencester - Gloucestershire
Regal, Lewis Lane
Tel: 01285 658755
Seats: 1:100, 2:100

Clacton - Essex
Flicks, Pier Avenue
Tel: 01255 429627/421188
Seats: 1:625, 2:135

Clevedon - Avon
Curzon, Old Church Road
Tel: 01275 871000
Seats: 392

Clitheroe - Lancashire
Grand, York Street
Tel: 01200 423278
Seats: 400

Colchester - Essex
Odeon, Head Street
X
Tel: 0870 50 50 007
Website: www.odeon.co.uk
Seats: 1:120, 2:168, 3:206, 4:119, 5:166, 6:305, 7:130, 8:207

Coleford - Gloucestershire
Studio, High Street
Tel: 01594 833331
Seats: 1:200, 2:80

Consett - Co Durham
Empire, Front Street
XE
Tel: 01207 218171
Seats: 535

Cosham - Hants
Carlton, High Street
Tel: 023 92376635
Seats: 1:441 X, 2:118, 3:107

Coventry - West Midlands
Odeon, Sky Dome, Croft Road
X
Tel: 0870 50 50 007
Website: www.odeon.co.uk
1:228, 2:415, 3:180, 4:359, 5:174, 6:137, 7:115, 8:163, 9:172

Showcase, Gielgud Way, Walsgrave
Tel: 0247 660 2111
Website:
www.showcasecinemas.co.uk
Seats: 4,413 (14 screens)

Warwick Arts Centre, University of Warwick, Gibbet Hill Road, CV4 7AL
X
Tel: 0247 652 4524/3060
Website:
www.warwickartscentre.co.uk
Seats: 240

Crawley - West Sussex
UGC, Crawley Leisure Park, London Road
XE
Tel: 01293 537415/0870 902 0411
Website: www.ugccinemas.co.uk
Seats: 1:236, 2:421, 3:186, 4:551, 5:186, 6:129, 7:129, 8:318, 9:173, 10:231, 11:184, 12:156, 13:173, 14:173, 15:70

Crewe - Cheshire
Apollo, High Street
Tel: 01270 255708
Website: www.apollocinemas.co.uk
Seats: 1:107, 2:110, 3:91

Cromer - Norfolk
Regal, Hans Place
Tel: 01263 513311
Seats: 1:129, 2:136, 3:66, 4:55

Crookham - Hants
Globe, Queen Elizabeth Barracks
Tel: 01252 876769
Seats: 340

Crosby - Merseyside
Plaza, Crosby Road North, Waterloo
Tel: 0151 474 4076
Seats: 1:600, 2:92, 3:74

Darlington - Co Durham
Arts Centre, Vane Terrace (P/T)
XE
Tel: 01325 483168/483271/486555
Seats: 100

Odeon, Northgate
Tel: 0870 50 50 007
Website: www.odeon.co.uk
Seats: 1:579, 2:182, 3:124

Dartington – Devon
Barn Theatre, Arts Society, The Gallery, TQ9 6DE (P/T)
X
Tel: 01803 865864/863073
Seats: 208

Deal - Kent
Flicks, Queen Street
Tel: 01304 361165
Seats: 1:162, 2:99

Derby - Derbyshire
Metro Cinema, Green Lane, DE1 1SA
XE
Tel: 01332 340170/347765
Seats: 128

Showcase, Foresters Park, Osmaston Park Road at Sinfin Lane
X
Tel: 01332 270300
Website:
www.showcasecinemas.co.uk
Seats: 2,557 (11 screens)

UCI, Meteor Centre 10, Mansfield Road
X
Tel: 0870 0102030
Website: www.uci-cinemas.co.uk
Seats: 1:191, 2:188, 3:188, 4:191,

5:276, 6:276, 7:191, 8:188, 9:188, 10:191

Dereham - Norfolk
Hollywood, Market Place
Tel: 01362 691133/691718
Website: www.hollywoodcinemas.net
Seats: 1:147, 2:95, 3:57

Devizes - Wiltshire
Palace, Market Place
Tel: 01380 722971
Seats: 253

Didsbury – Greater Manchester
UGC, Parrs Wood Entertainment Complex, Kingsway, East Didsbury
XE
Tel: 0161 434 0909/0870 907 0742
Website: www.ugccinemas.co.uk
Seats: 1:592, 2:261, 3:181, 4:214, 5:235, 6:214, 7:186, 8:350, 9:193, 10:277, 11:145

Doncaster - South Yorkshire
Civic Theatre, Waterdale (P/T)
Tel: 01302 62349
Seats: 547

Odeon, Hallgate
X
Tel: 0870 50 50 007
Website: www.odeon.co.uk
Seats: 1:975, 2:159, 3:161

Warner Village, Doncaster Leisure Park, Bawtry Road
Tel: 01302 371313/371020
Seats: 1:224, 2:212, 3:252, 4:386, 5:252, 6:212, 7:224

Dorchester - Dorset
Plaza, Trinity Street
Tel: 01305 262488
Seats: Premiere: 208, Century: 92

Dorking - Surrey
Dorking Halls (P/T)
Tel: 01306 881717
Seats: 198

Douglas - Isle of Man
Palace Cinema
Tel: 01624 76814
Seats: 1:319, 2:120

Summerland Cinema
Tel: 01624 25511
Seats: 200

Dover - Kent
Silver Screen, White Cliffs Experience, Gaol Lane
Tel: 01304 228000
Seats: 110

Dronfield – South Yorks
Civic Hall (P/T)
Tel: 01246 418573
Seats: 200

Dudley - West Midlands
Limelight Cinema, Black Country Living Museum
Tel: 0121 557 9643
Seats: 100

Showcase, Castlegate Park, off Birmingham New Road
Tel: 01384 246500/246540
Website:
www.showcasecinemas.co.uk
Seats: 2,850 (14 screens)

Durham – Co Durham
Gala, Claypath
X
Tel: 0191 332 4041
Seats: 118

Eastbourne - East Sussex
Curzon, Langney Road
Tel: 01323 731441
Seats: 1:530, 2:236, 3:236

UGC, Sovereign Harbour Retail Park, Pevensey Bay Road
XE
Tel: 01323 470070/0870 1555159
Website: www.ugccinemas.co.uk
Seats: 1:322, 2:312, 3:271, 4:254, 5:221, 6:221

East Grinstead - West Sussex
King Street Picturehouse, Atrium Building, King Street
Tel: 01342 321666
Seats: 1:240, 2:240

Eastleigh - Hants
Point Dance and Arts Centre, Town Hall Centre, Leigh Road (P/T)
Tel: 023 8065 2333
Seats: 264

Elland - North Yorkshire
Rex, Coronation Street
X
Tel: 01422 372140
Website: www.nm-cinemas.co.uk
Seats: 294

Ely - Cambridgeshire
The Maltings, Ship Lane (P/T)
Tel: 01353 666388
Seats: 200

Epsom - Surrey
Odeon, Upper High Street
X
Tel: 0870 50 50 007
Website: www.odeon.co.uk
Seats: 1:320, 2:210, 3:271, 4:246, 5:172, 6:298, 7:242, 8:392

Playhouse, Ashley Avenue (P/T)
XE
Tel: 01372 742555/6
Seats: 300

Esher - Surrey
Odeon, High Street
Tel: 0870 50 50 007
Website: www.odeon.co.uk
Seats: 1:524 X, 2:114, 3:114 X, 4:113 X

Exeter - Devon
Northcott Theatre, Stocker Road (P/T)
Tel: 01392 54853
Seats: 433

Odeon, Sidwell Street
Tel: 0870 50 50 007
Website: www.odeon.co.uk
Seats: 1:684, 2:120, 3:105, 4:324

Phoenix, Gandy Street (P/T)
Tel: 01392 667080
Seats: 180

Picturehouse, Bartholomew Street West
Tel: 01392 435522
Website: www.picturehouse-cinemas.co.uk
Seats: 1:220, 2:156

Exmouth - Devon
Savoy, Rolle Street
Tel: 01395 268220
Seats: 1:204, 2:100, 3:70

Fakenham - Norfolk
Hollywood, The Market Place
X
Tel: 01328 856 466
Website: www.hollywoodcinemas.net
Seats: 1:118, 2:88, 3:60

Falmouth - Cornwall
Arts Centre, Church Street (P/T)
Tel: 01326 212300
Seats: 199

Farnham - Surrey
Redgrave Theatre, Brightwell (P/T)
X
Tel: 01252 727 720
Seats: 362

Faversham - Kent
New Royal, Market Place
Tel: 01795 535551
Seats: 448

Felixstowe - Suffolk
Palace, Crescent Road
Tel: 01394 282787
Seats: 1:150, 2:90

Folkestone - Kent
Silver Screen, Guildhall Street
Tel: 01303 221230
Seats: 1:435, 2:106

Forest, Guernsey - Channel Islands
Mallard Cinema, Mallard Hotel, La Villiaze
Tel: 01481 64164
Seats: 1:154, 2:54, 3:75, 4:75

Frome - Somerset
Westway, Cork Street
Tel: 01373 465685
Seats: 304

Gainsborough - Lincolnshire
Trinity Arts Centre, Trinity Street (P/T)
X
Tel: 01427 810710
Seats: 210

Gateshead - Tyne and Wear
UCI, Metro Centre
Tel: 0191 493 2022/3
Website: www.uci-cinemas.co.uk
Seats: 1:200, 2:200, 3:228, 4:256, **5: 370, 6:370, 7:256, 8:228, 9:200, 10:200, 11:520**

Gerrards Cross - Buckinghamshire
Odeon, Ethorpe Crescent
Tel: 0870 50 50 007
Website: www.odeon.co.uk
Seats: 1:325, 2:212

Gloucester - Gloucestershire
Guildhall Arts Centre, Eastgate Street
X
Tel: 01452 505086/9
Seats: 1:120, 2:150(P/T)

New Olympus Theatre, Barton Street (P/T)
Tel: 01452 505089
Seats: 375

UGC, Peel Centre, St. Anns Way, Bristol Road
XE
Tel: 01452 331181/08701 555174
Website: www.ugccinemas.co.uk
Seats: 1:354, 2:354, 3:238, 4:238, 5:219, 6:219

Godalming - Surrey
Borough Hall (P/T)
Tel: 01483 861111
Seats: 250

Goole - Humberside
The Gate, Dunhill Road (P/T)
Tel: 01405 720219
Seats: 90

Grantham - Lincolnshire
Paragon, St Catherine's Road
X
Tel: 01476 570046
Seats: 1:270, 2:160

Grays - Essex
Thameside, Orsett Road (P/T)
Tel: 01375 382555
Seats: 303

Great Yarmouth - Norfolk
Hollywood, Marine Parade
Tel: 01493 842043/852600
Website: www.hollywoodcinemas.net
Seats: 1:500 X, 2:296, 3:250 X, 4:250 X

Grimsby - Lincolnshire
Odeon, Freeman Street
Tel: 01472 342878/349368
Website: www.odeon.co.uk
Seats: 1:392, 2:229, 3:126

Whitgift Film Theatre, Grimsby College (P/T)
Tel: 01472 88117
Seats: 200

Guildford - Surrey
Odeon, Bedford Road
Tel: 0870 50 50 007
Website: www.odeon.co.uk
Seats: 1:422, 2:353, 3:269, 4:269, 5:293, 6:144, 7:108, 8:126, 9:126

Hailsham - East Sussex
Pavilion, George Street (P/T)
Tel: 01323 841414
Seats: 203

Halstead - Essex
Empire, Butler Road
Tel: 01787 477001
Seats: 320

Halton - Buckinghamshire
Astra, RAF Halton (P/T)
Tel: 01296 623535
Seats: 570

Hanley - Staffordshire
Forum Theatre, Stoke-on-Trent City Museum, Bethesda Street (P/T)
Tel: 01782 232799
Seats: 300

Harlow - Essex
Odeon, The High
Tel: 0870 50 50 007
Website: www.odeon.co.uk
Seats: 1:399, 2:217, 3:179

Playhouse, The High (P/T)
XE
Tel: 01279 431945
Seats: 330

UGC, Queensgate Centre, Edinburgh Way
E
Tel: 01279 436014/0870 907 0713
Website: www.ugccinemas.co.uk
Seats: 1:356, 2:260, 3:240, 4:234, 5:233, 6:230

Harrogate - North Yorkshire
Odeon, East Parade
Tel: 0870 50 50 007
Website: www.odeon.co.uk
Seats: 1:298, 2:242, 3:101, 4:76, 5:329

Hartlepool - Cleveland
Warner Village, The Lanyard, Marina Way
Tel: 01429 261 177/263 263
Seats: 1:303, 2:345, 3:160, 4:204, 5:431, 6:204, 7:160

Harwich - Essex
Electric Palace, King's Quay Street (P/T)
Tel: 01255 553333
Seats: 204

Haslemere - Surrey
Haslemere Hall, Bridge Road (P/T)
Tel: 01428 661793
Seats: 350

Hastings - East Sussex
Odeon, Queens Road
Tel: 0870 50 50 007
Website: www.odeon.co.uk
Seats: 1:125, 2:172, 3:151, 4:127

St Mary-in-the-Castle Arts Centre, Pelham Crescent (P/T)
Tel: 01424 781624
Seats: 590

Hatfield - Herts
UCI, The Galleria, Comet Way
Tel: 0870 010 2030
Website: www.uci-cinemas.co.uk

Seats: 1:172, 2:235, 3:263, 4:167, 5:183, 6:183, 7:260, 8:378, 9:172

Havant - Hants

Arts Centre, East Street (P/T)
X
Tel: 023 92472700
Seats: 130

Haverhill - Suffolk

Arts Centre, Town Hall, High Street (P/T)
Tel: 01440 714140
Seats: 210

Hayling Island - Hants

Hiads Theatre, Station Road (P/T)
Tel: 02392 466363
Seats: 150

Haywards Heath - West Sussex

Clair Hall, Perrymount Road (P/T)
Tel: 01444 455440/454394
Seats: 350

Heaton Moor - Greater Manchester

Savoy, Heaton Moor Road
Tel: 0161 432 2114
Seats: 476

Hebden Bridge - West Yorkshire

Picture House, New Road
XE
Tel: 01422 842807
Seats: 493

Helmsley - North Yorkshire

Helmsley Arts Centre, The Old Meeting House (P/T)
Tel: 01439 771700
Seats: 131

Helston – Cornwall

Flora, Wendron Street
Tel: 01326 573377
Seats: 80

Hemel Hempstead - Herts

Odeon, Leisure World, Jarmans Park
XE
Tel: 0870 50 50 007
Website: www.odeon.co.uk
Seats: 1:130, 2:183, 3:183, 4:317, 5:261, 6:431, 7:166, 8:161

Henley-on-Thames - Oxfordshire

Kenton Theatre, New Street (P/T)
X
Tel: 01491 575698
Seats: 240

Regal, Broma Way, off Bell Street
Tel: 01491 414150
Seats: 1:152, 2:101, 3:85

Hereford - Hereford & Worcs

Odeon, Commercial Road
Tel: 01432 272554
Website: www.odeon.co.uk
Seats: 336

The Courtyard Theatre and Arts Centre, Edgar Street (P/T)
X
Tel: 01432 359252
Seats: 1:364, (Studio:)124

Herne Bay - Kent

Kavanagh, William Street
X
Tel: 01227 362228
Seats: 1:135, 2:93

Hexham - Northumberland

Forum, Market Place
Tel: 01434 601144
Seats: 207

High Wycombe - Buckinghamshire

thefilmworks, Crest Road, Cressex
X
Tel: 0870 010 2030
Seats: 1:388, 2:388, 3:284, 4:284, 5:202, 6:202

Hoddesdon - Herts

Broxbourne Civic Hall, High Street (P/T)
Tel: 01992 441946/31
Seats: 564

Hollinwood - Greater Manchester

Roxy, Hollins Road
Tel: 0161 681 1441/4000
www.roxycinema.co.uk
Seats: 1:470, 2:130, 3:260, 4:260, 5:320, 6:96, 7:140

Holmfirth – West Yorks

Picturedrome
X
Tel: 01484 689759

Horsham - West Sussex

Arts Centre (Ritz Cinema and Capitol Theatre), North Street
Seats: 1:423 (P/T), 2:170, 3: not known
(Scheduled to re-open summer 2003)

Horwich - Lancashire

Leisure Centre, Victoria Road (P/T)
Tel: 01204 692211
Seats: 400

Hucknall - Notts

Byron, High Street
Tel: 0115 963 6377
Seats: 430

Huddersfield – West Yorkshire

UCI, McAlpine Stadium, Bradley Mills Road
Tel: 0870 0102030
Website: www.uci-cinemas.co.uk
Seats: 1:375, 2:296, 3:296, 4:268, 5:268, 6:176, 7:176, 8:148, 9:148

Hull - Humberside

Odeon, Kingston Street
X
Tel: 0870 50 50 007
Website: www.odeon.co.uk
Seats: 1:169, 2:169, 3:148, 4:170, 5:458, 6:272, 7:132, 8:148, 9:108, 10:88

Screen, Central Library, Albion Street HU1 3TF
XE
Tel: 01482 327600
Seats: 247

UCI, St Andrew's Quay, Clive Sullivan Way
X
Tel: 0870 0102030
Website: www.uci-cinemas.co.uk
Seats: 1:166, 2:152, 3:236, 4:292, 5:292, 6:236, 7:152, 8:166

UGC, Kingswood Leisure Park, Ennerdale Link Road
XE
Tel: 01482 835035/08709 070721
Website: www.ugccinemas.co.uk
Seats: 1:165, 2:211, 3:253, 4:498, 5:253, 6:211, 7:165, 8:165, 9:98

Hunstanton - Norfolk

Princess Theatre, The Green (P/T)
Tel: 01485 532252
Seats: 467

Huntingdon - Cambridgeshire

Cineplex, Prince Street
Cineworld, Towerfields, Abbot's Ripton Road
Tel: 01480 412255
Website: www.cineworld.co.uk
Seats: 1:224, 2:126, 3:90, 4:125, 5:110, 6:317, 7:284, 8:208, 9:208, 10:101

Ilfracombe - Devon

The Landmark Theatre, Wilder Road (P/T)
Tel: 01271 324242
Seats: 175

Pendle Stairway, High Street
X
Tel: 01271 863260
Seats: 382

Ilkeston - Derbyshire
Scala, Market Place
Tel: 0115 932 4612
Seats: 500

Ipswich – Suffolk
Film Theatre, Corn Exchange, King Street, IP1 1DH
XE
Tel: 01473 433100
Website: www.ipswich-ents.co.uk
Seats: 1:220, 2:40

Odeon, St Margaret's Street
Tel: 0870 50 50 007
Website: www.odeon.co.uk
Seats: 1:510, 2:313, 3:281, 4:210, 5:210

UGC, Cardinal Park, Grafton Way
XE
Tel: 01473 254978/0870 907 0748
Website: www.ugccinemas.co.uk
Seats: 1:168, 2:186, 3:168, 4:270, 5:179, 6:510, 7:238, 8:398, 9:186, 10:168, 11:83

Keighley - West Yorkshire
Picture House
Tel: 01535 602561
Website: www.nm-cinemas.co.uk
Seats: 1:364, 2:95

Kendal - Cumbria
Brewery Arts Centre, Highgate, LA9 4HE (S/O)
XE
Tel: 01539 725133
Seats: 1:192, 2:115, Theatre (P/T) 250

Keswick - Cumbria
Alhambra, St John Street
X
Tel: 017687 72195
Seats: 270

Kettering - Northants
Odeon, Pegasus Court, Wellingborough Road
X
Tel: 0870 50 50 007
Website: www.odeon.co.uk
Seats: 1:173, 2:123, 3:229, 4:345, 5:103, 6:81, 7:103, 8:307

Kingsbridge - Devon
The Reel Cinema, Fore Street
Tel: 01548 856636
Seats: 162

King's Lynn - Norfolk
Arts Centre, King Street (P/T)
Tel: 01553 764864/765565
Seats: 314

Majestic, Tower Street
Tel: 01553 772603
Seats: 1:450, 2:123, 3:400

Kirkby in Ashfield - Nottinghamshire
Cineplex
Seats: 200
(Ex-Regent, scheduled to re-open by August 2003)

Knutsford - Cheshire
Studio, Civic Centre, Toft Road
X
Tel: 01565 633005
Website: www.macclesfield.gov.uk
Seats: 400

Lancaster - Lancashire
Regal, King Street
Tel: 01524 64141
Seats: 1:250, 2:246

The Dukes Cinema, Moor Lane, LA1 1QE (P/T)
XE
Tel: 01524 598500
Seats: 307

Leamington Spa - Warwicks
Apollo, Portland Place
Tel: 01926 427448
Website: www.apollocinemas.co.uk
Seats: 1:309 X, 2:199 X, 3:138, 4:112 X
(Two additional screens to open by December 2003)

Royal, Spa Centre, Newbold Terrace
Tel: 01926 887726/888997
Seats: 208

Leeds - West Yorkshire
Cottage Road Cinema, Headingley
Tel: 0113 275 2001
Website: www.lounge-cinema.co.uk
Seats: 468

Hyde Park Picture House, Brudenell Road
Tel: 0113 275 2045
Website: www.leedscinema.com
Seats: 360

Lounge, North Lane, Headingley
X
Tel: 0113 275 2001
Website: www.lounge-cinema.co.uk
Seats: 691

Showcase, Gelderd Road, Birstall
X
Tel: 01924 420622
Website: www.showcasecinemas.co.uk
Seats: 4,250 (16 screens)

Ster Century, The Light, Headrow
X
Tel: 0870 240 3696
Website: www.stercentury.co.uk
Seats: 1:143, 2:142, 3:193, 4:189, 5:205, 6:236, 7:153, 8:192, 9:260, 10:260, 11:260, 12:328, 13:328

Warner Village, Cardigan Fields, Kirkstall Road
Tel: 0870 240 6020
Seats: 1:345, 2:124, 3:166, 4:245, 5:252, 6:245, 7:166, 8:124, 9:345

Leicester - Leicestershire
Odeon, Aylestone Road, Freemens Park
XE
Tel: 0870 50 50 007
Website: www.odeon.co.uk
Seats: 1:129, 2:165, 3:154, 4:239, 5:230, 6:362, 7:332, 8:230, 9:239, 10:154, 11:165, 12:127

Phoenix Arts
21 Upper Brown Street
LE1 5TE (P/T)
XE
Tel: 0116 255 4854/255 5627
Seats: 274

Piccadilly, Abbey Street
Tel: 0116 262 0005
Seats: 1:250, 2:180

Piccadilly, Green Lane Road
Tel: 0116 251 8880
Seats: 1:440, 2:120, 3:80

Warner Village, Meridian Leisure Park, Lubbesthorpe Way, Braunstone
Tel: 0116 282 7733/289 4001
Seats: 1:423, 2:158, 3:189, 4:266, 5:306, 6:266, 7:202, 8:158, 9:423

Leighton Buzzard - Bedfordshire
Theatre, Lake Street (P/T)
Tel: 01525 378310
Seats: 170

Leiston - Suffolk
Film Theatre, High Street
Tel: 01728 830549
Seats: 288

Letchworth - Herts
Broadway, Eastcheap
Tel: 01462 681 223
Seats: 1:488, 2:176 X, 3:174 X

Leyburn - North Yorkshire
Elite, Railway Street (P/T)
Tel: 01969 624488
Seats: 173

Lincoln - Lincolnshire
Odeon, Brayford Wharf
Tel: 0870 50 50 007
Website: www.odeon.co.uk
Seats: 1:169, 2:163, 3:410, 4:160, 5:169, 6:213, 7:265, 8:360, 9:102

Littlehampton – West Sussex
Windmill Theatre, Church Street (P/T)
Tel: 01903 722224
Seats: 252

Liverpool - Merseyside
Odeon, Allerton Road
Tel: 0151 724 3550/5095
Website: www.odeon.co.uk
Seats: 490

Odeon, London Road
Tel: 0870 50 50 007
Website: www.odeon.co.uk
Seats: 1:482, 2:154, 3:157, 4:149, 5:211, 6:128, 7:132, 8:123, 9:191, 10:132

Philharmonic Hall, Hope Street (P/T)
X
Tel: 0151 709 2895/3789
Seats: 1,627

Picturehouse at FACT, Wood Street
Tel: 0151 707 4450
Website: www.picturehouse-cinemas.co.uk
Seats: 1:360, 2:244, 3:104

Showcase, East Lancashire Road, Norris Green
X
Tel: 0151 549 2021
Website:
www.showcasecinemas.co.uk
Seats: 3,415 (12 screens)

UGC, Edge Lane Retail Park, Binns Road
XE
Tel: 0151 252 0551/08701 555146
Website: www.ugccinemas.co.uk
Seats: 1:356, 2:354, 3:264, 4:264, 5:220, 6:220, 7:198, 8:200

Woolton, Mason Street
X
Tel: 0151 428 1919
Seats: 256

Longridge - Lancashire
Palace, Market Place
X
Tel: 01772 785600
Seats: 200

Loughborough - Leicestershire
Curzon, Cattle Market
Tel: 01509 212261
Seats: 1:418, 2:303, 3:199, 4:186, 5:140, 6:80

Louth - Lincolnshire
Playhouse, Cannon Street
Tel: 01507 603333
Seats: 1:215, 2:158 X, 3:78 X

Lowestoft - Suffolk
Hollywood, London Road South
Tel: 01502 588355/564567
Website: www.hollywoodcinemas.net
Seats: 1:200 X, 2:175, 3:65 X, 4:40 X

Marina Theatre, The Marina (P/T)
Tel: 01502 573318
Seats: 751

Ludlow - Shropshire
Assembly Rooms, Mill Street (P/T)
X
Tel: 01584 878141
Seats: 320

Luton - Bedfordshire
Artezium, Arts and Media Centre
Tel: 01582 707100
Seats: 96

Cineworld, The Galaxy, Bridge Street
Tel: 01582 401092/400705
Website: www.cineworld.co.uk
Seats: 1:114, 2:75, 3:112, 4:284, 5:419, 6:212, 7:123, 8:217, 9:137, 10:213, 11:240

St George's Theatre
Central Library (P/T)
Tel: 01582 547440
Seats: 238

Lyme Regis - Dorset
Regent, Broad Street
X
Tel: 01297 442053
Seats: 400

Lymington - Hants
Community Centre, New Street (P/T)
Tel: 01590 676939
Seats: 110

Lytham St. Annes - Lancashire
Cinema 4, Pleasure Island, South Promenade
X
Tel: 01253 780085
Seats: 1:170, 2:92, 3:117, 4:105

Lynton – Devon
New Lynton Cinema, Lee Road
Tel: 01598 752 275
Seats: 100

Mablethorpe - Lincolnshire
Loewen, Quebec Road
Tel: 0150 747 7040
Seats: 1:203, 2:80

Maidenhead - Berkshire
thefilmworkds, Grenfell Island
Tel: 0870 0102030
Website: www.uci-cinemas.co.uk
Seats: 1:319, 2:246, 3:139, 4:113, 5:201, 6:179, 7:87, 8:146

Maidstone - Kent
Odeon, Lockmeadow
Tel: 0870 50 50 007
Website: www.odeon.co.uk
Seats: 1:86, 2:89, 3:127, 4:111, 5:240, 6:240, 7:398, 8:347

Malton – North Yorkshire
Ryedale Palace, The Lanes
Tel: 01653 600 008/698 899
Seats: 142

Malvern - Hereford & Worcs
Malvern Theatres, Grange Road
Tel: 01684 569256
Seats: 374, (Forum Theatre P/T) 800

Manchester - Greater Manchester
AMC, Great Northern Warehouse, Deansgate & Peter Street
Tel: 0161 817 3000
Website: www.amccinemas.co.uk
Seats: 1:411, 2:476, 3:236, 4:411, 5:164, 6:164, 7:102, 8:123, 9:125, 10:157, 11:243, 12: 254, 13: 157, 14:133, 15:123, 16:102

Cornerhouse, 70 Oxford Street, M1 5NH
XE
Tel: 0161 200 1500
Website: www.cornerhouse.org
Seats: 1:300, 2:170, 3:60

Odeon, Oxford Street
E
Tel: 0870 50 50 007
Website: www.odeon.co.uk

Seats: 1:617, 2:364, 3:143 X, 4:97, 5:201, 6:142 X, 7:86

Showcase, Hyde Road, Belle Vue
Tel: 0161 220 8765
Website: www.showcasecinemas.co.uk
Seats: 3,191 (14 screens)

TheFilmWorks, The Printworks, Exchange Square
X
Tel: 08 700 10 20 30
Website: www.thefilmworks.co.uk
Seats: 1 (IMAX):368, 2: 217, 3:122, 4:140, 5:140, 6:140, 7:122, 8:214, 9:120, 10:138, 11:228, 12:371, 13:422, 14:164, 15:140, 16:140, 17:322, 18:564, 19:122, 20:122

UCI, Trafford Centre, The Dome, Dumplington
X
Tel: 08700 10 20 30
Website: www.uci-cinemas.co.uk
Seats: 1:427, 2:427, 3:371, 4:301, 5:243, 6:243, 7:181, 8:181, 9:181, 10:181, 11:181, 12:181, 13:152, 14:152, 15:140, 16:140, 17:112, 18:112, 19:112, 20:112

Mansfield - Notts

Odeon, Mansfield Leisure Park, Park Lane
X
Tel: 0870 50 50 007
Website: www.odeon.co.uk
Seats: 1:390, 2:390, 3:246, 4:246, 5:221, 6:221, 7:193, 8:193

March – Cambridgeshire

Hippodrome, Dartford Road
Tel: 01354 653178
Seats: 96

Margate - Kent

Dreamland, Marine Parade
Tel: 01843 227822
Seats: 1:378, 2:376

Marple - Greater Manchester

Regent, Stockport Road
X
Tel: 0161 427 5951
Seats: 285

Market Drayton - Shropshire

Royal Festival Centre (P/T)
Seats: 165

Melton Mowbray - Leicestershire

Regal, King Street
Tel: 01664 562251
Seats: 226

Middlesbrough - Cleveland

UGC, Leisure Park, Marton Road
XE
Tel: 01642 247766/0870 907 0734
Website: www.ugccinemas.co.uk
Seats: 1:204, 2:151, 3:141, 4:271, 5:401, 6:204, 7:125, 8:141, 9:230, 10:271, 11:402

Middleton - Greater Manchester

Northend, Cheapside, off Rochdale Road
Tel: 653 7366

Milton Keynes - Buckinghamshire

Cineworld, Xscape, Marlborough Gate
XE
Tel: 01908 230 088
Website: www.cineworld.co.uk
Seats: 1:137, 2:234, 3:205, 4:170, 5:214, 6:281, 7:304, 8:158, 9:158, 10:316, 11:281, 12: 214, 13:170, 14: 205, 15: 234, 16:135

easycinema, The Point, Midsummer Boulevard
Website: www.easycinema.com
Seats: 1:156, 2:169, 3:250, 4:222, 5:222, 6:222, 7:222, 8:250, 9:169, 10:156

Minehead – Somerset

ABC, Summerwest World
X
Tel: 0870 50 50 007
Seats: 218

Morecambe – Lancashire

Apollo, Central Drive
Tel: 01524 426642
Website: www.apollocinemas.co.uk
Seats: 1:207, 2:207, 3:106, 4:106

Nailsea - Avon

Cinema, Scotch Horn Leisure Centre, Brockway (P/T)
Tel: 01275 856965
Seats: 250

Nantwich - Cheshire

Civic Hall, Market Street (P/T)
Tel: 01270 628633
Seats: 300

Newark - Notts

Palace Theatre, Appleton Gate (P/T)
Tel: 01636 655755
Seats: 351

Newbury - Berkshire

Corn Exchange, Market Place (P/T)
X
Tel: 01635 522733
Seats: 370

Newcastle-under-Lyme - Staffordshire

Warner Village, The Square, High Street
Tel: 01782 711666
Seats: 1:242, 2:236, 3:272, 4:319, 5:373, 6:206, 7:198, 8:241

Newcastle-upon-Tyne - Tyne and Wear

Odeon, The Gates Complex, Newgate Street
X
Tel: 0870 50 50 007
Website: www.odeon.co.uk
Seats: 1:436, 2:102, 3:273, 4:346, 5:130, 6:160, 7:199, 8:67, 9:120, 10:318, 11:157, 12: 230

Tyneside, 10-12 Pilgrim Street, NE1 6QG
XE
Tel: 0191 232 8289
Seats: 1:296, 2:122

Warner Village Cinemas, New Bridge Street
X
Tel: 0191 221 0202/0222
Seats: 1:404, 2:398, 3:236, 4:244, 5:290, 6:657, 7:509, 8:398, 9:248

Newport - Isle of Wight

Cineworld, Coppins Bridge
XE
Tel: 01983 550800
Website: www.cineworld.co.uk
1:300, 2:96, 3:202, 4:178, 5:152, 6:101, 7:84, 8:132, 9:169, 10:195, 11:263

Medina Movie Theatre, Mountbatten Centre, Fairlee Road (P/T)
XE
Tel: 01983 527 020
Seats: 419

Newton Abbot - Devon

Alexandra, Market Street
X
Tel: 01626 365368
Seats: 1:206, 2:127

Northampton – Northants

Forum Cinema, Lings Forum, Weston Favell Centre, NN3 4JR (P/T)
Tel: 01604 401006/402833
Seats: 270

UCI, Sol Central, Doddridge Street
Tel: 08 700 10 20 30
Website: www.uci-cinemas.co.uk
Seats: 1:444, 2:256, 3:167, 4:162, 5:198, 6:262, 7:418, 8:278, 9:181, 10:181

UGC, Sixfields Leisure Park, Weedon Road, Upton
XE
Tel: 01604 580880/08701 560564
Website: www.ugccinemas.co.uk
Seats: 1:452, 2:287, 3:287, 4:207, 5:207, 6:147, 7:147, 8:147, 9:147

North Shields – Tyne and Wear

UCI, Silverlink
X
Tel: 0870 0102030
Website: www.uci-cinemas.co.uk
Seats: 1:326, 2:156, 3:185, 4:198, 5:410, 6:198, 7:185, 8:156, 9:326

Northwich - Cheshire

Regal, London Road
Tel: 01606 43130
Seats: 1:797, 2::200

Norwich - Norfolk

Cinema City, St Andrew's Street, NR2 4AD
X
Tel: 01603 625145/622047
Seats: 230

Hollywood, Anglia Square
Tel: 01603 621903/767737
Website: www.hollywoodcinemas.net
Seats: 1:442, 2:197, 3:195 X

Ster Century, Level 4, Castle Mall
Tel: 01603 221 900
Website: www.stercentury.co.uk
Seats: 1:170, 2:143, 3:216, 4:324, 5:313, 6:294, 7:331, 8:126

UCI, Riverside
X
Tel: 0870 010 2030
Website: www.uci-cinemas.co.uk
Seats: 1:168, 2:349, 3:123, 4:138, 5:157, 6:269, 7:464, 8:247, 9:157, 10:138, 11:138, 12:156, 13:247, 14:212

Nottingham - Notts

Broadway, Nottingham Media Centre, 14 Broad Street, NG1 3AL
Tel: 0115 952 6600/952 6611
Website: www.broadway.org.uk
Seats: 1:379 E, 2:155 XE

Royal Centre, Theatre Square (P/T)
Tel: 0115 989 5555
Seats: 1,000

Savoy, Derby Road
Tel: 0115 947 2580/941 9123
Seats: 1:386, 2:128, 3:168

Screen Room, Broad Street, Hockley
Tel: 0115 924 1133
Seats: 21

Showcase, Redfield Way, Lenton
Tel: 0115 986 6766
Website: www.showcasecinemas.co.uk
Seats: 3,307 (12 screens)

Warner Village, The Cornerhouse, Forman Street
Tel: 0115 950 0163/5
Seats: 1:368, 4:108, 5:146, 6:146, 7:130, 8:237, 9:139, 10:590, 11:108, 12:146, 13:146, 14:130
(Screens 2 &3 not in use in summer 2003))

Nuneaton - Warwicks

Odeon, St. David's Way, Bermuda Park
Tel: 0870 50 50 007
Website: www.odeon.co.uk
Seats: 1:471, 2:386, 3:314, 4:314, 5:253, 6:253, 7:210, 8:210

Okehampton - Devon

Carlton, St James Street
Tel: 01837 52167
Seats: 380

Oxford - Oxfordshire

Odeon, George Street
Tel: 0870 50 50 007
Website: www.odeon.co.uk
Seats: 1:252, 2:252, 3:111, 4:140, 5:239, 6:129

Odeon, Magdalen Street
Tel: 0870 50 50 007
Website: www.odeon.co.uk
Seats: 1:647, 2:61

Phoenix Picturehouse, 57 Walton Street
X
Tel: 01865 512526
Website: www.picturehouse-cinemas.co.uk
Seats: 1:220, 2:105

Ultimate Picture Palace, Jeune Street
X
Tel: 01865 245288
Seats: 185

Oxted - Surrey

The Screen At The Plaza, Station Road West
X
Tel: 01883 722288
Seats: 442

Padstow - Cornwall

Cinedrome, Lanadwell Street
Tel: 01841 532344
Seats: 183

Paignton - Devon

Apollo, Esplanade
Tel: 01803 558822
Website: www.apollocinemas.co.uk
Seats: 1:360, 2:360, 3: 181, 4;181, 5:217, 6:85, 7:83, 8:77, 9:86

Penistone - South Yorkshire

Paramount, Town Hall
X
Tel: 01226 762004
Seats: 348

Penrith - Cumbria

Alhambra, Middlegate
X
Tel: 01768 862400
Seats: 1:167, 2:90

Rhegel Discovery Centre
Tel: 01768 868000
Seats: 258 (large screen format)

Penzance - Cornwall

Savoy, Causeway Head
Tel: 01736 363330
Seats: 1:200, 2:50, 3:50

Peterborough – Cambridgeshire

Broadway, 46 Broadway (P/T)
Tel: 01733 316100
Seats: 1,200

Showcase, Mallory Road, Boon Gate
X
Tel: 01733 555636
Website: www.showcasecinemas.co.uk
Seats: 3,365 (13 screens)

Pickering - North Yorkshire

Castle, Burgate
Tel: 01751 472622
Seats: 180

Plymouth - Devon

ABC, Derry's Cross
Tel: 01752 663300/225553
Seats: 1:582, 2:380, 3:115

Arts Centre, Looe Street
X
Tel: 01752 206114
Seats: 73

Warner Village, Barbican Leisure Centre, Shapters Road, Coxside
Tel: 01752 223435
Seats: 1:167, 2:189, 3:152, 4:185, 5:187, 6:132, 7:283, 8:442, 9:479, 10:258, 11:208, 12:131, 13:126, 14:197, 15:178

Pocklington – East Yorks

Oak House, Pocklington Civic Arts Centre, Market Place (P/T)
Tel: 01759 301547
Seats: 200

Poole - Dorset

The Cinema, Poole Centre for the Arts, Kingland Road
X
Tel: 01202 685222
Seats: 103

UCI, Tower Park, Mannings Heath
Tel: 0870 010 2030
Website: www.uci-cinemas.co.uk
Seats: 1:194, 2:188, 3:188, 4:194, 5:276, 6:276, 7:194, 8:188, 9:188, 10:194

Portsmouth - Hants

Odeon, London Road, North End
Tel:0870 50 50 007
Website: www.odeon.co.uk
Seats: 1:631, 2:227, 3:175, 4:259

Rendezvous
Lion Gate Building
University of Portsmouth (S/O)
Tel: 023 92833854
Seats: 90

UCI, Port Way, Port Solent
X
Tel: 0870 010 2030
Website: www.uci-cinemas.co.uk
Seats: 1:214, 2:264, 3:318, 4:264, 5:257, 6:190

Warner Village, Gunwharf Quays
X
Tel: 02392 827600/827644
1:230, 2:332, 3:430, 4:332, 5:230, 9:246, 10:175, 11:193, 12:377, 13:167, 14:155 (Screens 6 to 8 not in use)

Potters Bar - Herts

Wyllyotts Centre, Darkes Lane (P/T)
X
Tel: 01707 645005
Seats: 345

Preston – Lancashire

UCI, Riversway, Ashton-on-Ribble
X
Tel: 0870 0102030
Website: www.uci-cinemas.co.uk
Seats: 1:194, 2:188, 3:188, 4:194, 5:276, 6:276, 7:194, 8:188, 9:188, 10:194

Warner Village, The Capitol Centre, London Way, Walton-le-Dale
X
Tel: 01772 881100/882525
Seats: 1:180, 2:180, 3:412, 4:236, 5:236, 6:412, 7:192

Quinton - West Midlands

Odeon, Hagley Road West
Tel: 0121 422 2562/2252
Website: www.odeon.co.uk
Seats: 1:300, 2:236, 3:232, 4:121

Ramsey - Cambridgeshire

Grand, Great Whyte (P/T)
Tel: 01487 710221
Seats: 173

Ramsgate - Kent

Granville Premier, Victoria Parade (P/T)
Tel: 01843 591750
Seats: 1:210, 2:230

Reading - Berkshire

(see also Wokingham)

Film Theatre, Whiteknights (P/T)
Tel: 0118 986 8497
Seats: 409

The Hexagon, South Street (P/T)
Tel: 0118 960 6060
Seats: 450

Warner Village, Oracle Centre
Tel: 0870 240 6020
Seats: 1:134, 2:147, 3:251, 4:373, 5:191, 6:191, 7:232, 8:148, 9:118, 10:88

Redcar - Cleveland

Regent, The Esplanade
Tel: 01642 482094
Seats: 350

Redhill - Surrey

The Harlequin, Warwick Quadrant (P/T)
X
Tel: 01737 765547
Seats: 494

Redruth - Cornwall

Regal Film Centre, Fore Street
Tel: 01209 216278
Seats: 1:171, 2:121, 3:600, 4:95

Reigate - Surrey

Screen, Bancroft Road
Tel: 01737 223200
Seats: 1:139, 2:142

Rickmansworth - Herts

Watersmeet Theatre, High Street (P/T)
Tel: 01923 771542
Seats: 390

Rochdale - Greater Manchester

Odeon, Sandbrook Way, Sandbrook Park
Tel: 0870 50 50 007
Website: www.odeon.co.uk
Seats: 1:474, 2:311, 3:311, 4:236, 5:208, 6:208, 7:208, 8:165, 9:165

Rochester - Kent

UGC, Valley Park, Chariot Way, Strood
XE
Tel: 01634 719963/08701 560568
Website: www.ugccinemas.co.uk
Seats: 1:485, 2:310, 3:310, 4:217, 5:220, 6:199, 7:199, 8:92, 9:142

Rubery - West Midlands

UGC, Great Park
XE
Tel: 0121 4530465/0870 907 0726
Website: www.ugccinemas.co.uk
Seats: 1:165, 2:187, 3:165, 4:149, 5:288, 6:194, 7:523, 8:247, 9:400 10:149 11:187 12:165, 13:82

Rugby - Warwicks

Cineworld, Junction One Retail & Leisure Park, Junction One, Leicester Road
Tel: 01788 551110
Website: www.cineworld.co.uk
Seats: 1:222, 2:95, 3:131, 4:120, 5:311, 6:290, 7:202, 8:131, 9:96

Runcorn - Cheshire

Cineworld, Trident Park, Halton Lea
Tel: 01928 759811
Website: www.cineworld.co.uk
Seats: 1:127, 2:121, 3:94, 4:87, 5:317, 6:283, 7:164, 8:184, 9:214

Ryde - Isle of Wight

Commodore, Star Street
Tel: 01983 564064
Seats: 1:180, 2:180, 3:180

St Albans - Herts

Alban Arena, Civic Centre (P/T) XE
Tel: 01727 844488
Seats: 800

St Austell - Cornwall

Film Centre, Chandos Place
Tel: 01726 73750
Seats: 1:274, 2:134, 3:133, 4:70, 5:70

St Helens - Merseyside

Cineworld, Chalon Way West
Tel: 01744 616576
Website: www.cineworld.co.uk
Seats: 1:180, 2:139, 3:210, 4:180, 5:115, 6:103, 7:129, 8:94, 9:283, 10:302, 11:269

St Helier Jersey - Channel Islands

Cineworld, Waterfront Centre
Tel: 01534 756200
Website: www.cineworld.co.uk
Seats: 1:303, 2:203, 3:189, 4:124, 5:91, 6:117, 7:139, 8:207, 9:242, 10:172

Odeon, Bath Street
Tel: 0870 50 50 007
Website: www.odeon.co.uk
Seats: 1:409, 2:247, 3:184 X, 4:162 X

St Ives - Cornwall

Royal, Royal Square
Tel: 01736 796843
Seats: 1:409, 2:244, 3:213, 4:171

St Peter Port Guernsey - Channel Islands

Beau Sejour Centre
Tel: 01481 26964
Seats: 250

St Saviour Jersey - Channel Islands

Cine Centre, St Saviour's Road
Tel: 01534 871611
Seats: 1:400, 2:291, 3:85

Salford Quays – Greater Manchester

Warner Village, The Designer Outlet at the Lowry
Tel: 08702 40 60 20/0161 872 1707
Seats: 1:566, 3:318, 4:207, 5:44, 7:224, 8:314, 9:210 (Screens 2 & 6 not in use in summer 2003)

Salisbury - Wiltshire

Odeon, New Canal
Tel: 0870 50 50 007
Website: www.odeon.co.uk
Seats: 1:471, 2:276 X, 3:127 X, 4:111 X, 5:70

Sandwich - Kent

Empire, Delf Street
Tel: 01304 620480
Seats: 130

Scarborough - North Yorkshire

Futurist, Forshaw Road (P/T)
X
Tel: 01723 370742
Seats: 1,200

Hollywood Plaza, North Marine Road
Tel: 01723 365119
Seats: 275

Stephen Joseph Theatre, Westborough (P/T)
XE
Tel: 01723 370541
Seats: 165 (McCarthy Auditorium)

YMCA Theatre, St Thomas Street (P/T)
Tel: 01723 506750
Seats: 290

Scunthorpe - Humberside

Screen, Central Library, Carlton Street, DN15 6TX (P/T)
X
Tel: 01724 860190/860161
Seats: 253

UCI, The Parishes, Fenton Street
Tel: 08700 10 20 30
Website: www.uci-cinemas.co.uk
Seats: 1:245, 2:243, 3:292, 4:159, 5:172, 6:172, 7:202

Sevenoaks - Kent

Stag Cinemas, London Road
Tel: 01732 450175/451548
Seats: 1:126, 2:108

Shaftesbury - Dorset

Arts Centre, Bell Street (P/T)
Tel: 01747 854321
Seats: 160

Sheffield - South Yorkshire

The Showroom, Media and Exhibition Centre, Paternoster Row, S1 2BX
X
Tel: 0114 275 7727
Website: www.showroom.org.uk
Seats: 1:83, 2:110, 3:178, 4:282

Odeon, Arundel Gate
XE
Tel: 0870 50 50 007
Website: www.odeon.co.uk
Seats: 1:252, 2:229, 3:248, 4:113, 5:113, 6:129, 7:171, 8:148, 9:150, 10:120

UGC, Don Valley, Broughton Lane
XE
Tel: 0114 2421237/0870 9020420
Website: www.ugccinemas.co.uk
Seats: 1:143, 2:141, 3:164, 4:262, 5:262, 6:551, 7:691, 8:551, 9:262, 9:262, 10:262, 11:173, 12:193, 13:115, 14:197, 15:197, 16:197, 17:197, 18:93, 19:82, 20:82

Warner Village, Meadowhall Centre
X
Tel: 0114 256 9825
Seats: 1:200, 2:200, 3:97, 4:238, 5:200, 6:365, 7:195, 8:195, 9:73, 10:195, 11:323

Shepton Mallet - Somerset

Amusement Centre, Market Place (P/T)
Tel: 01749 3444688
Seats: 270

Sheringham - Norfolk

Little Theatre, Station Road (S/O)
Tel: 01263 822347
Seats: 198

Shrewsbury - Shropshire

Cineworld, Old Potts Way
Tel: 01743 340726/240350
Website: www.cineworld.co.uk
Seats: 1:224, 2:157, 3:226, 4:280, 5:135, 6:100, 7:81, 8:222

The Music Hall Film Theatre, The Square, SY1 1LH
Tel: 01743 281281
Seats: 100

Sidmouth - Devon

Radway, Radway Place
X
Tel: 01395 513085
Seats: 272

Sittingbourne - Kent

New Century, High Street
Tel: 01795 423984/426018
Seats: 1:300, 2:110

Skegness - Lincolnshire

ABC, Butlins Family Entertainment Resort, Roman Bank
Tel: 0870 50 50 007
Seats: 1:120, 2:120

Tower, Lumley Road
Tel: 01754 763938
Seats: 401

Skipton - North Yorkshire

Plaza, Sackville Street
X
Tel: 01756 793417
Website: www.nm-cinemas.co.uk
Seats: 320

Slough - Berkshire

UGC, Queensmere Centre
E
Tel: 01753 511299/0870 9070715
Website: www.ugccinemas.co.uk
Seats: 1:140, 2:130, 3:160, 4:354, 5:456, 6:194, 7:92, 8:144, 9:83, 10:74

Solihull - West Midlands
Cineworld, Mill Lane Arcade (Upper), Touchwood
X
Tel: 0121 711 5000/1025
Website: www.cineworld.co.uk
Seats: 1:100, 2:200, 3:144, 4:225, 5:155, 6:317, 7:432, 8:158, 9:125

UCI, Highland Road, Shirley
X
Tel: 0870 010 2030
Website: www.uci-cinemas.co.uk
Seats: 286 (2 screens), 250 (2 screens), 214 (2 screens), 178 (2 screens)

South Shields - Tyne and Wear
Customs House, Mill Dam
Tel: 0191 454 1234
Seats: 1:400, 2:160

Southampton - Hants
Harbour Lights Picturehouse, Ocean Village SO14 3TL
Website: www.picturehouse-cinemas.co.uk
Tel: 023 8033 5533
Seats: 1:325, 2:144

Odeon, Leisure World, West Quay Road
Tel: 0870 50 50 007
Website: www.odeon.co.uk
Seats: 1:540, 2:495, 3:169, 4:111, 5:99, 6:139, 7:270, 8:318, 9:331, 10:288, 11:102, 12:102, 13:138

UGC Ocean Way, Ocean Village
XE
Tel: 02380 232 880/08701 555132
Website: www.ugccinemas.co.uk
Seats: 1:421, 2:346, 3:346, 4:258, 5:258

Southend - Essex
Odeon, Victoria Circus
XE
Tel: 0870 50 50 007
Website: www.odeon.co.uk
Seats: 1:200, 2:264, 3:145, 4:221, 5:388, 6:260, 7:260, 8:197

Southport - Merseyside
Arts Centre, Lord Street (P/T
X
Tel: 01704 540004/540011
Seats: 400

SBC, Ocean Plaza, Marine Drive XE
X
Tel: 0870 240 4442
Seats: 1:108, 2:129. 3:407, 4:155, 5:116, 6:277, 7:242

Southwold - Suffolk
Electric Picture Palace, Blackmill Road (P/T)
Seats: 66

Spalding - Lincolnshire
The South Holland Centre, Market Place (P/T)
X
Tel: 01775 725031

Stafford - Staffordshire
Apollo, Newport Road
Tel: 01785 251277
Website: www.apollocinemas.co.uk
Seats: 1:305, 2:170, 3:164
(Two additional screens to open by December 2003)

Staines - Middlesex
Warner Village, Tilly's Lane
X
Tel: 08702 406 020
Seats: 1:139, 2:180, 3:179, 4:140, 5:269, 6:269, 7:174, 8:173, 9:318, 10:375

Stalybridge - Greater Manchester
Palace, Market Street
Tel: 0161 330 1993
Website: www.cosmoleisure.com
Seats: 414

Stanley - Co Durham
Lamplight Arts Centre
Tel: 01207 218899

Stamford - Lincolnshire
Arts Centre, St. Mary's Street
Tel: 01780 763203
Seats: 166

Stevenage - Herts
Cineworld, Stevenage Leisure Park, Six Hills Way
X
Tel: 01438 740944/740310
Website: www.cineworld.co.uk
Seats: 1:357, 2:289, 3:175, 4:148, 5:88, 6:99, 7:137, 8:112, 9:168, 10:135, 11:173, 12:286, 13:247, 14:234, 15:202, 16:180

Gordon Craig Theatre, Lytton Way (P/T)
Tel: 01438 766 866
Seats: 507

Stockport - Greater Manchester
Plaza Super Cinema, Mersey Square (P/T)
Tel: 0161 477 7779
Seats: 1,200

UGC, Grand Central Square, Wellington Road South
XE
Tel: 0161 4765996/08701 555 157
Website: www.ugccinemas.co.uk
Seats: 1:303, 2:255, 3:243, 4:243, 5:122, 6:116, 7:96, 8:120, 9:84, 10:90

Stockton - Cleveland
The Arc, Dovecot Street
Tel: 01642 666600/666606/666669
Seats: 130

Showcase, Aintree Oval, Teeside Leisure Park (A66/A19 Junction)
Tel: 01642 633222
Website:
www.showcasecinemas.co.uk
Seats: 3,400 (14 screens)

Stoke-on-Trent - Staffordshire
Film Theatre, College Road, ST4 2DE
Tel: 01782 411188/413622
Seats: 212

Odeon, Festival Park, Etruria Road
X
Tel: 0870 50 50 007
Website: www.odeon.co.uk
Seats: 1:197, 2:212, 3:364, 4:158, 5:165, 6:181, 7:560, 8:158, 9:101, 10:74

Stourport - Hereford & Worcs
Civic Centre, Civic Hall, New Street
Tel: 01562 820 505
Seats: 399

Stowmarket - Suffolk
Regal, Ipswich Street (P/T)
Tel: 01449 612825
Seats: 234

Stratford-on-Avon - Warwicks
Picturehouse, Windsor Street
X
Tel: 01789 415500
Seats: 1:208, 2:104

Street - Somerset
Strode Theatre, Strode College, Church Road, BA16 0AB (P/T)
XE
Tel: 01458 442846/46529
Seats: 400

Sunninghill - Berkshire
Novello Theatre, High Street (P/T)
Tel: 01990 20881
Seats: 160

Sutton Coldfield - West Midlands

Odeon, Birmingham Road
Tel: 0870 50 50 007
Website: www.odeon.co.uk
Seats: 1:582, 2:134 X, 3:109 X, 4:327 X

Swanage - Dorset

Mowlem, Shore Road (P/T)
Tel: 01929 422239
Seats: 411

Swindon - Wiltshire

Arts Centre, Devizes Road, Old Town (P/T)
E
Tel: 01793 614 837
Seats: 228

Cineworld, Greenbridge Retail & Leisure Park, Drakes Way
X
Tel: 01793 484322/420710
Website: www.cineworld.co.uk
Seats: 1:327, 2:282, 3:170, 4:154, 5:94, 6:102, 7:134, 8:105, 9:139, 10:129, 11:137, 12:263

UGC, Shaw Ridge Leisure Park, Whitehill Way
XE
Tel: 01793 881118/08701 555134
Website: www.ugccinemas.co.uk
Seats: 1:349, 2:349, 3:297, 4:297, 5:272, 6:166, 7:144

Wyvern, Theatre Square (P/T)
Tel: 01793 524481
Seats: 617

Switch Island - Merseyside

Odeon, Dunnings Bridge Road, Netherton
Tel: 0870 50 50 007
Website: www.odeon.co.uk
Seats: 1:369, 2: 228, 3:130, 4:149, 5:243, 6:156, 7:338, 8:228, 9:130, 10:149, 11:243, 12:156

Tamworth - Staffordshire

Palace, Lower Gungate (P/T)
Tel: 01827 57100
Seats: 325

UCI, Bolebridge Street
X
Tel: 0870 010 2030
Website: www.uci-cinemas.co.uk
Seats: 203 (8 screens), 327 (2 screens)

Taunton - Somerset

Odeon, Heron Gate, Riverside
X
Tel: 0870 50 50 007
Website: www.odeon.co.uk
Seats: 1:125, 2:372, 3:258, 4:304, 5:124

Tavistock - Devon

The Wharf, Canal Street (P/T)
Tel: 01822 611166
Seats: 212

Telford - Shropshire

UCI Cinemas, Telford Centre, Forgegate
X
Tel: 0870 010 2030
Website: www.uci-cinemas.co.uk
Seats: 1:194, 2:188, 3:188, 4:194, 5:276, 6:276, 7:194, 8:188, 9:188, 10:194

Tenbury Wells - Hereford & Worcs

Regal, Teme Street (P/T)
Tel: 01584 810971
Seats: 260

Tewkesbury - Gloucestershire

Roses Theatre, Sun Street (P/T)
Tel: 01684 295074
Seats: 375

Thirsk - North Yorkshire

Ritz, Westgate
X
Tel: 01845 524751
Seats: 238

Tiverton - Devon

Tivoli, Fore Street
Tel: 01884 252157
Seats: 304

Tonbridge - Kent

Angel Centre, Angel Lane (P/T)
Tel: 01732 359588
Seats: 306

Torquay - Devon

Central, Abbey Road
Tel: 01803 380001
Seats: 1:308, 2:122, 3:78, 4:42

Nickelodeon, Blue Walnut Restaurant, Walnut Road, Chelston (P/T)
Tel: 01803 605995
Seats: 25

Torrington - Devon

Plough Arts Centre, Fore Street
Tel: 01805 622552/3
Seats: 108

Totnes - Devon

Dartington Arts Centre, Dartington Hall (P/T)
Tel: 01803 863073
Seats: 185

Truro - Cornwall

Plaza, Lemon Street
Tel: 01872 272 894
Seats: 1:300, 2:198, 3:135, 4:70

Tunbridge Wells - Kent

Odeon, Knights Way, Pembury
Tel: 0870 50 50 007
Website: www.odeon.co.uk
Seats: 1:437, 2:271, 3:257, 4:221, 5:138, 6:271, 7:257, 8:221, 9:139

Trinity Theatre, Church Road (P/T)
Tel: 01892 678678/678670
Seats: 294

Uckfield - East Sussex

Picture House, High Street
Tel: 01825 763822/764909
Website: www.picturehouseuckfield.com
Seats: 1:150, 2:100, 3:100

Ulverston - Cumbria

Laurel & Hardy Museum, Upper Brook Street (P/T) (S/O)
Tel: 01229 52292/86614
Seats: 50

Roxy, Brogden Street
Tel: 01229 53797/56211
Seats: 310

Urmston - Greater Manchester

Curzon, Princess Road, Flixton
Tel: 0161 755 0550
Website: www.curzonmanchester.co.uk
Seats: 1:400, 2:134

Uxbridge - Middlesex

Odeon, The Chimes
Tel: 0870 50 50 007
Website: www.odeon.co.uk
Seats: 1:310, 2:414, 3:254, 4:251, 5:153, 6:193, 7:241, 8:189, 9:253

Wadebridge - Cornwall

Regal, The Platt
Tel: 01208 812791
Seats: 1:224, 2:98

Wakefield - West Yorkshire

Cineworld, Westgate Retail Park, Colinsway
X
Tel: 01924 332230
Website: www.cineworld.co.uk
Seats: 1:323, 2:215, 3:84, 4:114, 5:183, 6:255, 7:255, 8:183, 9:114, 10:84, 11:215, 12:323

Wallingford - Oxfordshire
Corn Exchange (P/T)
Tel: 01491 825000
Seats: 187

Walsall - West Midlands
Showcase, Bentley Mill Way, Junction 10, M6
X
Tel: 01922 22123
Website: www.showcasecinemas.co.uk
Seats: 2,870 (12 screens)

Walton on Thames - Surrey
The Screen at Walton, High Street
Tel: 01932 252825
Seats: 1:200, 2:140

Wantage - Oxfordshire
Regent, Newbury Street
Tel: 01235 771 155
Seats: 1:110, 2:87

Wareham - Dorset
Rex, West Street
Tel: 01929 552778
Seats: 151

Warrington - Cheshire
UCI, Westbrook Centre, Cromwell Avenue
X
Tel: 08700 102030
Website: www.uci-cinemas.co.uk
Seats: 1:186, 2:180, 3:180, 4:186, 5:276, 6:276, 7:186, 8:180, 9:180, 10:186

Watford - Herts
Warner Village, Woodside Leisure Park, Garston
Tel: 01923 682886/682244
Seats: 1:249, 2:233, 3:264, 4:330, 5:221, 6:208, 7:215, 8:306

Wellingborough - Northants
Castle, Castle Way, Off Commercial Way (P/T)
Tel: 01933 270007
Seats: 500

Wellington - Somerset
Wellesley, Mantle Street
Tel: 01823 666668/666880
Seats: 400

Wells - Somerset
Film Centre, Princes Road
Tel: 01749 672036/673195
Seats: 1:116, 2:113, 3:82

Welwyn Garden City - Herts
Campus West, The Campus, AL8 6BX (P/T)
Tel: 01707 357165
Seats: 300

Westgate-on-Sea - Kent
Carlton, St Mildreds Road
Tel: 01843 832019
Seats: Premiere: 297 X, Century: 56 X, Bijou: 32

Weston-Super-Mare - Avon
Odeon, The Centre
Tel: 0870 50 50 007
Website: www.odeon.co.uk
Seats: 1:581, 2:104, 3:120, 4:273

Playhouse, High Street (P/T)
Tel: 01934 23521/31701
Seats: 658

West Thurrock - Essex
UCI, Lakeside Retail Park
X
Tel: 0870 010 2030
Website: www.uci-cinemas.co.uk
Seats: 276 (2 screens), 194 (4 screens), 188 (4 screens)

Warner Village, Lakeside Shopping Centre
X
Tel: 01708 860 393
Seats: 1:382, 2:184, 3:177, 4:237, 5:498, 6:338, 7:208

Wetherby - West Yorkshire
Film Theatre, Caxton Street
Tel: 01937 580544
Seats: 156

Weymouth - Dorset
Cineworld, New Bond Street
X
Tel: 01305 768798
Website: www.cineworld.co.uk
Seats: 1:299, 2:218, 3:265, 4:102, 5:136, 6:187, 7:139, 8:132, 9:148

Whitby – North Yorkshire
Coliseum, Victoria Place
Tel: 01947 825000
Seats: 99

Whitehaven - Cumbria
Gaiety, Tangier Street
Tel: 01946 693012
Seats: 264

Rosehill Theatre, Moresby (P/T)
X
Tel: 01946 694039/692422
Seats: 208

Whitley Bay - Tyne and Wear
Playhouse, Marine Avenue (P/T)
Tel: 0191 252 3505
Seats: 746

Whitstable - Kent
Imperial Oyster, The Horsebridge, Horsebridge Road
Tel: 01227 770829
Seats: 144

Wigan - Greater Manchester
UGC, Anjou Boulevard, Robin Park, Robin Park Road, Newtown
XE
Tel: 01942 218005/08701 555 157
Website: www.ugccinemas.co.uk
Seats: 1:554, 2:290, 3:290, 4:207, 5:207, 6:163, 7:163, 8:163, 9:163, 10:207, 11:129

Wilmslow - Cheshire
Rex, Alderley Road (P/T)
Tel: 01625 522266
Seats: 838

Wimborne - Dorset
Tivoli, West Borough (P/T)
Tel: 01202 848014
Seats: 500

Winchester - Hants
The Screen at Winchester, Southgate Street
X
Tel: 01962 856009
Seats: 1:214, 2:170

Windsor - Berkshire
Arts Centre, St Leonards Road (P/T)
Tel: 01753 8593336
Seats: 108

Witney - Oxfordshire
Corn Exchange, Market Square (P/T)
Tel: 01993 703646
Seats: 207

Woking - Surrey
Ambassador Cinemas, Peacock Centre off Victoria Way
X
Tel: 01483 761144
Seats: 1:434, 2:447, 3:190, 4:236, 5:268, 6:89

Wokingham - Berkshire
Showcase, Loddon Bridge, Reading Road, Winnersh
X
Tel: 0118 974 7711
Website: www.showcasecinemas.co.uk
Seats: 2,980 (12 screens)

Wolverhampton - West Midlands

Cineworld, Bentley Bridge Leisure, Wednesfield Way, Wednesfield
Tel: 01902 306922/306911
Website: www.cineworld.co.uk
Seats: 1:103, 2:113, 3:151, 4:205, 5:192, 6:343, 7:379, 8:343, 9:184, 10:89, 11:105, 12:162, 13:143, 14:98

Light House, Chubb Buildings, Fryer Street
XE
Tel: 01902 716055
Seats: 1:242, 2:80

Woodbridge - Suffolk

Riverside Theatre, Quay Street
Tel: 01394 382174/380571
Seats: 280

Woodhall Spa - Lincolnshire

Kinema in the Woods, Coronation Road
Tel: 01526 352166
Seats: 1:290, 2:90

Hereford Worcester – Hereford & Words

Odeon, Foregate Street
Tel: 0870 50 50 007
Website: www.odeon.co.uk
Seats: 1:273, 2:175, 3:172, 4:67, 5:128 X, 6:95 X, 7:202 X

Warner Village, Friar Street
Tel: 01905 617806/617737
Seats: 1:234, 2:254, 3:330,4:249, 5:212, 6:92

Workington - Cumbria

Plaza, Dunmail Park Shopping Centre, Maryport Road
X
Tel: 01900 870001
Seats: 1:307, 2:229, 3:174, 4:95, 5:95, 6:95

Worksop - Notts

Regal, Carlton Road
Tel: 01909 482896
Seats: 1:326 (P/T), 2:154

Worthing - West Sussex

Connaught Theatre, Union Place
Tel: 01903 231799/235333
Seats: 1:512 (P/T), 2(Ritz): 220

Dome, Marine Parade
Tel: 01903 823112/200461
Website: www.worthingdome.com
Seats: 1:425, 2:120

Yeovil - Somerset

Cineworld, Yeo Leisure Park, Old Station Way
Tel: 01935 381880/472042
Website: www.cineworld.co.uk
Seats: 1:168, 2:314, 3:242, 4:184, 5:97, 6:117, 7:141, 8:152, 9:278, 10:202

York - North Yorkshire

City Screen, Coney Street
Tel: 01904 541144
Website: www.picturehouse-cinemas.co.uk
Seats: 1:226, 2:142, 3:135

Odeon, Blossom Street
Tel: 0870 50 50 007
Website: www.odeon.co.uk
Seats: 1:799, 2:111 X, 3:111 X

Warner Village, Clifton Moor Centre, Stirling Road
X
Tel: 01904 691147/691094
Seats: 1:128, 2:212, 3:316, 4:441, 5:185, 6:251, 7:251, 8:185, 9:441, 10:316, 11::212, 12:128

SCOTLAND

Aberdeen - Grampian

Belmont Picturehouse, Belmont Street
Tel: 01224 343536/343534
Seats 1:272, 2:146, 3:67

SBC The Lighthouse, Shiprow
Tel: 084560 20266
Seats: 1:321, 2:221, 3:180, 4:236, 5:219, 6:165, 7:190

UGC, Queens Link Leisure Park, Links Road
XE
Tel: 01224 572228/08701 550 502
Website: www.ugccinemas.co.uk
Seats: 1:160, 2:86, 3:208, 4:290, 5:560, 6:280, 7:208, 8:160, 9:160

Annan - Dumfries & Gall

Lonsdale Cinemas, Lady Street Leisure Centre, Moat Street
Tel: 01461 206901
Seats: 1:107, 2:57

Aviemore - Highlands

Speyside, Aviemore Centre
X
Tel: 01479 810624/810627
Seats: 721

Ayr - Strathclyde

Odeon, Burns Statue Square
Tel: 0870 50 50 007
Website: www.odeon.co.uk
Seats: 1:386, 2:164, 3:129, 4:449

Campbeltown - Strathclyde

Picture House, Hall Street (P/T)
Tel: 01586 553899
Seats: 265

Clydebank - Strathclyde

UCI, Clyde Regional Centre, Britannia Way
X
Tel: 0870 0102030
Website: www.uci-cinemas.co.uk
Seats: 1:202, 2:202, 3:230, 4:253, 5:390, 6:390, 7:253, 8:230, 9:202, 10:202

Coatbridge - Strathclyde

Showcase, Langmuir Road, Bargeddie, Bailleston
X
Tel: 01236 434 434
Website:
www.showcasecinemas.co.uk
Seats: 3,664 (14 screens)

Dumfries - Dumfries & Gall

Odeon, Shakespeare Street

Tel: 01387 253578
Website: www.odeon.co.uk
Seats: 360

Robert Burns Centre Film Theatre, Mill Road (P/T)
Tel: 01387 264808
Seats: 67

Dundee - Tayside

Dundee Contemporary Arts, Nethergate
Tel: 01382 432000
Seats: 1:217, 2:77

Odeon, Eclipse Leisure Park
X
Tel: 0870 50 50 007
Website: www.odeon.co.uk
Seats: 1:409, 2:234, 3:317, 4:182, 5:102, 6:479, 7:256, 8:294, 9:161, 10:118

Steps Theatre, Central Library, The Wellgate, DD1 1DB
Tel: 01382 432082
Seats: 250

UGC, Camperdown Park, Dayton Drive
XE
Tel: 01382 828793/0870 9020407
Website: www.ugccinemas.co.uk
Seats: 1:263, 2: 180, 3:109, 4:224, 5:512, 6:224, 7:130, 8:109, 9:79

Dunfermline - Fife

Odeon, Whimbrel Place, Fife Leisure Park
X
Tel: 0870 50 50 007
Website: www.odeon.co.uk
Seats: 1:265, 2:333, 3:265, 4:207, 5:137, 6:415, 7:265, 8:333, 9:207, 10:137

Dunoon - Strathclyde

Studio, John Street
Tel: 01369 704545
Seats: 1:188, 2:70

East Kilbride - Strathclyde

Arts Centre, Old Coach Road (P/T)
Tel: 01355 261000
Seats: 96

UCI, Olympia Shopping Centre, Rothesay Street, Town Centre
Tel: 0870 0102030
Website: www.uci-cinemas.co.uk
Seats: 1:319, 2:206, 3:219, 4:207, 5:207, 6:219, 7:206, 8:206, 9:219

Edinburgh - Lothian

Cameo, Home Street, Tollcross
X
Tel: 0131 228 4141
Seats: 1:253, 2:75, 3:66

Dominion, Newbattle Terrace, Morningside
Tel: 0131 447 2660/4771
Seats: 1:586, 2:317, 322:47, 4:67

Filmhouse, 88 Lothian Road, EH3 9BZ
XE
Tel: 0131 228 2688/6382
Seats: 1:280, 2:97, 3:73

Odeon, Clerk Street
Tel: 0870 50 50 007
Website: www.odeon.co.uk
Seats: 1:639, 2:292 X, 3:201 X, 4:261, 5:165

Odeon, Lothian Road
Seats: 800 (4 screens)
(Scheduled to open in September 2003)

Odeon, Westside Plaza, Wester Hailes Road
X
Tel: 0870 50 50 007
Website: www.odeon.co.uk
Seats: 1:414, 2:317, 3:317, 4:243, 5:227, 6:211, 7:189, 8:170

Ster Century, Ocean Terminal, Leith
X
Tel: 0131 553 0700
Website: www.stercentury.co.uk
Seats: 1:220, 2:155, 3:138, 4:138, 5: 155, 6: 220, 7: 372, 8: 322, 9: 145, 10:155, 11: 319, 12: 372

UCI, Kinnaird Park, Newcraighall Road
X
Tel: 0870 0102030
Website: www.uci-cinemas.co.uk
Seats: 170 (6 screens), 208 (4 screens), 312 (2 screens)

UGC, Fountain Park, Dundee Street
XE
Tel: 0131 2288788/0870 9020417
Website: www.ugccinemas.co.uk
Seats: 1:298, 2:339, 3:228, 4:208, 5:174, 6:159, 7:527, 8:248, 9:188, 10:194, 11:194, 12:177, 13:88

Warner Village, Omni, Greenside, Leith Walk
X
Tel: 08702 406020
Seats: 1:348, 2:274, 3:461, 4:188, 5:148, 6:93, 7:115, 8:175, 9:175, 10:76, 11:76,12: 76

Falkirk – Central
Cineworld, Central Retail Park, Old Bison Works, off Stewart Road/Queen's Street
X
Tel: 01324 617860
Website: www.cineworld.co.uk
Seats: 1:311, 2:218, 3:103, 4:128, 5:171, 6:253, 7:253, 8:171, 9:128, 10:103, 11:243, 12:232

FTH Arts Centre, Town Hall, West Bridge Street
Tel: 01324 506850

Fort William - Highlands

Studios 1 and 2, Cameron Square
Tel: 01397 705095
Seats: 1:128, 2:76

Galashiels - Borders

Pavilion, Market Street
Tel: 01896 752767
Seats: 1:335, 2:172, 3:147, 4:56

Glasgow - Strathclyde

Bombay, Lorne Road, Ibrox
Tel: 0141 419 0722

Glasgow Film Theatre, 12 Rose Street, G3 6RB
XE
Tel: 0141 332 6535/8128
Seats: 1:404, 2:144

Odeon, Renfield Street
X
Tel: 0870 50 50 007
Website: www.odeon.co.uk
Seats: 1:555, 2:152, 3:113, 4:173, 5:188, 6:231, 7:239, 8:249, 9:222

Odeon, Springfield Quay, Paisley Road
X
Tel:0870 50 50 007
Website: www.odeon.co.uk
Seats: 1:431, 2:131, 3:91, 4:200, 5:202, 6:280, 7:324, 8:131, 9:90, 10:194, 11:244, 12:258

UGC, The Forge, Parkhead
XE
Tel:0141 5564282/08701 555173
Website: www.ugccinemas.co.uk
Seats: 1:434, 2:434, 3:322, 4:262, 5:208, 6:144, 7:132

UGC, Renfrew Street, West Nile Street
XE
Tel: 0141 353 6699/0870 9070789
Website: www.ugccinemas.co.uk

Seats: 1:169, 2:157, 3:663, 4:192, 5:216, 6:137, 7:432, 8:195, 9:241, 10:180, 11:370, 12:195, 13:241, 14:180, 15:370, 16:83, 17:83, 18:173

Glenrothes - Fife
Kingsway, Church Street
Tel: 01592 750980
Seats: 1:294, 2:223

Greenock - Strathclyde
Waterfront, off Container Way
Tel: 01475 732201
Seats: 1:258, 2:148, 3:106, 4:84

Hamilton - Strathclyde
SBC Cinemas, Palace Grounds Road
Tel: 0870 240 4442
Seats: 1:459, 2:180, 3:193, 4:101, 5:101, 6:93, 7:148, 8:148, 9:93

Inverness - Highlands
Eden Court Theatre, Bishops Road
Tel: 01463 234234
Seats: 84

Warner Village, Inverness Business and Retail Park, Eastfield Way
Tel: 01463 711 175/147
Seats: 1:314, 2:352, 3:160, 4:203, 5:430, 6:203, 7:160

Irvine - Stathclyde
Magnum, Harbourside (S/O)
X
Tel: 01294 313010
Seats: 311

Kelso - Borders
Roxy, Horse Market
Tel: 01573 224609
Seats: 260

Kilmarnock - Strathclyde
Odeon, Queens Drive
X
Tel: 0870 50 50 007
Website: www.odeon.co.uk
Seats: 1:304, 2:304, 3:143, 4:183, 5:432, 6:183, 7:143, 8:199

Kirkcaldy – Fife
Adam Smith Theatre
Bennochy Road, KY1 1ET (P/T) XE
Tel: 01592 412929
Seats: 475

Kirkwall - Orkney
New Phoenix, Pickaquoy Centre, Muddisdale Road
Tel: 01856 879900
Seats: 244

Largs - Strathclyde
Vikingar Cinema, Greenock Road (S/O)
Tel: 01475 689777
Seats: 500

Livingston – West Lothian
The Circuit, McArthur Glen Designer Outlet, Almondvale North
X
Tel: 0870 240 4442
Seats: 1:402, 2:178, 3:140, 4:211, 5:254, 6:140, 7:140, 8:195

Millport - Strathclyde
The Cinema (Town Hall), Clifton Street (S/O)
Tel: 01475 530741
Seats: 250

Motherwell - Lanarkshire
Civic Theatre, Civic Centre (P/T)
Tel: 01698 66166
Seats: 395

Newton Stewart - Dumfries & Gall
Cinema, Victoria Street
Tel: 01671 403 333

Oban - Strathclyde
Highland Theatre, Highland Discovery Centre, George Street (P/T)
Tel: 01631 563794
Seats: 1:277, 2:25

Paisley - Strathclyde
Showcase, Phoenix Business Park, Linwood
Tel: 0141 887 0011
Website:
www.showcasecinemas.co.uk
Seats: 3,784 (14 screens)

Perth - Tayside
Playhouse, Murray Street
Tel: 01738 623126
Seats: 1:606, 2:56, 3:156, 4:144, 5:131, 6:113, 7:110

Pitlochry - Tayside
Regal, Athal Road (S/O)
Tel: 01796 2560
Seats: 400

Portree - Highland
Aros Cinema, Viewfield Road
Tel: 01478 613750
Seats: 400

Rothesay - Isle of Bute
MBC Cinema, Winter Gardens, Victoria Centre, Victoria Street
Tel: 01700 505462
Seats: 98

St Andrews - Fife
New Picture House, North Street
X
Tel: 01334 473509
Seats: 1:500, 2:120, 3:100

Saltcoats - Ayrshire
Apollo, Esplanade, Winton Circus
Tel: 01294 471777
Seats: 1:144, 2:144

Stirling - Central
Carlton, Allanpark
Tel: 01786 474137
Seats: 1:399, 2:289

MacRobert Arts Centre, University of Stirling, FK9 4LA (P/T)
XE
Tel: 01786 461081
Seats: 495

Stornoway - Western Isles
Twilights, Seaforth Hotel, James Street (P/T)
Tel: 01851 702740
Seats: 60

Thurso – Highland
All Star Factory, Ormlie Road
Tel: 01847 890890
Seats: 1:88, 2:152

WALES

Aberaman - Mid Glamorgan
Grand Theatre, Cardiff Road (P/T)
Tel: 01685 872310
Seats: 950

Abercwmboi - Mid Glamorgan
Capitol Screen
Tel: 01443 475766
Seats: 280

Aberdare - Mid Glamorgan
Coliseum, Mount Pleasant Street (P/T)
X
Tel: 01685 881188
Seats: 621

Aberystwyth - Dyfed
Arts Centre, Penglais, Campus, University of Wales (P/T)
Tel: 01970 623232
Seats: 125

Commodore, Bath Street
Tel: 01970 612421
Seats: 410

Bala - Gwynedd
Neuadd Buddug (P/T)
Tel: 01678 520 800
Seats: 372

Bangor - Gwynedd
Apollo, High Street
Tel: 01248 371080
Website: www.apollocinemas.co.uk
Seats: 1:248, 2:178

Theatr Gwynedd, Deiniol Road (P/T)
X
Tel: 01248 351707/351708
Seats: 343

Barry - South Glamorgan
Theatre Royal, Broad Street
Tel: 01446 735019
Seats: (two screens)

Bethesda - Gwynedd
Ogwen, High Street (P/T)
Tel: 01286 676335
Seats: 315

Blackwood - Gwent
Miners' Institute, High Street (P/T)
X
Tel: 01495 227206
Seats: 409

Blaenavon - Gwent
Workman's Hall, High Street (P/T)
Tel: 01495 792661
Seats: 80

Blaengarw – Mid Glamorgan
Workmen's Hall, Blaengarw Rd (P/T)
X
Tel: 01656 871911
Seats: 250

Brecon - Powys
Coliseum Film Centre, Wheat Street
Tel: 01874 622501
Seats: 1:164, 2:164

Bridgend - Mid Glamorgan
Odeon, McArthur Glen Designer Outlet
X
Tel: 0870 50 50 007
Website: www.odeon.co.uk
Seats: 1:428, 2:324, 3:252, 4:245, 5:219, 6:176, 7:154, 8:162, 9:110

Brynamman - Dyfed
Public Hall, Station Road
Tel: 01269 823232
Seats: 838

Brynmawr - Gwent
Market Hall, Market Square
Tel: 01495 310576
Seats: 320

Builth Wells - Powys
Castle Cinema, Wyeside Arts Centre, Castle Street
Tel: 01982 552555
Seats: 210

Cardiff - South Glamorgan
Chapter, Market Road
Canton, CF5 1QE
X
Tel: 029 20304 400
Seats: 1:194, 2:68

St David's Hall, The Hayes (P/T)
Tel: 029 20371236/42611
Seats: 1,600

Ster Century, Millennium Plaza
X
Website: www.stercentury.co.uk
Seats: 1:132, 2:146, 3:273, 4:372, 5:347, 6:271, 7:191, 8:118, 9:132, 10:252, 11:324, 12:323, 13:351, 14:173

UCI, Hemingway Road, Atlantic Wharf, Cardiff Bay
X
Tel: 0870 010 2030
Website: www.uci-cinemas.co.uk
Seats: 1:520, 2:353, 3:351, 4:313, 5:267, 6:267, 7:200, 8:200, 9:153, 10:153, 11:147, 12:147

UGC, Mary Ann Street
XE
Tel: 02920 667667/0870 9070739
Website: www.ugccinemas.co.uk
Seats: 1:132, 2:195, 3:195, 4:126, 5:155, 6:206, 7:248, 8:375, 9:478, 10:125, 11:154, 12:206, 13:248, 14:183, 15:183

Cardigan - Dyfed
Theatr Mwldan, Bath House Road (P/T)
X
Tel: 01239 621200
Seats: 210

Carmarthen - Dyfed
Lyric, King's Street (P/T)
Tel: 01267 232632
Seats: 740

Colwyn Bay – Clwyd
Theatr Colwyn, Abergele Road (P/T)
Tel: 01492 872000
Seats: 386

Cross Hands - Dyfed
Public Hall
Tel: 01269 844441
Seats: 300

Cwmaman - Mid Glamorgan
Public Hall, Alice Place (P/T)
Tel: 01685 876003
Seats: 344

Cwmbran - Gwent
Scene, The Mall
Tel: 016338 66621
Seats: 1:115, 2:78, 3:130

Ferndale - Mid Glamorgan
Cinema, Hall, High Street (P/T)
Seats: 190

Fishguard - Dyfed
Theatr Gwaun, West Street
Tel: 01348 873421/874051
Seats: 252

Harlech - Gwynedd
Theatr Ardudwy, Coleg Harlech (P/T)
Tel: 01766 780667
Seats: 266

Haverfordwest - Dyfed
Palace, Upper Market Street
Tel: 01437 767675
Seats: 500

Holyhead - Gwynedd
Empire, Stanley Street
Tel: 01407 761458
Seats: 160

Ucheldre Centre, Millbank Road (P/T)
X
Tel: 01407 763361
Seats: 170

Llandudno Junction - Gwynedd
Cineworld, Junction Leisure Park, Off Junction Way
Tel: 01492 580503
Website: www.cineworld.co.uk
Seats: 1:228, 2:100, 3:138, 4:107, 5:322, 6:292, 7:207, 8:138, 9:100

Llanelli - Dyfed
Entertainment Centre, Station Rd
Tel: 07000 001234
Seats: 1:516, 2:310, 3:122

Llantwit Major - Mid Glamorgan
St Donat's Arts Centre, St Donat's Castle
Tel: 01446 799099
Seats: 220

Maesteg - Mid Glamorgan
Town Hall Cinema, Talbot Street
Tel: 01656 733269
Seats: 170

Merthyr Tydfil - Mid Glamorgan
Castle
Tel: 01685 386669
Seats: 1:98, 2:198

Milford Haven - Dyfed
Torch Theatre, St Peters Road
Tel: 01646 695267
Seats: 297

Mold - Clwyd
Theatr Clwyd, County Civic Centre, CH7 1YA
X
Tel: 01352 756331/755114
Seats: 1:530, 2:129

Monmouth - Gwent
Savoy, Church Street
Tel: 01600 772467
Seats: 450

Nantgarw – Mid Glamorgan
Showcase, Treforest
Tel: 01443 846 908
Website: www.showcasecinemas.co.uk
Seats: 2,604 (12 screens)

Newport – Gwent
City Cinema, Bridge Street
Tel: 01633 224040
Seats: 1:406, 2:170, 3:117

UGC, Retail Park, Seven Styles Avenue
X
Tel: 01633 274272/08701 550516
Website: www.ugccinemas.co.uk
Seats: 1:199, 2:178, 3:123, 4:187, 5:267, 6:405, 7:458, 8:287, 9:180, 10:123, 11:211, 12:156, 13:77

Newtown - Powys
Regent, Broad Street
Tel: 01686 625917
Seats: 1:210, 2:40

Pontardawe - West Glamorgan
Arts Centre, Herbert Street
Tel: 01792 863722
Seats: 450

Pontypool - Gwent
Scala, Osborne Road
Tel: 0149 575 6038
Seats: 197

Pontypridd - Mid Glamorgan
Muni Screen, Gelliwastad Rd (P/T)
XE
Tel: 01443 485934
Seats: 400

Port Talbot - West Glamorgan
Apollo, Hollywood Park, Aberavon Sea Front, Princess Margaret Way
Tel: 01639 895552
Website: www.apollocinemas.co.uk
Seats: 1:118, 2:103, 3:258, 4:258, 5:118, 6:118

Porthcawl - Mid Glamorgan
Grand Pavilion (S/O) (P/T)
Tel: 01656 786996
Seats: 500

Porthmadog - Gwynedd
Coliseum, Avenue Road
Tel: 01766 512108
Website: www.coliseum-porthmadog.co.uk
Seats: 582

Pwllheli - Gwynedd
Neuadd Dwyfor/Town Hall Cinema (P/T)
Tel: 01758 613371
Seats: 450

Rhyl - Clwyd
Apollo, Children's Village, West Promenade
Tel: 01745 353856
Website: www.apollocinemas.co.uk
Seats: 1:206, 2:206, 3:117, 4:107, 5:107

Swansea - West Glamorgan
Taliesin Arts Centre, University College, Singleton Park, SA2 8PZ
XE
Tel: 01792 296883/295491
Seats: 328

UCI, Quay Parade, Parc Tawe
X
Tel: 01792 645005
Website: www.uci-cinemas.co.uk
Seats: 1:180, 2:188, 3:188, 4:194, 5:276, 6:276, 7:194, 8:188, 9:188, 10:180

Tenby - Dyfed
Royal Playhouse, White Lion Street
Tel: 01834 844809
Seats: 400

Treorchy - Mid Glamorgan
Parc and Dare Theatre, Station Road
Tel: 01443 773112
Seats: 794

Tywyn - Gwynedd
The Cinema, Corbett Square
X
Tel: 01654 710260
Seats: 368

Welshpool - Mid Glamorgan
Pola, Berriew Street
Tel: 01938 555715
Seats: 1:150, 2:40

Wrexham - Clwyd
Odeon, Plas Coch Retail Park, Plas Coch Road
X
Tel: 0870 50 50 007
Website: www.odeon.co.uk
Seats: 1:351, 2:188, 3:147, 4:251, 5:110, 6:110, 7:110

Ystradgynlais - Mid Glamorgan
Miners' Welfare and Community Hall, Brecon Road (P/T)
X
Tel: 01639 843163
Seats: 345

NORTHERN IRELAND

Antrim - Antrim

Cineplex, Fountain Hill
Tel: 028 94 469500
Seats: 1:312, 2:232, 3:132, 4:112

Armagh - Armagh

City Film House, Market Street
Tel: 028 37 511033
Seats: 1:225. 2:128, 3:197, 4:91

Ballymena - Antrim

IMC, Larne Link Road
Tel: 028 25 631111
Seats: 1:342, 2:261, 3:160, 4:160, 5:109, 6:112, 7:109

Bangor - Down

Cineplex, Valentine's Road, Castlepark
Tel: 028 91454729
Seats: 1:287, 2:196, 3:164, 4:112

Belfast - Antrim

Cineworld, Kennedy Centre, Falls Road
E
Tel: 028 90 600988
Seats: 1:296, 2:190, 3:178, 4:178, 5:165

Movie House, Yorkgate Shopping Centre
X
Tel: 028 90 755000
Seats: 1:314, 2:264, 3:248, 4:181, 5:172, 6:97, 7:97, 8:332, 9:72, 10:67, 11:67, 12:83, 13:83, 14:475

Queen's Film Theatre, 25 College Gardens, BT9 6BS
X
Tel: 028 90 244857/667687
Seats: 1:250, 2:150

Sheridan IMAX Cinema, Odyssey Pavilion, Queen's Quay
Tel: 028 9046 7000
Seats: 373

The Strand, Hollywood Road
Tel: 028 90 673500
Seats: 1:250, 2:193, 3:84, 4:98

UGC, Dublin Road
X
Tel: 02890 245700/08701 555176
Website: www.ugccinemas.co.uk
Seats: 1:436, 2:354, 3:262 X, 4:264 X, 5:252, 6:272, 7:187 X, 8:187 X, 9:169, 10:118 X

Warner Village Cinemas, The Pavillion, Odyssey Centre 2, Queens Quay
X
Tel: 02890 739134/08702 406020
1:405, 2:155, 3:155, 4:155, 5:476, 6:188, 7:188, 8:267, 9:294, 10:280, 11:246, 12:246

Carrickfergus - Antrim

Omniplex, Marina, Rogers Quay
Tel: 02893 351111
Seats: 1: 378, 2:232, 3:210, 4:153, 5:117, 6:128

Coleraine - Londonderry

Jet Centre, Riverside Park
Tel: 028 70 329909
Seats: 1:273, 2:193, 3:152, 4:104

Cookstown - Tyrone

Ritz, Burn Road
Tel: 02886 765182
Seats: 1:355, 2:200. 3:95, 4:100, 5:80

Dungannon - Tyrone

Global Cinemas, Oaks Centre, Oaks Road
Tel: 02887 727733
Seats: (6 screens)

Dungiven - Londonderry

St Canice's Hall, Main Street
Seats: 300

Enniskillen - Fermanagh

Ardhowen Theatre, Dublin Road (P/T)
Tel: 028 66325440
Seats: 295

Omniplex, Factory Road
Tel: 02866 324777
Seats: 1:300, 2:126, 3:104, 4:154, 5:254, 6:165, 7:78

Glengormley - Antrim

Movie House, Glenville Road
Tel: 028 90 833424
Seats: 1:309, 2:243, 3:117, 4:110, 5:76, 6:51

Kilkeel - Down

Vogue, Newry Road
Tel: 016937 63092
Seats: 295

Lisburn - Antrim

Omniplex, Governors Road
Tel: 028 92 663664
Seats: 1:489, 2:219, 3:161, 4:112, 5:176, 6:234, 7:142, 8:112, 9:84, 10:66, 11:66, 12:84, 13:97, 14:148

Londonderry - Londonderry

Orchard, Orchard Street
Tel: 028 71 267789
Seats: 1:132, 2:700 (P/T)

Strand, Quayside Centre, Strand Road
Tel: 028 71 373939/373900
Seats: 1:317, 2:256, 3:227, 4:227, 5:134, 6:124, 7:90

Lurgan - Armagh

Euroscreen International, Portadown Road
Tel: 028 3832 1997
Seats: 1:276, 2:180, 3:110, 4:90

Maghera - Londonderry

Movie House, St Lurach's Road
Tel: 028 796 43872/42936
Seats: 1:221, 2:117, 3:95

Newry - Down

Omniplex, Quays Shopping Centre, Albert Basin
Tel: 028 30256098
Seats: 1:470, 2:219, 3:168, 4:203, 5:203, 6:168, 7:219, 8:333, 9:122

Newtownards - Down

Movieland, Ards Shopping Centre
Tel: 028 9182 2000/01247 821000
Seats: 1:278, 2:238, 3:155, 4:155, 5:119, 6:119

Omagh - Tyrone

Studios 1-6, Gillyhooley Road
Tel: 02882 242034
Seats: (six screens)

Portrush - Antrim

Playhouse, Main Street
Tel: 028 7082 3917
Seats: 1:315, 2:65

COURSES

Listed here is just a small selection of film schools, educational establishments and companies which offer courses in film and television. The duration of the courses vary from half a day to several years, and are designed for all levels from beginners to professional film-makers.

Professionals will know which specialised course they are looking for, however, for beginners, care should be taken and a good starting point would be a one-day seminar or a short introductory course in the area chosen. Students may find, that before starting a course, they need to take a preliminary, possibly part-time evening course, to allow them to make the best of a short, expensive, specialist course. For example, before going on an "Avid Film Editing Course" on a Macintosh computer, it would be advisable to be very familiar with Macintosh computers and have done some film editing.

Film-making courses are frequently 100 per cent practical and film studies courses can be 100 per cent theoretical. However, many courses are a mixture and it is always advisable, if possible, to visit the organisation before enrolling, to clearly understand what the course entails, and to see how much equipment is available for student use. For all practical courses, the ratio of equipment to students, and the quality of the equipment and facilities should be checked.

For a full and more detailed search of courses from the Skillset/bfi database of over four thousand media and multimedia courses go to the webpage:

www.bfi.org.uk/mediacourses

Please note that inclusion in this listing does not constitute a recommendation. Compiled by Lavinia Orton

Academy of Radio, Film and Television

American Building
79A Tottenham Court Road
London W1T 4TD
Website: www.londonacademy.co.uk
Contact: Tracey Parkin
Tel: 020 8408 7158
email: help@londonacademy.co.uk
London Academy of Radio, Film & TV is aimed at people who are looking for a career and who want to update their existing skills. Courses are run on a day, evening and weekend basis and cover a variety of the skills needed to succeed in the world of radio, film and television

The Arts Institute at Bournemouth

School of Media
Wallisdown
Poole
Dorset BH12 5HH
Website: www.aib.ac.uk
Contact: Course Office
Tel: 01202 363228
Fax: 01202 537729
email: courseoffice@aib.ac.uk
Run BA Film and Animation Production Course

BBC Training and Development

Wood Norton
Evesham
Worcs WR11 4YB
Website: www.bbctraining.co.uk
Contact: Sally Keane
Tel: 0870 122 0216
Fax: 0870 122 0145
email: training@bbc.co.uk
Run a wide range of courses covering all aspects of Television, New Media, Broadcast Technology, Radio, Journalism and Health and Safety.

BBC Training and Development (BBC Trainees)

Room B102
Centre House
56 Wood Lane
London W12 7SB
Website: www.bbc.co.uk/jobs

Contact: Caroline Jackson
Tel: 020 8576 8820
Fax: 020 8576 4975
email: caroline.jackson.01@bbc.co.uk
Room B102
Centre House
56 Wood Lane
London W12 7SB
Website:
www.bbc.co.uk/jobs/bbctrainees
Contact: Jessica Bone
Tel: 020 8576 7984
Fax: 020 8576 4975
email: jessica.bone@bbc.co.uk
Contact: Neil Walker
Tel: 020 8576 7221
Fax: 020 8576 4975
email: neil.walker@bbc.co.uk
Room B106
Centre House
56 Wood Lane
London W12 7SB
Website: www.bbc.co.uk/designvision
Contact: Linda Mattock
Tel: 020 8225 8319/7344
Fax: 020 8576 4975
email: vision@bbc.co.uk
Room B106
Centre House
56 Wood Lane
London W12 7SB
Website: www.bbc.co.uk
Contact: Murray Furlong
Tel: 020 8576 7835
email: murray.furlong@bbc.co.uk

Birkbeck College
University of London
School of History of Art, Film and Visual Media
43 Gordon Square
London WC1H 0PD
Website: www.birkbeck.ac.uk/hafvm
Contact: Penny Luker-Brown, Mike Allen, Laura Mulvey
Tel: 020 7631 6112/6104/6102
Fax: 020 7631 6107
email: ma.cinema@bbk.ac.uk
Offers MA courses in History of Film and Visual Media by Reasearch, History of Film and Visual Media, History of Film and Visual Media and Mphil/Phd in Film and Television Studies

BKSTS – The Moving Image Society
Ealing Studios
Ealing Green
London W5 5EP
Website: www.bksts.com
Contact: Training Department
Tel: 020 8584 5220
Fax: 020 8584 5230
email: training@bksts.com
The BKST mission statement is: To encourage, sustain, educate, train and represent all those who, creatively or technologically, are involved – creatively or technologically - in the business of providing moving images and associated crafts in any form and through any media.

The Bournemouth Media School
Bournemouth University
Talbot Campus
Fern Barrow
Poole, Dorset BH12 5BB
Website: media.bournemouth.ac.uk
Contact: The Programme Administrator
Tel: 01202 595351
Fax: 01202 595099
email:
bmsugrad@bournemouth.ac.uk
The Media School at Bournemouth University is the largest centre in the UK for the study of Corporate & Marketing Communications, Journalism and Communication, Media Production and Computer Animation. It is a leading school for vocational higher education, applied research, consultancy and training - successfully preparing students for careers in the fast-growing media and communications sectors

Brighton Film School
Administration Office
13 Tudor Place
Dean Court Road
Rottingdean
East Sussex BN2 7DF
Website:
www.brightonfilmschool.org.uk
Contact: Meryl von Habsburg
Tel: 01273 302 166
Fax: 01273 302 163
email:
info@brightonfilmschool.org.uk

British Universities Film and Video Council
77 Wells Street
London W1T 3QJ
Website: www.bufvc.ac.uk
Contact: Sandra Houlton
Tel: 020 7393 1504
Fax: 020 7393 1555
email: events@bufvc.ac.uk
The BUFVC is a representative body which promotes the production, study and use of film and related media in higher education and research. It runs a number of one day courses throughout the year on topics such as Location Shooting, Copyright Clearance for Print, Broadcast and Multimedia Production and Production Techniques, Audio for the Web

Cardiff University
School of Journalism, Media and Cultural Studies
King Edward VII Avenue
Cardiff CF10 3NB
Website: www.cardiff.ac.uk/jomec
Contact: Rebecca Harris
Tel: 029 2087 4041
Fax: 029 2023 8832
email: HarrisRL@cardiff.ac.uk
The school is one of Britain's premier centres for teaching and research in journalism, media and cultural studies

Central Saint Martins College of Art and Design
Short Course Office
Southampton Row
London WC1B 4AP
Website: www.csm.linst.ac.uk
Contact: Chris Ball
Tel: 020 7514 7015
Fax: 020 7514 7016
email: shortcourse@csm.linst.ac.uk

The Children's Film Unit
South Way
Leavesden
Herts WD25 7LZ
Website: www.btinternet.com/~cfu/
Contact: Carol Rennie
Tel: 01923 354656
Fax: 01923 354656
email: cfilmunit@aol.com
The Children's Film Unit is an Educational Charity, which trains young people from the ages of ten to sixteen in all aspects of film-making

Cyfle Cyf
Gronant
Penrallt Isaf
Caernarfon
Gwynedd LL55 1NW
Website: www.cyfle.co.uk
Contact: Richard Morris Jones, Iona Williams, Sion Hughes
Tel: 01286 671000
Fax: 01286 678831
email: cyfle@cyfle.co.uk
Cyfle is the national training provider for the Television, Film and Interactive Media industry in Wales

University of Derby

Film and Video Department
Green Lane
Derby DE1 1RX
Website:
vertigo.derby.ac.uk.hitchcock
Contact: Martine Thoquenne
Tel: 01332 593065
Fax: 01332 622296
email:
m.m.b.thoquenne@out.derby.ac.uk

Edinburgh College of Art

School of Visual Communication
74 Lauriston Place
Edinburgh EH3 9DF
Website: www.eca.ac.uk
Contact: Noé Mendelle
Tel: 0131 221 6114
Fax: 0131 221 6100
email: viscom@eca.ac.uk
The centre concentrates on the criticial study and analysis of visual culture and the various theories used to interpret it

The Finishing School

National Film and Television School
Beaconsfield Studios
Station Road
Beaconsfield
Bucks HP9 1LG
Website: www.fschool.net
Contact: St John Walker
Tel: 01494 677 022, 01494 731 462
Fax: 01494 678 708
email: sjwalker@nftsfilm-tv.ac.uk
The Finishing School is a new industry accredited Digital Post-Production workshop and creative laboratory offering Effects and Animation Courses, Short Courses offering the latest software and hardware equipment, reserach and testing of new production and training techniques

First Film Foundation

9 Bourlet Close
London W1W 7BP
Website: www.firstfilm.co.uk
Contact: Jonathan Rawlinson
Tel: 020 7580 2111
Fax: 020 7580 2116
email: info@firstfilm.demon.co.uk
First Film Foundation was founded to help new writers, producers and directors to make their first film. The programmes includes: Information, Development and Training, Short Film Showcasing

Four Corners Film Workshop

113 Roman Road
Bethnal Green
London E2 0QN
Contact: Course Co-ordinator
Tel: 020 8981 4243/6111
Fax: 020 8983 7866
email: film@fourcorners.demon.co.uk

ft2 - Film and Television Freelance Training

Fourth Floor
Warwick House
9 Warwick Street
London W1R 5RA
Website: www.ft2.org.uk
Contact: Sharon Goode
Tel: 020 7734 5141
Fax: 020 7287 9899
email: info@ft2.org.uk
FT2 - Film and Television Freelance Training is the only national provider of training for people seeking to establish a freelance career in the junior construction, technical and production grades of the film and television industry

University of Glasgow

Department of Theatre, Film and Television Studies
Gilmorehill Centre
Glasgow G12 8QQ
Website: www.arts.gla.ac.uk/tfts
Contact: Dr Dimitris Eleftheriotis
Tel: 0141 330 3809
Fax: 0141 330 4142
email: d.eleftheriotis@tfts.arts.gla.ac.uk

Goldsmiths College

University of London
New Cross
London SE14 6NW
Website: www.goldsmiths.ac.uk
Contact: Admissions Office
Tel: 020 7919 7060 (PG Enquiries)
email: admissions@gold.ac.uk

Intermedia Film and Video (Nottingham) Ltd

19 Heathcote Street
Nottingham NG1 3AF
Website: www.intermedianotts.co.uk
Contact: Fred Broad
Tel: 0115 955 6909
Fax: 0115 955 9956
email: info@intermedianotts.co.uk
Intermedia is the leading Media Development Agency for the East Midlands. Through Production Support, Facilities, Training and Funding it provides a range of services for people working at all levels of the film, television, video and new media industries

International Film School Wales

University of Wales College, Newport
School of Art, Media and Design
Caerleon Campus
PO Box 179
Newport NP18 1YG
Website: www.ifsw.newport.ac.uk
Contact: Clive Myer
Tel: 01633 432677
Fax: 01633 432885
email: post.ifsw@newport.ac.uk
Contact: Gethin While
Tel: 01633 432679
Fax: 01633 432680
email: gethin.ifsw@newport.ac.uk
International Film School Wales (IFSW) is the nationally recognised institution for the promotion and development of the audiovisual culture of Wales through higher-level education, research and training. The moving image courses held at IFSW are BA Animation, BA Film & Video, BA Documentary and MA Film.

University of Kent at Canterbury

School of Drama, Film and Visual Arts
Rutherford College
Canterbury
Kent CT2 7NX
Website: www.ukc.ac.uk
Contact: Carolyn Smith
Tel: 01227 764000 (x 3177)
Fax: 01227 827846
email: cas3@ukc.ac.uk
Contact: Dr S.E. Cardwell
Tel: 01227 764000
Fax: 01227 827846

LCP (London College of Printing)

Developments at London Institute (DALI)
10 Back Hill
Clerkenwell
London EC1R 5LQ
Website: www.lcptraining.co.uk
Contact: Brenda Daly
Tel: 020 7514 6562
Fax: 020 7514 6563
email: dali@lcp.linst.ac.uk
Elephant and Castle
LondonSE1 6SB
Website: www.lcp.linst.ac.uk
Contact: Robert Ferguson
Tel: 020 7514 6578
Fax: 020 7514 6535

email: r.ferguson@linst.ac.uk
Although the origins were in printing LCP now encompasses film and TV, digital imaging, journalism, advertising, graphic design, retailing and e-commerce, photography, publishing and many related subjects

London College of Music and Media

Thames Valley University
St Mary's Road
Ealing
London
W5 5RF
Website: elgar.tvu.ac.uk
Tel: 020 8231 2304
Fax: 020 8231 2546
email: enquiries.lcm2@tvu.ac.uk
Offers training for careers in music and media

London Film Academy

The Old Church
52a Walham Grove
London SW6 1QR
Website:
www.londonfilmacademy.com
Contact: Daisy Gili
Tel: 020 7386 7711
Fax: 020 7381 6116
email: info@londonfilmacademy.com
LFA, a non-profit making trust founded in January 2002, is an innovative venture in professional film training for a new generation of film-makers. Students work in small groups, supported and guided by working professionals. LFA courses put theory into practice and teach principles on 16 mm film.

London Film School

24 Shelton Street
London
WC2H 9UB
Website: www.lfs.org.uk
Contact: The Director
Tel: 020 7836 9642 (School Secretary)
Fax: 020 7497 3718
email: film.school@lfs.org.uk
Formerly known as the London International Film School, the LFS remains world renowned for its professional training and its exceptional output of films and filmmakers.

London Metropolitan University

Communication Subject Area
Sir John Cass Department of Art, Media and Design
59-63 Whitechapel High Street
London E1 7PF
Website: www.londonmet.ac.uk
Contact: Elaine Pierson, Peter Hewitt or Course Enquiry Unit
Tel: 020 7320 1000/1974
Fax: 020 7320 1938
email: enqs@lgu.ac.uk

Metropolitan Film School

email: info@metfilmschool.co.uk,
Website: www.metfilmschool.co.uk
Tel: (0)845 658 4400
Fax: 020 7681 1819
The Metropolitan Film School aims to inspire new filmmakers, appreciators and story-tellers by delivering innovative, interactive courses in the comfort and convenience of local art house cinemas – all taught by industry professionals

National Film and Television School

Beaconsfield Studios
Station Road
Beaconsfield
Bucks HP9 1LG
Website: www.nftsfilm-tv.ac.uk
Contact: The Registry
Tel: 01494 731425/731413
Fax: 01494 674042
email: admin@nftsfilm-tv.ac.uk
The leading international centre for professional training in the film, television and related media industries. Offers full-time MA, diploma and project development programmes, a wide range of short courses for industry professionals, training in post-production effects and computer-based animation.

National Short Course Training Programme

National Film and Television School
Beaconsfield Studios
Station Road, Beaconsfield
Bucks, HP9 1LG
Website: www.nfts-scu.org.uk
Contact: Production Office
Tel: 01494 677903/671234
Fax: 01494 678708
email: info@nfts-scu.org.uk

Northern Film School

Leeds Metropolitan University
2 Queen Square
Leeds
LS2 8AF
Website: www.lmu.ac.uk/hen/aad/nfs
Contact: Ian Macdonald
Tel: 0113 283 1900
Fax: 0113 283 1901
email: nfs@lmu.ac.uk

Northern Visions Media Centre

4 Lower Donegall Street Place
Belfast BT1 2FN
Website: www.northernvisions.org
Contact: Marilyn Hyndman
Tel: 028 9024 5495
Fax: 028 9032 6608
email: info@northernvisions.org

University of Nottingham

Institute of Film Studies
Nottingham
NG7 2RD
Website: www.nottingham.ac.uk
Contact: Professor Mark Jancovich
Tel: 0115 951 4250
Fax: 0115 951 4270
email: m.jancovich@nottingham.ac.uk

Oxford Film and Video Makers

The Old Boxing Club
54 Catherine Street
Oxford OX4 3AH
Website: www.ofvm.org
Contact: Richard Duriez
Tel: 01865 792 731
email: office@ofvm.org

PACT (Producers Alliance for Cinema and Television)

45 Mortimer Street
London W1W 8HJ
Website: www.pact.co.uk
Contact: Rebecca Fitzgerald
Tel: 020 7331 6000
Fax: 020 7331 6700
email: training@pact.co.uk
Founded in 1991, Pact is the UK trade association that represents and promotes the commercial interests of independent feature film, television, animation and interactive media companies. Runs a number of traning initiatives

Raindance Ltd

81 Berwick Street
London W1F 8TW
Website: www.raindance.co.uk
Contact: Elliot Grove
Tel: 020 7287 3833
Fax: 020 7439 2243
email: info@raindance.co.uk
Dedicated to fostering and promoting independent film in the UK and around the world, Raindance combines Film Training Courses, Rawtalent Productions, Raindance, Raindance East and Raindance Kids Film Festivals, Raindance Film Magazine, and hosts the prestigious British Independent Film Awards

Ravensbourne College of Design and Communication

Short Course Unit
Walden Road
Chislehurst
Kent BR7 5SN
Website:
www.rave.ac.uk/shortcourses/
Contact: Lorraine Ceuppens
Tel: 020 8325 8323
Fax: 020 8325 8323
email: short.courses@rave.ac.uk
Walden Road
Chislehurst
Kent
BR7 5SN
Website: www.ravensbourne.ac.uk
Contact: Admissions Office
Tel: 020 8289 4900
Fax: 020 8325 8320
email: info@rave.ac.uk

University of Reading

Department of Film, Theatre and Television
Bulmershe Court
Woodlands Avenue
Earley
Reading RG6 1HY
Website: www.rdg.ac.uk/FD
Contact: Alison Butler, Alastair Phillips
Tel: 0118 931 8878
Fax: 0118 931 8873
email: e.a.silvester@reading.ac.uk
The Department of Film, Theatre & Television offers film and theatre study opportunities at undergraduate and postgraduate level. Bachelor of Arts, Master of Arts in Film, Drama, Theatre, Television, Performanc

Retford International College

11 Grove Street
Retford
Notts DN22 6PJ
Contact: Jean Bryant
Tel: 01777 707371
Fax: 01777 860374
email: retcol@msn.com

University of Stirling

Department of Film and Media Studies
Stirling FK9 4LA
Website: www-fms.stir.ac.uk
Contact: Dr Gillian Doyle
Tel: 01786 467520
Fax: 01786 466855
email: stirling.media@stir.ac.uk
Founded in 1978 the Department was one of the earliest centres dedicated to the study of film and media. It has since grown into the largest of its kind in Scotland and one of the leading departments in the UK

University of Wales, Aberystwyth

Department of Theatre, Film and Television Studies
Parry-Williams Building
Penglais Campus
Aberystwyth
SY23 2AJ
Website: www.aber.ac.uk/tfts
Contact: Dr Mikel J. Koven
Tel: 01970 621 605
Fax: 01970 622 831
email: mik@aber.ac.uk
Contact: Nigel Orrillard
Tel: 01970 621698
Fax: 01970 622258
email: nno@aber.ac.uk
The Department, established in 1973, offers a variety of practical, design and academic courses relating to the study of Theatre, Performance, Television, Film, Media and Communication through the medium of both English and Welsh, at undergraduate and postgraduate level

University of Warwick

Department of Film and Television Studies
Faculty of Arts
Coventry CV4 7AL
Website: www.warwick.ac.uk
Contact: Elaine Lenton
Tel: 024 7652 3511
Fax: 024 7652 4757
email: E.J.Lenton@warwick.ac.uk

University of the West of England, Bristol (Bristol, UWE)

Faculty of Art, Media and Design
Bower Ashton Campus
Kennel Lodge Road
Off Clanage Road
Bristol BS3 2JT
Website: www.uwe.ac.uk/amd
Contact: Dan Harvey
Tel: 0117 344 4721
Fax: 0117 344 4745
email: amd.enquiries@uwe.ac.uk

Women's Independent Cinema House

40 Rodney Street
Liverpool L1 9AA
Contact: Ann Carney
Tel: 0151 707 0539/8314
Fax: 0151 707 8314
email: mediawitch@hotmail.com

DISTRIBUTORS (NON-THEATRICAL)

Companies here control UK rights for non–theatrical distribution (for domestic and group viewing in schools, hospitals, airlines and so on).

For an extensive list of titles available non–theatrically with relevant distributors' addresses, see the *British National Film & Video Catalogue*, available for reference from the *bfi* National Library and major public libraries. Other sources of film and video are listed under Archives and Film Libraries and Workshops.

4Learning

c/o Channel 4 Television
124 Horseferry Road
London SW1P 2TX
Tel: 08701 246 444
Fax: 08701 246 444
email:
4learning.sales@channel4.co.uk
Website: www.channel4.com/learning
Channel 4 educational resources for teachers, parents and students

Amber Films

5-9 Side
Newcastle upon Tyne NE1 3JE
Tel: 0191 232 2000
Fax: 0191 230 3217
email: amberside@btinternet.com
Website: www.amber-online.com
*Amber was established in 1969 with the specific intention of creating a film and photographic practice in relation to the working class communities of the North East of England.
From its foundation it has pursued a policy of integrating production, exhibition and distribution.
Throughout its 30 year history, it has pioneered experimental partnerships between film makers, photographers, writers and local communities in the North East of England.
Distribution of films produced by Amber, recent titles include Like Father

Arts Council Film and Video Library

Concord Video and Film Council
22 Hines Road
Ipswich 1P3 9BG
Tel: 01473 726012
Fax: 01473 274531
email: concordvideo@btinternet.com
Website:
www.btinternet.com/~concordvideo
Lydia Vulliamy
Concord Video and Film Council are distributors for many of the Arts Councils documentaries

Arts Council South West

Bradninch Place
Gandy Street
Exeter EX4 3LS
Tel: 01392 218188
Fax: 01392 229229
Website: www.artscouncil.org.uk
Clare Frank, Ruth Bint: Information Advisers
Team Video Productions

AVP

School Hill Centre
Chepstow NP16 5PH
Tel: 01291 625439
Fax: 01291 629671
email: info@avp.co.uk
Website: www.avp.co.uk
AVP was founded in 1969 to produce and publish educational resources, at that time audio-visual and later video material. AVP became active in educational computing in 1983 and since then has become a leading supplier of educational software to schools in the UK

BBC Videos for Education and Training

Woodlands
80 Wood Lane
London W12 0TT
Tel: 020 8433 2541
Fax: 020 8433 2916

bfi Distribution

21 Stephen Street
London W1T 1LN
Tel: 020 7957 8938
Fax: 020 7580 5830
email: bookings@bfi.org.uk
Website: www.bfi.org.uk
Handles non-theatrical 16mm, 35mm, video and DVD. Subject catalogues available. Film bookings on behalf of non-theatrical users such as film societies, film clubs, and educational users may be placed through this unit. Catalogues of animation, avant-garde or documentary shorts are available, as well as current lists of DVD films available for film society use

Boulton-Hawker Films

Hadleigh
near Ipswich
Suffolk IP7 5BG
Tel: 01473 822235
Fax: 01473 824519
Educational films and videos: health education, social welfare, home economics, P.S.E., P.E., Maths, biology, physics, chemistry, geography

BUFVC (British Universities Film & Video Council)

77 Wells Street
London W1T 3QJ
Tel: 020 7393 1500
Fax: 020 7393 1555
email: ask@bufvc.ac.uk
Website: bufvc.ac.uk
Geoffrey O'Brien, Assistant Director
Videocassettes for sale direct from above address. Film hire via Concord Video and Film Council. The BUFVC maintains an Off-Air Recording Back-Up Service available to any educational institution in BUFVC membership holding an Educational Recording Agency licence

Canalot

222 Kensal Road
London W10 5BN
Tel: 020 8960 5536
Fax: 020 8960 9784
email: Chris Thomas, Billy Ridgers
Producer and distributor of educational video resources

Carlton Archive Sales

Carlton Television
Lenton Lane
Nottingham NG7 2NA
Tel: 0115 964 5476
Fax: 0115 964 5202
email: archive.sales@carltontv.co.uk
Website: www.carltonarchive.co.uk
James McDonald

Chain Production Ltd
2 Clanricarde Gardens
London W2 4NA
Tel: 020 7229 4277
Fax: 020 7229 0861
Website: chainproduction.com
Specialist in European films and world cinema, cult classics, handling European Film Libraries with all rights to over 1,000 films - also clip rights and clip search

Cinenova: Promoting Films by Women
113 Roman Road
Bethnal Green
London E2 0QN
Tel: 020 8981 6828
Fax: 020 8983 4441
email: enquiries@cinenova.org.uk
Website: www.cinenova.org
Shona Barrett, Distribution
Laura Hudson: Development
Cinenova acts as a champin for the equality of women behind the camera, taking the diversity of women's voices to a global audience. It is committed to the acquisition, promotion, distribution and exhibition of films and videos directed by women and to provide the context to support women's film

Concord Video and Film Council
22 Hines Road
Ipswich IP3 9BG
Tel: 01473 726012
Fax: 01473 274531
email: concordvideo@btinternet.com
Website: www.concordvideo.co.uk
Lydia Vulliamy
Videos and films for hire/sale on domestic and international social issues - counselling, development, education, the arts, race and gender issues, disabilities, etc - for training and discussion. Also incorporates Graves Medical Audio Visual Library and Arts Council Film and Video Library

CTVC Video
Hillside Studios
Merry Hill Road
Bushey
Watford WD2 1DR
Tel: 020 8950 4426
Fax: 020 8950 1437
email: ctvc@ctvc.co.uk
Website: www.ctvc.co.uk
Christian, moral and social programmes

Derann Film Services
99 High Street
Dudley
West Mids DY1 1QP
Tel: 01384 233191/257077
Fax: 01384 456488
email: Website: www.derran.co.uk
Website: email: derek@derann.co.uk
D Simmonds, S Simmonds
8mm package movie distributors; video production; bulk video duplication; laser disc stockist

Education Distribution Service
Education House
Castle Road
Sittingbourne
Kent ME10 3RL
Tel: 01795 427614
Fax: 01795 474871
email: info@edist.co.uk
Lin Gates/Barry Wiles
Distribution library for many clients including film and video releases. Extensive catalogue available

Educational and Television Films
247A Upper Street
London N1 1RU
Tel: 020 7226 2298
Fax: 020 7226 8016
email: zoe@etvltd.demon.co.uk
Website: www.etvltd.demon.co.uk
Zoe Moore, Jack Amos
Established in 1950, ETV has amassed a wide and varied range of documentary archive materia from the ex-Socialist world, with particular emphasis on the ex-Soviet Union, the former eastern Block countries and China. Material is also held from Vietnam, Cuba, Chile, Afghanistan and the other Arab Nations. ETV also houses material from the British Labour Movement and the Spanish Civil War

Einstein Network
67-74 Saffron Hill
London EC1N 8QX
Tel: 020 7693 7777
Fax: 020 7693 7788
email: info@einstein-network.com
Website: www.einstein-network.com
Einstein Network is committed to producing TV programmes for companies

Euroview Management Services Limted
PO Box 80
Wetherby
Yorks LS23 7EQ
Tel: 01937 541010
Fax: 01937 541083
email: euroview@compuserve.com
Website: www.euroview.co.uk

Filmbank Distributors
Warner House
98 Theobalds Road
London WC1X 8WB
Tel: 0207 984 5950
Fax: 0207 984 5951
email: sbryan@filmbank.demon.co.uk
Website: www.filmbank.co.uk
Bookings Department
Filmbank represents all of the major film studios for the non-theatrical market (group screenings) and distributes titles on video, dvd and 16mm film

Granada Learning/SEMERC
Granada Television
Quay Street
Manchester M60 9EA
Tel: 0161 827 2927
Fax: 0161 827 2966
email: info@granada-learning.co
Website: Paula Warwick
Granada Learning Ltd is the Uk's leading publisher of educational software. Its extensive range of CD-ROMs spans the syllabus of primary and secondary schools to meet the requirements of learners of all ages and abilities, including those with special educational needs. Granada Learning recently acquired Letts Educational, the UK's leading provider of educational textbooks and revision guides for the home market, and BlackCat, the UK's market-leading supplier of educational tools and applications for younger children

IAC (Institute of Amateur Cinematographers)
24c West Street, Epsom
Surrey KT18 7RJ
Tel: 01372 739672
Fax: 01372 739672
email: iacfilmvideo@compuserve.com
Website: www.theiac.org.uk
Janet Smith

Imperial War Museum
Film and Video Archive (Loans)
Lambeth Road
London SE1 6HZ
Tel: 020 7416 5293/4
Fax: 020 7416 5299
email: film@iwm.org.uk
Website: www.iwm.org.uk
Toby Haggith, Matthew Lee

Documentaries, newsreels and propaganda films from the Museum's film archive on 16mm, 35mm and video

Leeds Animation Workshop (A Women's Collective)
45 Bayswater Row
Leeds LS8 5LF
Tel: 0113 248 4997
Fax: 0113 248 4997
email: law@leedsanimation.demon.co.uk
Website: www.leedsanimation.demon.co.uk
Terry Wragg
Milena Dragic, Jane Bradshaw, Stephanie Munro, Janis Goodman, Milena Dragic
Producers and distributors of animated films on social issues

London Television Service
21-25 Saint Anne's Court
London W1F 0BJ
Tel: 020 74341121
Fax: 020 77340619
email: Website: www.londontv.com
Website: email: lts@londontv.com
John Ridley(General Manager)

National Educational Video Library
Arfon House
Bontnewydd
Caernarfon
Bangor
Gwynedd LL57 7UD
Tel: 01286 676001
Fax: 01286 676001
email: tryfannevl@aol.com
Website: John Lovell
Supply of educational videotapes

National Film and Television School
Beaconsfield Studios
Station Road
Beaconsfield
Bucks HP9 1LG
Tel: 01494 731344
Fax: 01494 674042
email: rjenkins@nftsfilm-tv.ac.uk
Website: www.nftsfilm-tv.ac.uk
Richard Jenkins, Hemant Sharda

Open University Worldwide
Walton Hall
Milton Keynes MK7 6AA
Tel: 01908 659083
Fax: 01908 858787
email: s.l.mccormack@open.ac.uk
Website: www.ouw.co.uk
Sarah McCormack

Royal Danish Embassy
55 Sloane Street
London SW1X 9SR
Tel: 020 7333 0200
Fax: 020 7333 0270
email: ionamb@um.dk
Website: www.denmark.org.uk
Annette Lundgaard, Cultural Attaché

RSPCA
Wilberforce Way
Southwater
West Sussex RH12 9RS
Tel: 0870 7540229
Fax: 0870 7530229
email: publications@rspca.org.uk
Website: www.rspca.org.uk
Micheala Miller

Sheila Graber Animation Limited
50 Meldon Avenue
South Shields
Tyne and Wear NE34 0EL
Tel: 0191 455 4985
Fax: 0191 455 3600
email: sheila@graber.demon.co.uk
Website: www.graber-miller.com
Over 70 animated shorts available - 16mm, video and computer interactive featuring a range of 'fun' educational shorts on art, life, the universe and everything. Producers of interactive CD-Roms

Shotlist
Educational Broadcasting Services Trust
36-38 Mortimer Street
London W1N 7RB
Tel: 020 7765 4635 / 5087 / 5714.
Fax: 020 7580 6246
email: order@shotlist.co.uk
Website: www.shotlist.co.uk
Shotlist is a bank of subject-specific video materials for Higher Education teaching and research. They may also be of interest to companies and individuals seeking resources for study or training.

Television Trust for the Environment (TVE)
Prince Albert Road
London NW1 4RZ
Tel: 020 7586 5526
Fax: 020 7586 4866
email: tve-uk@tve.org.uk
Website: www.tve.org.uk
An independent, non-profit organisation, the mission of the Television Trust for the Environment (TVE) is to act as a catalyst for the production and distribution of films on environment, development, health and human rights issues

The Short Film Bureau
74 Newman Street
London, W1T 3EL
Tel: 020 7207 636 2400
Fax: 020 7207 636 8558
email: info@shortfilmbureau.com
Website: www.shortfilmbureau.com
Kim Leggatt
Specialising in the promotion and distribution of short films for theatrical and non-theatrical release world wide. The Bureau also runs a script consultancy service for short films which looks at helping the writer rework their projects to maximise commercial success

THE (Total Home Entertainment)
National Distribution Centre
Rosevale Business Park
Newcastle-under-Lyme
Staffs ST5 7QT
Tel: 01782 566566
Fax: 01782 565617
email: alex.heath@the.co.uk
Website: www.the.co.uk
Alex Heath
Exclusive distributors for Visual Corp, ILC, Quantum Leap, Mystique, Prime Time, IMS, Wardvision, Academy Media, Empire, RWP (over 6,000 titles) (see also Video Labels)

The University of Westminster
School of Media, Arts and Design
Harrow Campus, Watford Road
Northwick Park HA1 3TP
Tel: 020 7911 5944
Fax: 020 7911 5943
email: cdm@wmin.ac
Website: www.wmin.ac.uk/media
Professor Brian Winston

Training Services
Brooklands House
29 Hythegate
Werrington
Peterborough PE4 7ZP
Tel: 01733 327337
Fax: 01733 575537
email:
tipton@training.services.demon.co.uk
Website:
www.trainingservices.demon.co.uk
Christine Tipton
Distribute programmes from the following producers:
Aegis Healthcare
Angel Productions
Barclays Bank Film Library

John Burder Films
Career Strategies Ltd

TV Choice Ltd

PO Box 597,
Bromley,
Kent BR2 0YB, UK
Tel: 0208 464 7402
Fax: 0208 464 7845
email: tvchoiceuk@aol.com
Website: www.tvchoice.uk.com
TV Choice has a catalogue of over 100 films covering a wide range of subjects from business and technology to the environment and history. They include documentaries, dramas and drama-documentaries.

Uniview Worldwide Ltd

PO Box 20,
Hoylake,
Wirral CH48 7HY
Tel: Tel. 0151 625 3453
Fax: Fax 0151 625 3707
email: sales@uniview.com
Website: www.uniview.co.uk
Gill Campbell

Vera Media

30-38 Dock Street
Leeds LS10 1JF
Tel: 0113 242 8646
Fax: 0113 242 8739
email: vera@vera-media.co.uk
Website: www.vera-media.co.uk
Al Garthwaite
Catherine Mitchell

Video Arts

Dumbarton House
68 Oxford Street
London W1N 0LH
Tel: 020 7637 7288
Fax: 020 7580 8103
Video Arts produces and exclusively distributes the John Cleese training films; Video Arts also distributes a selection of meeting breaks from Muppet Meeting Films TM as well as Tom Peters programmes (produced by Video Publishing House Inc) and In Search of Excellence and other films from the Nathan/Tyler Business Video Library

Viewtech Educational Media

7-8 Falcons Gate
Northavon Business Centre
Dean Road, Yate
Bristol BS37 5NH
Tel: 01454 858055
Fax: 01454 858056
email: info@viewtech.co.uk
Website: www.viewtech.co.uk
Simon Littlechild
Distributors of British and overseas educational, health, training/safety video games as well as new CD-ROM titles. Act as agent for the promotion of British productions overseas. Free catalogue

WFA

9 Lucy Street
Manchester M15 4BX
Tel: 0161 848 9782/5
Fax: 0161 848 9783
email:wfa@timewarp.co.uk
Website: www.wfamedia.co.uk
Chloe Beattie

DISTRIBUTORS (THEATRICAL)

3mv Vision
[Manga Entertainment]
3rd floor
7 Holyrood Street
London SE1 2EL
Tel: 020 7378 8866
Fax: 020 7378 8855
email: info@3mv.com
Cheryl Hutchinson

Amber Films
5 & 9 Side
Newcastle-upon-Tyne NE1 3JE
Tel: 0191 232 2000
Fax: 0191 230 3217
email: amberside@btinternet.com
Website: www.amber-online.com
Distribution of films produced by Amber, recent titles include Like Father.

Arrow Films Distributors
18 Watford Road
Radlett
Herts WD7 8LE
Tel: 01923 858306
Fax: 01923 859673
email: neil@arrowfilms.co.uk
Website: www.arrowfilms.co.uk
Neil Agran
2002 releases:
Du Rififi Chez Les Hommes - 16 Aug
Recent releases:
Mrs Caldicot's Cabbage War

Artificial Eye Film Company
14 King Street
London WC2E 8HR
Tel: 020 7240 5353
Fax: 020 7240 5242
Website: www.artificial-eye.com
Robert Beeson
2002 releases:
Va savoir - 4 Jan
Heftig & Begeistret - 8 Feb
Comédie de L'innocence - 8 March
L'Emploi du Temps - 5 April
Vou Para Casa - 17 May
Roberto Succo - 7 June
Une Hirondelle a fait Le Printemps - 26 July
Zhantai - 2 August
Raye Makhfi - 13 Sept
Små Ulykker - 20 Sept
Laissez-passer - 8 November
Lundi Matin - 6 Dec
11 '09' 01 September 11 - 27 Dec
Recent/forthcoming releases:
Divine Intervention - 17 January 2003
Japon - 21 February 2003
The Son (Le Fils) - 14 March 2003
Russian Ark - 4 April 2003
Werckmeister Harmonies - 18 April 2003
Pure - 2 May 2003
Dolls - 30 May 2003
Springtime in a Small Town - 13 June 2003
Unknown Pleasures – Jul 2003
Sex is Comedy – Jul 2003
Time of the Wolf - Oct 2003

Axiom Films
12 D'Arblay Street
London W1V 3FP
Tel: 020 7287 7720
Fax: 020 7287 7740
email: mail@axiomfilms.co.uk
Website: www.axiomfilms.co.uk
2002 releases:
Tosca - 10 May
Recent releases:
Life and Debt - 28 Feb 2003
El Bola - 4 April 2003

bfi Distribution
21 Stephen Street
London W1T 1LN
Tel: 020 7957 8935
Fax: 020 7580 5830
email: bookings.films@bfi.org.uk
Website: www.bfi.org.uk
Margaret Deriaz/Christine Whitehouse
2002 releases:
Throne of Blood/Kumonosu-jo – 4 Jan
Hidden Fortress/Kakushi Toride No San-Akunin - 20 Jan
If.... - 1 March
Mother India - 3 May
High Society - 31 May
Get Carter - June
Cabaret - 21 June
To Sleep With Anger - 28 June
A Night at the Opera/A Day at the Races - 12 July
Freaks - 27 Sept
Saturday Night and Sunday Morning - 11 Oct
Mughal-E-Azam - 25 Oct
Sans Soleil - 20 Nov
Recent releases:
Death in Venice
The Leopard
Day of Wrath
Kirikou
Le Cercle rouge
Monsieur Hulot's Holiday

Blue Dolphin Film & Video
40 Langham Street
London W1W 7AS
Tel: 020 7255 2494
Fax: 020 7580 7670
email: info@bluedolphinfilms.com
Website: www.bluedolphinfilms.com
Joseph D'Morais
Handle MGM/UA catalogue for theatrical distribution in the UK as well as Blue Dolphin theatrical releases.
2002 releases
Hehesder - 2 Aug
Recent/forthcoming releases:
Fogbound - Apr 2003
Ten Minutes Older: The Trumpet – Oct 2003

Blue Light
231 Portobello Road
London W11 1LT
Tel: 020 7792 9791
Fax: 020 7792 9871
email: kevan@bluelight.co.uk
Kevan Wilkinson, Alain De La Mata
(See also Made in Hong Kong)
Recent releases:
Avalon – Nov 2002

Bollywood Films
384 D Northolt Road
South Harrow
Middlesex HA2 8EX
Tel: 020 8933 6551
Fax: 020 8933 6552
Recent releases:
Kaante – Feb 2003
American Chai – July 2003

Boudicca
8 Cotton's Gardens
London E2 8DN
Tel: 020 7613 5882
Fax: 020 7613 5882
email: sales@boudiccafilms.com
Website: www.boudiccafilms.com
Ray Brady
Recent releases:
Love Life,

Boy Meets Girl
Kiss Kiss Bang Bang
Releases in 2003:
Day of the Sirens
Cold Dark

Brian Jackson Films Ltd

39/41 Hanover Steps
St George's Fields
Albion Street
London W2 2YG
Tel: 020 7402 7543
Fax: 020 7262 5736
email: brianjfilm@aol.com
Brian Jackson
Specialising in classic feature films for children.

Buena Vista International (UK)

3 Queen Caroline Street
Hammersmith
London W6 9PE
Tel: 020 8222 1000
Fax: 020 8222 2795
Website: www.bvimovies.com
Daniel Battsek
2002 releases:
Iris - 18 Jan
In the Bedroom - 25 Jan
Monsters, Inc - 8 Feb
The Conversation - 1 March
The Shipping News - 1 March
Abril Despedaçado - 8 March
Hearts in Atlantis - 8 March
The Royal Tenenbaums - 15 March
Return to Never Land - 22 March
Kate & Leopold - 5 April
The Count of Monte Cristo - 19 April
Snow Dogs - 31 May
The Musketeer - 21 June
Bad Company - 12 July
Heaven - 9 Aug
Spy Kids 2 Islands of Lost Dreams - 16 Aug
Reign of Fire - 23 Aug
Insomnia - 30 Aug
The Importance of Being Earnest - 6 Sept
Signs - 13 September
Lilo & Stitch - 4 Oct
The Rookie - 11 Oct
Halloween Resurrection - 25 Oct
Rabbit-Proof Fence - 8 Nov
The Quiet American - 29 Nov
The Santa Clause 2 - 29 November
Dirty Pretty Things - 13 Dec
Sweet Home Alabama -20 December
Chicago - 26 Dec
Recent/forthcoming releases:
Four Feathers –July 2003
The Pirates of the Caribbean – Aug 2003
Calendar Girls – Sep 2003
Finding Nemo – Oct 2003
Kill Bill – Oct 2003
Cold Mountain – Dec 2003

Cinefrance

12 Sunbury Place
Edinburgh EH4 3BY
Tel: 0131 225 6191
Fax: 0131 225 6971
email: info@cinefrance.co.uk
Website: www.cinefrance.co.uk
2002 release:
Le Roi Danse - 5 July
Recent/forthcoming releases:
Pot Luck (L'auberge Espagnole) – May 2003
Fluss Der Zeit – July 2003
Kelthoum's Daughter

Circuit Films

5 Warner House
43-49 Warner Street
London EC1R 5ER
Tel: 0777 1857652
email: kate@circuitfilms.com
Website: www.circuitfilms.com
Kate Gerova
2003 release:
Rain

City Screen

Hardy House
16-18 Beak Street
London W1F 9RD
Tel: 020 7734 4342
Fax: 020 7734 4027
email: enquiries@picturehouses.co.uk
Website: www.picturehouses.co.uk
Maya Nakamura
2002 releases:
AKA - 11 Oct
Recent releases:
Perfume de violetas – Jan 2003
Three Brothers – Feb 2003
Elling – Mar 2003

Columbia TriStar Films (UK)

Europe House
25 Golden Square
London W1R 6LU
Tel: 020 7533 1111
Fax: 020 7533 1105
Website: www.columbiatristar.co.uk
2002 releases:
Metropolis - 11 Jan
Saving Silverman - 11 Jan
Black Hawk Down - 18 Jan
The Glass House - 25 Jan
Funny Girl - 15 Feb
Thir13en Ghosts - 15 March
Pauline & Paulette - 12 April
Panic Room - 3 May
Dark Blue World - 10 May
Not Another Teen Movie - 24 May
Pollock - 24 May
Rollerball - 28 June
Spider-Man - 14 June
Dogtown and Z-Boys - 5 July
Stuart Little 2 - 19 July
Sunshine State - 26 July
Men in Black II - 2 Aug
The Sweetest Thing - 30 Aug
Two Can Play That Game - 13 Sept
The New Guy - 20 Sept
xXx - 17 Oct
Mr. Deeds - 1 Nov
Da Wan - 15 Nov
Enough - 29 Nov
Eight Crazy Nights - 6 Dec
Grateful Dawg - 13 Dec
Recent/forthcoming releases:
Terminator 3: Rise of the Machines – Aug 2003
Hollywood Homicide – Aug 2003
Winged Migration – Sep 2003
Bad Boys 2 – Oct 2003
Mona Lisa Smile – Jan 2004

Contemporary Films

24 Southwood Lawn Road
Highgate
London N6 5SF
Tel: 020 8340 5715
Fax: 020 8348 1238
email:
inquiries@contemporaryfilms.com
Website:
www.contemporaryfilms.com
Eric Liknaitzky
Primarily handle archival material and classic titles.
2002 release:
Pather Panchali - 3 May

Entertainment Film Distributors

Eagle House
108-110 Jermyn Street
London SW1Y 6HB
Tel: 020 7930 7744
Fax: 020 7930 9399
2002 releases:
Gosford Park - 1 Feb
Ali - 15 Feb
Life as a House - 15 March
Blade II - 29 March
John Q - 26 April
I am Sam - 10 May
Monster's Ball - 7 June
Before You Go - 21 June
Jason X - 19 July
Austin Powers in Goldmember - 26 July
Unconditional Love - 13 Sept
My Big Fat Greek Wedding - 20 Sept
Boat Trip - 4 Oct
S1mone - 25 Oct
They - 1 Nov

Lord of the Rings The Two Towers - 18 Dec
Recent/forthcoming releases:
Gangs of New York – Jan 2003
Far From Heaven - Mar 2003
Ripley's Game – May 2003
The Texas Chainsaw Massacre – Oct 2003
The Lord of the Rings: The Return of the King – Dec 2003

Eros International

Unit 23
Sovereign Park
Coronation Road
London NW10 7QP
Tel: 020 8963 8700
Fax: 020 8963 0154
email: eros@erosintl.co.uk
Website: www.erosentertainment.com
2002 releases:
Company - April
Hum Tumhare Hain Saham - May
Na Tum Jaano Na Hum - May
Devdas - June
Om Jai Jagdish - July
Shakti The Power - September
Karz - December
Recent releases:
Dum - January 2003
Khushi - February 2003
Ex Aurek Guaran - March 2003
Armaan - May 2003
Chalte Chalte - June 2003
Shahruch Khan
Rani Mukherjee
Forthcoming release:
Darna Mana Hai – Jul 2003

Feature Film Company

see Winchester Film Distribution

FilmFour Distributors

FilmFour Distributors were wound down in 2002. Listed here are the last films that were released by the company
2002 releases:
Monsoon Wedding - 4 Jan
Charlotte Gray - 22 February
Bully – 1 March
Invincible - 29 March
K-Pax - 12 April
The Warrior - 3 May
Crush - 7 June
Birthday Girl - 28 June
Once Upon a Time in the Midlands - 6 Sept

Gala

26 Danbury Street
Islington
London N1 8JU
Tel: 020 7226 5085
Fax: 020 7226 5897
Sue Porter/Lizzie Frith
2002 releases:
O Invasor - 13 Sept
Goyangireul Butakhae - 26 Dec
Recent releases:
L'afrance - 2003
The Three Marias – 2003

Guerilla Films

35 Thornbury Road
Isleworth
Middlesex TW7 4LQ
Tel: 020 8758 1716
Fax: 020 8758 9364
Website: www.guerilla-films.com
email: david@guerilla-films.com
David Wilkinson
Fully independent distribution company concentrating on the release of British films.
2002 releases:
Beginner's Luck - 21 June
Offending Angels 19 April
Two Men Went to War - 1 Nov
Recent/forthcoming releases:
Puckoon – April 2003
Nine Dead Gay Guys – Sep 2003

GVI (Gurpreet Video International)

26 Balfour Industrial Estate
Balfour Road
Southall
Middlesex
Tel: 020 8813 8059
Fax: 020 8813 8062

Helkon SK Film Distribution

see Redbus Film Distribution

Ian Rattray

10 Wiltshire Gardens
Twickenham
Middlesex TW2 6ND
Tel: 020 8296 0555
Fax: 020 8296 0556
email: ianrattray@blueyonder.co.uk
(Also handles bookings on behalf of Gala, Millennium, Arrow, Rockcity Film Distributors and releases for Ratpack Films)
2002 releases:
Christie Malry's Own Double Entry - 16 August
Recent/forthcoming releases:
Most Fertile Man in Ireland
Emotional Backgammon
The Boy David Story

ICA Projects

12 Carlton House Terrace
London SW1Y 5AH
Tel: 020 7766 1416
Fax: 020 7306 0122
email: sara@ica.org.uk
Website: www.ica.org.uk
Sara Squire
2002 releases:
Promises - 11 Jan
Atanarjuat the Fast Runner - 1 Feb
Peau d'homme coeur de bête - April
Hotel - 5 April
Delbaran - 19 April
Everything Put Together - 14 June
Et Là-Bas, Quelle Heure est-il? - 21 June
Riri Chou-Chou No Subete - 30 Aug
10 - 27 Sept
Abouna - 22 Nov
Recent releases:
The Man Without a Past - Jan 2003
Derrida - Jan 2003
In This World - March 2003
Thomas Punchon - May 2003
Mon-Rak Transistor - June 2003
The Clay Bird – July 2003
Forthcoming releases:
Crimson Gold – Sep 2003
All Tomorrow's Parties – Jan 2004
Osama – Mar 2004

Icon Film Distributors

The Quadrangle, 4th Floor
180 Wardour Street
London W1F 8FX
Tel: 020 7494 8100
Fax: 020 7494 8151
Website: www.iconmovies.co.uk
Georgia Kaufman
2002 releases:
We Were Soldiers - 8 March
Y tu mamá también - 12 April
Swimf@n - 20 Sept
Sweet Sixteen - 4 Oct
Anita & Me - 22 Nov
Recent releases:
Rules Of Attraction
Open Hearts
Whale Rider
Blackball
Wilbur
Gladiatress
Bright Young Things
Butterfly Effect
Singing Detective
Forthcoming releases:
Blackball – Sep 2003
Bright Young Things – Oct 2003
Dogville – Feb 2004

Indy UK

13 Mountview
Northwood
Middlesex HA6 3NZ
Tel: 01923 820330/820518
Fax: 0870 1617339
email: ssp@indyuk.co.uk
Stuart St Paul
Recent release:
Devil's Gate - 2002

Kino Kino!

24c Alexandra Road
London N8 0PP
Tel: 020 8881 9463
Fax: 020 8881 9463
Website: www.kinokino.co.uk
email: kinokino@boltblue.com
Recent releases:
Brother
Happy Days
A Place on Earth
Hands

Life Films

1 Blake House
Admirals Way
London E14 9UJ
Tel: 020 7515 9666
Fax: 020 7515 9966
email: info@lifefilms.co.uk
Website: www.lifefilms.co.uk
Specialise in the sub-distribution of urban films.

Lux

3rd Floor
18-26 Shacklewell Lane
London E8 2EZ
Tel: 020 7503 3980
Fax: 020 7503 1606
email: info@lux.org.uk
Website: www.lux.org.uk
Distributor of artists' film and video works.

Made in Hong Kong

231 Portobello Road
London W11 1LT
Tel: 020 7792 9791
Fax: 020 7792 9871
Website:
www.madeinhongkong.co.uk
Kevan Wilkinson
(See also Blue Light)
Specialise in Hong Kong cinema

Maiden Voyage Pictures

The Basement
18 Cleveland Street
London W1T 4HZ
Tel: 07968 005961
email: enquiries@
maidenvoyagepictures.com
Website:
www.maidenvoyagepictures.com
Bjorn Ricketts
Recent release:
La Comunidad – Jul 2003

Metro Tartan Distribution Ltd

Atlantic House
5 Wardour Street
London W1D 6PB
Tel: 020 7494 1400
Fax: 020 7439 1922
Website: www.tartanvideo.com
Laura De Casto
2002 releases:
Trois Huit - 1 Feb
Bangkok: Dangerous - 22 Feb
Akai hashi no shita no nurui mizu - 15 March
Le Pornographe - 19 April
Lucía Y El Sexo - 10 May
Shi Qi Sui De Dan Che - 28 June
ivansxtc. - 19 July
La Spagnola - 9 Aug
Hundstage - 6 September
Jian Gui - 27 Sept
L.I.E. - 29 Sept
My Kingdom - 11 Oct
Bundy - 22 Nov
Trouble Every Day - 27 Dec
Recent/forthcoming releases:
Bad Guy – Jul 2003
Vendredi Soir – Aug 2003
Sixteen Years of Alcohol – Sep 2003

Metrodome Distribution

33 Charlotte Street
London W1T 1RR
Tel: 020 7153 4421
Fax: 020 7153 4401
Website: www.metrodomegroup.com
Metrodome Distribution is part of the Metrodome Group.
2002 releases:
Last Orders - 11 Jan
The Fluffer - 1 Feb
Musíme Si Pomáhat - 31 May
Impostor - 14 June
Tape - 12 July
Lovely & Amazing - 2 Aug
The Wash - 9 Aug
Donnie Darko – 25 Oct
Recent/forthcoming releases:
Lilya 4-Ever – April 2003
The Hard Word – Sep 2003
Spellbound – Oct 2003
My Life Without Me – Nov 2003

Millennium Film Distributors

via Ian Rattray (see above)
2002 releases:
Ali Zaoua - 22 March
Grégoire Moulin Contre L'Humanité - 7 June

Millivres Multimedia

Unit M, 32-34 Spectrum House
London NW5 1LP
Tel: 020 7424 7461
Fax: 020 7424 7401
email: info@millivres.co.uk
Website:
www.millivresmultimedia.co.uk
Kim Watson
Recent releases include:
Girls Can't Swim
Criminal Lovers

Miracle Communications

38 Broadhurst Avenue
Edgware
Middx HA8 8TS
Tel: 020 8958 8512
Fax: 020 8958 5112
email:
martin@miracle63.freeserve.co.uk
Website: Martin Myers
2002 releases:
The Mystic Masseur - 29 March
Revelation - 12 April
Dancing at the Blue Iguana -21 June
Villa Des Roses - 11 Oct
The War Bride - 29 Nov
Recent releases:
Trembling Before G-d – May 2003
Other World – June 2003

Momentum Pictures

2nd Floor
184-192 Drummond Street
London NW1 3HP
Tel: 020 7388 1100
Fax: 020 7383 0404
email:
sam.nichols@momentumpictures.co.uk
Website:
www.momentumpictures.co.uk
Sam Nichols
2002 releases:
Soul Survivors - 11 Jan
Made - 25 Jan
Just Visiting - 8 Feb
La Stanza Del Figlio - 15 Feb
Crossroads - 29 March
The Business of Strangers - 3 May
Slackers - 10 May
No Man's Land - 17 May
Novoçaine - 5 July
Hijack Stories - 19 July
Scratch - 5 Sept
National Lampoon's Van Wilder - 27 Sept
My Little Eye - 4 Oct
Morvern Callar - 1 Nov
Bowling For Columbine - 15 Nov
Recent/forthcoming releases:
Standing in the Shadows of Motown – Jul 2003
Confidence – Aug 2003
Camp – Sep 2003

New Line International

4th Floor
Turner House
16 Great Marlborough Street
London W1F 7HS
Tel: 020 7693 0977
Fax: 020 7693 0978
email: paul.saunter@turner.com

Website: www.newline.com
Paul Saunter
Releases of current New Line productions are handled in the UK by Entertainment Film Distributors.

New Realm
25 Margaret Street
London W1W 8RX
Tel: 020 7436 7800
Fax: 020 7436 0690
Ancilliary distribution

Oasis Cinemas and Film Distribution
20 Rushcroft Road
Brixton
London SW2 1LA
Tel: 020 7733 8989
Fax: 020 7733 8790
email: mail@oasiscinemas.co.uk

Optimum Releasing
9 Rathbone Place
London W1T 1HW
Tel: 020 7637 5403
Fax: 020 7637 5408
email: info@optimumreleasing.com
Website: www.optimumreleasing.com
2002 releases
Muhammad Ali, the Greatest - 8 Feb
La Chambre des Officiers - 22 March
Le Placard - 17 May
Biggie and Tupac - 24 May
Betty Fisher et Autres Histories - 14 June
Lawless Heart - 28 June
What's the Worst That Could Happen? - 28 June
Nueve Reinas - 19 July
Lost in La Mancha - 2 Aug
Tortilla Soup - 23 Aug
Recent/forthcoming releases:
Personal Velocity – Mar 2003
Nowhere in Africa – April 2003
Mostly Martha – May 2003
Broken Wings – June 2003
Igby Goes Down – June 2003
Roger Dodger – Aug 2003
XX/XY – Oct 2003
Spirited Away – Sep 2003
Comandante
Animal Factory

Pathé Distribution
Kent House
14-17 Market Place
Great Titchfield Street
London W1W 8AR
Tel: 020 7323 5151
Fax: 020 7631 3568
Website: www.pathe.co.uk
2002 releases
Mulholland Dr. - 4 Jan
Rat Race - 11 Jan
L'Anglaise et le Duc - 15 Feb
Dinner Rush - 29 March
24 Hour Party People - 5 April
Italiensk For Begyndere - 26 April
Dust - 3 May
Dog Soldiers - 10 May
Sur Mes Lèvres - 24 May
Thunderpants - 24 May
Killing Me Softly - 21 June
Comment J'ai Tué Mon Père - 28 June
Amen. - 12 July
Resident Evil Genesis - 12 July
The Abduction Club - 19 July
Hable Con Ella - 23 Aug
Ma Femme est une Actrice - 27 Sept
Astérix & Obélix Mission Cleopatre - 18 Oct
À La Folie Pas Du Tout - 22 Nov
Deathwatch - 6 Dec
Recent/forthcoming releases:
Buffalo Soldiers – Jul 2003
Gerry – Aug 2003
It's All About Love – Nov 2003

Peccadillo Pictures Ltd
9 Kent House
Sewardstone Road
London E2 9JL
email: info@peccadillopictures.com
Website: www.peccadillopictures.com
Tel: 020 7729 5225
Fax: 020 7729 3071
2002 releases:
Club Le Monde - 11 Oct
Recent/forthcoming releases:
Ma Vie – Jul 2003
Food of Love – Aug 2003

Ratpack Film Ltd
Bookings via Ian Rattray (see above)
Forthcoming releases:
Jeremy Hardy Versus the Israeli Army – Jul 2003
The Boy David Story – Sep 2003

Redbus Film Distribution
Ariel House
74a Charlotte Street
London W1T 4QT
Tel: 020 7299 8800
Fax: 020 7299 8801
email: ali@redbusgroup.com
Website: www.helkon-sk.com
Ali King
Formerly known as Helkon SK
2002 releases:
The Mothman Prophecies - 1 March
Sidewalks of New York - 5 April
Bend it Like Beckham - 12 April
A Walk to Remember - 13 Sept
Recent/forthcoming releases:
Welcome to Colinwood
The Hunted
Bollywood Queen – Sep 2003
Cabin Fever – Oct 2003

Salvation Films
Dewhurst House
Winnett Street
London W1D 6JY
Tel: 020 7494 1186
Fax: 020 7287 0153
Website: www.salvation-films.com
Nigel Wingrove
2002 release:
The Bunker - 27 Sept

ScreenProjex
13 Manette Street
London W1D 4AW
Tel: 020 7287 1170
Fax: 020 7287 1123
Website: www.screenprojex.com
2002 release:
Club Le Monde - 11 Oct

Soda Pictures
33/34 Great Pulteney Street
London W1F 9NP
Tel: 020 7851 0755
Fax: 020 7434 1240
Website: www.sodapictures.com
Edward Fletcher
Recent/forthcoming releases:
Balzac and the Litle Chinese Seamstress - 9 May 2003
El Bonaerense – Aug 2003
The Cuckoo – Nov 2003

Squirrel Films Distribution
119 Rotherhithe Street
London SE16 4NF
Tel: 020 7231 2209
Fax: 020 7231 2119
email: ostochman@sandsfilms.co.uk
Website: www.sandsfilms.co.uk

Twentieth Century Fox Film Co
20th Century House
31-32 Soho Square
London W1V 6AP
Tel: 020 7437 7766
Fax: 020 7734 3187
Website: www.fox.co.uk
2002 releases:
Behind Enemy Lines - 4 Jan
Shallow Hal - 26 Jan
From Hell - 8 Feb
Don't Say a Word - 22 Feb
Ice Age - 22 March
Waking Life - 19 April
Hart's War - 24 April
Roadkill - 26 April
Star Wars Episode II Attack of the Clones - 16 May
Unfaithful - 7 June
Kissing Jessica Stein - 21 June
Minority Report - 4 July

The Crocodile Hunter Collision Course - 26 July
Black Knight - 23 Aug
Windtalkers - 30 Aug
Road to Perdition - 20 Sept
Xingfu Shiguang - 27 Sept
One Hour Photo - 4 Oct
High Crimes - 25 Oct
28 Days Later... - 31 Oct
Super Troopers - 15 Nov
Die Another Day - 22 Nov
Joe Somebody - 29 Nov
Like Mike - 13 Dec
The Dancer Upstairs - 6 Dec
Recent/forthcoming releases:
Brown Sugar – Jul 2003
Agent Cody Banks – Jul 2003
Legally Blonde 2 – Aug 2003
Alien – Director's Cut – Oct 2003
The League of Extraordinary Gentlemen – Oct 2003
In America – Oct 2003

UGC Films

34 Bloomsbury Street
London WC1B 3QJ
Tel: 020 7631 4683
Fax: 020 7323 9817
email: info@ugcfilms.co.uk
Gemma Spector
2002 releases:
All or Nothing - 18 Oct
8 Women - 29 Nov
Recent/forthcoming releases:
Summer Things - June 2003
Goodby Lenin - July 2003
Swimming Pool - Aug 2003

UIP (United International Pictures (UK))

12 Golden Square
London W1A 2JL
Tel: 020 7534 5200
Fax: 020 7636 4118
Website: www.uip.co.uk
2002 releases:
The Last Castle - 4 Jan
Nobody Someday - 4 Jan
Domestic Disturbance - 11 Jan
Long Time Dead - 18 Jan
Vanilla Sky - 25 Jan
D-Tox - 1 Feb
A Beautiful Mind - 22 Feb
Ali G Indahouse - 22 March
Jimmy Neutron Boy Genius - 22 March
E.T. The Extra-Terrestrial - 29 March
The Scorpion King - 19 April
About a Boy - 26 April
40 Days and 40 Nights - 31 May
Big Fat Liar - 28 June
Spirit: Stallion of the Cimarron - 5 July
The Sum of all Fears - 16 Aug
The Guru - 23 Aug
The Bourne Identity - 6 Sept
Frailty - 6 Sept
Clockstoppers - 11 Oct
Red Dragon - 11 Oct
K-19 The Widowmaker - 25 Oct
Changing Lanes - 1 Nov
Orange County - 8 Nov
The Curse of the Jade Scorpion - 6 Dec
Hey Arnold! The Movie - 20 Dec
Recent/forthcoming releases:
Hulk – July 2003
Sinbad – July 2003
Tomb Raider 2 – Aug 2003
Love Actually – Nov 2003
Peter Pan – Dec 2003
The Cat in the Hat – April 2004

Warner Bros.

98 Theobalds Road
London WC1X 8WB
Tel: 020 7984 5000
Fax: 020 7984 5211
Website: www.warnerbros.co.uk
Nigel Sharrocks
2002 releases:
The Affair of the Necklace - 11 Jan
Rock Star - 11 Jan
Training Day - 1 Feb
Ocean's Eleven - 15 Feb
Queen of the Damned - 12 April
Collateral Damage - 5 April
Showtime - 3 May
The Majestic - 24 May
The Time Machine - 31 May
Amadeus: The Director's Cut - 26 July
Murder By Numbers - 28 June
Scooby-Doo - 12 July
Eight Legged Freaks - 9 Aug
The Adventures of Pluto Nash - 30 Aug
Divine Secrets of the Ya-Ya Sisterhood - 27 Sept
Juwanna Mann - 4 Oct
Powerpuff girls - 18 Oct
Possession - 25 Oct
Harry Potter and the Chamber of Secrets - 8 Nov
Blood Work - 27 Dec
Recent/forthcoming releases:
What a Girl Wants – Aug 2003
Young Adam – Sep 2003
The Matrix: Revolutions – Nov 2003
The Whole Ten Yards – Jan 2004
Exorcist: The Beginning – Mar 2004

Winchester Film Distribution

19 Heddon Street
London W1B 4BG
Tel: 020 7851 6500
Fax: 020 7851 6505
email: mail@winchesterent.co.uk
Website: www.winchesterent.com
2002 releases:
Lava - 25 Jan
Baise-moi - 23 May
Lighthouse - 19 July
Lantana - 16 Aug
Slap Her, She's French - 18 Oct
Recent/forthcoming releases:
Undercover Brother – Feb 2003
Double Whammy – Jul 2003
The Man Who Sued God – Aug 2003
Triggermen – Nov 2003
Scorched – Jan 2004

Winstone Film Distributors

18 Craignish Avenue
Norbury
London SW16 4RN
Tel: 020 8765 0240
Fax: 020 8765 0564
email: winstonefilmdist@aol.com
Mike.G.Ewin, Sara Ewin
Winstone handle theatrical distribution of films from the catalogues of Carlton International and Canal + Image. Also handle releases on behalf of Metro Tartan Distribution.
2002 release:
Living in Hope - 7 June

Yash Raj Films International Ltd

3rd Floor Wembley Point
1 Harrow Road
Middlesex HA9 6DE
Tel: 0870 739 7345
Fax: 0870 739 7346
email: ukoffice@yashrajfilms.com
Website: www.yashrajfilms.com
Avtar Panesar, Apoorva Mehta
Recent/forthcoming releases:
Koi... Mil Gaya – Aug 2003

FACILITIES

4MC Ltd
142 Wardour Street
London W1F 8ZU
Tel: 020 7878 7800
Fax: 020 7878 7800
Sally Hart-Ives
Website: www.4mc.co.uk
Telecine transfer from 35mm, Super 16mm, 16mm and Super 8mm to all video formats with full grading, blemish concealment and image restoration service. Video mastering, reformatting and duplication to and from any format; standards conversion service including motion compensation via the Alchemist Ph. C. digital converter. Also landlines for feeds to the BT Tower and commercials playouts. Laserdisc pre-mastering and full quality assessment. Packaging. Duplcation, Content Restoration, Sound Mastering, HD editing, HD duplication and HD conversion

Abbey Road Studios
3 Abbey Road
St John's Wood
London NW8 9AY
Tel: 020 7266 7000
Fax: 020 7266 7250
email: bookings@abbeyroad.com
Website: www.abbeyroad.com
Colette Barber
Studio 1: Neve VRP 72 channel, capacity 100 orchestra, 120 piece choir, 44ft screen, 2 x isolation rooms, large client lounge, shower room, private office.
Studio 2: Neve VRP 60 channel, capacity 55 musicians.
Studio 3: SSL 9000 J series 96 channel mixing console. Full range 5.1monitoring.
Penthouse: Neve Capricorn Digital mixing console with CSX film panel.
2 mobile location recording units; Audio post production: mastering, re-mastering, editing, 5.1 audiopreparation and restoration, CD preparation, copying; Abbey Road Interactive: design and digital video studio.

AFM Lighting Ltd
Waxlow Road
London NW10 7NU
Tel: 020 8233 7000
Fax: 020 8233 7001
email: info@afmlighting.com
Website: www.afmlighting.com
Ian Sherborn
Lighting equipment and crew hire; generator hire

After Image Facilities
32 Acre Lane
London SW2 5SG
Tel: 020 7737 7300
Website: www.after.arc.co.uk
email: Jane Thorburn, Mark Lucas
Website: Full broadcast sound stage - Studio A (1,680 sq ft, black, chromakey, blue, white cyc) and insert studio (730 sq ft hard cyc). Multiformat broadcast on-line post production. Special effects - Ultimatte/blue screen

Air Studios
Lyndhurst Hall, Lyndhurst Road
Hampstead
London NW3 5NG
Tel: 020 7794 0660
Fax: 020 7794 8518
email: info@airstudios.com
Website: www.airstudios.com
Alison Burton
Lyndhurst Hall: capacity 500 sq m by 18 m high with daylight; 100 plus musicians; four separation booths. Full motion picture scoring facilities. Neve 88R 96 channel console with encore automation. 5.1monitoring. Studio 1: capacity 60 sq m with daylight; 40 plus musicians. Neve/Focusrite72 channel console with GML automation. 5.1 monitoring. Studio 2: mixing room with SSL8000G plus series console and Ultimation. 5.1 monitoring. Film and TV dubbing facilities: two suites equipped with AMS Logic II consoles; 24 output; Audiofile SC. 5.1 monitoring. Exabyte back-up. Third suite with AMS Logic III console. Foley stage and ADR facilities.

Angel Recording Studios
311 Upper Street
London N1 2TU
Tel: 020 7354 2525
Fax: 020 7226 9624
email: angel@angelstudios.co.uk
Website: www.angelstudios.co.uk
Lucy Jones
Two large orchestral studios with Neve desks, and one small studio. All with facilities for recording to picture

Anvil Post Production Ltd
Denham Studios
North Orbital Road, Denham
Uxbridge
Middx UB9 5HL
Tel: 01895 833522
Fax: 01895 835006
email: reception@anvil-post.com
Website: www.anvil-post.com
Contact: Roger Beck (Director)
Sound completion service; re-recording, ADR, post-sync, Fx recording, transfers, foreign version dubbing; non-linear and film editing rooms, neg cutting, off-line editing, production offices

ARRI Lighting Rental
20a The Airlinks,
Spitfire Way,
Heston,
Middx TW5 9NR
Tel: 020 8561 6700
Fax: 020 8569 2539
email: Tim Ross
Website: www.arri.com
Lighting equipment hire

Associated Press Television News
The Interchange
Oval Road
Camden Lock
London NW1 7DZ
Tel: 020 7482 7400
Fax: 020 7413 8302
email: aptn_broadcast_services@ap.org
Website: www.aptn.com
APTN Broadcast Services provides camera crews, editing, satellite uplink, space segment and delivery - from

anywhere in the world, direct to a broadcaster's door

Barcud Derwen

Cibyn
Caernarfon
Gwynedd LL55 2BD
Tel: 01286 684300
Fax: 01286 684379
email: barcud@barcudderwen.com
Website: www.barcudderwen.com
Video formats: 1C
Beta SP
D2 OB Unit 1: up to 7 cameras 4VTR
OB Unit 2: up to 10 cameras 6VTR
DVE
Graphics Betacam units. Studio 1: 6 500 sq ft studio with audience seating and comprehensive lighting rig.
Studio 2: 1
500 sq ft studio with vision/lighting control gallery and sound gallery. Three edit suites; two graphics suites

Bell Media

Lamb House
Church Street
Chiswick Mall
London W4 2PD
Tel: 020 8996 9960
Fax: 020 8996 9966
email: Contact Paul Campbell(Managing Director)
Website: www.bell-media.com
email: name@bell-media.com

Black Island Studios

Alliance Road
London W3 ORA
Tel: 020 8956 5600
Fax: 020 8956 5604
email: info@islandstudios.net
Website: www.islandstudios.net
Steve Guidici

Blue Post Production

58 Old Compton Street
London W1D 4UF
Tel: 020 7437 2626
Fax: 020 7439 2477
email: info@bluepp.co.uk
Website: www.bluepp.co.uk
Contact: Ashley Ransen, Facilities Manager
Digital Online Editing with Axial edit controllers, Quantel Edit Box , Flame, Sound Studio with pro tools offline/online Avid version II
Davinci Spirt
Mastergrade Suite

BUFVC

77 Wells Street
London W1T 3QJ
Tel: 020 7393 1500
Fax: 020 7393 1555
email: ask@bufvc.ac.uk
Website: www.bufvc.ac.uk
Geoffrey O'Brien, Assistant Director
16mm video steenbeck and 16mm viewing facilities. Seminar room for up to 30 people with video/data protection facilities

Capital FX

2nd Floor
20 Dering Street
London W1S 1AJ
Tel: 0207 4939998
Fax: 0207 4939997
email: ian@capital-fx.co.uk
Website: www.capital-fx.co.uk
Contact: Ian Buckton(Operations Director)
Graphic design and production, laser subtitling, opticals effects and editing

Capital Studios

13 Wandsworth Plain
London SW18 1ET
Tel: 020 8877 1234
Fax: 020 8877 0234
Central London: 3,000 and 2,000 sq ft fully equipped broadcast standard television studios. 16x9/4x3 switchable, two on-line edit suites (D3, D2, D5, Digital Betacam & Beta SP). Avid on/off line editing. Multi track and digital sound dubbing facilities with commentary booth. 'Harriet' graphics suite. BT lines. All support facilities. Car park. Expert team, comfortable surroundings, immaculate standards

CFS in soho

26 Berwick Street
London W1F 8RG
Tel: 020 7734 4543
Fax: 020 7734 6600
email:
cfsinsoho@colourfilmservices.co.uk
Website:
www.colourfilmservices.co.uk
Contact: GrahamTolley

Chromacolour International Ltd

Unit 5 Pilton Estate
Pitlake
Croydon
Surrey CRO 3RA
Tel: 020 8688 1991
Fax: 020 8688 1441
email: sales@chromacolour.co.uk
Website: www.chromacolour.co.uk
Contact: Joanne Hogan
Animation supplies/equipment

Cinebuild

Studio House
34 Rita Road
Vauxhall
London SW8 1JU
Tel: 020 7582 8750
Fax: 020 7793 0467
email: cinebuild@btclick.com
Website: www.cinebuild.sageweb.co.uk
Special effects: rain, snow, fog, mist, smoke, fire, explosions; lighting and equipment hire. Studio: 200 sq m

Cinecontact

27 Newman Street
London W1T 1AR
Tel: 020 7323 1690
Fax: 020 7323 1215
Sunny Dimitriadou
Documentary film-makers. Avid post production facilities

Cinesite (Europe) Ltd

Medius House
2 Sheraton Street
London W1F 8FH
Tel: 020 7973 4000
Fax: 020 7973 4040
email: Website: www.cinesite.com
Utilising state-of-the-art technology, Cinesite provides expertise in every area of resolution-free digital imaging, digital and physical special effects for feature films. Our creative and production teams offer a full spectrum of services from the storyboard to the final composite, including digital effects and shoot supervision. Credits include: Harry Potter and The Prisoner of Azkaban, Shanghai Knights, Harry Potter and The Chamber of Secrets, Die Another Day, Tomb Raider, Band of Brothers

Colour Film Services

10 Wadsworth Road
Perivale
Middx UB6 7JX
Tel: 020 8998 2731
Fax: 020 8997 8738
email:
johnward@colourfilmservices.co.uk
Website:
www.colourfilmservices.co.uk
D.John Ward

Connections Communications Centre
Palingswick House
241 King Street
Hammersmith
London W6 9LP
Tel: 020 8741 1766
Fax: 020 8563 1934
email: info@cccmedia.co.uk
Website: www.cccmedia.co.uk
Jacqueline Davis
Bill Hammond (Facilities)
Production Equipment
BETA SP, DV, DVCPRO, SVHS cameras. Wide range of lighting and sound including SQN stereo mixer and portable D.A.T.
Post Production Equipment
Avid Xpress Deluxe Non-Linear Edit system. BETA SP 3 machine suite with computerised edit controller SVHS on-line and off-line editing
Final Cut Pro and AVID media composer

Corinthian Television Facilities (CTV)
Chiswick Park
London W4 5AN
Tel: 020 8100 1000
Fax: 020 8100 1000
Website: www.ctv.co.uk
OBs: Multi-camera and multi-VTR vehicles. Post Production: 3 suites, 1 SP component, 2 multi-format with 1 D2 Abekas A64 A72
Aston and colour caption camera. Studios: 2 fully equipped television studios (1 in St John's Wood 1in Piccadilly Circus)
1-5 camera

De Lane Lea Ltd
75 Dean Street
London W1lD 3PU
Tel: 020 7432 3800
Fax: 020 7432 3838
email: info@delanelea.com
Website: www.delanelea.com
Peter Joly, Managing Director
Anna/Mica
2 high speed 16/35mm Dolby stereo dubbing theatres with Dolby SR; high speed ADR and FX theatre (16/35mm and NTSC/PAL video); Synclavier digital FX suite; digital dubbing theatre with Logic 2 console; 3 x AudioFile preparation rooms; sound rushes and transfers; video transfers to VHS and U-Matic; Beta rushes syncing. 24 cutting rooms/offices. See also under studios

Denman Productions
5 Holly Road
Twickenham TW1 4EA
Tel: 020 8891 3461
Fax: 020 8891 6413
email: Website: www.denman.co.uk
Website: Anthony Gambier-Parry
Video and film production, including 3D computer animation and web design

Depot Studios
Bond Street
Coventry CV1 4AH
Tel: 024 76 525074
Fax: 024 76 634373
email: info@depotstudios.org.uk
Website: www.depotstudios.org.uk
Contact: Anne Forgan, Matthew Taylor
A creative media centre run by Coventry City Council offering training, equipment hire, events and production support to community groups and individuals. Facilities include Avid Xpress and Adobe Premiere non linear editing, production kit including Beta SP, DVCam and Mini DV cameras, a 24 track recording studio and six workstations running Flash, Dreamweaver, Director, Photoshop and Bryce

Digital Audio Technology
Phoenix Sound
Engineeers Way
Wembley
Middlesex HA9 ODT
Tel: 020 8903 6668
Fax: 020 8903 8571
email: info@digitalauiotech.com
Website: digitalaudiotech.com
Ian Silvester
Providing a one-stop solution to all your digital audio requirements for music, film, television and DVD productions

The Digital Cinema at VTR 64 Dean Street
London W1V 5HG
Tel: 020 7437 0026
Fax: 020 7494 0059
email: alan.church@filmfactory.com
Website: www.filmfactory.com
Alan Church, Simon Giles
The Film Factory is one of London's major feature film post-production facilities specialising in high-resolution digital effects. Credits include Deep Blue Sea, Tea With Mussolini, Lost in Space, The Wings of the Dove, Love is the Devil, Gormenghast and Seven Years in Tibet. Produce visual effects, digital opticals, titles, computer animation and visual effects and supervision. Title sequences include: The Adventures of Pinocchio, Best Laid Plans, Photographing Fairies, Bent, Saving Grace, Cousin Bette, Up 'n' Under, Tube Tales, I Want You and Pandaemonium. Company also has tape-to-film transfer service and full 35mm digital scanning and recording service

Diverse Post
6 Gorleston Street
London W14 8XS
Tel: 020 7603 4567
Fax: 020 7603 2148
email: Louise@diversepost.tv
Website: www.diversepost.tv
Louise Townsend
TV post-production. Diverse Post offers a comprehensive range of post production services; from rushes dubbing, through Avid off line, online, audio dubbing, grading, subtitling and deliverables

Dolby Laboratories
Wootton Bassett
Wiltshire SN4 8QJ
Tel: 01793 842100
Fax: 01793 842101
email: gce@dolby.co.uk
Website: www.dolby.com
Graham Edmondson
Cinema processors for replay of Dolby Digital, Dolby Digital Surround Ex and Dolby SR (analogue) film soundtracks. Sound consultancy relating to Dolby film production, distribution and exhibition. Signal processing equipment for production and broadcast of Dolby Surround, Dolby Digital and Dolby E formats for TV, DVD, and broadcast applications. Audio noise reduction equipment

Dubbs
25-26 Poland Street
London W1F 8QN
Tel: 020 7629 0055
Fax: 020 7287 8796
email: sales@dubbs.co.uk
Website: www.dubbs.co.uk
David Wilson, Sales Manager
Lauren McCready, Business

Development
Dubbs offers a complete video duplication and Digital Media facility, open 7 days a week, 24 hours a day. With a complete range of digital video duplication facilities, Dubbs provides a flexible, reliable, quality of service. Dubbs Digital Media boasts two dedicated DVD authoring systems, Sonic Solutions Creator and Fusion. In addition, Spruce and Digital Rapids allow real-time video encoding to Mpeg, Quicktime, WMV, Real, AVI, and audio formats. Dubbs also offers DVD and CD replication, and a printing and packaging service.

Dukes Island Studios

Dukes Road
Western Avenue
London W3 OSL
Tel: 0208 956 5600
Fax: 0208 956 5604
email: info@islandstudios.net
Website: www.islandstudios.net
Steve Guidici

Edinburgh Film Workshop Trust

56 Albion Road
Edinburgh EH7 5QZ
Tel: 0131 656 9123
email: post@efwt.demon.co.uk
Website: www.efwt.demon.co.uk
David Halliday, Angus Ferguson
Beta SP production; 16mm Arri, 6-plates and rostrum, broadcst quality video animation and non-linear editing; off-line editing. Animation and video training, consultancy and project development. Specialists in enviornment, health and welfare

Edric Audio-visual Hire

34-36 Oak End Way
Gerrards Cross
Bucks SL9 8BR
Tel: 01753 481400
Fax: 01753 887163
Website: www.edric-av.co.uk
James Hunter
Audiovisual and video production facilities

Elstree Light and Power

Millennium Studios
Elstree Way
Borehamwood
Herts WD6 1SF
Tel: 020 8236 1300
Fax: 020 8236 1333
email: elp@elstree-online.co.uk
Website: www.elstree-online.co.uk/elp
Tony Slee

Eon Productions Limited

Eon House
138 Piccadilly
London W1J 7NR
Tel: 020 7493 7953
Fax: 020 7408 1236
email: chris.brisley@eon.co.uk
Chrissy Brisley
22 seater screening theatre
35 mm double-head projection
multi system video/DVD equipment
Dolby Digital Sound
Full computer projection facility
power point presentation

Eye Film and Television

9/11a Dove Street
Norwich NR2 1DE
Tel: 01603 762551
Fax: 01603 762420
email: production@eyefilmandtv.co.uk
Website: www.eyefilmandtv.co.uk
Lucy Bolton
Production crews, Avid Non Linear and Final Cut Pro on and offline systems

Faction Films

26 Shacklewell Lane
London E8 2EZ
Tel: 020 7690 4446
Fax: 020 7690 4447
email: faction@factionfilms.co.uk
Website: www.factionfilms.co.uk
Mark Casebow
2xAvid MC1000 composer; 1 on-line, 1 off-line - for hire; Sony VX1000 digi-cam; Sony Hi-8; HHB Portadat; Production office space available for hire. Tape Transfer facilities

Film Work Group

Top Floor, Chelsea Reach
79-89 Lots Road
London SW10 0RN
Tel: 020 7352 0538
Fax: 020 7351 6479
email: Loren Squires, Nigel Perkins
Website: Video and Film post-production facilities. AVID on-line (2:1) and off-line editing. 36 gigs storage, Digital Animation Workstations (draw, paint, image, modification, edit). 3 machine Hi-Band SP and mixed Beta SP/Hi-Band with DVE. 2 machine Lo-Band off-line with sound mixing. 6 plate Steenbeck. Special rates for grant aided, self-funded and non-profit projects

FinePoint Broadcast

Hill House, Furze Hill
Kingswood
Surrey KT20 6EZ
Tel: 0800 970 2020
Fax: 0800 970 2030
email: hire@finepoint.co.uk
Website: www.finepoint.co.uk
Colin Smith, hire co-ordinator
Roger Wedlake, chief engineer
Broadcast equipment hire. Cameras, lenses, control units, high speed cameras, disc recorder, cables, VTRs, edit controllers, digital video effects, vision mixers, monitors, sound kit

FrameStore

9 Noel Street
London W1F 8GH
Tel: 020 7208 2600
Fax: 020 7208 2626
email: steph.bruning@framestore.co.uk
Website: www.framestore.co.uk
Full service digital video facility - Spirit Datacine, Ursa Diamond Telecine, 4 Inferno, 4 x Henry Infinity, Flame, Digital Editing, Avid, Softimage, Maya, After Effects, Commotion, Photoshop, Final Cut Pro, Premiere, Combustion

Frontline Television Services

35 Bedfordbury
Covent Garden
London WC2N 4DU
Tel: 020 7836 0411
Fax: 020 7379 5210
Website: www.frontline-tv.co.uk
Tracy Thomas
Extensive edit, duplication, computer animation and multimedia facilities - 5 Avid Media Composers, Avid Symphony, DS, Linear Digital Betacam Suite. Low volume, low cost, quick turnaround duplication. 2D and 3D animation and graphics. Multimedia facilities including encoding.

Goldcrest Post Production Facilities Ltd

Entrance 1 Lexington Street
36/44 Brewer Street
London W1F 9LX
Tel: 020 7439 7972
Fax: 020 7437 5402
email: mailbox@goldcrest-post.co.uk

Website: www.goldcrest.org
Raju Raymond/Poppy Quinn
Theatre 1 with Otari Elite + consol, Dolby SRD, Fairlight on FX3.48 DFW film + video projection; ADR & FX recording, built in Foley surfaces and extensives props;
Theatre 2 with Otari Elite + consol, Dolby SRD, video projection, ADR + FX recording, built in Foley surfaces & extensive props;
Theatre 3 with Protools TDM Mix + Harrison series 12 + video projection; ADR + FX recording, built in Foley surfaces and extensive props;
All theatres equipped with ISDN link; Sound Transfer Bay for all film and video formats with Dolby SRD; Rank Cintel MKIIC Telecine enhanced 4:2:2, Pogle and secondary colour correction.
On and offline Avid suites, Lightworks cutting rooms, production offices and luxury apartments

Hillside

Merry Hill Road
Bushey
Herts WD23 1DR
Tel: 020 8950 7919
Fax: 020 8421 8085
email: enquiries@hillside-studios.co.uk
Website: www.hillside-studios.co.uk
David Hillier
Production and Post-Production facilities to Broadcast standards. 1500 sq ft studio with 16 x 9 switchable cameras and Digital Mixer. Smaller studio and single camera location units available. Sounds Studios and Dubbing Suite, Non-Linear and Digital Editing. Graphics, Set Design and Construction. Offices, restaurant and parking

Hull Time Based Arts

42 The High Street
Hull HU1 1PS
Tel: 01482 586340/216446
Fax: 01482 589952
email: lab@timebase.org
Website: www.timebase.org
Walter van der Cruijsen
Avid Media Composer 9000XL non-linear editing suite with 1:1 compression, digital I/O and Commotion 2.1 compositing software, Avid Media Composer 1000 editing suite with 2:1 compression, G4 with Final Cut Pro, ProTools Audio Suite, Multimedia authoring, DVC Pro, DVCam and DV cameras, DAT recorder, Data projector and all ancillary video equipment available. Special rates for non commercial projects

Humphries Video Services

Unit 2, The Willow Business Centre
17 Willow Lane
Mitcham
Surrey CR4 4NX
Tel: 020 8648 6111/0207 636 3636
Fax: 020 8648 5261
email: sales@hvs.co.uk
Website: www.hvs.co.uk
David Brown, Jago Michell, Richard Meredith
Video cassette duplication: all formats, any standard. Standards convertors. Macrovision anti-copy process, CD and DVD Authoring/Replication labelling, shrink wrapping, packaging and mail out services, free collections and deliveries in central London. Committed to industrial and broadcast work

Interact Sound

160 Barlby Road
London W10 6BS
Tel: 020 8960 3115
Fax: 020 8964 3022
email: info@interact-sound.co.uk
Sandie Wirtz
Spacious digital and analogue dubbing theatres. Dolby stereo, SR-D. DTS compatable. Large screen film and video projection. 5 digital audio edit suites. Rooms available for production offices. Mixers: Aad Wirtz, Lee Taylor and John Falcini

ITN

200 Gray's Inn Road
London WC1X 8XZ
Tel: 020 7430 4134
Fax: 020 7430 4655
email: Martin Swain
Website: Martin Swain, Jenny Mazzey
2400 sq ft studio; live or recorded work; comprehensive outside source ability; audience 65; crews; video transfer; Westminster studio; graphics design service using Flash Harry, Paintbox etc; Training offered; Sound and dubbing; tape recycling; experienced staff

Lee Lighting

Wycombe Road
Wembley
Middlesex HAO 1QD
Tel: 020 8900 2900
Fax: 020 8902 5500
Website: www.lee.co.uk
Film/TV lighting equipment hire

Light House Media Centre

The Chubb Buildings
Fryer Street
Wolverhampton WV1 1HT
Tel: 01902 716044
Fax: 01902 717143
email: raj@light-house.co.uk
Website: www.light-house.co.uk
Contact: Technical department
Three machine U-Matic edit suite (hi-band - BVE 900, lo-band BVE 600) VHS/U-Matic/Betacam/ENG kits, also animation and chroma keying

Lighthouse

9-12 Middle Street
Brighton BN1 1AL
Tel: 01273 384222
Fax: 01273 384233
email: info@lighthouse.org.uk
Website: www.lighthouse.org.uk
Technical Department
A training and production centre, providing courses, facilities and production advice. Avid off- and online edit suites. Apple Mac graphics and animation workstations. Digital video capture & manipulation. Output to/from Betacam SP. SVHS offline edit suite. Post Production and Digital Artists equipment bursaries offered three times a year

MAC Sound Hire

1-2 Attenburys Park
Park Road
Altrincham
Cheshire WA14 5QE
Tel: 0161 969 8311
Fax: 0161 962 9423
email: info@macsound.co.uk
Website: www.macsound.co.uk
Professional sound equipment hire

The Machine Room

54-58 Wardour Street
London WID 4JQ
Tel: 020 7292 8506
Fax: 020 7287 3773
email: david.atkinson@themachineroom.co.uk
Website: www.themachineroom.co.uk
David Atkinson

Mersey Film and Video (MFV)

13 Hope Street
Liverpool L1 9BQ
Tel: 0151 708 5259
Fax: 0151 707 8595
email: info@mersey-film-video.co.uk
Website: www.mfv.merseyside.org
Joanne Toomey,
Producer/Development Manager
Patrick Hall (Resources Co-Ordinator)
Production facilities for: BETA SP, DVCPro, Hi8, MiniDV SVHS and VHS - full shooting kits for all. Wide range of grip and lighting equipment. All format tape duplication and tape stock. Guidance and help for funding, finance, budgets production

Metro Broadcast

6-7 Great Chapel Street
London W1F 3FF
Tel: 020 7434 7700
Fax: 020 7434 7701
email: info@metrobroadcast.co.uk
Website: www.metrobroadcast.co.uk
Mark Cox
Broadcast Hire and Crewing:
Digital Beta, Beta SX, Beta SP, DVC Pro, DV Cam, Mini DV, Hi-Def CiniAlta
Avid: MCO, film Composers, 9000, NT or MAC
Duplication: Alchemists standards conversions from/to all formats.
Technical assessment. Format include: D1, D2, D3, Digital Beta, Beta SX, DVC Pro, DV Cam, Mini DV, CD ROM, DVD

The Mill/Mill Film

40/41 Great Marlborough Street
London W1V 1DA
Tel: 020 7287 4041
Fax: 020 7287 8393
email: inb@mill.co.uk
Website: www.mill.co.uk
Emma Shield
Post Production for commercials and feature films using Spirit, Ursa, Inferno, Flame, Softimage, Henry, Harry and digital editing

Millennium Studios

Elstree Way
Borehamwood
Herts WD6 1SF
Tel: 020 8236 1400
Fax: 020 8236 1444
email: Kate Tufano
Website: Sound stage 80'x44'x24' with 6'x44'x11' balcony flying and cyc grid. In house suppliers of: lighting; generators; rigging; photography; crew catering and fully licensed bar

Mosaic Pictures Ltd

8-12 Broadwick Street
London W1V 1FH
Tel: 020 7437 6514
Fax: 020 7494 0595
email: info@mosaicfilms.com
Website: www.mosaicfilms.com
Deborah Weavers, Facilities Manager
Avid Symphony, 6 Avid offline suites, DV Camera Hire, Video Transfer Suite, Final Cut Pro, DV Post-Production expertise, Video encoding for the Web, Digibeta/16mm Aaton Cameramen, meeting room, production offices

The Moving Picture Company

127 Wardour Street
London W1V 4AD
Tel: 020 7494 7964
Fax: 020 7434 2641
Video formats: D1, D2, Digital Betacam, Betacam SP, 1 C format hi-/lo-band.
Editing: 3xD1/Disk based edit suites, Sony 9100 and Abekas A84 (8 layers) A57 DVE, A64, A60 and A66 Disks; A72 and Aston Motif caption generator. Video Rostrum and Colour Caption Camera
Non Linear Offline Editing: 1 x Avid 4000 with Betacam SP. 35/16mm cutting room
Telecine: 2 URSA Gold 4 x 4 with Pogle DCP/Russell Square Colour Correction Jump Free, Low Speed/Silk Scan Options, Matchbox Stills Store, Key Code, noise reduction
SFX: Discreet Logic 2 x Flame, 1 x Flint and Quantel 2 x Henry
3D: Hardware: 7 x SGI systems (3 x High Impacts and 4 x Indigo 2 Extremes). Software: Alias Poweranimator, Custom Programming and Procedural Effects, Matador, 3D Studio Paint, Elastic Reality and Pandemonium.
Rendering: SGI Challenge and Onyx (x2). Digital Film: High resolution 35mm digital film post production, comprising 7 x Kodak Cineon, 1 x Discreet Logic Inferno and Matador. Filmtel TM video tape to 35mm transfer. Mac: Disk or ISDN input of artwork. File transfer, Photoshop and Illustrator and stills output to 35mm or high resolution 5 x 4 transparencies
Studio: 47' x 30' with L cyc

Oasis Television

6-7 Great Pulteney Street
London W1F 9NA
Tel: 020 7434 4133
Fax: 020 7494 2843
email: sales@oasistv.co.uk
Website: www.oasistv.co.uk
Pat Gale, Ray Nunney, Helen Leicester
14 online suites (including digital linear, analogue linear, Jaleo Digital, Non-linear, Avid Online). 2 fully digital audiodubbing suites. 11 Avid and Lightworkds offline services. 5 graphics suites C2D and 3D, including illusion), standards conversion. Full duplication facilities multimedia

Oxford Film and Video Makers (OFVM)

The Old Boxing Club
54 Catherine Street
Oxford OX4 3AH
Tel: 01865 792731
Fax: 01865 792732
email: office@ofvm.org
Website: www.ofvm.org
Richard Duriez: Office Administrator
Geron Swann: Centre Director
Gary Shenton: Production Development
OFVM is an independent centre for film and digital media offering: A range of training courses
Production development and support.Local screening opportunities. Post production facilities for hire

Panavision Grips

Metropolitan Centre
Bristol Road
Greenford
Middx UB6 8UQ
Tel: 020 8839 7333
Fax: 020 8578 1536
email: enquiries@panavision.co.uk
Website: www.panavision.co.uk
Mark Furssedonn
Grip equipment and studio hire

Pinewood Studios

Sound Dept
Pinewood Road
Iver Heath
Bucks SL0 0NH

Tel: 01753 656301
Fax: 01753 656014
email: graham_hartstone@pinewood-studios.co.uk
Website: www.pinewood-studios.co.uk
Graham Hartstone
Two large stereo dubbing theatres with automated consoles, all digital release formats. 35mm and Digital dubbing. Akai DD8 dubbers & recorders, Broadband connectivity, ADR & Foley recording. Large ADR/Fx recording theatre, 35mm or AVID AUDIOVISION, removable drives, Protools, ISDN Dolbyfax with timecode in aux data. Digital dubbing theatres with AMS/NEVE Logic 2 and AudioFile Spectra 16. Preview theatre 115 seats. Formats 35/70mm Dolby SR.D, DTS and SDDS. Comprehensive transfer bay. Stereo Optical Negative transfer including Dolby SR.D, SDDS and DTS. Cutting rooms

The Pierce Rooms

Pierce House
London Apollo Complex
Queen Caroline Street
London W6 9QU
Tel: 020 8563 1234
Fax: 020 8563 1337
email: meredith@pierce-entertainment.com
Website: www.pierce-entertainment
Meredith Leung, Studio Manager
Complete surround sound facilities: surround sound to picture recording. Foley and mixing. Large and accurate main control room - Neve VR 72-60 console with flying fader automation, recall and digital surround automation. Dynaudio M4-surround sound monitoring. Separate digital preproduction room. Permanent tie lines to Apollo theatre for studio quality live recordings. In house team of engineers and programmers; 24 hour maintenance; private parking

Salon Post-Productions

12 Swainson Road
London W3 7XB
Tel: 020 8746 7611
Fax: 020 8746 7613
email: hire@salonrentals.com
Website: www.salonrentals.com
Editing Equipment rental - non linear systems including Avid Film Composer & Lightworks, hard disk storage, BetaSP and DAT etc
Film equipment - including 35mm and 16mm Steenbecks and all editing accessories and supplies. Edit suites in Acton or delivered to any location. Digital sound editing systems include Audiovision, Protools

Sheffield Independent Film

5 Brown Street
Sheffield S1 2BS
Tel: 0114 272 0304
Fax: 0114 279 5225
email: admin.sif@workstation.org.uk
Website: www.sifmediaa.org.uk
Dave Woodcock, Enquiries
Daren Eagles, General Manager
Sheffield Independent Film houses several independent media production companies and provides film and video facilities including Aaton XTR+ 16mm kit, DV and BetaSP cameras, AVID and FCP post-production and a 1200 sq.ft studio

Shepperton Sound

Shepperton Studios
Studios Road
Shepperton
Middx TW17 0QD
Tel: 01932 572676
Fax: 01932 572396
email: sheppertonsound@dial.pipex.com
Website: www.sheppertonstudios.com
Tania Robertson
Three Dubbing Theatres (16mm, 35mm, video) Post-sync, and footsteps; effects, theatre, in-house sound transfers

Shepperton Studios

Studios Road
Shepperton
Middx TW17 0QD
Tel: 01932 562611
Fax: 01932 568989
email: sheppertonstudios@dial.pipex.com
Website: Cutting rooms; 16mm, 35mm viewing theatres

Soho Images

8-14 Meard Street
London W1V 3HR
Tel: 020 7437 0831
Fax: 020 7734 9471
email: sohogroup.com
Website: www.sohoimages.com
Zahida Bacchus
Kodak endorsed laboratory offers full processing of 16/35mm film, 24 hours rushes, computerised in-house negative cutting, cinema commercials, broadcast and features bulk prints, archive and restoration. Facilities include: 8/16/35mm Telecine transfers with Wet-Gate. Spirit DataCine with POGAL Platinum, URSA Gold with DCP, Rank Cinitels' with up-grades. Sound suite using Instant Sync, InDaw and SADIE. Broadcast standards conversions, aspect ration conversions, edit suites, Avid Symphony Universal with 24P, 3D and Animation, Flame, Henry and Edit Box

SVC

142 Wardour Street
London WIF 8ZO
Tel: 020 7734 1600
Fax: 020 7437 1854
Website: www.svc.co.uk
Catherine Langley
Video Post Production including the following: Datacine, Inferno, Flame, 2 Infinitys; Henry, Computer Animation and Motion Control

Tele-Cine

Video House
48 Charlotte Street
London W1P 1LX
Tel: 020 7208 2200
Fax: 020 7208 2250
email: telecine@telecine.co.uk
Website: www.telecine.co.uk
Wendy Bleazard
Digital linear and non linear editing; telecine; audio post production; DVD authoring; video compression; fibre and satellite communications; duplication

Terry Jones PostProductions Ltd

Goldcrest International
65-66 Dean Street
London W1D 4PL
Tel: 020 7434 1173
Fax: 020 7494 1893
email: terryjonespost@btconnect.com
Website: www.terryjonespostproductions.com
Terry Jones
Lightworks V.I.P. editing suites. Experiencd and creative, award winning editors handling commercials, documentaries, features and corporate work

Twickenham Film Studios

St Margaret's
Twickenham
Middx TW1 2AW
Tel: 020 8607 8888
Fax: 020 8607 8889
Website:
www.twickenhamstudios.com
Gerry Humphreys (Post Production)
Caroline Tipple (Stages)
Two dubbing theatres; ADR/Foley theatre; 40 cutting rooms; Lightworks, Avid, 16/35mm. Three stages, offices, art departments, workshop, prop rooms

Videolondon Sound

16-18 Ramillies Street
London W1F 7LW
Tel: 020 7734 4811
Fax: 020 7494 2553
email:
info@videolondonsoundstudios.co.uk
Website:
www.videolondonsoundstudios.co.uk
Clifford Judge
Five sophisticated sound recording studios with comprehensive digital audio postproduction facilities

Videosonics Cinema Sound

68a Delancey Street
London NW1 7RY
Tel: 020 7209 0209
Fax: 020 7419 4470
email: info@videosonics.com
Website: www.videosonics.com
2 x All Digital THX Film Dubbing Theatres. Dolby Digital and SR 35 mm, 16mm and Super 16mm. All aspect ratios, all speeds. Video Projection if required Theatre I: AMS-Neve Logic II console (112 channels) with 24track Audiofile. Theatre II (Big Blue): AMS-Neve DFC console (224 channels) with 2 x 24 track Audio files. 3 x additional television Sound Dubbing Suites, 2 with AMS-Neve digital consoles, 1 x SSL console. 6 x Digital Audio Editing rooms, 35mm film editing, Facilities for Lightworks and Avid 2 x Foley and ADR Studios. A total of 14 AMS Audiofiles. Parking by arrangement. Wheelchair Access

VTR Ltd

64 Dean Street
London W1V 5HG
Tel: 020 7437 0026
Fax: 020 7439 9427
email: info@vtr.co.uk
Website: www.vtr.co.uk
Anthony Frend
VTR is one of London's major digital non-linear post production facilities specialising in commercials, corporates and promos. Facilities include: 2 x Spirit DataCines the world's first real-time high resolution film scanner for 35mm, 16mm and super 16mm; Ursa Gold telecines with Pogle Platinum and full range of Ursa optical effects incl. Kaleidoscope; Inferno and Flame for resolution independent special effects for TV and cinema. 3x Henry Infinity for non-linear digital editing and effects. 3D Computer Graphics and Animation with Maya Software; Flint RT, 3 x Macs; dubbing, ISDN and playout facilities. Domino (digital film effects) see under 'The Film Factory at VTR.'
a) The VTR Ltd entry
b) The Film Factory at VTR entry - now read as Digital Cinema at VTR.

Windmill Lane Pictures

4 Windmill Lane
Dublin 2
Ireland
Tel: (353) 1 6713444
Fax: (353) 1 6718413
email: info@windmillane.com
Website: www.windmilllane.com
Liz Murphy
Telecine, digital on-line, AVID off-line, Henry, Flame, Flint, EFP Crews and number 4 Audio Studio
London W1V 3AW
Tel: 020 7434 1121
Fax: 020 7734 0619
email: sound@worldwidegroup.ltd.uk
Website: worldwidegroup.ltd.uk

FESTIVALS

Listed below by country of origin are a selection of international film, television and video festivals with contact names and brief synopses. Compiled by Jose De Esteban

AUSTRALIA

FlickerFest International Short Festival

4-12 January 2003
Bondi Pavillion
PO BOX 7416
Bondi Beach, NSW 2026
Tel: +61 (02) 99017070
email: info@flickerfest.com.au
Website: www.flickerfest.com.au
Bronwyn Kidd, Festival Director
Australia's premiere international short film festival, it consists of a main competitive programme of international and Australian shorts, which then tour nationally to all major cities and regional centres; an Online Festival (computer generated and digital short films) and other activities including seminars and forums

Melbourne International Film Festival

23 July-10 August 2003
PO Box 2206
Fitzroy Mail Centre
Melbourne, Vic 3065
Tel: +613 9417 2011
Fax: +613 9417 3804
email:
miff@melbournefilmfestival.com.au
Website:
melbournefilmfestival.com.au
James Hewison, Executive Director
A showcase for the latest developments in Australian and international filmmaking offering a wide range of features and shorts, documentaries, animation and experimental films.

Sydney Film Festival

6-20 June 2003
PO Box 950
Glebe, NSW 2037
Tel: +61 (02) 9660 3844
Fax: +61 (02) 9692 8793
email: info@sydfilmfest.org
Website: www.sydneyfilmfestival.org
A celebration of World Cinema screening features, documentaries, shorts, animation, video, experimental work and retrospectives as well as forums and lectures with local and international industry professionals,critics and academics. Prix UIP is awarded by the audience to the best European film screened in the Contemporary World Cinema strand. Also Audience Awards for Best Documentary, Best Short and Best feature film

AUSTRIA

Viennale - Vienna International Film Festival

17-29 October 2003
Siebensterngasse 2
A-1070 Vienna
Tel: +431 526 5947
Fax: +431 523 4172
email: office@viennale.at
Website: www.viennale.at
Hans Hurch, Director
Festival for the general public, which premieres Austrian and international films of all genres and in all formats. FIPRESCI-Prize to a debut or follow-up film; Short Film Prize and the "Standard Readers' Prize" for a film in the festival without an Austrian distribution deal

BELGIUM

Festival du Film De Bruxelles

25 March-4 April 2003
Maliestraat 13
1050 Elsene
Tel: (32) 2 533 3420
email: info@fffb.be
Website: www.fffb.be
Competitive festival promoting films from Europe and Belgium, showing about 100 features and 120 shorts. European features and shorts eligible to compete for Golden and Silver Iris Awards. Sections include Kaleidoscope of the World Cinema, Belgian Focus, Night of the Short Film, tributes and retrospectives.

Festival International du Film Fantastique

12-27 March 2004
Rue de la Comptesse de Flandre 8
Gravin van Vlaanderenstraat 8
Tel: +32[0]2 201 1713
Fax: +32[0]2 201 1409
email:peymet@bifff.org
Webb:www.bifff.org
Competitive festival presenting over 100 features in the field of fantasy, horror, science-fiction, thrillers, cult and underground. In addition, the festival puts the spotlights on every art form related to the genre: painting, sculpture, literature,music,video, facial make-up, body painting, fashion, video games and theatre.

Flanders International Film Festival

7-18 October 2003
Leeuwstraat 40b
B-9000 Ghent
Tel: +32 9 242 8060
Fax: +32 9 221 9074
email: info@filmfestival.be
Webb: www.filmfestival.be
Jacques Dubrulle, General Secretary
Largest competitive showcase in Belgium, presenting some 190 features and 100 short films from all over the world. The festival focuses on the "Impact of Music on Film", a fixed section in which 15 films compete for three prizes

BOSNIA and HERZEGONIVA

Sarajevo Film Festival

15-23 August 2003
Art Services
Sarajevo Film Festival
Hamdije Kresevljakovica 13
71000 Sarajevo Bosnia and Herzegovina
Tel: 387 (33) 209-411/263-380
Fax: 387 (33) 221-516
email: info-sff@sff.ba
Website: www.sff.ba
Paula Gordon, Festival Manager
The festival promotes recent contemporary film production and to

support the distribution of independent films in Bosnia and Herzegovina. The event also aims 'to establish Sarajevo as a new venue where film directors, actors, producers and distributors can meet, exchange ideas and initiate new projects'.

BRAZIL

Festival do Rio BR - Rio de Janeiro Film Festival

25 September-9 October 2003
Rua Voluntários dá Pátria 53/4th Floor
97 Botafogo
Rio de Janeiro 22270-000
Tel: +55 21 25790352
Fax: +55 21 25393580
email: films@festivaldoriobr.com.br
Website: www.festivaldoriobr.com.br
Ilda Santiago, Executive Director
Largest film festival in Brazil and Latin America. With prizes for Best feature, short and documentary. Also 'Premio UIP' for the best European Film voted by audiences.

Mostra BR de Cinema -São Paulo International Film Festival

17-30 October 2003
Rua Antonio Carlos, 288-2nd andar
Cep 01309-010 Cerqueira Cesar-SP
Tel: (55 11) 3141 2548/3141 1068
Fax: (55 11) 3266 7066
email: info@mostra.org
Website: www.mostra.org
Leon Cakoff, Festival Director
A cultural, non-profit event for international films. The festival's main sections are: The New Filmmakers Competition and International Perspective.

BURKINA FASO

FESPACO-Panafrican Film and TV Festival of Ouagadougou

26 February-5 March 2005
01 BP 2505
Ouagadougou 01
Tel: (226) 30 75 38
Fax: (226) 31 25 09
email: sg@fespaco.bf
Website: www.fespaco.bf
Baba Llama, General Delegate
The Panafrican Film and Television Festival is the largest competitive showcase in Africa.Featuring African diaspora and African filmmakers, whose work has been produced during the three years preceding the biennial festival and not shown before at FESPACO.

CANADA

Atlantic Film Festival

12-20 September 2003
PO Box 36139
220-5600 Sackville Street
Halifax,
Nova Scotia B3J 1L2
Tel: (1) 902 422 3456
Fax: (1) 902 422 4006
email: festival@atlanticfilm.com
Website: www.atlanticfilm.com
Lia Rinaldo, Programme Director
Atlantic premieres new works from the Atlantic region and Canada. Other programmes include International Perspectives (a selection of films from Celtic and Nordic countries); Different Takes; The Late Shifts and the special children's series.

Banff Television Festival

8-13 June 2003
1350 Railway Avenue
Canmore, Alberta, T1W 3E3
Tel: (1) 403 678 9260
Fax: (1) 403 678 9269
email: info@banfftvfest.com
Website: www.btvf.com
Festival for television programme producers and on-line content creators. The conference schedule features over 60 hours of workshops, plenary sessions, keynote speakers, master classes, market simulations and pitching opportunities. There is also the international Banff Rockie Awards programme competition.

Festival des Films du Monde - Montreal World Film Festival

27 August-7 September 2003
1432, de Bleury Street
Montreal,Quebec H3A 2J1
Tel: (1) 514 848 3883
Fax: (1) 514 848 3886
email: info@ffm-montreal.org
Website: www.ffm-montreal.org
Serge Losique, Festival President
Competitive festival with films from more than seventy countries. It includes the following sections: Cinema of Europe, Cinema of the Americas (divided in three sub-sections:Panorama Canada, Cinema of the USA, Latin American Cinema), Cinema of Asia, Cinema of Africa, Cinema of Oceania and Documentaries of the World.

Festival International de Nouveau Cinéma et des Nouveaux Médias de Montréal

9-19 October 2003
3530 Boulevard Saint-Laurent blvd, suit 304
Montreal
Quebec H2X 2V1
Tel: (1) 514 847 1242
email: montrealfest@fcmm.com
Website: www.fcmm.com
'Innovation and exploration are the guiding principles of the FCMM's programming'. The festival is divided in four categories: Feature Film and Video, Documentary, Short and New Media

Hot Docs Canadian International Documentary Festival

25 April- 4 May 2003
517 College Street
Suite 420,Toronto
Ontario, M6G 4A2
Tel: (1) 416 203 2155
Fax: (1) 416 203 0446
email: info@hotdocs.ca
Website: www.hotdocs.ca
Hot Docs is North America's largest documentary festival with a selection of over 100 documentaries from Canada and the rest of the world. The festival has a reputation for providing 'a full range of professional development market and networking opportunities for documentary professionals'.

Ottawa International Student Animation Festival

16-19 October 2003
2 Daly Avenue, Suite 120
Ottawa
Ontario K1N 6E2
Tel: (1) 613 232 8769
Fax: (1) 613 232 6315
email: neall@magma.ca
Website: www.awn.com/ottawa
Kelly Neall, Managing Director
Presenting a special screening entitled 'Essential Viewing' featuring all the 'must see' films for any animation fan. This year with retrospectives on Martha Colburn and Oscar Grillo.

Toronto International Film Festival

9-18 September 2004
2 Carlton Street, Suite 1600
Toronto, Ontario M5B IJ3
Tel: (1) 416 967 7371

Fax: (1) 416 967 9477
email: tiffg@torfilmfest.ca
Website: www.bell.ca/filmfest
Piers Handling, Festival Director
Non-competitive showcase for feature films and shorts not previously shown in Canada.The festival also includes some American premieres, retrospectives and national cinema programmes.

Vancouver International Film Festival

25 September-10 October 2003
Suite 410, 1008 Homer Street
Vancouver, BC V6B 2X1
Tel: (1) 604 685 0260
Fax: (1) 604 688 8221
email: viff@viff.org
Website: www.viff.org
Alan Franey, Director
One of the largest festivals in Canada. The competitive sections include: Dragons and Tiger: The Cinemas of East Asia, Canadian Images, Nonfictions features, Cinema of Our Time and Spotlight on France. The VIFF also presents a Trade Forum, which brings together roundtable experts on film and television for discussions and seminars

COLOMBIA

Festival Internacional de Cine y Television de Cartagena

28 February- 7 March 2003
Calle San Juan de Dios
Baluarte de San Francisco Javier
A.A. 1834, Cartagena
Tel: (57) 5 660 1702
email: info@festicinecartagena.com
Website: www.festicinecartagena.com
Victor Nieto, Festival Director
The most senior film festival in Latin America. It covers: Iberoamerican short and feature films; international showcase; Colombian Television; Cinema , Television, Video and Cable markets; telefestival ; seminars and conferences

CROATIA

See Docs in Dubrovnik

June
Art Radionica Lazareti
Pobijana 8
20000 Dubrovnik
Tel: (385) 20 423 497
Fax: (385) 20 421 114
email: art-lazareti@du.tel.hr
Website: www.filmfest.dk/dubrovnik
Sister festival to Balticum Film & TV Festival in Bornholm, Denmark. It focuses on documentaries made in South East Europe, the countries around the Baltic Sea and in European Film Schools. It also organises seminars, workshops and professional meetings to promote and stimulate both the culture and production of documentaries

World Festival of Animated Films

14-19 June 2004
Koncertna Direkcija Zagreb
Kneza Mislava 18
10000 Zagreb
Tel: (385) 1 45 01 190/191/192
Fax: (385) 1 46 11 807
email: animafest@kdz.hr
Website: www.animafest.hr
Dragan Svaco, Director
Competitive showcase for animated productions of any genre made for cinema, television or internet with a running time ranging from 30 seconds to 30 minutes.

CUBA

International Festival of New Latin American Cinema

2-12 December 2003
Calle 2, no.411 e/17y19
10400 Vedado
Habana
Tel: (53) 7 552 841
Fax: (53) 7 334 273
email: festival@icaic.inf.cu
Website: www.habanafilmfestival.com
A selection of Latin American films and videos, unpublished scripts and posters competing for the Coral Awards. It also includes first long feature films and videos by Latin American and Caribbean filmmakers in the category of FIRST WORKS. Other sections: Latin American Panorama, Documentary Information, Made in Cuba, Tributes, Retrospectives, Contemporary International Scene, New Latin American Film Market, seminars, books and specialised magazines launchings

CZECH REPUBLIC

Karlovy Vary International Film Festival

4-12 July 2003

Film Servis Festival Karlovy Vary
Panská 1
110 00 Prague
Tel: (420) 221 411 011/022
Fax: (420) 221 411 033
email: festival@kviff.com
Website: www.iffkv.cz
Jiri Bartoska, President
Situated in the old 19th century spa town, the festival includes a non-specialised international competition of feature films; an international competition of full-length and short documentaries; non-competitive informative film programmes and restrospectives. There is no video section in the official festival programme

DENMARK

Copenhagen Gay & Lesbian Film Festival

17-26 October 2003
Danish Film Institute
Gothersgade 55
DK-1123 Copenhagen R
Tel: (45) 3374 3406
Fax: (45) 3374 3403
email: info@cglff.dk
Website: www.cglff.dk
Simon Verheij, Organiser
Oldest film festival in Copenhagen. It is a competitive showcase of feature, documentary, short and experimental works

Odense International Film Festival

11-16 August 2003
Vindegade 18
5100 Odense
Tel: (45) 6613 1372
Fax: (45) 6592 4318
email: off.ksf@odense.dk
Website: www.filmfestival.dk
Odense is the birthplace of the world-famous writer of fairy-tales Hans Christian Andersen, so it does not come as a surprise if the film festival there pays special tribute to fairy-tales and artistic imagination. The event is an independent short film festival with both an international and a national competition. It admits films and videos from all genres not exceding a lengh of 30 minutes.

National Film Festival

26 March-4 April 2004
St. Kannikestr, 6
DK 1169 Kobenhavak
Tel: +45 3312 0005
email: info@natfilm.dk

Website: www: filmfest.dk
The biggest international film event in Denmark is a very successful platform for domestic distributors, with an Audience prize that secures theatrical release. The festival also provides special support for young Danish filmmakers

EGYPT

Cairo International Film Festival

7-17 October 2004
17 Kasr El Nil Street
Cairo
Tel: (202) 392 3962
Fax: (202) 393 8979
email: info@cairofilmfest.com
Website: www.cairofilmfest.com
Hussein Fahmi, President
The festival's competitive section is only for films that have not competed at other international film festivals. Out of competition the festival includes the following sections: Festival of Festivals, Informative, Retrospective, Tribute and Film Market

FINLAND

Midnight Sun Film Festival

11-15 June 2003
Malminkatu 36
00100 Helsinki
Tel: (358) 9 685 2242
Fax: (358) 9 685 2242
email: office@msfilmfestival.fi
Website: www.msfilmfestival.fi
Held in the village of Sodankylä, in the heart of Finnish Lapland, some 120 kilometers above the Arctic Circle, the festival can loosely be divided into three sections: films by the most famous film directors of all times, pearls of the new cinema and silent movies with live music. Films are screened in three venues for 24 hours a day

Tampere Film Festival

3-7 March 2004
Box 305
33101 Tampere
Tel: (358) 3 213 5681
Fax: (358) 3 223 0121
email: office@tamperefilmfestival.fi
Website: www.tamperefilmfestival.fi
Jukka-Pekka Laakso, Director
In addition to the short film competitions the festival screens several special programmes such as Cinema Africa and Indian Independent Documentaries made by women

Tough Eye International Turku Animated Film Festival

14-18 May 2003
Linnankatu 54
20100 Turku
Tel: (358) 10 553 5258
Fax: (358) 10 553 5273
email: info@tough-eye.com
Website: www.tough-eye.com
An animated film competition that offers hundreds of short animations from all over the world. The festival, which takes place in every other year, shows over forty screening programmes, including the Timeless Competition, the Timeless Panorama and the Tough Eye Selection

FRANCE

Cinéma du Réel - International Documentary Film Festival

5-14 March 2004
Bibliothèque Publique d'Information
Centre Pompidou
25, rue du Renard
75197 Paris Cedex 04
Tel: (33) 1 44 78 44 21
Fax: (33) 1 44 78 12 24
email: cinereel@bpi.fr
Website: www.bpi.fr
Suzette Glenadel, General Delegate
This year the International Festival of Visual Anthropology and Social Documentation presents an international competition of 20 to 25 recent and previously unreleased films, a French competition of films shot in 2003 and a selection of non-competitive films about Argentina

Festival des Trois Continents

26 November-3 December 2002
19 A, Passage Pommeraye
BP 43302
44033 Nantes Cedex 1
Tel: (33) 2 40 69 74 14
Fax: (33) 2 40 73 55 22
email: festival@3continents.com
Website: www.3continents.com
Marie-Annick Ranger, General Delegate
The Festival of the Three Continents presents feature-length fiction films from Africa, Asia, Latin and Black America. The event includes a competitive section, tributes to directors and actors, and panoramas

Festival du Cinéma Américain

5-14 September 2003
36, rue Pierret
92200 Neuilly-sur-Seine
Tel: (33) 1 46 40 55 00
Fax: (33) 1 46 40 55 39
email: info-deauville@deauville.org
Website: www.festival-deauville.com
Competition and panorama of American productions only.

Festival du Court Métrage Clermont-Ferrand

31 January-8 February 2003
La Jetée
6, place Michel-de-l'Hospital
63058 Clermont-Ferrand Cedex 1
Tel: (33) 4 73 91 65 73
Fax: (33) 4 73 92 11 93
email: info@clermont-filmfest.com
Website: www.clermont-filmfest.com
The world's premier cinema event dedicated to international and national short films. It offers retrospectives and various thematic programmes, including a Market.

Festival du Film Britannique de Dinard

2-5 October 2003
2, Boulevard Féart
35800 Dinard
Tel: (33) 2 99 88 19 04
Fax: (33) 2 99 46 67 15
email:
fest.film.britain.dinard@wanadoo.fr
Website: www.festivaldufilm-dinard.com
Thierry de la Fournière, President
Competitive festival with retrospectives and exhibitions. It also promotes meetings between French and English producers.

Festival International de Films de Femmes

21-30 March 2003
Maison des Arts
Place Salvador Allende
94000 Créteil
Tel: (33) 1 49 80 38 98
Fax: (33) 1 43 99 04 10
email: filmsfemmes@wanadoo.fr
Website: www.filmsdefemmes.com
Jacki Buet, Programme Director
Competitive for feature films, documentaries and shorts directed by one or more women, or a mixed team

Festival International du Film d'Amiens

7-16 November 2003

MCA - 2, place Léon Gontier
80 000 Amiens
Tel: (33) 3 2271 3570
Fax: (33) 3 2292 5304
email: contact@filmfestamiens.org
Website: www.filmfestamiens.org
Jean-Pierre Garcia, Director
The festival's goal is threefold: a quality cultural event, a meeting point for professionals and a diverse audience. It shows full-length or short films, fiction, animation, and documentaries.

Festival International du Film d'Animation

2-7 June 2003
JICA/MIFA
18 avenue du Tresum
BP 399
74013 Annecy Cédex
Tel: (33) 04 50 10 09 00
Fax: (33) 04 50 10 09 70
email: info@annecy.org
Website: www.annecy.org
Competition for animated shorts, features, TV films and commercials produced in the previous 2 years.

Festival International du Film de Cannes

12-23 May 2004
Departement Films
3, rue Amelie
F-75007 Paris
Tel: (33) 1 53 59 61 71
Fax: (3)3 1 53 59 61 70
email maria.sjoberg@festival-cannes.fr
Website: www.festival-cannes.org
Competitive section for feature films and shorts (up to 15 mins) produced in the previous year, which have not been screened outside country of origin nor been entered in other competitive festivals. Non-competitive section: Un Certain Regard & Cinefondation. Other non-competitive events taking place are: **Directors' Fortnight and International Critic's Week**
Contacts:
email: quinzaine@club-internet.fr
email: critique@club-internet.fr

Festival International du Film Policier

10-13 April 2003
Le Public Système Cinéma
36 rue Pierret
92200 Neuilly-sur-Seine
Tel: (33) 1 46 40 55 00
Fax: (33) 1 46 40 55 39
email: cognac@pobox.com
Website: cognac-france.com/polar
Competitive for thriller films (police movies, thrillers, film noirs, court movies, and investigations), which have not been commercially shown in France or participated in festivals in Europe

Gérardmer-Festival du Film Fantastique

28 January-1 february 2004
Le Public Système Cinéma
40, rue Anatole France
92594 Levallois-Perret Cédex
Tel: (33) 1 41 34 20 33
Fax: (33) 1 41 34 20 77
email: presse@gerardemer-fantasticart.com
Website: www.gerardmer-fantasticart.com
Formerly held in Avoriaz.
Competitive for international fantasy feature films (science-fiction, horror and supernatural)

MIP-TV

10-14 October 2003
Reed MIDEM Organisation
179, avenue Victor Hugo
75116 Paris
Tel: (33) 1 41 90 45 84
Fax: (33) 1 44 90 45 70
email:
andre.vaillant@reedmidem.com
Website: www.miptv.com
André Vaillant, Programme Director
An international television programme market held in Cannes. It focuses on content programming for the television industry worldwide. The trade show serves professionals working in TV broadcasting, programmes production and/or distribution, video and the Internet, advertising, licensing and merchandising, consultancy, service companies and new media

Rencontres Cinématographiques Franco-Américaines

June
Avignon Film Festival
10, Montée de la Tour
30400 Villeneuve-les-Avignon
Tel: +33 4 90 25 93 23
Fax: +33 4 90 25 93 24
French-American Center of Provence
44 Hudson St. 2nd Floor
10013 NY
Tel: +212 343 2675
Fax: +212 587 1950
email: jhr2001@aol.com
Website: www.avignonfilmfest.com
The French-American Film Workshop brings together independent filmmakers from USA and France. New independent films are celebrated. With retrospectives and round-tables

Sunny Side of the Doc

25-28 June 2003
Docs Services
23, rue François Simon
13003 Marseille
Tel: (33) 495 04 44 80
Fax: (33) 491 84 38 34
email:
contact@sunnysideofthedoc.com
Website:
www.sunnysideofthedoc.com
Yves Jeanneau, General Commissioner
International documentary market serving as an interface between professionals of the industry from 40 countries whether they be producers, distributors, broadcasters or commissioning editors

GERMANY

Feminale - International Women's Film Festival

2-6 October 2004
Internationales FrauenFilmFestival
Maybachstr, 111
50670 Cologne
Tel: (0049) 221 1300225
Fax: (0049) 221 1300281
email: press@feminale.de
Website: www.feminale.de
Second largest festival of this kind in the world. The Feminale offers a forum that introduces film and video productions made by women to a broad public. Its diverse programme includes the sections: Horizons-Debut Competitions, Panorama, Zoom-In, Queer Looks, Portrait, Girl's Focus and Animation

Filmfest Hamburg

19-26 September 2003
FilmFest Hamburg GmbH
Steintorweg 4
20099 Hamburg
Tel: (49) 40 399 190 00
Fax: (49) 40 399 190 010
email: info@filmfesthamburg.de
Website: www.filmfesthamburg.de
Josef Wutz, Director
Working in close cooperation with the Bitfilm-Festival for digital film and new media the Hamburg Film Festival has added two new sections to its programme: The Four

Dimesion/DVD-Straight to Filmfest, which presents outstanding productions that did not made it to the big screen but appeared directly on DVD, and Children's Filmfest, to introduce young audience to animation films

FilmFest München

28 June-5 July 2003
Internationale Müenchner Filmwochen
Sonnenstrasse 21
80331 Munich
Tel: (49) 89 3819 040
Fax: (49) 89 3819 0427
email: programmkoordination@filmfest-muenchen.de
Website: filmfest-muenchen.de
The Munich International Film Festival presents new cinematic discoveries from around the world, highlights from the big studios and major companies as well as the best works by international young directors. The extensive programme of international, European and German Premieres is rounded out with Retrospectives, Portraits, Tributes, Special Screenings and the traditional sections of World Cinema, American Independents, Made in Germany – German Films, German TV Movies and Children's Film Fest

International FilmFest Emden/Aurich/Norderney

11-18 June 2003
An der Berufsschule 3
26721 Emden
Tel: (49) 4921 915 532
Fax: (49) 4921 915 599
email: filmfest@uhs-emden.de
Website: www.filmfest-emden.de
Audience festival with three competitions: Bernhard-Wicki-Award for feature films, the German Trade Union Film Award, and the Short Film Award. It presents about 50 feature (mainly new production, however also film history, documentaries, experimental films and films on specific themes) as well as some 50 shorts and animation films. Focuses on the most recent films from north-western Europe, above all British productions and New German Cinema

International Film Festival Mannheim-Heidelberg

20-29 November 2003
Collini-Center, Galerie
68161 Mannheim
Tel: (49) 621 102 943
Fax: (49) 621 291 564
email: ifmh@mannheim-filmfestival.com
Website: www.mannheim-filmfestival.com
Dr Michael Koetz, Director
New talents compete in the two main sections International Competition and International Discoveries. A selection of around 35 new feature films that have never been premiered, mainly fiction films but also cinematographically interesting documentaries and short films

Internationale Filmfestspiele Berlin - Berlin International Film Festival

5-15 February 2004
Potsdamer Strasse 5
10785 Berlin
Tel: (49) 30 25 920 202
Fax: (49) 30 25 920 299
email: info@berlinale.de
Website: www.berlinale.de
Dieter Kosslick, Executive Director
Competition for international feature films and shorts. Includes a section, Perspektive Deutsches Kino, on current German film production and a separate competition programme for children (Kinderfilmfest), consisting of features, shorts/animation and live action

Internationales Leipziger Fesztival für Dokumentar- und Animationsfilm

14-19 October 2003
DOK Filmwochen GmbH
Grosse Fleischergasse 11
04109 Leipzig
Tel: (49) 341 980 3921
Fax: (49) 341 980 6141
email: info@dokfestival-leipzig.de
Website: www.dokfestival-leipzig.de
Fred Gehler, Director
Committed to animations and documentaries, this year's edition will look at Soviet-Russian documentary film and pay tribute to Peter Schamoni. The festival includes as well the familiar items First Flush and The Most Shockin Local Short Night, which will be fronting a cult event comprising one day and one night of young film

Nordische Filmtage Lübeck - Nordic Film Days Lübeck

30 October-2 November 2003
Hansestadt Lubeck-Bereich Kunst and Kultur
Dr. Ada Kadelbach
Schrildstr 12
23539 Lübeck
Tel: (49) 451 122 41 00/01
Fax: (49) 451 122 41 06
email: info@filmtage.luebeck.de
Website: www.filmtage.luebeck.de
Festival of Scandinavian and Baltic films. A competition for feature, children's, documentary and Nordic countries' films

Oberhausen International Short Film Festival

29 april-4 May 2004
Grillostrasse 34
46045 Oberhausen
Tel: (49) 208 825 2652
Fax: (49) 208 825 5413
email: info@kurzfilmtage.de
Website: www.kurzfilmtage.de
Lars Henrik Gass, Director
With its excellent archive, distribution, publications and 'the meticulousness with which its programme is compile' the Oberhausen festival activily works to promote and ensure a lively existence for the Short Film. Special attention is paid to the shorts' position regarding social reality, cultural differences and aesthetic innovation

Prix Europa

11-18 October 2003
Sender Freies Berlin
14046 Berlin
Tel: (49) 30 30 31 16 10
Fax: (49) 30 30 31 16 19
email: prix-europa@sfb.de
Website: www.prix-europa.de
Susanne Hoffmann, Project Manager
Competition for fiction, non-fiction, current affairs, multicultural matters on television, documentary and drama. Open to all broadcasting organisations and producers in Europe

GREECE

International Thessaloniki Film Festival

21-30 November 2003
40 Paparigopoulou St.
11473 Athens
Tel: (30) 210 645 3669
Fax: (30) 210 644 8143
email: coordination@filmfestival.gr
Website: www.filmfestival.gr
Dedicated to the promotion of independent cinema from all over the world, the event features the International Section for first or

second features (Golden Alexander for Best Film; Special Jury Award Silver Alexander); panorama on Greek films; New Horizons programme; the Balkan Survey; numerous retrospectives and tributes to leading figures in the world of films; exhibitions and special events.

Kalamata International Documentary Film Festival

19-25 October 2003
125-127 Kifisas Avenue
11524 Athens
Tel: (30) 010 699 0660
Fax: (30) 010 699 0905
email: festival@documentary.gr
Website: www.documentary.gr
Kostas Skouras, Managing Director
The festival awards the following prizes: Golden and Silver 'Olive' Awards; Special Award; Award 'Eri Rotzokou'. It also organises a competitive Student Documentary section. Parallel events include: honorary tributes, exhibition of cinematographic giant posters, exhibition of Doc photos and music entertainment

HONG KONG

Hong Kong International Film Festival

8-23 April 2003
Film & Media Arts Office
22nd Floor, 181 Queen's Road Central
Hong Kong
Tel: +852 2970 3300
Hong Kong Arts Development TelT
Fax: +852 2970 3011
email: hkiff@hkiff.org.hk
Website: www.hkiff.org.hk
Non-competitive for feature films, documentaries and short films from around the world, which have been produced in the previous two years. Also a local short film and video competition; a FIPRESCI Award for Young Asian cinema and a showcase for the historical development of Hong Kong cinema.

INDIA

International Film Festival of India

9-19 October 2003
Directorate of Film Festivals
Siri Fort Auditorium Complex
August Kranti Marg, Khel Gaon
110049 New Delhi
Tel: (91) 11 4615953/4697167
Fax: (91) 11 4623430
email: dffiffi@bol.net.in
Website: mib.nic.in/dff
With an Indian Panorama section for 21 feature and 21 non-feature films distinguised by their thematic and aesthetic excellence. The festival main objective is to promote Indian films in international film festivals in India and abroad

International Film Festival of Kerala

12-19 December 2003
Golf Links road, Jawahar Nagar
Kowdiar, Thiruvananthapuram
695003 Kerala
Tel: +91 471 2312214/2310323
Fax: +91 471 2310322
email: chitram@md3.vsnl.net.in
Website: www.keralafilm.com
'*To see to feel and to feel to think*' is the motto of this festival. The competitive section is especially designed for films from Asia, Africa and Latin America whereas the non-competitive section includes Indian Cinema, World Cinema, Homages and Retrospectives

IRAN

International Short Film Festival

20-25 October 2003
Iranian Young Cinema Society
Gandhi Ave, 19th Street, No 20
P.O. Box 15175-163
Tehran
Tel: (98) 21 877 3114
Fax: (98) 21 879 5675
email: info@shortfilmfest-ir.com
Website: www.shortfilmfest-ir.com
International competition with the following categories: experimental, animation, documentaries and fiction. The festival also pays tributes to short films from other countries and organises special programmes.

IRELAND

Cork International Film Festival

12-19 October 2003
10 Washington Street
Cork
Tel: +353 21 427 1711
Fax: +353 21 427 5945
email: info@corkfilmfest.org
Website: www.corkfilmfest.org
Michael Hannignan, Director
Ireland's oldest (1956) and biggest film event, featuring the best of international cinema and serving as a platform for new Irish cinema. The festival is also committed to screening other forms of film production such as animation, experimental, student works, and digital work. The programme includes retrospectives, seminars and industry events

Dublin Film Festival

Ten days in mid-April
Sth William St.
Dublin 2
Tel: +353 1 679 2937
Fax: +353 1 679 2939
email: info@dublinfilmfestival.net
Website: www.dublinfilmfestival.net
Andrea Corbett, Chief Executive
A non-competititive, audience orientated showcase for new cinema, internationalist in scope and with a progressive cultural remit

ISRAEL

Haifa International Film Festival
21-28 October 2003
142 Hanassi Avenue
34633 Haifa
Tel: +97 24 835 3521/8353522
Fax: +97 24 838 4327
email: haifaff@netvision.net.il
Website: www.haifaff.co.il
Eliane Auerbach
The biggest annual meeting for professionals associated with the film industry in Israel. It is a competitive showcase for foreign and Israeli feature films, short films, documentaries and TV dramas.

Jerusalem Film Festival

10-19 July 2003
PO Box 8561, Wolfson Gardens
Hebron Road
91083 Jerusalem
Tel: +972 2 565 4333
Fax: +972 2 565 4335/4
email: jer-cin@jer-cin.org.il
Website: www.jer-cin.org.il
Lia Van Leer, Director
A showcase for the finest in recent international cinema, documentaries, animation, avant garde, retrospectives, special tributes and homages, Mediterranean and Israeli cinema. Three international awards: Wim van Leer's In Spirit of Freedom focused on human rights, Mediterranean Cinema and Jewish Theme

ITALY

Festival dei Popoli
28 November-4 December 2003
Borgo Pinti 82 rosso
50121 Firenze
Tel: (39) 055 244 778
Fax: (39) 055 241 364
email: fespopol@dada.it
Website: www.festivaldeipopoli.org
Maria Bonsanti, Head of Hospitality Office
Competitive and non-competitive sections for documentaries on sociological, historical, political and anthropological subjects as well as music, art and cinema produced during the year preceding the festival. The films for the competitive section should not have been screened in Italy before.

Festival Internazionale Cinema Giovanni - Torino Film Festival
13-21 November 2003
Via Monte di Pietà 1
10121 Torino
Tel: (39) 011 562 3309
Fax: (39) 011 562 9796
email: info@torinofilmfest.org
Website: www.torinofilmfest.org
Stefano Della Casa, Director
Competitive sections for international features, shorts and documentaries. 'Spazio Italian' open solely to Italian fiction and videos and 'Spazio Torino' reserved to filmmakers and videomakers, born or residing in Turin and the Piedmont region

Festival Internazionale di Film con Tematiche Omosessuali
22-29 April 2004
L'Altra Communicazione
Piazza San Carlo 161
10123 Turin
Tel: (39) 011 534 888
Fax: (39) 011 535 796
email: loredanaleconte@iol.it
Website: www.tglff.com
Lesbian and gay themed festival. Competitive for features, shorts and documentaries. Also retrospectives and special showcases for both cinema and television work

Giffoni Film Festival
19-26 July 2003
C/o Cittadella del Cinema
84095 Giffoni Valle Piana
Tel: (39) 089 802 3111
Fax: (39) 089 802 3210
email: giffonif@giffoniff.it
Website: www.giffoniff.it
Claudio Gubitosi, Director
Also refered to as the Giffoni's Children Film Festival, it presents children's films with and without strong themes to the young. Out of competition activities include a debate and study section called 'Y Generation', previews and Animated Nights

Le Giornate del Cinema Muto - Pordenone Silent Film Festival
11-18 October 2003
c/o La Cineteca del Friuli
Via G. Bini, Palazzo Gurisatti
33013 Gemona
Tel: (39) 0432 980458
Fax: (39) 0432 970542
email: info.gcm@cinetecadelfriuli.org
Website: www.cinetecadelfriuli.org
David Robinson, Director
The principal presentation of this year's programme is 'Distant, Difficult and Dangerous: The Life and Films of Merian C. Cooper', which includes an exhibition of original Merian C. Cooper materials. Other sections are: Mozhukhin: The Paths of Exile; The Griffith Project 7; Films produced in 1913; Saving the Silents 3; East of the Sun, West of the Moon; Films from Thailand, and The Pioners of the Balkan Cinema: The Manaki brothers.

MIFED - Cinema & Television International Multimedia Market
9-13 November 2003
Palazzina FMI,
Largo Domodossola 1
20145 Milan
Tel: +39 02 48 5501
Fax: +39 02 48 550420
email: mifed@fmi.it
Website: www.mifed.com
International market for companies working in the film, television, and home videos industries

Mostra Internazionale d'Arte Cinematografica - Venice International Film Festival
27 August- 6 September 2003
Palazzo del Cinema
Lungomare Marconi
30126 Lido de Venezia
Tel: (39) 041 521 8878
Fax: (39) 041 522 7539
email: cinema@labiennale.org
Website: www.labiennale.org
Moritz de Hadeln, Director
The oldest film Festival worldwide (1932 -), whose programme includes a competition for feature film and short films.This year's edition pays homage to Katharine Hepburn and Great Italian producers

Mostra Internazionale del Nuovo Cinema - Pesaro Film Festival
21-29 June 2003
Via Villafranca 20
00185 Rome
Tel: +39 06 445 6643
Fax: +39 06 491 163
email: info@pesarofilmfest.it
Website: www.pesarofilmfest.it
Pedro Armocida, General Delegate
Particularly concerned with the work of new directors, emergent cinemas and innovation at every level. The festival is devoted each year to an specific country or culture. It also organises a special event on Italian cinema

Noir In Festival - International Mystery Festival
A week in December
Studio Coop.
Via Panaro, 17
00199 Rome
Tel: +3906-860 3111
Fax: +3906-862 13298
email: noir@noirfest.com
Website: www.noirfest.com
Giorgio Gosetti, Director
With a competitive and a non-competitive section, the festival aims to promote and diffuse the mystery genre (crime story, suspense, thriller, horror, fantasy, spy story, whodunnit...) in Italy and abroad. It presentes previews, retrospectives, meetings and seminars

Prix Italia
13-20 September 2003
RAI Radio Televisione Italiana
Via Monte Santo, 52
00195 Rome
Tel: (39) 06 377 12349
Fax: (39) 06 372 9583
email: prixitalia@rai.it
Website: www.prixitalia.rai.it
Luciano Pinelli, Director
Competitive for television and radio productions from national broadcasting organisations. Prizes are awarded for quality productions in the fields of drama (single plays and serials), documentaries (culture and current affairs), performing arts (television) and music (radio).

Taormina International Film Festival

11-19 July 2004
Palazzo Firenze
Via Pirandello 31
98039 Taormina
Tel: (39) 942 21142
Fax: (39) 942 23348
email: info@taoarte.it
Website: www.taorminafilmfest.it
Competitive for features. Emphasis on new directors and a great panorama of European, African and American films

JAPAN

Tokyo International Film Festival

1-9 November 2003
Ginza Bldg, 1-6-5 Ginza
Chou-Ku
Tokyo 104-0061
Tel: +81 3 3563 6305
Fax: +81 3 3563 6310
email: info@tiff-jp.net
Website: www.tiff-jp.net
The festival programme offers a competition of feature films which are either the first, second or third film by the director; Special Screenings showing 'the newest and hottest films'; Winds of Asia, focusing on Asian films and introducing works by enthusiastic Asian filmmakers; symposia with creators of game software, commercials, visual arts and Nippon Cinema Classics

Tokyo Video Festival

14 February 2004
c/o Victor Co of Japan Ltd
1-7-1 Shinbashi
Victor Bldg, Minato-ku
Tokyo 105
Tel: (81) 3 3289 2815
Fax: (81) 3 3289 2819
Website: www.jvc-victor.co.jp/english/tvf/index-e.html
Nobuhiko Obayashi, Director
Worldwide video contest for amateurs and professionals alike. The only requirement for a work to be accepted is that it has to be shot with a video camera and be no longer than 20 minutes. Any theme can be addressed. Past entries have dealt with personal opinions and experience, dreams, daily life and creation

Yamagata International Documentary Film Festival

A week in October
ID Kawadacho Bldg, 3 fl.
7-6 Kawadacho
Shinjuku-Ku
Tokyo 162-0054
Tel: (81) 3 5362 0672
Fax: (81) 3 5362 0670
email: mail@tokyo.yidff.jp
Website:
www.city.yamagata.yamagata.jp/yidff
Sponsored by the city of Yamagata, this is a biennial festival whose main activities include International Competition, Jurors' Films, New Asian Currents, Japanese Panorama, Classic Japanese Film Screenings and Retrospective. The website also offers a link to Documentary Box, a journal devoted to covering recent trends in making and thinking about documentaries

KOREA

Pusan International Film Festival

2-10 October 2003
Yachting Center, #208
1393 Woo 1- Dong
Haeundae-Gu, Pusan 612-797
Tel: 82-51 747 3010-1
Fax: 82-51 747 3012
email: program@piff.org
Website: www.piff.org
The first international film festival ever to be held in Korea, it acts as a window for Asian Cinema and offers a Korean Panorama in order to promote emerging talents from Asia. The festival accepts features, experimental films, documentaries shorts and animation

MALTA

Golden Knight International Amateur Film & Video Festival

November
Malta Amateur Cine Circle
PO Box 450
Marsa
Tel: +356 222 345/236173
Fax: +356 225 047
email: macc@global.net.mt
Website: www.global.net.mt/macc
The festival is divided in three sections: Amateur, Film School Student and Open. Productions should be a maximum of 30 minutes. Golden, Silver and Bronze Trophies are awarded

MONACO

Festival de Television de Monte Carlo

30 June-5 July 2003
4, boulevard du Jardin Exotique
MC 98000 Monaco
Tel: (377) 93 10 40 60
Fax: (377) 93 50 70 14
email: info@tvfestival.com
Website: www.tvfestival.com
Laurent Puons, Admin. Director
The Monte Carlo International Television Festival replaces the Monte Carlo Television Market & Festival previously held in February. Its aim is 'to use TV as an exceptional means of bringing people together and enriching their culture'. Prizes are awarded to short news, current affairs, 24-hour news programmes, TV films and mini-series, drama and comedy series and to a European producer

THE NETHERLANDS

Cinekid

12-19 October 2003
Korte Leidesedwarsstraat 12
1017 RC Amsterdam
Tel: (31) 20 531 7890
Fax: (31) 20 531 7899
email: info@cinekid.nl
Website: www.cinekid.nl
The festival provides an overview of the best international children's film, television and new media productions. It is aimed at young people from 4 to 16, who can also try out the latest CD-Roms and participate in interactive workshops

International Documentary Film Festival Amsterdam

20-30 November 2003
Kleine-Gartmanplantsoen 10
1017 RR Amsterdam
Tel: (31) 20 627 3329
Fax: (31) 20 638 5388
email: info@idfa.nl
Website: www.idfa.nl
IDFA holds competitions for documentaries and videos. It also presents a Forum for co-financed European documentaries and awards the Joris Ivens prize

International Film Festival Rotterdam

21 January-1 February 2004

PO Box 21696
3001 AR Rotterdam
Tel: (31) 10 890 9090
Fax: (31) 10 890 9091
email: tiger@filmfestivalrotterdam.nl
Website:
www.filmfestivalrotterdam.com
Simon Fiedl, Sandra den Hamer, Directors
One of the largest and most popular film festivals, its main programme includes the Tiger Awards Competition, international and European premieres. Other highlights include retrospectives on different genres and directors and World Cinema Tour

Netherlands Film Festival
24 September-3 October 2003
Stichting Nederlands Film Festival
PO Box 1581
3500 BN Utrecht
Tel: (31) 30 230 3800
Fax: (31) 30 230 3801
email: info@filmfestival.nl
Website: www.filmfestival.nl
Doreen Boonekamp, Director
Screening a selection of new Dutch features, shorts, documentaries, animation and TV drama. Also retrospectives, seminars, talkshows, Cinema Militans Lecture and Holland Film Meeting

World Wide Video Festival
8-25 May 2003
Keizersgracht 462
1016 PJ Amsterdam
Tel: (31) 20 420 7729
Fax: (31) 20 421 3828
email: wwvf@wwvf.nl
Website: www.wwvf.nl
Tom van Vliet, Director
Multi-media art festival, which accepts CD-ROMs and websites.

NEW ZEALAND

Auckland International Film Festival
11-27 July 2003
The New Zealand Film Festival Trust
PO Box 9544
Marion Square
Wellington
Tel: (64) 4 385 0162
Fax: (64) 4 801 7304
email: festival@nzff.co.nz
Website: www.enzedff.co.nz
The festival and its Wellington sibling (same contact) include feature and short films, documentaries, video and animation. The NZ Film Festival Trust also organises other events: Dunedin International Film Festival, Travelling Festival Circuit and Christchurch International Film Festival. Details of these can also be found on this same website

NORWAY

Norwegian International Film Festival
17-24 August 2003
PO Box 145
5501 Haugesund
Tel: (47) 52 734 430
Fax: (47) 52 734 420
email: info@filmfestivalen.no
Website: www.filmfestivalen.no
The festival main programme is devoted to feature films for theatrical release and its participation is devoted to film and cinema professionals, students and members of the press. The annual market, called New Nordic Films, is an opportunity for international distributors and TV companies to see new Nordic features and to meet Nordic filmmakers, producers, agents, buyers and distributors

Oslo International Film Festival
Ten days in November
Dronningers Gt. 16
N-0152 Oslo
Tel: (47) 22 20 07 66
Fax: (47) 22 20 18 03
email: info@oslofilmfestival.com
Website: www.pluto.no/filmfestival
Tommy Lordahl, Director
Regular programme includes screening of feature and short films, with special focus on American independents, new European cinema and films from Asia, documentaries on filmmaking, music, history and personal stories

POLAND

Krakow Film Festival
28 May-2June 2003
c/o Apollo-Film
ul. Pychowicka 7
30-364 Krakow
Tel: (48) 12 267 13 55
Fax: (48) 12 267 23 40
email: festiwal@apollofilm.pl
Website: www.cracowfilmfestival.pl
Krzysztof Gierat, Director
Also known as the International and National Documentary and Short Film Festival, the event is dedicated to documentary, animation and other short film forms. The festival grants an international life achievement award, called the Dragon of Dragons Special Prize. It also features retrospectives of national cinematography, artistic schools and directors

PORTUGAL

International Animated Film festival of Espinho-Cinanima
10-16 November 2003
Rua 62, 251
Apartado 743
4500-901 Espinho
Tel: +351 22 734 1350
Fax: +351 22 733 1358
email: cinanima@mail.lelepac.pt
Website: www.cinanima.pt
Festival for the promotion of animation art, comprising a competitive and non-competitive programme and including retrospectives, exhibitions, debates and animation workshops.

Fantasporto-Oporto International Film Festival
20-28 February 2004
Rua Aníbal Cunha
84 - sala 1.6
4050-048 Porto
Tel: +351 2 2207 6050
Fax: +351 2 2207 6059
email: info@fantasporto.online.pt
Website: www.fantasporto.online.pt
Biggest film festival in Portugal and one of the most respected in Europe along with Sitges and Brussels. This year the festival will pay attention to the 'Orient Express' new section, dedicated to Asian Cinema. The official competition sections remain the Fantasy Cinema and the Directors Week, complemented by some retrospectives and sidebars

International Film Festival of Troia
6-15 June 2003
Troia International Film Festival
Forum Luisa Todi
Av. Luisa Todi, 65
2900-461 Setubal
Tel: +35 1 265 525 908
Fax: +35 1 265 525 681
email: geral@festroia.pt
Website: www.festroia.pt
Presenting full-length films, the

competitive section only accepts works from countries producing up to 25 films per year. The Information Section (non-competitive) includes retrospectives distinguished by their artistic or historic importance and deserving public recognition

RUSSIA

St. Pertersburg Film Festival

23-29 June 2003
10 Kamennoostrovsky Av.
St. Petersburg 197101
Tel: (7) 812 237 0304
Fax: (7) 812 394 5870
email: info@filmfest.ru
Website: www.filmfest.ru
Russia's largest non-competitive festival for recent outstanding works of international and Russian origin

Moscow International Film Festival

20-29 June 2003
Interfest
10/1 Khoklhovsky per.
Moscow 109028
Tel: (095) 917 2486
Fax: (095) 916 0107
email: info@miff.ru
Website: www.miff.ru
Renat Davletiarov, general Director
Although the festival has a definitive Russian perspective, it still offers international competition screenings, retrospectives, films from CIS and the Baltics, Medium Forum and Forum for Young Filmmakers

SINGAPORE

Singapore International Film Festival

17 April-3 May 2003
45A Keong Saik Road
Singapore 089149
Tel: (65) 6738 7567
Fax: (65) 6738 7578
email: filmfest@pacific.net.sg
Website: www.filmfest.org.sg
Screening over 300 films consisting of features, shorts and animations. The festival focuses on South-east Asian cinema as well as Indonesian and Malaysian emerging productions

SLOVAKIA

Art Film Festival Trencianske Teplice

20-28 June 2003
Art Film, n.f.
Konventna 8
81103 Bratislava
Tel: (421) 2 5441 9481
Fax: (421) 2 5441 1679
email: festival@artfilm.sk
Website: www.artfilm.sk
Taking place in an spa town, the festival views 'cinema as an art form rather than as a commodity or advertising tool'. Accordingly, this event shows in competition features, shorts and full-length documentaries with emphasis on innovative forms and visual means

SOUTH AFRICA

Cape Town International Film Festival

Three weeks in April and May or in November
University of Cape Town
Private Bag, Rondebosch
7700 Cape Town
Tel: (27) 21 423 8257
Fax: (27) 21 423 8257
email: filmfest@hiddingh.uct.ac.za
Website:
www.netribution.co.uk/festivals
Trevor Steele Taylor, Director
Oldest film festival in South Africa. It screens features, documentaries and short films on 35mm, 16mm or video. Emphasis on the independent, the transgressive and the iconoclastic. Major profile of South African production

Encounters South African International Documentary Festival

Cape Town: 20 July-3 August 2003
Johannesburg: 1-10 August 2003
10 Buiten Street
Cape Town 8001
Tel: (27) 21 448 0608
Fax: (27) 21 448 1065
email: info@encounters.co.za
Website: www.encounters.co.za
Peter Eaton, Programmer
A joint venture with Switzerland, aimed at promoting documentary filmmaking and exchange between South African and Swiss filmmakers.

Southern African Film & Television Market

14-23 November 2003
SABC Building
209 Beach Road, Sea Point
Cape Town
Tel: (27) 21 430 8160
Fax: (27) 21 430 8186
email: info@sithengi.co.za
Website: www.sithengi.co.za
Michael Auret, Chief Executive Officer
The core programmes of this media event are the *Product Market*, which deals with the buying and selling of completed product, and The *Pitching Forum*, which aims to bring about the buying and selling of ideas. This event includes also the Sithengi Film Festival, showcasing films made by or with indigenous peoples worldwide, and RestFest, a festival of digital filmmaking

SPAIN

L'Alternativa-Festival de Cine Independiente de Barcelona

14-22 November 2003
Centre de Cultura Contemporania
Montalegre 5
08001 Barcelona
Tel: +34 93 306 4100
Fax: +34 93 301 8251
email: alternativa@cccb.org
Website: alternativa.cccb.org
A platform for the promotion and distribution of films (shorts, animations, documentaries and features) which due to their innovative characteristics are unable to find a way into main exhibition and distribution circuits

Bilbao International Festival of Documentary & Short Films

18-27 November 2003
Colón de Larreátegui 37-4
Apdo. 579
48009 Bilbo
Tel: (34) 94 424 8698
Fax: (34) 94 424 5624
email: info@zinebi.com
Website: www.zinebi.com
Competitive for animation, fiction and documentaries (up to 30 mins). The festival presents a selection of the best shorts produced in the Basque Country, Spain and Latin America

Donostia-San Sebastian International Film Festival

18-27 September 2003
PO BOX 397
20080 Donostia-San Sebastian
Tel: (34) 943 481 212
Fax: (34) 943 481 218
email: films@sansebastianfestival.com

Website;
www.sansebastianfestival.ya.com
Website:
www.sansebastianfestival.ya.comMike l Olacirequi, Festival Director
The main activities are the Official Competition and the informative section 'Zabaltegi', which presents newly released films of different formats, lengths, styles and genres. Other sections: Made in Spain, Horizontes Latinos, 'En Construccion' and Restrospectives

Huesca Film Festival

5-14 June 2003
Avda. Parque, 1-2
22002 Huesca
Tel: (34) 974 212 582
Fax: (34) 974 210 065
email: info@huesca-filmfestival.com
Website: www.huesca-filmfestival.com
An international short film contest with a great deal of Iberoamerican cinema and a Sample of European Cinema to name but a few sections. The festival programme for 2004 will include a retrospective on French actor Jean Gabin while Chile will be the guest country

International Film Festival For Young People

20-28 November 2003
Paseo de Begona, 24, Entlo.
PO BOX 76
33205 Gijón
Tel: (34) 98 534 3739
Fax: (34) 98 535 4152
email: festivalgijon@telecable.es
Website: www.gijonfilmfestival.com
Also known as the Gijon International Film Festival, its purpose is to show films featuring youngsters and their concern with life. The established programme includes the Official Sections for features and shorts, Enfants Terribles, an Informative Section for young and older spectators, comprising Outlines, Cycles and Retrospectives

Semana Internacional de Cine de Valladolid

24 October-1 November 2003
Teatro Calderón
Calle Leopoldo Cano, s/n 4th fl.
PO BOX 646
47003 Valladolid
Tel: (34) 983 426 460
Fax: (34) 983 426 461
email: festvalladolid@seminci.com
Website: www.seminci.com
Fernando Lara, Director
The Valladolid International Film Festival consists of the following sections: Official, presenting a panorama of current international cinema; Meeting Point, a parallel non-competitive showcase of fiction films worthy of special attention for their subject matter or style; Time History, consisting of documentaries that deal with moments of history; and Tributes, devoted to the presentation and analysis of directors, genres, styles, schools or a national cinema. There is also the screening of almost all the Spanish films (with English subtitles) of the preceding 12 months

Sitges-Festival Internacional de Cinema de Catalunya

27 November-7 December 2003
Av. Josep Tarradellas
135, Esc. A, 3r. 2a.
08029 Barcelona
Tel: (34) 3 93 419 3635
Fax: (34) 3 93 439 7380
email: info@cinema.sitges.com
Website: www.sitges.com
A specialised competitive event for fantasy films and shorts (up to 30 mins), retrospectives, animation, videos and exhibitions.

ST. BARTH

St. Barth Film Festival and 'Cinéma Caraibe'

25-30 April 2003
BP 1017
St. Jean 97012
St Barthelemy Cedex
Tel: (590) 27 80 11
Fax: (590) 29 74 70
email: elgreaux@wanadoo.fr
Website: www.stbarthff.org
Ellen Lampert-Gréaux, General Delegate
The festival celebrates Caribbean culture and offers a meeting place for regional filmmakers to screen and discuss their work.

SWEDEN

Göteborg Film Festival

23 January-2 February 2003
Olof Palmes plats
413 04 Göteborg
Tel: (46) 31 339 30 00
Fax: (46) 31 41 00 63
email: goteborg@filmfestival.org
Website:
www.goteborg.filmfestival.org
Jannike Ahlund, Director
The major competitive international film event in Scandinavia (Sweden, Norway, Denmark, Finland & Iceland) and a meeting place for the Nordic film industry. The Nordic Event offers exclusive previews of the latest Nordic films with English subtitles, only open to representatives from film festivals and the film industry worldwide. The Cinemix presents a great number of seminars, lectures and debates on film, both in Swedish and English

Stockholm International Film Festival

13-23 November 2003
PO Box 3136
103 62 Stockholm
Tel: (46) 8 677 5000
Fax: (46) 8 20 0590
email: info@filmfestivalen.se
Website: www.filmfestivalen.se
The Stockholms Trettonde Internationella is a competitive showcase for innovative feature films, with a focus on American Independents. It offers a retrospective and presents a summary of Swedish films released during the year. Also, as part of the festival, Internet users can watch ten competing international short films and vote for the best one. The winning film will receive the World Wide Winner award at the final prize ceremony in Stockholm.

Uppsala International Short Film Festival

20-26 October 2003
Box 1746
751 47 Uppsala
Tel: (46) 18 120 025
Fax: (46) 18 121 350
email: info@shortfilmfestival.com
Website: www.shortfilmfestival.com
Sofia Lindskog, Director
Sweden's premiere presents more than 200 sound and silent shorts (fiction, animation, experimental films and documentaries). The programme includes the International Competition, retrospectives, Nordic films-The Video section, Children's Film Fest and the Film School Day

SWITZERLAND

Festival International de Films de Fribourg

21-28 March 2004

Rue Nicolas de Praroman 2
Case Postale
1701 ribourg
Tel: +41 26 347 42 00
Fax: +1 26 347 42 01
email: info@fiff.ch
Website: www.fiff.ch
Competition for movies and documentaries of varying lengths from Africa, Asia and Latin America. The festival also organises non-competitive sections (tributes, focus on, retrospectives) for films which have seldom or never been shown in Switzerland

Locarno International Film Festival

6-16 August 2003
Via Luini 3a
6601 Locarno
Tel: (41) 91 756 2121
Fax: (41) 91 756 2149
email: info@pardo.ch
Website: www.pardo.ch
Irene Bignardi, Artistic Director
Situated at the base of the Alps, near the Italian border, Locarno has been hosting one of the most distinguished film festivals worldwide since 1946. Its main programme consists of an International Competition (reserved for full-length features with a special focus on films which introduce new schemes and styles) and a new separate Video Competition selecting the most innovative and original video or digital productions. Other regular activities include Piazza Grande ('classic entertainement with an edge'), Filmmakers of the Present; Leopards of Tomorrow (short film output of young directors); Appellations Suisse (a bouquet of Swiss films); retrospectives and the Critics' Week (www.criticsweek.filmjournalist.ch)

Rose d'Or Festival

13-18 April 2004
Bigger Prix Ltd
PO Box 5511
3001 Bern
Tel: (41) 31 318 3737
Fax: (41) 31 318 3736
email: info@rosedor.com
Website: www.rosedor.ch
George Luks, General Delegate
The Golden Rose of Montreux hosts international awards for light entertainment television programming (comedy, sitcoms, variety, music and game shows, arts and specials) from around 40 countries. It is also a business rendezvous for the onscreen entertainment community, who can attend the established conferences and choose to view TV programmes from the Videokiosk

VIPER-International Festival for Film, Video and New Media

21-25 October 2003
St. Alban-Rheinweg 64
4052 Basel
Tel: (41) 61 283 27 00
Fax: (41) 61 283 27 05
email: information@viper.ch
Website: www.viper.ch
Conny E. Voester, Festival Director
The most important media art festival in the country. It presents new international innovative and experimental productions on films, videos, CD-ROMs and Internet. Two competitions: International Competition for Film & Video and National Competition for Film & Video

Visions du Réel - Nyon International Documentary Film Festival

28 April-4 May 2003
Festival International de Cinéma
18, rue Juste Olivier
CP 593
1260 Nyon
Tel: (41) 22 365 44 55
Fax: (41) 22 365 44 50
email: docnyon@visionsdureel.ch
Website: www.visionsdureel.ch
Jean Perret, Festival Director
International competition screening independent documentaries of all sorts: experimental films, essays, diaries, family films, major reports, historical inquiries, classic narratives and fragmentary stories

TAIWAN

Taipei Golden Horse Film Festival

Late November-early December
3F, 37, Kaifeng St.
Taipei 100, Taiwan, ROC
Tel: (886) 2 2388 3880
Fax: (886) 2 2370 1616
email: tghffctt@ms14.hinet.net
Website: www.goldenhorse.org.tw
Wei-jan Liu, Coordinator
This festival was set up by the government in an effort to stimulate and revitalise the local filmmaking industry. The event is divided in two parts: the Golden Horse Awards Chinese language Film Competition(including Mandarin, Cantonese, Taiwanese, and Shangai dialects) and the non-competitive Annual Golden Horse International Film Exhibition, featuring retrospectives and special programmes

TANZANIA

Festival of the Dhow Countries

28 June-12 July 2003
ZIFF
PO BOX 3032
Zanzibar
Tel: (255) 4 747 411499
Fax: (886) 4 747 419955
email: ziff@ziff.or.tz
Website: www.ziff.or.tz
Imruh Bakari, Festival Director
Established in 1998 as the Zanzibar International Film Festival (ZIFF), the event now promotes an extensive programme of films, music and performing arts from Africa, India, Gulf States and Indian Ocean Island-the Dhow Countries. Sidebars include women's events, chidren's panorama, workshops and seminars

TUNISIA

Carthage International Film Festival

October/November
The JCC Managing Committee
PO Box 1039-1045
Tunisia
Tel/Fax: +21 61 26 0323
Website: www.tunisieinfo.com/Jcc98/
Official competition open to Arab and African short and feature films.It also has an Information Section, International Film Market(MIPAC) and workshops

TURKEY

International Istanbul Film Festival

12-27 April 2003
Istanbul Foundation for Culture and Arts
Istiklal Caddesi Luvr Apt. No. 146
80070 Beyoglu
Istanbul
Tel: (90) 212 334 0700
Fax: (90) 212 334 0702

email: film.fest@istfest-tr.org
Website: www.istfest.org
The Istanbul Festival focuses on features films dealing with arts (literature, theatre, cinema, music, dance and plastic arts). Showing over 200 films from five continents, the festival includes popular night screenings

UNITED KINGDOM

Animated Encounters

24-27 April 2003
Watershed Media Centre
1 Canon's Road
Harbourside
Bristol BS1 5TX
Tel: (44) 117 927 5102
Fax: (44) 117 930 9967
email: info@animated-encounters.org.uk
Website: www.animated-encounters.org.uk
Also known as the Bristol International Animated Festival, it consists of four days of screenings, seminars and parties with a dedicated Industry day, New British and International programmes, Desert Island Flicks and a range of special events

Bath Film Festival

16 October-2 November 2003
7 Terrace Walk
Bath BA1 1LN
Tel/Fax: (44) 1225 401149
email: info@bathfilmfestival.org
Website: www.bathfilmfestival.org
A non-competitive festival screening titles which do not make it to the town of Bath.It also includes a number of classic re-releases and participatory events (workshops, seminars, performances) and the Spools in Schools education programme

Birmingham Film and TV Festival

20-26 March 2004
9 Margaret Street
Birmingham B3 3BS
Tel: (44) 121 212 0999s
Fax: (44) 121 212 0666
email: info@film-tv-festival.org.uk
Website: www.film-tv-festival.org.uk
The BFTV Festival celebrates the moving image through a selection of previews, retrospective and archive screenings. It also organises events debating topical issues in moving image production and exhibition. Specialised strands include Movie Mahal, which focuses on South Asian films, and programmes on digital media

Bite the Mango

20-26 September 2003
National Museum of Photography, Film & Television
Pictureville
Bradford BD1 1NQ
Tel: +44 (0)870 7010 200
Fax: +44 (0)127 4723 155
email: talk.nmpft@nmsi.ac.uk
Website: www.bitethemango.org.uk
Lisa Kavanagh, Director
A celebration of Asian and Black cinema

Bradford Film Festival

14-29 March 2003
National Museum of Photography, Film & Television
Pictureville
Bradford BD1 1NQ
Tel: +44 (0)870 7010 200
email: talk.nmpft@nmsi.ac.uk
Website:
www.bradfordfilmfestival.org.uk
Lisa Kavanagh, Director
Non-competitive festival focusing on widescreen cinemascope, IMAX, cinerama and world cinema

Brief Encounters: Bristol Short Film Festival

12-16 November 2003
Watershed Media Centre
1 Canon's Road
Harbourside
Bristol BS1 5TX
Tel: (44) 117 927 5102
email: info@brief-encounters.org.uk
Website: www.brief-encounters.org.uk
A showcase of the best in regional, national and international short films alongside industry seminars, masterclasses, special events and a Gala Awards Ceremony. Open to all producers and directors of short films (up to 30 mins), including animation, documentary, drama and experimental

Cambridge Film Festival

10-20 July 2003
Arts Picture House
38-39 St. Andrews Street
Cambridge CB2 3AR
Tel: (44) 1223 578944
Fax: (44) 1223 578956
email: festival@cambarts.co.uk
Website:
www.cambridgefilmfestival.org.uk
Non-competitive festival screening new world cinema selected from international festivals. Also featuring director retrospectives, short film programmes, thematic seasons and revived classics; conference for independent exhibitors and distributors, public debates and post-screening discussions

Cardiff Screen Festival

14-22 November 2003
10 Mount Stuart SQ.
Cardiff CF10 5EE
Tel: +44 02920 333 300
email: sarah@sgrin.co.uk
Website:
www.cardiffscreenfestival.co.uk
Sarah Howells, Festival Manager
Formally the International Film Festival of Wales, the event offers premiere screenings, special guest appearances and debates on everything from soaps to the future of broadcasting. A celebration of film, TV and media from Wales and beyond

Celtic Film and Television Festival

April 2004
249 West George St.
Glasgow
Scotland G2 4QE
Tel: +44 (0) 141 302 1737
Fax: +44)0) 141 302 1738
email: jude@theceltic.org
Website: www.celticfilm.co.uk
Jude Sharvin, Festival Producer
Competition for films, television, radio and new media programmes whose subject matter has particular relevance to the Celtic regions and countries (Brittany, Cornwall, Ireland, Scotland and Wales)

Chichester Film Festival

21 August-7 September 2003
Chichester Cinema
New Park Road
Chichester
West Sussex PO19 1XN
Tel: (44) 1243 786650
Fax: (44)1243 539853
email: ellen@chichestercinema.org
Website: www.chichestercinema.org
A non-competitive festival that focuses on previews and retrospectives. Special emphasis on UK and other European productions. There is also a five-category international short film (up to 16 mins) competition

Cinemagic-Northern Ireland's World Screen Festival for Young People
4-14 December 2003
3rd Floor, Fountain House
17-21 Donegall Place
Belfast BT1 5AB
Tel: (44) 28 9031 1900
Fax: (44) 28 9031 9709
email: info@cinemagic.org.uk
Website: www.cinemagic.org.uk
Nicki Fulcher, Programmer
A competitive festival for international shorts, feature films and television programmes for young people aged between 4 and 18. It includes big movie premieres, practical workshops, directors discussions, masterclasses with industry professionals and special events

Edinburgh International Film Festival
13-24 August 2003
Filmhouse
88 Lothian Road
Edinburgh EH3 9BZ
Tel: +44 (0) 131 228 4051
Fax: +44 (0) 131 229 5501
email: info@edfilmfest.org.uk
Website: www.edfilmfest.org.uk
Shane Danielsen, Artistic Director
A unique showcase of new international cinema with special attention to British production. Programme sections: Focus on British Film; Retrospective; Gala (World, European and British premieres); Rosebud (first and second time directors); Director's Focus; Reel Life (illustrated lectures by filmmakers); Documentary; Mirrorball (music video); short films and animation

Festival of Fantastic Films
29-31 August 2003
95 Meadowgate Road
Salford
Manchester M6 8EN
Tel: (44) 161 707 3747
Fax: (44) 161 792 0991
email: AnthonyFEdwards@aol.com
Website: www.fantastic-films.com
Tony Edwards
The Annual Convention of the Society of Fantastic Films celebrates a century of science fiction and fantasy films, with guests of honour, interviews, signing panels, dealers, talks and a retrospective film programme. There is also an international competition for independently produced feature-length and short films

FILMSTOCK International Film Festival
1-15 June 2003
24 Guildford Street
Luton LU1 2NR
Tel: (44) 01582 752908
Fax: (44) 01582 423347
email: contact@filmstock.co.uk
Website: www.filmstock.co.uk
Justin Doherty, Neil Fox, Festival Directors
According to the organisers 'FILMSTOCK is more than a film festival. It is about cinema in its entirety and aims to fuse the joy of movie-going with the art of filmmaking in one simultaneous experience'

Foyle Film Festival
21-30 November 2003
The Nerve Centre
7-8 Magazine St
Derry BT48 6HJ
Tel: (44) 2871 276 432
Fax: (44) 2871 371 738
email: competition@nerve-centre.org.uk
Website: www.foylefilmfestival.com
Northern Ireland's major annual film event. There are four competition categories (Best film, Best Irish short, Best international short, and Best animated short) plus a separate On-Line competition for films under 10 minutes (Live Action and Flash Animation categories)

French Film Festival UK
7 November-1 December 2003
12 Sunbury Place
Edinburgh EH4 3BY
Tel: (44) 131 225 6191
Fax: (44) 131 225 6971
email: fff@frenchfilmfestival.org.uk
Website: www.frenchfilmfestival.org.uk
Richard Mowe, Director
The only British festival devoted exclusively to 'le cinéma français'. The programme falls in two categories: Panorama, devoted to the best names in French Cinema and New Waves, showcasing first and second-time directors. Held in Edinburgh, Glasgow, Aberdeen, Dundee and London

Frightfest
22-25 August 2003
C/o Ian Rattray Films
10 Wiltshire Gardens
Twickenham
Middlesex
London TW2 6ND
Tel: 020 8296 0555
Fax: 020 8296 0556
Website: www.frightfest.co.uk
Ian Rattray
Held in London over the August Bank Holiday at the Prince Charles Cinema, the festival is a fantasy event, which shows some 16 feature films from all over the world

Media Guardian Edinburgh International Television Festival (MGEITF)
22-24 August 2003
1st Floor
17-21 Emerald Street
London WC1N 3QN
Tel: (44) 207 430 1333
Fax: (44) 207 430 2299
email: info@mgeitf.co.uk
Website: www.mgeitf.co.uk
Sarah Barnett, Director
Now in its 28th year, the festival is a four-day forum featuring prominent industry voices. Attended by over 1700 delegates, the event covers a range of topics from policy to programme-making issues

Human Rights Watch International Film Festival
10-20 March 2003
2ns Floor, 2-12 Pentonville Rd.
London N1 9HF
Tel: +44 (0)20 7713 19 25
Fax: +44 (0)20 7713 18 00
email: hrwuk@hrw.org
Website: www.hrw.org/iff
A non-competitive festival showcasing features, shorts and documentaries with human rights themes from around the world

Italian Film Festival
4-17 April 2003
82 Nicolson Street
Edinburgh EH8 9EW
Tel: (44) 131 668 2232
Fax: (44) 131 668 2777
email: italianinstitute@btconnect.com
Website: italcult.net/edimburgo/ici-frame_events.htm (archives)
A unique event in the UK, throwing an exclusive spotlight on 'il cinema italiano'. The festival presents documentaries, shorts, new film and new talents. It travels to Aberdeen, Dundee, Edinburgh, Glasgow and London

IVCA Awards
One day in March
IVCA
Business Communication Centre
19 Pepper Street, Glengall Bridge

London E14 9RP
Tel: (44) 207 512 0571
Fax: (44) 207 512 0591
email: info@ivca.org
Website: www.ivca.org
The International Visual Communication Awards runs a competitive event for non-broadcast industrial/training films and videos, covering all aspects of the manufacturing and commercial world. Categories include Website, Editing, Documentary, Animation, Graphics and Special Effects, Direction, Script and Drama

KinoFilm: Manchester's International Short Film Festival

20-26 October 2003
42 Edge Street
Manchester M4 1HN
Tel: (44) 161 288 2494
Fax: (44) 161 281 1374
email: kino.fest@good.co.uk
Website: www.kinofilm.org.uk
John Wojowski, Director
Focusing on the British New Wave and International Panorama, the festival also includes: KinoLatino, Kino Horror, Going Underground and Magic Carpet. Awards for Best British and International; Best Student and Low Budget; Best Animation; Best Screenplay and Best Documentary

Latin American Film Festival

Two weeks in September
Website:www.latinamericanfilmfestival.co.uk
email:
info@latinamericanfilmfestival.co.uk
Competitive showcase for features, shorts, documentaries and videos from Latin America

Leeds International Film Festival

2-12 October 2003
Town Hall
The Headrow
Leeds LS1 3AD
Tel: (44) 113 247 8389
Fax: (44) 113 247 8397
email: filmfestival@leeds.gov.uk
Website: www.leedsfilm.com
Chris Fell, Director
Competition for feature films by new directors (Leeds New Directors Awards), Fiction and Animated Shorts (Louis le Prince International). Over 10 strands including Evolution (interactive and online), Eureka (European Films), Film Festival Fringe, Voices of Cinema and Fanomenon (Cult Films)

London Lesbian and Gay Film Festival

2-16 April 2003
National Film Theatre
South Bank
London SE1 8XT
Tel: (44) 207 815 1323
Fax: (44) 207 633 0786
email: anna.dunwoodie@bfi.org.uk
Website: www.outuk.com/llgff
Anna Dunwoodie, Festival Administrator
Organised by the British Film Institute, the festival is not only 'a celebration of cinema and queer-maker's contribution to the art form', it is also a unique opportunity to enjoy the astounding diversity of films reflecting gay and lesbian culture. On a national tour from April to September

Out Of Sight- International Film And Television Archive Festival

3-7 April 2003
Broadway
14-18 Broad Street
Nottingham NG1 3AL
Tel: (44) 115 952 6600
Fax: (44) 115 952 6622
email: info@broadway.org.uk
Website: www.broadway.org.uk
An annual week-end on British Silent Cinema investigating British film production before 1930, organised by the Broadway Cinema in Nottingham and the BFI National and Television Archive

Raindance Film Festival

24 October-7 November 2003
81 Berwick Street
London W1F 8TW
Tel: (44) 207 287 3833
Fax: (44) 207 439 2243
email: info@raindance.co.uk
Website: www.raindance.co.uk
Fostering and promoting independent film in the UK and abroad, the festival offers Film Training Courses, Rawtalent Productions, Raindance East and Raindance Kids. It also hosts the prestigious British Independent Film Awards

Sand-Swansea Animation Days

26-29 November 2003
Taliesin Arts Centre
Swansea, Wales
Tel: +44 (0) 01792 481028
email: dmc@sihe.ac.uk
Website: www.sand2003.org.uk
Felicity Blastland, Director
International digital event, which features world leaders in 3D animation, computer games, VR and AI with their most recent work. The Sand festival is also a meeting place to exchange ideas and create new project opportunities

Sheffield International Documentary Festival

13-19 October 2003
The Workstation
15 Paternoster Row
Sheffield S1 2BX
Tel: (44) 114 276 5141
Fax: (44) 114 272 1849
email: info@sidf.co.uk
Website: www.sidf.co.uk
Brent Woods, Festival Director
A platform for the best in British and international documentary film and television, the festival is both a public film event and an industry gathering, with screenings and discussions on the new developments in documentary. A selection of films travels to cinemas in the UK from November to February each year

The Times *bfi* London Film Festival

22 October- 6 November 2003
National Film Theatre
South Bank
London SE1 8XT
Tel: (44) 207 815 1322
Fax: (44) 207 633 0786
email: sarah.lutton@bfi.org.uk
Website: www.lff.org.uk
Sarah Lutton, Programme Coordinator
Britain's premier film festival, presented by the British Film Institute, it screens the best in new cinema from all over the world. It also includes previews of international feature films, shorts and videos. Selected highlights from the festival go on tour to regional film theatres from November to December

Viva! Spanish Film Festival

13-23 March 2003
Cornerhouse
70 Oxford Street
Manchester, M1 5NH
Tel: +44 (1) 161 200 1516
email: viva@cornerhouse.org
Website: www.cornerhouse.org
The UK's only Spanish Film Festival offers quality premieres, specially

imported new releases, special guests, parallel events and academic conferences. The festival tours to major cities, among others, Newcastle, Edinburgh, Cardiff, Dublin and London

Wildscreen
10-15 October 2004
Anchor Road
Bristol BS1 5TT
Tel: (44) 117 915 7217
Fax: (44) 117 915 7105
email: info@wildscreen.org.uk
Website: www.wildscreen.org.uk
Biennial international festival of moving images from the natural world, covering all aspects of screen-based natural history communications, including the Internet, interactive media and film formats such as Imax. The festival offers seminars, screenings, discussions, training workshops, trade show for delegates and the general public. The Panda Awards Competition is open to film, TV and interactive productions from anywhere in the world

Wow! Wales One World Festival
5 March-21 April 2004
Taliesin Arts Centre
University of Wales Swansea
Swansea, Wales
Tel/Fax: +44 (0) 1239 615066
email: sa3657@eclipse.co.uk
Website: wowfilfestival.org
David Gilliam, Festival Director
Presenting films that are currently under-represented on Welsh screens, the festival showcases a programme of top quality works from Africa, Asia and Latin America

URUGUAY

Montevideo International Film Festival
Two weeks in April
Cinemateca Uruguaya
Lorenzo Carnelli 1311
11200 Montevideo
Tel: (598) 2 709 7637
Fax: (598) 2 707 6389
email: cinemuy@chasque.apc.org
Website: www.festival.org.uy
A competitive festival devoted to short, feature length, documentary, fiction, experimental, Latin American and international films

Montevideo International Film Festival for Children and Young People
Twelve days in July
Cinemateca Uruguaya
Lorenzo Carnelli 1311
11200 Montevideo
Tel: (598) 2 709 7637
Fax: (598) 2 707 6389
email: cinemuy@chasque.apc.org
Website: www.cinemateca.org.uy
The festival presents an overview of new film productions for children and adolescents, facilitating access to the best and most diverse material for young people

USA

AFI Fest: American Film Institute Los Angeles International Film Festival
6-16 November 2003
American Film Institute
2021 N. Western Avenue
Los Angeles, CA 90027-1657
Tel: (1) 323 856 7707
Fax: (1) 323 462 4049
email: afifest@afi.com
Website: www.afifest.com
The festival presents over 140 films through an International Competition of first-and second-time filmmakers as well as regional showcases of international cinema: Asian New Classics, European Film Showcase, Latin Cinema Series and American Directions

American Black Film Festival
18-22 June 2003
c/o Film Life
100 Sixth Avenue, 15th floor
New York, NY 10013
Tel: (1) 212 219 7267
email: abff@thefilmlife.com
Website: www.abff.com
Jeff Friday, Director
Considered as the 'Black Holliwood's annual retreat and international film market', the festival presents independent film premieres, workshops, panels, networking, parties and Film Life Awards

American Film Market
19-26 February 2003
9th Floor, 10850 Wilshire Blvd
Los Angeles, CA 90024
Tel: (1) 310 446 1000
Fax: (1) 310 446 1600
email: info@afma.com
Website: www.afma.com/AFM
Jonathan Wolf, Managing Director
The largest motion picture trade event in the world, held in Los Angeles

Asian American International Film Festival
20-29 June 2003
Asian CineVision
133 W. 19th Street, 3rd Floor
New York, NY 10011
Tel: (1) 212 989 1422
Fax: (1) 212 727 3584
email: info@asiancinevision.org
Website: www.asiancinevision.org
Diane Lee, Festival Director
Proudly known as 'The First Home to Asian American Cinema', the festival is a leading showcase for Asian American film and video arts. A selection of the festival's entries travels on a 10-month tour to major US cities

Chicago International Film Festival
2-16 October 2003
32 West Randolph St.
Chicago, IL 60601
Tel: (1) 312 425 9400
Fax: (1) 312 425 0944
email: info@chicagofilmfestival.com
Website: www.chicagofilmfestival.com
Sophia Wong Boccio, Managing Director
North America's oldest competitive international film festival (1964 -) presents the latest in world cinema with new works by both veteran masters and talented newcomers. The highest prize for best film is the Gold Hugo Award

Cleveland International Film Festival
20-30 March 2003
Cleveland Film Society
2510 Market Avenue
Cleveland OH 44113
Tel: +1 216 623 3456
Fax: +1 216 623 0103
email: cfs@clevelandfilm.org
Website: www.clevelandfilm.org
A competitive showcase of about 80 contemporary American and international feature films plus nearly 100 shorts. The programme also includes films from Eastern Europe, American Independent, retrospectives and cinema for children

Columbus International Film and Video Festival
Mid-October
Film Council of Greater Columbus

5701 North High Street, #204
Worthington, OH 43085
Tel/Fax: (1) 614 841 1666
email: info@chrisawards.org
Website: www.chrisawards.org

Also known as The Chris Awards, it specialises in honouring documentary, animation, drama, CD-ROMs/Interactive, information film and video productions. The festival also includes categories for the arts, entertainment, education and business

Fort Lauderdale International Film Festival

22 October-16 November 2003
1314 East Las Olas Blvd. #007
Fort Lauderdale, FL 33301
Tel: (1) 954 760 9898
Fax: (1) 954 760 9099
email: info@fliff.com
Website: www.fliff.com
Bonnie Leigh Adams, Senior Prog. Director
The longest festival in the world (37 days) and one of the most important regional film festivals in the US, where over 100 films (features, documentaries, art on film series, shorts, animation) are screened from Boca Raton to Miami

Hawaii International Film Festival

30 October-9 November 2003
1001 Bishop Street
Pacific Tower, Suite 745
Honolulu, Hawaii 96813
Tel: (1) 808 528 3456
Fax: (1) 808 528 1410
email: info@hiff.org
Website: www.hiff.org
Chuck Boller, Executive Director
A State-wide event, taking place on the six Hawaiian islands, the festival presents 100 features, documentaries and shorts premieres, experimental films representing social and ethnic issues and first features by new directors. The event is also unique in discovering works from Asia made by Asians, films about the Pacific made by Pacific Islanders and films by Hawaii filmmakers presenting Hawaii in a culturally accurate way

Human Rights Watch International Film Festival

11-26 June 2003
350 Fith Av. 34th Floor
New York, NY 10018-3299
Tel: (1) 212 216 1264
Fax: (1) 212 736 1300
email: hrwny@hrw.org
Website: www.hrw.org/iff
A leading venue for fiction, documentary and animated films and videos, concentrating equally on artistic merit and human rights content. Screenings are usually followed by discussions with the filmmakers and Human Rights Watch (HRW) staff. The festival also awards a prize in the name of cinematographer and director Nestor Almendros, who was an active supporter of HRW's cause. In 1996, the event expanded to London (see entry under United Kingdom for details)

Independent Feature Film Market

21-26 September 2003
104 West 29th Street
12th Floor
New York, NY 10001-5310
Tel: (1) 212 465 8200
Fax: (1) 212 465 8525
email: mbond@ifp.org
Website: www.ifp.org
This is the longest running market devoted to emerging American independent film talents seeking domestic and foreign distribution. It is the market for innovative projects in development, outstanding documentaries and startling works of fiction

Miami Film Festival

30 January-8 February 2004
Film Society of Miami
444 Brickell Avenue, Suite 229
Miami, FL 33131
Tel: (1) 305 348 5555
email: info@miamifilmfestival.com
Website: www.miamifilmfestival.com
With its new section 'Miami Encuentros' to support Iberoamerican filmmakers, the festival has become a well-known gateway for Spanish-language films in the US

New York Film Festival

3-19 October 2003
Film Society of Lincoln Center
70 Lincoln Center Plaza
New York, NY 10023
Tel: (1) 212 875 5638
Fax: (1) 212 875 5636
Website: www.filmlinc.com
The non-competitive event, this year celebrating its 41st anniversary, screens features, shorts, documentaries, animations and experimental works

Palm Springs International Festival of Short Films

16-22 September 2003
1700 E. Tahquitz Canyon Way, #3
Palm Springs, CA 92262
Tel: (1) 760 322 2930
Fax: (1) 760 322 4087
email: info@psfilmfest.org
Website: www.psfilmfest.org
Also known as the Nortel Networks PSIFF, the festival is said to have captured 'Hollywood's attention as a scouting ground for new film-making talent' and has become an 'absolute must-attend for those in the business of buying and selling short films'

Portland International Film Festival

14 February-1 March 2003
Northwest Film Center
1219 SW Park Avenue
Portland, OR 97205
Tel: (1) 503 221 1156
Fax: (1) 503 294 0874
email: info@nwfilm.org
Website: www.nwfilm.org
Oregon's major film event, the festival offers approximately 100 feature and short films from over 30 countries

San Francisco International Film Festival

17 April-1 May 2003
30 Mesa St., Ste. 110
The Presidio
San Francisco, CA 94129
Tel: (1) 415 561 5000
Fax: (1) 415 561 5099
email: sffs@sffs.org
Website: www.sffs.org/festival
A showcase for approximately 200 new shorts, documentaries, animation, experimental works and television productions, eligible for the Golden Gate Award competition

San Francisco International Lesbian & Gay Film Festival

22 May-15 June 2003
Frameline
346 Ninth St. Suit 300
San Francisco, CA 94103-2636
Tel: (1) 415 703 8650
Fax: (1) 415 861 1404
email: info@frameline.org
Website: www.frameline.org
The largest and oldest festival of its kind, whose mission is 'to support, develop and promote lesbian, gay, bisexual, transgender and queer visibility through media arts'. It presents features, shorts, documentaries, videos and experimental work

Seattle International Film Festival

22 May-15 June 2003
911 Pine St., 6th Floor
Seattle, WA 98101
Tel: (1) 206 464 5830
Fax: (1) 206 264 7919
email: SIFF_PR@seattlefilm.com
Website: www.seattlefilm.com
Darryl Macdonald, Director
The biggest and most attended film Festival in the country, it includes gala premieres, new films from first-time and well-known directors, previews, special archival programmes, post-film Q&A sessions and forums

Starz Denver International Film Festival

9-19 October 2003
Denver Film Society
1725 Blake Street
Denver, CO 80202
Tel: (1) 303 595 3456
Fax: (1) 303 595 0956
email: dfs@denverfilm.org
Website: www.denverfilm.org
Non-competitive event which presents over 175 films focusing on new international feature releases, independently produced fiction films and documentaries, experimental videos and children's films

Sundance Film Festival

16-26 January 2003
PO Box 3630
Salt Lake City, UT 84110
Tel: (1) 801 328 3456
Fax: (1) 801 575 5175
email: institute@sundance.org
Website: www.sundance.org
Jill Miller, Managing Director
Part of Robert Redford's Sundance Institute since 1985, the festival is recognised internationally as a showcase for the best in American Independent cinema. It is a competitive event for US and International narrative feature, full-length documentary, and short films. Its programme also includes the Native Forum section (films written and directed by Indegenous filmmakers), an Animation section, an Online Festival, special retrospectives and seminars

Telluride Film Festival

29 August-1 September 2003
379 State Street
Portsmouth, NH 03801
Tel: (1) 603 433 9202
Fax: (1) 603 433 9206
email: Mail@telluridefilmfestival.org
Website: www.telluridefilmfestival.com
Although concentrating mainly on features, Telluride also organises three programmes of shorts. It is open to professional and non-professional filmmakers working in all film forms: documentary, narrative, animation and experimental

US International Film & Video Festival

Early June
713 S. Pacific Coast Highway, SuitA
Redondon beach, CA 90277-4233
email:
filmfestivalinfo@filmfestawards.com
Website: www.filmfestawards.com
International awards competition for television, industrial and informational productions

WorldFest-Houston International Film Festival

16-25 April 2004
9494SW Freeway, 5th floor
Houston, Texas 77074
Tel: (1) 713 965 9955
email: mail@worldfest.org
Website: www.worldfest.org
Part marketplace part film festival, the event is totally dedicated to independent feature and short films. It offers 11 major areas of competition and awards, including documentary, film & video production, TV & cable production, experimental, shorts, TV commercials, screenplays, music video, new media, feature films and students' films

FUNDING

The dust of the recent years upheavals has almost settled and the UK funding landscape is beginning to stabalise at least for the time being. Check websites of organisations you wish to approach beforehand to confirm contact details. Compiled by David Reeve

Funding

ADAPT (Access for Disabled People to Arts Premises Today)

The ADAPT Trust
Wellpark
120 Sydney Street
Glasgow G31 1JF
Tel: 0141 556 2233
Fax: 0141 556 7799
email: adapt.trust@virgin.net
Director: Stewart Coulter
Charitable trust providing advice and challenge funding to arts venues - cinemas, concert halls, libraries, heritage and historic houses, theatres, museums and galleries - throughout Great Britain. ADAPT also provides a consultancy service and undertakes access audits and assessments. Grants and Awards for 2003/2004 advertised as available

ADAPT NI

Cathedral Quarter Managed Workspace
109-113 Royal Avenue
Belfast BT1 1FF
Tel: 028 9023 1211
Fax: 028 9024 0878
email: caroline@adaptni.org
Website: www.adaptni.org
ADAPT NI aims to promote Universal Accessibility in all Arts, Heritage, Leisure and Community venues by providing training, advice and support. This includes accessibility audits, technical advice, information and training on how proposed or existing premises can better accommodate people of all abilities. ADAPT has developed a programme of activities and events, which involve disabled and non-disabled people at all levels in a way, which is relevant to the objectives of the organisation. ADAPT primary remit covers arts and community centres, theatres, concert halls, libraries, museums and public galleries, leisure centres and other buildings where arts and social activities take place, ADAPT aims to improve accessibility in the future, not just in terms of built environment but in the widest sense of access through projects, which encourage awareness, participation, integration and employment

AIR (Animator In Residence)

National Museum of Photography, Film and Television
Bradford BD1 1NQ
Tel: 0870 70 10 200
email: Tom.Hillenbrand@bfi.org.uk
Website: www.a-i-r.info
Adam Pugh
Professional animator residencies based at the bfi London IMAX cinema are awarded to animators who have graduated within the last 5 years. Here they will develop their own original idea for a short animated film into a proposal for Channel 4 television's animation department, who will consider a full commission of the final production. Animators receive advice from a professional producer, £1600 materials budget, and a £3000 grant

Awards For All

Tel: 0845 600 2040
email: info@awardsforall.org.uk
Website: www.awardsforall.org.uk
Awards for All is a grants programme supported by the Heritage Lottery Fund, the Arts Council England, Sport England, the New Opportunities Fund and the Community Fund. It funds projects that enable people to take part in art, sport, heritage and community activities, as well as projects that promote education, the environment and health in the local community. They cannot award grants to companies which aim to distribute a profit or individuals. Awards for All operates through nine regional offices in England. There are similar programmes running in Northern Ireland, Scotland and Wales. They award grants of between £500 and £5,000. Contact 0845 600 2040 or visit the website for further information".

Awards For All England
Awards for All is a national programme operating through nine regional offices in England. Each region has some areas of special emphasis it wishes to focus on.
North East: 0191 2551100
North West: 01925 626800
Yorkshire and the Humber: 0113 224 5300
East Midlands: 0115 934 9304
West Midlands: 0121 200 3511
Eastern: 01223 449009
London: 020 7587 6600
South West: 01392 849705
South East: 01483 462943

Awards for All in Northern Ireland
Tel: 028 9055 9090
Fax: 028 9055 1444

Awards for All in Scotland
Tel: 0141 242 1200
Fax: 0141 223 8620

Awards for All in Wales
Tel: 01686 611740
Fax: 01686 621534

British Council

Web and Information Team
Film and Literature Department
British Council
10 Spring Gardens
London SW1A 2BN
Tel: 020 7389 3166
Fax: 020 7389 3175
Email:
filmandliterature@britishcouncil.org
Website: www.britfilms.com
Britain's International agency for cultural and educational relations. Assists in the co-ordination and shipping of films to festivals, and in some cases can provide funds for the film-maker to attend when invited. Publishers of the annual British Films Catalogue and the portal website, the

Directory of International Film and Video Festivals, and the directory of British Film Directors

Cineworks

Glasgow Media Access Centre
3rd Floor
34 Albion Street
Glasgow G1 1LH
Tel: 0141 553 2620
Fax: 0141 553 2660
email: info@cineworks.co.uk
Website: www.cineworks.co.uk
David Smith - Cineworks Co-ordinator
Cineworks is Scotland's entry level short film scheme commissioning five original projects each year in the fields of animation, documentary and drama with budgets of £10,000 or £15,000. It is run by the Glasgow Media Access Centre in partnership with the Edinburgh Mediabase and funded by Scottish Screen, The UK Film Council's New Cinema fund and BBC Scotland. The five films are premiered at the Edinburgh International Film Festival before being distributed by Scottish Screen and Cineworks

Community Fund

Corporate Office
St Vincent House
16 Suffolk Street
London SW1Y 4NL
Tel: 020 7747 5299
email: enquiries@community-fund.org.uk
Website: www.community-fund.org.uk
International Grants: 020 7747 5294
Research Grants: 020 7747 5360
Wales: 01686 611700
Northern Ireland: 028 9055 1455
Scotland: 0141 223 8600
Strategic Grants: 0115 934 2950
North East: 0191 255 1133
North West: 01925 626800
Yorkshire and the Humber: 0113 224 5300
East Midlands: 0115 934 9300
West Midlands: 0121 200 3512
Eastern: 01223 449000
London: 020 7587 6609
South East: 01483 462 941
South West: 01392 849700
Community Fund distributes money raised by the National Lottery to support charities and voluntary and community groups throughout the UK and to UK agencies working abroad. Their main aim is to help meet the needs of those at greatest disadvantage in society and to improve the quality of life in the community. See website for full regional contact details and information about previously funded projects

Edinburgh Mediabase

25a South West Thistle Street Lane
Edinburgh EH2 1EW
Tel: 0131 220 0220
Fax: 0131 220 0017
email: info@edinburghmediabase.com
Website: www.edinburghmediabase.com
Edinburgh Mediabase is a resource facility for anyone interested in film, digital video or new media. It allows budding film-makers the chance to access to good facilities Mediabase helps with everything from scriptwriting classes to broadcast quality digital cameras, professional edit suites and a monthly screening at the Cameo Cinema in Edinburgh called The Blue Room. Mediabase runs script award competitions such as: Cineworks (in partnership with Glasgow Media Access Centre), a short film production scheme designed to nurture new film-making talent, Small Wonders, a training and production scheme set up to discover new talent and Forty8ight Hours, a no-budget video production competition run in conjunction with the monthly Blue Room screening event. Mediabase also provides information and advice to members on everything from funding for their projects to careers in the creative industries

Kraszna-Krausz Foundation

122 Fawnbrake Avenue
London SE24 0BZ
Tel: 020 7738 6701
Fax: 020 7738 6701
email: info@k-k.org.uk
Website: www.k-k.org.uk
Andrea Livingstone, Administrator
The Foundation offers small grants to assist in the development of new or unfinished projects, work or literature where the subject specifically relates to the art, history, practice or technology of photography or the moving image (defined as film, television, video and related screen media). The Foundation also sponsors annual book awards, with prizes for books on the moving image (film, television, video and related media) alternating with those for books on still photography. Books that have been published in the previous two years can be submitted from publishers in any language. The prize money is around £10,000, with awards in two categories. The next awards for books on photography will be in 2004

Nicholl Fellowships in Screenwriting

Academy of Motion Picture Arts and Sciences
8949 Wilshire Boulevard
Beverly Hills, CA 90211
USA
Tel: 001 310 247 3059
email: nicholl@oscars.org
Website: www.oscars.org/nicholl
Annual Screenwriting Fellowship Awards

The Isle of Man Film and Television Fund

Isle of Man Film Commission
Department of Trade & Industry
Hamilton House
Peel Road
Douglas Isle of Man
Tel: 01624 687173
Fax: 01624 687171
email: filmcomm@dti.gov.im
Website: www.gov.im/dti/iomfilm
The Isle of Man Film and Television Fund has been established to make available equity investment to film and television productions shooting wholly or partly on the Isle of Man. Offers up to 25% of the budget as direct equity investment with no upper or lower limits. Additionally, television projects will be able to apply for production credits where the project is being funded wholly or in part by a recognised broadcaster. To qualify for investment your project should be able to be filmed wholly or in part on the Isle of Man (a minimum of 50% principal photography on the Isle of Man), be capable of spending at least 20% of the below the line budget with local service providers, be otherwise fully funded, have a sales agent and/or a distributor attached and have a completion bond in place

The Prince's Trust

Head Office
18 Park Square East
London NW1 4LH
Tel: 020 7543 1234
FreeFax: 0800 842 842
Fax: 020 7543 1200

email: info@princes-trust.org.uk
Website: www.princes-trust.org.uk
The Prince's Trust helps young people to succeed. It provides long term support to 14-30 year olds, who have the potential, but few of the opportunities. It enables them to develop confidence and skills, get a job and start their own businesses.

Arts Funding

The Arts Council of England and the 10 Regional Arts Boards merged to form a single organisation in April 2002, and from 17 February 2003 the organisation has been known as Arts Council England. It has a national office and nine regional offices. Between 2003 and 2006 they will invest £2 billion of public funds in the arts in England, including funding from the National Lottery.

National Office

Arts Council England

14 Great Peter Street
London SW1P 3NQ
Tel: 020 7333 0100
Fax: 020 7973 6590
email: enquiries@artscouncil.org.uk
Website: www.artscouncil.org.uk
For information about current initiatives and opportunities, please check the website

Regional Offices

Arts Council England, East

Eden House
48-49 Bateman Street
Cambridge CB2 1LR
Tel: 01223 454400
Fax: 0870 242 1271
email: east@artscouncil.org.uk
Funds artists' films and videos. Arts Council England, East covers the following area: Bedfordshire, Cambridgeshire, Essex, Hertfordshire, Norfolk, Suffolk; and unitary authorities of Luton, Peterborough, Southend-on-Sea, and Thurrock. Arts Council England, East, now has a regional screen agency, Screen East, which is responsible for funding film and video production in the region.

Arts Council England, East Midlands

St Nicholas Court
25-27 Castle Gate
Nottingham NG1 7AR
Tel: 0115 989 7520
Fax: 0115 950 2467
email:
eastmidlands@artscouncil.org.uk
Funds artists' films and videos. Arts Council England, East Midlands covers the following area: Derbyshire, Leicestershire, Lincolnshire (excluding North and North East Lincolnshire), Northamptonshire, Nottinghamshire; and unitary authorities of Derby, Leicester, Nottingham, and Rutland. Arts Council England, East Midlands, now has a regional screen agency, EM-Media, which is responsible for funding film and video production in the region.

Arts Council England, London

2 Pear Tree Court
London EC1R 0DS
Tel: 020 7608 6100
Fax: 020 7608 4100
email: london@artscouncil.org.uk
Funds artists' films and videos. Arts Council England, London covers the following area: Greater London. Arts Council England, London, now has a regional screen agency, Film London, which is responsible for funding film and video production in the region

Arts Council England, North East

Central Square
Forth Street
Newcastle upon Tyne NE1 3PJ
Tel: 0191 255 8500
Fax: 0191 230 1020
TextFax: 0191 255 8500
email: northeast@artscouncil.org.uk
Funds artists' films and videos. Arts Council England, North East covers the following area: Durham, Northumberland; metropolitan authorities of Gateshead, Newcastle upon Tyne, North Tyneside, South Tyneside, Sunderland; and unitary authorities of Darlington, Hartlepool, Middlesbrough, Redcar and Cleveland, and Stockton-on-Tees. Arts Council England, North East, now has a regional screen agency, Northern Film & Media, which is responsible for funding film and video production in the region

Arts Council England, North West

Manchester House
22 Bridge Street
Manchester M3 3AB
Tel: 0161 834 6644
Fax: 0161 834 6969
email: northwest@artscouncil.org.uk
Funds artists' films and videos. Areas covered: Cheshire, Cumbria and Lancashire, and the metropolitan districts of Bolton, Bury, Knowsley, Liverpool, Manchester, Oldham, Rochdale, St. Helens, Salford, Sefton, Stockport, Tameside, Trafford, Wigan, and Wirral, and the non-metropolitan districts of Blackburn with Darwen, Blackpool, Halton, and Warrington. Arts Council England, North West, now has a dedicated regional screen agency, North West Vision, which is responsible for funding film and video production in the region

Arts Council England, South East

Sovereign House
Church Street
Brighton BN1 1RA
Tel: 01273 763000
Fax: 0870 242 1257
email: southeast@artscouncil.org.uk
Funds artists' films and videos. The new South East region covers Buckinghamshire, East Sussex, Hampshire, Isle of Wight, Kent, Oxfordshire, Surrey, and West Sussex, and the unitary authorities of Bracknell Forest, Brighton and Hove, Medway, Milton Keynes, Portsmouth, Reading, Slough, Southampton, West Berkshire, Windsor and Maidenhead and Wokingham. Arts Council England, South East, now has a regional screen agency, Screen South, which is responsible for funding film and video production in the region.

Arts Council England, South West

Bradninch Place
Gandy Street
Exeter EX4 3LS
Tel: 01392 218188
Fax: 01392 229229
email: southwest@artscouncil.org.uk
Funds artists' films and videos. Areas covered: Cornwall, Devon, Dorset (excluding Borough of Christchurch), Gloucestershire, Somerset; non-metropolitan districts of Bath and North East Somerset, Bristol, North Somerset, Plymouth, South

Gloucestershire, and Torbay. Arts Council England, South West, now has a regional screen agency, South West Screen, which is responsible for funding film and video production in the region

Arts Council England, West Midlands

82 Granville Street
Birmingham B1 2LH
Tel: 0121 631 3121
Fax: 0121 643 7239
email:
westmidlands@artscouncil.org.uk
Funds artists' films and videos. Area covered: Shropshire, Staffordshire, Warwickshire, Worcestershire; metropolitan authorities of Birmingham, Coventry, Dudley, Sandwell, Solihull, Walsall, Wolverhampton; and unitary authorities of Herefordshire, Stoke-on-Trent, Telford and Wrekin. Arts Council England, West Midlands, now has a regional screen agency, Screen West Midlands, which is responsible for funding film and video production in the region

Arts Council England, Yorkshire

21 Bond Street
Dewsbury
West Yorkshire WF13 1AX
Tel: 01924 455555
Fax: 01924 466522
email: yorkshire@artscouncil.org.uk
Funds artists' films and videos. Area covered: North Yorkshire; metropolitan authorities of Barnsley, Bradford, Calderdale, Doncaster, Kirklees, Leeds, Rotherham, Sheffield, Wakefield; and unitary authorities of East Riding of Yorkshire, Kingston upon Hull, North Lincolnshire, North East Lincolnshire, and York. Arts Council England, Yorkshire, now has a regional screen agency, Screen Yorkshire, which is responsible for funding film and video production in the region.

Arts Council of Northern Ireland

Arts Development Department
MacNeice House,
77 Malone Road
Belfast BT9 6AQ
Tel: 028 9038 5200
Fax: 028 9066 1715
email: nmckinney@artscouncil-ni.org
Website: www.artscouncil-ni.org
With effect from 1 April 2002 The Arts Council of Northern Ireland delegated its responsibility for film finance to the Northern Ireland Film & Television Commission (see separate entry). Check www.artscouncil-ni.org for details of other funds

Arts Council of Wales

9 Museum Place
Cardiff CF10 3NX
Tel: 029 20 376500
Fax: 029 20 221447
email: info@artswales.org.uk
Website: www.artswales.org.uk
The Arts Council of Wales (ACW) is responsible for funding and developing the arts in Wales. It became accountable to the National Assembly for Wales on 1 July 1998 when responsibility was transferred from the Secretary of State for Wales. Check their website for further information and funding opportunities

Scottish Arts Council

12 Manor Place
Edinburgh EH3 7DD
Tel: 0845 603 6000/ hard of hearing prefix number with 18001
Fax: 0131 225 9833
email: help.desk@scottisharts.org.uk
Website: www.sac.org.uk
The Scottish Arts Council is one of the main channels for Government funding for the arts in Scotland, receiving its funding from the Scottish Executive. They also distribute National Lottery funds received from the Department for Culture, Media and Sport. Check their website for details of the funds

Public Funding

UK Film Council

10 Little Portland Street
London W1W 7JG
Tel: 020 7861 7861
Fax: 020 7861 7862
email: info@filmcouncil.org.uk
Website: Websites:
www.ukfilmcouncil.org.uk
Contact: Iain Hepplewhite - Head of Communications
www.firstlightmovies.com
www.bfc.co.uk
General enquiries: 020 7861 7924
Tina McFarling - Head of Industry Relations
The UK Film Council is the key strategic body with responsibility for advancing the film industry and film culture in the UK. Funded by Government through the Department for Culture, Media and Sport, The UK Film Council has two broad aims:
To help develop a sustainable UK film industry;
To develop film culture by improving access to, and education about, the moving image.
The UK Film Council provides public funding for a range of initiatives supporting film development, production, training, distribution, exhibition, education and culture, which are focused on achieving these key aims. The UK Film Council also funds the bfi, the British Film Office in Los Angeles, the Cinema Marketing Agency and Film Education's National Schools Film Week. It also supports the New Producers Alliance, the European Film Awards, the Grierson Awards and the Dinard Festival for British Film. The UK Film Council receives £55 million (a combination of Grant-in-aid and Lottery money) a year to enable it to meet 13 key objectives set by the Government. Three production funds have been set up with an overall budget of £60 million over three years to spend on film production and development - **the Premiere Fund** (£30 million), **the New Cinema Fund** (£15 million) and **the Development Fund** (£15 million). The UK Film Council also has a **Training Fund** (£1 million a year) expanding training for scriptwriters and producer/film-makers and works in partnership with Skillset, the Sector Skills Council for the audio-visual industries. In

addition, a grant-funded programme supported by £1 million of Lottery funds called First Light" offers children and young people the opportunity to experience filmmaking and display their talents using low-cost technology."
As a strategic body The UK Film Council has created a £6 million a year Regional Investment Fund for England (RIFE) which is available to support cultural and industrial film initiatives in the English regions and works to a joined-up UK-wide agenda with the national film agencies, Scottish Screen, Sgrîn Cymru Wales and the Northern Ireland Film and Television Commission. The UK Film Council also continues to administer Lottery funds to the film production franchises set up by the Arts Council of England in 1997 and awarded to The Film Consortium, Pathé Pictures and DNA Films. For up-to-date information on The UK Film Council and its funds visit www.ukfilmcouncil.org.uks

Northern Ireland Film And Television Commission

Third Floor Alfred House
21 Alfred Street
Belfast BT2 8ED
Tel: 028 9023 2444
Fax: 028 9023 9918
email: info@niftc.co.uk
Website: www.niftc.co.uk

The Northern Ireland Film and Television Commission (NIFTC) offers loans to production companies for the development and production of feature films or television drama series or serials that are intended to be produced primarily in Northern Ireland. On 1 April 2002 The Arts Council of Northern Ireland delegated its responsibility for film finance to the NIFTC. The hand-over, for a three-year pilot period will see 13 per cent of the Arts Council's National Lottery funding allocated annually to NIFTC. See their website for further information

Scottish Screen

2nd Floor
249 West George Street
Glasgow G2 4QE
Tel: 0141 302 1700
Fax: 0141 302 1711
email: info@scottishscreen.com
Website: www.scottishscreen.com

Scottish Screen develops, encourages and promotes every aspect of film, television and new media in Scotland. Working with the Scottish Executive, their mission is to establish Scotland as a major screen production centre and project Scottish culture to the world

Production Development

Scottish Screen currently has various film schemes in partnership with a range of other bodies.

Cineworks
is a new entrant production scheme partly supported by Scottish Screen to offer opportunities for filmmakers to make their first professional films. An extensive development and training programme is included. All types of work including animation and documentary are eligible. Included in the scheme is a partnership with the Fax to produce very low budget digital shorts. For further information see the separate entry for Cineworks in the Funding section

Tartan Shorts
is a joint initiative with BBC Scotland to create an opportunity for Scotland's filmmaking talent to make cinematic short films. The scheme has been running for several years and each year, three projects are awarded up to a maximum of £65,000 to produce a 35mm film. Each film should be approximately 9 minutes duration.

New Found Land
is a collaboration with the Scottish Media Group and the National Lottery to enable new filmmakers to work on longer form drama. Six half-hour projects are commissioned and shot using new digital technology, with budgets of approximately £50,000. New Found Land is now running every 2 years in conjunction with New Found Films

New Found Films
is a new production scheme offering emerging Scottish talent a first step into feature film production. For 2003 two 90-minute films with budgets of £200,000 will go into production. Development and production finance will be provided by Scottish Television, Grampian Television and the National Lottery Fund. New Found Films is now running every 2 years in conjunction with New Found Land

Four Minute Wonders
is a music production scheme whereby each month around £5,000 can be won to develop and produce a video based on a new piece of music. The new track will be uploaded to the 4minutewonders.com web site at the beginning of each month

ALT-W
is an initiative supporting Scotland's new media development and promotes creative entrepreneurial talent. Production grants of up to £2,500 are available for innovative digital productions that can be delivered via the web. For further details visit: www.ALT-W.com.

Tartan Smalls
offers an opportunity for new talent to work in the children's arena, or existing talent (without previous children's experience) to enter this exciting creative genre. This scheme will create new and exciting work for an audience of 6-13 years. Three projects are short-listed with a budget of £40,000. Projects should not exceed 9 minutes in duration.

This Scotland
is a documentary production scheme for new and existing talent and will commission single documentaries within one overall strand. The scheme is co-produced by Scottish TV, Grampian TV and Scottish Screen.

Bridging the Gap
is a documentary scheme aimed at Scottish based filmmakers. This scheme aims to bridge the gap between training/graduation and a first broadcast. The scheme is a collaboration between Edinburgh College of Art and Angus Digital Media Centre and is sponsored by Scottish Screen and Scottish Enterprise Tayside. Five twenty-five minute films are chosen for training and mentoring with a budget of £16,000.

Other Funding

Outside of the various schemes, Scottish Screen occasionally will invest in one-off short film projects.

Development

Development funding can be sought under the Seed Fund or through Script Development Funding/Project Development Funding).

The **Seed Fund** is intended to

encourage feature film projects at the early stages of development, typically where a project is insufficiently developed to be eligible for an award under the Lottery-funded Script Development scheme. It is open to both companies and individuals. The maximum award is £5,000 and takes the form of a loan repayable if the project goes into production. Applications are considered on a monthly basis

Scottish Screen National Lottery Production Funding

From 7 April 2000, Scottish Screen assumed responsibility for allocating National Lottery funds for all aspects of film production in Scotland. This represents about £3m per year for film production.

Other National Lottery funding programmes operated by the Scottish Arts Council remain open to film and video projects and organisations. Contact SAC for further details. The various funding programmes operated by Scottish Screen are as follows:

Feature Film Production Finance
Funding is available up to £500,000 per project for feature films (including feature length documentaries) aimed at theatrical distribution.

Short Film Production Funding
Applications for under £25,000 are accepted on a continuous basis. Short films requesting in excess of £25,000 will be considered by the full Lottery Panel on specified dates.

Script Development Funding
Funding between £2,500 and £25,000 is available to projects which would benefit from further development of the script prior to packaging and financing. The project will be already at first draft or at the very least full treatment stage (including sample scenes where appropriate). The Scheme is aimed at projects which can make a robust case that this level of investment will materially advance the treatment or script towards the stage where it can attract the interest of financiers and/or key players.

Project Development Funding
Funding up to £75,000 is available for second-stage development of feature films. This is aimed at projects already at a relatively advanced stage. It will support elements such as script polish, preparation of schedule and budget, casting etc. Applications for under £25,000 are accepted on a continuous basis.

Distribution and Exploitation Support
Funding of up to £25,000 is available for completed feature films to support print and advertising costs associated with the commercial exploitation of the film in the UK marketplace. Funding may also be applied to overseas sales and marketing of completed features.

Company Development Programme
Finance of up to £75,000 is available as working capital funding into companies to support a slate of film, television and multi-media projects and to develop the commercial success of that company.

Short Film Award Schemes
On an annual, basis, Scottish Screen will consider applications, of up to £60,000 from outside bodies to operate short film production schemes. Previous examples included Cineworks operated by the Glasgow Media Access Centre.

Twenty First Films - Low Budget Film Scheme
This scheme offers support for low budget features (including feature documentaries) with budgets up to around £600,000.

Sgrîn, Media Agency for Wales

The Bank, 10 Mount Stuart Square
Cardiff Bay
Cardiff CF10 5EE
Tel: 029 2033 3300
Fax: 029 2033 3320
email: sgrin@sgrin.co.uk
Website: www.sgrin.co.uk
Head of Production - Judith Higginbottom
Short Film and New Talent Manager - Gaynor Messer Price
Lottery Manager - Anneli Jones
Sgrîn, Media Agency for Wales, is the primary organisation for film, television and new media in Wales. Sgrîn distributes lottery funding for film in Wales. Sgrin also runs short film schemes and a script reading service for those resident in Wales, and provides funding support for cinema venues, both public and private, cultural and interpretive printed and audiovisual material which complements and promotes exhibition programmes, and events. Guidelines and deadlines are available on request. The European Union Media Antenna is located at Sgrin, as is the New Media Group Wales and the Wales Screen Commission location service. For more information please visit www.sgrin.co.uk

Regional Screen Agencies

These agencies were established to develop and promote moving image culture in each region.

EM-MEDIA

35 - 37 St Mary's Gate
Nottingham NG1 1PU
Tel: 0115 934 9090
Fax: 0115 950 0988
email: anna.dawson@em-media.org.uk
Website: www.em-media.org.uk
Chief Executive: Ken Hay
Head of Education and Training Anna Dawson
EM Media is the regional screen agency for the East Midlands (Derbyshire, Leicestershire, Lincolnshire, Northamptonshire, Nottinghamshire and Rutland). It aims to develop a vibrant regional media culture and industry across a range of areas, from supporting feature and short film production, offering talent and business support, to locations advice, education initiatives, independent cinema and training. Investment funds include RIFE (Regional Investment Fund for England) Lottery and Treasury on behalf of the UK Film Council, and a range of European funds for production and training activities. EM Media seeks to invest in organisations and projects which meets one or more of its priorities. Further information can be found at www.em-media.org.uk

Film London

20 Euston Centre
Regent's Place
London NW1 3JH
Tel: 020 7387 8787
Fax: 020 7387 8788
email: info@filmlondon.org.uk
Website: www.filmlondon.org.uk
Adrian Wooton, Chief Executive Officer
Gill Henderson, Head of Industry and Cultural Development
Sue Hayes, Film Commissioner
Daniela Kirchner, Head of Information and Strategy
On 1st April 2003 the London Film Commission (LFC) and the London Film and Video Development Agency (LFVDA) were brought together to form Film London, the new single strategic agency for the development of film and the screen sector in London. Film London is an independent company supported by the UK Film Council and other funders. It has a board chaired by the film producer Sandy Lieberson. Film London will provide an integrated service in production and business support, training, film locations, cinema education and exhibition.

East London Moving Image Initiative (ELMII)

This initiative builds on the successful East London Film Fund and is primarily aimed at business support and project development for companies and individuals based in the East London region. The project is coordinated through the LFVDA and has eleven culturally diverse partners, including four London boroughs and local media businesses. There will be small awards available through local London Borough production schemes. For further details check the LFVDA website.

London Borough Production Awards

Also visit the site for details of London Borough production awards such as the Croydon Film And Video Awards, Enfield Film Fund, Newham Film Fund, Tower Hamlets Film Fund, Waltham Forrest Production Fund and the Wandsworth Film Fund

London Film and Video Development Agency

(See Film London)

Northern Film & Media

Central Square
Forth Street
Newcastle upon Tyne NE1 3PJ
Tel: 0191 269 9200
Fax: 0191 269 9213
email: info@northernmedia.org
Website: www.northernmedia.org
Chief Executive: Tom Harvey
Northern Film & Media has been set up to strategically invest in the content and media industry in the North East (County Durham, Northumberland, Tees Valley and Tyne & Wear) and aims to build a vibrant and sustainable film, media and digital content industry and culture in the North. Northern Film & Media offers a range of funding schemes covered by five strands: the development of people, content, companies, audiences, and networks. Northern Film & Media also offers advice and support on production services and locations to content production companies interested in basing their projects in the region.

North West Vision
Unit 203a
The Tea Factory
Wood Street
Liverpool L1 4DQ
Tel: 0151 708 9858
Fax: Contact North West Vision
email: info@northwestvision.co.uk
Website: www.northwestvision.co.uk
Chief Executive: Alice Morrison
North West Vision is the media development agency for the North West region (Cheshire, Cumbria, Greater Manchester, Lancashire and Merseyside) established in April 2002 to provide a single support structure for a whole raft of cultural and industrial moving image initiatives. The agency provides funding for film and television projects and practitioners based in the North West, locations support, crewing resources, advice on post-production and facilities, support for various cultural initiatives such as arthouse cinemas and festivals, and help and advice for emerging and established filmmakers throughout the region. The fund will cover three strands: Production Development, Audience Development, and Individual & Organisational Development. NB. The telephone and fax numbers for North West Vision have changed. Call the above number for a recorded message or check the website for up to date details.

Screen East

1st Floor
2 Millennium Place
Norwich NR2 1TF
Tel: 01603 776920
Fax: 01603 767191
email: info@screeneast.co.uk
Website: www.screeneast.co.uk
Chief Executive: Laurie Hayward
Screen East is the regional agency dedicated to developing, supporting and promoting every aspect of film, television and the moving image in the east of England (Bedfordshire, Cambridgeshire, Essex, Hertfordshire, Norfolk and Suffolk). Supported and funded by The UK Film Council through the Regional Investment Fund for England (RIFE) programme. RIFE is being implemented to strengthen film

industry and culture in the regions, giving more opportunities to audiences, new and established filmmakers and media businesses. Screen East's activities encompass the following areas: Production, Locations, Company Development, Training, Screenwriter Development, Exhibition, and Archives. Check their website for further information

Screen South

Folkestone Enterprise Centre
Shearway Business Park
Shearway Road
Folkestone
Kent CT19 4RH
Tel: 01303 298 222
Fax: 01303 298 227
email: info@screensouth.org
Screen South is the regional screen agency for the South East of England (Kent, Buckinghamshire, Oxfordshire, Hampshire, Surrey, Berkshire, East and West Sussex and the Isle of Wight). It is driving the development of a dynamic film & media industry and culture in the South through advocacy and the distribution of funds from the UK Film Council initiative Regional Investment In Film in England. Screen South are a resource that helps people get their ideas off the ground, whether they want to make a documentary, learn how to write successful scripts, set up a film festival or shoot a major movie here. In 2002-3 Screen South invested over £600,000 in the region, developing talented people; sustainable regional companies; creative content and new audiences, all adding up to creating a regional film culture. Check the Screen South website for further information www.screensouth.org.

Screen West Midlands

31-41 Bromley Street
Birmingham B9 4AN
Tel: 0121 766 1470
Fax: 0121 766 1480
email: info@screenwm.co.uk
Website: www.screenwm.co.uk
Chief Executive: Krysia Rozanska
Screen West Midlands is the regional agency working to support, promote and develop all screen media in the West Midlands. Their aim is to create a sustainable screen industry throughout the whole of the region; Birmingham and the Black Country, Herefordshire, Shropshire, Staffordshire, Warwickshire and Worcestershire. Whether film, television or new media related they can provide friendly and accurate advice for almost any enquiry and have two strands of funding: Production Development and Sector Development. Check their website, email them or call for further information

Screen Yorkshire

40 Hanover Square
Leeds LS3 1BQ
Tel: 0113 294 4410
Fax: 0113 294 4989
email: info@screenyorkshire.co.uk
Website: www.screenyorkshire.co.uk
Lead Officer: Jo Spreckley
Screen Yorkshire is the strategic agency for film, broadcast and the moving image sector in Yorks and the Humber. The aim is to lead the region's screen media industry to business growth and success by maximising opportunity, creating employment and promoting the vibrant creativity of the region

South West Screen

St Bartholomews
Lewins Mead
Bristol BS1 5BT
Tel: 0117 952 9977
Fax: 0117 952 9988
email:
firstname.surname@swscreen.co.uk
Website: www.swscreen.co.uk
Chief Executive: Caroline Norbury
Chair: Jeremy Payne
South West Screen is the regional organisation for film, video, television and digital media in the South West (Bristol, Cornwall, Devon, Dorset, Somerset, Wiltshire, and Gloucestershire). It offers advice and funding initiatives for: low-budget short and feature-length production; experimental and cross-genre cinema; exhibition projects. Check their website or call for further information

European and Pan-European Sources

Eurimages

Council of Europe
Palais de l'Europe
67075 Strasbourg Cédex
France
Tel: (33) 3 88 41 26 40
Fax: (33) 3 88 41 27 60
Website:
www.coe.int/T/E/Cultural_Co-operation/Eurimages/
Provides financial support for feature-length fiction films, documentaries, distribution and exhibition. Applications for co-production from the UK can only be accepted if a UK producer is a fourth co-producer in a tripartite co-production or the third in a bipartite, and provided the combined co-production percentage of all non-member states involved in the co-production does not exceed 30 per cent for multilateral co-productions and 20% for bi-lateral co-productions

Europa Cinemas

54, rue Beaubourg
F-75 003 Paris, France
Tel: (33) 1 42 71 53 70
Fax: (33) 1 42 71 47 55
email: europacinema@magic.fr
Website: www.europa-cinemas.org
Contact: Claude-Eric Poiroux, Fatima Djoumer
The objectives of this programme are to increase the programming of European film in film theatres, with European non-national films taking priority, to encourage European initiatives by exhibitors aimed at young audiences and to develop a network of theatres to enable joint initiatives at a national and European level

FilmFörderung Hamburg

Friedensalle 14-16
22765 Hamburg
Germany
Tel: 00 (49) 40 39837-0
Fax: 00 (49) 40 39837-10
email: filmfoerderung@ffhh.de
Website: www.ffhh.de
Executive Director: Eva Hubert
Subsidies available for: script development; pre-production; co-production and distribution. Producers of cinema films can apply for a subsidy amounting to at most

50 per cent of the overall production costs of the finished film. Foreign producers can also apply for this support. It is recommended to co-produce with a German partner. 150 per cent of the subsidy must be spent in Hamburg and part of the film should be shot in Hamburg. Financial support provided by the FilmFörderung Hamburg can be used in combination with other private or public funding, including that of TV networks

MEDIA Programme

MEDIA Plus Programme

European Commission, Directorate General X:
Education and Culture
rue de la Loi, 200
1049 Brussels, Belgium
Tel: (32) 2 299 11 11
Fax: (32) 2 299 92 14
email: eac-media@cec.eu.int
Website:
europa.eu.int/Comm/avpolicy/media/index_en.html
Head of Programme: Jacques Delmoly

The MEDIA Plus Programme (2001 - 2006) is a European Union initiative that aims at strengthening the competitiveness of the European audiovisual industry with a series of support measures dealing with the training of professionals, development of production projects, distribution and promotion of cinematographic works and audiovisual programmes. The programme was introduced in January 2001 as a follow- up to the MEDIA 2 programme. MEDIA Plus is managed by the Directorate General for Education and Culture at the European Commission in Brussels. It is managed on a national level by a network of 38 offices called the MEDIA Desks and Antennae

Programme Contents

MEDIA Training
The programme offers funding to training providers for vocational training initiatives. The Commission supports courses covering subjects including economic, financial and commercial management, use of new technologies, and scriptwriting techniques. MEDIA-supported courses are open to all MEDIA member state nationals. For details on how to participate in these courses, contact your local Desk, Antenna or Service.

MEDIA Development
The programme offers financial support to European independent production companies to develop new fiction, documentary, animation or multimedia projects. Financial support is offered to catalogues of projects (through the "slate funding" scheme) or to single projects. The amounts awarded will not exceed 50% of development budgets. If the project co-financed by MEDIA Plus goes into production the company has an obligation to reinvest the amount awarded by MEDIA in the development of their next project or projects. Companies may apply for funding at any time within the life of a Call for Proposals, which is usually published in autumn and lasts until summer next year. Please contact your local MEDIA Desk or Antenna for details.

MEDIA Distribution
The programme runs several schemes to support theatrical distribution and sales of European films. The Selective Scheme funds promotional campaigns of European non-national films. Distributors must apply in groupings of a minimum of three territories. The Automatic schemes for distributors and sales agents are based on their performance on the European market (admissions of European non-national films) and allow them to reinvest the funds generated through MEDIA support in minimum guarantees and/or P&A costs. A similar scheme is in preparation for video and DVD publishing. Non-repayable grants of up to E500,000 are available to TV producers for programmes that involve at least two European broadcasters. MEDIA Plus also provides support to networks of cinemas for the promotion and marketing of European films (e.g. Europa Cinemas). There are fixed deadlines for this funding.

MEDIA Promotion
The programme offers financial support to encourage all kinds of promotional activities designed to facilitate European producers and distributors' access at major European and international events. It supports European film festivals and festival networks. There are fixed deadlines running throughout the year.

MEDIA Pilot Projects
The programme offers support for initiatives involving the use of digital technologies in the following areas:
Distribution: creation of digital interactive audio-visual services providing access to European content in a multilingual form.
Exhibition: activity to stimulate the introduction of digital technologies for the theatrical distribution and exhibition of European audio-visual works. Promotion: creation and co-ordination of a dynamic index of all European audio-visual content produced, to be made available through on-line access.

MEDIA i2i Initiative
Support for companies who raise finance through bank discounting. MEDIA Plus offers European producers 50,000 Euro per project to subsidise the costs of insurance policies, the completion guarantee and financing costs. Producers can submit several projects. The maximum contribution to one company is 100,000 Euro. Independent European production companies who either raised finance from a bank or financial institution which is a partner of the EIB Group, or received Slate Funding under the MEDIA Plus Programme are eligible.

Contact Details

Members of the UK MEDIA team listed below should be the first point of contact for UK companies or organisations seeking information and advice on the MEDIA Plus programme. Guidelines and application forms for all schemes are available from their website: http://www.mediadesk.co.uk. However, all completed application forms should be sent directly to the MEDIA Programme office in Brussels, details of which you will find below.

UK MEDIA Desk

Fourth Floor
66-68 Margaret Street
London W1W 8SR
Agnieszka Moody
Tel: 020 7323 9733
Fax: 020 7323 9747
email: england@mediadesk.co.uk

MEDIA Service Northern Ireland

Third Floor
Alfred House
21 Alfred Street
Belfast BT2 8ED
Cian Smyth
Tel: 02890 232 444
Fax: 02890 239 918
email: media@niftc.co.uk
Website: www.mediadesk.co.uk

MEDIA Antenna Scotland

249 West George Street
Glasgow G2 4QE
Emma Valentine
Tel: 0141 302 1776
Fax: 0141 302 1778
email: scotland@mediadesk.co.uk
Website: www.mediadesk.co.uk

MEDIA Antenna Wales

The Bank
10 Mount Stuart Square
Cardiff Bay
Cardiff CF10 5EE
Gwion Owain
Tel: 02920 333 304
Fax: 02920 333 320
email: antenna@sgrin.co.uk

MEDIA Office in Brussels

MEDIA Programme
European Commission
DG-EAC (B-100 04/22)
Rue Belliard 100
B-1049 Brussels
Belgium
Head of Unit: Jacques Delmoly
Head of Development: Domenico Raneri
Head of Distribution: Hughes Becquart
Head of Training: Judith Johannes
Head of Promotion/Festivals: Elena Braun

INTERNATIONAL SALES

Action Time
35-38 Portman Square
London W1H 0NU
Tel: 020 7486 6688
Fax: 020 7612 7524
email: info@actiontime.co.uk
Website: www.action-time.com
Action Time has a catalogue of entertainment programming including lifestyle, comedy reality and game shows

Alibi Films International
35 Long Acre
London WC2E 9JT
Tel: 020 7845 0400
Fax: 020 7836 6919
email: info@alibifilms.co.uk
Website: www.alibifilms.co.uk
Roger Holmes
Alibi is active in feature film financing, international sales and distribution and the production of feature film, television drama and children's programming. Titles include: One More Kiss (1999), One of the Hollywood Ten (2000), The Most Fertile Man in Ireland (2001) and The Hard Word (2002)

APTN (Associated Press Television News)
The Interchange
Oval Road, Camden Lock
London NW1 7DZ
Tel: 020 7482 7400
Fax: 020 7413 8327
Website: www.aptn.com
N. Parsons, David Simmons
International TV news, features, sport, entertainment, documentary programmes and archive resources. APTN have camera crews globally situated as well as in-house broadcasting and production facilities

AV Pictures Ltd
3rd Floor,
102 Dean Street
London W1D 3TQ
Tel: 020 7758 1484
Fax: 020 7758 1491
email: info@avpictures.co.uk
Vic Bateman
International sales agent for independent producers of commercial films. Titles include: Dog Soldiers and School For Seduction

Axiom Films
12 D'Arblay Street
London W1V 3FP
Tel. 020 7287 7720
Fax. 020 7287 7740
email: mail@axiomfilms.co.uk
Website: www.axiomfilms.co.uk
Douglas Cummins
Features include Mullet (2001), Beneath Clouds (2002), Tosca (2002), The Bank (2001), Small Cuts (2001), El Bola (2002) and Life and Debt (2002)

BBC Worldwide
Woodlands
80 Wood Lane
London W12 0TT
Tel: 020 8433 2000
Fax: 020 8749 0538
Website: www.bbcworldwide.com
International programming distribution, videos for education and training, co-production and library footage sales.

Beyond Films
3rd Floor
22 Newman Street
London W1T 1PH
Tel: 020 7636 9611
Fax: 020 7636 9622
email: hilary-davis@beyond.com.au
Website: www.beyond.com.au
Hilary Davis, Stephen Kellher, Nick Kilcoyne
Film titles include: Strictly Ballroom, Love & Other Catastrophes, Love Serenade, Kiss or Kill, Heaven's Burning, SLC Punk, Orphans, Two Hands, Paperback Hero, The Business of Strangers, The Hard Word, Lantana, Crackerjack, Three Blind Mice

bfi Archival Footage Sales
21 Stephen Street
London W1T 1LN
Tel: 020 7957 8934
Fax: 020 7580 5830
email: footage.films@bfi.org.uk
Website: www.bfi.org.uk
Jan Faull
Simon Brown
Material from the largest collection of film footage in Britain - the bfi's National Film and Television Archive. Television, films, documentaries, newsreels and animation are all covered with over 350,000 titles to choose from, including material dating back to 1895. The first stop for serious research on the subjects that have shaped the past century. Research facilities available

bfi Sales
21 Stephen Street
London W1T 1LN
Tel: 020 7957 8909
Fax: 020 7580 5830
email: sales.films@bfi.org.uk
Website: www.bfi.org.uk
John Flahive, Film Sales Manager
Laurel Warbrick-Keay, Film Sales Co-ordinator
Sales of bfi-produced features, shorts and documentaries, archival and acquired titles including: early features by Peter Greenaway and Derek Jarman; Free Cinema; shorts by famous directors including Ridley Scott, Stephen Frears and Sally Potter; shorts by new directors including Lynne Ramsay, Sean Ellis and Tinge Krishnan; and from the archives - South (1919) and The Edge of the World

Boudicca
8 Cotton's Gardens
London E2 8DN
Tel: 020 7613 5882
Fax: 020 7613 5882
email: sales@boudiccafilms.com
Website: www.boudiccafilms.com
Ray Brady
British independent sales and distribution company set up by producer/director Ray Brady.

British Home Entertainment
5 Broadwater Road
Walton-on-Thames
Surrey KT12 5DB
Tel: 01932 228832
Fax: 01932 247759
email:
cw@britishhomeentertainment.co.uk
Website:
www.britishhomeentertainment.co.uk

Clive Williamson
Video distribution and TV marketing company. Titles include An Evening with the Royal Ballet, Othello, The Mikado, The Soldier's Tale, Uncle Vanya, King and Country, The Hollow Crown and The Merry Wives of Windsor

Capitol Films

23 Queensdale Place
London W11 4SQ
Tel: 020 7471 6000
Fax: 020 7471 6012
Website: www.capitolfilms.com
International film production, financing and sales company. Recent titles include Gosford Park (2001), Ghost World (2001), Spider (2002) and Anything Else (2003)

Carlton International

35-38 Portman Square
London W1H 0NU
Tel: 020 7224 3339
Fax: 020 7486 1707
Website: www.carltonint.co.uk
Head of Sales: Judith Howton
International TV programme and film sales agent, representing Carlton Television, Central Television, HTV, ITN Productions and Meridian Broadcasting as well as a growing number of independent production companies.
Carlton's collection includes over 1500 films and over 18,000 hours of television programming and incorporates the ITC Library aquired by Carlton International in 1999. The ITC Library includes such celebrated films as The Eagle has Landed,The Big Easy,The Boys from Brazil, On Golden Pond, Farewell My Lovely, Sophie's Choice and The Last Seduction. It also features a huge array of classic TV series including The Saint, The Prisoner, Randall and Hopkirk (Deceased) and Space 1999, and popular children's programmes including Gerry Anderson's Thunderbirds, Joe 90 and Captain Scarlet. Carlton's collections also include the Rohauer Library (classic silent films), the Korda Library (many classic British films of the 1930s), the Romulus Library (films produced by John Woolf's company), and the Rank Library (a major library of British films dating from the 1930s to the 1980s).

Channel Four International

124 Horseferry Road
London SW1 2TX
Tel: 020 7396 4444
Fax: 020 7306 8363
Website: www.c4international.com
Managing Director: Paul Sowerbutts
Handles Channel 4 television material and incorporates the Film Four catalogue.

Chatsworth Television Distributors

97-99 Dean Street
London W1D 3TE
Tel: 020 7734 4302
Fax: 020 7437 3301
email: info@chatsworth-tv.co.uk
Website: www.chatsworth-tv.co.uk

Cobalt

4th Floor
5-7 Carnaby Street
London W1F 9PB
Tel: Tel. 020 7292 2800
Fax: Fax. 020 7292 2830/40
Website: www.cobaltmg.com
Titles include Shade

Columbia TriStar International Television

Sony Pictures, Europe House
25 Golden Square
London W1R 6LU
Tel: 020 7533 1000
Fax: 020 7533 1246
European TV production and network operations and international distribution of Columbia TriStar's feature films and TV product

Cumulus Distribution

Sanctuary House
45-53 Sinclair Road
London W14 0NS
Tel: Tel. 020 7300 6624
Fax: Fax. 020 7300 6529
Website: www.entercloud9.com
Subsidiary of Cloud 9 Screen Entertainment. Titles include The Tribe and Revelations

DLT Entertainment UK Ltd

10 Bedford Square
London WC1B 3RA
Tel: 020 7631 1184
Fax: 020 7636 4571
John Bartlett, John Reynolds, Gary Mitchell
Specialising in comedy and drama production and sales. Recent titles include: My Family (4 series), Meet My Folks and As Time Goes By for BBC Television

Documedia International Films Ltd

19 Widegate Street
London E1 7HP
Tel: 020 7625 6200
Fax: 020 7625 7887
Distributors of innovative and award winning drama specials, drama shorts, serials, tele-movies and feature films; documentary specials and series; for worldwide sales and co-production

Endemol UK

Shepherds Building Central
Charecroft Way
London W14 0EE
Tel: 0870 333 1700
Website: www.endemoluk.com
Licensing and distributing international rights to Endemol programmes and formats

Entertainment Rights

100 Hammersmith Road
Colet Court
London W6 7JP
Tel: 020 8762 6200
Fax: 020 8762 6299
Website:
www.entertainmentrights.com
Claire Derry

Fremantle International Distribution

FremantleMedia Enterprises
1 Stephen Street
London W1T 1AL
Tel: 020 7691 6000
Fax: 020 7691 6060
Email: fidsales@fremantlemedia.com
Website: www.fremantlemedia.com
Managing Director: Brian Harris
Executive Vice President: Joe Abrams

Goldcrest Films International

65/66 Dean Street
London W1D 4PL
Tel: 020 7437 8696
Fax: 020 7437 4448
Major feature film production, sales and finance company. Recent films include Space Truckers, Clockwatchers and To End All Wars starring Robert Carlyle. Library titles include The Mission, The Killing Fields and Name of the Rose

Granada International

48 Leicester Square
London WC2H 7FB
Tel: 020 7493 7677
Fax: 020 7491 1441
email: int.info@granadamedia.com
Website:
www.granadamedia.com/international
Nadine Nohr, Managing Director

Granada International is responsible for more than 15,000 hours of animation, reality, factual, drama, comedy, natural history, wildlife, entertainment and lifestyle programming. Granada International is part of Granada plc.

HanWay Films
24 Hanway Street
London W1T 1UH
Tel: 020 7290 0750
Fax: 020 7290 0751
Website: www.hanwayfilms.com
Theirry Wase-Bailey
Specialised film sales company. Titles include Rabbit-Proof Fence, Young Adam, The Dreamers

High Point
25 Elizabeth Mews
London NW3 4UH
Tel: Tel. 020 7586 3686
Fax: Fax. 020 7586 3117
email: info@highpointfilms.co.uk
Website: www.highpointfilms.co.uk
Titles include Ken Russell's The Fall of the House of Usher and Twin Sisters (2003)

Hollywood Classics
8 Cleveland Gardens
London W2 6HA
Tel: 020 7262 4646
Fax: 020 7262 3242
email: info@hollywoodclassics.com
Website: www.hollywoodclassics.com
Melanie Tebb
Hollywood Classics has offices in London and Los Angeles and sells back catalogue titles of major Hollywood studios for theatrical release in all territories outside North America. Also represents an increasing library of European and independent American titles and has all rights to catalogues from various independent producers

IAC Film
Greencoat House
15 Francis Street
London SW1P 1DH
Tel: 020 7592 1620
Fax: 020 7592 1627
email: general@iacholdings.co.uk
Fred Hedman

Icon Entertainment International
The Quadrangle, 4th Floor
180 Wardour Street
London W1V 3AA
Tel: 020 7494 8100
Fax: 020 7494 8151
Website: www.icon-online.com
Nick Hill, CEO
Andy Mayson, COO
Simon Crowe, Head of Sales
Caroline Johnson, Head of Marketing
Forthcoming titles include Jindabyne (Ray Lawrence) The Passion (Mel Gibson)

Indigo
116 Great Portland Street
London W1W 6PJ
Tel: 020 7612 1700
Fax: 020 7612 1705
email: info@indigofilm.com
Website: www.indigofilm.com
David Lawley, Managing Director

London Films
71 South Audley Street
London W1Y 5FF
Tel: 020 7499 7800
Fax: 020 7499 7994
Website: www.londonfilms.com
Andrew Luff
Founded in 1932 by Alexander Korda. Co-productions with the BBC include Poldark and I Claudius. More recent series include Lady Chatterley directed by Ken Russell and The Scarlet Pimpernel starring Richard E.Grant

Myriad Pictures
Cavendish House
51-55 Mortimer Street
London W1W 8HJ
Tel: 020 7580 9200
Fax: 020 7290 0844
Website: www.myriadpictures.com
Georgina Mortimer
Myriad Pictures is involved in the financing, production and worldwide sales of major motion pictures and television programming. Recent features include Imagining Argentina, Eulogy, The Good Girl, Van Wilder, People I Know, Jeepers Creepers 2

NBD Television
Unit 2, Royalty Studios
105 Lancaster Road
London W11 1QF
Tel: 020 7243 3646
Fax: 020 7243 3656
email: distribution@nbdtv.com
Website: www.nbdtv.com
Nicky Davies Williams, Andrew Winter, Sales Manager, Matt Cowley, Sales Executive
Company specialising in music and light entertainment

Orbit Media Ltd
80a Dean Street
London W1D 3SN
Tel: 020 7287 4264
Fax: 020 7287 0984
Website: www.orbitmedia.co.uk
Chris Ranger, Jordan Reynolds
Specialises in vintage product from the first decade of American TV: The Golden Years of Television 1960s and '70s film catalogue. Classic comedy packages

Paramount Television
49 Charles Street
London W1J 5EW
Tel: 020 7318 6400
Fax: 020 7491 2086
Website: www.paramount.com
Stephen Tague
Television sales office

Peakviewing Transatlantic
Suite 6, Avionics House
Quedgeley Enterprise Centre
Nass Lane
Quedgley
Gloucestershire GL2 4SN
Tel: 01452 722202
Fax: 01452 723302
email: info@peakviewing.co.uk
Website: www.peakviewing.co.uk

Photoplay Productions
21 Princess Road
London NW1 8JR
Tel: 020 7722 2500
Fax: 020 7722 6662
Kevin Brownlow, Patrick Stanbury
TV production company. Resoration and presentation of silent films. Archive of silent era cinema.

Portman Film and Television
21-25 St. Anne's Court
London W1F OBJ
Tel: 020 7494 8024
Fax: 020 7494 8046
email: sales@portmanfilm.com
Website: www.portmanfilm.com
Tristan Whalley

Renaissance Films
34-35 Berwick Street
London W1F 8RP
Tel: 020 7287 5190
Fax: 020 7287 5191
email: info@renaissance-films.com
Website: www.renaissance-films.com
Angus Finney, Managing Director
Claire Taylor, Head of International Sales
Sophie Janson, Head of Development & Acquisitions
Michaela Piper, Head of Marketing & Publicity

RM Associates
Shepherds West
Rockley Road
London W14 0DA
Tel: 020 7605 6600
Fax: 020 7605 6610
Website: www.rmassociates.co.uk
RM Associates work with numerous broadcasters and independent producers to bring together a comprehensive catalogue of music and arts programming available for television and video worldwide.

S4C International
50 Lambourne Crescent
Llanishen
Cardiff CF4 5DU
Tel: 029 20 741440
Fax: 029 20 754444
email: international@s4c.co.uk
Website: www.s4ci.com
Rhianydd Darwin, Head of International Sales
Huw Walters, Head of Co Productions
The commercial arm of S4C, the fourth television channel in Wales - distribution and co-production, including documentary and animation titles

Safir Films Ltd
49 Littleton Rd
Harrow
Middx HA1 3SY
Tel: 020 8423 0763
Fax: 020 8423 7963
email: lsafir@attglobal.net
Lawrence Safir
Hold rights to numerous Australian, US and UK pictures, including Sam Spiegel's Betrayal

Screen Ventures
49 Goodge Street
London W1T 1TE
Tel: 020 7580 7448
Fax: 020 7631 1265
email: info@screenventures.com
Website: www.screenventures.com
Christopher Mould
Specialise in international film, TV and video licensing of music, drama and arts featuring such artists as John Lennon, Bob Marley and Nirvana. Worldwide sales representation for international record companies and independent producers. Screen Ventures is also an independent producer of television documentaries and music programming.

Short Film Bureau
74 Newman Street
London W1T 3EL
Tel: 020 7636 2400
Fax: 020 7636 8558
email: sales@shortfilmbureau.com
Website: www.shortfilmbureau.com
Dawn Sharpless
International sales agent for short films. Sells to traditional outlets such as terrestrial, cable and satellite television, as well as new media such as DVD, Broadband, narrowband and WAP

SMG
3 Waterhouse Square
138-142 Holborn
London EC1N 2NY
Tel: 020 7882 1000
Fax: 020 7882 1020
Website: www.smg.plc.uk
The televison division of SMG incorporates Scottish Television, Grampian Television, Ginger Television and SMG TV Productions.

Southern Star
45-49 Mortimer Street
London W1N 7TD
Tel: 020 7636 9421
Fax: 020 7436 7426
Website: www.southernstargroup.com
Southern Star is an international television rights group. The companies within the group are:
Carnival (Films & Theatre)
Pavilion International
Delta Ventures
Production Finance & Management
Independent Wildlife
Harlequin Films & Television
Oxford Scientific Films

Sullivan Entertainment
Suites 30-32, Savant House
63-65 Camden High Street
London NW1 7JL
Tel: Tel. 020 7383 5192
Fax: Fax. 020 7383 0627
email: info@sullivan-ent.co.uk
Website: www.sullivan-ent.co.uk
Muriel Thomas
International sales office of Canadian production company and distributor.

Twentieth Century Fox Television
31-32 Soho Square
London W1V 6AP
Tel: 020 7437 7766
Fax: 020 7439 1806
Website: www.fox.co.uk
Stephen Cornish, Vice President
Randall Broman, Director of Sales
TV sales and distribution. A News Corporation company

TWI
McCormack House
3 Burlington Lane
London W4 2TH
Tel: 020 8233 5300
Fax: 020 8233 5301
Website: www.imgworld.com
The world's largest independent producer and distributor of sports programmes, TWI is owned by IMG Group and specialises in sports and factual programming (including BAFTA-winning titles). Titles include: Trans World Sport, Futbol Mundial, PGA European Tour productions, ATP Tour highlights, West Indies Test Cricket, Oddballs, A-Z of Sport, Goal!, The Olympic Series, Century and The Whitbread Round The World Race

Universal Pictures International (UPI)
Prospect House
80-110 New Oxford Street
London WC1A 1HB
Tel: 020 7079 6000
Fax: 020 7079 6500
Website: www.unistudios.com

VCI
Demon Music Group
4th Floor
Holden House
57 Rathbone Place
London W1P 1AB
Tel: 020 7396 8888
Fax: 020 7470 6655
Website: www.vci.co.uk
Paul Hembury, programming and acquisitions director
A wholly owned subsidiary of VCI PLC, responsible for all overseas activities. Distributes a wide variety of product including music, sport, children's, fitness, documentary, educational, special interest and features

Vine International Pictures
VIP House
Greenacres
New Road Hill
Downe
Orpington Kent BR6 7JA
Tel: 01689 854 123
Fax: 01689 850 990
email: info@vine-international.co.uk
Website: www.vine-international.co.uk
Marie Vine, Barry Gill
Sale of feature films such as Rainbow, The Pillow Book, The Ox and the Eye, Younger and Younger, The Prince

of Jutland, Erik the Viking, Let Him Have It, Trouble in Mind. Forthcoming titles include Jericho Mansions

Walt Disney Television International

3 Queen Caroline Street
Hammersmith
London W6 9PA
Tel: 020 8222 1000
Fax: 020 8222 2795
Website: www.disney.co.uk
MD: Etienne de Villiers
VP, Sales & Marketing: Keith Legoy
International television arm of major US production company.

Warner Bros International Television

98 Theobalds Road
London WC1X 8WB
Tel: 020 7494 3710
Fax: 020 7287 9086
Website: www.wbitv.com
Richard Milnes, Donna Brett, Tim Horan, Ian Giles
TV sales, marketing and distribution. A division of Warner Bros Distributors Ltd, a Time Warner Entertainment Company

Winchester Film & Television Sales Ltd

19 Heddon Street
London W1B 4BG
Tel: 020 7851 6500
Fax: 020 7851 6505
email: mail@winchesterent.co.uk
Website: www.winchesterent.com
Billy Hurman
Winchester Entertainment encompasses Winchester Films, handling feature film finance and sales, and Winchester Television, producer and sales agent of children's TV properties.
Titles include; Last Orders, Shooting Fish, Heartbreakers, Harv The Barbarian, Red Dwarf, Wheels On The Bus, Bounty Hamster.

The Works

Portland House
4 Great Portland Street
London W1W 8QJ
Tel: Tel. 020 7612 1080
Fax: Fax. 020 7612 1081
Website: www.theworksltd.com
Aline Perry, CEO
Rebecca Kearey, Head of Marketing
Joy Wong, Head of International Sales
Formerly known as The Sales Company, now owned by Civilian Content. Recent titles include Bend It Like Beckham, In This World, Bright Young Things, Country of My Skull and 24 Hour Party People

LABORATORIES

Bucks Laboratories Ltd
714 Banbury Avenue
Slough
Berks SL1 4LR
Tel: 01753 501500
Fax: 01753 691762
Website: www.bucks.co.uk
Darren Fagg
Comprehensive lab services in Super 35mm and 35mm, Super 16mm and 16mm, starting Sunday night. West End rushes pick up unit 10.30 pm. Also day bath. Chromakopy: 35mm low-cost overnight colour reversal dubbing prints. Photogard: European coating centre for negative and print treatment. Chromascan: 35mm and 16mm video to film transfer

CFS in Soho
26 Berwick Street
London W1F 8RG
Tel: 020 7734 4543
Fax: 020 7734 6600
email:
cfsinsoho@colourfilmservices.co.uk
Website:
www.colourfilmservices.co.uk
Contact: GrahamTolley

Colour Film Services Group
10 Wadsworth Road
Perivale
Middx UB6 7JX
Tel: 020 8998 2731
Fax: 020 8997 8738
email:
johnward@colourfilmservices.co.uk
Website:
www.colourfilmservices.co.uk
D. John Ward
Film Laboratory: full 16mm and 35mm colour processing laboratory, with Super 16mm to 35mm blow up a speciality. Video Facility: broadcastt standard wet gate telecines and full digital edit suite. Video duplication, CD mastering and archiving to various formats. Superscan: unique tape to film transfer system in both Standard Resolution and High Resolution. Sounds Studios: analogue and digital dubbing, track laying, synching, voice overs and optical transfer bay

Deluxe Laboratories Limited
North Orbital Road
Denham, Uxbridge
Middlesex UB9 5HQ
Tel: 01895 832323
Fax: 01895 832446
Website: www.bydeluxe.com
Terry Lansbury
Deluxe London, together with Deluxe Hollywood, Deluxe Toronto and Deluxe
Italia are subsidiaries of Deluxe Entertainment Services Division, which
forms part of the Rank Group. Comprehensive World-wide laboratory services
to the Motion picture and Commercial industries. London and Toronto
include video transfer suites. Toronto has complete sound and dubbing
suites. Part of the London operation is Capital FX, an established Digital and Optical Effects Company, offering a wide variety of facilities for Film
and TV post-production.

Film and Photo Ltd*
13 Colville Road
South Acton Industrial Estate
London W3 8BL
Tel: 020 8992 0037
Fax: 020 8993 2409
email: info@film-photo.co.uk
Website: www.film-photo.co.uk
Managing Director: Tony Scott
Post production motion picture laboratory. 16/35mm Colour & B/W reversal dupes. 16/35mm b/w neg/pos. 35mm E6 camera reversal processing. Tape to film transfers. Nitrate restoration/preservation

Film Lab North Ltd
Croydon House
Croydon Street
Leeds LS11 9RT
Tel: 0113 243 4842
Fax: 0113 2434323
email: hnd@filmlabnorth.co.uk
Website: www.filmlabnorth.co.uk
Howard Dawson
Full service in 16mm colour Negative Processing, 16mm colour printing, 35mm colour printing video transfer. Super 16mm a speciality - Plus 35mm colour grading and printing

Hendersons Film Laboratories
18-20 St Dunstan's Road
South Norwood
London SW25 6EU
Tel: 020 8653 2255
Fax: 020 8653 9773
email: sales@hensersonsfilmlabs.com
Website: www.hendersonsfilmlab.com
Hendersons offers a comprehensive lab service in 16mm and 35mm colour and black and white. Reversal a speciality as is the preservation of nitrate film footage

Sky Photographic Services Ltd
Ramillies House
Ramillies Street
London W1V 2EL
Tel: 0207 4342266
Fax: 0207 4340828
email: info@skyphoto.demon.co.uk
Website: www.sky-photographic.co.uk
Mike Sherry, Managing Director

Soho Images
8-14 Meard Street
London W1V 3HR
Tel: 020 7437 0831
Fax: 020 7734 9471
email: sohogroup.com
Website: www.sohoimages.com
Soho Laboratories offer day and night printing and processing of 16mm (including Super 16mm) and 35mm colour or b/w film

Technicolor Film Services

Technicolor Ltd
Bath Road
West Drayton
Middx UB7 0DB
Tel: 020 8759 5432
Fax: 020 8759 6270
Website: www.technicolor.com
Mike Howell
West End pick-up and delivery point:
F.M.F.
52 Berwick Street
London W1F 8SL
Tel: 020 7287 5596
Technicolor is a worldwide film and telecine operation, with laboratories in Hollywood, London, Rome, New York and Montreal. It offers a 24 hour service covering all film formats - 16mm, 35mm and 65mm large screen presentation. The extensive sound service operation complements customers' requirements by offering transfers to all digital formats. The newly created Technicolor Imaging is designed to service feature, commercial and 16mm drama/documentary markets. Five telecine suites accommodate two ITK Millennium telecines, URSA and two high grade Rank Cintel machines. Other services include feature mastering, drama finishing, sound laybacks, DVD video and audio pre-mastering all available under the same secure roof making Technicolor Europe's largest and most comprehensive film processing laboratory

Todd-AO UK

13 Hawley Crescent
London NW11 8NP
Tel: 020 7284 7900
Fax: 020 7284 1018
Website: www.todd-ao.co.uk
Roger Harlow
Complete 35mm, Super 16 and 16mm film processing laboratory and sound transfer service with full video post-production facility including Digital Wet Gate Telecines, D3, Digital Betacam, Betacam SP and other video formats. On-line editing, duplication and standards conversion. Sync sound and A+B roll negative to tape transfer, neg cutting service

University of East Anglia

East Anglian Film Archive
Norwich NR4 7TJ
Tel: 01603 592664
Fax: Fax 01603 593475
email: eafa@uea.ac.uk
Website: www.uea.ac.uk/eafa
Phil Butcher
The East Anglian Film Archive specialises in small gauge film work, including:-
Blow up film printing of Standard 8mm, Super 8mm, and 9.5mm to 16mm. Also centre perforation 17.5mm.
Transfer to video and DVD of Standard 8mm, Super 8mm, and 9.5mm
Conservation of Standard 8mm, Super 8mm, 9.5mm, centre perforation 17.5mm, and 35mm
Digital restoration service

LIBRARIES

This section provides a directory of libraries that have collections of books, periodicals, papers and other materials covering film and television. It includes a selection of libraries of academic institutions with graduate and post-graduate degree courses in the media and other organisations. Please contact the organisations directly or check websites (where available) for further details. Most of these collections are intended for student and teaching staff use: permission for access should always be sought from the Librarian first. Compiled by Ayesha Khan

bfi National Library

21 Stephen Street
London WIT 1LN
Tel: 020 7255 1444
020 7436 0165 (Information)
Fax: 020 7436 2338
The bfi National Library offers access to the world's largest collection of information on film and television. As a major national research collection the main priority is to provide comprehensive coverage of British film and television, but the collection itself is international in scope.

bfi National Library holdings

Books
Over 46,000 books covering all aspect of film and television ranging from reference books and biographies to published scripts, academic texts and broadcasting policy studies.
Periodicals
There are over 5,000 indexed periodical titles in the collection and over 400 are received every year from 45 countries.
Newspaper Cuttings
Over two million newspaper cuttings, mainly UK published, dating back to the 1930s. Most cuttings are stored on microfiche and are indexed according to film or programme title, personality, event, country and subject.
Scripts
Over 20,000 unpublished scripts, including production and post-production, and a number of television scripts. Translations used for earphone commentaries at the National Film Theatre are also held.
Publicity Materials
A wide range of materials is available from press releases to campaign books from the turn of the century, and festival catalogues dating back to the 1934 Venice Film Festival.
Unpublished Materials
Extensive collections of papers donated by individuals and organisations (including the British Board of Film Classification and BECTU).
Audio Tapes
The Library offers three main collections; 200 interviews from on-stage events at the National Film Theatre from 1962 onwards; the Denis Gifford Collection; and a major Oral History Project organised by BECTU.
CD-ROMs
Along with other indexes and CD-ROMs the bfi's CD-ROM film Index International provides filmographic data and periodical references relating to over 100,000 feature films from around the world.
SIFT (Summary of Information on Film and Television) Database
Access to the bfi's unique and extensive database dedicated to film and television is available in the Library. SIFT users can call up information on more than 500,000 films, television programmes and videos, plus one million personalities. 150,000 organisations and 6,000 events.

Access to the bfi National Library's holdings

The Reading Room
All of the collections are available for reference only in the Reading Room. Access to the Reading Room is available to either Day Pass holders or holders of the Library Annual Pass. The Majority of materials are stored in stacks, which are not open to users, but most can be consulted in the Reading Room. The book catalogue can be browsed in advance at www.bfi.org.uk/library/olib. Certain categories of material can only be consulted in the Special Collection study room. Staff are on hand and full details are available in the Reading Room to support users and help them get the best out of the collections.
Special Collections Unit
If you wish to consult unpublished materials or originals of press book publicity then this must be done in the Special Collections Unit at Stephen Street. It is necessary to book an appointment in advance, please ring 020 7957 4772 or email speccoll@bfi.org.uk.
Information Services
Collection information and providing answers to enquiries and research requests is an important part of the work of the bfi National Library. Further details can be found at www.bfi.org.uk/library/services. Charges are applicable for many requests.
Reading Room opening hours

Monday	10.30am - 5.30pm
Tuesday	10.30am - 8.00pm
Wednesday	1.00pm - 8.00pm
Thursday	10.30am - 8.00pm
Friday	10.30am - 5.30pm

Closed at weekends

Institutional pass:	£50.00
Annual Library pass:	£35.00
NFT Members pass:	£28.00
Annual Discount passes	£22.00*
Weekly pass	£15.00
Day pass	£ 6.00**

*Available to Senior Citizens, Registered Disabled and Unemployed upon proof of eligibility. Students may also apply for a discounted library pass.
**Available to anyone. Spaces may be reserved by giving 48 hours notice.
For more information on Institutional and Annual membership and to subscribe please call 020 7815 1374.
Enquiry Lines
The Enquiry Line is available for short enquiries. Frequent callers subscribe to an information service. The line is open from 10.00am to 5.00pm Monday to Friday - 020 7255 1444.

Aberdeen

Aberdeen University Library
Meston Walk
Aberdeen
Grampian AB24 3UE
Tel: 01224 272590
email: library@abdn.ac.uk
Website:
www.abdn.ac.uk/diss/library/
Contact: Librarian

Bath
Bath Spa University College
Sion Hill Library
8 Somerset Place
Bath BA1 5HB
Tel: 01225 875648
Website:
www.bathspa.ac.uk/departments/library
Contact: Helen Rayner (Campus Librarian)

Belfast
Belfast Central Library
Royal Avenue
Belfast
Co. Antrim BT1 1EA
Tel: 012890 509150
Contact: Librarian

Northern Ireland Film and Television Commission (Digital Film Archive)
3rd Floor Alfred House
21 Alfred Street
Belfast BT2 8ED
Tel: 44 28 902 32 444
Fax: 44 28 902 39 918
email: info@NIFTC.co.uk
Website: www.nifc.co.uk
Contact: Information Officer
Resources: Archive of moving images about Northern Ireland 1897-2000

Birmingham

Birmingham University Library
Information Services
Franchise Street
Perry Barr
Birmingham B42 2SU
Tel: 0121 331 5300
Fax: 0121 331 6543
Website: www.bham.ac.uk
Contact: Dean of Information Services

University of Central England
Birmingham Institute of Art & Design
Library Services
Corporation Street
Gosta Green
Birmingham B4 7DX
Tel: 0121 331 5860
Fax: Tel: 0121 331 5861
Website: http://library.uce.ac.uk
Contact: Subject Librarian

Vivid - Birmingham's Centre for Media Arts
Unit 311 The Big Peg
120 Vyse Street, Jewellery Quarter
Birmingham B18 6ND
Tel: 0121 233 4061
Fax: 0121 212 1784
email:info@vivid.org.uk
Website: www.vivid.org.uk
Contact: Marian Hall, Facilities Manager
Resources: Small library and archive of use to practitioners

Bradford
Bradford College
Grove Library
Great Horton Road
Bradford BD7 1AY
Tel: 01274 753156
Fax: 01274 389410
Website:
www.bradfordcollege.ac.uk/college/facilities/collfac/libraries
Contact: David Hawksworth (Art and Design Librarian)

National Museum of Film and Photography
Pictureville
Bradford BD1 1NQ
Tel: 01274 203377
Fax: 01274 772325
Website: www.nmpft.org.uk
Email: b.binder@nmsi.ac.uk
Contact: Enquiries

Brighton

Brighton Public Library
Vantage Point
New England Street
Brighton BN1 2GW
Tel: 01273 296961/57/69
Fax: 01273 296965
Email: blibrary@hotmail.com
Website: www.brighton-hove.gov.uk/bhc/libraries/

University of Brighton Faculty of Art, Design and Humanities
St Peter's House Library
16-18 Richmond Place
Brighton BN2 9NA
Tel: 01273 643221
Fax: 01273 607532
Website:
www.brighton.ac.uk/lis/lstpeter.
Contact: Information Services Manager

Bristol

Bristol City Council
Leisure Services
Central Library, Reference Library,
College Green
Bristol BS1 5TL
Tel: 0117 927 6121
Fax: 0117 922 6775
Contact: Head of Reference & Information Services

University of Bristol
University Library
Tyndall Avenue
Bristol BS8 1TJ
Tel: 0117 928 8000
Fax: 0117 925 5334
email: jez.conolly@bristol.ac.uk
Website: www.bris.ac.uk/is/
Contact: Jez Conolly (Subject Librarian)

University of Bristol Theatre Collection
Department of Drama
Cantocks Close
Bristol BS8 1UP
Tel: 0117 928 7836
Fax: 0117 928 7832
email: theatre-collection@bristol.ac.uk
Website: www.bristol.ac.uk/theatrecollection
Contact: Jo Elsworth

University of the West of England, Bristol
Faculty of Art, Media and Design Library
Bower Ashton Campus
Kennel Lodge Road
Bristol BS3 2JT
Tel: 0117 9344 4750
Fax: 0117 9344 4771
email: geoff.cole@uwe.ac.uk
Website: www.uwe.ac.uk/library
Contact: Geoff Cole, Campus/Subject Librarian, Art, Media and Design

Canterbury

Canterbury Christ Church College Library
North Holmes Road
Canterbury
Kent CT1 1QU
Tel: 01227 767700 ext. 2514
Website: http://.library/cant.ac.uk
Contact: Faculty Liaison Librarian

Kent Institute of Art & Design at Canterbury
New Dover Road
Canterbury
Kent CT1 3AN
Tel: 01227 769371
Fax: 01227 817500
email: librarycant@KIAD.ac.uk
Website: www.kiad.ac.uk
Kathleen Godfrey: Campus Librarian

Templeman Library
University of Kent at Canterbury
Templeman Library
Canterbury
Kent CT2 7NU
Tel: 01227 764000 ext.3573
Fax: 01227 823984
Website: www.ukc.ac.uk/library
Contact: Derek whitaker (Subject Librarian)

Cardiff

Cardiff University
Architecture Library
Bute Building
King Edward VII Avenue
Cardiff CF10 3NB
Tel: 02920 875975
Fax: 02920 874926
Website: www.cardiff.ac.uk/infos/centres/architecture
Contact: Librarian

Coleg Glan Hafren
Trowbridge Road
Rumney
Cardiff CF3 1XZ
Tel: 029 20 250250
Fax: 029 20 250339
Website: www.glan-hafren.ac.uk
Contact: Director of Learner and Learning Services

Carlisle

Cumbria Institute of the Arts Library
Brampton Road
Carlisle, Cumbria CA3 9AY
Tel: 01228 400312
Fax: 01228 514491
Website: www.cumbriacad.ac.uk
Contact: Librarian

Cheltenham

University of Gloucestershire
Pittville Learning Centre, Learning and Information Services
Pittville Campus
Albert Road, Pittville
Cheltenham
Gloucestershire GL52 3JG
Tel: 01242 532254
email: ajeffrey@glos.ac.uk
Website: www.glos.ac.uk
Contact: Annabel Jeffrey (Senior Information Advisor, Media and Design)

Chester

Chester College
Learning Resources
Park Gate Road
Chester CH1 4BJ
Tel: 01244 375444
Fax: 01244 392820
Website: www.chester.ac.uk/~smilne/
email: enquiries@chester.ac.uk
Contact: Fiona McLean (Subject Librarian)

Chislehurst

Ravensbourne College of Design and Communication Library
Walden Road, Chislehurst
Kent BR7 5SN
Tel: 020 8289 4919
email: library@rave.ac.uk
Website: www.rave.ac.uk
Contact: Librarian

Colchester

Colchester Institute
Sheepen Road
Colchester CO3 3LL
Tel: 01206 518642
Fax: 01206 518643
Website: www.colch-inst.ac.uk
Contact: Enquiries

University of Essex
Albert Sloman Library
Wivenhoe Park
Colchester CO4 3SQ
Tel: 01206 873192
Fax: 01206 872289
email: libcomment@essex.ac.uk
Website: libwww.essex.ac.uk

Coventry

Coventry City Library
Smithford Way
Coventry CV1 1FY
Tel: 024 76832336
Fax: 024 76832440
email: covinfo@discover.co.uk
Contact: Librarian

Lanchester Library
Frederick Lanchester Building
Coventry University
Gosford Street
Coventry CV1 5DD
Tel: 024 7688 7575
Fax: 024 7688 7543
email: s.silvester@coventry.ac.uk
Website: www.library.coventry.ac.uk
Contact: Stephanie Silvester (Subject Librarian, Arts, Design and Media)

University of Warwick Library
Gibbet Hill Road
Coventry CV4 7AL
Tel: 024 7652 4103
Fax: 024 7652 4211
Website: library.warwick.ac.uk
Contact: Librarian
Resources: Collection of German film programme from the 1930s

Derby

University of Derby
Briatannia Mill Learning Centre
Mackworth Road
Derby DE22 3BL
Tel: 01332 594050
Website:
lib.derby.ac.uk/library/homelib.html

Doncaster

Doncaster College
Church View Learning Resource Centre, Church View
Doncaster DN1 1RF
Tel: 01302 553816
Fax: 01302 553831
Website:
www.don.ac.uk/facilities/lrc.htm
email: janet.east@don.ac.uk
Contact: Janet East (Librarian)

Nova Film and Videotape Library
62 Ascot Avenue, Cantley
Doncaster DN4 6HE
Tel: 0870 765 1094
email: info@novaonline.co.uk
Website: www.novaonline.co.uk
Contact: Gareth Atherton
Resources: Non-fiction and archive film and contemporary videos.

Dorking

Surrey Performing Arts Library
Denbies Wine Estate
London Road
Dorking, Surrey RH5 6AA
Tel: 01306 875453
Fax: 01306 875074
email: performing.arts@surreycc.gov.uk

Website: www.surreycc.gov.uk/libraries
Contact: Enquiries
Resources: Scripts

Douglas

Douglas Corporation
Douglas Public Library
Ridgeway Street, Douglas
Isle of Man IM1 1EP
Tel: 01624 623021 ext. 251
Fax: 01624 662792
email: j.bowring@douglas.org.im
Contact: John Bowring (Librarian)

Dundee

Duncan of Jordanstone College of Art and Design Library
University of Dundee
Perth Road
Dundee DD1 4HT
Tel: 01382 345255
Fax: 01382 229283
email: dojlib@dundee.ac.uk
Website: www.dundee.ac.uk/library
Contact: College Librarian
Resources: Few scripts

Edinburgh

Edinburgh College of Art Library Service
Lauriston Place
Edinburgh
Scotland EH3 9DF
Tel: 0131 221 6034
Fax: 0131 221 6033
Website: www.lib.eca.ac.uk
Contact: Subject Librarian, Art and Design

Edinburgh University Library
George Square
Edinburgh EH8 9LG
Tel: 0131 650 1000
Fax: 0131 667 9780
email: library.ed.ac.uk
Website: www.lib.ed.ac.uk
Contact: Enquiries

Napier University
Merchiston Learning Centre
10 Colinton Road
Edinburgh
Scotland EH10 5DT
Tel: 0131 455 2582
Fax: 0131 455 2377
email: nulis.enquiry@napier.ac.uk
Website: nulis.napier.ac.uk
Contact: Information Services Advisor

National Library of Scotland
George IV Bridge
Edinburgh
Scotland EH1 1EW
Tel: 0131 226 4531
Fax: 0131 466 2804
Website: www.nls.uk
email: enquiries@nls.uk
Contact: Stephen Holland (Head of Collection Development)

Egham

Royal Holloway University of London Library
Egham Hill
Egham
Surrey TW20 OEX
Tel: 01784 443823
email: library@rhul.ac.uk
Website: www.lb.rhul.ac.uk
Contact: Librarian

Epsom

Surrey Institute of Art and Design
Epsom Library and Learning Resources Centre, Ashley Road
Epsom, Surrey KT18 5BE
Tel: 01372 202458
Fax: 01372 202457
Website: www.surrat.ac.uk/whoweare/learning_libraries.html
email: jseabourne@surrat.ac.uk
Contact: Jan Seabourne (site Librarian)

Exeter

Exeter University Library
Stocker Road
Exeter, Devon EX4 4PT
Tel: 01392 263861
Fax: 01392 263871
Website: www.ex.ac.uk/ library/
Contact: Librarian

University of Plymouth
Information and Learning Services – Exeter Campus
Earl Richard Road North
Exeter
Devon EX4 6HU
Tel: 01392 475059
Fax: 01392 475053
Website: www.plymouth.ac.uk
Contact: Enquiries

Farnham

Surrey Institute of Art & Design, University College
Farnham Campus
Falkner Road
The Hart, Farnham
Surrey GU9 7DS
Tel: 01252 722441
Fax: 01252 892616
Website: www.surrat.ac.uk
Contact: Institute Librarian
Registered users only

Gateshead

Gateshead Libraries and Arts Department
Central Library
Prince Consort Road
Gateshead
Tyne and Wear NE8 4LN
Tel: 0191 477 3478 ext 44
Fax: 0191 477 7454
Contact: Arts manager Ednie Wilson

Glasgow

Glasgow Caledonian University Library and Information Centre
Glasgow Caledonian University
Cowcaddens Road
Glasgow G4 0BA
Tel: 0141 331 3859
Website: www.lib.gcal.ac.uk
Contact: Enquiries

Glasgow City Libraries
Mitchell Library
North Street
Glasgow G3 7DN
Tel: 0141 287 2933
Fax: 0141 287 2933
Website: www.mitchellibrary.org
email: arts@gcl.glasgow.gov.uk
Contact: General Services Librarian

Scottish Screen Archive
1 Bowmont Gardens
Glasgow G12 9LR
Tel: 0141 337 7400
Fax: 0141 337 7413
email: archive@scottishscreen.com
Website: www.scottishscreen.com
Contact: Janet McBain (Archive Curator)
Resources: Production/Information Access to the Shiach Script library with over 100 feature and short film scripts. Video, publications resource. Internet site, National Archive collection of factual documentary material reflecting Scotland's social and cultural history. Available to broadcasters, programme makers, educational users and researchers. Distribution of Scottish shorts with back catalogue

University of Glasgow
The Library
Hillhead Street
Glasgow G12 8QE
Tel: 0141 330 6704
Fax: 0141 330 4952
Website: www.lib.gla.ac.uk
email: library@lib.gla.ac.uk
Contact: Subject Librarian

Gravesend

VLV - Voice of the Listener and Viewer Ltd
101 King's Drive
Gravesend
Kent DA12 5BQ
Tel: 01474 352835
Fax: 01474 351112
email: vlv@btinternet.com
Website: www.vlv.org.uk
Contact: VLV Librarian
Resources: VLV holds archives of the former Broadcasting Research Unit (1980-90) and British Action for Children's Television (1988-95). Access to these and VLV's own archive, which includes all VLV responses to government and public consultations and transcripts of most VLV conferences since 1984, can be arranged in Gravesend for a small fee

Hatfield

University of Hertfordshire Learning and Information Services
College Lane
Hatfield
Hertfordshire AL10 9AB
Tel: 01707 284678
Website: www.herts.ac.uk/lis/

Huddersfield

Kirklees Cultural Services
Central Library
Princess Alexandra Walk
Huddersfield HD1 2SU
Tel: 01484 221967
Fax: 01484 221974
Contact: Reference Librarian

Hull

University of Lincoln
Hull School of Art and Design
Learning Support Centre
Queens Gardens
Hull HU1 3DQ
Tel: 01482 462166
Fax: 01482 462101
Contact: Centre Manager

Keele

Keele Library Information Services
Keele University
Keele
Staffs ST5 5BG
Tel: 01782 583535
Fax: 01782 711553
Website: www.keele.ac.uk/depts/li/
email: libhelp@keele.ac.uk
Contact: Jim Linnell (Humanities subject Librarian)

Kingston Upon Thames

Kingston University Library Services
Knights Park Learning Resources Centre
Knights Park
Kingston Upon Thames
Surrey KT1 2QJ
Tel: 020 8547 7057
Fax: 020 8547 8039
email: library@kingston.ac.uk
Website: www.kingston.ac.uk/library_media/index.htm
Contact: Faculty Librarian (Design)

Kingston Museum & Heritage Service
Room 46 North Kingston Centre
Richmond Road
Kingston upon Thames
Surrey KT2 5PE
Tel: 020 8547 6738 or 6755
Website: www.kingston.gov/museum.muybridge
Contact: Paul Hill (Curator)
Resources: Eadweard Muyridge Collection. Pre-cinema images and artefacts

Lancaster

Lancaster University Library
Bailrigg
Lancaster LA1 4YH
Tel: 01524 592516
Website: libweb.lancs.ac.uk
email: library@lancs.ac.uk
Contact: Helen clash (Assistant Librarian)

Leeds

Leeds City Libraries
Central Library
Municipal Buildings
Calverley Street
Leeds, West Yorkshire LS1 3AB
Tel: 0113 247 8247
Fax: 0113 247 8247
email: artandmusic@leeds.gov.uk
Contact: Librarian

Leeds College of Art and Design
Vernon Street
Leeds LS2 8PH
Tel: 0113 202 8096
Fax: 0113 202 8150
Website: www.leeds-art.ac.uk
Contact: Library Manager

Leeds Metropolitan University
The Learning Centre
Leslie Silver Building
Woodhouse Lane
Leeds LS1 3HE
Tel: 0113 283 5968
email: infodesk.lc@lmu.ac.uk
Website: www.lmu.ac.uk/lis/lss
Contact: Learning Adviser, Art Architecture and Design

Leicester

De Montfort University Library
Kimberlin Library, The Gateway
Leicester LE1 9BH
Tel: 0116 2577042
Fax: 0116 2577043
Website: www.library.dmu.ac.uk
Contact: Assistant Librarian (Media Studies)

Leicester Reference and Information Library
Bishop Street
Leicester LE1 6AA
Tel: 0116 2995401
email: central.eference@leicester.gov.uk
Contact: Librarian
Resources: Burchell Collection of books, journals and memorilbilia

University of Leicester
Centre For Mass Communication Research
University Road
Leicester LE1 7RH
Tel: 0116 2523863
Tel: Fax: 0116 2523874
email: cmcr@le.ac.uk
email: Website: www.le.ac.uk/cmcr/
Contact: Enquiries

University of Leicester Library
PO Box 248
University Road
Leicester LE1 9QD

Tel: 0116 252 5288
Fax: 0116 252 2066
email: libdesk@le.ac.uk
Website: www.le.ac.uk/library
Contact: Brian Marshall (Information Librarian)
Resources: Collection supporting Mass communication studies

Liverpool

Aldham Roberts Learning Resource Centre
Liverpool John Moores University
Mount Pleasant
Liverpool L3 5UZ
Tel: 0151 231 3701
Fax: 0151 707 1307
Website: cwis.livjm.ac.uk/lea/aldham
Contact: Senior Information Officer (Media, Critical and Creative Arts)

Liverpool City Libraries
William Brown Street
Liverpool L3 8EW
Tel: 0151 2335835
email: refbt.central@liverpool.gov.uk
Contact: Librarian

Liverpool Hope University College
Hope Park
Liverpool L16 9LB
Tel: 0151 291 2000
Fax: 0151 291 2037
Website: www.hope.ac.uk
Contact: Director of Learning Resources

University of Liverpool
Sydney Jones Library
Chatham Street
Liverpool L69 3DA
Tel: 0151 794 2679
Fax: 0151 794 2681
Website: www.liv.ac.uk/library/
Contact: Enquiries

London

Barbican Library
Barbican Centre
Silk Street, London EC2Y 8DS
Tel: 020 7638 0569
Fax: 020 7638 2249
email: barbicanlib@corplondon.gov.uk
Website: www.cityoflondon.gov.uk/libraries
Contact: Librarian

British Universities Film & Video Council Library
77 Wells Street
London W1T 3QJ
Tel: 020 7393 1500
Fax: 020 7393 1555
email: library@bufvc.ac.uk
Website: www.bufvc.ac.uk
Luke McKernan, Head of Information
Resources: Scientific Film Association papers, BKSTS book collection, Slade Film History Register, Reuters Television newsreel documents

Brunel University Library
Twickenham Campus
300 St Margarets Road
Twickenham Tw1 1PT
Tel: 020 8891 0121 ext. 2205
Fax: 020 8891 8240
email: library@brunel.ac.uk
Website: www.brunel.ac.uk/depts/lib
Contact: Penny Lyndon (Subject Librarian)

Camberwell College of Arts Library
CCA
Peckham Road
London SE5 8UF
Tel: 020 7514 6349
Fax: 020 7514 6324
Contact: College Librarian
Resources: Special Collection of original letters, papers and ephemera Camden Public Libraries

Swiss Cottage Library
88 Avenue Road
London NW3 3HA
Tel: 020 7974 6522
Fax: 020 7974 6532
email: swisscottagelibrary@camden.gov.uk
Contact: Librarian

Central St Martins College of Art
Library and Learning Resources
Southampton Row
London WC1B 4AP
Tel: 020 7514 7037
Fax: 020 7514 7033
Contact: Library Manager

English and Media Centre
18 Compton Terrace
London N1 2UN
Tel: 020 7359 8080
Fax: 020 7354 0133
email: info@englishandmedia.co.uk
Website: www.englishandmedia.co.uk
Contact: Administrator
Resources: collections aimed specifically at Secondary and FE teachers and students

Harrow Library Services
Gayton Library
Gayton Road
Harrow
Middlesex HA1 2HL
Tel: 020 8427 6012/6986
Website: www.harrow.gov.uk/council/departments/libraries/libraryhome.asp
email: library@harrow.gov.uk
Contact: Lending Librarian

London Borough of Sutton
Sutton Library
St Nicholas Way
Sutton
Surrey SM1 1EA
Tel: 020 8770 4765
Fax: 020 8770 4777
Website: www.sutton.gov.uk/ifl/librarie/index.htm
email: Sutton.music@sutton.gov.uk
Contact: Enquiries

Institute of Education Library (London)
Information Services
20 Bedford Way
London WC1H OAL
Tel: 020 7612 6080
Fax: 020 7612 6093
email: lib.enquiries@ioe.ac.uk
Contact: Librarian

London College of Fashion
20 John Princes Street
London W1G 0BJ
Tel: 020 7514 7453
Fax: 020 7514 7580
Website: www.lcf.linst.ac.uk
Contact: Library Manager

London College of Printing
Back Hill Library School of Media
10 Back Hill, Clerkenwell
London EC1R 5LQ
Tel: 020 7514 6882
Fax: 020 7514 6886
Website: www.linst.ac.uk/library
Contact: LIbrarian

London Metropolitan University
Learning Centre, London North Campus
236-250 Holloway Road
London N7 6PP
Tel: 020 7753 5170
Contact: Librarian
Resources: includes London Guildhall University collections

London Metropolitan University Television Services
Academic Services,

Calcutta House,
Old Castle Street
London E1 7NT
Tel: 020 7320 1008
Fax: 020 7320 1100
Website: www.londonnet.ac.uk
Contact: Head of TV production

Middlesex University
Learning Resources
Cat Hill
Barnet EN4 8HT
Tel: 020 8411 5111
Fax: 020 8411 5105
Website: www.ilrs.mdx.ac.uk/
Contact: Librarian

Middlesex University Information and Learning Resources
Bounds Green Road
London N11 2NQ
Tel: 020 8362 5240
Fax: 020 84116150
Contact: Subject Librarian

Royal College of Art
Kensington Gore
London SW7 2EU
Tel: 020 7590 4224
Fax: 020 7590 4500
Website: www.rca.ac.uk
email: library@rca.org.uk
Contact: Library Desk

Royal Television Society
Holborn Hall
100 Grays Inn Road
London WC1X 8AL
Tel: Fax: 020 7430 0924
Fax: 020 7430 0924
email: info@rts.org.uk
Website: www.rts.org.uk
Contact: Archivist

Slade School of Fine Art Library
University College London
Gower Street
London WC1E 6BT
Tel: 020 76792313
Fax: 020 76797801
email: slade.enquiries@ucl.ac.uk
Contact: Art Librarian
For UCL staff and students

Thames Valley University
Learning Resources Centre
St Mary's Road
Walpole House
Ealing
London W5 5RF
Tel: 020 8231 2246
Website: www.tvu.ac.uk/lrs
Contact: Humanities Librarian

University of East London – School of Art and Design
Docklands Learning Resources Centre
University Way
London E16 2RD
Tel: 020 8223 7444
Website: www.uel.ac.uk/lss
Contact: Art and Film Subject Specialist

University of London Library
Senate House
Malet Street
London WC1E 7HU
Tel: 020 7862 8461
Fax: 020 7862 8480
Website: www.ull.ac.uk
Contact: Enquiries

University of London: Goldsmiths' College Library
Lewisham Way
London SE14 6NW
Tel: 020 7919 7150
Fax: 020 7919 7165
email: library@gold.ac.uk
Website: www.gold.ac.uk/infos/lib/
Contact: Subject Librarian: Media & Communications

University of London: School of Oriental and African Studies (Art Library)
Thornhaugh Street
Russell Square
London WC1H 0XG
Tel: 020 7898 4163
Fax: 020 7898 4159
Website: www.soas.ac.uk/library
email: libenquiry@soas.ac.uk
Contact: Y. Yasumura (Principal Assistant Librarian)

University of Surrey Roehampton
Roehampton Institute London
Learning Resources Centre
Roehampton Lane
London SW15 5SZ
Tel: 020 8392 3770
Fax: 020 8392 3559
email:
enquiry.desk@roehampton.ac.uk
Website:
www.roehampton.ac.uk/support/infoserv/index.asp
Contact: Enquiries

University of Westminster
Harrow Learning Resources Centre
Watford Road
Northwick Park
Harrow HA1 3TP
Tel: 020 7911 5885
Fax: 020 7911 5952
Website: www.wmin.ac.uk/harlib
Contact: Library Manager

Westminster Reference Library
35 St Martins Street
London WC2H 7HP
Tel: 020 7641 4638
Fax: 020 7641 4640
email: pcollins@westminster.gov.uk
Website:
www.westminster.gov.uk/libraries/special/perform.cfm
Arts Librarian
Contact: Peter Collins

Wimbledon School of Art
Learning Resources Centre
Merton Hall Road
London SW19 3QA
Tel: 020 8408 5027
Website: www.wimbledon.ac.uk
Contact: Subject Librarian

Loughborough

Loughborough University
Pilkington Library
Loughborough LE11 3TU
Tel: 01509 222360
Fax: 01509 223993
Website: www.lboro.ac.uk/library/
Contact: Barbara Whetnall (Academic Librarian)

Luton

University of Luton Learning Resources
Park Square
Luton LU1 3JU
Tel: 01582 743262
Fax: 01582 489325
Website: lrweb.luton.ac.uk
Contact: Jane Drage (Research Librarian)

Maidstone

Kent Institute of Art & Design at Maidstone
Oakwood Park
Maidstone
Kent ME16 8AG
Tel: 01622 757286
Fax: 01622 62110
Website:
www.kiad.ac.uk/library/set.htm
Contact: College Librarian

Manchester

Manchester Arts Library
Central Library

St Peters Square
Manchester M2 5PD
Tel: 0161 234 1974
Fax: 0116 1234 1961
Website:
www.manchester.gov.uk/libraries/central/arts
email:
arts@libraries.manchester.gov.uk
Contact: Arts Librarian

Manchester Metropolitan University Library
All Saints Building
Oxford Road
Manchester M15 6BH
Tel: 0161 247 6116/6108
Fax: 0161 247 6849
Website: mmu.ac.uk/services/library
email: humsocsci-lib-enq@mmu.ac.uk
Contact: Subject Librarian

North West Film Archive
Manchester Metropolitan University
Minshull House
47-49 Chorlton Street
Manchester M1 3EU
Tel: 0161 247 3097
Fax: 0161 247 3098
email: n.w.filmarchive@mmu.ac.uk
Website: www.nwfa.mmu.ac.uk
Contact: Enquiries
Resources: Moving image archive

Middlesbrough

University of Teeside
Library and Information Services
Borough Road
Middlesbrough TS1 3BA
Tel: 01642 342100
Fax: 01642 342190
Website: www.tees.ac.uk
Contact: Enquiries

Milton Keynes

Open University Library
Walton Hall
Milton Keynes MK7 6AA
Tel: 01908 659001
Fax: 01908 653571
Website: oulib1.open.ac.uk
email: lib-help@open.ac.uk
Contact: Enquiries

Newcastle upon Tyne

University of Northumbria
City Campus Library
Sandyford Road
Newcastle Upon Tyne NE1 8ST
Tel: 0191 227 4736
Fax: 0191 227 4563
Website: www.unn.ac.uk
Contact: Senior Officer, Information Services Department

Newport

University of Wales College, Newport
Library and Learning Resources
Caerleon Campus
PO Box 179
Newport
Wales NP18 3YG
Tel: 01633 432102
Fax: 01633 432108
email: library@newport.ac.uk
Website: library.newport.ac.uk
Contact: Art, Media and Design Librarian

Northumberland

Northumberland Morpeth Library
Gas House Lane
Morpeth
Northumberland NE61 1TA
Tel: 01670 534518
Fax: 01670 534513
Website:
www.northumberland.gov.uk
Contact: The Adult Services Librarian

Norwich

Anglia Polytechnic University
Norwich School of Art and Design Library
St George Street
Norwich NR3 1BB
Tel: 01603 610561 ext.3073
Fax: 01603 615728
Website: www.nsad.ac.uk
email: info@nsad.ac.uk
Contact: Jan McLachlan (Assistant Librarian)

East Anglian Film Archive
The Archive Centre
Martineau Lane
Norwich NR1 2DQ
Tel: 01603 592664
Fax: 01603 458553
email: eafa@uea.ac.uk
Website: www.uea.ac.uk/eafa
Contact: Assistant Archivist

University of East Anglia Library
Norwich, Norfolk NR4 7TJ
Tel: 01603 592421
Fax: 01603 259490
Website: www.lib.uea.ac.uk
email: library@uea.ac.uk
Contact: Film Studies Librarian

Nottingham

Nottingham Central Library
Angel Row
Nottingham NG1 6HP
Tel: 0115 9152811
Website:
www.nottinghamcity.gov.uk/libraries
email:
arts.library@nottinghamcity.gov.uk
Contact: Enquiries

Nottingham Trent University Library
The Boots Library
Goldsmith Street
Nottingham NG1 5LS
Tel: 0115 848 2175
Fax: 0115 848 2286
Website: www.ntu.ac.uk/lis
Contact: Information Specialist (Art & Design)

University of Nottingham
Hallward Library
University Park
Nottingham NG7 2RD
Tel: 0115 951 4561
Fax: 0115 951 4558
Website:
www.nottingham.ac.uk/library
Contact: Humanities Librarian

Oxford

University of Oxford
Bodleian Library
Broad Street
Oxford OX1 3BG
Tel: 01865 277162
Fax: 01865 277112
Website: www.bodley.ox.ac.uk
Contact: Enquiries

Plymouth

College of St Mark and St John Library
Derriford Road
Plymouth
Devon PL6 8BH
Tel: 01752 761145
email: libraryenquiries@marjon.ac.uk
Website: www.marjon.ac.uk/library
Contact: Resources Librarian

Poole

Arts Institute at Bournemouth Library
Wallisdown
Poole
Dorset BH12 5HH

Tel: 01202 363256
Fax: 01202 537729
email: library@arts-instit-bournemouth.ac.uk
Contact: Paul Briglin (Arts Librarian)

Bournemouth University Library
Talbot Campus
Fern Barrow
Poole
Dorset BH12 5BB
Tel: 01202 595083
Fax: 01202 595475
Website: www.bournemouth.ac.uk/library
Contact: Subject Librarian

Portsmouth

Portsmouth University Library
Frewen Library
Cambridge Road
Portsmouth
Hampshire PO1 2ST
Tel: 02392 843228
Fax: 02392 843233
email: library@port.ac.uk
Website: www.libr.port.ac.uk
Contact: Enquiries

Preston

University of Central Lancashire Library and Learning Resources Centre
St Peters Square
Preston
Lancashire PR1 2HE
Tel: 01772 892269
Website: www.uclan.ac.uk/library/libhom1.htm
Contact: Information Office

Reading

BBC Written Archives Centre
Caversham Park
Reading RG4 8T2
Tel: 0118 948 6281
Fax: 0118 946 1145
email: wac.enquiries@bbc.co.uk
Website: www.bbc.co.uk/thenandnow
Contact: Written Archivist

Reading University Library
Whiteknights
PO Box 223
Reading RG6 6AE
Tel: 0118 931 8770
Fax: 0118 931 6636
email: library@rdg.ac.uk
Website: www.rdg.ac.uk/libraries
Contact: Liaison Librarian for Film, Theatre and Television

Redhill

Reigate School of Art, Design and Media Library
Claremont Road
Redhill
Surrey RH1 2JX
Tel: 01787 772611 ext. 1253
email: fharries@staff.es.org.uk
Contact: Fina Harries (Libraries and Learning Centres Manager)

Rochdale

Rochdale Metropolitan Borough Libraries
Wheatsheaf Library
Wheatsheaf Centre
Baillie Street, Rochdale
Lancashire OL16 1JZ
Tel: 01706 864914
Fax: 01706 864992
Contact: Librarian

Rochester

Kent Institute of Art and Design
Rochester Campus Library
Fort Pitt
Rochester
Kent ME1 1DZ
Tel: 01634 820334
Fax: 01634 820300
Website: www.kiad.ac.uk/library/set.htm
email: libraryroch@kiad.ac.uk
Contact: Librarian

Salford

University of Salford, Information Services Division (Library)
Peru Street
Salford
Greater Manchester M3 6EQ
Tel: 0161 295 6084
Website: www.isd.salford.ac.uk
Contact: Information Officer
Resources: Scripts, DVDs and Computer Games (PC Games and Playstation 2)

Sheffield

Sheffield Hallam University Learning Centre
Psalter Lane
Sheffield S11 8UZ
Tel: 0114 225 2727
Fax: 0114 225 2717
Website: www.shu.ac.uk/services/lc/psalter/index.html
email: lc-psalter@shu.ac.uk
Contact: Enquiries

Sheffield Libraries & Information Services
Arts and Social Sciences Section
Central Library
Surrey Street
Sheffield S1 1XZ
Tel: 0114 273 4747
Fax: 0114 2735009
email: sheffield.cas@dial.pipex.com
Contact: Librarian

Southampton

Southampton Institute
Mountbatten Library
East Park Terrace
Southampton
Hampshire SO14 0YN
Tel: 02380 319486
Fax: 02380 31967
Website: www.solent.ac.uk/library/
email: jenny.gran@solent.ac.uk
Contact: Jenny Grant (Information Librarian)

University of Southampton
Avenue Campus
Highfield
Southampton
Hants S017 1BF
Tel: 01703 593521
Fax: 01703 593007
Contact: Assistant Librarian, Arts
Resources: Personal papers, pressbooks

Southport

Southport College Library
Mornington Road
Southport
Merseyside PR9 0TT
Tel: 01704 500606
Fax: 01704 392794
email: library@southport.ac.uk
Contact: Enquiries

Stoke-on-Trent

Staffordshire University Library and Information Service
Thompson Library
College Road
Stoke-On-Trent
Staffordshire ST4 2XS
Tel: 01782 294771/294809
email: llrse@staffs.ac.uk
Contact: Librarian

Sunderland

City Library and Art Centre
Fawcett Street
Sunderland SR1 1RE
Tel: 0191-514 1235
Fax: 0191-514 8444
email:
enquiry.desk@sunderland.gov.uk
Contact: Librarian

Sunderland University Library
Langham Tower
Ryhope Road
Sunderland SR2 7EE
Tel: 0191 515 2900
Fax: 0191 515 2423
Contact: Librarian

Totnes

Dartington College of Arts
Library and Learning Resources Centre
Dartington Hall Estate
Totnes, Devon TQ9 6EJ
Tel: 01803 861651
Fax: 01803 861666
Website:
www.dartington/ac/uk/studentsup/llrc.htm
email: library@dartington.ac.uk
Contact: Richard Taylor (Deputy Librarian)

Wakefield

University of Leeds
Bretton Hall Campus
National Arts Education Archive
West Bretton
Wakefield WF4 4LG
Tel: 01924 832020
Fax: 01924 832077
Website: http;//naea.leeds.ac.uk
Contact: Sonja Kielty (Assistant Curator)

Warrington

Warrington Collegiate Institute
The Library, Padgate Campus
Crab Lane, Warrington WA2 ODB
Tel: 01925 494284
Website: www.warr.ac.uk
Contact: Librarian

Winchester

King Alfred's College
Martial Rose Library
Sparkford Road, Winchester
Hampshire SO22 4NR
Tel: 01962 827306
email: libenquires@wkac.ac.uk
Website: www.lrc.wkac.ac.uk
Contact: Librarian

Winchester School of Art Library
Park Avenue, Winchester
Hampshire SO23 8DL
Tel: 02380 269824
Fax: 02380 269826
email: wsaenqs@soton.ac.uk
Website: www.library.soton.ac.uk
Contact: Site Librarian

Wolverhampton

Light House Media Centre
Media Reference Library
Chubb Buildings
Fryer Street
Wolverhampton WV1 1HT
Tel: 01902 716055
Fax: 01902 717143
email: richard@light-house.co.uk
Website: www.light-house.co.uk
Contact Richard Carr (Library Administrator)

University of Wolverhampton

Harrison Learning Centre
St Peters Square
Wolverhampton WV1 1RH
Tel: 01902 322300
Fax: 01902 322194
Website: www.wlv.ac.uk/lib
Contact: Art and Design Librarian

Wolverhampton Libraries and Information Services
Central Library
Snow Hill
Wolverhampton WV1 3AX
Tel: 01902 716055
Fax: 01902 552024
Contact: Librarian

Worcester

Worcester College of Technology, School of Art and Design
Barbourne Road
Worcester WR1 1RT
Tel: 01905 725647
email: llane@art.wortech.ac.uk
Website: www.wortech.ac.uk
Contact: Lisa Lane (Librarian)

York

York St John College

Library and Information Services
Lord Mayors Walk
York YO31 7EX
Tel: 01904 716700
Fax: 01904 612512
Website: www.yorksj.ac.uk/library
Contact: Librarian
Resources: Holds the Yorkshire Film Archive

ORGANISATIONS (EUROPE)

The following is a list of some of the main pan–European film and television organisations, entries for countries of the European Union and the various MEDIA II projects instigated by the European Commission

Pan-European Organisations

ACE (Ateliers du Cinéma Européen/European Film Studio)*

68 rue de Rivoli
75004 Paris
France
Tel: (33) 1 44 61 88 30
Fax: (33) 1 44 61 88 40
email: jessica.ace@wanadoo.fr
Director: Sophie Bourdon
ACE is a year-long training-through-projects and development programme designed for independent European cinema producers who have already produced at least one feature film. The selected producers then remain part of the ACE Producers' Network

AGICOA (Association de Gestion Internationale Collective des Oeuvres Audio-Visuelles)

rue de St-Jean 26
1203 Geneva
Switzerland
Tel: (41) 22 340 32 00
Fax: (41) 22 340 34 32
email:info@agicoa.org
Website:www.agicoa.org
Hein Endlich, Managing Director

Centre for Cultural Research

Dahlmannstr, 26
53113 Bonn
Germany
Tel: (49) 228 211058
Fax: (49) 228 217493
email: zentrum@kulturforsdhung.de
Website: www.kulturforsdung.de
Prof Andreas Johannes Wiesand
Research, documentation, and advisory tasks in all fields of the arts and media, especially with 'European' perspectives. Participation in arts and media management courses at university level. Produces publications and supports the founding scretariat of the European Institute for Comparative Cultural Policy and the Arts (ERICArts) with members in 25 European countries (www.ericarts.org)

EURIMAGES

Council of Europe
Palais de l'Europe
avenue de l'Europe
67075 Strasbourg Cédex, France
Tel: (33) 88 41 26 40
Fax: (33) 88 41 27 60
email: Website:
www.culture.coe.fr/eurimages
Contact: Executive Secretary
Founded in 1988 by a group of Council of Europe member states. Its objective is to stimulate film and audio-visual production by partly financing the co-production, distribution and exhibition of European cinematographic and audio-visual works. Eurimages now includes 24 member states

European Academy for Film & Television

rue Verte 69
1210 Brussels, Belgium
Tel: (32) 2 218 66 07
Fax: (32) 2 217 55 72
Permanent Secretary: Dimitri Balachoff
The purpose of the Academy, a non-profit making association, is the research, development and disclosure of all matters relating to cinema and television chiefly in the European continent, and also in other continents, taking into account artistic, commercial, cultural, economic, financial, historical, institutional, pedagogical, trade union and technical aspects.
Quarterly newsletter, ACANEWS

European Audio-visual Observatory

76 allée de la Robertsau
67000 Strasbourg, France
Tel: (33) 3 88 144400
Fax: (33) 3 88 144419
email: obs@obs.coe.int
Website: www.obs.coe.int/
Executive Director: Wolfgang Closs.
A European institution working within the framework of the Council of Europe, which provides vital information on the European television, film, video, DVD and multimedia industries in the fields of
Markets
Production and financing
Legal topics
The European Audiovisual Observatory has 36 members : 35 states and the European Union. It collects its information from a Europe-wide network of correspondents. It's products and services, which are available to government authorities and representatives of the audiovisual industry, include :
Print Publications :
Regular publications :
The Yearbook – Film, Television, Video and Multimedia in Europe
FOCUS – World Film Market Trends
IRIS – monthly legal newsletter
IRIS PLUS
ii. Special Reports
Online publications : available on the Observatory website.
Online services :
Yearbook Online Premium Service
IRIS ONLINE
Databases available free of charge on the Observatory website :
LUMIERE : Database on admissions for films released in Europe
http://lumiere.obs.coe.int/web/EN/search.php
KORDA : Database on public funding for the film and audiovisual sector in Europe
http://korda.obs.coe.int/web/en/
IRIS MERLIN : Database on legal information relevant to the audiovisual sector in Europe.
http://merlin.obs.coe.int/search.php
Participation in conferences and seminars : see programme on the Observatory website

European Broadcasting Union (EBU)

Ancienne Route 17a
1218 Grand-Saconnex
Geneva, Switzerland
Tel: (32) 2 218 66 07
Fax: (32) 2 217 55 72
email: Fax: (41) 22 717 2200
Website: www.ebu.ch/
Jean-Pierre Julien
The EBU is a professional association of national broadcasters with 117 members in 79 countries. Principal activities: daily exchange of news, sports and cultural programmes for television (Eurovision) and radio (Euroradio); Tv coproductions; technical studies and legal action in the international broadcasting sphere

European Co-production Association

c/o France 2
22 avenue Montaigne
75387 Paris Cedex 08
France
Tel: (33) 1 4421 4126
Fax: (33) 1 4421 5179
A consortium of, at present, six European public service television networks for the co-production of television programmes. Can offer complete finance. Proposals should consist of full treatment, financial plan and details of proposed co-production partners. Projects are proposed to the ECA Secretariat or to member national broadcasters

European Coordination of Film Festivals

64 rue Philippe le Bon
1000 Bruxelles
Tel: (32) 2 280 13 76
Fax: (32) 2 230 91 41
email: cefc@skypro.be
Website: www.eurofilmfest.org
Marie José Carta
A network of 150 audio-visual festivals in Europe to promote the diversity of the European moving image through collaboration projects such as touring programmes, staff exchanges, reserach and conferences on the socio-economic impact of film festivals, electronic subtitling and sponsorship, the quarterly newsletter (EuroFilmFest). The Coordination is funded by MEDIA

European Film Academy (EFA)

Kurfurstendamm 225
D-10719 Berlin
Germany
Tel: (49) 30 88 71 67 - 0
Fax: (49) 30 88 71 67 77
email: efa@europeanfilmacademy.org
Website:
www.europeanfilmacademy.org
Chairman: Nik Powell,
Director: Marion Döring

European Film College

Carl Th. Dreyers Vej 1
DK 8400 Ebeltoft
Tel: (45) 8634 0055
Fax: (45) 8634 0535
email: administration@efc.dk
Website: www.efc.dk
The European Film College was founded in 1993 with the overall goal of contributing to of a vibrant film culture and a successful film industry in Europe. The EFC provides education and training in all aspects of the audiovisual media to undergraduates, professionals and the general public

European Institute for the Media (EIM)

Kaistrasse 13
40221 Düsseldorf, Germany
Tel: (49) 211 90 10 40
Fax: (49) 211 90 10 456
Head of Research: Runar Woldt
Head of East-West: Dusoun Rejic
Acting Head of Library, Documentation and Statistics Centre: Helga Schmid
A forum for research and documentation in the field of media in Europe. Its activities include: research into the media in Europe with a political, economic and juridicial orientation; the organisation of conferences and seminars such as the annual European Television and Film Forum; East-West Co-operation Programme; the development of an advanced studies programme for students and media managers. Publication of the Bulletin in English/French/German, quarterly on European media development, and of the Ukrainian and Russian Bulletin as well as research reports. Officers in Kiev and Moscow. Organises the European Media Summer School, an annual course on media development for advanced students and professionals, and facilitates an information request service

Euroscript

Screenwriters' Centre
Suffolk House
1-8 Whitfield Place
London W1P 5SF
Tel: 020 7387 5880
Fax: 020 7387 5880
email: euroscript@netmatters.co.uk
Website: euroscript.co.uk
Paul Gallagher, Director
Euroscript started as a project of the European Union's MEDIA II programme. Euroscript offers support and distance learning material to help EU screenwriters develop scripts and run screenwriters' groups. Euroscript is a continuous distance training project to develop and promote EU scripts

EUTELSAT (European Telecommunications Satellite Organisation)

Tour Maine-Montparnasse
avenue du Maine 33
75755 Paris Cédex 15, France
Tel: (32) 2 280 13 76
Fax: (32) 2 230 91 41 Fax: (33) 1 45 38 37 00
Website: www.eutelsat.org/
Vanessa O'Connor
EUTELSAT operates a satellite system for intra-European communications of all kinds. Traffic carried includes Television and Radio channels, programme exchanges, satellite newsgathering, telephony and business communications

Fédération Européenne des Industries Techniques de l'Image et du Son (FEITIS)

avenue Marceau 50
75008 Paris
France
Tel: (49) 30 88 71 67 - 0
Fax: (33) 1 47 23 70 47
A federation of European professional organisations representing those working in film and video services and facilities in all audio-visual and cinematographic markets

Federation Internationale de la Press e Cinématographique (International Federation of Film Critics) (FIPRESCI)

Schleissheimer Str 83
D-80797 Munich
Tel: (49) 89 18 23 03
Fax: (49) 89 18 47 66
Klaus Eder, General Secretary

Fédération Internationale des Producteurs de Films Indépendants (FIPFI)
avenue Marceau 50
75008 Paris,
France
Tel: (33) 1 4421 4126
Fax: (33) 1 4421 5179
A consortium of, at present, six European public service television networks for the co-production of television programmes. Can offer complete finance. Proposals should consist of full treatment, financial plan and details of proposed co-production partners. Projects are proposed to the ECA Secretariat or to member national broadcasters

FIAD (Fédération Internationale des Associations de Distributeurs de Films)
74 avenue Kléber
75016 Paris
Tel: (33) 1 56 90 33 00
Fax: (32) 1 56 90 33 01
email: film.paris@wanadoo.fr
Website: www.eurofilmfest.org
Président: Gilbert Grégoire
Président d'honneur: M.Luc Hemelaer
Vice Président: MM Stephan Hutter, Antonio Llorens Olive
Secrétaire Général: Antoine Virenque
Represents the interests of film distributors

FIAT/IFTA (International Federation of Television Archives)
email: office@fiatifta.org
Website: www.fiatifta.org
President:
Emmanuel Hoog (INA, France)
Vice Presidents:
Peter Dusek (ORF, Austria)
Branko Bubenik (HRT, Croatia)
Dominique Saintville (INA, France)
General Secretary:
Steve Bryant (BFI, UK)
FIAT membership is mainly made up of the archive services of broadcasting organisations. It also encompasses national archives and other television-related bodies. The aim of the association is to set up local seminars and a worldwide conference annually. Information of the activities of the association is published on the website

IDATE (Institut de l'audio-visuel et des télécommunications en Europe)
BP 4167
34092 Montpelier Cédex 5
France
Tel: (33) 4 67 14 44 44
Fax: (33) 4 67 14 44 00
email: info@idate.fr
Website: www.idate.org
Jean-Dominique Séval: Marketing and Commercial Director

Institut de Formation et d'Enseignement pour les Métiers de l'Image et du Son (FEMIS)
rue Francoeur 6
75018 Paris
France
Tel: (33) 1 42 62 20 00
Fax: (33) 1 42 62 21 00
High level technical training in the audio-visual field for French applicants and those from outside France with a working knowledge of French. Organises regular student exchanges with other European film schools

Institut de Journalisme Robert Schuman - European Media Studies
rue de l'Association 32-34
1000 Brussels
Belgium
Tel: (32) 2 217 2355
Fax: (32) 2 219 5764
Anne de Boeck
Postgraduate training in journalism. Drawing students from all over Europe, it offers nine months intensive training in journalism for press, radio and television

International Cable Communications Council
boulevard Anspach 1, Box 34
1000 Brussels
Belgium
Tel: (32) 2 211 94 49
Fax: (32) 2 211 99 07
International body gathering European, Canadian, North American and Latin American cable television organisations

International Federation of Actors (FIA)
Guild House
Upper St Martin's Lane
London WC2H 9EG
Tel: 0171 379 0900
Fax: 0171 379 8260
Website: ISETU/FISTAV
Trade union federation founded in 1952 and embracing 60 performers' trade unions in 44 countries. It organises solidarity action when member unions are in dispute, researches and analyses problems affecting the rights and working conditions of film, television and theatre actors as well as singers, dancers, variety and circus artistes. It represents members in the international arena on issues such as cultural policy and copyright and publishes twice yearly newsheet FOCUS

(International Secretariat for Arts, Mass Media and Entertainment Trade Unions/International Federation of Audio-Visual Workers)
IPC, boulevard Charlemagne 1
PO Box 5
1040 Brussels, Belgium
Tel: (32) 2 238 09 51
Fax: (32) 2 230 00 76
General Secretary: Jim Wilson
Caters to the special concerns of unions and similar associations whose members are engaged in mass media, entertainment and the arts. It is a clearing house for information regarding multi-national productions or movement of employees across national borders, and acts to exchange information about collective agreements, legal standards and practices at an international level. It organises conferences, has opened a campaign in support of public service broadcasting, and has begun initiatives ranging from defending screen writers to focusing on the concerns of special groups

Pilots
Pau Claris 115, 5è, 4a
E-8009 Barcelona
Tel: (34) 93 487 37 73
Fax: (34) 93 487 39 52
email: pilots@intercom.es
Website: www.acpilots.com
Roger Gregory, UK Contact
Tel: 01926 491934
Fax: 01926 491212

Telefilm Canada/Europe
5 rue de Constantine
Paris 75007
Tel: (33) 1 44 18 35 30
Fax: (33) 1 4705 72 76

email: tfcsheila@attglobal.net
Website: www.telefilm.gc.ca
Director: Sheila de La Varende
Canadian government organisation financing film and television productions. European office provides link between Canada, UK and other European countries

UK Eureka Unit

Department of Trade and Industry
3rd Floor
151 Buckingham Palace Road
London SW1W 9SS
Tel: 020 7215 1618
Fax: 020 7215 1700
email: graham.crew@dti.gsi.gov.uk
Website:
www.globalwatchonline.com/eureka
A pan-European inititative to encourage industry-led, market-driven collaborative projects aimed at producing advanced technology products, processes and services

UNIC (Union Internationale des Cinémas)

15 Rue de Berri
75008 Paris
France
Tel: (33) 1 42-89-31-50
Fax: (33) 1 42-89-31-40
email: email; unicine@club-internet.fr
Horteuse de Labriffe, General Delegate
Defends the interests of cinema exhibitors worldwide, particularly in matters of law and economics. It publishes UNIC News and a Bulletin. Also provides statistical information and special studies concerning the exhibition sector, to members and others

URTI (Université Radiophonique et Télévisuelle Internationale)

General Secretariat
116, avenue du Président Kennedy
75786 Paris Cedex 16
France
Tel: (33) 1 42 30 39 98
Fax: (33) 1 40 50 89 99
email: President: Roland Faure
A non-governmental organisation recognised by UNESCO and founded in 1949, URTI is an association of professionals in the audio-visual field from all over the world. Promotes cultural programmes and organisation of projects including the International Grand Prix for Creative Documentaries, the Young Television Prize at the Monte Carlo International Television Festival, the Grand Prix for Radio (since 1989)

Austria

Animotion Films Vienna

Animationsfilm Wien
Theresiengasse 20/1/15,
A-1180 Vienna
Austria
Tel/Fax: (+43 1) 941 38 50
email: husi@chello.at
Hubert Sielecki

Association of Audio-visual and Film Industry

Wiedner Haupstrasse 63
1045 Wien
PO Box 327
Tel: (43) 1 50105/3010
Fax: (43) 1 50105/276
email: film@fafo.at
Website: www.fafo.at
Elmar A. Peterlunger

Austrian Film Commission

Stiftgasse 6
A-1070 Vienna
Tel: (43) 1 526 33 23-0
Fax: (43) 1 526 68 01
email: office@afc.at
Website: www.afc.at
Martin Schweighofer
The Austrian Film Commission is an export and promotion agency. The organisation, financed by public funds, offers a wide variety of services for Austrian producers and creative artists, it acts as consultant whenever its productions are presented in international festivals, and it provides members of the profession in all sectors with comprehensive information as to current activity in the Austrian film industry. It is the aim of all activities to enhance the perception of Austrian film-making abroad. In addition to the major festivals in Berlin, Cannes, Venice and Toronto, the Austrian Film Commission currently provides support for more than 300 international film festivals and markets. The catalogue Austrian Films published annually, offers an overview, divided in sections, of current Austrian film-making. Others publications: the Austrian Film Guide designed to provide quick access to the Austrian film industry and the newsletter Austrian Film News

Austrian Film Institute

Spittelberggasse 3
A-1070 Wien
Tel: (43) 1 526 97 30 - 400
Fax: (43) 1 526 97 30 - 440
email: office@filminstitut.or.at
Website: www.filminstitut.or.at
Andreas Hruza

Austrian Professional Audiovision Organizers and Movie Theaters Association/Fachverband der Lichtspieltheater und Audiovisionsveranstalter*

Wiedner Hauptstraße 63
A-1045 Vienna
Tel: (43 1) 501 05-3471
Fax: (43 1) 501 05-3526
email: kinos@wko.at
Website: www.diekinos.at
Kurt Kaufmann

Cine Tirol (Film Commission & Fund)

c/o Tirol Werbung
Johannes Köck, Sabine Aigner
Maria-Theresien-Straße 55,
A-6010 Innsbruck
Tel: Tel.: (43 512) 5320-0
Fax: (43 512) 5320-100
email: cinetirol@tirolwerbung.at
Website: www.cinetirol.com

Filmakademie Wien

Universität für Musik und darstellende Kunst
Institut für Film und Fernsehen
Metternichgasse 12
1030 Wien
Tel: (43) 1 711 55 2902
Fax: (43) 1 711 55 2999
email: weidinger@mdw.ac.at
Website: www.mdw.ac.at
Anneliese Weidinger

Filmfonds Wien (Vienna Film Fund)

Stiftgasse 6
A -1070 Vienna
Tel: (43) 1 526 50 88
Fax: (43) 1 526 50 88
email: office@filmfonds-wien.at
Website: www.filmfonds-wien.at
Dr Peter Zawrel
The objectives of the Vienna Film Fund are strengthening and consolidating Vienna as a city of film and audiovisual media in international media and also saving the cultural diversity of Europe. Therefore it is essential for the Vienna Film Fund to help subsidize culture, economy and employment in the film industry of Vienna, Austria and all of Europe. It is also an important assignment of the fund to promote the Austrian Film. The fund gives subsidies to film-producers in different phases of production:

project-development (including script-writing), production, distribution and taking part in film festivals. Cultural, economic and artistic merit of the project are important. The European, and especially the Viennese or Austrian culture should attract interest in movie making. While producing a movie you have to spend at least 100% of the financial contribution of the Vienna Film Fund for film production facilities and skills existing in Vienna, employing local creative staff and filmmakers and/ or having an onscreen-promotion of the city as a location.
You can get subsidies for feature-films for cinema (projection time at least 70 minutes), documentaries and movies for children for cinema (at least 59 minutes) and TV-movies.

Metternichgasse 12

A-1030 Vienna
Tel: (43 1) 711 55-2902
Fax: (43 1) 711 55-2999
email: weidinger@mdw.ac.at
Website: www.mdw.ac.at
Wolfgang Glück

Österreichisches Filmmuseum

Augustinerstrasse 1
A-1010 Vienna
Tel: (43 1) 533 70 54 29
Fax: (43 1) 533 70 56 25
email: st.stejskal@filmmseum.at
Website: www.filmmuseum.at
Alexander Horwath

Belgium

Cinémathèque Royale de Belgique/Royal Film Archive

Rue Ravenstein 23
1000 Brussels
Tel: (32) 2 507 83 70
Fax: (32) 2 513 12 72
email: filmarchive@ledoux.be
Website: www.ledoux.be/
Gabrielle Claes
Film preservation. The collection can be consulted on the Archive's premises for research purposes. Edits the Belgian film annual
Commission de Selection des Films

Film Museum Jacques Ledoux

Rue Baron Horta 9
1000 Brussels
Tel: (32) 2 507 83 70
Fax: (32) 2 513 12 72
email: filmmuseum@ledoux.be
Gabrielle Claes
Permanent exhibition of the prehistory of cinema. Five screenings per day - three sound, two silent. Organises one double festival a year: L'Age d'Or Prize and prizes for the distribution of quality films in BelgiumFlanders Image is the official organisation for the promotion of Flemish audiovisual productions outside Belgium

Flanders Image

Handelskaai 18 B3
B-1000 Brussels, Belgium
Tel: 32/2/226 06 30
Fax: 32/2/219 19 36
email: flandersimage@vaf.be
Website: www.flanders-image.com
Christian De Schutter, Veerle Creve
A division of the Flemish Audiovisual Fund (VAF), Flanders Image is your prime source for all information on audiovisual production in Flanders, Belgium. It is also in charge of the promotion of Flemish audiovisual product

Ministère de la Communauté francaise de Belgique

Service général de l'Audiovisuel et des Multimèdias
Boulevard Léopold II 44
1080 Brussels
Tel: (32) 2 413 33 42
Fax: (32) 2 413 20 68
email: veronique.pacco@cfwb.be
Website: www.cfwb.be/av
Véronique Pacco
Assistance given to the production of documentaries, short and long features by independent producers

Radio-Télévision Belge de la Communauté Française (RTBF)

Blvd Auguste Reyers 52
1044 Brussels
Tel: (32) 2 737 21 11
Fax: (32) 2 737 25 56
Website: www.rtbf.be
Administrateur Général: Jean-Louis Stalport
Public broadcaster responsible for French language services

Vlaams Audiovisueel Fonds (Flemish Audiovisual Fund, VAF)

Handelskaai 18 B3
B-1000 Brussels, Belgium
Tel: 32/2/226 06 30
Fax: 32/2/219 19 36
email: info@vaf.be
Website: www.vaf.be
Luckas Vander Taelen, Rudy Verzyck
The Flemish Audiovisual Fund (VAF) supports audiovisual production in, as well as international co-productions with Flanders. Its aims are threefold: to develop a sustainable Flemish audiovisual industry, to encourage and support upcoming audiovisual talent and to promote productions

VRT

Auguste Reyerslaan 52
1043 Brussels
Tel: (32) 2 741 3111
Fax: (32) 2 734 9351
email: info@vrt.be
Website: www.vrt.be
Managing Director: Tony Mary
Radio: Frans Ieven
Television: Aimé Van Hecke
Public television and radio station serving Dutch speaking Flemish community in Belgium

Denmark

Danish Film and Television Workers Union

Kongens Nytorv 21
Baghuset 3. sal
1050 Copenhagen K
Tel: (45) 33 14 33 55
Fax: (45) 33 14 33 03
email: faf@filmtv.dk
Website: www.filmtv.dk
Susanne Baekgaard
Trade union which organises film, video and television workers, and maintains the professional, social, economic and artistic interests of its members. Negotiates collective agreements for feature films, documentaries, commercials, negotiating contracts, copyright and authors' rights. Also protection of Danish film production

Danish Film Institute/Archive and Cinemateque

Gothersgade 55
DK - 1123 Copenhagen K
Tel: (45) 3374 3400
Fax: (45) 3374 3403
email: mus@dfi.dk
Website: www.dfi.dk
Dan Nissen, Director
The Archive and Cinematheque, founded in 1941, is one of the world's

oldest film archives. It has a collection of 31,000 titles from almost every genre and country, and has daily screenings. There is also an extensive library of books and pamphlets, periodicals, clippings, posters and stills

Danmarks Radio (DR)
Morkhojvej 170
2860 Soborg
Tel: (45) 35 20 30 40
Fax: (45) 35 20 26 44
email: dr@dr.dk
Website: www.dr.dk
Public service television and radio network

Ministry of Culture
Nybrogade 2
Box 2140
DK-1015 København K
Tel: (45) 3392 3370
Fax: (45) 3391 3388
email: kum@kum.dk
Website: www.kulturnet.dk

Producenterne
Kronprinsensgade 9B
1114 Copenhagen K
Tel: (45) 33 14 03 11
Fax: (45) 33 14 03 65
The Danish Producers' Association of Film, Television, Video and AV

Finland

AVEK - The Promotion Centre for Audio-visual Culture in Finland
Hietaniemenkatu 2
FIN - 00100 Helsinki
Tel: (358) 9 43152350
Fax: (358) 9 43152388
email: avek@avek.kopiosto.fi
Website: www.kopiosto.fi/avek
AVEK was established in 1987 to promote cinemas, video and television culture. It is responsible for the management of funds arising from authors' copyright entitlements and is used for authors' common purposes (the blank tape levy). AVEK's support activities cover the entire field of audio-visual culture, emphasis being on the production support of short films, documentaries and media art. The other two activity sections are training of the professionals working in the audio-visual field and audiovisual culture in general

Finnish Film Archive/Suomen Elokuva-arkisto
Pursimiehenkatu 29-31 A
PO Box 177
FIN-00151
Helsinki
Tel: (358) 9 615 40 00
Fax: (358) 9 615 40 242
email: sea@sea.fi
Website: www.sea.fi
Matti Lukkarila
Stock: 10,000 feature film titles; 30,000 shorts and spots; 18,000 video cassettes; 20,000 books and scripts; 330,000 different stills, 110,000 posters; and 40,000 documentation files. The archive arranges regular screenings in Helsinki and other cities. Documentation, database, publications (Finnish national filmography)

Finnish Film Foundation
Kanavakatu 12
Fin-00160 Helsinki
Tel: (358) 9 6220 300
Fax: (358) 9 6220 3050
email: keskus@ses.fi
Website: www.ses.fi
Rauha Petähäniemi
Film funding for script, development and production of feature film and documentaries. Audio post production and auditorio services. Distribution and screening support. International activities (cultural export and promotion of Finnish Film)

France

Bibliothèque du Film (BIFI)
100 rue du Faubourg Saint-Antoine
75012 Paris
Tel: Tel : (33) 01 53 02 22 30·
Fax: Fax : (33) 0153 02 22 39
email: Website: www.bifi.fr
Website: Contact: Laurent Billia
Documentation
Contact: Marc Vernet

Centre National de la Cinématographie (CNC)
rue de Lübeck 12
75016 Paris
Tel: (33) 1 45 05 1440
Fax: (33) 1 47 55 04 91
email: Website: www.cnc.fr/
Website: Director-General: Dominique Wallon, Press, Public & Internal Relations: Patrick Ciercoles
A government institution, under the auspices of the Ministry of Culture. Its areas of concern are: the economics of cinema and the audio-visual industries; film regulation; the promotion of the cinema industries and the protection of cinema heritage. Offers financial assistance in all aspects of French cinema (production, exhibition, distribution etc). In 1986, the CNC was made responsible for the system of aid offered to the production of films made for television. These include fiction films, animated films and documentaries. The aim here corresponds to one of the principal objectives of public sector funding, where support is given to the French television industry while the development of a high standard of television is encouraged

Chambre Syndicale des Producteurs et Exportateurs de Films Francais
rue du Cirque 5
75008 Paris
Tel: (33) 1 42 25 70
Fax: (33) 1 42 25 94 27
email: cspeff@wanadoo.fr
Pascal Rogard, General Secretary
National federation of French cinema production

Cinémathèque Française - Musée du Cinéma
4, rue de Longchamp
75016 Paris
Tel: (33) 1 53 65 74 57
Fax: (33) 1 53 65 74 97
email: cinematec-jz@magic.jz
Website: www.cinemathequefrancaise.com
Marianne de Fleury
Founded in 1936 by Henri Langlois, Georges Franju and Jean Mitry to save, conserve and show films. Now houses a cinema museum, screening theatres, library and stills and posters library

Fédération Nationale des Distributeurs de Films
74 avenue Kléber
75016 Paris
Tel: (33) 1 56 90 33 00
Fax: (33) 1 56 90 33 01
email: film.paris@wanadoo.fr
President: M. Marin Karmitz
Délégué général : M. Antoine Virenque
Déléguée générale chargée des relations extérieures : Mme Julie Lorimy.
National federation of film distributors

Fédération Nationale des

Industries Techniques duCinéma et de l'Audio-visuel

(FITCA)
36 rue Washington
75008 Paris
Tel: (33) 1 43 59 11 70
email: fitca@wanadoo.fr
Website: www.fitca-france.com
A federation of technical trade associations which acts as intermediary between its members and their market. Maintains a database on all technical aspects of production, and helps French and European companies find suitable partners for research and development or commercial ventures

Forum des images (ex Vidéothèque de Paris)

Forum des Halles
2, Grande Galerie
Porte Saint-Eustache
75001 Paris
Tel: 01 44 76 62 00
Website: www.vdp.fr/

France 2

avenue Montaigne 22
75008 Paris
Tel: (33) 1 44 21 42 42
Fax: (33) 1 44 21 51 45
Website: www.france2.fr
France's main public service terrestrial television channel

Institut National de l'Audiovisuel (INA) *

4, avenue de l'Europe
94366 Bry-sur-Marne Cédex
Tel: (33) 1 49 83 20 00
Fax: (33) 1 49 83 25 80
email: Website: www.ina.fr/
Television and radio archive; research into new technology; research and publications about broadcasting; production of over 130 first works for television and 15 major series and collections. INA initiates major documentaries and cultural series involving partners from Europe and the rest of the world

Les Archives du Film du Centre National de la Cinématographie

7 bis rue Alexandre Turpault
78390 Bois d'Arcy
Tel: (33) 1 30 14 80 00
Fax: (33) 1 34 60 52 25
email: michelle.aubert@cnc.fr
Website: www.cnc.fr
Michelle Aubert
The film collection includes some 64,000 titles, mostly French features, documentaries and shorts from 1895 to date through the new legal deposit for films which includes all categories of films shown in cinemas including foreign releases. Since 1991, a special pluriannual programme for copying early films, including nitrate film, has been set up. So far, some 1,000 titles have been restored including the whole of the Lumière brothers film production from 1895 to 1905 which covers 1,400 short titles. A detailed catalogue of the Lumiére production is available in print and CD-Rom. Enquiries and viewing facilities for film are available on demand

TF1

1 Quai du Point du Jour
92656 Boulogne, Cédex
Tel: (33) 1 41 41 12 34
Fax: (33) 1 41 41 29 10
email: Website: www.tf1,fr
Privatised national television channel

Germany

ARD (Arbeitsgemeinschaft der öffentlich rechtlichen Rundfunkanstalten der Bundesrepublik Deutschland)

Programme Directorate of Deutsches Fernsehen
Arnulfstrasse 42
Postfach 20 06 22
80335 Munich
Tel: (49) 89 5900 01
Fax: (49) 89 5900 32 49
email: info@das-erste.de
Website: www.daserste.de
Christian Blankenburg
One of the two public service broadcasters in Germany, consisting of 9 independent broadcasting corporations (after a recent merger in Berlin-Brandenberg)

Beauftragter der Bundesregierung für Anglelengesheiten der Kultur und de Medien*

Postfach 170290
53108 Bonn
Tel: 01 44 76 62 00
Tel: (49) 1888 681 3594
Fax: (49) 1888 681 3885
email:
FriedrichWilhelm.moog@bkm.brni.bund400.de
Website: www.vdp.fr/

BVDFP (Bundesverband Deutscher Fernseh - produzenten)

Widenmayerstrasse 32
80538 Munich
Tel: (49) 89 21 21 47 10
Fax: (49) 89 228 55 62
Trade association for independent television producers

Deutsches Filmmuseum

Schaumainkai 41
60596 Frankfurt/Main
Tel: (49) 69 21 23 88 30
Fax: (49) 69 21 23 78 81
email: info@deutsches-filmmuseum.de
Website: www.deutshes-filmmuseum.de
Prof. Walter Schobert, Director
Hans-Peter Reichmann, Exhibitions/Archives
Ulrike Stiefelmayer, Filmtheatre

Export-Union des Deutschen Films (EXU)

Sonnenstr. 21
80331 München
Tel: (49) 89 599 787-0
Fax: (49) 89-599 787-30
email: export-union@german-cinema.de
Website: www.german-cinema.de
Board of Directors: Jochem Strate, Antonio Excoustos, Rolf Bahr, Michel Weber
Managing Director: Christian Dorsch
PR Manager: Susanne Reinker

FFA (Filmförderungsanstalt)

Presse- und Öffentlichkeitsarbeit
Grosse Präsidentensrasse 9
10178 Berlin
Tel.: 49 (0)30-27577-0
Fax.: 49 (0)30-27577-111
email: presse@ffa.de
Website: www.ffa.de
Rolf Bahr, - Directors General
The German Federal Film Board (FFA), incorporated under public law, is the biggest film funding institution in the country. Its mandate is the all-round raising of standards of quality in German film and cinema and the improvement of the economic structure of the film industry. The annual budget of about 105 million Deutschmarks (53,7 million Eruo) is granted by a levy raised from all major German cinemas and video providers and money of TV-stations. The administrative council of 29 members is a representative cross

section of the German film industry including members of the government's upper and lower house as well as public and private TV stations. Funding is offered in the following areas: full-length features, shorts, screenplays, marketing, exhibition, additional prints and professional training. The Export-Union des Deutschen Films e.V. largely represents the FFA's interests abroad

FilmFörderung Hamburg GmbH

Friedensalle14-16
22765 Hamburg
Tel: 00 (49) 40 39837-0
Fax: 00 (49) 40 39837-10
email: filmfoerderung@ffhh.de
Website: www.ffhh.de
Executive Director: Eva Hubert
Subsidies available for: script development; pre-production; co-production and distribution. Producers of cinema films can apply for a subsidy amounting to at most 50 per cent of the overall production costs of the finished film. Foreign producers can also apply for this support. It is recommended to co-produce with a German partner. 150 per cent of the subsidy must be spent in Hamburg and part of the film should be shot in Hamburg. Financial support provided by the FilmFörderung Hamburg can be used in combination with other private or public funding, including that of TV networks

Filmmuseum Berlin - Deutsche Kinemathek

Potsdamer Strasse 2
10785 Berlin
Tel: (49) 030 300 903
Fax: (49) 030 300 903-13
email: Website: www.filmmuseum-berlin.de
Website: Hans Helmut Prinzler
German Film Archive with collection of German and foreign films, cine-historical documents and equipment (approx. 10,000 films, over 12 million photographs, around 20,000 posters, 15,000 set-design and costume sketches, projectors, camera and accessories from the early days of cinema to the 80s). Member of FIAF

FSK (Freiwillige Selbstkontrolle der Filmwirtschaft)

Kreuzberger Ring 56
65205 Wiesbaden
Tel: (49) 611 77 891 0
Fax: (49) 611 77 891 39
email: fsk@spio-fsk.de
Website: www.spio-fsk.de
Film industry voluntary self-regulatory body. Activities are: to examine together with official competent representatives which films can be shown to minors under 18 year olds and under; to discuss the examination of films with youth groups; to organise seminars on the study of film, videos and new media

Kunsthochschule für Medien Köln (Academy of Media Arts)

Peter-Welter-Platz 2
50676
Cologne
Tel: (49) 221 201890
Fax: (49) 221 2018917
email: Website: www.khm.de
The first academy of Arts in Germany to embrace all the audio-visual media. It offers an Audio-visual Media graduate programme concentrating on the areas of Television/Film, Media Art, Media Design and Art and Media Science

ZDF Germany Television

ZDF
55100 Mainz
Tel: (49) 6131 702060
Fax: (49) 6131 706822
email: aa@zdf.de
Website: www.zdf.de
Germany's national public service television broadcaster

Greece

ERT SA (Hellenic Broadcasting Corporation)

Messoghion 402
15342 Aghia Paraskevi
Athens
Tel: (30) 1 639 0772
Fax: (30) 1 639 0652
Website: www.ert.gr
National public television and radio broadcaster, for information, education and entertainment

Greek Film Archive

Kanari 1 str
Athens 106 71
Tel: (30) 1 3612046
Fax: (30) 1 3628468
The Greek Film Archive is a non-profit making cultural organization whose aim is to gather together, preserve and present both Greek and international films. The Greek Film Archive came into being through the activities of the Athens Film Association, set up in 1950 by the Union of Film Critics in Athens

Greek Film Centre

10 Panepistimiou Avenue
10671 Athens
Tel: (30) 1 210 3678500
Fax: (30) 1 210 3648269
email: info@gfc.gr
Website: www.gfc.gr
Amanda Livanou
Corporation that belongs to the broader public sector, is supervised by the Greek Ministry of Culture and is subsidised by the Greek State. Its goals are the protection, support and development of film in Greece and the promotion of greek films both domestically and internationally.

Ministry of Culture

Cinema Department
Boulinas Street 20
10682 Athens
Tel: (30) 1 322 4737

Ireland

An Chomhairle Ealaíon/The Arts Council

70 Merrion Square
Dublin 2
Tel: (353) 1 6180200
Fax: (353) 1 6761302
email: info@artscouncil.ie
Website: www.artscouncil.ie/
The Arts Council/An Chomhairle Ealaion, is the Irish Government's development agency for the arts. The Council promotes creative experiment in film through support to film-makers through various bursaries, awards and schemes which aim to encourage artistic innovation and research. The Council also supports the film production organisations (FilmBase, Cork Film Centre, Galway Film Centre), who encourage training, short film production and information provision, especially for the emerging film-maker. The Council promotes film exhibition through support for resource organisations (Film Institute of Ireland, Access Cinema) and through support for major festivals (Cork, Dublin, Galway Film Festivals) and niche festivals (Fresh, Dark Light, Lesbian and Gay, Junior Dublin Film Festival). The Arts Council is concerned with general best practice in film exhibition and through its cultural cinema initiative (partners include the Irish Film Board and the

Northern Ireland Film and Television Commission) is enhancing the physical environment for film exhibition and promoting excellence in cultural cinema programming. The Council co-partners the Framework Animation Scheme with An Bord Scannán na hÉireann, RTÉ and SPLANC! - the Irish language arts documentary scheme with TG4

Bord Scannán na hÉireann/Irish Film Board

Rockfort House
St. Augustine Street
Galway
Tel: (353) 91 561398
Fax: (353) 91 561405
email: info@filmboard.ie
Website: www.filmboard.ie
Chief Executive: Rod Stoneman
Teresa McCRane, Head of Business Affairs
Brendan McCarthy, Head of Production and Development
Moira Horgan, Head of Marketing
Rebecca O'Flanagan, Development Manager
Naoise Barry, Location Services Manager
Paddy McDonald, Business Officer
Louise Ryan, Information Co-ordinator
Katie Lowry, Development Assistant
Jill McGregor, Schemes and Applications Co-ordinator
Mags O'Sullivan, Marketing Assistant

Film Censor's Office

16 Harcourt Terrace
Dublin 2
Tel: (353) 1 7996100
Fax: (353) 1 676 1898
email: johnkelleher@ifco.gov.ie
John Kelleher
The Official Film Censor is appointed by the Irish Government to consider and classify all feature films and videos distributed in Ireland

Film Institute of Ireland

Irish Film Centre
6 Eustace Street, Temple Bar
Dublin 2
Tel: (353) 1 679 5744/677 8788
Fax: (353) 1 677 8755
email: info@ifc.ie
Website: www.fii.ie/
The Film Institute promotes film culture through a wide range of activities in film exhibition and distribution, film/media education, various training programmes and the Irish Film Archive. Its premises, the Irish Film Centre in Temple Bar, are also home to Film Base, MEDIA Desk, The Junior Dublin Film Festival, The Federation of Irish Film Societies, and Hubbard Casting. The Building has conference facilities, a bar cafe and a shop as well as 2 cinemas seating 260 and 115

RTE (Radio Telefis Eireann)

Donnybrook
Dublin 4
Tel: (353) 1 208 3111
Fax: (353) 1 208 3080
Website: www.rte.ie
Public service national broadcaster

Italy

ANICA (Associazione Nazionale Industrie Cinematografiche e Audiovisive)

Viale Regina Margherita 286
00198 Rome
Tel: (39) 06 4425961
email: anica@anica.it
Website: www.anica.it/
Gino de Dominicis
Trade association for television and movie producers and distributors, representing technical industries (post-production companies/dubbing/studios/labs); home video producers and distributors; television and radio broadcasters

Film Museum

Palazzo Dugnani
Via D Manin 2/b
Milan
Tel: (353) 1 6180200
Fax: (353) 1 6761302
Gianni Comencini
Film archive, film museum. Set up to promote the preservation of film as art and historical document, and to promote the development of cinema art and culture

Fininvest Television

Viale Europa 48
20093 Cologno Monzese, Milan
Tel: (39) 2 251 41
Fax: (39) 2 251 47031
email: Adriano Galliani
Major competitor to RAI, running television channels Canale 5, Italia Uno and Rete Quattro

Fondazione Cineteca Italiana

Villa Reale, Via Palestro 16
20121 Milan
Tel: (353) 1 6180200
Fax: (353) 1 6761302
email: Fax: (39) 2 798289
Website: email: info@cinetecamilano.it
Website: www.cinetecamilano.it

Museo Nazionale del Cinema

Via Montebello 15
10124 Turin
Tel: (39) 11 8125658
Website: www.museonazionaledelcinema.org
Giuliano Soria, Paolo Bertetto, Sergio Toffetti, Donata Pesenti Campagnoni, Luciana Spina. The museum represents photography, pre-cinema and cinema history. Its collections include films, books and periodicals, posters, photographs and cinema ephemera

RAI (Radiotelevisione Italiana)

Viale Mazzini 14
00195 Rome
Tel: (39) 6 361 3608
Fax: (39) 6 323 1010
email: Website: www.rai.it
Italian state broadcaster

Surproduction S.A.S

Via del Rosso Fiorentiono 2/b
50142 Firenze
Tel: (39) 055 712127
Fax: (39) 055 712127
email: contact@surproduction.com
Website: surproduction.com
Bruno Spinazzola

Luxembourg

Luxembourg

Cinémathèque Municipale - Ville de Luxembourg
rue Eugène Ruppert 10
2453 Luxembourg
Tel: (352) 4796 2644
Fax: (352) 40 75 19
Official Luxembourg film archive, preserving international film heritage. Daily screenings every year 'Live Cinema' performances - silent films with music. Member of FIAF, (13,000 prints/35mm, 16mm, 70mm)

RTL Group

Blvd Pierre Frieden 45
1543 Luxembourg
Tel: (352) 42 1 42 1
Fax: (352) 42 1 42 2760
email: firstname.lastname@Rtlgroup.com

Website: www.rtlgroup.com
Anette Rey, Head of PR. Director of Corporate Communications: Roy Addison. Radio, television; productions and rights, internet

The Netherlands

Mediapark, Studiocentrum
Kamer 2326
1202 KV Hilversum
Tel: (31) 35 6231166
Fax: (31) 6280051
email: a.overste@wxs.nl
Director: Andries M. Overste
Trade association for independent television producers (currently 14members)

Ministry of Education, Culture and Science (OCW)
Film Department
PO Box 25000
2700LZ Zoetermeer
Tel: (31) 079 323 23 23
Fax: (31) 079 323 23 20
email: info@minocw.nl
Website: www.minocw.nl
Rob Docter, Séamus Cassidy
The film department of the Ministry is responsible for the development and maintenance of Dutch film policy. Various different organisations for production, distribution, promotion and conservation of film are subsidised by this department

Netherlands Public Broadcasting
PO Box 26444
1202 JJ Hilversum
Tel: (31) 35 67 79222
Fax: (31) 35 67 73586
email: louis.heinsman@omroep.nl
Website: www.omroep.nl
Louis Heinsman
Public corporation co-ordinating three-channel public television (plus five channels and internet activities)
Filmmuseum
PO Box 74782
1071 AA Amsterdam
Tel: (31) 20 589 1400
Fax: (31) 20 683 3401
email: info@filmmuseum,nl
Website: www.filmmuseum.nl
Film museum with three public screenings each day, permanent and temporary exhibitions, library, film café and film distribution

Portugal

Cinemateca Portuguesa - Museu do Cinema (Portuguese Film Archive - Museum of Cinema)
Rua Barata Salgueiro, No 39
1269-059 Lisboa
Portugal
Tel: 351 21 359 62 00
Fax: 351 21 352 31 80
email: cinemateca@cpmc.pt
Website: www.cinemateca.pt/
João Bénard da Costa, President
National film museum and archive, preserving, restoring and showing films. Includes a public documentation centre, a stills and posters archive

Instituto Português da Arte Cinematográfica e Audiovisual (IPACA)
Rua S Pedro de Alcântara 45-1o
1250 Lisbon
Tel: (351) 1 346 66 34
Fax: (351) 1 347 27 77
email: President: Zita Seabra, Vice-Presidents: Paulo Moreira, Salvato Telles de Menezes
Assists with subsidies, improvement, regulation and promotion of the television and film industry

RTP (Radiotelevisão Portuguesa)
Avenida 5 de Outubro 197
1094 Lisbon Cedex
Tel: (351) 1 793 1774
Fax: (351) 1 793 1758
Website: www.rtp.pt
Maria Manuela Furtado
Public service television with two channels: RTP1 - general, TV2 - cultural and sports. One satellite programme, RTP International, covering Europe, USA, Africa, Macau

Spain

Academia de las Artes y de las Ciencias Cinematográficas de España
General Oraá 68
28006 Madrid
Tel: (34) 1 563 33 41
Fax: (34) 1 563 26 93

Filmoteca Española
Caalle Magdalena 10
28012
Madrid
Tel: 34 91 369 21 18

ICAA (Instituto de la Cinematografia y de las Artes Audio-visuales)
Ministerio de Cultura
Plaza del Rey No1
28071 Madrid
Tel: (34) 1 532 74 39
Fax: (34) 1 531 92 12
Enrique Balmaseda Arias-Dávila
The promotion, protection and diffusion of cinema and audiovisual activities in production, distribution and exhibition. Gives financial support in these areas to Spanish companies. Also involved in the promotion of Spanish cinema and audio-visual arts, and their influence on the different communities within Spain

TVE Canales Tematicos
Edificio Prado del Rey - 3a planta
Office 3/014,
Prado Del Rey
28223 Madrid
Tel: (34) 1 5 346 31 83
Fax: (34) 1 5 346 31 12
email: Website: www.rtve.es/
Teresa Moreno, Acquistions Executive
National public service broadcaster, film producer and distributor

Sweden

Oberoende Filmares Förbund (OFF)/Independent Film Producers Association
Box 27 121
102 52 Stockholm
Tel: (46) 8 665 12 21
Fax: (46) 8 663 66 55
email: kansliet@off.se
Website: www.off.se
OFF is a non-profit organisation, founded 1984, with some 300 members. OFF promotes the special interests of filmmakers and independent Swedish producers of documentaries, short and feature films. Our purpose is twofold: to raise the quality of Swedish audiovisual production and to increase the quantity of domestic production. OFF works on many levels. The organisation partakes in public debate, organises seminars, publishes a quarterly newsletter, does lobby-work on a national level besides nordic and international networking. OFF aids its producers with legal counsel as well as copyright, economic and insurance policy advisement

Statens biografbyrå
Box 7728
103 95 Stockholm
Tel: (46) 8 24 34 25
Fax: (46) 8 21 01 78
email:
registrator@statensbiografbyra.se
Website: www.statensbiografbyra.se
Gunnel Arrbäck, Director
The Swedish National Board of Film Classification (Statens biografbyrå) was founded in 1911. Films and videos must be approved and classified by the Board prior to showing at a public gathering or entertainment. For videos intended for sale or hire, there is a voluntary system of advance examination

Svenska Filminstitutet (Swedish Film Institute)
Box 27 126
Filmhuset
Borgvägen 1-5
S-10252 Stockholm
Tel: (46) 8 665 11 00
Fax: (46) 8 661 18 20
email: andreas.tornblom@sfi.se
Website: www.sfi.se
Andreas Törnblom, Head of the Information Department
The Swedish Film Institute is the central organisation for Swedish cinema. Its activities are to: support the production of Swedish films of high merit; promote the distribution and exhibition of quality films; preserve films and materials of interest to cinematic and cultural history and promote Swedish cinematic culture internationally

Sveriges Biografägareförbund
Box 1147
S 171 23 Solna
Tel: (946) 8 735 97 80
Fax: (946) 8 730 25 60
The Swedish Exhibitors Association is a joint association for Swedish cinema owners

Sveriges Filmuthyrareförening upa
Box 23021
S-10435 Stockholm
Tel: (946) 8 441 55 70
Fax: (946) 8 34 38 10
email: Kay Wall
The Swedish Film Distributors Association is a joint association for film distributors

Swedish Women's Film Association
Po Box 27182
S-10251 Stockholm
Visitors address: Filmhuset, Borgvägen 5
Tel: (46) 8 665 1100/1293
Fax: (46) 8 666 3748
Anna Hallberg
Workshops, seminars, festivals and international exchange programme

MEDIA Programme

MEDIA Plus Programme
European Commission, Directorate General X:
Information, Communication, Culture, Audio-visual
rue de la Loi, 200
1040 Brussels, Belgium
Tel: (32) 2 299 11 11
Fax: (32) 2 299 92 14
Head of Programme: Jacques Delmoly

The MEDIA Plus Programme (2001 - 2005) is an European Union initiative that aims at strengthening the competitiveness of the European audiovisual industry with a series support measures dealing with the training of professionals, development of production projects, distribution and promotion of cinematographic works and audiovisual programmes. The programme was introduced in January 2001 as a follow up to the old MEDIA 2 programme. MEDIA Plus is managed by the Directorate General for Education and Culture at the European Commission in Brussels. It is managed on a national level by a network of 31 offices called the MEDIA Desks, Antennae or Service.

Programme Contents

MEDIA Training
- the programme offers funding for pan-European training initiatives. The Commission supports courses covering subjects such as economic, financial and commercial management, use of new technologies and scriptwriting techniques. These courses are open to all EU nationals. For details on how to participate on these courses, your local Desk, Antenna or Service, will supply you with details.

MEDIA Development
- the programme offers financial support to European independent production companies to develop new fiction, documentary, animation or multimedia projects. Financial support is offered to catalogues of projects (through the "slate funding" scheme) or to one project at a time. The amounts awarded will not exceed 50% of development budgets. If the project co-financed by MEDIA Plus goes into production, the company has an obligation to reinvest the same amount in the development of one or more production projects. Companies may apply for funding at any time of the year.

MEDIA Distribution
- the programme supports the distribution and broadcasting of audiovisual works (fiction, documentary, animation, interactive programmes) and of European films in movie theaters, on video, on digital disc and on television. It also provides support to networks of cinemas for the promotion and marketing of European films. There are fixed deadlines for this funding.

MEDIA Promotion
- the programme offers financial support to encourage all kind of promotional activities designed to facilitate European producers and distributors' access and participate at major European and international events. There are fixed deadlines running throughout the year.

Contact Details

Members of the UK MEDIA team listed below should be the first point of contact for UK companies or organisations seeking information and advice on the MEDIA Plus programme. Guidelines and application forms for all schemes are available from them or downloadable from their web-site: www.mediadesk.co.uk. However, all completed application forms should be sent directly to the MEDIA Programme office in Brussels, details of which you will find below.

MEDIA Desk UK
66-68 Margaret Street
London W1W 8SR
Tel: 020 7323 9733
Fax: 020 7323 9747

email: england@mediadesk.co.uk
Website: www.mediadesk.co.uk
Agnieszka Moody, Director

MEDIA Antenna Wales

C/o SGRÎN,
The Bank, 10 Mount Stuart Square,
Cardiff CF 10 5EE
Tel: 02920 333 304
Fax: 02920 333 320
email: wales@mediadesk.co.uk
Website: www.mediadesk.co.uk/wales
Gwion Owain

MEDIA Antenne Scotland

249 West George Street,
Glasgow
UK-G2 4QE.
Tel: 0141 302 1776/7
Fax: 0141 302 1778
email: media.scotland@scottishscreen.com
Website: www.mediadesk.co.uk
Emma Valentine

MEDIA Services Northern Ireland

21 Ormeau Avenue,
Belfast, UK-BT2 8HD
Tel: 02890 232 444
Fax: 02890 239 918
email: media@nifc.co.uk
Website: www.mediadesk.co.uk/northernireland
Cian Smyth

MEDIA Plus Office in Brussels

MEDIA Plus Programme,
European Commission,
DG Education and Culture, C3,
100, Rue Belliard,
B-1040 Brussels,
Tel: 00 322 295 84 06
Fax: 00 322 299 9214
Website:
europa.eu.int/comm/avpolicy/media/index_fr.html
Head of Unit : Jacques Delmoly
Development : Jean Jauniaux
Training: Gisela Gauggel-Robinson

MEDIA Plus Programme

European Commission, Directorate General
EAC (Education and Culture)
Culture, audiovisual policy and sport
rue de la Loi, 200
1049 Brussels, Belgium
Tel: (32) 2 295 84 06
Fax: (32) 2 299 92 14
email: eac-media@cec.eu.int
Website:
europa.eu.int/comm/avpolicy/media/index/en.html
Head of Programme: Jacques Delmoly
The MEDIA Plus Programme (2001 - 2005) is an European Union initiative that aims at strengthening the competitiveness of the European audiovisual industry with a series support measures dealing with the training of professionals, development of production projects, distribution and promotion of cinematographic works and audiovisual programmes. The programme was introduced in January 2001 as a follow up to the old MEDIA 2 programme. MEDIA Plus is managed by the Directorate General for Education and Culture at the European Commission in Brussels. It is managed on a national level by a network of 36 offices called the MEDIA Desks, Antennae or Service

CARTOON

(European Association of Animation Film)
314 Boulevard Lambermont
B - 1030 Brussels
Belgium
Tel: 00 32 2 245 1200
Fax: 00 32 2 245 4689
email: cartoon@skynet.be
Website: www.cartoon-media.be
Contact: Corinne Jennart, Marc Vendeweyer
CARTOON, based in Brussels, is a European animation network which organises the annual CARTOON FORUM, co-ordinates the grouping of animation studios and runs specialist training courses in animation

EUROPA CINEMAS

54 rue Beaubourg
F - 75 003 Paris
France
Tel: 00 33 1 42 71 53 70
Fax: 00 33 1 42 71 47 55
email: europacinema@magic.fr
Website: www.europa-cinemas.org
Contact: Claude-Eric Poiroux, Fatima Djoumer
The project encourages screenings and promotion of European films in a network of cinemas in European cities. It offers financial support for screening European films, for promotional activities and for special events

MEDIA SALLES

Via Soperga, 2
I - 20 127 Milan
Tel: 00 39 02 6698 4405"
Fax: 00 39 02 669 1574
email: infocinema@mediasalles.it
Website: www.mediasalles.it
Secretary General, Elisabetta Brunella
MEDIA SALLES with Euro Kids Network is an initiative aimed at consolidating the availability of 'cinema at the cinema' for children and young people in Europe, and at raising the visibility of European film to a younger audience

ORGANISATIONS

Listed below are the main trade/government organisations and bodies relevant to the film and television industries in the UK. This is followed by a separate list of Regional Arts Boards and Regional Film Commissions. Finally, a small selection of organisations from the US concludes this section

Advertising Association
Abford House
15 Wilton Road
London SW1V 1NJ
Tel: 020 7828 2771/828 4831
Fax: 020 7931 0376
email: aa@adassoc.org.uk
Website: www.adassoc.org.uk
Philip Spink
The Advertising Association is a federation of 25 trade bodies representing the advertising and promotional marketing industries including advertisers, agencies, media and support services

Advertising Producers' Association (APA)
26 Noel Street
London W1F 89T
Tel: 020 7434 2651
Fax: 020 7434 9002
email: info@a-p-a.net
Website: www.a-p-a.net
Stephen Davies, Chief Executive
The APA represents production companies making TV and cinema commercials. It regulates agreements with agencies and with crew and provides a telephone advice service on production and legal matters and other services for members

Advertising Standards Authority (ASA)
Brook House
2 Torrington Place
London WC1E 7HW
Tel: 020 7580 5555
Fax: 020 7631 3051
Website: www.asa.org.uk

AFMA Europe
49 Littleton Road
Harrow
Middx HA1 3SY
Tel: 020 8423 0763
Fax: Tel: 020 8423 7963
email: lsafir@afma.com
Website: www.afma.com
Chairman: Lawrence Safir

AIM (All Industry Marketing for Cinema)
22 Golden Square
London W1F 9JW
Tel: 020 7437 4383
Fax: 020 7734 0912
email: sfd@sfd.demon.co.uk
Peter Dobson
Unites distribution, exhibition and cinema advertising in promoting cinema and cinema-going. Funds Film Education, holds Cinema Days for regional journalists, markets cinema for sponsorship and promotional ventures and is a forum for cinema marketing ideas. In 2001, AIM and the UK Film Council jointly established the Cinema Marketing Agency with a remit to increase and broaden further the UK cinema audience

Amalgamated Engineering and Electrical Union (Amicus - AEEU)
Hayes Court,
West Common Road,
Bromley,
Kent BR2 7AU
Tel: 020 8462 7755
Fax: 020 8462 4959
Website: www.aeeu.org.uk
Trade union representing - among others -people employed in film and TV lighting/electrical/electronic work

AMPS (Association of Motion Picture Sound)
28 Knox Street
London W1H 1FS
Tel: 020 7723 6727
Fax: 020 7723 6727
email: info@amps.net
Website: www.amps.net
Brian Hickin
Promotes and encourages science, technology and creative application of all aspects of motion picture sound recording and reproduction, and seeks to promote and enhance the status of those therein engaged

APRS - The Professional Recording Association
PO Box 22
Totnes
Devon TQ9 7YZ
Tel: 01803 868600
Fax: 01803 868444
email: info@aprs.co.uk
Website: www.aprs.co.uk
Peter Filleul, Acting Executive Director

Arts Council England
14 Great Peter Street
London SW1P 3NQ
Tel: 020 7333 0100
Fax: 020 7973 6590
email: enquiries@artscouncil.org.uk
Website: www.artscouncil.org.uk
Gary Thomas
(See English Regional Arts Councils in this section)

Arts Council of Wales
9 Museum Place
Cardiff CF10 3NX
Tel: 029 20 376500
Fax: 029 20 395284
email: info@artswales.org.uk
Website: www.artswales.org.uk
Anneli Jones, Strategic Unit
Lottery funding is available for the development and production of film projects. Responsibility for film funding is in the process of being partially delegated to Sgrin Cymru Wales

ASIFA
International Animated Film Association
94 Norton Gardens
London SW16 4TA
Tel: 020 8679 3270
Fax: 020 8679 3270
email: uk@asifa.net
Website: uk@asifa.net
Pat Raine Webb
A worldwide association of individuals who work in, or make a contribution to, the animation industry, including students. Activities include involvement in UK

and international events and festivals, an Employment Databank, Animation Archive, children's workshops. The UK group provides an information service to members and a news magazine

Association for Media Education in Scotland (AMES)

c/o D Murphy
24 Burnett Place
Aberdeen AB24 4QD
Tel: 01224 277113
email: d@murphy47.freeserve.co.uk
Des Murphy

Audio Visual Association

Herkomer House
156 High Street
Bushey
Herts WD2 3DD
Tel: 020 8950 5959
Fax: 020 8950 7560
email: multimedia@visual-arena.co.uk
Mike Simpson FBIPP

Australian Film Commission (AFC)

c/o 99-101 Regent Street
London W1R 7HB
Tel: (61) 2 9321 6444
Fax: (61) 2 9357 3631
email: marketing@afc.gov.au
Website: www.afc.gov.au/
Pressanna Vasudevan

Authors' Licensing & Collecting Society

Marlborough Court
14-18 Holborn
London EC1 N 2LE
Tel: 020 7395 0600
Fax: 020 7395 0660
email: alcs@alcs.co.uk
Website: www.alcs.co.uk
The ALCS is the British collecting society for all writers. Its principal purpose is to ensure that hard-to-collect revenues due to authors are efficently collected and speedily distributed. These include the simultaneous cable retransmission of the UK's terrestrial and various international channels, educational off-air recording and BBC Prime. Contact the ALCS office for more information

BAFTA (British Academy of Film and Television Arts)

195 Piccadilly
London W1V OLN
Tel: 020 7734 0022
Fax: 020 7734 1792
Website: www.bafta.org
Amanda Berry, Chief Executive
BAFTA was formed in 1947 by Britain's most eminent filmmakers as a non-profit making company. It occupies a pivotal, unique position in the industry with a clear aim to promote excellence in film, television and interactive entertainment. BAFTA is a diverse organisation: it is a charity and a members' club; it undertakes a number of educational and training activities (including scholarships and workshops) and has an active and successful trading arm. Membership is available to those who have a minimum of three years professional experience in the film, television or interactive entertainment industries (or any combination of these), who are able to demonstrate significant ccontribution to the industry. BAFTA has facilities for screenings, conferences, seminaars and discussion meetings. Its awards for film and television are annual televised events. There are also awards for childrens' programming and interactive entertainment. The Academy has branches in Manchester, Glasgow, Cardiff, Los Angeles and New York

BARB (Broadcasters' Audience Research Board)

2nd Floor
18 Dering Street
London W1R 9AF
Tel: 020 7529 5531
Fax: 020 7529 5530
Website: www.barb.co.uk
The main source of television audience research in the United Kingdom is supplied by BARB (Broadcasters Audience Research Board Limited). The company represents the major UK broadcasters, the British Broadcasting Corporation (BBC), the Independent Television Association (ITVA), Channels 4 and 5, BSkyB and The Institute of Practitioners in Advertising (IPA). BARB was created in August 1980 when the BBC and ITV decided to have a mutually agreed source of television audience research. BARB became operational in August 1981

BECTU (Broadcasting Entertainment Cinematograph and Theatre Union)

373-377 Clapham Road
London SW9 9BT
Tel: 020 7346 0900
Fax: 020 7346 0901
email: info@bectu.org.uk
Website: www.bectu.org.uk
General Secretary: Roger Bolton

BKSTS - The Moving Image Society

Suite 104, G Block
Pinewood Studios
Iver Heath
Buckinghamshire SLO ONH
London W5 5ED
Tel: 01753 656656
Fax: 01753 657016
email: info@bksts.com
Website: www.bksts.com

British Academy of Composers and Songwriters

2nd Floor
British Music House
26 Berners Street
London W1T 3LR
Tel: 020 7636 2929
Fax: 020 7636 2212
email: info@britishacademy.com
Website: www.britishacademy.com
Julian Lancaster

British Amateur Television Club (BATC)

The Villa
Plas Panteidal
Aberdyfi
Gwynedd LL35 ORF
Tel: 01654 767702
email: memsec@batc.org.uk
Website: www.batc.org.uk
Pat Hellen
Non-profit making organisation run entirely by volunteers. BATC publish a quarterly technical publication CQ-TV which is available via subscription

British Association of Picture Libraries and Agencies

18 Vine Hill
London EC1R 5DZ
Tel: 020 7713 1780
Fax: 020 7713 1211
email: enquiries@bapla.org.uk
Website: www.bapla.org.uk
Chief Executive: Linda Royles

British Board of Film Classification (BBFC)

3 Soho Square
London W1D 3HD
Tel: 020 7440 1570
Fax: 020 7287 0141
email: webmaster@bbfc.co.uk
Website: www.bbfc.co.uk

Under the 1909 Cinematograph Films Act, local authorities were made responsible for safety in cinemas and also for what was shown. In 1912, the British Board of Film Censors was set up by the film industry to establish uniformity in film classification across the UK. The British Board of Film Censors became the British Board of Film Classification in 1985. The Board classifies films on behalf of local authorities and films cannot be shown in public in the UK unless they have a BBFC certificate or the relevant local authorisation. Local Authorities can, and sometimes do, overrule BBFC classification decisions. The Video Recordings Act 1984 requires that videos and video games which come under the Act must carry a BBFC classification if they are sold or rented in the UK. The BBFC is funded entirely from the fees charged for classification.

British Broadcasting Corporation (BBC)

Television Centre
Wood Lane
London W12 7RJ
Tel: 020 8743 8000
Website: www.bbc.co.uk
The BBC provides two national television networks, five national radio networks, as well as local radio and regional radio and television services. They are funded through the Licence Fee. The BBC is a public corporation, set up in 1927 by Royal Charter. Government proposals for the future of the BBC were published in a White Paper in July 1994. The BBC also broadcasts overseas through World Service Radio and Worldwide Television, but these are not funded through the Licence Fee

British Cinema and Television Veterans

22 Golden Square
London W1F 9AD
An association open to all persons employed in the United Kingdom or by United Kingdom companies in the cinema and/or broadcast television industries in any capacity other than as an artiste, for a total of at least thirty years

British Copyright Council

29-33 Berners Street
London W1T 3AB
Tel: 01986 788 122
Fax: 01986 788847
Website: www.britishcopyright.org.uk
Janet Ibbotson
Provides liaison between societies which represent the interest of those who own copyright in literature, music, drama and works of art, making representation to Government on behalf of its member societies

The British Council

Films and Television Department
11 Portland Place
London W1N 4EJ
Tel: 020 7389 3065
Fax: 020 7389 3041
Website: www.britcoun.org
www.britfilms.com
The British Council is Britain's international network for education, culture and technology. It is an independent, non-political organisation with offices in over 100 countries. Films and Television Department acts as a clearing house for international festival screenings of British short films and videos, including animation and experimental work. Using its extensive 16mm library, and 35mm prints borrowed from industry sources, it also ensures British participation in a range of international feature film events. The department arranges seminars overseas on themes such as broadcasting freedom and the future of public service television. It publishes the International Directory of Film and Video Festivals (biennial) and the annual British Films Catalogue. a 15-seat Preview Theatre (16mm, 35mm, video) is available for daytime use by UK filmmakers

British Design & Art Direction (D&AD)

9 Graphite Square
Vauxhall Walk
London SE11 5EE
Tel: 020 7840 1111
Fax: 020 7840 0840
email: info@dandad.co.uk
Website: www.dandad.org
Professional association and charity representing design and advertising communities

British Educational Communications and Technology Agency (Becta)

Milburn Hill Road
Science Park
University of Warwick
Coventry CV4 7JJ
Tel: 024 7641 6994
Fax: 024 7641 1418
email: Becta@becta.org.uk
Website: www.becta.org.uk
Becta is the Government's lead agency for ICT in education. It supports the UK Government and national organisations in the use and development of ICT in education to raise standards, widen access, improve skills and encourage effective management

British Federation of Film Societies (BFFS)

The Ritz Building
Mount Pleasant Campus
Swansea Institute of Higher Education
Swansea SA1 6ED
Tel: 01792 481170
email: info@bffs.org.uk
email: bffs-admin@sihe.ac.uk
Website: www.bffs.co.uk
Susan Hurford, Adminstration Manager
The BFFS exists to promote the work of some 300 film societies in the UK

British Film Designers Guild

24 St Anslem's Place
London W1Y 1FG
Tel: 020 7499 4336
Fax: 020 7499 4336
Promotes and encourages activities of all members of the art department. Full availability and information service open to all producers

British Film Institute

21 Stephen Street
London W1T 1LN
Tel: 020 7255 1444
Fax: 020 7436 7950
Website: www.bfi.org.uk
Amanda Nevil, Director
Founded in 1933, the BFI was incorporated by Royal Charter in 1983; it is the UK national agency with responsibility for encouraging the arts of film and television and conserving them in the national interest

British Institute of Professional Photography

Fox Talbot House
Amwell End
Ware
Herts SG12 9HN
Tel: 01920 464011
Fax: 01920 487056
email: bipp@compuserve.com
Website: www.bipp.com
Company Secretary: Alex Mair

British Interactive Multimedia Association Ltd
5/6 Clipstone Street
London W1P 7EB
Tel: 020 7436 8250
Fax: 020 7436 8251
email: enquiries@bima.co.uk
Website: www.bima.co.uk
Janice Cable, Administrator
Established in 1985, the British Interactive Media Association (BIMA) is the trade association representing the diverse interests of the UK interactive industry

The British Phonographic Industry Ltd (BPI)
Riverside Building
County Hall
Westminster Bridge Road
London SE1 7JA
Tel: 020 7803 1300
Fax: 020 7803 1310
email: general@bpi.co.uk
Website: www.bpi.co.uk
Andrew Yeates, Director General

British Recording Media Association
Orbital House
85 Croydon Road
Caterham
Surrey CR3 6PD
Tel: 01883 334495
Fax: 01883 334490
email: brma@admin.co.uk
Elaine Cole
Trade association for the manufacturers of blank recording media

British Screen Advisory Council (BSAC)
13 Manette Street
London W1D 4AW
Tel: 020 7287 1111
Fax: 020 7306 0329
email:bsac@bsacouncil.co.uk
Website: www.bsac.uk.com
Director: Fiona Clarke-Hackston, Chairman: David Elstein
BSAC brings together high level executives and specialists from both the traditional and new sectors to develop industry-wide views and to represent these views to policymakers

British Society of Cinematographers (BSC)
PO Box 2587
Gerrards Cross
Bucks SL9 7WZ
Tel: 01753 888052
Fax: 01753 891486
email: BritCinematographers@compuserve.com
Website: www.bscine.com
Frances Russell

Broadcasting Press Guild
Tiverton
The Ridge
Woking
Surrey GU22 7EQ
Tel: 01483 764895 or 0208 624 9052
Fax: 01483 765882 or 0208 624 9096
email: torin.douglas@bbc.co.uk
Richard Last, Membership Secretary
Torin Douglas, Branch Secretary

Broadcasting Research Unit
VLV Librarian
101 King's Drive
Gravesend
Kent DA12 5BQ
Tel: 01474 352835
Fax: 01474 351112
email: vlv@btinternet.com
Website: www.vlv.org.uk
Linda Forbes
The Broadcasting Research Unit was an independent Trust researching all aspects of broadcasting, development and technologies, which operated from 1980-1991. Its publications and research are now available from the above address

Broadcasting Standards Commission
7 The Sanctuary
London SW1P 3JS
Tel: 020 7808 1000
Fax: 020 7233 0397
The Broadcasting Standards Commission will become part of Ofcom at the end of 2003

BUFVC (British Universities Film and Video Council)
77 Wells Street
London W1T 3QJ
Tel: 020 7393 1500
Fax: 020 7393 1555
email: ask@bufvc.ac.uk
Website: www.bufvc.ac.uk
Luke McKernan, Head of Information
The BUFVC is a representative body which promotes the production, study and use of film and related media in higher education and research. It was founded in 1948 as the British Universities Film Council.The Council receives core grant support from the Joint Information Systems Committee (JISC) of the Higher Education Funding Councils via the Open University

BVA (British Video Association)
167 Great Portland Street
London W1W 5PE
Tel: 020 7436 0041
Fax: 020 7436 0043
email: general@bva.org.uk
Website: www.bva.org.uk/
Lavinia Carey
The BVA was established in 1980 to represent the interests of publishers and rights owners of pre-recorded home entertainment on video. The BVA is the most authoritative source of video industry statistical information. In April each year we publish the BVA Yearbook with detailed analysis of the previous year's VHS and DVD retail data, rental transactions, market shares and consumer usage and attitudinal feedback

Cable Communications Association
5th Floor
Artillery House
Artillery Row
London SW1P 1RT
Tel: 020 7222 2900
Fax: 020 7799 1471
Chief Executive: Bob Frost
Represents the interests of cable operators, installers, programme providers and equipment suppliers. For further information on cable, see under Cable and Satellite

Campaign for Press and Broadcasting Freedom
Second Floor
23 Orford Road
Walthamstow
London E17 9NL
Tel: 020 8521 5932
Fax: 020 8521 5932
email: freepress@cpbf.org.uk
Website: www.cpbf.org.uk
A broad-based membership organisation campaigning for more diverse, accessible and accountable media in Britain, backed by the trade union movement. The CPBF was established in 1979. Its bi-monthly journal Free Press examines current ethical, industrial and political developments in media policy and practice. CPBF acts as a parliamentary lobby group on censorship and media reform

Carlton Screen Advertising
12 Golden Square
London W1F 9JE
Tel: 020 7534 6363

Fax: 020 7534 6227
Website: www.carltonscreen.com
www.pearlanddean.com

Celtic Film and Television Festival

249 West George Street
Glasgow G2 4QE
Tel: 0141 302 1737
Fax: 0141 302 1738
email: mail@celticfilm.co.uk
Website: www.celticfilm.co.uk
Frances Hendron, Chief Executive

Central Office of Information (COI)

Films and Video
Hercules Road
London SE1 7DU
Tel: 020 7261 8495
Fax: 020 7261 8877
Ian Hamilton
COI Films and Video is responsible for government filmmaking on informational themes. The COI organises the production of a wide range of TV commercials and trailers, documentary films, video programmes and CD ROMs. It uses staff producers, and draws on the film and video industry for production facilities

Children's Film and Television Foundation (CFTF)

Elstree Film and Television Studios
Borehamwood
Herts WD6 1JG
Tel: 020 8953 0844
Fax: 020 8953 0860
email: annahome@cftf.onyxnet.co.uk
Anna Home, Chief Executive
The Children's Film and Television Foundation started as the Children's Film Foundation 50 years ago. Originally it made a large number of films for Saturday morning matinees. It now finances script development for children's and family films and television projects. Funding is on a loan basis. Films from the Foundation's library are available for hiring at a nominal charge in 35mm, 16mm and video formats

Church of England Communications Unit

London Diocesan House,
36 Causton Street,
London, SW1P 4AU
Tel: 020 7932 1240
Fax: 020 7233 8670
email: eric.shegog@dlondon.org.uk
Responsible for liaison between the Church of England and the broadcasting and film industries. Advises the C of E on all matters relating to broadcasting

Cinema Advertising Association (CAA)

12 Golden Square
London W1F 9JE
Tel: 020 7534 6363
Fax: 020 7534 6227
email: Website: www.adassoc.org.uk
Website: www.pearlanddean.com
www.carltonscreen.com

Cinema Exhibitors' Association (CEA)

22 Golden Square
London W1R 3PA
Tel: 020 7734 9551
Fax: 020 7734 6147
email: cea@cinemauk.ftech.co.uk
Contact : John Wilkinson, Annette Bradford and Elaine Pearce
Exhibition was the first sector of the film industry to organise nationally, in 1912. Following a merger with the Association of Independent Cinemas (AIC) it became the only association representing cinema exhibition. CEA members comprise over 90% of UK commercial cinemas, including independents, regional film theatres and cinemas in local authority ownership. CEA represents its members' interests with the industry and to local, national and European Government. It is closely involved in legislation which could affect exhibitors (current and proposed) emanating from UK Government and the European Commission. CEA produces guidelines for its members in areas such as Disability Access & Employment and Fire Risk. Its Executive Board meets regularly to decide on CEA policy and CEA Branches around the UK, which also meet regularly, relay feedback and comment to the Board.

Cinema Marketing Agency

(See AIM)
Cinema & Television Benevolent Fund (CTBF)
22 Golden Square
London W1F 9AD
Tel: 020 7437 6567
Fax: 020 7437 7186
email: infor@ctbf.co.uk
Website: www.ctbf.co.uk
Sandra Bradley

Cinema Theatre Association

44 Harrowdene Gardens
Teddington
Middx TW11 0DJ
Tel: 020 8977 2608
Fax: Website: www.cinema-theatre.org.uk
email: Adam Unger
The Cinema Theatre Association was formed in 1967 to promote interest in Britain's cinema building legacy, in particular the magnificent movie palaces of the 1920s and 1930s. It is the only major organisation committed to cinema preservation in the UK. It campaigns for the protection of architecturally important cinemas and runs a comprehensive archive. The CTA publishes a bi-monthly bulletin and the magazine Picture House

Comataidh Craolaidh Gaidhlig (Gaelic Broadcasting Committee)

4 Harbour View, Cromwell Street
Stornoway
Isle of Lewis HSI 2DF
Tel: 01851 705550
Fax: 01851 706432
email: admin@ccg.org.uk
Website: www.ccg.org.uk
The Gaelic Television Fund and Comataidh Telebhisein Gaidhlig was set up under the provisions of the Broadcasting Act 1990. Funds made available by the Government were to be paid to the ITC for the credit of the fund to be known as the Gaelic Television Fund. The Fund was to be managed by the body known as the Gaelic Television Committee. Under the Broadcasting Act 1996 the Gaelic Television Fund was redesignated as the Gaelic Broadcasting Fund and the Gaelic Television Committee became the Gaelic Broadcasting Committee

Commonwealth Broadcasting Association

17 Fleet Street
London EC4 1AA
Tel: 020 7583 5550
Fax: 020 7583 5549
email: cba@cba.org.uk
Website: www.cba.org.uk
Elizabeth Smith, Secretary General

Critics' Circle

51 Vartry Road,
London N15 6PS
Website: www.criticscircle.org.uk
President: Charles Osborne

Deaf Broadcasting Council

70 Blacketts Wood Drive
Chorleywood, Rickmansworth
Herts WD3 5QQ

Tel: 01923 284538
Fax: 01923 283127
email: rmyers@waitrose.com
Website: deafbroadcastcouncil.org.uk
Ruth Meyers

Defence Press and Broadcasting Advisory Committee

Room G27
Ministry of Defence
Metropole Building
Northumberland Avenue
London WC2N 5BP
Tel: 020 7218 2206
Fax: 020 7218 5857
Website: www.dnotice.org.uk
Secretary: Rear Admiral Nick Wilkinson
The Committee is made up of senior officials from the Ministry of Defence, the Home Office and the Foreign & Commonwealth Office and representatives of the media. It issues guidance, in the form of DA Notices, on the publication of information which it regards as sensitive for reasons of national security

Department for Education and Employment (DFEE)

Sanctuary Buildings
Great Smith Street
London SW1P 3BT
Tel: 020 7925 5000
Fax: 020 7925 6000
email: info@dfee.gov.uk
Website: www.dfee.gov.uk

Draft Zero

Medius House (LG Floor)
2 Sheraton Street
London W1F 8BH
Tel: 0870 366 6966
Fax: 07092 371 565
email: email: info@draft zero .com
Website: www.draftzero.com.
Nick Crittenden
A training and consultancy organisation that focuses on screenplay development for film, TV, radio and multimedia projects. It provides a development programme for screenwriters and modular short courses for industry personnel working in development aimed at producers, directors, development executives, script readers, script editors as well as screenwriters

The Directors' and Producers' Rights Society

Victoria Chambers
16-18 Strutton Ground
London SW1P 2HP
Tel: 020 7227 4757
Fax: 020 7227 4755
email: info@dprs.org
Website: www.dprs.org
Suzan Dormer, Chief Executive
The Directors' and Producers' Rights Society is a collecting society which administers authorials rights payments on behalf of British film and television Directors

Em-Media

35-37 St Mary's Gate
Nottingham NG1 1PU
Tel: 0115 950 9599
Fax: 0115 950 0988
email: info@em-media.org.uk
Website: www.em-media.org.uk
Ken Hay, Chief Executive

Equity

Guild House
Upper St Martin's Lane
London WC2H 9EG
Tel: 020 7379 6000
Fax: 020 7379 7001
email: info@equity.org.uk
Website: www.equity.org.uk
General Secretary: Ian McGarry

European Captioning Institute

Thurston House
80 Lincoln Road
Peterborough PE1 2SN
Tel: 0207 323 4657
Fax: 0207 323 4658

Federation Against Copyright Theft (FACT)

7 Victory Business Centre
Worton Road
Isleworth
Middx TW7 6DB
Tel: 020 8568 6646
Fax: 020 8560 6364
email: contact@fact-uk.org.uk
Website: www.fact-uk.org.uk
DNL Lowe, Director General
Spencer MOTT, Director of Operations
FACT, Federation Against Copyright Theft, is an investigative organisation funded by its members to combat counterfeiting, piracy and misuse of their products. The members of FACT are major companies in the British and American film, video and television industries. FACT is a non-profit making company limited by guarantee. FACT assists all statutory law enforcement authorities and will undertake private criminal prosecutions wherever possible

Federation of Entertainment Unions (FEU)

1 Highfield
Twyford
Nr Winchester
Hants SO21 1QR
Tel: 01962 713134
Fax: 01962 713134
email: harris.s@btconnect.com
Steve Harris
The FEU represents 170,000 people working across the media and entertainment industries in the UK. It is a lobbying and campaigning group which meets regularly with statutory bodies and pressure groups ranging from the BBC, Ofcom, and the Film Council through to the Voice of the Listener and Viewer. The Federation comprises Equity, Broadcasting Entertainment Cinematograph and Theatre Union, Musicians' Union, National Union of Journalists, the Professional Footballers' Association Writers' Guild of Great Britain and Amicus (Electricians Section). It has three standing committees covering Film and Electronic Media, European Affairs and Training

The Feminist Library

5a Westminster Bridge Road
London SE1 7XW
Tel: 020 7928 7789
email: feministlibrary@beeb.net
Website:
www.gn.apg.org/womeninlondon
The Feminist Library provides information about women's studies, courses, and current events. It has a large collection of fiction and non-fiction books, pamphlets, papers etc. It holds a wide selection of journals and newsletters from all over the world and produces its own quarterly newsletter. Social events are held and discussion groups meet every other Tuesday. The library is run entirely by volunteers. Membership library. Open Tuesday (11.00am-8.00pm) Wednesday (3.00pm -5.00pm) and Saturday (2.00-5.00pm). A writers' group meets alternate Sunday afternoons (writers' group and discussion group are women only)

Film Archive Forum

c/o British Universities Film & Video Council (BUFVC)
77 Wells Street
London W1T 3QJ
Tel: 020 7393 1500
Fax: 020 7393 1555

email: faf@bufvc.ac.uk
Website: www.bufvc.ac.uk
Luke McKernan, Chair

Film Artistes' Association (FAA)

373-377 Clapham Road
London SW9 9BT
Tel: 020 7436 0900
Fax: 020 7436 0901
email: smacdonald@bectu.org.uk
Spencer MacDonald
The FAA represents extras, doubles, stand-ins. Under an agreement with PACT, it supplies all background artistes in the major film studios and within a 40 mile radius of Charing Cross on all locations

Film Distributors' Association (FDA)

22 Golden Square
London W1F 9JW
Tel: 020 7437 4383
Fax: 020 7734 0912
email: info@fda.uk.net
Website: www.launchingfilms.com
Chief Executive: Mark Batey
Film Distributors' Association is the trade body for UK theatrical film distributors. It promotes the generic interests of distributors and offers a range of services to its member companies and others.

Film Education

2nd Floor
21-22 Poland Street
London W1V 3DD
Tel: 020 7851 9450
Fax: 020 7439 3218
email: postbox@filmeducation.org
Website: www.filmeducation.org
Ian Wall

Film London

20 Euston Centre
Regent's Place
London NW1 3JH
Tel: 020 7387 8787
Fax: 020 7387 8788
email: info@filmlondon.org.uk
Website: www.filmlondon.org.uk
Adrian Wooton, Chief Executive Officer
Gill Henderson, Head of Industry and Cultural Development
Sue Hayes, Film Commissioner
Daniela Kirchner, Head of Information and Strategy
On 1st April 2003 the London Film Commission (LFC) and the London Film and Video Development Agency (LFVDA) were brought together to form Film London, the new single strategic agency for the development of film and the screen sector in London. Film London is an independent company supported by the Film Council and other funders. It has a board chaired by the film producer Sandy Lieberson. Film London will provide an integrated service in production and business support, training, film locations, cinema education and exhibition

The Film Office

The Old Town Hall
Patriot Square
Bethnal Green
London E2 9NP
Tel: 020 8980 8771
Fax: 020 8981 2272
email: info@thefilmoffice.fsnet.co.uk
Website: www.filmoffice.co.uk
Works in association with local authorities in London to assist with filming in London locations

Film Unit Drivers Guild

136 The Crossways
Heston
Middlesex TW5 OJR
Tel: 020 8569 5001
Fax: 020 8569 6001
email: letstalk@fudg.uk.com
Website: www.fudg.com
L. Newell

First Film Foundation

9 Bourlet Close
London W1P 7PJ
Tel: 020 7580 2111
Fax: 020 7580 2116
email: info@firstfilm.demon.co.uk
Website: www.firstfilm.co.uk
First Film Foundation is a charity that exisits to help new British writers, producers and directors make their first feature film by providing a range of unique, educational and promotional programmes. FFF also provides impartial practical advice on how to develop a career in the film industry

FOCAL International Ltd (Federation of Commercial Audio-Visual Libraries)

Pentax House, South Hill Avenue
South Harrow
Middx HA2 ODU
Tel: 020 8423 5853
Fax: 020 8933 4826
email: info@focalint.org
Website: www.focalint.org
Commercial Manager: Anne Johnson

German Federal Film Board and Export Union of Germany Cinema

Top Floor
113-117 Charing Cross Road
London W2H ODT
Tel: 020 7437 2047
Fax: 020 7439 2947
email: Iris Kehr
UK representative of the German Federal Film Board (Filmförderungsanstalt), the government industry organisation, and the German Film Export Union (Export Union des Deutschen Films), the official trade association for the promotion of German films abroad. For full details see entries under Organisations (Europe)

Grierson Memorial Trust

c/o Ivan Sopher & co
5 Elstree Gate
Elstree Way
Borehamwood
Herts WD6 1JD
Tel: 020 8207 0602
Fax: 020 8207 6758
email: admin@greirsontrust.org
Website: www.griersontrust.org
Jeanette Lipscombe, Trust Adminstrator

Guild of British Camera Technicians

Panavision Building
Metropolitan Centre
Bristol Road
Greenford
Middlesex UB5 8GD
Tel: 020 8813 1999
Fax: 020 8813 2111
email: admin@gbct.org
Website: www.gbct.org
Christine Henwood, Office Manager
Rachel Conisbee, Database Manager

Guild of British Film Editors

72 Pembroke Road
London W8 6NX
Tel: 020 7602 8319
Fax: 020 7602 8319
email:
secretarygbfe@btopenworld.com
Sally Fisher, Secretary

Guild of Stunt and Action Co-ordinators

72 Pembroke Road
London W8 6NX
Tel: 020 7602 8319
Fax: 020 7602 8319
email: stunts.uk@btinternet.com
Sally Fisher

To promote the highest standards of safety and professionalism in film and television stunt work

Guild of Television Cameramen

1 Churchill Road
Whitchurch, Tavistock
Devon PL19 9BU
Tel: 01822 614405
Fax: 01822 615785
Website: www.gtc.org.uk
Sheila Lewis
The Guild was formed in 1972 'to ensure and preserve the professional status of the television cameramen and to establish, uphold and advance the standards of qualification and competence of cameramen'. The Guild is not a union and seeks to avoid political involvement

Guild of Vision Mixers

147 Ship Lane
Farnborough
Hants GU14 8BJ
Tel: 01252 514953
Fax: 01252 514953
Website: visionmixers.tv
Peter Turl
The Guild aims to represent the interests of vision mixers throughout the UK and Ireland, and seeks to maintain the highest professional standards in vision-mixing

IAC (Institute of Amateur Cinematographers)

24c West Street
Epsom
Surrey KT18 7RJ
Tel: 01372 739672
Fax: 01372 739672
email: iacfilmvideo@compuserve.com
Website: www.theiac.org.uk
Janet Smith, Admin Secretary

Imperial War Museum Film and Video Archive

Lambeth Road
London SE1 6HZ
Tel: 020 7416 5299
Fax: 020 7416 5379
email: film@iwm.org.uk
Website: www.iwm.org.uk
See entry under Archives and Film Libraries

Incorporated Society of British Advertisers (ISBA)

44 Hertford Street
London W1J 7AE
Tel: 020 7499 7502
Fax: 020 7629 5255
email: info@isba.org.uk
Website: www.isba.org.uk
Joe Lamb, Communications Manager

Incorporated Society of Musicians (ISM)

10 Stratford Place
London W1C 1AA
Tel: 020 7629 4413
Fax: 020 7408 1538
email: membership@ism.org
Website: www.ism.org
Chief Executive: Neil Hoyle

Independent Television Commission (ITC)

The ITC will become part of Ofcom at the end of 2003

Institute of Practitioners in Advertising (IPA)

44 Belgrave Square
London SW1X 8QS
Tel: 020 7235 7020
Fax: 020 7245 9904
Website: www.ipa.co.uk
The representative body for UK advertising agencies. Represents the collective views of its member agencies in negotiations with Government departments, the media and industry and consumer organisations

Intellect

Russell Square House
10 - 12 Russell Square
London WC1B 5EE
Tel: 020 7331 2000
Fax: 020 7331 2040/56
email: info@intellectuk.org
Website: www.intellectuk.org
Intellect is the trade body for the UK based information technology, telecommunications and electronics industry

International Association of Broadcasting Manufacturers (IABM)

Broad Oaks
Parish Lane
Farnham Common
Slough SL2 3JW
Tel: 01753 645682
Fax: 01753 645682
email: info@iabm.org.uk
Website: www.iabm.org.uk
Secretariat: Brenda White

International Federation of the Phonographic Industry (IFPI)

IFPI Secretariat
54 Regent Street
London W1R 5PJ
Tel: 020 7878 7900
Fax: 020 7878 7950
email: info@ifpi.org
Website: www.ifpi.org
Director General: Nicholas Garnett

International Institute of Communications

3rd Floor, Westcott House,
35 Portland Place,
London W1B 1AE
Tel: 020 7323 9622
Fax: 020 7323 9623
email: enquiries@iicom.org
Website: www.iicom.org

International Intelligence on Culture

4 Baden Place
Crosby Row
London SE1 1YW
Tel: 020 7403 7001
Fax: 020 7403 2009
email: enquiry@intelculure.org
Website: www.intelculture.org
Information Service
International Intelligence on Culture is a dynamic consultancy which brings together a highly-experienced multi-national group of experts to work with and for the international cultural sector. Our activities include: policy intelligence; research; consultancy; training; and information services. Our email, journal and web-based subscriber service International Cultural Compass will keep you up-to-date with international developments, policies and programmes relating to culture. Meanwhile our training sessions and information service can develop your awareness of existing opportunities, and how to access them and of key issues in the field.

ITV Network Ltd

200 Gray's Inn Road
London WC1X 8HF
Tel: 020 7843 8000
Fax: 020 7843 8160
email: dutyoffice@itv.co.uk
Website: www.itv.co.uk
Director of Programmes: J.Nigel Pickard

IVCA (International Visual Communication Association)

Business Communication Centre
19 Pepper Street, Glengall Bridge
London E14 9RP
Tel: 020 7512 0571
email: info@ivca.org
Website: www.ivca.org

Chief Executive: Wayne Drew
The IVCA is the largest European Association of its kind, representing a wide range of organisations and individuals working in the established and developing technologies of visual communication. With roots in video, film and business events industries, the Association has also developed significant representation of the new and fast growing technologies, notably business television, multimedia, interactive software and the internet. It provides business services for its members: legal help, internet service, insurance, arbitration etc. and holds events/seminars for training, networking and for all industry related topics

Kraszna-Krausz Foundation

122 Fawnbrake Avenue
London SE24 0BZ
Tel: 020 7738 6701
Fax: 020 7738 6701
email: info@k-k.org.uk
Website: www.k-k.org.uk
Andrea Livingstone, Administrator
The Foundation offers small grants to assist in the development of new or unfinished projects, work or literature where the subject specifically relates to the art, history, practice or technology of photography or the moving image (defined as film, television, video and related screen media). The Foundation also sponsors annual book awards, with prizes for books on the moving image (film, television, video and related media) alternating with those for books on still photography.

London Film and Video Development Agency (LFVDA)

See Film London

London Film Commission

See Film London

Lux

3rd Floor
18 Shacklewell Lane
London E8 2EZ
Tel: 020 7503 3980
Fax: 020 7503 1606
email: ben@lux.org.uk
Website: www.lux.org.uk
LUX is a not-for-profit organisation established to promote and support artists' moving image work both in the UK and internationally. While LUX represents the collection of the former Lux Centre, it does not run a cinema, a gallery, offer equipment hire, post-production facilities or training courses

Mechanical-Copyright Protection Society (MCPS)

29/33 Berner Street
London W1T 3AB
Tel: 020 8664 4500
Fax: 020 7306 4380
email: first name . last name @ mcps.co.uk
Website: www.mcps.co.uk
Contact: The Media Licensing Department
The Mechanical-Copyright Protection Society Ltd currently represents around 16,300 composers, songwriters and music publishers whenever their copyright musical works are recorded. Acting as an agent on behalf of its members, MCPS negotiates agreements with those who wish to record and distribute product containing copyright musical works. MCPS collects and then distributes "mechanical" royalties generated from the copying of music onto many different formats (CD, video, computer games etc). MCPS is a wholly owned subsidiary of the Music Publishers Association.

Medialex - Legal & Business Training

15 Sandycombe Road
Kew
Richmond
Surrey TW9 2EP
Tel: 020 8940 7039
Fax: 020 8758 8647
email: info@medialex.co.uk
Industry approved Media Law seminars designed for the film and television industry including copyright, contracts, industry agreements, music copyright, internet and new media

Mediawatch-uk

3 Willow House
Kennington Road
Ashford
Kent TN24 ONR
Tel: 01233 633936
Fax: 01233 633836
email: info@mediawatchuk.org
Website: www.mediawatchuk.org
Director: John C Beyer

Mental Health Media

356 Holloway Road
London N7 6PA
Tel: 020 7700 8171
Fax: 020 7686 0959
email: info@mhmedia.com
Website: www.mhmedia.com
Mental Health Media produces and sells videos and multimedia resources which educate and inform about mental health and distress. We also provide media skills training and support to users and professionals

Metier

Glyde House
Glydegate
Bradford BD5 0BQ
Tel: 01274 738 800
Fax: 01274 391 566
Chief Exec: Duncan Sones
A National Training Organisation, developing National and Scottish Vocational Qualifications for occupations in performing and visual arts, arts administration, front-of-house, arts development & interpretation and technical support functions in the arts and entertainment sector. It is responsible for strategic action to improve the quality, availability and effectiveness of vocational training within its industrial sector

Music Publishers Association Ltd

3rd Floor
20 York Buildings
London WC2N 6JU
Tel: 020 7389 0665
Fax: 020 7839 7776
email: pbrindley@mpaonline.org.uk
Website: www.mpaoline.org.uk
Paul Brindley, Communications Consultant

Music Video Producers' Association (MVPA)

26 Noel Street
London W1F 8GT
Tel: 020 7434 2651
Fax: 020 7434 9002
email: michael@a-p-a.net
Website: www.a-p-a.net
Stephen Davies
The MFVPA represents production companies making music promos. It advises on agreements and provides a telephone advice service to members on production and legal matters

Musicians' Union (MU)

60-62 Clapham Road
London SW9 0JJ
Tel: 020 7582 5566
Fax: 020 7793 9185
email: info@musiciansunion.org.uk

Website: Media Department
Contacts: Howard Evans, Marilyn Stoddart
Represents the interests of virtually all professional musicians in the UK. The media department deals with all music related issues involving film and TV: day to day working and interpretation of the MU/PACT agreement, synchronisation of audio recordings and advertisements and film and rights clearances. Queries regarding video, DVD, promotional filming, EPK's, contractors, musicians, composers and arrangers

National Association for Higher Education in the Moving Image (NAHEMI)

Sir John Cass Department of Art
London Guildhall University
31 Jewry Street
London EC3N 2EY
Tel: 020 8566 5673
email: yossibal@aol.com
Yossi Balanescu
A forum for debate on all aspects of film, video and multi media production in Higher Education. The Association has links with industry and government which represents in the UK which offer a major practical study in film, video, television and new media

National Campaign for the Arts

Pegasus House
37-43 Sackville Street
London W1S 3EH
Tel: 020 7333 0375
Fax: 020 7333 0660
email: nca@artscampaign.org.uk
Website: www.artscampaign.org.uk
Director: Victoria Todd

National Film and Television School

Beaconsfield Studios, Station Road
Beaconsfield
Bucks HP9 1LG
Tel: 01494 671234
Fax: 01494 674042
email: admin@nftsfilm-tv.ac.uk
Website: www.nftsfilm-tv.ac.uk
Director Full Time Programme, Roger Crittenden
The National Film and Television School provides advanced training and retraining to professional standards in all major filmmaking disciplines. Graduates are entitled to BECTU membership on entering employment. It is an autonomous non-profit making organisation funded by the Department for Culture, Media and Sport and the film and television industries. See also under Courses.

National Film Trustee Company Limited (NFTC)

4th Floor
66-68 Margaret Street
London W1W 8SR
Tel: 020 7580 6799
Fax: 020 7636 6711
email: alun@nftc.co.uk
Website: www.nftc.co.uk
Alun Tyers (Director)

National Museum of Photography Film & Television

Bradford BD1 1NQ
Tel: 0870 7010200
Fax: 01274 723155
email: talk.nmpt@nmsi.ac.uk
Website: www.nmpft.org.uk
Bill Lawrence, Head of Film
The world's only museum devoted to still and moving pictures, their technology and history. Host to three annual film festivals - Bradford Film Festival, Bite the Mango and BAF! - and home to three cinemas, including the world's only public Cinerama and Europe's first IMAX film system. TV Heaven offers 700 landmark programmes for viewing on demand while Insight: Collections and Research Centre is home to the national coollection of TV receivers and cameras, cinematography and a library of television commercials and film posters

National Screen Service

Unit 1
Perivale Industrial Park
Horsenden Lane South
Greenford
Middlesex UB6 7RU
Tel: 020 8991 2121
Fax: 020 8991 5757
Pat Walton

National Union of Journalists

Headland House
308-312 Grays Inn Road
London WC1X 8DP
Tel: 020 7278 7916 Direct line to Broadcasting Office: 0171 843 3726
Fax: 020 7837 8143
email: paulm@nuj.org.uk
Paul McLaughlin, National Broadcasting Organiser
Represents nearly 5,000 journalists working in broadcasting in the areas of news, sport, current affairs and features. It has agreements with all the major broadcasting companies and the BBC. It also has agreements with the main broadcasting agencies, WTN, Reuters Television and PACT

Neilsen EDI

Sixth Floor
Endeavour House
189 Shaftesbury Ave
London WC2H 87J
Tel: 020 7170 5200
Fax: 020 7 170 5201
Website: www.entdata.com
Dave Thurston, Managing Director
Nielsen EDI provides the film industry with official box office information. The London office currently tracks all films for all distributors from 865 theatres, covering 4,600 playdates per week across the U.K. and Ireland

NESTA (The National Endowment for Science, Technology and the Arts)

Fishmongers' Chambers,
110 Upper Thames Street
London, EC4R 3TW
Tel: Tel 020 7645 9500 Enquiry Line: 020 7645 9538
Fax: 020 7645 9501
email: nesta@nesta.org.uk
Website: www.nesta.org.uk
Chief Executive: Jeremy Newton

New Producers Alliance (NPA)

9 Bourlet Close
London W1W 7BP
Tel: 020 7580 2480
Fax: 020 7580 2484
email: queries@npa.org.uk
Website: www.newproducer.co.uk
The NPA is the national membership and training organisation for independent new producers and filmmakers. It provides access to contacts, information and advice regarding film production to over 1,000 members, ranging from film students and first timers to highly experienced feature filmmakers, major production companies and industry affiliates. Members services include; specialised producer training programmes from entrance' to advanced' levels; ongoing events, masterclasses, seminars, networking evenings, practical workshops and preview screenings; free advice services including legal and tax &

accountancy; monthly newsletter and online members' directory

Ofcom
Office of Communications
Riverside House
2A Southwark Bridge House
London SE1 9HA
Website: www.ofcom.org.uk

Office for National Statistics
1 Drummond Gate
London SW1V 2QQ
Tel: 0845 601 3034
Fax: 01633 652747
Website: www.statistics.gov.uk
email: info@statistics.gov.uk
The Office for National Statistics (ONS) is the government department that provides statistical and registration services. ONS is responsible for producing a wide range of key economic and social statistics which are used by policy makers across government to create evidence-based policies and monitor performance against them. ONS also builds and maintains data sources both for itself and for its business and research customers. It makes statistics available so that everyone can easily assess the state of the nation, the performance of government and their own position

The Official UK Charts Company
3rd Floor
Century House
100 Oxford Street
London W1D 1LN
Tel: 020 7436 3000
Fax: 020 7436 8000
email: info@theofficialcharts.com
Website: www.theofficialcharts.com
Sophie Clark

Office of Fair Trading
Fleetbank House
2-6 Salisbury Square
London EC4Y 8JX
Tel: 08457 22 44 99
email: enquires@oft.gsi.gov.uk
Website: www.oft.gov.uk
The Office of Fair Trading (OFT) currently enforces UK competition legislation in the film and television sectors. It also has a specific role relating to the supply of films for exhibition in cinemas. Following a report by the Monopolies and Mergers Commission (MMC) in 1994, the OFT is responsible for ensuring that the adverse public interest findings of the MMC are remedied. Under the Broadcasting Act 1990, the OFT also has three specific roles in relation to the television industry. In his report published in December 1992, the Director General of Fair Trading assessed the Channel 3 networking arrangement. The OFT also has a role in reviewing news provision for ITV and since January 1993 the OFT has had to monitor the BBC's progress towards a statutory requirement to source 25 per cent of its qualifying programming from independent producers

PACT (Producers Alliance for Cinema and Television)
45 Mortimer Street
London W1W 8HJ
Tel: 020 7331 6000
Fax: 0020 7331 6700
email: enquiries@pact.co.uk
Website: www.pact.co.uk
Chief Executive: John McVay

Pearl & Dean
3 Waterhouse Square
138-142 Holborn
London EC1N 2NY
Tel: 020 7882 1100
Fax: 020 7882 1111
Website: www.pearlanddean.com

Performing Right Society (PRS)
29-33 Berners Street
London W1T 3AB
Tel: 020 7580 5544
Fax: 020 7306 4455
email: musiclicence@prs.co.uk
Website: www.prs.co.uk
PRS is a non-profit making association of composers, authors and publishers of musical works. It collects and distributes royalties for the use, in public performances, broadcasts and cable programmes, of its members' copyright music and has links with other performing right societies throughout the world

Phonographic Performance (PPL)
1 Upper James Street
London W1F 9DE
Tel: 020 7534 1000
Fax: 020 7534 1111
Jill Drew
PPL (Phonographic Performance Limited) represents over 3,000 record companies - 14,000 labels and licenses the broadcast and public performance of their repertoire - recordings in every genre of music. We collect and distribute revenues from radio stations, pubs, clubs and thousands of users of sound recordings on behalf of member companies as well as some 25,000 performers

Production Managers Association (PMA)
Ealing Studios
Ealing Green
Ealing
London W5 5EP
Tel: 020 8758 8699
Fax: 020 8758 8658
email: pma@pma.org.uk
Website: www.pma.org.uk
C.Fleming

The Production Guild of Great Britain
Pinewood Studios
Pinewood Road
Iver Heath
Bucks SL0 0NH
Tel: 01753 651767
Fax: 01753 652803
email: info@productionguild.com
Website: www@productionguild.com
Lynne Hames (Administrator)

Radio, Electrical and Television Retailers' Association (RETRA)
Retra House
St John's Terrace
1 Ampthill Street
Bedford MK42 9EY
Tel: 01234 269110
Fax: 01234 269609
email: retra@tetra.co.uk
Website: www.retra.co.uk
Fred Round

The Royal Photographic Society
Milsom Street
Bath, Avon BA1 1DN
Tel: 01225 462841
Fax: 01225 448688
email: rps@rps.org
Website: www.rps.org
A learned society founded for the promotion and enjoyment of all aspects of photography. Contains a specialist Film and Video Group, secretary John Tarby, FRPS, with a regular journal, meetings and the opportunity to submit productions for the George Sewell Trophy and the Hugh Baddeley Trophy; and an Audiovisual group, secretary Brian Jenkins, LRPS, offering an extensive programme of events, seminars and demonstrations, and the bi-monthly

magazine AV News. Membership open to both amateur and professional photographers

Royal Television Society

Holborn Hall
100 Grays Inn Road
London WC1X 8AL
Tel: 020 7430 1000
Fax: 020 7430 0924
email: info@art.org.uk
Website: www.rts.org.uk
Dep. Exec. Director: Claire Price
The Television Society was formed on 7 September 1927, nine years before the first public service broadcast from Alexandra Palace. The Society was granted its Royal title in 1966 and now represents over 4,000 members from the entire spectrum of the broadcasting industry. No longer just an engineering society, RTS members can now be found in all parts of the ever widening industry. In order to serve its members nationwide, the Society has Regional Centres, each running its own programme of lectures and social functions throughout the year

Scottish Arts Council

12 Manor Place
Edinburgh EH3 7DD
Tel: 0131 226 6051
Fax: 0131 225 9833
email: help.desk@scottisharts.co.uk
Website: www.sac.org.uk
Director: Graham Berry
The Scottish Arts Council is an executive non-departmental public body (NDPB) which is one of the main channels for Government funding for the arts in Scotland, receiving its funding from the Scottish Executive. It also distributes National Lottery funds received from the Department for Culture, Media and Sport. As a non-departmental public body it is independent from, but accountable to, the Scottish Executive. It funds a range of arts organisations for annual programmes of work. In addition, it makes project and lottery grants to individual artists and arts organisations

Scottish Screen

Second Floor
249 West George Street
Glasgow G2 4QE
Tel: 0141 302 1700
Fax: 0141 302 1711
email: info@scottishscreen.com
Website: www.scottishscreen.com
Chief Executive: Steve McIntyre

Screenwriters' Workshop

Suffolk House
1-8 Whitfield Place
London W1T 5JU
Tel: 020 7387 5511
Fax: 020 7387 5511
email: screenoffice@tiscali.co.uk
Website: www.lsw.org.uk
Katharine Way

The Script Factory

Welbeck House
66/67 Wells Street
London W1T 3PY
Tel: 020 7323 1414
Fax: 020 7323 9464
email: general@scriptfactory.co.uk
Website: www.scriptfactory.co.uk
Briony Hanson, Co-Director
The Script Factory is a script development organisation which fills the gap between screenwriters and the film industry. It is a major provider of screenwriter and development training for the UK FILM COUNCIL; stages performed readings of screenplays in development; and produces a high profile series of masterclasses with filmmakers who have included Robert Altman, Spike Lee, Mira Nair, and Thomas Vinterberg, both across the UK and at international film festivals

Sgrîn (Media Agency for Wales)

The Bank, 10 Mount Stuart Square
Cardiff Bay
Cardiff CF10 5EE
Tel: 029 2033 3300
Fax: 029 2033 3320
email: sgrin@sgrin.co.uk
Website: www.sgrin.co.uk
Chief Executive: J. Berwyn Rowlands

The Short Film Bureau

74 Newman Street
London, W1T 3EL
Tel: 020 7207 636 2400
Fax: 020 7207 636 8558
email: info@shortfilmbureau.com
Website: www.shortfilmbureau.com
Contact: Kim Leggatt

SKILLSET

The Sector Skills Council for the Audio Visual Industries
80-110 New Oxford Street
London WC1A 1HB
Tel: 020 7520 5757
Fax: 020 7520 5758
email: info@skillset.org
Website: www.skillset.org
www.skillsformedia.com

Society of Authors' Broadcasting Group

84 Drayton Gardens
London SW10 9SB
Tel: 020 7373 6642
Fax: 020 7373 5768
email: jhodder@societyofactors.org
Website: www.societyofauthors.org
Jo Hodder
Specialities: Radio, television and film scriptwriters

Society of Cable Telecommunication Engineers (SCTE)

Fulton House Business Centre
Fulton Road, Wembley Park
Middlesex HA9 0TF
Tel: 020 8902 8998
Fax: 020 8903 8719
email: office@scte.org.uk
Website: www.scte.org.uk
Mrs Beverley K Allgood FSAE

The Society for Screen-Based Learning

9 Bridge Street
Tadcaster LS24 9AW
North Yorkshire
Tel: 01937 530520
Fax: 01937 530520
email: josie.key@learningonscreen.u-net.com
Website:
www.learningonscreen.org.uk
The Society is a meeting place, a skills forum, a resource for all those who want to exploit screen-based media in their roles as managers, trainers, lecturers, teachers, producers and communicators in the field of education, training, government and commerce

Society of Television Lighting Directors

STLD Secretary
c/o 11 Bloomfield Crescent
Ilford
Essex IG2 6DR
Website: www.stld.org.uk
The Society provides a forum for the exchange of ideas in all aspects of the TV profession including techniques and equipment. Meetings are organised throughout the UK and abroad. Technical information and news of members' activities are published in the Society's magazine

TAC (Welsh Independent Producers)

Gronant
Caernarfon

Gwynedd LL55 1NS
Tel: 01286 671123
Fax: 01286 678890
email: email post@teledwyr.com
Website: www.teledwyr.com
Dafydd Hughes

UK Film Council

10 Little Portland Street
London W1N 7JG
Tel: 020 7861 7861
Fax: 020 7861 7862
email: info@film.council.org.uk
Website: www.filmcouncil.org.uk
Contact: Iain Hepplewhite - Head of Communications
Tina McFarling - Head of Industry Relations
John Woodward, Chief Executive
The UK Film Council, the Government-backed film agency (not just film funding) is responsible for the creation of a sustainable film industry and developing education and film culture in the UK.
On April 1 2000 the UK Film Council took responsibility for the British Film Commission, the Arts Council of England's Lottery Film Department, British Screen Finance and the British Film Institute's Production Department. The British Film Institute continues to run as an independent body funded by the UK Film Council. The UK Film Council channels £55 million a year of into the industry - a combination of Lottery and Government grant in aid funding. Three production funds have been set up with an overall budget of £20 million a year to spend on film production and development - the Premiere Fund (£10m), the New Cinema Fund (£5m) and the Development Fund (£5m). The UK Film Council also has a Training Fund (£1 million a year) expanding training for scriptwriters and producer/film-makers in partnership with Skillset, the National Training Organisation for the film industry. In addition, a grant-funded programme supported by £1 million of Lottery funds called "First Light" offering children and young people the opportunity to experience film-making and display their talents using low-cost technology has been launched. As a strategic body the UK Film Council has created the £6 million a year Regional Investment Fund for England (RIFE) which is available to support cultural and industrial film initiatives in the English regions. The UK Film Council has also developed a joined-up UK-wide agenda with its sister organisations the national organisations Scottish Screen, Sgrîn, and the Northern Ireland Film Commission. The UK Film Council also continues to administer Lottery funds to the film production franchises set up by the Arts Council of England in 1997 and awarded to The Film Consortium, Pathé Pictures and DNA Films

UK Film Council International

10 Little Portland Street
London W1W 7JG
Tel: 020 7861 7860
Fax: 020 7861 7864
email: info@bfc.co.uk
Website: www.bfc.co.uk
Formerly known as the British Film Commission. Originally established in 1991, The BFC is now a division of the Film Council, funded through the department of Culture, Media and Sport. Its remit is to attract inward investment by promoting the UK as an international production centre to the film and television industries and encouraging the use of Britain's locations, services, facilities and personnel. Working with the UK Screen Agencies, the BFC also provides a bespoke information service to producers worldwide and assists those filming in the UK both before and during the shoot

Variety Club of Great Britain

Variety Club House
93 Bayham Street
London NW1 OAG
Tel: 020 7428 8100
Fax: 020 7428 8111
email: info@varietyclub.org.uk
Website: www.varietyclub.org.uk
Ginny Martin

The Video Standards Council

Kinetic Business Centre
Theobald Street
Borehamwood
Herts WD6 4PJ
Tel: 0208 387 4020
Fax: 0208 387 4004
Website: www.videostandards.org.uk
The VSC was established in 1989 as a non-profit making body set up to develop and oversee a Code of Practice and Code of Practice Rules designed to promote high standards within the video industry. The Code and Rules have subsequently been expanded to promote high standards within the computer and video games industry

VLV - Voice of the Listener and Viewer Ltd

101 King's Drive
Gravesend
Kent DA12 5BQ
Tel: 01474 352835
Fax: 01474 351112
email: vlv@btinternet.com
Website: www.vlv.org.uk
Linda Forbes

Women in Film and Television (UK)

6 Langley Street
London WC2H 9JA
Tel: 020 7240 4875
Fax: 020 7379 1625
email: info@wftv.org.uk
Website: www.wftv.org.uk
Emily Compton

Writers' Guild of Great Britain

15 Britannia Street
London WC1X 9JN
Tel: 020 7833 0777
Fax: 020 7833 4777
email: admin@writersguild.org.uk
Website: www.writersguild.org.uk
Bernie Corbett, General Secretary

Yorkshire/Yorkshire Media Industries Partnership*

Yorkshire Screen Commission
The Workstation
15 Paternoster Row
Sheffield S1 2BX
Tel: 0114 279 6511
Fax: 0114 279 6511
email: liz.ysc@workstation.org.uk
Liz Rymer, Acting CEO

English Regional Arts Boards

On 1 April 2002 The Arts Council of England and the 10 English Regional Arts Boards joined together to form a single development organisation for the arts in England. At the same time, regional boundaries were redrawn to complement existing Government Office boundaries and the three RABs in the south of England formed two new regional arts councils covering the same area.

For up to date details look up the Regional Arts Online website: www.arts.org.uk

Arts Council England
14 Great Peter Street
London SW1P 3NQ
Tel: 020 7333 0100
Fax: 020 7973 6590
email: enquiries@artscouncil.org.uk
Website: www.artscouncil.org.uk

Arts Council England, East
Eden House
48-49 Bateman Street
Cambridge CB2 1LR
Tel: 01223 454400
Fax: 0870 242 1271
email: email info@eearts.co.uk
Website: www.arts.co.uk
Arts Council England, East covers the following area:
Bedfordshire, Cambridgeshire, Essex, Hertfordshire, Norfolk, Suffolk; and unitary authorities of Luton, Peterborough, Southend-on-Sea, Thurrock

Arts Council England, East Midlands
St Nicholas Court
25-27 Castle Gate
Nottingham NG1 7AR
Tel: 0115 989 7520
Fax: 0115 950 2467
email: eastmidlands@
artscouncil.org.uk
Website: www.arts.co.uk
Arts Council England, East Midlands covers the following area:
Derbyshire, Leicestershire, Lincolnshire (excluding North and North East Lincolnshire), Northamptonshire, Nottinghamshire; and unitary authorities of Derby, Leicester, Nottingham, Rutland

Arts Council England, East Midlands
2 Pear Tree Court
London EC1R 0DS
Tel: 020 7608 6100
Fax: 020 7608 4100
email: london@artscouncil.org.uk
Website: www.arts.co.uk
Arts Council England, London covers the following area:
Greater London

Arts Council England, North East
Central Square
Forth Street
Newcastle upon Tyne NE1 3PJ
Tel: 0191 255 8500
Fax: 0191 230 1020
email: northeast@artscouncil.org.uk
Website: www.arts.co.uk
Arts Council England, North East covers the following area:
Durham, Northumberland; metropolitan authorities of Gateshead, Newcastle upon Tyne, North Tyneside, South Tyneside, Sunderland; and unitary authorities of Darlington, Hartlepool, Middlesbrough, Redcar and Cleveland, Stockton-on-Tees

Arts Council England, North West
Manchester House
22 Bridge Street
Manchester M3 3AB
Tel: 0161 834 6644
Fax: 0161 834 6969
email: information.n.w@
artscouncil.org.uk
Website: www.arts.org.uk
Arts Council England, North West covers the following area:
Cheshire, Cumbria, Lancashire; metropolitan authorities of Bolton, Bury, Knowsley, Liverpool, Manchester, Oldham, Rochdale, St Helens, Salford, Sefton, Stockport, Tameside, Trafford, Wigan, Wirral; and unitary authorities of Blackburn with Darwen, Blackpool, Halton, Warrington

Arts Council England, South East
Sovereign House
Church Street
Brighton BN1 1RA
Tel: 01273 763000
Fax: 0870 242 1257
email: southeast@artscouncil.org.uk
Website: www.arts.co.uk
Arts Council England, South East covers the following area:
Buckinghamshire, East Sussex, Hampshire, Isle of Wight, Kent, Oxfordshire, Surrey, West Sussex; and unitary authorities of Bracknell Forest, Brighton & Hove, Medway Towns, Milton Keynes, Portsmouth, Reading, Slough, Southampton, West Berkshire, Windsor and Maidenhead, Wokingham
Arts Council England, South West covers the following area:
Cornwall, Devon, Dorset, Gloucestershire, Somerset, Wiltshire; unitary authorities of Bath and North East Somerset, Bournemouth, Bristol, North Somerset, Plymouth, Poole, South Gloucestershire, Swindon, Torbay

Arts Council England, South West
England, South West
Bradninch Place
Gandy Street
Exeter EX4 3LS
Tel: 01392 218188
Fax: 01392 229229
email: southwest@artscouncil.org.uk
Arts Council England, South West covers the following area:
Cornwall, Devon, Dorset, Gloucestershire, Somerset, Wiltshire; unitary authorities of Bath and North East Somerset, Bournemouth, Bristol, North Somerset, Plymouth, Poole, South Gloucestershire, Swindon, Torbay

Arts Council England, South West
82 Granville Street
Birmingham B1 2LH
Tel: 0121 631 3121
Fax: 0121 643 7239
email: westmidlands@
artscouncil.org.uk
Website: www.arts.co.uk
Arts Council England, West Midlands covers the following area:
Shropshire, Staffordshire, Warwickshire, Worcestershire; metropolitan authorities of Birmingham, Coventry, Dudley, Sandwell, Solihull, Walsall, Wolverhampton; and unitary authorities of Herefordshire, Stoke-on-Trent, Telford and Wrekin

Arts Council England, Yorkshire
21 Bond Street
Dewsbury
West Yorkshire WF13 1AX

Tel: 01924 455555
Fax: 01924 466522
email: email info@yarts.co.uk
Website: www.arts.co.uk
Arts Council England, Yorkshire covers the following area: North Yorkshire; metropolitan authorities of Barnsley, Bradford, Calderdale, Doncaster, Kirklees, Leeds, Rotherham, Sheffield, Wakefield; and unitary authorities of East Riding of Yorkshire, Kingston upon Hull, North Lincolnshire, North East

UK Film Commissons and Film Offices

Bath Film Office
Trimbridge House
Trim Street
Bath BA1 2DP
Tel: 01225 477711
Fax: 01225 477279
email:
bath_filmoffice@bathnes.gov.uk
Website: www.visitbath.co.uk
Maggie Ainley, Film Commissioner

Comisean Fiolm na Gaidhealtachd's nan Eilean Alba (Scottish Highlands & Islands Film Commission)
Inverness Castle
Inverness 1V2 3EG
Tel: 01463 710221
Fax: 01463 710848
email: trish@scotfilm.org
Website: www.scotfilm.org
Trish Shorthouse, Jenny Yeomans

Screen Yorkshire
40 Hanover Square
Leeds LS3 1BQ
Tel: 0113 294 4410
email: ysc@workstation.org.uk
Website: www.ysc.co.uk
Yorkshire Screen Commission is now part of the new regional screen agency called Screen Yorkshire For locations, crewing and all kinds of production advice contact production liaison:
Kaye Elliott, Emma Waite

East Midlands Screen Commission
EM Media
35-37 St Mary's Gate
Nottingham NG1 3AL
Tel: 0115 9349090
Fax: 0115 9500988
email: emsc@emsc.org.uk
Webite: www.emsc.org.uk
Contacts: Phil Nodding, Emily Lappin, Kath Anderson

Eastern Screen
Anglia TV
Norwich NR1 3JG
Tel: 01603 767077
Fax: 01603 767191
email: info@easternscreen.com
Website: Web: www.eastern-screen.co.uk
Contacts: David Shepheard, Sarah Wheller

Edinburgh Film Focus
Castlecliff
25 Johnston Terrace
Edinburgh EH1 2NH
Tel: 0131 622 7337
Fax: 0131 622 7338
email: info@edinfilm.com
Website: www.edinfilm.com
George Carlaw, Ros Davis, Heather MacIntyre, Lucy Quinton

F.T.C. - Lancashire
Unit G14
Preston Technology Management Centre
Marsh Lane
Preston
Lancashire PR1 8UQ
Tel: 01772 889090
Fax: 01772 889091
email: lftvo@hotmail.com
Lynda Banister

Film and Television Commission @ North West England
109 Mount Pleasant
Liverpool L3 5TF
Tel: 015 1708 8099
Fax: 015 1708 9859
email: ftc@northwestengland.co.uk
Helen Bingham: Director of Marketing & Information,Andrew Patrick, Jane Arnold
Area: Cheshire, Greater Manchester, Lancashire, Merseyside

Glasgow Film Office
City Chambers
Glasgow G2 1DU
Tel: 0141 287 0424
Fax: 0141 287 0311
email: film.office@drs.glasgow.gov.uk
Website: www.glasgowfilm.org.uk
Lenny Crooks, Director

Isle of Man Film Commission
First Floor, Hamilton House
Peel Road, Douglas
Isle of Man 1M1 5EP
Tel: 01624 687173
Fax: 01624 687171
email: filmcomm@dti.gov.im
Website: www.gov.im/dti/iomfilm
Hilary Dugdale, Project Manager

Lanarkshire Screen Locations
Dept of Planning & Environment
North Lanarkshire Council
Kildonan Street
Coatbridge ML5 3LN
Tel: 01236 812 387

Fax: 01236 431 068
email: lesliea@northlan.gov.uk
Website: Alan J. Leslie
Covers North Lanarkshire, South Lanarkshire

Liverpool Film Office

4th Floor, Pioneer Buildings
67 Dale Street
Liverpool L2 2NS
Tel: 0151 291 9191
Fax: 0151 291 9199
email: lfo@liverpool.gov.uk
Website: filmliverpool.com
Lynn Saunders, Film Office Manager

Mid Wales Screen Commission

Mid Wales Office
6G Parc Gwyddoniaeth
Cefn Llan
Aberystwyth
Ceredigion SY23 3AH
Tel: 01970 617995
Fax: 01970 617942
Mathew Parry
Film Liaison Manager

North Wales Film Commission

Mentee, Deiniol Road
Bangor
Gwynedd LL57 2UP
Tel: 01286 679685
Fax: 01286 673324
email: fil@gwynedd.gov.uk
Website: Hugh Edwin Jones, Peter Lowther
Area film liaison office for information on filming in the county of Gwynedd and Anglesey. Information provided on locations, facilities and crew

Northern Film and Media Office

Central Square
Forth Street
Newcastle-upon-Tyne NE1 3PJ
Tel: 0191 269 9200
Fax: 0191 269 9213
email: first.name@nfmo.co.uk
Website: www.nsc.org.uk
Tom Harvey, Chief Executive
Michael Chaplin, Chair
Chief Executive: Tom Harvey

Northern Screen Commission

Central Square
Forth Street
Newcastle Upon Tyne NE1 3PJ
Tel: 019 1269 9212
Fax: 019 1269 9213
email: nsc@nfmo.co.uk
Website: Contacts: Dr Paul Mingard, Gayle Mason
Area: Cumbria, Durham, Teeside, Tyne & Wear, Northumberland

Northern Ireland Film and Television Commission

3rd Floor
Alfred House
21 Alfred Street
Belfast BT2 BED
Tel: 01232 232444
Fax: 01232 239918
email: info@nifc.co.uk
Website: www.nifc.co.uk
The Northern Ireland Film Commission promotes the growth of film and television culture and the industry in Northern Ireland

Screen East Locations

South Way
Leavesden
Hertfordshire WD2 7LZ
Tel: 01923 495 051
Fax: 01923 333007
email: locations@screeneast.co.uk
Website: www.filmlink.org.uk
Chris Holt, Head of Locations

Screen South

The Metropole Galleries
The Leas
Folkestone Kent CT2 2LS
Tel: 01303 851 320
email: firstname@screensouth.org
Gina Fegan, Chief Executive
Graham Benson, Chair

Screen West Midlands

31-41 Bromley Street
Birmingham B9 4AN
Tel: 0121 766 1470
Fax: 0121 766 1480
email: info@screenwm.co.uk
Website: www.screenwm.co.uk
Chief Executive: Krysia Rozanska

Screen West Screen

59 Prince Street
Bristol BS1 4QH
Tel: 0117 377 6066
Fax: 0117 377 6067
email:
firstname.surname@swscreen.co.uk
Caroline Norbury, Chief Executive
Jeremy Payne, Chair

South Wales Film Commission

The Media Centre
Culverhouse Cross
Cardiff Cf5 6XJ
Tel: (029) 2059 0240
Fax: (029) 2059 0511
email:
southwalesfilm@compuserve.com
Website: www.southwalesfilm.com
Yvonne Cheal, Commissioner

South West Scotland Screen Commission

Gracefield Arts Centre
28 Edinburgh Road
Dumfries DG1 1JQ
Tel: 01387 263666
Fax: 01387 263666
email: screencom@dumgal.gov.uk
Website: www.sw-scotlandscreen.com
Belle Doyle

Southern Screen Commission

Town Hall
Bartholomew Square
Brighton BN1 1JA
Tel: 01273 384211
Fax: 01273 384211
email: southernscreen@pavilion.co.uk
Website: Philippe Chandless
Southern Screen promotes and markets locations, personnel and services in the South East to the film and television industries

Tayscreen.com

Dundee Contemporary Arts
152 Nethergate
Dundee DD1 4DY
Tel: 01382 432321
Fax: 01382 432252
email: info@tayscreeen.com
Website: www.tayscreen.com
Julie Craike

Wales Film Commission

6G Science Park
Cefn Llan
Aberystwyth
Ceredigion SY23 3AH
Tel: 01970 627186
Fax: 01970 617942
email: enquiry@
walesscreencommission.co.uk
Website:
www.walesscreencommission.co.uk
Rachel Whitfield
Mid Wales Film Commission seeks to promote the use of Mid Wales facilities and locations for the production of films, television programmes and commercial

US Organisations

American Film Institute

2021 North Western Avenue
Los Angeles, CA 90027
Tel: (323) 856-7600
Fax: Fax (323) 467-4578
Website: www.AFI.com
Communications Office
Tel: (323) 856 7667
Fax: (323) 856 7798
Dedicated to advancing and preserving the art of film, television and other forms of the moving image

AMPAS (Academy of Motion Picture Arts & Sciences)

8949 Wilshire Boulevard
Beverly Hills
CA 90211
Tel: (1) 310 247 3000
Fax: (1) 310 859 9619
Organisation of producers, actors and others which is responsible for widely promoting and supporting the film industry, as well as for awarding the annual Oscars

Hollywood Foreign Press Association

292 S. La Cienega Blvd, #316
Beverly Hills
CA 90211
Tel: (1) 310 657 1731
Fax: (1) 310 657 5576
Journalists reporting on the entertainment industry for non-US media. Annual event: Golden Globe Awards - awarding achievements in motion pictures and television

The Museum of Television and Radio

25 West 52 Street
New York, NY 10019
Tel: (1) 212 621 6600/6800
Fax: (1) 212 621 6715
The Museum (formerly The Museum of Broadcasting) collects and preserves television and radio programmes and advertising commercials, and makes them available to the public. The collection, which now includes nearly 60,000 programmes, covers 70 years of news, public affairs programmes, documentaries, performing arts, children's programming, sports, and comedy. The Museum organises exhibitions, and screening and listening series

PR COMPANIES

The Associates
39-41 North Road
London N7 9DP
Tel: 020 7700 3388
Fax: 020 7609 2249
email: info@associates.co.uk
Website: www.the-associates.co.uk
Lisa Richards - Director
Film and video publicity specialists
Personnel:
Richard Larcombe - Managing Director
Rachael Marshall - Account Executive
Lisa DeBell - Account Services
Taryn Anderson - Financial Controller
Mike Brennan - writer/researcher

Avalon Public Relations
4a Exmoor Street
London W10 6BD
Tel: 020 7598 7222
Fax: 020 7598 7223
email: edt@avalonuk.com
Edward Thomson
Specialist entertainment based pr agency providing services from pr and unit publicity to transmission publicity and media launches

Blue Dolphin PR and Marketing
40 Langham Street
London W1N 5RG
Tel: 020 7255 2494
Fax: 020 7580 7670
email: traceyhislop@bluedolphinfilms.com
Website: www.bluedolphinfilms.com
PR and marketing arm of Blue Dolphin Films that specialises in key areas, such as film, video, television and music

The Braben Company
18b Pindock Mews
London W9 2PY
Tel: 0207 289 1616
Fax: 0207 289 1166
email: firstname@braben.co.uk
Website: Web: www.braben.co.uk
CEO: Ms. Sarah Braben
Managing Director: Matt Bourn
Braben Company was launched in 1994 and is a leading PR consultancy for the media and entertainment industries. Today the company has an extensive portfolio of clients in television, film and video, publishing, radio and new media, providing corporate, trade and consumer communications

Byron Advertising, Marketing and PR
Byron House
Wallingford Road
Uxbridge
Middx UB8 2RW
Tel: 01895 252131
Fax: 01895 252137
Les Barnes

Emma Chapman Publicity
2nd Floor
18 Great Portland Street
London W1W 8QP
Tel: 020 7637 0990
Fax: 020 7637 0660
email: emma@ecpub.com
Contact: Emma Chapman

CJP Public Relations Ltd
Park House
8 Grove Ash
Mount Farm
Milton Keynes MK 1B2
Tel: 01908 275271
Fax: 01908 275 272
email: t.chalmers@cjppr.co.uk
Website: www.cjppr.co.uk
Theo Chalmers

Max Clifford Associates
109 New Bond Street
London W1Y 9AA
Tel: 020 7408 2350
Fax: 020 7409 2294
Website:
www.maxcliffordassoc.demon.co.uk
email: max@mcapr.demon.co.uk
Max Clifford

Dennis Davidson Associates (DDA)
Royalty House
72-74 Dean Street
London W1D 3SG
Tel: 020 7534 6000
Fax: 020 7437 6358
email: info@ddapr.com
Dennis Davidson, Graham Smith, Jackie Page

emfoundation
the Old Truman Brewery
91-95 Brick Lane
London E1 6QN
Tel: 020 7247 4171
Fax: 020 7247 4170
email: info@emfoundation.co.uk
Website: emfoundation.co.uk
Keeley Naylor
emfoundation is a publicity & events management consultancy which was founded in 1998

FEREF Limited
14-17 Wells Mews
London W1A 1ET
Tel: 020 7580 6546
Fax: 020 7631 3156
email: robinbehling@feref.co.uk
Website: www.feref.com
Peter Andrews, Robin Behling, Brian Bysouth, Chris Kinsella

Franks PR Lynne
327-329 Harrow Road
London W9 3RB
Tel: 020 7724 6777
Fax: 020 7724 8484
Website: www.lynnefranks.com
Julian Henry

HPS-PR Ltd
Park House
Desborough Park Road
High Wycombe
Bucks, HP 123 DJ
Tel: 01494 684300
Fax: 01494 440952
email: r.hodges@hps-pr.co.uk
Ms Ray Hodges, MCam MIPR

JAC Publicity
1st Floor, Playhouse Court
64 Southwark Bridge Road
London SE1 0AS
Tel: 020 7261 1211
Fax: 020 7261 1214
email: susie@jac-ltd.com
Claire Forbes

Richard Laver Publicity
3 Troy Court
Kensington High Street
London W8 7RA
email: richardlaver@btconnect.com
Tel: 020 7937 7322
Richard Laver

McDonald and Rutter

34 Bloomsbury Street
London WC1B 3QJ
Tel: 020 7637 2600
Fax: 020 7637 3690
email: info@mcdonalddrutter.com
Website: www.mcdonaldrutter.com
Charles McDonald, Jonathan Rutter

Porter Frith Publicity & Marketing

26 Danbury Street
London N1 8JU
Tel: 020 7359 3734
Fax: 020 7226 5897
Sue Porter, Liz Frith

Premier Public Relations

91 Berwick Street
London W1F ONE
London W1 F 8QQ
Tel: 020 7292 8330
Fax: 020 7734 2024
email: (firstname)@prempr.co.uk
Website: www.prempr.co.uk
Lawrence Atkinson (Film)
Harriet Warburton (Corporate); Jane Gibbs (International); Melissa Hall-Smith (Television)
James Knox (Home Entertainment)
Managing Directors: Ginger Corbett, Sara Keene and Chris Paton

SSA Public Relations

Chesham House
150 Regent Street
London W1B 5ST
Tel: 020 7432 0336
Fax: 020 7432 0342
email: kfouchestssa@aol.com
Website: www.ssapr.com
Karine Fouchet
S.S.A Public Relations is a full service public relations firm that provides trade and consumer publicity for a wide range of corporate and entertainment clients. The company specialises in key areas, representing television and theatrical film production and distribution companies

Sue Hyman Associates

St. Martin's House
59 St. Martin's Lane
London WC2N 4JS
Tel: 020 7379 8420/9944
Fax: 020 7379 4944
email: sue.hyman.@btinternet.com
Sue Hyman

Town House Publicity

45 Islington Park Street
London N1 1QB
Tel: 020 7226 7450
Fax: 020 7359 6026
email: thp@townhousepublicity.co.uk
Website:
www.townhousepublicty.co.uk
Mary Fulton

UpFront Television Ltd

39-41 New Oxford Street
London WC1A 1BN
Tel: 020 7836 7702
Fax: 020 7836 7701
email: upfront@btinternet.com
Website:
www.celebritiesworldwide.com
Claire Nye
Richard Brecker

Warren Cowan/Phil Symes Associates

35 Soho Square
London W1V 5DG
Tel: 020 7439 3535
Fax: 020 7439 3737

Stella Wilson Publicity

130 Calabria Road
London N5 1HT
Tel: 020 7354 5672
Fax: 020 7354 2242
email: stella@starmaker.demon.co.uk
Stella Wilson

PRESS CONTACTS

19

(Monthly)
IPC Magazines
King's Reach Tower
Stamford Street
London SE1 9LS
Tel: 020 7261 6410
Fax: 020 7261 7634
Website: www.ipcmedia.com
Editor(s): April Joyce, Samantha Warwick
Film: Corrine Barraclough
Magazine for young women.
Lead time: 8 weeks
Circulation: 187,740

Arena

(Monthly)
Third Floor, Block A
Exmouth House
Pine Street
London EC1V 0JL
Tel: 020 78687500
Fax: 020 7689 0900
Website: www.emapmagazines.co.uk
Magazine for men covering general interest, film, literature, music and fashion.
Lead time: 6-8 weeks
Circulation: 100,000

Ariel

(Weekly, Tues)
Room 129, Henry Wood House
3 and 6 Langham Place
London W1A 1AA
Tel: 020 7765 3623
Fax: 020 7765 3646
email: claire.barrett@bbc.co.uk
Website: www.ariel.gateway.bbc.co.uk
Editor: Andrew Harvey
Deputy Editors: Sally Hillier and Cathy Loughran
BBC staff magazine.
Lead time: Tuesday before publication
Circulation: 24,000

Art Monthly

Britannia Art Publications Ltd.
4th Floor
28 Charing Cross Road
London WC2H 0DB
Tel: 020 7240 0389
Fax: 020 7497 0726
email: info@artmonthly.co.uk
Website: www.artmonthly.co.uk
Editor: Patricia Bickers
Deputy Editor: Andrew Wilson
Aimed at artists, art dealers, teachers, students, collectors, arts administrators, and all those interested in contemporary visual art. Includes a review section covering exhibitions and books.
Lead time: 4 weeks
Circulation: 4,000 plus

Asian Times

(Weekly, Tues)
Ethnic Media Group
Whitchapel Technical Centre, Unit 2
65 Whitechapel Road
London E1 1DU
Tel: 020 7650 2000
Fax: 020 7650 2001
email: asiantimes@easterneyeuk.co.uk
Website: www.ethnicmedia.co.uk
Editor: Amar Singh
National weekly newspaper for Britain's English-speaking Asian Community.
Press Day: Friday
Circulation: 30,000

The Big Issue

(Weekly, Mon)
1-5 Wandsworth Road
Vauxhall
London SW8 2LN
Tel: 020 7526 3200
Fax: 020 7526 3201
email: editorial@bigissue.com
Website: www.bigissue.com
Editor-in-Chief: A. John Bird
Managing Editor: Matt Ford
Deputy Editor (Arts): Lorna Russell
Film: Leslie Falperin
General interest magazine, with emphasis on homelessness. Sold by the homeless.
Lead time: Tues, 3 weeks before
Circulation: ABC figure 122,059

Black Filmmaker

Suite 13
5 Blackhorse Lane
London E17 6DS
Tel: 020 85319111
email: bfm@teleregion.co.uk
Website: www.blackfilmmakermag.com
Editor: Menelik Shabazz
Deputy Editor: Marsha Prescod
Magazine focusing on black film and television.

Broadcast

(Weekly, Fri)
EMAP Media
33-39 Bowling Green Lane
London EC1R 0DA
Tel: 020 7505 8000
Fax: 020 75058504
Editor: Conor Dignam
email: bcasted@media.emap.co.uk
Website: www.broadcastnow.co.uk
Broadcasting industry news magazine with coverage of TV, radio, cable and satellite, corporate production and international programming and distribution.
Press day: Wed.
Lead time: 2 weeks C
irculation: 13,556

The Business of Film

(Monthly)
41-42 Berners Street
London W1T 3NB
Tel: 020 7372 9992
Fax: 020 73729993
email: elspeth@thebusinessoffilm.com
Website: www.thebusinessoffilm.com
Publisher/Editor: Elspeth Tavares
Aimed at film industry professionals - producers, distributors, exhibitors, investors, financiers.
Lead time: 2 weeks

Caribbean Times

(Weekly, Mon)
Ethnic Media Group
Whitchapel Technical Centre, Unit 2
65 Whitechapel Road
London E1 1DU
Tel: 020 7650 2000
Fax: 020 7650 2001
email: caribbeantimes@ethnicmedia.co.uk
Website: www.ethnicmedia.co.uk
Editor: Michael Eboda
Tabloid dealing with issues pertinent to community it serves.
Press day: Fri
Circulation: 25,000

City Life
(Fortnightly)
164 Deansgate
Manchester M60 2RD
Tel: 0161 211 2708
Fax: 0161 839 1488
email: editorial@citlife.co.uk
Website: www.citylife.co.uk
Editor: Luke Bainbridge
Film editor: Danny Moran
What's on in and around Greater Manchester.
Circulation: 20,000

Company
(Monthly)
National Magazine Company Ltd.
National Magazine House
33 Broadwick Street
London W1F 9EP
Tel: 020 73123775
Fax: 020 73123797
email: company.mail@natmags.co.uk
Website: www.natmags.co.uk and www.company.co.uk
Editior: Sam Baker
Arts Writer: Ali Harris
Glossy magazine for women aged 18-30.
Lead time: 10 weeks
Circulation: 330,373

Cosmopolitan
(Monthly)
National Magazine Company Ltd.
National Magazine House
72 Broadwick Street
London W1V 2BP
Tel: 020 7439 5000
Fax: 02074376886
email: cosmo.mail@natmags.co.uk
Website: www.natmags.co.uk and www.cosmopolitan.co.uk
Editor: Lorraine Candy
Lyifestyle magazine for women aged 18-35.
Lead time: 12 weeks
Circulation: 463,058

Creation International
(Monthly)
Hardware Creations Ltd.
48 The Broadway
Maidenhead
Berkshire SL6 1PW
Tel: 01628773935
email: dick@hardwarecreations.tv
Editor: Dick Hobbs
Film, television, new media publication.
Circulation: 12,000

Creative Review
(Monthly)
Centaur Publishing
St. Giles House
50 Poland Street
London W1V 4AX
Tel: 020 79704000
Fax: 020 7970 4099
Website: www.mad.co.uk/cr/index.asp
Editor: Patrick Burgoyne
Publisher: Jess MacDermot
Trade paper for creative people covering film, advertising and design. Film reviews, profiles and technical features.
Lead time: 4 weeks
Circulation: 19,000

Daily Mail
Associated Newspaper Holdings
Northcliffe House
2 Derry Street
London W8 5TT
Tel: 020 7938 6000
Showbusiness Dpt.: 020 79386362
Fax: 020 79384890
Website: www.dailymail.co.uk
Editor: Paul Dacre
Managing Director: Guy Zitter
Entertainment Collumnist: Baz Bamigboye
Film: Christopher Tookey
TV: Peter Paterson
National daily tabloid newspaper.
Circulation: 2,163,676

The Daily Star
Express Newspapers PLC
Ludgate House
245 Blackfriars Road
London SE1 9UX
Tel: 020 792227373
Fax: 020 7922 7962
email: dailystarnewsdesk@dailystar.co.uk
Website: www.dailystar.co.uk
Editor: Peter Hill
National tabloid daily newspaper.
Circulation: 672,949

Daily Telegraph
Telegraph Group Ltd.
1 Canada Square
Canary Wharf
London E14 5DT
Tel: 020 7538 5000
Fax: 020 7538 6242
Website: www.telegraph.co.uk
Editor: Charles Moore
Film critic: Sukdev Sandhu
Arts Editor: Sarah Crompton
Media Correspondent: Tom Leonard
TV & Entertainment Editor: Marsha Dunstan
National broadsheet daily newspaper.
Lead time: 1 week
Circulation: 1,214,000

Diva
(Monthly)
Diva Magazine
Unit M
Spectrum House
32-34 Gordon House Road
London NW5 1LP
Tel: 020 7424 7400
Fax: 020 7424 7401
email: edit@divamag.co.uk
Website: www.divamag.co.uk
Editor: Gillian Rodgerson
Magazine on lesbian news and culture.
Lead times: 4-6 weeks
Circulation: 35,000

Eastern Eye
(Weekly, Thurs)
Ethnic Media Group
Whitchapel Technical Centre, Unit 2
65 Whitechapel Road
London E1 1DU
Tel: 020 7650 2000
Fax: 020 7650 2001
Editor: Amar Singh
Community news and perspectives on British Asian culture. Includes media reviews and indepth features on sports, music, and the arts.
Circulation: 35,000

The Economist
(Weekly)
25 St James's Street
London SW1A 1HG
Tel: 020 7830 7000
Fax: 020 79300458
email: inquires@economist.com
Website: www.economist.com
Editor: Bill Emmott
Culture Correspondant: Edmund Fawcett
International coverage of major political, social and business developments with arts section.
Press day: Wed
Circulation: 838,030

Elle
(Monthly)
Hachette Filipacchi UK Ltd.
64 North Row
London W1K 7LL
Tel: 020 71507000
Fax: 020 71507001
email: sarahbailey@hf-uk.com
Website: www.hachettefilipacchi.co.uk
Editor: Sarah Bailey
General Manager: Julie Harris
Glossy magazine aimed at 18-35 year old career women.
Lead time: 3 months
Circulation: 220,000

Empire
(Monthly)
Empire Magazine
4th Floor
Mappin House
4 Winsley Street
London W1W 8HF
Tel: 020 74361515
Fax: 020 73438703
email: empire@emap.com
Website: www.empireonline.co.uk
Editor: Colin Kennedy
Quality film monthly incorporating features, interviews and movie news as well as reviews of all new movies and videos.
Lead time: 3 weeks
Circulation: 161,503

Evening Standard
(Mon-Fri)
Associate Newspaper Holdings Plc.
Northcliffe House
2 Derry Street
Kensington
London W8 5TT
Tel: 020 7938 6000
Fax: 02079372648
Website: www.eveningstandard.co.uk
Editor: Veronica Wadley
Film: Neil Norman
Media editor: Victor Sebestyen
London weekday evening paper.
Circulation: 438,136

The Express
Express Newspapers Ltd.
Hamilton House
1 Temple Avenue
London EC4
Tel:020 7928 8000
Fax: 020 7620 1654
email: editor@express.co.uk
Website: www.express.co.uk
National daily tabloid newspaper
Circulation: 941,790

The Express on Sunday
Express Newspapers Ltd.
Hamilton House
1 Temple Avenue
London EC4
Tel:020 7928 8000
Fax: 020 7620 1654
email: editor@express.co.uk
Website: www.express.co.uk
Editor: Rosie Boycott
Film: Chris Peachment
TV: Nigel Billen
National Sunday tabloid newspaper.
Circulation: 894,204

The Face
(Monthly)
Endeavour House
189 Shaftesbury Avenue
London WC2H 8JG
Tel: 02072955000
email: editorial@theface.co.uk
Website: www.theface.co.uk
Film: Alex Rainer
Visual-orientated youth culture magazine: emphasis on music, fashion and films.
Lead time: 4 weeks
Circulation: 100,744

FHM
(Monthly)
Endeavour House
189 Shaftesbury Avenue
London WC2H 8JG
Tel: 020 78598657
Fax: 020 78598670
email: jacqui.tangney@emap.com
Website: www.fhm.co.uk
Editor: Dave McLaughlin
Deputy Editor: Chris Mooney
Men's lifestyle magazine.
Lead time: 6 weeks
Circulation: 755,000

Film Review
(Monthly + 4 specials)
Visual Imagination Ltd.
9 Blades Court, Deodar Road
London SW15 2NU
Tel: 020 8875 1520
Fax: 020 8875 1588
email: filmreview@visimag.com
Website: www.visimag.com/filmreview
Editor: Neil Corry
Reviews of films on cinema screen and video; star interviews and profiles; book and CD reviews.
Lead time: 1 month
Circulation: 50,000

Film Waves
(Quarterly)
Obraz Productions Ltd
PO Box 420 Edgware HA8 OXA
Tel: 020 8951 1681
email: filmwaves@filmwaves.co.uk
Website: www.filmwaves.co.uk
Editor/Publisher: Marco Zee-Jotti
Magazine for low/no-budget filmmakers

Financial Times
1 Southwark Bridge
London SE1 9HL
Tel: 020 7873 3000
Fax: 020 7873 3076
Website: www.ft.com
Editor: Andrew Gowers
Deputy Editor: Chrystia Freeland
National Broadsheet Newspaper giving financial information.
Circulation: 316,578

Gay Times
(Monthly)
Milliveres Prowler Ltd
Spectrum House
32-34 Gordon House Road
London NW5 1LP
Tel: 020 7424 7400
Fax: 020 7424 7401
email: edit@gaytimes.co.uk
Website: www.gaytimes.co.uk
Arts editor: James Cary Parkes
Britain's leading gay magazine. Extensive film, television and arts coverage
Lead time: 6-8 weeks
Circulation: 65,000

The Guardian
119 Farringdon Road
London EC1R 3ER
Tel: 020 7278 2332
Fax: 020 7837 2114
email: userhelp@guardian.co.uk
Website: www.guardian.co.uk
Editor: Alan Rusbridger
Media Editor: Charlie Burgess
National broadsheet daily newspaper.
Circulation: 407,870

Harpers & Queen
(Monthly)
National Magazine House
72 Broadwick Street
London W1F 9EP
Tel: 020 7439 5000
Fax: 020 7439 6886
email:
rebecca.broadley@natmags.co.uk (PA to Editor)
Website: www.harpersandqueen.co.uk
Editor: Lucy Yeomans
Arts & Films: Sarah Buys
Glossy magazine for women.
Lead time: 12 weeks
Circulation: 88, 049

Heat
Endeavour House
189 Shaftsbury Avenue
London WC2H 8JG
Tel: 020 7859 8657
Fax: 020 7598670
Website: www.emap.com
email: heat@ecm.emap.com
Film Editor: Charles Grant
TV Editor: Boyd Hilton

The Herald
200 Renfield Street
Glasgow
Scotland
G2 3QB
Tel: 01413027000
Fax: 01413027171
email: arts@theherald.co.uk
Website: www.theherald.co.uk

Editor: Harry Reid
Film critic: William Russell
TV editor: Ken Wright
Scottish daily newspaper
Circulation: 107,527

The Hollywood Reporter

(Daily and Weekly international, Tues)
US Office:
VNU Business Publications
5055 Wilshire Blvd
Los Angeles
CA 90036-4396
UK Office:
50-51 Bedford Row
London WC1R 4LR
Tel: 020 78228301
Fax: 020 72429137
email:
hollywoodreporter@galleon.co.uk
Website: www.hollywoodrepoter.com
Editor-in-Chief/Publisher: Robert J. Dowling
Editor: Howard Burns
TV Editor: Andrew Grossman
Film Editor: Gregg Kiday
Showbusiness trade paper.
Circulation: 39,000

Home Entertainment Week

(Weekly, Fri)
Bleeding Edge
3rd Floor, Jordon House
47 Brunswick Place
London N1 6EB
Tel: 020 7608 6767
Fax: 020 7608 6768
email: jhayward@columbus-group.co.uk
Website: www.heweek.co.uk
Editor: Peter Dodd
Video trade publication for rental and retail.
Lead time: Monday before publication
Circulation: 7,613

i-D Magazine

(Monthly)
US Office:
116 East 27th Street/ Floor 6
New York
NY 10016
Tel: 212 4471400
Fax: 212 4475231
UK Office:
Universal House
124 Tabbernacle Street
London EC2A 4SA
Tel: 020 7490 9710
Fax: 020 7251 2225
email: idedit@fwpubs.com
Website: www.idonline.com
Editor: Julie Lasky
Film & TV: David Cox
Youth/fashion magazine with film features
Lead time: 6-8 weeks
Circulation: 65,000

Illustrated London News

(2 pa)
20 Upper Ground
London SE1 9PF
Tel: 020 7805 5555
Fax: 020 7805 5911
email: iln@ilng.co.uk
Website: www.ilng.co.uk
Editor: Alison Booth
News, pictorial record and commentary, and a guide to coming events
Lead time: 8-10 weeks
Circulation: 30,000

In Camera

(Quarterly)
Kodak House
Entertainment Imaging
P.O Box 9b
Thanmes Ditton
Surrey KT7 OBR
Tel: 01442 844875
Fax: 01442 844987
Website: www.kodak.com
Editor: Martin Pearce
Business editor: Elisabete Perazzi
Journal for motion picture industry, primarily for cinematographers, but also for other technicians and anyone in the industry
Lead time: 4 weeks
Circulation: 45,000

The Independent on Sunday

Independent House
191 Marsh Wall
London E14 9RS
Tel: 020 7005 2000
Fax: 020 7005 2627
email: newseditor@independent .co.uk
Website: www.independent.co.uk
National broadsheet Sunday newspaper.
Lead time: 2 weeks
Circulation: 227,959

The Independent

Independent House
191 Marsh Wall
London E14 9RS
Tel: 020 7293 2000
Fax: 020 7293 2047
email: newseditor@independent.co.uk
Website: www.independent.co.uk
Editor(s): Simon Kelner & Janet Street-Porter
National broadsheet daily newspaper.
Circulation: 224,897

International Connection

Brave New World International Ltd.
Orchardton House
Auchencairn
Dumfries & Galloway
DG7 1QL
Tel: 08451306249
Fax: 08456588329
email: susan@bnw.demon.co.uk
Website: www.filmtvdir.com
Editor: Lauren Courtney
Publisher: Susan Foster
Film and TV industry business magazine.

Interzone

(Monthly)
David Pringle
C/o Interzone
217 Preston Drove
Brighton BN1 6FL
Tel: 01273 504710
email: interzone@cix.co.uk
Website: www.sfsite.com/interzone
Editor/Publisher: David Pringle
Film: Nick Lowe
Science-fiction and fantasy magazine.
Lead time: 8 weeks
Circulation: 10,000

The List

(Fortnightly, Thur)
14 High Street
Edinburgh EH1 1TE
Tel: 0131 550 3050
Fax: 0131 557 8500
email: mail@list.co.uk
Website: www.list.co.uk
Film editor: Paul Dale
TV: Brian Donaldson
Glasgow/Edinburgh events guide
Lead time: 1 week
Circulation: 18,000

Mail on Sunday

Associated Newspaper Holdings Ltd.
Northcliffe House
2 Derry Street
London W8 5TT
Tel: 020 7938 6000
Fax: 020 79384890
Website: www.mailonsunday.co.uk
Editor: Peter Wright
Film: Sebastian Faulks
TV critic: Jaci Stephen
National Sunday tabloid newspaper.
Press day: Fri/Sat
Circulation: 2,325,618

Marie Claire

(Monthly)
13th Floor Kings Reach Tower
Stamford Street
London SE1 9LS
Tel: 020 704445000

Fax: 020 7261 5277
Website: www.ipcmedia.com
Editor: Marie O'Riordan
Women's magazine
Lead time: 3 months
Circulation: 457,034

Media Week

(Weekly, Thur)
Quantum House
19 Scarbrook Road
Croydon CR9 ILX
Tel: 020 85654326
Fax: 020 8565 4394
email: mweeked@mediaweek.co.uk
Website: www.mediaweek.co.uk
Editor: Tim Burrowes
Deputy Editor: Mike Butcher
News magazine aimed at the advertising and media industries.
Press day: Wed
Circulation: 13,209 ABC

The Mirror

Mirror Group Newspapers Ltd.
1 Canada Square
Canary Wharf
London E14 5AP
Tel: 020 7293 3000
Fax: 020 72932435
email: feedback@mirror.co.uk
Website: www.mirror.co.uk
Editor: Piers Morgan
Film/TV Editor: Nicola Methuen
Film Critic: Kevin O'Sullivan
National tabliod daily newspaper with daily/weekly film and television column.
Circulation: 1,841,000
incorporating The Daily Record (Scottish daily newspaper)

Movie Club News

Orchardton House
Auchencairn
Dumfries & Galloway
DG7 1QL
Tel: 0845 1306249
Fax: 0845 658 83429
email: edit@bnw.demon.co.uk
Website: www.review.uk.com
Circulation: 60,000

New Musical Express

(Weekly, Wed)
25th Floor
King's Reach Tower
Stamford Street
London SE1 9LS
Tel: 08704445000
Fax: 020 7261 5185
Website: www.nme.com
Editor: Conor McNicholas
Film/TV editor: John Mulvey
Rock music newspaper
Lead time: Mon, 1 week before press day
Circulation: 121,001

New Statesman and Society

(Weekly, Fri)
7th Floor,
Victoria Station House
191 Victoria Street
London SW1E 5NE
Tel: 020 7828 1232
Fax: 020 7828 1881
email: info@newstatesman.co.uk
Website: www.newstatesman.co.uk
Editor: Peter Wilby
Art Director: David Gibbons
Independent radical journal of political, social and cultural comment.
Press day: Mon
Circulation: 26,000

News of the World

News Group Newspapers Ltd.
1 Virginia Street
London E1 9XR
Tel: 020 77824000
Fax: 020 75839504
email: ricky.sutton@news-of-the-world.co.uk
Website: www.newsoftheworld.co.uk
Editor: Ricky Sutton
Films: Johnathon Ross
TV critic: Charles Catchpole
National Sunday tabloid newspaper.
Press day: Sat
Circulation: 4,003,000

The Observer

(Weekly, Sun)
119 Farringdon Road
London EC1R 3ER
Tel: 020 7278 2332
Fax: 020 7713 4250
email: media@guardian.co.uk
Website: observer.guardian.co.uk
Arts editor: Jane Ferguson
Film critic: Philip French
TV: Mike Bradley
National daily broadsheet newspaper.
Lead time: 1 week
Press day: Fri
Circulation: 450,831

The PACT Magazine

Producers Alliance for Cinema and Television
C21 Media
Top Floor, 25 Phipp Street
London EC2 A4NP
Tel: 020 7729 7460
Fax: 020 7729 7461
email: Louise@c21media.net
Website: www.pact.co.uk
Editor: Louise Bateman
PACT members' monthly.
Circulation:2,000

The People

(Weekly, Sunday)
1 Canada Square
Canary Wharf
London E14 5AP
Tel: 020 7510 3000
Fax: 020 7293 3280
Website: www.people.co.uk
Editor: Mark Thomas
National Sunday newspaper.
Press day: Sat
Circulation: 1,400,000

Picture House

(Annual)
Cinema Theatre Association
c/o Neville C Taylor
Flat 1, 128 Gloucester Terrace
London W2 6HP
Tel: 01444 246893
email: nevtaylor@freeuk.com
Editor: Allen Eyles
Documents the past and present history of cinema buildings.
Lead time: 8 weeks
Circulation: 2,000

Pink Paper The

(Weekly, Thur)
2n Floor Medius House
63-69 New Oxford Street
London WC1A 1DG
Tel: 020 7845 4300
Fax: 020 78454309
email: editorial@pinkpaper.co.uk
Website: www.pinkpaper.com
Editor: Tristan Reid Smith
Assistant Editor: Simon Swift
Film/TV: Simon Swift
Britain's national lesbian and gay newspaper.
Lead time: 14 days
Circulation: 53,780[d]

PIX

c/o BFI Publishing
21 Stephen Street
London W1T 1LN
Tel: 020 7957 4789
Fax: 020 7636 2516
Editor/Designer: Ilona Halberstadt
A counterpoint of images and critical texts, PIX brings together experimental, independent and commercial cinema from all over the world and explores its relation to other arts.

Pocket Films

Rosedale House
Rosedale Road
Richmond

Surrey TW9 2SZ
Tel: 020 8939 9017/07931741419
email: pocketfilms@yahoo.com
Editor: Tony Franks
Two publications: The London Cinema Map (published quarterly) and Pocket Films (published weekly, scheduled re-launch Autumn 2002). The London Cinema Map is a visual guide to the location of the capital's 100-plus cinemas.
Circulation: Up to 200,000

Press Gazette

19 Scarbrook Road
Croydon
Surrey CR9 1LX
Tel: 020 8565 4473
Fax: 020 8565 4395
email: pged@app.co.uk
Website: www.pressgazette.co.uk
Editor: Ian Reeves
Weekly magazine covering all aspects of the media industry: journalism; advertising; broadcast; freelance.
Press day: Thurs
Circulation: 8,500

Q

(Monthly)
1st Floor
Mappin House
4 Winsley Street
London W1W 8HF
Tel: 020 74361515
Fax: 020 73479305
email: Qmagazine@Q4music.com
Website: www.qonline.co.uk
Editor: Paul Rees
Specialist music magazine for 18-45 year olds. Includes reviews of new albums, films and books
Lead time: 2 months
Circulation: 212,607

Radio Times

(Weekly, Tues)
80 Wood Lane
London W12 0TT
Tel: 0870 6084455
Fax: 020 8433 3923
email: radio.times@bbc.co.uk
Website: www.radiotimes.com
Editor: Gill Hudson
Films: Barry Norman
Weekly guide to UK television, radio and satellite programmes.
Lead time: 14 days
Circulation: 1,406,152

Regional Film & Video

(Monthly)
Flagship Publishing
48-50 York Street
Belfast BT15 1AS
Tel: 028 9031 9008
Fax: 028 9072 7800
email:
rfvnewscopy@flagshipmedia.co.uk
Website: www.4rfv.co.uk
Editor: Gavin Bell
Film and Video Trade Newspaper.
Circulation: 12,000

Satellite TV Europe

Highbury – WV
53-79 Highgate Road
London NW5 1TW
Tel: 020 73311000
Fax: 020 73311273
email: mail@satellitetvtoday.com
Website: www.satellitetvtoday.com
Editor: Paul Hirons
Circulation: 100,000

The Scotsman

The Scotsman Publications Ltd.
Barclay House
108 Holyrood Road
Edinburgh EH8 8AS
Tel: 0131 620 8620
Fax: 0131 620 8616
email: Jmcgurk@scotsman.com
Website: www.scotsman.com
Editorial Director: John McGurk
Assistant Editor: Charlotte Ross
Arts Editor: Andrew Eaton
Film Editor: Alistair Mackay
Scottish daily newspaper.
Circulation: 77,057

Scotland on Sunday

The Scotsman Publications Ltd.
Barclay House
108 Holyrood Road
Edinburgh EH8 8AS
Tel: 0131 620 8620
Fax: 0131 620 8616
Website: www.scotsman.com
email: Jmcgurk@scotsman.com
Arts & Film Editor: Fiona Leith
Scottish Sunday newspaper.
Lead time: 10 days
Circulation: 110,000

Screen Digest

(Monthly)
Lyme House Studios
38 Georgiana Street
London NW1 0EB
Tel: 020 7424 2820
Fax: 020 7580 0060
email: editorial@screendigest.com
Website: www.screendigest.com
Managing director: Allan Hardy
Editor: David Fisher
Executive editor: Ben Keen
Deputy editor: Mark Smith
International industry news digest and research report covering film, television, cable, satellite, video and other multimedia information. Has a centre page reference system every month on subjects like law, statistics or sales.

Screen Finance

(Fortnightly)
Informa Media
Mortimer House
37-41 Mortimer Street
London W1T 3JH
Website: www.infomamedia.com
Tel: 020 70174248
Fax: 020 7017 4289
Editor: Tim Adler
Detailed analysis and news coverage of the film and television industries in the UK and Europe
Lead time: 1-3 days

Screen International

(Weekly, Thur)
EMAP Media
33-39 Bowling Green Lane
London EC1R 0DA
Tel: 020 7505 8000
Fax: 020 7505 8117
email:
Leo.Barraclough@media.emap.co.uk
Website: www.screendaily.com
Managing Editor: Leo Barraclough
Features: Leo Barraclough
International trade magazine for the film, television, video, cable and satellite industries. Regular news, features, production information from around the world
Press day: Tue
Features lead time: 3 months
Circulation: 10,000

Screen

(Quarterly)
The Gilmorehill Centre
University of Glasgow
Glasgow G12 8QQ
Tel: 0141 330 5035
Fax: 0141 330 3515
email: screen@arts.gla.ac.uk
Website: www.screen.arts.gla.ac.uk
Editorial Assistant: Caroline Beven
Journal of essays, reports, debates and reviews on film and television studies. Organises the annual Screen Studies Conference
Circulation: 1,400

SFX

Future Publishing
99 Baker Street
London W1M 1FB
Tel: 0207 3172600
Fax: 0207 4865678
email: sfx@futurenet.co.uk

Website: www.sfx.co.uk
Editor: Dave Golder
Circulation: 39,603

Shivers

(Monthly)
Visual Imagination Ltd
9 Blades Court
Deodar Road
London SW15 2NU
Website: www.visimag.com
Tel: 020 8875 1520
Fax: 020 8875 1588
Editor: David Miller
Horror film reviews and features.
Lead time: 1 month
Circulation: 30,000

Sight and Sound

(Monthly)
British Film Institute
21 Stephen Street
London W1T 1LN
Tel: 020 7255 1444
Fax: 020 7436 2327
Editor: Nick James
Incorporating 'Monthly Film Bulletin'. Includes regular columns, feature articles, a book review section and review/synopsis/credits of every feature film theatrically released, plus a brief listing of every video
Copy date: 4th of each month
Circulation: 24,300

South Wales Argus

Cardiff Road
Maesglas
Newport
Gwent NP20 3QN
Tel: 01633 810000
Fax: 01633 777202
email: kevin.ward@gwent-wales.co.uk
Website: www.thisisgwent.co.uk
Editor: Gerry Keighley
Deputy Editor: Kevin Ward
Film & TV editor: Lesley Williams
Regional evening newspaper
Lead time: 2 weeks
Circulation: 32,569

The Spectator

(Weekly, Thur)
56 Doughty Street
London WC1N 2LL
Tel: 020 7405 1706
Fax: 020 7242 0603
email: editor@spectator.co.uk
Website: www.spectator.co.uk
Editor: Boris Johnson
Arts editor: Elizabeth Anderson
Film: Mark Steyn
TV: James Delingpole and Simon Hoggart
Independent review of politics, current affairs, literature and the arts.
Press day: Wed
Circulation: 60,000

Stage Screen & Radio

(10 issues a year)
BECTU
373-377 Clapham Road
London SW9 9BT
Tel: 020 73460900
Fax: 020 73460901
email: info@bectu.org.uk
Website: www.bectu.org.uk
Editor: Janice Turner
Journal of the film, broadcasting, theatre and entertainment union BECTU. Reporting and analysis of these industries and the union's activities plus coverage of technological developments.
Lead time: 4 weeks
Circulation: 34,600

The Stage

(Weekly, Thurs)
The Stage Newspaper Ltd.
47 Bermondsey Street
London SE1 3XT
Tel: 020 7403 1818
Fax: 020 7357 9287
email: editor@thestage.co.uk
Website: www.thestage.co.uk
Editorial Assistant: Alex Whitelaw
TV: Joanna Taylor
Weekly trade paper covering all aspects of entertainment.
Circulation: 40,198 ABC

Starburst

(Monthly + 4 Specials + German language version)
Visual Imagination
9 Blades Court
Deodar Road
London SW15 2NU
Tel: 020 8875 1520
Fax: 020 8875 1588
email: starburst@visimag.com
Website: www.visimag.com/starburst
Group Editor: Stephen Payne
Editor: Gary Gillat
Magazine covering science fiction, fantasy and horror films, television and video.
Lead time: 1 month
Circulation: 45,000

Stardust

(Monthly)
Magna Publishing Co. (UK) Ltd.
Wembley Point
2nd Floor
1 Harrow Road
Wembley
Middlesex HA9 6DE
Tel: 02087955318
Fex: 02087955328
email: stardustmag@aol.com
Editor: Ashwin Varde
Magazine focusing on Indian cinema.
Circulation: 207,787

Stills Audio Motion

SAM Publications
15 Marden Road
Staplehurst
Kent TN12 0NF
Tel: 0158 089 1683
Fax: 0158 089 0143
email: stillsaudiomotion@talk21.com
Editor: Steve Bergson

The Sun

PO Box 481
1 Virginia Street
London E1 9XP
Tel: 020 7782 4000
Fax: 020 7488 3253
Website: www.thesun.co.uk
Editor: Rebecca Wade
Showbiz Editor: Victoria Newton
TV Features: Beth Adams
National daily tabloid newspaper
Circulation: 3,875,329

Sunday Mirror

Mirror Group Newspapers Ltd.
1 Canada Square
Canary Wharf
London E14 5AP
Tel: 020 7293 3000
Fax: 020 72932435
email: feedback@mirror.co.uk
Website: www.mirror.co.uk
Film critic: Quentin Falk
TV: David Rowe, Pam Francis
National Sunday tabloid newspaper.
Circulation: 2,268,263

Sunday Telegraph

Telegraph Group Ltd.
1 Canada Square
Canary Wharf
London E14 5AP
Tel: 020 7538 5000
Fax: 020 7538 6242
email: starts@telegraph.co.uk
Website: www.telegraph.co.uk
Arts: Susannah Herbert
Film: Jenny McCartney
TV: John Preston
National Sunday broadsheet newspaper.
Circulation: 886,377

Sunday Times

1 Pennington Street
London E98 1TT
Tel: 020 7782 5000
Website: www.the-times.co.uk
Editor: John Witherow

National broadsheet Sunday newspaper.
Press day: Wed
Circulation: 1,314,576

Talking Pictures

(Quarterly)
1 Orchard Cottages
Colebrook
Plympton
Plymouth PL7 4AJ
Tel: 01752 347200
email: valis23a@aol.com
Website: www.talkingpix.co.uk
Editor: Nigel Watson
Online magazine (formerly Talking Pictures) devoted to a serious yet entertaining look at film, computer entertainment, television and video/DVD.

Tatler

(Monthly)
Vogue House
1 Hanover Square
London W1S 1JU
Tel: 020 7499 9080
Fax: 020 74931345
Website: www.tatler.co.uk
Editorial Director: Vassi Chamberlain
Arts Editor: Camila Long
Features Editor: Kate Bernard
Smart society magazine favouring profiles, fashion and the arts.
Lead time: 3 months
Circulation: 88,235

Telegraph Magazine

Telegraph Group Ltd.
1 Canada Square
Canary Wharf
London E14 5DT
Tel: 020 7538 5000
Fax: 020 75386242
Website: www.telegraph.co.uk
TV films: Jessamy Calkin
Supplement to Saturday edition of the Daily Telegraph
Lead time: 6 weeks
Circulation: 1,300,000

Television

(10 p.a.)
Royal Television Society
Holborn Hall
100 Gray's Inn Road
London WC1X 8AL
Tel: 020 7430 1000
Fax: 020 7430 0924
email: info@rts.org.uk
Website: www.rts.org.uk
Editor: Steve Clarke
Television trade magazine
Lead time: 2 weeks
Circulation: 4,000

Televisual

(Monthly)
St. Giles House
50 Poland Street
London W1F 7AX
Tel: 020 7970 6446
Fax: 020 7970 6733
email: tvlcirc@centaur.co.uk
Website: www.televisual.com
Editor: Mundy Ellis
Features Editor: James Hamilton
Monthly business magazine for production professionals in the business of moving pictures
News lead time: 1 month
Features lead time: 2 months
Circulation: 6,000

Time Out

(Weekly, Tues)
Universal House
251 Tottenham Court Road
London W1P 7AB
Tel: 020 7813 3000
Fax: 020 7813 6001
Website: www.timeout.co.uk
Editor: Laura Lee Davis
Film: Geoff Andrew, Tom Charity
TV: Alkarim Jivani
London listings magazine with cinema and television sections.
Listings lead time: 8 days
Features lead time: 1 week
Circulation: 100,000 plus

The Times Educational Supplement Scotland

(Weekly, Fri)
Scott House
10 South St Andrew Street
Edingburgh EH2 2AZ
Tel: 0131 557 1133
Fax: 0131 558 1155
email: scoted@tes.co.uk
Website: www.tes.co.uk/scotland
Editor: Olga Wojtas
Press day: Wed
Circulation: 10,000

The Times Educational Supplement

(Weekly, Fri)
Admiral House
66-68 East Smithfield
London E1 1BX
Tel: 020 7782 3000
Fax: 020 7782 3333
email: editor@tes.co.uk
Website: www.tes.co.uk
Editor: Bob Doe
Deputy Editor: David Budge
Review editor, Friday magazine: Geraldine Brennan
Press day: Tuesday
Lead itme for reviews: copy 14-21 days
Circulation: 157,000

The Times Higher Educational Supplement

(Weekly, Fri)
Admiral House
66-68 East Smithfield
London E1 1BX
Tel: 020 7782 3000
Fax: 020 7782 3333
email: editor@thes.co.uk
Editor: John O'leary
Deputy Editor: Gerard Kelly
Press day: Wed
Lead time for reviews: copy 10 days before publication
Circulation: 26,666

The Times Literary Supplement

(Weekly, Fri)
Admiral House
66-68 East Smithfield
London E1W 1BX
Tel: 020 7782 3000
Fax: 020 7782 3100
email: lettersethe-tls.co.uk
Website: www.the-tls.co.uk
Arts editor: Will Eaves
Press day: Tues
Lead time: 2 weeks
Circulation: 35,000

The Times

1 Pennington Street
London E98 1TT
Tel: 020 7782 5000
Website: www.the-times.co.uk
Editor: Robert Tomson
Film/video critic: Geoff Brown
Film writer: David Robinson
TV: Matthew Bond
National daily newspaper
Circulation: 747,054

Total Film

Future Publishing
99 Baker Street
London W1M 1FB
Tel: 020 7317 2600
Fax: 020 74865678
email: totalfilm@futurenet.co.uk
Website: www.futurenet.co.uk
Editor: Matt Mueller

Tribune

(Weekly, Fri)
9 Arkwright Road
London NW3 6AN
Tel: 020 7433 6410
Fax: 020 74336419
email: mail@tribuneweekly.com
Website: www.tribuneweekly.com

Editor: Mark Seddon
Review editor: Caroline Rees
Political and cultural weekly that covers issues concerning the labour and trade union movements.
Lead time: 14 days
Circulation: 10,000

TV Times

(Weekly, Tues)
IPC Media
King's Reach Tower
Stamford Street
London SE1 9LS
Website: www.ipcmedia.com
Tel: 020 7261 7000
Fax: 020 7261 7777
Editor: Mike Hollinsworth
Film editor: David Quinlan
Weekly magazine of listings and features serving viewers of trestrial, satellite and radio programmes.
Lead time: 6 weeks
Circulation: 981,311

TV Zone

(Monthly + 4 specials)
Visual Imagination Limited
9 Blades Court
Deodar Road
London SW15 2NU
Tel: 020 8875 1520
Fax: 020 8875 1588
email: tvzone@visimag.com
Website: www.visimag.com/tvzone
Editor: Tom Spilsbury
Magazine of cult television, past, present and future, with emphasis on science fiction and fantasy
Lead time: 1 month
Circulation: 45,000

Uncut

IPC Magazines Ltd
King's Reach Tower
Stamford Street
London SE1 9LS
Tel: 020 7261 6992
Fax: 020 7261 5573
Website: www.uncut.net
Editor: Allan Jones
Art Editor: Kerrin Hands
Circulation: 40,167

Variety

(Weekly, Mon) and Daily (Mon-Fri)
7th Floor
88 Theobalds Road
London WC1X 8RR
Tel: 020 7611 4580
Fax: 020 7611 4591
email: news@reedbusiness.com
Website: www.variety.com
International Sales Director: Lionel O'Hara
European editor: Adam Dawtrey
International showbusiness newspaper
Press day: Thurs
Circulation: 36,000

Viewfinder

(4 p.a.)
BUFVC
77 Wells Street
London W1T 3QJ
Tel: 020 7393 1500
Fax: 020 7393 1555
email: ask@bufvc.ac.uk
Website: www.bufvc.ac.uk
Editor: Hetty Malcom-Smith
Periodical for people in higher education and further education and research, includes articles on the production, study and use of film, television and related media. Also includes supplement Media Online Focus Deadlines: 25 January, 24 April, 24 August, 25 October
Lead time: 6 weeks
Circulation: 5,000

Vogue

(Monthly)
Conde Nast Publications Ltd.
Vogue House
Hanover Square
London W1R 0AD
Tel: 020 7499 9080
Fax: 020 7493 1345
email: voguemagaizne@codenast.com
Website: www.vogue.com
Editor: Alexandra Shulman
Films: Susie Forbes
Glossy magazine for women
Lead time: 12 weeks
Circulation: 201,187

The Voice

(Weekly, Monday)
Vee Tee Ay (Media) Resources Ltd.
Nu Vox House
Coldharbour Lane
London SW9 8PL
Tel: 020 7737 7377
Fax: 020 7274 8994
email: mail@the-voice.co.uk
Website: www.voice-online.net
Editor in chief: Mike Best
Arts: Diedre Forbes
Britain's leading black newspaper with mainly 18-35 age group readership. Regular film, television and video coverage. Supplements include W2W and Young Voices.
Press day: Friday
Circulation: 40,000

What's On In London

(Weekly, Tues)
180 Pentonville Road
London N1 9LB
Tel: 020 7278 4393
Fax: 020 7837 5838
Website: www.whatsoninlondon.co.uk
Editor: Michael Darvell
Films & Video: Rachel Holdsworth
Publisher: E G Shaw
London based weekly covering cinema, theatre, music, arts, books, entertainment and video
Press day: Friday
Lead time: 10 days
Circulation: 35,000

What's On TV

(Weekly, Tues)
King's Reach Tower
London SE1 9LS
Tel: 020 7261 7769
Fax: 020 7261 7739
email: colin.touch@ipcmedia.com
Editor: Colin Tough
Publisher: Rachel Pearce
TV listings magazine
Lead time: 3 weeks
Circulation: 1,676,000

BBC Radio

1Xtra
Broadcasting House
London W1A 1AA
Tel: 020 7224 2424
email: 1xtra@bbc.co.uk
Website: www.bbc.co.uk/1xtra
Radio Station playing Hip Hop, RnB, Garage,Dance Hall, Drum & Bass ect.

BBC Radio 1
London W1N 4DJ
Tel: 08700 100 100
Text: 81199
email: one.world@bbc.co.uk
Website: www.bbc.co.uk/readio1

BBC Radio 2
Broadcasting House
London W1A 1AA
Tel: 020 7224 2424
Website: www.bbc.co.uk/radio2

BBC Radio 3
Broadcasting House
London W1A 1AA
Tel: 020 7224 2424
Website: www.bbc.co.uk/radio3

BBC Radio 4
Broadcasting House
London W1A 1AA
Tel: 020 7224 2424
Website: www.bbc.co.uk/radio4
Controller: Helen Boaden
Talk shows including Women's Hour.

BBC Radio 5 Live
Room 2605
Television Centre
Wood Lane
London W12 7RJ
Tel: 08700 100 500
Website: www.bbc.co.uk/fivelive
BBC's sport station.

BBC 6 Music
BBC Western House
London W1A 1AA
Tel: 020 7224 2424
email: 6music@bbc.co.uk
Website: www.bbc.co.uk/6music
Pop and rock music from the contemporary to the classic.

BBC 7
Room 1003
BBC Broadcasting House
London W1A 1AA
Tel: 0207 7224 2424
email: bbc7@bbc.co.uk
Website: www.bbc.co.uk/bbc7
One of the BBC's new digital radio networks.

BBC Asian Network
PO Box 869
Birmingham B5 7ZA
Tel: 08459440445
Website:
www.bbc.co.uk/asiannetwork
See website for contacts for individual presenters/shows
BBC's station for UK Asian communities.

BBC Radio Berkshire
PO Box 104.4
Reading
Berkshire RG4 8TZ
Tel: 0118 946 4200
Fax: 0118 946 4555
email: radio.berkshire@bbc.co.uk
Website: www.bbc.co.uk/berkshire
Editor: Marianne Bell

BBC Radio Bristol
Broadcasting House
Whiteladies Road
Bristol BS8 2LR
Tel: 0117 973 2211
email: radio.bristol@bbc.co.uk
Website: www.bbc.co.uk/bristol

BBC Radio Cambridgeshire
104 Hills Road
Cambridge
CB2 1LD
Tel: 01223259696
Fax: 01223589870
email: cambs@bbc.co.uk
Website:
www.bbc.co.uk/cambridgeshire
Editor: David Martin

BBC CWR (Coventry & Warwickshire)
Hold Court
1 Greyfriars Road
Coventry CV1 2WR
Tel: 024 7686 0086
email:
coventry.warwickshire@bbc.co.uk
Website:
www.bbc.co.uk/coventrywarwickshire
Editor: Keith Beech

BBC Radio Cleveland
Broadcasting House
Newport Road
Middlesbrough TS1 5DG
Tel: 01642 225211
Fax: 01642 219 837
email: bbcradiocleveland@bbc.co.uk
Website: www.bbc.co.uk/cleveland
Managing Editor: Andrew Glover

BBC Radio Cornwall
Phoenix Wharf
Truro
Cornwall TR1 1UA
Tel: 01872 275421
Fax: 01872 240679
email: radio.cornwall@bbc.co.uk
Website: www.bbc.co.uk/cornwall
Managing Editor: Pauline Causey

BBC Radio Cumbria
Annetwell Street
Carlisle
Cumbria CA3 8BB
Tel: 01228 592 444
Fax: 01228 640 079
email: radio.cumbria@bbc.co.uk
Website: www.bbc.co.uk/cumbria
Editor: Nigel Dyson

BBC Radio Derby
PO Box 104.5
Derby DE1 3HL
Tel: 01332 361111
Fax: 01332 290794
email: radio.derby@bbc.co.uk
Website: bbc.co.uk/radioderby
Managing Editor: Simon Cornes

BBC Radio Devon
Broadcasting House
Seymour Road
Mannamead
Plymouth PL3 5YQ
Tel: 01752 260323
Fax: 01752 234599
email: john.lilley@bbc.co.uk
Website: www.bbc.co.uk/devon
Editor: John Lilley

BBC Radio Foyle
Northland Road
Derry/Londonderry BT48 7GD
Tel: 028 7137 8600
email: foyle@bbc.co.uk
Website:
www.bbc.co.uk/northernierland
Manager: Ana Leddy

BBC Essex
PO Box 765
Chelmsford
Essex CM2 9XB
Tel: 01245 616000
Fax: 01245 492983
email: essex@bbc.co.uk
Website: www.bbc.co.uk/essex
Station Manager: Margaret Hyde

BBC Radio Gloucester
London Road
Gloucester
GL1 1SW
Tel: 01452 308 585
Fax: 01452 309 491
email: radio.gloucester@bbc.co.uk
Website: www.bbc.co.uk/gloucester
Editor: Mark Hurrell

BBC GMR
PO Box 951
Oxford Road
Manchester M60 1SD
Tel: 0161 200 2000
Fax: 0161 228 6110
email: gmr@bbc.co.uk
Website: www.bbc.co.uk/gmr
Editor: Steve Taylor

BBC Radio Guernsey
Broadcasting House
Bulwer Avenue
St. Sampson's
Guernsey GY2 4LA
Tel: 01481 200 600
Fax: 01481 200 373
email: radio.guernsey@bbc.co.uk
Website: www.bbc.co.uk/guernsey
Editor: Rod Holms

BBC Hereford & Worcester
Hylton Road
Worcester WR2 5WW
Tel: 01905 748485
43 Broad Street
Hereford HR4 9WW
Tel: 01432355252
email: bbch@bbc.co.uk
Website:
www.bbc.co.uk/herefordandworcester

BBC Radio Humberside
9 Chapel Street
Hull HU1 3NU
Tel: 01482 323232
Fax: 01482 226409
email: radio.humberside@bbc.co.uk
Website: www.bbc.co.uk/humberside
Editor: Helen Thomas

BBC Radio Jersey
18 Parade Road
St Helier
Jersey JE2 3PL
Tel: 01534 87000
email: radio.jersey@bbc.co.uk
Website: www.bbc.co.uk/jersey
Editor: Denzil Dudley

BBC Radio Lancashire
20-26 Darwen Street
Blackburn
Lancs BB2 2EA
Tel: 01254 262411
Fax: 01254 680821
email: radio.lancashire@bbc.co.uk
Website: www.bbc.co.uk/lancashire
Editor: John Clayton

BBC Radio Leeds
Broadcasting House
Woodhouse Lane
Leeds LS2 9PN
Tel: 0113 224 7300
Fax: 0113 242 0652
email: radio.leeds@bbc.co.uk
Website: www.bbc.co.uk/leeds
Editor: Richard Whitaker

BBC Radio Leicester
Epic House/9th Floor
Charles Street
Leicester LE1 3SH
Tel: 0116 251 6688
Fax: 0116 251 1463
email: radioleicester@bbc.co.uk
Website:
www.bbc.co.uk/leicester@bbc.co.uk
Editor: Liam McCarthy

BBC Radio Lincolnshire
PO Box 219
Lincoln LN1 3BQ
Tel: 01522 511411
Fax: 01522 511058
email: radio.lincolnshire@bbc.co.uk
Website: www.bbc.co.uk/lincolnshire
Editor: Charlie Partridge

BBC Radio London
PO Box 94.9
Marylebone High Street
London W1A 6FL
Tel: 020 7224 2424
email: yourlondon@bbc.co.uk
Website: www.bbc.co.uk/london
Editor: David Robey

BBC Radio Kent
The Great Hall
Mount Pleasant Road
Tunbridge Wells
Kent TN1 1QQ
Tel: 01892 670 000
Fax: 01892 675 644
email: radio.kent@bbc.co.uk
Website: www.bbc.co.uk/kent

BBC Radio Merseyside
55 Paradise Street
Liverpool L1 3BP
Tel: 0151 708 5500
Fax: 0151 794 0988
email: radio.merseyside@bbc.co.uk
Website: www.bbc.co.uk/merseyside
Editor: Mick Ord

BBC Radio Newcastle
Broadcasting Centre
Barrack Road
Newcastle Upon Tyne NE99 1RN
Tel: 0191 232 4141
Fax: 0191 232 5082
email: radio.newcastle@bbc.co.uk
Website: www.bbc.co.uk/newcastle
Editor: Sarah Drummond

BBC Radio Norfolk
Norfolk Tower
Surrey Street
Norwich NR1 3PA
Tel: 01603 617411
Fax: 01603 633692
email: radionorfolk@bbc.co.uk
Website: www.bbc.co.uk/norfolk
Editor: David Clayton

BBC Radio Northampton
Broadcasting House
Abington Street
Northampton NN1 2BH
Tel: 01604 239100
Fax: 01604 230709
email:
radionorthhampton@bbc.co.uk
Website:
www.bbc.co.uk/northhampton
Editor: David Clargo

BBC Radio Nottingham
London Road
Nottingham NG2 4UU
Tel: 0115 955 0500
Fax: 0115 955 0501
email: radio.nottingham@bbc.co.uk
Website: www.bbc.co.uk/nottingham
Editor: Mike Bettison

BBC Radio Oxford
269 Banbury Road
Oxford OX2 7DW
Tel: 01865889092
Fax: 08459311555
email: oxford.online@bbc.co.uk
Website: www.bbc.co.uk/oxford
Editor: Phil Ashworth

BBC Radio Scotland
Queen Margaret Drive
Glasgow G12 8DG
email: enquiries.scot@bbc.co.uk
Website: www.bbc.co.uk/scotland
/radioscotland

BBC Radio Sheffield
54 Shoreham Street
Sheffield S1 4RS
Tel: 0114 2731177
Fax: 0114 2675454
email: radio.sheffield@bbc.co.uk
Website: www.bbc.co.uk/sheffield
Editor: Gary Keown

BBC Radio Shropshire
2-4 Boscobel Drive
Harlescott
Shrewsbury SY1 3TT
Tel: 017143 248484
Fax: 01743 271702
email: radio.shropshire@bbc.co.uk
Website: www.bbc.co.uk/shropshire
Editor: Tim Pemberton

BBC Radio Solent
Havelock Road
Southhampton SO14 7PW
Tel: 02380632811

Fax: 02380339648
email: radio.solent@bbc.co.uk
Website: www.bbc.co.uk/solent
Editor: Mia Costello

BBC Radio Stoke
Cheapside
Hanley
Stoke-on-Trent ST1 1JJ
Tel: 01782 208080
Fax: 01782 289115
email: radio.stoke@bbc.co.uk
Website: www.bbc.co.uk/stoke
Editor: Sue Owen

BBC Southern Cournties Radio
Broadcasting House
Guildford
Surrey GU2 7AP
Tel: 01483 306306
Fax: 01483 304952
email: southerncounties.radio@bbc.co.uk
Website: www.bbc.co.uk/southerncounties
Editor: Mike Hapgood

BBC Somerset Sound
Broadcasting House
Park Street, Taunton
Somerset TA1 4DA
Tel: 01823 348920
Fax: 01823 332539
email: somerset.sound@bbc.co.uk
Website: www.bbc.co.uk/somerset
Assistant Editor: Simon Clifford

BBC Radio Suffolk
Broadcasting House
St. Matthew's Street
Ipswich
Suffolk IP1 3EP
Tel: 01473250000
Fax: 01473210997
email: radiosuffolk@bbc.co.uk
Website: www.bbc.co.uk/suffolk
Managing Editor: Gerald Main

BBC Radio swindon
PO Box 1234
Swindon
Tel: 01793 513626
Fax: 01793 513650
email: radio.swindon@bbc.co.uk
Website: www.bbc.co.uk/swindon
Editor: Tony Worgan

BBC Three Counties Radio
1 Hastings Street
Luton LU1 5XL
Tel: 01582 637400
Fax: 01582 401467
email: 3cr@bbc.co.uk
Website: www.bbc.co.uk/3cr
Editor: Mark Norman

BBC Radio Ulster
PO Box 1116
Belfast BT2 7AJ
Tel: 08700100222
Website: www.bbc.co.uk/northernireland/radioulster

BBC Radio Wales
Broadasting House
Llandaff
Cardiff CF2 2YQ
Tel: 02920322000
email: radiowales@bbc.co.uk
Website: www.bbc.co.uk/radiowales

BBC Radio Wiltshire
PO Box 1234
Trowbridge & Salisbury
Tel: 01793 513626
Fax: 01793 513650
email: radio.wiltshire@bbc.co.uk
Website: www.bbc.co.uk/wiltshire
Editor: Tony Worgan

BBC Radio WM
PO Box 206
Birmingham B5 7SD
Tel: 0121 432 8888
Fax: 0121 414 8817
email: radio.wm@bbc.co.uk
Website: www.bbc.co.uk/wm
Editor: Keith Beech

BBC World Service
231CB Bush House
Strand
London W12 O2Y
Tel: 020 7557 2941
Fax: 020 7557 1912
email: worldservice.press@bbc.co.uk
Website: www.bbc.co.uk/worldservice

BBC Radio York
20 Bootham Row
York YO30 7BR
Tel: 01904641351
email: northyourkshire.radio@bbc.co.uk
Website: www.bbc.co.uk/york
Editor: Matt Youdale

Independent Radio

Capital FM Network
30 Leicester Square
London WC2H 7LA
Tel: 0207 766 6000
Fax: 0207 7666 1000
email: nicky.tranter@capitalradio.com
Website: www.capitalfm.com
Managing Director: Andria Vidler
Including Stations for London, Birmingham, Hampshire, South Wales, Sussex, Manchester and Kent.

Capital Gold Network
30 Leicester Square
London WC2H 7LA
Tel: 0207 766 6000
Fax: 0207 7666 1000
Website: www.capitalgold.com
Managing Director: Lyn Long

Century FM Network
Century House
Waterfront Quays
Salford Quays
Manchester M5 2XW
Tel: 0161 400 0105
Fax: 0161 400 1105
Managing Director: Nick Davidson
Including stations in Nottingham, Manchester, Gateshead and Fareham.

Classic FM
7 Swallow Place
Oxford Circus
London W1B 2AG
Tel: 0207 343 9000
Website: www.classicfm.co.uk

Virgin 1215 AM
1 Golden Square
London W1F 9DJ
Tel: 020 7434 1215
Fax: 020 7434 1197
Website: www.virgin.com

Xfm Network
30 Leicester Square
London WC2H 7LA
Tel: 0207 766 6000
Fax: 0207 766 6100
Website: www.xfm.com
Managing Director: Graham Bryce

Independent Television Companies

Anglia Television
Anglia House
Norwich NR1 3JG
Tel: 01603 615151
Fax: 01603 761245
email: dutyoffice@angliatv.co.uk
Website: www.anglia.tv.co.uk
Includes regional centres in Cambridge, Chelmsford, Ipswich, Nothampton, Luton, Peterborough and Milton Keynes.

Border Television
Television Centre
Carlisle CA1 3NT
Tel: 01228 525101
Fax: 01228 541384
Website: www.border-tv.com

Carlton Television
35-38 Portman Square
London W1H 6NU
Tel: 020 7486 6688
Fax: 020 7486 1132
email: dutyoffice@carltontv.vo.uk
Website: www.carlton.com

Central Independent Television (East)
Carlton Studios
Lenton Lane
Nottingham NG7 2NA
Tel: 0115 986 3322
Fax: 0115 964 5018
Website: www.carlton.com

Central Independent Television (South)
9 Windrush Court
Abingdon Business Park
Abingdon
Oxon OX14 1SA
Tel: 01235 554123
Fax: 01235 524024
Website: www.carlton.com

Channel Five Broadcasting
22 Long Acre
London WC2E 9LY
Tel: 020 7550 5555
Fax: 020 7550 5554
email: dutyoffice@channel5.co.uk
Website: www.five.tv

Channel Four Television
124 Horseferry Road
London SW1P 2TX
Tel: 020 7396 4444
Fax: 020 7306 8353
Website: www.channel4.co.uk

Channel Television
Guernsey Office:
Television House
Bulwer Avenue
St Sampsons
Guernsey GY2 4LA
Tel: 01481 41888
Fax: 01481 41889
email: broadcast.gsy@channeltv.co.uk
Jersey Office:
The Television Centre
La Pouquelaye
St Helier
Jersey JE1 3ZD
Tel: 01534 816816
Fax: 01534 816817
email: broadcast@channeltv.co.uk
London Office:
Channel Television Ltd.
Unit 16A/3rd Floor
Enterprise House
59-65 Upper Ground
London SE1 9PQ
Tel: 020 7633 9902
Fax: 020 7401 8982
Website: www.channeltv.co.uk
Managing Director: Michael Lucas

GMTV
London Television Centre
Upper Ground
London SE1 9LT
Tel: 020 7827 7000
Fax: 020 7827 7249
email: malcolm.douglas@gmtv.co.uk
Website: www.gmtv.co.uk

Grampian Television
The Television Centre
Craigshaw Business Park
West Tullos AB12 3QH
Tel: 01224 848848
email:
viewer.enquiries@grampiantv.co.uk
Website: www.grampiantv.co.uk
North Tonight; Crossfire; News Programmes

Granada Television
Quay Street
Manchester M60 9EA
Tel: 0161 832 7211
Fax: 0161 827 2029
Albert Dock
Liverpool L3 4BA
Tel: 0151 709 9393
White Cross
Lancaster LA1 4XQ
Tel: 01524 606688
36 Golden Square
London W1R 4AH
Tel: 0171 734 8080
Bridgegate House
5 Bridge Place
Lower Bridge Street
Chester CH1 1SA
Tel: 01244 313966
email: duty.office@granadatv.co.uk
Website: www.granadatv.co.uk

HTV Wales
Television Centre
Culverhouse Cross
Cardiff CF5 6XJ
Tel: 01222 590590
Fax: 01222 590759
Website: www.htvwales.com

HTV West
Television Centre
Bath Road
Bristol BS4 3HG
Tel: 0117 9722722
Fax: 0117 972 3122
Website: www.htvwest.com
HTV News; The West This Week, West Eye View

Independent Television News (ITN)
200 Gray's Inn Road
London WC1X 8XZHF
Tel: 020 7833 3000
Fax: 020 7430 4868
Website: www.itn.co.uk

Meridian Broadcasting
TV Centre
Northam Road
Southampton SO14 0PZ
Tel: 023 8022 2555
Fax: 023 8071 2081
email: dutyoffice@meridiantv.com
Website: www.meridiantv.com

S4C
Parc Ty Glas
Llanishen
Cardiff CF4 5DU
Tel: 01222 747444
Fax: 01222 754444
email: s4c@s4c.co.uk
Website: www.S4c.co.uk
Head of Press and Public Relations: David Meredith

Scottish TV
200 Renfield Street
Glasgow G2 3PR
Tel: 0141 300 3000
Fax: 0141 332 9274
email:
viewer.enquiries@scottishtv.co.uk
Website: www.scottishtv.co.uk

Tyne Tees Television
The Television Centre
City Road
Newcastle upon Tyne NE1 2AL
Tel: 0191 261 0181
Fax: 0191 232 2302

Website: www.tynetees.tv

Ulster Television
Havelock House
Ormeau Road
Belfast BT7 1EB
Tel: 01232 328122
Fax: 01232 246695
Website: www.utvlive.com

Westcountry Television
Western Wood Way
Language Science Park
Plymouth PL7 5BQ
Tel: 01752 333333
Fax: 01752 333033
Website: www.itv.com/westcountry

Yorkshire Television
The Television Centre
Kirkstall Road
Leeds LS3 1JS
Tel: 0113 243 8283
Fax: 0113 243 3655
Website: www.yorkshire-television.tv

BBC Television

British Broadcasting Corporation
Television Centre
Wood Lane
London W12 7RJ
Tel: 020 8743 8000
Website: www.bbc.co.uk/tv
Direector General: Greg Dyke

BBC East Midlands Today
London Road
Nottingham NG2 4UU
Tel: 0115 955 0500
Fax: 0115 902 1984
email: emt@bbc.co.uk
Website:
www.bbc.co.uk/midlandstoday

BBC Look East
St. Catherine's Close
All Saints Green
Norwich NR1 3ND
Tel: 01603 619331
Fax: 01603 284455
104 Hill Road
Cambridge CB2 1LD
Tel: 01223 259696
Fax: 01223 460823
email: look.east@bbc.co.uk
Website: www.bbc.co.uk/lookeast

Look North
Broadcasting Centre
Barrack Road
Newcastle Upon Tyne NE99 2NE
Tel: 0191 232 1313
email:
looknorth.notheast.cumbria@bbc.co.uk
Editor: Andrew Lambert
Broadcasting House
Woodhouse Lane
Leeds LS2 9PX
Tel: 0113 244 1188
Fax: 0113 244 2131
email: look.north@bbc.co.uk
Website: www.bbc.co.uk/looknorth
Editor: Jake Fowler

Midlands Today
BBC West Midlands
Pebble Mill
Brimingham B5 7QQ
Tel: 0121 432 8888
email: midlandstoday@bbc.co.uk
Website:
www.bbc.co.uk/midlandstoday
Head of regional and local programmes: David Holdsworth
Editor: Chas Watkins

North West Tonight
New Broadcasting House
Oxford Road
ManchesterM60 1SJ
Tel: 0161 200 2020
email: nwt@bbc.co.uk
Website:
www.bbc.co.uk/northwesttonight
Head of regional and local programmes: Martin Brooks

Points West
Broadcasting House
Whiteladies Road
Bristol BS8 2LR
Tel: 0117 973 2211
Fax: 0117 974 1537
email: pointswest@bbc.co.uk
Website: www.bbc.co.uk/pointswest
Editor(s): Jane Kinghorn & Stephanie Marshall

South East Today
The Great Hall
Mount Pleasant Road
Tunbridge Wells TN1 1QQ
Tel: 01892 675580
Fax: 01892 549118
email: southeasttoday@bbc.co.uk
Website:
www.bbc.co.uk/southeasttoday
Acting Editor: Graham Majin

South Today
Havelock Road
Southhamption SO14 7PU
Tel: 02380 226201
Fax: 02380 339931
email: south.today@bbc.co.uk
Website: www.bbc.co.uk/southtoday
Editor: Lee Desty

Spotlight
BBC South West
Broadcasting House
Seymour Road
Plymouth PL3 5BD
Tel: 01752 229201
Fax: 01752 234595
email: spotlight@bbc.co.uk
www.bbc.co.uk/spotlight
Editor: Simon Read

For more regional and personnel details see the Television Companies section.

News and Photo Agencies

Associated Press
12 Norwich Street
London EC4A 1BP
Tel: 020 7353 1515
Fax: 020 7583 0196
email: info@ap.org
Website: www.ap.org

Central Office of Information
Hercules House
London SE1 7DU
Tel: 020 7928 2345
Fax: 020 7928 5037
Website: www.coi.gov.uk

Central Press Features
5th Floor
BUP Building
Temple Way
Bristol BF99 7HD
Tel: 0117 934 3604
Fax: 0117 934 3642
email: sam.bush@central-press.co.uk
Website: www.central-press.co.uk

Fleet Street News Agency
68 Exmouth Market
London EC1R 4RA
Tel: 020 7278 5661
Fax: 020 7278 8480

News Team International
Stratford House
Stratford Place
Camp Hill
Birmingham B12 0HT
Tel: 0121 246 5511
Fax: 0121 246 5100
Provides material from the West Midlands and Manchester Region.

Press Association
292 Vauxhall Bridge Road
London SW1V 1AE
Tel: 020 7963 7000
Northern Headquarters:
The Bishop's Manor
Market Place
Howden
E. Yorks DN14 7BL
email: information@pa.press.net
Website: www.pa.press.net/

Reuters Ltd
85 Fleet Street
London EC4P 4AJ
Tel: 020 7250 1122
Fax: 020 7542 7921
Website: www.reuters.com
Chief Executive: Tom Glocer
Incompassing Bridge News for business information.

Scotland News and Features
TFI
8 Rossie Place
Edinburgh EH7 5SG
Tel: 0131 244 2709

Solo
49 Kensington High Street
London W8 5ED
Tel: 020 7376 2166
Fax: 020 7938 3165
Feature and news material from Associated Newspapers and IPC Magazines.

Wales News Service
Womanby Street
Cardiff CF1 2UD
Tel: 01222 666 366
Fax: 01222 664181

United Press International
Prince Consort House
27-29 Albert Embankment
London SE1 7TJ
Tel: 020 7820 4180
Fax: 0207 8204 4190
Website: www.upi.com
UPI London Editor: Dr. Hussain Hindawi

PREVIEW THEATRES

BAFTA
195 Piccadilly
London W1J 9LN
Tel: 020 734 0022
Fax: 020 7734 1009
email: pollyc@bafta.org
Website: www.bafta.org
Polly Collins
Formats: Twin 35mm all aspect ratios. Dolby A, SR, SRD, DTS sound. 35 Double head mono, twin/triple track stereo plus Dolby Matrix. 16mm and super 16mm, 16 double head stereo plus Dolby Matrix. BARCO G-10 ELM Data Video Projector VHS, Lo Band U-matic, Beta, Beta SP, Digi Beta + DVD. Interfaces for most PC outputs, SVGA, MAC etc. 35mm slides single, with a remote control, Audio, RGB Video Tie Lines in Theatre. ISDN 3. Catering by Roux Fine Dining. Seats: Princess Anne Theatre, 213 Run Run Shaw Theatre, 30 (not all formats available), Function Room, up to 200
Disabled access: ramp, lift and other facilities

British Film Institute
21 Stephen Street
London W1P 2LN
Tel: 020 7957 8976
Fax: 020 7436 7950
email: roger.young@bfi.org.uk
Website: www.bfi.org.uk
Picture Formats: All aspect ratios
Film Speeds: 16fps-30fps
Formats: 35mm: Mono/Dolby A/SR/SRD+EX
16mm: Mono/Dolby A/SR
Video Projection: VHS/SVHS/U-Matic/Beta SP/DVD/Laserdisc
Hospitality Room
Disabled Access
Seats: 1: 36
Seats 2: 36

BUFVC
77 Wells Street
London W1T 3QJ
Tel: 020 7393 1500
Fax: 020 7393 1555
email: services@bufvc.ac.uk
Website: bufvc.ac.uk
Geoffrey O'Brien, Assistant Director
Formats: Viewing rooms equipped with 16mm double-head, Betacam, SVHS, VHS, lo-band and hi-band U-Matic, Betamax, Phillips 1500
Seats: 20-30 max

Century Preview Theatres
31-32 Soho Square
London W1V 6AP
Tel: 020 7753 7135
Fax: 020 7753 7138
email: projection@foxinc.com
Nick Ross
Picture Formats: 1.1:37, 1.1:66, 1.1:85, Super 35, Scope
Sound Formats: (CP 500) Mono, Dolby A, SR, SR-D+EX. DTS. Double Head 6 TRK (Magnetic) 2000 ft. Also: Spotlighting, microphones, lecturns, for conventions. Most video formats using DLP
Seating Capacity: 73

Chapter Cinema
Market Road
Canton
Cardiff CF5 1QE
Tel: 01222 311050
Fax: 01222 313431
email: chaptercinema@easynet.co.uk
Website: www.chapter.org.uk
Tony Whitehead, Cinema Programmer
Formats: 35mm optical, 16mm optical/sep mag, high quality video projection, U-Matic/VHS - all standards. Beta SP PAL2 Channel infra-red audio amplification/simultaneous translation system in both screens. Reception space, bars and restaurant
Seats: 1:194, 2:68

Columbia TriStar Films UK
Sony Pictures Europe House
25 Golden Square
London W1R 6LU
Tel: 020 7533 1095
Fax: 020 7533 1105
Formats: 35mm optical (SDDS, Dolby SR" + "A" type)/double head SVA Mag

Computer Film Company
19-23 Wells Street
London W1P 3FB
Tel: 020 7344 8000
Fax: 020 7344 8001
email: charlie.dodiya@framestore-cfc.com
Website: www.framestore-cfc.com
Charlie Dodiya
Picture Formats: 1.1:33, 1.1:66, 1.1:85, Super 35, Scope. Variable speeds, reverse projection if required. Sound Formats: Mono, Dolby A, SR, SRD. Video VHS + Beta + DVD. Bar area

The Curzon Minema
45 Knightsbridge
London SW1X 7NL
Tel: 020 7235 4226
Fax: 020 7235 3426
email:info@minema.com
Website: www.minema.com
Formats: 35mm and 16mm, video and AV presentations

Curzon Soho
93-107 Shaftesbury Avenue
London W1D 5DY
Tel: 020 7734 2255
Fax: 020 7734 1977
email:
rob.kenny@curzoncinemas.com
Website: www.curzoncinemas.com
Robert Kenny
Picture Formats: 1.1:33, 1.1:66, 1.1:85, Scope. Kodak slide projection, Video Projection: Beta SP, Digi-Beta, Powerpoint Capable, Analogue Projector, PA on request, all theatres to THX standard

De Lane Lea
75 Dean Street
London W11D 3PU
Tel: 020 7432 3800
Fax: 020 7432 3838
email: dll@delanelea.com
Website: www.delanelea.com
Picture Formats: 35mm. 1.1:33, 1.1:66, 1.1:85. Super 35, Scope
Sound Formats: Mono, Dolby, A + SR with double-head capacity (magnetic) 6,4,3 track stereo

Edinburgh Film & TV Studios
Nine Mile Burn
Penicuik EH26 9LT
Tel: 01968 672131
Fax: 01968 672685
Website:

www.edinburghfilmstudios.co.uk
Formats: 16mm and 35mm double-head stereo, U-Matic, VHS
Seats: 100

Eon Theatre

Eon House
138 Piccadilly
London W1J 7NR
Tel: 020 7493 7953
Fax: 020 7408 1236
email: chris.brisley@eon.co.uk
Chris Brisley
Projection 35mm. Picture Formats: 1.1:33 & 1.1:85 Scope
Sound Formats: Mono, Dolby, A&S-R, DVD

FilmFour Ltd

77-78 Charlotte Street
London W1P 1X
Tel: 020 7868 7700
Fax: 020 7868 7767
Website: www.filmfour.com
Picture Formats: 35mm, 16mm, 16mm super. 1.1:33. 1.1:66, 1.1: 85, Scope
Sound Formats: Mono, Dolby, A+SR, SRD, Double headed (magnetic) (3 Track)

Filmhouse

88 Lothian Road
Edinburgh EH3 9BZ
Tel: 0131 228 6382
Fax: 0131 229 6482
email: admin@filmhousecinema.com
Website: www.ffilmhousecinema.com
Gwen Orr

Foresight Preview Theatre

Beaumont House
Kensington Village
Avonmore Road
London W14 8TS
Tel: 020 7348 1065
35mm Optical (Dolby A, SR, SRD), 35mm Sep Mag (Monon & Stereo) VHS, Umatic, Betacam, DVD Large Screen Television, Slides, OHP and Multimedia presentation
Seats: 55-70

ICA

The Mall
London SW1Y 5AH
Tel: 020 7766 1413
Fax: 020 7306 0122
email: hires@ica.org.uk
Website: www.ica.org.uk
Cinema 1: 185 seats
35mm film changeover projection.
Beta sp pal, VHS pal, DVD pal/ntsc multiregion, LD pal/ntsc.
Playback in Dolby Pro-logic, stereo or mono.
Data projection up to SXGA, native XGA resolution.
CD and cassette playback/recording.
Stage area with 2 point lighting
Facilities available with notice:
Vocal pa from table mics for conference.
35mm slide projection.
Radio mic
Lecturn
Additional video formats
Cinema 2: 45 seats.
35mm film projection from tower.
16mm film projection.
1:33 1:66 1:85 2:35 combined optical prints only
Video projection.
Barco cine 7 CRT projector. Flat or anamorphic video
Beta sp pal, VHS pal/ntsc/secam, DVD pal/ntsc multi region (NO recordable DVD's playable)
CD & cassette playback
Infra red hearing support with induction loop
Facilities available with notice:
35mm slide projection
Additional video formats
Data projection using LCD projector brought in.

Imperial War Museum

(Corporate Hospitality)
Lambeth Road
London SE1 6HZ
Tel: 020 7416 5293
Fax: 020 7416 5229
email: film@iwm.org.uk
Website: www.iwm.org.uk
Toby Haggith
Formats: 35mm and 16mm; Betacam, U-Matic, SVHS and VHS. Catering by arrangement. Large Exhibit Hall, capacity: 1,000 Disabled access
Seats: Cinema: 200

King's Lynn Arts Centre

27/29 King Street
King's Lynn
Norfolk PE30 1HA
Tel: 01553 765565
Fax: 01553 762141
Website: www.kingslynnarts.org.uk
Formats: 16mm, 35mm
Seats: 349

Mr Young's Screening Rooms

14 D'Arblay Street
London W1V 3FP
Tel: 020 7437 1771
Fax: 020 7734 4520
email: enquires@mryoungs.com
Website: www.mryoungs.com
Contact: Reuben
Formats: 35mm, Super 35mm, U-Matic, VHS, Betacam SP, Dolby stereo double-head optical and magnetic Dolby SR. Large screen video projection. Bar area, catering by request. Theatres non-smoking
Seats: 1: 42, 2: 25, 3:45

Picture Production Company

19-20 Poland Street
London W1F 8QF
Tel: 020 7439 4944
Fax: 020 7434 9140
email: sales@theppc.com
Website: www.theppc.com

Pinewood Studios

Sound Department - Preview Theatres
Pinewood Road
Iver Heath
Bucks SL0 0NH
Tel: 01753 656296
Fax: 01753 656014
email: helen_wells@pinewood-studios.co.uk
Website: www.pinewood-studios.co.uk
Contact: Helen Wells
Formats: 35mm, 70mm, Dolby SR, SR.D, DTS, SDDS. Compot, Commag, Sepmag. Separate timecode digital sound screening by arrangement. Screen width 34ft. Disabled access. Lounge available.
Seats: 115 seats

Planet Hollywood

13 Coventry Street
London W1
Tel: 020 7437 7827
Fax: 020 7439 7827
Website: www.planet-hollywood.demon.co.uk
Formats: 35mm, 70mm, SVHS/VHS, U-Matic, Laser Disc, Lucasfilm Ltd THX Sound Sytem, Dolby CP200 + SRD/DTS digital stereo. Super 35mm with separate magnetic tracks and remote volume control. Microphone facilities. Lifts for the disabled available
Seats: Cinema: 75, Dining area: 85, 120 (standing)

RSA

8 John Adam Street
London WC2N 6EZ
Tel: 020 7839 5049
Fax: 020 7321 0271
email: Conference@rsa-uk.demon.co.uk
Website: www.rsa.org.uk

The Great Room
Video Formats: SVHS, Beta SP. Other formats by arrangement.
Barcographics 8100 Projector for Video and Data Projection. Loop system for hard of hearing, disabled access to all rooms. Full catering available: Seats: 202

Screen West

John Brown Publishing
136-142 Bramley Road
London W10 6SR
Tel: 020 7565 3102
Fax: 020 7565 3077
email: sarah.alliston@jbcp.co.uk
Website: www.screenwest.co.uk
Sarah Alliston
Enquiries: Sarah Alliston
State of the art preview theatre with luxury seating for 74 people. Formats: 35mm, Super 35mm, Double Head, Beta, VHS, PC. Surround Sound: Optical, Magnetic, Digital (SRD and DTS). and full catering facilities in the adjoining function room

The Screening Room at MPC

The Moving Picture Company
127 Wardour Street
London W1V 0NL
Tel: 020 7494 7879
Fax: 020 7287 9698
email: screening@moving-picture.co.uk
Website: www.moving-picture.co.uk
Contact: Paul Roberts, Chief Film Technician
Mark Wiseman, Senior Film Technician
74 Seat wheelchair accessible professional Screening Room and reception foyer.
35mm Sondor Film Projectors, all aspect ratios inc. Super 35.
Split screen comparisons and interlocking projectors possible.
Variable speed playback (2fps - 30fps) with full auditorium control.
Magnetic 6track,3track,SVA with or without SR noise reduction.
DLP digital projection from all formats by arrangement.
HD projection available by arrangement for additional charge

Shepperton Studios

Studios Road
Shepperton
Middx TW17 0QD
Tel: 01932 562611/572350
Fax: 01932 568989
email: sheppertonstudios@dial.pipex.com
Formats: 35mm double-head and married, Dolby A + SR,
Seats: (35mm) 17

Total Film

99 Baker Street
London W1M 1FB
Tel: 020 7317 2600 or 07788 847190
Fax: 020 7317 0275
email: totalfilm@futurenet.co.uk
Graham Singleton
Fully air conditioned screening room facility with Crestron touch screen remote for computer generated presentations and adjacent boardroom facilities. Format: 35mm print, Betacam and VHS through an overhead CRT with line doubler. Ernemann 15-laser audio projector with both scope and flat lenses. Sony Betacam SP player and professional JVC HRH 507MS VCR with overhead CRT projector. Sound delivery by Sony Digital Camera System with Dolby SR set-up & installed by Dolby Laboratories
Seats: 24

Twentieth Century Fox

Executive Theatre
31-32 Soho Square
London W1V 6AP
Tel: 020 7735 7135
Fax: 020 7735 7138
email: projection@foxinc.com
Peter Holland
Picture formats: 1.1:85, 1:1:66 Scope, Super 35 + DLP Video Projection
Sound formats (CP500) Mono, Dolby A, SR, SR-D-EX, 3 Track Mag

Twickenham Film Studios

St Margaret's
Twickenham
Middx TW1 2AW
Tel: 020 8607 8888
Fax: 020 8607 8889
Website: www.twickenhamstudios.com
Gerry Humphreys
Formats: 35mm.
Seats: 31

UIP International Theatre

UIP House
45 Beadon Road
Hammersmith
London
Tel: 0208 563 4336 (Nina Carter bookings) Tel: 0208 563 4143 (George Frith Projectionists)
email: george-frith@uip.com email: nina-carter@uip.com
George Frith, Chief Projectionist
Picture Formats: 1.1:33, 1.1:66, 1.1:85, Scope
Sound Formats: Mono, Dolby, A+SR, SRD +EX, DTS, SDDS, Double head (magnetic). Mono, SVA, 6 Track
Video: VHS, U-Matic, Beta SP

Warner Bros

98 Theobalds Road
London WC1X 8WB
Tel: 020 7984 5272
Website: www.warnerbros.co.uk

Watershed Media Centre

1 Canons Road
Bristol BS1 5TX
Tel: 0117 9276444
Fax: 0117 9213958
email: info@watershed.co.uk
Formats: Super 8mm
Super 16mm (C1) double-head

PRODUCTION COMPANIES

Aardman Animations
Gas Ferry Road
Bristol BS1 6UN
Tel: 0117 984 8485
Fax: 0117 984 8486
Website: www.aardman.com

Absolutely Productions
Craven House
Suite 226
121 Kingsway
London WC2B 6PA
Tel: 00 44 (0)20 7930 3113
Fax: 00 44 (0)20 7930 4114
email: info@absolutely-uk.com
Website: www.absolutely-uk.com

Acacia Productions Ltd
80 Weston Park
London N8 9TB
Tel: 020 8341 9392
Fax: 020 8341 4879
email: acacia@dial.pipex.com
Website:
www.acaciaproductions.co.uk
Edward Milner

Action Time
1 Heathcock Court
415 Strand
London WC2R 0NS
Tel: 020 7836 0505
Indpendent producer, programmes include: Catchphrase, Crazy Cottage, Game of War, Spellbound, The Mole

Addictive TV
The Old House
39a North Road
London N7 9DP
Tel: 020 7700 0333
Fax: 020 7700 0303
email: mail@addictive.com
Website: www.addictive.com
Jim Walters

Adventure Pictures
6 Blackbird Yard
Ravenscroft Street
London E2 7RP
Tel: 020 7613 2233
Fax: 020 7256 0842
email: mail@adventurepictures.co.uk
Website: www.sallypotter.com

After Image Ltd
32 Acre Lane
London SW2 5SG
Tel: 020 737 7300
Website: www.after.arc.co.uk
Jane Thornburn

Alibi Productions
35 Long Acre
London WC2E 9JT
Tel: 020 7845 0420
Fax: 020 7379 7039
email: rogerholmes@alibifilms.co.uk
Website: www.alibifilms.co.uk
Roger Holmes

Alomo Productions
c/o FremantleMedia Ltd
1 Stephen Street
London W1P 1PJ
Tel: 020 7691 6000
Website: www.fremantlemedia.com
Part of FremantleMedia's UK production division which comprises Thames Television, Talkback Productions, Regent Productions and Alomo Productions, all producing a diverse range of programming for the UK's terrestrial and satellite channels

Amber Films
5 & 9 Side
Newcastle-upon-Tyne NE1 3JE
Tel: 0191 232 2000
Fax: 0191 230 3217
email: amberside@btinternet.com
Website: www.amber-online.com
Pat McCarthy
Amber was established in 1969 with the specific intention of creating a film and photographic practice in relation to the working class communities of the North East of England. From its foundation it has pursued a policy of integrating production, exhibition and distribution.Recent titles include Like Father, Eden Valley and The Scar

Angelic Pictures
21a Colebrooke Row
Angel
Islington
London N1 8AP
Tel: 020 7359 9514
Fax: 020 7359 9153
email: rslw1@hotmail.com
Website: www.angelicpictures.co.uk
Rebecca Wilson

Anglia Television Limited
Anglia House
Norwich NR1 3JG
Tel: 01603 615151
Fax: 01603 631032
Website: www.anglia.tv.com

Anglo American Pictures
Ealing Studios
Ealing Green
London W5 5EP
Tel: 07802 666 693
email: admin@anglo-ap.com
Website:
www.angloamericanpictures.com
Chris Barfoot
Current features in development:
Beansidhe (Curse of the Black Witch)
Fall of the Roman Empire

Anglo/Fortunato Films
170 Popes Lane
London W5 4NJ
Tel: 020 8932 7676
Fax: 020 8932 7491
Luciano Celentino

The Animation Station
Leisure and Tourism Department
Cherwell District Council
Bodicote House
Bodicote, Banbury
Oxon OX15 4AA
Tel: 01295 221730
Fax: 01295 270797
email: animation.station@cherwell-dc.gov.uk
Website: www.animationstation.co.uk
ClintonOsborne. Multimedia Arts Development Officer

Animha Productions
121 Roman Road
Linthorpe
Middlesbrough TS5 5QB
Tel: 01642 813 137
email: info@animha.com
Website: www.animha.com
Dave Brunskill

Antelope South Ltd
Drounces
White Chimney Row
Westbourne
Emsworth PO10 8RS
Tel: 01243 370 806
Fax: 01243 376 985

email: mick.csaky@antelope.co.uk
Website: www.antelope.co.uk
Mick Csáty

Arcane Pictures
46 Wetherby Mansions
Earl Court Square
London SW5 9DI
Tel: 020 7244 6590
Fax: 020 7565 4495
email: info@arcanepictures.com
Website: www.arcanepictures.com
Meg Thomson

Archer Street Ltd
Studio 5
10-11 Archer Street
London W1D 7AZ
Tel: 020 7439 0540
Fax: 020 7437 1182
Contact: Andy Paterson
Recent production: Girl with a pearl earring

Ariel Productions Ltd
11 Albion Gate
Hyde Park Place
London W2 2LF
Tel: O2O7 262 7726
Fax: O2O7 262 7726
email:ottoplaschtes@lycos.co.uk
Otto Plaschkes

Arlington Productions Ltd
Cippenham Court
Cippenham Lane
Cippenham, Nr Slough
Berkshire SL1 5AU
Tel: 01753 516767
Fax: 01753 691785

Ashford Entertainment Corporation Ltd
20 The Chase
Coulsdon
Surrey CR5 2EG
Tel: 020 8645 0667
email: info@ashford-entertainment.co.uk
Website: www.ashford entertainment.co.uk
Frazer Ashford

Assembly Film & Television Ltd
Riverside Studios
Crisp Road, Hammersmith
London W6 9RL
Tel: 020 8237 1075
Fax: 020 8237 1071
email:
judithmurrell@riversidestudios.co.uk
Website: www.chrysalis.co.uk
William Burdett-Coutts

Richard Attenborough Productions
Twickenham Studios
St Margaret's
Twickenham TW1 2AW
Tel: 020 8607 8873
Fax: 0208744 2766
Judy Wasdell

AV Pictures Ltd
102 Dean Street
3rd London W1D 3TQ
Tel: 020 7758 1484
Fax: 020 7758 1491
email: info@avpictures
Vic Bateman, Jane Carolan

Bard Entertainments Ltd
7 Denmark Street
London WC2H 8LZ
Tel: 020 7240 7144
Fax: 020 7240 7088
email:
office@bardentertainments.co.uk
Recent productions: Revengers Tragedy, American Counsins, Kin

Peter Batty Productions
Claremont House
Renfrew Road
Kingston
Surrey KT2 7NT
Tel: 020 8942 6304
Fax: 020 8336 1661

Bazal
46-47 Bedford Square
London WC1B 3DP
Tel: 020 7462 9000
Fax: 020 7462 9998
Independent producer, programmes include: Ready Steady Cook, Can't Cook Won't Cook

BBC Films Ltd
1 Mortimer Street
London W1T 3JA
Tel: 020 7765 0251
Fax: 020 7765 0278
Website: www.bbc.co.uk/bbcfilms
Recent production: Out of Control

The Big Group
91 Princedale Road
London W11 4HS
Tel: 020 7229 8827
Fax: 020 7243 146
email: ed.riseman@biggroup.co.uk
Website: www.biggroup.co.uk
Ed Riseman

Black Coral Productions
2nd Floor
241 High Road
London E17 7BH
Tel: 020 8520 2881
Fax: 020 8520 2358
email: bcp@coralmedia.co.uk
Lazell Daley, Managing Director, Producer

Blue Dolphin Film & Video
40 Langham Street
London W1N 5RG
Tel: 020 7255 2494
Fax: 020 7580 7670
Website: www.bluedolphinfilms.com

Blue Heaven Productions Ltd
116 Great Portland Street
London W1W 6PJ
Tel: 020 7436 5552
Fax: 020 7426 0888
Christine Benson

Braunarts
The Beehive
226a Gipsy Road
London SE27 9RB
Tel: 020 8670 9917
Fax: 020 8670 9917
email: terry@braunarts.com & gabi@braunarts.com
Website: www.braunarts.com
Contact: Gabi Braun & Terry Braun

Breakthrufilms
BreakThru Films Ltd
2nd Floor
Highgate Business Centre
33 Greenwood Place
London NW5 1LB
Tel: 020 7428 3974
Fax: 020 7428 3963
email: hugh@breakthrufilms.co.uk
Website: www.breakthrufilms.co.uk
Alan Dewhurst Producer
HughWelchman Producer
Tom Truscott
Feature films/Animation production company

Brook Lapping Productions
6 Anglers Lane
London NW5 3DG
Tel: 020 7482 3100
Fax: 020 7284 0626
Anne Lapping

Buena Vista Productions
Centre West
3 Queen Caroline Street
Hammersmith
London W4 9PE
Tel: 020 8222 1000
Fax: 020 8222 2795

John Burder Films
37 Braidley Road
Meyrick Park

Bournemouth BH2 6JY
Tel: 01202 295 395
email: burderfilms@aol.com
Website: www.johnburder.co.uk

Buxton Raven Productions Ltd
102 Clarence Road
London E5 8HB
Tel: 020 8986 0063
Fax: 020 8986 2708
email: jb@buxtonraven.com
Website: buxtonraven.com
Jette Bonnevie, Jens Ravn

Cactus
Cactus TV
The Chrysalis Building
Bramley Road
London W10 6SP
Tel: 020 7465 6161
Indpendent producer, programmes include: It's Anybody's Guess, King of the Castle

Capitol Films
23 Queensdale Place
London W11 4SQ
Tel: 020 7471 6000
Fax: 020 7471 6012
email: films@capitolfilms.com
Website: www.capitolfilms.com

Carey Films Ltd
5 Henshaw Lane
Yeadon
Leeds LS19 7RW
Tel: 00 44 (0)113 250 6411
Fax: 00 44 (0)113 210 9426
email: owen@careyfilms.com
Website: www.careyfilms.com

Carnival (Films and Theatre) Ltd
12 Raddington Road
Ladbroke Grove
London W10 5TG
Tel: 020 8968 0968
Fax: 020 8968 0155
email: info@carnival-films.co.uk
Website: www.carnival-films.co.uk

Cartwn Cymru
Ben Jenkins Court
19a High Street
Llandaf
Cardiff CF5 2DY
Tel: 02920 575999
Fax: 02920 575919
email: production@cartwn-cymru.demon.co.uk
Contact: Naomi Jones
Recent production: Other World

Catalyst Television
Brook Green Studios
186 Shepherd's Bush Road
London W6 7LL
Tel: 020 7603 7030
Fax: 020 7603 9519

Celador Films
39 Long Acre
London WC2E 9LG
Tel: 020 7845 6998
Fax: 020 7836 1117
email: Imackinnon@celador.co.uk
Website: celador.co.uk
ivana MacKinnon

Celador Productions
39 Long Acre
London WC2E 9JT
Tel: 020 7240 8101
Fax: 020 7836 1117
Paul Smith
Indpendent producer, programmes include: The People Versus, Who Wants To Be A Millionaire?, Winning Lines

CF1 CYF
Uppercliff House
Uppercliff Close
Penarth CF64 1BE
Tel: 02920 400820
Fax: 02920 400821
email: CF1CYF@hotmail.com
Website: www.fearmovie.com

Channel X
22 Stephenson Way
London NW1 2HD
Tel: 020 7387 3874
Fax: 020 7387 0738
email: mail@channelx.co.uk
Indpendent producer, programmes include: XYZ, Shooting Stars, Families at War

Chatsworth Television
97-99 Dean Street
London W1D 3DE
Tel: 020 7734 4302
Fax: 020 7437 3301
email: television@chatsworth-tv.co.uk
Website: www.chatsworth-tv.co.uk
Malcolm Heyworth, Managing Director
Indpendent producer, programmes include: Treasure Hunt, Interceptor, The Crystal Maze, Wine Hunt

The Children's Film Unit
South Way
Leavesden
Herts WD25 7LZ
Tel: 01923 354656
Fax: 01923 354656
email: cfilmunit@aol.com
Website: www.btinternet.com/~cfu
Carol Rennie

Chrysalis Visual Entertainment
The Chrysalis Building
13 Bramley Road
London W10 6SP
Tel: 020 7221 2213
Fax: 020 7465 6159
Website: www.chrysalis.co.uk
Charlotte Boundy

Cinema Verity Productions Ltd
11 Addison Avenue
London W11 4QS
Tel: 020 7460 2777
Fax: 020 7371 3329

Civilian Content plc
4th Floor
Portland House
4 Great Portland Street
London W1N
Tel: 020 7612 0030
Fax: 020 7612 0031
email: contact@civilancontent.com
Website: www.civiliancontent.com
Richard Holmes, Managing Director

Colstar International Television Limited
78 York Street
London W1H 1DP
Tel: 020 7625 6200
email: mediadoc@aol.com
Steve Goddard, Head of International Licensing and Co-Productions
General feature films, short films television serials and specials, children's programming, animation, documentaries on science and wildlife, politics and world history, humanities, biographies, the arts, sport and adventure

The Comedy House
91 Berwick Street
London W1F 0NE
Tel: 020 7292 8370
Fax: 020 7292 8372
John Goldstone, Producer

Company Pictures
Suffolk House
1/8 Whitfield Place
London W1T 5JU
Tel: 020 7380 3900
Fax: 020 7380 1166
email: enquiries@companypictures.co.uk
Website: www.companypictures.co.uk

Company of Wolves
Computer Film Company
5th Floor, 19-23 Wells Street
London, W1P 3FP

Tel: 020 7344 8090
Fax: 020 7344 8091
cofwolves@aol.com
Recent production: The Actors

Connections Communications Centre Ltd

Palingswick House
241 King Street
Hammersmith
London W6 9LP
Tel: 020 8741 1766
Fax: 020 8563 1934
email: @cccmedia.co.uk
Website: www.cccmedia.co.uk
Jacqueline Davis

Cosgrove Hall Films

8 Albany Road
Chorlton-cum-Hardy
Manchester M21 0AW
Tel: 0161 882 2500
Fax: 0161 882 2555
email: animation@chf.co.uk
Website: www.chd.uk.com
Susan Ennis, Head of Production

Judy Couniham Films Ltd

12a Newburgh Street
London W1V 1LG
Tel: 020 7287 4329
Fax: 020 7287 2303

Covent Garden Films

67 Palfrey Place
London SW8 1AR
Tel: 00 44 (0)20 7820 7555
Fax: 00 44 (0)20 7820 7591
email: simon@coventgardenfilms.com
Website: www.coventgardenfilms.com

Dakota Films

4a Junction Mews
London W2 1PN
Tel: 020 7706 9407
Fax: 020 7402 6111
email: info@dakota-films.demon.co.uk

Dan Films Ltd

32 Maple Street
London W1T 6HB
Tel: 020 7916 4771
Fax: 020 7916 4773
email: office@danfilms.com
Website: www.danfilms.com
Jason Newmark (Producer)

DAT Productions

134 Cricklewood Lane
London NW2 2DP
Tel: 020 8450 5665
Fax: 020 8208 1979
email: cathy@datproductions.co.uk
Website: www.datproductions.co.uk
Cathy Ferrett

De Warrenne Pictures Ltd

St. Anne's House
Diadem Court
Soho
London W1D 3EF
Tel: 020 7734 7648
Fax: 070 9236 7853
email: info@dewarrenne.com
Website: www.dewarrenne.com
Tom Waller

Different Films

P.O. Box 564
London WC2H 8Lz
Tel: 0845 4 58 57 90
Fax: 0845 4 58 57 91
email: info@differentfilms.co.uk
Website: www.differentfilms.co.uk
Douglas M Ray

Dirty Hands Productions

2nd Floor
6-10 Lexington Street
London W1F OLB
Tel: 020 7287 7410
Fax: 020 7734 7131

Diverse Productions

Gorleston Street
London W14 8XS
Tel: 020 7603 4567
Fax: 020 7603 2148
email: info@diverse.tv
Website: www.diverse.co.uk
Established in 1982, Diverse is an independent factual programme maker

DNA Films

3rd Floor
75-77 Margaret Street
London W1N 8HB
Tel: 020 7291 8010
Fax: 020 7291 8020
email: info@dnafilms.com
Website: www.dnafilms.com
Joanne Smith

Domino Films

7 King Harry Lane
St Albans AL3 4AS
Tel: 01727 750153
email: Jo@dominofilms.co.uk
Joanna Mack

The Drama House

Coach Road Cottages
Little Saxham
Bury St Edmunds 1P29 5LE
Tel: 01284 810521
Fax: 01284 811425
email: jack@dramahouse.co.uk
Website: www.dramahouse.co.uk
Jack Emery

Dramatis Personae

19 Regency Street
London SW1P 4BY
Tel: 020 7834 9300
email: nathan.silver@htlworld.com
Nathan Silver

Ecosse Films

Brigade House
8 Parsons Green
London SW6 4TN
Tel: 020 7371 0290
Fax: 020 7736 3436
email: info@ecossefilms.com
Website: www.ecossefilms.com
Sophie Grumbar, Assistant to Managing Director
Jessica Amory, Office Manager

Edinburgh Film & Video Productions

Traquair House
Innelleithen
Peeblessairl EH44 6PW
Tel: 01896 831188
Fax: 01896 831198
Robin Crichton

Edric Audio Visual

34-36 Oak End Way
Gerrards Cross
Buckinghamshire SL9 8BR
Tel: 01753 481416
Fax: 01753 887163
email: robin@edic-av.co.uk
Website: www.edric-av.co.uk
Robin Congdon, Managing Director

Endboard Productions

114a Poplar Road
Bearwood
Birmingham B66 4AP
Tel: 0121 429 9779
Fax: 0121 429 9008
email: Sunandan@endboard.com
Website: www.endboard.com
Sunandan Walia, Director

Eon Productions Limited

Eon House
138 Piccadilly
London W1J 7NR
Tel: 020 7493 7953
Fax: 020 7408 1236
email: chris.brisley@eon.co.uk
Website: www.jamesbond.com
Contact: Katherine McCormack
Recent production: Die Another Day

Equilibrium Films

28 Sheen Common Drive
Richmond TW10 5BN
Tel: 020 7602 1989/07930
Fax: 020 7602 1989
John Miles

Extreme International
The Coach House
Ashford Lodge
Halstead
Essex C09 2RR
Tel: 01787 479000
Fax: 01787 479111
email: xdream@dream.co.uk
Website:
www.extremeinternational.com
Alistair Gosling

Festival Film and Television Ltd
Festival House
Tranquil Passage
Blackheath Village
London SE3 OBJ
Tel: 020 8297 9999
Fax: 020 8297 1155
email: info@festivalfilm.com
Website: www.festivalfilm.com
Ray Marshall

Figment Films Ltd
3rd Floor
75-77 Margaret Street
London W1W 8BH
Tel: 020 7291 8030
Fax: 020 7291 8040
email: figment@globalnet.co.uk
Website: www.figmentfilms.com

Film and General Productions
4 Bradbrook House
Studio Place
London SW1X 8EL
Tel: 020 7235 4495
Fax: 020 7245 9853
email: cparsons@filmgen.co.uk
Clive Parsons

Film and Music Entertainment Ltd
34 Bloomsbury Street
London WC1B 3QJ
Tel: 020 7636 9292
Fax: 020 7636 9229
email: info@fame.uk.com
Website: www.fame.uk.com
Contact: Mike Downey, Sam Taylor
Recent production: Deathwatch

FilmFour Ltd
124 Horseferry Road
London SW1P 2TX
Tel: 020 7396 4444
Website: www.channel4.com/film
Tessa Ross, Head of FilmFour

Firedog Films
20 The Chase
Coulsdon
Surrey, CR5 2NF
Tel: 020 8693 3477
email: email info@firedogfilms.co.uk
Website: www.firedogfilms.co.uk
Jonathan Martin

The First Film Company
38 Great Windmill Street
London W1V 7PA
Tel: 020 7439 1640
Fax: 020 7437 2062

Flashback Television Ltd
11 Bowling Green Lane
London EC1R OBD
Tel: 020 7490 8996
Fax: 020 7490 5610
email: mailbox@flashbacktv.co.uk
Website: www.flashbacktv.co.uk
In production since 1982 Flashback Television is an independent production company specialising in factual programmes

Flashlight Films
10 Golden Square
London W1R 3AF
Tel: 020 7436 6060
Fax: 020 7287 4232
email: kate@flashlightfilms.com
Kate Hagar, Aaron Simpson
Website: www.flashlightfilms.com

Focus Films
The Rotunda Studios
Rear of 116-118 Finchley Road
London NW3 5HT
Tel: 020 7435 9004
Fax: 020 7431 3562
email: focus@pupix.demon.co.uk
Website: www.focusfilms.co.uk
David Pupkewitz

Mark Forstater Productions
27 Lonsdale Road
London NW6 6RA
Tel: 020 7624 1123
Fax: 020 7624 1124

Fox Searchlight Pictures
Twentieth Century-Fox Film Co Ltd
Twentieth Century House
31-32 Soho Square
London W1V 6AP
Tel: 020 7437 7766
Fax: 020 7734 2170
Website: www.fox.co.uk

Fragile Films
95-97 Dean Street
London W1N 3XX
Tel: 020 7287 6200
Fax: 020 7287 0069
email: fragile@fragilefilms.com
Recent production: Hope Springs

Freedom Pictures
10 Rylett Crescent
Shepherds Bush
London W12 9RL
Tel: 0468 855746
Fax: 020 8743 6981
email:
timewhite@freedompictures.co.uk
Tim White

Fulcrum TV
254 Goswell Road
London EC1V 7RE
Tel: 020 7253 0353
Fax: 020 7490 0206
email: info@FulcrumTV.com
Website: www.FulcrumTV.com
Sandra Leeming, Production Manager

Global Vision Networ
Elstree Film Studios
Borehamwood
Hertfordshire WD6 1JG
Tel: 020 8324 2333
Fax: 020 8324 2700
email: info@gvn.co.uk
Website: www.gvn.co.uk

Goldcrest Films International
65-66 Dean Street
London W1D 4PL
Tel: 020 7437 8696
Fax: 020 7437 4448

GranadaWild
1-5 Whiteladies Road
Clifton
Bristol BS8 1NU
Tel: 0117 9745800
Fax: 0117 9733531
email: rosemary.ballingall@
granadamedia.com
Contact Rosemary Ballingall

Greenpoint Films
7 Denmark Street
London WC2H 8LZ
email: info@greenpointfilms.co.uk
Ann Scott

Gruber Films
eOffice no. 2
Sheraton Street
London W1F 8BH
Tel: 08703 66 93 13
email:
grichard.holmes@gruberfilms.com
Website: www.gruberfilms.com

Gullane Entertainment PLC
Stoneham Gate
Stoneham Lane
Eastleigh S050 9NW

Tel: 023 8064 9200
Fax: 023 8064 9201
Website: www.gullane.com

HAL Films Ltd
Elsley House
24-30 Great Tichfield Streeet
London W1P 7AD
Tel: 020 75358300
Website: www.miramax.com

Halas & Batchelor
The Halas & Batchelor Collection Ltd
Southerham House
Southerham
Lewes
East Sussex BN8 6JN
Tel: 01273 488 322
Fax: 01273 488 322
email: vivien@haba.demon.co.uk
Website: www.halasandbatchelor.com
Vivien Halas

Hammer Film Productions Ltd
92 New Cavendish Street
London W1W 6XJ
Tel: 020 7637 2322
Fax: 020 7323 2307
email: firstname@hammerfilms.com
Website: www.hammerfilms.com
Terry Ilott

Harbour Pictures
11 Langton Street
London SW10 OJL
Tel: 020 7351 7070
Fax: 020 7352 3528
email: info@harbourpictures.com
Website: www.harbourpictures.com
Nick Barton, Suzanne Mackie
Recent production: Calendar Girls

Hartswood Films
Twickenham Studios
The Barons, St Margarets
Twickenham
Middx TW1 2AW
Tel: 020 8607 8736
Fax: 020 8607 8744
Debbie Vertue

Hat Trick Productions
10 Livonia Street
London W1F 8AF
Tel: 020 7434 2451
Fax: 020 7287 9791
Website: www.hattrick.com
Denise O'Donoghue
Indpendent producer, programmes include: Confessions, Have I Got News For You, The Best Show in the World...Probably, Whatever You Want, Whose Line is it Anyway?

Hot Property Films Ltd
27 Newman Street
London W1T 1PP
Tel: 020 7323 9466
Fax: 020 7323 9467
email: janine@hotpropertyfilms.com
Website: www.hotpropertyfilms.com
Contact: Janine Marmot

Michael Hurll Television
3rd Floor
Beaumont House
Kensington Village
Avonmore Road
London W14 8TS
Tel: 020 7605 1200
Fax: 020 7605 1201

IBT Productions Ltd
3-7 Euston Centre
Regent's Place
London NW1 3JG
Tel: 020 7874 7650
Fax: 020 7874 7644
email: mail@ibt.org.uk
Website: www.ibt.org.uk

Icon Entertainment International Ltd
The Quadrangle , 4th Floor
180 Wardour Street
London W1V 3AA
Tel: 020 7494 8100
Fax: 020 7494 8151

Illuminations Films/Koninck
19-20 Rheidol Mews
Rheidol Terrace
London N1 8NU
Tel: 020 7288 8400
Fax: 020 7359 1151
email: griff@illumin.co.uk
Website: www.illumin.co.uk
Keith Griffiths

Illuminations Television
19-20 Rheidol Mews
Rheidol Terrace
London N1 8NU
Tel: 020 7288 8400
Fax: 020 7359 1151
email: illuminations@illumin.co.uk
Website: www.illumin.co.uk
Illuminations was founded in 1982 as one of the first independent production companies working for Channel 4 Television

Imaginary Films
75 East Road
London N1 6AH
Tel: 020 7490 1724
Fax: 020 7490 1764
email: anna@boudiccafilms.com
Website: boudicafilms.com
Ray Brady
Recent production: Day of the Siren

Impact Pictures Ltd
3 Percy Street
London W1T 1DE
Tel: 020 7636 7716
Fax: 020 7636 7814
email: production@impactpix.com
Jeremy Bolt, Judy Goldberg

InFilm Productions Ltd
37 Arteslan Road
London W2
Tel: 020 7792 5152
Fax: 020 7792 5153
email: infilm@infilmproductions.com
Website: www.infilmproductions.com
Dorothy Berwin, Paul Augarde

Intermedia
9-13 Grosvenor Street
London W1K 4QA
Tel: 020 7495 3322
Fax: 020 7495 3993
email: info@intermediafilm.co.uk
Website: www.intermediafilm.co.uk

J&M Entertainment Ltd
2 Dorset Square
London NW1 6PX
Tel: 020 7723 6544
Fax: 020 7724 7541
email: sales@jment.com
Website: ww.jment.com
Julia Palau

Bill Kenwright Films
BKL House
106 Harrow Road
London W2 1RR
Tel: 020 7446 6200
Fax: 020 7446 6222
email: info@kenwright.com
Website: www.kenwright.com
Bill Kenwright, Liz Holford

King Rollo Films
Dolphin Court
High Street
Honiton
Devon EX14 1HT
Tel: 01404 45218
Fax: 01404 45328
email: admin@kingrollofilms.co.uk
Clive Juster

Landseer Productions
140 Royal College Street
London NW1 0TA
Tel: 020 7485 7333
Fax: 020 7485 7573
email: mail@landseerfilms.com
Website: www.landseerfilms.com

Large Door Productions
3 Shamrock Street
London SW4 6HF
Tel: 020 7627 4218
email: ldoor@demon.co.uk
John Ellis

Little Bird Co
9 Grafton Mews
London W1P 5LG
Tel: 020 7380 3980
Fax: 020 7380 3981
email: info@littlebird.co.uk
Website: www.littlebird.ie

Little Dancer
Avonway
Naseby Road
London SE19 3JJ
Tel: 020 8653 9343
Fax: 020 8286 1722
email: Littledancerfilm@aol.com
Robert Smith

London Films
71 South Audley Street
London W1K 1JA
Tel: 020 7499 7800
Fax: 020 7499 7994
email: luff@londonfilms.com
Website: www.londonfilms.com
Andrew Luff

Malachite Productions
East Kirkby House
Spilsby
Lincolnshire PE23 4BX
Tel: 01790 763538
Fax: 01790 763409
email: info@malachite.co.uk
Website: www.malachite.co.uk
Charles Mapleston

Malone Gill Productions Ltd
27 Campden Hill Road
London W8 7DX
Tel: 020 7937 0557
Fax: 0207 376 1727
email: malonegill@aol.com
Georgina Denison

Jo Manuel Productions Ltd
11 Keslake Road
London NW6 6DG
Tel: 020 8930 0777
Fax: 020 8933 5475

Maya Vision International Ltd
43 New Oxford Street
London WC1A 1BH
Tel: 020 7836 1113
Fax: 020 7836 5169
email: info@mayavisionint.com
Website: www.mayavisionint.com
John Cranmer

Media Darlings Ltd
2/78 Greencroft Gardens
London NW6 3JQ
Tel: 020 7372 5020
Fax: 020 7372 0407
email: enquiries@mediadarlings.net
Michelle Kastly

The Media Trust
3-7 Euston Centre
Regent's Place
Off Euston Road
London NW1 3JG
Tel: 020 7874 7600
Fax: 020 7874 7644
email: info@mediatrust.org
Website: www.mediatrust.org

Mentorn Films
138-140 Wardour Street
London W1V 3AV
Tel: 020 7287 4545
email: mentorn@mentorn.co.uk
Website: www.mentorn.co.uk
Indpendent producer, programmes include: Challenge Anneka, Quisine, Robot Wars

Merchant Ivory Productions
46 Lexington Street
London W1R 3LH
Tel: 020 7437 1200/439 4335
Fax: 020 7734 1579
email: miplondon@merchantivory.demon.co.uk
Website: www.merchantivory.com
Paul Bradley

The Mersey Television Company
Campus Manor
Childwall Abbey Road
Liverpool L16 0JP
Tel: 0151 722 9122
Fax: 0151 722 6839
email: admin@merseytv.com
Website: www.merseytv.

Millennium Pictures
Suite 77
2 Landsdowne Row
Berkley Square
London W1J 6HL
Tel: 020 7413 9171
Fax: 020 7493 4935
email: daniel@figuero.freeserve.co.uk
Website: www.figuero.co.uk

Minerva Picture Company Ltd
6 Meard Street,
London W1F 0EG
Tel/Fax: 020 8964 4451
email: minervapic@aol.com

Mirage Enterprises Ltd
Old Chapel Studios
19 Fleet Road
London NW3 2QR
Tel: 020 7284 5588

Miramax International
Elsey House
24-30 Great Titchfield Street
London W1W 8BF
Tel: 020 7535 8300
Fax: 020 7535 8301
Website: www.miramax.com
David Aukin

Momentum Productions
32 Newman Street
LondonW1T 1PU
Tel: 020 7631 0666
Fax: 020 7631 0676
email: production@momentum.co.uk
Website: www.momentum.co.uk
Guy Meyer/Darren Cavanagh

Mosaic Films Ltd
2nd Floor
8-12 Broadwick Street
London W1V 1FH
Tel: 020 7437 6514
Fax: 020 7494 0595
email: info@mosaicfilms.com
Website: www.mosaicfilms.com
Contact: Colin Luke (London)

MW Entertainments
48 Dean Street
Soho
London W1D 5BF
Tel: 020 7734 7707
Fax: 020 7734 7727
email: contact@michaelwhite.co.uk

Noel Gay Television
Shepperton Studios
Studios Road
Shepperton
Middx TW17 OQD
Tel: 01932 592485
Fax: 01932 592172

Nova Productions
62 Ascot Avenue, Cantley
Doncaster DN4 6HE
Doncaster DN3 3AF
Tel: 0870 765 1021
Fax: 0870 125 7917
email: info@novaonline.co.uk
Website: www.novaonline.co.uk
Andrew White, Maurice White, Gareth Atherton
Film, television and graphics production company, specialising in documentary, entertainment, special event and music promo production. Producer of programmes released on

sell-through video on its own label via subsidiary Nova Home Entertainment and on other labels. Game Show format development and graphic production. Also training, promotional and multi-camera OB production for broadcast and non-broadcast

Orbit Media Ltd
80a Dean Street
London W1D 3SN
Tel: 020 7287 4264
Fax: 020 7287 0984
Website: www.orbitmedia.co.uk
Jordan Reynolds

Orlando TV Productions
Up-the-Steps
Little Tew
Chipping Norton
Oxon OX7 4JB
Tel: 01608 683218
Fax: 01608 683364
email: orlando.tv@btinternet.com
Website: www.orlandodigital.co.uk
Mike Tomlinson, Madelaine Westwood

Oxford Film and Video Makers
The Old Boxing Club
54 Catherine Street
Oxford OX4 3AH
Oxford OX3 9HY
Tel: 01865 792731 or 01865 792732
Fax: 01865 742901
email: office@ofvm.org
Website: www.ofvm.org

Oxford Film & Television
6 Erskine Road
London NW3 3AJ
Tel: 020 7483 3637
Fax: 020 7483 3567
email: email@oftv.co.uk
Website: www.oftv.co.uk
Vanessa Phillips, Head of Factual Programmes

Oxford Scientific Films
Lower Road
Long Hanborough
Oxford OX8 8LL
Tel: 01993 881881
Fax: 01993 882808
email: photo.library@osf.uk.com
Website: www.osf.uk.com

Paladin Invision Ltd
8 Barb Mews
London W6 7PA
Tel: 0207 371 2123
Fax: 0207 371 2160
Website: www.pitv.com
Clive Syddall
A multi Emmy-Award winning company specialising in Anglo-American co-productions of quality, popular factual programming including history, science, current affairs, religion and music and arts programming

paradogs Ltd
1st floor
17 - 25 Cremer St
London E2 8HD
Tel: 020 7613 3001
email: paradogs@pinkpink.demon.co.uk
Website: www.paradogs.org.uk
Steven Eastwood, Director/producer

Parallax Pictures
7 Denmark Street
London WC2H 8LS
Tel: 020 7836 1478
Fax: 020 7497 8062
email: info@parallaxpictures.co.uk
Website: www.parallaxpictures.co.uk
Sally Hibbin

Paranoid Celluloid
Keepers Cottage
Wennington
Abbots Ripton
Huntingdon
Cambridgeshire PE18 0JB
Tel: 00 44 (0)1487 773 255
Fax: 00 44 (0)1487 773 640
email: adammason@paranoid-celluloid.com
Website: www.paranoid-celluloid.com

Pathé Pictures
Kent House
Market Place
London W1N 8AR
Tel: 020 7323 5151
Fax: 020 7636 7594

Peakviewing Transatlantic
The Wheelhouse
Bonds Mill
Stonehouse
Gloucestershire GL10 3RF
Tel: 01453 826300
Fax: 01453 826303
email: info@peakviewing.co.uk
Website: www.peakviewing.co.uk

Photoplay Productions
21 Princess Road
London NW1 8JR
Tel: 020 7722 2500
Fax: 020 7722 6662

Picture Palace Films Ltd
13 Egbert Street
London NW1 8LJ
Tel: 020 7586 8763
Fax: 020 7586 9048
email: info@picturepalace.com
Website: www.picturepalace.com
Malcolm Craddock, Katherine Hedderly

Pilton Pictures
30 Ferry Road Avenue
Edinburgh EH4 4BA
Tel: 0131 343 1151
Fax: 0131 343 2820
email: office@piltonvideo.freeserve.co.uk
Website: www.piltonvideo.org.uk

Planet 24 Productions
35-38 Portman Square
London W1H ONU
Tel: 020 7486 6268
Fax: 020 7612 0679
Website: www.planet24.com
Indpendent producer, programmes include: The Big Breakfast

Praxis Films
PO Box 290
Market Rasen
Lincs LN3 6BB
Tel: 01472 399976
Fax: 01472 399976
email: info@praxisfilms.com
Website: www.praxisfilms.com
Sue Waterfield

Prominent Features
34 Tavistock Street
London WC2E 7PB
Tel: 020 7497 1100
Fax: 020 7497 1133
email: 101322.552@compuserve.com
Steve Abbott

Sarah Radclyffe Productions
5th Floor
83-84 Berwick Street
London W1V 3PJ
Tel: 020 7437 3128
Fax: 020 7437 3129
email: srpltd@globalnet.co.uk
Sarah Radclyffe, Bill Godfrey

Ragdoll Limited
Pinewood Studios
Pinewood Road
Iver Heath
Bucks SL0 0NH
Tel: 01753 631800
Fax: 01753 631831
email: pinewood@ragdoll.co.uk
Website: ragdoll.co.uk
Liz Queenan

Raw Charm
Ty Cefn

Rectory Road
Cardiff CF1 1QL
Tel: 029 20 641511
Fax: 029 20 668220
email: pam@rawcharm.co.uk
Website: www.rawcharm.tv
Pamela Hunt

Recorded Picture Co
24 Hanway Street
London W1P 9DD
Tel: 020 7636 2251
Fax: 020 7636 2261
Jocelyn Jones
Production Company:
Recorded Picture Company
24 Hanway Street
London W1P 9DD, England
Tel: +44 (0)20 7636 2251
Fax: +44 (0)20 7636 2261
info@recordedpicture.com
Contact: Jocelyn Jones
Recent production: Young Adam

Redwave Films
31-32 Soho Square
London W1V 6AP
Tel: 020 7753 7200
Fax: 020 7753 7201

The Reel Thing Ltd
20 The Chase
Coulsdon
Surrey CR5 2EG
Tel: 020 8668 8188
email: info@reelthing.tv
Website: www.reelthing.tv
Frazer Ashford

Regent Productions
c/o FremantleMedia Ltd
1 Stephen Street
London W1P 1PJ
Tel: 020 7691 6000
Fax: 020 7691 6100
Website: www.fremantlemedia.com
Part of FremantleMedia's UK production division which comprises Thames Television, Talkback Productions, Regent Productions and Alomo Productions, all producing a diverse range of programming for the UK's terrestrial and satellite channels

Revolution Films
9A Dallington Street
London EC1V 0BQ
Tel:020 7566 0700
Fax: 020 7566 0701
email@revolution-films.com

Richmond Light Horse Productions Ltd
3 Esmond Court
Thackeray Street
London W8
Tel: 020 7937 9315
Fax: 020 7938 4024
Euan Lloyd

Rocket Pictures
1 Blythe Road
London W14 OHG
Tel: 020 7603 9530
Fax: 020 7348 4830
Luke Lloyd Davies

RSPB Film
The Lodge, Sandy
Bedfordshire SG19 2DL
Tel: 01767 680551
Fax: 01767 683262
email: mark.percival@rspb.org.uk
Website: www.rspb.org.uk
Mark Percival

Sands Films
119 Rotherhithe Street
London SE16 4NF
Tel: 020 7231 2209
Fax: 020 7231 2119
email: ostockman@sandsfilms.co.uk
Website: www.sandsfilms.co.uk
Olivier Stockman
Sands Films specialises in independent, medium size budget films for the cinema

Scala Productions
15 Frith Street
London W1D 4RE
Tel: 020 7734 7060
Fax: 020 7437 3248
email: scalaprods@aol.com
Nik Powell, Anna Wulff

Scottish Television Enterprises
Cowcaddens
Glasgow G2 3PR
Tel: 0141 300 3000
Fax: 0141 300 3030
Darrel James, Managing Director

Screen Production Associates
10 Courthope Road
London NW3 2LB
Tel: (44) 020 7267 9953
Fax: (44) 020 7267 9953
email: piersjackson@screenpro.co.uk
Website: www.screenpro.co.uk

Screen Ventures
49 Goodge Street
London W1T 1TE
Tel: 020 7580 7448
Fax: 020 7631 1265
email: infro@screenventures.com
Website: www.screenventures.com

Siriol Productions
Phoenix Buildings
3 Mount Stuart Square
Butetown
Cardiff CF10 5EE
Tel: 02920 488400
Fax: 02920 485962
email: robin.lyons@siriol.co.uk
Website: www.siriolproductions.com
Robin Lyons, Managing Director

Sirius Pictures
12 Elmley Street
Plumstead
London SE18 7NT
Tel: 00 44 (0)20 8854 1206
Fax: 00 44 (0)20 8854 1206
email: info@siriuspictures.co.uk
Website: www.siriuspictures.co.uk
Production Company:
Sirius Pictures
12 Elmley Street
London SE18 7NJ, England
Tel/Fax: +44 (0)20 8854 1206
carrie@siriuspictures.co.uk
www.siriuspictures.co.uk
Contact: Carrie Holliman

SKA Productions Ltd
1 Horse and Dolphin Yard
London W1V 7LG
Tel: 020 7434 0869
Fax: 020 7437 3245

Skreba
Union Hall
29 Union Street
London SE1 1SC
Tel: 020 7357 9924
Fax: 020 7357 9920

Sky Pictures
BSky B, 6 Centaurs Park
Grant Way, Syon Lane
Isleworth
Middlesex TW7 5QD
Tel: 020 7941 5588
Fax: 0207 941 5599

Sly Fox Films Limited
6 York Buildings
London WC2N 6JN
Tel: 020 7839 1000
Fax: 020 7839 6486
email: linda@slyfoxfilms.com
Linda James

Smoking Dogs Films
26 Shacklewell Lane
London E.8 2EZ
Tel: 020 7249 6644
Fax: 020 7249 6655
email: info@smokingdogsfilms.com
John Akomfrah, Lina Gopaul, David Lawson

Soho Communications
2 Percy Street
London W1T 1DD
Tel: 020 7637 5825
Fax: 020 7436 9740
email: Jstaton@dircon.co.uk
Website: sohocommunications.com
Jon Staton

Sony Pictures Europe UK Ltd
Sony Pictures Europe House
25 Golden Square
London W1R 6LU
Tel: 020 7533 1111
Fax: 020 7533 1105

Specific Films
25 Rathbone Street
London W1T 1NQ
Tel: 020 7580 7476
Fax: 020 7494 2676
email: info@specificfilms.com
Michael Hamlyn

Spice Factory
81 The Promenade
Peacehaven
Brighton
East Sussex BN10 8LS
Tel: 01273 585275
Fax: 01273 585304
email: info@spicefactory.co.uk
Alex Marshall/Emily Kyriakides

Stagescreen Productions
12 Upper St Martin's Lane
London WC2H 9JY
Tel: 020 7497 2510
Fax: 020 7497 2208
email: stgescreenProds@aol.com
Jeffrey Taylor

Sterling Picture
53 Great Portland Street
London W1W 7LG
Tel: 020 7323 6810
Fax: 020 7323 6811
email: admin@sterlingpictures.com
Website: www.sterlingpictures.com

Talent Television
2nd Floor Regent House
235 Regent Street
London W1B 2EH
Tel: 020 7434 1677
Fax: 020 7434 1577
email: entertainment@talenttv.com
John Kaye Cooper, Managing Director

Talisman Films Limited
5 Addison Place
London W11 4RJ
Tel: 020 7603 7474
Fax: 020 7602 7422
email@talismanfilms.com
Richard Jackson, Andrew Lawton

TalkBack Productions Ltd
20-21 Newman Street
London W1T 1PG
Tel: 020 7861 8000
Fax: 020 7861 8001
Website: www.talkback.co.uk
Part of FremantleMedia's UK production division which comprises Thames Television, Talkback Productions, Regent Productions and Alomo Productions, all producing a diverse range of programming for the UK's terrestrial and satellite channels
Indpendent producer, programmes include: They Think It's All Over, Never Mind the Buzzcocks

Taylor Cartoon Films Richard
River View, Waterloo Drive
Clun, Craven Arms
Shropshire SY7 8JD
Tel: 01588 640 073

Telescope Pictures Ltd
Twickenham Film Studios
Saint Margarets, Twickenham
Middlesex TW1 2AW
Tel: 020 8607 8888
Fax: 020 8607 8889
email: telescopepics@aol.com

Teliesyn
Chapter Arts Centre
Market Road
Cardiff CF5 1QE
Tel: 029 2030 0876
Fax: 029 2030 0877
email: ebost:tv@teliesyn.demon.co.uk
Website: www.teliesyn.co.uk

Testimony Films
12 Great George Street,
Bristol BS1 5RS
Tel: 0117 925 8589
Fax: 0117 925 7668
email:
stevehumphries@testimonyfilms.com
Website: www.testimonyfilms.com
Steve Humphries

The Illuminated Film Company
115 Gunnersbury Lane
Acton
London W3 8HQ
Tel: 020 8896 1666
Fax: 020 8896 1669
email: info@illuminatedfilms.com
Website: www.illuminatedfilms.com
Iain Harvey

Thames Television
c/o FremantleMedia Ltd
1 Stephen Street
London W1T 1AL
Tel: 020 7691 6000
Fax: 020 7691 6100
Website: www.thamestv.co.uk
Part of FremantleMedia's UK production division which comprises Thames Television, Talkback Productions, Regent Productions and Alomo Productions, all producing a diverse range of programming for the UK's terrestrial and satellite channels

Thin Man Films
9 Greek Street
London W1D 4DQ
Tel: 020 7734 7372
Fax: 020 7287 5228
Claire Broughton

Tiger Aspect Productions
5 Soho Square
London W1V 5DE
Tel: 020 7434 6700
Fax: 020 7434 1798
email: pictures@tigeraspect.co.uk
Website: www.tigeraspect.co.uk
Independent television producers, working across a broad range of genre including comedy, drama, entertainment and factual programming

TKO Communications
PO Box 130, Hove
East Sussex BN3 6QU
Tel: 01273 550088
Fax: 01273 540969
email: jkruger02@aol.com

Toledo Pictures
3rd Floor, 75-77 Margaret Street
London W1N 7HB
Tel: 020 7291 8050
Fax: 020 7291 8060
email: adam.tudhope@dnafilms.com
Adam Tudhope, Assistant to Duncan Kenworthy

Trademark Films
Phoenix Theatre
110 Charing Cross Road
London WC2H OJP
Tel: 020 7240 5585
Fax: 020 7240 5586
email: mail@trademarkfilms.co.uk

Trans World International
TWI House
23 Eyot Gardens
London W6 9TR
Tel: 020 8233 5400
Fax: 020 8233 5401

Transatlantic Films
Studio 1
3 Brackenbury Road
London W6 OBE
Tel: 020 8735 0505
Fax: 020 8735 0605
email: mail@transatlanticfilms.com
Website: www.transatlanticfilms.com
Corisande Albert, Revel Guest

Turn On TV
Sun House
2-4 Little Peter Street
Manchester M15 4PS
Tel: 0161 834 1440
Fax: 0161 831 9452
email: post@turnontv.demon.co.uk
Website: www.turnontv.co.uk
Cathy Barratt

Twentieth Century-Fox Productions Ltd
20th Century House
31-31 Soho Square
London W1V 6AP
Tel: 020 7437 7766
Fax: 020 7734 3187

Twenty Twenty Television
Suite 2, Grand Union House
29 Kentish Town Road
London Nw1 9NX
Tel: 020 7284 2020
Fax: 020 7284 1810

Tyburn Film Productions Ltd
Cippenham Court
Cippenham Lane
Cippenham, Nr Slough
Berkshire SL1 5AU
Tel: 01753 516767
Fax: 01753 691785

United Artists Films (an MGM company)
10 Stephen Mews
London W1P 1PP
Tel: 020 7333 8877
Fax: 020 7333 8878

Universal Pictures International
Oxford House
76 Oxford Street
London W1N 0H9
Tel: 020 7307 1300
Fax: 020 7307 1301

Universal Pictures Ltd
1 Hamilton Mews
London W1V 9FF
Tel: 020 7491 4666
Fax: 020 7493 4702

Upfront Television Ltd
39-41 New Oxford Street
London WC1A 1BN
Tel: 020 7836 7702
Fax: 020 7836 7701
email: upfront@btinternet.com
Website:
www.celebritiesworldwide.com
Claire Nye

Vera Productions Ltd
3rd Floor
66/68 Margaret Street
London W1W 8SR
Tel: 020 7436 6116
Fax: 020 7436 6117/6016
email: racheail@vera.co.uk
Contact: Elaine Morris

Vine International Pictures
21 Great Chapel Street
London W1V 3AQ
Tel: 020 7437 1181
Fax: 020 7494 0634
email: vine@easynet.co.uk
Website: www.vine-international.co.uk

Vixen Films
13 Aubert Park
Highbury
London N5 1TL
Tel: 020 7359 7368
Fax: 020 7359 7368
email: tg@tgraham.demon.co.uk

Viz
4 Bank Street
Inverkeithing
Fife KY11 1LR
Tel: 01383 412811
Fax: 01383 418103
email: grigorfilm@aol.com
Murray Grigor

Walsh Bros Ltd
24 Redding House, Harlinger Street
King Henry's Wharf
London SE18 5SR
Tel: 020 8858 6870/020 8854 5557
Fax: 020 8858 6870
email: walshbros@mail.com
John Walsh

Warner Bros Productions Ltd
Warner Suite, Pinewood Studios
Iver Heath, Bucks SL0 0NH
Tel: 01753 654 545
Fax: 01753 655 703
email: Rbutton0993@aol.com
Contact: Roy Button
Recent production: Harry Potter and the Chamber of Secrets

Warner Bros International Television
Warner House
7th Floor
98 Theobalds Road
London WC1X 8WB
Tel: 020 7984 5439
Fax: 020 7984 5421

Warner Sisters Film & TV Ltd, Cine Sisters Ltd
The Cottage
Pall Mall Deposit
124 Barlby Road
London W10 6BL
Tel: 020 8960 3550
Fax: 020 8960 3880
email: sisters@warnercine.com

West-Coast Productions Ltd
27 Morrab Road
Penzance, Cornwall TR18 4EZ
Tel: 01736 350 019
email: antalkovacs@hotmail.com
Website; www.west-coastproductions.co.uk

David Wickes Productions
10 Abbey Orchard Street
Westminster
London SW1P 2LD
Tel: 020 7222 0820
Fax: 020 7222 0822
email: wickesco@aol.com
David Wickes, Heide Wilsher

Winchester Entertainment plc
19-21 Heddon Street
London,W1B 4BG
Tel: 020 7851 6500
Fax: 020 7851 6506
email: gsmith@winchesterent.co.uk
Website: www.winchesterent.com
Chief Executive: Gary Smith

Working Title Films
Oxford House
76 Oxford Street
London W1D 1BS
Tel: 020 7307 3000
Fax: 020 7307 3002
email: tony.davis@unistudios.com
Recent productions: Johnny English, Love Actually

World Productions
Eagle House
50 Tiarshall Street
London W1F 9BQ
Tel: 020 7734 3536
Fax: 020 7758 7070
email: info@world-productions.com
Website: www.world-productions.com

WTTV
77 Shaftesbury Avenue
London W1D 5DU
Tel: 020 7494 4001
Fax: 020 7255 8600

Yellow Productions Ltd
7 Thackley End
119 Banbury R
Oxford OX2 6LB
Tel: 0777 5713363
Fax: 01865 516566
email: info@yellowuk.biz
Website; www.yellowuk.biz
Recent production: Cargo

Xingu Films
12 Cleveland Row, St James
London SW1
Tel: 020 7451 0600
Fax: 020 7451 0601
Recent production: Cheeky

Zenith Group
43-45 Dorset Street
London W1H 4AB
Tel: 020 7224 2440
Fax: 020 7224 3194
email: general@zenith.tv.co.uk
Website: www.zenith.tv.co.uk
The Zenith Group comprises Zenith Productions and Zenith North. Between them the two companies produce a wide range of programmes for terrestrial, satellite and cable television and feature films for worldwide theatrical distribution

Zenith North
11th Floor
Cale Cross House
156 Pilgrim Street
Newcastle upon Tyne NE1 6SU
Tel: 0191 261 0077
Fax: 0191 222 0271
email: zenithnorth@dial.pipex.com
Website: www.zenith.tv.co.uk

Zephyr Films Limited
24 Colville Road
London W11 2BS
Tel: 020 7221 8318
Fax: 020 7221 9289
email: pippa@zephyr-1.dircon.co.uk

Zooid Pictures Limited
66 Alexander Road
London N19 5PQ
Tel: 020 7281 2407
Fax: 020 7281 2404
email: pictures@zooid.co.uk
Website: www.zooid.co.uk

PRODUCTION STARTS

With the advent of digital technology it is getting increasingly difficult to track and trace Production Starts (see statistical commentary). The list here is made up of feature-length films intended for theatrical release with a significant British involvement (whether creative, financial or UK-based) which went into production between January and December 2002. The production start date, distributor and release information is given where known up to 1 June 2003.

3 Blind Mice
2 March
Souris Verte, KCraft & Co., Take 4, Baker Street Media
Budget: £3.20m
Dir: Mathias Ledoux
with Edward Furlong, Emilia Fox, Chiwetel Ejiofor, Elsa Zylberstein, Peter Wight
Country: UK/France

16 Years of Alcohol
2 June
Tartan Works, Scottish Screen, Fortissimo Film Sales,
Budget: £0.50m
Dir: Richard Jobson
with Kevin McKidd, Laura Fraser, Susan Lynch, Ewen Bremner
Distributor: Metro Tartan Distributors **Country:** UK

Absolon
GFT Entertainment, Hannibal Pictures
Budget: £4.5m
Dir: David Barto
withChristopher Lambert, Lou Diamond Phillips, Kelly Brook, Ron Perlman, Roberta Angelica
Country: UK/Canada

The Actors
May
FilmFour, Company of Wolves, Four Provinces Films, Senator Film AG, Bord Scannán na hÉireann, Section 481
Budget: £15m
Dir: Conor McPherson
with Michael Caine, Dylan Moran, Michael Gambon, Lena Headey, Miranda Richardson
Distributor: Momentum Pictures
Country: UK/Germany/Ireland/US

AKA
2002
Third Rock, presented by Film Council, in association with Bard Entertainments
Dir: Roy Duncan
with Matthew Leitch, Diana Quick, George Asprey, Lindsey Coulson, Blake Ritson, Peter Youngblood Hills
Distributor: City Screen
Country: UK

American Cousins
14 January
Little Wing Productions, Scottish Screen, Glasgow Film Fund
Budget: £3m
Dir: Don Coutts
with Danny Nucci, Gerald Lepkowski, Shirley Henderson, Vinny Pastore, Dan Hedaya
Country: UK

Ashes & Sand
25 February
Open Road Films
Budget: £3m
Dir: Bob Blagden
with Lara Belmont, Nick Moran, Victoria Scarborough
Country: UK

Baltic Storm
5 November
Top Story Filmproduction GmbH, Filmförderung in Berlin-Brandenburg, Filmförderungsanstalt , Smile Entertainment, NordMedia, Norddeutscher Rundfunk, ARTE, IAC Film
Budget: £3.80m
Dir: Reuben Leder
with Greta Scacchi, Jürgen Prochnow, Donald Sutherland, Dieter Laser, Jürgen Schornagel, Barbara Schöne, Herb Andress **Country:** UK

Bitter Sweet
aka Hwerow Hweg
2002
West-Coast Productions Ltd
Budget: £?
Dir: Antal Kovacs
with Helen Rulel
Country: UK

Bl,.M
aka Ulysees
22 September
Stalheim, What's the Story
Budget: £2.2m
Dir: Sean Walsh
with Stephen Rea, Angeline Ball, Hugh O'Connor, Patrick Bergin, Alan Devlin, Phelim Drew, Maria Lennon, Alvaro Lucchesi, Eoin McCarthy, Dearbhla Molly
Country: UK/Ireland

Blackball
14 October
Midfield Films, Inside Track, Icon Entertainment International, The Isle of Man Film Commission
Budget: £4m
Dir: Mel Smith
with Paul Kaye, James Cromwell, Alice Evans, Bernard Cribbins, Johnny Vegas, Imelda Staunton, Vince Vaughn
Country: UK

Blue Butterfly
24 March
Galafilm Productions, Global Arts
Budget: £1.7m
Dir: Léa Pool
with Michael E Rodgers, James Watson, Lynsey Baxter, Oliver Cotton, Sam Ellis
Country: UK/Canada

The Bone Hunter
14 October
Palm Tree (UK)
Budget: £1.7m
Dir: Robbie Moffat
with Michael E Rodgers, James Watson, Lynsey Baxter, Oliver Cotton, Sam Ellis
Country: UK

Bright Young Things
2nd November
revolution Films, Doubting Hall, The Film Consortium, Vision View, Icon Entertainment
Budget: £7.6m
Dir: Stephen Fry
with Emily Mortimer, Stephen Campbell Moore, David Tennant, Fenella Woolgar, James McAvoy, Michael Sheen, Guy Henry
Country: UK

The Bum's Rush
18 November
Hero Films, Motlys, Vision View Scottish Screen, The Glasgow Film Office, Momentum Pictures, The Norwegian Film Fund
Budget: £2.8
Dir: Stewart Svaasand
with Jamie Sives, Kevin McKidd, Iain Robertson, Neve McIntosh, Dougray Scott, James Cosmo, Ewan Stewart, Jimmy Chisholm
Distributor: Momentum Pictures
Country: UK/Norway

The Calcium Kid
1September
WT2
Budget: £4m
Dir: Alex de Rakoff
with Orlando Bloom, Billie Piper, Michael A. Pena, Omid Djalili, David Kelly, Chris Eubank
Country: UK

Calendar Girls
24 June
Harbour Pictures
Budget: £8m
Dir: Nigel Cole
with Helen Mirren, Julie Walters, John Alderton, Linda Bassett, Annette Crosbie, Ciaran Hinds, Celia Imrie, Geraldine James, Penelope Wilton
Country: UK

Chaos and Cadavers
9 August
Matador Films, Zodiac Pictures International, Azuro Financing
Budget: £2.2m
Dir: Niklaus Hilber
with Nick Moran, Keeley Hawes, Steve Huison, Ian McNeice, John Bennett, Rik Mayall
Country: UK/Switzerland

Cheeky
22 October
Xingu Films, Europa Corp.
Budget: £3.9m
Dir: David Thewlis
with David Thewlis, Trudie Styler, Johnny Vegas, Ian Hart, Lesley Sharp, Ruth Sheen, Sean Ward
Country: UK/France

Cloud Cuckoo Land
14 January
Airborne Productions
Budget: £1.5m
Dir: Matt Dickinson
with Steve Varden, Derek Jacobi, Rosalind Blessed, Kriss Dosanjh, Boo Pearce, Jane Wall
Country: UK

Cold Mountain
December
Miramax Film, Mirage Enterprises, Bona Fida Productions
Budget:
Dir: Anthony Minghella
with Jude Law, Nicole Kidman, Renee Zelleger, Natalie Portman, Philip Seymour Hoffman, Giovanni Ribisi, Brendan Gleeson, Donald Sutherland, Jena Malone, Kathy Baker, Ray Winstone, Ethan Suplee, James Gammon, Charlie Hunnam, Lucas Black, Eileen Atkins
Distributor: Miramax **Country:** UK/US

The Day I Will Never Forget
2002
Channel Four
Budget: £?
Dir: Kim Longinotto
Documentary
AD Country: UK

Day of the Sirens
April
Imaginary Films
Budget: £?
Dir: Ray Brady
with Saeed Jaffrey, Galit Hershkovitz Celia Meiras, Carmine Mancuso, Shivani Ghai, Michael Chomiak, Des Backhouse-Brady, Rik Mayall
Country: UK

Devil's Gate
3 January
Alchemist Films
Budget: £2m
Dir: Stuart St. Paul
with Laura Fraser, Callum Blue, Luke Aikman, Roger Ashton-Griffiths, Tom Bell
Country: UK

Die Another Day
14 January
Eon Productions
Budget: £62.5m
Dir: Lee Tamahori
with Pierce Brosnan, Halle Berry, Rosamund Pike, Toby Stephens, Rick Yune, Michael Madsen, Judi Dench, Samantha Bond, John Cleese, Michael Kitchen
20th Century Fox International
Country: UK/US

Dominator The Movie
2002
Renga Media, Sci-Fi Channel Europe
Budget: £
Dir: Tony Luke
Animation
with the voices of Dani Filth, Ingrid Pitt, Mark Radcliffe, Marc Riley, Doug Bradley, Liza Goddard, Alex Cox, Seera Backhouse, Tara Harley
Country: UK

Don't Look Back
14 January
New Forest Pictures
Budget: £1m
Dir: Nicholas A.J. Sherard
with Oliver Tobias, Stephen Marcus, Jennifer Calvert, Charlotte Rogers, Kevin Howarth
Country: UK

Dot the I
21 April
Summit Entertainment, Arcane Pictures, Alquimia Cinema
Budget: £3m
Dir: Matthew Parkhill
with Gael Garcîa, Natalia Verbeke, James D'Arcy
Country: UK/US/Spain

The Dreamers
18 July
Recorded Picture Company, Peninsular Films, Fiction Cinematografica
Budget: £6m
Dir: Bernardo Bertolucci
with Michael Pitt, Louis Garrel, Eva Green
Country: UK/France/Italy

Emile
18 November
Raven West Films, Meltemi Entertainment
Budget: £7m
Dir: Carl Bessai
with Ian McKellen, Deborah Unger
Country: UK/Canada

Fallen Angels
3 May
Avrio Filmworks
Budget: £?
Dir: Ian David Diaz
with Esme Eliot, Michael Ironside,

Kai Wiesinger, Jeff Fahey
AD Country: UK

Fakers
December
Kleparski & Bee, Janes Films
Budget: £1.7m
Dir: Richard Janes
with Matthew Rhys, Kate Ashfield, Tony Haygarth, Art Malik
Country: UK

Finding Fortune
13 April
Palm Tree Productions
Budget: £1.5m
Dir: Robbie Moffat
with Ilaria, Victoria Prichard, Jason Harvey
Country: UK

The Football Factory
18 November
Vertigo Films
Budget: £0.50m
Dir: Keith Boak
with Dougray Scott
Country: UK

Girl With a Pearl Earring
November
Archer Street, DeLux Productions S.A., Pathé Productions Ltd. , Inside Track, Film Council, Lion's Gate Films
Budget: £11.5m
Dir: Peter Webber
with Colin Firth, Scarlett Johansson, Tom Wilkinson, Judy Parfitt, Cillan Murphy
Country: UK/Luxembourg/US

Good Luck, Bad Fortune
11 March
Mint Marche Entertainment, Chaplins of London
Dir: Chris McCarthy
with Peter McNeill, Leslie Foster, Dan Knightley
Country: UK

Gladiatress
11 November
Mission Pictures, Stock Productions, Icon Entertainment International
Budget: £3.5m
Dir: Brian Grant
with Sally Phillips, Doon Mackichan, Fiona Allen, David Hayman, Anna Wilson-Jones, Ronan vibert, Marcia Warren, Pam Ferris, Oliver Ford Davies
Country: UK

The Great Goose Caper
6 November
Voice Pictures, Productions Colin Neale, Studio Eight Productions, Téléfilm Canada, Equity Investment Program, CTF - Licence Fee Program, Alberta Foundation for the Arts, Harold Greenberg Fund, Government of Canada Tax Credit Programme, Canadian Film or Video Production Team
Budget: £3.40m
Dir: Nicholas Kendall
with Chevy Chase, Kari Matchett, Joan Plowright, James Purefoy, Isabella Fink
Country: UK/Canada

Happy Day
9 March
Toby Davis
Budget: ££35,000
Dir: Toby Davis
with Paula Brooke, Oliver Franks, Christopher Nabb, Angelique Talio
Country: UK

Hwerow Hweg
(See Bitter Sweet)

Hoover Street Revival
2002
Baker Street Media, BBC Films, Film Council New Cinema Fund, Haut et Court
Dir: Emily Young
Documentary
Distributor: Metro Tartan Distributors **Country:** UK/France

I Am David
17 June
David Productions, Walden Media
Budget: £5m
Dir: Paul Feig
with Ben Tibber, Joan Plowright, James Caviezel
Country: UK/US

The I Inside
5 June
MDP Worldwide, VIP Medienfonds, MDP Filmproduktion
Budget: £6.2m
Dir: Roland Suso Richter
with Ryan Phillippe, Sarah Polley, Piper Perabo, Stephen Rea, Stephen Lang, Robert Sean Leonard, Peter Egan, Stephen Graham, Rakie Ayola
Country: UK/US/Germany

IBrotha
7 July
Square Systems Solutions, iBrotha Productions
Budget: £
Dir: Jake Barnes
with Neil Rayment, Paulette Phillips, Nick Owen
Country: UK

If Only
10 November
If Only Production Services Ltd
Dir: Gil Junger
with Jennifer Love Hewitt, Paul Nicholls, Tom Wilkinson, Diana Hardcastle, Lucy Davenport
Country: UK/US

In the Cut
22 July
Red Turtle, Pathé International (Paris), Screen Gems
Dir: Jane Campion
with Meg Ryan, Mark Ruffalo, Jennifer Jason Leigh, Sharrieff Pugh
Country: UK

Intermission
14 January
Company of Wolves, Independent Film Channel, Parallel Film Productions, Bord Scannán na hÉireann, Section 481
Budget: £2.5m
Dir: John Crowley
with Colin Farrell, Colm Meaney, Cillian Murphy, Kelly MacDonald, Shirley Henderson
Country: UK/Ireland

In This World
2002
Film Consortium Ltd, Dallington Films Limited, BBC Films , Presented in association with Film Council , Works, Revolution Films
Dir: Michael Winterbottom
with Jamal Udin Torabi, Enayatullah, Imran Paracha, Hiddayatullah, Jamau, Wakeel Khan, Lal Zarin
AD Country: UK

I'll Be There
12 July
Morgan Creek Productions
Budget: £4m
Dir: Craig Ferguson
with Craig Ferguson, Charlotte Church, Jemma Redgrave, Ralph Brown, Ian McNeice, Stephen Noonan, Joss Ackland, Imelda Staunton
Distributor: Warner Bros Distributors (UK) **Country:** UK/US

I'll Sleep When I'm Dead
23 September
Will & Company Productions,

Revere Pictures, Seven Arts
Budget: £6m
Dir: Mike Hodges
with Clive Owen, Charlotte Rampling, Jonathan Rhys Meyers, Malcolm McDowell, Jamie Foreman, Ken Stott, Sylvia Syms
Country: UK/US

JM Barrie's Neverland
June
FilmColony, Miramax Films
Budget: £10m
Dir: Marc Foster
with Johnny Depp, Kate Winslet, Julie Christie, Dustin Hoffman, Radha Mitchell, Kelly Macdonald, Paul Whitehouse, Ian Hart
Country: UK/US

Jericho Mansions
30 September
Spice Factory
Budget: £3.86m
Dir: Alberto Sciamma
with James Caan, Jennifer Tilly, Geneviève Bujold, Maribel Verdú, Peter Keleghan, Suzan Glover
Country: UK

Jester Till
February
Scala Productions, Illuminated Film Company Ltd., Munich animaton, MotionWorks
Budget: £
Dir: Eberhard Junkersdorf
Animation
with the voice of Lee Evans
Country: UK/Germany/Belgium

Johnny English
15 April
Working Title Films, Rogue Male Films, Ltd.,
Budget: £15m
Dir: Peter Howitt
with Rowan Atkinson, Natalie Imbruglia, John Malkovich, Ben Miller
Distributor: United International Pictures (UK) Ltd **Country:** UK/US/France

Kiss of Life
13 October
Baker Street Media, Haut et Court, Take Five, Wild Horses Films, Haut et Court, Autonomous,Film Council, BBC Films, France 3 Cinéma, Gimages Films, Gimages 6, Film Council New Cinema Fund
Budget: £2m
Dir: Emily Young
with Ingeborga Dapkunaite, Peter Mullan, David Warner, Millie Findlay, James E. Martin, Gemma Jones
Country: UK/France

Lara Croft and the Cradle of Life: Tomb Raider
26 August
Paramount British Pictures
Budget: £65m
Dir: Jan De Bont
with Angelina Jolie, Gerard Butler, Ciaran Hinds, Chris Barrie, Noah Taylor, Djimon Hounsou, Til Schweiger
Country: UK

The Last Horror Movie
2002
Prolific Films, Snakehair Productions, MTM-I
Budget: £1m
Dir: Julian Richards
with Kevin Howarth, Mark Stevenson, Antonia Beamish, Chris Adamson, Christabel Muir
Country: UK

LD 50
27 October
Four Horsemen Films
Budget: £5.2m
Dir: Simon De Selva
with Katherine Towne, Melanie Brown, Tom Hardy, Leo Bill, Philip Winchester, Stephen Lord, Toby Fisher, Ross McCall, Tanya Emery
Country: UK

Leo
3 March
Scala Productions, Freewheel Productions
Budget: £?
Dir: Mehdi Norowzian
with Joseph Fiennes, Elisabeth Shue, Dennis Hopper, Sam Shepard, Deborah Unger, Jake Webber, Davis Sweat, Donnie Wahlberg, Mary Stuart Masterson
Country: UK

Lighthouse Hill
aka Flight of Fancy
9 February
Carnagy Films, Cirrus
Budget: £2.4m
Dir: David Fairman
with Jason Flemyng, Kirsty, Mitchell, Kulvinder Ghir, Frank Finlay, Julie T. Wallace, John Sessions, Annabelle Apsion, Samantha Janus, Maureen Lipman, Samantha Beckinsale
Country: UK

Live Forver
2002
Passion Pictures, Horsebridge Productions Limited, Film Council, BBC, Helkon SK
Budget: £?
Dir: John Dower
Documentary
Distributor: Helkon SK **Country:** UK

Living in Hope
2002
Fluidity Films
Budget:
Dir: John Miller
with Tom Harper, Paul Foster, Liam McMahon, Bennet Thorpe, Robin Edwards, Naomie Harris, Jade Ball, Lorraine Chase, Norman Bowler, Joseph Rye
Distributor: Winstone Film Distributors **Country:** UK

Love Actually
6 September
Universal Pictures, Working Title Films, DNA Films Limited
Budget: £20m
Dir: Richard Curtis
with Hugh Grant, Martine McCutcheon, Emma Thompson, Laura Linney, Liam Neeson, Alan Rickman, Colin Firth, Rowan Atkinson, Bill Nighy, Keira Knightley
Country: UK

Loving Glances
19 June
FAME Film & Entertainment, Yodi Movie Craftsmen, Serbian Ministry of Culture, European Co-Production Fund (UK)
Budget: £1m
Dir: Srdjan Karanovic
with Senad Alihodzic, Ivana Bolanca, Jelena Dokic, Gorica Popovic, Milena Dravic
Country: UK/Germany/Serbia

Luger
22 September
Luger The Movie, Stray Dog Films
Budget: £0.6m
Dir: Gustavo Martinez-Schmidt
with Gary Douglas, Ian Wright, Stefan Booth, Nabil Elouahabi, Jonathan McGuiness
Country: UK

Luminal
18 February
Dreyco Productions, Imago
Budget: £2m
Dir: Andrea Vecchiato

with Denis Lavant, Jameela Mustchin, Maria Papas, Thomas Orange, Jo Reynolds
Country: UK/Italy

The Magic Roundabout
October
Films Action, bolexbrothers/SPZ Pathe Pictures
Budget: £12.80m
Dir: Dave Borthwick
with voices of Jim Broadbent, Joanna Lumley, Kylie Minogue, Robbie Williams, Ray Winstone Richard O'Brien
Distributor: Pathé Distribution
Country: UK/France/Switzerland

Mandancin
11 November
Festival Films, 1A Productions, Saltire Films
Dir: Norman Stone
with Alex Ferns, Tom Georgeson, Kenneth Cranham, James Cosmo, Jenny Foulds, Cas Harkins, Gerald Lepkowski
Country: UK

Masked & Anonymous
17 June
Spitfire Pictures, Destiny Film Productions, BBC Films, Fate Productions Ltd., Fateful Productions
Budget: £3.2m
Dir: Larry Charles
with Jeff Bridges, Penelope Cruz, Bob Dylan, John Goodman, Jessica Lange, Luke Wilson, Angela Bassett, Marin Cheech, Richard C. Sarafian, Laura Harring
Country: UK/US

Moonlight
6 June
Spice Factory, Staccato Films, DeLux Productions S.A. Peppermint
Dir: Paula van der Oest
with Andrew Howard, Jemma Redgrave, Johan Leysen, Laurien van den Broeck, Howard Bussemaker
Country: UK/Netherlands/Luxembourg/ Germany

The Mother
17 June
Free Range Films, BBC Films
Budget: £2m
Dir: Roger Mitchell
with Anne Reid, Daniel Craig, Steven Mackintosh, Cathryn Bradshaw, Peter Vaughan, Oliver Ford Davies, Anna Wilson-Jones
Country: UK

The Motorcycle Diaries
30 September
South Fork Pictures, Tu Vas Voir, FilmFour, Senator Film AG, Wildwood Enterprises
Budget: £10m
Dir: Walter Salles
with Gael García, Rodrigo De La Serena, Mia Maestro, Mercedes Morán, Jean-Pierre Noher
Country: UK/US/France/Germany

Mrs Richie
December
Nomadic Pictures, Prophecy Entertainment
Dir: Paul Johansson
with Gena Rowlands, Kevin Zegers, Brenda James, Justin Chatwin (I), Heather Wahlquist
Country: UK/Canada

Ned Kelly
29 April
WTA, Endymion Films
Budget: £20m
Dir: Gregor Jordan
with Heath Ledger, Orlando Bloom, Geoffrey Rush, Naomi Watts, Laurence Kinlan, Philip Baranttini, Joel Edgerton, Kiri Paramore, Emily Browning, Kris McQuade
Country: UK/Australia/US

Neil's Party
2002
2:3:5
Budget: £1.2m
Dir: Stephen Pidgeon
with Andrew Kelly, Lauren Bigby, Bryn Lucas, Alex Hardy, Geraint Rees
Country: UK

Nicholas Nickleby
29 April
United Artists, Hart-Sharp Entertainment, Cloud Nine Entertainment
Budget: £6.8m
Dir: Doug McGrath
with Charlie Hunnam, Jamie Bell, Nathan Lane, Christopher Plummer, Jim Broadbent, Tom Courtenay, Alan Cumming, Phil Davis, Edward Fox, Romola Garai
Distributor: 20th Century Fox International (UK) **Country:** UK/US

Nine Lives
8 April
A&A Films
Budget: £2m
Dir: Andrew Green
with Rosie Fellner, Vivienne Harvey, Paris Hilton, Patrick Kennedy, David Nicolle, Ben Peyton, James Schlesinger, Lex Shrapnel, Amelia Warner
Country: UK

The Night We Called it a Day
14 October
Scala Productions, Ocean Pictures
Budget: £3.70m
Dir: Paul Goldman
with Dennis Hopper, Melanie Griffith, Portia De Rossi, Joel Edgerton, Rose Byrne
Country: UK/Australia

Octane
3 June
Four Horsemen Films, DeLux Productions, Random Harvest Pictures
Budget: £8m
Dir: Marcus Adams
with Madeleine Stowe, Norman Reedus, Bijou Phillips, Jonathan Rhys Meyers, Mischa Barton
Country: UK/Luxembourg

Oh Marbella
9 September
VF - Versatile Films
Dir: Piers Ashworth
with Rik Mayall, Lara Belmont, Tom Bell, Mike Reid
Country: UK

One for the Road
30 September
East Midlands Media Intitiative, Film Council New Cinema Fund, FilmFour Lab
Budget: £0.69m
Dir: Chris Cooke
with Robert Procter, Greg Chisholm, Mark Devenport, Hywel Bennett, Julie Legrand, Micaiah Dring, Penn Linfield
Country: UK

One Love
October
Take 4 TV Partnerships, One Love Films, Exposed Films, Euromax, Film Council, Baker Street Media presented in association with BV International Pictures
Budget: £1.60m
Dir: Rick Elgood, Don Letts
with Ky-mani Marley, Cherine Anderson, Vas Blackwood, Idris Elba, Winston Bell, Carl Bradshaw
Country: UK/Norway

Piazza of the Five Moons
2002
Martinelli Film Co. Ltd, Spice Factory, Blue Star, Box! Film/Istituto Luce
Budget: £6.40m
Dir: Renzo Martinelli
with Donald Sutherland
Country: UK/Italy/Germany

The Poet
17 August
Film Line, Meltemi Entertainment, MediaFonds 1, Eclypse Filmpartner
Budget: £3.15m
Dir: Paul Hills
with Laura Harring, Dougray Scott, Jürgen Prochnow, Andrew Lee-Potts
Country: UK/Germany/Austria

The Prodigal
July
Tiger Films, FusionTristar International
Budget: £1.3m
Dir: Ben Sampays
with Kevin Quinn, Jon-Paul Gates, Ivana Basic, Peter Lochburn, Peter Stenson
Country: UK

Pure
January
Little Wing Productions, Kudos Productions
Budget: £3m
Dir: Gillies MacKinnon
with Molly Parker, David Wenham, Keira Knightley, Harry Eden, Karl Johnson, Geraldine McEwan, Gary Lewis, Marsha Thomason, Kate Ashfield, Julia Deakin
Distributor: Artificial Eye Film Company **Country:** UK

The Real Thing
4 November
Wide Eye Films, Grosvenor Park, Peter Stockhaus Filmproduktion, Octagon Films Ltd.
Dir: David Gleeson
Country: UK/Ireland/Germay

The Republic of Love
December
Dan Films
Budget: £2.50m
Dir: Deepa Mehta
with Bruce Greenwood, Emilia Fox, Edward Fox, Lloyd Owen, Claire Bloom
Country: UK

Rivers and Tides
aka Fluss der Zeit
Mediopolis Film, Skyline Productions, WDR/ARTE, YLE, FilmFernsehFonds Bayern, Scottish Arts Council Lottery Fund, Scottish Screen National Lottery, Filmförderung in Berlin-Brandenburg
Budget: £2m
Dir: Jason Wulfsohn
Documentary
Distributor: Cinéfrance **Country:** UK/Germnay/Finland

S Club Seeing Double
December
Double Vision Film Ltd, Mediapro, Columbia Pictures Corporation, 19 Entertainment
Budget:
Dir: Nigel Dick
with Tina Barrett, Jon Lee, Bradley McIntosh, Jo O'Meara, Hannah Spearritt, Rachel Stevens, David Gant, Joseph Adams, Cristina Piaget, Merixell Santamaria
Country: UK/Spain

Sandmother
22 April
Focus Films, Persistence Pictures, Imaginarium, South African Film Finance Corporation, First Look Media
Budget: £2m
Dir: Jason Wulfsohn
with Scott Bairstow, Rachel Shelley, Warwick Grier, Patrick Shai, Paddy Lister, Adrienne Pearce
Country: UK/Canada/Zaire/US

Shanghai Knights
18 March
Touchstone Pictures, Spyglass Entertainment
Budget: £40.96m
Dir: David Dobkin
with Jackie Chan, Owen Wilson, Donnie Yen Chi-Dan
Distributor: Buena Vista International (UK) **Country:** UK/US

Skagerrak
22 April
Nimbus Film ApS, BBC Films, Danmarks Radio-TV Fiktion, DFI Filmvaerkstedet, Egmont Entertainment, Scottish Screen, Film i Väst, Glasgow Film Office
Budget: £3m
Dir: Søren Kragh-Jacobsen
with Iben Hjejle
Country: UK/Germany/Sweden

Song For a Raggy Boy
1July
Subotica Films, Moviefan, Copenhagen, Zoma Films UK, Lolafilms, Bord Scannán na hÉireann, Danske Filminstitut, Zentropa Entertainments ApS, Eurimages Conseil de l'Europe
Budget: £2.4m
Dir: Aisling Walsh
with Aidan Quinn, Iain Glen, Marc Warren, Dudley Sutton, Alan Devlin
Country: UK/Denmark/Spain

Solid Air
30 October
Elemental Films, Momentum Pictures, Scottsh Screen, Glasgow Film Fund
Budget: £0.9m
Dir: May Miles Thomas
with Maurice Roeves, Brian McCardie, Kathy Kiera Clarke, Gary Lewis, James Cosmo
Distributor: Momentum Pictures
Country: UK

Stella Street
18 November
Stella Street, Absolutely Productions, Columbia TriStar Motion Picture Company
Budget: £0.6m
Dir: Peter Richardson
with Phil Cornwell, John Sessions, Ronni Ancona
Country: UK/US

Suzie Gold
October
Green Wolf Films, Pathé Distribution, Inside Track, Film Council, Sky Movies Originals, Isle of Man Film Commission
Budget: £3.50m
Dir: Ric Cantor
with Summer Phoenix
Country: UK

Swimming Pool
2002
Fidélité Productions, Headforce Limited, France 2 Cinéma, Gimages Films, Foz, Canal+
Budget: £3.7m
Dir: François Ozon
with Charlotte Rampling, Ludivine Sagnier, Charles Dance, Marc Fayolle, Jean-Marie Lamour, Mireille Mossé, Michel Fau, Jean-Claude Lecas
Distributor: UGC Films UK
Country: UK/France

Sylvia Plath Project
14 January
Ruby Films, BBC Films, The Film Council
Budget: £8m
Dir: Christine Jeffs
with Gwyneth Paltrow, Daniel Craig
Country: UK

Team One
14 December
Imaginary Films
Budget: £0.9m
Dir: Roy Brady
with Adrian Rayment, Neil Rayment, Gordon Alexander, Buster Reeves, Silvio Simac, Jonathan Lomas, Jamie Cho
Country: UK

This Little Life
26 May
Common Features Ltd, BBC Films, Film Council, Yorkshire Media Production Agency, Northern Production Fund
Budget: £3.5m
Dir: Sarah Gavron
with Kate Ashfield, David Morrisey, Peter Mullan, Siân Reeves
Country: UK

Through the Looking Glass
13 March
Workshop Presents
Budget: £65,000
Dir: Craig Griffith
with Paul McCarthy, Jonathan Rhodes
Country: UK

To Kill a King
20 January
Natural Nylon Entertainment, IAC Holdings, Corsan Productions, Screenland Movieworld
Budget: £14m
Dir: Mike Barker
with Tim Roth, Dougray Scott, Rupert Everett, Olivia Williams, James Bolam, Corin Redgrave, Barry Lynch
Distributor: Pathé Distribution
Country: UK/Germany

Touching the Void
22 July
Darlow Smithson, FilmFour, Film Council, Channel Four,Public Broadcasting Service
Dir: Kevin Macdonald
Documentary
Country: UK/US

Tulse Luper Suitcase; A Personal History of Uranium
June 2002
Kasander Film Company, DeLux Productions S.A., Seagull Productions, Focus Film (Budapest), GAM Film, Net Entertainment A.G., Studio "12 A"
Budget: £2.21m
Dir: Peter Greenaway
with J.J. Feild, Drew Mulligan, Yorick van Wageningen, Kevin Tighe, Scot Williams, Tom Bower, Caroline Dhavernas, Michèle, Steven Mackintosh, Nigel Terry
Country: UK/Netherlands/Luxemborug/Spain/Hungary/Germany

Underworld
2 September
Subterranean Productions, Underworld Productions, Laurin Productions
Dir: Len Wiseman
with Kate Beckinsale, Scott Speedman, Bill Nighy, Michael Sheen, Erwin Leder, Shane Brolly, Robbie Gee, Sophia Myles, Wentworth Miller
Country: UK/Germany/Hungary/US

The Virgin of Liverpool
4 August
Mob Film Company, Senator Film AG
Budget: £2m
Dir: Lee Donaldson
with Ricky Tomilson, Johnny Vegas, Imelda Staunton, Paul Barber, Tom Georgeson, Claire Hackett, Rob Jarvis, Jake Abraham, Ian Puleston-Davies
Country: UK/Germany

Wanted
aka Crime Spree
24 April
GFT Entertainment, Studio 8, Hannibal Pictures
Budget: £5.50m
Dir: Brad Mirman
with Gérard Depardieu, Harvey Keitel, Johnny Hallyday, Saïd Taghmaoui, Renaud, Stéphane Freiss, Albert Dray, Joanne Kelly, Richard Bohringer, Abe Vigoda
Country: UK/Canada

The Water Giant
21 April
Barryfilms, Medienbeteiligungs und Produktions
Budget: £12.66m
Dir: John Henderson
with Bruce Greenwood, Rena Owen, Daniel Magder, Phyllida, Shane Rimmer, Tom Jackson, Joe Pingue
Country: UK/New Zealand/Germany

What a Girl Wants
aka American Girl
5 June
Warner Bros., Gaylord Films, Di Novi Pictures
Budget: £13m
Dir: Dennie Gordon
with Amanda Bynes, Kelly Preston, Colin Firth, Anna Chancellor, Johnathan Pryce, Eileen Atkins, Oliver James, Christine Cole
Country: US/UK

Wilbur Wants To Kill Himself
14 January
Zentropa Entertainments ApS, Sigma Films, Scottish Screen, Glasgow Film Fund, Danske Filminstitut, TV-2 Danmark, Nordisk Film- och TV-Fond
Budget: £?
Dir: Lone Scherfig
with Jamie Sieves, Adrian Rawlins, Shirley Henderson, Lisa McKinlay, Mads Mikkelsen, Julia Davis, Susan Vidler
Country: UK/Denmark, Norway

Wondrous Oblivion
19 August
APT Film and Television, Kuhn & Co.
Budget: £3.5m
Dir: Paul Morrison
with Delroy Lindo, Emily Woof, Sam Smith, Stanley Townsend
Distributor: Momentum Pictures
Country: UK

Young Adam
15 March
Recorded Picture Company, Sigman Productions, Sveno, Film Council, Scottish Screen
Budget: £4.5m
Dir: David MacKenzie
with Ewan McGregor, Tilda Swinton, Peter Mulan, Emily Mortimer
Country: UK

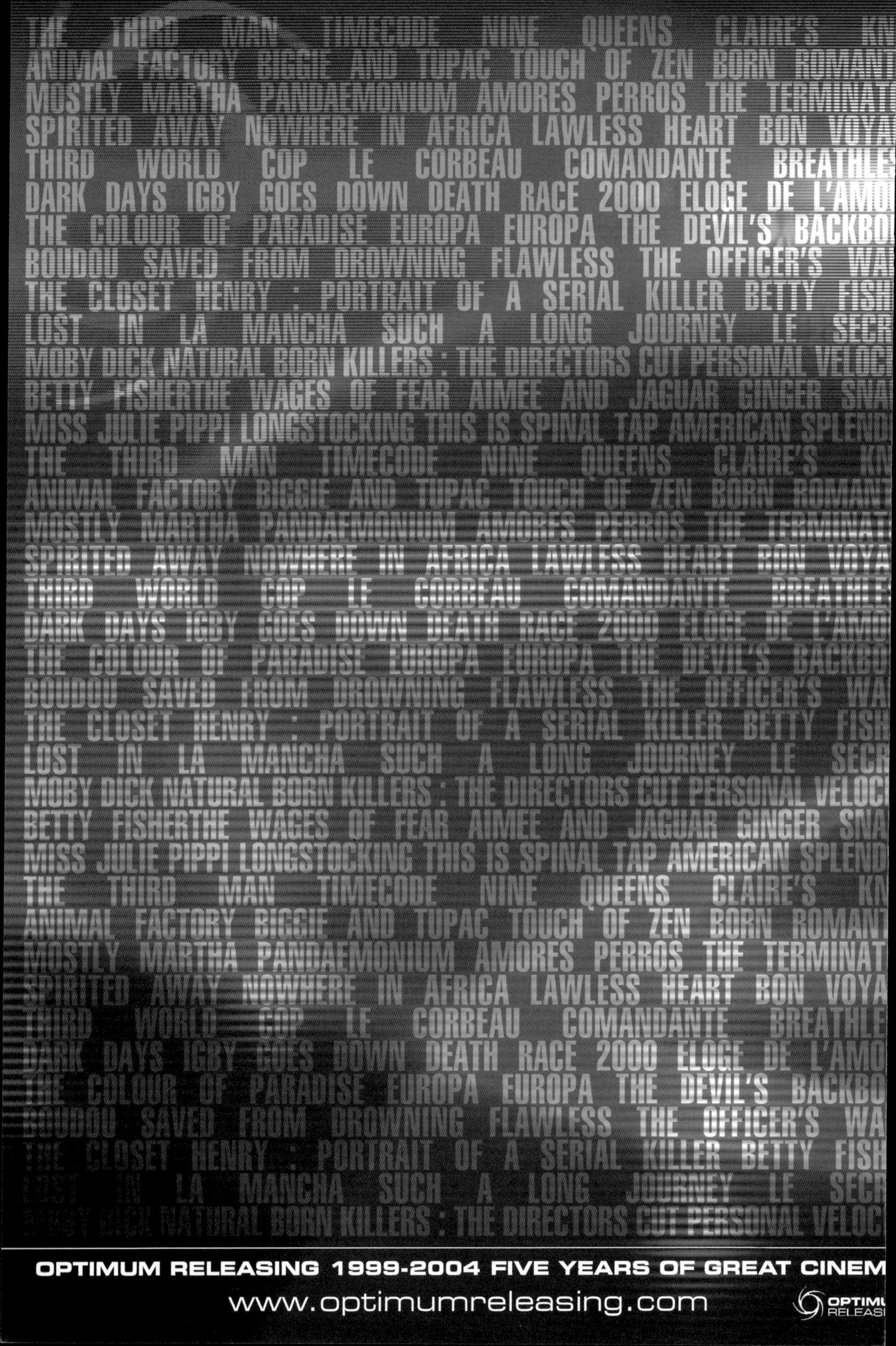
THE THIRD MAN TIMECODE NINE QUEENS CLAIRE'S KN
ANIMAL FACTORY BIGGIE AND TUPAC TOUCH OF ZEN BORN ROMANT
MOSTLY MARTHA PANDAEMONIUM AMORES PERROS THE TERMINAT
SPIRITED AWAY NOWHERE IN AFRICA LAWLESS HEART BON VOYA
THIRD WORLD COP LE CORBEAU COMANDANTE BREATHLES
DARK DAYS IGBY GOES DOWN DEATH RACE 2000 ELOGE DE L'AMO
THE COLOUR OF PARADISE EUROPA EUROPA THE DEVIL'S BACKBO
BOUDOU SAVED FROM DROWNING FLAWLESS THE OFFICER'S WA
THE CLOSET HENRY : PORTRAIT OF A SERIAL KILLER BETTY FISH
LOST IN LA MANCHA SUCH A LONG JOURNEY LE SECR
MOBY DICK NATURAL BORN KILLERS : THE DIRECTORS CUT PERSONAL VELOC
BETTY FISHERTHE WAGES OF FEAR AIMEE AND JAGUAR GINGER SNA
MISS JULIE PIPPI LONGSTOCKING THIS IS SPINAL TAP AMERICAN SPLEND
THE THIRD MAN TIMECODE NINE QUEENS CLAIRE'S KN
ANIMAL FACTORY BIGGIE AND TUPAC TOUCH OF ZEN BORN ROMANT
MOSTLY MARTHA PANDAEMONIUM AMORES PERROS THE TERMINAT
SPIRITED AWAY NOWHERE IN AFRICA LAWLESS HEART BON VOYA
THIRD WORLD COP LE CORBEAU COMANDANTE BREATHLE
DARK DAYS IGBY GOES DOWN DEATH RACE 2000 ELOGE DE L'AMO
THE COLOUR OF PARADISE EUROPA EUROPA THE DEVIL'S BACKBO
BOUDOU SAVED FROM DROWNING FLAWLESS THE OFFICER'S WA
THE CLOSET HENRY : PORTRAIT OF A SERIAL KILLER BETTY FISH
LOST IN LA MANCHA SUCH A LONG JOURNEY LE SECR
MOBY DICK NATURAL BORN KILLERS : THE DIRECTORS CUT PERSONAL VELOC
BETTY FISHERTHE WAGES OF FEAR AIMEE AND JAGUAR GINGER SNA
MISS JULIE PIPPI LONGSTOCKING THIS IS SPINAL TAP AMERICAN SPLEND
THE THIRD MAN TIMECODE NINE QUEENS CLAIRE'S KN
ANIMAL FACTORY BIGGIE AND TUPAC TOUCH OF ZEN BORN ROMANT
MOSTLY MARTHA PANDAEMONIUM AMORES PERROS THE TERMINAT
SPIRITED AWAY NOWHERE IN AFRICA LAWLESS HEART BON VOYA
THIRD WORLD COP LE CORBEAU COMANDANTE BREATHLE
DARK DAYS IGBY GOES DOWN DEATH RACE 2000 ELOGE DE L'AMO
THE COLOUR OF PARADISE EUROPA EUROPA THE DEVIL'S BACKBO
BOUDOU SAVED FROM DROWNING FLAWLESS THE OFFICER'S WA
THE CLOSET HENRY : PORTRAIT OF A SERIAL KILLER BETTY FISH
LOST IN LA MANCHA SUCH A LONG JOURNEY LE SECR
MOBY DICK NATURAL BORN KILLERS : THE DIRECTORS CUT PERSONAL VELOC
OPTIMUM RELEASING 1999-2004 FIVE YEARS OF GREAT CINEM
www.optimumreleasing.com

RELEASES

Listed here are feature-length films, both British and foreign which had a theatrical release in the UK between January and December 2002. Films released during the latter half of 2001 and still on release in 2002 are shown italicised.

Entries quote the title, distributor, UK release date, certificate, country of origin, director/s, leading players, production company/ies, duration, gauge (other than 35 mm) and the Sight and Sound reference (or Film Monthly Bulletin reference in the case or re-releases) if available.

Box office totals are provided and also take into account films still on release in 2003 (ie those released in November or December 2002). Opening weekend information is also included.

Films with some or total UK involvement are highlighted with monetary symbols representing the nations of the co-producers. * denotes re-release

Credits are taken from the SIFT database compiled by Filmographic Services of the bfi National Film Library. Additional research by Elena Marcarini

Films released in the UK in 2002

10

Dir Abbas Kiarostami
12 (France/Iran) 2002
ICA Projects – 27 September
Screenplay **Abbas Kiarostami**
DOP **Abbas Kiarostami**
Editor **Abbas Kiarostami**
Music **Peyman Yazdanian**
AKBARI, Mania [driver]
MAHER, Amin [Amin]
ARABSHAHI, Roya [.]
TALEIDZADEH, Katayoun [.]
SHARBAF, Mandana [.]
MORADI, Amene [.]
©2002 MK2 s.a./Abbas Kiarostami
Marin Karmitz and Abbas Kiarostami present
92 mins 48 seconds
Locations – Tehran, Iran
Subtitles
Sight and Sound .v12.n10.October 2002 p.57-58

Box Office:	**£308**
Screen	**1**
Screen average	**£308**

11 '09' 01 September 11

€ £ $
Dir [1] **Samira Makhmalbaf**
Dir [2] **Claude Lelouch**
Dir [3] **Youssef Chahine**
Dir [4] **Danis Tanovic**
Dir [5] **Idrissa Ouédraogo**
Dir [6] **Ken Loach**
Dir [7] **Alejandro González Iñárritu**
Dir [8] **Amos Gitai**
Dir [9] **Mira Nira**
Dir [10] **Sean Penn**
Dir [11] **Shohei Imamura**
12A (France/Egypt/UK/MexicoUS) 2002
Artificial Eye Film Company – 27 December
11 short films about the September 11 2001 attacks on the World Trade Centre and the Pentagon.
©2002 StudioCanal France
Galatée Films presents
a Galatée Films StudioCanal production
134 mins 5 seconds
Documentary.
Sight and Sound .v13.n1.January 2003 p.32-33,44-46

Box Office:	**£3,200***
	£30,298**
Screens	**3**
Screen average	**£1,067**

*(*total box office in 2002)*
*(** cumulative box office for 2002/03)*

23rd March 1931 Shaheed

Box Office:	**£86,823**
Opening weekend	**£35,242**
Screens	**21**
Screen average	**£1,678**

24 Hour Party People

£
Dir Michael Winterbottom
18 (UK) 2001
Pathé Distribution – 5 April
Prod Andrew Easton
Screenplay Frank Boyce Cottrell
DOP Robby Müller
Editor Trevor Waite
COOGAN, Steve Tony Wilson
ALLEN, Keith Roger Ames
BRYDON, Rob Ryan Letts
CILENTI, Enzo Pete Saville
COOK, Ron Derek Ryder
COGHILL, Chris Bez
CONSIDINE, Paddy Rob Gretton
CUNNINGHAM, Danny Shaun Ryder
GORMAN, Dave John the postman
HARRIS, Sean Ian Curtis
© 2001 24 Hour Films Limited
The Film Consortium and United Artists present
in association with Film Council and FilmFour
a Revolution Films production in association with Baby Cow
a Michael Winterbottom film
117 mins 1 seconds
Locations – Manchester, High Peak Estate, Derbyshire
Sight and Sound .v12.n5.May 2002 p.55-56

Box Office:	**£1,035,114**
Opening weekend	**£265,428**
Screens	**118**
Screen average	**£2,249**

28 Days Later...

£
Dir Danny Boyle
18 (UK) 2001
20th Century Fox International (UK) – 1 November
Prod Andrew Macdonald
Screenplay Alex Garland
DOP Anthony Dod Mantle
Editor Chris Gill
Music John Murphy
MURPHY, Cillian Jim
HARRIS, Naomie Selena
BURNS, Megan Hannah
GLEESON, Brendan Frank
ECCLESTON, Christopher Major Henry West
PALMER, Alex activist
STOPPANI, Bindu de activist
HILTUNEN, Jukka activist
SCHNEIDER, David scientist
SEDGWICK, Toby infected priest
©2001 DNA Films Ltd
Fox Searchlight Pictures with DNA Films and The Film Council present
113 mins 3 seconds
Locations/Studios London
Sight and Sound .v12.n12.December 2002 p.59-60
Box Office: £ 6,243,656
Opening weekend £1,500,079
Screens 318
Screen average £4,717

40 Days and 40 Nights

$ € £ Can$
Dir Michael Lehmann
15 (US/France/UK/Canada) 2001
United International Pictures (UK) Ltd – 31 May
Prod Tim Bevan, Eric Fellner, Michael London
Screenplay Robert Perez
DOP Elliot Davis
Editor Nicholas C. Smith
Music Rolfe Kent
HARTNETT, Josh Matt Sullivan
SOSSAMON, Shannyn Erica Sutton
SHAW, Vinessa Nicole
COSTANZO, Paulo Ryan
GYLLENHAAL, Maggie Sam
MARONNA, Michael (C) bagel guy
FITZGERALD, Glenn Chris
GROSS, Mary mom
ANDERSON, Stanley Father Maher
TRESE, Adam John Sullivan
©2001 Miramax Films and Universal Pictures and StudioCanal present a Working Title production in association with MiLo Productions
95 minutes 30 seconds
Locations – San Francisco
Sight and Sound .v12.n6.June 2002 p.42-43
Box Office: £ 5,259,975
Opening weekend £1,027,578
Screens 324
Screen average £3,172

* The 5,000 Fingers of Dr. T.

Dir Roy Rowland
(US) 1952
NFT – 29 March
Prod Stanley Kramer
Screenplay Allan Scott, Ted Geisel
DOP Franz Planer
Editor Al Clark
Music Frederick Hollander
HAYES, Peter Lind Zabladowski
HEALY, Mary Mrs. Collins
CONRIED, Hans Dr. Terwilliker
RETTIG, Tommy Bart
HEASLEY, John Whitney
HEASLEY, Robert Judson
CRAVAT, Noel Sgt. Lunk
KULKY, Henry Stroogo
Stanley Kramer Productions
88 mins
Monthly Film Bulletin.v21.n245.June 1954 p.84
Box Office: £1,470

À La Folie Pas Du Tout

aka: He Loves Me... He Loves Me Not
Dir Laetitia Colombani
12 (France) 2002
Pathé Distribution – 22 November
Prod Charles Gassot
DOP Pierre Aïm
Editor Véronique Parnet
Music Jérôme Coullet
TAUTOU, Audrey Angélique
Le BIHAN, Samuel Loïc
CARRÉ, Isabelle Rachel
GUILLEMIN, Sophie Héloise
SIBONY, Clément David
NAVARRE, Elodie Anita
SAVIN, Eric Julien
VILERS, Vania police chief
GARAY, Michèle Claire Belmont
CYLER, Catherine Jeanne
©2002 Téléma/TF1 Films Production
Charles Gassot presents
a Téléma/TF1 Films Production production
with the participation of TPS Cinéma
in association with cofimage 12
95 mins 27 seconds
Locations – Bordeaux
Sight and Sound .v12.n12.December 2002 p.47-48
Box Office: £116,818*
£137,679**
Opening weekend £32,917
Screens 15
Screen average £2,194
*(*total box office in 2002)*
*(** cumulative box office for 2002/03)*

Aankhen

Box Office: £ 213,622
Screens 22
Screen average £3,998

Aap Mujhe Achche Lagne Lage

Dir Vikram Bhatt
1 (India) 2001
Spark Ent – 19 April
ROSHAN, Hrithik character
PATEL, Amisha
ASGAR, Ali
HIRJEE, Vrajesh
THANDA, Jasbir
KHAN, Mushtaq
PANDEY, Hemant
KUMAR, Kiran
GROVER, Gulshan
SAPRU, Preeti
Box Office £190,046
Opening weekend £79,537
Screens 22
Screen average £3,615

A.B.C. Africa

Abbas Kiarostami
(Iran) 2001
bfi Bookings – 18 January
©2001 Abbas Kiarostami Productions
83 mins
Documentary
Box Office: £8,566

The Abduction Club

€ £
Dir Stefan Schwartz
12 (UK/Germany/France/Ireland) 2001
Pathé Distribution – 19 July
Prod Neil Peplow, Yves Marmion, Richard Holmes, David Collins
Screenplay Bill Britten, Richard Crawford
DOP Howard Atherton
Editor Pamela Power
Music Shaun Davey
EVANS, Alice Catharine Kennedy
LaPAINE, Daniel Garrett Byrne
MYLES, Sophia Anne Kennedy
RHYS, Matthew James Strang
CUNNINGHAM, Liam John Power
WOODWARD, Edward Lord Fermoy

MALAHIDE, Patrick Sir Myles
ARTHUR, John Robert Kennedy
MURPHY, Tom Knox
BYRNE, Terry Mary Nugent's father
Pathé Fund Ltd/Vierte Beteiligung KC Medien AG & Co. KG
Pathé Pictures presents
in association with The Film Council and Le Studio Canal+
a Gruber/UGC YM/Samson production
in association with KC Medien
96 mins 6 seconds
Sight and Sound .v12.n7.July 2002 p.38

Box Office:	**£61,593**
Opening weekend	**£29,940**
Screens	**49**
Screen average	**£509**

Abouna

aka: Our Father
Dir Mohamat-Saleh Hardoun
(France/Chad) 2002
ICA Projects – 22 November

Prod Guillaume de Seille
Screenplay Mahamat-Saleh Haroun
DOP Abraham Haile Biru
Editor Sarah Taouss Matton

MOUSSA, Ahidjo Mahamat Tahir Brahim
AGUID, Hamza Moctar Amine Brahim
HAROUN, Zara Achta Brahim, the mother
KHALIL, Mounira the mute girl
BOULAMA, Hassan Hassan
NGARADE, Diego Moustapha Uncle Adoum
ISSA, Garba the teacher
LAMKO, Koulsy Mr Brahim, the father
MAHAMAT, Ramada the teacher's wife
SOSSAL, Mahamat the teacher's assistant
©2002 Duo Films/Goï-Goï Productions
Duo Films Goï-Goï Productions present
with the support of Commission Européenne, Fonds Européen de Développement,
ARTE France, Ministère Français de la Culture, Centre National de la Cinématographie, Ministère des Affaires Étrangères, Fonds Sud, Fonds Francophone de Production Audiovisuelle du Sud, Agence Intergouvernementale de la Francophonie and CIRTEF, TVT
85 mins Subtitles
Sight and Sound .v12.n12.December 2002 p.36-38

Box Office:	**£18,000**

About a Boy

$ € £
Dir Paul Weitz, Chris Weitz
12 (German/US/France/UK) 2001
United International Pictures (UK) Ltd – 26 April

Prod Jane Rosenthal, Robert De Niro, Brad Epstein, Tim Bevan, Eric Fellner
Screenplay Peter Hedges, Chris Weitz, Paul Weitz
DOP Remi Adefarasin
Editor Nick Moore
Music Badly Drawn Boy

GRANT, Hugh Will
COLLETTE, Toni Fiona
WEISZ, Rachel Rachel
BROOK, Isabel Angie
SMALL, Sharon Christine
SMURFIT, Victoria Suzie
HOULT, Nicholas Marcus
COOK, Madison Imogen
COOK, Jordan Imogen
HUTCHISON, Nicholas John
©2002 KALIMA Productions GmbH & Co. KG
Universal Pictures and StudioCanal present
[StudioCanal territory: StudioCanal and Universal Pictures present]
a Tribeca/Working Title production
a Paul Weitz and Chris Weitz film
101 mins 8 seconds
Locations – London
Studios – Shepperton
Sight and Sound .v12.n5.May 2002 p.36

Box Office:	**£16,935,159**
Opening weekend	**£3,747,966**
Screens	**446**
Screen average	**£8,404**

Abril Despedaçado

aka: Behind the Sun
Dir Walter Salles
12 (Brazil/Switzerland/France) 2001
Buena Vista International (UK) – 8 March

Prod Arthur Cohn
Screenplay Walter Salles, Sérgio Machado, Karim Aïnouz
DOP Walter Carvalho
Editor Isabelle Rathéry
Music Antônio Pinto

DUMONT, José father
SANTORO, Rodrigo Tonho
ASSEMANY, Rita mother
VASCONCELOS, Luiz Carlos Salustiano
ANTONIO, Flavia Marco Clara
RAMOS LACERDA, Ravi Pacu
JUNQUEIRA, Caio Inácio
SOUZA PONTES, Everaldo de (C) old blind man
LOUREIRO, Mariana widow
HOLANDA, Servilio de Isaias
© 2001Videofilmes/Dan Valley AG/Bac Films
an Arthur Cohn production
a Videofilmes, Haut et Court, Bac Films, Dan Valley AG co-production
91 mins 57 seconds
Sight and Sound .v12.n3.March 2002 p.20-23

Box Office:	**£152,333**
Opening weekend	**£25,892**
Screens	**8**
Screen average	**£3,237**

The Adventures of Pluto Nash

Dir Ron Underwood
PG (US/Australia) 2001
Warner Bros Distributors (UK) – 30 August

Prod Martin Bregman, Michael Bregman, Louis A. Stroller
Screenplay Neil Cuthbert
DOP Oliver Wood, Dean Semler
Editor Paul Hirsch, Alan Heim
Music John Powell

MURPHY, Eddie Pluto Nash
QUAID, Randy Bruno
DAWSON, Rosario Dina Lake
PANTOLIANO, Joe Mogan
MOHR, Jay Anthony 'Tony' Francis
GUZMÁN, Luis Felix Laranga
REBHORN, James Belcher
BOYLE, Peter Rowland
YOUNG, Burt Gino
NUÑEZ Jr, Miguel A. Miguel
©2002 Village Roadshow Films (BVI) Limited (all other territories)
Castle Rock Entertainment presents
in association with Village Roadshow
Pictures and NPV Entertainment
a Bregman production
a Ron Underwood film
94 mins 40 seconds
Locations – Montreal
Sight and Sound .v12.n11.November 2002 p.52

Box Office:	**£161,184**
Opening weekend	**£87,480**
Screens	**159**
Screen average	**£550**

The Affair of the Necklace

Dir Charles Shyer
12 (US) 2001
Warner Bros Distributors (UK) – 11 January

Prod	Charles Shyer, Redmond Morris, Andrew A, Kosove, Broderick Johnson
Screenplay	John Sweet
DOP	Ashley Rowe
Editor	David Moritz
Music	David Newman
SWANK, Hilary	Jeanne St Rémy de Valois
PRYCE, Jonathan	Cardinal Louis de Rohan
BAKER, Simon	Retaux de Vilette
BRODY, Adrien	Nicolas de la Motte
COX, Brian	Minister Breteuil
RICHARDSON, Joely	Marie-Antoinette
WALKEN, Christopher	Cagliostro
BROOKE, Paul	Monsieur Böhmer
EYRE, Peter	Monsieur Bassenge
KUNZ, Simon	Minister of Titles

©2001 Affair Productions LLC
Alcon Entertainment presents
a Charles Shyer film
117 mins 26 seconds
Locations – Prague, Paris
Sight and Sound .v12.n2.February 2002 p.38

Box Office:	**£40,394**
Opening weekend	**£13,896**
Screens	**23**
Screen average	**£604**

L'Afrance

Dir Alain Gomis
12 (France) 2001
Gala Film Distributors – 5 July

Prod	Edouard Mauriat, Anne-Cécile Berthomuau
DOP	Pierre Stoeber
Editor	Favrice Rouaud
Music	Patrice Gomis
MBENGUE, Djolof	El Hadj
ZINGG, Delphine	Myriam
GUESMI, Samir	Khalid
SOWIÉ, Théophile Moussa	Demba
DHEM, Bass	Chérif
MENDY, Albert	Oumar
NDIAYE 'DOSS', Thierno (C)	El Hadj's father
ABOSSOLO, Emile	.
N'DIAYE, Oumar	Papis
BEYLER, Louis	teacher

©2001 Mille et Une Productions
Mille et Une Productions
Edouard Mauriat & Anne-Cécile Bertomeau
present
with the support of Centre National de la Cinématographie
90 mins 51 seconds
Sight and Sound.v12.n8.August 2002 p.36

Box Office:	**£23,719**

Agni Varsha

Box Office:	**£14,891**
Opening weekend	**£8,054**
Screens	**12**
Screen Average	**£671**

AKA

£
Dir Duncan Roy
18 (UK) 2001
City Screen Ltd – 11 October

Prod	Richard West
Screenplay	Duncan Roy
DOP	Scott Taylor, Steve Smith, Claire Vinson, Ingrid Domeij
Editor	Lawrence Catford, Jackie Ophir, Jon Cross
LEITCH, Matthew	Dean Page
QUICK, Diana	Lady Francine Gryffoyn
ASPREY, George	David Glendenning
COULSON, Lindsey	Georgie Page
RITSON, Blake	Alexander Gryffoyn
YOUNGBLOOD HILLS, Peter	Benjamin, 'Ben'
BELL, Geoff	Brian Page
STURTON, Camille	Hannah Yelland
LEE, Daniel	Jamie Page
NIGHY, Bill	Uncle Louis Gryffoyn

©2002 Third Rock Ltd
Third Rock Ltd, Film Council and Julian Hayward present
a Third Rock production in association with Bard Entertainments
123 mins 12 seconds
Sight and Sound .v12.n12.December 2002 p.38-39

Box Office:	**£6,404**
Opening weekend	**£6,404**
Screens	**3**
Screen average	**£2,135**

Akai hashi no shita no nurui mizu

Dir Shohei Imamura
15 (Japan) 2000
Metro Tartan Distributors – 15 March

Prod	Hisa Ilno
Screenplay	Shohei Imamura, Motofumi, Daisuke Tengan
DOP	Shigeru Komatsubara
Editor	Hajime Okayasu
Music	Shinchiro Ikebe
YAKUSHO, Koji	Yosuke Sasano
SHIMIZU, Misa	Saeko Aizawa
BAISHO, Mitsuko	Mitsu Aizawa
KITAMURA, Kazuo	Taro
FUWA, Mansaku	Gen
NATSUYAGI, Isao	Masayuki Uomi
KITAMURA, Yukiya	Shintaro Uomi
KOJIMA, Hijiri	Miki Tagami
NEGISHI, Toshie	Tomoko Sasano
SAKAMOTO, Sumiko	Masako Yamada

©2001Nikkatsu/Imamura Productions/Vap Inc/Eisei Gekijo/Maru
Nikkatsu Corporation presents
119 mins 43 seconds
Locations – Japan
Sight and Sound .v12.n4.April 2002 p.63

Box Office:	**£34,022**
Opening weekend	**£6,151**
Screens	**4**
Screen average	**£1,538**

Ali

Dir Michael Mann
15 (US) 2001
Entertainment Film Distributors Ltd – 15 February

Prod	Jon Peters, Paul Ardaji, Kitman A. Ho, Michael Mann, James Lassiter
Screenplay	Stephen J. Rivele, Christopher Wilkinson, Eric Roth, Michael Mann
DOP	Emmanuel Lubezki
Editor	William Goldenberg, Stephen Rivkin, Lynzee Klingman
Music	Lisa Gerrard, Pieter Bourke
SMITH, Will	Cassius Clay/ Muhammad Ali
FOXX, Jamie	Drew 'Bundini' Brown
VOIGHT, Jon	Howard Cosell
VAN PEEBLES, Mario	Malcolm X
SILVER, Ron	Angelo Dundee
WRIGHT, Jeffrey	Howard Bingham
WILLIAMSON, Mykelti (C)	Don King
PINKETT SMITH, Jada (C)	Sonji Roi
GAYE, Nona	Belinda
MICHELE, Michael (C)	Veronica Porsche

©2001 Columbia Pictures

Industries, Inc
Initial Entertainment Group presents
in association with Columbia Pictures
a Peters Entertainment, Forward Pass Production
in association with Lee Caplin/Picture Entertainment Corporation
and Overbrook Films
a Michael Mann film
159 mins
Locations – Los Angeles. Miami, Houston, New York, Chicago, Accra, Maputo
Sight and Sound .v12.n3.March 2002 p.34-35

Box Office:	**£4,473,530**
Opening weekend	**£125,573**
Screens	**17**
Screen average	**£7,387**

Ali G Indahouse

$ € £
Dir Mark Mylord
15 (UK/France/US/Germany) 2001
United International Pictures (UK) Ltd – 22 March

Prod	Tim Bevan, Eric Fellner, Dan Mazer
Screenplay	Sacha Baron Cohen, Dan Mazer
DOP	Ashley Rowe
Editor	Paul Knight
COHEN, Sacha Baron	Ali G/Borat
GAMBON, Michael	Prime Minister
DANCE, Charles	David Carlton
BRIGHT, Kellie	Julie
FREEMAN, Martin	Ricky C
MITRA, Rhona	Kate Hedges
NEW, Barbara	Nan
RIVERA, Emilio	Ricco
LaPIANA, Gina	hoochie 1
PAULEY, Dana	hoochie 2

©2001 KALIMA Productions GmbH & Co. KG
Universal Pictures StudioCanal
Working Title Films present
a WT2 production
in association with TalkBack Productions
88 mins 2 seconds
Locations – Manchester, Staines, London, Los Angeles, California/
Studios – Bray Film Studios
Sight and Sound .v12.n5.May 2002 p.37

Box Office:	**£10,296,604**
Opening weekend	**£3,231,673**
Screens	**396**
Screen average	**£8,161**

Ali Zaoua

Dir Nabil Ayouch
(France/Morroco/Belgium) 2000
Millennium Film Distributors – 22 March
Prod – Jean Cottin, Etienne Comar, Antoine Voituriez
Screenplay – Nathalie Saugeion, Nabil Ayouch
DOP Vincent Mathias
Editor – Jean Robert Thomann
Music – Krishna Lévy

KBAB, Mounïm	Kwita
HANSALI, Mustapha	Omar
MOUSSOUNE, Hicham	Boubker
ZHAYRA, Abdelhak	Ali Zaoua
TAGHMAOUI, Saïd	Dib
AYOUCH, Amal	Madame Zaoua
MAJD, Mohamed	Hamid, the fisherman
IBRAHIMI, Hicham	sailor
OULD HAJJAJ, Nadia	high school girl
LOTFI, Abdelkader	hardware store owner

©2000 Playtime/TF1 International/Ali'n Productions/Alexis Films
Playtime presents
a Playtime, TF1 International, Ali'n Productions, Alexis Films, Ace Editing
co-production
with the participation of Canal+, TPS Cinéma, Gimages 3
with the support of Commission du Fonds d'Aide du Centre Cinématographique
Marocain, Centre du Cinéma et de l'Audiovisuel de la Communauté Française
de Belgique, Fonds Sud du Ministère des Affaires Etrangères
a film by Nabil Ayouch
95 mins seconds
Locations/Studios
Sight and Sound .v11.n10.October 2001 p.39-40

Box Office:	**£2,074**
Opening weekend	**£2,074**
Screens	**2**
Screen average	**1,037**

All or Nothing

€ £
Dir Mike Leigh
18 (France/UK) 2001
UGC Films UK – 18 October

Prod	Alain Sarde, Simon Channing Williams
Screenplay	Mike Leigh
DOP	Dick Pope
Editor	Lesley Walker
Music	Andrew Dickson
SPALL, Timothy	Phil Bassett
MANVILLE, Lesley	Penny Bassett
GARLAND, Alison	Rachel Bassett
CORDEN, James	Rory Bassett
SHEEN, Ruth	Maureen
BAILEY, Marion	Carol
JESSON, Paul	Ron
KELLY, Sam	Sid
HUNTER, Kathryn	Cécile
HAWKINS, Sally	Samantha

©2002 Untitled 01 Ltd/Les Films Alain Sarde
Alain Sarde presents
Thin Man Films
a Simon Channing Williams production
128 mins 9 seconds
Locations – London, Kent
Sight and Sound .v12.n11.November 2002 p.38

Box Office:	**£672,605**
Opening weekend	**£164,291**
Screens	**55**
Screen average	**£2,987**

* Amadeus: The Director's Cut

Dir Milos Forman
PG (US) 1984
Warner Bros Distributors (UK) – 26 July

Prod	Saul Zaentz
Screenplay	Peter Shaffer
DOP	Miroslav Ondrícek
Editor	Nena Danevic, Michael Chandler
Music	Wolfgang Amadeus Mozart
ABRAHAM, F. Murray	Antonio Salieri
HULCE, Tom	Wolfgang Amadeus Mozart
BERRIDGE, Elizabeth	Constance Mozart
CALLOW, Simon	Emanuel Schikaneder
DOTRICE, Roy	Leopold Mozart
EBERSOLE, Christine	Katerina Cavalieri
JONES, Jeffrey	Emperor Joseph II
KAY, Charles	Count Orsini-Rosenberg
BAKER, Kenny	parody commendatore
BARTLETT, Lisabeth	Papagena

Saul Zaentz Company
178 mins
Locations/Studios Czechoslovakia
Monthly Film Bulletin. v52.n612.January 1985 p.14-15

Box Office:	**£145,234**
Opening weekend	**£19,801**
Screens	**8**
Screen average	**£2,475**

Amen.

Dir Costa-Gavras
PG (France/Germany) 2001
Pathé Distribution – 12 July

Prod Claude Berri
Screenplay Costa-Gavras, Jean-Claude Grumberg
DOP Patrick Blossier
Editor Yannick Kergoat
Music Armand Amar

TUKUR, Ulrich Kurt Gerstein
KASSOVITZ, Mathieu Riccardo Fontana
MÜHE, Ulrich the doctor
DUCHAUSSOY, Michel the cardinal
CARAMITRU, Ion Count Fontana
IURES, Marcel the pope
THUN, Friedrich von Gerstein's father
SCHMIDT, Antje Mrs Gerstein
MacINNES, Angus Tittman
ZISCHLER, Hanns Grawitz

©2002 Katharina/renn Productions/Vierte Beteiligung KC Medien AG & Co. KG Munich/TF1 Films Production
Claude Berri presents
a Katharina/Renn Productions co-production
TF1 Films production in association with KC Medien and with the participation of Canal+
a film by Costa-Gavras

131 mins 2 seconds
Locations – Romania
Sight and Sound .v12.n8.August 2002 p.37

Box Office:	**£71,208**
Opening weekend	**£9,528**
Screens	**3**
Screen average	**£3,176**

L'Anglaise et le Duc

Dir Eric Rohmer
PG (France/Germany) 2000
Pathé Distribution – 15 February

Prod Françoise Etchegarry
Screenplay Eric Rohmer
DOP Diane Baratier
Editor Mary Stephen

DREYFUS, Jean-Claude Prince Philippe, Duke of Orléan
RUSSELL, Lucy Grace Elliott
LIBOLT, Alain Duke of Biron
VÉRY, Charlotte Pulcherie, the cook
ROSETTE Fanchette
COBIANT, Léonard Marquis de Champcenetz
MARTHOURET, François Dumouriez
MORIN, Caroline Nanon
DUBIEL, Helena Madame Meyler
LE DOYEN, Laurent Miromesnil Section officer

©2001 Pathé Image/C.E.R./France 3 Cinéma/KC Medien/Pathé Distribution
Pathé Image, C.E.R., KC Medien, FR3 Cinéma with the participation of Canal+
present a film produced by Françoise Etchegaray

128 mins 57 seconds
Locations – Ateliers de Bercy
Sight and Sound .v12.n2.February 2002 p.36-37,47-48

Box Office:	**£129,405**
Opening weekend	**£19,158**
Screens	**7**
Screen average	**2,737**

Anita & Me

£

Dir Metin Hüseyin
12A (UK) 2002
Icon Film Distribution – 22 November

Prod Paul Raphaeil
Screenplay Meera Syal
DOP Cinders Forshaw
Editor Annie Kocur
Music Nitin Sawhney

BEDI, Kabir Yeti
BEESLEY, Max Hairy Neddy
BHASKAR, Sanjeev Papa
BREWSTER, Anna Anita Rutter
BURKE, Kathy Deidre Rutter
DHARKER, Ayesha (C) Mama
DJALILI, Omid Uncle Amman
FREEBORN, Alex Sam Lowbridge
REDGRAVE, Lynn Mrs Ormerod
SEGAL, Zohra Nanima

©2002 Take 3.1, 3.2, 3.3, 3.4 Partnerships
Portman Film, The Film Council & BBC Films present
in association with East Midlands Media Initiative
and Icon Film Distribution
A Starfield production
in association with Take 3 TV Partnership
and Chest Wigs and Flares Productions

92 mins 22 seconds
Locations – Nottingham
Sight and Sound .v12.n12.December 2002 p.39-40

Box Office:	**£1,747,644***
	£1,850,977**
Opening weekend	**£453,613**
Screens	**226**
Screen average	**£2,007**

*(*total box office in 2002)*
*(** cumulative box office for 2002/03)*

Annarth

Gurpreet Video Int – 1 November

Box Office	**£7,340**
Opening weekend	**£2,920**
Screens	**5**
Screen average	**£584**

Astérix & Obélix Mission Cleopatre

Dir Alain Chabat
PG (France/Germany) 2002
Pathé Distribution – 11 October

Prod Claude Berri
Screenplay Alain Chabat
DOP Laurent Dailland
Editor Stéphane Pereira
Music Philippe Chany

DEPARDIEU, Gérard Obélix
CLAVIER, Christian Astérix
DEBBOUZE, Jamel Numerobis
BELLUCCI, Monica Cleopatra
CHABAT, Alain Julius Caesar
RICH, Claude Panoramix
DARMON, Gérard Amonbofis
BAER, Édouard Otis
DIEUDONNÉ Caius Ceplus
DIOUF, Mouss Baba

©2002 Katharina/Renn Productions / TF1 Films Production - Chez Wam
[logo] Pathé
Claude Berri presents
a co-production of Katharina/Renn Productions, TF1 Films Production - Chez Wam
in association with CP Medien Erste, Zweite and Vierte Beteiligung KC Medien
AG & Co. KG Munich
with the participation of Canal+
and the participation of the Centre National de la Cinématographie
a Katharina/Renn Productions production

107 mins 53 seconds
Locations – Morocco, France
Subtitles
Sight and Sound .v12.n11.November 2002 p.38-39

Box Office:	**£47,000**
Opening weekend	**£1,357**
Screen	**5**
Screen average	**£271**

Atanarjuat the Fast Runner

Dir Zacharias Kunuk
15 (Canada) 2001
ICA Projects – 1 February

Prod Paul Apak Angilirq, Norman Cohn, Zacharias Kunuk
Screenplay Paul Apak Angilirq
DOP Norman Cohn
Editor Zacharias Kunuk, Norman Cohn, Marie-

Christine Sarda
Music Chris Crilly
UNGALAAQ, Natar Atanarjuat
IVALU, Sylvia Atuat
ARNATSIAQ, Peter Henry Oki
TULUGARJUK, Lucy Puja
IVALU, Madeline Panikpak
QULITALIK, Pauloosie Qulitalik
IPKARNAK, Eugene Sauri
INNUKSUK, Pakak Amaqjuaq
IRNGAUT, Neeve Uluriaq
ULAYURULUK, Abraham Tungajuaq
©2001 Igloolik Isuma Productions Inc
Igloolik Isuma Productions present a National Film Board of Canada co-production
Produced by Igloolik Isuma Productions Inc
in co-production with National Film Board of Canada
Produced with the participation of National Film Board of Canada, Canadian Television Fund created by the Government of Canada and the
Canadian cable industry, Telefilm Canada: Equity Investment Program,
CTF: License Fee Program, Channel 24 Igloolik, Vision TV, Aboriginal Peoples Television Network, Government of Canada Film Tax Credit
additional assistance from Government of the Northwest Territories,
Baffin Business Development Centre, Kakivak Association, Canada Council,
Nunavut Tunngavik Inc,First Air, CBC
168 mins seconds
Sight and Sound .v12.n3.March 2002 p.35-36
Box Office: **£2,157**
Opening weekend **£560**
Screens **1**
Screen average **£560**

Austin Powers in Goldmember

Dir Jay Roach
12 (US) 2002
Entertainment Film Distributors Ltd – 26 July
Prod Suzanne Todd, Jennifer Todd, Demi Moore, Eric McLeod, John Lyons, Mike Myers
Screenplay Mike Myers, Michael McCullers
DOP Peter Deming
Editor Jon Poll, Greg Hayden
Music George S. Clinton
MYERS, Mike Austin Powers/ Dr Evil/ Goldmember/ Fat Bastard
KNOWLES, Beyoncé Foxxy Cleopatra
GREEN, Seth Scott Evil
YORK, Michael Basil Exposition
WAGNER, Robert Number Two
STERLING, Mindy Frau Farbissina
TROYER, Verne (C) Mini Me
CAINE, Michael Nigel Powers
SAVAGE, Fred Number Three
©2002 New Line Productions, Inc.
New Line Cinema presents
a Gratitude International, Team Todd/Moving Pictures production
94 mins 26 seconds
Locations – Los Angeles
Sight and Sound
Sound.v12.n9.September 2002 p.54-55
Box Office: **£23,428,992**
Opening weekend **£5,585,978**
Screen **446**
Screen average **£12,525**

Avalon

Dir Mamoru Oshii
12 (Japan) 2000
Blue Light – 8 November
Prod Atsushi Kubo, Andrzej Gutowski, Andrzej Widelski
Screenplay Kazunori Ito, Neil Gaiman
DOP Grzegorz Kedzierski
Editor Hiroshi Okuda
FOREMNIAK, Malgorzata Ash
GUDEJKO, Jerzy Murphy
BISKUPSKI, Dariusz Bishop
SWIDERSKI, Bartek stunner
KOWALSKI, Wladyslaw Game Master
BARGIELOWSKA, Katarzyna receptionist
SAPRYK, Alicja Gill
BREITENWALD, Michal Murphy of Nine Sisters
KASZ, Zuzanna ghost
SZYSZKOWSKI, Adam player A
©2000 Mamoru Oshii/Avalon Project
Bandai Visual, Media Factory, Dentsu, Nippon Herald Films present
a DEIZ production
106 mins 20 seconds Subtitles
Sight and Sound .v12.n12.December 2002 p.41-42
Box Office: **£7,758**
Opening weekend **£4,922**
Screens **1**
Screen average **£4,922**

* Awara Pagal Deewana

Gurpreet Video International – 21 June
Box Office: **£66,596**
Opening weekend **£25,370**
Screen **15**
Screen average **£1,691**

* Bab Al-Hadid

aka: Cairo Station
Dir Youssef Chahine
(Egypt) 1958
NFT – 12 July
Screenplay Abdel Hay Adib
DOP Alvize Orfanelli
Editor Kamal Abul Ela
Music Fouad el-Zahiry
Mike & His Skyrockets
SHAWKI, Farid
ROSTOM, Hind
CHAHINE, Youssef
el-BAROUDY, Hassan
KHALIL, Abdel Aziz
WASFI, Naima
KHALIL, Said
NAGDI, Abdel Ghani
el-HAKIM, Loutfi
Gabriel Talhami
86 mins
No reference
Box Office: **£7,628**

Bad Company

Dir Joel Schumacher
12 (US) 2001
Buena Vista International (UK) – 12 July
Prod Jerry Bruckheimer, Mike Stenson
Screenplay Jason Richman, Michael Browning
DOP Dariusz A. Wolski
Editor Mark Goldblatt, Robert K. Lambert
Music Trevor Rabin
HOPKINS, Anthony Gaylord Oakes
ROCK, Chris Jake Hayes/Kevin Pope
MACHT, Gabriel Seale
STORMARE, Peter Adrik Vas
SLATTERY, John Roland Yates
WASHINGTON, Kerry Julie
BEAUVAIS-NILON, Garcelle (C) Nicole
SMITH, Brooke Officer Swanson
MARSH, Matthew Dragan Adjanic
HALL, Irma P. Mrs Banks
©2002 Touchstone Pictures/Jerry Bruckheimer Inc
Touchstone Pictures and Jerry

Bruckheimer Films present
a Joel Schumacher film
116 mins 40 seconds
Locations – New York, Prague
Sight and Sound .v12.n8.August 2002 p.38

Box Office:	**£1,475,324**
Opening weekend	**£382,949**
Screens	**288**
Screen average	**£1,330**

Badhaai Ho Badhaai

Gurpreet Video International – 14 June

Box Office:	**£ 52,860**
Opening weekend	**£22,395**
Screens	**16**
Screen average	**£1,400**

Baise-moi

Dir Virginie Despentes, Coralie Trinh Thi
18 (France) 2000
Winchester Film Distribution – 3 May

Prod	Philippe Godeau
Screenplay	Virginie Despentes, Coralie Trinh Thi
DOP	Benoît Chamaillard, Julien Pamart
Editor	Aïlo Auguste, Francine Lemaître, Véronique Rosa

BACH, Karen	Nadine
ANDERSON, Raffaëla	Manu
BEUGNOT, Céline	blonde woman at pool table
NIANE, Adama	man playing pool
LANDRY, Christophe	Claudy
	man at counter
SAAD, Tewfik	barman
McCARTY, Delphine	the flatmate
EMBAREK, Ouassini	Radouan
TOPOU, Patrick-Kodjo	Wanted
NAHOUM, Simon	Wanted's friend

©2000 Pan-Européenne Production/Ciné Valse
Toute Première Fois presents with the participation of Canal+
a film by Virginie Despentes and Coralie Trinh Thi
76 minutes 51 seconds
Subtitles

Box Office:	**£123,499**
Opening weekend	**£16,381**
Screens	**6**
Screen average	**£2,730**

Bangkok: Dangerous

Dir Oxide Pang
18 (Thailand) 2000
Metro Tartan Distributors – 22 February

Prod	Nonzee Nimibutr
Screenplay	Oxide Pang, Danny Pang
DOP	Decha Srimantra
Editor	Oxide Pang, Danny Pang
Music	Orange Music

MONGKOLPISIT, Pavari	Kon
RATANASOPHA, Premsinee	Fon
TIMKUL, Patharawarin	Aom
INTARAKANCHIT, Pisek	Joe

©2001 Film Bangkok, a division of BEC-TERO Entertainment
present a Pang Bros production
Dolby Digital
105 mins 54 seconds
Sight and Sound .v12.n3.March 2002 p.36-37

Box Office:	**£19,800**
Opening weekend	**£4,203**
Screens	**2**
Screen average	**£2,102**

A Beautiful Mind

Dir Ron Howard
12 (US) 2001
United International Pictures (UK) Ltd – 22 February

Prod	Brian Grazer, Ron Howard
Screenplay	Akiva Goldsman
DOP	Roger Deakins
Editor	Mike Hill, Dan Hanley
Music	James Horner

CROWE, Russell	John Forbes Nash Jr
HARRIS, Ed	William Parcher
CONNELLY, Jennifer	Alicia Larde Nash
BETTANY, Paul	Charles Herman
GOLDBERG, Adam	Sol
HIRSCH, Judd	Helinger
LUCAS, Josh (C)	Hansen
RAPP, Anthony	Bender
PLUMMER, Christopher	Doctor Rosen
CARDONE, Vivien	Marcee

©2001 Universal Studios/DreamWorks LLC
DreamWorks Pictures, Universal Pictures, Imagine Entertainment present
a Brian Glazer production
135 mins 26 seconds
Locations – New Jersey, New York
Sight and Sound .v12.n3.March 2002 p.37-38

Box Office:	**£ 8,118,615**
Opening weekend	**£186,862**
Screens	**24**
Screen average	**£7,786**

* Beauty and the Beast

Dir Kirk Wise, Gary Trousdale
U (US)
(1991)
Buena Vista – 4 January

Prod	Don Hahn
Screenplay	Linda Woolverton
Editor	John Carnochan, Ellen Keneshea

ORBACH, Jerry	voice of Lumière
OGDEN STIERS, David	voice of Cogsworth
LANSBURY, Angela	voice of Mrs Potts
WHITE, Richard	voice of Gaston
O'HARA, Paige	voice of Belle
BENSON, Robby	voice of Beast
MICHAEL, Bradley	voice of Pierce Chip
EVERHART, Rex	voice of maurice
CORTI, Jesse	voice of Lefou
SMITH, Hal	voice of Philippe

a Buena Vista release of a Walt Disney Pictures production
105 mins
Sight and Sound .v3.n1.January 1993 p.64.
Re-released in 2002 in the IMAX format
Box Office £359,110

Opening weekend	**£44,797**
Screens	**3**
Screen average	**£14,932**

Before You Go

£
Dir Lewis Gilbert
15 (UK) 2001
Entertainment Film Distributors Ltd – 21 June

Prod	Eoin O'Callaghan
Screenplay	Shelagh Stephenson
DOP	Nic Morris
Editor	John Wilson
Music	Debbie Wiseman

WALTERS, Julie	Teresa
HANNAH, John	Mike
WHALLEY, Joanne (C)	Mary
HAMILTON, Victoria	Catherine
HODGE, Patricia	Violet Heaney
WILKINSON, Tom	Frank
ROSS, Hugh	Mr Berry
CROWLEY, Dermot	Father Cunningham
STEELE, Theo Fraser	young doctor
BIGGINS, John	Dougie

©2001 Entertainment Film Distributors Ltd/Pacificus Productions/Big Fish Films Ltd
Entertainment Film Distributors and Capitol Films present in association with
Arkangel Productions and The Isle

of Man Film Commission
a Pacificus production in association with Big Fish Films
a Lewis Gilbert film
95 mins 17 seconds
Locations – Port Lewaigue, Maughold, Castleton, Isle of Man
Studios – Twickenham Film Studios
Sight and Sound .v12.n8.August 2002 p.39

Box Office:	**£ 134,102**
Opening weekend	**£58,387**
Screens	**65**
Screen average	**£898**

Beginner's Luck

£

Dir Nicholas Cohen, James Callis
(UK) 2001
Guerilla Films – 21 June

Prod	Harriet Evans-Lombe
Screenplay	Nick Cohen, James Callis
DOP	Chris Preston
Editor	Alistair Waterson

DELPY, Julie	Anya
BERKOFF, Steven	Bob
CAZENOVE, Christopher	Andrew Fontaine
FIELDING, Fenella	Aunt Emily
BERTOLOT, Jean Yves	Javaad
CALLIS, James	Mark
REDHILL, Tom	Jason Keritos
LOWE, Rosanna	Hettie Burton
BELCHER, Sarah	Alex
LOWDELL, Amelia	Sophie Emmett

©2001 Late Night Pictures
Late Night Pictures presents
in association with Angel Eye Films
a film by Nick Cohen and James Callis
90 mins
Sight and Sound .v12.n6.June 2002 p.36

Box Office:	**£2,819**
Opening weekend	**£1,913**
Screens	**1**
Screen average	**£1,913**

Behind Enemy Lines

Dir John Moore
12 (US) 2001
20th Century Fox International (UK) – 4 January

Prod	John Davis
Screenplay	David Veloz, Zak Penn
DOP	Brendan Galvin
Editor	Paul Martin Smith
Music	Don Davis

WILSON, Owen	Lieutenant Chris Burnett
HACKMAN, Gene	Admiral Reigart
MACHT, Gabriel	Stackhouse
ALMEIDA, Joaquim de	Piquet
KEITH, David	O'Malley
KRUPA, Olek	Lokar
MASHKOV, Vladimir	Tracker
WHITFIELD, Charles Malik	Rodway
PIERSON, Geoff	Admiral Donnelly
RUSSOM, Leon	Ed Burnett

©2001 Twentieth Century Fox Film Corporation
Twentieth Century Fox presents
a Davis Entertainment Company production
105 mins 37 seconds
Locations – Slovakia
Sight and Sound v12.n2.February 2002 p.39-40

Box Office:	**£ 2,822,056**
Opening weekend	**£903,589**
Screens	**319**
Screen average	**£2,833**

Bend it Like Beckham

£ €

Dir Gurinder Chadha
12 (Germany/UK) 2001
Helkon SK – 12 April

Prod	Deepak Nayar, Gurinder Chadha
Screenplay	Gurinder Chadha, Guljit Bindra, Paul Mayeda Berges
DOP	Jong Lin
Editor	Justin Krish
Music	Craig Pruess

NAGRA, Parminder (C)	Jess Bhamra
KNIGHTLEY, Keira	Jules Paxton
RHYS MEYERS, Jonathan	Joe
KHER, Anupam	Mr Bhamra
PANJABI, Archie	Pinky Bhamra
LEWIS, Shaznay	Mel
HARPER, Frank	Alan Paxton
STEVENSON, Juliet	Paula Paxton
KHAN, Shaheen	Mrs Bhamra
CHANA, Ameet	Tony

©2001 Kintop Pictures/Bend It Films/Road Movies/Roc Media
Kintop Pictures presents
in association with The Film Council and Filmförderung Hamburg
and with the participation of BSkyB and British Screen
and in association with HelkonSK, The Works and Future Film Financing
a Kintop Pictures, Bend It Films, Roc Media, Road Movies co-production
a Gurinder Chadha film
112 mins 14 seconds
Locations – London, Hamburg
Sight and Sound.v12.n5.May 2002 p.38-39

Box Office:	**£11,551,538**
Opening weekend	**£2,001,795**
Screens	**384**
Screen average	**£5,213**

Betty Fisher et Autres Histories

Dir Claude Miller
15 (France/Canada) 2001
Optimum Releasing – 14 June

Prod	Annie Miller, Yves Marmion
Screenplay	Claude Miller
DOP	Christine Pollock
Editor	Véronique

KIBERLAIN, Sandrine	Betty Fisher
GARCIA, Nicole	Margot Fisher
SEIGNER, Mathilde	Carole Novacki
MERVIL, Luck	François Diembélé
BAER, Édouard	Alex Basato
FREISS, Stéphane	Edouard
JACQUES, Yves	René the Canadian
ZEM, Roschdy	Dr Jérôme Castang
ABITEBOUL, Michaël	.
HAVILAND, Consuelo de	Madame Barsky

©2001 UGC YM/Les Films de la Boissière/Go Films International Inc/France 2 Cinéma
UGC YM and Les Films de la Boissière present
a French-Canadian co-production [of]
UGC YM, Les Films de la Boissière, Go Films
Co-produced by France 2 Cinéma with the participation of Canal+ and sofica Sofinergie 5
101 mins
Locations – Paris region
Sight and Sound .v12.n6.June 2002 p.18-20

Box Office:	**£72,576**
Opening weekend	**£19,220**
Screens	**12**
Screen average	**£1,602**

Bhookamp

Box Office	**£830**
Opening weekend	**£370**
Screens	**2**
Screen average	**£185**

Big Fat Liar

Dir Shawn Levy
PG (US/Germany) 2002
United International Pictures (UK) Ltd – 28 June

Prod	Mike Tollin, Brian Robbins
Screenplay	Dan Schneider

DOP Jonathan Brown
Editor Stuart Pappé, Kimberly Ray
Music Christophe Beck
MUNIZ, Frankie Jason Shepherd
GIAMATTI, Paul Marty Wolf
BYNES, Amanda Kaylee
DETMER, Amanda Monty Kirkham
MAJORS, Lee Vince
FAISON, Donald (C) Frank Jackson/Kenny Trooper
OH, Sandra Mrs Caldwell
HORNSBY, Russell Marcus Duncan
FRENCH, Michael Bryan Harry Shepherd
TUCCI, Christine Carol Shepherd
©2002 Mediastream Zweite Film GmbH & Co. Productions KG
Universal Pictures presents
a Tollin/Robbins production
in association with Mediastream Film
87 mins
Locations – Los Angeles
Sight and Sound .v12.n7.July 2002 p.39-40

Box Office:	**£1,227,242**
Opening weekend	**£406,105**
Screens	**214**
Screen average	**£1,898**

Big Shot's Funeral

Box Office	**£1,474**
Opening weekend	**£971**
Screens	**3**
Screen average	**324**

Biggie and Tupac

£
Dir Nick Broomfield
15 (UK) 2001
Optimum Releasing – 24 May
Prod Michele D'Acosta
DOP Joan Churchill
Music Christian Henson
BROOMFIELD, Nick
POOLE, Russell
HICKEN, David
GARLAND, Billy
WALLACE, Voletta
MOPREME
HACKIE, Kevin
WRIGHT Sr, Reggie
ALEXANDER, Frank
FLORES, Sonia
©2001 Lafayette Films Ltd a Lafayette Film produced for Channel 4
107 mins 56 seconds
Documentary
Sight and Sound .v12.n6.June 2002 p.37

Box Office:	**£93,835**
Opening weekend	**£19,536**
Screens	**6**
Screen average	**3,256**

Birthday Girl

$ £
Dir Jez Butterworth
15 (UK/US) 2001
FilmFour Distributors – 28 June
Prod Steve Butterworth, Diana Phillips, Eric Abraham
Screenplay Tom Butterworth, Jez Butterworth
DOP Oliver Stapleton
Editor Christopher Tellefsen
Music Stephen Warbeck
KIDMAN, Nicole Nadia
CHAPLIN, Ben John Buckingham
CASSEL, Vincent Alexei
KASSOVITZ, Mathieu Yuri
EVANS, Kate Clare
MANGAN, Stephen bank manager
ARMSTRONG, Xander Robert Moseley
PHILLIPS, Sally Karen
McINNES, Jo (C) waitress
MILLER, Ben concierge
©2001 Miramax Film Corp/FilmFour Ltd/Portobello Pictures Ltd
FilmFour and HAL Films in association with Mirage Enterprises present
a film by Jez Butterworth
93 mins 12 seconds
Locations – UK and Australia
Sight and Sound .v12.n7.July 2002 p.40-41

Box Office:	**£783,575**
Opening weekend	**£237,165**
Screens	**133**
Screen average	**£1,783**

Black Hawk Down

Dir Ridley Scott
15 (US) 2001
Columbia TriStar Films (UK) – 18 January
Prod Jerrry Bruckheimer, Ridley Scott
Screenplay Ken Nolan, Mark Bowden, Steven Zaillian, Stephen Gaghan
DOP Slawomir Idziak
Editor Pietro Scalia
Music Hans Zimmer
HARTNETT, Josh Ranger Staff Sgt Matt Eversmann
McGREGOR, Ewan Ranger Specialist Danny Grimes
SIZEMORE, Tom Ranger Lt Col Danny McKnight
BANA, Eric Delta Sgt First Class Norm ' Hoot' Hooten
FICHTNER, William Delta Sgt First Class Jeff Sanderson
BREMNER, Ewen Spec Sgt Shawn Nelson
SHEPARD, Sam Major General William F. Garrison
CASSEUS, Gabriel Ranger Spec Mike Kurth
COATES, Kim Delta Master Sgt Tim 'Griz' Martin
DANCY, Hugh Ranger Sgt First Class Kurt Schmid
©2001 Revolution Studios Distribution LLC/Jerry Bruckheimer Inc
Revolution Studios and Jerry Bruckheimer Films present
in association with Scott Free
a film by Ridley Scott
144 mins seconds
Locations – Morocco
Sight and Sound .v12.n2.February 2002 p.40-41

Box Office:	**£5,871,115**
Opening weekend	**£1,772,920**
Screens	**406**
Screen average	**£4,367**

Black Knight

Dir Gil Junger
PG (US) 2001
20th Century Fox International (UK) – 23 August
Prod Arnon Milchan, Darryl J. Quarles, Michael Green, Paul Schiff
Screenplay Darryl J. Quarles, Peter Gaulke, Gerry Swallow
DOP Veli Steiger
Editor Michael R. Miller
Music Randy Edelman
LAWRENCE, Martin Jamal Walker
WILKINSON, Tom Sir Knolte
THOMASON, Marsha Victoria
REGAN, Vincent Sir Percival
CONWAY, Kevin King Leo
MITCHELL, Daryl Steve
JENSEN, Erik Derek
CAREY, Helen The Queen
COUNTRYMAN, Michael Phillip
WEEGAR, Jeannette Princess Regina
©2001 Twentieth Century Fox Film Corporation/Monarchy Enterprises B.V./
Regency Entertainment (USA), Inc.
Twentieth Century Fox and Regency Enterprises present
a New Regency/Runteldat Entertainment/The Firm production
95 mins 27 seconds

Locations – Wilmington, North Carolina
Sight and Sound .v12.n9.September 2002 p.55-56

Box Office:	**£518,610**
Opening weekend	**£167,084**
Screens	**172**
Screen average	**£971**

Blade II

Dir Guillermo del Toro
18 (US/Germany) 2001
Entertainment Film Distributors Ltd – 29 March

Prod	Peter Frankfurt, Wesley Snipes, Patrick Palmer
Screenplay	David S. Goyer
DOP	Gabriel Beristain
Editor	Peter Amundson
Music	Marco Beltrami
SNIPES, Wesley	Blade
KRISTOFFERSON, Kris	Whistler
PERLMAN, Ron	Reinhardt
VARELA, Leonor	Nyssa
REEDUS, Norman	Scud
KRETSCHMANN, Thomas	Damaskinos
GOSS, Luke	Nomak
SCHULZE, Matthew (C)	Chupa
JOHN JULES, Danny (C)	Asad
YEN, Donnie (C)	Snowman

©2001 Linovo Productions GmbH & Co. KG
New Line Cinema presents
an Amen Ra production in association with Imaginary Forces
a Guillermo Del Toro film
116 mins 42 seconds
Locations – Prague
Sight and Sound.v12.n6.June 2002 p.38-39

Box Office:	**£9,118,147**
Opening weekend	**£2,540,226**
Screens	**345**
Screen average	**£7,363**

Blood Work

Dir Clint Eastwood
15 (US) 2001
Warner Bros Distributors (UK) – 27 December

Prod	Clint Eastwood
Screenplay	Brian Helgeland
DOP	Tom Stern
Editor	Joel Cox
Music	Lennie Niehaus
EASTWOOD, Clint	Terry McCaleb
DANIELS, Jeff	Buddy Noone
De JESÚS, Wanda	Graciela Rivers
LIFFORD, Tina	Jaye Winston
RODRIGUEZ, Paul	Detective Ronaldo Arrango
WALSH, Dylan	Detective John Waller
HUSTON, Anjelica	Dr Bonnie Fox
LUCERO, Mason	Raymond
BECKER, Gerry	Mr Toliver
HOFFMAN, Rick	James Lockridge

©2002 Warner Bros.
Warner Bros. Pictures presents
a Malpaso production
110 mins 20 seconds
Locations – Southern California
Sight and Sound .v13.n1.January 2003 p.35-36

Box Office:	**£61,053*** **£223,063****
Opening weekend	**£61,053**
Screens	**57**
Screen average	**£1,071**

*(*total box office in 2002)*
*(** cumulative box office for 2002/03)*

Bloody Sunday

£ €
Dir Paul Greengrass
15 (UK/Ireland) 2001
Granada Media – 25 January

Prod	Mark Redhead
Screenplay	Paul Greengrass
DOP	Ivan Strasburg
Editor	Clare Douglas
Music	Dominic Muldoon
NESBITT, James	Ivan Cooper
PIGOTT-SMITH, Tim	Major General Ford
FARRELL, Nicholas	Brigadier Patrick MacLellan
McSORLEY, Gerard	Chief Superintendent Lagan
CLARKE, Kathy Kiera	Frances
GILDEA, Allan	Kevin McCorry
CROSSAN, Gerard	Eamonn McCann
MOULDS, Mary	Bernadette Devlin
McCALLION, Carmel	Bridget Bond
VILLIERS, Chris (C)	Major Steele

©2001 Granada/Hell's Kitchen/Film Council
Feature Film Company presents
a Granada film
in association with Film Council, Portman Film and Bord Scannán na hÉireann/The Irish Film Board
a Granada Film/Hell's Kitchen production
110 mins 12 seconds
Locations – Northern Ireland and Republic of Ireland
Sight and Sound .v12.n3.March 2002 p.39

Box Office:	**£5,087**
Opening weekend	**£3,171**
Screens	**3**
Screen average	**£1,057**

Boat Trip

Dir Mort Nathan
15 (Germany/US) 2001
Entertainment Film Distributors Ltd – 4 October

Prod	Andrew Sugerman, Brad Krevoy, Gerhard Schmidt, Frank Hübner
Screenplay	Mort Nathan, William Bigelow
DOP	Shawn Maurer
Editor	John Axmess
Music	Robert Folk
GOODING Jr, Cuba	Jerry
SANZ, Horatio	Nick
FOX, Vivica A.	Felicia
SANCHEZ, Roselyn	Gabriella
GODIN, Maurice	Hector
SHAYE, Lin	Sonya
GUNTON, Bob	captain
SILVSTEDT, Victoria	Inga
ROUNDTREE, Richard	Felicia's dad
MOORE, Roger	Lloyd

©2002 ApolloMedia GmbH & Co. 5. Filmproduktion KG and IWP International West Pictures GmbH & Co. Erste Produktions KG
Motion Picture Corporation of America and International West Pictures and ApolloMedia present
a Brad Krevoy and Germund Films production
a film by Mort Nathan
93 mins 49 seconds
Locations – Germany, Istanbul and Greece
Sight and Sound .v12.n12.December 2002 p.42-43

Box Office:	**£1,005,410**
Opening weekend	**£425,325**
Screens	**256**
Screen average	**1,661**

The Bourne Identity

Dir Doug Liman
12 (US/Germany) 2001
United International Pictures (UK) Ltd – 6 September

Prod	Doug Liman, Patrick Crowley, Richard N. Gladstein
Screenplay	Tony Gilroy, William Blake Herron, David Self
DOP	Oliver Wood
Editor	Saar Klein
Music	John Powell
DAMON, Matt	Jason Bourne
POTENTE, Franka	Marie Kreutz
COOPER, Chris	Ted Conklin
OWEN, Clive	The Professor
COX, Brian	Ward Abbott
AKINNUOYE-AGBAJE, Adewale	

	Nykwana Wombosi
MANN, Gabriel	Zorn
GOGGINS, Walton	research technician
HAMILTON, Josh	research technician
STILES, Julia	Nicolette

©2001 Kalima Productions GmbH & Co KG
Universal Pictures presents
a Hypnotic and Kennedy/Marshall production
a Doug Liman film
118 mins 35 seconds
Locations – Paris, Prague
Sight and Sound .v12.n9.September 2002 p.56-57

Box Office:	**£7,848,011**
Opening weekend	**£2,150,511**
Screens	**419**
Screen average	**£5,132**

Bowling For Columbine

Dir Michael Moore
15 (Canada/Germany/US) 2002
Momentum Pictures – 15 November

Prod	Michael Moore, Kathleen Glynn, Jim Czarnecki, Charles Bishop, Michael Donovan
Editor	Durt Engfehr
Music	Jeff Gibbs

MOORE, Michael
HESTON, Charlton
MANSON, Marilyn
CLARK, Dick
NICHOLS, James
STONE, Matt
GLASSNER, Barry
CASTALDO. Richard
©2002 Iconolatry Productions Inc., and Alliance Atlantis Company/VIF Babelsberger Filmproduktion GmbH & Co. Zweite KG
Alliance Atlantis and United Artists present
a Salter Street Films, VIF 2 production
a Dog Eat Dog Films production
a film by Michael Moore
123 mins 53 seconds
Documentary
Sight and Sound .v12.n11.November 2002 p.20-23

Box Office:	**£1,036,076*** **£1,619,829****
Opening weekend	**£157,898**
Screens	**28**
Screen average	**£5,639**

*(*total box office in 2002)*
*(** cumulative box office for 2002/03)*

* Brighton Rock

£
Dir John Boulting
PG (UK) 1947
bfi Bookings – 17 May

Prod	Roy Boulting
Screenplay	Graham Greene, Terence Rattigan
DOP	Harry Waxman
Editor	Peter Graham Scott
Music	Hans May
ATTENBOROUGH, Richard	Pinkie Brown
BADDELEY, Hermione	Ida Arnold
HARTNELL, William	Dallow
STOCK, Nigel	Cubitt
WATSON, Wylie	Spicer
MARSH, Carol	Rose
WILLIAMS, Harcourt	Prewitt
WINTER, Virginia	Judy
PURDELL, Reginald	Fran
CARNEY, George	Phil Corkery

Associated British Picture Corporation presents
The Boulting Brothers' production
92 mins
Studios – Welwyn Studios
Monthly Film Bulletin.v14.n168.December 1947 p.170

Box Office:	**£15,687**
Opening weekend	**£1,798**
Screens	**1**
Screen average	**£1,798**

Bully

Dir Larry Clark
18 (France/US) 2001
FilmFour Distributors – 1 March

Prod	Don Murphy, Fernando Sulichin, Chris Hanley
Screenplay	Zachary Long, Roger Pullis
DOP	Zachary Long, Steve Gainer
Editor	Andrew Hafitz
RENFRO, Brad	Mario 'Marty' Puccio
PHILLIPS, Bijou	Alice 'Ali' Willis
MINER, Rachel	Lisa Connelly
PITT, Michael	Donny Semenec
GARNER, Kelli	Heather Swallers
FRANZESE, Daniel	Cousin Derek Dzvirko
FITZPATRICK, Leo	Derek Kaufman, the hitman
STAHL, Nick	Bobby Kent
PAULDING, Nathalie	Claudia
SUTTA, Jessica	blonde

©2001 StudioCanal France
StudioCanal in asociation with Lions Gate Films present
a Muse/Blacklist Films production in association with Gravity Entertainment
a film by Larry Clark
112 mins 15 seconds
Sight and Sound .v12.n3.March 2002 p.24-26

Box Office:	**£163,528**
Opening weekend	**£39,673**
Screens	**17**
Screen average	**£2,334**

Bundy

£ **$**
Dir Matthew Bright
18 (UK/US) 2002
Metro Tartan Distributors – 22 November

Prod	Hamish McAlpine, Michael Muscal
Screenplay	Stephen Johnston, Matthew Bright
DOP	Sonja Rom
Editor	Paul Heiman
Music	Kennard Ramsey
REILLY BURKE, Michael	Ted Bundy
BLISS, Boti Ann	Lee
McCARTHY, Julianna	professor
TISDALE, Jennifer	pretty girl
SANTOS, Michael	man at the window
WOOSTER, Anna Lee	girl attacked on street
BRASS, Steffani (C)	Julie
DICKSON, Tricia	Vincennes
SISTO, Meadow	Welch
DaRE, Eric	male partygoer

©2002 Tartan Films Ltd./First Look Media
Tartan Films and First Look Media present
a Tartan Films production
98 mins 54 seconds
Locations – California
Sight and Sound .v12.n12.December 2002 p.43p.43

Box Office:	**£10,304**
Opening weekend	**£1,398**
Screens	**3**
Screen average	**£466**

The Bunker

£
Dir Rob Green
15 (UK) 2001
Salvation Films Limited – 27 September

Prod	Daniel Figuergo
Screenplay	Clive Dawson
DOP	John Pardue
Editor	Richard Milward
Music	Russell Currie

BOORMAN, Charley Private 1st Class Engels
CARLISLE, John Private Mirus
DAVENPORT, Jack Lance Corporal Ebert
FAIRBANK, Christopher Sergeant Heydrich
FLEMYNG, Jason Corporal Baumann
KUNZ, Simon Lieutenant Krupp
MARSAN, Eddie Private 1st Class Kreuzmann
POTTS, Andrew Lee Private Neumann
TIERNAN, Andrew Lance Corporal Schenke
HAMNETT, Nicholas Private 1st Class Engels
©2000 Millennium Pictures plc
Millennium Pictures presents
a Daniel Figuero production
a Rob Green film
91 mins 32 seconds
Locations – Buckinghamshire
Studios – Twickenham Film Studios
Sight and Sound .v12.n10.October 2002 p.37
Box Office: **£3,744**
Opening weekend **£3,744**
Screens **7**
Screen average **£535**

The Business of Strangers

Dir Patrick Stettner
15 (US) 2001
Momentum Pictures – 3 May
Prod Susan A. Stover, Robert H.Nathan
Screenplay Patrick Stettner
DOP Teo Maniaci
Editor Keiko Deguchi
Music Alexander Lasarenko
CHANNING, Stockard Julie Styron
STILES, Julia Paula Murphy
WELLER, Frederick Nick Harris
TESTA, Mary receptionist
HALLETT, Jack Mr Fostwick
GIAMATTI, Marcus Robert
FITZPATRICK, Buddy waiter
LUDWIG, Salem man at pool
RATNER, Shelagh airport announcer
©2001 i5 Films LLC
an i5 Films production in association with Headquarters
83 mins 32 seconds
Sight and Sound .v12.n5.May 2002 p.34-35+39-40
Box Office: **£93,279**
Opening weekend **£16,083**
Screens **15**
Screen average **£1,072**

Butterfly Man

£

Dir Kaprice Kea
15 (UK) 2002
De Warrenne Pictures – 6 December
Prod Tom Waller
Screenplay Kaprice Kea
DOP Mark Duffield
Editor Atisthan Sangawut, William Watts
Music Stephen Bentley-Klein
LAING, Stuart Adam
NAKPRASITTE, Mamee Em
PAWARO, Phra Supachai the monk
MITCHELL, Kirsty Kate
PERMCHALAD, Pyroat old man in Bangkok
VATCHARAYON, Vasa Noi
MAGEE, Francis Joey
ALBERT, Phusa Sao
JAISHUN, Jantima travel agent
JEROH, Police Corporal police inspector
©2002 De Warrenne Pictures (UK) Ltd.
De Warrenne Pictures presents
a Tom Waller production
a Kaprice Kea film
95 mins
Locations – Thailand, Koh Samui, Koh Phangan
Sight and Sound .v13.n1.January 2003 p.36-37
Box Office: **£4,830**
Opening weekend **£4,830**
Screens **3**
Screen average **£1,610**

* Cabaret

Dir Bob Fosse
(US) 1972
bfi Bookings – 21 June
Prod Cy Fever
Screenplay Jay Allen
DOP Geoffrey Unsworth
Editor David Bretherton
Music John Kander
MINNELLI, Liza Sally Bowles
YORK, Michael Brian Roberts
GRIEM, Helmut Maximilian von Heune
WEPPER, Fritz Fritz Wendel
BERENSON, Marisa Natalia Ladauer
NEUMANN-VIERTEL, Elisabeth Fräulein Schneider
VITA, Helen Fräulein Kost
RICHTHOFEN, Sigrid von Fräulein Mayr
VESPERMANN, Gerd Bobby
WOLTER, Ralf Herr Ludwig
©1972 ABC Pictures Corp./Allied Artists Pictures Corporation
Allied Artists Pictures Corporation and ABC Pictures Corp. present
an ABC Pictures Corporation production
a Feuer & Martin production of...
123 mins
Monthly Film Bulletin.v39.n461.June 1972 p.108
Box Office: **£41,907**
Opening weekend **£2,037**
Screens **1**
Screen average **£2,037**

La Chambre des Officiers

aka The Officers Ward
Dir François Dupeyron
15 (France) 2000
Optimum Releasing – 22 March
Prod Michèle Pétin, Laurent Pétin
Screenplay François Dupeyron
DOP Tetsuo Nagata
Editor Dominique Faysse
CARAVACA, Éric Adrien
PODALYDÈS, Denis Henri
DERANGÈRE, Grégori Pierre
AZÉMA, Sabine Anaïs
DUSSOLLIER, André (C) the surgeon
RENAULD, Isabelle Marguerite
PAILHAS, Géraldine Clemence
PORTAL, Jean-Michel Alain
TRÉJAN, Guy the minister
GUILLEBON, Xavier de Louis
©2001 ARP/France 2 Cinéma
Michèle and Laurent Petin present
an ARP production
in co-production with France 2 Cinéma
with the participation of Canal+
a film by François Dupeyron
131 mins 53 seconds
Sight and Sound.v12.n4.April 2002 p.52
Box Office: **£61,723**
Opening weekend **£10,020**
Screens **5**
Screen average **£2,004**

Changing Lanes

Dir Roger Michell
15 (US) 2001
United International Pictures (UK) Ltd – 1 November
Prod Scott Rudin
Screenplay Chap Taylor, Michael Tolkin
DOP Salvatore Totino
Editor Christopher Tellefsen
Music
AFFLECK, Ben Gavin Banek
JACKSON, Samuel L. Doyle Gipson
COLLETTE, Toni Michelle

POLLACK, Sydney Andrew Delano
HURT, William sponsor
PEET, Amanda Cynthia Banek
STAUNTON, Kim Valerie Gipson
SLOAN, Tina Mrs Delano
JENKINS, Richard Walter Arnell
WALKER, Akil Stephen Gipson
©2002 Paramount Pictures
Paramount Pictures presents
a Scott Rudin production
a Roger Michell film
98 mins 49 seconds
Locations – New York
Sight and Sound .v12.n11.November 2002 p.36-37+40

Box Office:	**£2,972,343**
Opening weekend	**£808,268**
Screens	**311**
Screen average	**£2,599**

Charlotte Gray

$ £ €
Dir Gillian Armstrong
15 (UK/US/Germany) 2001
FilmFour Distributors – 22 February

Prod	Sarah Curtis, Douglas Rae
Screenplay	Jeremy Brock
DOP	Dion Beebe
Editor	Nicholas Beauman
Music	Stephen Warbeck

BLANCHETT, Cate Charlotte Gray
CRUDUP, Billy Julien Levade
GAMBON, Michael Levade
PENRY-JONES, Rupert Peter Gregory
FLEET, James Richard Cannerley
CRUTTENDEN, Abigail Daisy
McDOUGALL, Charlotte Sally
HANDS, Robert Borowski
GOODMAN-HILL, Tom businessman at party
GOODMAN-HILL, Tom businessman at party
©2001 FilmFour presents in association with Senator Film
an Ecosse Film production and a Pod Films production
a film by Gillian Armstrong
121 mins 10 seconds
Locations – St. Antonin-Noble-Val, London and the Home Counties
Studios – Pinewood Studios
Sight and Sound .v12.n3.March 2002 p.10-11

Box Office:	**£1,567,185**
Opening weekend	**£450,229**
Screens	**217**
Screen average	**£2,075**

Chicago

Dir Rob Marshall
12A (US/Germany) 2001
Buena Vista International (UK) – 27 December

Prod	Martin Richards
Screenplay	Bill Condon, Larry Gelbart
DOP	Dion Beebe
Editor	Martin Walsh
Music	John Kander

ZELLWEGER, Renée Roxie Hart
ZETA-JONES, Catherine Velma Kelly
GERE, Richard Billy Flynn
LATIFAH, Queen Matron Mama Morton
REILLY, John C. Amos Hart
LIU, Lucy Kitty Baxter
DIGGS, Taye bandleader
FEORE, Colm Harrison
BARANSKI, Christine Mary Sunshine
WEST, Dominic Fred Casely
©2002 Kalis Productions GmbH & Co. KG
a Miramax Films presentation
a Miramax Films production
a Zadan/Meron production
a Producer Circle Co. production
113 mins 22 seconds
Locations – Toronto
Sight and Sound .v13.n2.February 2003 p.41-42

Box Office:	**£113,386***
	£16,351,670**
Opening weekend	**£113,386**
Screens	**1**
Screen average	**£113,386**

*(*total box office in 2002)*
*(** cumulative box office for 2002/03)*

Chop Suey

Dir Bruce Weber
(US) 2001
NFT – 5 April

Prod	Nan Bush
Screenplay	Bruce Weber, Maribeth Edmonds
DOP	Lance Acord, Douglas Cooper, Jim Fealy
Editor	Angelo Corrao
Music	John Leftwich

JOHNSON, Peter
FAYE, Frances
FLETCHER, Herbie and Dibi (C)
FLETCHER, Christian and Nathan (C)
GRACIE and Family, Rickson (C)
MITCHUM, Robert
THESIGER, Sir Wilfred (C)
VINCENT, Jan Michael (C)
VREELAND, Diana
SHEPHERD, Teri
Just Blue Films
Nan Bush and Just Blue Films present
a film by Bruce Weber
98 mins
Sight and Sound .v12.n6.June 2002 p.39-40

Box Office:	**£2,624**
Opening weekend	**£2,624**
Screens	**1**
Screen average	**£2,624**

Chor Machaaye Shor

Box Office	**£38,797**
Opening weekend	**£19,684**
Screens	**13**
Screen average	**£1,514**

Christie Malry's Own Double Entry

£ €
Dir Paul Tickell
18 (Netherlands/Luxembourg/UK) 2001
Ian Rattray Films Ltd – 16 August

Prod	Kees Kasander
Screenplay	Simon Bent
DOP	Reiner van Brummelen
Editor	Chris Wyatt
Music	Luke Haines

MORAN, Nick Christie Malry
STUKE, Neil Headlam
ASHFIELD, Kate Carol
SBRAGIA, Mattia Leonardo da Vinci
MAZZARELLA, Marcello Pacioli
LAZZARO, Salvatore Giacomo
ALBELLI, Sergio Duke Ludovici
GIUFFRIDA, Francesco Salai
FIELD, Shirley Anne Christie's mother
SULLIVAN, Peter Wagner
Movie Masters BV/Delux Productions SA/Woodline Productions Ltd
Bob Hubar Denis Wigman Kees Kasander present
a Moviemasters C.V. production in association with
The Kasander Film Company & Delux Productions S.A., Woodline Productions
with the support of The Luxembourg Filmfund and Innocap
a Paul Tickell film
94 mins 48 seconds
Locations – London, Luxembourg
Sight and Sound .v12.n10.October 2002 p.37-38

Box Office:	**£ 1,600**

Clockstoppers

Dir Jonathan Frakes
(US) 2001
United International Pictures (UK) Ltd – 11 October

Prod	Gale Anne Hurd, Julia

Pistor
Screenplay Rob Hedden, David J. Stem, David N. Weiss
DOP Tim Suhrstedt
Editor Peter E. Berger, Jeff W.Canavan
Music Jamshied Sharifi
BRADFORD, Jesse Zak Gibbs
GARCES, Paula Francesca
STEWART, French Dr Earl DOPler
BIEHN, Michael Henry Gates
THOMAS, Robin George Gibbs, dad
MUTAMBIRWA, Garikayi Meeker
SWEENEY, Julia Mom
LETHERMAN, Lindze Kelly Gibbs
GEORGE, Jason Winston Richard
KIM, Linda Jay
©2002 Paramount Pictures
Paramount Pictures and Nickelodeon Movies present a Valhalla Motion Pictures and Nickelodeon Movies production
94 mins 5 seconds
Locations – Los Angeles
Sight and Sound .v12.n11.November 2002 p.41-42
Box Office: £584,655
Opening weekend £196,802
Screens 216
Screen average £911

Club Le Monde

£

Dir Simon Rumley
18 (UK) 2000
ScreenProjex – 11 October
Prod Simon Rumley, Piers Jackson
Screenplay Simon Rumley
DOP Stimon Starling
Editor Eddie Hamilton
Music Ed Butt
GORTON, Brad Mike
AINSLEIGH, Daniel Steve
McKENZIE, Allison Ali
STEELE, Dawn Jacqui
CONNOLLY, Tom Anthony
HALSTEAD, Tom Patrick
BADLAND, Annette Stella
KARLSEN, Gunilla Irene
MAUDSLEY, Tony Mosh
PIKE, Emma Yaz
©2002 Screen Production Associates Limited/2M Films Partnership
Club Le Monde limited
79 mins 15 seconds
Locations – London
Sight and Sound .v12.n11.November 2002 p.42
Box Office: £8,800
Opening weekend £4,168
Screens 18
Screen average £232

Collateral Damage

Dir Andrew Davis
15 (US) 2000
Warner Bros Distributors (UK) – 5 April
Prod Steven Reuther, David Foster, Peter MacGregor-Scott
Screenplay David Griffiths, Peter Griffiths, Nicholas Meyer
DOP Adam Greenberg
Editor Dennis Virkler, Dav Hoenig
Music Graeme Revell
SCHWARZENEGGER, Arnold Gordy Brewer
KOTEAS, Elias Brandt
NERI, Francesca Selena
CURTIS, Cliff Claudio, 'The Wolf'
SANDOVAL, Miguel Phipps
LENNIX, Harry (C Dray
LEGUIZAMO, John Felix
TURTURRO, John Armstrong
MILHOAN, Michael ack
FROST, Lindsay Anne Brewer
©2001Warner Bros/Bel Air Pictures LLC
Warner Bros. Pictures presents in association with Bel-Air Entertainment a David Foster production an Andrew Davis film
108 mins 42 seconds
Locations – Los Angeles, Mexico
Sight and Sound .v12.n4.April 2002 p.28-29
Box Office: £1,164,046
Opening weekend £434,639
Screens 270
Screen average £1,610

Comédie de L'innocence

Dir Raúl Ruiz
PG (France) 2001
Artificial Eye Film Company – 8 March
Prod Martine de Clermont-Tonnerre
Screenplay Françoise Dumas, Raoul Ruiz
DOP Jacques Bouquin
Editor Mireille Hannon
Music Jorge Arrigada
HUPPERT, Isabelle Ariane d'Orville
BALIBAR, Jeanne Isabella Stirner
BERLING, Charles Serge
SCOB, Édith Laurence
HUGON, Nils Camille d'Orville
CLERMONT-TONNERRE, Laure de Hélène
PODALYDÈS, Denis Pierre d'Orville
BRONNER, Chantal Martine
MARENGO, Bruno Alexandre, Camille's friend
La BAUME, Nicolas de lawyer
©2000 Mact Productions/TF1 International/Les Films du Camélia
Martine and Antoine de Clermont-Tonnerre, Mact Productions present a Mact Productions, TF1 International, Les Films du Camélia with the participation of Canal+ and with the support of Procirep
103 mins
Locations – Paris
Sight and Sound .v12.n3.March 2002 p.32-33,42
Box Office: £73,265
Opening weekend £13,420
Screens 4
Screen average £3,355

Comment J'ai Tué Mon Père

Dir Anne Fontaine
15 (France/Spain) 2001
Pathé Distribution – 28 June
Prod Philippe Carcassonne
Screenplay Jacques Fieschi, Anne Fontaine
DOP Jean-Marc Fabre
Editor Guy Lecorne
Music Jocelyn Pook
BOUQUET, Michel Maurice
BERLING, Charles Jean-Luc
RÉGNIER, Natacha Isa
CASAR, Amira Myriem
GUILLON, Stéphane Patrick
KOUNDÉ, Hubert Jean-Toussaint
ROCHER, Karole Laetitia
MICLA, Marie prostitute
EVANS, Nicole patient
LEHEMBRE, Philippe homeless person/elderly patient
Ciné B/Cinéa/France 2 Cinéma/P.H.F. Films
Philippe Carcassonne presents a French-Spanish co-production of Ciné.B, Cinéa, France 2 Cinéma, P.H.F. Films with the participation of Canal+ and sofica Sofinergie 5
98 mins 20 seconds
Locations – Paris, Versailles
Sight and Sound .v12.n6.June 2002 p.56
Box Office: £36,029
Opening weekend £7,257
Screens 5
Screen average £1,451

Comissar Shakespeare

Box Office £1,099

Opening weekend £1,099
Screens 1
Screen average £1,099

Company (India)

Box Office £43,469
Opening weekend £15,676
Screens 11
Screen average £1,425

*The Conversation

Dir Francis Ford Coppla
PG (US)
(1974)
Buena Vista International (UK) – 1 March

Prod Francis Ford Coppola
Screenplay Francis Ford Coppola
DOP Bill Butler, Haskell Wexler
Editor Richard Chew
Music David Shire

HACKMAN, Gene Harry Caul
CAZALE, John Stan
GARFIELD, Allen Bernie Moran
FORREST, Frederic Mark
WILLIAMS, Cindy Ann
HIGGINS, Michael Paul
MacRAE, Elizabeth Meredith
GARR, Teri Amy Fredericks
FORD, Harrison Martin Stett
WHEELER, Mark receptionist

©2001 Paramount Pictures Corporation
The Directors Company presents a Coppola Company production, filmed in San
Francisco through the facilities of American Zoetrope
113 mins
Locations – San Francisco
Monthly Film Bulletin.v41.n486.July 1974 p.145-146

Box Office: £23,644
Opening weekend £ N/A
Screens N/A
Screen average £ N/A

The Count of Monte Cristo

$ £ €

Dir Kevin Reynolds
PG (US/UK/Ireland) 2001
Buena Vista International (UK) – 29 March

Prod Roger Birnbaum, Gary Barber, Jonathan Glickman
Screenplay Jay Wolpert
DOP Andrew Dunn
Editor Stephen Semel, Chris Womack
Music Edward Shearmur

CAVIEZEL, Jim (C) Edmond Dantès
PEARCE, Guy Fernand Mondego
HARRIS, Richard Abbé Faria
FRAIN, James Villefort
DOMINCZYK, Dagmara Mercédès
WINCOTT, Michael Dorléac
GUZMÁN, Luis Jacopo
McCRORY, Helen Valentina Villefort
JONES, Freddie Colonel Villefort
ADAMSON, Christopher Maurice

©2001 Spyglass Entertainment Group L.P.
Touchstone Pictures and Spyglass Entertainment present
a Birnbaum/Barber production
a Kevin Reynolds film
130 mins 58 seconds
Locations – Ireland, Malta
Studios – Mediterranean Film Studios
Sight and Sound Sight and Sound.v12.n5.May 2002 p.41

Box Office: £1,433,043
Opening weekend £47,675
Screens 59
Screen average £808

The Crocodile Hunter Collision Course

Dir John Stainton
PG (US/Australia) 2001
20th Century Fox International (UK) – 26 July

Screenplay Holly Goldberg Sloan
DOP David Burr
Editor Suresh Ayyar, Bob Blasall
Music Mark McDuff

IRWIN, Steve himself
IRWIN, Terri herself
SZUBANSKI, Magda Brozzie Drewitt
WENHAM, David Sam Flynn
HULME, Lachy Agent Bob Wheeler
YOUNG, Aden Ron Buckwhiler
RANSOM, Kenneth Agent Vaughan Archer
BEAHAN, Kate Jo Buckley
VIDLER, Steve (C) Deputy Director
Harley Ansell
BASTONI, Steve Deputy Director
Reynolds

©2002 Metro-Goldwyn-Mayer Pictures Inc
Metro-Goldwyn-Mayer Pictures presents
a Best Picture Show Company/Cheyenne Enterprises production
a John Stainton film
89 mins 29 seconds
Sight and Sound .v12.n9.September 2002 p.57

Box Office: £1,392,548
Opening weekend £ 266,803
Screens 258
Screen average £1,034

Crossroads

Dir Tamra Davis
PG (US) 2001
Momentum Pictures – 29 March

Prod Ann Carli
Screenplay Shonda Rhimes
DOP Erc Edwards
Editor Melissa Kent
Music Trevor Jones

SPEARS, Britney Lucy
MOUNT, Anson Ben
SALDANA, Zoë Kit
MANNING, Taryn Mimi
AYKROYD, Dan Pete, Lucy's dad
CATTRALL, Kim Caroline, Lucy's mum
LONG, Justin Henry
JOHNSON, Beverly Kit's mom
TURPIN, Bahni Ms Jenson
Kool Mo Dee (C) bar owner

©2001 Filmco Enterprises, Inc
Paramount Pictures and Zomba Films present in association with MTV Films
a film by Tamra Davis
93 mins 22 seconds
Locations – Louisiana, Nevada, California
Sight and Sound.v12.n4.April 2002 p.42

Box Office: £5,421,768
Opening weekend £1,126,053
Screens 373
Screen average £3,019

Crush

$ £ €

Dir John McKay
15 (UK/Germany/US) 2001
FilmFour Distributors – 7 June

Prod Lee Thomas
Screenplay John McKay
DOP Henry Braham
Editor Anne Sopel
Music Kevin Sargent

MacDOWELL, Andie Kate
STAUNTON, Imelda Janine
CHANCELLOR, Anna Molly
DOUGHTY, Kenny Jed
PATERSON, Bill Reverend Gerald Farquhar Marsde
HOLDAWAY, Caroline Pam
ROBERTS, Joe Brendan
COLE, Josh (C) young police constable

POWELL, Gary	sergeant
BURGESS, Christian	Kate's Frenchman

©2001 Film Four Limited
FilmFour presents in association with Film Council, Senator Film and Industry Entertainment
a Pipedream Pictures production
112 mins
Locations Chipping Campden, Cotswolds, London
Sight and Sound .v12.n6.June 2002 p.40

Box Office:	**£169,724**
Opening weekend	**£32,441**
Screens	**24**
Screen average	**£1,352**

The Curse of the Jade Scorpion

Dir Woody Allen
12A (US/Germany) 2001
United International Pictures (UK) Ltd – 6 December

Prod	Letty Aronson
Screenplay	Woody Allen
DOP	Fei Zhao
Editor	Alisa Lepselter
ALLEN, Woody	C.W. Briggs
AYKROYD, Dan	Chris Magruder
HUNT, Helen	Betty Ann Fitzgerald
MARKINSON, Brian	Al
SHAWN, Wallace	George Bond
OGDEN STIERS, David	Eli Voytak 'Voltan' Polgar
THERON, Charlize	Laura Kensington
BERKLEY, Elizabeth	Jill
GERETY, Peter	Ned
SCHUCK, John	Mize

©2001 Gravier Productions Inc/VCL Licensing GmbH
DreamWorks Pictures presents in association with VCL
a Gravier production
101 mins 38 seconds
Locations – New York
Sight and Sound .v13.n1.January 2003 p.39-40

Box Office:	**£95,667**
Opening weekend	**£35,183**
Screens	**25**
Screen average	**£1,407**

D-Tox

Dir Jim Gillespie
18 (US/Germany/Canada) 2001
United International Pictures (UK) Ltd – 1 February

Prod	Ric Kidney, Brian Grazer, Karen Kehela
Screenplay	Ron L.Brinerhoff
DOP	Dean Semler
Editor	Steve Mirkovich, Tim Alverson
Music	John Powell
STALLONE, Sylvester	Jake Malloy
BERENGER, Tom	Hank
DUTTON, Charles S. (C)	Chuck Hendricks
FLANERY, Sean Patrick	Conner
FULFORD, Christopher	Frank Slater
LANG, Stephen	Jack
MEYER, Dina	Mary Donahue
PATRICK, Robert	Pete Noah
PROSKY, Robert	'Gramps' McKenzie
VANCE, Courtney B.	Willie Jones

©2001 Universal Studios/Dritte Beteiligung KC Medien AG & Co. KG
Universal Pictures presents in association with KC Medien/Capella
96 mins 14 seconds
Sight and Sound.v12.n4.April 2002 p.43

Box Office:	**£82,381**
Opening weekend	**£44,260**
Screens	**65**
Screen average	**£681**

Da Wan

aka Big Shot's Funeral
Dir Xiaogang Feng
PG (Hong Kong/China) 2001
Columbia TriStar Films (UK) – 15 November

Prod	Buting Yang
Screenplay	Li Shaoming, Kang Shi, Ziaogang
DOP	Li Zhang
Editor	Ying Zhou
Music	Bao San
GE You	Yo Yo
SUTHERLAND, Donald	Don Tyler
KWAN, Rosamund (C)	Lucy
YING Da	Louis Wang
MAZURSKY, Paul	Tony

©2001 Columbia Pictures Film Production Asia Limited
China Film Group, Hua Yi Brothers & Taihe Film
Investment Corporation, Columbia Pictures Film Production (Asia) Ltd present in association with China Film Co-production Company
100 mins 40 seconds
Locations – Beijing
Sight and Sound .v13.n1.January 2003 p.34-35

Box Office:	**£1,474**
Opening weekend	**£971**
Screens	**3**
Screen average	**£324**

The Dancer Upstairs

aka Pasos de Baile
Dir John Malkovich
(Spain/US) 2001
20th Century Fox International (UK) – 6 December

Prod	Andrés Vicentre Gómez, John Malkovich
Screenplay	Nicholas Shaespeare
DOP	Jos'Luis Alcaine
Editor	Mario Battistel
Music	Alberto Iglesias
BARDEM, Javier	Agustín Rejas
MORANTE, Laura	Yolanda
BOTTO, Juan Diego	Sucre
MÍNGUEZ, Elvira	Llosa
LENCASTRE, Alexandra	Sylvina
COTTON, Oliver	General Merino
CINTRA, Luís Miguel	Calderón
MANRIQUE, Javier	Clorindo
FOLK, Abel	Ezequiel/Durán
BERGANZA, Marie-Anne	Laura

©2001 Lolafilms S.A.
an Andrés Vicente Gómez production
for Mr. Mudd in association with Antena 3 Televisíon, Vía Digital
a film by John Malkovich
133 mins
Oporto & Quito, Portugal, Ecuador, Spain
Sight and Sound .v12.n12.December 2002 p.44

Box Office:	**£230,986 ***
	£327,634**
Opening weekend	**£61,622**
Screens	**24**
Screen average	**£2,568**

*(*total box office in 2002)*
*(** cumulative box office for 2002/03)*

Dancing at the Blue Iguana

$ £
Dir Michael Radford
18 (US/UK) 2000
Miracle Communications – 21 June

Prod	Michael Radford, Sheila Kelley, Damian Jones, Graham Broadbent, Etchie Stroh, Ram Bergman, Dana Lustig
Screenplay	Michael Radford, David Linter
DOP	Ericson Core
Editor	Roberto Perpignani
Music	Tai Bergman, Renato Neto
AYANNA, Charlotte	Jessie
HANNAH, Daryl	'Angel', Becky Willow
KELLEY, Sheila	'Stormy', Marie Hughes
KOTEAS, Elias	Sully, Stormy's brother
MASHKOV, Vladimir	Sacha
OH, Sandra	'Jasmine', Cathy
TILLY, Jennifer	'Jo', Ellen Taylor

WISDOM, Robert Eddie Hazel
BROWN, W. Earl Bobby
HOGAN, Chris Dennis
©2000 Impro-duction Ltd
Moonstone Entertainment present
a Bergman Lustig/Dragon/Gallery production
a Michael Radford film
123 mins 26 seconds
Locations – Los Angeles
Sight and Sound .v12.n7.July 2002 p.41-42

Box Office:	**£18,419**
Opening weekend	**£10,467**
Screens	**24**
Screen average	**£436**

Dark Blue World

aka Tmavomodry Svet

£ €

Dir Jan Sverák
12 (Czech Republic/ UK/Germany/ Denmark/Italy) 2001
Columbia TriStar Films (UK) – 10 May

Prod	Eric Abraham, Jan Sverák, Iva Procházková, Jaroslav Kucera
Screenplay	Zdenek Sverák
DOP	Vladimir Smutny
Editor	Alois Fisárek
Music	Ondrej Soukup

VETCHY, Ondrej	Lieutenant Frantisek 'Franta' S
HADEK, Krystof	Karel Vojtisek
FITZGERALD, Tara	Susan Whitmore
KAISER, Oldrich	Machaty
ASSMANN, Hans-Jorg	Doctor Blaschke
DANCE, Charles	Wing Commander Bentley
NOVOTNY, David	Mrtvy
RYBOVÁ, Linda	Hanicka
DULAVA, Jaromír	Kanka
KANTOR, Lukás	Tom Tom

©2001 Tmavomodry svet s.r.o. (Dark Blue World)
Eurimages [logo]
A Czech-German co-production
State Fund of the Czech Republic for the Support and Development of Czech Cinematography
in co-production with Helkon Media, Phoenix Film Investments, Fandango and Czech Television
Biograf Jan Sverak, Portobello Pictures present
112 mins 21 seconds
Locations – Czech Republic, Germany
Sight and Sound .v12.n5.May 2002 p.42

Box Office:	**£198,538**
Opening weekend	**£45,753**
Screens	**40**
Screen average	**£1,144**

* A Day at the Races

Dir Sam Wood
U (US) 2001
bfi Bookings – 12 July

Prod	Lawrence Weingarten, Irving Thalberg
Screenplay	Robert Pirosh, George Oppenheimer, George S. Kaufman, Al Boasberg, Leon Gordon
DOP	Leonard Smith
Editor	Frank E. Hull
Music	Bronislau Kaper, Walter Jurmann

MARX, Groucho	Dr Hugo Z. Hackenbush
MARX, Chico	Tony
MARX, Harpo	Stuffy
JONES, Allan	Gil Stewart
O'SULLIVAN, Maureen	Judy Standish
DUMONT, Margaret	Mrs Emily Upjohn
CEELEY, Leonard	Whitmore
DUMBRILLE, Douglas (C)	Morgan
MUIR, Esther	Cokey Flo Marlowe
RUMANN, Sig (C)	Dr Leopold Steinberg

©1937 Metro-Goldwyn-Mayer Corporation
Metro-Goldwyn-Mayer presents
a Sam Wood production
109 mins
Monthly Film Bulletin.v4.n43.July 1937 p.145

Box Office:	**£3,524**

Deathwatch

£ €

Dir Michael Bassett
15 (Germany/UK) 2001
Pathé Distribution – 6 December

Prod	Sam Taylor, Mike Downey, Frank Hübner
Screenplay	Michael J. Bassett
DOP	Hubert Taczanowski
Editor	Anne Sopel
Music	Curt Cress, Chris Weller

BELL, Jamie	Charlie Shakespeare
CONROY, Ruaidhrí	Colin Chevasse
FOX, Laurence	Captain Bramwell Jennings
LIEBRECHT, Torben	Friedrich
KELLY, Dean Lennox	Willie McNess
MARSHALL, Kris (C)	Barry Starinski
MATHESON, Hans	Jack Hawkstone
O'CONOR, Hugh	Anthony Bradford
RHYS, Matthew	Doc
SERKIS, Andy	Thomas Quinn

©2002 ApolloMedia GmbH & Co. 5. Filmproduktion KG/ApolloProMedia GmbH & Co. 1. Filmproduktion KG/Warpic Limited
Odysey Entertainment presents
an ApolloMedia, ApolloProMedia, Film and Music Entertainment co-production
a Sam Taylor/Mike Downey/Frank Hübner production
a German-UK co-production
94 mins 36 seconds
Locations – Czech Republic
Sight and Sound .v13.n1.January 2003 p.40

Box Office:	**£967,748**
Opening weekend	**£334,657**
Screens	**193**
Screen average	**£1,734**

Deewangee

Box Office	**£115,541**
Opening weekend	**£51,934**
Screens	**15**
Screen average	**£3,462**

Delbaran

Dir Abolfazl Jalili
PG (Ireland/Japan/Netherlands) 2001
ICA Projects – 19 April

Prod	Abolfazl Jalili, Shozo Ichiyama
Screenplay	Abolfazl Jalili
DOP	Mohammad Ahmadi
Editor	Abolfazl Jalili

ALIZADEH, Kaeem
EBRAHIMI, Ramatoallah
HASHEMIAN, Hosein
MAHDAVI, Ahmad
EBRAHIMZADEH, Ebrahim
SHAMSI, Teymour
BIRJANDI, Kobra
KAFI, Haser
MOHAMADI, Saïd
NASARI, Jalal
©2001 Office Kitano/Film-e-Aval
Office Kitano and Bandai Visual present
a T-Mark and Film-e-Aval production
with financial support from the Hubert Bals Fund of the International Film Festival Rotterdam
an Abolfazl Jalili film
96 mins 57 seconds
Subtitles

Sight and Sound .v12.n5.May 2002 p.42-43
Box Office: **£7,734**

Devdas
Dir Sanjay Leela Bhansali
PG (India) 2001
Eros International – 12 July
Prod Bharat Shah
Screenplay Prakash Kapadia, Sanjay Leela Bhansali
DOP Binod Pradhan
Editor Bela Segal
Music Prakash Patel, Yogesh Pradhan
KHAN, Shahrukh (C) Devdas
DIXIT, Madhuri Chandramukhi
RAI, Aishwarya 'Paro' Parvati
SHROFF, Jackie Chunnilal
KHER, Kiron Sumitra, Paro's mother
JAYKAR, Smita (C) Kaushalya, Devdas' mother
TALSANIA, Tiku Dharamdas
GHATGE, Vijayendra Zamindar Bhuvan
GUNAJI, Milind Kalibabu
KHARE, Ananya Kumud
Bharat Shah presents
a Mega Bollywood Pvt. Ltd. production
181 mins 47 seconds
Sight and Sound .v12.n9.September 2002 p.58
Box Office: **£1,742,553**
Opening weekend **£466,370**
Screens **54**
Screen average **£8,636**

Die Another Day
$ £
Dir Lee Tamahori
12A (UK/US) 2002
20th Century Fox International (UK) – 22 November
Prod Michael G. Wilson, Barbara Broccoli
Screenplay Neal Purvis, Robert Wade
DOP David Tattersall
Editor Christian Wagner, Andrew MacRitchie
Music David Arnold
BROSNAN, Pierce James Bond
BERRY, Halle Jinx
STEPHENS, Toby Gustav Graves
PIKE, Rosamund Miranda Frost
YUNE, Rick Zao
TSANG, Kenneth (C) General Moon
LEE, Will Yun Colonel Moon
ECHEVARRÍA, Emilio Raoul
BOND, Samantha Moneypenny
SALMON, Colin Charles Robinson
©2001 2 Danjaq, LLC/United Artists Corporation
Albert R. Broccoli's Eon Productions Limited presents
132 mins 46 seconds
Locations – Iceland, Hawaii
Studios – Pinewood Studios
Sight and Sound .v13.n1.January 2003 p.41-42
Box Office: **£31,392,839***
£36,044,960**
Opening weekend **£9,122,344**
Screens **430**
Screen average **£21,215**
*(*total box office in 2002)*
*(** cumulative box office for 2002/03)*

Dil Hai Tumhaara
Box Office £313,644
Opening weekend **£92,397**
Screens **23**
Screen average **£4,017**

Dil Vil Pyar Vyar
Box Office £45,775
Opening weekend **£17,308**
Screens **10**
Screen average **£1,731**

Dinner Rush
Dir Bob Giraldi
15 (US) 2000
Pathé Distribution – 29 March
Prod Louis DiGiaimo, Patti Greaney
Screenplay Rick Shaughnessy, Brian Kalata
DOP Tim Ives
Editor Allyson C. Johnson
Music Alexander Lasarenko
AIELLO, Danny Louis Cropa
BALLERINI, Edoardo Udo
WU, Vivian Nicole
McGLONE, Mike Carmen
ACEVEDO, Kirk Duncan
BERNHARD, Sandra Jennifer Freely
CORBETT, John Ken
HARRIS, Jamie Sean
PHOENIX, Summer Marti
DRAPER, Polly Natalie
©2001 Dinner Rush LLC
[US release: An Access Motion Picture Group release
An Entertainment Capital Group company]
Giraldi Suarez DiGiaimo Productions presents
a film by Bob Giraldi
97 mins 55 seconds
Locations – New York
Sight and Sound .v12.n4.April 2002 p.43-44
Box Office: **£204,532**
Opening weekend **£33,309**
Screens **20**
Screen average **£1,665**

Dirty Pretty Things
$ £
Dir Stephen Frears
(UK/US) 2002
Buena Vista International (UK) – 13 December
Prod Tracey Seaward, Robert Jones
Screenplay Steven Knight
DOP Chris Menges, Ivan Strasburg
Editor Mick Audsley
Music Nathan Larson
EJIOFOR, Chiwetel Okwe
TAUTOU, Audrey Senay
LOPEZ, Sergi (C) Sneaky
OKONEDO, Sophie Juliette
WONG, Benedict Guo Yi
BURIC, Zlatko Ivan
DOSANJH, Kriss Asian businessman
ADURAMO, Israel mini cab driver
AJIBADE, Yemi mini cab driver
KARANJ, Nizwar mini cab driver
©2002 Miramax Film Corp
Miramax Films and BBC Films present
a Celador Films production
a film by Stephen Frears
94 mins
Locations – London
Studios – Shepperton Studios
Sight and Sound .v12.n12.December 2002 p.32-34
Box Office: **£415,449***
£829,099**
Opening weekend **£141,865**
Screens **50**
Screen average **£2,837**
*(*total box office in 2002)*
*(** cumulative box office for 2002/03)*

Divine Secrets of the Ya-Ya Sisterhood
Dir Callie Khouri
1 (US) 2002
Warner Bros Distributors (UK) – 27 September
Prod Bonnie Bruckheimer, Hunt Lowry
Screenplay Callie Khouri
DOP John Bailey
Editor Andrew Marcus
Music T Bone Burnett
BULLOCK, Sandra Sidda Lee Walker
BURSTYN, Ellen Vivi
FLANAGAN, Fionnula (C) Teensy
GARNER, James Shep Walker
JUDD, Ashley younger Vivi
KNIGHT, Shirley Necie
MACFADYEN, Angus Connor McGill
SMITH, Maggie Caro

JONES, Cherry Buggy
McKENZIE, Jacqueline younger Teensy
©2002 Warner Bros./Gaylord Films LLC
Warner Bros. Pictures presents
in association with Gaylord Films
an All Girl production
116m 26 seconds
Locations – Louisiana
Sight and Sound .v12.n11.November 2002 p.43
Box Office: £304,094
Opening weekend £124,269
Screens 201
Screen average £618

Dog Soldiers

$ £ €
Dir Neil Marshall
15 (UK/US/Luxembourg) 2001
Pathé Distribution – 10 May
Prod Christopher Figg, Tom Reeve, David E. Allen
Screenplay Neil Marshall
DOP Sam McCurdy
Editor Neil Marshall
Music Mark Thomas
PERTWEE, Sean Wells
McKIDD, Kevin Cooper
CLEASBY, Emma Megan
CUNNINGHAM, Liam Ryan
LOCKYER, Thomas Bruce
MORFITT, Darren Spoon
ROBSON, Chris Joe
SIMPSON, Leslie Terry
LANDINI, Tina camper
CONWAY, Craig camper
©2001 Dog Soldiers Ltd
Kismet Entertainment Group, The Noel Gay Motion Picture Company present
in association with Victor Film Company
a Carousel Picture Company production
with the support of the Luxembourg Film Fund
104 mins 50seconds
Locations – Luxembourg, Scotland
Sight and Sound .v12.n5.May 2002 p.43-44
Box Office: £2,070,441
Opening weekend £681,348
Screens 313
Screen average £2,177

Dogtown and Z-Boys

Dir Stacy Paralta
15 (US) 2001
Columbia TriStar Films (UK) – 5 July
Prod Agi Orsi
Screenplay Stacy Peralta, Craig Stecyk
DOP Peter Pilafian
Editor Paul Crowder
Music Terry Wilson, Paul Crowder
Zephyr Skateboard Team appearance
ADAMS, Jay appearance
ALVA, Tony appearance
BINIAK, Bob appearance
CONSTANTINEAU, Paul appearance
KUBO, Shogu appearance
MUIR, Jim appearance
OKI, Peggy appearance
PERALTA, Stacy appearance
PRATT, Nathan appearance
©2001 Vans Off the Wall Productions
Vans Off the Wall Productions present
an Agi Orsi production
90 mins 42 seconds
Documentary
Sight and Sound .v12.n7.July 2002 p.42-43
Box Office: £102,083
Opening weekend £15,703
Screens 9
Screen average £1,745

Domestic Disturbance

Dir Harold Becker
12 (US) 2001
United International Pictures (UK) Ltd – 11 January
Prod Donald De Line, Jonathan D. Krane
Screenplay Lewis Colick
DOP Michael Seresin
Editor Peter Honess
Music Mark Mancina
TRAVOLTA, John Frank Morrison
VAUGHN, Vince Rick Barnes
POLO, Teri Susan
O'LEARY, Matt Danny Morrison
BUSCEMI, Steve Ray Coleman
LASHLY, James Jason
TILNEY, Rebecca Laurie
MOONEY, Debra Theresa
JONES, Leland L. Coach Mark
SANTIAGO-HUDSON, Ruben Sergeant Edgar Stevens
©2001 Paramount Pictures Corporation
Paramount Pictures presents
a De Line Pictures and Jonathan D. Krane production
a Harold Becker film
89 mins 17 seconds
Locations – North Carolina
Sight and Sound .v12.n3.March 2002 p.42-43
Box Office: £982,460
Opening weekend £402,837
Screens 221
Screen average £1,823

Donnie Darko

Dir Richard Kelly
15 (US) 2001
Metrodome Distribution Ltd – 25 October
Prod Sean McKittrick, Nancy Juvonen, Adam Fields
Screenplay Richard Kelly
DOP Steven Poster
Editor Sam Bauer, Eric Strand
Music Michael Andrews
GYLLENHAAL, Jake Donnie Darko
MALONE, Jena Gretchen Ross
BARRYMORE, Drew Karen Pomeroy
DUVAL, James Frank
GRANT, Beth Kitty Farmer
GYLLENHAAL, Maggie Elizabeth Darko
McDONNELL, Mary Rose Darko
OSBORNE, Holmes Eddie Darko
ROSS, Katharine Dr Lilian Thurman
SWAYZE, Patrick Jim Cunningham
©2001 Pandora Inc
Pandora presents
a Flower production
a Richard Kelly film
113 mins 11 seconds
Locations – Los Angeles
Sight and Sound .v12.n10.October 2002 p.34-35+39
Box Office: £1,345,515*
£1,557,294**
Opening weekend £191,348
Screens 37
Screen average £5,172
*(*total box office in 2002)*
*(** cumulative box office for 2002/03)*

Don't Say a Word

Dir Gary Fleder
15 (US/Australia) 2001
20th Century Fox International (UK) – 22 February
Prod Arnon Milchan, Arnold Kopelson, Anne Kopelson
Screenplay Anthony Peckham, Patrick Smith Kelly, Christine Roum, David Stewart, Andrew Klavan
DOP Amir Mokri
Editor William Steinkamp, Armen Minasian
Music Mark Isham
DOUGLAS, Michael Dr Nathan Conrad
BEAN, Sean Patrick B. Koster
MURPHY, Brittany Elisabeth Burrows
McCOLE BARTUSIAK, Skye Jessie Conrad
TORRY, Guy Martin J. Dolen

ESPOSITO, Jennifer Detective Sandra Cassidy
DOYLE, Shawn Russel Maddox
ARGO, Victor Sydney Simon
GOODE, Conrad Max J. Dunlevy
SCHULZE, Paul Jake
©2001 DSAW Film Partnership (rest of the world)
Regency Enterprises and Village Roadshow Pictures present
in association with NPV Entertainment
a Kopelson Entertainment/New Regency/Furthur Films production
113 mins 26 seconds
Locations – Toronto, New York
Sight and Sound .v12.n1.January 2002 p.41
Box Office: **£1,858,460**
Opening weekend **£597,896**
Screens **273**
Screen average **£2,190**

* Du Rififi Chez Les Hommes

Dir Jules Dassin
(France/Italy)
(1955)
Arrow Film Distributors Ltd – 16 August
Prod Henri Berard, Pierre Cabaud, René Bezard
DOP Philippe Agostini
Editor Roger Dwyre
Music Georges Auric
SERVAIS, Jean Tony le Stephanois
MÖHNER, Carl Jo le Suedois
MANUEL, Robert Mario
DASSIN, Jules César
NOËL, Magali Viviane
SABOURET, Marie Mado
DARCY, Janine Louise
GRASSET, Pierre Louis
HOSSEIN, Robert Remi
LUPOVICI, Marcel Pierre
Indusfilm, Prima Film, Société Nouvelle Pathé-Cinéma (Paris)
110 mins seconds
Studios – Photosonor (Courbevoie)
Monthly Film Bulletin.v22.n259.August 1955 p.119
Box Office: **£11,819**
Opening weekend **£11,819**
Screens **4**
Screen average **£2,955**

Dragonfly

Dir Tom Shadyac
12A (US) 2001
Columbia TriStar Films (UK) – 7 June
Prod Mark Johnson, Tom Shadyac, Roger Birnbaum, Gary Barber
Screenplay David Seltzer, Brandon Camp, Mike Thompson
DOP Dean Semler
Editor Don Zimmerman
Music John Debney
COSTNER, Kevin Joe Darrow
MORTON, Joe Hugh Campbell
RIFKIN, Ron Charlie Dickinson
HUNT, Linda Sister Madeline
THOMPSON, Susanna Emily Darrow
VARGAS, Jacob pilot
BATES, Kathy Mrs Belmont
BAILEY Jr, Robert Jeffrey Reardon
SMITH, Jacob Ben
THOMAS, Jay Hal
©2002 KALIMA Productions GmbH & Co. KG
Universal Pictures and Spyglass Entertainment present
a Gran Via/Shady Acres production
104 mins 4 seconds
Locations Chicago, Los Angeles, Kauai
Sight and Sound.v12.n6.June 2002 p.41-42
Box Office: **£179,415**
Opening weekend **£80,209**
Screens **198**
Screen average **£405**

Dust

£ €
Dir Milcho Manchevski
18
(UK/Germany/Italy/Macedonia/US) 2001
Pathé Distribution – 3 May
Prod Chris Auty, Vesna Jovanoska, Domenico Procacci
Screenplay Milcho Manchevski
DOP Barry Ackroyd
Editor Nic Gaster
Music Kiril Dzajkovski
FIENNES, Joseph Elijah
WENHAM, David Luke
LESTER, Adrian Edge
BROCHET, Anne Lilith
KUJACA, Nikolina Neda
MURPHY, Rosemary Angela
JOVANOVSKI, Vlado teacher
BILAL, Salaetin the major
FARMIGA, Vera Amy
ROSS, Matthew (C) Stitch
©2001 ©2001 History Dreams/ena Film/Fandango
The Film Consortium presents
a History Dreams/ena Film/Fandango production
with Shadow Films
in association with South Fork Pictures
with the support of The Film Council and Filmstiftung Nordrhein-Westfalen
and Ministerstvo za kultura na Republika Makedonija
with the participation of BSkyB and British Screen
123 mins 49 seconds
Locations – New York, Macedonia, Cologne
Sight and Sound .v12.n5.May 2002 p.44-45
Box Office: **£3,680**
Opening weekend **£1,058**
Screens **3**
Screen average **£353**

Ealing 100 Anniversary Tour

Box Office: **£60,353**
Opening weekend **£3,038**
Screens **1**
Screen average **£3,038**

Eight Crazy Nights

Dir Seth Kearsley
12A (US) 2001
Columbia TriStar Films (UK) – 6 December
Prod Adam Sandler, Jack Giarraputo, Allen Covert
Screenplay Brooks Arthur, Allen Covert, Brad Issacs, Adam Sandler
Editor Amy Budden
Music Ray Ellis, Marc Ellis, Teddy Castellucci
SANDLER, Adam voice of Davey Stone/Whitey Duv
SANDLER, Adam voice of Eleanore Duvall/deer
TITONE, Jackie (C) voice of Jennifer
STOUT, Austin voice of Benjamin
NEALON, Kevin voice of Mayor Stewey Dewey
SCHNEIDER, Rob voice of Chinese waiter/narrato
CROSBY, Norm voice of judge
LOVITZ, Jon voice of Tom Baltezor
BANKS, Tyra voice of Victoria's Secret gown
CLARK, Blake voice of Radio Shack walkie-tal
©2002 Columbia Pictures Industries, Inc.
Columbia Pictures presents
a Happy Madison production
76 mins 4 seconds
Sight and Sound .v13.n1.January 2003 p.43-44
Box Office: **£97,748**

Opening weekend £48,440
Screens 83
Screen average £584

Eight Legged Freaks

Dir Ellory Elkayem
12 (US/Australia) 2002
Warner Bros Distributors (UK) – 9 August

Prod Dean Devlin, Bruce Berman
Screenplay Jesse Alexander, Ellory Elkayem
DOP John Bartley
Editor David J. Siegel
Music John Ottaman
ARQUETTE, David Chris McCormick
WUHRER, Kari Sheriff Sam Parker
TERRA, Scott Mike Parker
DOUG, Doug E. Harlan Griffith
JOHANSSON, Scarlett Ashley Parker
OVERTON, Rick Deputy Pete Willis
RIPPY, Leon Mayor Wade
CZUCHRY, Matt Bret
JONES, Jay Arlen Leon
RYAN, Eileen Gladys
©2002 Village Roadshow Films (BVI) Limited [all other territories]
Warner Bros. Pictures presents in association with Village Roadshow Pictures and NPV Entertainment
an Electric Entertainment production
99 mins 12 seconds
Locations – Australia
Sight and Sound .v12.n9.September 2002 p.60
Box Office: £3,604,113
Opening weekend £1,031,494
Screens 400
Screen average £2,579

L'Emploi du Temps

Dir Laurent Cantet
PG (France) 2001
Artificial Eye Film Company – 5 April

Prod Caroline Benjo
Screenplay Robin Campillo, Laurent Cantet
DOP Pierre Milon
Editor Roobin Campillo, Stéphanie Léger
Music Jocelyn Pook
RECOING, Aurélien Vincent Renault
VIARD, Karin Muriel Renault
LIVROZET, Serge Jean Michel
MANGEOT, Jean-Pierre Vincent's father
MANGEOT, Monique Vincent's mother
KALSCH, Nicolas Julien
CANTET, Marie Alice
CANTET, Félix Félix
LE JOUBIOUX, Olivier Stan
SASSIER, Maxime Nono
©2001 Haut et Court/Arte France Cinéma/Havas Images/Rhône-Alpes Cinéma
Haut et Court presents in co-production with Arte France Cinéma, Rhône-Alpes Cinéma, Havas Images with the participation of Canal+, Centre National de la Cinématographie, Région Rhône-Alpes, sofica Sofinergie 5
a film by Laurent Cantet
134 mins 2 seconds Subtitles
Sight and Sound.v12.n4.April 2002 p.44-45
Box Office: £153,829
Opening weekend £21,266
Screens 6
Screen average £3,544

The End Son

Box Office £12,340
Opening weekend £1,907
Screens 1
Screen average £1,907

Enough

Dir Michael Apted
15 (US) 2001
Columbia TriStar Films (UK) – 29 November

Prod Irwin Winkler, Rob Cowan
Screenplay Nichoolas Kazan
DOP Rogier Stoffers
Editor Rick Shaine
Music David Arnold
LOPEZ, Jennifer Slim
CAMPBELL, Billy Mitch
LEWIS, Juliette Ginny
FUTTERMAN, Dan Joe
WARD, Fred Jupiter
COBBS, Bill Jim Toller
KOBER, Jeff FBI agent
YOUNG, Bruce A. instructor
ALLEN, Tessa Gracie
MAHER, Christopher Phil
©2001 ©2002 Columbia Pictures Industries Inc
Columbia Pictures presents
an Irwin Winkler production
a Michael Apted film
115 mins 8 seconds
Locations – Los Angeles, San Francisco, Seattle
Sight and Sound .v12.n12.December 2002 p.47
Box Office: £1,008,335
Opening weekend £340,600
Screens 238
Screen average £1,431

Et Là-Bas, Quelle Heure est-il?

Dir Ming-Liang Tsai
(France/Taiwan/Italy) 2001
ICA Projects – 21 June

Prod Bruno Pesery
Screenplay Ming-Liang Tsai, Pi-Ying Yang
DOP Benoît Delhomme
Editor Sheng-Chang Chen
LEE Kang-Sheng Hsiao-Kang
CHEN Shiang-Chyi Shiang-Chyi
LU Yi-Ching Hsiao-Kang's mother
MIAO Tien Hsiao-Kang's father
LIAO Ching-Kuo sorcerer
TSAI Chao-Yi (C) clock store owner
CHEN Hsu-Fei video tapes vendor
LEE Yo-Hsin vendor's customer
HSU Yue-Yin sorceress
©2001 ©2001 Arena Films/Arte France Cinéma
Arena Films presents in association with Homegreen Films
an Arena Films production in association with Homegreen Films, Arte France Cinéma, with the participation of Centre National de la Cinématographie, Alia Film, TelePiù
116 mins
Subtitles
Sight and Sound .v12.n7.July 2002 p.57
Box Office: £7,263

* E.T. The Extra-Terrestrial

Dir Steven Spielberg
U (US) 1982
United International Pictures (UK) Ltd – 29 March

Prod Steven Spielberg, Kathleen Kennedy
Screenplay Melissa Mathison
DOP Allen Daviau
Editor Carol Littleton
Music John Williams
WALLACE, Dee (C) Mary
THOMAS, Henry Elliott
COYOTE, Peter 'Keys'
MacNAUGHTON, Robert Michael
BARRYMORE, Drew Gertie
MARTEL, K.C. Greg
FRYE, Sean Steve
HOWELL, Tom (C) Tyler
ELENIAK, Erika pretty girl
O'DELL, David schoolboy
©2001 Universal Pictures
115 mins

Locations – Northridge, California
Monthly Film Bulletin.v49.n587.December 1982 p.282-283
Box Office: £2,063,690

Everything Put Together

Dir Marc Forster
(US) 2000
ICA Projects – 14 June

Prod Sean Furst
Screenplay Adam Forgash, Catherine Lloyd Burns, Marc Forster
DOP Roberto Forster
Editor Matt Chessé
Music Thomas Kippel

MITCHELL, Radha Angie
LOUIS, Justin Russ, Angie's husband
MULLALLY, Megan Barbie
BURNS, Catherine Lloyd Judith
MALLOY, Matt Dr Reiner
HICKS, Michele April
BOONE Junior, Mark (C) Bill
GEESON, Judy Angie's mother
RUCK, Alan Kessel
McCLEISTER, Tom Dr Miller

Furst Films presents
85 mins
Sight and Sound .v12.n7.July 2002 p.43-44
Box Office: £1,254

Das Experiment

Dir Oliver Hirschbiegel
18 (Germany) 2001
Metrodome Distribution Ltd – 22 March

Prod Norbert Preuss, Marc Conrad, Fritz Wildfever, Ulrike Leibfried
Screenplay Mario Giordano, Christoph Darnstädt, Don Bohlinger
DOP Rainer Klausmann
Editor Hans Funck
Music Alexander van Bubenhein

BLEIBTREU, Moritz Tarek Fahd, No 77
BERKEL, Christian Robert Steinhoff, No 38
STOKOWSKI, Oliver Günther Schütte, No 82
MÖHRING, Wotan Wilke Joe Maier, No 69
SZASZ, Stephan prisoner No 53
DAL, Polat prisoner No 40
RICHTER, Danny prisoner No 21
MÜLLER, Ralf prisoner No 15
RUDOLF, Markus prisoner No 74

©2001 Typhoon Film/Fanes Film
a Typhoon Film and Fanes Film production with Senator Film Produktion
in co-production with SevenPictures
supported by Filmstiftung Nordrhein-Westfalen, FilmFernsehFonds Bayern, Filmförderungsanstalt, BKM
a Oliver Hirschbiegel film
118 mins 49 seconds
Locations – North Rhine-Westphalia
Subtitles
Sight and Sound .v12.n3.March 2002 p.44

Box Office:	**£59,722**
Opening weekend	**£15,649**
Screens	**12**
Screen average	**£1,304**

Fatma

Dir Khaled Ghorbal
(Tunisia/France) 2001
NFT – 11 March

Prod Lofti Layouni, Francine, Jean-Baptiste
Screenplay Khaled Ghorbal
DOP Jean-Luc L'Huillier
Editor Andrée Davanture
Music Foued Ghorbal

JENDOUBI, Awatef Fatma
GUIDER, Nabila Samira
AOUM, Bagdadi Aziz
SAFTA, Amel Radhia
MAILLARD, Huguette
GARREL, Maurice

an MK2 Diffusion release (in France) of an Amilcar Films/Mandala Prods. co-production
124 mins
No Sight and Sound reference
Box Office: £3,340

Filhaal

Box Office £68,208	
Opening weekend	**£20,410**
Screens	**14**
Screen average	**£1,458**

The Fluffer

Dir Richard Glatzer
18 (US) 2000
Metrodome Distribution Ltd – 1 February

Prod Victoria Robinson, John R. Sylla
Screenplay Wash West
DOP Mark Putnam
Editor John Binninger
Music The Bowling Green, John Vaughn

GURNEY, Scott Michael 'Mike' Rossini/'Johnny
CUNIO, Michael Sean McGinnis
DAY, Roxanne Babylon
NEGRON, Taylor Tony Brooks
RIEHLE, Richard Sam Martins
BAGLEY, Tim Alan Dieser
PORTER, Adina Silver
MADERA, Ruben Hector Flores
HOLLAND, Josh Brian
COTTRELL, Mickey aunty at bar/Ralph Shifflett

©2001 Fluff and Fold LLC
93 mins 57 seconds
Sight and SoundSight and Sound.v12.n2.February 2002 p.43-44

Box Office:	**£61,755**
Opening weekend	**£8,961**
Screens	**4**
Screen average	**£2,240**

Frailty

Dir Bill Paxton
15 (US/Germany) 2001
United International Pictures (UK) Ltd – 6 September

Prod David Kirschner, David Blocker, Corey Sienega
Screenplay Brent Hanley
DOP Bill Butler
Editor Arnold Glassman
Music Brian Tyler

PAXTON, Bill Dad
McCONAUGHEY, Matthew 'Fenton Meiks', Adam Meiks
BOOTHE, Powers Agent Wesley J. Doyle
ASKEW, Luke Sheriff Smalls
SUMPTER, Jeremy young Adam Meiks
O'LEARY, Matt young Fenton Meiks
CHEETWOOD, Derk Agent Griffin Hull
CRIDER, Melissa Becky, sheriff's receptionist
KREIS, Levi Fenton Meiks
DAVIDSON, Alan Brad White

©2001 Cinedelta Internationale Film-produktionsgesellschaft mbH & Co. 1 Beteiligungs KG
Lions Gate Films presents
a David Kirschner production
in association with American Entertainment Co.
in association with Cinerenta/Cinedelta
99 mins 43 seconds
Locations – Los Angeles
Sight and Sound .v12.n10.October 2002 p.39

Box Office	**£192,118**
Opening weekend	**£85,415**
Screens	**100**
Screen average	**£854**

* Freaks

Dir Tod Browning
(US) 1932
bfi Bookings – 27 September

Prod Tod Browning
Screenplay Willis Goldbeck, Leon Gordon
DOP Merritt B. Gerstad
Editor Basil Wrangell

FORD, Wallace Phroso
HYAMS, Leila Venus
BACLANOVA, Olga Cleopatra
ATES, Roscoe Roscoe
VICTOR, Henry Hercules
EARLES, Harry Hans
EARLES, Daisy Frieda
DIONE, Rose Madame Tetrallini
HILTON, Daisy Siamese twin
HILTON, Violet Siamese twin

Metro-Goldwyn-Mayer
61 mins
No S&S reference
Box Office: £9,623

From Hell

Dir Albert Hughes
18 (US) 2001
20th Century Fox International (UK) – 8 February

Prod Don Murphy, Jane Hamsher
Screenplay Terry Hayes, Rafael Yglesias
DOP Peter Deming
Editor Dan Lebental, George Bowers
Music Trevor Jones

DEPP, Johnny Fred Abberline
GRAHAM, Heather Mary Kelly
HOLM, Ian Sir William Gull
COLTRANE, Robbie Peter Godley
RICHARDSON, Ian Sir Charles Warren
FLEMYNG, Jason Netley
CARTLIDGE, Katrin Dark Annie Chapman
HARVEY, Terence Ben Kidney
LYNCH, Susan Liz Stride
RHYS, Paul Dr Ferral

©2001 Twentieth Century Fox Film Corporation
Twentieth Century Fox presents an Underworld Pictures/Don Murphy and Jane Hamsher/Amy Robinson production
122 mins 12 seconds
Locations – Prague
Sight and Sound .v12.n3.March 2002 p.45

Box Office: £3,140,575
Opening weekend £891,862
Screens 235
Screen average £3,795

*Funny Girl

Dir William Wyler
U (US) 1968
Columbia TriStar Films (UK) – 15 February

Prod Ray Stark
Screenplay Isobel Lennart
DOP Harry Stradling
Editor Maury Winetrobe, William Sands
Music Walter Scharf

STREISAND, Barbra Fanny Brice
SHARIF, Omar Nick Arnstein
MEDFORD, Kay Rose Brice
FRANCIS, Anne Georgia James
PIDGEON, Walter Florenz Ziegfeld
ALLEN, Lee Eddie Ryan
QUESTEL, Mae Mrs. Strakosh
MOHR, Gerald Branca
FAYLEN, Frank Keeney
LAWRENCE, Mittie Emma

Rastar Productions, Columbia Pictures Corporation
147 mins
Monthly Film Bulletin .v36.n422. March 1969 p.48

Box Office: £12,686
Opening weekend £1,352
Screens 2
Screen average £676

* Get Carter

£

Dir Mike Hodges
18 (UK) 1971
bfi Bookings – June

Prod Michael Klinger
Screenplay Mike Hodges
Editor John Trumper
Music Roy Budd

CAINE, Michael Jack Carter
EKLAND, Britt Anna Fletcher
OSBORNE, John Cyril Kinnear
HENDRY, Ian Eric Paice
MOSLEY, Bryan Cliff Brumby
MOFFAT, Geraldine Glenda
WHITE, Dorothy Margaret
ARMSTRONG, Alun Keith
EDWARDS, Glynn Albert Swift
BECKLEY, Tony Peter

Metro-Goldwyn-Mayer
112 mins
Monthly Film Bulletin .v38.n447.April 1971 p.73

The Glass House

Dir Daniel Sackheim
15 (US) 2001
Columbia TriStar Films (UK) – 25 January

Prod Neal H. Moritz
Screenplay Wesley Strick
DOP Alar Kivilo
Editor Howard E. Smith
Music Christopher Young

SOBIESKI, LeeLee Ruby Baker
LANE, Diane Doctor Erin Glass
SKARSGÅRD, Stellan Terry Glass
DERN, Bruce Alvin Begleiter
BAKER, Kathy Nancy Ryan
MORGAN, Trevor Rhett Baker
NOTH, Chris (C) Uncle Jack
O'KEEFE, Michael Dave Baker
WILSON, Rita Grace Baker
O'CONNOR, Gavin Don Whitworth

©2000 Columbia Pictures Industries, Inc.
Columbia Pictures presents an Original Film release
106 mins 11 seconds
Locations – Los Angeles
Sight and Sound .v12.n2.February 2002 p.44

Box Office: £118,674
Opening weekend £69,371
Screens 119
Screen average £583

Gosford Park

$ £

Dir Robert Altman
15 (UK/US) 2001
Entertainment Film Distributors Ltd – 1 February

Prod Robert Altman, Bob Balaban, David Levy
Screenplay Julian Fellowes
DOP Andrew Dunn
Editor Tim Squyres
Music Patrick Doyle

SMITH, Maggie Constance Trentham
GAMBON, Michael William McCordle
SCOTT THOMAS, Kristin Sylvia McCordle
RUTHERFORD, Camilla Isobel McCordle
DANCE, Charles Raymond Stockbridge
SOMERVILLE, Geraldine Louisa Stockbridge
HOLLANDER, Tom Lieutenant Commander Anthony Me
WIGHTMAN, Natasha Lavinia Meredith
NORTHAM, Jeremy Ivor Novello
MACDONALD, Kelly Mary Maceachran
OWEN, Clive Robert Parks
MIRREN, Helen Mrs Wilson
ATKINS, Eileen Mrs Croft
WATSON, Emily Elsie
BATES, Alan Jennings
JACOBI, Derek Probert
GRANT, Richard E. George

SWIFT, Jeremy — Arthur
THOMPSON, Sophie — Dorothy
©2001 Film Council/Zestwick Limited/Sandcastle 5 Productions, Inc
Capitol Films and the Film Council present in association with USA Films
a Sandcastle 5 production in association with Chicagofilms and Medusa Film
136 mins 59 seconds
Studios – Shepperton Studios
Sight and Sound .v12.n2.February 2002 p.45-46

Box Office:	**£12,259,248**
Opening weekend	£837,169
Screens	156
Screen average	£5,366

Goyangireul Butakhae

Dir Jae-eun Jeong
PG (Korea) 2001
Gala Film Distributors – 27 December

Prod — Ki-min Oh
Screenplay — Jae-eun Jeong, Ji-seong Park
DOP — Yeong-hwan Choi
Editor — Hyun-mi Lee
Music — M&F

BAE Doo-na — Yoo Tae-hee
LEE Yo-won — Shin Hae-joo
OK Ji-yeong — Seo Ji-young
LEE Eun-sil — Biryu the twin
LEE Eun-ju — Onjo the twin
OH Tae-kyung — Uhm Chan-yong
KIM Hwa-young
a Masulpiri production
Presented by iPictures, Terasource Venture Capital
in association with Korean Film Commission, Intz.com
111 mins 21 seconds
Subtitles
Sight and Sound.v13.n2.February 2003 p.62,64

Box Office:	**£3,276**
Opening weekend	**£3,276**
Screens	**2**
Screen average	**£1,638**

Grateful Dawg

Dir Gillian Grisman
12 (US) 2000
Columbia TriStar Films (UK) – 13 December

Prod — Gillian Grisman
Editor — Josh Baron
Music — Dave 'dB' Dennison, John Cutler

GARCIA, Jerry — guitar/banjo/vocals
GRISMAN, David — mandolin/banjo
CRAVEN, Joe — percussion/violin
KERWIN, Jim — bass
BLEETSTEIN, Rob — interviewee
CLEMENTS, Vassar — interviewee
CRAVEN, Joe — interviewee
DENNISON, 'dB' Dave — interviewee
FLECK, Bela — interviewee
KOONS GARCIA, Deborah — interviewee
©2000 Acoustic Disc/11th Hour Productions and Entertainment, Inc
Acoustic Disc presents
a film by Gillian Grisman
80 mins
Documentary
Sight and Sound

Box Office:	**£534**
Opening weekend	£294
Screens	1
Screen average	£294

Grégoire Moulin Contre L'Humanité

Dir Artus de Penguern
15 (France) 2001
Millennium Film Distributors – 7 June

Prod — Cyrile Justin-Colbeau, Jean-Baptiste Dupont, Yves Rolland
Screenplay — Artus de Penguern, Jérôme
DOP — Vincent Mathias
Editor — Corinne Cahour, Christophe Marthoud, Claude-France
Music — Benoît Pimont

ARBILLOT, Pascale — Odile Bonheur/Emma i n 'Madame B
VITALI, Elisabeth — Hélène
DULÉRY, Antoine — Emmanuel Lacarrière
BÉNUREAU, Didier — Jean-François
DEGUY, Marie-Armelle — Solange
RIABOUKINE, Serge — taxi driver
BERLAND, François — Gustave, owner of Bar Penalty
CORNILLAC, Clovis — Jacky
MAGNAN, Philippe — Jérôme
ROUBAKHA, Rémy — policeman
©2001 LGM/Litswa/M6 Films/Rhône-Alpes Cinéma/SFP Cinéma
LGM presents
in co-production with M6 Films, Litswa, SFP Cinéma, Rhône-Alpes Cinéma
with the participation of TPS Cinéma, M6, Gimages 4
with the participation of la Région Rhône-Alpes and Centre National de la Cinématographie
a film by Artus de Penguern
90 mins 49 seconds
Sight and Sound .v12.n7.July 2002 p.45

Box Office:	**£1,894**
Opening weekend	**£1,894**
Screens	**2**
Screen average	**£947**

Gunaah

Box Office	**£15,743**
Opening weekend	**£7,150**
Screens	**12**
Screen average	**£596**

The Guru

$ £ €

Dir Daisy von Scherler Mayer
15 (US/Germany/France/UK) 2001
United International Pictures (UK) Ltd – 23 August

Prod — Tim Bevan, Eric Fellner
Screenplay — Tracey Jackson, Shekhar Kapur
DOP — John De Borman
Editor — Cara Silverman, Bruce Green
Music — David Carbonara

GRAHAM, Heather — Sharrona
TOMEI, Marisa — Lexi
MISTRY, Jimi — Ramu Gupta
McKEAN, Michael — Dwain
MIHOK, Dash — Rusty
MARWA, Emil — Vijay
GUTTMAN, Ronald — Edwin
McCOURT, Malachy — Father Flanagan
NAIDU, Ajay — Sanjiv
GILLETTE, Anita — Mrs McGee
©2001 KALIMA Productions GmbH & Co. KG
Universal, Studio Canal and Working Title present
a Working Title production
a Daisy Von Scherler Mayer film
94 mins 43 seconds
Locations – New York
Sight and Sound .v12.n10.October 2002 p.40

Box Office:	**£6,497,236**
Opening weekend	**£1,521,984**
Screens	**368**
Screen average	**£4,136**

Haan maine Bhi Pyar Kiya

Box Office	**£405,108**
Opening weekend	**£27,982**
Screens	**16**
Screen average	**£1,749**

Hable Con Ella

aka: Talk to Her
Dir Pedro Almodóvar
15 (Spain) 2002
Pathé Distribution – 23 August

Screenplay — Pedro Almodóvar

DOP	Javier Aguirresarobe
Editor	José Salcedo
Music	Alberto Iglesias
CÁMARA, Javier	Benigno
GRANDINETTI, Darío	Marco Zuloaga
WATLING, Leonor	Alicia
FLORES, Rosario	Lydia
FUENTES, Mariola	Nurse Rosa
CHAPLIN, Geraldine	Katerina Bilova
BAUSCH, Pina	"Cafe Müller" ballet dancer
AIRAUDO, Malou	"Cafe Müller" ballet dancer
ÁLVAREZ, Roberto	doctor
ANAYA, Elena	Angela

©2001 ©2002 El Deseo S.A.
El Deseo S.A. presents
with the participation of A3TV and Vía Digital
a production of El Deseo S.A.
a film by Almodóvar
112 mins 59 seconds
Locations – Paris, Marid
Sight and Sound .v12.n7.July 2002 p.24-27

Box Office:	**£1,461,569**
Opening weekend	**£174,757**
Screens	**57**
Screen average	**£3,066**

Hahesder

aka: Time of Favor
Dir Joseph Cedar
12 (Israel) 2001
Blue Dolphin Film & Video – 2 August

Prod	David Mandil, Eyal Shiray
Screenplay	Joseph Cedar
DOP	Ofer Inov
Editor	Tova Asher
Music	Yonatan Bar-Giora
AVNI, Aki	Menachem
TINKERBELL	Michal Meltzer
ALTERMAN, Edan	Pini
DAYAN, Assi	Rabbi Meltzer
SELEKTAR, Micha	Itamar
WOLF, Amnon	Mookie
MIMRAM, Shimon	Benny
KLAUSNER, Uri (C)	Sivan
KALDERON, Shemuel	Doron

©2001Hahesder Ltd
Cinema Factory, Israel Film Fund, Yes present
a film by Joseph Cedar
102 mins 10 seconds
Sight and Sound .v12.n9.September 2002 p.78

Box Office:	**£15,276**
Opening weekend	**£6,637**
Screens	**1**
Screen average	**£6,637**

Halloween Resurrection

Dir Rick Rosenthal
15 (US) 2001
Buena Vista International (UK) – 25 October

Prod	Paul Freeman
Screenplay	Larry Brand, Sean Hood
DOP	David Geddes
Editor	Robert A. Ferretti
Music	Danny Lux
RHYMES, Busta (C)	Freddie Harris
KAJLICH, Bianca	Sara Moyer
NICHOLAS, Thomas Ian	Bill Woodlake
MERRIMAN, Ryan	Myles Barton
McCRACKIN, Daisy	Donna Chang
SACKHOFF, Katee	Jen Danzig
KAY, Billy	Scott
KIRBY, Luke	Jim Morgan
THOMAS, Sean Patrick	Rudy Grimes
BANKS, Tyra	Nora Winston

©2002 Miramax Film Corp.
a Dimension Films release
Moustapha Akkad presents
a Nightfall production of a Rick Rosenthal film
89 mins 22 seconds
Locations – Vancouver
Sight and Sound .v12.n11.November 2002 p.44,46

Box Office:	**£1,364,212**
Opening weekend	**£520,171**
Screens	**319**
Screen average	**£1,631**

Happy Man

Aka: Szczesliwy Czlowiek
Dir Malgorzata Szumowska
(Poland) 2000
NFT – 31 May

Prod	Jerzy Wojciech Has
Screenplay	Malgorzata Szumowska
DOP	Marek Gajczak, Michal Englert
Editor	Jacek Drosio
Music	Zygmunt Konieczny
JANKOWSKA-CIESLAK, Jadwiga	the mother
HAJEWSKA-KRZYSZTOFIK, Malgorzata	Marta
JANKOWSKI, Piotr	Jan
GANCARCZYK, Roman	Rudy
GRABKA, Mieczyslaw	Rajmund
HUDZIAK, Andrzej	.
KALETA, Zbigniew	.
KOZIKOWSKA, Beata	.
KOMOROWSKA, Elzbieta	

Metro-Goldwyn-Mayer
86 minutes
No Sight and Sound Reference

Box Office:	**£3,287**

Hardball

Dir Brian Robbins
PG (US/Germany) 2001
United International Pictures (UK) Ltd – 21 June 2002

Prod	Tina Nides, Mike Tollin, Brian Robbins
Screenplay	John Gatins
DOP	Tom Richmond
Editor	Ned Bastille
Music	Mark Isham
REEVES, Keanu	Conor O'Neill
LANE, Diane	Elizabeth Wilkes
HAWKES, John	Ticky Tobin
SWEENEY, D.B.	Matt Hyland
McGLONE, Mike	Jimmy Fleming
BRIM, Sterling	Sterling
ELLIS Jr, A. Delon	Miles Pennfield II
GRIFFITH, Julian	Jefferson Albert Tibbs
HEARNE, Bryan C.	Andre Ray Peters
JORDAN, Michael	Jamal

©2001 MFP Munich Film Partners GmbH & Co. GHS Productions KG
Paramount Pictures presents in association with
Fireworks Pictures
a Nides/McCormick production
a Tollin/Robbins production
106 mins 9 seconds
Locations – Chicago
Sight and Sound.v12.n6.June 2002 p.43–4

Box Office:	**£166,290**
Opening weekend	**£79,864**
Screens	**106**
Screen average	**£753**

Harry Potter and the Chamber of Secrets

$ £ €
Dir Chris Columbus
PG (US/UK/Germany) 2002
Warner Bros Distributors (UK) – 15 November

Prod	David Heyman
Screenplay	Steve Kloves
DOP	Roger Pratt
Editor	Peter Honess
Music	John Williams
RADCLIFFE, Daniel	Harry Potter
GRINT, Rupert	Ron Weasley
WATSON, Emma	Hermione Granger
BRANAGH, Kenneth	Gilderoy Lockhart
CLEESE, John	Sir Nicholas, 'Nearly Headless
COLTRANE, Robbie	Rubeus Hagrid
DAVIS, Warwick	Professor Flitwick
GRIFFITHS, Richard	Uncle Vernon Dursley
HARRIS, Richard	Albus Dumbledore
ISAACS, Jason	Lucius Malfoy

©2002 MIRACLE Productions GmbH & Co. KG
Warner Bros. Pictures presents a Heyday Films/1492 Pictures production a Chris Columbus film
160m 40 seconds
Locations/Studios
Sight and Sound .v13.n1.January 2003 p.47-49

Box Office:	**£54,138,718**
Opening weekend	**£18,871,829**
Screens	**524**
Screen average	**£36,015**

Hart's War

Dir Gregory Hoblit
15 (US) 2001
20th Century Fox International (UK) – 24 May

Prod	David Ladd, David Foster, Gregory Hoblit, Arnold Rifkin
Screenplay	Billy Ray, Terry George, Jeb Stuart
DOP	Alar Kivilo
Editor	David Rosenbloom
Music	Rachel Portman
WILLIS, Bruce	Colonel William A. McNamara
FARRELL, Colin	Lieutenant Thomas W. Hart
HOWARD, Terrence	Lieutenant Lincoln A. Scott
HAUSER, Cole	Staff Sergeant Vic W. Bedford
IURES, Marcel	Colonel Werner Visser
ROACHE, Linus	Captain Peter A. Ross
COCHRANE, Rory	Sergeant Carl S. Webb
WESTON, Michael	Pfc W. Roy Potts
SHANNON, Vicellous (C)	Lieutenant Lamar T. Archer
CAMPBELL, Scott Michael	Corporal Joe S. Cromin

©2001 Metro-Goldwyn-Mayer Pictures Inc
Metro-Goldwyn-Mayer Pictures presents
a David Ladd Films, David Foster Productions, Cheyenne Enterprises production
a Gregory Hoblit film
125 mins 7 seconds
Locations – Prague
Sight and Sound .v12.n5.May 2002 p.45-46

Box Office:	**£300,136**
Opening weekend	**£129,484**
Screens	**170**
Screen average	**£762**

Hathyar

Box Office	**£46,108**
Opening weekend	**£20,574**
Screens	**9**
Screen average	**£2,286**

Hatouna Mehuheret

aka: Late Marriage
Dir Dover Kosashivili
1 (Israel/France) 2001
Distrib – 18 January

Prod	Marek Rozenbaum
Screenplay	Dover Kosashvili
DOP	Dani Schneor
Editor	Yael Perlov
Music	Joesph Bardanashvili
ASHKENAZI, Lior	Louie Zaza
ELKABETZ, Ronit	Judith
MOSHONOV, Moni	Yasha
KOSASHVILI, Lili	Lili
STEINOVITS LAOR, Aya	Ilana
CAMBOS, Rozina	Magouly
CHEN, Simon	Simon
KUGMAN, Sapir	Madona
DORON, Dina	Luba
KANEVSKI, Leonid	Otary

©2001Transfax Film Production/Arte France Cinéma/Morgane Production
Transfax Film Production, Morgane Production, Israel Film Fund, Keshet Broadcasting, Arte France Cinéma with the support of The Fund for the Promotion of Israeli Films, Le Centre National de la Cinématographie present
100 mins seconds
Locations/Studios
Sight and Sound .v12.n3.March 2002 p.48-49

Box Office:	**£21,813**

Hearts in Atlantis

Dir Scott Hicks
12 (US/Australia) 2001
Buena Vista International (UK) – 8 March

Prod	Kerry Heysen
Screenplay	William Goldman
DOP	Piotr Sobocinski
Editor	Pip Karmel
Music	Mychael Danna
HOPKINS, Anthony	Ted Brautigan
YELCHIN, Anton	Bobby Garfield
DAVIS, Hope	Liz Garfield
BOOREM, Mika	Carol Gerber
MORSE, David	adult Bobby Garfield
TUDYK, Alan	Monte man
BOWER, Tom	Len Files
WESTON, Celia	Alanna Files
LeFEVRE, Adam	Don Biderman
ROTHHAAR, Will	Sully-John

©2001 Village Roadshow Films (BVI) Limited (All other territories)
Castle Rock Entertainment presents in association with Village Roadshow Pictures and NPV Entertainment
a Scott Hicks film100 mins 52 seconds
Locations – Richmond, Virginia
Sight and Sound .v12.n3.March 2002 p.46

Box Office:	**£282,685**
Opening weekend	**£110,793**
Screens	**146**
Screen average	**£759**

Heaven

Dir Tom Tykwer
15 (Germany/US/France) 2001
Buena Vista International (UK) – 9 August

Prod	Anthony Minghella, William Horberg, Maria Köpf, Stefan Arndt, Frédérique Dumas
Screenplay	Krzysztof Kieslowski, Krzystof Piersiewicz
DOP	Frank Griebe
Editor	Mathilde Bonnefoy
BLANCHETT, Cate	Philippa
RIBISI, Giovanni	Filippo
GIRONE, Remo	Filippo's father
SBRAGIA, Mattia	Maggiore Pini
Di STASIO, Alberto	the public prosecutor
SANTOSPAGO, Stefano	Marco Vendice
SPERDUTI, Alessandro	Ariel
VETTORAZZO, Giovanni	the inspector
BARRA, Gianfranco	the lieutenant
RIOTTA, Vincent (C)	chief guard

©2001 created by Miramax Film Corp/X Filme Creative Pool
95 mins
Sight and Sound .v12.n8.August 2002 p.34-35,39-40

Box Office:	**£233,690**
Opening weekend	**£78,207**
Screens	**39**
Screen average	**£2,005**

Heftig & Begeistret

aka: Cool and Crazy
Dir Knut Erik Jensen
15 (Nowary/Sweden/Finland) 2000
Artificial Eye Film Company – 8 February

Prod	Tom Remlov, Jan-Erik Gammleng
Editor	Aslaug Holm
Berlevåg Mannsangforening	themselves

©2000 Norsk Film AS
Norsk Film AS and Barentsfilm AS

present
a film by Knut Erik Jensen
104 mins 41 seconds
Documentary
Subtitles
Sight and Sound .v12.n2.February 2002 p.42-43
Box Office: **£63,527**
Opening weekend **£6,446**
Screens **2**
Screen average **£3,223**

Hey Arnold! The Movie

Dir Tuck Tucker
U (US) 2001
United International Pictures (UK) Ltd – 20 December
Prod Albie Hecht, Craig Bartlett
Screenplay Craig Bartlett, Steve Viksten
Editor Christopher Hink
Music Jim Lang
KLEIN, Spencer voice of Arnold
SMITH, Francesca Marie (C) voice of Helga/deep voice
SMITH, Francesca Marie (C) voice of Helga/deep voice
CASTELLANETA, Dan voice of grandpa/Nick Vermicell
MacNEILLE, Tress voice of grandma/Mayor Dixie/Re
SORVINO, Paul voice of Scheck
LEIGH, Jennifer Jason voice of Bridget
LLOYD, Christopher voice of coroner
SCHIAVELLI, Vincent voice of Mr Bailey
LaMARCHE, Maurice voice of Big Bob/head of security
©2002 Paramount Pictures/Viacom International Inc
Paramount Pictures and Nickelodeon Movies present
a Snee-Oosh production in association with Nickelodeon Studios
75 mins 53 seconds
Animation
Sight and Sound .v13.n2.February 2003 p.45-46
Box Office: **£113,047*** **£358,812****
Opening weekend £35,881
Screens 152
Screen average £236
*(*total box office in 2002)*
*(** cumulative box office for 2002/03)*

High Crimes

Dir Carl Franklin
12 (US) 2002
20th Century Fox International (UK) – 25 October
Prod Arnon Milchan, Janet Yang, Jesse B'Franklin
Screenplay Yuri Zeltser, Cary Bickley
DOP Theo van de Sande
Editor Carole Kravetz-Aykanian
Music Graeme Revell
JUDD, Ashley Claire Kubik
FREEMAN, Morgan Charlie Grimes
CAVIEZEL, Jim (C) Tom Kubik', Ronald Chapman
SCOTT, Adam Lieutenant Embry
PEET, Amanda Jackie
DAVISON, Bruce Brigadier General Marks
BOWER, Tom Mullins
HERNÁNDEZ, Juan Carlos Major Hernández
GASTON, Michael Major Waldron
CICCOLELLA, Jude Colonel Farrell
©2002 Twentieth Century Fox Film Corporation/Monarchy Enterprises S.a.r.l./
Regency Entertainment (USA), Inc.
Twentieth Century Fox and Regency Enterprises present
a New Regency/Manifest Film Company/Monarch Pictures production
[end]
In association with Epsilon Motion Pictures
115 mins 3 seconds
Locations – Abilene, San Francisco, Los Angeles
Sight and Sound .v12.n11.November 2002 p.46-47
Box Office: **£404,425**
Opening weekend **£208,727**
Screens **241**
Screen average **£866**

* High Society

Dir Charles Walters
(US) 1956
bfi Bookings – 31 May
Prod Sol C. Siegel
Screenplay John Patrick
DOP Paul C. Vogel
Editor Ralph E. Winters
Music Cole Porter
CROSBY, Bing C.K. Dexter-Haven
KELLY, Grace Tracy Samantha Lord
SINATRA, Frank Mike Connor
HOLM, Celeste Liz Imbrie
LUND, John George Kittredge
CALHERN, Louis Uncle Willie
BLACKMER, Sidney Seth Lord
ARMSTRONG, Louis himself
GILLMORE, Margalo Mrs Seth Lord
REED, Lydia Caroline Lord
Metro-Goldwyn-Mayer
106 minutes
Monthly Film Bulletin .v23.n275.December 1956 p.150
Box Office: **£48,277**
Opening weekend **£5,277**
Screens **3**
Screen average **£1,759**

Hijack Stories

£ €
Dir Oliver Schmitz
(Germany/UK/France) 2000
Momentum Pictures – 19 July
Prod Christoph Meyer-Wiel
Screenplay Oliver Schmitz
DOP Michael Amathieu
Editor Oliver Schmitz
Music Martin Todsharow
KGOROGE, Tony Sox
SEIPHEMO, Rapulana Zama
MATSEMELA, Percy Fly
NDEBELE, Makhaola Joe
MOTSHEGWA, Moshidi Grace
McARTHUR, Emily Nicky
SEIAKE, Owen Dan
MATLHABO, Harold 'Speedy' Kenneth
LAMOLA, George Steve
WHITEHEAD, Robert casting director
©2000 Schlemmer Film GmbH/Xenos Pictures Limited
Christoph Meyer-Wiel and Philippe Guez present
a Schlemmer Film, Septième Production in co-production with Xenos Pictures and Paradis Films
With the participation of Deutsche Bank, British Screen and BSkyB, FilmBüro NW
Script development funded by Department of Arts Culture Science and
Technology (DACST)
94 mins
Johannesburg, Soweto
Sight and Sound .v11.n5.May 2001 p.51
Box Office: **£4,015**
Opening weekend **£1,739**
Screens **3**
Screen average **£580**

Une Hirondelle a fait Le Printemps

aka: Girl From Paris
Dir Christian Carion
15 (France/Belgium) 2001
Artificial Eye Film Company – 26 July
Prod Christophe Rossignon

Screenplay Christian Carion, Éric Assous
DOP Antoine Héberlé
Editor Andréa Sedlacková
Music Philippe Rombi

SERRAULT, Michel Adrien Rochas
SEIGNER, Mathilde Sandrine Dumez
ROUSSILLON, Jean-Paul Jean Farjon
PIERROT, Frédéric Gérard Chauvin
BERMAN, Marc Stéphane
BETTE, Françoise Sandrine's mother
ROSSIGNON, Christophe business farmer
CHALOSSE, Roland barman
VARAS dell'AQUILA, Achiles Francisc barfly
PASQUALE, Henri card player 1

©2001 Nord-Ouest Productions/StudioCanal France/Artémis Productions/Rhône-Alpes Cinéma/Mars Films
Nord-Ouest presents in co-production with StudioCanal, Artémis Productions, Rhône-Alpes Cinéma, Mars Films, M.S. Productions
with the participation of Canal+, Cofimage 12, La Région Rhône-Alpes
with the support of La Fondation Gan pour le Cinéma, La Procirep in association with Lazennec
103 mins 9 seconds
Locations – Paris, Vercos
Sight and Sound .v12.n7.July 2002 p.44

Box Office: **£1126,183**
Opening weekend **£11,629**
Screens **7**
Screen average **£1,661**

Hotel

£ €
Dir Mike Figgis
(UK/IT) 2001
ICA Projects – 5 April

Prod Annie Stewart, Mike Figgis, Etchie Stroh
Screenplay Heathcote Williams
DOP Patrick Alexander Stewart
Editor Adam Barton
Music Mike Figgis, Anthony Marinelli

BEESLEY, Max Antonio
BENTIVOGLIO, Fabrizio very important doctor
BOVELL, Brian cardinal
BURROWS, Saffron Duchess of Malfi
CAVALLOTTI, Elisabetta abducted hotel guest
CERVI, Valentina hotel maid
DiCENZO, George Boris
DI STEFANO, Andrea assassin
FARRON, Nicola hotel guest
FULFORD, Christopher Steve Hawk

©2001 Hotel Productions Limited
Moonstone Entertainment Inc presents
a United Kingdom/Italy co-production
Co-produced by Hotel Productions Limited and Cattleya Srl
a Red Mullet film
109 mins
Locations – Venice
Sight and Sound .v12.n5.May 2002 p.46

Box Office: **£4,963**

How Harry Became A Tree

Box Office £38,674
Opening weekend **£969**
Screens **1**
Screen average **£969**

Huit Femmes

aka: 8 Women
Dir François Ozon
(France/Italy) 2001
UGC Films UK – 29 November

Prod Olivier Delbosc, Marc Missonnier
Screenplay François Ozon, Marina de Van
DOP Jeanne Lapoirie
Editor Laurence Bawdin
Music

DARRIEUX, Danielle Mamy
DENEUVE, Catherine Gaby
HUPPERT, Isabelle Augustine
BÉART, Emmanuelle Louise
ARDANT, Fanny Pierrette
LEDOYEN, Virginie Suzon
SAGNIER, Ludivine Catherine
RICHARD, Firmine Madame Chanel
LAMURE, Dominique Marcel

©2001 Fidélité Productions/Mars Films/France 2 Cinéma
Fidélité Productions presents in co-production with
France 2 Cinéma, Mars Films in association with
Gimages 5, BIM Distribuzione
with the participation of Canal+ and Centre National de la Cinématographie
a film by François Ozon
103 mins
Sight and Sound .v12.n12.December 2002 p.46

Box Office: **£523,470**
Opening weekend **£113,126**
Screens **40**
Screen average **£2,828**

Hum Hain Pyaar Mein

Box Office £4,259
Opening weekend **£3,331**
Screens **5**
Screen average **£666**

Hum Kisi Se Kum Nahi

Box Office **£170,625**
Opening weekend **£68,968**
Screens **22**
Screen average **£3,135**

Hum Pyar Tumhi Se Kar Baithe

Box Office £10,943
Opening weekend **£5,020**
Screens **7**
Screen average **£717**

Hum Tumhare Hain Sanam

Box Office **£671,215**
Opening weekend **£241,110**
Screens **28**
Screen average **£8,611**

Humraaz

Box Office **£97,660**
Opening weekend **£47,095**
Screens **24**
Screen average **£1,962**

Hundstage

aka: Dog Days
Dir Ulrich Seidl
18 (Austria/Germany) 2001
Metro Tartan Distributors – 6 September

Prod Helmut Grasser, Philippe Bober
Screenplay Ulrich Seidl, Veronika Franz
DOP Wolfgang Thaler
Editor Andrea Wagner, Christof Schertenleib

HOFSTÄTTER, Maria Anna, the hitch-hiker
MRVA, Alfred Hruby, the alarm systems man
FINSCHES, Erich Walter, the old man
LEHNER, Gerti Walter's housekeeper
WEIß, Franziska Klaudia, the young girl
WANKO, Rene Mario, Klaudia's boyfriend
MARTINI, Claudia the ex-wife
RATHBONE, Victor the ex-husband
BAKONYI, Christian the masseur
JIRKU, Christine the teacher

©2001 Allegrofilm
The Coproduction Office presents
an Allegro Film produktion
a film by Ulrich Seidl
127mins 10 seconds

Locations – Vienna
Sight and Sound .v12.n9.September 2002 p.52-53,58,60
Box Office: £14,568
Opening weekend £2,791
Screens 2
Screen average £1,396

I am Sam

Dir Jessie Nelson
12 (US/Germany) 2001
Entertainment Film Distributors Ltd – 10 May

Prod	Jessie Nelson, Richard Solomon, Marshall Herskovitz, Edward Zwick
Screenplay	Kristine Johnson, Jessie Nelson
DOP	Elliot Davis
Editor	Richard Chew
Music	John Powell
PENN, Sean	Sam Dawson
PFEIFFER, Michelle	Rita Harrison
WIEST, Dianne	Annie Cassell
FANNING, Dakota	Lucy Diamond Dawson
SCHIFF, Richard	Turner
DEVINE, Loretta	Margaret Calgrove
HUTCHISON, Doug	Ifty
DERN, Laura	Randy Carpenter
DeSANTIS, Stanley	Robert
CHAO, Rosalind	Lily

©2001 "Sam" Filmproductions GmbH & Co. KG
New Line Cinema presents
a Bedford Falls Company/Red Fish, Blue Fish Films production
132 mins 9 seconds
Locations – Los Angeles
Sight and Sound .v12.n4.April 2002 p.45-46
Box Office: £519,421
Opening weekend £151,079
Screens 121
Screen average £1,249

Ice Age

Dir Chris Wedge
U (US) 2001
20th Century Fox International (UK) – 22 March

Prod	Lori Forte
Screenplay	Michael J. Wilson, Peter Ackerman
Editor	John Carnochan
Music	David Newman
ROMANO, Ray	voice of Manfred
LEGUIZAMO, John	voice of Sid
LEARY, Denis	voice of Diego
VISNJIC, Goran	oice of Soto
BLACK, Jack	voice of Zeke
STRONG, Tara (C)	voice of Roshan
Cedric 'The Entertainer'	voice of rhinos
ROOT, Stephen	voice of rhinos
BADER, Diedrich	voice of sabre-tooth tigers
TUDYK, Alan	voice of sabre-tooth tigers

©2001 Twentieth Century Fox Film Corporation
Twentieth Century Fox presents
a Blue Sky production
81 mins 1 seconds
Sight and Sound .v12.n5.May 2002 p.47
Box Office: £15,058,648
Opening weekend £3,029,738
Screens 423
Screen average £7,163

* If....

£
Dir Lindsay Anderson
(UK) 1968
bfi Bookings – 1 March

Prod	Michael Medwin, Lindsay Anderson
Screenplay	David Sherwin
DOP	Miroslav Ondrícek
Editor	David Gladwell
Music	Marc Wilkinson
McDOWELL, Malcolm	Mick Travers (Crusaders)
WOOD, David	Johnny (Crusaders)
WARWICK, Richard	Wallace (Crusaders)
NOONAN, Christine	The Girl (Crusaders)
WEBSTER, Rupert	Bobby Philips (Crusaders)
SWANN, Robert	Rowntree (Whips)
THOMAS, Hugh	Denson (Whips)
CADMAN, Michael	Fortinbras (Whips)
SPROULE, Peter	Barnes (Whips)
JEFFREY, Peter	Headmaster (Staff)

©1968 Memorial Enterprises, Paramount Pictures Corporation
111 mins
Locations – Cheltenham College
Monthly Film Bulletin.v36.n421.February 1969 p.2
Box Office: £19,090
Opening weekend £3,921
Screens 2
Screen average £1,961

Ikingut

Dir Gisli Snær Erlingsson
U (Iceland/Norway/Denmark) 2001
NFT – 6 September

Prod	Fridrik Thór Fridriksson
Screenplay	Jón Steinar Ragnarsson
DOP	Sigurdur Sverrir Pálsson
Editor	Sigvaldi J. Kárason, Skule Eriksen
Music	Vilhjálmur Gudjónsson

JÓNSSON, Hjalti Rúnar
NAKINGE, Hans Titus
GESTSSON, Palmi
RAGNARSSON, Magnús
KRISTOFERSDOTTIR, Freydis
GUDMUNDSSON, Finnur
ÓLAFSDÓTTIR, Elva Osk
EINARSSON, Pétur
JÓNSDÓTTIR, Sigurveig
HANSSON, Gunnar
an Icelandic Film Corp. production, in association with Filmhuset and Zentropa Prods.
international sales: La Fete, Montreal
85 mins
No reference
Box Office: £1,061

The Importance of Being Earnest

$ £
Dir Oliver Parker
U (US/UK) 2001
Buena Vista International (UK) – 6 September

Prod	Barnaby Thompson
Screenplay	Oliver Parker
DOP	Tony Pierce-Roberts
Editor	Guy Bensley
Music	Charlie Mole
EVERETT, Rupert	Algy
FIRTH, Colin	Jack
O'CONNOR, Frances	Gwendolen
WITHERSPOON, Reese	Cecily
DENCH, Judi	Lady Bracknell
WILKINSON, Tom	Dr Chasuble
MASSEY, Anna	Miss Prism
FOX, Edward	Lane
GODFREY, Patrick	Merriman
KAY, Charles	Gribsby

©2001 Important Films Limited/The Film Council
Miramax Films and Ealing Studios present in association with the Film Council and Newmarket Capital Group
a Fragile film
97 mins 52 seconds
Locations – London
Studios – Ealing
Sight and Sound .v12.n9.September 2002 p.61-62
Box Office: £3,519,574
Opening weekend £554,413
Screens 215
Screen average £2,579

Impostor

Dir Gary Fleder
15 (US) 2001
Metrodome Distribution Ltd – 14 June

Prod Marty Katz, Daniel Lupi, Gary Fleder, Gary Sinise
Screenplay Caroline Case, Ehren Kruger, David Twhohy, Mark Protosevich
DOP Robert Elswit
Editor Armen Minasian, Bob Ducsay
Music Mark Isham

SINISE, Gary Spence Olham
STOWE, Madeleine Maya Olham
D'ONOFRIO, Vincent Major Hathaway
SHALHOUB, Tony Nelson Gittes
GUINEE, Tim Doctor Carone
PEÑA, Elizabeth midwife
DOURDAN, Gary Captain Burke
CROUSE, Lindsay chancellor
PHIFER, Mekhi Cale
BECK, Jason gang boy 2

©2001 Miramax International/Dimension Films presents
a Marty Katz production
In association with Mojo Films
a Gary Fleder film

95 mins 30 seconds
Locations – Los Angeles, Eagle Mountain, Phoenix, Arizona
Sight and Sound .v12.n8.August 2002 p.40-41

Box Office: **£46,556**
Opening weekend **£23,177**
Screens **65**
Screen average **£357**

In the Bedroom

Dir Todd Field
15 (US) 2001
Buena Vista International (UK) – 25 January

Prod Graham Leader, Ross Katz, Todd Field
Screenplay Bob Festinger, Todd Field
DOP Antonio Calvache
Editor Frank Reynolds
Music Thomas Newman

SPACEK, Sissy Ruth Fowler
WILKINSON, Tom Matt Fowler
STAHL, Nick Frank Fowler
MAPOTHER, William Richard Strout
WISE, William Willis Grinnel
WESTON, Celia Katie Grinnel
TOMEI, Marisa Natalie Strout
ALLEN, Karen Marla Keyes
WELLS, Frank T. Henry
MURRAY, W. Clapham Carl

©2001 GreeneStreet Films LLC
Miramax Films and GreeneStreet Films present
Good Machine production
a film by Todd Field

130 mins 57 seconds
Locations – Knox County, Maine, Lincoln County, Maine
Sight and Sound .v12.n1.January 2002 p.44-45

Box Office: **£916,686**
Opening weekend **£87,294**
Screens **16**
Screen average **£5,456**

Insomnia

Dir Christopher Nolan
15 (US) 2001
Buena Vista International (UK) – 30 August

Prod Paul Junger Witt, Edward L. McDonnell, Broderick Johnson, Andrew A. Kosove
Screenplay Hilary Seitz
DOP Wally Pfister
Editor Dody Dorn
Music David Julyan

PACINO, Al Will Dormer
WILLIAMS, Robin Walter Finch
SWANK, Hilary Ellie Burr
TIERNEY, Maura Rachel Clement
DONOVAN, Martin Hap Eckhart
KATT, Nicky Fred Duggar
JACKSON, Jonathan Randy Stetz
DOOLEY, Paul Chief Charles Nyback
ZEMEN, Oliver 'Ole' pilot
HOLDEN, Larry Farrell

©2002 Insomnia Productions L.P.
Alcon Entertainment presents
a Witt/Thomas Section Eight production

118 mins
Locations – Vancouver, Squamish, Stewart, Port Alberni, Alaska
Sight and Sound .v12.n9.September 2002 p.62,64

Box Office: **£5,208,171**
Opening weekend **£1,159,754**
Screens **264**
Screen average **£4,393**

Invincible

$ £ €

Dir Werner Herzog
12 (Germany/Ireland/UK/US) 2001
FilmFour Distributors – 29 March

Prod Jim Lemley
Screenplay Michael Brant, Derek Haas, Jefery Levi
DOP John Stokes
Editor Keith Salmon
Music Rupert Parkes

ROTH, Tim Erik Jan Hanussen
AHOLA, Jouko Zishe Breitbart
GOURARI, Anna Marta Farra
RAABE, Max master of ceremonies
WEIN, Jacob Benjamin Breitbart
WÖHLER, Gustav Peter (C) Alfred Landwehr
KIER, Udo Count Helldorf
GOLDER, Herbert Rabbi Edelmann
BART, Gary Yitzak Breitbart
KRÖßNER, Renate Mother Breibart

©2001 Werner Herzog Filmproduktion/Tatfilm/Little Bird/FilmFour
FilmFour presents a Werner Herzog Filmproduktion/Tatfilm production in association with Little Bird and Jan Bart Productions

132 mins 56 seconds
Sight and Sound .v12.n4.April 2002 p.38-39,46

Box Office: **£13,572**
Opening weekend **£4,761**
Screens **12**
Screen average **£397**

Iris

$ £

Dir Richard Eyre
15 (UK/US) 2001
Buena Vista International (UK) – 18 January

Prod Robert Fox, Scott Rudin
Screenplay Richard Eyre, Charles Wood
DOP Roger Pratt
Editor Martin Walsh
Music James Horner

DENCH, Judi Iris Murdoch
BROADBENT, Jim John Bayley
WINSLET, Kate young Iris Murdoch
BONNEVILLE, Hugh young John Bayley
WILTON, Penelope Janet Stone
AUBREY, Juliet young Janet Stone
BRON, Eleanor principal
MORANT, Angela hostess
HAYES, Siobhan check-out girl
BAKEWELL, Joan BBC presenter

©2001 Fox Iris Productions Limited/Intermedia Film Equities Limited/
BBC Films
Intermedia Films, BBC Films, Miramax Films present
a Mirage Enterprises/Robert Fox/Scott Rudin production of a Richard Eyre film

90 mins 34 seconds
Locations – London, Oxford, Southwold, Suffolk
Studios – Pinewood Studios
Sight and Sound .v12.n2.February 2002 p.46-47

Box Office:	**£4,226,477**
Opening weekend	**£378,749**
Screens	**84**
Screen average	**£4,509**

ivansxtc.

Dir Bernard Rose
18 (US)
(1999)
Metro Tartan Distributors – 19 July

Prod	Lisa Enos
Screenplay	Bernard Rose, Lisa Enos
DOP	Bernard Rose, Ron Forsythe
Editor	Bernard Rose
HUSTON, Danny	Ivan Beckman
WELLER, Peter	Don West
ENOS, Lisa	Charlotte White
DUCKMAN, Joanne	Marcia Beckman
FEATHERSTONE, Angela	Amanda Hill
FEENEY, Caroline (C)	Rosemary Kramer
GOLINO, Valeria	Constanza Veo
KRENTZMAN, Adam	Barry Oaks
MARKEL, Heidi Jo	Francesca Knight
MERENDINO, James	Danny McTeague

©1999 Two Lobsters Inc
Rhino Films presents
an Enos/Rose production in association with
Alternative Investments of Michigan
92 mins 39 seconds
Sight and Sound .v12.n8.August 2002 p.41-42

Box Office:	**£140,341**
Opening weekend	**£17,415**
Screens	**6**
Screen average	**£2,903**

Italiensk For Begyndere

Dir Lone Scherfig
15 (Germany) 2001
Pathé Distribution – 26 April

Prod	Ib Tardini
Screenplay	Lone Scherfig
DOP	Jørgen Johansson
Editor	Gerd Tjur
BERTHELSEN, Anders W. (C)	Andreas
STØVELBÆK, Anette	Olympia
JØRGENSEN, Ann Eleonora	Karen
GANTZLER, Peter	Jørgen Mortensen
KAALUND, Lars	Hal-Finn
JENSEN, Sara Indrio	Giulia
MYNSTER, Karen-Lise	Kirsten, bank official
WÖLCK, Rikke	nurse
STEENTOFT, Elsebeth	verger
MEJDING, Bent	Reverend Wredmann

©2001 Zentropa Entertainment
Zentropa Entertainments6 presents
DOGME XII
with support from DR (Marianne Moritzen) and the Danish Film Institute (Vinca Wiedemann, Gert Duve Skovlund)
112 mins 9 seconds
Subtitles
Sight and Sound .v12.n4.April 2002 p.47

Box Office:	**£374,324**
Opening weekend	**£58,479**
Screens	**24**
Screen average	**£2,437**

Jaani Dushman-Ek Anokhi Kahani

Box Office	**£29,218**
Opening weekend	**£12,166**
Screens	**11**
Screen average	**£1,106**

Jason X

Dir James Issac
15 (US) 2000
Entertainment Film Distributors Ltd – 19 July

Prod	Noel Cunningham
Screenplay	Todd Farmer
DOP	Derek Underschultz
Editor	David Handman
Music	Harry Manfredini
DOIG, Lexa	Rowan
RYDER, Lisa	KAY-EM 14
CAMPBELL, Chuck	Tsunaron
POTTS, Jonathan	Professor Lowe
MENSAH, Peter	Sergeant Brodski
ADE, Melyssa	Janessa
JOHNSON, Melody	Kinsa
WILLIAMS, Philip	Crutch
JORDAN, Derwin	Waylander
TIEFENBACH, Dov	Azrael

©2000 New Line Productions Inc
[logos] New Line Cinema/Crystal Lake
New Line Cinema presents
a Sean S. Cunningham production
a Jim Isaac film91 mins 34 seconds
Locations – Toronto
Sight and Sound .v12.n8.August 2002 p.42

Box Office:	**£480,031**
Opening weekend	**£233,090**
Screens	**155**
Screen average	**£1,504**

Jee Aayan Nu

Box Office	**£38,061**
Opening weekend	**£10,227**
Screens	**11**
Screen average	**£930**

Jeena Sirf Merre Liye

Box Office	**£105,779**
Opening weekend	**£41,704**
Screens	**15**
Screen average	**£2,780**

Jian Gui

Dir Danny Pang
15 (Hong Kong/S) 2002
Metro Tartan Distributors – 27 September

Prod	Lawrence Cheng
Screenplay	Jojo Hui, Pang Brothers,
DOP	Decha Srimantra
Editor	Pang Brothers
LEE Sin-Je (C)	Wong Ka-Man
CHOU, Lawrence	Lo Wah
RUJINANON, Chutcha	Chiu Wai-Ling
LO, Candy	Mun's sister
PNG, Pierre	Dr Eak
CHEN, Edmund	Dr Lo
SO Yut-Lai	Ying Ying
KO Yin-Ping	Mun's grandmother
WANG Sue-Yuen	Ling's mother
YUEN, Ben	Mr Ching

©2002 Applause Pictures/Raintree Pictures present
an Applause Pictures production
99 mins 17 seconds
Sight and Sound .v12.n11.November 2002 p.43-44

Box Office:	**£125,211**
Opening weekend	**£21,389**
Screens	**12**
Screen average	**£1,782**

Jimmy Neutron Boy Genius

Dir John A. Davis
U (US) 2001
United International Pictures (UK) Ltd – 22 March

Prod	Steve Oedekerk, John A. Davis, Albie Hecht
Screenplay	John A. Davis, David N. Weiss, David J. Stem, Steve Oedekerk
Editor	Jon Michael Price, Gregory Perler
Music	John Debney
CAVANAGH, Megan	voice of Mom/VOX
DeCARLO, Mark	voice of Dad/pilot/arena guard
DERRYBERRY, Debi	voice of Jimmy
GARCIA, Jeff	voice of Sheen
GOEN, Bob	voice of newscaster
HART, Mary	voice of newscaster
LAWRENCE, Carolyn	voice of Cindy Vortex
MARTIN, Andrea	voice of Miss

	Fowl
MILO, Candi	voice of Nick Brittany/PJ
PAULSEN, Rob	voice of Carl/Carl's Mom and Da

©2001 Paramount Pictures/Viacom International Inc
Paramount Pictures and Nickelodeon Movies present
an O Entertainment and Nickelodeon production
82 mins 41 seconds
Sight and Sound .v12.n4.April 2002 p.47-48

Box Office:	**£2,726,104**
Opening weekend	**£541,453**
Screens	**384**
Screen average	**£1,410**

Joe Somebody

Dir John Pasquin
PG (US) 2001
20th Century Fox International (UK) – 29 November

Prod	Arnold Kopelson, Anne Kopelson, Matthew Gross, Ken (C) Atchity, Brian Reilly
Screenplay	Peter Tolan
DOP	Daryn Okada
Editor	David Finfer
Music	George S. Clinton
ALLEN, Tim	Joe Scheffer
BOWEN, Julie	Meg Harper
LYNCH, Kelly	Callie Scheffer
GERMANN, Greg	Jeremy
PANETTIERE, Hayden	Natalie Scheffer
WARBURTON, Patrick	Mark McKinney
BELUSHI, Jim (C)	Chuck Scarett
MARINO, Ken (C)	Rick Raglow
BODISON, Wolfgang	Cade Raymond
CONAWAY, Cristi	Abby Manheim

©2001 Twentieth Century Fox Film Corporation/Regency Entertainment (USA) Inc/Monarchy Enterprises S.a.r.l.
Fox 2000 Pictures and Regency Enterprises present
a Kopelson Entertainment production
a John Pasquin film
98 mins 20 seconds
Locations – Minneapolis
Sight and Sound .v13.n2.February 2003 p.47-48

Box Office:	**£3,254**
Opening weekend	**£2,030**
Screens	**10**
Screen average	**£203**

John Q

Dir Nick Cassavetes
15 (US) 2001
Entertainment Film Distributors Ltd – 26 April

Prod	Mark Burg, Oren Koules
Screenplay	James Kearns
DOP	Rogier Stoffers
Editor	Dede Allen
Music	Aaron Zigman
WASHINGTON, Denzel	John Quincy Archibald
DUVALL, Robert	Lieutenant Frank Grimes
WOODS, James	Doctor Turner
HECHE, Anne	Rebecca Payne
GRIFFIN, Eddie	Lester
ELISE, Kimberly	Denise Archibald
HATOSY, Shawn	Mitch
LIOTTA, Ray	Chief Monroe
THORNTON, David	immy Palumbo
SUPLEE, Ethan	Max

©2001 New Line Productions Inc
New Line Cinema presents
a Burg/Koules production
115 mins 59 seconds
Locations – Toronto
Sight and Sound .v12.n6.June 2002 p.44-45

Box Office:	**£866,051**
Opening weekend	**£306,517**
Screens	**197**
Screen average	**£1,556**

Just Visiting

aka: Les Visiteurs en Amérique
Dir Jean-Marie Poiré
PG (US/France) 2001
Momentum Pictures – 8 February

Prod	Patrice Ledoux, Ricardo Mestres
Screenplay	Christian Clavier, Jean-Marie Poiré, John Hughes
DOP	Veli Steiger
Editor	Michael A. Stevenson
Music	John Powell
RÉNO, Jean	Thibault, Count of Malfete
APPLEGATE, Christina	Princess Rosalind/Julia Malfete
CLAVIER, Christian	André le Pate
ROSS, Matthew (C)	Hunter
REID, Tara	Angelique
WILSON-SAMPRAS, Bridgette (C)	Amber
AYLWARD, John	Byron
PLIMPTON, George	Dr Brady
McDOWELL, Malcolm	wizard
AISTROPE, Martin	barfly 3

©2001 Gaumont
Hollywood Pictures present
88 mins 17 seconds
Locations – Chicago
Studios – Shepperton Studios
Sight and Sound .v12.n3.March 2002 p.46-47

Box Office:	**£726,158**
Opening weekend	**£121,414**
Screens	**239**
Screen average	**£508**

Juwanna Mann

Dir Jesse Vaughan
12A (US) 2001
Warner Bros Distributors (UK) – 4 October

Prod	**James G. Robinson, Bill Gerber, Steve Oedekerk**
Screenplay	**Bradley Allenstein**
DOP	**Reynaldo Villalobos**
Editor	**Seth Flaum**
Music	**Wendy Melvoin, Lisa Coleman**
NUNEZ Jr, Miguel A. (C)	Jamal Jefferies/Juwanna Mann
FOX, Vivica A.	Michelle Langford
POLLAK, Kevin	Lorne Daniels
DAVIDSON, Tommy	Puff Smokey Smoke
WAYANS, Kim	Latisha Jansen
Ginuwine	Romeo
Lil' Kim	Tina Parker
LEWIS, Jenifer	Aunt Ruby
CORLEY, Annie	Coach Rivers
REISS, Tammi	Vickie Sanchez

©2001 Morgan Creek Productions Inc
James G. Robinson presents
a Morgan Creek production
91 mins 6 seconds
Locations – North Carolina
Sight and Sound .v12.n12.December 2002 p.48-49

Box Office:	**£23,209**
Opening weekend	**£14,273**
Screens	**22**
Screen average	**£649**

K-19 The Widowmaker

**$** £ € Can$
Dir Kathryn Bigelow
12 (US/Germany/UK/Canada) 2002
United International Pictures (UK) Ltd – 25 October

Prod	Kathryn Bigelow, Joni Sighvatsson, Christine Whitaker, Edward S. Feldman, Mathias Deyle
Screenplay	Christopher Kyle, Tom Stoppard
DOP	Jeff Cronenweth
Editor	Walter Murch
Music	Klaus Badelt
FORD, Harrison	Captain Alexei Vostrikov
NEESON, Liam	Captain Mikhail Polenin

SARSGAARD, Peter	Vadim Radtchenko
ACKLAND, Joss	Marshal Zelentstov
SHRAPNEL, John	Admiral Bratyeev
SUMPTER, Donald	Dr Savran
WOODWARD, Tim	Partonov
NICOLSON, Steve	Demichev
ISYANOV, Ravil	Suslov
CAMARGO, Christian	Pavel

©2002 IMF Internationale Medien und Film GmbH & Co. 2 Produktions KG
Paramount Pictures and Intermedia Films present
a National Geographic/Palomar Pictures/First Light/IMF production [end]
Developed in association with Working Title Films
Produced with the assistance of the Nova Scotia Film Industry Tax Credit
138 mins 8 seconds
Locations – Toronto, Halifax, Canada, Moscow
Sight and Sound .v12.n11.November 2002 p.48-49

Box Office:	**£844,665**
Opening weekend	**£352,163**
Screens	**321**
Screen average	**£1,097**

K-Pax

Dir Iain Softley
12 (US/Germany) 2001
FilmFour Distributors – 12 April

Prod	Lawrence Gordon, Lloyd Levin, Robert F. Colesberry
Screenplay	Charles Leavitt
DOP	John Mathieson
Editor	Craig McKay
Music	Edward Shearmur
SPACEY, Kevin	Prot/Robert Porter
BRIDGES, Jeff	Dr Mark Powell
WOODARD, Alfre	Claudia Villars
McCORMACK, Mary	Rachel Powell
GERETY, Peter	Sal
WILLIAMS, Saul	Ernie
KELLY, David Patrick	Howie
WESTON, Celia	Mrs Archer
NAIDU, Ajay	Doctor Chakraborty
FERRELL, Conchata	Betty McAllister

©2001 Internationale Medien und Film GmbH & Co. 2 Produktions KG
Intermedia Films and Universal Pictures present
a Lawrence Gordon production
an Iain Softley film
120 mins 35 econds
Locations – Los Angeles, New York
Sight and Sound.v12.n4.April 2002 p.48-49

Box Office:	**£1,588,410**
Opening weekend	**£567,349**
Screens	**280**
Screen average	**£2,026**

Kaante

Box Office	**£398,912**
Opening weekend	**£108,747**
Screens	**30**
Screen average	**£3,625**

* Kakushi Toride No San-Akunin

Dir Akira Kurosawa
PG (Japan)
(1958)
bfi Bookings – 1 February

Prod	Masumi Fujimoto
Screenplay	Ruyzo Kikushima, Hideo Oguni, Shinobu, Akira Kurosawa
DOP	Kazuo Yamasaki
Music	Masaru Sato
MIFUNE, Toshiro	General Rokurota Makabe
UEHARA, Misa	Princess Yuki
CHIAKI, Minoru	Tahei
FUJIWARA, Kamatari	Matakichi
SHIMURA, Takashi	General Izumi Nagakura
FUJITA, Susumu	General Heiei Tadokoro
MIYOSHI, Eiko	lady-in-waiting
HIGUCHI, Toshiko	farmer's daughter
UEDA, Kichijiro	girl-dealer
MITSUI, Koji	soldier

©2001 Toho Co., Ltd
139 mins
Monthly Film Bulletin.v28.n327.April 1961 p.43

Box Office:	**£20,861**
Opening weekend	**£1,725**
Screens	**1**
Screen average	**£1,725**

Kate & Leopold

Dir James Mangold
12 (US) 2001
Buena Vista International (UK) – 5 April

Prod	Cathy Konrad
Screenplay	James Mangold, Steven Rogers
DOP	Stuart Dryburgh
Editor	David Brenner
Music	Rolfe Kent
RYAN, Meg	Kate McKay
JACKMAN, Hugh	Leopold, Duke of Albany
SCHREIBER, Liev	Stuart Bessler
MEYER, Breckin	Charles 'Charlie' McKay
LYONNE, Natasha	Darci
WHITFORD, Bradley	J. Camden
WHITEHEAD, Paxton	Uncle Millard
GRAY, Spalding	Doctor Geisler
STAMBERG, Josh	Bob, the colleague
SUSSMAN, Matthew	Phil, the ad executive

©2001 Miramax Film Corp
Miramax Films present
a Konrad Pictures production
118 mins 1 seconds
Locations – New York
Sight and Sound.v12.n4.April 2002 p.49-50

Box Office:	**£547,520**
Opening weekend	**£204,325**
Screens	**212**
Screen average	**£964**

Kehta Hai Dil Bar Bar

Box Office £45,969

Opening weekend	**£14,939**
Screens	**12**
Screen average	**£1,245**

Killing Me Softly

$ £
Dir Kaige Chen
18 (US/UK) 2001
Pathé Distribution – 21 June

Prod	Lynda Myles, Joe Medjuck, Michael Chinich
Screenplay	Kara Lindstrom
DOP	Michael Coulter
Editor	Jon Gregory
Music	Patrick Doyle
GRAHAM, Heather	Alice Loudon
FIENNES, Joseph	Adam Tallis
McELHONE, Natascha	Deborah Tallis
THOMSEN, Ulrich	Klaus
HART, Ian	Daniel, senior police officer
HUGHES, Jason	Jake
MARKHAM, Kika	Mrs Blanchard
ROBBINS, Amy	Sylvie
BANNERMAN, Yasmin	Joanna Noble
PALMER, Rebecca R.	Michelle

©2001 Noelle Entertainment Limited (All other territories)
Metro-Goldwyn-Mayer and The Montecito Picture Company present
a Chen Kaige film
100 mins 17 seconds
Locations – London, Cumbria
Studios – Shepperton
Sight and Sound .v12.n7.July 2002 p.46

Box Office:	**£69,330**
Opening weekend	**£22,344**
Screens	**33**
Screen average	**£677**

Kin

£ zmk
Dir Elaine Proctor
15 (UK/Zambia) 2001
Winchester Film Distribution – 30 August

Prod	Margaret Matheson
Screenplay	Elaine Proctor
DOP	Amelia Vincent
Editor	Nicholas Gaster
Music	Justin Adams

OTTO, Miranda	Anna
WASHINGTON, Isaiah	Stone
CHAMELEON, Chris	Marius
KANDJOZE, Moses	Naniserri
HEVITA, Ndondoro	old man
COETZER, Susan	Katinka
STEFANUS, Martin	Pahere
TJIUMA, Cornelius	Chohorerwa
MOSHESH, Nthati	Kata
FOUCHÉ, Bart	Rob

©1999 Bard (Kin) Limited
Bard Entertainments presents with the participation of BSkyB and British
Screen and The Arts Council of England
90mins 34secs
Locations – Namibia
Sight and Sound.v12.n11.November 2002 p.47-48

Box Office:	**£310**
Opening weekend	**£147**
Screens	**3**
Screen average	**£49**

Kissing Jessica Stein

Dir Charles Herman-Wurmfeld
15 (US) 2001
20th Century Fox International (UK) – 21 June

Prod	Eden H. Wurmfeld, Brad Zions
Screenplay	Heather Juergensen, Jennifer Westfeldt
DOP	Lawrence Sher
Editor	Kristy Jacobs Maslin, Greg Tillman
Music	Marcelo Zarvos

WESTFELDT, Jennifer	Jessica Stein
JUERGENSEN, Heather	Helen Cooper
COHEN, Scott (C)	Josh Meyers
HOFFMAN, Jackie	Joan
MASTRO, Michael	Martin
ELROD, Carson	Sebastian
HAMM, Jon	Charles
BAKER, David Aaron	Dan Stein
FELDSHUH, Tovah	Judy Stein
WURMFELD, Esther	Grandma Esther

©2001 Twentieth Century Fox Film Corporation
Fox Searchlight Pictures presents an Eden Wurmfeld Films production and
a Brad Zions Films production in association with
Cineric & Michael Alden Productions
96 mins 39 seconds
Locations – New York, Connecticut
Sight and Sound .v12.n7.July 2002 p.46-47

Box Office:	**£629,598**
Opening weekend	**£102,234**
Screens	**32**
Screen average	**£3,195**

Kitne Door Kitne Paas

Box Office	**£72,780**
Opening weekend	**£31,093**
Screens	**12**
Screen average	**£2,591**

Koi Mere Dil Se Pooche

Box Office	**£52,798**
Opening weekend	**£18,143**
Screens	**12**
Screen average	**£1,512**

Kranti

Box Office	**£37,891**
Opening weekend	**£13,241**
Screens	**6**
Screen average	**£2,207**

Kuch Tum Kaho Kuch Hum Kahein

Box Office	**£24,628**
Opening weekend	**£12,680**
Screens	**13**
Screen average	**£975**

Kya Dil Ne Kaha

Box Office	**£39,255**
Opening weekend	**£18,838**
Screens	**16**
Screen average	**£1,177**

Kya Yehi Pyar Hai

Box Office	**£53,474**
Opening weekend	**£14,336**
Screens	**9**
Screen average	**£1,593**

* Kumonosu-jo

Dir Akira Kurosawa
PG (Japan)
(1957)
bfi Bookings – 4 January

Screenplay	Hideo Oguni, Shinobu Hashimoto, Ryuzo Kikushima, Akira Kurosawa
DOP	Asaichi Nakai
Music	Fumio Yanoguchi

MIFUNE, Toshiro	Taketoki Washizu
YAMADA, Isuzu	Asaji, his wife
SHIMURA, Takashi	Noriyasu Odagura
CHIAKI, Minoru	Yoshiaki Miki
KUBO, Akira	Yoshiteru, his son
SASAKI, Takamaru	Kuniharu Tsuzuki
TACHIKAWA, Yoichi	Kunimaru, his son
NANIWA, Chieko	sorceress
KIMURA, Isao	phantom soldier
MIYOSHI, Eiko	old servant

Toho Co., Ltd.
105 mins
Monthly Film Bulletin.v25.n293.June 1958 p.71

Box Office:	**£23,529**
Opening weekend	**£5,283**
Screens	**1**
Screen average	**£5,283**

L.I.E.

Dir Michael Cuesta
(US) 2001
Metro Tartan Distributors – 29 November

Prod	Linda Moran, René Bastian, Michael Cuesta
Screenplay	Stephen M. Ryder, Michael Cuesta
DOP	Romeo Tirone
Editor	Eric Carlson, Kane Platt
Music	Pierre Földes

COX, Brian	Big John Harrigan
DANO, Paul Franklin	Howie Blitzer
KAY, Billy	Gary Terrio
ALTMAN, Bruce	Marty Blitzer
COSTA, James	Kevin Cole
DONNELLY, Tony (C)	Brian
MASTERSON, Walter	Scott
DeBONIS, Marcia	guidance counsellor
LeFEVRE, Adam	Elliot, Marty's lawyer
CARANO, Michelle	newscaster

©2001 L.I.E.
an Alter Ego/Belladonna production
108 mins
Sight and Sound .v12.n12.December 2002 p.49

Box Office:	**£40,503**
Opening weekend	**£6,823**
Screens	**2**
Screen average	**£3,412**

Laissez-passer

Dir Bertraund Tavernier
12 (France/Germany/Spain) 2001
Artificial Eye Film Company – 8 November

Prod	Alain Sarde, Frédéric Bourboulon
Screenplay	Jean Cosmos, Bertrand Tavernier
DOP	Alain Choquart
Editor	Sophie Brunet

Music Antoine Duhamel
GAMBLIN, Jacques Jean-Devaivre
PODALYDÈS, Denis Jean Aurenche
DESGRANGES, Marie Simone Devaivre
KADY, Charlotte Suzanne Raymond
MARLON, Ged Jean-Paul Le Chanois
MORIER-GENOUD, Philippe Maurice Tourneur
PITARRESI, Maria Reine Sorignal
SCHILLING, Laurent Charles Spaak
BERKEL, Christian Dr Alfred Greven
SAMMEL, Richard (C) Richard Pottier
©2001 ©2001 Les Films Alain Sarde/Little Bear/France 2 Cinéma/France 3 Cinéma/KC Medien/Vertigo
Alain Sarde and Frédéric Bourboulon present
a Les Films Alain Sarde, Little Bear, France 3 Cinéma, France 2 Cinéma, KC
Medien (Germany), Vertigo (Spain) co-production
with the participation of Canal+ and Studio Images 3,4,5
a film by Bertrand Tavernier
170m 12 seconds
Locations – Paris, Tours, Macon, France
Sight and Sound .v12.n11.November 2002 p.49-50
Box Office: **£93,637**
Opening weekend **£14,244**
Screens **6**
Screen average **£2,374**

Lantana

Dir Ray Lawrence
15 (Australia/Germany) 2001
Winchester Film Distribution – 16 August
Prod Jan Chapman
Screenplay Andrew Bovell
DOP Mandy Walker
Editor Karl Sodersten
Music Paul Kelly
LaPAGLIA, Anthony Leon Zat
RUSH, Geoffrey John Knox
HERSHEY, Barbara Dr Valerie Somers
ARMSTRONG, Kerry Sonja Zat
BLAKE, Rachael Jane O'May
DYKSTRA, Russell Michael, mystery man
FARINACCI, Daniella Paula Daniels
PHELPS, Peter Patrick Phelan
PURCELL, Leah Claudia Weis
ROBBINS, Glenn Pete O'May
©2001 MBP Medien AG & MBP KG II/Australian Film Finance Corporation Limited/Jan Chapman Films Pty Ltd
MBP, Jan Chapman Films, Australian Film Finance Corporation present
121 mins 19 seconds
Locations – Sydney
Sight and Sound .v12.n9.September 2002 p.65-66
Box Office: **£1,165,894**
Opening weekend **£92,566**
Screens **16**
Screen average **£5,785**

The Last Castle

Dir Rod Lurie
15 (US) 2001
United International Pictures (UK) Ltd – 4 January
Prod Robert Lawrence
Screenplay David Scarpa, Graham Yost
DOP Shelly Johnson
Editor Michael Jablow, Kevin Stitt
Music Jerry Goldsmith
REDFORD, Robert Lieutenant General Eugene R. Ir
GANDOLFINI, James Colonel Winter
RUFFALO, Mark Clifford Yates
COLLINS Jr, Clifton Corporal Ramón Aguilar
LINDO, Delroy General James 'Jim' Wheeler
BURTON, Steve Captain Peretz
CALDERON, Paul Sergeant Major Dellwo
BALL, Samuel Duffy
CHILDS, Jeremy Cutbush
SCOTT, George W. Thumper
©2001 DreamWorks LLC
DreamWorks Pictures presents
a Robert Lawrence Productions Inc. production
131 mins 23 seconds
Locations – Nashville
Sight and Sound .v12.n1.January 2002 p.47-48
Box Office: **£341,569**
Opening weekend **£161,862**
Screens **158**
Screen average **£1,024**

Last Orders

£ €

Dir Frank Schepisi
15 (UK/Germany) 2001
Metrodome Distribution Ltd – 11 January
Prod Fred Schepisi
Screenplay Fred Schepisi
DOP Brian Tufano
Editor Kate Williams
Music Paul Grabowsky
CAINE, Michael Jack Dodds
COURTENAY, Tom Vic Tucker
HEMMINGS, David Lenny Tate
HOSKINS, Bob Ray 'Lucky' Johnson
MIRREN, Helen Amy Dodds
WINSTONE, Ray Vince Dodds/ Vincent Ian Pritcher
FEILD, J.J. young Jack
FITCH, Cameron young Vic
HEMMINGS, Nolan young Lenny
YUSEF, Anatol young Ray
©2001 Scala (Last Orders) Limited/MBP
MBP, Scala and Winchester Films present
an MBP and Scala production
a Fred Schepisi film
109 mins 57 seconds
Locations – London, Kent
Sight and Sound
Box Office: **£946,719**
Opening weekend **£100,560**
Screens **25**
Screen average **£4,022**

Lava

£

Dir Joe Tucker
18 (UK) 2001
Winchester Film Distribution – 25 January
Prod Michael Riley, Gregor Truter
Screenplay Joe Tucker
DOP Ian Liggett, Roger Eaton, Sam McCurdy
Editor St John O'Rorke
Music Simon Fisher-Turner
TUCKER, Joe Smiggy
HOLMES, James Phillip
STAPLETON, Nicola Julie
FOX, Grahame (C) Darrel
LEADBETTER, Mark Neville
EMPSON, Tameka Maxine
GRANTHAM, Leslie Mr Aladdin
BELL, Tom Eric
MYERS, Johann Curtis
TITUS, Dennis Claude
©2001 Orangetop Ltd
Feature Film Company presents an IAC Film & Television presentation of an Orangetop/ Walking Point/Sterling Pictures production in association with Visionview
99 mins 29 seconds
Locations – London
Sight and Sound .v12.n2.February 2002 p.48
Box Office: **£4,501**
Opening weekend **£1,316**
Screens **2**
Screen average **£658**

Lawless Heart

$ £

Dir Neil Hunter, Tom Hunsinger
15 (UK/US) 2001
Optimum Releasing – 28 June

Prod Martin Pope
Screenplay Neil Hunter, Tom Hunsinger
DOP Sean Bobbitt
Editor Scott Thomas
Music Adrian Johnston

NIGHY, Bill Dan
HENSHALL, Douglas Tim Marsh
HOLLANDER, Tom Nick
CÉLARIÉ, Clémentine Corinne
HADDINGTON, Ellie Judy
SMITH, Sukie Charlie
BUTLER, Josephine Leah
LAING, Stuart David
HURST, Sally Michelle
HALL, Dominic Darren

©2001 MP Productions (LH) Limited/October Productions Limited
Isle of Man Film Commission, British Screen, The Film Council and October Productions in association with Overseas Film Group present
a Martin Pope production

99 mins 51 seconds
Locations – Essex, Isle of Man
Sight and Sound .v12.n7.July 2002 p.10-11

Box Office:	**£321,262**
Opening weekend	**£39,417**
Screens	**10**
Screen average	**£3,942**

Legend Of the Bhagat Singh

Box office	**£36,559**
Opening weekend	**£10,834**
Screens	**9**
Screen average	**£1,204**

Life as a House

Dir Irwin Winkler
15 (US/Germany) 2001
Entertainment Film Distributors Ltd – 15 March

Prod Irwin Winkler, Rob Cowan
Screenplay Mark Andrus
DOP Vilmos Zsigmond
Editor Julie Monroe
Music Mark Isham

KLINE, Kevin George Monroe
SCOTT THOMAS, Kristin Robin Kimball
CHRISTENSEN, Hayden Sam
SHERIDAN, Jamey Peter Kimball
ROBARDS, Sam David Dokos
BAKULA, Scott Kurt Walker
MALONE, Jena Alyssa Beck
STEENBURGEN, Mary Coleen Beck
PANKOW, John Bryan Burke
SOMERHALDER, Ian Josh

©2001 'Life' Productions GmbH & Co. KG
New Line Cinema
New Line Cinema presents
an Irwin Winkler film

125 mins 12 seconds
Locations – Los Angeles
Sight and Sound .v12.n5.May 2002 p.48-49

Box Office:	**£13,199**
Opening weekend	**£7,914**
Screens	**25**
Screen average	**£317**

Lighthouse

£

Dir Simon Hunter
15 (UK)
(1999)
Winchester Film Distribution – 19 July

Prod Mark Leake, Tim Dennison
Screenplay Simon Hunter
DOP Tony Imi
Editor Paul Green
Music Debbie Wiseman

PUREFOY, James Richard Spader
SHELLEY, Rachel Dr Kirsty McCloud
ADAMSON, Chris Leo Rook
BROOKE, Paul Captain Campbell
WARRINGTON, Don Prison Officer Ian Goslet
DUNNE, Chris (C) Chief Prison Officer O'Neil
GOODY, Bob Weevil
KELMAN, Pat Spoons
McCABE, Peter Prison Officer Hopkins
MITCHELL, Norman Brownlow

©1999 Tungsten Pictures Ltd
a Winchester Films presentation
In association with the Arts Council of England with the participation of British Screen and BSkyB
a film by Simon Hunter

95 mins
Locations – Land's End, Hastings
Studios – Three Mills Island Studio
Sight and Sound .v12.n8.August 2002 p.43

Box Office:	**£5,536**
Opening weekend	**£2,594**
Screens	**3**
Screen average	**£865**

Like Mike

Dir John Schultz
PG (US) 2001
20th Century Fox International (UK) – 13 December

Prod Barry Josephson, Peter Heller
Screenplay Michael Elliot, Jordan Moffet
DOP Shawn Maurer
Editor Peter Berger, John Pace
Music Richard Gibbs

Lil Bow Wow Calvin Cambridge
CHESTNUT, Morris Tracy Reynolds
LIPNICKI, Jonathan Murph
FORSTER, Robert Coach Wagner
GLOVER, Crispin Stan Bittleman, head of the orphan
MEARA, Anne Sister Theresa
LEVY, Eugene Frank Bernard
SONG, Brenda Reg Stevens
PLEMMONS, Jesse Ox
PROSPER, Sandra Janet

©2002 Twentieth Century Fox Film Corporation
Twentieth Century Fox presents in association with NBA Entertainment
a Heller Highwater/Josephson Entertainment production

99 mins 55 seconds
Locations – Los Angeles, Philadelphia
Studios – Hollywood Center Studios
Sight and Sound .v12.n12.December 2002 p.50

Box Office:	**£ 781,554***
	£1,420,833**
Opening weekend	**£246,169**
Screens	**279**
Screen average	**£882**

*(*total box office in 2002)*
*(** cumulative box office for 2002/03)*

Lilo & Stitch

Dir Chris Sanders
U (US) 2001
Buena Vista International (UK) – 4 October

Prod Clark Spencer
Screenplay Chris Sanders, Dean DeBlois
Editor Darren Holmes
Music Alan Silvestri

SANDERS, Christopher Michael (C) voice of Stitch
CHASE, Daveigh voice of Lilo
CARRERE, Tia voice of Nani
RHAMES, Ving voice of Cobra Bubbles
OGDEN STIERS, David voice of Jumba
McDONALD, Kevin voice of Pleakley
LEE, Jason Scott voice of David

	Kawena
CALDWELL, Zoe	voice of Grand Councilwoman
RICHARDSON, Kevin Michael (C)	voice of Captain Gantu
MOOK, Kunewa	voice of hula teacher

©2002 Disney Enterprises Inc
Walt Disney Pictures presents
85 mins 9 seconds
Sight and Sound .v12.n10.October 2002 p.41

Box Office:	**£13,025,297**
Opening weekend	**£1,516,249**
Screens	**280**
Screen average	**£5,415**

Living in Hope

£
Dir John Miller
15 (UK) 2001
Winstone Film Distributors – 7 June

Prod	Guy de Beujeu
Screenplay	Guy de Beujeu
DOP	Terry Flaxton
Editor	Nick Packer
Music	Supertoys
HARPER, Tom	'Posh', Alistair
FOSTER, Paul	Footsie
McMAHON, Liam	Liam
THORPE, Bennet	Animal
EDWARDS, Robin	Harry
HARRIS, Naomie	Ginny
BALL, Jade	Michaela
CHASE, Lorraine	Doreen
BOWLER, Norman	dad
RYE, Joseph	rugby coach

©2001 Fluidity Films Ltd
Fluidity Films presents
a de Beaujeu/Miller production
86 mins 57 seconds
Locations/Studios
Sight and Sound .v12.n6.June 2002 p.45
Box Office:

* Loneliness of the Long Distance Runner

£
Dir Tony Richardson
15 (UK) 1962
bfi Bookings – 11 October

Prod	Tony Richardson
Screenplay	Alan Stillitoe
DOP	Walter Lassally
Editor	Antony Gibbs
Music	John Addison
REDGRAVE, Michael	governor
COURTENAY, Tom	Colin Smith
BUNNAGE, Avis	Mrs. Smith
McCOWEN, Alec	Brown
BOLAM, James	Mike
ROBINSON, Joe	Roach
WARD, Dervis	detective
JANE, Topsy	Audrey
FOSTER, Julia	Gladys
CAIRNCROSS, James	[Jones]

Made by Woodfall Films, Curzon Street, London
A British Lion-Bryanston Release through BLC
©1962 by Woodfall Film Productions Ltd.
86 mins 57 seconds
Locations/Studios
Sight and Sound .v12.n6.June 2002 p.45

Box Office:	**£5,286**
Opening weekend	**£559**
Screens	**1**
Screen average	**£559**

Long Time Dead

£
Dir Marcus Adams
15 (UK) 2001
United International Pictures (UK) Ltd – 18 January

Prod	James Gay-Rees
Screenplay	Eitan Arrusi, Daniel Bronzite, Chris Baker, Andy Day
DOP	Nic Morris
Editor	Lucia Zucchetti
Music	Don Davis
ABSOLOM, Joe	Rob
BELMONT, Lara	Stella
GUTTERIDGE, Melanie	Annie
HAAS, Lukas	Webster
HILLIER, James	Spence
NEWMAN, Alec	Liam
RAIDO, Mel	Joe
THOMASON, Marsha	Lucy
BELL, Tom	Becker
FEAST, Michael	Paul Brennan

©2001 WT2 Limited
Working Title Films in association with Film Council present
a WT2 production in association with Midfield Films
93 mins 54 seconds
Locations – London
Sight and Sound v12.n2.February 2002 p.49

Box Office:	**£1,774,552**
Opening weekend	**£580,487**
Screens	**233**
Screen average	**£2,491**

Lord of the Rings The Two Towers

Dir Peter Jackson
12A (US/New Zealand/Germany) 2001
Entertainment Film Distributors Ltd – 20 December

Prod	Barrie M. Osborne, Fran Walsh, Peter Jackson
Screenplay	Fran Walsh, Philippa Boyens, Stephen Sinclair, Peter Jackson
DOP	Andrew Lesnie
Editor	Michael Horton, Jabez Olssen
Music	Howard Shore
WOOD, Elijah	Frodo Baggins
McKELLEN, Ian	Gandalf
TYLER, Liv	Arwen
MORTENSEN, Viggo	Aragorn
ASTIN, Sean	Samwise 'Sam' Gamgee
BLANCHETT, Cate	Galadriel
RHYS-DAVIES, John	Gimli
HILL, Bernard	King Theoden
LEE, Christopher	Saruman
BOYD, Billy	Peregrin 'Pippin' Took

©2002 Lord Zweite Productions Deutschland Filmproduktion GmbH & Co. KG.
New Line Cinema presents
a Wingnut Films production
79 mins 10 seconds
Locations – New Zealand
Sight and Sound .v13.n2.February 2003 p.48,50-51

Box Office:	**£26,175,904*** **£57,586,715****
Opening weekend	**£13,063,560**
Screens	**501**
Screen average	**£26,075**

*(*total box office in 2002)*
*(** cumulative box office for 2002/03)*

Lost in La Mancha

£
Dir Keith Fulton, Louis Pepe
15 (UK) 2002
Optimum Releasing – 2 August

Prod	Lucy Darwin
Screenplay	Keith fulton, Louis Pepe
Editor	Jacob Bricca
Music	Miriam Cutler

GRISONI, Tony
PATTERSON, Philip
CLEITMAN, René
GILLIAM, Terry
PECORINI, Nicola
ESCOLAR, José Luis
PEREZ-SOLERO, Barbara
FERNÁNDEZ, Benjamín
CALDERWOOD, Andrea
COOPER, Ray
©2001 Quixote Films Limited
a Quixote Films and Low Key Pictures production
in aasociation with Eastcroft Productions
a film by Keith Fulton and Louis

Pepe
93 mins 4 seconds
Documentary
Sight and Sound .v12.n8.August 2002 p.43-44

Box Office:	**£233,383**
Opening weekend	**£42,824**
Screens	**10**
Screen average	**£4,282**

Love Come Down

Box Office	**£4,106**
Opening weekend	**£4,106**
Screens	**3**
Screen average	**£1,369**

Lovely & Amazing

Dir Nicole Holofcener
15 (US) 2001
Metrodome Distribution Ltd – 2 August

Prod	Anthony Bregman, Eric d'Arbeloff, Ted Hope
Screenplay	Nicole Holofcener
DOP	Harlan Bosmajian
Editor	Rob Frazen
Music	Craig Richey

KEENER, Catherine	Michelle Marks
BLETHYN, Brenda	Jane Marks
MORTIMER, Emily	Elizabeth Marks
GOODWIN, Raven	Annie Marks
ELLIS, Aunjanue	Lorraine
GREGG, Clark	Bill
GYLLENHAAL, Jake	Jordan
Le GROS, James (C)	Paul
NOURI, Michael	Dr Crane
MULRONEY, Dermot	Kevin McCabe

©2001 Blow Up Pictures LLC
Blow Up Pictures presents
a Good Machine production in association with Roadside Attractions
91 mins 5 seconds
Sight and Sound .v12.n9.September 2002 p.66-67

Box Office:	**£213,907**
Opening weekend	**£35,483**
Screens	**14**
Screen average	**£2,535**

Lucía Y El Sexo

aka Sex and Lucia
Dir Julio Medem
18 (France/Spain) 2001
Metro Tartan Distributors – 10 May

Prod	Fernando Bovaira, Enrique López Lavigne
Screenplay	Julio Medem
DOP	Kiko de la Rica
Editor	Iván Aledo, S,L. Igloo PC
Music	

VEGA, Paz	Lucía
ULLOA, Tristán	Lorenzo
NIMRI, Najwa	Elena
FREIRE, Daniel	Carlos/Antonio
CÁMARA, Javier	Pepe
ANAYA, Elena	Belén
LLANOS, Silvia	Luna
SUÁREZ, Diana	Manuela, Belén's mother
FERNÁNDEZ, Juan	chief
ZAPARDIEL, Charo	midwife

©2001 Sociedad General de Cine, S.A.
An Alicia Produce production for Sogecine
with the participation of Canal+ España
and the participation of Televisión Española and StudioCanal France
127 mins 48 seconds
Sight and Sound .v12.n5.May 2002 p.52-53

Box Office:	**£376,037**
Opening weekend	**£59,955**
Screens	**13**
Screen average	**£4,612**

Lundi Matin

aka: Monday Morning
Dir Otar Iosseliani
PG (France/Italy) 2002
Artificial Eye Film Company – 6 December

Prod	Martine Marignac
Screenplay	Otar Iosseliani
DOP	William Lubtchansky
Editor	Otar Iosseliani, Ewa Lenkiewicz
Music	Nicolas Zourabichvili

BIDOU, Jacques	Vincent
MOZZO, Arrigo	Carlo, Vincent's friend
KRAVZ-TARNAVSKY, Anne	Josephine, Vincent's wife
BLANCHET, Narda	Vincent's mother
TARIELACHVILI, Dato (C)	Nicolas, older son
LAMOUR-FLORI, Anna	Berthe, Nicolas' friend
LAIDOUNI-DENIS, Myriam	Michel's wife
PACHOD, Adrien	Gaston, younger son
CHANAL, Pascal	Michel
KINSKI, Radzlav	Vincent's father

Pierre Grise Productions/Rhône-Alpes Cinéma/Mikado
Pierre Grise Productions (France), Rhône-Alpes Cin'ma (France), Mikado (Italy)
with the participation of Centre National de la Cinématographie, Canal+,
Gimages 4, Cofimage 12, Région Rhône-Alpes
with the support of Eurimages and Procirep
present
127 mins 50 seconds
Locations – Rhône-Alpes, Venice, Italy
Sight and Sound .v12.n12.December 2002 p.52-53

Box Office:	**£25,730*** **£44,559****
Opening weekend	**£8,032**
Screens	**3**
Screen average	**£2,677**

*(*total box office in 2002)*
*(** cumulative box office for 2002/03)*

Ma Femme est une Actrice

Dir Yvan Attal
15 (France) 2001
Pathé Distribution – 27 September

Prod	Claude Berri
Screenplay	Yvan Attal
DOP	Rémy Chevrin
Editor	Jennifer Augé
Music	Brad Mehldau

GAINSBOURG, Charlotte	Charlotte
ATTAL, Yvan	Yvan
STAMP, Terence	John
LVOVSKY, Noémie	Nathalie
BATEAU, Laurent	Vincent
SAGNIER, Ludivine	Géraldine
ALLEN, Keith	David, the film director
McINNES, Jo (C)	David's assistant
LEBOUTTE, Valérie	sexy young woman

©2001 Katharina/Renn Productions - TF1 Films Production
Claude Berri presents
a co-production of Renn Productions, Katharina, TF1 Films Production
with the participation of Canal Plus
93 mins
Sight and Sound .v12.n10.October 2002 p.42

Box Office:	**£105,490**
Opening weekend	**£18,819**
Screens	**14**
Screen average	**£1,344**

Maa Tujhhe Salaam

Box Office	**£16,832**
Opening weekend	**£557**
Screens	**2**
Screen average	**£279**

Made

Dir Jon Favreau
15 (US) 2001
Momentum Pictures – 25 January

Prod	Vince Vaughn, Jon Favreau
Screenplay	Jon Favreau

DOP Christopher Doyle
Editor Curtiss Clayton
Music John O'Brien, Lyle Workman
FAVREAU, Jon Bobby
VAUGHN, Vince Ricky
COMBS, Sean (C) Ruiz
JANSSEN, Famke Jessica
LOVE, Faizon Horrace
O'HARA, David Welshman
PASTORE, Vincent (C) Jimmy
FALK, Peter Max
GOOSSEN, Joe referee
VEGA, Makenzie Chloe
©2001 Artisan Pictures Inc
94 mins 22 seconds
Locations – Los Angeles
Sight and Sound .v12.n2.February 2002 p.53
Box Office: £75,979
Opening weekend £29,488
Screens 23
Screen average £1,282

The Magdalene Sisters
Box Office £2,057,920
Opening weekend £78,151
Screens 31
Screen average £2,521

Maine Dil Tujhko Diya
Box Office £39,799
Opening weekend £17,441
Screens 8
Screen average £2,180

The Majestic
Dir Frank Darabont
PG (US/Australia) 2001
Warner Bros Distributors (UK) – 24 May
Prod Frank Darabont
Screenplay Michael Sloane, Frank Darabont
DOP David Tattersall
Editor Jim Page
Music Mark Isham
CARREY, Jim Peter Appleton/ Luke Trimble
BALABAN, Bob Majority Counsel Elvin Clyde
BRISCOE, Brent Sheriff Cecil Coleman
DeMUNN, Jeffrey Ernie Cole
DETMER, Amanda Sandra Sinclair
GARFIELD, Allen Leo Kubelsky
HOLBROOK, Hal Congressman Doyle
HOLDEN, Laurie Adele Stanton
LANDAU, Martin Harry Trimble
RIFKIN, Ron Kevin Bannerman
©2001 Village Roadshow Films (BVI) Limited (All other territories)
Castle Rock Entertainment presents in association with Village Roadshow and NPV Entertainment
a Darkwoods production
152 mins 31 seconds
Locations – Los Angeles, Northern California
Sight and Sound .v12.n5.May 2002 p.49-50
Box Office: £115,860
Opening weekend £39,541
Screens 52
Screen average £760

* Malpertuis Histoire D'une Maison Maudite
Dir Harry Kümel
(Belgium/France/Denmark) 1971
NFT – 19 July
Prod Pierre Levie, Paul Laffargue
Screenplay Jean Ferry
DOP Gerry Fisher
Editor Richard Marden
WELLES, Orson Cassavius
HAMPSHIRE, Susan Nancy/ Euryale/ Alice
BOUQUET, Michel Dideloo
CARRIÈRE, Mathieu Yann
CASSEL, Jean-Pierre Lampernis
PILON, Daniel Mathias Krook
RILLA, Walter Eisengott
GROEN, Dora van der Sylvie Dideloo
JANSSENS, Charles Philarète
VARTAN, Sylvie Bets
©1971 S.O.F.I.D.O.C., S.A. (Brussels)
a co-production of S.O.F.I.D.O.C., S.A. (Brussels) / Societe d'Expansion du Spectacle (Paris) / Artemis GmbH (Berlin)
a Pierre Levie and Paul Laffargue presentation
124 mins
Locations – Belgium
Monthly Film Bulletin.v44.n527.December 1977 p.262
Box Office: £2,942

Manic
Dir Jordan Melamed
15 (US) 2001
Metrodome Distribution Ltd – 22 November
Prod Trudi Callon, Kirk Hassig
Screenplay Michael Bacall, Blayne Weaver
DOP Nicholas Hay
Editor Madeleine Gavin, Gloria Rosa Vela
Music David Wingo, Michael Linnen
GORDON-LEVITT, Joseph Lyle Jensen
BACALL, Michael Chad
DESCHANEL, Zooey Tracy
LIGHTNING, Cody Kenny
HENSON, Elden Mike
RIVAS, Sara Sara
CHEADLE, Don Dr David Monroe
ROLLO, Adrienne emergency room nurse
BAIRD, Maggie Rebecca
WEAVER, Blayne Charlie
©2001 Manic LLC
Next Wave Films presents
a Manic production
a film by Jordan Melamed
101 mins 45 seconds
Locations/Studios
Sight and Sound.v12.n12.December 2002 p.52
Box Office:

The Mapmaker
Box Office £21,133
Opening weekend £3,916
Screens 5
Screen average £783

MeIn Stern
Dir Valeska Grisebach
(Austria/Germany) 2001
NFT –
Prod Anna Von Wagner
Screenplay Valeska Grisebach
DOP Bernhard Keller
Editor Anja Jalomonowitz
GLÄSER, Nicole Nicole
SCHÖPS, Christopher Schöps
GLÄSER, Monique Monique
RINKA, Sebastian Sebastian
JAHN, Anika Anika
SANDKE, Christina Mutter
ZÜHIKE, Daniel Daniel
SKIBBE, Paul Bräutigam
LICHELBERGER, Marcel Pfarrer
LEHMANN, Nicole ex-girlfriend
a PolyFilm release (in Austria) of a Filmakademie Wien (Austria)/Hochschule für Film & Fernsehen Konrad Wolf (Germany) production
international sales: Austrian Film Commission, Vienna, Austria
62 mins
Locations – New York, Los Angeles
Studios – Sony Pictures Studios
Sight and Sound .v12.n9.September 2002 p.67-68
Box Office: £2,721

Men in Black II
Dir Barry Sonnenfeld
PG (US) 2001
Columbia TriStar Films (UK) – 2 August
Prod Wlter F. Parkes, Laurie MacDonald

Screenplay Robert Gordon, Barry Fanaro
DOP Greg Gardiner
Editor Steven Weisberg, Richard Pearson
Music Danny Elfman
JONES, Tommy Lee Kay
SMITH, Will Jay
BOYLE, Lara Flynn Serleena
KNOXVILLE, Johnny Scrad/Charlie
DAWSON, Rosario Laura Vasquez
SHALHOUB, Tony Jeebs
TORN, Rip Zed
WARBURTON, Patrick Agent Tee
KEHLER, Jack Ben
CROSS, David Newton
©2002 Columbia Pictures Industries, Inc.
Columbia Pictures presents an Amblin Entertainment production in association with MacDonald/Parkes Productions a Barry Sonnenfeld film
87 mins 58 seconds
Locations – New York, Los Angeles
Studos – Sony Pictures Studios
Sight and Sound .v12.n9.September 2002 p.67-68
Box Office: **£22,212,394**
Opening weekend **£6,191,428**
Screens **512**
Screen average **£12,093**

Mere Yaar Ki Shaadi Hai

Box Office **£260,590**
Opening weekend **£70,492**
Screens **21**
Screen average **£3,357**

Metropolis

Dir Rintaro
PG (Japan) 2001
Columbia TriStar Films (UK) – 11 January
Screenplay Katsuhiro Otomo
Music Toshiyuki Mima
IMOTO, Yuka voice of Tima
KOBAYASHI, Kei voice of Kenichi
OKADA, Kohki voice of Rock
ISHIDA, Taro voice of Duke Red
TOMITA, Kousei voice of Shunsaku Ban
WAKAMOTO, Norio voice of Pero
TAKIGUCHI, Junpei voice of Dr Laughton
AONO, Takeshi voice of Ponkotz
IKEDA, Masaru voice of President Boon
YASHIRO, Syun voice of Notarlin
©2001 a Bandai Visual Co Ltd production
Produced by Metropolis Committee
107 mins 51 seconds
Animation
Sight and Sound .v12.n3.March 2002 p.49-50
Box Office: **£20,807**
Opening weekend **£2,279**
Screens **1**
Screen average **£2,279**

Minority Report

Dir Steven Spielberg
12 (US) 2001
20th Century Fox International (UK) – 4 July
Prod Gerald R. Molen, Bonnie Curtis, Walter F. Parkes, Jan De Bont
Screenplay Frank Scott, Jon Cohen, Gary Goldman, Ronald Shusett
DOP Janusz Kaminski
Editor Michael Kahn
Music John Williams
CRUISE, Tom Chief John Anderton
SYDOW, Max von Director Lamar Burgess
HARRIS, Steve Jad
McDONOUGH, Neal Fletcher
KILPATRICK, Patrick Knott
CAPSHAW, Jessica Evanna
COCA, Richard Pre-crime cop
CAMPBELL, Keith Pre-crime cop
WOLLER, Kirk B.R. Pre-crime cop
©2002 Twentieth Century Fox Film Corporation/DreamWorks LLC
Twentieth Century Fox and DreamWorks Pictures present a Cruise/Wagner/Blue Tulip/Ronald Shusett/Gary Goldman production a Steven Spielberg film
144 mins 59 seconds
Locations – Los Angeles, Washingon DC
Sight and Sound .v12.n8.August 2002 p.44-45
Box Office: **£20,685,587**
Opening weekend **£4,506,315**
Screens **426**
Screen average **£10,578**

Monsoon Wedding

Dir Mira Nair
15 (US/Italy/Germany/France) 2001
FilmFour Distributors – 4 January
Prod Caroline Baron, Mira Nair
Screenplay Sabrina Dhawan
DOP Declan Quinn
Editor Alllyson C. Johnson
Music Mychael Danna
SHAH, Naseeruddin Lalit Verma
DUBEY, Lillete (C) Pimmi Verma
SHETTY, Shefali Ria Verma
RAAZ, Vijay P.K. Dubey
SHOME, Tilotama Alice
DAS, Vasundhara Aditi Verma
KHARBANDA, Kulbhushan C.L. Chadha
DABAS, Parvin Hemant Rai
KHANNA, Kamini Shashi Chadha
KAPOOR, Rajat Tej Puri
©2001 Mirabai Films Inc
IFC Production presents in association with Key Films, Pandora Films and Paradis Films a Mirabai Films production of a Mira Nair film
113 mins 37 seconds
Sight and Sound .v12.n1.January 2002 p.50
Box Office: **£2,270,404**
Opening weekend **£130,466**
Screens **25**
Screen average **£5,219**

Monster's Ball

Dir Marc Forster
15 (US) 2001
Entertainment Film Distributors Ltd – 7 June
Prod Lee Daniels
Screenplay Milo Addica, Will Rokos
DOP Roberto Schaefer
Editor Matt Chessé
Music Asche and Spencer
THORNTON, Billy Bob Hank Grotowski
BERRY, Halle Leticia Musgrove
BOYLE, Peter Buck Grotowski
LEDGER, Heath Sonny Grotowski
COMBS, Sean (C) Lawrence Musgrove
DEF, Mos Ryrus Cooper
CALHOUN, Coronji Tyrell Musgrove
SIMPSON, Taylor Lucille
WITCHER, Gabrielle Betty
RULES, Amber Vera
©2001 Lions Gate Films, Inc
Lions Gate Films present a Lee Daniels Entertainment production
111 mins 30 seconds
Locations – New Orleans
Sight and Sound .v12.n6.June 2002 p.14-16
Box Office: **£2,67,371**
Opening weekend **£486,017**
Screens **173**
Screen average **£2,809**

Monsters, Inc

Dir Pete Docter
U (US) 2001
Buena Vista International (UK) – 8 February
Prod Darla K. Anderson
Screenplay Andrew Stanton, Daniel Gerson
Editor Jim Stewart
Music Randy Newman

GOODMAN, John — voice of James P. 'Sulley' Sull
CRYSTAL, Billy — voice of Mike Wazowski
GIBBS, Mary — voice of Boo
BUSCEMI, Steve — voice of Randall Boggs
COBURN, James — voice of Henry J. Waternoose
TILLY, Jennifer — voice of Celia
PETERSON, Bob — voice of Roz, 'Number 1'
RATZENBERGER, John — voice of Yeti
OZ, Frank — voice of Fungus
GERSON, Daniel — voice of Needleman/ Smitty

©2001 Disney Enterprises Inc/Pixar Animation Studios
Walt Disney Pictures presents
a Pixar Animation Studios film
95 mins 28 seconds
Locations/Studios
Sight and Sound .v12.n2.February 2002 p.54-55

Box Office: **£37,907,451**
Opening weekend **£9,200,257**
Screens **503**
Screen average **£18,291**

Morvern Callar

£ Can$
Dir Lynne Ramsay
15 (UK/Canada) 2001
Momentum Distribution – 1 November
Prod — Robyn Slovo, Charles Pattinson, George Faber
Screenplay — Lynne Ramsay, Liana Dognini
DOP — Alwin Kuchler
Editor — Lucia Zucchetti
MORTON, Samantha — Morvern Callar
McDERMOTT, Kathleen — Lanna
BURCHELL, Raife Patrick — boy in room 1022
CADAN, Dan — Dazzer
CALDER, Carolyn — Tequila Sheila
CARDWELL, Steven — welcoming courier
DICK, Bryan — guy with hat's mate
CARRETTE, El — gypsy taxi driver
FLANNIGAN, Andrew — overdose
HAMILTON, Des (C) — Him

©2001 Morvern Callar Productions Limited
Alliance Atlantis and BBC Films presents in association with Film Council,
Scottish Screen and Glasgow Film Fund
a Company Picture production
97m 36 seconds
Locations – London, Oban, Scotland, Almeria, Spain
Sight and Sound .v12.n11.November 2002 p.50

Box Office: **£358,115*** **£386,902****
Opening weekend **£82,014**
Screens **17**
Screen average **£4,824**
*(*total box office in 2002)*
*(** cumulative box office for 2002/03)*

* Mother India

Dir Mehboob
U (India) 1957
bfi Bookings – 3 May
Screenplay — Vajahat Mirza, S.Ali Raza
DOP — Faredoon A. Irani
Editor — Shamsudin Kadri
Music — Naushad
NARGIS — Radha
DUTT, Sunil — Birju
KUMAR, Rajendra — Ramu
KUMAR, Raaj — Shyamu
LAL, Kanhaiya (C) — Sukhi-lala
MAA, Jilloo — Sundar Chachi
KUMKUM — Champa
CHANCHAL — Rupa
NAIK, Sheela — Kamala
MUQRI — Shambhu

Mehboob Productions
160 mins
Monthly Film Bulletin.v25.n294.July 1958 p.85

Box Office: **£13,506**
Opening weekend **£3,769**
Screens **5**
Screen average **£754**

The Mothman Prophecies

Dir Mark Pellington
12 (US) 2001
Helkon SK – 1 March
Prod — Tom Rosenberg, Gary Lucchesi, Gary Goldstein
Screenplay — Richard Hatem, Becky Johnston, Alan Cross, Ernest Marrero, Lewis Klahr
DOP — Fred Murphy
Editor — Brian Berdan
Music — Tomandandy
GERE, Richard — John Klein
LINNEY, Laura — Connie Mills
PATTON, Will — Gordon Smallwood
MESSING, Debra — Mary Klein
JENNEY, Lucinda — Denise Smallwood
BATES, Alan — Alexander Leek
EIGENBERG, David — Ed Fleischman
TRACEY, Bob — Cyrus Bills
EMANUEL, Ron — Washington Post reporter
STOVIAK, Tom (C) — real estate agent

©2001 Lakeshore Entertainment Corp.
Lakeshore Entertainment and Screen Gems present
a Lakeshore Entertainment Production
118 mins 39 seconds
Locations – Pittsburgh
Sight and Sound .v12.n3.March 2002 p.50,52

Box Office: **£2,512,158**
Opening weekend **£762,516**
Screens **286**
Screen average **£2,666**

Mr. Deeds

Dir Steven Brill
12A (US) 2001
Columbia TriStar Films (UK) – 1 November
Prod — Sid Ganis, Jack Giarraputo
Screenplay — Tim Herlihy, Adam Sandler, Steven Brill
DOP — Peter Lyons Collister
Editor — Jeff Gourson
Music — Teddy Castellucci
SANDLER, Adam — Longfellow Deeds
RYDER, Winona — Babe Bennett
GALLAGHER, Peter — Chuck Cedar
HARRIS, Jared — Mac McGrath
COVERT, Allen — Marty
AVARI, Erick — Cecil Anderson
TURTURRO, John — Emilio Lopez
DANTE, Peter — Murph
FERRELL, Conchata — Jan
PRESNELL, Harve — Preston Blake

©2002 Columbia Pictures Industries, Inc
Columbia Pictures and New Line Cinema presents
a Happy Madison production
in association with Out of the Blue Entertainment
96 mins 27 seconds
Locations – Los Angeles, New York
Sight and Sound .v12.n12.December 2002 p.53-54

Box Office: **£3,766,510**
Opening weekend **£879,441**
Screens **293**
Screen average **£3,002**

* Mughal-E-Azam

Dir K.Asif
PG (India) 1960
bfi Bookings – 25 October
Prod — K. Asif
Screenplay — K. Asif, Aman
DOP — R.D. Mathur
Editor — Dharamvir
Music — Naushad
PRITHVIRAJ (C) — Emperor Akbar

MADHUBALA	Anarkali
KUMAR, Dilip	Prince Salim
KHOTE, Durga	Maharani Jodha Bai
SULTANA, Nigar	Bahar
AJIT	Durjan Singh
KUMAR	sculptor
MURAT (C)	Maan Singh
BAI, Jillo (C)	.
VIJAYALAXMI (C)	.

Sterling Investment Corp. (P) Ltd presents
197 mins 33 seconds
Subtitles
Sight and Sound .v12.n12.December 2002 p.55

Box Office:	**£4,501**
Opening weekend	**£1,515**
Screens	**3**
Screen average	**£505**

* Muhammad Ali, the Greatest

Dir William Klein
PG (France)1975
Optimum Releasing – 8 February

DOP	William Klein
Editor	Francine Grubert, Eva Zora, Isabelle Rathéry, Emmanuelle Le Ray
Music	Mickey Baker, Umban, Le Wac

a Delpire Advico Films Paris New-York co-production
115 mins 42 seconds
Documentary
In Black & White/Colour
Partly Subtitled
Sight and Sound .v12.n3.March 2002 p.52

Box Office:	**£3,762**
Opening weekend	**£1,673**
Screens	**1**
Screen average	**£1,673**

Mujhe Dosti Karoge

Box Office £831,000

Opening weekend	**£204,490**
Screens	**32**
Screen average	**£6,390**

Mulholland Dr.

Dir David Lynch
15 (US/France) 2001
Pathé Distribution – 4 January

Prod	Mary Sweeney, Alain Sarde, Neal Edelstein, Michael Polaire, Tony Krantz, Joyce Eliason
Screenplay	David Lynch
DOP	Peter Deming
Editor	Mary Sweeney
Music	Angelo Badalamenti
THEROUX, Justin	Adam Kesher
WATTS, Naomi	Betty Elms/ Diane Selwyn
HARRING, Laura Elena (C)	Rita/ Camilla Rhodes
MILLER, Ann	Coco Lenoix
HEDAYA, Dan	Vincenzo Castigliane
PELLEGRINO, Mark	Joe
BRISCOE, Brent	Detective Domgaard
FORSTER, Robert	Detective Harry McKnight
TOWNE, Katharine	Cynthia
GRANT, Lee	Louise Bonner

©2001 Le Studio Canal Plus
Alain Sarde presents
a Les Films Alain Sarde/Asymmetrical production
a film by David Lynch
146 mins 27 seconds
Studios – Paramount Studios
Sight and Sound .v12.n1.January 2002 p.50-51

Box Office:	**£1,231,719**
Opening weekend	**£134,798**
Screens	**27**
Screen average	**£4,993**

Mullet

Box Office £1,539

Opening weekend	**£1,539**
Screens	**1**
Screen average	**£1,539**

Murder By Numbers

Dir Barbet Schroeder
15 (US) 2001
Warner Bros Distributors (UK) – 28 June

Prod	Richard Crystal, Barbet Schroeder, Susan Hoffman
Screenplay	Tony Gayton, Henry Bean
DOP	Luciano Tovoli
Editor	Lee Percy
Music	Clint Mansell
BULLOCK, Sandra	Cassie Mayweather
GOSLING, Ryan	Richard Haywood
PITT, Michael	Justin Pendleton
BRUCKNER, Agnes	Lisa Mills
PENN, Chris	Ray
CALL, R.D.	Captain Rod Cody
CHAPLIN, Ben	Sam Kennedy
VERICA, Tom	Al Swanson
BRENN, Janni	Ms Elder
VICKERY, John	restaurant manager

©2002 Castle Rock Entertainment
Castle Rock Entertainment presents
a Schroeder/Hoffman production
a Barbet Schroeder film
120 mins 7 seconds
Locations – Los Angeles, San Luis Obispo
Sight and Sound .v12.n7.July 2002 p.48-49

Box Office:	**£2,645,048**
Opening weekend	**£729,164**
Screens	**325**
Screen average	**£2,244**

Musíme Si Pomáhat

aka: Divided We Fall
Dir Jan Hrebejk
PG (Czech Republic) 2000
Metrodome Distribution Ltd – 31 May

Prod	Ondrej Trojan
Screenplay	Petr Jachovsky
DOP	Jan Malír
Editor	Vladimir Barák
Music	Ales Brezina
POLÍVKA, Boleslav	Josef Cízek
KASSAI, Csongor	David Wiener
DUSEK, Jaroslav	Horst Prohaska
SISKOVÁ, Anna	Marie Cízková
PECHA, Jirí	Frantisek Simácek
HUBA, Martin	Dr Albrecht Kepke
STASOVÁ, Simona	Libuse Simácková
MAREK, Vladimir	SS officer
KODET, Jirí	Dr Fiser-Rybár
TESARÍK, Richard	captain

Total HelpArt T.H.A. Film and Television Company/Czech Television - Pavel Borovan's Creative Team production
122 mins 17 seconds
No Sight and Sound

Box Office:	**£120,035**
Opening weekend	**£10,313**
Screens	**5**
Screen average	**£2,063**

The Musketeer

$ £ €
Dir Peter Hyams
PG (UK/Germany/US/Luxembourg) 2001
Buena Vista International (UK) – 21 June

Prod	Moshe Diamant
Screenplay	Gene Quintano, Fabrice Ziolkowski
DOP	Peter Hyams
Editor	Terry Rawlings
Music	David Arnold
DENEUVE, Catherine	The Queen
SUVARI, Mena	Francesca
REA, Stephen	Cardinal Richelieu
ROTH, Tim	Febre
CHAMBERS, Justin	D'Artagnan
MORAN, Nick	Aramis
TREACHER, Bill	Bonacieux
MESGUICH, Daniel	King Louis

SPEIRS, Steven Porthos
KREMP, Jan Gregor (C) Athos
©2001 D'Artagnan Productions Ltd/ApolloMedia GmbH and Co. 3 Filmproduktion KG
Miramax Films and Universal Pictures, MDP Worldwide and Crystal Sky present
a D'Artagnan Productions Ltd, ApolloMedia, Q and Q Media and Carousel Picture Company production with the support of Film Fund Luxembourg
a Peter Hyams film
104 mins 20 seconds
Locations – Luxembourg
Sight and Sound .v12.n7.July 2002 p.49-50

Box Office:	**£432,443**
Opening weekend	**£131,338**
Screens	**310**
Screen average	**£424**

My Big Fat Greek Wedding

Dir Joel Zwick
PG (US/Canada) 2001
Entertainment Film Distributors Ltd – 20 September

Prod	Rita Wilson, Tom Hanks, Gary Goetzman
Screenplay	Nia Vardalos
DOP	Jeffrey Jur
Editor	Mia Goldman
Music	Chris Wilson, Alexander Janko

VARDALOS, Nia Toula Portokalos
CORBETT, John Ian Miller
CONSTANTINE, Michael Gus Portokalos
KAZAN, Lainie Maria Portokalos
MARTIN, Andrea Aunt Voula
FATONE, Joey Angelo
ELEUSINIOTIS, Christina Toula aged 6
VIEIRA, Kaylee schoolgirl
KALANGIS, John Greek teacher
ZOURAVLIOFF, Marita Toula aged 12
©2001 Big Wedding LLC
Gold Circle Films presents in association with Home Box Office and MPH Entertainment
a Playtone picture
95 mins 3 seconds
Sight and Sound .v12.n10.October 2002 p.44-45

Box Office:	**£13,569,577**
Opening weekend	**£1,503,436**
Screens	**341**
Screen average	**£4,409**

My Kingdom

£
Dir Don Boyd
18 (UK) 2001
Metro Tartan Distributors – 11 October

Prod	Neal Weisman, Gabriela Bacher
Screenplay	Nick Boyd, Nick Davies
DOP	Dewald Aukema
Editor	Adam Ross
Music	Deirdre Gribbin, Simon Fisher Turner

HARRIS, Richard Sandeman
REDGRAVE, Lynn Mandy
BELL, Tom Richard Quick
CATHERWOOD, Emma Jo
GILLEN, Aidan Detective Sergeant Barry Puttna
LOMBARD, Louise Kath
McGANN, Paul Dean, Kath's husband
MISTRY, Jimi Jughinder Singh, 'Jug'
NOI, Reece the boy, Kath's son
PILKINGTON, Lorraine Tracy
©2001 British Sky Broadcasting
Sky Pictures presents
a Close Grip Films/Primary Pictures production
a Don Boyd film
116 mins 19 seconds
Locations – Liverpool
Sight and Sound .v12.n10.October 2002 p.45-46

Box Office:	**£13,566**
Opening weekend	**£2,588**
Screens	**7**
Screen average	**£370**

My Little Eye

**$** £ € Can$
Dir Marc Evans
18 (UK/US/France/Canada) 2001
Momentum Pictures – 4 October

Prod	Jon Finn, Jane Villiers, David Hilton, Alan Greenspan
Screenplay	David Hilton, James Watkins
DOP	Hubert Tacznaowski
Editor	Marguerite Arnold
Music	bias

JOHNSON, Sean CW (C) Matt
LEMCHE, Kris Rex
O'REILLY, Stephen Danny
REGAN, Laura Emma
SKY, Jennifer Charlie
COOPER, Bradley Travis Patterson
MENNELL, Nick the cop
©2001 WT Venture LLC
Momentum Pictures, Universal Pictures, Studio Canal and Working Title Films present a WTΣ production
95 mins 16 seconds
Locations – Halifax, Nova Scotia, Dartmouth, Nova Scotia Celementsport, Nova Scotia
Sight and Sound .v12.n10.October 2002 p.26-28

Box Office:	**£2,693,396**
Opening weekend	**£839,633**
Screens	**255**
Screen average	**£3,293**

The Mystic Masseur

$ £
Dir Ismail Merchant
PG (UK/US) 2001
Merchant Ivory Productions Ltd + Miracle – 29 March

Prod	Nayeem Hafizka, Richard Hawley
Screenplay	Caryl Phillips
DOP	Ernie Vincze
Editor	Roberto Silvi
Music	Richard Robbins, Zakir Hussain

PURI, Om Ramlogan
FOX, James Mr Stewart
MANDVI, Aasif Ganesh Ransumair
BHASKAR, Sanjeev Beharry
DHARKAR, Ayesha Leela
MISTRY, Jimi Partap
SEGAL, Zohra Auntie
JAFFREY, Sakina Suruj Mooma
LAVEAU, Albert headmaster
MAHARAJ, Grace Mrs Cooper
©2001 Merchant Ivory Productions Ltd/Pritish Nandy Communications Ltd
Merchant Ivory Productions presents in association with Pritish Nandy Communications and Video Associates Ltd
a film by Ismail Merchant
117 mins 58 seconds
Locations – Trinidad and Tobago, Oxford
Sight and Sound .v12.n4.April 2002 p.51-52

Box Office:	**£42,235**
Opening weekend	**£15,789**
Screens	**25**
Screen average	**£632**

Na Tum Jaano Na Hum

Box Office	**£226,836**
Opening weekend	**£89,337**
Screens	**24**
Screen average	**£3,722**

National Lampoon's Van

Wilder

Dir Walt Becker
15 (US/Germany) 2001
Momentum Pictures – 27 September

Prod Robert L. Levy, Peter Abrams, Andrew Panay, Jonathon Komack Martin
Screenplay Brent Goldberg, David T. Wagner
DOP James Bagdonas
Editor Dennis M. Hill
Music David Lawrence
REYNOLDS, Ryan Van Wilder
REID, Tara Gwen Pearson
MATHESON, Tim Vance Wilder Sr
PENN, Kal Taj Mahal Badalandabad
HOLMES, Teck Hutch
COSGROVE, Daniel Richard Bagg
RICHMOND, Deon Mini Cochran
BURNS, Alex Gordon
RUTHERFURD, Emily Jeannie
McCLURG, Edie campus tour guide

©2001 Die Sechste World Media Productions GmbH & Co. Medien und Musik KG
[logo] Myriad Pictures
[logo] Tapestry Films
[logo] Artisan Entertainment
Myriad Pictures presents
In association with IN-Motion AG and WMF V
a Tapestry Films production
a Walt Becker film
92 mins 49 seconds
Sight and Sound .v12.n10.October 2002 p.59

Box Office: **£1,810,970**
Opening weekend **£707,783**
Screens **338**
Screen average **£2,094**

The New Guy

Dir Ed Decter
12 (US) 2001
Columbia TriStar Films (UK) – 20 September

Prod Gordon Gray, Mark Ciardi, Todd Garner
Screenplay David Kendall
DOP Michael D. Oshea
Editor David Rennie
Music Ralph Sall
DJ Qualls Dizzy Gillespie Harrison/'Gil H
DUSHKU, Eliza Danielle
DESCHANEL, Zooey Nora
LOVETT, Lyle Bear
MIXON, Jerod Kirk
DOUGLAS, Illeana Kiki Pierce
SHEN, Parry Glen
FULLER, Kurt Mr Undine
CARRY, Julius coach
GAINEY, M.C. Clem

©2001 Revolution Studios Distribution Company LLC
Revolution Studios presents
88 mins 25 seconds
Locations – Austin
Sight and Sound .v12.n10.October 2002 p.47-48

Box Office: **£47,496**
Opening weekend **£26,172**
Screens **53**
Screen average **£494**

* A Night at the Opera

Dir Sam Wood
U (US) 2001
bfi Bookings – 12 July

Screenplay George S. Kaufman, Morrie Ryskind
DOP Merritt
B.Gerstad
Editor William Le Vanway
Music Herbert Stothart
MARX, Groucho
MARX, Chico
MARX, Harpo
CARLISLE, Kitty (C)
KING, Walter
JONES, Allan

Metro-Goldwyn-Mayer Corporation
94 mins
Monthly Film Bulletin.v3.n26.February 1936 p.29

No Man's Land

€ £

Dir Danis Tanovic
15 (France/Italy/Belgium/UK/ Slovakia) 2001
Momentum Pictures – 17 May

Prod Frédérique Dumas-zajdela, Marc Baschet, Cedomir Kolar
Screenplay Danis Tanovic
DOP Walther Vanden Ende
Editor Francesca Calvelli
Music Danis Tanovic
DJURIC, Branko Chiki
BITORAJAC, Rene Nino
SOVAGOVIC, Filip Cera
SIATIDIS, Georges Marchand
VALCKE, Serge-Henri Captain Dubois
KREMER, Sacha Michel
ELOY, Alain Pierre
NADAREVIC, Mustafa old Serbian soldier
DIKLIC, Bogdan Serbian officer
CALLOW, Simon Colonel Soft

©2001 Noé Productions/Fabrica/Man's Films/Judy Counihan Films/Studio Maj/Casablanca
Noé Productions presents
in co-production with Fabrica Cinema (Italy), Man's Films (Belgium)
and with Counihan Villiers Productions (UK), Studio Maj/Casablanca (Slovania)
in collaboration with Le Centre du Cinéma et de l'Audiovisuel de la Communauté
Française de Belgique and Télédistributeurs Wallons
and Les Fonds Slovène du Cinéma
Supported by Eurimages, with the participation of British Screen, TPS Cinema,
Multivision, RAI Cinema, RTBF, Canal+ Belgique
With the contribution of of Fondazione MonteCinemaVerità Locarno
(Switzerland) as well as Direction du Développement et de la Coopération (DDC), Départment Fédéral des Affaires Etrangères (Switzerland)
a film by Danis Tanovic
97 mins 14 seconds
Locations – Slovenia
Sight and Sound .v12.n4.April 2002 p.51-52

Box Office: **£196,873**
Opening weekend **£29,948**
Screens **17**
Screen average **£1,762**

Nobody Someday

$ € £

Dir Brian Hill
15 (UK) 2001
United International Pictures (UK) Ltd – 4 January

Prod Caroline Levy
Screenplay Brian Hill
DOP Simon Niblett, Michael Timney
Editor Stuart Briggs
Music Guy Chambers
WILLIAMS, Robbie On-screen participant
CHAMBERS, Guy Band (Musical Director/ Keyboard
NUTTALL, Gary Band (Guitar)
EISLER, Fil Band (Guitar)
CHARLES, Yolanda Band (Bass Guitar)
SHARROCK, Chri Band (Drums)
WORALL, Claire Band (Keyboards/ Guitar)
NILES, Tessa Band (Backing Vocals)
KISSOON, Katie Band

(Backing Vocals)
©2001 Robert Williams
Century Films presents
in association with IE Music
a Brian Hill film
99 mins 1 second
Documentary
Sight and Sound .v12.n2.February 2002 p.56

Box Office:	**£70,971**
Opening weekend	**£15,224**
Screens	**8**
Screen average	**£1,903**

Not Another Teen Movie

Dir Joel Gallen
15 (US) 2002
Columbia TriStar Films (UK) – 24 May

Prod	Neal Moritz
Screenplay	Michael G. Bender, Adam Jay Epstein, Andrew Jacobson, Phil Beauman, Buddy Johnson
DOP	Reynaldo Villalobos
Editor	Steven Welch
Music	Theodore Shapiro
LEIGH, Chyler	Janey Briggs
EVANS, Chris	Jake Wyler
PRESSLY, Jaime	Priscilla
OLSEN, Eric Christian	Austin
KIRSHNER, Mia	Catherine
RICHMOND, Deon	Malik
JUNGMANN, Eric	Ricky
LESTER, Ron	Reggie Ray
McMAINS, Cody	Mitch Briggs
HUNTINGTON, Sam	Ox

©2001 Columbia Pictures Industries Inc
Columbia Pictures presents
an Original Film production
88 mins 52 seconds
Locations – Los Angeles
Sight and Sound .v12.n8.August 2002 p.46-47

Box Office:	**£1,837,413**
Opening weekend	**£635,805**
Screens	**223**
Screen average	**£2,851**

Novocaine

Dir David Atkins
15 (US) 2001
Momentum Pictures – 5 July

Prod	Paul Mones, Daniel M. Rosenberg
Screenplay	David Atkins
DOP	Vilko Filac
Editor	Melody London
Music	Steve Bartek
MARTIN, Steve	Frank Sangster
BONHAM CARTER, Helena	Susan Ivey
DERN, Laura	Jean Noble
KOTEAS, Elias	Harlan Sangster
CAAN, Scott	Duane
DAVID, Keith	Detective Lunt
THIGPEN, Lynne	Pat
ROSS, Chelcie	Mike
NOONAN, Polly	Sally
CERNY, JoBe	Pharmacist Wayne Ponze

©2001 ©2001 Artisan Film Investors Trust
Artisan Entertainment presents
a Paul Mones/Daniel M. Rosenberg production
a film by David Atkins
94 mins 40 seconds
Locations – Chicago
Sight and Sound .v12.n7.July 2002 p.50-51

Box Office:	**£42,704**
Opening weekend	**£10,780**
Screens	**10**
Screen average	**£1,078**

Nueve Reinas

Dir Favian Bielinsky
15 (Argentina) 2000
Optimum Releasing – 12 July

Prod	Pablo Bossi
Screenplay	Fabian Bielinsky
DOP	Marcelo Camorino
Editor	Sergio Zóttola
Music	César Lerner
DARÍN, Ricardo	Marcos
PAULS, Gastón	Juan
BRÉDICE, Leticia	Valeria
FONZI, Tomás	Federico
ABADAL, Ignasi	Vidal Gandolfo
AWADA, Alejandro	Washington
UGO, Antonio	D'Agostino
SERRANO, Roly	Castrito
BERENGUER, Elsa	Berta
TENENBAUM, Graciela	convenience store clerk

©2000 Patagonik Film Group
Patagonik Film Group presents
113 mins 57 seconds
Subtitles
Sight and Sound .v12.n8.August 2002 p.46

Box Office:	**£410,973**
Opening weekend	**£49,438**
Screens	**17**
Screen average	**£2,908**

O

Dir Tim Blake Nelson
(US) 2001
Buena Vista International (UK) – 13 September

Prod	Eric Gitter, Daniel L.Fried, Anthony Rhulen
Screenplay	Brad Kaaya
DOP	Russell Lee Fine
Editor	Kate Sanford
Music	Jeff Danna
PHIFER, Mekhi	Odin 'O' James
HARTNETT, Josh	Hugo Goulding
STILES, Julia	Desi Brable
HENSON, Elden	Roger Rodriguez
KEEGAN, Andrew	Michael 'Mike' Casio
PHOENIX, Rain (C)	Emily
HEARD, John	Dean Brable
JOHNSON, Anthony 'A.J.' (C)	Dell
SHEEN, Martin	Coach Duke Goulding
FREIHOFER, Chris	assistant coach

©2001 Miramax Film Corp.
[end]
a Chickie the Cop production in association with Daniel Fried Productions and Rhulen Entertainment
a film by Tim Blake Nelson
Developed with assistance of the Sundance Institute
95 mins
Locations – Charleston, South Carolina
Sight and Sound.v12.n2.February 2002 p.56-7

Box Office:	**£155,501**
Opening weekend	**£70,739**
Screens	**131**
Screen average	**£540**

Ocean's Eleven

Dir Steven Soderbergh
12 (US/Australia) 2001
Warner Bros Distributors (UK) – 15 February

Prod	Jerry Weintraub
Screenplay	Ted Griffin, Stephen Carpenter
DOP	Peter Andrews
Editor	Steve Mirrione
Music	David Holmes
CLOONEY, George	Danny Ocean
DAMON, Matt	Linus
GARCIA, Andy	Terry Benedict
PITT, Brad	Rusty Ryan
ROBERTS, Julia	Tess Ocean
AFFLECK, Casey	Virgil Malloy
CAAN, Scott	Turk Malloy
GOULD, Elliott	Reuben Tishkoff
MAC, Bernie	Frank Catton
REINER, Carl	Saul Bloom

©2001 Warner Bros.
Warner Bros. Pictures presents
in association with Village Roadshow Pictures and NPV Entertainment
a Jerry Weintraub/Section Eight production
116 mins 25 seconds
Locations – Las Vegas, Los Angeles, Bellagio Hotel

Sight and Sound .v12.n3.March 2002 p.53
Box Office: £26,473,267
Opening weekend £5,095,062
Screens 433
Screen average £11,767

Offending Angels

£
Dir Andrew Rajan
15 (UK) 2000
Guerilla Films – 19 April
Prod Andrew Rajan
Screenplay Andrew Rajan, Tim Moyler
DOP Alvin Leong
Editor Roger Burgess, Catherine Fletcher
Music Martin Ward
HARKER, Susannah Paris
LINCOLN, Andrew Sam
PARKES, Shaun Zeke
RAJAN, Andrew Baggy
O'GRADY, Paula Alison
BAILEY, Marion mentor/false mentor
COCHRANE, Michael mentor
DIX, Sophie Mandy
GALLAGHER, Sean Clive
HOPKINS, Jesse young Sam
©2001 Pants Productions Limited
Pants Productions presents
an Andrew Rajan film
93 mins 21 seconds
Sight and Sound .v12.n6.June 2002 p.47
Box Office: £89
Opening weekend £30
Screens 2
Screen average £15

Officer's Ward

Box Office £61,723
Opening weekend £10,020
Screens 5
Screen average £2,004

Om Jai Jagadish

Box Office £174,982
Opening weekend £47,106
Screens 23
Screen average £2,048

O Invasor

Dir Beto Brant
18 (US) 2001
Gala Film Distributors – 13 September
Prod Bianca Villar, Renato Ciasca
Screenplay Marçal Aquino, Beto Brant, Renato Ciasca
DOP Toca Seabra
Editor Manga Campion
Music Sabotage, Instituto
RICCA, Marco Ivan Soares
BORGES, Alexandre 'Giba', Gilberto
MIKLOS, Paulo Anísio
XIMENES, Mariana Marina, Estevãos daughter
MADER, Malu Cláudia
COUTO, Chris Cecilia, Ivan's wife
FREIRE, George Estevão
CORREA, Tanah Dr Araújo
CUETO, Jayme del Norberto
SABOTAGE Sabotage
©2001 Drama Filmes Ltda
a Drama Filmes production
co-produced by Tibet Filme, Consórcio Europa, Videofilmes, Quanta
96 mins 56 seconds
Sight and Sound .v12.n10.October 2002 p.58
Box Office: £10,568
Opening weekend £4,317
Screens 4
Screen average £1,079

Once Upon a Time in the Midlands

£ €
Dir Shane Meadows
15 (UK/Germany) 2001
FilmFour Distributors – 6 September
Prod Andrea Calderwood
Screenplay Paul Fraser, Shane Meadows
DOP Brian Tufano
Editor Peter Beston
Music John Lunn
CARLYLE, Robert Jimmy
IFANS, Rhys Dek
BURKE, Kathy Carol
HENDERSON, Shirley Shirley
TOMLINSON, Ricky Charlie
ATKINS, Finn Marlene
FELTZ, Vanessa Vanessa
PATTERSON, Vicki audience guest
THRESHER, Kelly Donna
SHIM, Andrew Donut
©2002 FilmFour Limited/Film Council
FilmFour in association with the Film Council and Senator Films presents
with the participation of EMMI
a Slate Films production in association with Big Arty
a Shane Meadows film
104 mins 21 seconds
Locations – Nottingham
Sight and Sound .v12.n9.September 2002 p.68
Box Office: £494,281
Opening weekend £129,920
Screens 74
Screen average £1,756

One Hour Photo

Dir Mark Romanek
15 (US) 2001
20th Century Fox International (UK) – 4 October
Prod Christine Vachon, Pamela Koffler, Stan Wlodkowski
Screenplay Mark Romanek
DOP Jeff Cronenweith
Editor Jeffrey Ford
Music Reinhold Heil, Johnny Klimek
WILLIAMS, Robin Seymour 'Sy' Parrish
NIELSEN, Connie Nina Yorkin
VARTAN, Michael Will Yorkin
COLE, Gary Bill Owens
DANIELS, Erin Maya Burson
GREGG, Clark Detective Paul Outerbridge
SEARCY, Nick repairman
SMITH, Dylan Jacob 'Jake' Yorkin
La SALLE, Eriq (C) Detective James Van Der Zee
KIM, Paul Hansen Yoshi Araki
©2002 Twentieth Century Fox
Fox Searchlight Pictures presents in association with
Catch 23 Entertainment
a Killer Films/Laughlin Park Pictures production
95mins 55 seconds
Locations – Los Angeles
Sight and Sound .v12.n10.October 2002 p.68
Box Office: £1,671,447
Opening weekend £420,500
Screens 190
Screen average £2,213

The One

Dir James Wong
15 (US) 2001
Columbia TriStar Films (UK) – 12 April
Prod Glen Morgan, Steven Chasman, James Wong
Screenplay Glen Morgan, James Wong
DOP Robert McLachlan
Editor James Coblentz
Music Trevor Rabin
LI, Jet (C) Gabriel Yulaw/Gabriel 'Gabe' Yu
LI, Jet (C) Lawless

LINDO, Delroy	Harry Roedecker/ attendant
GUGINO, Carla	Traci 'T.K.' Katherine/ Massie W
STATHAM, Jason	Ethan Funsch
MORRISON, James	Aldrich/' A' World inmate 1
BRUNO, Dylan (C)	Yates
STEINMETZ, Richard	D'Antoni
HARRIS, Harriet Sansom	Nurse Besson
NORRIS, Dean	Sergeant Siegel

©2001 Revolution Studios Distribution Company LLC
Columbia Pictures [logo]
Revolution Studios presents
a Hard Eight Pictures production
87.mins 11 seconds
Locations Los Angeles
Sight and Sound.v12.n5.May 2002 p.50-51

Box Office:	**£1,125,329**
Opening weekend	**£493,491**
Screens	**238**
Screen average	**£2,073**

Orange County

Dir Jake Kasdan
12 (US) 2001
United International Pictures (UK) Ltd – 8 November

Prod	Scott Rudin, Van Toffler, David Gale, Scott Aversano
Screenplay	Mike White
DOP	Greg Gardiner
Editor	Tara Timpone
Music	Michael Andrews
HANKS, Colin	Shaun Brumder
BLACK, Jack	Lance
O'HARA, Catherine	Cindy Beugler
FISK, Schuyler	Ashley
LITHGOW, John	Bud Brumder
RAMIS, Harold	Don Durkett, dean of admissions
ADAMS, Jane	Mona
MARSHALL, Garry	Arthur Gantner
IVEY, Dana	Vera Gantner
CHASE, Chevy	Principal Harbert

©2001 Paramount Pictures
Paramount Pictures presents
an MTV/Scott Rudin production
82 mins 19 seconds
Locations – Los Angeles
Sight and Sound .v12.n4.April 2002 p.54

Box Office:	**£364,532**
Opening weekend	**£167,051**
Screens	**162**
Screen average	**£1,031**

Panic Room

Dir David Fincher
15 (US) 2002
Columbia TriStar Films (UK) – 3 May

Prod	Gavin Polone, Judy Hofflund, David Koepp, Ceán Chaffin
Screenplay	David Koepp
DOP	Conrad W. Hall, Darius Khondji
Editor	James Haygood, Angus Wall
Music	Howard Shore
FOSTER, Jodie	Meg Altman
WHITAKER, Forest	Burnham
YOAKAM, Dwight	Raoul
LETO, Jared	Junior
STEWART, Kristen	Sarah Altman
MAGNUSON, Ann	Lydia Lynch
BUCHANAN, Ian	Evan Kurlander
BAUCHAU, Patrick	Stephan Altman
SCHULZE, Paul	Officer Keeney
WALKER, Andrew Kevin	sleepy neighbour

©2001 Columbia Pictures Industries Inc
Columbia Pictures presents
a Hofflund/Polone production
an Indelible picture
111 mins 49 seconds
Locations – Los Angeles, New York
Sight and Sound .v12.n5.May 2002 p.51

Box Office:	**£8,371,604**
Opening weekend	**£2,022,582**
Screens	**424**
Screen average	**£4,770**

*Pather Panchali

Dir Satyajit Ray
U (India)1955
Contemporary Films – 3 May

Screenplay	Satyajit Ray
DOP	Subrata Mitra
Editor	Dulal Dutta
Music	Ravi Shankar
BANERJEE, Kanu	Harihar, the father
BANERJEE, Karuna	Sarbajaya, the mother
BANERJEE, Subir	Apu, the son
DAS GUPTA, Uma	the older Durga
DEVI, Chunibala	ndira Thakrun
BANERJEE, Runki	the younger Durga
DEVI, Reba	Seja Thakrun
DEVI, Aparna	Nilmoni's wife
CHAKRAVARTI, Tulsi	Prasanna, the schoolteacher
MUKHERJEE, Binoy	Baidyanath Majumdar

Government of West Bengal
121 mins
Monthly Film Bulletin .v25.n289.February 1958 p.15

Box Office:	**£4,416**
Opening weekend	**£4,416**
Screens	**1**
Screen average	**£4,416**

Pauline & Paulette

Dir Lieven Debrauwer
PG (Belgium/Netherlands/France) 2001
Columbia TriStar Films (UK) – 12 April

Prod	Dominique Janne
Screenplay	Lieven Debrauwer, Jaak Boon
DOP	Michel van Laer
Editor	Philippe Ravoet
Music	Frédéric Devreese
PETERSEN, Ann	Paulette
GROEN, Dora van der	Pauline
BERGMANS, Rosemarie	Cécile
STÉPHANE, Idwig	Albert
BRUYN, Julienne de	Martha
BLEREAU, Camilia	butcher's wife
BUYL, Nanda	notary
CNUDDE, Magda	Marie-José
DEMEDTS, Jef	undertaker
TANGHE, Jenny	Marcella

©2001 K-Line/Staccato Films Amsterdam BV/K2/K-Star/VRT/RTBF/NCRV
Dominique Janne presents
with a support of Fonds Film in Vlaanderen
a co-production of K-Line, Staccato Films, K2, K-Star, R.T.B.F. (Télévision belge), VRT, NCRV
Produced with the assistance of Centre du Cinéma et de l'Audiovisuel de la Communauté Française de Belgique and télédistributeurs wallons
With the participation of Canal+ Vlaanderen and TF1 International
77 mins 56 seconds
Sight and Sound .v12.n4.April 2002 p.54-55

Box Office:	**£20,658**
Opening weekend	**£4,470**
Screens	**6**
Screen average	**£745**

Peau d'homme coeur de bête

Dir Hélène Angel
(France) 2001
ICA Projects – April

Screenplay	Hélène Angel

DOP Isabelle Razavet
Editor Laurent Rouan, Eric Renault
Music Philippe Miller
RIABOUKINE, Serge Francky Pujol
BLANCAN, Bernard Coco Pujol
CERVO, Pascal Alex Pujol
JANSEN, Maaïke Marthe
HINDERCHIED, Cathy Aurélie Pujol
GUINAND, Virginie Christelle Pujol
RICHARD, Jean-Louis Tac Tac
LECOMTE, Cyril Anthony
LONDEZ, Guilaine Annie
BRUNET, Marc Bibof
©2001 Why Not Productions/Arte France Cinéma
Why Not Productions present
a Why Not Productions, Arte France Cinéma co-production with the participation of Canal+, Centre National de la Cinématographie, sofica Gimages 2
a film by Hélène Angel98 mins
Sight and Sound.v12.n7.July 2002 p.51-52
Box Office: £1,875

Pitaah

Box Office **£22,059**
Opening weekend **£8,772**
Screens **10**
Screen average **£877**

Le Placard

aka: Closet
Dir Francis Veber
15 (France) 2001
Optimum Releasing – 17 May
Prod Alain Poiré, Patrice Ledoux
Screenplay Francis Veber
DOP Luciano Tovoli
Editor Georges Klotz
Music Vladimir Cosma
AUTEUIL, Daniel François Pignon
DEPARDIEU, Gérard Félix Santini
LHERMITTE, Thierry Guillaume
LAROQUE, Michèle Mademoiselle Bertrand
ROCHEFORT, Jean Kopel, company director
VANDERNOOT, Alexandra Christine
CREVILLÉN, Stanislas Franck
AUMONT, Michel Belone
GIVRY, Edgar Mathieu
ASHANTI, Thierry Victor
©2001 Gaumont/EFVE Films/TF1 Films Production
Gaumont presents
84 mins 52 seconds
Locations – Paris
Sight and Sound.v12.n5.May 2002 p.40
Box Office: **£435,432**
Opening weekend **£75,396**
Screens **24**
Screen average **£3,142**

Pollock

Dir Ed Harris
(US) 2000
Columbia TriStar Films (UK) – 24 May
Prod Fred Berner, Ed Harris, Jon Kilik, James Francis Trezza
Screenplay Barbara Turner, Susan J. Emshwiller
DOP Lisa Rinzler
Editor Kathryn Himoff
Music Jeff Beal
HARRIS, Ed Jackson Pollock
HARDEN, Marcia Gay Lee Krasner
BOWER, Tom Dan Miller
CONNELLY, Jennifer Ruth Kligman
CORT, Bud Howard Putzel
HEARD, John Tony Smith
KILMER, Val Willem DeKooning
KNOTT, Robert Sande Pollock
LEARY, David Charles Pollock
MADIGAN, Amy Peggy Guggenheim
©2001 Pollock Films, Inc
Sony Pictures Classics [logo]
Peter M. Brant and Joseph Allen in association with Ed Harris and Fred Berner
Films present a Brant-Allen Films production
123 mins 7 seconds
Locations – The Hamptons, New York
Sight and Sound .v12.n6.June 2002 p.48
Box Office: **£254,455**
Opening weekend **£38,550**
Screens **14**
Screen average **£2,754**

Le Pornographe

Dir Bertrand Bonello
18 (France/Canada) 2001
Metro Tartan Distributors – 19 April
Prod Carole Scottia
Screenplay Bertrand Bonello
DOP Josée Deshaies
Editor Fabrice Rouaud
Music Laurie Markovitch
LÉAUD, Jean-Pierre Jacques Laurent
RÉNIER, Jérémie Joseph
BLANC, Dominique Jeanne
MOUCHET, Catherine Olivia Rochet
MONTALEMBERT, Thibault de Richard
MARCON, André Louis
HOURI, Alice Monika
OVIDIE Jenny
LUCAS, Laurent Carles
SAVOFF, Ségolène .
©2001 Haut et Court/In Extremis Images
Haut et Court & In Extremis Images present
110 mins 30 seconds
Locations/Studios
Sight and Sound .v12.n4.April 2002 p.12-14
Box Office: **£5,573**
Opening weekend **£1,766**
Screens **2**
Screen average **£883**

Possession

$ £ €
Dir Neil LaBute
12 (US/UK) 2001
Warner Bros Distributors (UK) – 25 October
Prod Paula Weinstein, Barry Levinson
Screenplay David Henry Hwang, Laura Jones, Neil LaBute, Don MacPherson
DOP Jean Yves Escoffier
Editor Claire Simpson
Music Gabriel Yared
PALTROW, Gwyneth Dr Maud Bailey
ECKHART, Aaron Roland Michell
NORTHAM, Jeremy Randolph Henry Ash
EHLE, Jennifer Christabel LaMotte
HEADEY, Lena Blanche Glover
STEPHENS, Toby Dr Fergus Wolfe
HOLLANDER, Tom Euan
EVE, Trevor Professor Mortimer Cropper
HICKEY, Tom Professor Blackadder
CROWDEN, Graham Sir George Bailey
©Gramercy Films LLC/Warner Bros.
USA Films and Warner Bros. Pictures present
a Baltimore/Spring Creek Pictures production
in association with Contagious Films
102 mins 5 seconds
Studios – Shepperton Studios
Sight and Sound .v12.n11.November 2002 p.52-53

Box Office: £321,907
Opening weekend £85,004
Screens 54
Screen average £1,574

Powerpuff girls

Dir Craig McCracken
PG (US) 2001
Warner Bros Distributors (UK)– 18 October
Prod Donna Castricone
Screenplay Charlie Bean, Lauren Faust, Craig McCracken, Paul Rudish, Don Shank
Editor Rob DeSales
Music James L. Venable
CAVADINI, Catherine (C) voice of Blossom
STRONG, Tara (C) voice of Bubbles
DAILY, E.G. voice of Buttercup
JACKSON, Roger L. (C) voice of Mojo Jojo
KANE, Tom voice of Professor Utonium
KENNY, Tom voice of mayor/the narrator
HALE, Jennifer voice of Ms Keane
MARTIN, Jennifer voice of Sara Bellum
BENNETT, Jeff Glen (C) voice of Ace/Big Billy/Grubber
DeLISLE, Grey voice of Linda/woman at zoo
©2002 Cartoon Network
Warner Bros. Pictures presents
a Cartoon Network production
73 mins 41 seconds
Animation
Sight and Sound .v12.n11.November 2002 p.53-54
Box Office: £379,066*
£414,013**
Opening weekend £92,007
Screens 222
Screen average £414

*(*total box office in 2002)*
*(** cumulative box office for 2002/03)*

* The Private Life of Sherlock Holmes

$ £
Dir Billy Wilder
(US/UK) 1970
Blue Dolphin – 6 December
Prod Billy Wilder
Screenplay Billy Wilder, I.A.L. Diamond
DOP Christopher Challis
Editor Ernest Walter
Music Miklós Rózsa
STEPHENS, Robert Sherlock Holmes
BLAKELY, Colin Dr John H. Watson
HANDL, Irene Mrs Hudson
HOLLOWAY, Stanley first gravedigger
LACEY, Catherine old lady in wheelchair
LEE, Christopher Mycroft Holmes
PAGE, Geneviève Ilse von Hoffmanstal/ "Gabrielle
REVILL, Clive Nikolai Rogozhin
TOUMANOVA, Tamara Madame Petrova
MAUREEN, Mollie Queen Victoria
©1970 Phalanx Productions Inc/Mirisch Productions Inc
The Mirisch Production Company presents
a production of Mirisch Films Limited in association with Sir Nigel Films Ltd
125 mins

Locations – Inverness
Monthly Film Bulletin.v38.n444.January 1971 p.11
Box Office: £7,835

Promises

Dir Justine Shapiro
(US/PS/Israel) 2001
ICA Projects – 11 January
Prod
Screenplay
DOP
Editor
Music
Documentary
a Promises Film Project presentation106 mins
No Sight and Sound reference

Pyaar Deewana Hota Hai

Box Office £26.808
Opening weekend £6,989
Screens 5
Screen average £1,398

Queen of the Damned

Dir Michael Rymer
15 (US/Australia) 2002
Warner Bros Distributors (UK) – 12 April
Prod Jorge Saralegui
Screenplay Scott Abbott, Michael Petroni
DOP Ian Baker
Editor Danny Cooper
Music Richard Gibbs, Jonathan Davis
TOWNSEND, Stuart Lestat
MOREAU, Marguerite Jesse Reeves
Aaliyah Akasha
PEREZ, Vincent Marius
McGANN, Paul David Talbot
OLIN, Lena Maharet
MANON, Christian Mael
BLACK, Claudia Pandora
SPENCE, Bruce Khayman
NEWTON, Matthew Armand
©2002 Village Roadshow Films (BVI) Limited (all other territories)
Warner Bros. presents in association with Village Roadshow Pictures and NPV Entertainment
a Material production
101 mins 25 seconds
Locations – Melbourne
Sight and Sound .v12.n6.June 2002 p.49
Box Office: £1,590,568
Opening weekend £611,440
Screens 273
Screen average £2,240

The Quiet American

$ £ €
Dir Phillip Noyce
15 (US/Germany/UK) 2001
Buena Vista International (UK) – 29 November
Prod William Horberg, Staffan Ahrenberg
Screenplay Christopher Hampton, Robert Schenkkan
DOP Christopher Doyle
Editor John Scott
Music Craig Armstrong
CAINE, Michael Thomas Fowler
FRASER, Brendan Alden Pyle
DO Thi Hai Yen Phuong
SHERBEDGIA, Rade (C) Inspector Vigot
MA, Tzi Hinh
STANTON, Robert Joe Tunney
OSBORNE, Holmes Bill Granger
QUANG Hai General Thé
HOANG, Ferdinand Mr Muoi
PHAM Thi Mai Hoa Phuong's sister
©2002 IMF - Internationale Medien und Film GmbH & Co. 2 Produktions KG
A Mirage Enterprises, Saga Films, IMF production
100 mins 42 seconds
Locations – Ho Chi Minh City, Hoi An, Hinh Bin, Hanoi City, Sydney
Sight and Sound .v12.n12.December

2002 p.56,58
Box Office: **£1,323,045***
£2,231,737**
Opening weekend **£240,552**
Screens **97**

Screen average **£2,480**
*(*total box office in 2002)*
*(** cumulative box office for 2002/03)*

Raaz

Box Office **£31,231**
Opening weekend **£8,717**
Screens **7**
Screen average **£1,245**

Rabbit-Proof Fence

Aus$ £
Dir Phillip Noyce
PG (Australia/UK) 2001
Buena Vista International (UK) – 8 November
Prod Phillip Noyce, Christine Olsen, John Winter
Screenplay Christine Olsen
DOP Christopher Doyle
Editor John Scott, Veronika Jenet
Music Peter Gabriel
SAMPI, Everlyn Molly Craig
SANSBURY, Tianna Daisy Craig
MONAGHAN, Laura Gracie Fields
GULPILIL, David Moodoo
LAWFORD, Ningali Molly's mother
LAWFORD, Myarn Molly's grandmother
MAILMAN, Deborah Mavis
CLARKE, Jason Constable Riggs
BRANAGH, Kenneth Mr A.O. Neville
WANGANEEN, Natasha Nina, dormitory boss
©2002 Australian Film Finance Corporation Limited/The Premium Movie Partnership/South Australian Film Corporation/Jabal Films Pty Ltd
HanWay and Australian Film Finance Corporation present
a Rumbalara Films Olsen Levy production
in association with Showtime Australia
93 mins 30 seconds
Locations – Adelaide, Flinders Ranges, S. Australia
Sight and Sound .v12.n11.November 2002 p.54-55
Box Office: **£1,447,959***
£1,745,070**
Opening weekend **£221,758**
Screens **99**
Screen average **£2,240**
*(*total box office in 2002)*
*(** cumulative box office for 2002/03)*

Raja

Box Office **£126**
Opening weekend **£126**
Screens **1**
Screen average **£126**

Rat Race

Dir Jerry Zucker
12 (US) 2001
Pathé Distribution – 11 January
Prod Jerry Zucker, Janet Zucker, Sean Daniel
Screenplay Andy Breckman
DOP Thomas Ackerman
Editor Tom Lewis
Music John Powell
ATKINSON, Rowan Enrico Pollini
CLEESE, John Donald Sinclair
GOLDBERG, Whoopi Vera Baker
GOODING Jr, Cuba Owen Templeton
GREEN, Seth Duane Cody
LOVITZ, Jon Randy Pear
MEYER, Breckin Nick Schaffer
NAJIMY, Kathy Bev Pear
SMART, Amy Tracy Faucet
BERGERE, Jenica hotel clerk
©2001 Paramount Pictures
Paramount Pictures presents in association with Fireworks Pictures
an Alphaville/Zucker production
112 mins
Locations – Calgary, Los Angeles
Sight and Sound .v12.n2.February 2002 p.58-59
Box Office: **£4,,606,209**

Opening weekend **£1,004,783**
Screens **292**
Screen average **£3,441**

Raye Makhfi

aka Secret Ballot
Dir Babak Payami
U (Iran/Italy/Canada/China/ Netherlands) 2001
Artificial Eye Film Company – 13 September
Prod Marco Müller, Babak Payami
Screenplay Babak Payami
DOP Farzad Jodat
Editor Babak Karimi
Music Michael Galasso
ABDI, Nassim election agent
ABIDI, Cyrus soldier
©2001 Payam Films/Fabrica Cinema
Payam Films, Fabrica Cinema and Sharmshir present
105 mins 3 seconds
Sight and Sound .v12.n9.September 2002 p.20-22
Box Office: **£25,199**

Opening weekend **£3,399**
Screens **2**
Screen average **£1,700**

Red Dragon

Dir Brett Ratner
15 (US/Germany) 2001
United International Pictures (UK) Ltd – 11 October
Prod Dino De Laurentiis, Martha De Laurentiis
Screenplay Ted Tally
DOP Dante Spiontti
Editor Mark Hlfrich
Music Danny Elfman
HOPKINS, Anthony Hannibal Lecter
NORTON, Edward Will Graham
FIENNES, Ralph Francis Dolarhyde
KEITEL, Harvey Jack Crawford
WATSON, Emily Reba McClane
PARKER, Mary-Louise (C) Molly Graham
HOFFMAN, Philip Seymour Freddy Lounds
HEALD, Anthony Dr Chilton
DUKE, Bill police chief
LEUNG, Ken Lloyd Bowman
©2002 Mikona Productions GmbH & Co KG
Universal Pictures and Dino De Laurentiis present
in association with Metro-Goldwyn-Mayer Pictures
a Brett Ratner film
124 mins 32 seconds
Locations – Los Angeles
Sight and Sound .v12.n12.December 2002 p.58-59
Box Office: **£9,594,844**
Opening weekend **£3,180,493**
Screens **428**

Screen average **£7,431**

Reign of Fire

£ €
Dir Rob Bowman
12 (UK/Ireland/US) 2001
Buena Vista International (UK) – 23 August
Prod Richard D. Zanuck, Lili Fini Zanuck, Gary Barber, Roger Birnbaum
Screenplay Gregg Chabot, Kevin Peterka, Matt Greenberg, Zak Penn, Terry Hayes
DOP Adrian Biddle
Editor Thom Noble

Music Edward Shearmur
BALE, Christian Quinn Abercromby
McCONAUGHEY, Matthew Denton Van Zan
SCORUPCO, Izabella Alex Jensen
BUTLER, Gerard Dave Creedy
MOUTTER, Scott James Jared Wilke
KENNEDY, David Eddie Stax
SIDDIG, Alexander Ajay
DENNEHY, Ned Barlow
KEENAN, Rory Devon
MAYNARD, Terence Gideon
©2001 B & B Company
Touchstone Pictures/Spyglass Entertainment present
[end]
Produced with the support of investment incentives for the Irish Film Industry
provided by the Government of Ireland
a co-production between World 2000 Entertainment Limited and Reign of Fire Limited
World 2000/Grosvenor Park
a United Kingdom/Ireland co-production
101 mins 48 seconds
Locations – Dublin
Studios – Ardmore Studios
Sight and Sound .v12.n9.September 2002 p.71-72

Box Office:	**£3,369,183**
Opening weekend	**£932,168**
Screens	**365**
Screen average	**£2,554**

Resident Evil Genesis

£ €
Dir Paul Anderson
15 (Germany/UK/France) 2001
Pathé Distribution – 12 July
Prod Bernd Eichinger, Samuel Hadida, Jeremy Bolt, Paul W. S. Anderson
Screenplay Paul W. S. Anderson
DOP David Johnson
Editor Alexander Berner
Music Marco Beltrami, Marilyn Manson
JOVOVICH, Milla Alice
RODRIGUEZ, Michelle Rain
MABIUS, Eric Matt
PUREFOY, James Spence
CREWES, Martin Kaplan
SALMON, Colin One
McCLUSKEY, Ryan (C) Mr Grey
PEARCE, Oscar Mr Red
OVÉ, Indra Ms Black
BOLT, Anna Dr Green
©2002 Constantin Film Produktion GmbH/New Legacy Films Ltd
Constantin Film/Davis Films present
a Constantin Film/New Legacy Film production
In association with Davis Films and Impact Pictures
Supported by Filmboard Berlin Brandenburg, FFA, Filmfernsehfonds Bayern
100 mins 27 seconds
Locations – Berlin, London, Ontario
Sight and Sound .v12.n6.June 2002 p.50-51

Box Office:	**£2,768,130**
Opening weekend	**£801,628**
Screens	**264**
Screen average	**£3,036**

Return to Never Land

Dir Robin Budd
U (US) 2002
Buena Vista International (UK) – 22 March
Prod Christopher Chase, Michelle Robinson, Dan Rounds
Screenplay Temple Mathews, Carter Crocker
Editor Anthony F. Rocco, Daniel Lee
Music Joel McNeely
OWEN, Harriet voice of Jane/ young Wendy
WEAVER, Blayne voice of Peter Pan
BURTON, Corey voice of Captain Hook
BENNETT, Jeff voice of Smee/pirates
SOUCIE, Kath voice of Wendy
McDONOUGH, Andrew voice of Danny
REES, Roger voice of Edward
BRESLIN, Spencer voice of Cubby
PIERCE, Bradley voice of Nibs
BESWICK, Quinn voice of Slightly
©2001 Disney Enterprises Inc
Walt Disney Pictures presents
72 mins 22 seconds
Sight and Sound .v12.n4.April 2002 p.56,58

Box Office:	**£3,825,923**
Opening weekend	**£266,149**
Screens	**370**
Screen average	**£719**

Revelation

£
Dir Stuart Urban
15 (UK) 2001
Miracle Communications – 12 April
Prod Jonathan Woolf
Screenplay Stuart Urban
DOP Sam McCurdy
Editor Julian Rodd
Music Kirsty Whalley
STAMP, Terence Lord Magnus Martel
D'ARCY, James Jake Martel
WIGHTMAN, Natasha Mira
CUNNINGHAM, Liam Father Ray Connolly
WILLIAMS, Heathcote new age man
JACOBI, Derek librarian
IMRIE, Celia Harriet Martel
MOODY, Ron Sir Isaac Newton
KIER, Udo Grand Master
MEGHREBLIAN, Diran craftsman
©2001 Romulus Films Limited
Romulus presents
a Cyclops Vision production for Romulus Films
a Stuart Urban film
110 mins 55 seconds
Locations – Malta, France, Cornwall, London
Studios – Pinewood, Bray Film Studios
Sight and Sound .v12.n5.May 2002 p.52

Box Office:	**£18,678**
Opening weekend	**£8,527**
Screens	**44**
Screen average	**£194**

Riri Chou-Chou No Subete

Dir Iwai Shunji
15 (Japan) 2001
ICA Projects – 30 August
Prod
Screenplay Shunji Iwai
DOP Noboru Shinoda
Editor Shunji Iwai
Music Takeshi Kobayashi, Claude Debussy
ICHIHARA, Hayato Yuichi Hasumi
OSHINARI, Shugo Shusuke Hoshino
AOI, Yu Shiori Tsuda
ITO, Ayumi Yoko Kuno
MATSUDA, Kazusa Sumika Kanzaki, head of girl ga
HOSOYAMADA, Takahito Kentaro Sasaki, Music classmate
KAKU, Tomohiro Tadano

KASAHARA, Hideyuki Kyota Shimizu, kendo classmate
KATSUJI, Ryo Hitoshi Terawaki, kendo classma
SAWAKI, Tetsu .
©2001 Lily Chou-Chou Partners/Victor Company of Japan Ltd/Wowow/Tube Entertainment/Oorong-Sha/Rockwell Eyes
Rockwell Eyes presents
146 mins Subtitles
Sight and Sound .v12.n10.October 2002 p.36
Box Office: £15,900

Rishtey

Box Office £199,344
Opening weekend £96,255
Screens 23
Screen average £4,185

Road

Box Office £22,210
Opening weekend £7,572
Screens 6
Screen average £1,262

Roadkill

aka: Joy Ride
Dir John Dahl
15 (US) 2001
20th Century Fox International (UK) – 26 April
Prod J.J. Abrams, Chirs Moore
Screenplay Clay Tarver, J.J. Abrams
DOP Jeffrey Jur
Editor Scott Chestnut, Todd E.
Miller, Glen Scantlebury
Music Barco Beltrami
ZAHN, Steve Fuller Thomas
WALKER, Paul Lewis Thomas
SOBIESKI, LeeLee Venna
BOWMAN, Jessica Charlotte
STONE, Stuart Danny, Lewis' roommate
WALLACE, Basil car salesman
LECKNER, Brian Officer Keeney
WICKLIFFE, Mary Salt Lake City police desk clerk
SATTERTHWAITE, McKenzie asst Salt Lake City police desk
YOUNT, Dell gas station mechanic
©2001 Monarchy Enterprises S.a.r.l./Regency Entertainment (USA) Inc
Regency Enterprises presents
a New Regency/Bad Robot/Liveplanet production
in association with Epsilon Motion Pictures
96 mins 58 seconds
Locations – Los Angeles
Sight and Sound .v12.n4.April 2002 p.58-59
Box Office: £2,285,775

Opening weekend £784,853
Screens 266
Screen average £2,951

Road to Perdition

Dir Sam Mendes
15 (US) 2001
20th Century Fox International (UK) – 20 September
Prod Richard D. Zanuck, Dean Zanuck, Sam Mendes
Screenplay David Self
DOP Conrad L. Hall
Editor Jill Bilcock
Music Thomas Newman
HANKS, Tom Michael Sullivan
NEWMAN, Paul John Rooney
LAW, Jude Maguire
LEIGH, Jennifer Jason Annie Sullivan
TUCCI, Stanley Frank Nitti
CRAIG, Daniel Connor Rooney
HOECHLIN, Tyler Michael Sullivan Jr
AIKEN, Liam Peter Sullivan
BAKER, Dylan Alexander Rance
HINDS, Ciarán (C) Finn McGovern
©2001 Twentieth Century Fox Film Corporation/DreamWorks LLC
Twentieth Century Fox and DreamWorks Pictures present
a Zanuck Company production
116 mins 51 seconds
Locations – Chicago
Sight and Sound .v12.n10.October 2002 p.48-49
Box Office: £6,698,460

Opening weekend £256,035
Screens 32
Screen average £8,001

Roberto Succo

Dir Cédric Kahn
15 (France/Switzerland) 2001
Artificial Eye Film Company – 7 June
Prod Gilles Sandoz, Patrick Sobelman
Screenplay Cédric Kahn
DOP Pascal Marti
Editor Yann Dedet, Marie da
Costa, Juliette Garcias, Camille Maury, Eric Armbrouster, Anne Souriau
Music Julien Civange
CASSETTI, Stefano 'Kurt', Roberto Succo
BESCO, Isild Le Léa
DELL'ISOLA, Patrick Major Thomas
ALIBERTI, Viviana Swiss schoolteacher
PERRON, Estelle Céline Simon
SASSI, Leyla Cathy
DECASTEL, Catherine Patricia
CARBONINI, Olivia Etna bar hostess
VUILLEMIN, Basile Ludovic, child
RAUL, Brigitte child's mother
©2001 AGAT Films & Cie/Diaphana Films/Ex Nihilo/France 3 Cinéma/Gimages Dévéloppement/Vega Film
Agat Films & Cie presents
in co-production with Diaphana Films, Ex Nihilo, France 3 Cinéma, Gimages Dévéloppement, Vega Film
and the participation of Canal+, Gimages 3, Eurimages, Télévision Suisse Romande (TSR)
124 mins 58 seconds
Subtitles
Sight and Sound .v12.n6.June 2002 p.51-52
Box Office: £90,595
Opening weekend £14,373
Screens 6
Screen average £2,396

Rock Star

Dir Stephen Herek
15 (US) 2001
Warner Bros Distributors (UK) – 11 January
Prod Robert Lawrence, Toby Jaffe
Screenplay John Stockwell
DOP Veli Steiger
Editor Trudy Ship
Music Trevor Rabin
WAHLBERG, Mark Chris Cole
ANISTON, Jennifer Emily Poule
FLEMYNG, Jason Bobby Beers
OLYPHANT, Timothy Rob Malcolm
SPALL, Timothy Mats
WEST, Dominic Kirk Cuddy
BONHAM, Jason A.C.
PILSON, Jeff Jorgen
WYLDE, Zakk Ghode
ELIAS, Blas Donny Johnson
©2001 Warner Bros. and Bel Air Pictures LLC
Warner Bros. Pictures presents
in association with Bel-Air Entertainment
a Mayville Pictures/Robert Lawrence production
a Stephen Herek film
105 mins 7 seconds
Locations – Los Angeles, Seattle

Sight and Sound .v11.n12.December 2001 p.56-57

Box Office:	**£747,807**
Opening weekend	**£294,973**
Screens	**210**
Screen average	**£1,405**

Le Roi Danse

Dir Gérard Corbiau
15 (Belgium/Germany/France) 2000
Cinéfrance – 5 July

Prod Dominique Janne
Screenplay Jean-Claude Carrière
DOP Gérard Simon
Editor Ludo Troch, Philippe Ravoet, Jennifer Augé

MAGIMEL, Benoît Louis XIV
TERRAL, Boris Jean-Baptiste Lully
KARYO, Tchéky Molière
EMMANUELLE, Colette Queen Mother, Anne of Austria
BOIS, Cécile Madeleine
KEIM, Claire Julie
LEYSEN, Johan Cambert
STÉPHANE, Idwig Conti
TARDING, Emil young Louis XIV
FRANÇOIS, Jacques Cambefort

©2000 K-Star/MMC Independent/K-Dance/K2/France 2 Cinéma/RTL TV1
[at start]©K-Star/MMCI/K0-Dance/K2/France 2 Cinéma/RTL TV1
Dominique Janne presents
a production of K-Star, France 2 Cinéma
with the participation of Canal+ and support of Procirep
a co-production of MMC Independent, K-Dance
with the support of Filmstiftung Nordrhein-Westfalen, K2, RTL TV1
produced with the assistance of Centre du Cinéma et de l'Audiovisuel de la Communauté française de Belgique and télédistributeurs wallons
this film has been supported by Eurimages
a film by Gérard Corbiau

113 mins 48 seconds
Locations – South of France
Sight and Sound .v12.n9.September 2002 p.64-65

Box Office:	**£13,146**
Opening weekend	**£5,035**
Screens	**3**
Screen average	**£1,678**

Rollerball

Dir John McTiernan
15 (US/Germany/Japan) 2001
Columbia TriStar Films (UK) – 28 June

Prod Charles Roven, Beau St. Clair, John McTiernan, Norman Jewison
Screenplay Larry Ferguson, John Pogue, David Campbell Wilson
DOP Steve Mason
Editor John Wright
Music Eric Serra

KLEIN, Chris Jonathan Cross
RÉNO, Jean Petrovich
LL COOL J Marcus Ridley
ROMIJN-STAMOS, Rebecca (C) Aurora
ANDREWS, Naveen Sanjay
TAKTAROV, Oleg Denekin
HEMBLEN, David Serokin
HEYMAN, Paul English sports announcer
WRIGHT, Janet Coach Olga
BRYNIARSKI, Andrew Halloran

©2001 Metro-Goldwyn-Mayer Pictures Inc
Metro-Goldwyn-Mayer Pictures presents
in association with Mosaic Media Group
a John McTiernan film

98 mins 5 seconds
Locations – Montreal
Sight and Sound .v12.n8.August 2002 p.48-49

Box Office:	**£259,419**
Opening weekend	**£136,243**
Screens	**179**
Screen average	**£761**

The Rookie

Dir John Lee Hancock
U (US) 2001
Buena Vista International (UK) – 11 October

Prod Gordon Gray, Mark Ciardi, Mark Johnson
Screenplay Mike Rich
DOP John Schwartzman
Editor Eric L.Beason
Music Carter Burwell

QUAID, Dennis Jimmy Morris
GRIFFITHS, Rachel Lorri Morris
HERNANDEZ, Jay Joaquin 'Wack' Campos
GRANT, Beth Olline, Jimmy's mother
JONES, Angus T. Hunter
COX, Brian Jim Morris Sr
GONZALEZ, Rick Rudy Bonilla
LINDBERG, Chad Joe David West
SPIZZIRRI, Angelo Joel De La Garza
APPLEGATE, Royce D. Henry

©2002 Disney Enterprises Inc
Walt Disney Pictures present
a Gran Via production

127 mins 53 seconds
Locations – Austin
Sight and Sound .v12.n10.October 2002 p.49-50

Box Office:	**£28,190**
Opening weekend	**£16,570**
Screens	**79**
Screen average	**£210**

The Royal Tenenbaums

Dir Wes Anderson
15 (US) 2001
Buena Vista International (UK) – 15 March

Prod Wes Anderson, Barry Mendel, Scott Rudin
Screenplay Wes Anderson, Owen Wilson
DOP Robert Yeoman
Editor Dylan Tichenor
Music Mark Mothersbaugh

HACKMAN, Gene Royal Tenenbaum
HUSTON, Anjelica Etheline Tenenbaum
STILLER, Ben Chas Tenenbaum
PALTROW, Gwyneth Margot Tenenbaum
WILSON, Luke Richie Tenenbaum
WILSON, Owen Eli Cash
MURRAY, Bill Raleigh St. Clair
GLOVER, Danny Henry Sherman
CASSEL, Seymour Dusty
PALLANA, Kumar Pagoda

©2001 Touchstone Pictures
Touchstone Pictures present an American Empirical picture

109 mins 53 seconds
Locations – New York
Sight and Sound .v13.n1.January 2003 p.58

Box Office:	**£3,329,372**
Opening weekend	**£700,025**
Screens	**159**
Screen average	**£4,403**

*Le Rayon Vert

aka: The Green Ray
Dir Eric Rohmer
15 (France) 1986
NFT – 19 April

Prod Margaret Ménégoz
Screenplay Eric Rohmer
DOP Sophie Maintigneux
Editor Maria-Luisa Garcia
Music Jean-Louis

Valéro
RIVIÈRE, Marie Delphine
CHEMAKHI, Amira ., Paris
RICHEZ, Sylvie Sylvie, Paris
HEREDIA, Lisa (C) ., Paris
GERVAISE, Basile grandfather, Paris
GERVAISE, Virginie Virginie, Paris
HERNANDEZ, René René, Paris
RIVIÈRE, Dominique Dominique, Paris
JULLIEN, Claude Claude, Paris
JULLIEN, Alaric Alaric, Paris
Films du Losange (Paris)
Ministère Français de la Culture
Ministère des Postes et Télécommunication99 mins
Monthly Film Bulletin .v54.n638.March 1987 p.84-85
Box Office: £12,208

The Runaway Mummy

Box Office £6,976Opening weekend £1,433
Screens 1
Screen average £1,433

S1mone

Dir Andrew Niccol
PG (US) 2002
Entertainment Film Distributors Ltd – 25 October
Prod Andrew Niccol
Screenplay Andrew Niccol
DOP Edward Lachman
Editor Paul Rubell
Music Carter Burwell
PACINO, Al Viktor Taransky
KEENER, Catherine Elaine Christian
VINCE, Pruitt Taylor Max Sayer
MOHR, Jay Hal Sinclair
SCHWARTZMAN, Jason Milton
ANDERSON, Stanley Frank Brand
WOOD, Evan Rachel Lainey Christian
VON BARGEN, Daniel chief detective
Simone (C) herself
SALISBURY, Benjamin personal assistant
©2002 New Line Productions, Inc.
New Line Cinema presents
a Niccol Films production
117 mins 25 seconds
Locations – Los Angeles
Sight and Sound .v12.n11.November 2002 p.55-56
Box Office: £299,712

Opening weekend £147,372
Screens 161
Screen average £915

Saathiya

Box Office £288,004

Opening weekend £41,951
Screens 20
Screen average £2,098

* Sans Soleil

Dir Chris Marker
(France) 1982
bfi Bookings – 15 November
Prod Anatole Dauman
Screenplay Chris Marker
DOP Chris Marker
Editor Chris Marker
DELAY, Florence Sandor Krasna's letters read
STEWART, Alexandra S.K.'s letters read (Eng. version)
Argos-Films
100 mins
Monthly Film Bulletin.v51.n606.July 1984 p.195-196
Box Office: £15,290
Opening weekend £2,237

Screens 1
Screen average £2,237

The Santa Clause 2

Dir Michael Lembeck
U (US) 2002
Buena Vista International (UK) – 29 November
Prod Brian Reilly, Bobby Newmyer
Screenplay Don Rhymer, Cinco Paul, Ken Daurio, Ed Decter, John J. Strauss
DOP Adam Greenberg
Editor David Finfer
Music George S. Clinton
ALLEN, Tim Scott Calvin/Santa/toy Santa
REINHOLD, Judge Neil Miller
CREWSON, Wendy Laura Miller
MITCHELL, Elizabeth Carol Newman
KRUMHOLTZ, David Bernard
LLOYD, Eric Charlie Calvin
BRESLIN, Spencer Curtis
MUMY, Liliana Lucy Miller
WOODMAN, Danielle Abby
LaFLEUR, Art Tooth Fairy
©2002 Disney Enterprises, Inc.
Walt Disney Pictures presents
an Outlaw Productions/Boxing Cats Films production
104 mins 14 seconds
Locations – Vancouver
Sight and Sound .v13.n1.January 2003 p.50,52
Box Office: £7,918,945
Opening weekend £951,754
Screens 362
Screen average £2,629

* Saturday Night and Sunday Morning

£
Dir Karel Reisz
(UK)1960
bfi Bookings – 11 October
Prod Harry Saltzman, Tony Richardson
Screenplay Alan Stillitoe
DOP Freddie Francis
Editor Seth Holt
Music John Dankworth
FINNEY, Albert Arthur
FIELD, Shirley Anne Doreen
ROBERTS, Rachel Brenda
BAKER, Hylda Aunt Ada
ROSSINGTON, Norman Bert
PRINGLE, Bryan Jack
CAWDRON, Robert Robboe
MORRIS, Edna Mrs. Bull
WAGSTAFFE, Elsie Mrs. Seaton
PETTITT, Frank Mr. Seaton
Woodfall Film Productions
89 mins
Studios – Twickenham Film Studios
Monthly Film Bulletin .v27.n323.December 1960 p.166
Box Office: £7,436

Opening weekend £2,779
Screens 1
Screen average £2,779

Saving Silverman

Dir Dennis Dugan
15 (US/Australia/Canada) 2001
Columbia TriStar Films (UK) – 11 January
Prod Neal H. Moritz
Screenplay Greg DePaul, Hank Nelken
DOP Arthur Albert
Editor Debra Neil-Fisher, Patrick J. Don Vito
Music Mike Simpson
BIGGS, Jason Darren Silverman
ZAHN, Steve Wayne Le Fessier
BLACK, Jack J.D. McNugent
PEET, Amanda Judith Snodgrass-Fessbeggler
ERMEY, R. Lee Coach
DETMER, Amanda Sandy Perkus
DIAMOND, Neil himself
GASS, Kyle bar dude
ARMOUR, Norman minister
FOO, Colin old man
©2001 Columbia Pictures Industries, Inc
Columbia Pictures and Village

Roadshow Pictures present
in association with NPV Entertainment
an Original Film production
a film by Dennis Dugan
91 mins 48 seconds
Locations – Vancouver
Sight and Sound .v12.n3.March 2002 p.43
Box Office: **£43,370**
Opening weekend **£26,548**
Screens **40**
Screen average **£664**

Scooby-Doo

Dir Raja Gosnell
PG (US) 2001
Warner Bros Distributors (UK) – 12 July
Prod Charles Roven, Richard Suckle
Screenplay James Gunn
DOP David Eggby
Editor Kent Beyda
Music David Newman
PRINZE Jr, Freddie Fred Jones
GELLAR, Sarah Michelle Daphne Blake
LILLARD, Matthew Norville 'Shaggy' Rogers
ATKINSON, Rowan Emile Mondavarious
NUÑEZ Jr, Miguel A. voodoo maestro
FISHER, Isla Mary Jane
GRIVES, Steven N'Goo Tuana
FRAZIER, Stan Sugar Ray
DJ Homicide (C) Sugar Ray
©2002 Warner Bros
Warner Bros Pictures presents
a Mosaic Media Group production
a Raja Gosnell film
86 mins 22 seconds
Locations – Warner Roadshow Movie World, Theme Park (SE Queensland, Australia)
Sight and Sound .v12.n8.August 2002 p.49-50
Box Office: **£22,596,370**
Opening weekend **£5,129,109**
Screens **472**
Screen average **£10,867**

The Scorpion King

Dir Chuck Russell
12 (US) 2001
United International Pictures (UK) Ltd – 19 April
Prod Stephen Sommers, Sean Daniel, James Jacks, Kevin Misher
Screenplay Stephen Sommers, William Osborne, David Hayter
DOP John R. Leonetti
Editor Michael Tronick, Greg Parsons
Music John Debney
The Rock (C) Mathayus
BRAND, Steven Memnon
HU, Kelly Cassandra, the sorceress
HILL, Bernard Philos
HESLOV, Grant Arpid
FACINELLI, Peter Prince Takmet
MOELLER, Ralph Thorak
CLARKE DUNCAN, Michael (C) Balthazar
RICHMOND, Branscombe Jesup
REES, Roger King Pheron
©2001 KALIMA Productions GmbH & Co. KG
Universal Pictures presents
In association with WWF Entertainment
An Alphaville/Stephen Sommers/Misher Production
91 mins 14 seconds
Locations – Los Angeles, Palm Springs
Sight and Sound .v12.n6.June 2002 p.52-53
Box Office: **£5,166,806**
Opening weekend **£1,610,794**
Screens **408**
Screen average **£3,948**

Scratch

Dir Doug Pray
15 (US) 2001
Momentum Pictures – 30 August
Prod Brad Blondeim, Ernest Meza
DOP Robert Bennett
Editor Doug Pray
Music Mix Master Mike, Qbert
Allies, The (C) artist
Atrak artist
DJ Craze artist
Infamous artist
J-Smoke artist
Develop artist
Spictakular artist
Bullet Proof Space Travelers artist
DJ Marz artist
DJ Quest artist
©2001 Darkhorse Entertainment LLC
Intermedia Films and Ridgeway Entertainment present
a Firewalk Films production
a film by Doug Pray
91 mins 17 seconds
Sight and Sound .v12.n9.September 2002 p.72,74
Box Office: **£30,474**
Opening weekend **£2,930**
Screens **2**
Screen average **£1,465**

Shaeed-E-Azam

Box Office **£4,806**
Opening weekend **£1,536**
Screens **6**
Screen average **£256**

Shakti – The Power

Box Office **£305,609**
Opening weekend **£110,198**
Screens **33**
Screen average **£3,339**

Shallow Hal

Dir Bobby Farrelly, Peter Farrelly
12 (US/Germany) 2001
20th Century Fox International (UK) – 1 February
Prod Bradley Thomas, Charles B. Wessler, Bobby Farrelly, Peter Farrelly
Screenplay Sean Moynihan, Peter Farrelly, Bobby Farrelly
DOP Russell Carpenter
Editor Christopher Greenbury
Music Ivy
PALTROW, Gwyneth Rosemary Shanahan
BLACK, Jack Hal Larson
ALEXANDER, Jason Mauricio
VITERELLI, Joe Steve Shanahan
KIRBY, Rene Walt
McGILL, Bruce Reverend Larson
ROBBINS, Tony Tony Robbins
WARD, Susan Jill
GESNER, Zen Ralph
BURNS, Brooke Katrina
©2001 "Shallow Hal" Filmproduktion GmbH & Co. KG/Twentieth Century Fox Film Corporation
Twentieth Century Fox presents
a Conundrum Entertainment production
A Farrelly Brothers movie
In association with "Shallow Hal" Filmproduktion GmbH & Co. KG
113 mins 30 seconds
Locations – North Carolina
Sight and Sound .v12.n3.March 2002 p.54
Box Office: **£5,779,232**
Opening weekend **£1,277,183**
Screens **284**
Screen average **£4,497**

Shararat

Box Office **£2,809**
Opening weekend **£1,071**
Screens **5**
Screen average **£214**

The Shipping News

Dir Lasse Hallström
15 (US) 2001
Buena Vista International (UK) – 1 March
Prod Irwin Winkler, Linda Goldstein Knowlton, Leslie Holleran
Screenplay Robert Nelson Jacobs, Beth Henley, Laura Jones, Ronald Bass, Tom Epperson
DOP Oliver Stapleton
Editor Andrew Mondshein
Music Christopher Young
SPACEY, Kevin Quoyle
MOORE, Julianne Wavey Prowse
DENCH, Judi Agnis Hamm
GLENN, Scott Jack Buggit
IFANS, Rhys Beaufield Nutbeem
POSTLETHWAITE, Pete (C) Tert Card
BLANCHETT, Cate Petal
PINSENT, Gordon Billy Pretty
BEHR, Jason Dennis Buggit
PINE, Larry Bayonet Melville
©2001 Miramax Film Corp.
Miramax Films presents
an Irwin Winkler production
a Lasse Hallström film
117 mins 14 seconds
Locations – Nova Scotia, Trinity, Newfoundland
Sight and Sound .v12.n3.March 2002 p.55
Box Office: **£1,454,281**
Opening weekend **£96,694**
Screens **23**
Screen average **£4,204**

Shi Qi Sui De Dan Che

Dir Xiaoshuai Wang
PG (Taiwan/France/China) 2001
Metro Tartan Distributors – 28 June
Prod Peggy Chiao, Hsiao-Ming Hsü, Sanping Han
Screenplay Xiaoshuai Wang, Danian Tang, Peggy Chiao, Hsiao-Ming Hsü
DOP Jie Liu
Editor Hongyu Yang, Ju-Kuan Hsiao
CUI Lin Guei
LI Bin Jian
ZHOU Xun Qin
GAO Yuanyuan Xiao
LI Shuang Da Huan
ZHAO Yiwei father
PANG Yan mother
ZHOU Fangfei Rong Rong
XIE Jian manager
MA Yuhong accountant
Arc Light Films presents
an Arc Light Films production
co-produced by Pyramide Productions in association with Public Television Service Foundation, Eastern Television, Asiatic Films, Beijing Film Studio
113 mins 22 seconds
Sight and Sound .v12.n7.July 2002 p.38-39
Box Office: **£28,377**
Opening weekend **£5,065**
Screens **3**
Screen average **£1,688**

Shooters

$ £ €
Dir Colin Teague
18 (NetherlandsUK/US) 2001
Universal Pictures International – 25 January
Prod Margery Bone
Screenplay Gary Young, Andrew Howard, Louis Dempsey
DOP Tom Erisman
Editor Devin Whelan
Music Kemal Ultanur
DUNBAR, Adrian Max Bell
HOWARD, Andrew J
DEMPSEY, Louis Gilly
BUTLER, Gerard Jackie Junior
HUGHES, Jason Charlie Franklin
RHYS, Matthew Eddie
GRUFFUDD, Ioan Freddy Guns
SWEENEY, Jamie (C) Skip
LYNSKEY, Melanie Marie
FIELDING, Emma Detective Inspector Sarah Pryce
©2001 Geops Amsterdam B.V.
PFG Entertainment presents
a co-production of Coolbeans Films & Catapult Productions
95 mins 18 seconds
Locations – London
Sight and Sound .v12.n1.January 2002 p.56
Box Office: **£6,983**
Opening weekend **£4,187**
Screens **21**
Screen average **£199**

Showtime

Dir Tom Dey
12 (US/Australia) 2001
Warner Bros Distributors (UK) – 3 May
Prod Jorge Saralegui, Jane Rosenthal
Screenplay Keith Sharon, Alfred Gough, Miles Millar, Ben Ramsey, Vince McKewin, Marc Hyman, Gary Ross, John Hamburg
DOP Thomas Kloss
Editor Billy Weber
Music Alan Silvestri
DE NIRO, Robert Mitch Preston
MURPHY, Eddie Trey Sellars
RUSSO, Rene Chase Renzi
FAISON, Frankie R. (C) Captain Winship
SHATNER, William himself
HARRIS, Rachel teacher
FARID, Zaid captain, audition
BORSTEIN, Alex casting director
MANDEL, Holly producer
MANESH, Marshall convenience store owner
©2002 Village Roadshow Films (BVI) Limited (all other territories)
Warner Bros. Pictures presents in association with Village Roadshow Pictures and NPV Entertainment
a Material production in association with Tribeca Productions
95 mins 17 seconds
Locations – Los Angeles
Sight and Sound .v12.n6.June 2002 p.53-54
Box Office: **£1,756,167**
Opening weekend **£486,753**
Screens **307**
Screen average **£1,586**

Sidewalks of New York

Dir Edward Burns
15 (US) 2001
Helkon SK – 5 April
Prod Charles Gassot
Screenplay Laetitia, Caroline Thivel
DOP Pierre Aïm
Editor Véronique Parnet
Music Jérôme
BURNS, Edward Tommy
DAWSON, Rosario Maria
FARINA, Dennis Carpo
GRAHAM, Heather Annie
KRUMHOLTZ, David Ben
MURPHY, Brittany Ashley
TUCCI, Stanley Griffin
LEYDON CAMPBELL, Michael Gio/Harry
DAJANI, Nadia Hilary
THORNE, Callie Sue
©2001 Sidewalks, LLC
a Marlboro Road Gang production in association with Artists Production Group
107 mins 55 seconds

Locations – Bordeaux
Sight and Sound .v12.n1.January 2002 p.56-57
Box Office: **£120,217**

Opening weekend **£43,063**
Screens **32**
Screen average **£1,346**

Signs

Dir M.Night Shyamalan
12 (US) 2001
Buena Vista International (UK) – 13 September
Prod M.Night Shyamalan, Frank Marshall, Sam Mercer
Screenplay M. Night Shyamalan
DOP Tak Fujimoto
Editor Barbara Tulliver
Music James Newton Howard
GIBSON, Mel Graham Hess
PHOENIX, Joaquin Merrill Hess
CULKIN, Rory Morgan Hess
BRESLIN, Abigail Bo Hess
JONES, Cherry Officer Paski
SHYAMALAN, M. Night Ray Reddy
KALEMBER, Patricia Colleen Hess
SUTTON, Ted SFC Cunningham
WEVER, Merritt Tracey Abernathy
FLAHERTY, Lanny Mr Nathan
©2001 Touchstone Pictures
Touchstone Pictures presents
a Blinding Edge Pictures / Kennedy/Marshall production
a M. Night Shyamalan film
106 mins 26 seconds
Locations – Philadelphia
Sight and Sound .v12.n10.October 2002 p.50,52
Box Office: **£16,245,914**

Opening weekend **£3,767,713**
Screens **443**
Screen average **£8,505**

Skout Hansawwar

Dir Youssef Chahine
12 (Egypt/France) 2001
NFT – 31 May
Prod Humbert Balsan, Marianne Khoury, Gabriel Khoury
Screenplay Youssef Chanhine
DOP Pierre Dupouey
Editor Rachida Abdel Salam, Tamer Ezzat
Music Omar Khairat
LATIFA Malak
WAFIK, Ahmed Jean-Jacques Lamei
al-KHATIB, Magd grandmother
RUBI Paula
CHAABAN, Mostapha Nasser
BEDEIR, Ahmed Alphi
WAHAB, Zaki Abdel Ezz Eldine
MEHREZ, Ahmed Abbas
TORK, Hanan
SALAMA, Hani
a Misr Intl.,/Ognon Pictures/France 2 Cinema/Havas Image co-production
international sales: Flach Pyramide Intl., Paris
108 mins
Locations – Egypt
No Sight and Sound reference
Box Office: **£4,238**

Slackers

Dir Dewey Nicks
15 (US) 2001
Momentum Pictures – 10 May
Prod Neal H. Moritz, Erik Feig
ScreenplayDavid H. Steinberg
DOP James Bagdonas
Editor Tara Timpone
Music Joey Altruda, Venus Brown, Printz Board, Justin Stanley
SAWA, Devon Dave
SCHWARTZMAN, JasonEthan
KING, James Angela
SEGEL, Jason Sam
MARONNA, Michael (C) Jeff
VAN DOREN, Mamie Mrs Van Graaf
FLAHERTY, Joe Mr Leonard
TAYLOR YOUNG, Leigh (C) Valerie Patton
ANDERSON, Sam Charles Patton
PREPON, Laura Reanna
©2001 Alliance Atlantis Pictures International
['domestic version']
[logos] Screen Gems/Alliance Atlantis/Original Films
Screen Gems presents
in association with Alliance Atlantis
a Neal H. Moritz production
in association with Erik Feig Productions
a Dewey Nicks film
['international version']
[logos] Alliance Atlantis/Original Films
Alliance Atlantis presents
a Neal H. Moritz production
in association with Erik Feig Productions
a Dewey Nicks film
86 mins 42 seconds
Locations – Los Angeles
Sight and Sound .v12.n4.April 2002 p.60,62
Box Office: **£373,525**
Opening weekend **£152,078**
Screens **177**
Screen average **£859**

Slap Her, She's French

Dir Melanie Mayron
12 (Germany/US) 2001
Winchester Film Distribution – 18 October
Prod Beau Flynn, Jonathan King, Matthias Emcke
Screenplay Lamar Damon, Robert Lee King, Alan Ball
DOP Charles Minsky
Editor Marshall Harvey
Music David Michael Frank
PERABO, Piper Genevieve LePlouff/Clarissa Vog
McGREGOR, Jane Starla Grady
FORD, Trent Edwin 'Ed' Mitchell
WHITE, Julie Bootsie Grady
SMITH, Brandon Arnie Grady
JAMES, Jesse Randolph Scott Grady
AYCOX, Nicki Tanner Jennings
ADI, Alexandra Ashley Lopez y Lopez
CZUCHRY, Matt Kyle Fuller
COPPEN, Cristen Doreen Gilmore
©2001 IMF Internationale Medien und Film GmbH & Co. 2. Produktions KG
Constantin Film presents
in association with Bandeira and Key Entertainment
a Beau Flynn and Emcke/Augsberger production
an IMF 2 production
91 mins 51 seconds
Locations – Dallas
Sight and Sound .v12.n11.November 2002 p.56,58
Box Office: **£633,040**
Opening weekend **£210,321**
Screens **157**
Screen average **£1,340**

Slogans

Dir Gjergj Xjuvani
(France/Albania) 2001
NFT – 15 February
Prod Anne-Dominique Toussaint, Pascal Judelewicz
Screenplay Ylljet Alicka, Yves Hanchar, Gjergj
DOP Gérald Thiaville

Editor Didier Ranz
Music Denis Barbier
GORISHTI, Artur André
XHUVANI, Luiza Diana
QIRJAQI, Agim school director
HASKO, Birce (C) Sabaf
KANXHERI, Niko Selman Tosku
CELA, Festim Festim Tosku
NDRENIKA, Robert Llesh
LADI, Rita Lumé
BITRAKU, Marko Gjin
KUJOFSKA, Fadil Pashk
a Les Films des Tournelles release (in France) of a Les Films des Tournelles/Albanian General Vision presentation of a Les Films des Tournelles,
Roissy Films, Les Films en Hiver (France) / Albanian General Vision (Albania)
production
90 mins
No reference
Box Office: £3,457

Små Ulykker

Dir Annette K. Olesen
15 (Germany) 2001
Artificial Eye Film Company – 20 September
Prod Ib Tardini
Screenplay Kim Fupz Aarkeson
DOP Morten Søborg
Editor Nicolaj Monberg
Music Jeppe Kaas
KIIL, Jørgen John Olsen, father
RICH, Maria Würgler Marianne Olsen, younger daughter
PRIP, Henrik Tom Olsen, John's son
CHRISTENSEN, Jesper Søren Olsen, John's brother
FAURSCHOU, Jannie Eva Olsen, older daughter
BRO, Vigga Ulla Olsen, mother
MADSEN, Martin Politiken colleague
HYLDEGAARD, Jesper Anders, Tom's colleague
MYNSTER, Karen-Lise Hanne, Søren's wife
WILLE, Mads Michael young man
©2002 Zentropa Entertainments6
Zentropa Entertainments6 presents in collaboration with TV2 (Adam Price,
Camilla Hammerich) and with support of Det Danske Filminstitut (Gert Duve
Skovlund)
109 mins 13 seconds
Locations – Copenhagen
Sight and Sound .v12.n10.October 2002 p.44
Box Office: £35,611
Opening weekend £8,445
Screens 9
Screen average £938

Snow Dogs

Dir Brian Levant
PG (US) 2002
Buena Vista International (UK) – 31 May
Prod Jordan Kerner
Screenplay Jim Kouf, Tommy Swerdlow, Michael Goldberg
DOP Thomas Ackerman
Editor Roger Bondelli
Music John Debney
GOODING Jr, Cuba Ted Brooks
COBURN, James Thunder Jack
SISQÓ Doctor Rupert Brooks
NICHOLS, Nichelle Amelia Brooks
GREENE, Graham Peter Yellowbear
DOYLE-MURRAY, Brian Ernie
BACALSO, Joanna Barb
WALSH, M. Emmet George
PARE, Jean-Michel Olivier
BOLTON, Michael himself
©2001 ©2002 Disney Enterprises Inc
Walt Disney Pictures present
a Jordan Kerner production in association with Galapagos Productions
99 mins 23 seconds
Locations – Calgary, Vancouver, Miami
Sight and Sound .v12.n6.June 2002 p.54-55
Box Office: £3,055,269

Opening weekend £331,432
Screens 313
Screen average £1,059

Soul Survivors

Dir Stephen Carpenter
12 (US) 2001
Momentum Pictures – 11 January
Prod Neal H. Moritz, Stokely Chaffin
Screenplay Steve Carpenter
DOP Fred Murphy
Editor Janice Hampton, Todd Ramsay
Music Daniel Licht
AFFLECK, Casey Sean
BENTLEY, Wes (C) Matt
DUSHKU, Eliza Annabel
FEATHERSTONE, Angela Raven
SAGEMILLER, Melissa Cassie
WILSON, Luke Father Jude
HAMILTON, Allen Doctor Haverston
MORENO, Ken hideous dancer
PAOLI, Carl Deathmask
ROBERTSON, Barbara Margaret
©2001 Artisan Film Investors Trust
Artisan Entertainment presents
a Neal H. Moritz prouction
a Steve Carpenter film
85 mins 2 seconds
Locations – Chicago, Pacific Northwest
Sight and Sound .v12.n2.February 2002 p.59-60
Box Office: £392,549
Opening weekend £200,178
Screens 110
Screen average £1,820

La Spagnola

Dir Steve Jacobs
15 (Australia) 2001
Metro Tartan Distributors – 9 August
Prod Anna-Maria Monticelli
Screenplay Anna-Maria Monticelli
DOP Steve Arnold
Editor Alexandre De Franceschi
Music Cezary Skubiszewski
MARCELI, Lola Lola
ANSARA, Alice Lucia
BARTOLOME, Lourdes Manola
OFRIA, Silvio Bruno
PALOMARES, Simon Ricardo
THOMSON, Helen Wendy
MASELLI, Gabriella Maria
MASELLI, Gabriella Maria
CROCCOLO, Armida Maria's mother
RODGERS, Steve teacher
©2001 The Australian Film Commission/Special Broadcasting Service
Corporation/Wild Strawberries Pty Ltd
The Australian Film Commission and SBS Independent presents
a Wild Strawberries production
90 mins 25 seconds
Sight and Sound .v12.n8.August 2002 p.50,52
Box Office: £55,819
Opening weekend £13,081
Screens 3
Screen average £4,360

Spider-Man

Dir Sam Raimi
12 (US) 2001
Columbia TriStar Films (UK) – 14 June
Prod Laura Ziskin, Ian Bryce

Screenplay David Koepp
DOP Don Burgess
Editor Rob Murawski, Arthur Coburn
Music Danny Elfman
MAGUIRE, Tobey Spider-Man/Peter Parker
DAFOE, Willem Green Goblin/Norman Osborn
DUNST, Kirsten Mary Jane Watson
FRANCO, James Harry Osborn
ROBERTSON, Cliff Ben Parker
HARRIS, Rosemary May Parker
SIMMONS, J.K. J. Jonah Jameson
BECKER, Gerry Maximilian Fargas
NUNN, Bill Joseph 'Robbie' Robertson
BETTS, Jack Henry Balkan
©2002 Columbia Pictures Industries
Columbia Pictures presents
a Marvel Entertainment/Laura Ziskin production
121 mins 20 seconds
Locations – Los Angeles, New York
Sight and Sound .v12.n7.July 2002 p.36-37+52

Box Office:	**£29,025,619**
Opening weekend	**£9,426,969**
Screens	**509**
Screen average	**£18,521**

Spirit: Stallion of the Cimarron

Dir Kelly Asbury, Lorna Cook
U (US) 2001
United International Pictures (UK) Ltd – 5 July
Prod Mireille Soria, Jeffrey Katzenberg
Screenplay John Fusco
Editor Clare de Chenu
Music Hans Zimmer
DAMON, Matt voice of Spirit
CROMWELL, James voice of the colonel
STUDI, Daniel voice of Little Creek
BERNET, Chopper voice of Sergeant Adams
LeBEAU, Jeff voice of Murphy
RUBANO, John voice of soldier
McGONAGLE, Richard voice of Bill
LEVIN, Matthew voice of Joe
PAUL, Adam voice of Pete
CAIT, Robert voice of Jake
©2002 DreamWorks LLC
DreamWorks Pictures presents
83 mins 43 seconds
Animation
Sight and Sound .v12.n8.August 2002 p.52-53

Box Office:	**£1,869,021**
Opening weekend	**£719,681**
Screens	**384**
Screen average	**£1,874**

Spy Kids 2 Islands of Lost Dreams

Dir Robert Rodriguez
U (US) 2002
Buena Vista International (UK) – 16 August
Prod Elizabeth Avellán, Robert Rodriguez
Screenplay Robert Rodriguez
DOP Robert Rodriguez
Editor Robert Rodriguez
Music Robert Rodriguez, John Debney
BANDERAS, Antonio Gregorio Cortez
GUGINO, Carla Ingrid Cortez
VEGA, Alexa Carmen Cortez
SABARA, Daryl Juni Cortez
JUDGE, Mike Donnagon Giggles
MONTALBAN, Ricardo grandfather
TAYLOR, Holland grandmother
McDONALD, Christopher president of the USA
TREJO, Danny Machete
CUMMING, Alan Fegan Floop
©2002 Miramax Film Corp.
[logo] Dimension Films
[logo] Troublemaker Studios
a Robert Rodriguez movie
99 mins 46 seconds
Locations – Austin, Texas
Sight and Sound.v12.n10.October 2002 p.52-53

Box Office:	**£5,515,055**
Opening weekend	**£1,069,090**
Screens	**409**
Screen average	**£2,614**

La Stanza Del Figlio

aka: the Son's Room
Dir Nanni Moretti
1 (Italy/France) 2001
Momentum Pictures – 15 February
Prod Angelo Barbagallo, Nanni Moretti
Screenplay Linda Ferri, Nanni Moretti, Heidrun Shleef
DOP Giuseppe Lanci
Editor Esmeralda Calabria
Music Nicola Piovani
MORETTI, Nanni Giovanni
MORANTE, Laura Paola
TRINCA, Jasmine Irene
SANFELICE, Giuseppe Andrea
ORLANDO, Silvio Oscar, patient
ACCORSI, Stefano Tommaso, patient
BERTORELLI, Toni patient
DELLA SETA, Claudia Raffaella, patient
ABBATI, Stefano patient
CANTARELLI, Dario patient
©2001 Sacher Film s.r.l
Sacher Film presents a Sacher Film, Roma - Bac Films - Studio Canal+, Parigi co-production with the collaboration of RAI Cinema e Tele+ a film by Nanni Moretti
87 mins
Locations – Ancona
Sight and Sound .v12.n3.March 2002 p.56

Box Office:	**£292,251**
Opening weekend	**£44,334**
Screens	**9**
Screen average	**£4,926**

Star Wars Episode II Attack of the Clones

Dir George Lucas
PG (US) 2001
20th Century Fox International (UK) – 17 May
Prod Rick McCallum
Screenplay George Lucas, Jonathan Hales
DOP David Tattersall
Editor Ben Burtt
Music John Williams
McGREGOR, Ewan Obi-Wan Kenobi
PORTMAN, Natalie Senator Padmé Amidala
CHRISTENSEN, Hayden Anakin Skywalker
OZ, Frank Yoda
McDIARMID, Ian Supreme Chancellor Palpatine
McDIARMID, Ian Darth Sidious
AUGUST, Pernilla (C) Shmi Skywalker
BEST, Ahmed Jar Jar Binks
FORD DAVIES, Oliver Sio Bibble
MORRISON, Temuera Jango Fett
©2001 Lucasfilm Ltd
a Lucasfilm Ltd production
a Twentieth Century Fox release
Dolby Digital Surround EX/DTS/SDDS
142 mins 5 seconds
Locations – Australia, Tunisia, Italy
Sight and Sound .v12.n9.September 2002 p.8

Box Office:	**£37,539,932**
Opening weekend	**£11,386,209**
Screens	**467**
Screen average	**£24,382**

Stuart Little 2

Dir Rob Minkoff
U (US) 2001
Columbia TriStar Films (UK) – 19 July

Prod Lucy Fisher, Douglas Wick
Screenplay Bruce Joel Rubin
DOP Steven Poster
Editor Priscilla Nedd Friendly
Music Alan Silvestri
FOX, Michael J. voice of Stuart Little
GRIFFITH, Melanie voice of Margalo
LANE, Nathan voice of Snowbell
DAVIS, Geena Mrs Eleanor Little
LAURIE, Hugh Mr Frederick Little
LIPNICKI, Jonathan George Little
WOODS, James voice of Falcon
ZAHN, Steve voice of Monty the alley cat
HOELCK, Anna Martha Little
HOELCK, Ashley Martha Little
©2002 Columbia Pictures Industries, Inc
Columbia Pictures presents
a Douglas Wick/Lucy Fisher production
a Franklin/Waterman production
a film by Rob Minkoff
77 mins 38 seconds
Locations – Los Angeles, New York
Sight and Sound .v12.n9.September 2002 p.75

Box Office: **£11,186,038**
Opening weekend **£1,343,398**
Screens **473**
Screen average **£2,840**

The Sum of all Fears

Dir Phil Alden Robinson
12 (US/Germany) 2001
United International Pictures (UK) Ltd – 16 August

Prod Mace Neufeld
Screenplay Paul Attanasio, Daniel Pyne, Akiva Goldsman
DOP John Lindley
Editor Nicolas de Toth
Music Jerry Goldsmith
AFFLECK, Ben Jack Ryan
FREEMAN, Morgan DCI William Cabot
CROMWELL, James President Robert Fowler
SCHREIBER, Liev CIA Operative John Clark
MOYNAHAN, Bridget Dr Cathy Muller
BATES, Alan Richard Dressler
HINDS, Ciarán (C) President Nemerov
HALL, Philip Baker Defense Secretary Becker
RIFKIN, Ron Secretary of State Owens
McGILL, Bruce National Security Adviser Revel
©2002 MFP Munich Film Partners GmbH & Co. AZL Productions KG
Paramount Pictures presents a Mace Neufeld production
123 mins 44 seconds
Locations – Montreal, Quebec
Sight and Sound .v12.n8.August 2002 p.53-54

Box Office: **£4,779,623**

Opening weekend **£1,144,501**
Screens **346**
Screen average **£3,308**

Summer Love

Box Office £2,238
Opening weekend **£692**
Screens **1**
Screen average **£692**

Sunshine State

Dir John Sayles
15 (US) 2002
Columbia TriStar Films (UK) – 26 July

Prod Maggie Renzi
Screenplay John Sayles
DOP Patrick Cady
Editor John Sayles
Music Mason Daring
LEWIS, Alex Terrell Bernard
KING, Alan Murray Silver
DOUGLAS, Cullen Jefferson Cash
JAMES, Clifton Buster Bidwell
ASINOF, Eliot Silent Sam
McDANIEL, James Dr Reginald 'Reggie' Perry
BASSETT, Angela Desiree Perry
FALCO, Edie Marly Temple
WING, Amanda Krissy
HUTTON, Timothy Jack Meadows
©2002 Sony Pictures Classics Inc
Sony Pictures Classics in association with Anarchists' Convention presents
140 mins 35 seconds
Locations – Amelia Island, Florida
Sight and Sound .v12.n8.August 2002 p.54-55

Box Office: **£155,064**

Opening weekend **£25,888**
Screens **15**
Screen average **£1,762**

Super Troopers

Dir Jay Chandrasekhar
15 (US) 2001
20th Century Fox International (UK) – 15 November

Prod Richard Perllo
Screenplay Broken Lizard
DOP Joaquin Braca-Asay
Editor Jacob Craycroft, Jumbulingan, Kevin Heffernan
Music 38 Special
COX, Brian Captain John O'Hagan
VON BARGEN, Daniel Chief Grady
COUGHLAN, Marisa Ursula
CARTER, Lynda Governor Jessman
DE LUCIA, Amy Bobbi
LLOYD, John Bedford Mayor Timber
GAFFIGAN, Jim Larry Johnson
VIPPOLIS, André college boy 1
KERN, Joey college boy 2
AREND, Geoffrey college boy 3
©2001 wentieth Century Fox Film Corporation
Fox Searchlight Pictures presents a Jersey Shore production
Cataland Films, Arpad Productions a Broken Lizard film
100 m 1 min
Sight and Sound .v12.n10.October 2002 p.53

Box Office: **£530,120**
Opening weekend **£269,696**
Screens **192**
Screen average **£1,405**

Sur

Box Office £12,049
Opening weekend **£5,659**
Screens **9**
Screen average **£629**

Sur Mes Lèvres

aka: Read My Lips
Dir Jacques Audiard
15 (France) 2001
Pathé Distribution – 24 May

Prod Jean-Lous Livi, Philippe Carcassonne
Screenplay Tonino Benacquist, Jacques Audiard
DOP Matthieu Vadepied
Editor Juliette Welfling
Music Alexandre Desplat
CASSEL, Vincent Paul Angeli
DEVOS, Emmanuelle Carla Bhem
GOURMET, Olivier Marchand
BONAMY, Olivia Annie
PERRIER, Olivier Masson
ALANE, Bernard Morel
SAMIE, Céline Josie Marchand
DIOT, Pierre Keller
LORIQUET, François Jean-François

BOUTLEROFF, Serge Mammouth
©2001 Sédif/Ciné B/Pathé Image Production/France 2 Cinéma
Jean-Louis Livi & Philippe Carcassonne present
a co-production of Sédif, Ciné B, Pathé Image, France 2 Cinéma
with the participation of Canal+
and the support of Centre National de la Cinématographie CNC
a film by Jacques Audiard
118 mins 51 seconds
Locations – Paris
Sight and Sound .v12.n6.June 2002 p.34-35+50
Box Office: **£359,572**
Opening weekend **£49,511**
Screens **18**
Screen average **£2,751**

The Sweetest Thing

Dir Roger Kumble
15 (US) 2001
Columbia TriStar Films (UK) – 30 August
Prod Cathy Konrad
Screenplay Nancy M. Pimental
DOP Anthony B. Richmond
Editor Wendy Greene Brichmont, David Rennie
Music Edward Shearmur
DIAZ, Cameron Christina Walters
APPLEGATE, Christina Courtney Rockliffe
JANE, Thomas Peter Donahue
BLAIR, Selma Jane Burns
BATEMAN, Jason Roger Donahue
POSEY, Parker Judy Webb
ADAMS, Lillian Aunt Frida
ANKROM, Herbert wedding guest 3
ANTHONY, Bryan geeky guy
ASUMA, Linda brawling bridesmaid
©2002 Columbia Pictures Industries Inc
Columbia Pictures presents
a Konrad Pictures production
a film by Roger Kumble
88 mins 27 seconds
Locations – Los Angeles, San Francisco
Sight and Sound .v12.n10.October 2002 p.54
Box Office: **£2,275,212**
Opening weekend **£592,722**
Screens **307**
Screen average **£1,931**

Sweet Home Alabama

Dir Andy Tennant
12A (US) 2002
Buena Vista International (UK) – 20 December
Prod Neal H. Moritz, Stokely Chaffin
Screenplay Jay C. Cox, Andy Tennant, Rick Parks, Robert Harling
DOP Andrew Dunn
Editor Troy Takaki, Tracey Wadmore-Smith
Music George Fenton
WITHERSPOON, Reese Melanie Carmichael
LUCAS, Josh (C) Jake Perry
DEMPSEY, Patrick Andrew Hennings
BERGEN, Candice Kate
PLACE, Mary Kay Pearl Smooter
WARD, Fred Earl Smooter
SMART, Jean Stella Kay
EMBRY, Ethan Bobby Ray
LYNSKEY, Melanie Lurlynn
GAINS, Courtney Wade
©2002 Touchstone Pictures
Touchstone Pictures presents
a Neal H. Moritz production
108 mins 48 seconds
Locations/Studios
Sight and Sound .v13.n1.January 2003 p.53-54
2002 p.14-17
Box Office: **£2,058,108***
£5,386,165**
Opening weekend **£758,267**
Screens **337**
Screen average **£2,250**
*(*total box office in 2002)(** cumulative box office for 2002/03)*

Sweet Sixteen

£ €
18
(UK/Germany/Spain/France/Italy) 2002
Icon Film Distribution – 4 October
Prod Rebecca O'Brien
Screenplay Paul Laverty
DOP Barry Ackroyd
Editor Johathan Morris
Music George Fenton
COMPSTON, Martin Liam
FULTON, Annmarie Chantelle
RUANE, William Pinball
ABERCROMBY, Michelle Suzanne
COULTER, Michelle Jean
McCORMACK, Gary Stan
McKEE, Tommy Rab
McALEES, Calum Calum
RENNIE, Robert Scullion
McCARDIE, Martin Tony
©2002 Sixteen Films Ltd/Road Movies Filmproduktion GmbH/Tornasol Films S.A./ Alta Films S.A.
A Sixteen Films production with Road Movies Filmproduktion and Tornasol/Alta
Films in a British, German and Spanish co-production.
A Scottish Screen and BBC Films presentation with the support of Filmstiftung
Nordrhein-Westfalen and The Glasgow Film Office
and in association with Diaphana Distribution, Bim Distribuzione, Cinéart,
ARD/Degeto Film and WDR
Developed with financial assistance from the Scottish Screen National Lottery
Fund
105 mins 56 seconds
Locations – Greenock & Glasgow
Sight and Sound .v12.n10.October
Box Office: **£824,821**
Opening weekend **£144,388**
Screens **66**
Screen average **£2,188**

Swimf@n

$ £
Dir John Polson
12 (US/UK) 2001
Icon Film Distribution – 20 September
Prod John Penotti, Allison Lyon Segan, Joe Caracciolo
Screenplay Charles Bohl, Phillip Schneider
DOP Giles Nuttgens
Editor Sarah Flack
Music Louis Febré
BRADFORD, Jesse Ben Cronin
CHRISTENSEN, Erika Madison Bell
APPLEBY, Shiri Amy
BURTON, Kate Carla Cronin
CRAWFORD, Clayne Josh
RITTER, Jason Randy
DeBELLO, James Dante
HIGGINS, Michael Mr Tillman
GOODWIN, Kia Joy Rene
SANDOW, Nick (C) Detective John Zabel
©2002 GreeneStreet Films LLC
Twentieth Century Fox presents
a GreeneStreet Films/Cobalt Media Group/Furthur Films production
85 mins 32 seconds
Sight and Sound .v12.n10.October 2002 p.56-57
Box Office: **£911,829**
Opening weekend **£396,425**

Screens 324
Screen average £1,224

Tape

Dir Richard Linklater
15 (US) 2001
Metrodome Distribution Ltd – 12 July
Prod Gary Winick, Alex Alexanian
Screenplay Stephen Belber
DOP Maryse Alberti
Editor Sandra Adair
HAWKE, Ethan 'Vin' Vince
LEONARD, Robert Sean 'Jon' Johnny
THURMAN, Uma Amy Randall
©2001 Tape Productions Inc
The Independent Film Channel Productions present
an InDigEnt production
in association with Detour Filmproduction
86 mins 26 seconds
Sight and Sound .v12.n6.June 2002 p.55-56
Box Office:£109,367
Opening weekend £18,652
Screens 15
Screen average £1,243

*A Taste of Honey

£
Dir Tony Richardson
15 (US) 2002
bfi Bookings – 11 October
Prod Tony Richardson
Screenplay Shelagh Delaney, Tony Richardson
DOP Walter Lassally
Editor Anthony Gibbs
Music John Addison
TUSHINGHAM, Rita Jo
BRYAN, Dora Helen
MELVIN, Murray Geoffrey
STEPHENS, Robert Peter
DANQUAH, Paul Jimmy
BOLIVER, David Bert
KAYE, Moira Doris
SMITH, Herbert Shoe Shop Proprietor
SCARDEN, Valerie Customer
SCASE, Rosalie (C) Nurse
Woodfall Film Productions
100 mins
Monthly Film Bulletin.v28.n333.October 1961 p.140
Box Office: £5,161
Opening weekend £845
Screens 1
Screen average £845

They

Dir Robert Harmon
15 (US) 2002
Entertainment Film Distributors Ltd – 1 November
Prod Scott Kroopf, Tom Engelman
Screenplay Brendan William Hood
DOP Rene Ohashi
Editor Chris Peppe
Music Elia Cmiral
REGAN, Laura Julia Lund
BLUCAS, Marc (C) Paul
EMBRY, Ethan Sam
DOMINCZYK, Dagmara Terry, Sam's roommate
ABRAHAMS, Jon Billy
GOULD, Alexander young Billy
ZUROWSKI, Desiree Mary Parks
HILDRETH, Mark Troy
CHERRY, Jonathan Darren
LaCROIX, Peter David Parks
©2002 They Pictures, Inc.
Focus Features presents
in association with Dimension Films
a Radar Pictures production
89 mins 20 seconds
Locations – Vancouver
Sight and Sound .v13.n1.January 2003 p.54-55
Box Office: £409,665
Opening weekend £225,867
Screens 185
Screen average £1,221

Thir13en Ghosts

Dir Steve Beck
15 (US) 2001
Columbia TriStar Films (UK) – 15 March
Prod Gilbert Adler, Joel Silver, Robert Zemeckis
Screenplay Neal Marshall Stevens, Richard D'Ovidio, James Gunn, Todd Alcott
DOP Gale Tattersall
Editor Derek G. Brechin, Edward A. Warshcilka
Music John Frizzell
SHALHOUB, Tony Arthur Kriticos
LILLARD, Matthew Dennis Rafkin
ELIZABETH, Shannon Kathy Kriticos
ROBERTS, Alec Bobby Kriticos
BOURNE, J.R. Ben Moss
Rah Digga Maggie Jones
ABRAHAM, F. Murray Uncle Cyrus Kriticos
DAVIDTZ, Embeth Kalina Seyler
HARRISON, Matthew Damon
RUPP, Jacob Cyrus' assistant
©2001 Columbia Pictures Industries, Inc./Warner Bros.
Columbia Pictures and Warner Bros. Pictures present
a Dark Castle Entertainment production
90 mins 40 seconds
Locations – Vancouver
Sight and Sound .v12.n4.April 2002 p.62
Box Office: £2,121,543
Opening weekend £738,210
Screens 280
Screen average £2,636

Thunderpants

£ €
Dir Peter Hewitt
PG (UK/Germany) 2002
Pathé Distribution – 24 May
Prod Graham Broadbent, Damian Jones, Pete Hewitt
Screenplay Phil Hughes
DOP Andy Collins
Editor Michael Parker
Music Rupert Gregson-Williams
CALLOW, Simon Sir John Osgood
FRY, Stephen Sir Anthony Silk QC
IMRIE, Celia Miss Rapier
GIAMATTI, Paul Johnson J. Johnson
BEATTY, Ned Ed Sheppard
COOK, Bruce Patrick Smash
GRINT, Rupert Alan A. Allen
GALLAGHER, Bronagh Mrs Smash
McGUIRE, Victor Mr Smash
GODLEY, Adam Placido P. Placeedo
©2002 Pathé Fund Ltd/Erste, Zweite, Dritte and Vierte Beteiligung KC Medien AG & Co. KG
Pathé Pictures and Sky present
In association with The Film Council
A Mission Pictures production
In association with CP Medien
87 mins 24 seconds
Locations – London
Sight and Sound .v12.n5.May 2002 p.53-54
Box Office: £1,969,798
Opening weekend £430,913
Screens 356
Screen average £1,210

The Time Machine

Dir Simon Wells
PG (US) 2001
Warner Bros Distributors (UK) – 31 May
Prod Walter F. Parkes, David Valdes

Screenplay John Logan
DOP Donald M. McAlpine
Editor Wayne Wahrman
Music Klaus Badelt
PEARCE, Guy Alexander Hartdegen
MUMBA, Samantha Mara
ADDY, Mark Dr David Philby
GUILLORY, Sienna Emma
LAW, Phyllida Mrs Watchit
YOUNG, Alan flower store
MUMBA, Omero Kalen worker
ARIAS, Yancey Toren
JONES, Orlando Vox
IRONS, Jeremy Uber-Morlock
©2001 ©2002 DreamWorks LLC/Warner Bros. Pictures
Warner Bros. Pictures and DreamWorks Pictures present
a Parkes/MacDonald production
95 mins 4 seconds
Locations/Studios
Sight and Sound .v12.n7.July 2002 p.55-56
Box Office **£4,067,881**
Opening weekend **£808,389**
Screens **356**
Screen average **£2,271**

Time of Favor
Box Office **£15,276**
Opening weekend **£6,637**
Screens **1**
Screen average **£6,637**

* To Sleep With Anger
Dir Charles Burnett
12 (US)1990
bfi Bookings – 28 June
Prod Caldecot Chubb, Thomas S. Byrnes
Screenplay Charles Burnett
DOP Walt Lloyd
Editor Nancy Richardson
Music Stephen James Taylor
GLOVER, Danny Harry Mention
BUTLER, Paul Gideon
ALICE, Mary Suzie
LUMBLY, Carl Junior
McGEE, Vonetta Pat
BROOKS, Richard Babe Brother
RALPH, Sheryl Lee Linda
AYLER, Ethel Hattie
HARRIS, Julius Herman
RICHARDSON, Sy Marsh
SVS Films
102 mins
Sight and Sound .v12.n7.July 2002 p.28
Box Office: **£2,092**
Opening weekend **£958**
Screens **3**
Screen average **£319**

Tod Browning - Double Bill
Box Office **£15,045**
Opening weekend **£2,900**
Screens **2**
Screen average **£1,450**

Tortilla Soup
Dir Maria Ripoll
PG (US) 2001
Optimum Releasing – 23 August
Prod John Bard Manulis
Screenplay Ramón Menédez, Tom Musca, Vera Blasi
DOP Xaveir Pérez Grobet
Editor Andy Blumenthal
Music Bill Conti
ELIZONDO, Hector Martin Naranjo
OBRADORS, Jacqueline Carmen Naranjo
MELLO, Tamara Maribel Naranjo
RODRIGUEZ, Paul Orlando
MARIE, Constance Yolanda
JOAN, Joel Antonio Urgell
KINSKI, Nikolai Andy
MECHOSO, Julio Oscar Gómez
PEÑA, Elizabeth Letitia Naranjo
WELCH, Raquel Hortensia
©2001 Samuel Goldwyn Films LLC/Starz Encore Group LLC
Samuel Goldwyn Films presents in association with Starz Encore Entertainment
a Samuel Goldwyn Films production
103 mins 2 seconds
Sight and Sound .v12.n9.September 2002 p.78-79
Box Office: **£5,910**
Opening weekend **£1,198**
Screens **4**
Screen average **£300**

Tosca

£ €
Dir Benoît Jacquot
PG (France/UK/Germany/Italy) 2001
Axiom Films Limited – 10 May
Prod Daniel Toscan Du Plantier
Screenplay Benoît Jaquot
DOP Romain Winding
Editor Nadine Verdier, Celia Laftiedupont
Music Giacomo Puccini
GHEORGHIU, Angela Tosca
ALAGNA, Roberto Mario Cavaradossi
RAIMONDI, Ruggero Scarpia
CANGELOSI, David Spoletta
COLIBAN, Sorin Sciarrone
FISSORE, Enrico sacristan
MURARO, Maurizio Angelotti
HOWELL, Gwynne gaoler
SAVAGE-HANFORD, James shepherd
ROGOSCH, Karl-Heinz tax judge
©2001 Euripide Productions/Axiom Films/Integral Film GmbH/Veradia Film/
Seven Stars Systems/France 3 Cinéma/WDR/Tele+
Euripide Productions, Axiom Films Limited, Veradia Film, France 3 Cinéma,
Integral Film GmbH, Seven Stars Systems
in co-production with WDR/ARTE
in collaboration with Tele+
with the participation of Canal+, sofica France Télévision Images, Filmstiftung NRW
with the support of Eurimages
present
124 mins 46 seconds
Locations – Cologne
Sight and Sound .v12.n5.May 2002 p.54-55
Box Office: **£33,552**
Opening weekend **£6,725**
Screens **3**
Screen average **£2,242**

Training Day
Dir Antoine Fuqua
18 (US/Australia) 2001
Warner Bros Distributors (UK) – 1 February
Prod Jeffrey Silver, Bobby Newmyer
Screenplay David Ayer
DOP Mauro Fiore
Editor Conrad Buff
Music Mark Mancina
WASHINGTON, Denzel Alonzo Harris
HAWKE, Ethan Jake Hoyt
GLENN, Scott Roger
BERENGER, Tom Stan Gursky
YULIN, Harris Doug Rosselli
BARRY, Raymond J. Lou Jacobs
CURTIS, Cliff Smiley
Dr Dré (C) Paul
Snoop Dogg Blue
GRAY, Macy Sandman's wife
©2001 Village Roadshow Films (BVI) Limited (all other territories)
Warner Bros. presents in association with Village Roadshow Pictures and NPV Entertainment
an Outlaw production
121m 56 seconds
Locations – Los Angeles

Sight and Sound .v12.n2.February 2002 p.62-63

Box Office: £2,605,946
Opening weekend £739,718
Screens 264
Screen average £2,802

Trois Huit

Dir Philippe Le Guay
15 (France) 2001
Metro Tartan Distributors – 1 February

Prod Alain Rocca
Screenplay Philippe Le Guay
DOP Jean-Marc Fabre
Editor Emmanule Castro
Music Yann Tiersen
LAROCHE, Gérald Pierre
BARBÉ, Marc Fred
BALLET, Bernard Franck
CASSAGNE, Michel Alain
CARRIÈRE, Alexandre Danny
LAPALUS, Jean-François Mickey
LAHMER, Sabri Farid
MOUCHEL, Luce Carole
VERDI, Maria Pierre's mother
FRÉCON, Philippe Yvon

©2001 Les Productions Lazennec/StudioCanal/France 3 Cinéma
Lazennec presents
in co-production with Studio Canal and France 3 Cinéma
with the participation of Canal+
in association with sofica Studio Images 7

96 mins 48 seconds
Locations – Chalon-sur-Saone, France
Sight and Sound .v12.n2.February 2002 p.55

Box Office: £15,648
Opening weekend £2,569
Screens 2
Screen average £1,285

Trouble Every Day

Dir Claire Denis
18 (France/Germany) 2001
Metro Tartan Distributors – 27 December

Prod Georges Benayoun, Jean-Michel Rey, Philippe Liégeois
Screenplay Christine Gamay
DOP Agnès Godard
Editor Nelly Quettier
Music Tindersticks
GALLO, Vincent Shane Brown
VESSEY, Tricia June Brown
DALLE, Béatrice Coré
DESCAS, Alex Léo Semeneau
LOIRET-CAILLE, Florence (C) Christelle
DUVAUCHELLE, Nicolas Erwan
GARCIA, José Choart
LAPIOWER, Hélène Malécot
CLÉMENT, Aurore Jeanne
MARINI, Marilu Friessen

©2001 Messaoud/a Films, Rezo Productions, Arte France Cinéma, Dacia Films, Kinétique, Inc.
Georges Benayoun, Jean-Michel Rey, Philippe Liégeois present
a Messaoud/a Films, Rezo Productions, Arte France Cinéma, Dacia Films, Kinétique Inc co-production
with the participation of Canal+, Arte/ZDF, Rezo Films

101 mins 11 seconds
Sight and Sound .v13.n1.January 2003 p.56

Box Office: £9,187
Opening weekend £1,764
Screens 2
Screen average £882

Tumko Na Bhool Paayenge

Box Office £171,959
Opening weekend £75,912
Screens 19
Screen average £3,995

Tumse Achcha Kaun Hai

Box Office £13,259
Opening weekend £2,640
Screens 4
Screen average £660

Two Can Play That Game

Dir Mark Brown
15 (US) 2001
Columbia TriStar Films (UK) – 13 September

Prod Doug McHenry, Mark Brown, Paddy Cullen
Screenplay Mark Brown
DOP Alexander Gruszynski
Editor Earl Watson
Music
FOX, Vivica A. Shanté Smith
ANDERSON, Anthony Tony
ROBINSON, Wendy Raquel Karen
JONES, Tamala Tracye Edwards
MO'NIQUE Diedre
WISE, Ray Bill Parker
BROWN, Bobby Michael
WHITFIELD, Dondré T. (C) Dwain
UNION, Gabrielle Connie Spalding
CHESTNUT, Morris Keith Fenton

©2001 Screen Gems, Inc.
Screen Gems presents
a Doug McHenry production
in association with C4 Pictures
a film by Mark Brown

91min 5 seconds
Locations – Los Angeles
Sight and Sound .v12.n11.November 2002 p.58-59

Box Office: £43,740
Opening weekend £14,348
Screens 10
Screen average £1,435

Two Men Went to War

£

Dir John Henderson
PG (UK) 2002
Guerilla Films – 1 November

Prod Ira Trattner, Pat Harding
Screenplay Richard Everett, Christopher Villiers
DOP John Ignatius
Editor David Yardley
Music Richard Harvey
CRANHAM, Kenneth Sergeant Peter King
BILL, Leo Private Leslie Cuthbertson
LAVELLE, Rosanna Emma Fraser
LAW, Phyllida Faith
FLEET, James Major Bates
GLOVER, Julian Colonel Hatchard
VALENTINE, Anthony Sergeant Major
RYALL, David Winston ChurchillDudley
JACOBI, Derek Major Desmond Merton
SUTTON, Richard Private Horrocks

©2002 Two Men Went to War Partnership
Little Wing Films present
an Ira Trattner production

109 m 1 second
Locations – Surrey & Cornwall
Studios – Shepperton Studios
Sight and Sound .v12.n11.November 2002 p.59

Box Office: 16,168
Opening weekend £1,623
Screens 6
Screen average £271

Ultimate X

Box Office £64,247
Opening weekend £552
Screens 2
Screen average £276

Unfaithful

Dir Adrian Lyne
15 (US) 2002
20th Century Fox International (UK) – 7 June

Prod Adrian Lyne, Mac G.

Brown
Screenplay Alvin Sargent, William Broyles Jr, Stephen Schiff, Susannah Grant
DOP Peter Biziou
Editor Anne V. Coates
Music Jan A. P. Kaczmarek
GERE, Richard Edward Sumner
LANE, Diane Constance 'Connie' Sumner
MARTINEZ, Olivier Paul Martel
LOWE, Chad Bill Stone
BURTON, Kate Tracy
COLIN, Margaret Sally
SULLIVAN, Erik Per Charlie Sumner
CHIANESE, Dominic Frank Wilson
TAYLOR, Myra Lucretia Gloria
MONAGHAN, Michelle Lindsay
©2002 Twentieth Century Fox Film Corporation/Monarchy Enterprises S.a.r.l./
Regency Entertainment (USA), Inc.
Fox 2000 Pictures and Regency Enterprises present
an Adrian Lyne film
124 mins
Locations – New York
Sight and Sound .v12.n7.July 2002 p.56-57

Box Office:	**£3,723,712**
Opening weekend	**£779,335**
Screens	**288**
Screen average	**£2,706**

Va savoir

Dir Jacques Rivette
PG (France/Italy/Germany) 2001
Artificial Eye Film Company – 4 January
Prod Martine Marignac
Screenplay Pascal Bonitzer,

Christine Laurent, Jacques Rivette
DOP William Lubtchansky
Editor Nicole Lubtchansky
BALIBAR, Jeanne Camille Renard
BASLER, Marianne Sonia
FOUGEROLLES, Hélène de Dominique 'Do' Desprez
ROUVEL, Catherine Madame Desprez, Do's mother
CASTELLITTO, Sergio Ugo Bassani
BONNAFFÉ, Jacques Pierre Mauduit
TODESCHINI, Bruno Arthur Delamarche
BERRI, Claude autograph librarian
©2001 Pierre Grise Productions/France 2 Cinéma/VM Productions/Mikado/Kinowelt
Pierre Grise Productions in co-production with France 2 Cinéma, Mikado Films, Kinowelt with the participation of Canal+/Cofimage 12/Gimages 4/Centre National de la Cinématographie and the support of Eurimages/Procirep
154 mins 13 seconds
Locations – Paris
Sight and Sound .v12.n1.January 2002 p.36-37,57

Box Office:	**£135,637**
Opening weekend	**£17,907**
Screens	**6**
Screen average	**£2,985**

Vanilla Sky

Dir Cameron Crowe
15 (US) 2001
United International Pictures (UK) Ltd – 25 January
Prod Tom Cruise, Paula Wagner, Cameron Crow
Screenplay Cameron Crowe
DOP John Toll
Editor Joe Hutshing, Mark Livolski
Music Nancy Wilson
CRUISE, Tom David Aames
CRUZ, Penélope Sofia Serrano
RUSSELL, Kurt McCabe
LEE, Jason Brian Shelby
TAYLOR, Noah Edmund Ventura
DIAZ, Cameron Julie Gianni
SPALL, Timothy Thomas Tipp
SWINTON, Tilda Rebecca Dearborn
SHANNON, Michael Aaron
MITCHELL, Delaina David's assistant
©2001 Paramount Pictures
Paramount Pictures presents
a Cruise/Wagner-Vinyl Films production
a Cameron Crowe film
136 mins 4 seconds
Sight and Sound .v12.n2.February 2002 p.63-64

Box Office:	**£9,523,575**
Opening weekend	**£2,978,264**
Screens	**425**
Screen average	**£7,008**

Villa Des Roses

£ €
Dir Frank van Passel
12 (Belgium/UK/Netherlands/ Luxembourg) 2001
Miracle Communications – 11 October
Prod Dirk Impens, Rudy Verzyck
Screenplay Christophe Dirickx
DOP Jan Vancaillie
Editor Ludo Troch, Karin Vaerenberg
Music Paul M. van Brugge
DELPY, Julie Louise Créteur
DINGWALL, Shaun Richard Grünewald
HENDERSON, Shirley Ella
WALTER, Harriet Olive Burrell
WEST, Timothy Hugh Burrell
VERCRUYSSEN, Frank Aasgaard
DECLEIR, Jan Monsieur Brizand
PEA, Alfredo Mr Craxi
WHELAN, Gary Mr O'Connor
EXCOFFIER, Stéphane Jeanne de Keros
©2002 Favourite Films/Menuet/Dan Films/Isabella Films/Samsa Film
A Favourite Films/Dan Films/Isabella Films/Samsa Film production[end] a Belgium-UK-Dutch-Luxembourg co-production
With the support of Fonds Film in Vlaanderen, VRT, Canal+ Belgium, National Lottery, Centre du Cinéma et de l'Audiovisuel de la Communauté Française de Belgique British Screen, BskyB, European Co-production Fund Dutch Film Fund, Cobo-Fund, Thuiskopie Fonds
In co-production with NPS TelevisionFilm Fund Luxembourg Eurimages
118 mins 48 seconds
Locations – Luxembourg, Belgium
Sight and Sound .v12.n10.October 2002 p.60

Box Office:	**£4,891**
Opening weekend	**£2,807**
Screens	**8**
Screen average	**£351**

* Vivre Sa Vie Film en Douze Tablieaux

Dir Jean-Luc Godard
(France) 1962
bfi Bookings – 19 July
Prod Pierre Braunberger,
Screenplay Jean-Luc Godard
DOP Raoul Coutard
Editor Agnès Guillemot
Music Michel Legrand
KARINA, Anna Nana Kleinfrankenheim
REBBOT, Saddy (C) Raoul
LABARTHE, André S. Paul
SCHLUMBERGER, Gyulaine Yvette
HOFFMAN, Gérard the cook
MESSINE, Monique Elizabeth

PAVEL, Paul a journalist
DINEFF, Dimitri Dimitri, a youth
KASSOWITZ, Peter a young man
SCHLUMBERGER, Eric Luigi
Films de la Pléiade
85 mins
Monthly Film Bulletin.v30.n349.February 1963 p.19
Box Office: £31,169
Opening weekend £5,194
Screens 2
Screen average £2,597

Vou Para Casa

Dir Manoel de Oliveira
PG (Portugal/France) 2001
Artificial Eye Film Company – 17 May
Prod Paulo Branco
Screenplay Manoel de Oliveira
DOP Sabine Lancelin
Editor Valérie Loiseleux
PICCOLI, Michel Gilbert Valence
CHAPPEY, Antoine George, agent
BALDAQUE, Leonor Sylvia
SILVEIRA, Leonor Marie
TREPA, Ricardo guard
ARNOLD, Jean-Michel doctor
VAN, Adrien de Ferdinand
TESTUD, Sylvie Ariel
WALE, Andrew Stephen
DAUNEY, Robert Haines
©2001 Madragoa Filmes/Gemini Films/France 2 Cinéma
Paulo Branco presents
a film by Manoel de Oliveira
a co-production of Madragoa Filmes (Portugal), Gemini Films (France), France 2 Cinéma
with the participation of Centre National de la Cinématographie, Canal+,
Instituto do Cinema Audiovisual e Multimedia, RTP - Radiotelevisão Portuguesa
89 mins 39 seconds
Locations – Paris
Sight and Sound .v12.n5.May 2002 p.48
Box Office: £30,874
Opening weekend £4,490
Screens 1
Screen average £4,490

Waah Tera Kya Kehna

Box Office £5,963
Opening weekend £2,997
Screens 5
Screen average £599

Waking Life

Dir Richard Linklater
15 (US) 2001
20th Century Fox International (UK) – 19 April
Prod Anne Walker-McBay, Tommy Pallotta, Palmer West, Jonah Smith
Screenplay Richard Linklater
DOP Richard Linklater
Editor Sandra Adair
Music Tosca Tango Orchestra
BROOKS, Trevor Jack
LINKLATER, Lorelei
WIGGINS, Wiley
GILL, Glover
HICKS, Lara
ASBELL, Ames
MAHONEY, Leigh
NELSON, Sara
ATTAWAY, Jeanine
GROSTIC, Erik
©2001 Twentieth Century Fox Film Corporation
The Independent Film Channel Productions and Thousand Words present
a Line Research/Detour Filmproduction production
100m 40 seconds
Sight and Sound .v12.n2.February 2002 p.64
Box Office: £84,077
Opening weekend £11,223
Screens 9
Screen average £1,247

A Walk to Remember

Dir Adam Shankman
PG (US) 2001
Helkon SK – 13 September
Prod Denise Di Novi, Hunt Lowry
Screenplay Karen Janszen
DOP Julio Macat
Editor Emma E. Hickox
Music Mervyn Warren
WEST, Shane Landon Carter
MOORE, Mandy Jamie Sullivan
COYOTE, Peter Reverend Sullivan
HANNAH, Daryl Cynthia Carter
GERMAN, Lauren Belinda
CRAWFORD, Clayne Dean
THOMPSON, Al Eric
HUERTA, Paz de la Tracie
PARKS JORDAN, Jonathan Walker
LUTZ, Matt Clay Gephardt
©2001 Pandora, Inc.
A Warner Bros. Pictures presents
in association with Pandora
a Di Novi Pictures production
102 mins 5 seconds
Locations – North Carolina
Sight and Sound .v12.n8.August 2002 p.55-56
Box Office: £480,832
Opening weekend £246,860
Screens 263
Screen average £939

The War Bride

£ Can$
Dir Lyndon Chubbuck
PG (UK/Canada) 2001
Miracle Communications – 29 November
Prod Alistair MacLean-Clark, Douglas Berquist
Screenplay Angela Workman
DOP Ron Orieux
Editor Alan Strachan
Music John Sereda
FRIEL, Anna Lily
FRICKER, Brenda Betty
YOUNG, Aden Charlie Travis
COX, Julie Sophie
DEAN, Loren Joe Clark
PARKER, Molly Sylvia
McLAREN, Schyler Lindy
CAVE, Caroline Peggy
GAINEY, Keeley Moira
Harvest Pictures II Limited/DB Entertainment
Random Harvest Pictures presents
a Harvest Pictures Limited/DB Entertainment Inc production
in association with Vanguard Entertainment
107 mins 31 seconds
Locations – Canada, London
Sight and Sound .v12.n12.December 2002 p.60
Box Office: £5,933
Opening weekend £2,985
Screens 16
Screen average £187

The Warrior

£ € Rs
Dir Asif Kapadia
12 (UK/France/Germany/India) 2001
FilmFour Distributors – 3 May
Prod Bertrand Faivre
Screenplay Asif Kapadia, Tim Miller
DOP Roman Osin
Editor Ewa J. Lind
Music Dario Marianelli
KHAN, Irfan Lafcadia, the warrior
CHHIBBER, Puru Katiba, Lafcadia's son
ANNUDDIN, Sheikh Biswas, the warrior
MISHRA, Manoj warrior

KHAN, Nanhe warrior
SINGH, Chander warrior
MAAHAOR, Hemant warrior
GOSWAMI, Mandakini shawl seller
SHARMA, Sunita the girl
BAIG, Shauket clerk
©2001 FilmFour Limited
FilmFour presents a production from The Bureau
in association with Senator Films with the participation of British Screen
86 mins 16 seconds
Locations – Rajasthan, Himachal Pradesh, India
Sight and Sound .v12.n5.May 2002 p.22-24

Box Office:	**£147,365**
Opening weekend	**£30,134**
Screens	**19**
Screen average	**£1,586**

The Wash

Dir DJ Pooh
15 (US) 2001
Metrodome Distribution Ltd – 9 August
Prod DJ Pooh, Rick Freeman, Philip G. Atwell
Screenplay DJ Pooh
DOP Keith L. Smith
Editor Jack Hofstra
Music Camara Kambon
Snoop Dogg Dee Loc
Dr Dre (C) Sean
WALLACE, George Mr Washington
CONWELL, Angell Antoinette
BRUCE, Bruce DeWayne
ALBANO, Anthony Mafia Tony
TIC Maniac's homie 2
BENTLEY, Lamont C-Money
Bishop Don Magic Juan, The (C) himself
BUCKMAN, Thai Ashley
©2001 Lions Gate Films Inc
Lions Gate Films and Lithium Entertainment present
a film by D.J. Pooh
96 mins 39 seconds
Locations – Los Angeles
Sight and Sound .v12.n8.August 2002 p.56

Box Office:	**£85,748**
Opening weekend	**£33,677**
Screens	**41**
Screen average	**£821**

We Were Soldiers

Dir Randall Wallace
15 (US/Germany) 2001
Icon Film Distribution – 8 March
Prod Bruce Davey, Stephen McEveety, Randall Wallace
Screenplay Randall Wallace
DOP Dean Semler
Editor William Hoy
Music Nick Gennie-Smith
GIBSON, Mel Lieutenant Colonel Hal Moore
STOWE, Madeleine Julie Moore
KINNEAR, Greg Major Bruce Crandall
ELLIOTT, Sam Sergeant Major Basil Plumley
ELLIOTT, Sam Sergeant Major Basil Plumley
RUSSELL, Keri Barbara Geoghegan
PEPPER, Barry Joe Galloway
DUONG, Don Lieutenant Colonel Nguyen Huu
HURST, Ryan Sergeant Ernie Savage
BLUCAS, Marc (C) 2nd Lieutenant Henry Herrick
©2002 Motion Picture Production GmbH & Co Erste KG
[USA] Paramount Pictures and Icon Productions present [outside USA] Icon Productions and Paramount Pictures present
an Icon/Wheelhouse Entertainment productiona Randall Wallace film
138 mins 25 seconds
Locations – California, Georgia
Sight and Sound .v12.n4.April 2002 p.64

Box Office:	**£2,288,856**
Opening weekend	**£757,760**
Screens	**384**
Screen average	**£1,973**

What's the Worst That Could Happen?

Dir SamWeisman
15 (US) 2001
Optimum Releasing – 28 June
Prod Lawrence Turman, David Hoberman, Ashok Amritraj
Screenplay Matthew Chapman, Barry Fanaro
DOP Anastas Michos
Editor Garth Craven, Nick Moore
Music Tyler Bates
LAWRENCE, Martin Kevin Caffery
DeVITO, Danny Max Fairbanks
LEGUIZAMO, John Berger
HEADLY, Glenne Gloria
EJOGO, Carmen Amber Belhaven
MAC, Bernie Uncle Jack
MILLER, Larry Earl Radburn
DUNN, Nora Lutetia Fairbanks
SCHIFF, Richard Walter Greenbaum
FICHTNER, William Detective Alex Tardio
©2001 Metro-Goldwyn-Mayer Pictures Inc
Metro-Goldwyn-Mayer Pictures presents a Turman-Morrissey Company/Hyde Park Entertainment production a Sam Weisman film
98 mins 15 seconds
Locations – Boston
Sight and Sound .v12.n8.August 2002 p.57

Box Office:	**£160,838**
Opening weekend	**£69,194**
Screens	**82**
Screen average	**£844**

Windtalkers

Dir John Woo
15 (US) 2001
20th Century Fox International (UK) – 30 August
Prod John Woo, Terence Chang, Tracie Graham, Alison Rosenzweig
Screenplay John Rice, Joe Batteer
DOP Jeffrey Kimball
Editor Steven Kemper, Jeff Gullo, Tom Rolf
Music James Horner
CAGE, Nicolas Joe Enders
BEACH, Adam Ben Yahzee
STORMARE, Peter Hjelmstad
EMMERICH, Noah Chick
RUFFALO, Mark Pappas
VAN HOLT, Brian Harrigan
HENDERSON, Martin Nellie
WILLIE, Roger Charlie Whitehorse
O'CONNOR, Frances Rita
SLATER, Christian Pete 'Ox' Henderson
©2001 2 Metro-Goldwyn-Mayer Pictures Inc
Metro-Goldwyn-Mayer Pictures presents a Lion Rock production a John Woo film
134 mins
Locations – Hawaii
Sight and Sound .v12.n9.September 2002 p.79-80

Box Office:	**£885,752**
Opening weekend	**£388,212**
Screens	**294**
Screen average	**£1,320**

Xingfu Shiguang

Dir Yimou Zhang
PG (China) 2001
20th Century Fox International (UK) – 27 September
Prod Yu Zhao
Screenplay Guizi
DOP Yong Hou
Editor Ru Zhai
Music Bao San

ZHAO Benshan old Zhao
DONG Jie Wu Ying, blind girl
DONG Lihua chunky mama
FU Biao little Fu
LENG Qibin little fatty
LI Xuejian old Li
NIU Ben old Niu, 'Oxhead'
GONG Jinghua Aunty Liu
ZHANG Hongjie Lao Zhang
ZHAO Bingkun Lao Bai
A Sunflower presentation
Guangxi Studios
96 mins 47 seconds
Sight and Sound .v12.n9.September 2002 p.61
Box Office: **£8,703**
Opening weekend **£1,004**
Screens **1**
Screen average **£1,004**

xXx

Dir Rob Cohen
12A (US) 2002
Columbia TriStar Films (UK) – 18 October
Prod Neal H. Moritz
Screenplay Rich Wiles
DOP Dean Semler
Editor Chris Lebenzon, Paul Rubell, Joel Negrón
Music Randy Edelman
DIESEL, Vin Xander Cage
ARGENTO, Asia Yelena
CSOKAS, Marton Yorgi
JACKSON, Samuel L. Agent Augustus Gibbons
TREJO, Danny El Jefe
ROOF, Michael Toby Lee Shavers
EVERETT, Tom Senator Dick Hotchkiss
MÜLLER, Richy Milan Sova
DAEHN, Werner Kirill
JÁKL, Petr Kolya
©2002 Revolution Studios Distribution Company LLC
Revolution Studios presents
a Neal H. Moritz production
a Rob Cohen film
123 mins 55 seconds
Locations – Los Angeles
Sight and Sound .v12.n11.November 2002 p.60
Box Office: **£11,508,703**
Opening weekend **£3,435,891**
Screens **435**
Screen average **£7.899**

* Ya - Cuba

aka: I Am Cuba
Dir Mihail Kalatozov
(Soviet Union/Cuba) 1964
NFT **21 May**
Screenplay Yevgeni Yevtushenko, Enrique Pineda Barnet
DOP Sergei Urussevsky
Editor N. Glagoleva
Music Carlos Farinas
CORRIERI, Sergio Alberto
WOOD, Salvador .
GALLARDO, José Pedro
GARCÍA, Raúl Enrique
COLLAZO, Luz Maria Maria/Betty
BOUISE, Jean Jim
MORGAN, Alberto .
RODRIGUEZ, Celia Gloría
MIRABAL, Fausto .
YORK, Robert García American activist
©1964 Mosfilm
©1995 Milestone Film
a joint production of Mosfilm (USSR) and ICAIC (Cuba)
141 mins
Subtitles
Sight and Sound.v9.n8.August 1999 p.45-46
Box Office: **£2,612**
Opening weekend **£2,612**
Screens **1**
Screen average **£2,612**

Y tu mamá también

Dir Alfonso Cuarón
18 (Mexico) 2001
Icon Film Distribution – 12 April
Prod Jorge Vergara, Alfonso Cuarón
Screenplay Carlos Cuarón, Alfonson Cuarón
DOP Emmanuel Lubezki
Editor Alfonso Cuarón, Alex Rodríguez
Music Liza Richardson, Annette Fradera
VERDÚ, Maribel Luisa Cortés
GARCÍA BERNAL, Gael (C) Julio Zapata
LUNA, Diego Tenoch Iturbide
AURA, Marta Enriqueta 'Queta' Allende
BRACHO, Diana Silvia Allende de Iturbide
ECHEVARRÍA, Emilio Miguel Iturbide
LANGER, Verónica María Eugenia Calles de Huerta
RÍOS, Arturo Esteban Morelos
LÓPEZ MERCADO, Ana Ana Morelos
GRINBERG, Nathan Manuel Huerta
©2001 Producciones Anhelo
Jorge Vergara, Producciones Anhelo present
105 mins 40 seconds
Subtitles
Sight and Sound .v12.n4.April 2002 p.40
Box Office: **£1,621,560**
Opening weekend **£182,166**
Screens **38**
Screen average **£4,794**

Yeh Dil Aap Ka Huwa

Box Office £68,345
Opening weekend **£26,734**
Screens **17**
Screen average **£1,573**

Yeh Hai Jalwa

Box Office **£102,428**
Opening weekend **£34,657**
Screens **16**
Screen average **£2,166**

Yesil Isik

Box Office **£11,825**
Opening weekend **£2,451**
Screens **1**
Screen average **£2,451**

Zindagi Khoobsarat Hai

Box Office **£45,151**
Opening weekend **£17,645**
Screens **9**
Screen average **£1,961**

Zhantai

Dir Zhang Ke Jia
15 (Hong Kong/Japan/France/ Netherlands/ Switzerland) 2001
Artificial Eye Film Company – 2 August
Prod Ming Kit Li, Shozo Ichiyama
Screenplay Zhang Ke Jia
DOP Lik Wai Yu
Editor Jing Lei Kong
Music Hanno Yoshihiro
WANG Hong Wei Minliang
ZHAO Tao Ruijian
LIANG Jing Dong Chang Jun
YANG Tian Yi Zhong Pin
SONG Yong Ping .
WANG Bo Yao Eryong
©2000 Hu Tong Communication (O/B Jetwood Investment Ltd)/T-Mark Inc
Hu Tong Communication (Hong Kong) and T-Mark Inc (Japan) present
in association with Artcam International (France)
a film by Jia Zhang Ke
195 mins
Sight and Sound .v12.n8.August 2002 p.47-48
Box Office: **£5,502**
Opening weekend **£1,777**
Screens **2**
Screen average **£889**

SPECIALISED GOODS AND SERVICES

This section has been divided into four parts. The first part features services specialising in actors, audiences and casting. The second lists costume, make-up and prop services. The third section is a general section of specialised goods and services for the film, television and video industries including such items as film stock suppliers, effects units and music services. The final section combines legal and business services for the industry

Actors, Audiences and Casting

Avalon Publicity Limited
4a Exmoor Street
London W10 6BD
Tel: 020 7598 7222
Fax: 020 7598 7223
email: edt@avalonuk.com
Edward Thomson

Bromley Casting (Film & TV Extras Directory)
77 Widmore Road
Bromley BR1 3AA
Tel: 020 8466 8239
Fax: 020 8466 8239
email: admin@bromleycasting.tv
Website: www.bromleycasting.tv
Simon Allen
Providing quality background artisits to the UK film and TV industry

Celebrities Worldwide Ltd
39-41 New Oxford Street
London WC1A 1BN
Tel: 020 7836 7703/4
Fax: 020 7836 7701
email: info@celebritiesworldwide.com
Website:
www.celebritiesworldwide.com
Claire Nye
For celebrity contacts online. Website provides thousands of celebrity contacts online 24 hrs. By subscription

Downes Agency
96 Broadway
Bexleyheath
Kent DA6 7DE
Tel: 020 8304 0541
Fax: 020 8301 5591
email: downes@presentersagency.com
Website: www.presentersagency.com
Agents representing presenters and actors experienced in the fields of presentations, documentaries, commentaries, narrations, television dramas, feature films, industrial videos, training films, voice-overs, conferences and commercials

Lip Service Casting Ltd
60-66 Wardour Street
London W1F 0TA
Tel: 020 7734 3393
Fax: 020 7734 3373
email: bookings@lipservice.co.uk
Website: www.lipserve.co.uk
Susan Mactavish
Voiceover agency for actors, and voiceover casting agency

Costumes, Make-up and Props

Angels - The Costumiers
1 Garrick Road
London NW9 6AA
Tel: 020 8202 2244
Fax: 020 8202 1820
email: angels@angels.uk.com
Website: www.angels.uk.com
Richard Green
World's largest Costume Hire Company. Extensive ranges covering every historical period, including contemporary clothing, civil and military uniforms. Full in-house ladies and men's making service, millinery department, jewellry, glasses and watch hire. Branches also in Shaftesbury Avenue and Paris. Additional services:- experinced personal costumiers, designers office space, reference library and shipping department

Angels Wigs
40 Camden Street
London NW1 0EN
Tel: 020 7 387 0999
Fax: 020 7 383 5603
email: wigs@angels.uk.com
Ben Stanton

Cabervans
Caberfeidh
Cloch Road
Gourock
Nr. Glasgow PA19 1BA
Tel: 01475 638775
Fax: 01475 638775
Make-up and wardrobe units, dining coaches, motorhomes, 3 & 4 bay American artistes Unit cars, minibuses and 77 seat coaches

Hirearchy Classic & Contemporary Costume
45-47 Palmerston Road
Boscombe
Bournemouth
Dorset BH1 4HW
Tel: 01202 394465
email: hirearchy@aol.com
Website: www.hirearchy.co.uk
Paul Tarrant

Specialising in the hire of ladies and gents costumes from medieval to present day. Also accessories, make-up, wigs, militaria jewellery, textiles and luggage

Hothouse Models & Effects

10 St Leonard's Road
Park Royal
London NW10 6SY
Tel: 020 8961 3666
Fax: 020 8961 3777
email: info@hothousefx.co.uk
Website: www.hothousefx.co.uk
Jez Clarke, Greg Lawrence
Special effects, mechanical rigs, models, sculpture and atmospherics for film and television

The Image Co

Pinewood Studios
Iver Heath
Buckinghamshire SLO ONH
Tel: 01753 630066
Fax: 01753 639900
email: mail@image-company.com
John Prentice
Wardrobe costume badging service, prop and promotional clothing

Kevin Jones, Freelance Costume Assistant & Designer

32 Austen Walk
West Bromwich
West Midlands B71 1RD
Tel: (0121) 588 6801
Fax: (0121) 588 6801
email: KJ58@vodafone.net
Costume Assistant, Designer, dresser for films television, commercials, pop videos, promotions, product launches, fashion shows, theatre, tours

Neal Scanlan Studio

Elstree Film Studios
Borehamwood
Hertfordshire WD6 1JG
Tel: 0208 324 2620
Fax: 0208 324 2774

Robert Hale Flowers

Interior and Flower Designers
8 Lovell Street
York YO123 1BO
Tel: 01904 613044
Contact: Robert Hale
Suppliers and designers of interior flower decoration

Ten Tenths

106 Gifford Street
London N1 0DF
Tel: 020 7607 4887
Fax: 020 7609 8124
email: mike@tentenths.co.uk
Website: www.tentenths.co.uk
Mike Hallowes
Props service specialising in vehicles (cars, bikes, boats and planes) ranging from 1901 to present day - veteran, vintage, classic, modern - with complementary wardrobe facilities

Woodbridge Productions Ltd

PO Box 123
Hounslow
London TW4 7EX
Tel: 020 8574 7778
Fax: 0208 574 7778
email: info@woodbridgeproductions.co.uk
Website: woodbridgeproductions.co.uk
John Woodbridge
Covers all aspects of cosmetic and prosthetic make-up artistry

3rd Generation Sets

Manygate Lane
Shepperton
Middx TW17 9EG
Tel: 01932 226341
Fax: 01932 246336
email: Callum@hallifordstudios.com
Website: www.hallifordfilmstudios.com
Contact: Callum Andrews/Studio manager

Film Services

Aerial Cameras Systems Ltd

Innovation House
Douglas Drive
Godalming
Surrey GU7 1JX
Tel: 01483 426 767
Fax: 01483 413 900
email: info@aerialcamerasystems.com
Website: www.aerialcamerasystems.com
Matt Coyde

Agfa-Gevaert

Motion Picture Division
27 Great West Road
Brentford
Middx TW8 9AX
Tel: 020 8231 4301
Fax: 020 8231 4315
Philip Hill

Any Effects

64 Weir Road
London SW19 8UG
Tel: 0800 2983484
Fax: 020 8944 6989
email: jules@anyeffects.com
Website: www.anyeffects.com
Mechanical (front of camera) special effects. Pyrotechnics: simulated explosions, bullet hits. Fine models for close up camera work. Weather: rain, snow, fog, wind. Breakaways: shatterglass, windows, bottles, glasses, collapsing furniture, walls, floors. Specialised engineering rigs and propmaking service

Art Star

66 Josephine Avenue
London SW2 2LA
Tel: 07976 294 985
Fax: 07970 455 956
email: h_artstar@hotmail.com
Website: www.artsar.co.uk
Henrietta Cartwright
Small art consultancy supplying clients, including the BBC, advertising companies and interior decorators, with paintings and sculpture to meet their requirements

Riky Ash Falling For You

c/o 65 Britania Avenue
Nottingham NG6 OEA
Tel: 0115 849 3470
Website: www.fallingforyou.co.uk
Television and Film Stuntman, Stunt Coordinator, with over 250 television and film credits. Extensive work for TV, feature films, commercials, non-broadcast video, promotions and advertising

Audio Interactive Ltd

Pinewood Studios
Iver Heath
Buckinghamshire SLO ONH
Tel: 01753 651700
Dick Joseph
Sound for the Multimedia industry - two fully soundproofed production room, on-site composers and a library of 30,000 sound effects

Bennett Underwater Productions, Charlie

114 Addison Gardens
West Kensington
London W14 0DS
Tel: 020 7263 952
email: chazben@aol.com
Underwater services to the film and television industry, including experienced qualified diving personnel and equipment; underwater film and video, stills photography and scuba instruction. Advice, logistics and support offered

on an international scale. Registered HSE Diving contractor

Bionic Productions Ltd

Pinewood Studios
Pinewood Road
Iver
Bucks SLO ONH
Tel: 01753 653456
Fax: 01753 654507
On-site computer playback, and computer hire

Bonded Services

Aerodrome Way
Cranford Lane
Hounslow
Middx TW5 9QB
Tel: 020 8897 7973
Fax: 020 8897 7979
email: info@ftsbonded.com
Website: www.ftsbonded.com
Kim Erin Cowley, Head of Business Development
Inventory management, worldwide freight, courier services, technical facilities including film checking and tape duplication, storage and distribution

Boulton-Hawker Films

Hadleigh
near Ipswich
Suffolk IP7 5BG
Tel: 01473 822235
Fax: 01473 824519
Wide range of educational videos and CD-ROMs. Subject catalogues on request

C I Travel

Shepperton Studios
Shepperton, Studio 16
Middx TW17 0QD
Tel: 01932 592323
Fax: 01932 592417
email: steve.garner@citravel.co.uk
Website: www.citravel.co.uk
Steve Garner
Transport and travel services

Camera Associates Ltd

Pinewood Studios
Iver Heath
Buckinghamshire SLO ONH
Tel: 01753 631007
Dave Cooper
Film video and grip hire service. Workshop and repair service also available on the Pinewood lot

celluloid dreams

6 Silver Place
London W1F OJS
Tel: 01273 729 115
Fax: 01273 729 115
email: celluloiddreams@hotmail.com
Website:
homepage.mac.com/celluloiddreams

Cinetron Desgin

Shepperton Studios
Shepperton
Middx TW17 0QD
Tel: 01932 572611
Fax: 01932 568989
Utilising a prodigious hoard of archive treasures, celluloid dreams provides bespoke replica publicity posters for virtually any film. Also specialise in recreating classic posters to any new design specification from postcard prints to quadras

Concept 2 Media Ltd

Consett
Brays Lane
Hyde Heath
Amersham
Bucks HP6 5RU
Tel: 01494 772518
email: info@concept2media.co.uk
Website: www.concept2media.com
Stephen Lofthouse

Concert Lights UK

c/o Elstree Film Studios
Borehamwood
Herts WD6 1JG
Tel: 020 8953 1600
Work on Who Wants to be a Millionnaire for Celador Productions and a number of TV shows

Connections Communications Centre Ltd

Palingswick House
241 King Street
Hammersmith
London W6 9LP
Tel: 020 8741 1766
Fax: 020 8563 1934
email: @cccmedia.co.uk
Website: www.cccmedia.co.uk
Jacqueline Davis
A registered charity producing promotional and educational videos for the voluntary sector. Currently in production Travelling Forward a 25 minute documentary commissioned by the Thalidomide Society

Cool Million *

Mortimer House
46 Sheen Lane
London SW14 8LP
Tel: 020 8878 7887
Fax: 020 6878 8687

De Wolfe Music

Shropshire House
2nd Floor East
11/20 Capper Street
London WC13 6JA
Tel: 020 7631 3600
Fax: 020 7631 3700
email: warren@dewolfemusic.co.uk
Website: www.dewolfemusic.co.uk
Warren De Wolfe, Alan Howe

Diverse Design

Gorleston Street
London W14 8XS
Tel: 020 7603 4567
Fax: 020 7603 2148
email: danielcr@diverse.co.uk
Website: www.diverse.co.uk
Daniel Creasey (Head of Design)

Dynamic Mounts International

Shepperton Studios
Shepperton
Middx TW17 0QD
Tel: 01932 592348
Fax: 01932 592138
email: dmi@mega3.tv
Website: www.mega3.tv
Dan Gillham

EOS Electronics AV*

EOS House
Weston Square
Barry
South Glamorgan CF63 2YF
Tel: 01446 741212
Fax: 01446 746120
Specialist manufacturers of video animation, video time laspsing and video archiving equipment. Products: Supertoon Low Cost School Animation System, AC 580 Lo-band Controller, BAC900 Broadcast Animation Controller, LCP3 Compact Disc, Listening Posts

ETH Screen Music

17 Pilrig Street
Edinburgh EH6 5AN
Tel: 0131 553 2721
Harald Tobermann
Producer and publisher of original music for moving images. Complete creative team - composers, arrangers, musicians

The Film Game

Unit 30
Metropolitan Centre
3 Taunton Road
Greenford
Middlesex, UB6 8UQ
Tel: 020 7494 9922
Fax: 020 7494 9944
email : sales@filmgame.co.uk

James Rowlands/Nick Flynn
Leading supplier of motion picture film stock (available on sale or return) and an extensive range of consumables to compliment your every production requirement

The Film Stock Centre Blanx

68-70 Wardour Street
London W1F OTB
Tel: 020 7494 2244
Fax: 020 7287 2040
email: sales@fscblanx.co.uk
Rob Flood
A "Kodak @" reseller of motion picture film stock and stills film, Sony and all major brands of professional video tape stock, film consumables, professional audio products and data media. Open weekdays 8.30am to 7pm. Emergency callout service 0831 701407

Film Vault Search Service

Unit 7
The Boundary
Wheatley Road
Garsington
Oxford OX44 9EJ
Tel: 01865 361 000
Fax: 01865 361 500
email: mail@filmvault.co.uk
Website: www.filmvault.co.uk
Steve Cummings
The largest deleted video search service in the country. No charges for deposit or 'search fees'. Every video sold is checked against faults and is professionally cleaned, comes with the correct copyright, BBFC certificate and full guarantee

Focus International Transport Ltd

Shepperton Studios
Shepperton
Middx TW17 0QD
Tel: 01932 572339
Fax: 01932 568989
Transport services

Formatt Filters

Unit 30
Metropolitan Centre
3 Taunton Road
Greenford
Middlesex, UB6 8UQ
Tel: 020 8570 7701
Fax: 020 8570 7702
email: info@formatt.co.uk
Website: www.format.co.uk
Mark Blaker
Camera filters that match the precision of your finest lenses. Formatt Filters is renowed for the high quality and technical excellence of its camer filters and lighting gels

FSC Blanx

68 - 70 Wardour Street
London, W1F 0TB
Tel : 020 7494 2244
Fax : 020 7287 2040
email: email : sales@fscblanx.co.uk
Contact : Jessica Finisterre/ Lisa Renton/ Anna O'Leary
Friendly shop and sales team in th heart of Soho, selling every kind of broadcast video tape, professional audio tape, data media stock and consumables. Open at weekends

Fully Equipped & Formatt Filters

Unit 30
Metropolitan Centre
3 Taunton Road
Greenford
Middlesex, UB6 8UQ
Tel: 020 8578 7701
Fax: 020 8578 7702
email: info@fullyequipped.co.uk
Website: www.format.co.uk
Mark Blaker/John Sears/Rob Flood
Premier choice for all new and used equipment. Products include cameras, tripods, grip, lighting, sound & editing equipment. Our sales team combines 100 years of experience in the film & video industry

Harkness Hall Ltd

The Gate Studios
Station Road
Borehamwood
Herts WD6 1DQ
Tel: 020 8953 3611
Fax: 020 8207 3657
email: sales@harknesshall.com
Website: www.harknesshall.com
Andrew Robinson, Tony Dilley
Projection screens and complete screen systems, fixed and portable, front or rear, flat, curved, flying, roller etc. Curtain tracks, festoons, cycloramas, raise and lower equipment, stage equipment

Heliphotos Aerial Photography

Elstree Aerodrome
Elstree
Hertfordshire
Tel: 0208 207 6042

Kodak Limited

Entertainment Imaging
PO Box 66, Station Road
Hemel Hempstead
Herts HP1 1JU
Tel: 01442 845945
Fax: 01442 844458
Website: www.kodak.com/go/motion
Customer Service
Suppliers of the full range of Kodak colour negative and print films, including the new family of Vision colour negative films

Little Cinema Company Limited

72 New Bond Street
London W1S 1RR
Tel: 020 7385 5521
Fax: 020 7385 5524
email: sales@littlecinema.co.uk
Joanne van Praagh
Suppliers and installers of digital projection, sound, and control systems for screening rooms and private cinemas worldwide.

Marine Bio-images

1 Orchard Cottages
Coombe Barton
Shobrooke, Crediton
Devon EX17 1BS
Tel: 01363 775 278
Fax: 01363 775 278
email: email colin-m@marine-bio-images.com
Website: www.marine-bio-images.com
Contact: Colin Munro

Midland Fire Protection Services

256 Foleshill Road
Coventry CV6 5AY
Tel: 024 7668 5252 (mobile) 07836 651408
Fax: 024 7663 7575
Robin Crane
Specialists in fire and rescue cover for location, studio and stage work. Special services, firefighters, action vehicles, fully equipped fire and rescue appliances, 5,000 gallons of water storage systems available, throughout the UK 24 hour service

Moving Image Touring Exhibition Service (MITES)

Foundation For Art & Creative Technology (FACT)
88 Wood Street
Liverpool L1 4DX
Tel: 0151 707 4435
Fax: 0151 707 4432
email: mites@fact.co.uk
Website: www.mites.org.uk

Simon Bradshaw
Extensive exhibition equipment resource, DVD authoring and production, archive and digital mastering facility. Courses for artists, gallery curators, technicians and exhibitors concerned with the commissioning and presentation of moving image art works. Also development, advice, consultation services

The National Research Group

Tel: 020 7351 4370
Lucy McDonald

Oxford Scientific Films (OSF)

Lower Road
Long Hanborough
Oxford OX8 8LL
Tel: 01993 881 881
Fax: 01993 882 808/883969
email: enquires@osf.uk.com
Website: www.osf.uk.com
Sean Morris
ndependent production company specialising in blue-chip natural history documentaries for broadcast. 30 years of experience and innovation in specialist camera techniques. Extensive stills and stock footage libraries

Pirate Motion Control

St Leonards Road
London NW10 6ST
Tel: 020 8930 5000
Fax: 020 8930 5001
email: help@pirate.co.uk
Website: www.pirate.co.uk
Michael Ganss
Motion Control Studio for 16mm film and video. 12 axis rig & 3 motion controlled lighting dimmer circuits. Call for showreel

ProDigital Audio Services

3 George Street
West Bay
Dorset DT6 4EY
Tel: 01308 422 866
Sound equipment, service and maintenance. Specialises in location sound equipment for the film and television industry - particularly DAT recorders

Radcliffes Transport Services

3-9 Willow Lane
Willow Lane Industrial Estate
Mitcham
Surrey CR4 4NA
Tel: 020 8687 2344
Fax: 020 8687 0997
Specialist transport specifically for the film and television industry, both nationally and internationally. Fleet ranges from transit vans to 40' air ride articulated vehicles with experienced staff

The Screen Company

182 High Street
Cottenham
Cambridge CB4 8RX
Tel: 01954 250139
Fax: 01954 252005
email:
thescreencompany@onetel.net.uk
Website:
www.thescreencompany.co.uk
Pat Turner
Manufacture, supply and installation of all types of front and rear projection screens for video, slide, film and OHP

Screenwriters Store

The Screenwriter's Store Ltd.
Suite 121, Friars House
157-168 Blackfriars Road
London SE1 8EZ
United Kingdom
Tel: +44 (0)20 7261 1908
Fax: +44 (0)20 7261 1909
email: info@thesws.com
Website: www.thesws.com
Rinaldo Quacquarini/Johanna Reder
Opening Hours: Mon- Fri, 9.30am - 6pm (callers by prior arrangement only)
Europe's largest authorised reseller and distributor of screenwriting and production software, also selling seminars, consultancy. The website has over 100 popular screenplays in proper script format available for downloading

Snow-Bound

37 Oakwood Drive
Heaton
Bolton BL1 5EE
Tel: 01204 841285
Fax: 01204 841285
Suppliers of artificial snow and the machinery to apply it for the creation of snow/winter scenes. The product is life-like (not poly beads or cotton wool) adheres to any surface and is fire-retardent, non-toxic and safe in use, and eco-friendly

Studio Art

Elstree Film Studios
Boreham Wood
Hertfordshire WD6 1JG
Tel: 0208 324 2600
Fax: 0208 324 2601
Danny Rogers
Specialist manufacturers of signs, neon, props and graphics for features and television

Visionworks Internet Ltd

13 Chartfield Avenue
London SW15 6DT
Tel: 020 8789 4254
Fax: 020 8785 0520
Website:
www.visionworksinternet.com
Sandy Knight
Web design from basic level up to e-commerce

Zooid Pictures Limited

66 Alexander Road
London N19 5PQ
Tel: 020 7281 2407
Fax: 020 7281 2404
email: pictures@zooid.co.uk
Website: www.zooid.co.uk
Richard Philpott
For over 20 years, Zooid has been a one-stop media resources supplier and researcher for all copyright materials including film/video, stills, illustration, animation and sound, from archives, libraries, agencies, private collections and museums worldwide, for use in film, television, book publishing, CD-Rom, multimedia, presentations and on-line services. Zooid manage all aspects from first briefing through to licensing. Zooid use advanced digital technologies and license their management system, Picture Desk, to leading international publishers

Workspace Management Limited

Canalot Production Studios
222 Kensal Road
London W10 5BN
Tel: 020 89608580
Fax: 020 89608907
email: sarah.charrington@
workspacegroup.co.uk
Andrea Kolakasi, Studio Manager
Sarah Charrington, Assistant Manager
Large Media business complex housing over 90 companies

Legal and Business Services

Ashurst Morris Crisp
Broadwalk House
5 Appold Street
London EC2A 2HA
Tel: 0207 638 1111
Fax: 0207 972 7990
email: film.tv@ashursts.com
Website: www.ashursts.com
Tony Ghee, Charlotte Douglas, Vanessa Bertelli, Sergei Ostrovsky, Monica Keightley
Leading City law firm with a young and progressive media and telecommunications team. Advice is provided on all aspects of the film and television industry, including corporate, employment, property and tax issues. Clients include leading national broadcasters, cable network operators and a number of small independents

Barclays Bank Media Banking Centre
27 Soho Square
London W1A 4WA
Tel: 020 7445 5773
Fax: 020 7445 5802
email: john.m.dixon@barclayscorporate.com
John Dixon
Large business centre providing a comprehensive range of banking services to all aspects of the film and television industry

Deloitte & Touche
Hill House
1 Little New Street
London EC4A 3TR
Tel: 020 7936 3000
Fax: 020 7583 8517
Website: www.deloitte.co.uk
Gavin Hamilton-Deeley
Advisors to film, television and broadcasting organisations. Business plans and financial models for companies, tax planning and business advice for individuals, and information on legal and regulatory developments affecting the sector

Dorsey & Whitney
21 Wilson Street
London EC2M 2TD
Tel: 020 7588 0800
Fax: 020 7588 0555
London or Helene Freeman in New York
Dorsey & Whitney is an international law firm with 22 offices across the United States, Europe and Asia. As a team of seasoned lawyers who are intimately familiar with the dynamics of the creative industries, Dorsey & Whitney's Creative Industries Group provides tailor-made solutions designed to meet the needs of media and entertainment clients operating at national and international levels. The Group regularly calls upon the expertise of colleagues across many time zones, specialising in areas as diverse as intellectual property due diligence, acquisitions and sales, licensing, financing and tax planning. This depth of capability enables the Group to provide a seamless service to clients involved in the film, TV, video, DVD, music, fashion, advertising, publishing, sport and leisure, computer games and technology sectors

Film Finances
14/15 Conduit Street
London W1R 9TG
Tel: 020 7629 6557
Fax: 020 7491 7530
Website: www.filmfinances.com
Provide completion guarantees for the film and television industry

Henry Hepworth
Media Law Solicitors
5 John Street
London WC1N 2HH
Tel: 020 7242 7999
Fax: 020 7242 7988
A new specialist media and intellectual property practice with a distinctive high quality client base which is active across the entire spectrum of the copyright and intellectual property industries

The Media Law Partnership,
33 Prospect Road
London NW2 2JU
Tel: 020 7435 7127
Fax: 0870 1307486
email: as@medialaw.uk.com
Adam Sutcliffe
Offers experience in all aspects of the negotiation and drafting of agreements for film production, film financing and international co-productions, with an emphasis on concise and effective documents, and a practical 'business affairs' approach to legal matters for all those involved in the film-making and distribution process

Olswang
90 Long Acre
London WC2E 9TT
Tel: 020 7208 8888
Fax: 020 7208 8800
email: olsmail@olswang.co.uk
Website: www.olswang.co.uk

Richards Butler
110 Cannon Street
London EC4N 6AR
Tel: 020 7772 5763
Website: www.richardsbutler.com
Selina Short, Communications

STUDIOS

3 Mills Island Studios
Three Mill Lane
London E3 3DU
Tel: 020 7363 3336
Fax: 020 8215 3499
email: info@3mills.com
Website: www.3mills.com
Lisa Jarvis or Candice McDonald
16 Stages, 6 Rehearsal Rooms, Production Offices, Restaurant/Bar
Recent features:
28 Days Later; Dr Sleep; Pure; Lighthouse
Recent television:
Bad Girls, Dream Team, Gary Rhodes - Cookery Year, London's Burning, Mile High, Murphy's Law, Night & Day

BBC Television Centre Studios
Wood Lane
London W12 7RJ
Tel: 020 8700 100 883
email: bbcresources.co.uk
Website: bbcresources.com
National Call Centre
8 full-facility television studios
TC1 10,250 sq ft
TC3 8,000 sq ft
TC4 and TC8 8,000 sq ft (digital and widescreen capable)
TC6 8,000 sq ft (digital)
TC2, TC5 and TC7 3,500 sq ft
BBC Television Centre Studios*

Bray Studios
Down Place
Water Oakley
Windsor Road
Windsor SL4 5UG
Tel: 01628 622111
Fax: 01628 770381
email: b.earl@tiscali.co.uk
Studio manager: Beryl Earl
STAGES
1 (sound) 955 sq metres
2 (sound) 948 sq metres
3 (sound) 238 sq metres
4 (sound) 167 sq metres
FILM
Revelation
TELEVISION
Born and Bred II and III
Fimbles I and II

De Lane Lea Dean Street Studio
75 Dean Street
London W1V 5HA
Tel: 020 7439 1721/ 0171 432 3877 (direct line 24 hours)
Fax: 020 7437 0913
email: dll@delanelea.com
Website: www.delanelea.com
Studio manager: Dick Slade
STAGE
1 86 sq metres
40x23x18 SYNC
lighting rig, film and TV make-up rooms, one wardrobe, one production office, full fitted kitchen

Ealing Studios
Ealing Studios
Ealing Green
London W5 5EP
Tele: 020 8567 6655
Fax: 020 8758 8658
email: info@ealingstudios.com
Website: www.ealingstudios.com
STAGES:
1 (silent) = area 232m2
2 (sound) = 864m2
3A (sound) = 530m2
3B (sound) = 530m2
3A/B combined = 1,080m2
4 (model stage silent) = 390m2
5 (sound) = 90m2
FILMS:
Shaun Of The Dead
Bride and Prejudice
Just One Of Those Things
Notting Hill
TELEVISION:
Rodger Rodger (BBC)
Spooks (Kudos)
Red Cap (Stormy Film Productions)
The Royle Family (Granada)

Halliford Studios
Manygate Lane
Shepperton
Middx TW17 9EG
Tel: 01932 226341
Fax: 01932 246336
email: sales@hallifordstudios.com
Website: www.hallifordfilmstudios.com
Contact: Callum Andrews/Studio Manager
Stages:
A stage 60'*60' (18.27*18.27m) 334sq metres, 18'6" HIGH (5.63m)
B stage 60'*40' (18.27*12.18m) 223sq metres, 18'6" HIGH (5.63m)

Holborn Studios
49/50 Eagle Wharf Road
London N1 7ED
Tel: 020 7490 4099
Fax: 020 7253 8120
email: reception@holborn-studios.co.uk
Website: www.holbornstudios.com
Ian Barker, Studio manager
STAGES
4 2,470 sq feet
6 2,940 sq feet
7 2,660 sq feet
18 roomsets 3,125 sq feet
Also eight fashion studios, set building, E6 lab, b/w labs, Calumet in house, canal-side restaurant and bar

Lamb Studios
Lamb House
Church Street
Chiswick
London W4 2PD
Tel: 020 89969961
Fax: 020 89969966
Website: www.bell.com

Leavesden Studios
PO Box 3000
Leavesden
Herts WD2 7LT
Tel: 01923 685 060
Fax: 01923 685 061
Studio Manager: Daniel Dark
STAGES
A 32,076sq feet
B 28,116 sq feet
C 11,285 sq feet
D 11,808 sq feet
F 15,427 sq feet
G 14,036 sq feet
Flight Shed 1 35,776
Effects 15,367 sq feet
Back Lot 100 acres
180 degrees of clear and uninterrupted horizon
Further 200,000 sq.ft of covered space available
FILMS
GoldenEye, Mortal Kombat, Annihilation; Sleepy Hollow, Star Wars: Episode One - The Phantom Menance, An Ideal Husband

Magic Eye Film Studios
Magic Eye Film Studios
20 Lydden Road
London SW18 4LR
Tel: 020 8877 0800
Fax: 020 8874 7274
Website: www.magiceye.co.uk
email: info@magiceye.co.uk
Magic Eye offers five fully operational stages, ranging from 900 to 4,500 square feet. They all include production offices and make-up rooms. Several of the stages are also fully coved

Millennium Studios
Elstree Way
Herts WD6 1SF
Tel: 020 8236 1400
Fax: 020 8236 1444
Website: www.elstree-online.co.uk
Contact: Ronan Willson
'X' Stage: 327 sq metres sound stage with flying grid and cyc. Camera room, construction workshop, wardrobe, dressing rooms, edit rooms, hospitality suite and production offices are also on site

Pinewood Studios
Pinewood Road
Iver Heath
Bucks SL0 0NH
Tel: 01753 651700
Fax: 01753 656844
Website: www.pinewood-studios.co.uk
Managing Director: Steve Jaggs
STAGES
A 1,685 sq metres
(Tank: 12.2m x 9.2m x 2.5m)
B 827 sq metres
C 827 sq metres
D 1,685 sq metres
(Tank: 12.2m x 9.2m x 2.5m)
E 1,685 sq metres
(Tank: 12.2m x 9.2m x 2.5m)
F 698 sq metres
(Tank: 6.1m x 6.1m x 2.5m)
G 247 sq metres
H 300 sq metres
J 824 sq metres - dedicated TV Studio
K 824 sq metres
L 880 sq metres
M 880 sq metres
N/P 767 sq metres
R 1,780 sq metres
S 1,789 sq metres
South Dock (silent)
1,547 sq metres
Albert R Broccoli 007 (silent) 4,223 sq metres (Tank: 90.5m x 22.3m x 2.7m Reservoir: 15.3m x 28.7m x 2.7m)
Large Process 454 sq metres
Exterior Lot 50 acres, comprising formal gardens and lake, woods, fields, concrete service roads and squares
Exterior Tank 67.4m narrowing to 32m wide, 60.4 long, 1.06m deep. Capacity 764,000 gallons. Inner Tank: 15.5m x 12.2m x 2.7m. Backing 73.2m x 18.3m
Largest outdoor tank in Europe
FILMS
Die Another Day, Quills, Proof of Life, Tomb Raider, Revelation, Charlotte Gray, The Hours, Below, the World is Not Enough, the Mummy Returns
TELEVISION
Dinotopia, Jack and the Beanstalk - the Real Story, Wit, Hornblower, Thursday the 12th, Sam's Game, My Family

Riverside Studios
Crisp Road
Hammersmith
London W6 9RL
Tel: 020 8237 1000
Fax: 020 8237 1011
email:
jonfawcett@riversidestudios.co.uk
Website: www.riversidestudios.co.uk
Jon Fawcett
Studio One 529 sq metres
Studio Two 378 sq metres
Studio Three 130 sq metres
Plus preview cinema, various dressing rooms, offices, café
TELEVISION
T.F.I. Friday, 'Collins & McConies Movie Club', Channel 4 Sitcom Festival, 'This Morning with Richard Not Judy', Top of the Pops (2001) Riverside Studios*

Rotherhithe Studios
119 Rotherhithe Street
London SE16 4NF
Tel: 020 7231 2209
Fax: 020 7231 2119
email: ostockman@sands.films.co.uk
Website: sandsfilms.co.uk
O Stockman, C Goodwin
STAGES
1 Rotherhithe 180 sq metres
Pre-production, construction, post-production facilities, period costume making, props
FILMS
The Nutcracker Story (IMAX 3D)
The Children's Midsummer Night's Dream

Shepperton Studios
Studio Road
Shepperton
Middx TW17 0QD
Tel: 01932 562 611
Fax: 01932 568 989
email:
admin@sheppertonstudios.co.uk
Website: www.sheppertonstudios.co.uk
Paul Olliver
STAGES
A 1,668 sq metres
B 1,115 sq metres
C 1,668 sq metres
D 1,115 sq metres
E 294 sq metres
F 294 sq metres
G 629 sq metres
H 2,660 sq metres
I 657 sq metres
J 1,394 sq metres
K 1,114 sq metres
L 604 sq metres
M 259 sq metres
T 261 sq metres
R 948 sq metres
S 929 sq metres
FILMS
Dirty Pretty Things, Just Visiting, Possession, Killing Me Softly, Two Men Went To War, Shakespeare in Love; Elizabeth, Hilary & Jackie; Sliding Doors; Notting Hill; Love's Labour's Lost; End of the Affair

South West Film Studios
St Agnes
Cornwall TR5 OLA
Tel: (0)1872 554131
Fax: (0)1872 552880
email:
info@southwestfilmstudios.com
Website:
www.southwestfilmstudios.com
Kate Hughes
South West Film Studios is a new purpose built studio facility, located on the stunning north coast of Cornwall. It offers a complete package
for film productions, including sound stages, water stage, workshop and office spaces, all set in beautiful landscaped gardens. South West Film Studios offers a flexible approach, whether you require a production base for a location shoot or fully sound proofed stage facilities.
Stages
1A - 24m x 18m x 12m
1B - 24m x 18m x 12m including water tank 3 x 3 x 2.5m
1A/B combined 36m x 24m x 12m
Stage 2 - 21m x 21m x 11.5m

Stonehills Studios
Shields Road

Gateshead
Tyne and Wear NE10 0HW
Tel: 0191 495 2244
Fax: 0191 495 2266
Studio Manager: Nick Walker
STAGES
1 1,433 sq feet
2 750 sq feet
The North's largest independent television facility comprising of Digital Betacam Edit Suite with the BVE 9100 Edit Controller, and Abekas ASWR 8100 mixer, A57 DVE and four machine editing, including two DVW 500s. Also three Avid off-line suites, 2D Matador and 3D Alias graphics and a Sound Studio comprising a Soundtracs 6800 24-track 32 channel desk and Soundscape 8-track digital editing machine
TELEVISION
Germ Genie, BBC 2; The Spark, Border; Come Snow Come Blow, Granada

Teddington Studios

Broom Road
Teddington
Middlesex TW11 9NT
Tel: 020 8977 3252
Fax: 020 8943 4050
email: sales@teddington.co.uk
Website: www.teddington.co.uk
Sales and Client Liaison
STUDIOS
1 653 sq metres
2 372 sq metres
3 120 sq metres
TELEVISION
This is Your Life; Des O'Connor Tonight; Harry Hill; Brian Conley Show; Alistair McGowan, My Hero, Beast, Coupling

Twickenham Film Studios

St Margaret's
Twickenham
Middx TW1 2AW
Tel: 020 8607 8888
Fax: 020 8607 8889
Website:
www.twickenhamstudios.com
Gerry Humphreys, Caroline Tipple (Stages)
STAGES
1 702 sq metres
with tank 37 sq metres x 2.6m deep
2 186 sq metres
3 516 sq metres
2 x dubbing theatres; 1 x ADR/Foley theatre; 40 x cutting rooms; Lightworks, Avid 35/16mm
Films include
Before You Go
The Bunker

Westway Studios

8 Olaf Street
London W11 4BE
Tel: 020 7221 9041
Fax: 020 7221 9399
Steve/Kathy
STAGES
1 502 sq metres (Sound Stage)
2 475 sq metres
3 169 sq metres
4 261 sq metres

TELEVISION COMPANIES

Below are listed all British terrestrial television companies, with a selection of their key personnel, and in some cases programmes. A more comprehensive listing of programmes, producers and cast members can be found via the web pages of each company. Compiled by Anastasia Kerameos

BBC Television

British Broadcasting Corporation

Television Centre
Wood Lane
Shepherds Bush
London W12 7RJ
Tel: 020 8743 8000
Website: www.bbc.co.uk
BBC Broadcasting House
Potrland Place
London W1A 1AA
Tel: 020 7580 4468
BBC Drama
Television Centre
Wood Lane
London W12 7RJ
Tel: 020 8743 8000
Tel: 020 85761 1861 (publicity dept)
BBC Resources
Television Centre
Wood Lane
London W12 7RJ
Tel: 08700 100 883
Fax: 08700 100 884
email: bbcresources@bbc.co.uk
Website: www.bbcresources.co.uk
Managing Director: Michael Southgate
Head of BBC Post Production: Lesley McMahon
Head of BBC Studios: Richard Philipps
Head of Costume & Wigs: Alan Godleman
Head of Marketing & Customer Relations: Tania Waine
Head of Business Strategy: Sarah Mackey
HR Director: Rachel Currie
Director of Finance: Stephen Killick

BBC Worldwide

Woodlands
80 Wood Lane
London W12 0TT
Tel: 020 8433 2000
Fax: 020 8749 0538
email: bbcworldwide@bbc.co.uk
Website: www.bbcworldwide.com
Online Catalogue: www.bbcworldwidetv.com

Chairman: Gavyn Davies
Director General: Greg Dyke
Director of Radio & Music: Jenny Abramsky, CBE
Director, Television: Jana Bennett, OBE
Director, Factual and Learning: Glenwyn Benson
Director of World Service & Global News: Mark Byford
Director of Human Resources & Internal Communication: Stephen Dando
Director of Marketing & Communications: Andy Duncan
Director of Strategy & Distribution: Carolyn Fairbairn
Chief Executive of BBC Ventures Group: Roger Flynn
Chief Executive, BBC Worldwide: Rupert Gavin
Director of New Media and Technology: Ashley Highfield
Director of Nations & Regions: Pat Loughrey
Director of Sport: Peter Salmon
Director of News: Richard Sambrook
Director of Finance, Property & Business Affairs: John Smith
Director of Policy & Legal Division: Caroline Thomson
Director, Drama, Entertainment & CBBC Division: Alan Yentob
Controller, BBC One: Lorraine Heggessey
Controller, BBC Two: Jane Root
Controller, BBC Three: Stuart Murphy
Managing Editor, BBC Four: Nick Ware
Controller, Daytime: Alison Sharman
Controller Commissioning, Drama: Jane Tranter
Controller Commissioning, Entertainment: Jane Lush
Controller, Programme Acquisition: George McGhee
Controller, Factual TV: Glenwyn Benson
Commissioner, Factual, Current Affairs & Investigations: Peter Horrocks
Acting Commissioner, Factual, Documentaries & Contemporary: Tom Archer
Commissioner, Factual, Specialist: Emma Swain
Commissioner, Factual, Arts & Culture: Franny Moyle
Commissioner, Factual, Lifeskills: Seetha Kumar
Commissioner, Factual, New Media: Liz Cleaver
BBC Independent Executive: Elaine Bedell
Head of Interactive TV Programmes: Scott Gronmark
Business & Finance Director: Bal Samra
Head of Genre Management & Business Affairs, Drama: Felicity Milton
Head of Genre Management & Business Affairs, Entertainment: Claire Evans
Head of Genre Management & Business Affairs, Factual: Anne Sullivan
Head of Legal & Business Affairs, Programme Acquisition: Helen Fox
Controller, CBBC: Dorothy Prior
Head of Publicity: Vanda Rumney
Managing Director, BBC Resources: Mike Southgate
Controller Network Development, Nations & Regions: Colin Cameron
Head of Fictionlab: Richard Fell

BBC Broadcast Programme Acquisition

BBC TV Centre
Wood Lane
London W12 7RJ
Tel: 020 8225 6721
Fax: 020 8749 0893
Controller, Programme Acquisition: George McGhee
Head of Films: Steve Jenkins
Responsible for feature film acquisition.
Head of Series: Sue Deeks
Responsible for fiction series acquisition.
Business Development Manager:

Paul Eggington
Responsible for short fiction film acquisition.
Head of Legal and Business Affairs: Paul Fagan
Responsible for acquisitions business issues.

Regional Television

BBC East (Look East)
St Catherine's Close
All Saint's Green
Norwich, Norfolk NR1 3ND
moving Autumn 2003 to
The Forum
Millennium Plain
Norwich, Norfolk NR2 1TF
Tel: 01603 619331
Fax: 01603 667865
email: look.east@bbc.co.uk
Head, Regional & Local Programmes: Tim Bishop

BBC East Midlands
East Midlands Broadcasting Centre,
London Road,
Nottingham NG2 4UU
Tel: 0115 955 0500
Fax: 0115 902 1984
email: emt@bbc.co.uk
Head of Regional & Local Progs: Alison Ford

BBC London
35c Marylebone High Street
London W1U 4QA
Tel: 020 7224 2424
email: yourlondon@bbc.co.uk
Head of Regional & Local Programmes: Michael MacFarlane

BBC North
Broadcasting Centre
Woodhouse Lane
Leeds LS2 9PX
Tel: 0113 244 1188
Fax: 0113 243 9387
email: look.north@bbc.co.uk
Head of Regional & Local Programmes: Colin Philpott

BBC North East & Cumbria
Broadcasting Centre
Barrack Road
Newcastle upon Tyne NE99 2NE
Tel: 0191 232 1313
Fax: 0191 221 0112
email: look.north.northeast.cumbria@bbc.co.uk
Head of Regional & Local Programmes: Wendy Pilmer

BBC North West
New Broadcasting House
Oxford Road
Manchester M60 1SJ
Tel: 0161 200 2020
Fax: 0164 236 1005
email: nwt@bbc.co.uk
Head of Regional & Local Programmes: Martin Brooks

BBC Northern Ireland
Broadcasting House
Ormeau Avenue
Belfast BT2 8HQ
Tel: 028 9033 8000
Fax: 028 9033 8800
email: ni@bbc.co.uk
Controller: Anna Carragher

BBC Scotland
Broadcasting House
Queen Margaret Drive
Glasgow G12 8DG
Tel: 0141 338 2000
Fax: 0141 334 0614
email: enquiries.scot@bbc.co.uk
Controller, BBC Scotland: John McCormick
Edinburgh
Broadcasting House
Queen Street
Edinburgh EH2 1JF
Tel: 0131 225 3131
Aberdeen
Broadcasting House
Beechgrove Terrace
Aberdeen AB9 2ZT
Tel: 01224 625233

BBC South
Broadcasting House
Havelock Road
Southampton SO14 7PU
Tel: 0238 022 6201
email: south.today@bbc.co.uk
Head of Regional & Local Programmes: Eve Turner

BBC South East
The Great Hall
Mount Pleasant Road
Tunbridge Wells
Kent TN1 1QQ
Tel: 01892 670 000
email: southeasttoday@bbc.co.uk
Head of Regional & Local Programmes: Laura Ellis

BBC South West
Broadcasting House
Seymour Road
Plymouth PL3 5BD
Tel: 01752 229201
Fax: 01752 234595
email: spotlight@bbc.co.uk
Head of Regional & Local Programmes: Leo Devine

BBC Wales
Broadcasting House
Llandaff
Cardiff CF5 2YQ
Tel: 029 2032 2000
email: feedback.wales@bbc.co.uk
Controller, BBC Wales: Menna Richards
Broadcasting House
Meirion Road
Bangor
Gwynedd LL57 3BY
Tel: 01248 370880
Fax: 01248 351443

BBC West
Broadcasting House
Whiteladies Road
Bristol BS8 2LR
Tel: 0117 973 2211
email: pointswest@bbc.co.uk
Head of Regional & Local Programmes: Andrew Wilson

BBC West Midlands
BBC Pebble Mill
Birmingham B5 7QQ
moving late 2003 to
The Mailbox
Royal Mail Street
Birmingham B1 1XL
Tel: 0121 567 6767
Tel: 0121 432 8888
email: midlands.today@bbc.co.uk
Head of Regional & Local Progs: David Holdsworthy

Independent Television Companies

Anglia Television
Anglia House
Norwich NR1 3JG
Tel: 01603 615151
Fax: 01603 631032
Website: www.anglia.tv.co.uk
Email: pr@angliatv.co.uk
Fax: 01603 761245 (Press Office)
Regional Offices:
Cambridge
26 Newmarket Road
Cambridge CB5 8DT
Tel: 01223 357676
Chelmsford
64-68 New London Road
Chelmsford CM2 0YU
Tel: 01245 357676
Ipswich

Hubbard House
Civic Drive
Ipswich IP1 2QA
Tel: 01473 226157
Luton
16 Park Street
Luton LU1 2DP
Tel: 01582 729666
Milton Keynes
ADMAIL 3222
Milton Keynes MK2 2NA
Tel: 01908 691660
Northampton
77b Abington Street
Northampton NN1 2BH
Tel: 01604 624 343
Peterborough
6 Bretton Green Village
Rightwell, Bretton
Peterborough PE3 8DY
Tel: 01733 269440
Chairman: David McCall
Managing Director: Graham Creelman
Controller of Programmes: Neil Thompson
Controller of News: Guy Adams
Regional Programme Executive: Mike Talbot
Broadcast and Regional Affairs Executive: Jim Woodrow
Director of Programmes and Production: Malcolm Allsop
Director of Broadcasting: Bob Ledwidge
Head of Network Factual Programmes: Andrea Cornes
Part of the Granada Media Group and covering the east of England, Anglia Television produces around 8 hrs of news and other programmes per week for its own transmission. Anglia also produces programmes for the ITV Network and other broadcasters such as Channel 4.
Programmes include:
Anglia News, divided into East and West
Art in the Home, a collaboration with Suffolk-based Wingfield Arts foundation
Big Night Out, late night series
The Biz, arts programme
Bloody Crimes, a journey through a historical period of swashbuckling criminality and religious persecution, presented by Bryan McNerney
Brian Turner's All Star Cooking
Champions of the Future
Cover Story, current affairs series
Crime Night, on the policing process
Cutting the Odds, documentary special on cancer
A Date with Helen, single-subject daytime magazine strand
Eastern Promises, issue led strand
Go Fishing, remains the only terrestrial angling series made and broadcast in Europe
Going Home, a series of short films on returning home to lay personal issues to rest, presented by John Peel
Killer Queens, on the theme of strong female leaders in the region's history, presented by Rory McGrath
King & Country, re-invented for a wider audience
Party of Your Life (co-produced with Meridian)
Riddles on the Road, local history series presented by Bryan McNerney
Safe as Houses, on the housing market
Six of the Best, a one-off arts awards programme
Soccer Sunday
Stand-Up Britain, a search for an unknown regional comedian
Summertime Blues, documentary on the Bedforshire constabulary
Take a Leaf, daytime gardening show
Tall Tales & Antique Sales, this programme prooved so successful it was sold to the ITV Network as part of its new-look schedule for 2003
The Way we Were, one hundred years of pre-video family film intercut with contemporary personal commentary, presented by James Bolam
What's the Story, news-based quiz

Border Television

The Television Centre
Carlisle CA1 3NT
Tel: 01228 525101
Fax: 01228 541384
Website: www.border-tv.com
Chairman: James L. Graham
Managing Director: Douglas Merrall
Director of Programmes: Neil Robinson
Head of News: Ian Proniewicz
Covering 288,000 homes in Cumbria, Border Television's broadcast coverage extends from Peebles in the North, down to Seascale in the south and includes the Isle of Man., and viewers in the Border Television region watch more television than the national average. Border Television renewed its licence in 2001 and is required to produce/commission a minimum of 294 hrs of regional programming annually. It also producers material for the ITV Network, such as the award-winning series Innovators and other broadcasters including Channel 4.
Programmes include:
The Border, a co-production with Scottish Television
Border News
Dale, a profile of the West Cumbrian politician Dale Campbell-Savours (now Lord Allerdale)
The Force, programme look at at how rural police officers deal with crime
HomeLookaround, news magazine programme
In Pursuit of Valour, the story of the Border Regiment
Killer Birds, introduction to birds of prey presented by Dee Barron
Mirrors, Masks and Movies, profile of a Lakeland based special effects artist
Nitty and Gritty, children's series
Out From the Crowd, arts series aimed at a young adult audience
Out of Town, a series of walks along the North of England presented by Eric Robson
Rural Lives, current affairs series
Secret Kingdom, the history and hidden treasures of North Northumberland and Southeast Scotland
Spoon with a View, cookery series
Talking Sides, studio interviews combined with filmed documentaries on political issues
Trailblazing, programme exploring Cumbria by mountain bike
TV Guide to Life, studio based advice series
Web Works, series of short community led programmes

Carlton Television

101 St Martin's Lane
London WC2N 4RF
Tel: 020 7240 4000
Fax: 020 7240 4171
Website: www.carlton.com
Chairman: Michael Green
Carlton Television holds 5 ITV franchises: Carlton London Region (weekdays), Carlton Central Region, Carlton West Country Region, HTV Wales and HTV West. Most Carlton commissioning is now channeled through its subsidiary Carlton Productions - see below

Carlton Productions

35-38 Portman Square
London W1H 0NU
Tel: 020 7486 6688
Fax: 020 7486 1132
Chief Executive: Rupert Dilnott-Cooper
Director of Programmes and Managing Director, Carlton Productions: Steve Hewlett

Joint Managing Directors, Action Time Productions: Phil Trelease and Caroline Beaton
Managing Director, Planet 24 Productions: Mary Durkan
Managing Director of Content, Carlton Productions: Michael Foster
Controller, Business Affairs: Martin Baker
Director, Drama & Co-production: Jonathan Powell
Executive Producer, Drame: Sharon Bloom
Controller, Children's & Young People's Programmes: David Mercer
Controller, Light Entertainment: Mark Wells
Controller of Factual Entertainment: Nick Bullen
Controller of Sport: Gary Newbon
Head of Special Projects and Development: Sally Doganis
Director of Factual Group: Polly Bide
Director of Factual Programmes:Richard Clemmow
Controller, Digital Programmes: Peter Lowe
Supplier of popular programming across all genres. It includes entertainment producer Planet 24 (www.planet24.com) and game show format supplier Action Time (www.action-time.com).

Carlton Broadcasting Central Region

Website: www.itv.com/carltoncentral
West Midlands:
Central Court
Gas Street
Birmingham B1 2JT
Tel: 0121 643 9898
Fax: 0121 643 4897
East Midlands:
Carlton Studios,
Lenton Lane
Nottingham NG7 2NA
Tel: 0115 986 3322
Fax: 0115 964 5552
South Midlands:
9 Windrush Court
Abingdon Business Park
Abingdon OX14 1SA
Tel: 01235 554123
Fax: 01235 524024
Outside Broadcasting Facilities:
Carlton 021
Units 11-13 Gravelly Industrial Park,
Gravelly Hill,
Birmingham B24 8HZ
Tel: 0121 327 2021
Fax: 0121 327 7021
Website: www.carlton021.net
email: 021info@carltontv.co.uk
Managing Director: Ed Everest
Carlton Studios
Lenton Lane,
Nottingham NG7 2NA
Tel: 01159 863 322
Managing Director: Ian Squires
Head of Regional Affairs: Kevin Johnson
Editor, Central News East: Mike Blair
Head of Regional Programmes, Central: Duncan Rycroft
Finance Director of Carlton Broadcasting: Ian Hughes
Head of Presentation and Programme Planning: David Burge
Controller, News & Operations: Laurie Upshon
Controller, Sports: Gary Newbon
Head of News: John Boileau
Editor, Central News West: Dan Barton
Editor, Central News South: Ian Rumsey
Covering the East, West and South Midlands Carlton Central Television broadcasts to a population of over 9 million. It produces regional material for its own output as well as material for the ITV Network and other broadcasters.
Programmes include:
30 Minutes, current affairs half hour single subject series
50 Years of…
Airbase, "real life" observational documentary based at RAF Waddington in Lincolnshire
Baby Hospital
Central News (East, West, South, and in Summer), see www.itv.com/centralnews
Central Weekend, current affairs
Fire & Rescue, the Warwickshire Fire Service on rescue missions
Heart of the Country
Heart of the Coutnry Goes Wild
Guinness in the Garden, series featuring garden designer Bunny Guinness
It's Your Shout, debates on local and national issues
Jobfinder
Midlander of the Year
Peak Practice, drama series about a group of GPs in a small village
Pulling Power
Pulling Power: the Story of...
Renovation Street
Rock Legends
Scam, investigation into confidence tricks perpetrated on the internet
Sky High, aerial survey of the Midlands
Spotlight Asia, weekend current affairs programme
Waterworld, tales of the people who live and work on the Midlands canals
Young Offenders

Carlton Broadcasting London Region

101 St Martin's Lane,
London WC2N 4RF
Tel: 020 7240 4000
Fax: 020 7240 4171
Tel: 020 7347 3611 (Press Office)
email: dutyoffice@carltontv.co.uk
website: www.itv.com/carltonlondon
London Television Centre
Upper Ground
London SE1 9LT
Tel: 020 7620 1620
Fax: 020 7827 7500
Managing Director: Coleena Reid
Head of Regional Acquisitions and Planning: David Joel
Head of Regional Programmes: Emma Barker
Holds the weekday ITV licence for the areas of London and the South-East. Carlton Television London is required to produce/commission a minimum of 419 hours of regional programming annually. It also produces material for the ITV Network and other broadcasters.
Programmes include:
Ask Ken, viewers question London's Mayor
Bulls and Bears, finance program
Carlton Country
Carlton Debate, an annual programme on a single issue
Carlton Multicultural Achievement Awards, staged and broadcast
Children's Casualty, featuring the staff and patients at St Mary's Hospital in Paddington
City Survival Guide, useful help and information for city living
Evening Standard Film and Theatre Awards, coverage of the evening
First Edition, current affairs series
The Frock and Roll Years, London fashion
Guinness in the Garden
Late Night London, audience debate programme
Legends
London's Richest
London Tonight, news magazine
Metroland, a showcase for new documentary directors
Pulling Power, co-produced with Carlton in the Midlands
The Queen and Me, two part series to mark the Queen's Golden Jubilee year
Secret Life of Kids, documentary

featuring 6-12 year olds given cameras to film their own lives
Single Voices, series of monologues
Statutes and Monuments
Tall Stories, on London's towers, spires and landmarks
The Way We Were, chronicling social change in the last century

Carlton Broadcasting West Country Region

Western Wood Way
Langage Science Park
Plymouth PL7 5BQ
Tel: 01752 333333
Fax: 01752 333444
email: dutyoffice@carltontv.co.uk
Website:
www.itv.com/carltonwestcountry
Managing Director: Mark Haskell
Director of Programmes: Jane McCloskey
Controller of News: Phil Carrodus
Controller of Features and Programme Development: Caroline Righton
Controller, Technical Operations: Mark Chaplin
Controller of Business Affairs: Peter Gregory
Owned by Carlton, Westcountry Television has a network of seven regional studios together with the main studio and headquarters in Plymouth and broadcasts to Cornwall and Devon and to much of Dorset and Somerset.The company transmits to 1.7 million people who live in one of the most diverse regions in the UK, and WT is strongly committed to reflecting this diversity in its regional coverage. Westcountry Television is required to produce/commission a minimum of 628 hours of regional programming. The company also produces material for the ITV network and other broadcasters such as Channel 4

Programmes include:
Adrenalin Kitchen, behind the scenes at the Extreme Academy in Cornwall
Buried Treasures, antiques programme with expert tim Wonnacott
Celebrity South West
Coast to Coast, ron Bendell journeyed on a celebration of 25 years of the South West Coastal path
Cornish Brass, a portrait of Cornwall's brass bands
Country Lives
An Englishman's Castle, a look behind the scenes at Powderham Castle
Emergency, documentary coverage of the Royal Devon and Exeter Hospital's casualty unit
The Face of Change, cultural change in the region seen through personal stories
Illuminations, religious programme
Lenkiewicz the Legacy
A Little Bit of Heaven, documentary series on a children's hospice
Model Ambitions
Pulling Power
Seventy Years Under the Stars, celebrating the anniversary of the Minnack Theatre
Short Curcuits
Soccer Sunday
Special Report, current affairs investigations
Storm Warning, on the changing climate in the South West
Surf's Up
Taste of the West, in co-production with HTV West
A Touch of Frost, the life and philosophy of the artist Sir Terry Frost
Update, weekly news review for the hard of hearing
The View From Here, current affairs investigations
Westcountry Live, coverage of live stories
Westcountry Sunday Edition, current affairs led by Graham Smith
What on Earth
Without Trace, a special documentary profiling convicted murderer John Allen

Central Television

see Carlton Broadcasting Central Region

Channel Four Television

124 Horseferry Road
London SW1P 2TX
Tel: 020 7396 4444
Fax: 020 7306 8353
Website: www.channel4.com
Executive Members
Chief Executive and Director of Programmes: Mark Thompson
Managing Director: David Scott
Commercial Director: Andy Barnes
Director of Business Affairs: Janet Walker
Director of Strategy and Development: David Brook
Director of Television: Tim Gardam
Non-Executive Members
Chairman: Vanni Treves
Controller of Programme Acquisition: June Dromgoole
Controller, Broadcasting: Rosemary Newell
Managing Editor, Commissioning: Janey Walker
Head of Series (C4 & E4): Jay Kandola
Editor, Non Primetime Feature Films: Tim Highstead
Acting Head of News, Current Affairs: Dorothy Byrne
Commissioning Editor, News, Current Affairs: Dorothy Byrne
Editor, Investigations: Kevin Sutcliffe
Editor, Politics: Mark Rubens
Commissioning Editor, Indy Fund: Deborah Rayner
Head of Drama: John Yorke
Commissioning Editor, Drama: Lucy Richer
Editor, Series: Ben Stephenson
Head of Entertainment, Controller of E4: Danielle Lux
Head of Entertainment: John McHugh
Commissioning Editor, Entertainment: Katie Taylor
Head of Comedy & Comedy Films: Caroline Leddy
Commissioning Editor, Comedy: Iain Morris
Editor, Sitcoms: Robert Popper
Commissioning Editor, 4 Music: Jo Wallace
Head of Specialist Factual Group: Janice Hadlow
Head of Science & Education: Simon Andreae
Commissioning Editor, Education: Simon Dickson
Disability Advisor: Alison Walsh
Commissioning Editor, History: Hamish Mykura
Deputy Commissioning Editor, History: Ralph Lee
Commissioning Editor. Archaeology, Anthropology & Adventure: Charles Fumeaux
Editor, Arts: Janet Lee
Editor, Religion & Science: Aaqil Ahmed
Editor, Music & Performance: Jan Younghusband
Head of Documentaries: Peter Dale
Commissioning Editor Documentaries: Hilary Bell
Deputy Commissioning Editor, Documentaries: Sam Bickley
Editor, Independent Film and Video: Jess Search
Editor, Documentaries: Danny Cohen
Head of Factual Entertainment: Julian Bellamy
Head of Cross Platform Development: Peter Grimsdale

Deputy Head of Cross Platform Development: Debbie Searle
Editor, Factual Entertainment: Nav Raman
Editor, Factual Entertainment, Events: Sharon Powers
Head of Factual Entertainment & Featuers Group: Ben Frow
Editor, Features: Emma Westcott
Head of Features: Jo McGrath
Editor, Features: Ben Adler
Head of Nations & Regions: Stuart Cosgrove
Commissioning Editor, Nations & Regions: Steven D Wright
Head of Sport: David Kerr
Deputy Editor, Sport: Deborah Poulton
Commissioning Editor, 4Learning, Schools: John Richmond
Commissioning Editor, T4/Youth: Jo Wallace
Editorial Manager, Cultural Diversity: Mary Fitzpatrick
Manager, Commissioning & Suppliers: Helen Robertson
Producer, Talent Development: Charlotte Black
Channel 4 is a national service set up by Act of Parliament in 1982 as a non profit making corporation, funded principally by its revenue from advertising. Its remit is to: have a distinctive character of its own, and cater for interests not served by other channels; provide a diverse service including news, current affairs, education, religion and multicultural programming, all of which are to be an integral part of the peak-time programming strategy, reflect and respond to disability issues; place educational material at the heart of the schedule; play a central role in the UK film industry; and encourage a large and diverse independent production industry, within and outside London. With a handful of exceptions, C4 does not make programmes itself - it both commissions new material from production companies and buys in already completed programmes. In 2002, 67% of broadcast hours were made up of new programming, and C4 achieved 10% share of all viewing. In this year a reorganisation also took place to face financial challenges. FilmFour was restructured and production absorbed back into the main channel.
Programmes include:
Alt TV: The Luckiest Nut in the World
Andy Warhol: the Complete Picture, a three part biographical documentary
The Art Show, contemporary arts and culture series
The Autopsy, a controversial showing of an autopsy performed in front of an audience by Professor Gunther von Hagens at his Body Worlds exhibition
The Battle of Orgreave, film by Mike Figgis on the brutal encounter between miners and police during the miner's strike of 1983/4
Big Brother, reality television programme with housemates locked up in a big house
The Book Group, comedy drama series written, set, cast and made in Scotland
Brookside, soap opera set in Liverpool
Buried
Channel 4 News
Feltham Sings, the prisoners sing about their lives
House of War, documentary on the four-day uprising of Taliban prisoners
Indian Summer, a season of festivals, concerts, TV programmes to coincide with televised cricket matches
Jamie's Kitchen, vocational training opportunity for unemployed youth provided by chef Jamie Oliver reality TV style
Marrying a Stranger
Muslim and British
The Osbournes, a series on the Ozzy Osbourne family
Operatunity
The Salon
So Graham Norton, late night talk show hosted by Graham Norton
When She Died: Death of a Princess, specially commissioned opera composed by Jonathan Dove
White Teeth, comedy
Without Prejudice

Channel Television

Television Centre, La Pouquelaye
St Helier
Jersey JE1 3ZD
Tel: 01534 816816
Fax: 01534 816817
email: broadcast@channeltv.co.uk
Television House, Bulwer Avenue
St Sampson
Guernsey GY2 4LA
Tel: 01481 241888
Fax: 01481 241866
email: broadcast.gsy@channeltv.co.uk
Unit 16A, 3rd floor
Enterprise House
59-65 Upper Ground
London SE1 9PQ
Tel: 020 7633 9902
Fax: 020 7401 8982
email: broadcast@channeltv.co.uk
Website: www.channeltv.co.uk
Chief Executive: Huw Davies
Managing Director: Michael Lucas
Director of Resources and Transmission: Kevin Banner
Group Finance Director: David Jenkins
Director of Sales: Gordon de Ste Croix
Director of Business Development & Compliance: Rowan O'Sullivan
Director of Finance and Administration: Amanda Trotman
Owned by Yattendon Investment Trust and covering the Channel Islands (principally the Islands of Jersey, Guernsey, Alderney, Herm and Sark) with a population of 150,000, Channel Television produced 124 hours of regional programming over 2002. The regional programme service is centred around local events and current affairs and the station's main studios are based in Jersey with additional studios in Guernsey
Programmes include:
Broadway Dreams, documentary charting the progress of three Channel islanders studying at the Bristol Old Vic Theatre School
Cabinet or Committee?, special debate programme focused on Government reform proposed for Guernsey
Channel Report, regional news magazine
Crimeline, monthly crime stand
The Parish, 'fly on the wall' documentary following two channel Islands clergymen at work and at home
Puffin's Plaice, a children's entertainment series featuring the character Oscar Puffin
Report Sport, sports programme looking at the sport news making headlines in the Channel Islands region
Sark – a Secret Sea, documentary on the underwater world aroudn Sark
Seven Summits, a special programme celebrating the climbing achievements of Channel Television reporter Eric Blakeley
Spiritual Paths, on the emergence of new and different expressions of faith within the community
Victoria College – 150, Not Out,

marking the 150th anniversary of Jersey's Victoria College

five

22 Long Acre
London WC2E 9LY
Tel: 020 7550 5555
Fax: 020 7550 5554
Website: www.channel5.co.uk (www.five.tv)
Email: dutyoffice@channel5.co.uk
Chief Executive: Jane Lighting
Deputy Chief Executive and Director of Sales: Nick Milligan
Director of Programmes: Kevin Lygo
Director of Finance: Grant Murray
Director of Legal and Business Affairs: Colin Campbell
Director of Marketing: David Pullan
Director of Broadcasting: Ashley Hill
Director of Acquisitions: Jeff Ford
Senior Programme Controller: Chris Shaw
Controller of Factual: Dan Chambers
Controller of Sport: Robert Charles
Controller of Drama: Corrine Hollingworth
Controller of Factual Entertainment: Sue Murphy
Controller of Entertainment: Andrew Newman
Controller of Youth, Music and Interactive: Sham Sandhu
Controller of Children's: Nick Wilson

Channel 5 launched on 30 March 1997, as the UK's fifth terrestrial broadcaster. Before broadcasting could begin, however, 5 was faced with the Herculean task of retuning 9 million homes across the UK. Coverage has now extended to 86.6% of homes with a share average for 2002 of 6.3%. Channel 5 is owned by two shareholders, RTL Group 64.625% and United Business Media 35.375%. Under its remit, 51% of programming must be original, 51% must be of European origin, 25% must be independent commissions, there must a minimum of 11 hours news programming; and 62 hours per week of programming must be subtitled. In 2002 Channel 5 changed its name to five.

Programmes include:
5th Gear, motoring programme
9/11 – A Tale of Two Towers, documentary marking the first anniversary of the September 11th attack
9/11 – the Firemen's Story, documentary marking the first anniversary of the September 11th attack
Afghan Massacre
Ali G: Before he Got Massive, one of five's contemporary biography programmes
Ancient Murder Mystery, presented by Bettany Hughes
Animal Express, children's series
Art Now, series profiling practising artists
Britain's Worst Driver, presented by Quentin Willson
The Britney Spears Story
Detox Camp
Don't Blame the Koalas, comedy drama co-produced with Australia's Channel 9
Family Affairs, soap opera set in a London borough
Five News
Gaudi's Barcelona, two-part programme
Great Artists, the story of art in the Western world
The Greatest Heroes of History, documentary
Harry and Cosh
Hot Property, Alice Beer
House Doctor, Ann Maurice gives advice on how to tart up homes to owners desperate to sell
International King of Sports
It's Your Funeral, public figures discuss their own funeral arrangements and their attitudes towards life and death
Kings & Queens of England, twelve part series presented by Nigel Spivey
Kylie Spinning Around
The Lee Bowyer Story
Live with Chris Moyles
Make Way for Noddy, chidlren's series
Michael Jackson's Face, one of the Sunday Documentary strand programmes
A Mind to Kill, four part drama
Mission to the Deep, shipwrecks
Monkey Makes, children's series
The Most Evil Men in History, documentary
Mysteries of the Ancients, presented by Bettany Hughes
Park Life, a look at life for teenage worker at Alton Towers
Pop, music magazine show
Revealed, strand of history programmes with episodes ranging from The Hindenburg Mystery, to Dambusters, and The Brits Who Fought for Hitler
Silent and Deadly, documentary marking one hundred years of submarine warfare in Britain
Tate Modern and Picasso
The Tribe, older children's series
UK Undercover, current affairs
Ultimate, a strand of programmes on Aircraft, Carriers, Hovercrafts, Rollercoasters, Superplanes, Tanks, Crash texts and others
The Wright Stuff, daily live topical talk show

GMTV

London Television Centre
Upper Ground
London SE1 9LT
Tel: 020 7827 7000
Fax: 020 7827 7001/020 7827 7100
Website: gm.tv (or www.gmtv.co.uk)
Chairman: Charles Allen
Managing Director: Paul Corley
Director of Programmes: Peter McHugh
Managing Editor: John Scammell
Editor: Martin Frizell
Head of Press: Nicki Johnceline
Presenters: Clare Nasir, Eamonn Holmes, Fiona Phillips, Lorraine Kelly, Penny Smith, John Stapleton, Andrew Castle, Kate Garraway, Jenni Falconer, Ben Shepherd, Andrea McLean.

Owned by Carlton, Disney, Granada and the Scottish Media Group, each holding a 25% share, GMTV broadcasts nationally news and magazine programming, with features on life style and show business, on the ITV network from 6.00 am to 9.25 am. Weekday programming share for 2002 was 30.4%.

Grampian Television

Queen's Cross
Aberdeen AB15 4XJ
Tel: 01224 846846
Fax: 01224 846800
email: viewer.enquiries@grampian.co.uk
Website: www.grampiantv.co.uk
Managing Director: Derrick Thomson
Chairman: Dr Calum A MacLeod CBE

Part of the Scottish Media Group and covering the North of Scotland, including Aberdeen, Dundee and Inverness, Grampian TV broadcasts to an audience of 1.2 million viewers. During 2002, Grampian gained a 32% peak-time audience share. Grampian also produces material for the ITV Network and other broadcasters such as BBC1, Channel 4, and Nickelodeon.

Programmes include:
An t-Urlar Ur, profiling traditional

musicians in Scotland
Boiling Point, culinary quiz show (co-produced with Scottish Television)
Cairt-Turais, travel programme, presented by Angela MacEachen and Annabel MacLeod
Co is Cuin, archive-based, presented by Norman MacLeod
Comhla Rinn, in depth interviews
Crossfire, current affairs series
Desert Island Chefts, cookery programme
Eye to Eye, religious programme commissioned from Tern Television Productions
Ginger Nuts, a Hogmanay programme looking at red heads in Scottish history
Grampian Midweek, a weekly magazine covering social issues
New Found Land (co-production with Scottish Television), series of shorts made by new filmmakers
North Tonight, Grampian's flagship news programme
North Tonight Specials
The People Show, profiling unusual and charismatic individuals in the region
Scottish Legends, documentaries on iconic Scottish subjects (co-produced with Scottish Television)
Scottish Politician of the Year Awards (co-produced with Scottish Television)
This Scotland (co-production with Scottish Television) documentary films exploring aspects of contemporary life in Scotland
Slàinte, magazine programme dealing with issues in medicine, presented by Catriona Nicholson
The Week In Politics, a review of events in Parliament
Whelan Around, Charlie Whelan with guests on the golf course (co-produced with Scottish Television)

Granada Media

Main offices:
Granada Television Centre
Quay Street
Manchester M60 9EA
Tel: 0161 832 7211
Fax: 0161 827 2029
email:
officers.duty@granadamedia.com
Website: www.granadamedia.com
News centres:
London
4th Floor
48 Leicester Square
London WC2H 7FB
Tel: 020 7389 8555
Fax: 020 7930 8499
Granada News Centre
Albert Dock, Liverpool L3 4BA
Tel: 0151 709 9393
Fax: 0151 709 3389
Chester
Bridgegate House
5 Bridge Place
Lower Bridge Street
Chester CH1 1SA
Tel: 01244 313966
Fax: 01244 320599
Lancaster
White Cross, Lancaster LA1 4XQ
Tel: 01524 60688
Fax: 01524 67607
Blackburn
Daisyfield Business Centre
Appleby Street
Blackburn BB1 3BL
Tel: 01254 690099
Fax: 01254 699299
Granada Film
The London Television Centre
Upper Ground
London SE1 9LT
Tel: 020 7620 1620
Executive Chairman, Granada plc: Charles Allen, CBE
Group Finance Director, Granada plc: Henry Staunton
Commercial Director, Granada plc: Graham Parrott
Chief Executive, Granada Broadcasting and Enterprises: Mick Desmond
Chief Executive, Managing Director, Granada Content: Simon Shaps
Managing Director of Operations, Granada plc: Jules Burns
Managing Director, Granada Screen: John Willis
Creative Director, Granada Content: Andrea Wonfor
Director, Granada Media Entertainment: Marcus Plantin
Director of Programmes, Granada Content North: John Whiston
Director of Programmes, Granada Content South: Grant Mansfield
Commercial Director: Chris Pye
LWT Controller, Arts and Features: Melvyn Bragg
Financial Director: Grant Murray
Chief Operating Officer, Granada Content: John Cresswell
Managing Director, Granada Learning: Nigel Ward
Chief Operating Officer: Max Graesser
Operations Director, Broadcasting: Ian McCullouch
Director of Channels, Granada Content: Chris Griffin
Director of International Formats & Entertainment, Granada Content: Paul Jackson
Granada is the largest company in the UK commercial television sector, providing programmes for UK and international broadcasters. It currently owns seven ITV licenses – Granada TV, LWT (London Weekend Television), Yorkshire TV, Tyne Tees TV, Meridian Broadcasting, Anglia TV and Border Television, covering 15 million homes. In 2001 it restructured into two distinct divisions: Enterprises and Content.

Granada Television
email: duty.office@granadatv.co.uk
Web: www.granadatv.com
Managing Director: Brenda Smith
Controller of Programmes, Granada TV: Kieron Collins
Head of Regional Programmes: Eammon O'Neal
Editor, News and Current Affairs: Mark Alderton
Head of Regional Affairs: Jane Luca
Granada TV has held the ITV franchise for the North of England since the start of commercial television in the UK in 1956. Its transmission area includes Manchester and Liverpool, and stretches from the Lake District to Shropshire, and from the North Wales coast to the Pennines, serving a population of 6.2 million. During 2002, Granada TV broadcasted 491 hours of regional programming. It also makes programmes for the ITV Network and other broadcasters such as Channel 4.
Programmes include:
Back Page Football, discussion programme presented by Alistair Mann and James Cooper
Beyond the Baton, four part documentary series on the 2002 Commonwealth Game
Crimefile, looking at recent crimes committed in the region, presented by So Rahman
Granada Action, community service announcement slots for the voluntary and charity sectors
Granada Reports, news magazine programme
Granada Reports Special, one hour live debate on the issue of Race
Green and Reds, one-off series which looked at the North West's footballing connection with Ireland and Irish players who have played for Liverpool and Manchester United

The Holocaust Memorial, a special programme covering the memorial event held in Manchester's Bridgewater Hall
The Irish Connection, six-part series on transmigration between Ireland and the North West of England
Late Debate, debates on current news issues
Losing It, series investigating spirituality
Lunchtime Live
Mad About Motors, commissioned from MMA
Muck & Jeff, gardening advice and garden make-overs
Northern Exposure, documentary highlighting the work of independent filmmakers and their ambitions for national recognition
Our Barbara, documentary celebrating the life of Baroness Castle of Blackburn
Out of Town, Eric Robson introduced hidden gems of the northern countryside (co-production with Border and Tyne Tees Television)
Party Fever, commissioned from Strong Films, how people of the region choose to party
Soccer Sunday, sports programme presented by Alistair Mann
Special Delivery, eight part series following the experiences of couples who were having babies at Macclesfield General Hospital
Sunday Supplement, series highlighting political issues affecting the region
Supervets, commissioned from Key Productions
That Tony Wilson, documentary looking at Tony Wilson's contribution to the media and music industry, and the making of his film 24 Hour Party People
These Things Take Time, a documentary about the group The Smiths
This Is Music, a six part series on local musical talent
The Way We Used To…, six part series developed to showcase the work of the North West Film Archive and the Manchester Metropolitan University
The Works, looking at the impact of some of the new museums and art galleries in the region
Worksmart, community information announcements related to Health and Safety

HTV Wales

The Television Centre
Culverhouse Cross
Cardiff CF5 6XJ
Tel: 02920 590 590
Fax: 02920 597 183
email: info@htv.co.uk
Website: www.htvwales.com; www.itv1wales.com
Carmarthen Office:
Top Floor
19-20 Lammas Street
Carmarthen SA31 3AL
Tel: 01267 236 806
Fax: 01267 238 228
email: giles.smith@itv1wales.co.uk
Colwyn Bay Office:
Celtic Business Centres
Plas Eirias
Heritage Gate, Abergele Road, Colwyn Bay LL29 8BW
Tel: 01492 513888
Fax: 01492 513888
email: colwyn@itv1wales.co.uk
Swansea Office:
21 Walter Road
Swansea SA1 5NQ
Tel: 029 20 590746
email: richard.nosworthy@itv1wales.co.uk
Newtown Office:
St. David's House
Newtown
Powys SY16 1RB
Tel: 01686 623381
Fax: 01686 624816
email: rob.shelly@itv1wales.co.uk
Wrexham Office:
HTV Wales
Crown Buildings
31 Chester Street
Wrexham
Tel: 01978 261 462
email: paul.mewies@itv1wales.co.uk
Chairman HTV Wales: Clive Jones
Managing Director: Jeremy Payne
Controller and Director of Programmes: Elis Owen
Head of Features: Geraint Curig
Head of Drama Development: Peter Edwards
Head of Corporate Affairs: Iona Jones
Head of Press and Public Relations: Mansel Jones
Head of News: John G Williams
Head of Human Resources: Julia Cassley
Part of the Carlton Group and covering Wales, during 2001 HTV Wales broadcasted 615 hours of regional programming. It also makes programmes for the ITV Network and other broadcasters and S4C. The company is committed to producing range of its programmes in the Welsh language.
Programmes include:
Alien Nation, a comparison of West Country residents with their European counterparts in Bordeaux and Hannover
Barry Welsh is Coming, entertainment series
Crime Secrets, documentary series
The Ferret, consumer affairs programme
Fishlock's Wild Tracks, introduction to six walks in Wales
From War to Westminster, the story of Stefan Terlezki who arrived from the Ukraine after WWII and eventually became MP for Cardiff West
Fun in the Sun, a series on Tenby through a summer season
Heaven's Sound, visits to various religious sites in Wales
High Performance, arts programme
HTV News, flagship news programme
Jigsaw, profiles of arts personalities
Life and Debt, drama on the work of bailiffs in Wales
Melting Pot, social action series, portraying multi-cultural Wales
Nuts + Bolts, drama series
The Pop Factory, on the Welsh pop scene
Presenters, HTV's search for new talent throughout Wales
Screen Gems, a showcase for the work of new Welsh film directors and their short films
Sharp End, coverage of the Welsh political scene
Soccer Sunday
Surviving Hell, two–part series marking the 60th anniversary of the fall of Singapore(co-produced with Carlton West Country)
Talking Stones, interesting stories behind gravestones in Welsh cemeteries
Taste of Wales Food Awards
Tin Gods?, series questioning the reputation of Welsh heroes and heroines
Wales this Week, current affair programme
Waterfront, political programme presented by Jo Kiernan
West Eye View, investigative journalism

HTV West

Television Centre
Bath Road
Bristol BS4 3HG

Tel: 0117 972 2722
Fax: 0117 971 7685
email: reception@htv-west.co.uk
Website: www.htvwest.com; www.itv1west.com
Chairman: Clive Jones
Managing Director: Jeremy Payne
Director of Programmes: Jane McCloskey
Head of News & Regional Production Unit: Steve Egginton
Head of Features & Current Affairs: James Garrett
Owned by Carlton and covering the West of England.

Programmes include:
The A-Z of Rude Health, series exploring the sexual health of the region
Chris Chapman's West Country
Digital Shorts, showcase for new directors, developed in conjunction with South West Screen
The Good Health Guide, series offering general health advice
Hit Back, sports archive series
HTV News
Johnny Kingdom's Wild West
Punchbag, current affairs series
Sacred Sites, Carenza Lewis explores the region's spiritual heritage
Silence at Ramscliffe, an insight into the devastation of foot and mouth on a local farm, presented by Chris Chapman
Soccer Sunday
Three Weddings, documentary portrait of three weddings of different faiths
West Eye View, current affairs series
What on Earth, promotion of environmental campaign week (partly co-produced with Carlton West Country)

Independent Television News

200 Gray's Inn Road
London WC1X 8XZ
Tel: 020 7833 3000
Fax: 020 7430 4868
Website: www.itn.co.uk
Chairman: Mark Wood
Chief Executive: Stewart Purvis
Finance Director: Andrew Whitaker
ITN is the news provider nominated by the Independent Television Commission to supply news programme for the ITV network. Subject to review, this licence is for a ten year period from 1993. ITN also provides news for Channel 4, Channel 5 and for the Independent Radio News (IRN) network. ITN is recognised as one of the world's leading news organisation whose programmes and reports are seen in every corner of the globe. In addition to its base in London, ITN has permanent bureaux in Washington, Moscow, South Africa, the Middle East, Hong Kong, and Brussels as well as at Westminster and eight other locations around the UK. Other business concerns are ITN Archive, ITN Factual, and ITN International.
Editor of ITV News: David Mannion
Presenters: Sir Trevor McDonald, OBE, John Suchet, Mark Austin, Mary Nightingale, Katie Derham, Nicholas Owen
Programmes for ITV:
ITV Evening News
ITV Lunchtime News
ITV News At Ten
Morning and Afternoon Bulletins
Night-time Bulletins
Weekend Programmes
Editor of Channel 4 News: Jim Gray
Presenters: Jon Snow, Krishnan Guru-Murthy, Alex Thomson, Bridgid Nzekwu, Samira Ahmed
Programmes for Channel 4:
Channel 4 News
First Edition (aimed at 9-13 year olds)
Editor of five news: Gary Rogers
Presenters: Kirsty Young, Charlie Stayt, Rob Butler, Katie Ledger
Programmes for five:
five news
five news at noon
Hourly Bulletins, weekdays
Weekend Bulletins
Five News Early

ITV Network Centre

200 Gray's Inn Road
London WC1X 8HF
Tel: 020 7843 8000
Fax: 020 7843 8158
Website: www.itv.com
ITV is a federation of regional broadcasters. National coverage is achieved by 15 licensees, broadcasting in 14 regional areas : Anglia, Border, Carlton London, Carlton Central, Carlton West Country, Channel, Grampian, Granada, HTV, LWT, Meridian, Scottish Television, Ulster Television, Tyne Tees, Yorkshire. (London has two licencees, one for the weekday - Carlton and one for the weekend - LWT) In May 2002 the ITV licensees agreed a Charter for the Nations and the Regions with its regulator, the ITC. In autumn 2002 ITV1 was adopted as the lead channel brand in most ITV regions.
Director of Programmes: Nigel Pickard
Director of Programme Strategy: David Bergg
Controller News, Current Affairs, Arts & Religion: Steve Anderson
Controller Factual: Bridget Boseley
Controller Daytime: Liam Hamilton
Controller Network Children's and Youth Programmes: Steven Andrew
Controller Network Drama: Nick Elliot
Controller Network Acquisitions: Jeremy Boulton
Controller Network Entertainment: Claudia Rosencrantz

LWT (London Weekend Television)

The London Television Centre
Upper Ground
London SE1 9LT
Tel: 020 7620 1620
Website: www.lwt.co.uk
Chairman: Charles Allen
Chief Executive: Steve Morrison
Managing Director: Christie Swords
Controller of Arts: Melvyn Bragg
Director of Programmes: (awaiting appointment)
Controller of Drama: Michelle Buck
Controller of Entertainment: Duncan Gray
Controller of Factual Programmes: Jim Allen
Director of Production: Tamara Howe
Part of the Granada Media Group, LWT has the London Franchise for the weekend, beginning 17.15 on Fridays and ending 06.00 Mondays, As LWT can be picked up well beyond the London area, it serves a population of around 11 million. LWT is also a major supplier of programmes to the ITV Network and other broadcasters such as Channel 4, Channel 5 and BSkyB. LWT and Carlton TV are joint owners of the London News Network.

Programmes include:
Ant and Dec's Saturday Night Takeaway
Artworks, arts programme showcasing exhibitions and new releases in the capital
Blind Date
Boot Sale Challenge, contestants search for hidden treasures
Crimefighters, real life crime fighting
Des Res, homes and their owners
Doodlebug Summer, history series documenting the story of the V1

rockets of WWII (co-produced with Meridian)
Dream Ticket, regional travel programme
The End of the Week, late night discussion show hosted by Mariella Frostrup
I'm a Celebrity, Get Me Out of Here
Killer Queens, Rory McGrath presented the story of ruthless women, such as Boudicca, who helped shape Britain's history (co-produced with Anglia and Meridian)
The London Programme, covering the stories and issues of people who live and work in and around London
London's Scariest Mysteries, tales from London's past
London Tonight, local news programme
NYLON, documentary on New York and London
The Real A&E, documentary following the staff at St George's, Tooting
Royal Life, a unique insight into royal life in the capital across the centuries, presented by HRH Prince Michael of Kent and timed to coincide with the Queen's Jubilee
Sea to Source, series on the history of the Thames following the river from the North Sea to its source in Gloucestershire
Sin City, a history of bad behaviour in the capital, presented by historian Bettany Hughes
Soccer Sunday, sports programme
The South Bank Show, arts series produced and presented by Melvyn Bragg
Stand Up Britain, a collaboration with a number of ITV regions in the search for the best new regional comic in Britain
Stiletto Ghetto, upbeat take on London's growing lap dancing industry
This London, exploring different cultural styles through the themes of love, money, and work
The Week, Sunday lunchtime review of news stories from the previous week, presented by Phil Gayle
Whose London?, a unique year long project allowing 70 community groups to make films portraying part of their lives in London, culminating in an awards night

Meridian Broadcasting Ltd

Television Centre
Northam Road
Southampton SO14 0PZ
Tel: 023 8022 2555
Fax: 023 8033 5050
email: dutyoffice@meridiantv.com
Website: www.meridiantv.com
Regional news centres:
Maidstone
West Point
New Hythe
Maidstone
Kent ME20 6XX
Tel: 01622 882244
Fax: 01622 714000
Newbury
1-3 Brookway
Hambridge Lane
Newbury, Berks RG14 5UZ
Tel: 01635 522322
Fax: 01635 522620
Chairman: Charles Allen
Managing Director, Meridian: Lindsay Charlton
Controller of Regional Programmes: Mark Southgate
Director of News: Andy Cooper
Director of Commercial and Regional Affairs: Martin Morrall
Controller of Sport: Tony Baines
Controller of Network Factual: Trish Powell
General Manager: Jan Beal
Controller of Personnel: Peter Ashwood
Finance Controller: Sian Harvey
Part of the Granada Media Group, Meridian covers the South and South East of England, broadcasting to a population of 5.5 million. Meridian Broadcasting's main studio complex is in Southampton with additional studios at Maidstone, Newbury and Brighton. During 2002, the company broadcast more than 630 hrs of new programmes and also supplied material to other networks including Channel 4, Channel 5 and BBC.
Programmes include:
24 Hours, documentary series
7-Days, series looking at political issues
Bon Voyage, regional holiday series
Car as Art, Brian Sewell on the beauty of motor car design, at the Beaulieu Motor Museum
Country Ways
Focus, current affairs series
The Frame, arts series on a wide range of topics
Full Bloom, gardening programmes
Grass Roots
Great Country Houses
The Impossible Job, special programme on the retirement of the Archbishop of Canterbury
Let's Meet..., location-based interview series presented by Ann Diamond
Looking for Love, dating show
Lunchtime Live, studio chat show
Meridian Tonight, flagship news programme
Pilgrim's Way, Paul Heiney walking across the Meridian region from Winchester to Canterbury
The Queen and I, memories from the region's viewers of meeting the Queen
Screentime, showcasing the local movie scene and reviewing the latest releases
Soccer Sunday, Nationwide football
Southern Flavours, regional cookery show
Taped Up, featuring the work of young directors
Village Voices

S4C

Parc Ty Glas
Llanishen
Cardiff CF14 5DU
Tel: 029 2074 7444
Fax: 029 2075 4444
Lôn Ddewi
Caernarfon LL55 1ER
Tel: 01286 674622
email: s4c@s4c.co.uk
Website: www.s4c.co.uk
Chairman: Elan Closs Stephens
Chief Executive: Huw Jones
Director of Programmes: Huw Eirug
Managing Director, S4C Masnachol: Wyn Innes
Director of Channel Management: Emlyn Penny Jones
Director of Corporate Affairs: Alun Davies
Director of Animation: Chris Grace
Commissioning Editor, Factual Programmes: Cenwyn Edwards
Director of Finance and Human Resources: Kathryn Morris
Director of Engineering and IT: Arshad Rasul
S4C (Sianel Pedwar Cymru – Channel Four Wales) was established under the Broadcasting Act, 1980 and is responsible for providing a service of Welsh and English programmes on the Fourth Channel in Wales, with a remit that the majority of programmes shown between 18.30 and 22.00 should be in Welsh. In 2002 it broadcast roughly 40 hours of Welsh language programming per week. The remainder of its output, is provided by Channel 4 and is in English. 10 hours per week of Welsh programmes are provided by the BBC

and the rest are commissioned/purchased from independent producers. Since 1993 S4C has been directly funded by the Treasury and is responsible for selling its own advertising. In November 1998 S4C Digital was launched, which provides over 80 hours a week of Welsh language programming.

Programmes include:

9 Tan 9, comedy series written by Eilir Jones
Ar y Bocs, talent show
Ar y Stryd, two-part series on drugs and homelessness in Caernarfon and Bangor
Bandit, late night magazine programme for teenagers, presented by Ian Cottrell
Y Byd ar Bedwar – Yn ôl i'r Falklands, a special edition of the series, Tweli Griffiths takes two Welsh soldiers back to the islands
Byd Pws, Dewi Pws on his travels through varying countries
Cefn Gwlad, long standing series dealing with people and their communities
Y Clwb, Sunday afternoon sports magazine programme
Cofio'r Comin, special programme looking back at the protests at Greenham Common through the eyes of Welsh women
Côr Cymru, competition presenting choral singing in Wales
Da di Dil de, half hour comedy show featuring Dilwyn Pierce
Darn o Dir, drama showing youngsters' lives in rural areas
Dechrau Canu Dechrau Canmol, religious programme
Dudley, a food tour throughout Wales and beyond, presented by chef Dudley Newbery
Eisteddfod Arall, highlights of the Young Farmer's eisteddfod
Ffermio, farming programme broadcast during peak viewing hours
Hacio, youth current affairs programme
Hannes S4C yn 20 oed, celebration of the channel's twentieth birthday
Heliwr, detective series
Llafur Gwlad, on the importance of industry in rural Wales, presented by Professor Merfyn Jones
Nia, chat show presented by Nia Roberts
O4 Wal, a lifestyle programme aimed at the 30s age group looking at homes in Wales and beyond
Pacio, (HTV) travel programme presented by Kev Thame and Llyr Evans
Pawb a'i Farn, a chance for the Welsh public to question politicians
Pobol y Cwm (BBC), Welsh language TV soap
Porc Peis Bach, comedy series
Popty, music series
Rasus, harness racing series
Y Sioe Gelf, arts series
Rownd A Rownd, drama series
Tab?, late night programme on the sexual practices and experiences of the Welsh
Talcen Caled, drama series
Tweenies, broadcast in Welsh for the first time in 2002
Wedi 6, factual stories from around Wales
Welsh in a Week, fly-on-the-wall documentary series about people trying to learn Welsh in a week
Wyn Davies yn 60, programme celebrating the footballer's birthday

Scottish Television

200 Renfield Street
Glasgow G2 3PR
Tel: 0141 300 3000
Fax: 0141 300 3030
email: viewer.enquiries@scottishtv.co.uk
Website: www.scottishtv.co.uk
Chairman, SMG: Don Cruikshank
Chief Executive, SMG: Andrew Flanagan
Chief Executive, SMG Television: Donald Emslie
Managing Director, Scottish TV: Sandy Ross
Head of News and Current Affairs: Paul McKinney
Managing Director SMG Television Productions / Ginger Television: Elizabeth Partyke

Part of the Scottish Media Group, Scottish TV has held the ITV licence for Central Scotland since commercial television started in 1957. It remains the most watched station in Scotland, broadcasting to 3.4 million viewers. In addition to programmes for its own region, ST also makes programmes for the ITV Network and other broadcasters such as Channel 4.

Programmes include:

Air a' Bhòrd, Gaelic food and drink series
Air an Spot, Gaelic sporting quiz show
Artery, series profiling the arts in Scotland
Boiling Point, cookery programme presented by Dominic Diamond and Scottish chef John Quigley
Fàilte, Gaelic lifestyle magazine programme
High Road, drama series
The Home Show, presented by Kaye Adams and John Amabile
Jock Bottom, special documentary on Scottish international football, presented by Ali McCoist
Monday Night Live, sports discussion show
Moviejuice, cinema and video review show
Nochd Gun Chadal, Gaelic music-based magazine programme aimed at the 18-30s age group
Platform, political magazine program
The Ploughman's Pearls, special programme marking Burns' night, celebrating his music and poetry
Scotland Today, regional news magazine
Scotsport, sports programme
Scottish Action, social action programme
Scottish Legends, presented by comedian Bruce Morton
Scottish Passport, travel programme presented by Bryan Burnett and Cathy Macdonald
Seven Days, current affairs/political review programme
Sploaid, children's programme in Gaelic
Taggart, detective drama series
This Scotland, documentary series on aspects of contemporary life in Scotland
Whelan Around, chat on the golf course, with Charlie Whelan

Tyne Tees Television

The Television Centre
City Road
Newcastle Upon Tyne NE1 2AL
Tel: 0191 261 0181
Fax: 0191 261 2302
email: tyne.tees@granadamedia.com
feedback@tynetees.tv
Website: www.tynetees.tv
Chairman: Charles Allen
Managing Director: Margaret Fay
Controller of Programmes: Graeme Thompson
Engineering Manager: Dixon Marshall
Head of Operations: Howard Beebe
Head of Regional Affairs: Norma Hope
Head of Network Features: Mark Robinson
Managing Editor, News: Graham Marples
Editor - Current Affairs and Features:

Jane Bolesworth
Head of Sports: Roger Tames
Becoming part of the Granada Media Group in 1997 and covering the North East of England, TTTV has a transmission area stretching from Berwick in the North to Selby in the South and across to Alston in the West. Operating from studios and offices in Newcastle, Sunderland, Billingham, York, and Westminster, the company provides more than 11.5 hours of regional output each week. TTTV also produces material for the ITV network and other broadcasters such as Channel 4.

Programmes include:
Around the House, weekly political round up with Gerry Foley
The Black and White Knight, an hour-long tribute to Sir Bobby Robson
Bodytalk, series examining the ways we use parts of our bodies
A Dog's Life, fly-on-the-kennel-wall series
Durham – A First Class Story, sports documentary marking the tenth anniversary of Durham cricket club
The Great Ethiopian Run, Ian Payne's film capturing Brendan Foster's dream to stage the Great North Run in Ethiopia
Grundy's Wonders, John Grundy's examination of the North East landscape
Guilt, tabloid series
Inside Out, inmates and staff at an open prison in County Durham
Justice for Julie, investigative documentary exposing the need to abolish the ancient laws on double jeopardy
Late Night Legends, football talk show
Learn to Live, looking at the experiences of people who go back to college as adult learners
Mike Neville – A Life in Television, special tribute to mark 40 years of continuous daily broadcasting
North East Today, weekday daytime magazine
North East Tonight with Mike Neville, local news programme
Northstars, archive series chronicling the story of rock from its roots in the North East
Playing Away, travel guide for party-goers
Pub Stories, bar-room talk show
Soccer Sunday
The Tube – 20 Years On, short programme looking at the enduring impact of the iconic North East music series
When We Were Kids, chronicles the lives of eight people growing up in the north during the 50s and 60s
The Whole Nine Yards, garden makeover series
Your Town on the Telly, explores the news and events that has shaped the people of the North East over the past four decades presented by Pam Royle

Ulster Television

Havelock House
Ormeau Road
Belfast BT7 1EB
Tel: 028 90328122
Fax: 028 90246695
email: info@u.tv
Website: www.utv.co.uk
Chairman: John B McGuckian
Group Chief Executive: John McCann
Director of Television: A Bremner
Group Finance Director: JR Downey
Head of Press and Public Relations: Orla McKibbin
Head of News: Rob Morrison
Covering Northern Ireland, during 2002 UTV produced/commissioned 568 hours of local programmes for its own transmission.

Programmes include:
Health Check, health programme
Home, short film series
Insight, weekly current affairs programme
Jenny Bristow Cooks for the Seasons, cookery series
Journeys, religious series in six parts
Kelly, chat show
Lesser Spotted Ulster, regional documentary series
On the Threshold of Sanity, series of short films on mental health
School Around the Corner
School Choir of the Year, profiling choirs in primary, secondary, and grammar schools
The Strength Within, documentary on children with serious illnesses
UTV Live at Six, news programme
We Were Brothers, documentary marking Remembrance Sunday

Westcountry Television

see Carlton Broadcasting West Country Region

Yorkshire Television

The Television Centre
Kirkstall Road
Leeds LS3 1JS
Tel: 0113 243 8283
Fax: 0113 242 3867
Website: www.yorkshiretv.com

Regional offices:
Sheffield
Charter Square
Sheffield S1 4HS
Tel: 0114 272 3262
Fax: 0114 275 4134
Hull
23 Brook Street
The Prospect Centre
Hull HU2 8PN
Tel: 01482 24488
Fax: 01482 586028
Lincoln
88 Bailgate
Lincoln LN1 3AR
Tel: 01522 530738
Fax: 01522 514162
Immingham
Immage Studios
Margaret Street
Immingham
NE Lincs DN40 1LE
Tel: 01469 510 661
Fax: 01469 510 662
York
8 Coppergate
York YO1 1NR
Tel: 01904 610066
Fax: 01904 610067
Chairman: Charles Allen
Managing Director: David Croft
Director of Programmes: John Whinston
Controller of Features: Bridget Boseley
Director of Business Affairs Granada Content North: Filip Cieslik
Head of Site Services: Peter Fox
Controller of Programmes: Clare Morrow
Controller of Drama: Carolyn Reynolds
Controller of Comedy Drama and Drama Specials: David Reynolds
Controller of Drama, Yorkshire and Tyne Tees: Keith Richardson
Controller of Factual Programmes: Helen Scott
Head of Media Relations North: Sallie Ryle
Head of Regional Affairs: Sallie Ryle
Head of Engineering: John Nichol
Head of Business Affairs: Justine Rhodes
Head of Sales and Planning: Jim Richardson
Director of Finance, Granada Content North: Ian Roe
General Manager: John Surtees
Head of Personnel: Sue Slee
Part of the Granada Media Group since 1997 and covering Yorkshire, Humberside and Lincolnshire, Yorkshire Television broadcasts to a

population of 5.7 million. The main studio complex is in Leeds but there are regional offices in Sheffield, Hull, Grimsby, Lincoln, and York. Each year the regional programmes department produces over 900 hours of regional programmes for its own transmission. It also produces programmes for the ITV network and other channels, such as Channel 4.

Programmes include:

Alan Brazil Talks Sport, a sixt part debate show abou the issues facing the sporting world

Around the House, political programme

Attitude!, series where 16-24 year olds air their views on current topics of interest

Calendar, news magazine programme presented by Christa Ackroyd (then Christine Talbot) and Mike Morris

Cooking For Ages, a combination of cooking and history

Crimestoppers

Dales Diary, reflection of life in the Yorkshire Dales

Emmerdale, soap set in farming community (Steve Frost, producer)

Hardwick at Large, showcasing interesting people and stories around the region, presented by Alan Harwick

How They Caught, late night series made in collaboration with other regional programme makers

It's Your Call, daily community service announcements

The Joe Longthorne Story, two part series charting the entertainer's career

Ninety Minutes in Nepal, two films following the first ever football team, a youth team from Lincolnshire, to play in Nepal

Soccer Sunday, football highlights

A Stitch in Time, documentary celebrating the completion of the Leeds Tapestry

VIDEO/DVD LABELS

These companies acquire the UK rights to all or specialised forms of audio-visual product and arrange for its distribution on video or DVD at a retail level. Examples of titles released on each label are also listed. A listing of currently available titles, and also those available for hire only, can be found in the trade catalogue Videolog (published by Trade Service Information) which is updated on a monthly basis. Videolog is used by most retailers - so check with your local store first - and may also be held by your local reference library. Check the Film Links Gateway at www.bfi.org.uk for online sources of deleted videos and DVDs. Compiled by David Reeve

4 Front Video
see Universal Pictures Video

Abbey Home Media
435-437 Edgware Road
London W2 1TH
Tel: 020 7563 3910
Fax: 020 7563 3911
Action Man
Bump
Butt-Ugly Martians
Postman pat
Redwall
Superted
Tweenies

Academy Video
see bfi Video

Arrow Film Distributors
18 Watford Road
Radlett
Herts WD7 8LE
Tel: 01923 858306
Fax: 01923 869673
email: neil@arrowfilms.co.uk
Website: www.arrowfilms.co.uk
Neil Agran
Cinema Paradiso
La Bonne Annee
Rififi
Would I Lie to You

Art House Productions
39-41 North Road
Islington
London N7 9DP
Tel: 020 7700 0068
Fax: 020 7609 2249
Les Biches
Bicycle Thieves

Artificial Eye Film Company
14 King Street
London WC2E 8HR
Tel: 020 7240 5353
Fax: 020 7240 5242
email: video@artificial-eye.com
Website: www.artificial-eye.com
11'09"01 - September 11
Solaris
Beau Travail
Blackboards
Fanny and Alexander
Last Resort
The Piano Teacher
Three Colours Trilogy

BBC Worldwide Publishing
Woodlands
80 Wood Lane
London W12 0TT
Tel: 020 8433 2000
Fax: 020 8749 0538
Abigail's Party
Absolutely Fabulous
Alan Partridge
Doctor Who
The League of Gentlemen
The Office

bfi Video
21 Stephen Street
London W1T 1LN
Tel: 020 7957 8957
Fax: 020 7957 8968
email: video.films@bfi.org.uk
Website: www.bfi.org.uk/video
bfi Video, incorporating Connoisseur and Academy, releases over 300 titles (including DVDs) covering every decade of cinema, from the 1890s to the present. New releases are under the bfi Video label.
Bande à part
La Belle Et La Bete
Cathy Come Home
Un Chant D'amour
George Washington
Rashomon
Salo
Seven Samurai
South
Throne of Blood
Yojimbo

Blue Dolphin Film & Video
40 Langham Street
London W1W 7AS
Tel: 020 7255 2494
Fax: 020 7580 7670
Website: Website: www.bluedolphinfilms.com
Animal Farm - Special Edition
Crystal Voyager - Special Edition
Mindwalk
The Ninth Configuration - Special Edition
Texas Chainsaw Massacre - Special Edition

Blue Light
231 Portobello Road
London W11 1LT
Tel: 020 7792 9791
Fax: 020 7792 9871
Festen
Ma Vie En Rose

BMG Music Programming
Bedford House
69-79 Fulham High Street
London SW6 3JW
Tel: 020 7384 7500
Fax: 020 7384 8010
Mostly music related titles but some feature films.
Dawn of the Dead
The Harder They Come

Buena Vista Home Entertainment
3 Queen Caroline Street
Hammersmith
London W6 9PE
Tel: 020 8222 1000
Fax: 020 8222 2795
Distribute and market Walt Disney, Touchstone, and Hollywood Pictures product on video and DVD. Titles include:
Apocalypse Now Redux
Chocolat
Il Postino
Insomnia
Life is Beautiful

Carlton Visual Entertainment
5th Floor

35-38 Portman Square
London W1H 0NU
Tel: 020 7486 6688
Fax: 020 7612 7399
Website: www.carltonvideo.co.uk
Gerry Donohoe, Managing Director
Carlton Visual Entertainment is a leading independent video and DVD distributor specialising in classic film, TV, children's and special interest genres. As part of the Carlton Group it has access to the largest British owned film catalogue (encompassing the Rank, Korda, Rohauer, Romulus and ITC collections)

Channel 4 Video

124 Horseferry Road
London SW1P 2TX
Tel: 020 7306 8640
Fax: 020 7306 8044
Channel 4 programme releases, such as:
Black Books
Brass Eye
Spaced

Cherry Red Films

Unit 17
1st Floor
Elysium Gate West
126-128 New Kings Road
London SW6 4LZ
Tel: 020 7371 5844
Fax: 020 7384 1854
Release DVD versions of certain Visionary Film titles.
James Dean - The Rare Movies

Cinema Club

76 Dean Street
London W1D 3SQ
Tel: 020 7316 4488
Fax: 020 7316 4489
email: info@cinemaclub.co.uk
Website: www.cinemaclub.co.uk
Cinema Club is a low price VHS and DVD publishing division of Video Collection International.

Classic Pictures Entertainment

Shepperton Film Studios
Studios Road
Shepperton TW17 0QD
Tel: 01932 592016
Fax: 01932 592046
Website: www.classicpictures.co.uk
History and Nostalgia titles such as:
The Battle Of Britain
Muffin the Mule

Clear Vision

36 Queensway
Ponders End
Enfield
Middx EN3 4SA
Tel: 020 8805 1354
Fax: 020 8805 9987
Website: www.clearvision.co.uk
Ian Allan
Wrestling and TV Drama titles, including:
The Bill
Callan
Minder
World Wrestling Entertainment

Columbia TriStar Home Video

Sony Pictures Europe House
25 Golden Square
London W1R 6LU
Tel: 020 7533 1200
Fax: 020 7533 1015
The Basketball Diaries
Charlie's Angels
Lawrence of Arabia
Spider Man

Connoisseur Video

see bfi video

Contender Entertainment Group

48 Margaret Street
London W1W 8SE
Tel: 020 7907 3773
Fax: 020 7907 3777
The Avengers
Bad Girls
Farscape
Footballers' Wives
The Professionals
Spooks
Tractor Tom

Dreamworks Home Entertainment

Oxford House
76 Oxford Street
London W1D 1BS
Tel: 020 7307 1390
Fax: 020 7307 1346
American Beauty
Catch Me if You Can
Gladiator
Old Skool
Sea Biscuit
Shrek
Sinbad

Entertainment in Video

108-110 Jermyn Street
London SW1Y 6HB
Tel: 020 7930 7766
Fax: 020 7930 9399
Ali
Gosford Park
Lord of the Rings
My Big Fat Greek Wedding

Eros International

Unit 23
Sovereign Park
Coronation Road
London NW10 7QP
Tel: 020 8963 8700
Fax: 020 8963 0154
email: eros@erosintl.co.uk
Website: www.erosentertainment.com
Chori Chori Chupke Chupke
Dhadkan

Eureka Video

Unit 9 Ironbridge Close
Great Central Way
London NW10 0UF
Tel: 020 8459 8054
Fax: 020 8459 5162
E-mail: info@eurekavideo.co.uk
Website: www.eurekavideo.co.uk
Alexander Nevsky
Battleship Potemkin
The Birth of a Nation
Buster Keaton titles
M
Metropolis
Münchhausen
Yakuza trilogy

Feature Film Company

see Winchester Entertainment

FilmFour Video

Rental titles distributed through Pathe
Retail titles distributed through Video Collection International

Firefly Entertainment

Suite 5
9 North Audley Street
London W1K 6WF
Tel: 020 7659 0840
Fax: 020 7659 0850
email:
info@fireflyentertainment.co.uk
Website:
www.fireflyentertainment.co.uk
A sell-through video distributor of music, sport, special interest, comedy, children and programmes about film.

Fremantle Home Entertainment

1 Stephen Street
London W1T 1AL
Tel: 020 7691 6000
Fax: 020 7691 6079
Website:
www.fremantlemedia.com/homeentertainment
Arsenal
The Bill

Cabaret
Celtic
Chorlton and the Wheelies
Cinema Paradiso
Danger Mouse
Goodness Gracious Me
History of Football
Manchester City
Men Behaving Badly
Monkey
Notorious
Rafifi
Rainbow
Rebecca
Spellbound
Straw Dogs
The Water Margin
World of War

Granada Media

Commercial Ventures
200 Gray's Inn Road
London WC1X 8XZ
Tel: 020 7396 6000
Fax: 020 7316 3222
Website: www.granadavideo.com
Cold Feet
Darling Buds of May
The Royle Family

Green Umbrella Sport & Leisure

4 The Links
Old Woking Road
Old Woking
Surrey GU22 8BF
Tel: 01483 726969
Fax: 01483 721188
email: sales@greenumbrella.co.uk
Website: www.greenumbrella.co.uk
Jules Gammond
Sports and special interest videos and DVDs

guerilla films

35 Thornbury Road
Iselworth
Middlesex TW7 4LQ
Tel: 020 8758 1716
Fax: 020 8758 9364
Website: www.guerilla-films.com
David Nicholas Wilkinson
Fully independent distribution company. Includes films by Eric Rohmer, Barbet Shroeder, Jacques Rivette. Since 1999 it has concentrated on only releasing British films. Recent releases include:
Beginner's Luck
Two Men Went to War
Puckoon
Nine Dead Gay Guys

ICA Projects

12 Carlton House Terrace
London SW1Y 5AH
Tel: 020 7766 1416
Fax: 020 7306 0122
Website: www.ica.org.uk
Abouna
All About Lily Chou Chou
Atanarjuat
The Clay Bird
In This World
The Man Without a Past
Mon-rak Transistor
Ten

Icon Home Entertainment

180 Wardour Street
London W1F 8FX
Tel: 020 7494 8100
Fax: 020 7494 8141
Anita and Me
Felicia's Journey
Ghost World
Sweet Sixteen

Lace International

Lace House
39 Old Steine
Brighton BN1 1NH
Tel: 01273 202220
Fax: 01273 778973
Mostly sports titles.
On Any Sunday

Manga Entertainment

8 Kensington Park Road
London W11 3BU
Tel: 020 7229 3000
Fax: 020 7221 9988
Akira
Ghost in the Shell
Urotsukidoji - Legend Of The Overfiend

Medusa Communications & Marketing

51 Bancroft
Hitchin
Herts SG5 1LL
Tel: 01462 421818
Fax: 01462 420393
Video and DVD distributors for: Playboy; Hong Kong Legends; Medusa Pictures; Adult Channel, Danielle Steele titles

Metrodome Distribution

5th Floor
33 Charlotte Street
London W1T 1RR
Tel: 020 7153 4421
Fax: 020 7153 4446
101 Reykjavik
Chopper
Dagon
Donnie Darko
Last Orders
Lilya 4-Ever

MGM Home Entertainment (Europe) Ltd

5 Kew Road
Richmond
London TW9 2PR
Tel: 020 8939 9300
Fax: 020 8939 9314
Annie Hall
Die Another Day
Four Weddings And A Funeral
The Good, The Bad and The Ugly
The Great Escape
Kes
The Magnificent Seven
Manhattan

Millivres Multimedia

Unit M
Spectrum House
32-34 Gordon House Road
London NW5 1LP
Tel: 020 7424 7400
Fax: 020 7424 7401
Website: www.millivres.co.uk

Momentum Pictures Home Entertainment

2nd Floor
184-192 Drummond St
London NW1 3HP
Tel: 020 7391 6900
Fax: 020 7383 0404
Amélie
Bowling for Columbine
CSI - Crime Scene Investigation
The Elephant Man
Show Me Love
The Son's Room

Mosaic Entertainment

19-24 Manasty Road
Orton
Southgate
Peterborough PE2 6UP
Tel: 01733 363010
Fax: 01733 363011
Website: www.mosaicmovies.co.uk
Cube 2: Huyercube
Rasputin

Nova Productions

62 Ascot Avenue
Cantley
Doncaster DN4 6HE
Tel: 0870 765 1094
Fax: 0870 125 7917
email: library@novaonline.co.uk
Website: www.novaonline.co.uk
Contact Andrew White, Gareth Atherton
Sell-through video distributor, a subsidiary of Nova Productions, with a catalogue of specialist & local

interest documentaries and nostalgia programming. Britain's leading transport label, with releases on trains, trams, bus, cars, motorbikes and trolleybuses.

Odyssey Video
PO Box 32889
London N1 2WP
Tel: 020 8216 6993
Fax: 020 7704 6365
Ambush in Waco
A Place for Annie
Joan of Arc

Optimum Releasing
9 Rathbone Place
London W1T 1HW
Tel: 020 7637 5403
Fax: 020 7637 5408
Website: www.optimumreleasing.com
Amores Perros
Biggie and Tupac
Breathless
Kurt and Courtney
Lost in La Mancha
The Officer's Ward

Orbit Media Ltd
80a Dean Street
London W1D 3SN
Tel: 020 7287 4264
Fax: 020 7727 0515
email: enquiries@orbitmedia.co.uk
Website: www.orbitmedia.co.uk
Screen classics label, feature films and documentaries
Laurel and Hardy
Jack and the Beanstalk
Sherlock Holmes Library

Paramount Home Entertainment
45 Beadon Road
Hammersmith
London W6 0EG
Tel: 020 8741 9333
Fax: 020 8741 5690
Breakfast At Tiffany's
Chinatown
If
The Italian Job
Once Upon a Time in the West
Star Trek
Tomb Raider

Pathé Distribution
Kent House
14-17 Market Place
Great Titchfield Street
London W1W 8AR
Tel: 020 7323 5151
Fax: 020 7631 3568
Website: www.pathe.co.uk
24 Hour Party People
Pi
Talk to Her

Peccadillo Pictures
36b Shipton Street
London E2 7RU
Tel: 020 7729 5225
Fax: 020 7729 3074
Le Fate Ignoranti
The Iron Ladies
Lost and Delirious
Paris Was a Woman
The Wolves of Kromer

Quantum Leap
1a Great Northern Street
Huntingdon
Cambridgeshire PE29 7HJ
Tel: 01480 450006
Fax: 01480 456686
email: quantumleap@ukonline.co.uk
Website: www.qleap.co.uk
Kim Lyon
Special interest titles with subjects such as gardening, alternative health, sport etc.

Redbus
Ariel House
74a Charlotte Street
London W1T 4QJ
Tel: 020 7299 8800
Fax: 020 7299 8801
Website: www.redbus.com
Bend it Like Beckham
One Day in September
Spider

Screen Edge
St. Annes house
329 Clifdon Drive South
Lytham St. Annes
Lancashire FY8 1LP
Tel: 01253 712453
Fax: 01253 712362
Website: www.screenedge.com
Incorporates Screen Edge, Screen Edge Pink Japan, and the Visionary Labels.

Tartan Video
2nd Floor
14-18 Ham Yard
London W1D 7DT
Tel: 020 7494 1400
Fax: 020 7292 0521
email: info@tartanvideo.com
Website: www.tartanvideo.com
A Ma Soeur
Asia Extreme titles
Audition
Bangkok Dangerous
Bergman collection
Dark Water
Etre et Avoir
Irreversible
Secretary

Telstar Video Entertainment
see Firefly Entertainment

Twentieth Century Fox Home Entertainment
20th Century House
31-32 Soho Square
London W1V 6AP
Tel: 020 7753 8686
Fax: 020 7753 0120
Website: www.fox.co.uk
24
28 Days Later
Brazil
Once Upon a Time in the Midlands
Phone Booth
Solaris

Universal Pictures Video
1 Sussex Place
Hammersmith
London W6 9XS
Tel: 020 8910 5000
Fax: 020 8910 5404
Labels include Playback (nostalgia), 4 Front Video (low price), and Universal.
8 Mile
About a Boy
Bridget Jones' Diary
Trainspotting

Video Collection International
76 Dean Street
London W1D 3SQ
Tel: 020 7396 8888
Fax: 020 7396 8996/7
VCI runs as a label as well as a distributor. They cover feature films, television, children's programming, sport, music etc.
Brass Eye
Cold Feet
Coupling
Father Ted

Visionary Film
Incorporates Visionary Film, Visionary Documentary, Visionary Art Experimental and Visionary Music Video.
see Screen Edge

Walt Disney Video
see Buena Vista Home Entertainment

Warner Home Video
Warner House
98 Theobald's Road
London WC1X 8WB
Tel: 020 7984 6400

Fax: 020 7984 5001
Annie Get Your Gun
Bend It Like Beckham
A Clockwork Orange
Friends
Harry Potter titles
The Matrix
North by Northwest
Six Feet Under
The Sopranos
The Third Man
The West Wing
The Wicker Man
The Wizard of Oz

Warner Vision International

35-38 Portman Square
London W1H 6LR
Tel: 020 7467 2566
Fax: 020 7467 2564
Big Brother
Sex and the City
South Park

Winchester Entertainment

19 Heddon Street
London W1B 4BG
Tel: 020 7851 6500
Fax: 020 7851 6505
Labels include: Feature Film Company and Winchester Film Distribution.
Another Life

Yash Raj Films

Wembley Point
1 Harrow Road
Middlesex HA9 6DE
Tel: 0870 739 7345
Fax: 0870 739 7346
Hindi language titles
Daag
Mohabbatein

WEBSITES

**This section contains a small selection of useful websites which coincide with most of the sections in this book. For more detailed information visit the gateway film links section on the *bfi* website.
http://www.bfi.org.uk/gateway**

Archive and Film Libraries

Alexandra Palace TV Society
www.apts.org.uk

ARKive
www.arkive.org.uk

BFI National Film and TV Archive
www.bfi.org.uk/collections

British Association of Picture Libraries and Agencies (BAPLA)
www.bapla.org.uk

British Movietone News
movietone.com

British Pathe
www.britishpathe.com

British Universities Film and Video Council
www.bufvc.ac.uk/

Contemporary Films Archive
contemporaryfilms.com/archives/arc_set.htm

East Anglian Film Archive
www.uea.ac.uk/eafa/

FIAF: The International Federation of Film Archives
www.cinema.ucla.edu/FIAF/

FIAT: International Federation of Television Archives
camilla.nb.no/fiat

FOCAL
www.focalint.org

Footage.net
www.footage.net

France - La Vidéoteque de paris
www.vdp.fr/

Getty Images Creative
www.imagesbank.com

Hulton Archive
www.archivefilms.com

Huntley Film Archives
www.huntleyarchives.com

Imperial War Museum Film and Video Archive
iwm.org.uk/lambeth/film.htm

National Archive of Film Shorts
www.nafs.co.uk

National Museum of Photography Film & Television
www.nmsi.ac.uk/nmpft

North West Film Archive
www.nwfa.mmu.ac.uk

Scottish Film and Television Archive
www.scottishscreen.com

SEAPAVAA
members.nbci.com/archives/

South East Film and Video Archive
shs.surreycc.gov.uk/sefva.html

Tanmedia
www.tanmedia.co.uk

UK Film Archive Forum
www.bufvc.ac.uk/faf/html

Wales Film and Television Archive
Archif Ffilm a Theledu Cymru
www.sgrinwales.demon.co.uk/filmarchive.htm

Wessex Film and Sound Archive
www.hants.gov.uk/record-office/film.html

Awards

BAFTA
www.bafta.org

Berlin
www.berlinale.de

British Independent Film Awards
www.bifa.org.uk

Cannes
www.festival-cannes-fr

Edinburgh International Film Festival
www.edfilmfest.org.uk/

Emmys
www.emmys.org/

Emmys International
www.intlemmyawards.com/

European Film Awards
www.europeanfilmacademy.org

Alex Fung's Film Page
www.ncf.carleton.ca/~aw220/

Golden Globes
www.hfpa.com

Golden Rose of Montreux
www.rosedor.ch

Golden Rasberry Awards
www.razzies.com

Grierson Trust Awards
www.editor.net/griersontrust rman

International Film Academy
www.iifa.com

Karlovy Vary
www.iffkv.cz

Locarno
www.pardo.ch

Oscars
www.oscars.org/awards

Monte Carlo TV Festival
www.tvfestival.com/

Royal Television Society Awards
www.rts.org.uk/

Books

bfi Publishing
www.bfi.org.uk/bookvid

Oxford University Press
www.oup.co.uk

Routledge
www.routledge.com

bfi Film and Television Handbook
www.bfi.org.uk/handbook

Booksellers

Amazon
www.amazon.co.uk

Blackwell's
www.blackwell.co.uk/bookshops

Cinema Store
www.atlasdigital.com/cinemastore

Reel Posters
www.reelposter.com

Retro Sellers
www.retrosellers.com

Waterstones
www.waterstones.co.uk

UK BookWorld
www.ukbookworld.com

Zwemmer
www.zwemmer.com

Cable, Satellite and Digital

Cable/Satellite Guide
www.sceneone.co.uk/s1/TV

BSkyB
www.sky.co.uk

Freeview
www.freeview.co.uk

NTL
www.ntl.co.uk

SkyDigital
www.skydigital.co.uk

Telewest Communications
www.telewest.co.uk

Careers and Training

British Council Training and Careers Advice
www.britfilms.com/training

Film Education
www.filmeducation.org

Focal
www.focal.ch

Institut National de l'Audiovisual
www.ina.fr

Moving Image Gateway
www.bufvc.ac.uk/gateway

National Film and Television School
www.nftsfilm-tv.ac.uk

Skillset
www.skillset.org

skillsformedia
www.skillsformedia.com

Cinemas

Apollo Cinemas
www.apollocinemas.co.uk

Caledonian Cinemas
www.caledoniancinemas.co.uk

Cinema Admissions
www.dodona.co.uk

Cinemas in the UK
www.aber.ac.uk/~jwp/cinemas

The Cinema Theatre Association
cinema-theatre.org.uk

Cineworld
www.cineworld.co.uk

Film Finder
www.yell.co.uk/yell/ff/

Fox Movies
www.foxmovies.com

Mainline
www.screencinemas.co.uk

Odeon
www.odeon.co.uk

Picturehouse
www.picturehouse-cinemas.co.uk

Reeltime Cinemas
reeltime-cinemas.co.uk

Scoot
www.cinema.scoot.co.uk

Ster Century
www.stercentury.co.uk

Showcase Cinemas
showcasecinemas.co.uk

UCI (UK) Ltd
www.uci-cinemas.co.uk

UCG
www.ucg.fr

Vue Entertainment Group
www.myvue.com

Warner Village
warnervillage.co.uk

Courses

The American Intercontinental University
www.aiulondon.ac.uk

University of Bath
www.bath.ac.uk

Birkbeck College University of London
www.birkbeck.ac.uk

University of Birmingham
www.birmingham.ac.uk

Bournemouth University
www.bournemouth.ac.uk

University of Bradford
www.bradford.ac.uk

Brighton Film School
www.brightonfilmschool.org.uk

Bristol Animation Course
www.mediaworks.org.uk/animate

University of Bristol
www.bristol.ac.uk

Brunel University
www.brunel.ac.uk

Canterbury Christ Church College
www.cant.ac.uk

Coventry University
www.alvis.coventry.ac.uk

Cyber Film School
www.cyberfilmschool.com

De Montfort University Bedford
www.dmu.ac.uk/Bedford

De Montfort University Leicester
www.dmu.ac.uk/Leicester

University of Derby
www.derby.ac.uk

University of East Anglia
www.uea.ac.uk

University of East London
www.bradford.ac.uk

University of Exeter
www.ex.ac.uk

First Film Foundation
www.firstfilm.co.uk

University of Glasgow
www.arts.gla.ac.uk/tfts/

Glasgow Caledonian University
www.gcal.ac.uk

Global Film School
www.globalfilmschool.com

Goldsmiths College
www.goldsmiths.ac.uk

Kent Institute of Art and Design
www.kiad.ac.uk

University of Kent
www.ukc.ac.uk

King Alfred's College Winchester
www.wkac.ac.uk

Kingston University
www.kingston.ac.uk

University of Leicester
www.le.ac.uk

University of Liverpool
www.liv.ac.uk

Liverpool John Moores University
www.livjm.ac.uk

London Guildhall University
www.lgu.ac.uk

London Film Academy
www.londonfilmacademy.com

London Film School
www.lifs..org.uk

London School of Economics and Political Science
www.lse.ac.uk

University of Manchester
www.man.ac.uk

Middlesex University
www.mddx.ac.uk

Napier University
www.napier.ac.uk

National Film and Television School
www.nftsfilm-tv.ac.uk

National Short Course Training Programme
www.nfts-scu.org.uk

University of Newcastle upon Tyne
www.ncl.ac.uk/ncrif

Northern School of Film and Television
www.lmu.ac.uk

University of Northumbria at Newcastle
www.unn.ac.uk

Nova Camcorder School
www.novaonline.co.uk

University of Portsmouth
www.port.ac.uk

University of Reading
www.reading.ac.uk

College of Ripon and York St John
www.ucrysj.ac.uk

Raindance Ltd
www.raindance.co.uk

Roehampton Institute
www.roehampton.ac.uk

Royal College of Art
www.rca.ac.uk/Design

University of Salford
www.salford.ac.uk

University of Sheffield
www.sheffield.ac.uk

Sheffield Hallam University
www.shef.ac.uk

South Bank University
www.sbu.ac.uk

Staffordshire University
www.staffs.ac.uk

University of Stirling:Film and Media Studies Department
www-fms.stir.ac.uk

The University of Sunderland
www.sunderland.ac.uk

University of Sussex
www.sussex.ac.uk

Thames Valley University
www.tvu.ac.uk

Trinity and All Saints College
www.tasc.ac.uk

University of Wales College, Newport
http;//www.newport.ac.uk

University College Warrington
www.warr.ac.uk

University of Warwick
www.warwick.ac.uk

University of Westminster
www.wmin.ac.uk

University of Wolverhampton
www.wolverhampton.ac.uk

Databases/film reviews

625 Television Room
www.625.uk.com

All Movie Database
allmovie.com

Animation World Network
www.awn.com

Baseline
www.pkbaseline.com

Bib Online
www.bibnet.com

Box Office
www.entdata.com

Box Office Guru
www.boxofficeguru.com/

Brit Movie
www.britmovie.co.uk

Castnet
castnet.com

Classic Movies
www.geocities.com/Hollywood/9766

Classic TV
www.classic-tv.com

Cult TV
www.metronet.co.uk/cultv

European Cinema On-Line Database
www.mediasalles.it

FilmUnlimited
www.filmunlimited.co.uk

Film TV
www.film-tv.co.uk/

Highangle
www.highangle.co.uk

Hollywood Online
www.hollywood.com

InDevelopment
www.indevelopment.co.uk

Internet Movie Database
www.uk.imdb.com

The Knowledge
www.theknowledgeonline.com

The Location guide
www.thelocationguide.com

Media UK Internet Directory
www.mediauk.com/directory

Mandy's International Film and TV Production Directory
www.mandy.com

Moving Image Gateway
www.bufvc.ac.uk/gateway

Movie Map
www.visitbritain.com/moviemap/

Movie Page
www.movie-page.com

National Filmographies
www.rosland.freeserve.co.uk/filmbooks.htm

Netribution
www.netribution.co.uk

Popcorn
www.popcorn.co.uk

Production Base
www.productionbase.co.uk

Spotlight
www.spotlightcd.com
www.players-guide.com

TV Guide - Movies
www.tvguide.com/movies

TV Cream
tv.cream.org

UKTV
www.uktv.com

World Wide Box Office
www.worldwideboxoffice.com

Distributors (Non-Theatrical)

Central Office of Information
www.coi.gov.uk

CFL Vision
www.euroview.co.uk

Vera Media
www.vera.media.co.uk

Distributors (Theatrical)

Alibi Communications plc
www.alibifilms.co.uk

Alliance Releasing
www.alliance.

Artificial Eye Film Company
www.artificial-eye.com

BFI
www.bfi.org.uk

Blue Dolphin Film & Video
www.bluedolphinfilms.com

Blue Light
www.bluelight.co.uk

Boudicca
www.boudiccafilms.com

Buena Vista International (UK)
www.bvimovies.com

Cinefrance
www.cinefrance.co.uk

City Screen
www.picturehouses.co.uk

Columbia TriStar Films (UK)
www.columbiatristar.co.uk

Contemporary Films
www.contemporaryfilms.com

Eros International
www.erosentertainment.com

Film Distributors Association
www.launchingfilms.com

Guerilla Films
www.guerilla-films.com

ICA Projects
www.ica.org.uk

Icon Film Distributors
www.iconmovies.co.uk

Metro Tartan Distribution Ltd
www.tartanvideo.com

Metrodome Distribution
www.metrodomegroup.com

Millivres Multimedia
www.millivresmultimedia.co.uk

Momentum Pictures
www.momentumpictures. co.uk

New Line International
www.newline.com

Optimum Releasing
www.optimumreleasing.com

Pathé Distribution
www.pathe.co.uk

Redbus
www.helkon-sk.com

Salvation Films
www.salvation-films.com

ScreenProjex
www.screenprojex.com

Soda Pictures
www. sodapictures.com

Twentieth Century Fox Film Co
www.fox.co.uk

UIP (United International Pictures)
www.uip.com

Universal Studios
universalstudios.com

Warner Bros
www.warnerbros.com

Winchester Film Distribution
www.winchesterent.com

Yash Raj Films International Ltd
www.yashrajfilms.com

Facilities

Abbey Road Studios
www.abbeyroad.co.uk/

Cinesite (Europe) Ltd
www.cinesite.com

Communicopia Ltd
www.communicopia.co.uk

Connections Communications Centre
www.cccmedia.demon.co.uk

Dubbs
www.dubbs.co.uk

Edinburgh Film Workshop Trust
www.efwt.demon.co.uk

The Film Factory at VTR
www.filmfactory.com

FrameStore
www.framestore.co.uk

Hillside Studios
www.ctvc.co.uk

Hull Time Based Arts
www.htba.demon.co.uk

Lee Lighting
www.lee.co.uk

PMPP Facilities
www.pmpp.dircon.co.uk

Salon Post-Productions
www.salon.ndirect.co.uk

Tele-Cine
www.telecine.co.uk

VTR Ltd
www.vtr.co.uk

Festivals

Edinburgh International Film Festival
www.edfilmfest.org.uk

Film Festivals Servers
www.filmfestivals.com

Berlin
www.berlinale.de

Cannes
www.festival-cannes-fr

London Film Festival
www.lff.org.uk

Karlovy Vary International Film Festival
www.iffkv.cz

Sundance Film Festival
www.sundance.org

Film Societies

Film Societies
www.bffs.org.uk

Funding

Arts Council of England
www.artscouncil.org.uk

Arts Council of Northern Ireland
www.artscouncil-ni.org

Arts Council of Wales
www.ccc-acw.org.uk

British Council
www.britfilms.com

Kraszna-Krausz Foundation
www.k-k.org.uk

Scottish Screen
www.scottishscreen.com

Sgrin, Media Agency for Wales
www.sgrinwales.demon.co.uk

UK Media
www.mediadesk.co.uk

The UK Film Council
www.ukfilmcouncil.org.uk

English Regional Arts Boards
www.arts.org.uk

Northern Ireland Film Commission
www.nifc.co.uk/

Shooting people
shootingpeople.org

Scottish Screen
www.scottishscreen.com/

Sgrîn
www.sgrinwales.demon.co.uk

International Sales

BBC Worldwide
www.bbc.worldwide.com

BRITE (British Independent Television Enterprises)
www.brite.tv.co.uk

London Television Service
www.londontv.com

Pearson Television International
www.pearsontv.com

Twentieth Century Fox Television
www.fox.co.uk

Vine International Pictures
www.vineinternational.co.uk

Libraries

bfi National Library
www.bfi.org.uk/library

British Library
www.bl.uk/

COPAC
copac.ac.uk/copac/

Film Libraries - International
www.unesco.org/webworld/portal_bib/Library_Websites/Special/Film_Libraries/

Library Association
www.la-hq.org.uk

Public Libraries - Online Information and Queries answered online.
www.earl.org.uk

Organisations

American Film Institute
www.afionline.org/

Arts Council of England
www.artscouncil.org.uk

Authors Licensing and Collecting Society
www.alcs.co.uk

BBC
www.bbc.co.uk

British Council - British films
www.britfilms.com

British Film Commission
www.britfilmcom.co.uk

British Film Institute
www.bfi.org.uk

BKSTS - The Moving Image Society
www.bksts.demon.co.uk

BUFVC(British Universities Film and Video Council
www.bufvc.ac.uk

Department for Culture, Media and Sport (DCMS)
www.culture.gov.uk/

Directors' Guild of Great Britain
www.dggb.co.uk

EDI
www.entdata.com

Equity
www.equity.org.uk/

National Museum of Photography, Film and Television
www.nmsi.ac.uk/nmpft

Federation Against Copyright Theft – FACT
www.fact-uk.org.uk/

Film London
www.filmlondon.org.uk

New Producer's Alliance
www.npa.org.uk

PACT - Producers Alliance for Cinema and Television
www.pact.co.uk

Shooting People
www.shootingpeople.org

Scottish Screen
www.scottishscreen.com

Skillset
www.skillset.org

Women in Film and TV - the Organisation
www.wftv.org.uk

Organisations (Europe)

Association of European Film Institutes
www.filmeurope.co.uk

Cordis
www.cordis.lu

European Association of Animation Film
www.cartoon-media.be

European Audio-visual Observatory
www.obs.coe.int

EURIMAGES
www.culture.coe.fr/eurimages

Europa
www.europa.eu.int

European Broadcasting Union (EBU)
www.ebu.ch/

The European Coordination of Film Festivals EEIG
www.eurofilmfest.org

European Documentary Network
www.edn.dk

European Film Academy
www.europeanfilmacademy.org

EUTELSAT (European Telecommunications Satellite Organisation)
www.eutelsat.org

Idea
www.europa.eu.int/idea

Belgium - The Flemish Film Institute

www.vfi-filminsituutbe

Denmark - Danish Film Institute
www.dfi.dk

Finland - AVEK - The Promotion Centre for Audio-visual Culture in Finland
www.kopiostofi/avek

Finnish Film Archive
www.sea.fi

The Finnish Film Foundation
www.ses.fi/ses

France - Bibliothèque du Film (BIFI)
www.bifi.fr

TV France International
www.tvfi.com

Germany - Filmf^rderungsanstalt
www.ffa.de

Iceland - Icelandic Film Fund
www.centrum.is/filmfund

Ireland - Bord Scann·n na hÉ.ireann/Irish Film Board
www.iol.ie/filmboard

Film Institute of Ireland
www.iftn.ie/ifc

Poland - Polish Cinema Database
info.fuw.edu.pl/Filmy/

Portugal - Portuguese Film and Audiovisual Institute
www.nfi.no/nfi.htm

Scottish Screen
www.scottishscreen.com

Press Contacts

6degrees.co.uk
www.6degrees.co.uk

Empire
www.empireonline.co.uk

Filmwaves
www.filmwaves.co.uk

Film Unlimited
filmunlimited.co.uk

Flicks
www.flicks.co.uk

Guardian online
www.guardian.co.uk/guardian

Inside Out
www.insideout.co.uk

Movie Club News
www.movieclubnews.co.uk

Premiere
www.premieremag.com

Radio Times
www.radiotimes.beeb.com

Screen
www.arts.gla.ac

Screendaily
screendaily.com

Screen Digest
www.screendigest.com

Sight and Sound
www.bfi.org.uk/sightandsound

Sunday Times
www.sunday-times.co.uk

Talking Pictures
www.filmcentre.co.uk

Television
www.rts.org.uk

Time Out
www.timeout.co.uk/

Total Film
www.futurenet.co.uk

UK Government press releases
www.open.gov.uk/

Uncut
www.uncut.net

Variety
www.variety.com

Visimag
visimag.com

Preview Theatres

BAFTA
www.bafta.org

The Curzon Minema
www.minema.com

Mr Young's Screening Rooms
www.mryoungs.com

RSA
www.rsa.org.uk

The Screening Room
www.moving-picture.co.uk

Production Companies

Aardman Animations
www.aardman.com

British Film Commission
www.britfilmcom.co.uk

British Films Catalogue
www.britfilms.com/

Fox Searchlight Pictures
www.fox.co.uk

guerilla films
www.guerilla.u-net.com

Hammer Film Productions Limited
www.hammerfilms.com

imaginary films
www.imagfilm.co.uk

Mosiac Films Limited
www.mosaicfilms.com

New Producers Alliance
www.npa.org.uk

PACT
www.pact.co.uk

Zooid Pictures Limited
www.zooid.co.uk

Specialised Goods and Services

Ashurst Morris Crisp
www.ashursts.com

Bromley Casting (Film & TV Extras Agency)
www.showcall.co.uk

Hothouse Models & Effects
www.hothousefx.co.uk

MBS Underwater Video Specialists
www.eclipse.co.uk.mbs

Moving Image Touring Exhibition Service (MITES)
www.mites.org.uk

Olswang
www.olswang.co.uk

Studios

Capital FX
www.capital.fx.co.uk

Ealing Studios
www.ealingstudios.co.uk

Elstree Film Studios
www.elstreefilmstudios.co.uk

Hillside Studios
www.ctvc.co.uk

Millennium Studios
www.elstree-online.co.uk

Pinewood Studios
www.pinewood-studios.co.uk

Television Companies

625 Television Room
www.625.uk.com

TV Commissions

www.tvcommissions.com

TV Guides
www.link-it.com/TV
www.sceneone.co.uk/s1/TV

Episode Guides Page
epguides.com/

Anglia Television
www.anglia.tv.co.uk/

BBC
www.bbc.co.uk/

Border Television
www.border-tv.com/

Carlton Television
www.carltontv.co.uk/

Channel Four
www.channel4.com

Granada Television
www.granada.co.uk
HTV
www.htv.co.uk/

London Weekend Television (LWT)
www.lwt.co.uk/

Meridian Broadcasting Ltd
www.meridan.tv.co.uk/

S4C
www.s4c.co.uk/

Scottish Television
www.stv.co.uk/

Ulster Television
www.utvlive.com

Video Labels

British Videogram Association
www.bva.org.uk

Blockbuster Entertainment
www.blockbuster.com

DVD rental
www.movietrak.com

MovieMail
www.moviem.co.uk

Movies Unlimited
www.moviesunlimited.com

Videolog
www.videolog.co.uk

Workshops

City Eye
www.city-eye.co.uk

Edinburgh Film Workshop Trust
www.efwt.demon.co.uk

Hull Time Based Arts
www.htba.demon.co.uk

Pilton Video
www.piltonvideo.co.uk

The Place in the Park Studios
www.screenhero.demon.co.uk

Real Time Video
www.rtvideo.demon.co.uk

Vera Media
www.vera-media.co.uk

Vivid
www.wavespace.waverider.co.uk/~vivid/

WORKSHOPS

The selection of workshops listed below are generally non-profit distributing and subsidised organisations. Some workshops are also active in making audio-visual products for UK and international media markets

Amber Side Workshop
5-9 Side
Newcastle upon Tyne NE1 3JE
Tel: 0191 232 2000
Fax: 0191 230 3217
Website: www.amber-online.com
Murray Martin

Belfast Film Workshop
37 Queen Street
Belfast BT1 6EA
Tel: 01232 648387
Fax: 01232 246657

Black Media Training Trust (BMTT)
Workstation
15 Paternoster Row
Sheffield S12 BX
Tel: 01142 492207
Fax: 01142 492207
Contact: Carl Baker

Blaze the Trail Limited (Film & Television Training)
2nd Floor
241 High Street
London E17 7BH
Tel: 020 8520 4569
Fax: 020 8520 2358
email: bctraining@coralmedia.co.uk
Website: www.blaze-the-trail.com
The Course Coordinator

Chapter MovieMaker
Chapter Arts Centre
Market Road
Canton
Cardiff CF5 1QE
Tel: 029 2031 1050
Fax: 029 2031 3431
email: chaptercinema@easynet.co.uk
Website: www.chapter.org
Tony Whitehead

The Children's Film Unit
South Way
Leavesden
Herts WD25 7LZ
Tel: 01923 354656
Fax: 01923 354656
email: cfilmunit@aol.com
Website: www.btinternet.com/~cfu
Carol Rennie, Adminstrator

City Eye
Swaythling Neighbourhood Centre
Rear 200 Burgess Road
Swaythling
Southampton SO16 3AY
Tel: 023 80677167
Fax: 023 80 575717
email: admin@city-eye.co.uk
Website: www.city-eye.co.uk
David White, Camille Smith

Connections Communications Centre
Palingswick House
241 King Street
Hammersmith, London W6 9LP
Tel: 020 8741 1766
Fax: 020 8563 1934
email:
connections@cccmedia.demon.co.uk
Website: www.cccmedia.demon.co.uk
Jacqueline Davis

cre8 studios
Town Hall Studios
Regent Circus
Swindon SN1 1QF
Tel: 01793 463224
Fax: 01793 463223
email: keith@cre8studios.org.uk
Website:
www.swindon.gov.uk//index/leisure/artsandculture/cre8.htm
Keith Phillips

Cultural Partnerships
90 De Beauvoir Road
London N1 4EN
Tel: 020 7254 8217
Fax: 020 7254 7541
Brian Matcham, Chief Executive

Depot Studios
Bond Street
Coventry CV1 4AH
Tel: 024 76 525074
Fax: 024 76 634373
email: info@depotstudios.org.uk
Website: www.depotstudios.org.uk
Contact: Anne Forgan, Matthew Taylor

Edinburgh Film and Video Access Centre
25a South West
Thistle Lane
Edinburgh EH2 1EW
Tel: 0131 220 0220
Fax: 0131 220 0017
email: fva_Edinburgh@hotmail.com
Website: www.fvac.co.uk

Edinburgh Mediabase
25a SW Thistle Street Lane
Edinburgh EH2 1EW
Tel: 0131 220 0220
Fax: 0131 220 0017
email:
info@edinburghmediabase.com
email:
training@edinburghmediabase.com
Website:
www.edinburghmediabase.com
Paul Ryan

Exeter Phoenix
Media Centre
Bradninch Place
Gandy Street
Exeter
Devon EX4 3LS
Tel: 01392 667066
Fax: 01392 667596
email: media@exeterphoenix.org.uk
Website: www.exeterphoenix.org.uk
Jonas Hawkins

Film Work Group
Top Floor
Chelsea Reach
79-89 Lots Road
London SW10 0RN
Tel: 0171 352 0538
Fax: 0171 351 6479
Loren Squires, Nigel Perkins

First Take
Merseyside Innovation Centre
131 Mount Pleasant
Liverpool L3 5TF
Tel: 0151 708 5767
Fax: 0151 707 0230
email: all@first-take.demon.co.uk
Website: www.first-take.demon.co.uk
Mark Bareham, Lynne Harwood

Four Corners Film Workshop
113 Roman Road

Bethnal Green
London E2 0QN
Tel: 020 8981 6111
Fax: 020 8983 4441
email: film@fourcorners.demon.co.uk
Website: www.fourcornersfilm.org
Lyn Turner

Glasgow Media Access Centre

3rd Floor
34 Albion Street
Glasgow G1 1LH
Tel: 0141 553 2620
Fax: 0141 553 2660
email: admin@g-mac.co.uk
Website: www.g-mac.co.uk
Ian Reid, John Sackey, Blair Young, Stella Tobia, Cordelia Stephens

Hull Time Based Arts

42 The High Street
Hull HU1 1PS
Tel: 01482 216446
Fax: 01482 589952
email: timebase@htba.demon.co.uk
Website: www.timebase.org
Annabel McCourt, Dan Van Heeswyk

Intermedia Film and Video*

19 Heathcote Street
Nottingham NG1 3AF
Tel: 0115 955 6909
Fax: 0115 955 9956
email: info@intermedianotts.co.uk
Website:
www.emnet.co.uk/coda/intermedia/
Ceris Morris, Director

Jubilee Arts c/PLEX Project

Unit 1A Overend Street
West Bromwich
West Midlands B70 6EY
Tel: 0121 525 6861
Fax: 0121 525 6475
email: @jubart.demon.co.uk
Website: www.c-plex.co.uk

Knew productions

The Place in the Park Studios,
Belle Vue Road
Wrexham
North Wales LL13 7NH
Tel: 01978 358522
email: studio@knewmediaco.uk
Website: www.knewmedia.co.uk
Richard Knew

Leeds Animation Workshop (A Women's Collective)

45 Bayswater Row
Leeds LS8 5LF
Tel: 0113 248 4997
Fax: 0113 248 4997
Website:
www.leedsanimation.demon.co.uk
Jane Bradshaw, Terry Wragg, Stephanie Munro, Janis Goodman, Milena Dragic

London Deaf Access Project

1-3 Worship Street
London EC2A 2AB
Tel: 0171 588 3522 (voice) Tel: 0171 588 3528 (text)
Fax: 0171 588 3526
email: lucyf@bda.org.uk
Website: www.bda.co.uk
Lucy Franklin, Production Coordinator

Media Production Facilities

Bon Marche Centre
Ferndale Road
London SW9 8BJ
Tel: 020 7737 7152
Fax: 020 7738 5428
email: mpf@media-production.demon.co.uk
Website: www.media-production.demon.co.uk

The Media Workshop

City Museum and Art Gallery
Priestgate
Peterborough PE1 1LF
Tel: 01733 343119
Fax: 01733 341928
email: mediaworkshop@peterborough.gov.uk
Clifton Stewart, Media Development Coordinator

Mersey Film and Video (MFV)

13-15 Hope Street
Liverpool L1 9BQ
Tel: 0151 708 5259
Fax: 0151 707 8595
email: mfv@hopestreet.u-net.com
Website: www.mfv.merseyside.org

Migrant Media

Studio 401
Greenhealth Centre
31 Three Colts Lane
London EZ 6JB
Tel: 020 7729 9109
Fax: 020 7729 6909
email: info@injusticefilm.co.uk
Website: www.injusticefilm.co.uk
Ken Fero, Yesim Deveci

Moving Image Touring Exhibition Services (MITES)

Foundation For Art & Creative Technology (FACT)
88 Wood Street
Liverpool L1 4DX
Tel: 0151 707 4435
Fax: 0151 707 4432
email: mites@fact.co.uk
Website: www.mites.org.uk
Simon Bradshaw

Nerve Centre

7/8 Magazine Street
Derry BT48 6HJ
Northern Ireland
Tel: 02871 260562
Fax: 02871 371738
Website: www.nerve-centre.org.uk
Bernie McLaughlin, Aisling McGill

The Old Dairy Studios

156b Haxby Road
York YO3 7JN
Tel: 01904 641394
Fax: 01904 692052
Website: www.olddairystudios.co.uk

Oxford Film and Video Makers

The Old Boxing Club
54 Catherine St
Oxford OX4 3AH
Tel: 01865 792731 or 01865 792732
Fax: 01865 742901
email: office@ofvm.org
Website: www.ofvm.org

Panico London Ltd

PO Box 496
London WC1A 2WZ
Tel: 020 7485 3533
Fax: 020 7485 3533
email: panico@panicofilms.com
Website: www.panicofilms.com

Picture This Moving Image

40 Sydney Row
Spike Island Studios
Bristol BS1 6UU
Bristol BS2 0QL
Tel: 0117 925 7010
Fax: 0117 925 7040
email: info@picturethis.demon.co.uk
Website:
www.picturethismovingimage.co.uk
Josephine Lanyon, Director

Pilton Video

30 Ferry Road Avenue
Edinburgh EH4 4BA
Tel: 0131 343 1151
Fax: 0131 343 2820
email: info@piltonvideo.org
Website: www.piltonvideo.org
Hugh Farrell, Joel Venet, Eleanor Hill, Graham Fitzpatrick, Graham Drydale

Platform Films and Video

Unit 14, Pennybank Chambers
33-35 St Johns Square
London EC1M 4DS
Tel: 020 7278 8394

Fax: 020 7278 8394
email: platform.films@virgin.net
Chris Reeves

Real Time Video
The Arts and Media Centre
21 South Street
Reading RG1 4QU
Tel: 0118 901 5205
Fax: 0118 901 5206
email: info@real-time.org.uk
info@real-time.fsnet.co.uk
Website: www.real-time.org.uk
Clive Robertson

Screenwriters' Workshop
Suffolk House
1-8 Whitfield Place
London W1T 5JU
Tel: 0171 387 5511
Fax: 020 7387 5511
email: screenoffice@tiscali.co.uk
Website: www.lsw.org.uk
Katharine Way

Sheffield Independent Film
5 Brown Street
Sheffield S1 2BS
Tel: 0114 272 0304
Fax: 0114 279 5225
email: admin.sif@workstation.org.uk
Gloria Ward

Signals Media Arts
Victoria Chambers
St Runwald Street
Colchester CO1 1HF
Tel: 01206 560255
Fax: 01206 369086
email: admin@signals.org.uk
Website: signals.org.uk
Anita Belli

Swingbridge Video
Norden House
41 Stowell Street
Newcastle upon Tyne NE1 4YB
Tel/Fax: 0191 232 3762
email: Swingvid@aol.com
Contact: Hugh Kelly

Trilith
Corner Cottage, Brickyard Lane
Bourton, Gillingham
Dorset SP8 5PJ
Tel: 01747 840750/840727

Valley and Vale Community Arts Ltd
The Valley and Vale Media Centre,
Heol Dew, Sant
Betws
Mid Glamorgan CF32 8SU
Tel: 01656 729246/871911
Fax: 01656 729185/870507
Website: www.valleyandvale.co.uk

Vera Media
30-38 Dock Street
Leeds LS10 1JF
Tel: 0113 2428646
Fax: 0113 242 8739
email: vera@vera-media.co.uk
Website: www.vera-media.co.uk
Al Garthwaite, Catherine Mitchell

VET (Video Engineering & Training)
Lux Building
2-4 Hoxton Square
London N1 6NU
Tel: 020 7505 4700
Fax: 020 7505 4800
email: post@vet.co.uk
Website: www.vet.co.uk

Vivid
Birmingham's Centre for Media Arts ltd
Unit 311
The Big Peg
120 Vyse Street, Jewellery Quarter
Birmingham B18 6ND
Tel: 0121 233 4061
Fax: 0121 212 1784
email: info@vivid.org.uk
Website: www.vivid.org.uk
Yasmeen Baig-Clifford

West Yorkshire Media Services
Hall Place Studios
3 Queen Square
Leeds LS2 813U
Tel: 0113 283 1906
Fax: 0113 283 1906
email: m.spadafora@lmu.ac.uk
Website: www.hallplacestudios.com
Maria Spadafora

WFA
Media and Cultural Centre
9 Lucy Street
Manchester M15 4BX
Tel: 0161 848 9785
Fax: 0161 848 9783
email: wfa@timewarp.co.uk
Website: www.wfamedia.co.uk
Chloe Beattie

INDEX

A

E

G

H

M

N

O

P

Q

R

S

T

U

V

W

X

Y

Z